WORLD HISTORY
Perspectives on the Past

Authors

Steven L. Jantzen

Author of works on history, government, and classroom-tested teaching strategies; editor of social studies texts; former high-school teacher of government and history

Kenneth Neill

Author of textbooks on nineteenth- and twentieth-century world history; former history teacher; publisher/editor of *Memphis* magazine, Memphis, Tennessee

Larry S. Krieger

Social studies supervisor in Edison, New Jersey; coauthor of social studies textbooks and teaching materials; former world history teacher

The *Research Skills Handbook* and exercises for *Writing and Speaking about History* were developed by Virginia S. Wilson and James Allison Litle, instructors of History/Social Science at the North Carolina School of Science and Mathematics. Dr. Wilson is head of the Department of Humanities at the School of Science and Mathematics and also a part-time instructor in social studies methods at Duke University. Mr. Litle is a former department coordinator and former social studies teacher in the Duke Durham Enrichment School Program.

WORLD HISTORY
Perspectives on the Past

D.C. Heath and Company
Lexington, Massachusetts   Toronto, Ontario

Teacher Reviewers

Lolene Blake
Longmeadow High School
Longmeadow, Massachusetts

Spiro Cora
Wingfield High School
Jackson, Mississippi

John Dare
John Marshall Senior High School
Cleveland, Ohio

Michael J. Harkins
Community Unit School, District 300
Dundee, Illinois

Eileen Murray
St. Edmunds School
Tonawanda, New York

John Petretich
Boardman High School
Boardman, Ohio

Content Reviewers

Charmarie Jenkins Blaisdell   Associate Professor of History, Northeastern University, Boston, Massachusetts; specialist in European social and intellectual history; past president of the Sixteenth Century Studies Council

Joan Erdman   Professor of Anthropology, Columbia College, Chicago, Illinois; Research Associate, Committee of Southern Asian Studies, University of Chicago

J. Rufus Fears   Professor of Classics and Chair of the Department of Classical Studies, Boston University, Boston, Massachusetts

Thomas Spear   Professor of African History, Chair of African and Middle Eastern Studies, Williams College, Williamstown, Massachusetts

Leslie Swartz   Specialist in Chinese studies and director of Harvard East Asian Outreach Program, Boston, Massachusetts

Charles T. Wood   Fellow, Medieval Academy of America; Daniel Webster Professor of History, Dartmouth College, Hanover, New Hampshire; former member of the executive committees of both the New Hampshire School Boards Association and the New Hampshire Joint Educational Council

Chapter 36, *Latin America and Canada in the Modern World*, was written by Bert Bower, regional specialist and supervisor, Stanford Teacher Education Program. Mr. Bower is a former social studies teacher and curriculum developer for the Stanford Program in International and Cross Cultural Education—Latin America (SPICE).

Executive Editor	Phyllis Goldstein
Senior Editors	Martha Green,
	Susan Belt Cogley
Executive Designer	Will Tenney
Designers	Jane Miron,
	Cornelia Boynton
Production Coordinator	Maureen LaRiccia
Editorial Services	Elizabeth Grose,
	Marianna Frew
	Palmer

Published simultaneously in Canada

Printed in the United States of America

International Standard Book Number: 0-669-09149-9

3 4 5 6 7 8 9 0

Cover illustration: The Roman aqueduct at Segovia, Spain

Contents

BRITONS
YOU
JOIN YOUR COUNTRY'S ARMY!
GOD SAVE THE KING

Maps

Maps

Graphs, Charts, and Diagrams

Research Skills Handbook

Research Skills Handbook

Interpreting the Past

Historians are people who study the past. Some are professional historians who make their living by studying the past. Others may be history buffs who study the past for fun. Or historians can be people such as you—students enrolled in a history course.

Professional historians include people who teach and write about history. Many professional historians took part in preparing this book. They have done more than simply report the facts. In choosing what information to include, they have made judgments about what events are most important to your understanding of history. They have also interpreted those events to present them from a particular point of view.

The point of view a historian presents in a book or article is called the **thesis**. A historian supports the thesis, or point of view, with evidence. The thesis is very important in historical writing. It organizes and gives focus to a topic.

For example, the authors of this text chose to organize the first section of the chapter on ancient Egypt (pages 48–51) around this thesis: "The Nile River shaped Egyptian life." The section includes information that supports this thesis. That information includes how the Nile linked diverse lands, how it influenced farming, and how it influenced settlement patterns in ancient Egypt.

The thesis of the second section on ancient Egypt (pages 52–57) is: "Egypt's pharaohs ruled as gods." The section supports this thesis with information on how Egyptian pharaohs shaped Egyptian history.

Look for the thesis of the third section (pages 57–63). What information in the section supports the thesis?

The history of ancient Egypt is a long and rich one, spanning over 3,000 years of history. In a sense, a thesis narrows the field of study. No longer does a historian have to tell every fact known about a particular subject. Instead, the historian chooses appropriate facts to support his or her thesis statement.

- ◆ The point of view a historian presents in a book or article is called a **thesis**.

- ◆ *Example of Thesis:* The Nile River shaped Egyptian life.

- ◆ *Evidence:*
  The Nile linked diverse lands.
  Farmers relied on the Nile's floods.
  Egypt's villages and cities lay along the Nile.
  The surrounding desert affected life.
  Villages along the river formed political units.

Research Skills

Using Sources

Historians look for information in two kinds of sources: primary sources and secondary sources. **Primary sources** are historical documents written at the time of the events they describe. For example, an eyewitness account of a battle is a primary source. Primary sources include treaties, laws, constitutions, charters, court cases, proclamations, speeches, chronicles, eyewitness accounts, letters, and diaries. In each chapter of this book, the section entitled "Voice from the Past" presents a primary source.

Secondary sources are later accounts of historical events. Scholarly books and articles written by historians are considered secondary sources. This textbook is also a secondary source. Secondary sources can summarize and evaluate the information from many primary sources.

Historians look for three things when they read primary and secondary sources:

1. dates and facts
2. concepts
3. generalizations

Dates and facts are the necessary guideposts that provide order and continuity to the study of history. However, the real goal of a historian is to understand the basic generalizations and concepts of history.

A **concept** is a general idea that a person develops after thinking about a number of specific cases. For example, *book* is a concept that includes many different types, from comic books to textbooks to dictionaries. One of the key concepts in this book is *civilization*. The concept of civilization is defined on page 27, and many specific types of civilizations are presented in the rest of the book.

A **generalization** is a broad statement that brings together several concepts from different cases. For example, in studying the rise of ancient civilizations, a historian might look at Sumer, which arose in the Tigris-Euphrates River valley; Egypt in the Nile River valley; and China in the Yellow River valley. A generalization about the rise of civilization might then be: "Many early civilizations arose in river valleys."

It is important to understand the basic generalizations and concepts of the past. It is also important to interpret how those generalizations and concepts apply to the world in which we live today.

- ◆ **Primary sources** are historical documents written at the time of the events they describe.

- ◆ **Secondary sources** are later accounts of historical events.

- ◆ A **concept** is a general idea that a person develops after thinking about a number of specific cases.

- ◆ A **generalization** is a broad statement that brings together several concepts from different cases.

Artifacts, such as this crude hand axe, can also be primary sources.

Research Skills

Studying Different Kinds of History

History in its broadest sense includes the whole of the human experience. Most historians focus on one aspect or field of history. The following list explains some of the major fields of study that a historian might investigate.

Political history Political history deals with governments, laws, and political leaders. The study of pharaohs and how they ruled Egypt is part of political history. Textbooks often focus mainly on political history.

Military history Military history is the study of conflict, wars, weapons, and the strategy and tactics of warfare. It is also the study of how people resolve conflicts.

Social history Social history examines every part of a people's way of life—the kinds of tools they make, the art they produce, the foods they eat, even the way they view the world and the values they teach their children. When we look at the contributions made by various people to art, literature, and science, that is part of social history.

Intellectual history Intellectual history concentrates on the ideas that motivate and direct the actions of the society. Some of these ideas are clearly set forth by thinkers of the time. Others of these ideas are merely assumptions that most people of the time shared, without ever stating them directly. Religious and philosophical ideas fall under the general heading of intellectual history.

Economic history Economic history looks at the goods and services people buy and sell, the products they make, and the way they use the resources in their environment. Business, finance, and trade are also part of economic history.

As a student, you will be studying the events and ideas of the past. As a historian, you will be judging and evaluating those events and ideas to see what lessons for today they offer.

Social history includes information about marriage customs and families.

Research Skills

Using Books Effectively

The more a historian knows about the parts of a book, the more valuable that book becomes for study and research. Books are generally organized to present the facts as clearly as possible. *World History: Perspectives on the Past* is organized in the following way:

Title Page The title page gives the full title of the book, the authors' names, the publisher, and the place of publication.

Table of Contents The table of contents forms an outline of the book by listing the unit and chapter titles and the pages on which they begin. The table of contents for this book shows the student that there are 9 units and 37 chapters. The table of contents also includes lists of the tables, charts, illustrations, and maps found in the book. These lists help the reader find specific information.

Unit Opening This textbook contains nine units that group the chapters into historical periods. Each unit begins with a two-page overview that shows a photograph related to the period, lists the chapter titles, and introduces the major themes of the unit.

Chapter Opening Each chapter focuses on a specific theme, which is stated in the title. The chapter opens with a dramatic event related to that theme. The opener also lists the sections in the chapter.

Numbered Sections Each chapter has two to six numbered sections. These section headings summarize the major topics in the chapter.

Section Review At the end of each section is a Section Review that checks the student's knowledge of terms, people, places, and events in the section.

Pictures, Drawings, and Charts The pictures and drawings in this book enhance the content and should be studied along with the text material. Captions identify each picture and provide additional information for the reader.

Maps Maps are an important part of this text. They locate places, show the size of empires, and provide clues to geography. A map study question or activity appears in the caption for each map.

Special Features Several special features appear in each chapter. "Voice from the Past" presents primary source material. "Daily Life" features information on how people lived. "Footnotes to History" contains interesting facts as a sidelight to history.

Chapter Review Each chapter ends with a two-page chapter review. The review begins with a summary of the chapter and a timeline of major events in the chapter. Next comes a series of exercises, questions, and activities to help students understand the ideas covered in the chapter.

Research Skills Handbook At the conclusion of each unit is a Research Skills Handbook page that focuses on research, writing, and speaking skills.

Unit Review A Unit Review follows each Research Skills page. The unit review contains a series of questions that prepares readers for unit tests.

Historical Atlas The historical atlas is a series of eight maps, each showing the world at a certain period in history. Studying these maps helps the reader see what was going on in different parts of the world at a specific time.

Glossary The glossary lists all the boldfaced terms presented in the text and gives their definitions.

Index The index is an alphabetical listing of subjects, people, and events discussed or mentioned in the book with a listing of each page on which they appear.

Chapter Title

Chapter Sections

Event Related to Theme

Chapter **3**

3100 B.C. - 332 B.C. *Ancient Egypt*

This golden mask covered the face of Tutankhamon's mummy. Its ears are pierced for earrings. The vulture and the cobra on the headdress represent two Egyptian gods.

1. The Nile River shaped Egyptian life.
2. Egypt's pharaohs ruled as gods.
3. Egypt's way of life endured 3,000 years.

It was late fall in 1922. In northeastern Africa, the sun blazed hot in the Valley of the Kings, which lies in Egypt near a sweeping curve in the Nile River. British archaeologist Howard Carter had spent six years there moving ton upon ton of rock in search of tombs of ancient Egypt's last great rulers. More than 3,000 years had passed since these rulers had been laid to rest. Over the centuries, robbers had opened most of the tombs and taken their treasures. Still, Carter pressed on.

On November 26, 1922, Carter stood before a sealed door. If the wildest of Carter's dreams were true, behind the door lay the mummy and treasure of the ruler Tutankhamon (TOOT-ahngk-AH-mun). Carter made a small hole in the door and stuck a candle through. His report told what he saw.

47

Research Skills

Mastering Study Skills

Understanding and remembering what you read is the key to successful studying. Use the following steps to help you get the most from this and other books:

Preview the chapter Before reading the chapter, skim the chapter opening and summary. Pay careful attention to the titles of each section within the chapter. Look through the chapter for maps, graphs, and photographs. Make a mental note of the general content of the chapter.

Read the chapter carefully One way to get the most out of your reading is to turn each section heading into a *who, what, when, where,* or *why* question. As you read, look for the answers to your questions.

Take notes Jot down the answers to your questions in note format (page 90) or record the main ideas in outline format (page 256).

Reread the chapter Reread the chapter a second time without pausing to take notes. Because you are already familiar with the material, you will retain much more of the information and gain a better understanding of any section that may have seemed confusing to you.

Review the material Read the chapter summary carefully. Compare the main ideas listed there with your notes. Use the section, chapter, and unit reviews to test your knowledge of what you have read.

Using Headings to Take Notes

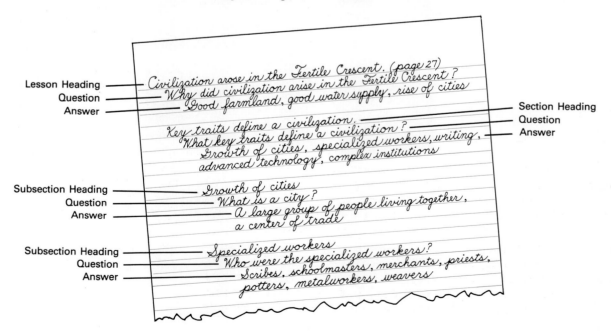

Lesson Heading — Civilization arose in the Fertile Crescent. (page 27)
Question — Why did civilization arise in the Fertile Crescent?
Answer — Good farmland, good water supply, rise of cities

Section Heading — Key traits define a civilization.
Question — What key traits define a civilization?
Answer — Growth of cities, specialized workers, writing, advanced technology, complex institutions

Subsection Heading — Growth of cities
Question — What is a city?
Answer — A large group of people living together, a center of trade

Subsection Heading — Specialized workers
Question — Who were the specialized workers?
Answer — Scribes, schoolmasters, merchants, priests, potters, metalworkers, weavers

Introduction

History is the record of all the hopes, achievements, defeats, victories, discoveries, ideas, and beliefs of human beings since they first appeared on earth. History records the wars, disasters, plagues, and famines that have befallen humankind. Yet history also shows that people are capable of acting with courage, kindness, wisdom, and brilliance.

Every group of people has its own history. To forget that history would be as devastating as loss of memory is to an individual. Knowing who you are means remembering who you were yesterday and all the days before that. The history of a group of people—whether that group is a family, a religious group, or a nation—is part of that group's identity.

As different groups meet, trade, fight, and make alliances, their histories blend into a larger history. Taken together, the histories of all groups make up the history of the largest group of all—humankind.

Stonehenge, a giant arrangement of stones in England, may be more than 3,500 years old. It may have been both a religious center and a huge calendar. On June 21, the longest day of the year, the sun rises directly over a special stone.

Historians need ways to measure time.

History would be impossible without some way of accurately measuring the passage of time. Dates allow historians to place events in correct sequence. Dates tell when such and such a person lived, how long a certain war lasted, how many years passed between two events. However, finding accurate dates is often one of the most difficult problems a historian faces.

People use different calendars.

What year is this? A person asking that question might well get one answer in the United States, another in Israel, and still a third in Saudi Arabia. All three answers would be right. Other answers—equally correct—might come from people in India or China.

How are specific numbers or dates assigned to the passing years? Different groups of people follow different customs. Take, for example, the year that people in the United States and Europe will call 2000. They use that number because the year will come approximately 2,000 years after the birth of Jesus. Some people call this system of dating "the Christian Era." Others call it "the Common Era" because it is widely used.

However, for many Jews, this same year will be called 5761 because, according to the Jewish traditions, God created the world 5,761 years before. The same year will be numbered 1378 by many Muslims because they begin counting from the founding of their religion in the year that Europeans and Americans label 622.

In the past, people had even more ways of recording the passage of time. Many groups of people numbered their years only by the reigns of kings (for example, "in the eighth year of King Philip's rule"). Others counted forward or backward from great religious festivals. Historians often must do a lot of detective work to determine accurate dates from such sources.

Years are labeled B.C. and A.D.

The dates given in this text are those of the Christian or Common Era. You will see that these dates fall into two groups, B.C. and A.D.

In the early part of the book, many of the dates are followed by the letters B.C. These letters stand for "before Christ" and mean that the event took place a certain number of years before the birth of Jesus. Thus, the year 500 B.C. was 500 years before the birth of Jesus, or almost 2,500 years ago. As dates get closer to the birth of Jesus, the numbers get smaller. For example, a person who was born in 378 B.C. might well have lived until 318 B.C. (How old would that person have been at death?)

If a year is labeled A.D., it took place after the birth of Jesus. The letters stand for "*anno domini*," a Latin phrase meaning "in the year of our Lord."

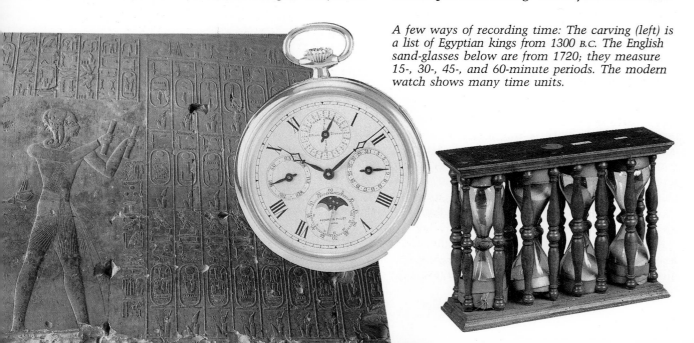

A few ways of recording time: The carving (left) is a list of Egyptian kings from 1300 B.C. The English sand-glasses below are from 1720; they measure 15-, 30-, 45-, and 60-minute periods. The modern watch shows many time units.

| 4th Century B.C. | | | 1st Century B.C. | 1st Century A.D. | | 3rd Century A.D. | | 19th Century A.D. | 20th Century A.D. | |

| 400 B.C. | 300 B.C. | 200 B.C. | 100 B.C. | 1 A.D. | 100 A.D. | 200 A.D. | 300 A.D. | 1800 A.D. | 1900 A.D. | 2000 |

B.C.　　　Birth of Jesus　　　A.D.

These dates usually are written with the letters first: A.D. 939. In this book, dates will be labeled A.D. only when other dates in the chapter are labeled B.C. If a year has no letters with it, you can assume it is A.D.

Historians use other time labels.

Besides numbering individual years, historians also group years into useful divisions:

A *decade* is 10 years.
A *century* is 100 years.
A *millenium* is 1,000 years.

We live in the twentieth century, but our years are labeled 19—. Why are these years called the *twentieth* century? Remember that years are numbered from the birth of Jesus. The years A.D. 1 to A.D. 100 were the first century. The years 101 to 200 were the second century, and so on. Therefore, when someone mentions the fifteenth century, you should think of the years from 1401 to 1500.

The same division into centuries is used for the period of time before the birth of Jesus. The years from 100 B.C. to 1 B.C. are the first century B.C. The years from 500 B.C. to 401 B.C. are the fifth century B.C. Thus, an event in 735 B.C. took place in the eighth century B.C.

Ages and eras are broad time periods.

Sometimes historians talk about periods of time called *ages* or *eras*. For example, certain times in history are known as the Bronze Age or the Middle Ages or the Age of Reason. Other time periods may be called the Modern Era or the Industrial Era.

An age or era is a broad zone of time. Historians use these words to describe time periods when people shared certain patterns of life and thought. Thus, the Stone Age is the period of time when people made many of their tools from stone. The Industrial Era is the period of time during which people have made many of their goods in factories by the use of machines.

It is impossible to give exact dates for the end of one age and the beginning of another. Transitions from one age to another are always gradual, never a sudden leap. For example, we live in the Industrial Era. Scholars may say that the Industrial Era began around the year 1800 in Europe and the United States. For some parts of the world, however, the Industrial Era began just a few years ago, when factories and machines began to influence life in those places.

As one age succeeds another, human ways of living change, but there is never a complete break. Old ways of doing things carry over into the new age. Every age has deep roots in the past.

Section Review

Define: (a) decade, (b) century, (c) millenium, (d) age, (e) era

Answer:

1. (a) What system do people in the United States use to number the passing years? (b) Why will the year A.D. 2000 be numbered 5761 by many Jews? (c) Why will that same year be numbered 1378 by many Muslims?
2. Which year in each of the following pairs is more recent? (a) 736 B.C. or 1288 B.C. (b) A.D. 12 or 416 B.C. (c) A.D. 1593 or A.D. 1750
3. How many years apart are (a) A.D. 100 and 400 B.C.? (b) 1000 B.C. and 3000 B.C.? (c) 1200 B.C. and A.D. 1900?
4. In what century is each of the following dates? (a) 697 B.C. (b) A.D. 2010 (c) A.D. 1435

Critical Thinking

5. Why are the dates for the beginning and end of an age or era only approximate?
6. (a) What label would you choose to describe the present period of history? (b) Would this term apply to all parts of the world or only to certain regions?

Unit I
The Beginnings of Civilization

Change came slowly in the early years of human prehistory and history. Yet the achievements of these times are the basis for our world today. During the prehistoric ages, people learned to make tools, use language, and raise food. Beginning about 3500 B.C., people started to build cities. With cities came many other developments— formal laws and governments, organized religions, a broad variety of jobs, and the keeping of written records.

At first, cities existed only in a few widely separated river valleys. The cities of Southwest Asia grew up in the valleys of the Tigris and Euphrates rivers. The rich kingdom of Egypt arose in the valley of the Nile. On the Indian subcontinent, carefully planned cities sprang up near the Indus River and then disappeared mysteriously. In northern China, the first cities were built in the valley of the Yellow River.

With these civilizations developed some of the world's major religions. Judaism arose in Southwest Asia, Buddhism in India, and Confucianism in China.

Some of these civilizations grew into mighty empires. The Han dynasty in China, Persian rulers in Southwest Asia, and the Mauryans in India all created empires that helped to preserve the achievements of their civilizations.

Persian emperor's audience hall, Persepolis

Chapter 1

300,000 *B.C.* - 3500 *B.C.*   ## *Prehistoric Cultures*

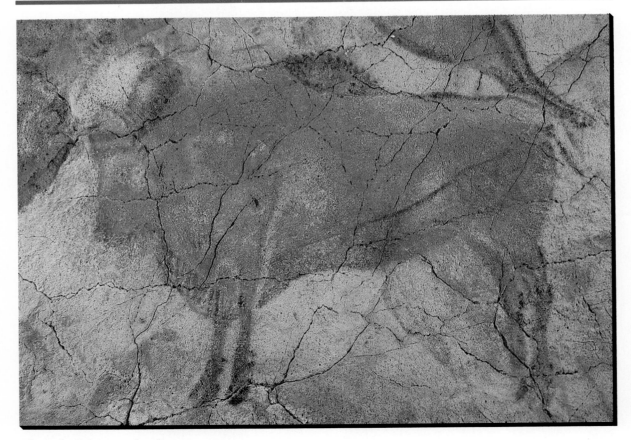

The Paleolithic people of Altamira lived by hunting. Their cave paintings reflect their careful observations of the animals on which they depended for food.

1. **Prehistory lacks written records.**

2. **Paleolithic people hunted and gathered.**

3. **Neolithic people learned to farm.**

In 1868, in a rugged, rock-strewn part of northeastern Spain, a hunting dog became trapped in a pile of boulders. The hunter shoved aside some of the stones to free the dog and found that the rock pile had covered the mouth of a cave.

The cave lay on a farm known as Altamira (AHL-tuh-**MIHR**-uh). It looked no different from many other caves in that part of Spain. However, in 1879, the owner of the land, Don Marcelino de Sautuola, decided to explore the cave. He was an amateur **archaeologist**. An archaeologist is a person who studies the remains of ancient societies.

Archaeologists look for tools, bones, artwork, jewelry, traces of housing, ashes from ancient campfires—anything that will give them clues to the way people lived in the long-vanished past. Don Marcelino hoped to find traces of early human beings in the cave.

While Don Marcelino searched the floor of the cave, his 12-year-old daughter, Maria, wandered farther into its long, winding passages. As she turned her lantern upward at the cave's low ceiling, Maria suddenly saw something that had been hidden from human eyes for thousands of years. Paintings of bison, horses, deer, wolves, and boars covered the ceiling. The red, black, and violet paints were still vivid. Maria shouted to her father. He too stared in awe. Soon afterward he told other archaeologists of the amazing discovery.

No one had imagined that ancient artists could paint such figures. Most scholars of the 1800's thought that ancient people did not have the ability, the intelligence, or the interest to create such works of art. As a result, Don Marcelino was mocked and criticized by many archaeologists. Some even charged him with fraud, saying he had had the paintings done.

Today's archaeologists, however, believe that the lifelike animals of the Altamira cave were painted by skilled artists who lived between 12,000 and 15,000 years ago. Other caves with similar paintings have been discovered in southern Europe. Carvings of animals and human figures have also been found. Even stone tools such as knife blades and arrowheads were often made in beautiful, leaflike shapes. It seems clear that the people who shaped these tools liked beauty for its own sake, just as people do today.

What can we learn of this very distant part of the human past? How much can anyone today really know about people who lived and died 15,000 years ago? The answer seems to be "not much—but more than you might think." Archaeologists have made a number of discoveries about the distant past, the period of time known as **prehistory**.

Prehistory lacks written records. 1

To reconstruct the human past, historians rely on written records. They examine old letters, diaries, legal documents, business ledgers, ancient clay tablets, scrolls of Chinese silk, bound books, inscriptions on stone monuments—in short, anything with written symbols.

However, writing is a comparatively recent invention. Human beings lived on earth for thousands of years before they learned to record their thoughts in writing. No one knows exactly when the first human beings appeared, but many scientists believe that the most ancient traces of *Homo sapiens* ("thinking man") go back 250,000 or 300,000 years. Of this vast stretch of time, written records cover only the last 5,000 years. Prehistory is the long, long period of time before written records.

In the absence of writings, scholars must look for other kinds of information about prehistoric times. Pieces of stone or bone that were used as tools are clues to early ways of life. A patch of ashes under several layers of soil may show where someone built a fire in ancient times. A place where the ground is slightly softer and darker than the earth around it may show where, long ago, someone put in a post to support a tent.

Sometimes prehistoric stone tools or ancient pieces of bone turn up on the surface of the ground, uncovered when wind or water wears the soil away. Sometimes people find these items by accident when plowing or digging a well. Sometimes archaeologists try to guess where early people might have lived and then dig there.

Much important information about ancient times is undoubtedly buried under our modern work places, housing developments, and shopping centers. Construction crews may uncover traces of ancient buildings when digging for a new subway. Archaeologists must then work quickly to study the clues before they are destroyed.

Dates are difficult to determine.

One of the most important questions archaeologists must answer is, "When did the group of people who made this item live?" Over the years, archaeologists have developed many ways of dating the material they find.

One way of determining dates is by carefully noting just where an object is found. When archaeologists find a prehistoric campsite, they slowly dig downward through layer after layer of soil. Obviously, the items they find in the bottom layer are the oldest of all. The items found closest to the surface are the newest.

Another method of dating is by comparing items from one site to those from another site.

Suppose someone finds a particular kind of arrowhead at a certain layer in a campsite in France. Later another archaeologist finds a similar arrowhead somewhere else. If the two arrowheads are very much alike, archaeologists may assume that both come from about the same time period.

Such methods can provide *relative* dates—that is, they can tell which of several items is the oldest, which is youngest, and which falls between. However, these methods do not give *absolute* dates. An absolute date is a number, such as 15,400 B.C. or A.D. 1000.

Archaeologists have found several ways of determining absolute dates. One of the best known is called the carbon 14 method. Carbon 14 is a form of radioactive carbon found in all living things. After a living thing dies, the carbon 14 slowly changes to regular carbon. Scientists know the rate at which this change takes place. By measuring how much carbon 14 remains, scientists can tell how long an animal or plant has been dead. Thus, if bits of burned wood or bone turn up at a prehistoric tent site, an archaeologist may be able to tell approximately how long ago the tent builders lived. Several other radioactive elements can be used in similar ways to provide absolute dates.

Archaeologists have also found other ways to pinpoint prehistoric dates. In parts of Europe, scientists have counted the layers of clay deposited year by year at the bottom of lakes. Elsewhere, especially in the southwestern United States, experts can measure dates by counting tree rings. By comparing pieces of wood from prehistoric sites with trees that are still living (some up to 4,000 years old), experts sometimes can tell when the ancient wood was cut.

Archaeologists make deductions about society and culture.

Like people today, prehistoric people lived in social groups. They lived in a network of relationships with other human beings, including family members, neighbors, or nearby groups with whom their paths crossed regularly. Such a network of people who interact with one another is called a **society**.

People who live and work together share many habits, ideas, skills, traditions, and values. All these habitual ways of thinking and acting make up the society's **culture**. Culture is the way of life that a group of people develops and passes on to its children. Every group of human beings—from the most ancient to the most modern, from the smallest to the largest—has a culture. A group's language, tools and skills, beliefs and traditions, ways of organizing itself, and much

An archaeologist in Mexico works painstakingly to remove ancient remains embedded in the rocky soil. Even jeweler's tools are used for this especially delicate work.

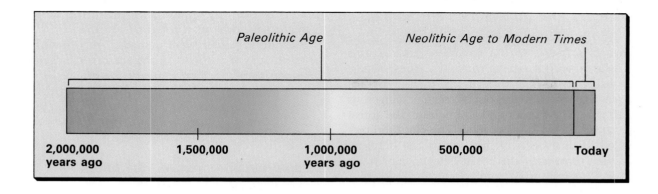

	Paleolithic Age			Neolithic Age to Modern Times	
2,000,000 years ago	1,500,000	1,000,000 years ago	500,000		Today

more are all part of its culture. Culture has been described as "a blueprint for living." From birth to death, most of human life is spent learning, following, and passing on this blueprint.

A single stone tool from prehistoric times tells little about ancient society or culture. However, archaeologists can find clues to social relationships in the way an ancient campsite was arranged. By investigating many, many items, they can begin to find cultural patterns. As you read the following sections, notice the way archaeologists have used clues to make deductions about ancient cultures.

Archaeologists have discovered an amazing amount of information from a wide variety of clues. Because many of the items that survive from prehistoric times are stone tools or bones of animals, archaeologists know a great deal about how ancient people got their food and made their tools. Archaeologists can also make fairly good guesses about prehistoric housing and the number of people who lived together. However, we know very little about prehistoric people's thoughts and feelings, their religious beliefs, or their ideas of right and wrong. Only by careful detective work can modern scholars put together a partial picture of an ancient way of life.

Section Review 1

Define: (a) archaeologist, (b) prehistory, (c) relative date, (d) absolute date, (e) society, (f) culture
Answer:
1. What is the main difference between the study of history and the study of prehistory?

2. How can archaeologists date their findings?
3. (a) What parts of prehistoric culture are best known from their remains? (b) What parts are least known?

Critical Thinking
4. (a) Suggest some reasons why finding the cave paintings of Altamira was more important than finding a large group of stone tools would have been. (b) Why do you think scholars were unwilling to believe Don Marcelino at first?

Paleolithic people hunted and gathered. 2

The earliest part of human prehistory is known as the Paleolithic (PAY-lee-uh-LITH-ik) Age, or the Old Stone Age. (*Paleo* comes from the Greek word for "old," and *lithos* was the Greek word for "stone.") Scholars call this period the Stone Age because people in those years used stone to make many of their basic tools. As the graph on this page shows, the Paleolithic Age was by far the longest part of humankind's past.

The Paleolithic period is sometimes also called the Ice Age. Several times in the past 2 million years, temperatures grew colder all over the world. Each time, huge ice sheets spread out from the polar regions. When these ice sheets were at their greatest extent, they covered much of northern Europe and North America. Then, when the weather warmed, the ice sheets retreated. These climate changes probably forced early people to learn to cope with a variety of conditions.

Hunters and gatherers were nomads.

Picture a grassy plain in eastern Africa at the edge of a forest, with a stream or lake nearby. It was in such a setting that the earliest people probably lived. The trees in the forest provided a place to rest at night, out of reach of dangerous animals. The plants and animals of the forest provided many kinds of food. The plain too provided food, especially meat from the herds of animals that grazed there. The lake provided water as well as fish, frogs, and other animal life.

By living where different environments met, early humans had a wide choice of food. If they failed to find one kind of food, they could look for another. Variety meant safety from starvation.

Women and children roamed through the tall grasses and clumps of trees to gather roots, berries, nuts, and seeds. Women were the plant specialists of the Old Stone Age. Their work probably provided most of the food people ate every day.

While the women gathered plant foods, small parties of men set out from the camp to track down game. They hunted everything from rabbits to elephants. The hunters' work supplied only a small share of the calories people needed each day. However, the protein in the meat they brought back was vital for good health.

Paleolithic people were **nomads**. They moved often in search of food. As the seasons changed or when game became scarce, they traveled to a new campsite. Probably they followed regular routes, revisiting the same places from year to year. In this way, they would come to know a broad stretch of territory very well.

People became skilled tool users.

Tools and the skills to use those tools make up a group's **technology**. Technology is an important part of a group's culture. Technology is the part of prehistoric culture that archaeologists know most about, because they have found the tools that early people used. In turn, the tools tell much about the skills people must have had.

Tools The earliest tools of the Old Stone Age are crudely made choppers. The toolmaker took a stone and knocked a few chips off one side to make a jagged edge. Such chopping tools probably were used to cut up game after hunters had made a kill. The latest tools of the Old Stone Age are beautifully made knife blades and spearheads that

About 10,000 years ago, someone used the stone at the left to start fires, striking it with flint to make a spark. Other prehistoric tools ranged from crude hand axes (lower right) to antler spears to finely worked arrowheads.

The stone at left is not a tool but rather the core that remained after an ancient toolmaker struck off many sharp flakes. The flakes (such as the one in the center) were used as scrapers. Sometimes people refined the edges of the points by more chipping to make them sharper.

took hours of expert chipping. People's tool-making skills improved greatly over the long period of time included in the Old Stone Age. The best tools clearly show the makers' pride in their work.

Undoubtedly, people of the Old Stone Age used a wide variety of materials to make tools. Besides stone, they used wood, bone, and hide. However, those materials decay, and so we know less about tools made from them.

The use of fire As hunters and gatherers moved from place to place, they learned to live in many kinds of environments. Ever so slowly, groups spread over the world. Prehistoric campsites in Europe and Asia show circles of ash, burned bones, and heat-cracked rocks. The people who lived in those camps had learned to use fire to help them survive in a cold climate.

Fire greatly changed the way people lived. Of course, it helped to protect them from cold. Just as important, it was a protection against dangerous

Footnote to History

One of the materials that prehistoric people used to make cutting tools was obsidian, a black glass formed naturally by volcanoes. A prehistoric toolmaker could make an obsidian blade that was as sharp as a modern surgeon's knife.

animals. It also provided light, so that people could continue to make tools, prepare food, and talk together after nightfall. Much later, people also learned to use fire to cook their food. Beginning with these ancient campfires, the hearth came to stand for home, for family, and for a warm welcome.

People lived in small groups.

The groups that gathered around these fires probably were fairly small. Groups who lived by hunting and gathering in more recent times usually lived in groups of 25 to 40 individuals. Most were probably blood relatives—parents, children, uncles, aunts, and cousins.

Such groups stayed small for two reasons. First, a given area of land would support only so many people. When a band grew too large to find food within a reasonable distance, people usually divided into two smaller groups and drifted apart. Second, quarrels were less likely to break out while groups stayed small. If individuals found they could not get along together, again the group might divide to prevent violence.

Language One of the most important social developments that took place in the Old Stone Age was the development of language. Although no one knows what Paleolithic languages were like, archaeologists are certain that Paleolithic people could speak. These people hunted large animals that could have been killed only by a group of hunters working together. Some of these hunts involved planning ahead to drive game into dead-end valleys or other areas that were natural traps. Such teamwork probably relied on language. No one knows exactly when people began to develop language, but it was an early and important achievement.

A society of equals Paleolithic hunters and gatherers lived with one another as equals. They had no place for kings, nobles, or chiefs. As nomads, they owned few possessions, and food from the hunt probably was shared with everyone in the group.

Of course, there were differences within the group. The best hunters probably enjoyed extra respect. The oldest members of the group undoubtedly supplied advice, based on their long experience, when food or water was hard to find.

Early hunters and gatherers may have built temporary shelters similar to this dwelling, called a scherm, made by the Kung of the Kalahari Desert.

Some clues to ancient societies come from studies of more recent groups of hunters and gatherers such as the Kung of Africa's Kalahari (KAH-luh-HAHR-ee) Desert and the Aborigines (AB-uh-RIHJ-uh-neez) of Australia. These people are quick to put down anyone who tries to win power over others. Scholars have found that equality and sharing are the rules for survival.

Paleolithic beliefs remain a mystery.

Beliefs and traditions are an important part of every group's culture, yet these are just the parts of Paleolithic culture about which we know the least. Without writing, people in the Old Stone Age could not leave explicit records of their thoughts and feelings. Again, archaeologists must look for other clues.

Hunting magic The cave paintings of Altamira and similar works found at Lascaux (las-KOH) are some of the most important clues to the thoughts of Paleolithic people. However, no one knows for certain how to interpret them. Most scholars assume that the ancient artists created their paintings as a form of magic. Animals as food were vital to the survival of hunters and gatherers. Perhaps people believed that painting a bison or a deer would magically bring the animals close. A few paintings actually show animals that have been speared. Perhaps these were meant to bring luck in the hunt.

The paintings are skillfully done, showing a beautiful sense of movement and line. Few hunters can have had the time or talent to become so skilled at painting. Thus these pictures probably were the work of specialists. The artist-magician may have worked for the whole group and been rewarded with gifts of food.

Treatment of the dead A few tantalizing clues suggest that these very early people may have thought about the question of life after death. In a cave in Iraq, archaeologists found a body that had been buried more than 40,000 years ago. The person had been laid to rest on a bed of pine boughs and bright flowers. Numerous other burials from Paleolithic times show that treasured objects and food were often placed in graves. These may be the first signs of belief in a soul that lives after the body dies.

Hunting and gathering worked well for thousands of years.

People today usually picture life in Paleolithic times as harsh, uncomfortable, and filled with danger. Admittedly, the lives of Paleolithic people often were cut short by accident, injury, or illness. It is true, too, that these people had few possessions because of their nomadic life. Still, in many ways, the hunters and gatherers of the Paleolithic Age lived well. Food was usually plentiful and their varied diet was a healthy one. Moreover, finding food took only a few hours of work each day. There was plenty of time left for storytelling, singing, dancing, and playing.

The hunting and gathering way of life served people well for thousands of years, but it had one great weakness. To be sure of a reliable food supply, hunters and gatherers needed large areas of land. As the number of people in the world slowly increased, less and less land was available for each group. Hunters and gatherers faced the threat of hunger. As a result, the stage was set for the next period of prehistory.

Section Review 2

Define: (a) nomad, (b) technology
Answer:
1. Why was the Paleolithic Age given its name?
2. How did Paleolithic people acquire their food?
3. (a) What conclusions have scholars drawn about the organization of Paleolithic societies? (b) About Paleolithic religious ideas?
4. How did an increasing population eventually cause a problem for hunters and gatherers?

Critical Thinking
5. List three developments of lasting importance that took place during the Paleolithic Age. Explain why you consider each important.

Voice from the Past · *Mysterious Markings*

About 30,000 years ago, a toolmaker in France used a piece of bone to sharpen the edge of stone tools by flaking off chips of rock. Evidently, the toolmaker kept this piece of bone for a long time, using it over and over. When archaeologists found the piece of bone and looked at it very carefully, they saw that it had been used in another way as well. The bone was covered with tiny scratches made over a long period of time, using different points. There was a total of 69 marks, which formed a snakelike pattern back and forth across the piece. Archaeologist Alexander Marschak writes:

It was almost as though someone, 25,000 years before the development of writing and arithmetic, was keeping a record of some process . . . The twists and turns [in the line of scratch marks] corresponded to the changing phases of the moon, all the full moons falling at the left, all the half-moons in the middle, and all the crescents at the right. The fit was perfect for an observational lunar notation.

1. What evidence does the archaeologist provide that this item was something like a calendar?
2. What other evidence from the Paleolithic Age might suggest that people then were capable of making a calendar?
3. Why might people have wanted a record of the phases of the moon?

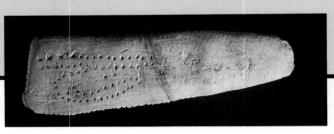

Neolithic people learned to farm.

3

Ten thousand years ago, there were fewer people in the whole world than there are today in New York City. Perhaps 10 million people were spread over the entire globe. By the standards of hunters and gatherers, however, the world was already becoming crowded. People began to look for ways to find more food.

This period of time, beginning about 10,000 years ago in Europe and Asia, is called the New Stone Age, or the Neolithic (NEE-uh-LITH-ik) Age. Compared to the Paleolithic Age, the Neolithic Age was a time of rapid change. Many of the discoveries that form the basis for modern life took place in the Neolithic Age. The most important of these discoveries were farming and herding.

Women began to plant seeds.

Wild plants had been an important source of food in the Paleolithic Age. As a result, people already knew a great deal about how plants grew. They knew where different kinds of plants thrived and when each kind ripened. Prehistoric people probably knew how to grow plants from seed long before anyone actually did so.

Because women probably did most of the gathering of plant foods in ancient times, many archaeologists think women were the first farmers. Some sort of farming may have begun while people were still nomads. Women may have sowed the seeds of favorite food plants near a regular campsite. In that way, when the group returned later, they would be able to find the plants easily.

As the world's population increased, wild food became scarcer. These little fields that were planted purposely became more and more important for a group's survival. People began to spend more time caring for their food plants. Children may have been set to work pulling up weeds so that the food plants had a better chance to grow. People also learned not to eat up all the seeds they raised but to save some seeds for planting next year.

Herders domesticated animals.

Just as early gatherers observed plants closely, early hunters were experts on animals. Gradually, some of these animals were tamed for human use. Which animals were tamed first varied from region to region.

In northern Europe, dogs were probably the first animals to be domesticated. Wild dogs may have hung around the edges of human camps in search of meat scraps. Perhaps people found dogs useful for giving warning when dangerous animals or strangers approached.

In Southwest Asia, sheep and goats were the earliest domestic animals. Many times, hunters must have killed a female animal and then found its young. If the hunters had no immediate need for more food, it would have been easy to keep the young animals and let them graze near the camp until they grew larger. Such half-wild, half-tame animals may have been the first herds that humans kept for food. The bones of domestic sheep have been unearthed in Southwest Asia at sites 10,000 years old (8000 B.C.). Pigs were domesticated about 8,500 years ago in that region, and cattle nearly 7,500 years ago. As game became scarcer, these animals became the main sources of meat.

People settled in permanent homes.

As people spent more and more time caring for their food plants, they began to settle near the fields they had planted. Instead of moving whenever the seasons changed or the herds of game migrated, people stayed in one place.

The Neolithic Age was the time when many settled villages sprang up. Farmers needed a place where the soil was fairly fertile. They also needed a steady supply of water. Therefore, most early settlements grew up around a spring or near a stream.

Jarmo A good example of an early farming village is the archaeological site of Jarmo in Southwest Asia. Jarmo is located in what is now Iraq and dates from about 6750 B.C.

How did the people of Jarmo live nearly 9,000 years ago? Evidence shows that the village was made up of about 25 mud houses. Each house had several rectangular rooms divided by mud

The Neolithic way of life spread to many parts of the world. These prehistoric houses are from a village in the islands north of Scotland.

walls. The houses were roofed with brush or reeds plastered with more mud. Jarmo probably was home to about 150 people.

The people of Jarmo did not have as healthy a diet as their ancestors who lived by hunting and gathering. In Jarmo, people grew barley and wheat. (Wild varieties of those grains grow in the nearby hills.) They also had peas and lentils to eat, but it is not clear whether they grew those plants or gathered them from the wild. For meat, the people of Jarmo raised goats and hunted gazelles, wild sheep, and wild pigs. From the number of shells found at Jarmo, it appears that villagers also ate a great many snails.

Çatal Hüyük Not all Neolithic settlements were as tiny as Jarmo. In what is now Turkey, archaeologists found the remains of a larger town, Çatal Hüyük (chuh-**TUL** hoo-**YOOK**). Indeed, with more than 3,000 people, Çatal Hüyük was almost a city.

The residents of Çatal Hüyük had many luxuries that other Neolithic groups lacked. For example, they had mirrors made of obsidian. They also had begun to work with metals, making beads and tubes of copper and lead.

Located high on a plateau, Çatal Hüyük stood in the midst of a region rich in minerals. The people of Çatal Hüyük built up a busy trade based on their mineral wealth. Traders also took finished goods made by Çatal Hüyük's skillful stonecutters. They shaped axes, knives, mirrors, bowls, bracelets and beads.

The town boasted a number of shrines. Some had figures of male and female gods. Others featured figures of stags or leopards. Still others had clay heads of bulls decorated with actual horns from wild cattle. As with the Paleolithic period, however, modern investigators cannot be sure how all these shrines fit together in the religious beliefs of Çatal Hüyük's people.

21

People developed new skills.

Farming required a different kind of technology from hunting and gathering. To the extent that people still hunted, they continued to need spears, arrows, and bows. However, they also needed tools to scratch and loosen the soil for planting. They needed sickles to harvest their grain and grinding tools to make the grain into flour. When archaeologists find those tools, they know that people were beginning to farm. As a result of these new needs, a number of important technological developments took place in the New Stone Age.

Pottery People who lived as hunters and gatherers found food as they needed it. When people began to live by farming, they harvested their crops once or twice each year. Suddenly, they faced the problem of storing food for use all year long. People needed to protect their harvest from dampness, insects, and also the hungry hordes of rats and mice who quickly moved into the new farming villages.

In many parts of the world, the answer to the food storage problem was pottery. The earliest farmers made containers of stone, wood, or basketry. Pottery jars, however, were easier and faster to make. Moreover, clay was available along many stream banks and riverbeds. The earliest potters shaped their lumps of clay into bowls and jars simply by molding the clay with their hands. Later, people learned to make smoother, rounder shapes by turning the clay on a wheel.

Once people learned to harden the clay by firing it in ovens, clay pots became an important part of everyday life. Broken pottery pieces are so common at ancient living sites that archaeologists often study the pottery to determine the date of the culture.

Ground stone tools Among the many changes that took place in the Neolithic period was a new way of making stone tools. Toolmakers no longer chipped or flaked pieces of stone to make a sharp edge. Instead, they began to grind and polish pieces of stone to sharpen them.

The new kinds of tools had several advantages. First, many of the toughest kinds of rock cannot be chipped or flaked. With grinding, people could use these harder kinds of rocks to make more durable tools. Second, when a ground tool becomes dull, it can be sharpened by regrinding. Thus, the same tool could be used for a much longer period of time. With the new, durable axes, farmers could cut trees and clear even more land for farming.

Farming began in many places.

The changeover from hunting and gathering to farming took place not once but many times. Archaeologists have found evidence that a number of groups learned independently to farm. In Southwest Asia, China, Southeast Asia, Central America, and other places—perhaps some yet undiscovered—people learned how to raise plants from seed. People became food producers rather than food finders.

In each place, early farmers began with foods that grew wild nearby. Thus, farmers in Southwest

This clay model from the Neolithic period shows a potter using a wheel to make jars for storing food. Potters used a variety of natural dyes to decorate their works.

Daily Life • *Spinning and Weaving*

At many Neolithic sites, tiny circular objects with holes in the center are a common find. To most modern people, these objects are mysterious, but any Neolithic child would have recognized them. They are spindle whorls, or weights that helped a spindle turn. The presence of these objects show that people were spinning thread. Archaeologists have also found loom weights, showing that people wove the thread into cloth. Plants such as cotton and flax (for making linen) and wool from sheep were probably the earliest sources of cloth.

Each village household probably made its own clothing, from raw fiber to finished garment. Family members sheared wool from the sheep, spun the wool into thread, wove the thread into cloth, and sewed the cloth into clothing.

Asia raised wheat and barley. In Central America, corn (or maize) became the main crop. In parts of Asia, farmers raised rice. Then, from each of the centers where farming was invented, the idea spread outward.

It is important to remember, however, that the change did not affect the whole world. None of the great changes of history affected everyone, everywhere, once and for all. Even today, a few isolated groups in the world still live by hunting and gathering. The Kung of the Kalahari Desert lived as hunters and gatherers until very recently. Some Inuit (**IN**-oo-it) of Alaska and northern Canada follow traditional ways and live by hunting. Although the number of hunters and gatherers grew fewer with each passing year, the spread of farming took thousands of years.

Farming led to population growth.

The slow, slow growth of the human population during the Paleolithic Age forced people to look for new ways of providing food. The discovery of farming and herding in the Neolithic Age seemed to solve that problem. But the new food supply had an unexpected result. After the discovery of farming, the world's population began to increase at a much faster pace.

Change piled upon change. The long time span of the Paleolithic Age had been marked by few changes. Beginning in the Neolithic Age, however, people in almost every generation found new ways of living. Many of the changes were tiny, but they added up. All the changes that took people from the nomadic life style of hunters and gatherers to today's giant cities follow step by step from the crucial discoveries made in the Neolithic Age.

Section Review 3

Define: (a) Neolithic Age, (b) obsidian, (c) spindle whorl
Identify: (a) Jarmo, (b) Çatal Hüyük
Answer:

1. How did the knowledge that people had developed as hunters and gatherers help them in becoming farmers and herders?
2. Why did farming lead to the development of villages?
3. How was Çatal Hüyük different from Jarmo?
4. (a) Describe two important advances in technology that took place in the Neolithic Age. (b) How was each related to farming?
5. Why did different types of farming develop in different parts of the world?
6. What was the long-term effect of farming on world population?

Critical Thinking

7. Suggest at least three ways that the change from hunting and gathering might have affected social life within a group. Explain your conclusions.

Summary

1. Prehistory lacks written records. Human beings lived for many thousands of years before they invented writing. Therefore, scholars learn about these prehistoric people through the physical remains of their culture rather than through written records. Archaeologists use scientific methods to determine when an object was made. Archaeologists then make deductions about prehistoric societies based on their investigations of remains and artifacts.

2. Paleolithic people hunted and gathered. The earliest part of prehistory is known as the Paleolithic Age, or Old Stone Age. Paleolithic people traveled from place to place in search of food. They lived in small family groups and made tools of stone, wood, bone, and hide. Eventually, they learned to use fire for cooking and warmth. Scholars believe they also had spoken languages and religions. Hunting and gathering became more difficult as the number of people increased.

3. Neolithic people learned to farm. The Neolithic Age, or New Stone Age, began about 10,000 years ago. During the Neolithic Age, people in many parts of the world gave up a nomadic way of life and settled down in permanent homes to farm. Scholars believe that farming began because early people could no longer find enough food by hunting and gathering. Since farming required a different kind of technology from hunting and gathering, Neolithic people invented pottery and improved their tools by learning to grind stone. The invention of farming marked the beginning of a rapid series of changes that led to modern life.

Reviewing the Facts

1. Define the following terms:
   a. archaeologist   d. culture
   b. prehistory   e. nomad
   c. society   f. technology
2. Explain the importance of each of the following names or places:
   a. Altamira   d. Paleolithic Age
   b. Jarmo   e. Neolithic Age
   c. Çatal Hüyük
3. (a) How can archaeologists sometimes determine which of two prehistoric events was the earlier? (b) How can archaeologists sometimes determine actual dates for prehistoric events?
4. How do scholars learn about the cultures of prehistoric people?
5. (a) Why did Paleolithic people move often? (b) Why did they live in small groups? (c) What were some of their religious beliefs?

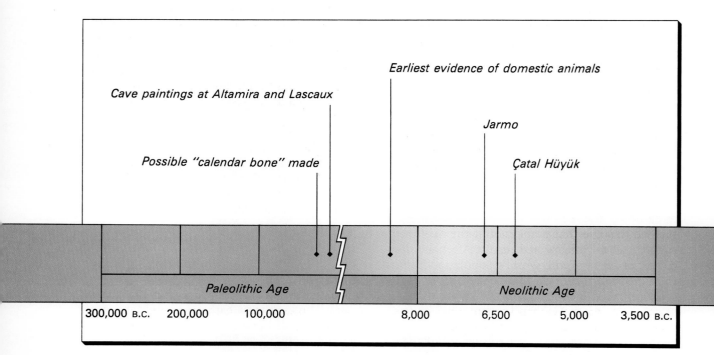

Earliest evidence of domestic animals

Cave paintings at Altamira and Lascaux

Jarmo

Possible "calendar bone" made

Çatal Hüyük

| | Paleolithic Age | | | Neolithic Age | |

300,000 B.C.   200,000   100,000   8,000   6,500   5,000   3,500 B.C.

6. Why did Neolithic people change to a settled way of life?
7. What differences in technology distinguish Neolithic from Paleolithic groups?

Thinking about History

1. The English philosopher Thomas Hobbes once described a life such as those led by the Paleolithic hunters as "solitary, poor, nasty, brutish, and short." In light of what you have read about Paleolithic societies, decide whether you agree or disagree with Hobbes. Perhaps you agree with parts of his description but not others. Explain your reactions.
2. The transition to Neolithic times has been called "the food-producing revolution." Why might the ability to raise one's own food be a revolutionary change for human beings? (Do any other living things produce their own food? How do they live?)
3. Suppose you traveled back in time to Jarmo or Çatal Hüyük. What modern idea, tool, or invention would be most useful to take with you. Explain your answer.

Writing and Speaking about History

1. A thesis is a position or an argument that the historian seeks to prove with supporting data. Write a thesis statement that tells why the study of history is valuable for you. Give several reasons to support your thesis.
2. List and categorize the kinds of evidence archaeologists examine to aid historians in analyzing prehistoric times.
3. Portray an archaeologist who has just discovered a remnant of a prehistoric group. Prepare an informal talk in which you identify what you have discovered and explain what the artifact reveals about the time period or people.

Practicing Skills

1. In 8000 B.C., the population of the world was about 10 million. In an almanac, find the present population of the world. What factors might account for a growth or decline in the population in an area?
2. (a) What do the letters A.D. tell about a date? (b) What do the letters B.C. tell about a date?

(c) How many years apart are 12,000 B.C. and A.D. 1967?
3. (a) What years does the third decade B.C. include? (b) What years does the fourteenth century A.D. include? (c) What years does the fourth millenium B.C. include?
4. (a) According to the time line on page 24, which came first: the cave paintings at Altamira or the settlement at Çatal Hüyük? (b) How many years passed between the earliest evidence of domestic animals and the end of the Neolithic Age?
5. The following table shows where and when some of the world's first farming villages arose. Locate each of the places on an outline map of the world. Then use the information to make a time line that extends from 8000 B.C. to A.D. 2000 in thousand-year increments.

Southwest Asia	9,500 years ago
Greece	8,000 years ago
North China	7,000 years ago
Egypt	6,500 years ago
Pakistan	6,000 years ago
Thailand	6,000 years ago
Mexico	4,000 years ago
Peru	4,000 years ago

Investigating History

1. Even in this century, a few groups of people in different parts of the world continued to follow a hunting and gathering way of life. Some of these groups were the Kung (Bushmen), the Tasaday, the Inuit, the Aborigines, and the Mbuti. Choose one of these groups and find out about their culture. How are they living today?
2. The cave art of Altamira and Lascaux has been published in many strikingly beautiful books. Look in your library for books on the art of the Upper Paleolithic period. What kinds of paints were used? What do the paintings tell about the natural environment of the time?

Decision Making in History

As an archaeologist, what criteria would you use to judge whether a site was a good place for an archaeological dig? What kinds of items would you have to find to justify the expense of working in that location?

Chapter 2

Civilizations and Empires in Southwest Asia

This panel from a wooden box about 18 inches long comes from Ur, an early city in Southwest Asia. The people in the top row are nobles; those in the bottom row are herders. The figures are made of shell, red limestone, and lapis lazuli (a blue semiprecious stone).

1. **Civilization arose in the Fertile Crescent.**

2. **Newcomers contributed to civilization.**

3. **Conquerors ruled ever larger empires.**

About 4,000 years ago, a boy sprinted down a city street, kicking up dust as he ran. The morning sun had just begun to rise above the walls of the city. Even so, the boy knew he was already late for school, which was called the *edubba.*

Historians know of this boy and his school from ancient clay tablets found in Southwest Asia, in what is now the country of Iraq. Part of one tablet tells of a student's typical day:

When I awoke early in the morning, I faced my mother and said to her, "Give me my lunch. I want to go to school." My mother gave me two rolls and I set out. In school, the monitor in charge said to me, "Why are you late?" Afraid and with pounding heart, I entered before my teacher and made a respectful curtsy.

The tablet goes on to tell of eight other offenses that the boy committed in school that day, including mistakes in his writing lesson and talking without permission. For each offense, a school official called "the man who holds the whip" lashed the boy across his bare back. In fact, the boy did so poorly in school that his father invited the schoolmaster home for dinner and gave him gifts to keep the boy from failing.

Civilization arose in the Fertile Crescent. 1

The boy and his schoolmates were studying to be scribes—that is, professional writers—in an ancient region known to historians as the Fertile Crescent. On the map on page 28, you can see an arc of land with its eastern end touching the Persian Gulf and its western end lying along the Mediterranean Sea. Inside this arc is some of the best land for farming in Southwest Asia. The region's curved shape and the richness of its land led scholars to call it the Fertile Crescent. (Today this area lies within the nations of Israel, Jordan, Syria, Lebanon, and Iraq.)

In the western part of the ancient Fertile Crescent, the Jordan River watered grapevines, olive trees, and cedar trees. In the eastern part, ducks nested among the marshes created by the Tigris (TY-gris) and Euphrates (yoo-FRAY-teez) rivers. Along the northern curve of the Fertile Crescent, streams flowed down from the mountains. Wherever rivers and streams flowed, people built their villages. In ancient times, the settled life of farmers and villagers was possible only in lands with good supplies of water.

The land where the schoolboy made his home lay at the eastern end of the Fertile Crescent, between the Tigris and Euphrates rivers. This region is known as Mesopotamia (MEHS-uh-puh-TAY-mee-uh), which in Greek means "land between the rivers."

The schoolboy belonged to a group of people known as the Sumerians (soo-MEHR-ee-uhnz). Their homeland, Sumer (SOO-muhr), was in the southern part of Mesopotamia, in the marshes near the Persian Gulf. Sumer was neither a city nor a country in the modern sense of those words. Rather, it was a collection of separate cities with a common way of life.

Although the cities fought and squabbled constantly, the Sumerian people shared a common culture. Historians believe the Sumerians built the world's first civilization. The next pages will describe what a civilization is and how Sumer was different from any settlements people had ever built before.

Key traits define a civilization.

Every group of people has its own culture—its own way of life including language, tools, customs, and rules. However, not all groups have a way of life that is considered a **civilization.** Civilization is one form of culture—a very complicated form.

The Sumerians stand out in history as the first group of people to become civilized. They developed a new way of life that set them apart from neighboring peoples.

Just what set the Sumerians apart from their neighbors? Historians and other social scientists have struggled with the problem of defining exactly what makes one group of people civilized and another group not. Most scholars agree that the following traits are essential for civilization.

The growth of cities One of the key traits for civilization is cities. (In fact, the word *civilization* comes from the Latin word for *city.*) By 3000 B.C., the Sumerians had built at least a dozen fair-sized cities. For example, Uruk may have had a population of 10,000, and it continued to grow to around 20,000 over the next 200 years. In Lagash, there were about 19,000 people and in Umma, about 16,000. People elsewhere in Asia, Europe, and Africa lived in farming villages, but none of those tiny communities could rightly be called a city.

A city is more than a large group of people living close together. Population size alone does not make a village into a city. One of the most important differences between a city and a village is that a city is a center of trade for a larger area.

Like their modern descendants, ancient city dwellers depended on trade. Farmers, merchants, and traders brought goods to market in the cities. The city dwellers themselves produced a variety of goods for exchange, including pots, tools, and jewelry. Each person specialized in a certain kind

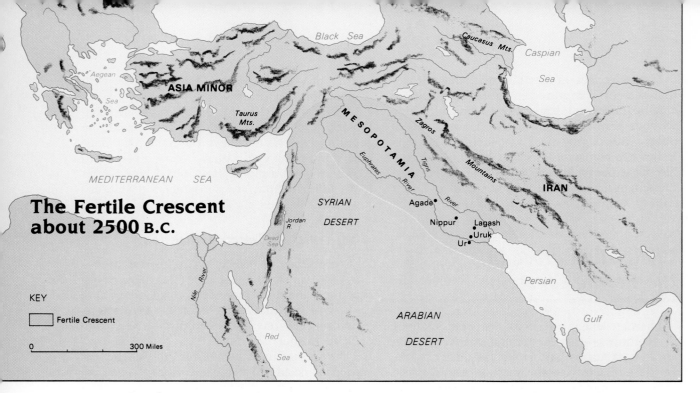

The Fertile Crescent about 2500 B.C.

KEY

Fertile Crescent

0   300 Miles

Map Study

What major rivers flow through the Fertile Crescent? Into what body of water do those rivers flow? What is the region between those rivers called? What region lies between the Black and Mediterranean seas?

of work and exchanged goods with other people who were also specialists. The importance of trade thus led to another key trait of civilization—specialized workers.

Specialized workers Think back on the Sumerian schoolboy who was studying to be a scribe. Day after day, scribes in Sumer wrote letters for people, copied down laws, and kept business records for merchants. Scribes were specialists. They traded their services for food, clothing, and roofs over their heads. Some of the other specialists in Sumer were schoolmasters, merchants, priests, and even "the man who holds the whip." Still others were potters, metalworkers, and weavers. Such skilled workers who make goods by hand are called **artisans.** Artisans became an important social group as cities developed.

In earlier human societies, nearly everyone had to spend most of the day getting food, either by hunting and gathering or by raising crops. In Sumer, for the first time in history, farmers were able to raise enough food to have a surplus. They could trade that extra food to a potter for clay pots or to a scribe in payment for writing a letter. Farmers also paid some of their surplus in taxes

to support the city government and the city temple with its priests.

Raising food was no longer a full-time job for everyone in the society. The ability to raise a surplus of food was the key that freed some people to do specialized jobs.

Writing Another essential trait of civilization also made its first appearance at Sumer—writing. Scholars call the Sumerians' way of writing **cuneiform** (kyoo-NEE-uh-fawrm) because of the letters' wedge-like shape. (In Latin, *cuneus* means "wedge.") The scribe's tool, called a stylus, was a sharpened reed with a wedge-shaped point. The scribe pressed the stylus into moist clay to create symbols. Then he laid the clay tablet in the sun to dry and harden.

Sumerians invented writing as a necessity of city life. Priests needed some way to keep track of the grain and other merchandise that moved in and out of the temple storehouses. Merchants needed accounts of debts and payments. The first written symbols, therefore, stood for commonly traded objects—a donkey, an ox, a sack of grain. These signs were called pictographs because they pictured the things they stood for.

Eventually, ideas became associated with certain pictures. For example, a house might also stand for the idea of protection or safety. Such signs are known as ideograms.

Still later, signs came to stand for certain sounds. Cuneiform signs did not stand for single sounds, as letters in the alphabet do today. Instead, each cuneiform sign stood for a whole syllable. Thus, a sign might stand for the word *mouth*, which in Sumerian was pronounced *ka*. In that form, the sign was a pictograph. But the same sign also stood for the sound *ka* when that sound was used in other words. By putting groups of signs together, scribes could write full sentences and express many ideas. They could create everything from financial records to poems.

Sumerian writing grew more and more efficient. The earliest tablets used about 2,000 different signs. By 3000 B.C., that number had been reduced to 800. By 2500 B.C., the number had been cut down even further to about 600 written signs. However, this was still such a large number that only a few people learned to read or write.

Advanced technology To their list of civilization's hallmarks, historians usually add another important trait—advanced technology. The Sumerians were skilled in many fields of science and technology. Many of the basic inventions on which humans depend originated in Sumer.

The wheel, the plow, and the sailboat seem like simple devices today. In Sumerian times, however, they were revolutionary. With the plow, farmers could raise more crops, creating the food surplus that Sumer's cities needed to exist. The wheel and the sailboat together vastly improved human ability to move goods over long distances for trade. All these devices were probably in daily use in Sumer by 3000 B.C.

Footnote to History

Sumerian schools taught the use of numbers as well as words. Sumerian mathematicians calculated everything in terms of the number 60. The symbol for 60, written 6 times, equaled 360, almost the number of days in a solar year. The Sumerians also divided circles into 360 parts (or degrees), which helped them measure angles for surveying and architecture. From this use of 60 comes today's circular clock divided into 60 minutes, each having 60 seconds.

Sumerian skill in metalworking shows in this golden helmet, dagger, and sheath from about 2450 B.C. Gold is too soft for use in battle, so these items were ceremonial.

The Sumerians were also skilled in working metal, although they were not the first people to make metal tools. People in Mesopotamia began using copper around 7000 B.C., at least 3,000 years before the Sumerians arrived. However, the Sumerians greatly increased the use of copper. They also used bronze, which is a mixture of copper and tin. Bronze is harder than pure copper and thus more useful for tools and weapons. After 2500 B.C., skilled metalworkers in Sumer's cities turned out bronze spearheads by the thousands. In fact, bronze eventually became so important in making tools of all kinds that the period of history beginning around 2800 B.C. at Sumer is often called the Bronze Age, just as earlier times were called the Stone Age.

Complex institutions As you might imagine, a bustling city required much more organization to run smoothly than did a tiny village or a group of wandering hunters. The long-lasting patterns of organization in a community are known as **institutions**. Complex institutions are another key trait of civilization.

Government is an example of an institution. For hunters and gatherers, family ties and group customs had supplied all the rules that were necessary. In cities, a new kind of government took shape. The ancient Sumerians were the first people to set up formal governments with officials and laws.

Organized religion is another type of institution. Villagers and hunters and gatherers had worshiped local gods and spirits. With the growth of cities, however, religion was organized in a new way. Most cities had great temples where dozens of priests took charge of religious duties. Priests often kept track of the yearly calendar, managed grain storehouses, and organized important rituals.

Thus, there are five key traits that set Sumer apart from all the human societies that existed before it: (1) the rise of cities; (2) specialized workers; (3) the use of writing; (4) advanced tools; and (5) complex institutions. All the later peoples who lived in this region of the world built upon these key Sumerian traits.

Sumerians faced geographic problems.

Sumer's civilization was shaped in part by the land in which the Sumerians lived. The Sumerians came to Mesopotamia about 4000 B.C. No one knows for sure where they came from. They found that the Tigris and Euphrates rivers flooded their new homeland at least once a year. As the floodwater receded, it left a thick bed of mud. In this rich, new soil, farmers could plant and harvest enormous quantities of wheat and barley.

Good soil was the advantage of living on the flat, swampy land of Sumer. There were three disadvantages.

The water problem The flooding of the rivers was dangerous because nobody could predict when it would happen. Sometimes it came as early as April, sometimes as late as June. Moreover, after the flood receded, the mud quickly dried out. Little or no rain fell, and the land became almost a desert. How could Sumerian farmers get enough water from the rivers during the dry summer months to make their barley grow?

The defense problem Sumer was a small region, only about the size of Massachusetts. It was also as flat as a tabletop. The villages were little clusters of reed huts standing in the middle of an open plain. With no natural barriers for protection, a Sumerian village was almost defenseless. Time

and again, nomadic herders from the nearby mountains and desert swooped down and stole the village's livestock and grain. How could the Sumerian villagers protect themselves?

The resource problem The natural resources of Sumer were extremely limited. Besides the fertile soil, there were huge reeds ten feet tall that grew in dense masses along the river's edge. With bundles of these reeds, people could make primitive boats and one-room huts. But they could not make hammers or axes. Without a good supply of stone, wood, and metal, what were the Sumerians to use for tools or buildings?

The solutions Over a period of 500 years (from about 3500 to 3000 B.C.), the Sumerians worked out ways to handle these problems. To help with the water problem, Sumerians dug irrigation ditches so that they could bring river water into the crop fields. To defend their settlements, they built city walls with mud bricks. To acquire more resources, Sumerians developed a broad trading network with the people of the mountains and the desert. Merchants from Sumer traded grain, cloth, and tools for stone, wood, and metal. By dealing with their problems, the Sumerians cleared the way for the growth of their civilization.

Sumerians created city-states.

Around each Sumerian city lay vast acres of barley and wheat. Each city and the surrounding countryside that it controlled was known as a **city-state.** These city-states included Ur, Kish, Nippur, Lagash, Uruk, and others.

Picture yourself in a field of grain with the mud-brick walls of Ur in the distance. It is early in the morning, but already the summer sun is almost too hot to bear. (By noon, it will be nearly 100°F.) All around, people are working barefoot in the irrigation ditches that run between patches of green plants. With stone hoes, the workers widen the ditches, bringing life-giving water into their fields from the reservoir a mile away. Without this elaborate irrigation network, the crops would die and the city-dwellers of Ur would starve.

Inside the city A broad dirt road leads from the fields up to the city's wall of mud bricks. Inside the city gate, the city dwellers go about their daily lives. A woman walks down a narrow lane with a jug of water balanced on her head.

Her dark hair is braided and coiled around her head. Her dress is a long, white cloth wrapped loosely around her, leaving her arms and one shoulder uncovered. Two men who pass wear skirtlike garments around their waists. Their hair falls down over their bare shoulders in wavy locks. Long, neatly trimmed beards hang low over their chests.

The dusty, unpaved streets are littered with garbage that people throw out their doorways. Most of the houses are small, windowless, one-story boxes packed tightly together along the street. However, a few wealthy families live in two-story houses with an inner courtyard. The courtyard allows some light and fresh air into these houses, but even rich people climb up to the flat roofs on summer nights to escape their stuffy rooms.

Trade The narrow streets finally open out onto a broad avenue where merchants squat under their awnings and trade a necklace for two or three sheep. This is the city's bazaar. People do not use coins to make purchases because money has not yet been invented. However, merchants and their customers know roughly how many pots of grain a farmer must give to buy a jug of wine. (This way of exchanging goods is called **barter**.) More complicated trades require the services of a scribe, who records on a clay tablet how much barley a certain farmer owes a certain merchant for a certain donkey.

The temple Farther down the main avenue stands Ur's tallest and most important building, the temple. Like a city within a city, the temple is surrounded by a heavy wall. Within the temple gate rises a massive, three-tiered structure known as a ziggurat (ZIHG-ur-aht), which means "mountain of god." Leading straight up the outside of the ziggurat is a flight of perhaps 100 mud-brick stairs. Every day, priests with shaved heads climb these stairs, sometimes dragging behind them a plump goat or sheep to sacrifice to Ur's gods.

The ziggurat was central to Sumerian cities.

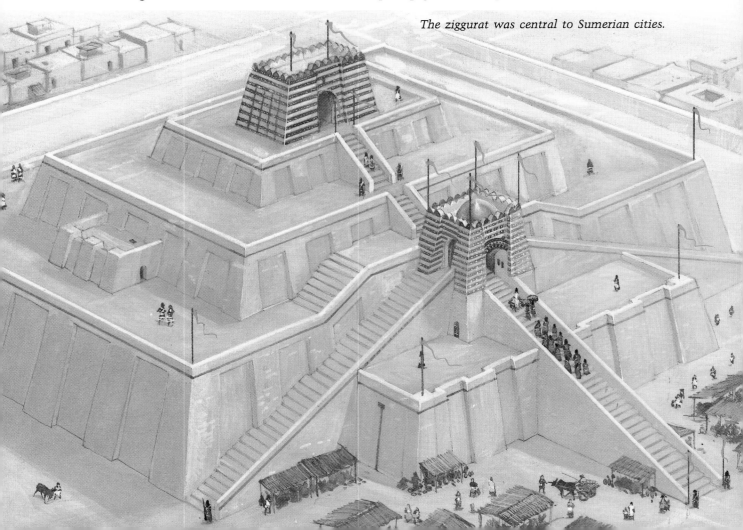

Sumerians believed in many gods.

Like many peoples in the Fertile Crescent, the Sumerians were **polytheists** (PAHL-ee-THEE-ists), believers in many gods. Anu (the god of heaven), Enlil (the god of clouds and air), and Ea (the god of water and floods) were the most powerful of their gods. Ranking slightly lower were the gods of the sun, moon, and stars. Then came those gods who inhabited the temple of a particular city-state. Next came the gods who dwelled in every Sumerian home. Lowest of all were demons known as Wicked Udugs, who caused disease, misfortune, and every kind of human trouble. Altogether, the Sumerians believed in roughly 3,000 gods.

Sumerians described their gods as doing many of the same things humans do—falling in love, having children, quarreling, and so on. Yet the Sumerians also believed that their gods were both immortal and all-powerful. The power of the gods was absolute. Humans were nothing but their servants. At any moment, the anger of the gods might strike, sending a fire, a flood, or an enemy army to destroy a city. To placate the gods, the people of Sumer built ziggurats and made rich offerings.

Sumerians worked hard to earn the gods' protection in this life, but they expected little help from the gods after death. The Sumerians believed that the souls of the dead went to the "land of no return," a dismal, gloomy place between the earth's crust and the ancient sea. No joy awaited souls there. According to a Sumerian poem about dead souls, "Dust is their fare and clay their food."

Priests and kings ruled Sumer.

Historians believe that Sumer's earliest governments were controlled by the temple priests. Only the priests knew how to please the city gods and thus keep Ur safe. The ziggurat was far more than a place of worship. It was like a city hall from which priests managed all the major industries of Sumer. They managed the irrigation system and told farmers when to plant and when to harvest. They also demanded a portion of every farmer's crop as taxes. Part of the tax was an offering to the gods, and the rest was used to feed the hundreds of laborers employed at the temple.

In time of war, however, the priests did not lead the city. Instead, the men of the city chose a tough fighter who could command the city's soldiers. At first, a commander's power ended as soon as the war was over. However, as wars between cities became more and more frequent, the commander gradually became a full-time ruler, or king. This ruler usually passed his power on to his sons.

After 3000 B.C., every Sumerian city had both a powerful group of priests and a king. Most cities then had two great buildings, the priests' temple and the royal palace.

Gudea was king of the Sumerian city-state of Lagash about 2100 B.C. He was a pious king who built a great temple to the chief god of Lagash.

Sumerian society had many classes.

With civilization came greater differences between groups in society—between the rich and the poor, noble and peasant, free person and slave. A village farmer who visited Ur would have noticed at once that the priests and nobles were much wealthier than the village leaders back home. Priests and kings made up the highest level in Sumerian society. Wealthy merchants ranked next. The vast majority of ordinary Sumerian people worked with their hands in fields and workshops.

At the lowest level of Sumerian society were the slaves. Some slaves were foreigners who had been captured in war. Others were Sumerians who had been sold into slavery as children to

This small statue of a Sumerian husband and wife from Nippur suggests both affection and equality within marriage.

pay the debts of their impoverished parents. By working obediently day and night, Sumerian slaves could hope to earn their freedom.

Social class affected the lives of both men and women. On the whole, Sumerian women could engage in most of the occupations of city life, from merchant to farmer to artisan. Women could also join the lower ranks of the priesthood. However, none of Sumer's written records mentions a female scribe. Therefore, scholars have concluded that girls were not allowed to attend the schools where upper-class boys learned to read and write. In spite of these limitations, however, women in Sumer possessed more rights than women in many later civilizations.

Warfare brought Sumer's downfall.

For 1,000 years (from 3000 to 2000 B.C.), the city-states of Sumer were almost constantly at war with one another. For a time, the king of Kish was the mightiest ruler in Mesopotamia. But Kish's power gave way to that of the city-state Uruk and then of Lagash, Umma, and Ur.

All these city-states had their brief moments of glory.

Sumerian civilization ended because the constant warfare weakened all the city-states so much that they could no longer ward off attacks from a different enemy. Nomadic raiders from the deserts and the hills looked with envy on the riches of the cities. Around 2000 B.C., these warriors scaled the walls of Ur, swept through the streets, and burst through the gates of the temple. Ur was left in ruins. A grief-stricken scribe speaks for the goddess Ningal in this poem:

Woe is me, my house is a ruined stable,
I am a herdsman whose cows have been scattered,
I, Ningal, like an unworthy shepherd on whose flock the weapon has fallen!
Woe is me, I am an exile from the city that has found no rest;
I am a stranger dwelling in a strange city.

Section Review 1

Define: (a) civilization, (b) scribe, (c) artisan, (d) cuneiform, (e) pictograph, (f) ideogram, (g) institution, (h) irrigation, (i) city-state, (j) barter, (k) ziggurat, (l) polytheist
Identify: (a) Fertile Crescent, (b) Mesopotamia, (c) Sumer
Answer:
1. Explain how life in a Sumerian city differed from life in a small farming village in the same region.
2. (a) What were the advantages and disadvantages of Sumer's natural environment? (b) Explain how Sumerians overcame the disadvantages.
3. Give a brief description of daily life in Sumer, mentioning the activities of at least one member of each social class.
4. Why was this period known as the Bronze Age?

Critical Thinking
5. (a) Writing was a key invention of the Sumerians. Do you think writing is still essential to modern civilization? Explain your answer. (b) Choose another of the Sumerians' inventions and explain how life today would have been different if that invention did not exist.

Newcomers contributed to civilization. 2

Around 2000 B.C., many groups of people were on the move through Southwest Asia and neighboring lands. These huge migrations involved thousands of people and lasted hundreds of years. The arrival of new groups brought a wave of warfare and conquest to the Fertile Crescent.

The Sumerians never recovered from the attacks on their cities around 2000 B.C. However, Sumerian civilization did not die. Each new set of rulers adapted the basic ideas of Sumerian civilization to meet their own needs. As kingdoms grew larger and larger, the Sumerian pattern of civilization spread more widely across Southwest Asia. At the same time, the newcomers also made contributions of their own to the development of civilization.

Babylonians wrote a code of laws.

The first conquerors came from the city of Babylon (BAB-uh-luhn), a little upstream from Sumer. The Babylonians (BAB-uh-LOHN-ee-uhnz)

Map Study
Describe the geographic area covered by the Babylonian empire.

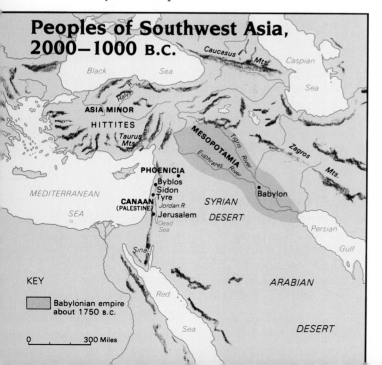

Peoples of Southwest Asia, 2000–1000 B.C.

KEY

Babylonian empire about 1750 B.C.

0   300 Miles

had been nomads, but they quickly adopted the civilized ways of the Sumerians they conquered. They built ziggurats, wrote cuneiform, irrigated fields, and organized society in the same manner as the Sumerians. Most important, by conquering almost all of Mesopotamia, the Babylonians spread civilization over a large area.

The major achievement of the Babylonians was a code of laws. This too was based on earlier Sumerian practices. Several Sumerian kings had set forth the laws of their city-states in writing. The Babylonian law code was more complete than the earlier ones. Moreover, it proclaimed the law not just for one city-state but for an entire **empire**. (An empire is a state that has conquered other lands and now rules them.)

The Babylonian law code was the work of one of history's truly great kings, Hammurabi (ham-uh-RAH-bee). The exact years of his reign are unknown. Toward the end of his life (roughly 1750 B.C.), Hammurabi ordered a scribe to chisel a record of his kingly deeds onto an eight-foot slab of black stone.

The stone boasts that Hammurabi gave justice to all the people he ruled. The central and most important part of the stone lists nearly 300 laws. Each one tells how a grievance between wife and husband, master and slave, merchant and customer, or neighbor and neighbor was to be settled. For example, these are five laws in the code:

> If a man destroys the eye of another man, they shall destroy his eye.
> If he breaks a man's bone, they shall break his bone.
> If he destroys the eye of a common man or breaks a bone of a common man, he shall pay one mina of silver.
> If a man knocks out a tooth of a man of his own rank, they shall knock out his tooth.
> If he knocks out a tooth of a common man, he shall pay one-third mina of silver.

To develop his law code, Hammurabi chose among the many laws of the different city-states he ruled, picking the rulings that seemed best to him. He had to get rid of disagreements and contradictions in the laws. That process is what sets a law *code* apart from a simple list of laws that were enacted one by one.

In this scene from the top of the stone on which Hammurabi's code was carved, the god of justice (seated) commands the king to write the laws.

Hammurabi's law code was important for the growth of justice in two ways. First, the laws were recorded in writing on the great stone, so that they were public knowledge. (Of course, that knowledge was limited to people who could read.) Second, Hammurabi's idea of justice required balance—an eye for an eye, a tooth for a tooth, a life for a life. Although many of the punishments seem harsh by modern standards, they at least fit the crime. A small crime did not lead to a great punishment.

Around 1550 B.C., 200 years after Hammurabi's rule, the Babylonian empire fell to nomadic warriors. For the next 700 years, the Fertile Crescent broke into small kingdoms as new peoples moved into the region. Small kingdoms and independent city-states sprang up across the region. Despite their small size, some of these groups made important contributions to civilization. Among these peoples were the Phoenicians (fuh-NIH-shuhnz) and the Jews.

Phoenicians invented the alphabet.

About 1100 B.C., the Phoenicians were the most powerful traders and merchants around the Mediterranean Sea. They did not rule a great empire, but they built a number of wealthy cities, something like the independent Sumerian city-states. The first Phoenician cities lay in what is now Lebanon. Later, however, the far-sailing Phoenicians settled widely around the Mediterranean Sea.

Wealth from trade The Phoenicians' wealth began in an unlikely way. Around their island city of Tyre (tire), millions of little snails washed up along the rocky shore. These snails were the resource from which the Phoenicians produced an intensely rich purple dye. To produce just one pound of dye, workers had to squeeze the drops from 60,000 smelly snail glands, a very costly process. All around the Mediterranean, the Phoenicians sold this rare dye at a fabulous price. Indeed, only a king's family could afford to wear "the royal purple" made at Tyre.

All in all, however, Phoenicia was poor in natural resources. Besides the snails, the only valuable item the land produced was fine, tall cedar trees that were in wide demand for building.

Thus, the Phoenicians turned to trade. In addition to purple dye and cedar, they traded goods they got from other lands, including wine, weapons, slaves, cloth, glass, precious metals, and ivory. Tyre competed fiercely with the other Phoenician city-states such as Byblos and Sidon for business that passed through Phoenician ports.

The Phoenicians' desire for trade made them excellent sailors. In narrow, single-sailed vessels equipped with long oars, they traveled all along the Mediterranean coasts of Europe and Africa. They even sailed past the Rock of Gibraltar into the stormy Atlantic Ocean. One Phoenician fleet may have circled the entire continent of Africa around 600 B.C. No other explorers are known to have attempted such a feat until 2,100 years later.

Between 1100 and 700 B.C., the Phoenicians founded trading colonies on almost every Mediterranean island. Perhaps as many as 300 Phoenician cities dotted Africa's Mediterranean coast. By far the greatest was Carthage, built on a fine natural harbor. (In later days, Carthage rivaled Rome in power.)

Phonecian	Greek	Modern
(symbols)	A	A
	B	B
	Γ	C
	Δ	D
	E	E
		F
		G
	Z	H
	H	
	θ	
	I	I
		J
	K	K
	Λ	L
	M	M
	N	N
	Ξ	O
	O	P
	Π	
	P	Q
	Σ	R
	T	S
	Y	T
		U
	X	V
		W
	Ω	X
		Y
		Z

The alphabet On their travels, Phoenician merchants needed a simplified kind of writing to keep business records. Cuneiform, with its 600 symbols, was much too cumbersome. Consequently, the Phoenicians discovered a way to keep records using just 22 symbols.

The Phoenician writing system first appeared around 900 B.C. Soon it was carried to trading centers all over the Mediterranean world. Later, the Greeks and Romans changed the shapes of the 22 letters and added 4 others, making the alphabet we know today. The word *alphabet*, in fact, comes directly from the first two letters of the Phoenician alphabet, *aleph* and *beth*.

The invention of the alphabet was immensely important. Unlike cuneiform, the Phoenician way of writing was a simple system that many people could master fairly quickly. True, the majority of the population still could not read or write. However, over the centuries, **literacy** (the ability to read and write) became more widespread. The growth of science and industry many years later would have been impossible without this spread of literacy.

Jews worshiped a single God.

Like the Phoenicians, the Jews were a small group of people in Southwest Asia. Also like the Phoenicians, their contribution to civilization was a large one.

Around 2000 B.C., a group of travelers left the Sumerian city-state of Ur. Among them, according to the Bible, was a man named Abraham and his wife, Sarah. Abraham, Sarah, and their family of nomadic herders gradually moved westward to the far end of the Fertile Crescent. After many years of travel, they came to a strip of land called Canaan (KAY-nuhn) near the Mediterranean Sea. This land was later known as Palestine. Such is the Biblical account of the beginnings of the Jewish people.

Monotheism The Jews were a small group who never wielded great political power in the ancient Fertile Crescent, but their influence on history was far-reaching. Unlike the other groups who dwelled around them, the Jews prayed only to one God. While other groups in the Fertile Crescent were polytheists, the Jewish people became **monotheists** (MAH-no-THEE-ists), from the Greek word *mono* meaning "one" and *theist* meaning "god-worshiper."

According to Jewish tradition as recorded in the Bible, the one true God was the creator of all things and the ruler of the universe. The God that Abraham worshiped was not limited to any particular geographic place, as the city gods of Mesopotamia were. Thus, the Jews carried their worship of God into whatever lands they visited, rather than taking up the worship of local gods.

The leadership of Moses Around 1650 B.C., drought and famine brought hard times to Canaan. Many groups of people, including the Jews, migrated toward Egypt. Even in dry years, Egypt had water from its great river, the Nile. According to the Bible, at first the Jews had positions of honor in the Egyptian kingdom. Later, however, the Egyptians made the Jews their slaves.

Sometime between 1300 and 1200 B.C., the Jews fled from Egypt. The man who led them out of slavery to seek a land of their own was Moses. From that time on, Moses has been considered the greatest leader in Jewish history.

According to the Bible, while the Jews journeyed across the Sinai Peninsula, Moses climbed to the top of a mountain to pray. There he spoke with God. When Moses came down from Mount Sinai, he brought two tablets of stone on which were written ten laws, the Ten Commandments of the Bible.

These commandments and the other teachings from God that Moses delivered to his people became the basis for the religious laws of Judaism. The Jews believed that the laws formed a covenant, or promise, between God and the Jewish people. God promised to protect the Jews, and they, in turn, promised to honor God's commandments.

The covenant was based on the idea that God is just, not arbitrary as the gods of Mesopotamia were. Moreover, by the laws set forth to Moses, God demanded a high standard of moral conduct from human beings. This emphasis on justice, morality, and an individual relationship with God set Judaism apart. These ideas marked the birth of a set of religious traditions the impact of which has lasted thousands of years.

Building the kingdom of Israel On the far side of the Sinai Desert, the Jews came once more to Canaan, the land they believed God had promised them. The southern part of this land around the Dead Sea was brown and desertlike. The northern part, watered by the Jordan River, was green with olive trees and palms. The Canaanites, who already lived in the area, fiercely resisted the newcomers for centuries.

The Jews decided that they needed a king to lead them to victories. From about 1020 to 922 B.C., the Jews were united under three able kings in succession—first Saul, then David, and finally Solomon. Their kingdom was called Israel, and its capital was the city of Jerusalem. This short time period—less than 100 years—was the time of Israel's greatest power and independence.

Daily Life · *Safeguarding a Letter*

Laws in Babylon required that every business transaction be written down. However, most people could not write, so they would hire a scribe to record their business deals on a clay tablet. The scribe would then make an envelope by pressing a lump of clay piecrust-thin, wrapping it around the tablet, and sealing the edges.

Why did a clay tablet need an envelope? The envelope kept the tablet tamperproof. The scribe wrote on the envelope exactly what he had written on the tablet within. The envelope served both as a copy of the agreement and as a kind of safe-deposit box for the original.

What prevented someone from simply breaking the envelope, changing the tablet, and making a new envelope? There were two things. First, clay shrinks when it dries. When both the envelope and the tablet were wet, both shrank equally. If a new wet envelope were wrapped around a dry tablet, only the envelope would shrink. Soon it would be too small for the tablet and would crack. Second, both people making the deal had to sign the tablet and the envelope. (Since most people could not write, they signed by pressing the damp clay with their own stamp made of carved stone.) Even if someone forged a whole new tablet and envelope, the other person's stamp would be missing.

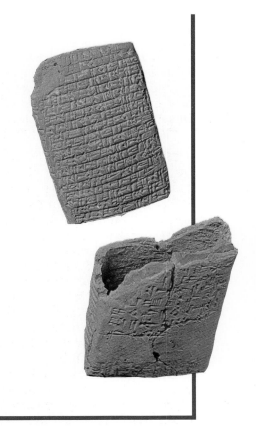

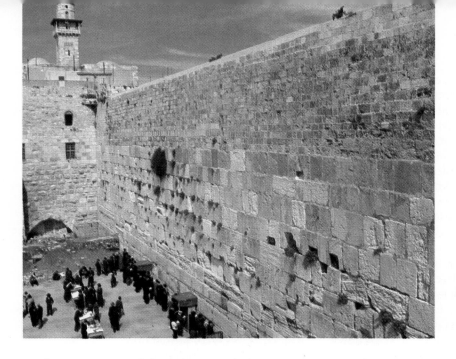

The Western Wall is all that remains of the Biblical temple in Jerusalem. Jews from all parts of the world come to pray at this sacred and historic site.

The most powerful of the Jewish kings was Solomon. At the height of his rule, Solomon set about building a temple to glorify God. The temple was to be a permanent home for the Ark of the Covenant, which held the tablets of Moses' law. The temple that Solomon built was not large, but it gleamed like a precious gem. Bronze pillars stood at its door. The temple was stone on the outside, but its inner walls were made of Lebanese cedar covered in gold. The main hall was richly decorated with brass and gold. Solomon also built a palace for himself that was even more costly than the temple.

These building projects required high taxes and badly strained the little kingdom's economy. After Solomon's death, the Jews in the northern part of the kingdom revolted. In 922 B.C., the kingdom split in two, Israel in the north and Judah in the south. Thereafter, the Jewish people were swept up in the waves of conquest and migration that made Southwest Asia a battleground of empires for centuries.

The prophets Although the Jewish kingdom was broken, the Jewish religion continued to develop under religious teachers known as **prophets.** The prophets believed that they were messengers sent to reveal God's will to the Jews. Prophets such as Isaiah (eye-**ZAY**-uh) and Jeremiah sternly warned the Jews that God would punish greed, wickedness, or the worshiping of idols. The prophets spoke fearlessly even to kings, demanding justice and ethical conduct.

Prophets taught that the Jews had a duty not only to worship God but also to live justly with one another. In the words of the prophet Micah, "It hath been shown to you, O man, what is good and what the Lord requires of you: Only to do justly, and to love mercy, and to walk humbly with thy God."

People learned to work with iron.

Although some of the important developments of civilization can be linked to particular groups, other changes cannot be pinned down to one group. The shift from bronze to iron as the chief metal for making tools is a change that cannot be linked to any single group. Like the earlier change from stone tools to bronze ones, the transition to iron had far-reaching effects.

From about 2800 to 1200 B.C., bronze was the basic metal used for tools and weapons. Bronze is a combination of copper and another metal, usually tin. Copper was not very hard to find in the Fertile Crescent and nearby lands, especially the island of Cyprus. Tin, however, must have come from a great distance, perhaps as far as western Britain or even Southeast Asia. Both copper and tin melt at lower temperatures than iron. Therefore, early metalworkers learned to make bronze long before they could build a fire that was hot enough to work with iron.

Between 1500 and 1200 B.C., people around the eastern end of the Mediterranean Sea learned the complicated process of smelting iron. However, the skill of ironworking was so rare that a piece of iron was sometimes worth 40 times as much as the same weight of silver.

Iron has a number of advantages over bronze. It is harder than bronze, so that an iron sword or spear could cut through the bronze shield of an enemy warrior. The most important advantage, though, is that iron is a very common metal. It is found nearly everywhere. No longer did people have to depend on copper and tin from distant lands. Once people had the skill to work with it, iron was much cheaper than bronze. Thus, people could use much more metal than earlier. Armies had more metal weapons, and artisans had more metal tools.

The shift from bronze to iron took hundreds of years. Gradually, from 1200 to around 700 B.C. in the Fertile Crescent, the Bronze Age came to an end and the Iron Age began. The use of iron gave urban civilizations a great advantage over less settled people who were not able to make metal weapons. In some ways, the use of iron paved the way for an age of empires.

Section Review 2

Define: (a) law code, (b) empire, (c) literacy, (d) monotheist, (e) covenant
Identify: (a) Babylonians, (b) Hammurabi, (c) Phoenicians, (d) Jews, (e) Abraham, (f) Canaan, (g) Moses, (h) Israel, (i) Jerusalem, (j) Solomon
Answer:
1. How did Sumerian civilization continue to be important, even after the Sumerians were conquered?
2. Explain why Hammurabi's code of law was outstanding for its day.
3. What advantages did the Phoenician alphabet have over cuneiform?
4. How was the Jewish religion revolutionary in ancient times?
5. (a) Why did people learn to work with bronze before learning to work with iron? (b) What were the advantages of iron over bronze?

Critical Thinking
6. After 700 B.C., the Fertile Crescent entered a period when great empires arose in the region. The invention of a convenient writing system and the use of law codes were two key elements that made large empires possible. Explain why each of those developments was essential to building an empire.

Conquerors ruled ever larger empires.   3

Although Southwest Asia in ancient times was a mixture of many peoples, the area was surprisingly united culturally. Modern scholars refer to it as "the cuneiform world." Empires came and went, but farming, irrigation, city life, and cuneiform writing remained. The culture that began in Sumer spread over a wide area, carried both by traders like the Phoenicians and by conquerors like the Babylonians.

In the years after 900 B.C., a series of empires united Southwest Asia. Each new empire seemed to rise out of the ashes of the old one. For a while, the new empire would grow larger and more powerful. Then it too would collapse and be replaced by another.

Map Study
Compare this map to the one on page 34. What territories did the Assyrians rule that the Babylonians did not?

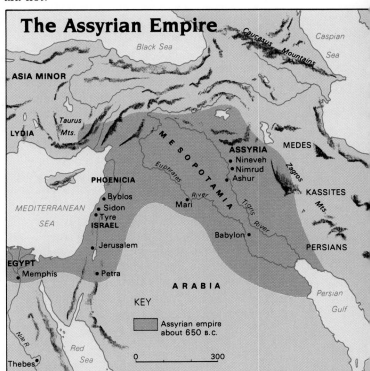

The Assyrian Empire

KEY

Assyrian empire about 650 B.C.

The mighty king of Assyria, Assurbanipal, lived in luxury at his palace in Nineveh. He reclines on a couch in the garden, while Assursharrat, his wife, sits at his feet.

The Assyrian empire rose and fell.

I am Assurbanipal, the Great King, the Mighty King, King of the Universe, King of Assyria, King of the World's Four Regions, King of Kings, Unrivaled Prince . . .

This was not just the idle boast of a vain king. When these words were carved in stone in 650 B.C., there was indeed a "king of kings." The empire of Assurbanipal (AH-soor-BAH-nee-pahl) spanned the Fertile Crescent from the Persian Gulf to the Mediterranean Sea.

The Assyrians (uh-SIHR-ee-uhnz) came from the northern part of Mesopotamia. Their farming villages in northern Mesopotamia had been attacked repeatedly by barbarians from the nearby mountains. Thus, over the centuries, the Assyrians learned to be tough fighters. Around 850 B.C., they began a campaign of conquest that made them, for a time, the greatest power in Southwest Asia.

Assyrian soldiers were well equipped for conquering an empire. They had iron swords and iron-pointed spears. Moreover, the Assyrians were the most disciplined army the world had yet seen. They were trained to march and fight in tightly organized columns and divisions led by commanders of different ranks.

With the precision of a machine, Assyrian soldiers marched shoulder to shoulder to within an arrow's shot of a city wall. At a signal from their commander, they stopped, strung their bows, and released a shower of arrows. Wave upon wave of arrows hissed over the walls of the besieged city. Meanwhile, other troops moved up to the city gates and hammered them with massive, iron-tipped battering rams. When at last the gates splintered, the Assyrians showed their victims no mercy. They tortured, killed, or enslaved the people of the city. To prevent later rebellions, the Assyrians uprooted conquered people from their homelands, sending great groups of captives to distant parts of the empire.

Between 850 and 650 B.C., the kings of Assyria conquered Syria, Palestine, and Babylonia. They extended their empire into North Africa by conquering Egypt. Cartloads of jewels and ivory, gold and silver rumbled into Nineveh (NIHN-uh-vuh), Assyria's capital city. Tribute from foreign kings was, after all, one of the great rewards of conquest.

Nineveh, on the Tigris River in Mesopotamia, was famous as the largest city of its day. It was about three miles long by one mile wide. In addition to the treasures of the empire, Nineveh also held the world's largest library. King Assurbanipal collected 25,000 clay tablets. Some were like foreign-language dictionaries, giving the same words in several languages. When archaeologists found the remains of the library, the tablets helped scholars decipher the cuneiform writing of ancient Mesopotamia.

The Assyrian army seemed invincible, and the Assyrian king was one of the most powerful rulers on earth. Yet Assurbanipal was almost the last of the mighty Assyrian kings. Assyrian power had spread too thin. Nineveh fell 21 years after Assurbanipal's death. In 612 B.C., the city's gates were rammed open by a combined army of Medes (meedz) and Chaldeans (kal-DEE-uhnz). The Assyrians' cruelty had made them many enemies who were pleased by their downfall. As the Jewish prophet Nahum wrote, "Nineveh is laid waste: who will bemoan her?"

The Chaldeans rebuilt Babylon.

Thus, around 600 B.C., Babylon again became the center of an empire, more than 1,000 years after Hammurabi had ruled there. After defeating the Assyrians, the Chaldeans made Babylon their capital. From there, they began to build up their own empire.

The wonders of Babylon Many who beheld the new Babylon marveled at its beauty. The chief builder of Babylon was a remarkable Chaldean king, Nebuchadnezzar (NEB-yuh-kuhd-NEZ-uhr), who ruled from 605 to 562 B.C. The walls of his palace were covered with shiny tiles arranged in bright patterns of blue, yellow, red, and white.

The most impressive part of the palace was the famous hanging gardens of Babylon. According to legend, one of Nebuchadnezzar's wives missed the flowering shrubs of her mountain homeland. To please her, the king had sweet-smelling trees and shrubs from the mountains planted on terraces that rose 75 feet above the flat plain of Babylon. Slaves watered the plants daily from pumps hidden inside towering columns. These gardens won the admiration of Greek visitors, who listed the garden as one of the Seven Wonders of the World.

Indeed, the entire city was a wonder. Its walls were so thick that, according to one report, a four-horse chariot could wheel around on top of them. To ensure that the world knew who ruled Babylon, even the bricks were inscribed: "I am Nebuchadnezzar, King of Babylon."

The stargazers of Babylon The highest building in Babylon was a great, seven-tiered ziggurat more than 300 feet high and visible for miles. At night, priests observed the stars from the top of this ziggurat and others in the city. They kept detailed records of how the stars and planets seemed to change position in the night sky. The rise of each constellation, or group of stars, marked the beginning of a new month on the Chaldean calendar.

The Chaldeans believed that the stars determined human destiny. Thus, to foretell the future from day to day, Chaldean priests observed a belt of 12 constellations called a zodiac. Nebuchadnezzar consulted the temple's star charts carefully in governing his kingdom.

The priest-astrologers of Babylon also watched the four phases of the moon. They concluded that every month should be divided into four weeks—one week for each change from new moon to half, half to full, full to half, and half to new. Their calculations were accurate to within a few minutes.

The Chaldeans' observations formed the basis for both astronomy and astrology. Much of their knowledge was passed on to the Greeks, who used it to develop many theories about Earth, the planets, and the stars.

The Jews' Babylonian captivity Like other emperors before him, Nebuchadnezzar followed a policy of taking conquered groups from their homelands and sending them to another part of the empire. People who were cut off from their homeland were less likely to rebel against the empire.

Among the peoples that Nebuchadnezzar conquered were the Jews. After a long siege, his armies captured Jerusalem in 586 B.C. They pillaged the temple and burned the city. Thousands of Jews fled to surrounding lands. Nebuchadnezzar's soldiers captured about 15,000 Jews and sent them as slaves to Babylon.

This period of time was vitally important in the history of Jewish monotheism. While other people worshiped the god of whatever city they

This reconstruction of a city gate shows the grandeur of Nebuchadnezzar's Babylon. Above the gate rose the famous Hanging Gardens.

Voice from the Past · *The Babylonian Captivity*

The Bible is a collection of writings that form the basis of both the Jewish and the Christian religions. Much of the material in the Bible is important for historic information as well as for religion. The following passage, Psalm 137, describes the feelings of the Jews after being taken captive to Babylon.

By the rivers of Babylon, there we sat down, yea, we wept, when we remembered Zion [their homeland].

We hanged our harps upon the willows in the midst thereof.

For there they that carried us away captive required of us a song; and they that wasted us required of us mirth, saying, Sing us one of the songs of Zion.

How shall we sing the Lord's song in a strange land?

If I forget thee, O Jerusalem, let my right hand forget her cunning.

If I do not remember thee, let my tongue cleave to the roof of my mouth; if I prefer not Jerusalem to my chief joy.

Remember, O Lord, the children of Edom [a people who joined forces with Nebuchadnezzar] in the day of Jerusalem; who said, Raze it [destroy it], raze it, even to the foundation thereof.

O daughter of Babylon, who art to be destroyed; happy shall he be, that rewardeth thee as thou hast served us.

Happy shall he be, that taketh and dasheth thy little ones against the stones.

1. What are the feelings of the Jews in their exile?
2. What are their captors asking of them, according to the psalm?
3. What do the Jews vow to do concerning Jerusalem?
4. What do the Jews expect and hope will happen to Babylon and its people?

ירושׁלים

---

lived in, the Jews held fast to their religion even apart from their homeland.

Nebuchadnezzar governed for 43 years. His empire fell shortly after his death. The fall of Babylon marked the end of the Mesopotamian empires. The empires that arose in the following centuries were much larger than Mesopotamia or even than the Fertile Crescent.

The Persians united a vast area.

The Assyrians had shown that it was possible to build an empire based on fear and harsh government. The giant empire that next arose in Southwest Asia showed that it was possible to build an empire based on tolerance and wise government. Beginning around 550 B.C., the Persians spread their rule from the Indus River to the Nile River and the Black Sea.

The rise of Persia The Persians' homeland lay east of the Fertile Crescent, among the mountains and plateaus of Iran. The rest of the world paid little heed to the Persians until 550 B.C. In that year, Cyrus (SYE-ruhs), king of the Persians, defeated several neighboring kingdoms. Suddenly, it was clear that a new power was arising in Southwest Asia.

In just 11 years, between 550 and 539 B.C., Cyrus conquered all of the Fertile Crescent and most of Asia Minor. His generosity toward conquered peoples was one reason for his astonishing success. When Cyrus's army marched into a city, there was no looting or burning. Instead of destroying the local temple, Cyrus was more likely to worship there himself. Cyrus believed that it was wise to let alone local customs and religions.

Knowing Cyrus's tolerance, Babylon peacefully opened its gates for him in 539 B.C. With great

42

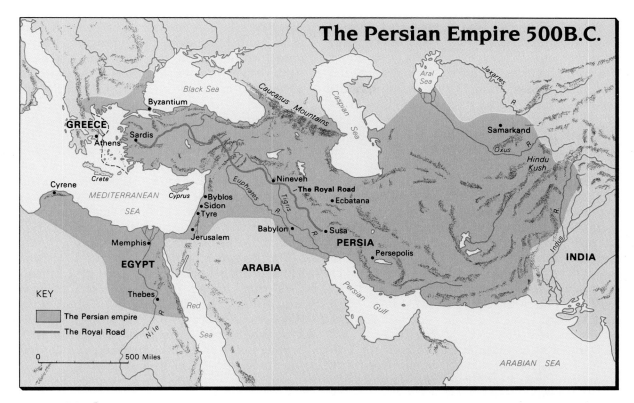

The Persian Empire 500 B.C.

Map Study

What river valley marked the easternmost end of the Persian empire? On what three continents did the empire hold land?

tact, Cyrus lifted up prayers of thanks for this bloodless victory to Babylon's chief god, Marduk. According to Persian accounts, "all the inhabitants of Babylon . . . princes and governors included, bowed to Cyrus and kissed his feet, jubilant and with shining faces."

As another act of generosity, Cyrus allowed the Jews to go back to Jerusalem in 538 B.C. and rebuild their city. The Jewish city flourished under Persian rule. It was during this period that many portions of the Bible were first put into writing.

In 530 B.C., Cyrus was killed in battle. His son, Cambyses (kam-**BYE**-seez), extended the Persian empire by conquering all of Egypt. After ruling only eight years, Cambyses died, probably from the infection of an accidental sword wound. Immediately, widespread rebellions broke out across the empire, showing how fragile Persian control really was.

Cambyses' successor, Darius (duh-**RYE**-uhs), had been a member of the king's bodyguard, an elite group of Persian soldiers known as the Ten Thousand Immortals. With their help, Darius won the throne and spent his first three years as king putting down revolts.

Darius extended Persian conquests in the east, leading armies up into the mountains of Afghanistan and down into the river valleys of India. The Persian empire was now immense. It embraced Egypt and Asia Minor in the west, part of India in the east, and the Fertile Crescent in the center.

Persian government How could this sprawling empire be governed? Darius's answer was to divide the empire into 20 provinces. The provinces were roughly equal to the homelands of the many groups of people within the Persian empire. Under Persian rule, the people of each province still practiced their own religion, spoke their own language, and to some extent followed their own laws. (This pattern of many groups—sometimes called "nationalities"—living by their own laws within one empire continued in Southwest Asia until the early 1900's.)

43

In each province of the Persian empire was a royal governor called a *satrap* (SAY-trap). Darius also appointed an army leader and a tax collector for each province. To make sure his satraps did not rebel against him, Darius sent inspectors known as the "King's Eyes and Ears" to all parts of his kingdom.

The Persian king used two other important tools to hold his empire together. One was an excellent road system and the other was standardized coinage.

The famous Royal Road of the Persian empire ran from Susa, the Persian capital, to Sardis in Asia Minor, a distance of 1,677 miles. An ordinary caravan took three months to travel this distance, but the king's messengers took only about a week. Royal riders dashed along the road. At 111 post stations spaced along the road, new riders on fresh horses took over for tired ones. With this system, royal commands reached all parts of the empire.

Darius's second idea, borrowed from the Lydians of Asia Minor, was to manufacture metal coins. For the first time, coins of a standard value circulated throughout most of the civilized world. People no longer had to weigh and measure bits of gold or silver to pay for their purchases. Like the road system, the wider use of money made trade much easier. Trade, in turn, helped to hold the empire together.

The teachings of Zoroaster By Darius's time, about 2,500 years had passed since the first Sumerian city-states had been built. During those years, people of the Fertile Crescent had suffered often from war, conquest, and famine. Why was there so much evil in the world? A Persian prophet named Zoroaster (ZOH-roh-AS-tuhr) offered an inspirational answer.

Scholars know almost nothing about the life of Zoroaster except that he lived around 600 B.C. His ideas, however, are well-known. Zoroaster taught that two spiritual armies fight for possession of a person's soul. One army is led by

Ahura-Mazda (AH-hoo-ruh-MAHZ-duh), god of truth and light. The other is commanded by Ahriman (AH-ree-muhn), god of evil and darkness. At the end of time, said Zoroaster, all souls would be judged according to the side they had chosen. Followers of Ahura-Mazda would be lifted into a paradise. Followers of Ahriman would suffer forever in a fiery pit.

This belief in a heaven and a hell was radically different from Sumer's gloomy vision of the afterlife. Zoroaster's religion was far more hopeful, because a person's own choice controlled his or her fate. Those who chose the side of goodness were not doomed to a dismal underworld.

The Persian empire lasted about 200 years. Through their tolerance and good government, the Persians brought political order to Southwest Asia. During this long period of comparative peace, the region's great cities prospered. Commerce flourished. Learning and the arts progressed. In other words, all the achievements of civilization were protected and allowed to grow.

Section Review 3

Define: (a) constellation, (b) astronomy, (c) satrap
Identify: (a) Assyria, (b) Assurbanipal,
(c) Chaldeans, (d) Babylon,
(e) Nebuchadnezzar, (f) Iran, (g) Persians,
(h) Cyrus, (i) Darius, (j) Zoroaster
Answer:
1. Explain how the Assyrians succeeded in conquering a great empire.
2. What were the achievements of the Chaldeans in the time of Nebuchadnezzar?
3. What important religious stand did the Jews take during their captivity in Babylon?
4. How was the Persian king Cyrus's way of building an empire different from that of Assyrian kings?
5. How was Zoroaster's philosophy different from earlier religions of Southwest Asia?

Critical Thinking
6. Suppose you lived in a city in Mesopotamia. Would you rather have lived there in the period of the independent Sumerian city-states or in the time of the Persian empire? Explain your answer.

Footnote to History

Satraps lived in luxurious palaces. The Persian name for a satrap's private hunting park was *paradise* (from which comes our own word for a heavenly place).

Chapter Review 2

Summary

1. Civilization arose in the Fertile Crescent. About 5,000 years ago, many groups of people throughout the world were living in small farming villages. In the Fertile Crescent of Southwest Asia, however, the people of Sumer developed a more complex way of life. They built cities in which people worked at a variety of trades. For the first time in history, farmers were able to raise enough food to have a surplus. The ability to raise a surplus freed people to do specialized jobs. Sumerian government and religion were highly organized. Sumerians invented a system of writing, and their technology was advanced for its day. These traits made Sumer the first civilization.

2. Newcomers contributed to civilization. Beginning around 2000 B.C., waves of new peoples swept through the Fertile Crescent. Each new group adopted the ways of life begun in Sumer and added their own ideas. The Babylonians' most famous achievement was a code of law. The Phoenicians invented a system of writing that evolved into our present-day alphabet. The Jews developed a religion based on belief in one God. Between 1500 and 1000 B.C., the Bronze Age gave way to the Iron Age.

3. Conquerors ruled ever larger empires. Between 900 and 350 B.C., the Assyrians, the Chaldeans, and the Persians each took a turn at ruling Southwest Asia. Each group of people imposed its culture and ruling style on the area. Some of the important developments during this time were the increased use of iron, the beginnings of astronomy, the use of money for trade, and the belief in an afterlife.

Reviewing the Facts

1. Define the following terms:
   a. civilization
   b. artisan
   c. cuneiform
   d. institution
   e. city-state
   f. barter
   g. polytheist
   h. empire
   i. literacy
   j. monotheist
   k. prophet

2. Explain the importance of each of the following names, places, or terms:
   a. Fertile Crescent
   b. Mesopotamia
   c. Bronze Age
   d. Iron Age
   e. Sumer
   f. Hammurabi
   g. Phoenicians
   h. Jews
   i. Moses
   j. Solomon
   k. Assyria
   l. Nebuchadnezzar
   m. Persians
   n. Cyrus
   o. Darius
   p. Zoroaster

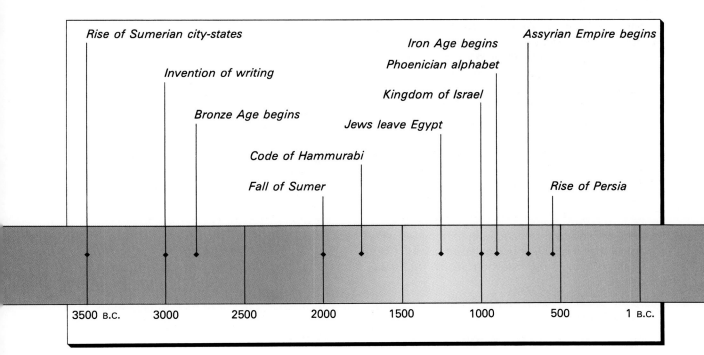

Rise of Sumerian city-states

Invention of writing

Bronze Age begins

Code of Hammurabi

Fall of Sumer

Jews leave Egypt

Kingdom of Israel

Phoenician alphabet

Iron Age begins

Assyrian Empire begins

Rise of Persia

| 3500 B.C. | 3000 | 2500 | 2000 | 1500 | 1000 | 500 | 1 B.C. |

3. (a) What are the key traits of a civilization? (b) Describe how each of those traits was present in Sumer.
4. (a) How were the city-states of Sumer different from both cities and countries as we know them? (b) How were Sumerian city-states governed?
5. Why is Hammurabi remembered as a great king?
6. What lasting contributions to civilization were made by each of the following groups? (a) the Phoenicians (b) the Jews (c) the Chaldeans
7. Explain how each of the following kings gained or held power over his empire. (a) Assurbanipal of Assyria (b) Cyrus of Persia (c) Darius of Persia

Thinking about History

1. Historians often describe the conflicts that took place in this period of Southwest Asia's history as war between "the desert and the sown"—that is, between the nomads and the farmers. (a) What are some examples of this conflict? (b) What strengths would each side have in war? (c) Explain why such conflict might arise. (Watch for other examples of this ancient pattern in later times.)
2. Reread the excerpt from Hammurabi's code of law on page 34. Do you agree or disagree with the statement, "Although this code was an outstanding example of justice for its day, it would fall short by today's standards"?
3. Suppose that today only a few specialists were able to read and write. List some effects this situation might have on our society.
4. Explain how the quote, "Necessity is the mother of invention," applies to the invention of writing and coins.

Writing and Speaking about History

1. Select a news story (from a newspaper or newsmagazine) to bring to class. Read the introductory paragraph and circle the *who, what, when, where, why,* and *how.* Using the paragraph as a model, write an introductory paragraph for a newspaper article that describes the significant accomplishments of one of the following people from this chapter:

Nebuchadnezzar	Abraham
Cyrus	David
Solomon	Saul
Darius	Isaiah

Hammurabi	Jeremiah
Moses	Assurbanipal
Zoroaster	

2. Separate the people in the preceding list into these two categories—prophets (or holy men) and kings (or rulers). Then write a generalization about the historic importance of one of the groups. (A generalization is a broad statement that is true in an overwhelming number of instances.) Use information about the individuals to support your generalization.
3. Pretend that one of the people listed above will address your class on the topic "my role in history." Prepare a brief oral presentation to introduce the individual to your class.

Practicing Skills

1. Use the time line on page 45 to put the following events from this chapter in the correct order.
   a. Iron Age
   b. rise of Persia
   c. Phoenician alphabet
   d. invention of writing
   e. rise of Assyria
2. Locate the Fertile Crescent on the map on page 28. Use geographic features such as deserts, mountains, seas, and rivers to define the boundaries of the Fertile Crescent.

Investigating History

1. The Hanging Gardens of Babylon were one of the Seven Wonders of the Ancient World. Use reference books to find out what the others were. Choose one and do further research. Write a brief description or make a drawing or model to show how that wonder may have looked.
2. On a computer, create a database file for important historic dates. Begin by selecting the key events from this chapter. Set up a field for the date, a field for the part of the world (Southwest Asia), and a field for a brief label for the event. For example, one entry might read: 3000 B.C.; Southwest Asia; First cities arise.

Decision Making in History

Suppose you were the conqueror of Mesopotamia. What alternatives would you have in dealing with the conquered peoples?

Chapter 3

3100 B.C. - 332 B.C. Ancient Egypt

1. **The Nile River shaped Egyptian life.**
2. **Egypt's pharaohs ruled as gods.**
3. **Egypt's way of life endured 3,000 years.**

This golden mask covered the face of Tutankhamon's mummy. Its ears are pierced for earrings. The vulture and the cobra on the headdress represent two Egyptian gods.

It was late fall in 1922. In northeastern Africa, the sun blazed hot in the Valley of the Kings, which lies in Egypt near a sweeping curve in the Nile River. British archaeologist Howard Carter had spent six years there moving ton upon ton of rock in search of tombs of ancient Egypt's last great rulers. More than 3,000 years had passed since these rulers had been laid to rest. Over the centuries, robbers had opened most of the tombs and taken their treasures. Still, Carter pressed on.

On November 26, 1922, Carter stood before a sealed door. If the wildest of Carter's dreams were true, behind the door lay the mummy and treasure of the ruler Tutankhamon (TOOT-ahngk-AH-mun). Carter made a small hole in the door and stuck a candle through. His report told what he saw.

At first I could see nothing . . . but presently as my eyes grew accustomed to the light, details of the room within emerged slowly from the mist, strange animals, statues, and gold—everywhere the glint of gold.

The wealth of gold within the tomb included four golden chariots, gilded couches, a golden throne with lions' heads carved in the arms, and much more. All these splendors had been created for Tutankhamon, who ruled Egypt for only a few short years. He became king at the age of 8 in about 1347 B.C. and died 9 years later in 1339 B.C., only 17 years old.

Carter had indeed found the tomb he sought, but where was the royal mummy? The young king's burial chamber lay behind yet another sealed door. When that door was opened, Carter's electric lamp revealed a breathtaking sight—a large, box-shaped shrine of gilded wood that filled the entire room. Nested within the large shrine were three smaller ones, and within the smallest shrine was a great stone coffin.

With a rope and tackle, Carter's crew of workers hoisted the heavy lid off the coffin. From inside, a golden face looked up at them through deep blue eyes of precious stones. Resting lightly on this gleaming mask was a fragile wreath of flowers, placed there by Tutankhamon's young widow. Carter later wrote,

Among all that regal splendour, that royal magnificence . . . there was nothing so beautiful as those few withered flowers . . . They told us what a short period 3,300 years really was.

The Nile River shaped Egyptian life.   1

Tutankhamon's reign was just a brief moment in ancient Egypt's long history. Egypt had already been a united kingdom for 1,700 years when young Tutankhamon came to the throne. The country he ruled was nearly as old as the city-states of Sumer.

Although Egypt existed at the same time as the cities of Sumer and the later empires of Southwest Asia, Egyptian civilization was very different from the ways of life that arose in the Fertile Crescent. Unlike Southwest Asia, Egypt was early united into a single country. That country survived, through good times and bad, for more than 3,000 years. At the center of Egypt's unity was the country's most important geographic feature, the Nile River. Indeed, the story of ancient Egypt begins with the story of the Nile.

The Nile linked diverse lands.

From the highlands of eastern Africa to the Mediterranean Sea, the Nile River meanders over 4,100 miles, making it the longest river in the world. The map on page 49 shows how it winds through Egypt, a thin ribbon of water in a parched desert land.

The cataracts For most of their history, ancient Egyptians knew only the lower part of the Nile—the last 750 miles before it empties into the sea. Their domain ended in the south at Aswan, where jagged granite cliffs pinch inward. The narrowing cliffs and boulders that have fallen from them turn the river into churning rapids called a **cataract** (KAT-uh-rakt). Riverboats cannot pass this spot, known as the First Cataract. (Five other cataracts lie farther upstream to the south.)

Upper Egypt and Lower Egypt Between the First Cataract and the Mediterranean lay two very different regions. Upper Egypt (to the south) was a skinny strip of land from the First Cataract to the point where the river split into many branches. Lower Egypt (to the north, near the sea) began about 100 miles before the river entered the Mediterranean Sea. At that point, branches of the river fanned out over a broad, marshy, triangular area of land. Such a region is called a **delta** (map, page 49).

A transportation link The Nile provided an easy, reliable system of transportation between Upper and Lower Egypt. Going from one end of Egypt to another required no more effort than climbing into a boat. The Nile flowed north, so northbound boats simply drifted with the current all the way from the First Cataract to the marshy flats of Lower Egypt. Southbound boats hoisted a wide sail. The prevailing winds of Egypt blew from north to south, carrying sailboats against the river current.

Farmers relied on the Nile's floods.

Every year in June, spring rains and melting snow from the mountains caused the Nile River to rise and spill over its banks. This flood was not a menace to the Egyptians. Rather, they depended on it.

The gift of the Nile When the river receded in October, it left behind a rich, wet deposit of fertile black mud. Year after year, Egyptian peasants knew they could count on the flooding Nile to provide this rich layer of soil in time for their next planting.

Before the scorching sun could dry out the soil, the peasants would hitch their cattle to plows and prepare their fields for planting. All summer and fall, they tended the wheat and barley plants. They watered their crops from an intricate network of irrigation ditches. At last came the welcome harvest. This cycle repeated itself year after year—flood, plant, harvest; flood, plant, harvest. As an ancient Greek historian named Herodotus (huh-**RAHD**-uh-tuhs) remarked in the fifth century B.C., Egypt was the "gift of the Nile."

Worshiping the Nile Egyptian farmers were much more fortunate than the villagers of Mesopotamia. Compared to the rampaging, unpredictable Tigris River, the Nile was as regular as clockwork. The Egyptians worshiped it as a god who gave them life and seldom turned against them. They felt secure in their well-being. With nature so much in their favor, Egyptians tended to approach life more confidently and optimistically than their neighbors in the Fertile Crescent.

Even so, life in Egypt had its risks. If the Nile's floodwaters were just a few feet lower than normal, the amount of fresh soil and water for crops was greatly reduced. Thousands of people might starve. If the floodwaters were a few feet higher than usual, the water would spread beyond the fields to the mud-brick villages nearby. The unwanted water might destroy houses, granaries, and the precious seeds that farmers needed for planting.

Thus, the Egyptians were careful to observe all the religious rituals that were supposed to please the gods and keep Egypt safe. In a religious festival on the Nile's banks, they sang: "Hail to thee, O Nile, that issues from the earth and comes to keep Egypt alive."

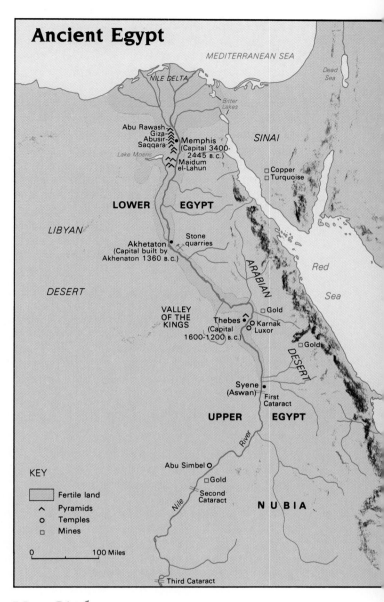

Ancient Egypt

Map Study
In which part of Egypt were most of the pyramids built? What resources did the Sinai contain?

Deserts shielded Egypt from attack.

All of Egypt's villages and cities were built along the Nile on a narrow strip of land made fertile by the river. Beyond that, on either side of the river, the land changed suddenly to desert. To the west stretched the sands of the Libyan Desert, a part of the Sahara. To the east along the Red Sea lay the Arabian Desert, which was even drier and more barren. The change from fertile land to desert was so abrupt that a person could stand with one foot in each. To the Egyptians, the desert stood for death and the river for life.

The vast and forbidding deserts forced Egyptians to stay close to their lifeline, the Nile. However, the deserts also shut out invaders. For much of its history, Egypt was spared the constant warfare that plagued the Fertile Crescent.

The only possible invasion route into Egypt lay across a narrow corridor called the Isthmus of Suez. In time, invaders would reach Egypt by way of this one geographic link with the outside world. However, for hundreds of years, the deserts kept Egypt secure from any serious attack.

Farm villages joined in nomes.

Egyptians lived in farming villages as far back as 6000 B.C., perhaps even earlier. During those times, they cleared and cultivated the land with stone tools. They domesticated cattle, goats, sheep, and donkeys. They worshiped the wild creatures that swam in the Nile—the hippopotamus and the crocodile. They tried to preserve bodies of the dead by heaping up mounds of sand around them in the desert.

Eventually, the villages united into agricultural districts called *nomes* (nohmz). Each nome had its own rituals, gods, and chieftain. Often people of rival nomes raided one another's territory.

By 3200 B.C., Egyptians were coming into contact with the people of Mesopotamia. Caravans loaded with goods for trade were traveling between the two regions. Even more important, whole groups of people seem to have moved freely from one region to another in search of better land for farming or grazing.

At the same time, important changes were taking place in Egypt. The first kings arose, uniting the territories of many nomes. Egyptians also developed their own system of writing. These ideas may have been borrowed, at least in part, from Mesopotamia. The period of Mesopotamian influence was soon over, however. From then on, Egyptian culture followed its own path, which was very different from Mesopotamia's.

Voice from the Past · *Seven Lean Years in Egypt*

Although the Nile was a dependable, life-giving force in ancient Egypt, the river sometimes withdrew its gifts. In the following account, the ruler Djoser (JOH-suhr) describes one such crisis.

I was in distress on the Great Throne, and those who are in the palace were in heart's affliction from a very great evil, since the Nile had not come in my time for a space of seven years. Grain was scant, fruits were dried up, and everything which they eat was short. Every man robbed his companion ... The infant was wailing; the youth was waiting; the heart of the old man was in sorrow ... The courtiers were in need. The temples were shut up.

[The ruler then tells of a vision that came to him in his sleep.]

I discovered the god standing over me ... I prayed to him in his presence ... His words were:

"I am Khnum, thy maker ... The Nile will pour forth for thee, without a year of cessation or laxness for any land. Plants will grow, bowing down under the fruit."

[Upon waking, the ruler went to the temple of Khnum. He made an offering to the god and prayed for the return of the Nile's floodwaters.]

1. Using the information in the account, describe in your own words what a drought meant for Egypt.
2. (a) How did the ruler handle the disaster? (b) How might a modern government handle a similar natural disaster today?

This wall painting from an Egyptian tomb shows a tax assessor measuring a field of grain to decide how much tax the farmer must pay. The farmer's wife and son bring refreshments while younger children stand nearby.

Menes united two kingdoms.

By 3200 B.C., the nomes of Egypt were divided into two groups under two kings. One king ruled Lower Egypt and wore a red crown. Another king ruled Upper Egypt and wore a tall white crown shaped like a bowling pin.

This carving shows the large figure of King Menes wearing the White Crown of Upper Egypt as he triumphs over his foes.

Then, about 3100 B.C., a strong-willed king of Upper Egypt named Menes (MEE-neez) united all of Egypt. As a symbol of his united kingdom, Menes created a double crown from the red and white crowns. Menes shrewdly established his capital near the spot where Upper and Lower Egypt met, about 100 miles from the Mediterranean Sea. The capital was called Memphis. Menes was the first of a long series of kings to rule over the united country of Egypt.

Section Review 1

Define: (a) cataract, (b) delta, (c) irrigation, (d) nome
Identify: (a) Howard Carter, (b) Tutankhamon, (c) Nile River, (d) Upper Egypt, (e) Lower Egypt, (f) Menes
Answer:
1. Why was the Nile's yearly flood important to Egyptian farmers?
2. How did the surrounding desert affect life in ancient Egypt?
3. How did Menes alter Egypt's political organization?

Critical Thinking
4. Ancient Egyptians worshiped the forces of nature as gods. Why would they have regarded the Nile River as one of their most important gods?

Egypt's pharaohs ruled as gods.　2

The kingdom Menes created held together remarkably well, long after Menes died. Members of Menes's family passed the double crown of Upper and Lower Egypt from father to son to grandson. Such a series of rulers from a single family is called a **dynasty**. When one ruling family died out or lost control, another took its place. Eventually, the history of ancient Egypt would consist of an amazing 31 dynasties, spanning 2,800 years.

Like the Nile flooding and receding, the fortunes of Egyptian kings rose and fell. When strong kings held Egypt together, the region prospered. When the king's control weakened, in-fighting broke out among the nobles of the nomes. Outsiders might spot this sign of weakness and take the opportunity to invade. A century or two of war and misery would follow. Then a strong king would take control of Egypt again. Over and over, strength followed weakness; prosperity followed ruin.

Religion glorified pharaohs in the Old Kingdom.

The history of Egypt's first two dynasties is little known, but records improve with the Third Dynasty. Historians call the period that began with the Third Dynasty the Old Kingdom. This period lasted roughly from 2660 to 2180 B.C. The Old Kingdom set the pattern for Egypt's culture for nearly 3,000 years.

The power of the pharaohs The kings of Egypt are known as **pharaohs** (FAIR-ohz). It is useful to have a special term for Egypt's kings, because they were much more than political leaders to their people. In fact, the role of the king was one of the most striking differences between Egypt and Mesopotamia. In Mesopotamia, kings were considered to be representatives of the gods. But to the ancient Egyptians, pharaohs *were* gods, almost as splendid and powerful as the gods of the heavens.

The god-king stood at the center of Egypt's religion as well as its government and army. Egyptians believed that the pharaoh bore full responsibility for the kingdom's well-being. It was the pharaoh who caused the sun to rise, the Nile to flood, and the crops to grow. It was the pharaoh's duty to foster truth and justice. All the good things of life came from the pharaoh. No wonder Egyptians obeyed the ruler's every word. Who would dare to disobey the commands of a god?

Immortality for the pharaoh Egyptians believed that their pharaoh ruled even after his death. He had an eternal spirit, or *ka* (kah), that continued to take part in the governing of Egypt.

In the Egyptian's mind, the ka remained much like a living pharaoh in its needs and pleasures. To provide for the pharaoh's eternal comfort, artists decorated the walls of his burial chamber with pictures of whatever he might need or like. A picture of many fat geese, for instance, would assure him of endless sumptuous meals. Images of loved ones and devoted servants would keep him company and see that his commands were carried out. The burial chamber was also stocked with such luxuries as fine jewelry, game boards covered with precious stones, and rich clothing. Inscriptions on the tomb walls recounted the pharaoh's achievements.

Even though the ka was a spiritual being, it needed to refresh itself occasionally by entering its human body. Thus, the Egyptians preserved the pharaoh's body by making it a mummy. Scholars still accept Herodotus's description of the process of mummification:

> First, they draw out the brains through the nostrils with an iron hook . . . Then with a sharp stone they make an incision in the side, and take out all the bowels . . . Then, having filled the belly with pure myrrh, cassia, and other perfumes, they sew it up again; and when they have done this they steep it in natron [a mineral salt], leaving it under for 70 days . . . At the end of 70 days, they wash the corpse, and wrap the whole body in bandages of waxen cloth.

The time of the pyramids Since pharaohs expected to reign forever, their tombs were even more important than their palaces. For the pharaohs of the Old Kingdom, home after death was an immense structure called a **pyramid**. The Old Kingdom was the great age of pyramid building in ancient Egypt.

The largest of the pyramids is the Great Pyramid at Giza, completed about 2556 B.C. Pyramids were not solid stone but contained chambers and passages. Often there were concealed doors and dead-end tunnels to frustrate robbers.

Air shaft

King's chamber

Queen's chamber

Grand gallery

Ascending passage

Descending passage

Escape shaft

Unfinished chamber

Today, standing at the foot of the Great Pyramid at Giza, millions of stunned visitors have asked themselves: "How could this mountain of stone have been built by people who had not even begun to use the wheel?" Each perfectly cut stone block weighs at least 2½ tons. Some weigh 15 tons. More than 2 million of these blocks are stacked with precision to a height of 481 feet. The entire structure covers more than 13 acres.

Scholars today no longer believe the famous story told by Herodotus that 100,000 slaves were whipped and driven for 20 years before the last stone of the Great Pyramid was lugged into place. Modern historians think that peasants, not slaves, built the pyramids. Moreover, they did the work willingly for the glory of their god-king. In fact, they needed the work to keep busy and well-fed during the flood season. For cutting and hauling stones, they were probably paid with grain from the king's storehouses. Without work on the royal tombs, temples, and palaces, they would have gone hungry during the flood season.

About 80 pyramids still stand in the Egyptian desert. However, the bodies of the pharaohs no longer rest there. Robbers probably stole the mummies long ago, together with armloads of dazzling treasures.

Footnote to History

Although the ancient Egyptians did not know about the wheel, they did know about the slippery nature of mud. Modern scholars think the Egyptians made huge mud-brick ramps beside the pyramid under construction. One team of workers splashed water over the ramp to make a slick surface. Another team hauled the great blocks of stone up the ramp.

The First Illness brought ruin.

Toward the end of the Old Kingdom, the power of the pharaohs declined. More and more power fell into the hands of nobles and officials. Local rulers struggled among themselves for power. Civil war tore Egypt apart.

Some scholars think that these troubles began with a change in climate. Less rain fell in the African highlands, causing the Nile's floodwaters to be too low. Crops died, and the threat of starvation hung over Egypt. Because Egyptians looked to the pharaoh as a god, they expected him to control the forces of nature. When he failed, the people began to doubt his authority.

The Egyptians called this period of weakness and turmoil the First Illness. From 2180 to 2080 B.C., poor harvests, lawlessness, and warfare plagued the region. One Egyptian wrote of this unhappy time:

> . . . The desert is spread over the land. The provinces are destroyed. Barbarians are come into Egypt from without . . . Laughter has disappeared forever. It is wailing that fills the land . . .

Royal power returned in the Middle Kingdom.

Law and order returned to Egypt under the strong kings of the Middle Kingdom (2080–1640 B.C.). Farming revived, trade grew, and the arts flourished. The pharaohs moved the country's capital from Memphis to Thebes and built two massive temples there.

Projects for the public good Some of the prosperity of the Middle Kingdom was brought about by pharaohs who seemed to care about the welfare of the common people. They made trade and transportation easier by having a canal dug all the way from the Nile to the Red Sea. With the wealth that new trade brought in, the pharaohs undertook other public projects. To improve farming, they ordered the building of huge dikes to trap and channel the Nile's floodwaters for irrigation. They also created thousands of new acres of farmland by draining the swamps of Lower Egypt. Harvests were again plentiful; peasants could enjoy a daily diet of bread and beer. One king of this period boasted,

> I was one who cultivated grain and loved the harvest god. The Nile greeted me and every valley. None was hungry in my years, none thirsted then. Men dwelt in peace through that which I wrought, and conversed of me.

Afterlife for commoners During this period, new religious beliefs also showed the increased importance of the common people. During the Old Kingdom, only the pharaoh had expected to live forever. During the Middle Kingdom, Egyptians came to believe that ordinary people had eternal souls as well. People of all classes planned for their burials, so that their place in the afterlife would be assured. This new belief took away some of the pharaoh's grandeur.

The Hyksos ruled during the Second Illness.

The prosperity of the Middle Kingdom did not last. A period known as the Second Illness ravaged the land for about 70 years. Civil war broke out again, leaving Egypt prey to enemies from outside the country. Invaders swept across the Isthmus of Suez into Egypt in horse-drawn chariots. The conquerors were Asian nomads known as the Hyksos (HIHK-sahs), which meant "the rulers of the uplands." They ruled much of Egypt from 1640 to 1570 B.C.

The proud Egyptians despised their less civilized rulers. However, the Egyptians learned several important new skills from the Hyksos. They learned how to make bronze, which was a harder metal than the copper they had used in the past for tools and weapons. They learned to wage war from horse-drawn chariots, shooting arrows from a powerful new kind of bow. And they learned new techniques in the gentler arts of spinning and weaving.

Around 1600 B.C., a series of warlike rulers began to restore Egypt's power. Among those who helped drive out the Hyksos was Queen Ahhotep (ah-HOH-tep), who took over when her husband died in battle. The inscriptions say of her, "She has pacified Upper Egypt and cast out its rebels."

The next pharaoh, Kamose (kah-MOH-suh), won a great victory over the hated Hyksos. Afterward, he described the battle this way:

*When day broke I pounced on the foe like
a falcon; at breakfast time I attacked him,
I broke down his walls, I slew his people,
I captured his women. My soldiers were
as lions with the spoils of the enemy; slaves,
flocks, fat and honey. They shared out their
property with merry heart.*

Kamose's successors drove the Hyksos completely out of Egypt and pursued them across the Sinai Peninsula into Palestine.

The New Kingdom was an age of empire.

Egypt now entered its third period of power and glory, the New Kingdom (1570–1075 B.C.). The kingdom was wealthier and more powerful than ever before. The buildings were larger and more lavishly decorated. (This was the period when Tutankhamon's tomb, with its wealth of gold, was built.) Showiness was the fashion throughout Egypt. Yet the art and architecture of the New Kingdom were not as creative nor as carefully crafted as in earlier periods.

The Egyptian empire The invasion of the Hyksos had shaken the Egyptians' confidence in the deserts as natural barriers for protecting the country. The pharaohs of the New Kingdom set out to strengthen Egypt by building an empire.

Equipped with bronze weapons and two-wheeled chariots, the Egyptians became conquerors themselves. The warlike pharaohs of the Eighteenth Dynasty (1570–1365 B.C.) set up a professional army including bowmen, charioteers, and infantry. The symbols of royal power had always been the red crown and the white crown. Now the pharaohs added a new piece of royal headgear—the blue crown, a war crown shaped like a battle helmet.

Rule by a queen Among the rulers of the New Kingdom, perhaps the most surprising was Hatshepsut (hat-**SHEP**-soot). This remarkable woman was one of Tutankhamon's ancestors. Although Egypt had several strong queens who wielded power through their fathers, sons, or husbands, custom decreed that the pharaoh be male. Nonetheless, Hatshepsut declared herself pharaoh around 1478 B.C., while her stepson, Thutmose (thoot-**MOH**-suh), was a mere child. On special occasions, she donned a man's kilt and attached

This statue of Hatshepsut shows her wearing the ceremonial beard of a pharoah. Tutankhamon's golden mask (page 47) has a similar beard.

the pharaoh's long, braided, ceremonial beard to her chin.

Hatshepsut ruled boldly for 22 years. Unlike most New Kingdom rulers, she was better known for encouraging trade than for waging war. Carved scenes on her great funeral temple show her officials on a trade expedition to the east African coast, buying myrrh, frankincense, ebony, ivory, and leopard skins.

Hatshepsut's death is still a mystery to historians. No one knows whether she died naturally or was murdered by her stepson, the impatient-to-rule Thutmose III.

A warrior pharaoh Thutmose III proved to be a more warlike ruler than his stepmother. Between the time he took power around 1450 B.C. and his death in 1425 B.C., he conducted 15 victorious invasions into Palestine and Syria. In addition, his armies pushed south as far as the Fourth Cataract and returned to Thebes with thousands of Nubian slaves.

Egypt was now a mighty empire. It controlled regions far beyond the Nile River valley and drew boundless wealth from them. Egypt had never before—nor has it since—commanded such power and wealth as during the reign of the pharaoh Thutmose III.

Meeting their match By 1300 B.C., Egyptian armies had crossed the Sinai Peninsula and conquered parts of Syria and Palestine. This advance brought the Egyptians face to face with the Hittites, a group of people who had moved into Asia Minor around 1900 B.C. during the great migrations of that period. In later years, the Hittite kingdom expanded southward into Palestine. After a series of confrontations, the Egyptian and Hittite armies met at the battle of Kadesh in 1288 B.C. There they fought each other to a standstill.

Eventually, the pharaoh and the Hittite king made a treaty promising "peace and brotherhood between us forever." For the rest of the century, the two kingdoms were allies. However, the Egyptians could no longer think of themselves as the only powerful rulers in the world. From this time on, Egypt's rulers had to deal with other powers and even to recognize some as their equals.

An age of builders Like the Old Kingdom with its pyramids, the New Kingdom was an age of great buildings. Because the pyramids of the Old Kingdom were too visible and easily robbed, rulers of the New Kingdom built their tombs beneath desert cliffs. The site they chose was the remote Valley of the Kings near Thebes in which Carter found the tomb of Tutankhamon. Besides royal tombs, the pharaohs of this period also built great palaces and magnificent temples. (Indeed, the word *pharaoh* means "great house" and comes from this time period. The word became a royal title because the ruler's own name was too sacred to use.)

One of the greatest builders of the New Kingdom (and Egypt's last great pharaoh) was Ramses (RAM-seez) II, who reigned for 67 years (1279–1212 B.C.). He lived to the age of 99 and was the father of 150 children. Ramses created the giant temple to Amon (AH-muhn), Egypt's chief god, at Karnak. He also built a massive temple at Abu Simbel (AH-boo SIHM-buhl). Ramses decorated his temples with gigantic statues of himself (the ears more than three feet long). Although these

Ramses II's great temple of Abu Simbel was cut into red sandstone cliffs above the Nile River.

buildings are huge and impressive, they are not as skillfully built as those of the Old Kingdom.

Egypt's power waned.

After 1200 B.C., the empire built by Thutmose III and ruled by Ramses II slowly came apart. Other strong civilizations were now rising to challenge Egypt's power. The tribes of Palestine often rebelled against their Egyptian overlords. Even the vast western desert no longer stopped tribes of Libyans from raiding Egyptian villages.

Shortly after Ramses' death, a great wave of invasions took place all around the eastern Mediterranean. Like the earlier invasions of 2000 B.C. that destroyed the city-states of Sumer, the invasions of 1200 B.C. destroyed many kingdoms.

Egyptian records speak of attacks by "the Peoples of the Sea." Little is known of these invaders, but the destruction they left behind was vast.

Both the Egyptian empire and the Hittite kingdom fell to these mysterious enemies.

Egypt never recovered its power. The warlike Assyrians spoke of Egypt's pharaoh as "a broken reed." Taking advantage of the kingdom's weakness, the Assyrians invaded and conquered Egypt in 671 B.C. A century and a half later, the Persians took over Egypt. From then on, Egypt passed from one foreign conqueror to the next. Even the conquerors, however, were struck with the grandeur of Egypt's past.

Section Review 2

Define: (a) dynasty, (b) pharaoh, (c) ka, (d) pyramid
Identify: (a) Hyksos, (b) Ahhotep, (c) Kamose, (d) Hatshepsut, (e) Thutmose III, (f) Ramses II, (g) Peoples of the Sea
Answer:
1. Explain why Egypt's pharaohs were unusually powerful rulers.
2. (a) Why were the pyramids even more important than palaces? (b) Describe the objects and paintings inside a pharaoh's burial chamber and explain what purposes they served.
3. Why did Egyptians give the name "First Illness" to the years around 2100 B.C.?
4. How did pharaohs of the Middle Kingdom help restore prosperity to Egypt?
5. (a) What was the "Second Illness" in Egypt? (b) How was it overcome?
6. (a) How was Egypt's wealth and power increased by Hatshepsut? (b) By Thutmose III?
7. What led to Egypt's downfall after the death of Ramses II?

Critical Thinking
8. When the Egyptians described times of suffering for their land, they called such times "illnesses." According to an Egyptian, what would have characterized a good or "healthy" time? You may wish to use some of the quotations from Egyptian sources in this section as examples.
9. Why might the Greek historian Herodotus have assumed that the pyramids had been built with slave labor, as mentioned on page 53? (Hint: Greeks in Herodotus' time had a democratic society.)

Egypt's way of life endured 3,000 years. 3

For 3,000 years, power passed from one pharaoh to another. Dynasties flourished and then died out. Invaders seized power and then lost it. Yet, in all that time, daily life for Egyptians changed very little. Each generation kept up the rituals and patterns of life that their parents had followed.

Nobles lived in luxury.

If you think of Egyptian society as a pyramid, the pharaoh stood at the top. Below the pharaoh and his family were the nobles. What was life like for the upper classes during Egypt's golden age?

Serving the pharaoh Nobles in Egypt did not lead an idle life. Many of the men spent busy days in the service of the pharaoh. They were governors, generals, tax collectors, and officials of all sorts. Others were priests, responsible for the upkeep and rituals of the great temples.

Women also served as government officials and priests. The Egyptians were better prepared for female leadership than were most ancient peoples, because women in Egypt held many of the same rights as men. For example, a wealthy or middle-class woman could own and trade property. She could propose marriage or seek divorce. If she were granted a divorce, she would be entitled to one third of the couple's property.

Home life At home, noble families enjoyed many luxuries. Imagine that you are going to a banquet at the home of a wealthy family. From the road you cannot see the single-story house. Only the mud-brick wall that surrounds it is

Footnote to History

By modern standards, many of the pharaoh's high officials and priests were very young. For example, a man named Bakenkhons became a priest at age 16, after spending several years as chief of the pharaoh's military stable. He soon rose to be a high priest. The Egyptians had good reason to appoint comparatively young people to high positions: The average life expectancy was only 36 years!

Every upper-class Egyptian home included a garden with a pool. The bronze mirror, folding chair, and cat figurine were other common objects that might be found in the homes of the wealthy.

visible. You enter through the main gate and cross an open courtyard to the garden where the children are chasing one another around a rectangular pool. Since the children are all under 12 years old, they wear no clothing. Both boys and girls wear golden ornaments around their necks, and the girls wear strings of beads around their waists.

Inside the house, the host and hostess greet you. Their clothes are made of soft, sheer cotton.

Both husband and wife wear their finest jewelry—golden earrings jiggling from their pierced ears and broad necklaces glittering with dozens of multicolored gems.

Servants bring in the food—bowls of figs, slabs of bread, platters of roasted duck and lamb. Everyone eats with their fingers and drinks wine from glass goblets. A harpist plays soft music in the background.

Social mobility Most of the wealthy Egyptians who led such pleasant lives had been born as nobles. Some, however, had been born to families of artisans or small shopkeepers. Still others had been born in families of peasant farmers or even slaves.

The way to rise in Egypt was through the pharaoh's service, especially through the army. A soldier who showed courage in battle might win a cash reward, called "the gold of valor." In time, he might become an officer. After a lifetime of service in the pharaoh's army, he would be rewarded with a small farm, livestock, and some peasants to work his land for him. His sons and grandsons could hold this land as their own, as long as one man in the family continued to serve in the army.

To win the highest posts, either in the army or in the government, people had to be able to read and write. Thus, most high positions went to people who had been born into families wealthy enough to send their children to school. But even humble village scribes taught their own children and perhaps some of their friends' children. In Egypt, unlike Sumer, girls as well as boys were permitted to study to become scribes. Once a person had the skill to read and write, many careers were open in the army, the royal treasury, the priesthood, and the pharaoh's court.

Peasants led a life of toil.

We know less about the peasants of Egypt than about the upper classes. Since the peasants' everyday lives were not considered very important, scribes recorded little about them. Most information about peasant life comes from wall paintings in tombs.

Those paintings show that peasants worked hard and had few comforts. Planting, cultivating, and harvesting in the hot sun were grueling work. Women worked beside men in the fields. Peasants did not even own the land they farmed. The land belonged to the pharaoh and was parceled out by royal officials. These officials hauled away a large share of the harvest as taxes.

Although farming was not possible during the flood season, this time of year rarely brought rest for the peasants. Instead, peasant men—and sometimes women—were called to work on the pharaoh's latest project. A tomb, dike, or canal required many workers.

Nonetheless, it seems that the peasants managed to enjoy life. They were usually left with enough to eat even after taxes. In this respect, they were better off than artisans such as toolmakers and jewelers, who might go hungry during hard times when no one needed their services. Peasants found time for music and games, and they sometimes joined their overseers in a great feast to celebrate the harvest. However, while the rich drank wine, peasants drank barley beer.

Daily Life · *Egyptian Cosmetics*

The dramatic, dark-lined eyes that look out at us from the artwork of ancient Egypt were the height of fashion 3,000 years ago. However, the dark lining was not just a beauty aid. It also softened the glare of the brilliant desert sun. The makeup, called *kohl,* was made from powdered stone—malachite for dark green and galena for black—mixed with water. Men and women applied it to their eyes with small sticks.

Oils were a key ingredient of many other cosmetics the Egyptians used. Some oils came from animal fats, and others were pressed from plant seeds. The Egyptians mixed oil with powdered red ocher (a kind of iron ore) to make lipstick, which they applied with a brush. They steeped flowers and fragrant woods in oil and rubbed the oil into their skin. Sometimes they decked their hairdos with cones of scented oil, which melted slowly in the heat. Like the eye makeup, these fragrant oils had a practical use. They protected skin, lips, and hair from the dry desert air. This glass fish at the right held sweet-smelling oil, and the other container held kohl.

Slaves were the lowest class.

Until the time of the New Kingdom, peasants made up the lowest class in Egypt. Then, during the New Kingdom's wars of conquest, thousands of slaves were brought to Egypt from Asia and Nubia, a land to the south of Egypt.

The most fortunate slaves worked in the homes of the rich. They perfomed every kind of service for their wealthy masters—giving them baths, combing their hair, cooking meals, watching their children, feeding their cattle. Through loyal service to a priest or noble, house slaves could hope someday to be granted their freedom.

Other slaves were not so lucky. Whole families of slaves were sent into the mountains of Upper Egypt to work in the gold mines. Often they felt

During the New Kingdom, slavery became common in Egypt. Many slaves were war captives. This slave is carrying a heavy cauldron.

the stinging lash of the overseer's whip. Men, women, and children dropped from exhaustion. According to one account,

> *There is no forgiveness or relaxation at all for the sick, or the maimed, or the old . . . but all with blows are compelled to stick to their labor until, worn out, they die in their servitude.*

Religion taught fairness and hope.

Laws did not forbid Egyptians to mistreat their slaves. However, Egyptian religion taught that it was morally wrong to do so. The Egyptians used the word **maat** (muh-AHT) to speak of the virtues of a good life. Maat was the idea of justice, right, truth, and order. To live according to maat meant always trying to act rightly and justly. Everyone, including the pharaoh, was supposed to uphold this ideal. The idea of maat influenced even the god-king's behavior.

Judgment by Osiris Egyptians believed they would be judged for their deeds when they died. Osiris (oh-SY-rihs), the powerful god of the dead, would weigh each dead person's heart. To win eternal life, the heart could be no heavier than a feather. Each soul was required to come before the great judge, Osiris, and say something like this:

> *Hail to Thee, Great God, Lord of Truth and Justice . . . I have not committed inequity against men. I have not oppressed the poor . . . I have not laid labor upon any free man beyond that which he wrought for himself . . . I have not defaulted, I have not committed that which is an abomination to the gods. I have not caused the slave to be ill-treated of his master . . .*

If the heart tipped the scale, showing that the person was lying, a fierce beast known as the Devourer of Souls would pounce on the impure heart and gobble it up. But if the soul passed this demanding test for purity and truth, it could live forever.

Scenes painted on the walls of tombs showed how Egyptians imagined their future life. Souls journeyed by boat to a pleasant, fertile land, much like Egypt itself. Children in the underworld would still quarrel and pull one another's hair.

A priest who has apparently suffered from polio brings an offering to the altar of a goddess. An attendant follows him.

Peasants would still drive oxen over the fields. The rich would continue to enjoy banquets. Nothing would be changed.

The power of the priests What hope was there for those Egyptians who had committed just one mistake—perhaps stealing a jar of grain? How could their souls escape the snapping jaws of the Devourer? They believed their only hope was to employ the services of a priest. Egypt's priests specialized in magical charms and chants to protect both the living and the dead from troubles of all kinds. Many of these prayers were recorded in a text known as the *Book of the Dead*, which was placed in the dead person's coffin.

Because Egyptians believed that their priests could influence the gods with their magic, priests had enormous power and prestige. In fact, in the New Kingdom, the priests probably controlled more land, more slaves, and more wealth than the pharaoh himself.

A *challenge to tradition* Around 1375 B.C., one pharaoh dared to challenge Egypt's religious traditions and also the power of the priests. The name of this bold pharaoh was Akhenaton (AH-kuh-NAH-tuhn).

When the sun rose every morning in the Egyptian sky, Akhenaton worshiped it as a god. This was nothing new. The sun had always been worshiped by Egyptians as one of their many gods. However, Akhenaton made the new and shocking claim that this sun-god, Aton, was the only true god in all the universe. Perhaps the pharaoh truly believed this claim, or perhaps his goal was to lessen the priests' power.

Akhenaton did everything in his power to convert Egyptian religion from polytheism to monotheism. He ordered the religious cults that worshiped the cat-god, the crocodile-god, the baboon-god, and all the other gods to shut down their temples and worship only Aton.

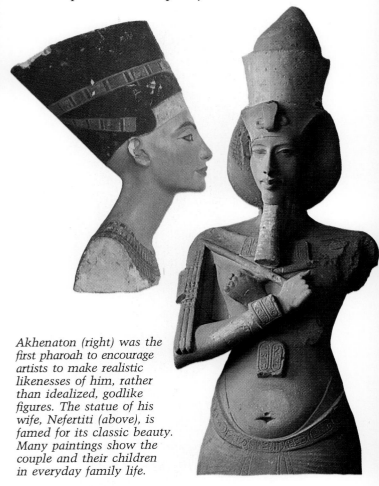

Akhenaton (right) was the first pharoah to encourage artists to make realistic likenesses of him, rather than idealized, godlike figures. The statue of his wife, Nefertiti (above), is famed for its classic beauty. Many paintings show the couple and their children in everyday family life.

Above all, people were commanded to stop worshiping Amon, god of air, wind, and the breath of life. The huge temples around Thebes were all dedicated to Amon. The high priests of Amon were the most powerful rulers in Egypt next to the pharaoh himself. Akhenaton ordered that all the offerings and taxes that had poured into Amon's temples now go to Aton's treasury. Naturally, the priests of Amon were furious.

Workers with chisels and hammers were sent all over Egypt to smash the name of Amon wherever it appeared. The pharaoh changed his own name, originally *Amon*hotep, to Akhen*aton,* meaning "He who serves Aton." Akhenaton then moved the royal capital from Thebes to a new city, which he named Akhet*aton,* "the Place of Aton's Power."

However, many Egyptians refused to abandon their old gods. They defied the pharaoh's laws by secretly worshiping Amon, Osiris, and their other favorites.

When Akhenaton died in 1362 B.C., the priests of Amon regained their power. The new pharaoh, who was only eight or nine years old, took the name Tutankh*amon,* moved the capital back to Thebes, and ordered the names and images of Aton to be destroyed. As a reward, when Tutankhamon died, the priests packed his tomb with the golden treasures that Howard Carter found nearly 3,300 years later.

Egyptians studied many subjects.

The breadth and richness of Egypt's culture impressed early visitors from Greece, Persia, and Mesopotamia. Even then, Egypt gave an impression of great age and secret wisdom that awed travelers from other lands. In many fields, Egypt richly deserved its reputation for knowledge.

Writing Crude pictographs had been the earliest form of writing in Egypt, but scribes quickly developed a better system. For most of ancient Egypt's history, scribes used a form of writing that we call **hieroglyphics** (HY-er-oh-GLIF-ihks). This term comes from the Greek words *hieros* and *glyphe,* meaning "sacred carving."

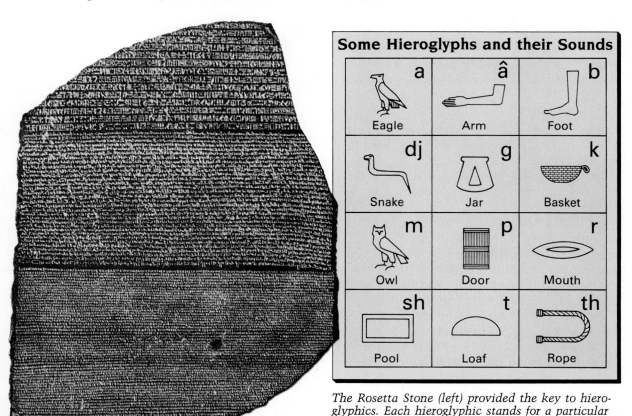

Some Hieroglyphs and their Sounds

a — Eagle	â — Arm	b — Foot
dj — Snake	g — Jar	k — Basket
m — Owl	p — Door	r — Mouth
sh — Pool	t — Loaf	th — Rope

The Rosetta Stone (left) provided the key to hieroglyphics. Each hieroglyphic stands for a particular sound, as the examples above show.

Soon after Egypt's decline, the ability to read hieroglyphics was lost and remained so for 15 centuries. In 1799, near the delta village of Rosetta, some French soldiers found a polished black stone inscribed with a message in three languages. One version was written in hieroglyphics, another was in a simpler form of hieroglyphics, and the third was in Greek. Ancient Greek was a well-known language, yet deciphering the hieroglyphics on the Rosetta Stone still took many years of work. A young Frenchman named Jean François Champollion (shahm-pohl-YAWN) became fascinated by hieroglyphics when he was only a child. By the time he was 16, he had mastered 8 ancient languages. In 1822, at the age of 32, he finally broke the code of the hieroglyphics.

Although hieroglyphics were first written on stone and clay, the Egyptians soon invented a better writing surface. They used the tall stalks of papyrus (puh-PY-ruhs), a reed that grew in the marshy delta. The Egyptians split the reeds into narrow strips, soaked them, and then pressed them into sheets of paperlike material. (The English word *paper* comes from *papyrus.*) Egypt's dry climate preserved papyrus for centuries. Modern scholars can still read writings that are more than 5,000 years old.

Numbers The government of Egypt needed a way of doing arithmetic for the purpose of assessing and collecting taxes. Out of this need, Egyptians invented a system of written numbers for counting, adding, and subtracting. The system was fairly clumsy for numbers greater than 100. To express the figure 999, a scribe had to write 27 symbols. (On the other hand, to express 1 million required only one symbol—a picture of a man striking his hands above his head as if to say, "How in the world could there be such a big number?")

Geometry and surveying One job of the pharaoh's officials was to assign plots of land to peasant families. Because of the Nile's flooding, this job had to be redone every year. The floodwaters wiped out all previous boundaries, and the land had to be measured and marked again. To save time and expense, Egyptians invented an efficient mathematical system for surveying and measuring areas. This method was the origin of geometry.

A calendar To be sure of a good crop, peasants needed to plant at exactly the right time of year.

Crops had to be ripe and harvested before the next flood. Therefore, the Egyptians developed a calendar to keep track of the time between floods. Officials had observed that a very bright star, now known as Sirius, began to appear above the eastern horizon just before the floods came. The time between one rising of Sirius and the next was 365 days. They divided this year into 12 months of 30 days each and added 5 days for holidays and feasting. This calendar was so accurate that it fell short of the true solar year by only six hours.

Medicine Egyptian doctors were the most famous in the ancient world. Their medical services were in demand at royal courts in many kingdoms around the Mediterranean Sea. Although Egyptian medical writings contain all sorts of magic charms and chants, Egyptian doctors also had much practical knowledge. They knew how to check a person's heart rate by feeling for a pulse in different parts of the body. They dealt with broken bones, wounds, and fevers. All in all, they approached their study of medicine in a remarkably scientific way.

Section Review 3

Define: (a) maat, (b) hieroglyphics, (c) papyrus

Identify: (a) Osiris, (b) Akhenaton, (c) Aton, (d) Amon, (e) Tutankhamon, (f) Rosetta Stone, (g) Champollion

Answer:
1. (a) What kinds of work might a noble do in ancient Egypt? (b) A peasant?
2. What beliefs influenced the morals of people in ancient Egypt?
3. How was the ability to read hieroglyphics regained in modern times after having been lost for 15 centuries?
4. (a) What practical need led the Egyptians to invent a system of numbers? (b) A branch of mathematics that formed the basis for modern geometry? (c) A calendar?

Critical Thinking
5. As god-kings, Egypt's pharaohs might have ruled through terror, but generally they did not. What attitudes and beliefs in Egypt acted as a check on the pharaohs?

Chapter Review 3

Summary

1. The Nile River shaped Egyptian Life. The Nile River flooded every year, leaving a blanket of rich soil on Egypt's land. The dependability of this pattern made Egypt an excellent farmland. Farming villages flourished as early as 6000 B.C., protected from invasion by the surrounding deserts. Eventually, groups of villages united to form small kingdoms. In 3100 B.C., all of Egypt was united under King Menes.

2. Egypt's pharaohs ruled as gods. Egypt's pharaohs were considered divine and immortal. Over the years, periods of weakness (known as "illnesses") alternated with periods of strength for Egypt. Around 1200 B.C., a wave of invasions began, leading to a decline from which ancient Egypt never recovered.

3. Egypt's way of life endured 3,000 years. Egyptian society was divided into social classes. Upper-class people generally held government jobs and lived in luxury. Peasants did the farming, and slaves served the rich. Egyptians of all classes were polytheists. Egyptian religion emphasized *maat*, or justice. Those who lived according to maat could expect eternal life in the afterworld. Among the Egyptians' cultural achievements were a system of writing and mathematics and a highly accurate calendar. They were also skilled in the field of medicine.

Reviewing the Facts

1. Define the following terms:
   - a. cataract
   - b. delta
   - c. dynasty
   - d. pharaoh
   - e. pyramid
   - f. maat
   - g. hieroglyphics
2. Explain the importance of each of the following names, places, or terms:
   - a. Upper Egypt
   - b. Lower Egypt
   - c. Nile River
   - d. Isthmus of Suez
   - e. Menes
   - f. Hyksos
   - g. Hatshepsut
   - h. Thutmose III
   - i. Ramses II
   - j. Peoples of the Sea
   - k. Osiris
   - l. Akhenaton
   - m. Tutankhamon
   - n. Champollion
3. How did the Nile's yearly cycle affect life in ancient Egypt?
4. (a) Describe the powers of the Egyptian pharaohs. (b) How was the pharaoh different from a Mesopotamian king?
5. (a) Describe the main groups that made up Egyptian society. (b) What skills were necessary for an Egyptian to move up in society?
6. What were some of the basic beliefs of Egyptian religion?
7. List some of the Egyptians' scientific achievements.

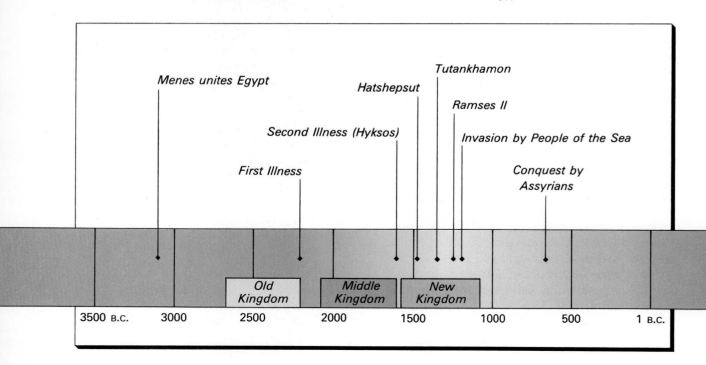

Menes unites Egypt

Tutankhamon

Hatshepsut

Ramses II

Second Illness (Hyksos)

Invasion by People of the Sea

First Illness

Conquest by Assyrians

| | Old Kingdom | Middle Kingdom | New Kingdom | |

3500 B.C. 3000 2500 2000 1500 1000 500 1 B.C.

Thinking about History

1. Many scholars characterize the ancient Egyptians as optimistic and confident, especially in comparison with the people of Mesopotamia. (a) What features have you seen that might justify this characterization? (b) What explanation can you offer for the Egyptians' basic optimism and confidence about life?

2. All cultures are a mixture of change and continuity. However, some cultures choose to emphasize change, using words like *progress, modern, revolutionary,* and *up-to-date.* Others choose to stress continuity with words like *tradition, time-honored,* and *customary.* (a) Do you think Egyptians emphasized change or continuity? Give reasons for your answer. (b) How would you describe American society today in this respect? Support your answer with specific examples.

3. Many historians question whether Akhenaton was a true monotheist or whether he had other motives for wanting his subjects to give up their many gods. What other motives might Akhenaton have had? What is your opinion about this historic controversy?

4. Geography greatly influenced the Egyptian people and the peoples of Mesopotamia. Compare the influence of geography on the two regions. How did geography shape life in each area?

Writing and Speaking about History

1. Choose one of the concepts listed below. Define that concept in a sentence or two. Indicate why it is important in the study of civilization.
    water availability
    religion
    government
    social structure
    trade

2. Divide a sheet of paper into two columns. Label one column *Sumer* and the other column *Egypt.* In each column, describe the concept you selected above as it applies to that civilization.

3. Use the information in your columns to compare and contrast Egypt and Sumer. In small groups, discuss how the civilizations were alike and how they were different.

4. Reread the section of this chapter that looks at the significance of the desert to Egyptian life (pages 49–50). Write a sentence that states the main idea of that section.

Practicing Skills

1. (a) Use the time line on page 64 to calculate about how many years each period in Egyptian history lasted. (b) How many years elapsed between the uniting of Egypt as a nation and the conquest of Egypt by the Assyrians?

2. Make a time line that contains the following events from Chapters 2 and 3. Use the time line to compare dates in Egyptian and Mesopotamian history.
    a. Old Kingdom
    b. rise of Sumerian city-states
    c. Assyrian empire begins
    d. Menes unites Egypt
    e. Fall of Sumer
    f. conquest of Egypt by Assyrians

3. (a) According to the map on page 49, how long is the Nile between the Second Cataract and the Nile Delta in Lower Egypt? (b) How does the map help explain why Egypt has been called "the gift of the Nile"?

Investigating History

1. Read about the life of Jean François Champollion and write a brief biographical report. Explain how he became interested in hieroglyphics and describe the steps that led him to deciphering the code.

2. The opening of Tutankhamon's tomb revealed a great variety of treasures. Look for books on Egyptian art that show some of these items. What kinds of treasures were revealed?

3. Egyptian hieroglyphics progressed from pictograms to ideograms and phonograms. Find out more about these different ways of writing. How does an alphabetic system differ from picture writing? Which system is more efficient in conveying ideas?

Decision Making in History

Evaluate the merits to Egyptians and Hittites of the peace treaty signed between the two groups during the New Kingdom. What provisions can countries make to ensure that a peace treaty will last?

Ancient India and China

The jagged peaks of the Himalayas dwarf the Buddhist monastery that stands amid them.

1. **A new culture arose in northern India.**

2. **Buddhism spread under Mauryan rulers.**

3. **Imperial government united China.**

4. **Ch'in and Han emperors strengthened China.**

The two wisest teachers of ancient India and China never heard of each other. The highest, most formidable mountain barrier in the world—the Himalayas (HIH-muh-**LAY**-uhz)—separated their two civilizations. Yet, by an odd coincidence, these two influential thinkers of ancient Asia were seeking the same goal at nearly the same time. Their common goal was to find wisdom and to know the truth about life. Born within a few years of each other, both wisdom seekers were probably in the prime of life about 525 B.C.

On the southern side of the Himalayas lived Siddhartha Gautama (sih-**DAHR**-tuh **GAW**-tuh-muh), later known as the Buddha. The Buddha preached his first sermon to five companions. They were so astonished by his wise and gentle words that they exclaimed: "Truly, O Buddha, Our Lord, thou has found the truth!" Thousands of Indians agreed and became his devoted followers.

At the same time, in China, a teacher named Confucius (kuhn-FYOO-shuhs) wandered from village to village offering lessons in wisdom to any family that served him a meal. Young students began writing down his witty replies to their questions. Where, they asked, could you find a perfectly wise person? Confucius said: "I do not expect to find a saint today. But if I find a gentleman, I shall be quite satisfied."

What did it mean to have wisdom? To be wise, said Confucius, was to respect your elders and rulers so that families and kingdoms could live in harmony. The Buddha, on the other hand, said that wisdom lay in giving up all selfish desires so that your soul might escape the pain of life and death. Confucius and the Buddha followed different paths to wisdom in part because each man expressed the ideas of his own civilization. This chapter tells the story of the two remarkable cultures that grew up on either side of the world's highest mountains.

A *new culture arose in northern India.* 1

A great landmass lies between the Himalayan Mountains and the Indian Ocean. Today that region includes the countries of India, Pakistan, and Bangladesh. Historically, however, this land has been divided many different ways. Therefore, when speaking of ancient times, historians generally refer to the entire region as India.

India's outline resembles a diamond-shaped kite. To the north (at the top of the imaginary kite), two mountain chains—the Hindu Kush on the west and the Himalayas on the east—meet at a point. This great wall of mountains separates India from the rest of Asia. As a result, India is sometimes called a **subcontinent** of Asia. Though rugged, the mountains are not impassable. Mountain passes like the 34-mile-long Khyber Pass have been used since prehistoric times by migrants and invaders coming into India.

South of the Himalayas lies an enormous flat and fertile plain formed by two rivers—the Indus River and the Ganges (GAN-jeez) River. These two rivers and the lands they water make up a large arc that stretches 2,000 miles across northern India. This arc is called the Indus-Ganges plain. Because the land is flat, easy to irrigate, and very fertile, this plain has always been the rich heartland of India.

The southern part of the Indian subcontinent (the bottom of the imaginary kite) is a peninsula that thrusts south into the Indian Ocean. The center of the peninsula is a high plateau cut by twisting rivers; this region is called the Deccan (DEK-uhn). Covered by dense forests or scrubby grasses, the Deccan is a harsh land.

A narrow border of lush, tropical land lies along the coasts of southern India. This coastal rim has a wet climate and rich soil. Valuable forests of teak and fragrant sandalwood have grown there since ancient times.

Throughout history, southern India often has been a land apart. Its culture remains very different from that of northern India, even though the two regions are united in one country today.

India's climate is dominated by seasonal winds called **monsoons**. From October to May, winter monsoons from the northeast blow dry air across the country. Then, in the middle of June, the winds shift. Spring monsoons blow from the southwest, carrying moisture from the ocean in great rain clouds. The people of India depend on these monsoons for rain to water their crops of wheat, rice, and cotton. If there is too little rain, plants wither in the fields and people go hungry. If there is too much rain, floods may sweep away whole villages. This climate pattern has shaped life for India's farmers since prehistoric times.

Cities flourished in the Indus valley.

India's first civilization developed on the rich plains of the northern subcontinent. The Indus River flows southwest from the Himalayas through what is now Pakistan. Like the Nile, the Tigris, and the Euphrates rivers, the Indus flooded each year. At each flood, the Indus spread a layer of rich silt across its valley, providing good soil for farming.

Well-planned cities Around 2500 B.C., while Egyptians were building the pyramids, people in

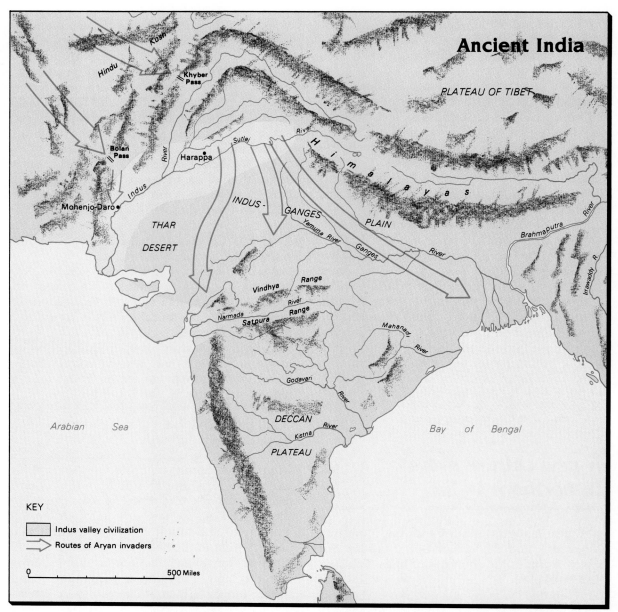

Ancient India

KEY

Indus valley civilization

Routes of Aryan invaders

0   500 Miles

Map Study

From what mountain range does the Ganges River flow? Describe the route by which the Aryan invaders arrived in India.

the Indus valley were laying the bricks for India's first cities. Archaeologists have found the ruins of about 100 settlements along the Indus.

The largest cities were Harappa (huh-**RAP**-uh) and Mohenjo-Daro (moh-**HEHN**-joh-**DAHR**-oh). Each city had a population of roughly 30,000. Although these two cities were 350 miles apart,

they were remarkably alike. Each was laid out neatly, with streets running north-south and east-west like a grid. Their mighty walls were built with oven-fired bricks, all of a standard size. To archaeologists, this regular pattern of building suggests that the cities were carefully planned by a strong central government.

The fine brickwork of Mohenjo-Daro shows in a pool for ritual bathing (left). Cattle such as the one shown on the seal (above) are still common in India today.

Many kinds of specialized buildings lay within the two cities. Each had huge public storehouses for grain, an arrangement that suggests a well-organized government. One large building in Mohenjo-Daro was clearly a bathhouse, with a great brick tub about the size of a swimming pool. Shops lay along main streets.

Housing Dozens of tiny, branching alleys ran off the wide main streets. The doors to people's homes opened out onto these mazelike alleys. Few windows looked out on the street, however. For fresh air, families went to inner courtyards or up stairways to their rooftops. Houses might be two or even three stories high.

The cities of the Indus valley show more concern with cleanliness and sanitation than any other cities of their time. Many houses had brick-floored bathing rooms from which dirty water drained through clay pipes into gutters. Citizens of Mohenjo-Daro disposed of their garbage through narrow slits conveniently cut into the walls of their houses. The garbage fell into containers neatly lined up on the street below.

Everyday life Most people lived by farming. They raised wheat, barley, and perhaps rice for food. They also grew cotton to make cloth. The Indus valley settlers had domesticated cattle, sheep, goats, pigs, and fowl as well as cats and dogs. Some scholars think they may also have tamed elephants.

Next to agriculture, trade was the most important source of prosperity. The Indus valley city dwellers left hundreds of small clay seals that merchants probably used to mark shipments of goods. Some of these seals have also been found in the ruins of ancient Mesopotamia. Apparently the merchants of Mohenjo-Daro and the merchants of Ur exchanged goods. Perhaps they exchanged ideas as well.

The people of the Indus valley cities worked at a variety of crafts. Archaeologists have found kilns for pottery, vats for dyeing cloth, and many different kinds of metal, including gold, silver, copper, bronze, and lead.

Archaeologists have also turned up relics of everyday pleasures. Little cubes stamped with dots on each side indicate that these early city dwellers enjoyed rolling dice. Children amused themselves with wheeled pull toys made of clay.

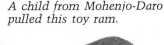

A child from Mohenjo-Daro pulled this toy ram.

The decline of the Indus valley civilization

Around 1750 B.C., the quality of building in the Indus valley cities became poorer. Mohenjo-Daro grew less and less prosperous. Gradually, the great cities fell into decay.

What happened? Some historians think that the Indus River changed course, as it has been known to do, so that its floods no longer fertilized the fields near the cities. Other scholars suggest that people wore out the valley's land. They overgrazed it, allowing their cattle and goats to eat the ground nearly bare. They overfarmed it, growing the same crops year after year. They overcut its trees, brush, and grass to build their houses and provide fuel for their cooking fires and kilns.

As the Indus valley civilization neared its end, around 1500 B.C., human enemies may have had a hand in the cities' downfall. A half-dozen groups of skeletons were found in the latest ruins of Mohenjo-Daro. Bones of men, women, and children lie together where they fell, seemingly never buried. Two skulls show injuries from a sword or axe. These signs of violence suggest that the city, already weakened by its slow decline, may have been abandoned after a devastating attack. Many historians believe the enemies were newcomers from the north side of the Himalayas.

Aryans moved in from the northwest.

Around 1500 B.C., nomads from central Asia trudged across the Khyber Pass and into the Indus valley. Some of the newcomers called themselves Aryans (AIR-ee-uhnz), which in their language meant "the nobles." Other central Asian groups, whose names and languages are unknown to us, probably drifted into India at the same time.

The newcomers were very different from the people they conquered. For one thing, the Indus valley people lived in cities and were chiefly farmers, artisans, and merchants. The Aryans were nomadic herders who counted their wealth in cattle. The Aryans did not move into the cities they conquered, but left them abandoned. It would be many years before the Aryans became city dwellers. Another major difference was that the Indus valley people were literate. The Aryans had no writing system. Instead, their priests preserved their culture from generation to generation by memorizing long hymns and poems. These poems were in the Aryan language, an early form of Sanskrit. Sanskrit remains a learned and sacred language in India today.

To escape the Aryans, some of the Indus valley people may have fled southward across the Vindhya (VIHN-dee-uh) Mountains to the Deccan. To this day, the people of southern India speak a different group of languages, known as the Dravidian language family.

Not all the Indus valley dwellers fled, however. Many remained as slaves to the newcomers. Although they were conquered, the people of the Indus valley had a lasting influence on Indian culture. Between 1500 and 500 B.C., a new society took shape in northern India. The cultures of the Indus valley dwellers and the Aryans blended into a uniquely Indian civilization. One product of that blending was the religion known today as Hinduism.

Hinduism shaped India's culture.

Hindu practices grew from the mingled beliefs of many groups in India. Figurines from the Indus valley seem to show early examples of some gods that were later important to Hindus. However, the earliest records of Hinduism—the long Sanskrit hymns that the priests memorized—are Aryan.

The Vedic Age When the Aryans migrated to India, they brought a rich collection of myths, or tales of their gods. They had gods of thunder, fire, earth, heaven, the moon, and the sun. Priests made offerings of food and drink to the gods. Everything in nature was believed to be in some way holy.

Footnote to History

Strange as it seems, English is distantly related to Sanskrit. Both are members of a large group of languages called the Indo-European language family. The relationship shows in the roots for some of the most basic words in any language—family terms.

English	Sanskrit
mother	matar
father	pitar
brother	bhratar
sister	svasar
daughter	duhitar
son	sunus

Aryan priests could sing from memory a great number of long and complicated hymns, each one suited to a different religious ritual. Some of these hymns may date back to 1500 B.C. Priests gathered the hymns into four collections called Vedas (VAY-duhz). The most ancient and important of these collections, the *Rig-Veda*, included 1,028 hymns of praise. It is probably the oldest set of scriptures still in active use. The Vedas were finally written down about A.D. 1400.

Millions of Indians today cherish the Vedas as sacred. Historians cherish them for a different reason. The Vedas are a most important clue to the history of India from 1500 to 500 B.C. This thousand-year period is called the Vedic Age.

The Upanishads Sometime around 400 B.C., the wisest Hindu teachers tried to interpret and explain the hidden meaning of the Vedic hymns. They discussed such questions as these: What is the nature of reality? What is morality? Is there eternal life? What is the soul? The teachers' comments were memorized by their students and later written down as a collection of essays known as the Upanishads (oo-PAN-ih-shadz). Most of our knowledge about Hindu beliefs comes from these writings. Here are the basic ideas expressed in the Upanishads.

1. The one true reality is Brahman, the mighty spirit that creates and destroys. Brahman reveals itself in millions of earthly shapes, from a mountain to a raindrop. Brahman is One, and yet expresses itself as Many.

Brahman is a unifying and all-powerful spirit. In European and American society, people tend to believe that human life is totally different from the life of a turtle or a butterfly. No, declares an ancient Hindu text, everything in nature is tied together by Brahman. The ancient text puts it poetically:

Thou art woman. Thou art man. Thou art the dark-blue bee and the green [parrot] with red eyes. Thou hast the lightning as a child. Thou art the seasons and the seas. Thou dost abide with all pervadingness, wherefrom all things are born.

2. One aspect of Brahman is the Self, or Soul, called Atman. Atman can be compared to particles of salt dissolved in a glass of water. You cannot see the salt, yet it is everywhere in the water— just as Atman is everywhere.

Although this painting was done in the 1700's, it celebrates a battle from the Mahabharata, *a great Hindu poem based on events that took place before 1000 B.C.*

3. Nothing that lives ever dies entirely. When a living thing dies, its inner self is reborn in another form. This passing of the inner self from body to body is known as **reincarnation.** To be reincarnated, say the Upanishads, is much like being given a new coat to wear:

Just as a man, having cast off old garments, puts on other, new ones, even so does the embodied one, having cast off old bodies, take on other, new ones.

4. All wise Hindus must seek to reach a state of perfect understanding called *moksha*. The inner self that attains moksha will never suffer another reincarnation. In moksha, the self disappears to merge with Brahman.

Castes structured Indian society.

During the Vedic Age, Indians began to develop a complicated set of divisions between groups of people. These social divisions were closely linked to the Hindu world view.

According to the *Rig-Veda*, four different groups of people had been created from the body of a Hindu god. First, the Brahmins were created from the god's mouth. They later became the priestly class and were the highest group in Indian society. (Note that a member of this class is a *Brahmin*, while the universal spirit is *Brahman*.) The second group, the Kshatriyas (kuh-**SHAHT**-ree-uhz), came from the god's arms. They were rulers and warriors. Third, the Vaishyas (**VYSH**-yuhz) were created from the god's legs. They were landowners, merchants, and artisans. The fourth group, the Shudras (**SHOO**-druhz), came from the god's feet. They were servants or slaves.

In reality, Hindu society was much more complicated than the myth suggested. There were hundreds of different groups, not just four. Over the years, these divisions in society became more and more defined. Eventually, each group had its own occupation, which was passed down from parent to child. People of each group ate only with each other and usually married only within their own group.

Hindus call these groups within their society *jatis*, a word that means "birth group." When Europeans came to India, they called the groups **castes** (kasts), from a Latin word that meant "pure."

Ritual purity was the basis for the ranking of castes. Hindus considered high castes purer than low castes. Priests were considered the purest group. Farmers were thought to be purer than people who make their living washing clothes. To share food or have any contact with a lower-ranking person was to risk contamination.

The very lowest group in society were those people outside the caste system—the outcastes or untouchables. Even lower than servants, untouchables could not so much as draw water from a caste well, lest their touch contaminate the water. They had to use separate wells or wait for a higher-ranking person to get water for them.

Why was one person born a Brahmin while another was born an untouchable? Hinduism explained it by saying that Brahmins, in former lives, had committed no bad deeds. An untouchable, on the other hand, must have done bad deeds in an earlier incarnation.

Hindus believed in an ethical law of cause and effect called *karma*. It operated as automatically as the law of gravity. By the law of karma, moral behavior in one life guaranteed rebirth in a higher caste. Immoral behavior, on the other hand, automatically dropped a reborn soul to a lower caste. Says a Hindu scripture: "Just as he acts, just as he behaves, so he becomes."

To earn a good rebirth, according to Hindu teachings, a person had to be a good member of his or her caste. Each caste had its particular *dharma*, or duty. Dharma is the set of duties and obligations of each caste. For example, a boy born into the warrior caste had to be willing to fight, kill, and be killed. A woman's dharma was to obey her father while she was a child, her husband after she married, and her sons if she was widowed. The individual's own wishes or talents made no difference. According to an ancient Hindu text, it is better to do one's own duty badly than to do another's duty well.

Section Review 1

Define: (a) subcontinent, (b) monsoon, (c) reincarnation, (d) moksha, (e) caste, (f) untouchable, (g) karma, (h) dharma
Identify: (a) Himalayas, (b) Indus River, (c) Harappa and Mohenjo-Daro, (d) Aryans, (e) Hinduism, (f) Vedas, (g) Upanishads, (h) Brahmins, (i) Kshatriyas, (j) Vaishyas, (k) Shudras
Answer:
1. What evidence has led historians to the following beliefs about India's first cities? (a) The cities were run by a strong central government. (b) People of the cities carried on trade with Sumer. (c) The people were skilled in a number of crafts. (d) The cities' downfall may have been caused by a slow decline, followed by an attack from outsiders.
2. How were the people of the Indus valley different from the Aryans who conquered them?
3. (a) Why are the Vedas of religious importance to many Indians? (b) Why are they important to historians?

4. (a) Explain how the ideas of Brahman, moksha, and reincarnation are all related in Hindu beliefs. (b) Explain how the ideas of reincarnation, karma, and caste are related.

Buddhism spread under Mauryan rulers. 2

Around 530 B.C., near the very end of the Vedic Age, a young man named Siddhartha Gautama challenged the ideas of the Brahmin priests. Even a lowborn person, he said, could gain enough wisdom in one lifetime to escape the cycle of death and rebirth.

The Buddha sought an answer to life's pain.

The date traditionally given for Gautama's birth is 563 B.C. The legends of his life are probably exaggerated. The stories say that Gautama was born into the warrior class and lived in luxury at his family's palaces near the foothills of the Himalayas. Pampered by his wealthy family, he never saw pain, suffering, or death. He married a beautiful woman who bore him a son.

Again according to legend, Gautama's comfortable life was shattered one day when he first saw proof of human suffering. While riding in his chariot, Gautama saw a man who was terribly sick, another who was old and feeble, and a third who had died. He realized that life was an endless cycle of pain and the only way to escape it was by seeking wisdom.

One night, when he was about 29, Gautama took a last look at his sleeping wife and son. Then he left his palace and joined a wandering, homeless band of five other wisdom seekers. For six years, Gautama tried to find wisdom through harsh discipline and suffering. For days at a time, he ate only a single grain of rice each day. His stomach became so empty that, by poking a finger into it, he could touch his backbone. Yet Gautama gained only pain, not wisdom. He decided, therefore, to seek wisdom in other ways.

At last, enlightenment came to him. After meditating deeply for many days in the shade

This Buddha on the island of Sri Lanka was cut from solid rock between A.D. 400 and 500.

of a tree, Gautama suddenly felt that the truth became clear to him. He rose and set out to teach others what he had learned. Thereafter, he was known as Buddha, a title meaning "the Enlightened One."

Buddhism taught nonviolence.

Buddha gave his first sermon to the five wisdom seekers who had been his companions. That sermon was a landmark in the history of world religions. Buddha taught the four main ideas that had come to him in his enlightenment, calling them the Four Noble Truths.

First Noble Truth Everything in life is suffering and sorrow.

Second Noble Truth The cause of all this pain is people's self-centered cravings and desires. People seek pleasure that cannot last and leads only to rebirth and more suffering.

Third Noble Truth The way to end all pain is to end all desires.

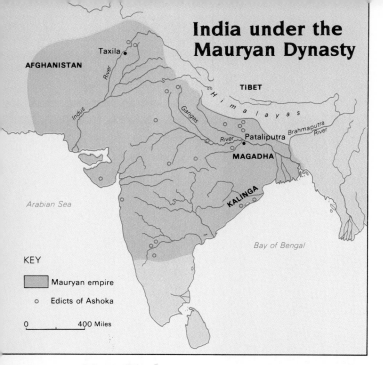

India under the Mauryan Dynasty

AFGHANISTAN
Taxila
Indus River
TIBET
Ganges
Himalayas
Brahmaputra River
River
Pataliputra
MAGADHA
KALINGA
Arabian Sea
Bay of Bengal

KEY

Mauryan empire

o Edicts of Ashoka

0   400 Miles

Map Study

Describe the extent of Ashoka's empire. What part of India remained outside his control?

Fourth Noble Truth People can overcome their desires and attain enlightenment by following the Eightfold Path.

The Eightfold Path was like a staircase. According to Buddha, those who sought enlightenment had to master one step at a time. The steps of the Eightfold Path were right knowledge, right purpose, right speech, right action, right living, right effort, right mindfulness, and right meditation. By following the Eightfold Path, anyone could attain *nirvana* (nur-VAHN-uh), Buddha's word for release from pain and selfishness.

Buddha taught his followers to treat all living things (humans, animals, and even insects) with loving kindness. A devout Buddhist was not even supposed to swat a mosquito.

Buddhists and Hindus both sought to escape from the woes of this world, but their paths of escape were very different. Unlike traditional Hinduism, Buddhism did not require complex rituals. Moreover, Buddha taught in everyday language, not in the ancient Sanskrit language of the Vedas and the Upanishads, which most Indians in 500 B.C. could no longer understand. Buddha's religion was also unique in its concern for all human beings—women as well as men, lowborn as well as highborn.

The Mauryan dynasty built an empire.

Buddha lived near the end of the Vedic Age, around 500 B.C. More than 1,000 years had passed since the fall of the Indus valley cities and the arrival of the Aryans. In all those years, no single ruler had united India's many kingdoms. In Buddha's time, a dozen families had carved the Ganges River valley into little states that were often at war. However, a change was coming. Soon India was to experience a new type of government that brought together large territories under a single king.

In 512 B.C., the armies of the great Persian king Darius I came through the Khyber Pass and conquered northwestern India. For almost 200 years, the Indus valley was ruled by a Persian satrap, or governor. For the first time since the Aryan invasions, Indians felt both the benefits (unity and order) and burdens (heavy taxes) of centralized control.

Then, in 326 B.C., the Greek empire builder Alexander the Great led his armies over the mountain passes into India. The Indus valley passed into Greek hands, but only for five years. When Alexander died, his empire died with him. His ambition to unify all of northern India was finally achieved by another young conqueror—an Indian ruler named Chandragupta Maurya (chuhn-druh-GUP-tuh MOW-ree-uh).

The rise of Chandragupta Around 322 B.C., the young warrior Chandragupta stirred up a revolt against a weak king and thus made himself ruler of the largest kingdom on the Ganges. Over the next 24 years (322–298 B.C.), Chandragupta's army of 9,000 elephants and 700,000 soldiers trampled neighboring kingdoms. He united all of northern India (the Indus valley, the Ganges valley, and the southern Himalayas) under his rule. Chandragupta and his descendants who followed him as kings are known as the Mauryan dynasty.

Chandragupta ruled by force and fear. He planted government spies everywhere to prevent plots against him. He trusted nobody. To avoid being poisoned at a meal, he made servants taste all his food. To avoid being murdered in bed, he slept in a different room every night. People he suspected of plotting revolt were tortured to death. After all, said a political manual of the time, "Government is the science of punishment."

74

Chandragupta was succeeded on the throne by his son, about whom little is known. However, Chandragupta's grandson, Ashoka (uh-SHOH-kuh), became the most famous member of the Mauryan dynasty. Ashoka became the complete opposite of his cruel grandfather.

Ashoka's rule Ashoka inherited the throne in 273 B.C. At first, he was as warlike as Chandragupta. His victory against southern tribes ended in the slaying of perhaps 100,000 captives.

The later chronicles say that news of this massacre filled Ashoka with remorse. He decided henceforth to rule according to Buddha's teachings of "peace to all beings." (In fact, Ashoka's acceptance of Buddhism probably took place gradually.) He sent an apology to the southern tribes and promised kind treatment in the future.

Throughout his empire, Ashoka ordered huge stone pillars to be erected. Each pillar was inscribed with a public announcement, or **edict**, of his new policies. Some edicts guaranteed righteous treatment for all Ashoka's subjects. Others urged the people of his empire to live righteously themselves.

Instead of spies, Ashoka employed "officials of righteousness" to look out for the welfare of

Voice from the Past · *An Edict of Ashoka*

The following is from one of the many edicts that King Ashoka had carved on a rock pillar. It was inscribed about 256 B.C.

The Kalinga country was conquered by the Beloved of the Gods [Ashoka] in the eighth year of his reign. One hundred and fifty thousand persons were carried away captive, one hundred thousand were slain, and many times that number died.

Immediately after the Kalingas had been conquered, the Beloved of the Gods became intensely devoted to the study, love, and teaching of Dharma [truth, moral goodness, and social duty].

The Beloved of the Gods is moved to remorse now, because the conquest of the Kalingas involved slaughter, death, and deportation.

But there is a more important reason for the King's remorse. Those who live there, including priests and holy persons of all sects—who all practiced obedience to superiors, parents, and teachers, and proper courtesy and firm devotion to friends, acquaintances, companions, relatives, slaves, and servants—all suffer from the injury, slaughter, and deportation inflicted on their loved ones. This weighs on the King's mind.

The King seeks to persuade even the forest peoples who have come under his rule to live according to Dharma. He reminds them, however, that he exercises the power to punish, in spite of his repentance, to discourage crimes.

This edict on Dharma has been inscribed so that my sons and great-grandsons who may come after me should not think new conquests worth achieving. Let their pleasure be pleasure in morality. For this alone is good, here and hereafter.

1. How does Ashoka explain his change of heart after the Kalinga war?
2. (a) What is dharma?
(b) What examples does the edict give of righteous behavior for people?
3. What statement shows that Ashoka respected all religions, not just Buddhism?
4. (a) Does Ashoka believe in punishing criminals? (b) Why or why not?
5. What was Ashoka's hope in posting this edict?

These lions stood atop a pillar set up by Ashoka about 250 B.C. The modern country of India has made this figure its badge.

Buddhism spread far beyond India and became a major world religion with millions of followers.

Ashoka was the last strong ruler of the Mauryan dynasty. In 180 B.C., only 50 years after Ashoka's death, the Mauryan empire was torn apart by rivalry among local princes. Again, India became a collection of small kingdoms. However, the basic form of Indian civilization—begun in the Indus valley and developed through Hinduism and Buddhism—was already established. This civilization proved strong enough to survive centuries of political disunity.

Section Review 2

Define: (a) nirvana, (b) dynasty, (c) edict
Identify: (a) Siddhartha Gautama, (b) Buddhism, (c) Chandragupta Maurya, (d) Ashoka
Answer:
1. (a) How did Buddhists hope to achieve enlightenment? (b) How was the Buddhist path to enlightenment different from the Hindu path?
2. During what years did the Mauryan dynasty rule India?
3. What were the great contributions of the following rulers? (a) Chandragupta (b) Ashoka

Critical Thinking
4. Both Hinduism and Buddhism accept that human life is filled with suffering. How do the two religions differ in their explanations of human suffering?

Imperial government united China. 3

The walls of China's first cities were built 1,500 years after the walls of Ur, 1,000 years after the great pyramids of Egypt, and 1,000 years after the tidy cities of the Indus valley. Though a late starter, the civilization begun on China's Yellow River 3,500 years ago outlasted all the others and continued into the twentieth century. What gave Chinese civilization its endurance and its unity? Part of the answer lies in China's geography.

Indians of every caste. Was anyone imprisoned unjustly? Was a family suffering because of flood or drought? The emperor instructed his officials to furnish necessary aid.

Ashoka sent hundreds of Buddhist missionaries to neighboring lands such as Ceylon (the modern Sri Lanka) and even to kingdoms as far away as Syria. Thanks largely to his encouragement,

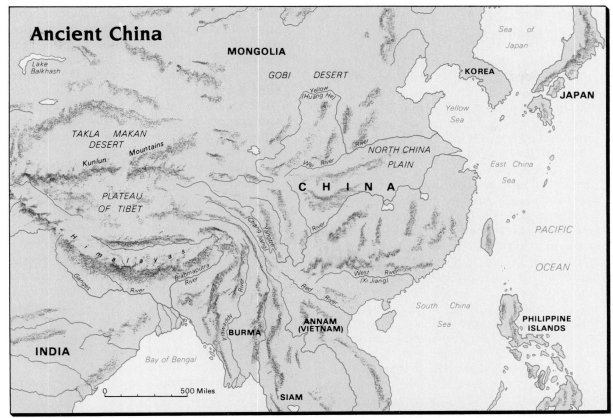

Ancient China

MONGOLIA

GOBI DESERT

Lake Balkhash

Sea of Japan

KOREA

JAPAN

Yellow (Huang He)

Yellow Sea

TAKLA MAKAN DESERT

Kunlun Mountains

Wei River

River

NORTH CHINA PLAIN

East China Sea

C H I N A

PLATEAU OF TIBET

Chang Jiang

Yangtze

River

PACIFIC

OCEAN

H i m a l a y a s

Brahmaputra River

River

West River (Xi Jiang)

Ganges River

River

Red River

South China Sea

PHILIPPINE ISLANDS

Irrawaddy

BURMA

ANNAM (VIETNAM)

INDIA

Bay of Bengal

0   500 Miles

SIAM

Map Study

What geographic barriers lie to the west and northwest of China? What are the two longest rivers that flow through China?

Geography isolated China.

Chinese civilization grew up in the valleys of two rivers, the Yellow River and the Yangtze River.* On the map on this page, notice that both these long, twisting rivers flow out of the towering highlands of Tibet. The rivers flow east until they reach a broad, flat pocket of land near the Pacific Ocean. This rich plain is cupped on the north, west, and south by hills and mountains. About 90 percent of China's land that is suitable for farming lies within this comparatively small region. This plain was China's heartland.

* This book uses the traditional system for writing Chinese names, sometimes called the Wade-Giles system. This system is used in many standard reference books and in all books on China published before 1979. The new *pinyin* system appears in some current publications, especially newspapers. For place-names, maps in this book show the pinyin form in parentheses after the traditional spelling.

Throughout China's long history, its political boundaries have expanded and contracted depending on the strength or weakness of its ruling families. Yet China remained a center of civilization with all that the word implies—cities, writing, organized government and religion, specialized crafts, and more. In the Chinese view, only barbarians (people who are not civilized) lived outside China's borders. Because the Chinese saw their country as the center of the civilized world, their own name for China was the Middle Kingdom.

Ancient China was isolated from all other civilizations. To its east lay the Pacific Ocean. To the west lay the forbidding Takla Makan Desert and the icy 14,000-foot Plateau of Tibet. To the southwest were the Himalayas. And to the north lived the warlike nomads of Mongolia. For the first 1,000 years of their history, the only foreigners the Chinese met were indeed barbarians.

Strong bonds held Chinese society together.

The culture that grew up in China had strong bonds that made for unity. From earliest times, the group seems to have been more important than the individual. Above all, people's lives were governed by their duties to two important authorities—their family and their king or emperor.

The family In China, the family was central to society. Everyone's role in the family was fixed from birth to death. The elderly had privileges and power; the young had practically none. The oldest man was in charge of all the family's goods and possessions. He also had final approval of the marriages that the women of the family arranged for his children and grandchildren. The oldest woman—usually the grandmother—had authority over all the younger women. Children were expected to obey their parents and grandparents without question. The most important virtue in Chinese society was respect for one's parents.

Women in Chinese society were treated as inferiors. They were expected to obey their fathers, their husbands, and later, their own sons. When a girl was between 13 and 16 years old, her marriage was arranged, and she moved permanently into the house of her husband. A young bride often entered her husband's household with fear and trembling, wondering how her mother-in-law would treat her. Only by bearing sons for her husband's family could a woman hope to improve her status. Eventually, of course, she might be able to rule over her own daughters-in-law.

The importance of family ties is shown by the fact that the Chinese were the first people known to use two names: a personal name and a family name (or surname). Among the Chinese, the first name is the family name. Thus, in a name such as Liu Pang, Liu is the family name and Pang is the personal name.

In China, the family was closely linked to religion. The spirits of family ancestors were thought to have the power to bring good fortune or disaster to living members of the family. The Chinese did not regard these spirits as mighty gods. Rather, the spirits were more like troublesome or helpful neighbors who demanded attention and respect. Every family paid respect to its ancestors and made sacrifices in their honor. Only sons could carry on the traditional religious duties, so sons were valued much more highly than daughters. (Also, only the ancestors in the father's family were so honored; the mother's family did not count.)

View of government In ancient China, a person's chief loyalty throughout life was to the family. Beyond this, people owed obedience and respect to the ruler of the Middle Kingdom, just as they did to their own grandfather. The ruler was like a super-grandfather who had supreme responsibility for the welfare of the Chinese people.

The Chinese believed that royal authority came from heaven. A just ruler had divine approval, known as the Mandate of Heaven. A wicked or foolish king could lose the Mandate of Heaven. The ancestral spirits might show their displeasure by causing a flood, riot, or other calamity. In that case, the Mandate of Heaven might pass to another noble family. This was the Chinese explanation for rebellion and civil war. The fall of one dynasty and the rise of another was never achieved without bloodshed.

Historians describe the rise and fall of dynasties as a cycle. Each dynasty rules vigorously for a while, then weakens and is replaced by a new ruling family. This pattern of strength, decline, and replacement is called the dynastic cycle.

Chinese history is marked by a succession of dynasties until dynastic rule was finally overthrown in the early 1900's. The first historic family to rule the Middle Kingdom (from about 1500 to 1027 B.C.) were the Shang (shahng) kings. The last Shang king was overthrown by the first Chou (jo) king. The Chou dynasty, the longest in Chinese history, lasted for eight centuries (from 1027 to 221 B.C.). It was followed by the shortest and cruelest dynasty, the Ch'in, which in turn was followed by the mighty Han dynasty. These four dynasties—Shang, Chou, Ch'in, and Han—span the first 1,900 years of China's history.

Civilization emerged in Shang times.

Archaeologists have found the remains of China's first civilization along the Yellow River. The river's color is indeed yellowish. From the western mountains, the water picks up a dusty, yellow soil called *loess* (les). The river spreads the loess like a layer of butter over the peasants' fields. Winds from the west bring more rich loess to keep the farmlands of the Middle Kingdom fertile.

The Yellow River is fearfully unpredictable. Its floods can be generous or ruinous. At its worst, when rains are unusually heavy, the river devours whole villages. (The great flood of 1887 killed nearly a million people.) Those who live near the Yellow River know well why it is nick-named "China's Sorrow." Yet the rich farmland constantly draws people back to the river valley.

Early cities China's first cities appeared near the Yellow River about 2000 B.C. Among the oldest and most important was Anyang (ahn-yahng). Anyang was one of the capitals of the Shang dynasty.

Unlike the cities of the Indus valley or the Fertile Crescent, Anyang was built mainly of wood. The city stood in a forest clearing. Nobles lived in large, rectangular wooden houses with thatched roofs. Average families lived in little cone-shaped huts or pit-houses.

Social classes Chinese society was sharply divided between nobles and peasants. Warrior-nobles owned the land. They served in the army and the government of the Shang king. They were skilled fighters with the horse, the chariot, and the bow and arrow. Noble families governed the scattered villages within the Shang lands,

sending tribute to the Shang ruler in exchange for local control.

Meanwhile, peasants tilled the soil for their overlords. In Shang times, the farmers had no plows, only wooden digging sticks and hoes and sickles made of stone. The soil was so rich, though, that it yielded two crops a year of millet, rice, and wheat.

A separate class in Chinese society was made up of people who were skilled in special crafts. At Anyang, these artisans lived outside the city walls. Their houses were smaller than those of the nobles but much more spacious and comfortable than those of the peasants.

Crafts Bronzework was the leading craft in which Shang artisans excelled. Beautiful bronze objects were used in religious rituals and were also symbols of royal power. Some of these objects were small and graceful, such as bronze bells. Others were massive caldrons, weighing almost a ton. The skills of the Shang bronzesmiths, say modern admirers, have never been surpassed.

In earliest Shang times, the Chinese also learned how to draw the fine threads from a silkworm's cocoon and weave them into a light, beautiful fabric. Nobles prided themselves on their finely embroidered silk shoes, which they esteemed as a symbol of civilization. Barbarians, after all, were known to go barefoot.

Shang bronzesmiths made the offering vessel (right) in the form of a tiger protecting a man. The ax (left) was used for beheadings.

A *writing system developed.*

The earliest evidence of Chinese writing comes from Shang times. At Anyang and other Shang cities, archaeologists have found hundreds of animal bones and tortoise shells with written symbols scratched on them. These strange objects are known as oracle bones because priests used them to foretell the future. The writing on the oracle bones showed that people 3,500 years ago were part of the same cultural tradition that continues in China today. Some of the characters are very much like those in a modern Chinese newspaper.

In the Chinese method of writing, each character stands for an idea, not a sound. Recall that many of the Egyptian hieroglyphs stood for sounds in their spoken language. Sumerian cuneiform and the Phoenician alphabet also corresponded to spoken language. In contrast, there were practically no links between China's spoken language and its written language. One could read Chinese without being able to speak a word of it. (This seems less strange when you think of our own number system. Both a French person and an American can understand the written equation $2 + 2 = 4$, but an American may not understand the spoken statement, *"Deux et deux font quatre."*)

The Chinese system of writing had one great advantage. People in all parts of China could learn the same system of writing, even if their spoken languages were very different. Thus, the Chinese written language was very important in unifying a large and diverse land.

The disadvantage of the Chinese system was the enormous number of written characters to be memorized. To be barely literate, a person needed to know at least 1,000 characters. To be a true scholar, one needed to know between 5,000 and 10,000 characters. For centuries, this severely limited the number of literate, educated Chinese. As a general rule, a noble's children learned to write, but a peasant's children did not.

Daily Life · *The World's Most Treasured Fabric*

According to legend, silk was discovered by the 14-year-old empress Hsi Ling-shi, who lived around 2500 B.C. Hsi Ling-shi was walking one day among the mulberry trees near the palace. A few days earlier, the trees had been covered with caterpillars eating the mulberry leaves. Now the caterpillars hung from the branches in mummylike cocoons.

Curious about the cocoons, Hsi Ling-shi plucked one from a branch and took it home. She dropped it in a pot of water and watched it soften into a loose, tangled web. When she picked up the web, she found she could unravel it like a skein of yarn to form a single long thread of silk.

The legend may or may not be true. The process of making silk became China's best-kept secret for the next 3,000 years. Foreign gold and silver poured into China from the silk trade. To pass on the secret of silk-making to the outside world was treason, punishable by death.

Anyone who has ever seen or worn a garment of pure silk knows why the Chinese had to guard their invention so jealously. Silk is petal soft and lighter than the sheerest cotton, yet it is the strongest natural fiber. A silk thread is stronger than some kinds of steel thread of equal thickness. Silk drapes and flows gracefully, and it can be dyed to richer hues than any other natural fabric.

The Chou dynasty ruled in troubled times.

In the long parade of dynasties that have ruled China, the Chou followed the Shang. No dramatic changes in civilization marked the change of dynasties. The Chou ruled much as the Shang had. The Chou ruled from around 1027 to 221 B.C. For the first 300 years of this long period, the Chou ruled a large empire including both eastern and western lands. The king's power was wielded locally by mighty lords, but final power still lay in the hands of the king.

Gradually, however, Chou rule weakened. In 771 B.C., the dynasty's weakness brought on a crisis. In this unhappy year, barbarians from the north and west sacked the city of Hao, the Chou capital. They murdered the Chou monarch, but a few members of the royal family escaped eastward to the city of Loyang (loh-yahng). Here in this new capital on the Yellow River, the Chou dynasty pretended to rule the Middle Kingdom for another 500 years.

In fact, the Chou kings at Loyang were almost powerless. Noble families, who supposedly owed allegiance to the king, could not be controlled. Trained as warriors, they sought every opportunity to pick fights with neighboring lords. As their power grew, these warlords claimed to be kings in their own territory. As a result, the later years of the Chou are often called "the time of the warring states."

In this time of bloodshed, traditional values collapsed. At the very heart of Chinese civilization was a love of order, harmony, and respect for authority. Now there was chaos, arrogance, and defiance. How could China be saved? Three solutions were offered by the Middle Kingdom's scholars and philosophers.

Confucius urged social harmony.

Foremost among these scholars was K'ung Chiu, or K'ung Fu-tzu (Master Kung). In English, he is better known as Confucius. Born in 551 B.C., Confucius was about 12 years younger than the Indian sage Gautama (Buddha).

Confucius led a scholarly life, devoting himself to the study of his three favorite subjects—history, music, and morals. To make a modest living, he offered lessons in wisdom to children of noble

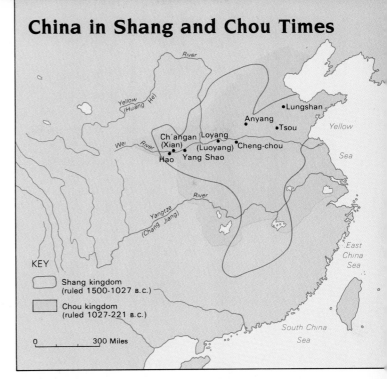

China in Shang and Chou Times

KEY

▢ Shang kingdom
(ruled 1500-1027 B.C.)

▢ Chou kingdom
(ruled 1027-221 B.C.)

0 _____ 300 Miles

Map Study

Which dynasty—the Shang or the Chou—controlled more land along China's coast? About how far is it from Loyang to Anyang? From Loyang to Tsou?

families. Charmed by his kindly humor, students apparently adored him. As he trudged along country roads, his students followed. The only record of his teachings are the writings of his students.

Confucius wanted to reform society by showing princes and dukes how to govern wisely. To govern well, he said, a prince must live virtuously. The people would then imitate their ruler's example, and peace and order would follow. "If a ruler himself is upright," Confucius said, "all will go well without orders. But if he himself is not upright, even though he gives orders they will not be obeyed."

Confucius was a traditionalist—a lover of old ideas, old values, and old customs. He urged people to uphold the great traditions and customs of the past, so that society would again be well ordered.

Although he valued religious traditions, he was more interested in human society than in the gods. Good manners and good morals were judged practically one and the same. Confucius taught, for example, this variation on the golden rule: "Do not do to others what you would not want

Taoists sought harmony with nature.

For Confucius, the *social* order (family and government) was most important. For another Chinese thinker named Lao Tzu (low dzu), only the *natural* order was important. If you seek order and harmony, said Lao Tzu, go up into the hills, sit by a stream, and observe a drifting cloud or a soft breeze. Observe that nothing in nature strives for fame, power, or even wisdom. The cloud, the breeze, and the stream move without effort because they follow the Tao (dow), meaning "the Way" or the universal force that guides all things.

Of all the creatures of nature, only humans fail to follow the Tao. They argue about questions of right and wrong, good manners and bad. According to Lao Tzu, such arguments are futile. A simple creature like a turtle is naturally wise because it does not argue, does not strive for personal glory. The turtle simply follows the Tao of its nature. Humans should do likewise, said Lao Tzu. The philosophy of Lao Tzu came to be known as Taoism. Chinese who adopted the Taoist philosophy withdrew from society to live close to nature.

Legalists urged harsh government.

A third group, the Legalists, believed that a highly efficient and powerful government was the key to restoring order. The Legalists taught that a ruler should provide rich rewards for people who carried out their duties well. Likewise, the disobedient should be harshly punished.

In practice, the Legalists stressed punishment more than rewards. For example, anyone caught outside his own village without a travel permit should have his ears or nose chopped off, said the Legalists.

The Legalists believed in controlling ideas as well as actions. They suggested that a ruler should burn all writings that might encourage people to think critically about government. After all, it was for the prince to govern and the people to obey.

Eventually, Legalist ideas gained favor with a prince of a new dynasty that replaced the Chou. A powerful ruler soon put an end to China's long period of disorder, as you will read in the next section.

There is no portrait of Confucius that was made during his own time. Like most later portraits, this one suggests his wisdom and kindness.

done to yourself." Most important, said Confucius, remember to respect your elders and your social superiors.

Confucius never won the high political position that he sought. Although he may have held some minor posts, no king ever accepted him as chief adviser. Confucius died in obscurity around 479 B.C. It was only much later, 350 years after his death, that millions of Chinese began to memorize his teachings.

Define: (a) Middle Kingdom, (b) Mandate of Heaven, (c) dynastic cycle, (d) loess

Identify: (a) Yellow River, (b) Yangtze River, (c) Tibet, (d) Mongolia, (e) Shang, (f) Chou, (g) Confucius, (h) Lao Tzu

Answer:

1. (a) What were the two important bonds that united early Chinese society? (b) What role did religion play in each of those bonds?
2. (a) In the Shang times, what kind of work was done by nobles? (b) By peasants? (c) By artisans?
3. (a) How did writing help to unite China? (b) Why was literacy in China long limited to the wealthy?
4. Why was the traditional way of life in China badly shaken during the late years of the Chou dynasty?
5. What were the basic ideas of the following? (a) Confucius (b) the Taoists (c) the Legalists

Critical Thinking

6. Reread the statement by Confucius on page 81 about the importance of a ruler's character. (a) How does that statement support the Chinese idea of the Mandate of Heaven? (b) In your opinion, how does that statement apply to leadership today?

Ch'in and Han emperors strengthened China.

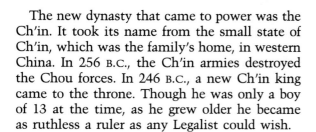

4

The new dynasty that came to power was the Ch'in. It took its name from the small state of Ch'in, which was the family's home, in western China. In 256 B.C., the Ch'in armies destroyed the Chou forces. In 246 B.C., a new Ch'in king came to the throne. Though he was only a boy of 13 at the time, as he grew older he became as ruthless a ruler as any Legalist could wish.

The Ch'in dynasty built an empire.

This proud ruler was Ch'in Shih Huang-ti (chin shir hwahng-tee), whose name meant "First Emperor." *Huang-ti* was a title that this ruler took

for himself in 221 B.C. In earlier times, it had been used only for gods. Because the title means someone even greater than a king, it is translated *emperor*. From this time on, the ruler of China was known as an emperor.

Shih Huang-ti stopped the petty wars that had sapped China's strength. He conquered the barbarians to the south of his kingdom and protected the northern border by building the Great Wall. Most important, he gave China a form of government that lasted more than 2,000 years. His dynasty was even responsible for giving China its name. Nevertheless, Ch'in Shih Huang-ti was hated by one and all. A later Chinese scholar described Shih Huang-ti as having a "high pointed nose, slit eyes, pigeon breast, wolf voice, tiger heart." Furthermore, he was "stingy, cringing, graceless." Nonetheless, Shih Huang-ti was an effective ruler.

Stamping out opposition The First Emperor concentrated all his energies on two tasks: destroying outside rival armies and destroying resistance to his rule from within. His goals were extreme and so were his methods.

His armies struck out in every direction, attacking barbarians north of the Yellow River and south as far as what is now Vietnam. Because of his conquests, the China of the Ch'in dynasty was roughly double the size of China under the Chou dynasty.

At the same time, the Ch'in emperor crushed political opposition within China. To destroy the power of rival warlords, he commanded all the noble families to live at the capital city under his watchful eye. This edict, according to tradition, uprooted 120,000 noble families. To put a stop to wars between states, the First Emperor wiped out the ancient borders of Lu, Ch'u, Ch'in, and other states, and drew new boundaries. China was carved into 36 administrative districts, each of which was controlled by officials from Ch'in.

To prevent criticism of his rule, the emperor ordered the burning of all books that were judged to be either useless or harmful. This included all poetry of the Chou dynasty and all political writings—every book valued by Confucian scholars. Only practical books about medicine and farming were to be spared.

To unite his empire, Shih Huang-ti ordered a gigantic network of highways to be built by peasant work gangs. He also set uniform standards

The Great Wall of China is the only human-made feature on Earth that is visible from the moon. Although Shih Huang-ti built the earliest unified wall, the wall as it exists today dates from the Ming dynasty (1368–1644).

for Chinese law, money, and weights and measures—even the length of cart axles. This last standard ensured that all vehicles fit the ruts of all Chinese main roads.

The Great Wall If scholars most hated Shih Huang-ti for his book burning, peasants most hated him for his Great Wall. This colossal wall, which still stands, was not entirely the idea of the First Emperor. Smaller walls had been built in Chou times to discourage attacks by northern barbarians. Mounted on tough war-horses, the barbarians could not ride through the walls, but of course they could and did ride around them. Shih Huang-ti decided to close the gaps and stretch a new wall so far to the west that an enemy would have to gallop halfway to Tibet to get around it.

Pushing wheelbarrows (a Chinese invention), about a million peasants collected, hauled, and dumped millions of tons of stone, dirt, and rubble. Slabs of cut stone on the outsides of the wall

enclosed a heap of pebbles and rubble on the inside. Each section of wall rose to a height of 20 to 25 feet. From the Yellow Sea in the east to the edge of the Gobi Desert in the west, the Great Wall twisted like a dragon's tail for a total distance of roughly 1,400 miles.

The wall builders worked neither for wages nor for love of empire. They worked because it was the law, and to break Ch'in law was death.

Footnote to History

Before his death in 210 B.C., Shih Huang-ti ordered the building of a great tomb for himself. The whole site was as big as a city. Within the burial mound were more than 7,500 life-size clay statues of warriors, charioteers, archers, and spearmen. This royal bodyguard came to light in 1974, in one of the greatest archaeological finds of the century.

An army of clay soldiers was buried with Shih Huang-ti in a tomb that covered as much ground as a small city. Archaeologists have roofed over areas as large as two football fields to protect the figures as they are excavated.

Many died anyway from the crushing labor and the freezing winter winds. According to legend, thousands of human bones lie within the wall.

The fall of the Ch'in The Ch'in dynasty was short-lived. Shih Huang-ti's son, though just as cruel as his father, was less able. After three years under the rule of this second Ch'in emperor, the peasants rebelled. One of their leaders, a peasant from the land of Han, marched triumphantly into the capital city. Thus, in 202 B.C., the Ch'in dynasty ended and the Han dynasty began.

Civilization flowered under the Han dynasty.

The Chinese think of the Han years as a time of glory, unity, and peace. The Chinese even call themselves "the people of Han." There were several reasons for the high reputation of the Han. First, though the emperor still had great power, the hated laws of the Ch'in emperors were revoked. Legalist thinkers were expelled from the imperial palace. Second, the Han ruled during a time when barbarians rarely threatened the Chinese. Third, scholars spoke highly of the Han

dynasty because these were the years when Confucius's teachings won widespread influence.

The most powerful of the Han emperors was Wu-ti, who ruled from 140 to 87 B.C. Wu-ti was known as the Martial Emperor because of his success in battle. Northern barbarians, the Huns, had earlier broken through the Great Wall and pitched their tents in one corner of the empire. But Wu-ti's armies drove them back beyond the wall. At the same time, the boundaries of the empire were extended westward to central Asia, south to Vietnam, and east into what is now Korea. The armies of the Han struck up to 2,000 miles from their emperor's palace.

Wu-ti and the Confucian scholars During Han rule, there was a renewal of learning. Scholars were again allowed to read the old Chinese classics, the poetry and history so loved by Confucius. Ch'in book burners had destroyed many ancient works, but a few scholars had hidden their classics. Others had memorized them. The most precious books were known as the "Five Classics" because, shortly before his death, Confucius was said to have collected the greatest writings of Chou times and organized them into five books. A sixth book, the *Analects*, contained Confucius's words of wisdom as recorded by his students.

China in Ch'in and Han Times

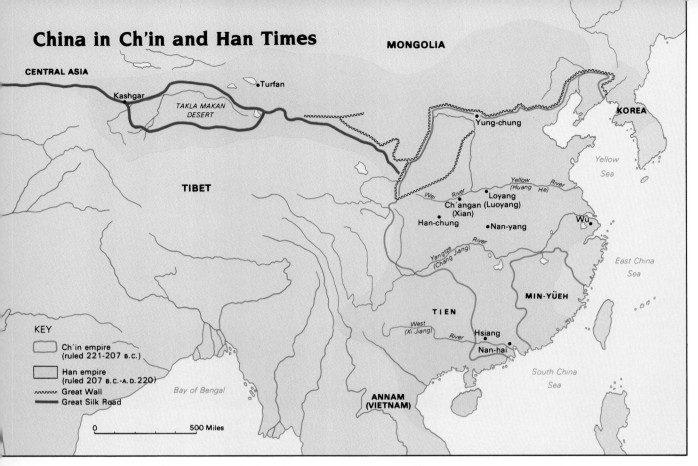

MONGOLIA

CENTRAL ASIA

KOREA

Turfan

Kashgar

TAKLA MAKAN
DESERT

Yung-chung

Yellow
Sea

TIBET

Yellow
(Huang
He)

River

Wei   River

Loyang

Ch'angan (Luoyang)
(Xian)

Han-chung

Nan-yang

Wu

East China
Sea

Yangtze
(Chang Jiang)

River

MIN-YÜEH

TIEN

West
(Xi Jiang)

River

Hsiang

Nan-hai

South China
Sea

KEY

Ch'in empire
(ruled 221-207 B.C.)

Han empire
(ruled 207 B.C.-A.D. 220)

Great Wall

Great Silk Road

Bay of Bengal

ANNAM
(VIETNAM)

0 ———— 500 Miles

Map Study

During which dynasty did part of Korea become subject to Chinese rule? What areas in the south and west did the Han dynasty add to its empire? What reason might Han emperors have had for wanting to rule the Takla Makan desert?

Wu-ti proclaimed Confucianism the official set of beliefs for his government. In 124 B.C., Wu-ti founded a national university to teach the Five Classics and other great writings of the past. Graduates who passed examinations on the Classics were chosen for high positions in Wu-ti's government. Soon the most powerful officials in China (outside the imperial family) were scholars who had mastered the Classics. In later years, these examinations were a key feature of Chinese government.

The Great Silk Road Wu-ti's conquests to the west of China encouraged the growth of overland trade. According to legend, Wu-ti sent a trusted Chinese official in search of a fresh supply of horses for his armies. Traveling far beyond the Great Wall, the official brought back reports that stunned Wu-ti. Far to the west, he had discovered foreigners (Persians) who were almost as civilized as the Chinese.

It was silk that first linked China with Persia and the rest of the civilized world. Camel caravans carried bundles of silk over a rocky, mountainous route that led past Tibet, across the Takla Makan desert, and into central Asia. This route was known as the Great Silk Road. After a journey of 4,000 miles, Chinese silk reached the great markets of Syria and Asia Minor at the eastern end of the Mediterranean Sea. By that time, the silk had changed hands many times, each time for a higher price.

Collapse of the Han dynasty In the years following Wu-ti's reign, China's prosperity declined. Chinese peasants suffered most in any time of troubles. They lived under a crushing burden of debts and taxes. In times of bad harvests or drought, many peasant families were forced to sell their children into slavery. Famine and plague stalked China's villages. Thousands of peasants fled into the mountains and became bandits.

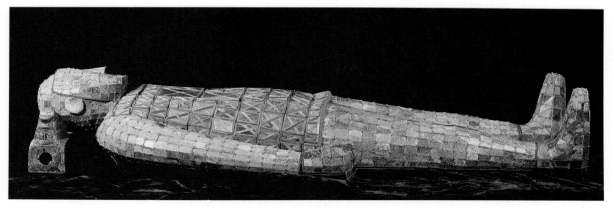

This burial suit is made of 3,000 pieces of jade sewn together with gold thread. It belonged to Liu Sheng, a Han prince who died in 113 B.C. The jade suit was expected to preserve his body for eternal life.

They joined secret societies, each known by a colorful name: the Red Eyebrows, the Green Woodsmen, the Yellow Turbans. Led by these rebels, the peasants revolted.

Twice the Han dynasty was overthrown, partly because of peasant discontent and partly because of rebellious and ambitious warlords. There were therefore two periods of Han rule. The Early Han dynasty lasted from 206 B.C. to A.D 8. The Later Han ruled from A.D. 25 to 220.

A period of peace followed the return of the Han to the throne, but soon the empire was in difficulties again. Cruel and corrupt officials gained power in the government. In the countryside, generals led armies in the emperor's name but, in fact, ruled for themselves. Peasants turned again to banditry. As disorder spread through China, the Han dynasty neared its end.

The spread of Buddhism During the late years of the Han dynasty, between 50 B.C. and A.D. 100, Buddhism became increasingly popular in China. Buddhism came to China with traders on the Great Silk Road or on trade vessels from the Indian Ocean.

In the villages of China, Buddhist monks taught that the Buddha had been a merciful god who came to earth to save human souls. Of course, Buddha himself, dead now for five centuries, had never claimed to be a god. Yet people in both India and China were carving statues of him and bowing before them. In the rocky hills of northern China, huge statues of Buddha were carved into sandstone cliffs and grottos. One such Buddha measured 50 feet from chin to topknot. (The topknot or bun of rolled hair was a Buddhist symbol for wisdom.)

In these bitter times for Chinese of all classes, the need for religious comfort was great. The worship of family ancestors continued, but people were also eager to embrace new beliefs. Millions of Chinese turned to the kindly Buddha. Thus, as the once glorious Han empire collapsed, the religion of Buddhism spread rapidly through the troubled land.

Section Review 4

Define: emperor
Identify: (a) Ch'in, (b) Shih Huang-ti, (c) the Great Wall, (d) Han, (e) Wu-ti, (f) the Five Classics, (g) the Analects, (h) the Great Silk Road
Answer:
1. (a) What were Shih Huang-ti's achievements as a ruler? (b) What methods did he use to reach his goals?
2. (a) How did Wu-ti encourage learning during his reign? (b) How did he expand China's foreign trade?
3. What circumstances encouraged the spread of Buddhism into China?

Critical Thinking
4. Use the idea of the dynastic cycle to describe the rule of the Han dynasty. What characteristics marked each stage of the dynasty's development?

Chapter Review 4

Summary

1. A new culture arose in northern India. India's first cities grew up in the Indus valley. Around 1500 B.C., these cities were conquered by Aryans from central Asia. The blending of Indian and Aryan culture produced the religion known today as Hinduism and a caste system of society.

2. Buddhism spread under Mauryan rulers. Around 550 B.C., a new religion known as Buddhism developed in India. Around 300 B.C., the Mauryan dynasty united most of India. The greatest of the Mauryans was Ashoka, who adopted Buddhism and devoted much of his reign to humane causes.

3. Imperial government united China. Chinese civilization began over 3,000 years ago on a plain crossed by the Yellow and Yangtze rivers. A tradition of respect and obedience toward family and government helped the Chinese form a stable society. The teachings of the Chinese scholar Confucius greatly supported these values. Other major schools of thought were the Taoists and the Legalists.

4. Ch'in and Han emperors strengthened China. The harsh Ch'in dynasty strengthened China and paved the way for a period of prosperity under the Han. Near the end of Han rule, during a time of civil strife, Buddhism spread to China.

Reviewing the Facts

1. Define the following terms:
   a. subcontinent   c. caste
   b. reincarnation   d. edict
2. Explain the importance of each of the following names, places, or terms:
   a. Himalayas   j. Yangtze River
   b. Indus River   k. Shang
   c. Mohenjo-Daro   l. Chou
   d. Aryans   m. Ch'in
   e. Vedas   n. Han
   f. Buddha   o. Confucius
   g. Chandragupta Maurya   p. Lao Tzu
   h. Ashoka   q. Shih Huang-ti
   i. Yellow River   r. Wu-ti
3. What signs have archaeologists found indicating that life in India was highly civilized as early as 2500 B.C.?
4. (a) How did Hinduism develop in India? (b) How is Hinduism related to Indian society?
5. (a) How did Buddhism develop in India? (b) What are the main teachings of Buddhism?
6. (a) What important part did Chandragupta Maurya play in India's history? (b) How did Ashoka affect life in India and in countries beyond India?

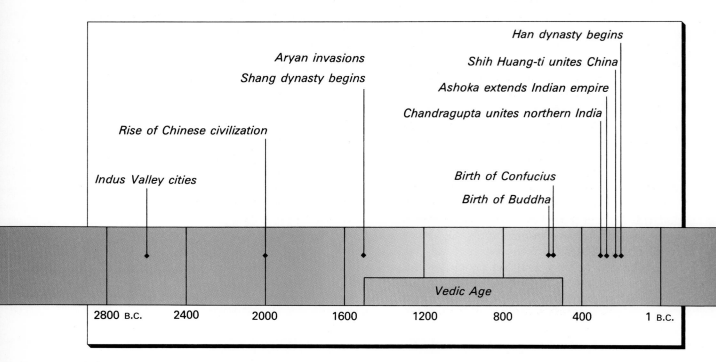

Han dynasty begins
Shih Huang-ti unites China
Aryan invasions
Ashoka extends Indian empire
Shang dynasty begins
Chandragupta unites northern India
Rise of Chinese civilization
Birth of Confucius
Indus Valley cities
Birth of Buddha

Vedic Age

2800 B.C.   2400   2000   1600   1200   800   400   1 B.C.

7. What were the keys to unity in earliest Chinese society?

8. Describe three different philosophies that emerged in China during the troubled years of the Chou dynasty.

9. How did Shih Huang-ti restore order to China?

10. (a) Why are the early years of the Han dynasty considered a golden era in the history of China? (b) What religious change took place in China during the later years of the Han dynasty?

Thinking about History

1. How were China and Sumer opposites in terms of geographic defenses?

2. How is the Indian idea of caste different from the idea of social classes in modern American society?

3. History shows many examples of conquerors being conquered themselves by the culture of the people they defeated. (a) How does this generalization apply to India's history? (b) What evidence from other world regions you have studied supports this generalization?

4. An Indian political philosopher in Mauryan times wrote, "Government is the science of punishment." What rulers and philosophers in both China and India would have agreed with that statement? What rulers and philosophers would have disagreed? Give evidence for your answers.

Writing and Speaking about History

1. Use the information on pages 67, 76–77, and 78–79 of the text to make a chart that describes geography and water availability in ancient China and India. To make your chart, divide a sheet of paper into two columns. Label one column *China* and the second column *India*. Down the side of your paper, make a column for each of the three features being compared.

2. Write a brief generalization about one of the three features above as it relates to China. (Example: Geography isolated ancient China.) Repeat the process for India. Give two supporting pieces of evidence for the generalization.

3. Prepare a one-minute speech explaining the concept of one of the following:
    right living according to Buddha
    right relationships according to Confucius

Practicing Skills

1. Make a bar graph that shows the relationship of these figures:
    1,000,000 peasants to build the Great Wall
    240,000 workers to build the Panama Canal
    80,000 workers to build the Transcontinental Railroad in the United States

2. Use the time line on page 88 to answer these questions: (a) About how old is Indian civilization? (b) About how old is Chinese civilization? (c) What was happening in India at the beginning of China's Shang dynasty? (d) What was happening in India about the same time that the Han dynasty was beginning in China?

3. A century is any period of 100 years. For about how many centuries did the following historic periods last? (a) India's Vedic Age (1500–500 B.C.) (b) China's Shang dynasty (1500–1027 B.C.) (c) China's Chou dynasty (1027–221 B.C.)

Investigating History

1. Writing was not only a form of communication in China; it also became an important art form. Look in the library for books on Chinese calligraphy (the art of decorative writing).

2. Interview people who speak Indo-European languages other than English. Ask them to provide in their language the family terms shown on page 70 and the numbers from one to ten. Compare your list with others in the class. How closely related to English is the language you researched?

3. In what countries are Hinduism and Buddhism important religions today? Make a world map highlighting these areas, using one color for Hinduism and another for Buddhism.

4. Shih Huang-ti's magnificent tomb was discovered in 1974, filled with statues of an entire army as well as other riches. A fine article on this discovery appears in *Smithsonian*, Volume 10, Number 8 (November 1979). Prepare a report on this striking archaeological find.

Decision Making in History

Evaluate Siddhartha Gautama's decision to leave family and friends. Knowing what he knew ten years later, do you think he would have made the same decision?

Research Skills

Notetaking

Taking notes is one of the best ways to remember information that you have heard in class or read in a book. Here are some helpful hints for taking notes from a lecture:

1. Keep a notebook for classroom discussions and lectures.
2. Date notes to identify lectures.
3. Write a title for the notes that states the general topic. Speakers often alert listeners to the main topic with words and phrases such as *my purpose is to show* and *today I will discuss.*
4. Write down the main ideas and supporting details of the lecture. Speakers signal main ideas and details with words and phrases such as *first, then, in summary, in conclusion, the reason for,* and *the result was.*
5. Use words and phrases, not complete sentences, to record notes. You can always clarify information later.
6. Skip several lines between topics. Add subheadings later.
7. Leave a blank page at the end of each set of notes. Use this page to review or summarize your notes.

Here are some helpful hints for taking notes from a textbook:

1. Keep a notebook for each subject.
2. Write down the chapter title and date.
3. Write down the main ideas of the chapter in your own words. Use chapter headings as clues to main ideas. Support main ideas with important details.
4. Be brief. Use words and phrases, not complete sentences.
5. Define the key boldfaced terms. Explain the importance of the key people, places, and events.
6. Develop a timeline of key events. Draw arrows connecting the events that have a direct cause and effect relationship.
7. Review your notes shortly after you have written them. If there is a chapter summary, read it carefully to make sure your notes cover points mentioned in the summary.
8. Write down questions or points you would like to have clarified.

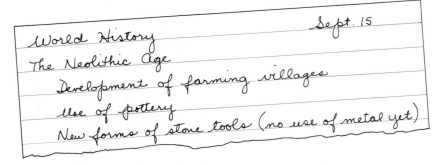

Unit Review I

1. Describe the relationship between or among each of the following sets of terms:
   a. technology
      culture
      civilization
   b. archaeologist
      artifact
      prehistory
   c. cuneiform
      hieroglyphics
   d. pyramid
      pharaoh
   e. Paleolithic
      Neolithic
   f. polytheist
      monotheist
   g. ideogram
      pictograph

2. What is the most important difference between history and prehistory?

3. With what civilization is each of the following people associated? What role did that person play in the civilization?
   a. Moses
   b. Nebuchadnezzar
   c. Hammurabi
   d. Cyrus the Great
   e. Menes
   f. Akhenaton
   g. Shih Huang-ti
   h. Confucius
   i. Ashoka
   j. Buddha

4. Describe the location and explain the importance of each of the following places:
   a. Jarmo
   b. Çatul Hüyük
   c. Mesopotamia
   d. Nile River
   e. Himalayas
   f. Mohenjo-Daro
   g. Yellow River

5. (a) What do the letters B.C. and A.D. stand for in a date? (b) How many years are there in a century?

6. Use the text as well as the timelines on pages 45, 64, and 88 to put the events in groups a–d in the correct chronological order.
   a. Rise of Chinese civilization
      Rise of Sumer
      Menes unites Egypt
   b. Old Kingdom in Egypt
      Aryan invasion of India
      Beginnings of Bronze Age
   c. Birth of Buddha
      Rise of Persia
      Conquest of Egypt by Assyrians
   d. Great age of pyramid building in Egypt
      Age of empire building in Egypt
      Second Illness in Egypt

7. Identify the specific culture or civilization with which each of the following facts or ideas is associated.
   a. constructed pyramids as royal tombs
   b. invented a system of writing known as cuneiform
   c. invented an alphabet that made use of 22 symbols
   d. worshipped one God only
   e. made observations about the stars that formed the basis for astronomy and astrology
   f. permitted women to have many of the same rights as men
   g. structured society according to a complicated division among groups of people
   h. lacked direct contact with other civilizations and believed peoples of other cultures were barbarians
   i. used metal coins of a standard value

8. Make a list of the key traits that define a civilization. Then, for each of the civilizations listed below, describe one of the traits as it relates to that civilization.
   a. Sumer
   b. Egypt
   c. Babylon
   d. Phoenicia
   e. Persia
   f. Hindu India
   g. Shang China

9. Describe the origins and beliefs of three of the following religions:
   a. Confucianism
   b. Buddhism
   c. Judaism
   d. Hinduism
   e. Taoism

10. Many of the civilizations you read about in this unit developed around rivers. Make a list of these civilizations. Then describe how the river provided the civilization with advantages. What problems arose as a result of the river?

Unit II
The Mediterranean World

The civilization of Greece and Rome gave birth to many of the most prized ideals of the modern world. In government, the Greeks developed the ideas of democracy and individual worth. Greek science encouraged the use of human reason. Greek art and architecture established standards of beauty based on balance, scale, and proportion. As they founded cities around the Mediterranean Sea, the Greeks spread their ideas far beyond their homeland.

The Romans were not such original thinkers as the Greeks, but they were fearsome conquerors and skilled empire builders. They took up Greek culture and extended it to new lands as their empire spread. Their own great contribution was law—a single law that united many peoples and gave new meaning to the idea of citizenship.

During the period of Roman rule, a new religion, Christianity, arose. Beginning in the land of Palestine, Christianity spread throughout Roman lands. Christianity too united many peoples, this time by bonds of faith.

Even after the Roman empire fell, the heritage of Greco-Roman culture lived on. Its achievements became central elements in Western civilization.

Temple of Poseidon, Cape Sunion, Greece

Chapter 5

2000 B.C. - 323 B.C. *Ancient Greece*

An acropolis was a fortified hilltop at the heart of a Greek city-state. Here the acropolis of Athens is dominated by the ruins of the Parthenon (at right).

1. Greek culture grew up around the Aegean Sea.

2. Greek city-states competed for power.

3. Athens led Greece in its golden age.

4. Alexander's conquests spread Greek culture.

On a June morning in 480 B.C., the male citizens of Athens hiked up a steep hill outside their city. Thousands—perhaps even 10,000— took their seats on rows of stone benches on the hillside. This was the day of decision for Athens. A colossal Persian army, rumored to number more than 2 million soldiers, was marching toward the city. At the same time, a fleet of 1,000 Persian ships was sailing along the coast of Greece.

In size, Athens was no match for the Persian empire. Athens was a Greek city-state of 250,000 people controlling a 117-square-mile plain. The Persian empire, on the other hand, stretched from the Indus River (in what is now Pakistan) to the shores of the Mediterranean and the Black seas. Should the people of Athens fight or run? The citizens on the hill had to decide.

"Pray silence for Themistocles (thee-MIHS-toh-kleez), son of Neocles!" a voice shouted. From the speaker's platform, a stout, bullnecked man addressed the crowd. Themistocles argued that it would be foolish for Athenian soldiers to try to save their city from the Persians. If need be, let the Persians enter the city and burn it. Send the women, old men, and children to safety on a nearby island. Meanwhile, let all men of fighting age row out to meet the Persian fleet with the 200 new Athenian warships. Even though their ships might be outnumbered five to one, said Themistocles, this was the Greeks' only chance.

Naturally, there was strong opposition to this plan. Many Athenians could not bear the thought of allowing the Persians to destroy their city. In the end, though, Themistocles convinced a majority of the citizens to vote his way.

Almost three months later, Persian soldiers walked into a near-empty Athens and burned it to the ground. They destroyed the buildings of Athens, but they could not destroy its spirit. While their city lay in ruins, the Athenians won a complete victory at sea and forced the Persians to withdraw. (You will read the full story of this heroic encounter later in the chapter.) When the stunned Persians finally left Greece, the city of Athens rose from its ashes more glorious than ever before.

We can rejoice with the Greeks that their civilization was not destroyed in 480 B.C. The culture that developed in Greece had a huge influence over what historians call *Western civilization.* This civilization had its roots in Greece, continued its development in Europe, and eventually spread to the Americas.

In this chapter, we will see how the Greeks overcame a rather harsh environment to build a remarkable society. The story of Greek civilization is the story of individual thinkers, artists, writers, mathematicians, soldiers, athletes, and political leaders who contributed to the future of civilization. The setting for this story is Greece's many city-states, each with its own style of life. Perhaps the greatest tragedy of ancient Greece is that wars between city-states opened the land to conquest by foreign empires. Yet, although the Greek city-states disappeared, Greek culture spread by way of those empires to many distant lands.

Greek culture grew up around the Aegean Sea. 1

In ancient times, Greece was not a united country but a collection of lands and islands where Greek-speaking people lived. The mainland of the ancient Greeks was a rugged peninsula that jutted out into the part of the Mediterranean Sea known as the Aegean (ee-JEE-uhn) Sea. The rest of Greek territory consisted of lands on the coast of Asia Minor and hundreds of islands in the Aegean and Ionian (eye-OH-nee-uhn) seas.

Geography shaped Greek civilization.

Physically, Greece is a land of rough mountains, narrow valleys, and no navigable rivers. However, it has a long coastline with many inlets and bays. This combination of physical features had several effects on Greek character and history.

The sea The sea shaped Greek civilization just as rivers shaped the ancient civilizations of the Fertile Crescent, Egypt, India, and China. In fact, some writers have said that the Greeks did not live *on* a land but *around* a sea.

The Aegean Sea and the neighboring Ionian and Black seas were the links that united the Greek people. The "watery ways," as the Greek poet Homer called them, were the best and sometimes the only route between most parts of Greece.

Sea travel was also a link with other societies. The Greek islands formed handy stepping stones across the Aegean Sea. Even in small ships and without compasses, Greek sailors could go from one island to another to reach the older, richer civilizations of Asia and Egypt. Sea travel and trade were vital to the Greeks because their homeland was poor in resources.

The land About three fourths of Greece is covered with mountains, the highest of which is Mount Olympus, the towering, snow-capped "home of the gods." These mountains divide Greece into a number of different regions. In ancient times, rugged terrain made transportation difficult. For example, the city-state of Sparta was only about 60 miles from Olympia, the site of the Olympic games. Yet it took Spartans nearly a week to travel that distance.

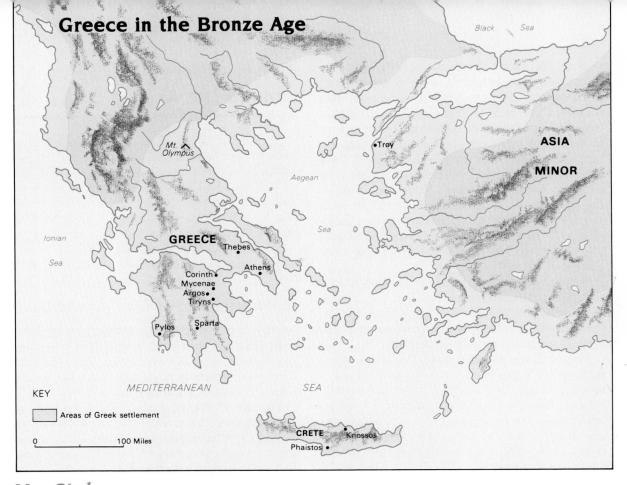

Greece in the Bronze Age

Black Sea

Mt Olympus

•Troy

Aegean

ASIA

MINOR

Ionian

Sea

GREECE

Thebes

Sea

Athens

Corinth•
Mycenae•
Argos•
Tiryns•

Pylos•   Sparta•

MEDITERRANEAN   SEA

KEY

Areas of Greek settlement

0   100 Miles

CRETE   •Knossos
Phaistos •

Map Study

Name four seas on which Greek sailors would have sailed in the Bronze Age.
About how far is it from Mycenae to Troy?

The mountains significantly influenced Greek political life. It was very difficult to unite the country under one government. Therefore, the Greeks were content to live in a collection of small independent communities. To most Greeks, home was their own valley and the mountains that enclosed it. It was a small world but one in which self-reliance and individualism could thrive.

Tiny but fairly fertile valleys covered about one fourth of the Greeks' land. These valleys were watered by small streams, not large rivers. Thus, the Greeks had no need for the kind of large-scale irrigation, controlled by powerful priests and kings, that shaped the river valley civilizations.

Greece was never able to feed a large population. It is estimated that no more than 2 million people lived in ancient Greece at one time. Even this small population could not expect the land to support a life of luxury. Fruits and vegetables could grow in only a few places. Meat was rare because the country lacked grasslands to feed large herds of cattle or flocks of sheep. The three principal Greek crops were grains, grapes, and olives. As a result, the Greek diet was light and simple. For instance, a Greek soldier might march through the mountains all morning and fight a battle in the afternoon on a day's meal of a few olives and a small loaf of barley bread.

The climate Climate was the third important environmental influence on Greek civilization. Greece has a Mediterranean climate. Temperatures are moderate, and rain falls only in winter. The Greek way of life, at least for men, was an outdoor life. Men spent almost all their leisure time at the *agora* (AG-uh-ruh) or marketplace, at the gymnasium, in political meetings, at the theater, and at civic and religious celebrations. All these public events took place outdoors.

The open gatherings, combined with the small settlements, meant that most people in a city-state knew one another. Citizens met often to discuss public issues and to exchange news. For the Greeks, taking an active part in civic life became both a duty and a virtue.

Rich cultures arose in the Bronze Age.

The first great civilizations in the Aegean area developed during the Bronze Age, the period roughly between 2000 and 1200 B.C. Rich towns and palaces flourished both on the mainland of Greece and on the island of Crete.

Cretan civilization Long and slender, Crete is the largest of the islands near Greece. The civilization that grew up on Crete is often called the Minoan (muh-NOH-uhn) civilization, from the name *Minos* (MY-nahs), a legendary king of Crete.

During the Bronze Age, Crete carried on a lively trade with Greece and other Aegean lands. With their wealth, the rulers of Crete built themselves great, sprawling palaces with many wings and dozens upon dozens of rooms. Some palaces even had clay pipes that carried running water. Around the palaces clustered prosperous towns connected by good roads.

The Cretans left records in two different types of writing, known as Linear A and Linear B. Both types were a puzzle to scholars for many years. Then a brilliant linguist, Michael Ventris, deciphered Linear B. Ventris began trying to crack the code of the mysterious language when he was 14. He finally succeeded at age 30 and surprised historians by proving it was Greek.

Was the civilization of Bronze Age Crete a branch of the civilization on the Greek mainland at the same time? Or were there two different civilizations, one on the mainland and one on Crete? No one can yet answer that question.

The prosperity of Crete ended abruptly sometime between 1400 and 1200 B.C. All over the island, the walls of the mighty palaces fell. Some show signs of raging fires. A mystery remains: Did human hands tear down the walls, or were they leveled by a terrible earthquake? No one knows for sure. Either way, Crete was devastated.

Mainland Greece in the Bronze Age Around 2000 B.C., groups of Greek-speaking people moved into mainland Greece and began to settle there. They were part of the large wave of migrations that swept lands from India to the Fertile Crescent and beyond around that time. The mainland Greeks of the Bronze Age are often known as Mycenaeans (MY-suh-NEE-uhnz), from the name of their leading city, Mycenae (my-SEE-nee).

Mycenae was built to withstand almost any attack. It was located on a steep, rocky ridge and was surrounded by a protective wall up to 20 feet thick. From the citadel of Mycenae, a warrior-king ruled the surrounding villages and farms.

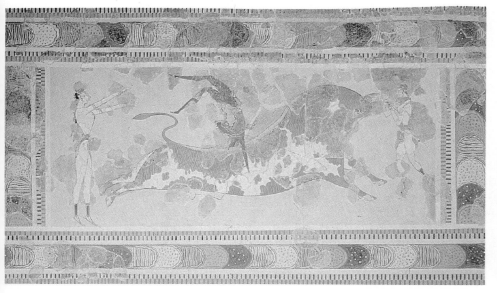

At the Minoan court, young men and women took part in the sport of dancing or leaping over bulls, as shown in this picture. Such rituals may have led to the legend that King Minos of Crete sacrificed young captives to the Minotaur, a monster that was half human and half bull.

Similar palace-forts dotted the southern part of Greece. In each lived a proud, warlike ruler. These kings dominated Greece from about 1600 to 1200 B.C.

Bronze Age society The nobles who lived within the fortresses enjoyed a life of surprising splendor. They feasted in great halls 35 feet wide and 50 feet long. In the center of the hall, a fire blazed on the circular hearth that was ten feet across. During banquets, the firelight glittered from a dazzling variety of gold and silver pitchers, bowls, and cups. When the royal Mycenaeans died, they were buried with their richest treasures. The body of one child was completely covered with a golden suit.

This enormous wealth was won by warrior-kings who led their armies in search of plunder. Trade was also a source of wealth, but Bronze Age trade often was close to piracy.

The warrior kings were only a tiny group at the top of Bronze Age society. The kings had weapons of bronze and jewelry of gold, but ordinary people still used tools of stone and wood. Most people lived as farmers, but there were also weavers, goatherds, shepherds, stonemasons, bakers, metalworkers, nurses, and more.

The Trojan War War was the main business of Greece's Bronze Age kings. Their most famous war was the siege of the great seaport of Troy in Asia Minor. Stories from this war were told hundreds of years later by the Greek poet Homer. According to Homer, a Greek army besieged and destroyed Troy because a Trojan youth had stolen Helen, the beautiful wife of a Greek king.

For many years, historians thought that Homer's stories were imaginary. However, a German archaeologist named Heinrich Schliemann (SHLEE-muhn) thought otherwise. As a boy, Schliemann read Homer's poems over and over. He became determined to find Troy. In 1871, using clues from Homer, Schliemann began to dig for Troy at a site in northwestern Asia Minor. He and his crew unearthed nine layers of city life as well as 8,700 pieces of gold jewelry.

Schliemann's discoveries at Troy, together with the ruins of Mycenae and other cities, showed that Homer's poems had some basis in fact. The Trojan War was probably a great Mycenaean raid against a rival trading city. It took place sometime around 1200 B.C., and it was the last of the Bronze Age Greeks' triumphs.

Dark Ages interrupted civilization.

Not long after the Trojan War, Mycenaean civilization collapsed. Around 1200 B.C., palace after palace was attacked and burned. At Mycenae, a layer of ashes covered the entire palace site, the silent remains of a terrible fire. These were the same years that the Egyptians and Hittites suffered under the attacks of the mysterious "Peoples of the Sea." A tablet from one Mycenaean citadel says, "The watchers are guarding the coast." But guards could not save Mycenaean civilization from destruction.

The Dorian migrations Into this war-torn countryside moved a new group of people, the Dorians (DAWR-ee-uhnz). The Dorians spoke a dialect of Greek and were distant relatives of the Bronze Age Greeks.

The Dorians were far less advanced than the Mycenaean Greeks. Dorian pottery and tools show little skill. The Dorians were not good traders either, and trade came to a standstill with their arrival. Most important to historians, the skill of writing was lost in this time of destruction. There is a 400-year gap in written Greek history from 1150 to 750 B.C. This period is known as Greece's Dark Ages. Without written records, little is known of the Dark Ages, but important events took place during these years.

The poems of Homer Lacking writing, the Greeks of the Dark Ages relied on the spoken word to pass on knowledge to their children. Bards (wandering poets) told stories that glorified the old heroes of Mycenae and Troy. A single tale might last many evenings around a hearth. Such long, heroic poems are called **epics**. The greatest of the bards, according to Greek tradition, was a blind old man named Homer.

We know almost nothing about Homer except his poems. He may have lived as early as 900 B.C. or as late as 750 B.C. His two great epic poems are the *Iliad* (IHL-ee-uhd) and the *Odyssey* (AHD-ih-see).

The *Iliad* is the story of heroes at war. All the action takes place outside the walls of Troy, at the very end of the Trojan War. However, Homer does not explain how the Greek army won the war. He was not interested in groups, only in individuals. Throughout the *Iliad*, the battles that matter are private duels between great heroes, not clashes between armies.

The Greeks' love of athletics showed in their art. The vase above features a chariot race, and the small picture at left shows a weight lifter working out. The "Discus Thrower" (far left) captures both grace and force.

Homer's second epic, the *Odyssey*, concerns the adventures of Odysseus (oh-**DIHS**-ee-uhs), a Greek hero. According to the *Odyssey*, Odysseus spends the ten years after the Trojan War in a series of adventures on his way home. Only through never-failing cunning is he able to survive.

The heroic ideal Listening to Homer's tales, the Greeks of the Dark Ages learned a powerful ideal called **arete** (**AR**-eh-tee). Simply stated, arete meant to strive for excellence, to show courage, and to win fame and honor.

Homer's heroes competed constantly for glory. The two most renowned heroes of the *Iliad* are Hector, Troy's greatest champion, and Achilles (uh-**KIHL**-eez), the Greek champion. In a dramatic scene, Andromache (an-**DRAHM**-uh-kee), Hector's wife, begs him not to fight Achilles:

> *"O Hector, your courage will be your destruction; and you have no pity on your little son or on me, who will soon be your widow. For soon all the Greeks will attack you and kill you; and if I lose you, it would be better for me to die . . ."*
>
> *Then tall Hector of the shining helmet answered, "Wife, I too have thought upon all this. But I would feel deep shame if like a coward I stayed away from battle. All my life I have learned to be brave and to fight always in the front ranks of the Trojans, winning glory for myself . . ."*

Hector's answer gives us an insight into the ideal of arete. Confronted with the likelihood of death and tragedy for his family, Hector chooses to live and die by the heroic code. In the following battle, the merciless Achilles slays Hector.

The Olympic games In war, Greek heroes sought glory in battle. In peace, they sought glory in athletic competitions. The most famous games, the Olympics, were held every four years beginning in 776 B.C. Young charioteers, boxers, wrestlers, runners, and javelin throwers came from all parts of Greece to compete on a grassy field at Olympia.

Footnote to History

According to later legends, it was Odysseus's clever scheme that finally brought down the walls of Troy. The Greeks built a gigantic, hollow wooden horse and left it outside Troy's gates. The Trojans convinced themselves the horse must be an offering to the gods and would protect Troy. They dragged the Greek "gift" into the city. Later that night, Greek warriors who had hidden inside the horse's belly leaped out and opened Troy's gates, letting in the Greek army.

The games lasted five days. The most eagerly awaited event was known as the pentathlon (pehn-**TATH**-luhn). The pentathlon was considered the supreme contest of athletic skill. Contestants took part in five events—a broad jump, a discus hurl, a javelin throw, a stadium sprint (about 200 yards), and a wrestling match. The victor was crowned with the coveted Olympic prize, a wreath of olive leaves. As with the Homeric heroes, the true prize was honor and fame.

Greeks worshiped humanlike gods.

The Olympic games, like many other contests in ancient Greece, were held in part to honor the gods. The Greeks imagined their gods to be very much like humans in most ways. The Greek gods struggled with human passions and weaknesses—love, hate, anger, jealousy. They quarreled constantly with one another. However, unlike humans, the gods were immortal. The 12 most powerful gods and goddesses were believed to gather atop a snow-capped mountain in northern Greece, Mount Olympus. The Greeks also honored local gods and household spirits.

The Greeks developed a rich set of myths or stories about their gods. Through these myths, the Greeks sought to understand the mysteries of nature and the power of human passions.

The Greeks did not develop a powerful priestly class, as the Egyptians and Sumerians did. Instead, priests in Greece were ordinary officials. Serving as a priest was not a lifelong career. Rather, it was only one of many civic duties for a Greek citizen. Thus, religion in ancient Greece was closely linked to government and to civic pride.

Section Review 1

Define: (a) agora, (b) bard, (c) epic, (d) arete, (e) pentathlon, (f) myth
Identify: (a) Aegean Sea, (b) Ionian Sea, (c) Black Sea, (d) Minoan civilization, (e) Mycenaean civilization, (f) Trojan War, (g) Homer, (h) Dorians, (i) Dark Ages, (j) the *Iliad*, (k) the *Odyssey*, (l) the Olympics
Answer:
1. How was ancient Greek society influenced by each of the following geographic factors? (a) the sea (b) the land (c) the climate

2. Describe the society that existed in Greece and on nearby islands in the Bronze Age.
3. How did the Dorian migrations affect Greek civilization?
4. Why were Homer's poems important to Greek society?
5. How was the Greek religion different from the religions of Egypt and the Fertile Crescent?

Critical Thinking
6. (a) What evidence suggests that writing was a skill limited to a small group of specialists in Mycenaean society? (b) Suggest a comparable skill that might be lost today in a society destroyed by war, and explain the consequences of the loss.

Greek city-states competed for power. 2

After 750 B.C., the Greeks began to recover from the Dark Ages. This period was marked by the rise of the city-states, for which the Greek word was **polis** (**PAHL**-uhs). (This is the root of such words as *police, politics,* and *politician*.)

A polis included a city and its surrounding countryside. Most city-states controlled between 50 and 500 square miles of territory, although the largest, Sparta, controlled about 4,000 square miles.

The Greeks expected all citizens to share in the discussion of public matters. They held meetings in the agora or on a fortified hilltop called an *acropolis* (uh-**KRAHP**-uh-lihs). The Greeks knew that such general discussion was only possible with a fairly small population. Thus, the ideal polis, to Greek political thinkers, had between 5,000 and 10,000 citizens. (Only free adult men were counted as citizens, however; women, children, slaves, and foreigners living in the city made the whole population of a polis much larger.)

The polis was the central force in Greek life. Citizenship was based on the ideal of human beings as free and rational individuals. Civic decisions were made by open debate, not by a pharaoh or an emperor. In Greece, the freedom to express ideas and the willingness of leaders to listen were not only acceptable but expected.

Power passed from kings to citizens.

Clearly, Greece in the time of the city-states was very different from Greece in the time of the warrior-kings that Homer described. During the Dark Ages, the kings had lost their power. In general, rule passed into the hands of a small group of noble families. Such a government is called an **aristocracy** (AR-uh-STAHK-ruh-see). Yet aristocratic rule soon proved oppressive and unjust. The nobles made laws to suit themselves and forced small farmers into slavery for debts.

A new kind of army Ordinary citizens became dissatisfied with aristocratic rule. The power of those small farmers and artisans was growing because of another change that had taken place in Greece. In the age of Homer, only kings and nobles were warriors. Only the rich could afford great bronze spears, shields, breastplates, and chariots. During the Dark Ages, however, iron became the most important metal for weapons and armor. Not only is iron harder than bronze, but it also is more common and therefore cheaper. Soon, even ordinary citizens could afford iron weapons and armor.

A whole new kind of army developed as a result of the use of iron. Now every citizen was expected to be a soldier for his polis. These soldiers, called **hoplites,** fought on foot. They stood side by side, each man with a spear in one hand and a shield in the other. As the hoplites faced their enemy, the shields formed a solid wall bristling with spears. This fearsome group of soldiers was known as a **phalanx** (FAY-lanks). In its day, the Greek phalanx was the most powerful fighting machine in the world.

The rise of tyrants It was impossible for rulers to ignore the power of these citizen-soldiers. In many city-states, farmers who had lost their lands and debt-ridden artisans joined in revolt against the nobles. Often the rebels were led by a man from the nobility, perhaps someone who had lost out in a feud among the nobles themselves. With the support of the citizens, such men won power in many city-states.

The ambitious men who came to power through these rebellions were known as **tyrants.** Hated by the nobles, the tyrants usually worked to help the small farmers and artisans. Sometimes tyrants took lands from the defeated aristocrats and divided the property among the poor. To increase their popularity and impress their neighbors, tyrants were great builders. Many Greek cities gained forts, harbors, and temples under a tyrant's rule.

During the time of the tyrants, many Greek city-states also founded **colonies.** Groups of citizens moved abroad to islands and harbors around the Mediterranean. These new settlements were separate city-states, but they retained ties of loyalty to their home city. Colonies became an important source of trade and wealth for many Greek cities.

Some city-states passed from one tyrant to the next, as competing groups took power. Other cities, however, found new ways of governing. Among these city-states were two of the most powerful, Sparta and Athens.

Teamwork was clearly essential in the Greek phalanx. In the Greek polis, every citizen was a soldier.

Greece and Its Colonies

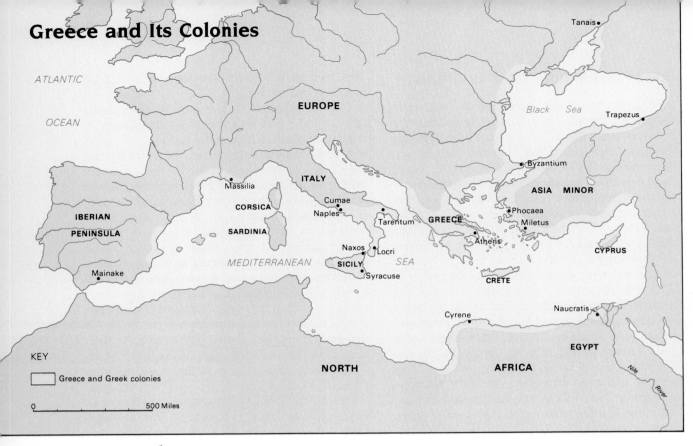

Map Study

Between 750 and 550 B.C., Greek colonies spread around the Mediterranean Sea. What settlement controlled the mouth of the Black Sea?

Sparta built an army state.

Sparta was located in the southern part of Greece, in the large land area known as the Peloponnesus (PEHL-uh-puh-NEE-sus). As the map on page 105 shows, this stretch of land is nearly cut off from the rest of Greece by the Gulf of Corinth.

While other city-states founded colonies abroad, Sparta looked no farther than the fertile fields of neighboring Messenia (muh-SEE-nee-uh). About 725 B.C., the Spartans conquered the Messenians and took over their land.

The Spartans treated the Messenians almost as slaves. Messenians became *helots* (HEL-uhts), peasants forced to stay on the land they worked. Each year, the Spartans demanded half of the Messenians' yearly crop. Around 600 B.C., the Messenians, who outnumbered the Spartans eight to one, revolted. The Spartans put down the revolt, but just barely. From then on, the Spartans lived in fear of a helot uprising. The Spartans concluded that the only way to survive was to make their city-state overwhelmingly strong. Spartan citizens devoted their lives to serving their polis, especially in the army.

To strengthen their city-state, the Spartans adopted a harsh set of laws known as the Code of Lycurgus (ly-KUR-gus). According to legend, Lycurgus gave Sparta its laws, then starved himself to death to save food for his polis. Whether or not the story is true, it shows the Spartan values of self-discipline and endurance.

Footnote to History

Although the Spartans lived on the work of the helots, the Spartan masters certainly did not live in luxury. According to legend, a foreign visitor who shared a meal with the Spartan army remarked after eating the usual dinner of black porridge, "Now I know why the Spartans do not fear death."

102

Spartan babies were examined at birth to see if they were healthy. If not, they were left in the hills to die. All fit children stayed with their mothers until their seventh birthdays. Then the boys were sent to army barracks, and their training began. They wore one light tunic, winter or summer, and usually went barefoot. Their beds were hard benches. For food, they had meager servings of coarse black porridge. They were expected to get extra food by stealing from nearby farms, though they would be whipped if caught. Such schooling produced tough soldiers who could fend for themselves in enemy territory.

At the age of 20, a Spartan man was allowed to marry. He continued, though, to live in the barracks for another ten years. After completing full-time military service, men remained on active reserve for another 30 years. Their lives of discipline, loyalty, and training made the Spartan phalanx almost unbeatable.

Spartan girls also led hardy lives. Unlike girls in other city-states, Spartan girls ran, wrestled, and played sports. As adults, they managed the family estates while their husbands served the polis. Spartan women had every right except the vote. As a result of their freedom, they were considered scandalous by other Greeks.

From around 600 until 371 B.C., the Spartans had the most powerful army in Greece. However, they paid a high price for their power. They created little literature, art, or architecture. The Spartans valued duty, strength, and discipline over individuality, beauty, and freedom of thought.

Athens turned to democracy.

In outlook and values, the city-state of Athens stood in sharp contrast to Sparta. An ambassador from Corinth, a city located halfway between the two rivals, once compared the Spartans to the Athenians while he was speaking to the Spartan assembly. With typical Greek frankness, he told the Spartans that even though they had the strongest army in Greece, they were overly cautious and generally lacking in any excitement of the mind. Athenians, he said, were always eager to learn new ideas. They had been educated to think and act as free people.

Like other city-states, Athens went through a power struggle between rich and poor. However,

Athenians avoided civil war by making timely reforms. Two of the leading reformers were Solon (SO-luhn) and Cleisthenes (KLYS-thuh-neez). These reforms created a **democracy**, a government in which all citizens took part.

Solon's reforms By 594 B.C., conflict between the rich aristocrats who ruled Athens and the poor farmers who made up most of its population had reached a boiling point. To prevent civil war, the aristocrats asked a middle-aged poet, philosopher, and merchant named Solon to head the government. Solon was well-known for his fairness, and the Athenians gave him full power to reform the laws. Solon's first acts were aimed at improving Athens's economy.

1. He canceled all debts and freed those who had been enslaved for debt.
2. He made farming profitable. The soil of Athens was too poor for grain but good for grapevines and olive trees. Solon refused to allow farmers to sell grain abroad, thus encouraging them to grow more wine grapes and olives. Olive oil and wine became the base of a rich trade for the Athenians.
3. He encouraged industry by requiring every father to teach his son a trade. This gave Athens a better mixture of agriculture and industry. Athenian pottery, for example, was sold all around the Mediterranean Sea.

Solon's political reforms were just as important as his economic ones.

1. He allowed every male citizen to attend the assembly. All important matters were debated there and decided by vote.
2. He began a new legal system in which any citizen could bring charges against anyone who had committed a wrong. Thus, if a citizen saw a crime committed against a slave, the citizen could bring a charge, even though the slave could not. The idea that all citizens were responsible for justice was revolutionary.

After 22 years in power, Solon refused a popular request that he become ruler for life. Instead, he went on an extended tour of Egypt and Asia Minor.

The reforms of Cleisthenes About 60 years later, another Athenian leader, Cleisthenes, introduced further reforms. Beginning in 508 B.C., he convinced the Athenians to enact a series of laws that made Athens a full democracy.

103

Cleisthenes increased the power of the Athenian assembly. He also created the Council of Five Hundred to propose laws and advise the assembly. Members of this council were chosen by lot, so that every citizen had an equal chance of serving.

After all these reforms, Athenians enjoyed nearly a complete democracy. However, it is important to remember that only about one fifth of the people in Athens were citizens. The rest were slaves, foreigners, and women. Women in Athens had no part in government and very little part in its intellectual life.

The Greeks turned back the powerful Persians.

Danger of a helot revolt caused the Spartans to be inhumanly tough. Danger of revolution among poverty-stricken farmers caused Athens to become a democracy. The greatest danger of all—invasion by Persian armies—spurred Athens and Sparta alike to their greatest glory.

The full story of the Persian Wars comes down to modern times in the writings of a Greek scholar named Herodotus (huh-**RAHD**-uh-tuhs). His *History of the Persian Wars* was new and remarkable. Unlike the scribes of Babylon and Egypt, Herodotus did not set out to glorify the deeds of kings.

Instead, he wanted to investigate the past, find out the truth, and report it. He did allow many tall tales to slip into his work, but Herodotus is still justly called the first true historian.

The first invasion The Persian Wars began in Ionia, a thin strip of coastland in what is now Turkey. Greeks had long been settled there, but around 520 B.C., the Persians conquered the area. The Greeks of Ionia submitted to Persian rule for a generation but then revolted. Athens sent ships and soldiers to the Ionians' aid. After the Persian king Darius defeated the rebels, he vowed to destroy Athens in revenge.

In 490 B.C., a Persian fleet carried 25,000 men across the Aegean Sea and landed a little northeast of Athens on a plain called Marathon. There, 10,000 Athenians, neatly bunched into phalanxes, were waiting for them. Shoulder to shoulder, singing as they ran, the Athenians charged. The casualties reportedly numbered 6,400 Persians and only 192 Athenians.

Though the Athenians were victorious, their city was now defenseless. Sailing along the coast, the Persian ships could reach Athens before the Greeks could march overland to defend it. Someone had to race back to Athens to tell people there how badly the Persians had been defeated. Otherwise, the citizens might surrender the city without a fight. A young runner named Pheidippides (fye-**DIP**-uh-deez) stripped off his clothes

Daily Life • Athenian Pottery

"We like beautiful things but don't spend a fortune on them," a leading Athenian remarked about the people of his city. Some of the loveliest objects in Greece, and throughout the Mediterranean for that matter, were easily affordable to almost every family in Athens. These objects were the graceful Athenian vases or pots.

The pottery was made and purchased for practical use as mixing bowls, pitchers, drinking cups, wine jars, and water jars. Different shapes were designed to serve different purposes. Often, Athenians bought new pottery for celebrations, and the scenes on the pottery showed the event they were celebrating—a marriage, an athletic contest, or a voyage.

Athenian potters were dedicated to high quality and beauty in their craft. They proudly signed their finest works. Their products have become a symbol for perfection in art.

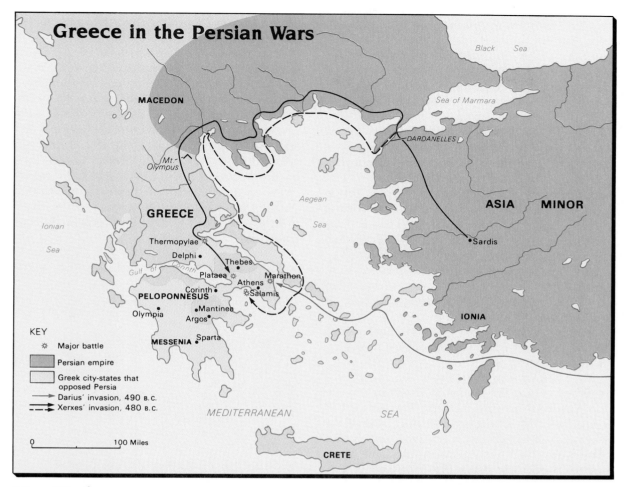

Greece in the Persian Wars

KEY

☼ Major battle

▨ Persian empire

▢ Greek city-states that opposed Persia

→ Darius' invasion, 490 B.C.

⟶⟶ Xerxes' invasion, 480 B.C.

0   100 Miles

Map Study

Which Persian ruler took a direct sea route to invade Greece? Which ruler brought both a fleet and a land-based army? What two battles did his army fight? What battle did his fleet fight?

and ran 26 miles over the rocky ground from Marathon to Athens. With his last breath, he gasped, "Rejoice, we conquer." Then he collapsed and died. Persian ships arrived much later, saw the situation was hopeless, and sailed away.

The second invasion Ten years later, in 480 B.C., Darius the Great was dead. His son and successor, Xerxes (ZURK-seez), was determined to crush Greece. Xerxes assembled an enormous invasion force of ships and men.

Xerxes' army was like a marching exhibit of all the peoples of the Persian empire. There were Ethiopians in lion skins carrying spears tipped with gazelle horn. Arab soldiers followed him on camels. Scythians from Russia were known

by their pointed caps. The Persians sported leather jerkins and fish-scale armor. Xerxes' army was many times larger than any force the Greeks could muster.

The Greeks were badly divided. Some city-states decided to fight the Persians. Others thought it wiser to let Xerxes destroy Athens and return home. Some Greeks actually fought on the Persian side. Thus, Xerxes' army met no resistance as it marched down the eastern coast of Greece. Then, about 85 miles northeast of Athens, Xerxes came to a narrow mountain pass at Thermopylae (ther-MOP-ih-lee). Here he found 7,000 Greeks, including 300 Spartans, blocking his way.

105

Xerxes expected to smash this small army with ease, but he underestimated the Spartans. For three days, the ground at Thermopylae ran red with Persian blood. Finally, a Greek traitor told the Persians about a secret path around the cliffs. Defeat for the Greeks was now inevitable.

The Spartan commander, Leonidas, told the Greeks from other city-states to retreat to safety. He and his Spartans would hold the pass as long as possible and die with honor at Thermopylae. The Persians killed them all. The Spartans' valiant sacrifice made a great impression on all Greeks.

In Athens, the citizens began to plan for the city's defense. It was then that Themistocles convinced Athenians to evacuate their city and pin all their hopes on victory at sea (page 94).

Early one September morning, 310 Greek ships (more than half rowed by Athenians) headed out to sea to face the Persians. Straight ahead was the island of Salamis (SAL-uh-mihs). To the left and right, blocking both ends of the channel, were masses of Persian ships. The Greeks appeared to be trapped.

But Themistocles knew the waters around Salamis better than the foreigners. The channel was too narrow to permit the large Persian fleet to maneuver well. Suddenly, the huge size of the Persian fleet turned into a terrible disadvantage. With lusty shouts, Athenian oarsmen drove straight for the wooden hulls of the enemy. Battering rams protruded from Greek ships below the waterline. These rams punched holes in the Persian ships. The great Persian fleet sank, ship by ship, in the channel.

Xerxes watched it happen. He had set his golden throne upon a rocky height to enjoy seeing the Greeks crushed. Instead, he saw his own navy destroyed. After the battle, Xerxes left Greece hurriedly with about half his army. The remaining half of the Persian army was defeated by the Spartans at a third great battle, which took place on the plain of Plataea (pluh-TEE-uh). Thus ended the second Persian invasion of Greece.

Consequences of the Persian Wars Athens basked in the glory of the Persian defeat. Athens alone had challenged Persian power from the beginning. Athenian heroes had fallen first in Ionia, then at Marathon. Athenian ships had fought at Salamis. The city of Athens, burned to ashes, had suffered the most damage. The Athenians claimed to be the war's greatest heroes.

Their pride in themselves and their city soared to new heights.

After the war, Athens became the leader of an alliance of 140 city-states called the Delian (DEE-lee-uhn) League. The purpose of the league was to ward off further Persian attacks. Soon, though, Athens began to use its powerful navy to control the other members of the league. City-states were forced to join the league and pay yearly dues to Athens. The Delian League thus became just another name for an Athenian empire.

The prestige of victory and the wealth of empire set the stage for a dazzling outburst of creativity in Athens. The city was entering its brief, brilliant golden age.

Section Review 2

Define: (a) polis, (b) acropolis, (c) aristocracy, (d) hoplites, (e) phalanx, (f) tyrant, (g) colony, (h) helot, (i) democracy

Identify: (a) Sparta, (b) Messenia, (c) Lycurgus, (d) Athens, (e) Solon, (f) Cleisthenes, (g) Darius, (h) Herodotus, (i) Marathon, (j) Themistocles, (k) Thermopylae, (l) Xerxes, (m) Gulf of Salamis, (n) Plataea, (o) Delian League

Answer:
1. Why was the polis important to Greeks?
2. How did the Iron Age help ordinary citizens gain power in Greece?
3. How was the rule of tyrants generally different from that of aristocrats?
4. (a) Why was revolt a constant threat in Sparta? (b) How did the Spartans respond to this threat?
5. (a) Why was revolt a threat in early Athens? (b) How did the Athenians respond to this threat?
6. How did the end of the Persian Wars affect the people of Greece, especially the Athenians?

Critical Thinking
7. Choose one of Solon's reforms and explain why it was important to making Athens a democracy.
8. At several major battles in the Persian Wars, there were nearly as many Greeks fighting for the Persians as against them. From your reading, what reasons can you suggest for this division among the Greeks?

Athens led Greece in its golden age. **3**

During Athens's golden age, the arts of drama, sculpture, poetry, philosophy, architecture, and science all reached new heights. For 50 years (from 480 to 430 B.C.), Athens set off sparks of genius in all directions.

Pericles sought glory for Athens.

Among those who evacuated Athens before the Persians arrived in 480 B.C. was a teenager named Pericles (PEHR-uh-kleez). His aristocratic father, a leader of the Athenian assembly, had fought in the Battle of Salamis. When the Persians were finally driven out, much of Athens had been burned. In this bleak, war-scarred city, Pericles prepared to become Athens's leader.

Pericles first attended meetings of the assembly at the age of 20. Soon, his great talent for public speaking won him fame. He did not try to excite his audience but only to reason with them. His arguments made sense to aristocrats, farmers, and artisans alike.

In 461 B.C., the assembly elected Pericles one of Athens's ten generals. He was reelected year after year and became, in effect, the leader of Athens. This one man so dominated the life of Athens for 32 years (461–429 B.C.) that the period often is called the Age of Pericles.

Pericles had three goals: (1) to strengthen Athenian democracy; (2) to build a commercial empire; and (3) to glorify Athens.

To strengthen democracy, Pericles increased the number of public officials who were paid salaries. In earlier times, many public jobs were unpaid, and therefore only the wealthier citizens could afford the time to hold such offices. Under Pericles, members of the Council of Five Hundred, jurors, and all sorts of other public officials were paid for their work. Thus, even the poorest citizens could afford to serve if elected or chosen by lot.

Through the Delian League, Pericles tried to enlarge the wealth and power of Athens. He used money from the league's treasury to make Athens's navy the strongest in the Mediterranean. The navy safeguarded Athenian commerce and settled disputes between league members.

Pericles, shown in his war helmet, was Athens's leading statesman in the city's golden age.

Pericles also used money from the empire to beautify Athens. He persuaded the Athenian assembly (without the league's approval) to vote huge sums of Delian League money to buy gold, ivory, and marble. Still more money went to a small army of artisans who worked for 15 years (447–432 B.C.) on building one of architecture's noblest works, the Parthenon (PAHR-thuh-nahn).

Art flourished in Athens.

The Parthenon was not novel in style. It was built in the traditional style that had been used in Greek temples for 200 years. Neither was it especially large—228 feet by 101 feet. What made it one of the masterpieces of all time was its excellent craftsmanship and design.

Within the temple stood a giant statue of Athena, goddess of wisdom and protector of Athens (which was named for her). Pericles had entrusted much work on the temple, including the statue of Athena, to his friend Phidias (FIHD-ee-us), a sculptor. The great statue of the goddess stood

The Parthenon achieved classical perfection in proportion and symmetry.

about 39 feet tall. A golden helmet crowned her head above her ivory face. A golden robe fell in great folds over her golden sandals. A graceful ivory hand rested on a huge golden shield.

Phidias and the other sculptors of the golden age of Athens aimed to create figures that were graceful, strong, and perfectly formed. Their faces showed neither laughter nor anger, only serenity. Greek sculptors also tried to capture the grace of the human body in motion. Their standards of order, balance, and proportion became the standard for classical art in Western civilization.

Nearly all the great sculpture and architecture of Periclean Athens was created for the polis.

Marble, bronze, and gold went into public temples, not private homes. A great bronze statue of Athena stood above the harbor, the tip of her bronze spear visible far out to sea. The many shrines and temples that the Persians had destroyed were rebuilt, more beautiful than ever.

The importance that Athenians gave to fine public architecture is shown by the temple of Athena Nike (*nike* meant "victory"). This temple was built while Athens was fighting for its life against Sparta. Money was short, and war casualties and plague carried off workers. Yet all through the 30 years of war, the Athenians struggled to complete the temple.

Pillars supported the roofs of the great Greek temples. The three classical styles for the tops (or capitals) of the columns were the Doric, the Ionic, and the Corinthian.

The Greeks invented drama.

Like the Parthenon, Athens's theatrical productions were both an expression of civic pride and a tribute to the gods. Writing plays to be performed on stage was a new form of art. Drama as we know it was a Greek invention.

Early in the spring, Athenians rose at dawn and walked to the city's outdoor theater to watch a festival honoring the god of wine, Dionysus. Just as athletes competed in the Olympic games, playwrights competed in this festival. A group of citizens judged the plays and awarded the winner a simple prize: a wreath of ivy.

In the Age of Pericles, two writers dominated these contests. First came Aeschylus (ES-kih-lus), who won the ivy wreath 13 times. Aeschylus shared deeply in Athens's glory; he himself had fought at Marathon and probably at Salamis. He probably wrote more than 80 plays, of which only 7 survive. The second great dramatist, Sophocles (SAHF-uh-kleez), won his first dramatic contest by beating the great Aeschylus in 468 B.C. All together, Sophocles wrote about 100 plays, including the most famous Greek drama of all, *Oedipus* (EHD-uh-puhs).

Greek plays were partly acted and partly chanted. A chorus of singers would comment on the action of the play, helping the plot along. The actors wore masks to identify their roles. The large protruding lips of each mask served as a megaphone to help carry the actor's voice to the back rows.

Both Sophocles and Aeschylus wrote the type of drama known as **tragedy**. To qualify as tragedy, a play had to portray men and women of strong character whose very strength led to their downfall. There was no such thing as a meek hero.

In classic tragedy, strength led the hero to pride, and pride inevitably led to an unforgivable sin. And always, in tragic drama, the gods punished the hero for sinning. The audience who saw these plays left the theater both saddened and uplifted— sad for the fate of mankind and uplifted by the nobility and courage the characters displayed.

Public drama was more than entertainment to the Athenians. It was a form of public education. The plays dealt with great issues that were important to the polis—the power of leaders, the power of the people, questions of justice and morality, questions of war and peace, and the duties owed to the gods, the family, and the city.

The Greek theater at Delphi was set on a hillside with nature as its backdrop. Actors wore masks such as the one at right to show their roles.

For most Greek women, household chores were the main activity. However, Spartan women such as the runner above took part in athletic contests. Sappho, the woman shown on the vase, was considered one of the finest Greek poets.

Drama was so important to public life in Athens that citizens were sometimes paid to attend the plays, just as they were paid for holding public office. As part of their civic duty, wealthy citizens bore the cost for producing the plays.

Athens prospered in the golden age.

The Parthenon and the amphitheater were surrounded by a teeming city. How did it feel to live in such a place?

Athens reeked with the odor of the pigpens most familes kept in their backyards. Foul smells mingled with the raucous noise of the agora. Here merchants in outdoor stalls advertised their goods by shouting. The sound of clanging metal from nearby workshops added to the din. Athens was a city of small shopowners and artisans who specialized in every kind of craft: shoe making, sword making, pottery making, wine making, and so on. The shops were owned by foreigners as well as by Athenian citizens.

Free men and slaves worked side by side in a typical shop and might be given the same meager wages. There were perhaps 100,000 slaves in the city-state of Athens in the 400's, roughly one third the population. Most of them were non-Greeks captured in war. A rich family might own as many as 50 slaves. Even a poor citizen was likely to own one or two. Because poor citizens and slaves dressed much alike, however, it was almost impossible to distinguish them from one another.

The voices in the marketplace were mostly male. A woman's voice rarely was heard outside the home. Cooking meals, nursing babies, and weaving cloth were expected to consume all of a woman's time. If she stepped outside to buy fish at the market, her face was supposed to be veiled. She could not own or inherit land. She had very few legal rights and could not appeal to a jury in her own defense. Unlike her brothers, who started going to school at the age of six, she was educated at home. When she married, she lived in the part of her husband's house reserved for women. She was supposed to retreat there whenever her husband entertained male guests at home.

Most Athenian families lived in tiny, plain dwellings with thin, mud-brick walls. Typical furniture was a few tables and chairs. Often, a family's most valued possessions were the painted pieces of pottery in which they stored their wine and olive oil. The red and black vases made in Athenian workshops were famous throughout the Mediterranean world. In the Age of Pericles, they were Athens's chief export.

Despite its physical discomfort, Athens was in many ways a splendid city. Like the heroes in Sophocles' plays, however, the proud citizens of Athens were soon to suffer a tragic fate.

Sparta defeated Athens in war.

Tension between Athens and Sparta had been building for years. Many people in both cities thought war was inevitable. Instead of trying to avoid war, leaders began to press for a war to begin while they thought their own city had the advantage. Finally, in 431 B.C., the Spartans marched into Athenian territory. They swept over the countryside, burning the Athenians' local food supply.

Athens itself, however, seemed safe. Years before, Pericles had taken the precaution of building the Long Walls, two great ramparts that protected the roadway from Athens to the sea. Thus, Athens was safe from starvation as long as ships could sail into port with food from Athenian colonies as far away as the Black Sea.

Athens was the strongest sea power, but Sparta was the strongest land power. As the leading Athenian general, Pericles did not try to defeat the Spartans on land. Instead, his strategy was to avoid battles with the superior Spartan army and to use Athens's great navy to strike Sparta's territory from the sea.

From the earliest battles, an Athenian named Thucydides (thyoo-SID-ih-deez) wrote about the war in a journal. We still rely on his *History of*

Voice from the Past · *Pericles' Funeral Oration*

In the winter of 431 B.C., Athens honored its war dead with a public funeral. As part of the ceremony, Pericles spoke in praise of the dead and the city for which they had died. His speech is the best expression of the Athenians' pride in their polis.

Our constitution does not copy the laws of neighboring states. Instead, others copy what we do. Our plan of government favors the many instead of the few; that is why it is called a democracy. As for laws, we offer equal justice to everyone. As for social standing, advancement is open to everyone, according to ability. High position does not depend on wealth, nor does poverty bar the way . . .

We take pleasure in the arts, but without extravagance, and in knowledge, but without being soft . . . Our public leaders have their own businesses, as well as politics, to take care of. Our ordinary citizens see to their own livelihoods but are also capable of making political decisions. Unlike other nations, we Athenians do not call a man who takes no part in public life quiet or unambitious; we call such a man useless . . .

In short, our polis is the school of all Greece . . . This is the Athens for which these men nobly fought and died, because they could not bear the thought of losing such a city.

1. How does Pericles define a democracy?
2. According to Pericles, in what aspects of life should a citizen take an interest to lead a full life?
3. (a) How does Pericles describe Athens's position in Greece? (b) What evidence does he offer of its leadership?

the *Peloponnesian War* to understand how this war ruined Athens and weakened all of Greece.

Disaster for Athens Two events were particularly deadly to Athens—a plague and a disastrous military defeat in far-off Sicily. The plague struck in 430 B.C., in the second year of the war. While Spartan soldiers were again laying waste to Athens's farmland, Athenians sought safety behind the city walls. Overcrowding made Athens vulnerable to a frightful plague that killed roughly one third of the population, including Pericles. Thucydides himself fell sick and barely survived.

The second disaster took place in 415 B.C., after the war had gone on for 16 years. The Athenian assembly sent a huge fleet carrying 27,000 soldiers to the island of Sicily, near Italy. Their goal was to destroy the polis of Syracuse, one of Sparta's wealthiest allies. The expedition met overwhelming defeat in 413 B.C. Thucydides reported, "They were destroyed with a total destruction—their fleet, their army—there was nothing that was not destroyed, and few out of many returned home."

Somehow, a terribly weakened Athens managed to fend off Spartan attacks for another nine years. But in 404 B.C., Athens and its allies surrendered. The Spartans then forced the Athenians to join in tearing down the Long Walls, symbol of Athens's strength.

Cultural changes After 27 years of war, Athens had lost its fleet, its empire, its power, and its wealth. It had also lost its self-confidence. This loss of spirit was perhaps the most serious of all for the people of Athens.

Confidence in democratic government began to falter. One leader after another proved weak, corrupt, or traitorous. The assembly began to change its decisions with every shift of the political winds. Leaders and generals were in constant danger of exile if a new speaker persuaded the assembly to turn on them.

Oddly enough, the crisis in public confidence was accompanied by an artistic outburst. As people turned to their private lives, art began to reflect their joys and sorrows. For the first time, the faces of bronze and marble statues began to show emotion.

Drama also underwent a change. It was during the Peloponnesian War that a playwright named Aristophanes (AR-is-TAHF-uh-neez) wrote the first great comedies of the stage. In them, he made fun of the politics, people, and ideas of his time. Athenians laughed at his biting jokes. The fact that Athenians could listen to such criticism of themselves, even in the midst of a great war, showed that the spirit of freedom and public discussion still lived.

Philosophers searched for truth.

In the years after the Peloponnesian War, yet another aspect of Greek culture reached new heights. In this time of questioning and uncertainty, several great thinkers were determined to seek for truth, no matter where the search led them. The name that the Greeks gave to such thinkers was *philosopher*—literally, "one who loves wisdom." The Greek philosophers questioned even the most basic and widely accepted ideas of their time.

Greek thinkers based their philosophy on two original assumptions. First, they assumed that the universe was put together in an orderly way. Land, sky, and sea were all subject to the same laws. These laws were absolute and unchanging. Second, the Greeks assumed that people could understand these laws through reason.

Socrates One of Greece's greatest philosophers fell victim to the frustrations aroused by Athens's defeat in the Peloponnesian War. He was an old Athenian soldier and stonecutter named Socrates (SAHK-ruh-teez). Socrates was not a handsome man, and his clothes and grooming left much to be desired. His agile mind, however, made up for his homely appearance.

Stopping a young man on the street, Socrates would ask if he knew where certain merchandise could be bought. After the youth answered easily, Socrates would ask if he knew where goodness and virtue could be found. No, the youth would reply, he did not know where one could find those. More questions would follow. Soon, Socrates and the young man would be deeply examining some idea like truth or goodness or beauty. (This way of teaching by asking questions is still called the Socratic method.)

Socrates questioned all the accepted values of Athens—democracy, patriotism, religion. He taught that people must examine their ideas by the demanding standards of truth and reason. Those who understood Socrates admired him deeply. The majority of citizens, however, could

This painting, "The Death of Socrates," was painted by the French artist Jacques Louis David in 1787, more than 2,000 years after Socrates died. What impression does the painting give of Socrates?

not understand this strange old man. The bitterness of a long war made them suspicious.

In 399 B.C., when Socrates was 70 years old, he was brought to trial. The father of one of his pupils accused him of "corrupting the youth of Athens" and failing to revere "the gods that the state recognizes." The 501 jurors at his trial listened to Socrates speak in his own defense. He said that his teachings were good for Athens because they forced people to think about their values and actions. In fact, he suggested that the city should give him a pension.

By a majority of 60 votes, the jury voted Socrates guilty as charged. The penalty was death. Friends visited Socrates in prison and pleaded with him to flee into exile. He calmly explained the flaws in their reasoning and drank the slow-acting poison made from hemlock. Athens thus lost one of its greatest citizens.

Plato Among those who had visited Socrates in prison was a brilliant, wealthy idealist named Plato (**PLAY**-toh). He was 28 years old when Socrates died, and the death convinced him that the average citizens of a democracy (who condemned Socrates) were unable to govern wisely.

Plato left Athens in bitterness after Socrates' death. He returned later, however, and established his own school. Plato's school, called the Academy, continued for 900 years.

Unlike Socrates, Plato was a writer as well as a teacher. In his early works, he wrote down the conversations of Socrates as he remembered them. Sometime between 385 and 380 B.C., Plato wrote his most famous work, *The Republic*. In it, he set forth his vision of a perfectly governed society. It was certainly no democracy.

In an ideal community, he wrote, all citizens would fall naturally into three groups. The most common type would be best suited for working as farmers and artisans. A more gifted type had minds and bodies fine enough to be trusted as warriors. Only the third and rarest type should belong to the ruling class. From this highest category, the person with the greatest insight and intellect ought to be chosen philosopher-king. This person might be either a woman or a man.

What mattered most was that the state be ruled by its greatest philosopher.

Plato's writings dominated philosophic thought in Europe for nearly 1,500 years. His only rivals in importance were his own teacher, Socrates, and his own pupil, Aristotle (AR-ihs-tot'l).

Aristotle One of the brightest students at Plato's Academy was a physician's son named Aristotle. Few minds in history were as hungry for knowledge as his. He wanted to know about morals, music, mathematics, biology, botany, geology, medicine, politics, art, drama, language, geography, education, and law. He studied with Plato for 20 years.

Aristotle insisted that every truth followed logically from other truths. You could not miss a step, jumping from truth A to truth C. In the middle, you needed truth B to link the other truths. Aristotle developed a set of logical statements known as a syllogism (SIHL-uh-jihz-uhm). A syllogism consists of three logically related statements. Here is an example:

1. All people are mortal.
2. Socrates was a person.
3. Therefore, Socrates was mortal.

This rigid system for organizing and testing ideas was important for developing rational, scientific thought.

Section Review 3

Define: (a) classical art, (b) tragedy, (c) philosopher, (d) syllogism
Identify: (a) Pericles, (b) the Parthenon, (c) Athena, (d) Phidias, (e) Aeschylus, (f) Sophocles, (g) Peloponnesian War, (h) Thucydides, (i) Aristophanes, (j) Socrates, (k) Plato, (l) the Academy, (m) *The Republic,* (n) Aristotle
Answer:
1. How did Pericles strengthen Athens's position as a leader in Greece?
2. (a) How were the Parthenon and other works of art and architecture examples of Athenian values? (b) How was drama important to the polis?
3. How were the lives of Greek girls and women different from the lives of the boys and men?
4. (a) What were the key events of the Peloponnesian War? (b) What were its results?

5. (a) What topics did Socrates consider important for discussion? (b) How did his views lead to his execution?
6. (a) Why did Plato reject democracy? (b) What type of society did he advocate?
7. How did Aristotle aid the development of scientific thinking?

Critical Thinking
8. (a) Are historians justified in calling this period of Greek history a golden age? Give reasons for your answer. (b) Write a short definition of a golden age that would apply to other civilizations. (Save your definition for reference in later chapters.)
9. How were the assumptions of the Greek philosophers about the universe different from the ideas of earlier civilizations such as the Egyptians and the Sumerians?

Alexander's conquests spread Greek culture. 4

In the years after Athens's defeat by Sparta in 404 B.C., the Greek city-states continued to fight one another. First one polis and then another rose to power, but none was able to bring peace or unity to Greece.

By 350 B.C., the greatest threat to Greek freedom came from a little-known kingdom north of classical Greece called Macedon (MAS-uh-dahn). The Macedonians were a tough, Greek-speaking people who lived in mountain villages, not city-states. Other Greeks looked down on them as uncivilized. They had no great philosophers, sculptors, or writers. However, they did have shrewd and fearless kings.

Philip built Macedon's power.

In 359 B.C., the shrewdest of all the Macedonians, Philip II, became Macedon's new king. Though only 23 years old, Philip knew what he wanted. First, he aimed to unite Greece under his leadership. After that, he planned to invade the Persian empire.

From 356 to 338 B.C., Philip used a combination of war, diplomacy, bribery, and trickery to defeat the Greek city-states one by one. In their continuing squabbles, Philip played them off against one another with great skill. Finally, in 338 B.C., Philip defeated Athens and its ally Thebes at Chaeronea (KAIR-uh-NEE-uh). These two were the last powerful city-states to stand against him. (Sparta was still independent, but it was now so small and weak that it could do nothing against Philip.) The victory at Chaeronea gave Philip control of all Greece.

Although Philip treated Thebes harshly, he was lenient with Athens. One reason for his mild treatment of the Athenians was his respect for Athens as the leader of Greek culture. In fact, around 343 B.C., he had invited Aristotle to tutor the heir to the Macedonian throne, 13-year-old Alexander.

After Chaeronea, Philip began to ready his army for an invasion of Asia. But in 336 B.C., at a great wedding feast for his daughter, Philip was murdered by a Macedonian nobleman. The assassin had a personal grudge against Philip but may also have been in the pay of the Persian king.

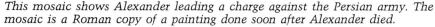

Alexander conquered a vast empire.

Philip's son, Alexander, was 20 years old in 336 B.C., when he became king of Macedon. Having studied with Aristotle for seven years, Alexander was steeped in the best traditions of Greek thought. He kept a copy of the *Iliad* under his pillow. He was also a seasoned army commander. He had put down a rebellion in Thrace when he was 16 and commanded a section of Philip's army at Chaeronea when he was 18.

Alexander's conquests Alexander soon showed he meant to keep all that his father had won. When Thebes rebelled, he destroyed the city and sold the survivors into slavery. The other Greek cities, intimidated, quickly fell into line. Then Alexander was free to carry out Philip's plan to invade Asia.

In 334 B.C., Alexander crossed the Dardanelles and set off on a march of conquest that went on for 8 years and covered a route of 20,000 miles. First, he conquered Asia Minor and the eastern coast of the Mediterranean. Then he

This mosaic shows Alexander leading a charge against the Persian army. The mosaic is a Roman copy of a painting done soon after Alexander died.

The Empire of Alexander the Great

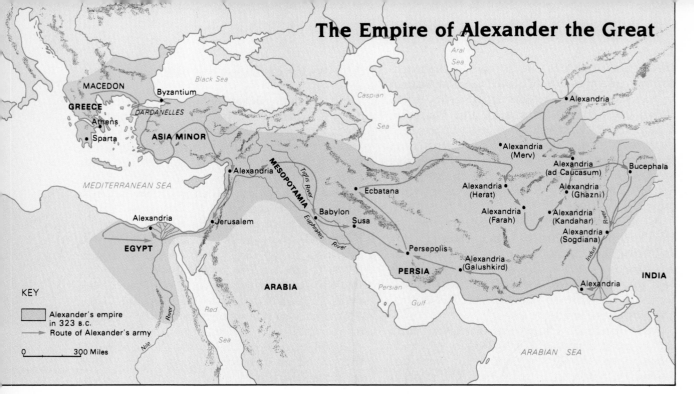

Map Study

What narrow body of water did Alexander cross to reach Asia Minor? Where did he go after capturing Jerusalem? Where did Alexander build a city to honor Bucephalus, his favorite war horse?

marched into Egypt in 332 B.C. The Egyptians welcomed him as a liberator from Persian rule.

From Egypt, Alexander moved north and east into the heart of the Persian empire around Babylon. Here he smashed the Persian forces. The Persian king, Darius III, fled. Alexander marched into Babylon in triumph. Shortly afterward Darius was murdered by one of his satraps. By 330 B.C., Alexander had become the Great King of Persia.

Alexander continued east, into lands even beyond the reaches of the Persian empire. He conquered the Indus River valley and wanted to go farther. His weary army, however, had faced parching deserts, monsoon rains, and the terrifying war elephants of the Indian armies. The soldiers threatened mutiny, and Alexander turned back.

The army fought its way back, crossing some of the harshest deserts in the world. Shortly after Alexander returned to Babylon, he caught a fever that grew steadily worse. When it was clear he was dying, his loyal Macedonian soldiers filed through the palace past his bedside to bid him farewell. Two days later, on June 18, 323 B.C., Alexander died. He was not yet 33.

The breakup of Alexander's empire Immediately after his death, Alexander's empire broke apart. His three strongest generals each grabbed a piece of it. Ptolemy (TAH-luh-mee) took control of Egypt. Seleucus (suh-LOO-kuhs) took Asia Minor and the Fertile Crescent. Antigonus (an-TIHG-uh-nus) took Macedon.

In Greece itself, individual city-states like Athens and Sparta never recovered their glory. Instead, the city-states grouped themselves into leagues. These leagues and the kingdoms founded by the generals fought with one another almost constantly until a new power farther west—the Romans—came on the scene to rule them all.

Greek culture spread in the Hellenistic Age.

The widespread lands conquered by Alexander were not politically united. However, they developed a common culture known as Hellenism, strongly influenced by Greek civilization. The word *Hellenism* derives from the Greeks' name for their own country, Hellas.

A *blending of cultures* Everywhere Alexander had gone, he had established governments run by Greek administrators. Long after Alexander's death, this Greek ruling class continued to spread Greek influence under later kings and queens. The conquered peoples exchanged coins bearing the profile of Alexander the Great. Their public buildings were fashioned in the Greek style. For two centuries after Alexander's conquests, the Hellenizing process affected all lands touching the Mediterranean Sea.

The heart of Hellenism lay in the great cities that Alexander had conquered or founded. Alexander founded more than 70 cities, many of which he named Alexandria in honor of himself. The greatest Alexandria was on Egypt's Nile delta. In its harbor stood a gigantic lighthouse, an estimated 370 feet tall, which greeted ships from all over the Mediterranean. One of the Seven Wonders of the Ancient World, the lighthouse symbolized Alexandria's role as the new center of Mediterranean trade. A huge library containing more than 500,000 papyrus scrolls symbolized Alexandria's fame as the center of learning.

Hellenism was a rich blend of many cultures. In Alexandria, it was part Greek, part Jewish, and part Egyptian. Farther east, it was a blend of Persian and Greek. Although Greek independence was snuffed out by Philip and Alexander, much of Greek creativity was still alive. Hellenistic art, architecture, philosophy, sculpture, and literature showed the influence of many traditions, but its roots were clearly Greek.

Triumphs in science Perhaps the Hellenistic Age's greatest triumphs were in the sciences. Alexander himself had led the way. Even as his armies crossed Asia, he had writers keep records of the plants, animals, weather, and geographic features they found. (Remember, he had been Aristotle's pupil.) Later, the establishment of libraries, the exchange of manuscripts and ideas between cities, and the weakening of ancient Greek religion led to a flowering of science. Two of its geniuses were Euclid (YOO-klihd) and Archimedes (AHR-kih-MEE-deez).

Euclid opened a school of geometry in Alexandria. In his most lasting work, the *Elements*, he logically organized the findings of Greek geometry. The book was used as a geometry textbook in Islamic and European universities well into the 1900's.

Archimedes studied in Euclid's school at Alexandria. He worked with levers, inclined planes, wedges, screws, wheels, and pulleys to find out what laws governed their motions. He discovered that people can use levers to lift objects much larger than themselves. In fact, he once boasted, "Give me a place to stand, and I can move the Earth."

Building on the knowledge of Archimedes, Hellenistic scientists could have started an industrial revolution. They built a force pump, pneumatic machines, and even a steam engine. But they never seem to have considered producing large numbers of these machines. In an age when slaves were plentiful, labor-saving devices had little appeal.

By 150 B.C., Hellenism was losing its strength. A new city, Rome, was at the same time growing and gaining strength. Like Athens, Rome lay on the Mediterranean Sea, but far to the west. Through Rome, the lands of western Europe would soon be introduced to Greek-style drama, architecture, sculpture, literature, religion, and philosophy. These ideas became the heart of Western civilization. How that happened is part of the story told in the next two chapters.

Section Review 4

Define: Hellenism
Identify: (a) Macedon, (b) Philip II, (c) Battle of Chaeronea, (d) Alexander the Great, (e) Ptolemy, (f) Seleucus, (g) Antigonus
Answer:
1. (a) How did Philip II win control of Greece? (b) What was the attitude of both Philip and Alexander toward Greek culture?
2. (a) Describe Alexander's route during his great march of conquest. (b) What happened to Alexander's empire after his death?
3. What changes did Alexander bring to the societies he conquered?
4. (a) What was the importance of Euclid's book, the *Elements*? (b) How did Archimedes build on Euclid's contribution?

Critical Thinking
5. "Alexander's achievements, though brilliant, did not last long." (a) Give evidence to support this statement. (b) Give evidence to refute the statement.

Summary

1. Greek culture grew up around the Aegean Sea. Bronze Age cultures on Crete and mainland Greece laid the foundation for later Greek culture. Greek life was also shaped by the mountainous land, the mild climate, and the sea. Adventures of the heroes and gods of the early Greeks have come down to us in the form of epic poems.

2. Greek city-states competed for power. Two of the most powerful city states were Athens and Sparta. Spartans valued military strength above all, whereas Athenians encouraged individualism and creativity. Athens gradually developed a democratic government. After playing an important role in defeating the invading Persian army, Athens became the powerful leader of an alliance of Greek city-states called the Delian League.

3. Athens led Greece in its golden age. Pericles, leader of Greece for 32 years, helped the city grow in military and economic strength. He glorified the city by supporting the work of architects, sculptors, and dramatists. Although Athens's confidence was much shaken by a war with Sparta, the struggle sparked great achievement in the area of philosophy.

4. Alexander's conquests spread Greek culture. Two kings of Macedon, Philip and Alexander, conquered Greece as well as a vast empire beyond. A combination of Greek culture with other cultures, called Hellenism, spread throughout this empire. The Hellenistic Age was marked by important advances in science as well as the arts.

Reviewing the Facts

1. Define the following terms:

   a. epic
   b. arete
   c. polis
   d. aristocracy
   e. hoplite
   f. phalanx
   g. tyrant
   h. colony
   i. democracy
   j. tragedy

2. Explain the importance of each of the following names, dates, places, or terms:

   a. Crete
   b. Mycenae
   c. Trojan War
   d. Homer
   e. Athens
   f. Sparta
   g. Solon
   h. Cleisthenes
   i. Herodotus
   j. 490 B.C.
   k. Peloponnesian War
   l. Pericles
   m. 431–404 B.C.
   n. Aeschylus
   o. Sophocles
   p. Socrates
   q. Plato
   r. Aristotle
   s. Philip II
   t. Alexander the Great
   u. 323 B.C.

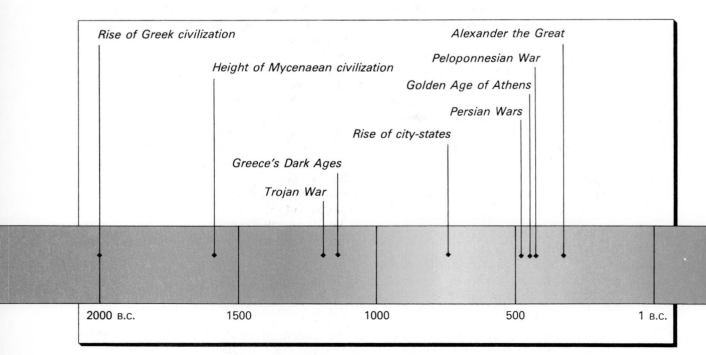

Rise of Greek civilization

Height of Mycenaean civilization

Greece's Dark Ages

Trojan War

Rise of city-states

Alexander the Great

Peloponnesian War

Golden Age of Athens

Persian Wars

2000 B.C.   1500   1000   500   1 B.C.

3. What major changes took place in Greek political organization between 1200 and 500 B.C.?
4. What Greek ideals were expressed both in Homer's poems and in the Olympic games?
5. What were Sparta's strengths and weaknesses?
6. How did Athens move from aristocratic rule to democracy?
7. Why is the period between 480 and 430 B.C. known as a golden age for Athens?
8. How did the disunity of the Greek city-states lead to their conquest by Philip?
9. How did Greek culture become influential across a broad area outside Greece?

Thinking about History

1. In what ways might ancient Athens be considered more democratic than the United States today? In what ways might it be considered less democratic than the United States?
2. Choose one individual mentioned in this chapter and describe how that person fulfilled some of the ideals of Greek culture.

Writing and Speaking about History

1. The introduction to this chapter on pages 94–95 discusses the impact on Western civilization of Greece's victory over Persia. State the thesis of this discussion in your own words.
2. Make a chart that describes the Egyptian and Athenian concepts of government, slavery, and religion. Divide a sheet of paper into two columns. Label one column *Egypt* and the second column *Athens*. Down the side of your paper, make a column for each of the three concepts being compared. Fill in the columns with information from the text.
3. Use the information in your chart to formulate a thesis statement that shows how Egyptian society differed from Athenian society. (Example: Religion was more important to Egyptians because they worshiped the pharaoh as a god.)
4. Place the people listed in Exercise 2 on page 118 in one of the following categories:
    Political
    Military
    Cultural
Prepare a short speech in which you nominate one of these people for the World Hall of Fame.

Practicing Skills

1. Following the Persian defeat at Marathon, Pheidippides ran 26 miles to tell Athenians of the victory. Use the map on page 116 to compare and contrast this distance to the distance between Athens and the following cities founded by Alexander the Great. What do these distances tell you about the size of Alexander's empire?
    a. Alexandria, Egypt
    b. Alexandria, Galushkind
    c. Alexandria, Sogdiana
    d. Bucephala
2. Compare the map of Alexander's empire on page 116 with a modern world map in the atlas section of this book. What present-day countries lie within the boundaries of Alexander's empire?
3. Copy the time line on page 118 on a separate sheet of paper. Add the following events from this chapter to the timeline. Use approximate dates.
    a. fall of Crete
    b. Homer
    c. Solon's reforms
    d. rise of Philip II

Investigating History

1. Heinrich Schliemann's discoveries at Troy and Mycenae included great hoards of golden treasures. Look in the library for information on Schliemann's life and achievements, as well as photographs of the riches he found.
2. Read some of the myths that the Greeks developed about their gods. Who were the 12 Olympic deities, and what was each associated with?
3. Look for examples of Greek-style architecture in your own community or nearby. If possible, take photographs to illustrate examples and bring the pictures to class.
4. Homer's *Iliad* and *Odyssey* have both been translated into English. Locate a copy of one of these epics in the library. Find passages to read to the class that illustrate *arete*. What other Greek ideals do the epics demonstrate?

Decision Making in History

Evaluate Themistocles' decision to abandon Athens and the Spartans' decision to stand to the last soldier at Thermopylae from each of the following viewpoints: (a) a government official (b) a soldier

The Roman Republic

In the years when Rome's power was spreading around the Mediterranean Sea, warfare was almost a way of life for Romans.

1. The Romans founded their city.

2. The Roman republic spread its power.

3. Republican government collapsed in Rome.

According to an ancient Roman myth, the war god Mars fathered twin sons, Romulus and Remus. Their mother was a Latin princess, Rhea Silvia. A jealous Latin king feared that the twins might some day claim his throne, so he ordered them placed in a basket and set afloat on Italy's Tiber River. The king assumed they would drown. Miraculously, a she-wolf found the half-starved infants and fed them with her own milk. Soon after, a shepherd discovered the babies and brought them up as his sons.

As young men, Romulus and Remus decided to build a city near the spot where they had been abandoned as babies. In the rolling land near the Tiber, each brother chose a hilltop and claimed leadership of the new city. Soon they were quarreling bitterly over their rival claims. In the heat of anger, Romulus struck his brother and killed him. The hilltop Romulus had chosen, the Palatine (PAL-uh-TYN), became the center of the new city. The city itself was called Rome, taking its name from the triumphant and murderous brother.

After a long reign, the myth continues, Romulus disappeared one day during a thunderstorm. A dark cloud enveloped him and lifted him up to heaven. Romulus, now a god, later came back to earth to speak to an old comrade. "Go tell the Romans," he said, "it is heaven's will that my Rome shall be capital of the world. Let them learn to be soldiers. Let them know and teach their children that no power on earth can stand against Roman arms."

Although this story is a myth, it has historic value (as many myths do). It tells how Romans in the days of Rome's greatness viewed themselves and their world. By 27 B.C., Rome had indeed become capital of the world—at least, of the world known to the people of Italy. Rome's ships controlled the entire Mediterranean Sea. Its armies exacted taxes and tribute from people on three continents—Africa, Asia, and Europe.

In the years of Rome's growth, Romans overcame the enemies who surrounded them. At the same time, they developed an effective government and an outstanding system of law. At last, however, disputes among groups of Romans gave way to civil war. The Roman government in which many men had a voice gave way to rule by a single man. This chapter will trace the development of Rome from a small village to "capital of the world."

The Romans founded their city. 1

The map on this page shows the long Italian peninsula. Shaped like a high-heeled boot, it seems ready to kick the nearby island of Sicily. To the east of Italy lies Greece. To the west stretch the southern coasts of modern-day France and Spain. To the south, only 80 miles from Sicily, lies the coast of Africa.

Geography was important to Rome's success. The Italian peninsula is near the midpoint of the

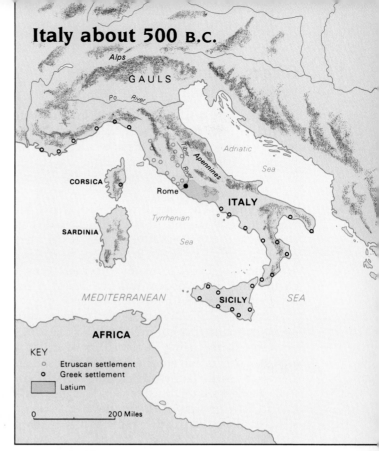

Map Study

What mountains lie north of Italy? Where were most of the Greek settlements in Italy?

Mediterranean, dividing the sea into an eastern and a western half. Rome itself is located midway between the Alps and Italy's southern tip. Thus, the city is a central point within a central peninsula. Rome occupies an ideal position from which to send out ships and armies in all directions. Moreover, the city was built about 15 miles inland from the sea, at the first convenient place for crossing the Tiber River. Thus, many key trade routes between northern and southern Italy met at Rome.

Italy's land is mountainous but not as rugged as the land of Greece. The snow-capped peaks of the Alps sharply separate Italy from the rest of Europe. There are, however, passes through the Alps by which invaders and migrating groups could reach the peninsula. A lower mountain range, the Apennines (AP-uh-nynz), runs down the length of Italy. Especially on the western side of the Apennines, the country in ancient times was rolling, wooded, and fertile.

Greeks, Latins, and Etruscans battled for Italy.

The earliest settlers of the Italian peninsula arrived in prehistoric times. Around 1000 B.C., Italy's prehistoric period drew to a close. Over the next 500 years, the region's culture was shaped by three dominant groups: the Latins, the Greeks, and the Etruscans.

The Latins The Latins wandered across the Alps into Italy around 1000 B.C. They settled on either side of the Tiber River, a region that they called Latium (**LAY**-shee-uhm). Rome began as a settlement of Latin shepherds, no more than a cluster of round wooden huts perched atop the 300-foot Palatine Hill.

According to the Roman myth, Romulus built his wall around this hill in 753 B.C. At that time, however, Rome barely deserved to be called a city. Its farmers and shepherds lived very simply and wore coarse, homespun clothing. Only a few trade goods from the outside world reached their village. The growth of Rome into a city would soon be influenced greatly by the other two groups that settled in Italy, the Greeks and the Etruscans (ih-**TRUHS**-kuhnz).

The Greeks Between 750 and 600 B.C., settlers from Greece established about 50 colonies on the coast of southern Italy and Sicily. The numerous Greek colonies prompted the Latins to call this area *Magna Graecia*, or Greater Greece. These prosperous and commercially active cities brought all of Italy, including Rome, into closer contact with Greek civilization.

The Etruscans A third group of settlers, the Etruscans, entered northern Italy between 1200 and 800 B.C. Historians have never been sure where the Etruscans originated, but evidence suggests they may have come from Asia Minor.

The Etruscans were much more civilized than their Latin neighbors. The Etruscans had a writing system, which the Latins did not. (Etruscan letters were adapted from the Greek alphabet, which the Greeks in turn had adapted from the Phoenicians.) However, linguists have not yet deciphered the Etruscan language, and so their writings remain unread.

The Etruscans had a great cultural influence on the Latins. Eventually, the Latin settlers of Rome adopted the Etruscan alphabet. Roman buildings show the influence of Etruscan architecture. Etruscans also helped to develop Rome's trade. Several of Rome's kings were of Etruscan background, having migrated to Rome from Etruscan cities.

Romans borrowed religious ideas.

Both the Greeks and the Etruscans had a great influence on the development of Roman religious ideas. Like the Greeks, the Romans were polytheists, believing in many gods and spirits. Unlike Greek gods, however, many early Roman gods had no names or personalities. Instead, they were spirits linked with daily cares such as guarding

Etruscan women had considerable freedom and equality, as suggested by this sculpture from the tomb of a married couple. Wives and husbands were partners, and children bore the names of both parents.

children's food, protecting the household, and keeping grain supplies safe.

From the Etruscans, Romans learned the practice of "taking the auspices," which literally meant "watching birds in flight." It was auspicious (a good sign) if, before a battle, a vulture or eagle soared overhead. There were also other ways of trying to interpret the will of the gods, including looking at the liver of a slaughtered animal.

Knowledge of Greek gods filtered into Rome through traders. The Romans gave their own names to these gods but kept the legends and personalities of the Greek divinities. The almighty Greek god Zeus became the almighty Roman god Jupiter. The Greek goddess Hera became the Roman goddess Juno.

Romans overthrew their kings and established a republic.

In its early years, Rome was ruled by kings. During the years of royal rule between about 600 and 509 B.C., Rome changed from a collection of hilltop villages to a city. Kings ordered the construction of many of Rome's first temples and public buildings. By royal order, the swampy valley below the Palatine Hill was drained, making a public meeting place. In later years, this valley, known as the Forum (FAWR-uhm), became the heart of Roman political life, as the agora was the heart of the Greek polis.

According to legend, the son of the last king of Rome attacked a Roman woman, Lucretia. The outraged Romans rose in revolt and overthrew the prince's father. Then, the Romans declared they would never again be ruled by a king. Henceforth, any Roman who plotted to make himself king could be killed without trial.

In 509 B.C., Rome set up a **republic,** a government in which citizens who have the right to vote choose their leaders. The word *republic* comes from a Latin phrase, *res publica,* which simply means "public affairs." For the Romans, a republic was not a democracy, because the right to vote and other political rights were not shared by all citizens. Rather, in the Roman republic, various groups struggled for power, sometimes resorting to violence. To understand how the Roman republic worked, we must look first at Rome's social organization.

Romans valued family ties.

Throughout Rome's history, the character of its citizens was influenced by a group of values called "the ways of the fathers." The Romans emphasized discipline, strength, and loyalty. A person with these qualities was said to have the important virtue of **gravitas** (weightiness or seriousness). The Romans honored strength more than beauty, power more than grace, usefulness more than elegance, and steadiness more than quickness of mind. The sober, weighty quality of gravitas left its mark on all aspects of Roman society, from its government to its art.

At the heart of Roman society was the family. By law and custom, power to rule the early Roman household belonged exclusively to one person— the eldest man, known as the *pater familias* (PAY-tur fuh-MIHL-yuhs), or "father of the family." The pater familias had complete power over his family. He controlled all family property. He could sell a family member into slavery or even kill any member of his household without penalty. Usually, of course, the pater familias acted as the protector of his family. It was he who spoke for the family in public assemblies or in the law courts. The pater familias in each household also acted as its chief priest.

Although the pater familias was the legal head of the family, Roman women were in charge of the daily running of the household. A woman in Rome had much greater freedom than in Athens. She was a citizen, with the right to own property and testify in court. She ate meals with her husband, even though he reclined on a couch while she sat upright on a chair. She often advised her husband on business and politics. She did not, however, have the key right, the right to vote. Officially, the Roman woman was expected to remain in the background.

Society was divided into classes.

Not all families were equal in Roman society. Although all male Roman citizens could take part in politics, the city was dominated by a small group of families. Romans of this upper class claimed that their ancestors had been *patres,* or "fathers," who founded Rome. These specially privileged families were known as the **patrician** (puh-TRIH-shuhn) class. They claimed that their ancestry gave them the authority to make laws for Rome and its people.

The common farmers, artisans, and merchants were known as **plebeians** (plih-BEE-uhnz). The plebeians were free citizens with a number of rights, including the right to vote. However, they had far less power than the patricians, who held nearly all important political offices.

Birth alone (not merit or wealth) determined every Roman's social and political status. The line between the patrician and plebeian classes was extremely rigid. In the early years of the republic, for example, marriage between the two classes was forbidden by law.

Rome built a mighty army.

The constant threat of war forced both patrician and plebeian men in Rome to lead double lives as farmers and soldiers. All male citizens were required to serve in the army, and no one could hold public office until he had first served ten years as a soldier.

Learning to fight Roman-style meant being part of a massive military unit called a legion. The Roman legion was made up of 4,000 to 6,000 heavily armed foot soldiers (infantry). A group of soldiers on horseback (cavalry) cooperated with each legion. Every legion was divided into 60 smaller groups, each of which was known as a century.

In battle, the Roman legion proved superior to the Greek phalanx because the legion was more flexible. The wall-like phalanx could move effectively in only two directions—forward and backward. But each century in a legion could move independently. Under a skillful general, a Roman legion could surround and outflank its foes. The legions were the fighting force that spread Rome's power around the Mediterranean.

Daily Life · *The Roman Toga*

Practicality has never been a requirement of fashion. The Roman toga (TOH-guh) was an uncomfortable garment. It was hot in summer, cold in winter, and clumsy for just about any activity but standing still. The toga was, however, practical in one way: It was easy to make, since it involved no sewing. Not even a buttonhole was needed. An adult's toga was basically a large wool blanket, measuring about 18 by 7 feet. It was draped around the body in a variety of ways, without the use of buttons or pins.

In the early days of the Roman republic, both women and men wore togas. Women eventually wore more dresslike garments, called *stolas,* with separate shawls. For men, however, the toga remained in fashion with very little change.

Soon after the republic was formed, the toga became a symbol of Roman citizenship. Different styles of togas indicated a male citizen's place in society. For example, a young boy would wear a white toga with a narrow purple band along the border. When his family decided he was ready for adult responsibilities, he would don a pure white toga. On that day, usually when he was about 16, his family would take him to the Forum, where he would register as a full citizen. For the rest of his life, he would wear a toga at the theater, in court, for religious ceremonies, and on any formal occasion. At his funeral, his body would be wrapped in a toga to mark him, even in death, as a Roman citizen.

Section Review 1

Define: (a) republic, (b) gravitas, (c) pater familias, (d) toga, (e) patrician, (f) plebeian, (g) legion, (h) century

Identify: (a) Italy, (b) Rome, (c) Romulus, (d) Palatine Hill, (e) Alps, (f) Tiber River, (g) Apennines, (h) Latins, (i) Etruscans, (j) Forum

Answer:

1. How did geography help Rome?
2. Why was each of the following groups important to Rome's development? (a) Latins (b) Greeks (c) Etruscans
3. What were the values of early Roman society?
4. (a) How was the Roman household organized? (b) What was the role of women in the household? (c) What freedoms did women have in the family and in society?
5. How was the army closely linked to Roman society as a whole?

Critical Thinking

6. Choose one of the earlier civilizations you have studied, such as Egypt or Greece. How did the values of Roman society differ from those of the other society?

The Roman republic spread its power. 2

For 500 years, the Romans governed their city and surrounding farmland as a republic. The history of these five centuries may be divided into two periods of almost equal length.

In the first two-and-a-half centuries (509–265 B.C.), Roman troops battled for mastery of the Italian peninsula. At the same time, in Rome itself, plebeians forced patricians to surrender some of their power.

Footnote to History

Part of a Roman soldier's pay was a special allowance to buy salt. The Latin word for salt was *sal,* and the special allowance was called the *salarius,* from which we get the English word *salary.*

The second half of the republic's history (265–44 B.C.) was marked by civil war, the rising power of army leaders, and the eventual triumph of Julius Caesar. Yet even while Romans fought among themselves, they extended Roman rule around the Mediterranean Sea.

Plebeians slowly won more power.

For centuries, Roman coins bore the letters *SPQR,* which stood for *Senatus Populusque Romanus*—the senate and the Roman people. Together, these two groups were the heart of Roman government. This simple phrase masked years of bitter struggle between patricians (who controlled the Roman senate) and plebeians (who made up the majority of the population).

Conflict between patrician and plebeian After the Romans drove out their kings in 509 B.C., patricians controlled Rome's government. Plebeians were barred by law from holding most important positions in government. Only patricians could command the armies, serve as high priests, or hold the highest political offices. As the years passed, however, plebeians won a greater share of political power.

According to tradition, in 494 B.C., thousands of disgruntled plebeians walked out of the city and camped on a neighboring hillside. They refused to fight in the Roman army unless the patricians agreed to reforms. Between 494 and 287 B.C., the plebeians used this tactic several times. Each time, they won new rights.

Plebeians gradually won the right to hold many political offices that had once been open only to patricians. Laws that had hurt the plebeians were slowly abolished. Enslavement for debt was ended. Plebeians and patricians could marry. Because both sides were willing to compromise, the result was a government in which power was shared.

Twelve Tables Among the first victories of the plebeians was the creation of a written law code. Roman law rested heavily on custom. When laws were unwritten, patrician officials often interpreted the law to suit themselves. Consequently, plebeians demanded that the laws of Rome be published.

In 451 B.C., a special group of ten officials took on the task of writing down Rome's laws. The laws were carved on 12 great tablets, or tables,

125

At Roman family meals, the husband reclined on a couch while the wife sat in a chair. The food came from busy shops like the one at the left, which had fruit, chickens, and rabbits.

and hung in the Forum. They became the foundation for later Roman law. Although the laws were sometimes harsh, the Twelve Tables established the idea that all free citizens had a right to the protection of the law. Thus, the Twelve Tables helped to settle the conflict between patricians and plebeians.

Rome achieved a balanced government.

By about 275 B.C., Roman writers boasted that Rome had achieved a balanced government. They meant that their government was partly a monarchy (government by a king), partly an aristocracy (government by nobles), and partly a democracy (government by the people). The Romans believed that this mixture gave them the best features of all kinds of governments.

The office of consul In place of a king, Rome had two officials called **consuls**. The consuls took over many of the powers that the kings had once held. They commanded Rome's army and directed its government. They had the power of life and death over citizens in wartime and great powers in peacetime as well.

The consuls' power was limited, however, by two rules. First, a consul's term was only one year long, and the same person could not be elected consul again for ten years. Second, one consul could always overrule, or **veto**, the other's decisions. (In Latin, *veto* means "I forbid.")

The powerful senate The **senate** was the aristocratic branch of Rome's government. Tradition said that Romulus had named 100 patricians to advise him, thus creating the first senate. Later, the number of senators increased, and plebeians could also be members. Membership was for life. Therefore, the senate provided continuity and stability in the government. It exercised enormous influence over both foreign and domestic policy.

The power of the people The democratic side of Roman government was the assembly. All citizen-soldiers were members of this branch of government. In the early days of the republic, the assembly had little power in comparison to the consuls and the senate. Over the years, however, the powers of the assembly increased. Eventually, its decisions gained the force of law.

The office of dictator In times of crisis, the republic could turn to another type of political leadership, the **dictator**. A man who was named dictator had absolute power to make laws and command the army, but his power lasted for only six months. Dictators were chosen by the consuls and then elected by the senate.

126

The Roman ideal of a dictator is shown by the story of Cincinnatus (SIN-sih-NAY-tus). In 458 B.C., when Rome's armies were in peril, the senate named Cincinnatus dictator. Cincinnatus was plowing his four-acre farm when messengers brought him the news. He left his plow, defeated Rome's enemies, and stepped down as dictator within 15 days. Then he returned to his farm to finish his plowing.

Rome won control of Italy.

Political struggles between patricians and plebeians were remarkably bloodless during these years. Outside the city walls, however, the blood of both classes was spilled over Italian hills and fields as Rome's legions subdued Italy. City by city, the Romans defeated other Latin groups and the Etruscans. Roman power grew slowly but steadily. And then, Rome suffered a smashing defeat.

The sack of Rome by the Gauls In 390 B.C., Rome's walls were successfully stormed by marauding Gauls (gawlz), a people from the Po River valley, north of the Apennines. The Gauls sacked Rome, leaving it in ruins. Then, the Romans were forced to pay a humiliating bribe to persuade the Gauls to leave.

The Romans recovered rapidly, though. They built a stronger, larger wall around their city. The reconstructed Rome spanned 1,000 acres, making it the largest city in Italy. Foreign troops would not sack the city again for 800 years.

War with the Greeks Eventually, Romans controlled all of the Italian boot except its heel and toe. For centuries, those southern regions of Italy had been colonized by the Greeks.

The Greek cities watched the rise of Roman power with alarm. In 282 B.C., Greek colonists sought aid from Pyrrhus (PIHR-uhs), a king in western Greece. A brilliant general, Pyrrhus brought 20,000 soldiers to fight the Romans. Twice Pyrrhus's army slammed into the Roman legions and drove them from the field. In each battle, however, the Greek army suffered terrible losses. Pyrrhus learned a bitter lesson of warfare (and of life): You can win every battle and still lose the war. In 275 B.C., the Romans drove Pyrrhus's tired and decimated troops back to Greece. Ever since, a victory gained at too high a price has been known as a "Pyrrhic victory."

Rome governed Italy skillfully.

After 275 B.C., the Romans were masters of all Italy except the Po Valley in the north, which was still held by the Gauls. Different parts of the conquered territory were subject to different laws and treatment from Rome.

Latin neighbors on the Tiber were treated as full citizens of Rome. They could marry other Romans, vote in assemblies, and appeal for justice in a Roman court.

In territories farther from Rome, conquered peoples were given the status of half-citizens. They enjoyed all the rights of a Roman citizen except the privilege to vote.

All other conquered groups fell into a third category, allies of Rome. Allies were required to contribute troops to the Roman army. They were forbidden to make treaties of friendship with any state but Rome. An allied city was free, however, to govern its own people without any Roman interference.

Unlike the Athenians, the Romans were willing to extend their citizenship to people outside Rome itself. The new citizens became partners in Rome's growth. This policy helped Rome to succeed in building a long-lasting empire, where Athens had failed.

With most of Italy unified behind it, Rome was now ready to enter the second stage of its astonishing rise to power. In the 250 years after 275 B.C., Roman power spread far beyond Italy.

Rome fought with Carthage.

After the decline of Athens, trade in the Mediterranean region was dominated by two wealthy cities, both on the northern coast of Africa. One was Alexandria in Egypt, still ruled by the Ptolemies. The other was Carthage, the former Phoenician colony. Like Rome, Carthage had the advantage of a location near the midpoint of the Mediterranean coast.

In 264 B.C., Rome and Carthage went to war for control of Sicily and the western Mediterranean. Thus began the first of three periods of struggle known as the Punic (PYOO-nik) Wars. *Punic* comes from the Latin word for Phoenicia.

Let us compare the two cities and their capacity for making war. With a population of 250,000, Carthage was about three times the size of Rome.

Carthage had a huge navy of 500 ships. Overseas trade had made Carthage an immensely wealthy city. Each year, it collected the equivalent of almost 1 million pounds of gold in tariffs and tribute. With this great wealth, Carthage employed the people of neighboring Numidia as **mercenaries**, soldiers who fight in any country's army for pay.

Rome's resources in ships and wealth seemed meager by comparison. In fact, at the beginning of the First Punic War, Rome had no navy whatsoever. Rome's power had always rested entirely on its armies. However, this great disadvantage was offset by three advantages. First, Rome could draw on a reserve of more than 500,000 troops made available through its conquests in Italy. Second, Rome's citizen troops were generally more loyal and reliable than the mercenaries employed by Carthage. Third, warfare was a Roman specialty. Over the centuries, Romans had directed much of their energy toward winning wars. All of Carthage's energies, on the other hand, had been aimed at winning wealth through trade.

Luck also seemed to favor the Romans. Toward the beginning of the first war, a Carthaginian warship washed up on the Italian shore. Needing a fleet in a hurry, the Romans hastily built 140 ships by copying the Carthaginian design. Unlike the Carthaginian model, however, each Roman warship was equipped with a long gangplank. When not in use, this gangplank was lashed upright to the mast. Attached to the bottom of the gangplank was an iron hook, shaped like a bird's beak and called a raven. When a Roman ship drew alongside a Carthaginian vessel, the gangplank crashed down between the two. Its beak stuck deep in the Carthaginian deck, binding the ships together. Roman soldiers then rushed over the gangplank.

By this means, the Romans won their first two naval battles against the African master of the Mediterranean. Carthage later avenged itself with several shattering victories of its own on land and sea.

The First Punic War dragged on for 23 punishing years before Carthage's last fleet was defeated and sunk in 241 B.C. The defeat marked the end of Carthage as a sea power. Rome took over the rich, grain-growing island of Sicily as the chief prize of victory.

Hannibal sought revenge on Rome.

From 241 to 218 B.C., Carthage and Rome each had other interests. Rome was bent on driving the Gauls out of northern Italy. Carthage set out to win much of southern Spain, which it then turned into a rich colony.

In 218 B.C., however, the uneasy peace between the two cities was broken. The mastermind behind this Second Punic War was a Carthaginian leader named Hannibal, one of the great military geniuses of all time. He was only a boy of nine when his father, a general, made him swear that he would always hate Rome and seek to destroy it. Hannibal grew to manhood on the southern coast of Spain. Here he observed his father's masterful tactics for fighting Spanish tribes and gained experience with troops of his own.

Hannibal's invasion of Italy When Hannibal was 29 years old, in 218 B.C., he assembled an army of 50,000 infantry, 9,000 calvary, and 60 elephants to try to capture Rome itself. He led his army on a long trek from Spain across France and up into the dizzying heights of the Alps. Desertions, battles with Gallic tribes, and blizzards in the mountains killed more than half his men and most of his elephants.

Rome assembled an army to fight this invader, but Hannibal destroyed it. A second Roman army, larger than the first, was also routed. In 216 B.C., a third army of 86,000 Romans found Hannibal's reinforced army of 50,000 men camped at Cannae on the eastern coast of Italy. By brilliant maneuvering, Hannibal drew the attacking army into a deadly trap. In this battle—Hannibal's greatest victory—between 40,000 and 70,000 Romans died.

For the next 13 years, Hannibal marched his armies at will up and down the Italian peninsula. The Romans did not dare to challenge him again in open battle. His soldiers lived off the land, seizing crops and cattle, pillaging farmhouses. However, they could not capture Rome itself. Its walls were too high and their own forces too small even to make the attempt. For years, Hannibal waited for Carthage to send him reinforcements. For years, he waited for Rome's allies to revolt and join his own armies. For years, Hannibal was disappointed.

The Battle of Zama Finally Rome found a general whose boldness and brilliance were nearly

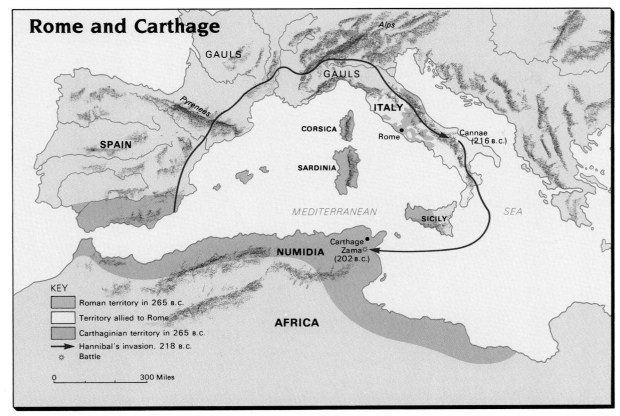

Rome and Carthage

GAULS

Alps

GAULS

ITALY

Pyrenees

SPAIN

CORSICA

Rome

Cannae
(216 B.C.)

SARDINIA

MEDITERRANEAN

SEA

SICILY

Carthage
Zama
(202 B.C.)

NUMIDIA

KEY

Roman territory in 265 B.C.

Territory allied to Rome

Carthaginian territory in 265 B.C.

Hannibal's invasion, 218 B.C.

Battle

0   300 Miles

AFRICA

Map Study

How far was Carthage from Rome? Where did Hannibal begin his march to invade Rome? What two mountain ranges did he cross on his way?

equal to Hannibal's. His name was Scipio (SIP-ee-oh). Scipio attacked Carthage itself, forcing Hannibal to rush home to the rescue. The great Carthaginian, unbeaten on European soil, was soundly thrashed by Scipio at the Battle of Zama in 202 B.C. (Hannibal survived and governed Carthage for seven years. He later killed himself to avoid capture by Rome.)

Thus ended the Second Punic War. Zama is one of the few battles that may truly have changed the course of history. Quite possibly, if Hannibal had been the victor, Carthage and not Rome would have become the greatest empire in the world. Because Rome was victorious, it was Rome that passed on its laws, its government, and its culture to Western civilization.

Scipio, in honor of his victory, was named *Africanus* (conqueror of Africa). In the terms of peace, Rome allowed Carthage to keep its lands in northern Africa but nothing more.

Rome made conquests to the east.

Rome now dominated the western half of the Mediterranean Sea. During the next 70 years, Romans also conquered the eastern half.

After the death of Alexander the Great in 323 B.C., his empire had been divided among his generals. Their descendants still ruled the lands around the eastern Mediterranean. The Antigonid dynasty ruled Macedon, the Ptolemaic dynasty ruled Egypt, and the Seleucid dynasty ruled most of what had been the Persian empire. These three—and a few other small kingdoms—were almost constantly at war with one another.

Greece lay nearest Rome, and it was the first to feel Rome's heavy hand. At first, Roman armies marching into Macedon looked like protectors of Greek freedom. The Greeks rejoiced when, in 197 B.C., the Romans freed them from the rule of Philip V of Macedon. Once settled in Greece, however, the Romans interfered in Greek politics, crushing all opposition to rulers favored by Rome.

As time passed, the exercise of Roman power in the east became increasingly ruthless. A few Greek city-states tried to free themselves from Rome's tightening grip, but the effort failed. Rome singled out Corinth for punishment as an example to the others. In 146 B.C., its people were massacred or enslaved, its walls wrecked, and its homes and temples burned. The once lovely city was reduced to an ash heap.

Rome finally destroyed Carthage.

In the same year, 146 B.C., Carthage was destroyed. By the time of the Third Punic War (149–146 B.C.), Carthage was no longer a threat to Rome. Yet it was still a prosperous city, and some Romans were filled with hate each time they thought of it. The Roman most responsible for this needless war was a senator named Cato (KAY-toh). Over and over, Cato ended his speeches with the same vindictive message: *"Carthago delenda est"* ("Carthage must be destroyed").

In 149 B.C., Rome forced war on Carthage, seizing on the excuse that Carthage had warred with neighboring Numidia without Rome's permission. The Carthaginians barricaded themselves in their beloved city. For three years, they withstood a Roman siege. Finally, under the leadership of Scipio Aemilianus (uh-MIHL-ee-AY-nuhs)—the grandson of Scipio Africanus—the Roman army broke into Carthage and set it afire. Carthage flamed and smoked for six days, while fighting raged from street to street. Watching the city burn, the Roman general wept. "This is a glorious moment," he said to a friend, "but I am seized with foreboding that someday the same fate will befall my own country." He was right, but Rome's downfall did not come for another 556 years.

Legend says that after Carthage was destroyed, the Romans plowed salt into the soil, so that not even crops would spring up again for Rome's hated rival. The legend, however, is untrue.

After the Third Punic War, Rome continued to expand eastward. In 133 B.C., the western tip of Asia Minor dropped peacefully into Roman hands as the gift of a dying king. This king of Pergamum had welcomed Roman aid against the Seleucids. Dying without an heir, he left his kingdom to Rome. Thus, Rome's Mediterranean empire stretched from Asia Minor to Spain.

Map Study

What territory had Rome gained by 133 B.C. in the region of Asia Minor? Name a city shown on this map that was not under Roman control.

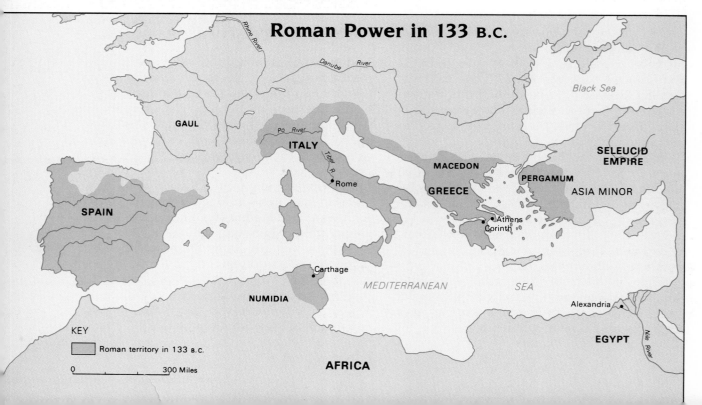

Roman Power in 133 B.C.

Section Review 2

Define: (a) consul, (b) veto, (c) senate, (d) assembly, (e) dictator, (f) mercenary
Identify: (a) SPQR, (b) Twelve Tables, (c) Cincinnatus, (d) Gauls, (e) Pyrrhus, (f) Carthage, (g) Punic Wars, (h) Hannibal, (i) Battle of Zama, (j) Scipio Africanus, (k) Scipio Aemilianus
Answer:

1. (a) Why were many plebeians dissatisfied with Rome's government in the early years of the republic? (b) How did they win reforms? (c) What changes did they bring about in Roman government?
2. Why did Romans consider that they had a balanced government?
3. Once Rome had conquered most of Italy, how did the Roman government win the support of the conquered people?
4. (a) At the start of the Punic Wars, why might Carthage have appeared the stronger power? (b) Why was Rome, in fact, the victor?
5. Why was the Battle of Zama a major turning point in history?
6. (a) Why did the Greeks at first welcome Roman armies? (b) Why did the Greek attitude change?

Critical Thinking

7. (a) How was the Roman republic different from a democracy? (b) What features of the republic were democratic?
8. (a) Give two examples of Rome's increasing ruthlessness as its empire grew. (b) How did Rome's treatment of conquered people outside Italy differ from that of the groups Rome conquered within Italy?

Republican government collapsed in Rome. 3

Carthage was not the only loser of the Punic Wars. Rome was also hurt in many ways. Thousands of men and boys who left their farms to fight in a Roman legion never came back. Those who did return found conditions in Italy drastically changed.

The gap between rich and poor grew.

Hannibal's armies had destroyed farms, homes, and villages. Returning soldiers could rarely afford to rebuild. Many small farmers sold their ruined acres to wealthy citizens. These new landowners treated farming strictly as a business. On their huge estates, known as *latifundia*, they found that raising cattle was more profitable than growing grain. (After the First Punic War, cheap wheat from Sicily had flooded Italian markets.) Labor for the latifundia was cheap because Rome's many wars brought thousands of chained captives to work as slaves.

Battle-scarred farmers could not return to their old way of life. Their land was gone, owned now by wealthy strangers, worked by slaves. Where could uprooted veterans go? Thousands of them sought new homes in or around Rome. They sought city jobs but seldom found them. Wealthy Romans preferred owning slaves to hiring free workers. This new class of urban, landless poor was called the **proletariat** (PROH-leh-**TAIR**-ee-uht). The people of this class were the poorest of Romans. Without work or hope, they became a dangerous and discontented mob within the city. From this time on, riots were a constant danger in Rome.

While poor farmers lost their land, the rich were corrupted by wealth. Winning a war always meant an opportunity for collecting loot. A victorious general might take a share of the spoils for himself and send the rest to the Roman treasury. After one year's victories, for example, Scipio Africanus displayed in the Roman Forum 123,000 pounds of silver that his army had brought back from Spain and Carthage.

Captured booty was proudly paraded through Roman streets during special holidays called "triumphs." The typical triumph consisted of a victorious general, dressed in purple-trimmed toga and golden crown, riding through a triumphal arch to the cheers of the crowd. He was followed by wagons of loot and bands of veterans.

The spoils of war brought dramatic changes in patrician life. Modest homes turned into ornately furnished mansions. There might be urns from Babylon, silk from China, gold from Carthage, and marble from Athens. While their dress remained rather simple, the rich learned to love exotic foods and lavish entertainment.

Slavery became widespread.

The luxury of the rich depended on the labor of slaves. In Rome's slave market, a tablet around the neck of a foreign captive identified his or her special skills and place of origin. Every year, thousands of unhappy captives were inspected and sold. As a result of the First Punic War alone, 75,000 formerly free men and women became Roman slaves. By the year 100 B.C., slaves formed perhaps one third of Rome's total population.

Low-priced slaves, unskilled and uneducated, were assigned to heavy labor in Roman mines, on cattle farms, in vineyards, and in shipyards. The more expensive slaves, usually from Greece and Asia Minor, worked in Roman households as cooks, teachers, musicians, private secretaries, and messengers. In one mansion, a rich Roman kept 11 highly educated Greek slaves just to recite the poems of Homer at his banquets.

Romans lived with the ever-present danger of a massive slave uprising. As the Roman slogan went, "Every slave we own is an enemy we harbor." Three times between 138 and 70 B.C., thousands of slaves rebelled against their masters. The third uprising was by far the most threatening. It was led by the slave Spartacus, who had been trained as a gladiator (a person who fought other warriors or wild beasts as a form of public entertainment). Spartacus raised an army of 70,000 slaves and ravaged the Italian countryside from 73 to 71 B.C. They fought desperately for their freedom, beating the Roman army nine times before their revolt was crushed. About 6,000 of Spartacus's followers were crucified.

The Gracchi attempted reforms.

The worst threat to the Roman republic, however, came from the Roman citizens themselves. The richest families of the city, plebeian as well as patrician, competed for political power. It was a more violent kind of politics than the old struggle between patricians and plebeians. After the Punic Wars, political arguments and rivalries often were settled by bloodshed.

Two brothers, Tiberius and Gaius Gracchus (GRAK-us), attempted to reform Rome's government. The elder brother, Tiberius, was elected to the political office of **tribune** in 133 B.C. Tribunes were officials who spoke on behalf of the plebeians. They were elected by the assembly. Tiberius spoke eloquently about the plight of the landless, dispossessed farmers. "The wolves and the bears have dens to rest and sleep," said Tiberius. "But the men who fight their country's battles have nothing . . . You fight and die only for the wealth and luxury of others. You are called the masters of the world, but you do not have a single clod of earth to call your own." What could be done for these unfortunate citizens? Give them land, said Tiberius. Limit the size of large estates, and distribute lands to the poor people of Rome.

To a poor man, Tiberius's program seemed only fair. To a rich landowner, it seemed like robbery. Tiberius further alarmed the rich by seeking to be reelected as tribune, something never before attempted. On election day, some senators and their followers clubbed Tiberius to death and flung his body into the Tiber.

Gladiators fought to the death in Roman arenas. Political leaders used such games to entertain the proletariat and prevent rebellions.

Ten years later (123 B.C.), the murdered man's younger brother, Gaius Gracchus, was elected tribune. Gaius made the office of tribune the most powerful position in Rome. By his eloquence and political skill, he pushed through a series of laws designed to weaken the senate. He planned programs to deal with unemployment.

The senate's opposition to the younger Gracchus's reforms again led to open violence. Gaius was declared an enemy of the state. The senate offered a large reward for his head. Gaius and his supporters took refuge on one of Rome's hills, where they were attacked by a band of senators with their slaves and foreign mercenaries. Gaius died in the battle. Later, the senate executed 3,000 of his followers.

Army leaders took political power.

After the death of the Gracchi, two army leaders muscled their way to power. First came Marius, whose victories against German tribes made him immensely popular with the people. Then came Sulla, the strong-armed champion of the senate.

Marius and his army saved Rome from a frightening invasion of Germanic tribes in 105 B.C. As a result, he was elected consul five times in a row, breaking the tradition that a consul could not be reelected for ten years. Marius blamed the weakness of Rome's defenses on its dwindling number of citizen-soldiers. Only landowners could serve in the army, and too many farmers had been forced off the land. To make

Voice from the Past · *The Perils of Success*

The Roman historian Sallust lived between 86 and 35 B.C., when Rome was already the greatest power in the Mediterranean region. Sallust had strong views on the course of Roman history, especially on changes he believed had taken place in the character of the Romans.

[In Rome's early years,] good morals were cultivated at home and in the field; there was the greatest harmony and little or no greed; justice and integrity prevailed . . . [Citizens] were lavish in their offerings to the gods, thrifty at home, loyal to their friends. By boldness in warfare and justice in peace, they watched over themselves and their country . . .

But when our country had grown great . . . then Fortune began to grow cruel and to bring confusion into all our affairs. Those who had found it easy to bear hardship and dangers . . . found leisure and wealth, desirable under other circumstances, a burden and a curse. Hence, the lust for money first, then for power, grew upon [Romans]; these were, I may say, the root of all evils. For greed destroyed honor, integrity, and all other noble qualities; taught in their place insolence, cruelty, to neglect the gods, to set a price on everything. Ambition drove many men to become false; to have one thought locked in the breast, another ready on the tongue; to value friendships and enmities not on their merits but by the standard of self-interest, and to show a good front rather than a good heart. At first these vices grew slowly . . . Finally, when the disease had spread like a deadly plague, the state was changed and a government that had been second to none in equity and excellence became cruel and intolerable.

1. According to Sallust, how did Romans show their good moral character in early times?
2. What two evils did Sallust believe were the root of Rome's later problems?
3. To sum up Sallust's ideas, make two lists of words. In the first list, include words that he might have used to describe the early Romans. In the second list, include words he might have used to describe Romans of his own day.
4. Do you agree with Sallust that hard times sometimes bring out better qualities in people than times of prosperity? Explain your answer.

EXEO·OMNIB

up for this loss of manpower, Marius allowed the city's poor to enlist in the army. The new recruits received weapons and armor from the state, unlike the self-equipped citizen-soldiers.

These new soldiers signed up for a period of 16 years—much of their adult lives. In other words, they became professional soldiers. As such, they were willing to fight for any army leader who rewarded them with land and gold. After Marius, Roman armies did not fight for the republic. They fought instead for the military leader who used his political power to give them weapons, food, and loot. More often than not, these leaders used their armies to advance their own political ambitions. It was now possible for rival politicians, each supported by his own army, to win power by force of arms.

In 88 B.C., Marius commanded one army while his rival, Sulla, commanded another. Over the next six years, both leaders used their armies to march against Rome. Each held power for a while and slaughtered the supporters of his opponent. Each forced his own laws on Rome. Sulla, who returned to power in 82 B.C., abolished the six-month limit to a dictator's term and had himself named dictator until he chose to step down. Both Sulla and Marius died peacefully in bed, somehow escaping the violent deaths they had dealt to others. But their pattern of using the army to gain political power outlived them both.

Julius Caesar rose to power.

Among those whom Sulla intended, but failed, to kill was a 20-year-old patrician named Gaius Julius Caesar (SEE-zuhr). Caesar escaped an early death because he understood the uses of money. He bribed Sulla's soldiers to spare his life.

Caesar had little money of his own, but like other ambitious Romans of his day, he knew that the quickest way to wealth was to govern one of Rome's provinces—Spain, Sicily, Gaul, Asia Minor, Macedon, or Africa. A provincial governor could amass a small fortune from just one year's collection of taxes, bribes, and war booty. The position of governor was seldom given to the best administrator. It went instead to the politician who won the good will of the senate and the Roman people.

For more than 20 years, Caesar played hard at the game of Roman politics. In the Forum, he charmed crowds with his brilliant speeches. In his country villa, he threw lavish parties for influential politicians.

To support his extravagant lifestyle, Caesar borrowed huge sums from a man whose well-deserved nickname was Crassus the Rich. Crassus invested in Caesar's political career as a gambler might invest in a racehorse. The gamble paid off handsomely when Caesar was appointed governor of a province in Spain. Caesar collected enough booty there in one year to enrich himself, his soldiers, and Crassus.

The First Triumvirate In 60 B.C., Caesar and Crassus joined forces with Pompey, a popular general. The three men agreed to support one another's political interests. To cement their alliance, Pompey married Caesar's daughter, Julia. With the help of his two allies, Caesar was elected consul in 59 B.C.

Julius Caesar

For the next ten years, the three men ruled Rome. The senate and assembly were bribed and bullied into following their decisions. They were known as the **triumvirate** (try-UHM-vuhr-iht), a Latin word meaning "rule of three."

The conquest of Gaul Abiding by ancient tradition, Caesar served only one year as consul. Then he assigned himself the governorship of Gaul. (See the map on page 130.) For eight years, he led his legions in a series of grueling but successful wars in western Europe. He pushed north into the dense woodlands and fertile valleys of central Gaul. He even crossed the English Channel and battled the barbaric tribes who lived in Britannia (present-day England). Back on the continent, he crossed the Rhine River to meet the onslaught of Germanic tribes. According to the historian Plutarch, Caesar's army killed a third of the people in the land it conquered.

Caesar was a tough and dauntless fighter. He drove himself and his troops relentlessly. Carrying 60-pound packs, Caesar's soldiers might march 50 miles in a day. At the day's end, each soldier pulled a shovel from his pack and dug his share of a trench to protect a camp more than one mile square. Inside, two legions (about 9,000 men) could eat and sleep safely before the next day's ordeal. Dinner in Caesar's army was meager: a few handfuls of grain and a cup of sour wine. Caesar himself ate no better. Because he shared fully in the hardships of the march, he won his men's enduring loyalty and devotion.

Never forgetting politics, Caesar sent back regular dispatches to Rome, telling of his victories. Collected into six books, these writings became one of the classics of Latin literature, Caesar's *Commentaries on the Gallic Wars.*

Caesar made himself ruler of Rome.

News from Gaul caused two reactions in Rome. The poorer citizens, who generally adored Caesar, loved him all the more for his conquests. But senators, alarmed at his immense popularity, feared for their own power. By 50 B.C., the triumvirate of Caesar, Crassus, and Pompey had come apart. Crassus was dead, killed in battle while commanding Roman troops in Asia. Pompey had become Caesar's rival rather than his ally. With Pompey's approval, the senate ordered Caesar to disband his legions and return to Rome.

Crossing the Rubicon Caesar's next move led inevitably to civil war. On the night of January 10, 49 B.C., he rode south across the Rubicon River in Italy, the southern limit of his military command. His troops followed loyally behind. Thus, Caesar defied the senate's order and directly challenged Pompey. To this day, "crossing the Rubicon" means making a decision from which there is no return.

Caesar's army marched swiftly through northern Italy and occupied Rome. Pompey barely managed to escape, fleeing eastward to rally his own armies. A year later (48 B.C.), Caesar's troops defeated Pompey's at Pharsalus in Greece. Pompey sailed to Alexandria in Egypt, hoping to win support there for his next campaign against Caesar. Instead, the young pharaoh ordered Pompey to be greeted warmly—and then murdered. When Caesar arrived in Alexandria, he was presented with Pompey's head as a gift. Caesar grieved at the sight, remembering that Pompey had once been both his ally and his son-in-law.

Becoming absolute ruler When Caesar returned to Rome in 46 B.C., he commanded the support of both his armies and the masses. In 44 B.C., the senate appointed him dictator for ten years.

As absolute ruler, Caesar made several sweeping changes. He granted Roman citizenship to many people in provinces outside Italy. Then he expanded the senate to 900 men, adding many of his loyal followers from other parts of Italy and from Gaul. This change made the senate more representative of Rome's empire, but it angered the powerful patricians because it gave Caesar control of the senate.

Some of Caesar's other actions would have pleased the Gracchi. He ordered landowners who used slave laborers to substitute free men for at

Footnote to History

According to legend, while Caesar was in Egypt, a large oriental rug was brought into his quarters. Rolled up inside it was Egypt's 21-year-old queen, the elegant and intelligent Cleopatra. She had herself smuggled into Caesar's presence because she was at war with her brother, the pharaoh. Although Caesar had a wife in Rome, he married Cleopatra under Persian law. With Roman help, Cleopatra defeated her brother and ruled Egypt.

least one third of their work force. He set up a public works program to create more jobs. He also founded 20 colonies in Spain, France, Switzerland, Africa, and elsewhere to provide land for Rome's landless poor. These programs cut by more than half the number of Romans who lived on government grain handouts.

The calendar Caesar's most lasting reform was to set up a new calendar. He replaced the old Roman calendar, linked to the phases of the moon, with a new solar calendar worked out by the scholars of Alexandria. The new calendar was called the Julian calendar. It counted 365 days in a year and 1 extra day every fourth year. Because the Romans thought February unlucky, they made it the shortest month. The seventh month, July, was named after Julius Caesar, because it included his birthday. The Julian calendar was used in most of Europe until 1582, when slight changes were made for even greater accuracy.

Caesar's death On March 15, 44 B.C., Caesar walked to the Theater of Pompey, where the senate was meeting. Waiting for him were a number of senators with knives hidden beneath their togas.

The chief conspirators, Brutus and Cassius, had been generously pardoned by Caesar for their earlier support of Pompey. Brutus, especially, had been Caesar's friend since then. Even so, both men were still troubled by Caesar's ambitions and his disregard for the old constitution of the republic. They feared that he would make himself king. (According to the ancient laws, you may recall, anyone who plotted to become king could be killed without trial.)

As Caesar approached, the conspirators pressed up against him, pretending to discuss urgent business. Suddenly they struck. Stabbed countless times, Caesar groaned his last words to his old friend Brutus, *"Et tu, Brute!"* ("And you, also, Brutus!") Thus died one of history's most remarkable men.

Civil war followed Caesar's death.

Caesar's assassins thought they had saved the Roman republic. By that time, however, the republic was almost as dead as Caesar himself. Two civil wars (Marius against Sulla and Caesar against Pompey) had crippled the former power of the patricians. Soon after Caesar's death, a third civil war broke out. The final victor of this conflict proved to be an even more astute politician than Julius Caesar. His name was Octavian (ahk-TAY-vee-uhn).

The Second Triumvirate Octavian was Caesar's grandnephew and adopted son. When Caesar was murdered in 44 B.C., Octavian was a frail, sickly youth of 18. Octavian's chief rival, Mark Antony, had been Caesar's trusted comrade. Compared to the young Octavian, Antony was a robust, mature leader and an experienced general.

There was little trust between the two men. For a time, however, they agreed to cooperate in destroying Caesar's enemies. Teaming up with Lepidus, a powerful politician, Antony and Octavian led armies into Rome and forced the assembly to grant them power to rule the state. For ten years (43–33 B.C.), Caesar's three avengers acted together as the Second Triumvirate.

Their vengeance was indeed cruel. A list was drawn up of more than 100 senators and 2,000 businessmen to be killed. One of those murdered was Cicero (SIHS-uh-roh), the senate's greatest orator. Although Cicero had not plotted to kill Caesar, he often had spoken in defense of the republic and against absolute rule. As for Caesar's chief murderers, Brutus and Cassius, they both committed suicide by falling on their own swords after their armies were routed by Antony in 42 B.C. at the Battle of Philippi in Greece.

War between Octavian and Antony The Second Triumvirate ended like the first, in jealousy and violence. Octavian defeated Lepidus and forced him to retire, but Antony's position still seemed secure.

Antony had married Octavian's sister as a political gesture. But while commanding Roman troops in Asia Minor, Antony met the bewitching Cleopatra. (She came to greet him on a barge rowed with silver oars and adorned with purple sails.) Egypt's queen wooed and won Antony as she had won Caesar. Antony sent back word to Rome that he was divorcing Octavian's sister and marrying Cleopatra. In the senate, Octavian accused Antony of plotting to rule Rome from the foreign city of Alexandria. Rome braced itself for a third civil war, this one between Antony and Octavian.

The two forces clashed in a naval battle off the west coast of Greece. In the Battle of Actium (31 B.C.), the fleet commanded by Antony and

This cameo shows Octavian (Augustus) after he was well established as Rome's sole ruler.

Cleopatra was defeated by Octavian's navy. The couple later committed suicide. To make his triumph even sweeter, Octavian made Egypt another province of Rome.

Octavian became sole ruler.

Like Caesar before him, Octavian was now the sole ruler of Rome. The powers in his hands were as great as a king's or emperor's. However, Octavian remembered what happened to his grand-uncle, Caesar. As a politician, Octavian was more cautious than Caesar, and therefore he lived longer. Instead of seeking a crown, Octavian took only the title of "first citizen."

In 27 B.C., the senate begged Octavian to accept the title of Augustus (aw-GUS-tus). The word means "exalted one" and was normally reserved for the gods. Octavian offered token resistance and then graciously accepted the honor. Afterward, he was known by his honorary title, Augustus, rather than Octavian.

The Roman state under Augustus was no longer ruled by the senate and the assembly as a republic. It was ruled by one man as an empire. However, the senate and the assembly continued to meet and transact business in the old ways. Augustus continued to address the senate as if, at any time, it could strip him of his power and titles.

The senators were not fools. They understood that Augustus held the real power while they held almost none, yet they played along. After all, only by flattering and supporting Augustus could they hope to win appointment to a rich government post in the provinces. Besides, what could they hope to achieve by plotting to overthrow him? Nothing but another civil war, perhaps ending in their own deaths. Thus, Roman politicians found it convenient to let the ancient republic die while pretending that it still lived.

Octavian was to rule Rome for 41 years. His reign marked the beginning of the longest period of peace and prosperity that Rome ever knew.

Section Review 3

Define: (a) latifundia, (b) proletariat, (c) gladiator, (d) tribune, (e) triumvirate
Identify: (a) Spartacus, (b) the Gracchi, (c) Marius, (d) Sulla, (e) Julius Caesar, (f) First Triumvirate, (g) Cleopatra, (h) Brutus, (i) Octavian, (j) Second Triumvirate, (k) Mark Antony, (l) Cicero
Answer:
1. How did victory in the Punic Wars change Roman society?
2. How did slavery undermine Roman society?
3. What reforms did the Gracchi try to make?
4. How were military leaders able to gain political power in Rome?
5. (a) What tactics did Julius Caesar use in his rise to power? (b) What groups supported Caesar? (c) What groups opposed him?
6. (a) Why did Octavian and Mark Antony join forces? (b) How did Rome come under the rule of one man?

Critical Thinking
7. (a) What event do you think was the turning point in Rome's change from a republic to one-man rule? (b) Give two reasons to support your answer.

137

Summary

1. The Romans founded their city. Rome grew up at a location with many geographic advantages. Its early culture was influenced by Latins, Greeks, and Etruscans. At first, Rome was ruled by kings, but in 509 B.C. it became a republic. Roman society was divided into two classes, patricians and plebeians. Over the years, plebeians gradually won more and more rights. By about 275 B.C., Rome claimed to have achieved a balanced form of government.

2. The Roman republic spread its power. Between 509 and 265 B.C., plebeians won increasing political power, leading to a government that blended elements of monarchy, aristocracy, and democracy. Also by 265 B.C., Rome had won control of Italy. At that point, Rome began to expand around the Mediterranean, starting with the defeat of Carthage and extending eastward to Greece and Asia Minor.

3. Republican government collapsed in Rome. The Punic Wars and the spread of slavery brought great changes to Rome. Many Romans became landless and jobless. Political struggles became increasingly violent, and army leaders won control of the government. In 44 B.C., Julius Caesar became sole ruler of the Roman empire. After Caesar's assassination, Octavian held power, becoming king in all but name.

Reviewing the Facts

1. Define the following terms:

   a. republic
   b. gravitas
   c. patrician
   d. plebeian
   e. consul
   f. veto
   g. senate
   h. dictator
   i. mercenary
   j. proletariat
   k. tribune
   l. triumvirate

2. Explain the importance of each of the following names, dates, places, or terms:

   a. Rome
   b. Italy
   c. Latins
   d. Etruscans
   e. 509 B.C.
   f. pater familias
   g. Carthage
   h. Twelve Tables
   i. Punic Wars
   j. Hannibal
   k. Battle of Zama
   l. 146 B.C.
   m. the Gracchi
   n. Julius Caesar
   o. 49 B.C.
   p. 44 B.C.
   q. Cleopatra
   r. Brutus
   s. Octavian (Augustus)
   t. Mark Antony

3. Explain how each of the following factors influenced life in early Rome.

   a. the geography of Italy
   b. Latin, Greek, and Etruscan settlers
   c. the existence of social classes
   d. the constant threat of war

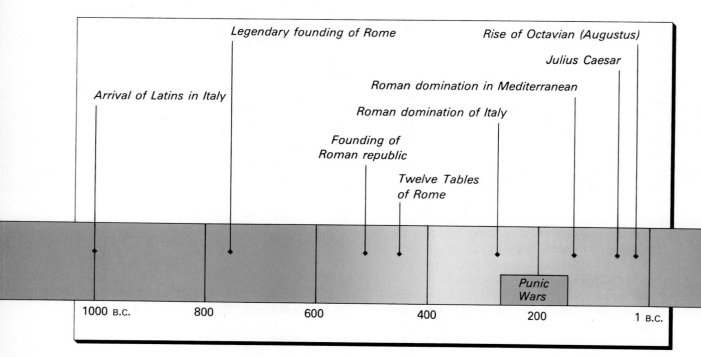

Arrival of Latins in Italy

Legendary founding of Rome

Rise of Octavian (Augustus)

Julius Caesar

Roman domination in Mediterranean

Roman domination of Italy

Founding of Roman republic

Twelve Tables of Rome

Punic Wars

1000 B.C.   800   600   400   200   1 B.C.

4. (a) What was the conflict between patricians and plebeians in the earliest days of the Roman republic? (b) How was the conflict reduced?
5. Describe the structure of Rome's government during the republic. In your discussion, include both the powers and the limitations of each part of the government.
6. How did Rome use its idea of citizenship to unify the lands it won in Italy?
7. (a) How was Rome strengthened by the Punic Wars? (b) How was the Roman republic weakened by the Punic Wars?
8. How was the rise of rulers such as Marius, Sulla, and Julius Caesar different from that of early leaders of the republic?
9. How did Octavian (Augustus) become sole ruler of Rome?

Thinking about History

1. Marius changed Rome's army from citizen-soldiers into professional soldiers. (a) What do you think were the advantages that Rome gained from this change? (b) What do you think were the drawbacks of the new kind of army? (c) In your opinion, did the advantages outweigh the disadvantages? Explain your answer.
2. Why were the Twelve Tables a major triumph for plebeians?
3. Compare the structure of the Roman republic to that of the United States government. What similarities and differences do you see?
4. Compare the way Rome governed the people it conquered (page 127) with the methods used by the Assyrian conquerors of Mesopotamia (page 40). How did the Roman methods ensure a long-lasting empire?
5. Make a list of all the ways Rome changed once it conquered an empire. What Roman values suffered?

Writing and Speaking about History

1. In chart form, describe the population, navy, army, and resources of Carthage and Rome during the Punic Wars (pages 127–128).
2. Use the information from your chart to write a paragraph that compares and contrasts Rome and Carthage in the Punic Wars. Make sure your paragraph has a topic sentence and clearly states how the two empires were alike.
3. Write a news story on the assassination of Julius Caesar. In your introductory paragraph, state *who, what, where, when, why,* and *how.* Expand on these topics in subsequent paragraphs.

Practicing Skills

1. In 100 B.C., slaves comprised one third of Rome's population. Using *Historical Statistics of the United States,* find the percentage of the slave population in this country in 1750, 1820, and 1860. Speculate on the consequences of the various percentages.
2. (a) Use the time line on page 138 to calculate about how many years elapsed between the founding of the Roman republic and Roman domination of Italy. (b) How many years passed between Roman domination of Italy and the spread of Roman power to the Mediterranean? (c) What part of this period did Rome devote to fighting the Punic Wars?
3. Use the map on page 129 to compare the distance between Carthage and Rome with the length of Hannibal's invasion route. Why do you suppose Hannibal chose the longer, more dangerous route?
4. Use maps (pages 96 and 121) and the text to compare the geography of Italy and Greece. How did the geography of the two countries differ? How did geography influence each country?

Investigating History

1. Read Shakespeare's play *Julius Caesar.* What view does the play present of Caesar? Who are the heroes of the play, in your opinion?
2. Select a prosecutor, a defender, and a jury to hold a trial to decide whether Brutus and Cassius were murderers or were acting in defense of the Roman republic.
3. Use reference books on Roman myths to find out the names and descriptions of some of the most important Roman gods and goddesses. What Greek god or goddess does each resemble?

Decision Making in History

Evaluate the consequences of Julius Caesar's decision to cross the Rubicon. What would you have done under similar circumstances?

Chapter 7

29 B.C. – A.D. 476

The Roman Empire

The Colosseum in Rome was a center for gladiatorial combats. Its shape is used today for many football stadiums.

1. **Augustus's rule began the Pax Romana.**
2. **Romans extended Greek culture.**
3. **Christianity spread through the empire.**
4. **Rome's empire declined and fell.**

In A.D. 80, tens of thousands of spectators poured into Rome's new sports arena, the Colosseum (KAHL-uh-SEE-uhm). To celebrate its opening, spectacles were held every day for 100 days. The Colosseum was the largest building of its kind in the ancient world. A tribute to Roman engineering, it was built so tightly that its arena could be filled with water for mock naval battles.

From the outside, the Colosseum looked truly colossal. Its 160-foot-high walls had 4 tiers of windows, columns, and arches. The Colosseum's 80 entrances were set in the bottom row of arches. As many as 50,000 spectators with numbered tickets entered through 76 of these entrances. Two entrances were reserved for Emperor Titus and his party. The last two were reserved for the gladiators themselves.

Once inside, spectators climbed sloping ramps to their seats. The bottom tier featured boxes for the emperor, state priests, and senators. Above them, in rows of marble seats, sat distinguished citizens, members of the middle class, favored slaves, and foreigners, in that order. In the fourth tier, on wooden benches sat women and the poor. No matter where people sat, however, there was a clear view of the arena below. Overhead was a tremendous colored awning that could be rolled out on cables to shield the audience against sun and rain.

The show started early in the morning and lasted all day. Sometimes it opened with a contest between comics, but it soon became bloody. Mornings were devoted to animal shows. Tigers, lions, bears, elephants, and giraffes from distant parts of the empire were released into the arena to fight to the death. In the afternoon, professional gladiators fought animals or one another. Most gladiators were slaves, prisoners of war, or condemned criminals. But others, including a few women, were free Romans who chose to gamble their lives for a short span of glory and public adoration.

The Romans had adopted gladiator contests from the Etruscans. For the Etruscans, such contests had had religious importance. For the Roman government, however, the bloody entertainments in the Colosseum served a political purpose. They were one way to entertain the thousands of unemployed—and potentially dangerous—people who flocked to the city of Rome.

In many ways, the Colosseum is symbolic of the entire Roman empire. From the outside, both were awesome in their size and strength. Within, both combined bravery, honor, and glory with cruelty, sensationalism, and violence.

Rome was at the peak of its power from the time of Augustus's rule to A.D. 180. Then it began a long and uneven decline to the collapse of the western empire in A.D. 476. In the first part of this 500-year period, Rome advanced in architecture, law, philosophy, and literature. At the same time, faith in a new religion, Christianity, spread widely through the empire. Gradually, however, the Roman empire lost the strength to fight off its enemies. In the end, a barbarian king ruled in Rome, and Rome's culture was transferred to a new capital city in the east, Constantinople.

Augustus's rule began the Pax Romana. 1

Pax (paks) is the Latin word for peace. For 207 years (27 B.C.–A.D. 180), peace was the chief gift that Rome gave the people it ruled. Though legions still fought on the borders of the empire, the immense territory within those borders was largely free of war. This period of peace and prosperity is known as the *Pax Romana*.

The borders of the empire during the Pax Romana measured 10,000 miles and enclosed an area of more than 3 million square miles, about the size of the United States today. The empire extended north to Scotland in the British Isles, south to the Sahara in Africa, east to Mesopotamia in Asia, and west to the Atlantic Ocean. The population of the empire during this period was between 70 and 90 million people. The city of Rome itself was home to about 1 million people.

Augustus set up sound government.

Augustus was perhaps Rome's ablest emperor. He built the foundation for the Pax Romana through a number of far-sighted actions. He encouraged trade, glorified Rome by a splendid building program, and created a system of government that survived for centuries.

Just as important, Augustus set the tone for the empire by extolling the old values of simplicity, sober conduct, and patriotism. Augustus dressed in homemade white togas and lived in a small house on the Palatine Hill.

Trade and transportation In Augustus's time, a silver coin called a denarius (dih-NAIR-ee-uhs) circulated throughout the empire. (It looked very much like an American quarter.) Having a common coinage made trade between different parts of the empire much easier.

Footnote to History

As the adopted son of Julius Caesar, Augustus used *Caesar* as one of his titles. Over the years, the word came to mean an emperor or ruler. So powerful did the word become that, nearly 2,000 years later, the ruler of Germany was called "kaiser" and the ruler of Russia "czar."

Augustus also realized that it hurt trade to tax goods as they moved across each province's border. Therefore, he eliminated all such taxes, making Roman lands one large economic empire rather than a group of states with a single capital.

To improve transportation and to bind his empire together more tightly, Augustus began a program of highway construction. Continuing his work, later emperors turned Roman highways into one of the most lasting monuments of their civilization. Roman roads were as impressive in their own way as the pyramids of Egypt. By A.D. 100, there were 50,000 miles of major roads and more than 200,000 miles of secondary roads connecting the cities of the empire.

A *public building program* Marvels such as Rome's roads and bridges were possible through the use of an amazing new building material: concrete. The Romans had learned to mix lime mortar, pour it into a wooden mold, and wait for it to become as hard as stone. Concrete formed the backbone of Rome's bold architecture. The Romans used concrete and decorated its surface with more costly materials, such as marble.

Augustus, however, never bragged about his use of cement. He liked to boast that he had turned Rome from a city of brick into a city of marble. He commissioned Greek artists and architects to build temples similar to the Parthenon throughout the city. During Augustus's reign, Rome began to look like a world capital.

The *civil service* Under Augustus, Rome became the center of an efficient imperial government. Augustus left the senators their titles and money-making positions in the provinces, but he gave much of the real work of running the empire to plebeians and even slaves.

Augustus set up a **civil service**, with salaried, experienced workers to take care of Rome's grain supply, road repairs, the postal system, and all the other work of running an empire. People of all ranks served in this civil service. Hardworking, loyal freedmen (former slaves) won many of the highest and most influential positions. Because these men had a rare opportunity to improve their lot, they served Augustus well.

Peace continued after Augustus died.

Because Augustus had been a sickly youth, his enemies had hoped he would not rule long. But Augustus was more durable than he had looked. He died at the age of 76 in A.D. 14. By that time, he had ruled Rome for 41 years.

When Augustus died, the senate promptly hailed his adopted son and chosen successor, Tiberius (tye-BIHR-ee-uhs), as the new ruler. Tiberius and the three emperors after him are known as the Julian emperors because they were descended from the family of Julius Caesar. None of them, however, matched Augustus or Julius Caesar in boldness or skill.

Water supplies were a problem for many Roman cities. Aqueducts such as this one at Segovia, Spain, brought water from distant mountain lakes.

In the years of the Pax Romana, some of Rome's emperors were conscientious, intelligent, and able. Some were corrupt, cruel, or incompetent. One or two were probably insane. (Caligula, for example, appointed his horse consul and talked to statues in the Forum.) Yet the senate and the Roman people put up with each of them and even worshiped them. The system of government set up by Augustus proved to be more stable and effective than its individual leaders.

The problem of succession Rome's emperors never satisfactorily solved the problem of succession. When an emperor died, who was to take his place? Was it to be a person chosen by the senate or a person chosen by the dying emperor himself? Should the favorite candidate of one of the provincial armies be appointed? Or should the Praetorian (pree-TOH-ree-uhn) Guard—the army of 9,000 men stationed in Rome—impose its choice on the empire by force?

At one time or another, each of these methods was tried. Since there was no fixed rule of succession, every time an emperor died there was a potential crisis. When the emperor Nero committed suicide, for example, provincial armies and the Praetorian Guard took turns proclaiming a new emperor, then promptly murdering him, and installing another. In 18 months (A.D. 68–69), Rome had 4 emperors.

The Good Emperors The succession problem was temporarily solved by the men known to history as the Five Good Emperors, or the Adoptive Emperors. When Domitian (doh-MEE-shuhn) was assassinated in A.D. 96, the senate chose Nerva emperor. Nerva made only one vital contribution to the Pax Romana. He adopted as his heir a respected army leader, Trajan (TRAY-juhn). When Nerva died in 98, Trajan was peacefully accepted by armies and senate alike as emperor. Trajan then adopted a distant relative, Hadrian (HAY-dree-uhn), as his successor. Hadrian adopted Antoninus Pius, and Antoninus, in turn, adopted Marcus Aurelius (aw-REE-lee-us), who ruled until the year A.D. 180.

Voice from the Past · A *Roman Citizen*

"*Civis Romanus sum*" (I am a Roman citizen). Aside from being a proud boast, this statement guaranteed a person the protection of Roman law and also some important privileges in traveling and doing business within the empire. Around A.D. 150, a Greek writer named Aelius Aristides described the idea of Roman citizenship.

Most wonderful of all is your noble idea of citizenship. There is nothing on earth like it. For you have divided all the people of the empire . . . into two groups. The more cultured, better born, and more influential everywhere you have declared Roman citizens. . . . All others are mere subjects. No barrier of sea or land cuts one off from citizenship . . . Everything lies open to everybody, and no one who is worthy to be trusted with public office is considered a foreigner . . .

You have not made Rome a target of envy by letting no one else share in it . . . You have made the word "Roman" apply not to a city but to a universal people . . . As a result, there are many people in each city who are . . . fellow citizens of yours . . . You have no need to keep troops in those cities; the greatest and most influential men everywhere keep watch over their own native places for you. You have a double hold on those cities—from here [Rome] and through the Roman citizens in each.

1. (a) Is everyone within the empire a Roman citizen? (b) What groups in each city are citizens?
2. What military advantage for Rome results from Rome's policy, according to the writer?
3. What benefits might come to a city from being ruled by local people who had become Roman citizens instead of by officials from Rome itself?
4. Do you think this was a wise and fair policy for Rome to follow? Explain.

The Roman Empire at Its Height

KEY

Roman empire in A.D.120

Gades -Roman name
(Cadiz) -Modern name

0 — 500 Miles

Map Study

Rome's empire reached its greatest size under Emperor Trajan in A.D. 117. His successor, Hadrian, strengthened its borders. He ordered the building of the wall shown below to keep out barbarians. Where was it located?

Thus, for 85 years, 5 emperors succeeded one another without bloodshed. Although historians call the whole group the Good Emperors, three were perhaps better than good. Trajan, Hadrian, and Marcus Aurelius came close to greatness.

Even during Marcus Aurelius's lifetime, the Pax Romana was severely tested and strained. A dreadful disease—possibly the plague—swept across the eastern provinces into Rome itself, where it killed 2,000 people in a single day. German tribes overwhelmed Roman legions along the Danube River, the empire's northern frontier. After Marcus Aurelius's death in A.D. 180, the Pax Romana collapsed, marking the end of Rome's golden age.

Section Review 1

Define: (a) civil service, (b) succession
Identify: (a) Colosseum, (b) Pax Romana, (c) Augustus, (d) the Julian emperors, (e) the Good Emperors

144

1. Describe three ways in which Augustus contributed to Rome's success as the center of a great empire.
2. (a) Why was the death of an emperor often followed by violence of some kind? (b) How did the five Good Emperors temporarily solve this problem?
3. Name two events that weakened the empire during the last years of the Pax Romana.

Critical Thinking

4. How might the growth of a civil service make the individual character of a ruler less important to the empire?

Romans extended Greek culture. 2

Under the Roman empire, hundreds of territories were knitted into a single political state. Cities grew in lands where cities had never been known before. Those cities looked very much alike because they had the same model: Rome. Governing lands as different as Britannia and Judaea, Gaul and northern Africa, was in itself a great achievement. The government in one province was set up much like that in another. Goods moved untaxed over Roman roads. Those goods were paid for with Roman coinage. Latin, the language of Rome, could be understood throughout the empire. People who could read shared in a growing body of Latin literature.

The Romans were proud of their ability to rule, but they acknowledged Greek leadership in the fields of art, architecture, literature, and philosophy. Educated Romans learned the Greek language. Emperors and wealthy citizens copied Greek architecture and hired Greek sculptors. The Pax Romana spread Greek as well as Roman achievements. The blend of these two cultures sometimes is called "Greco-Roman" culture.

New schools of philosophy arose.

The tradition of Greek philosophy had continued since the days of Socrates, Plato, and Aristotle. Meanwhile, over the years, traditional Roman religion had lost its meaning for many Romans. In the later years of the Roman republic and the early years of the empire, the Romans turned increasingly to two philosophies.

Epicureanism Epicurus (ep-ih-KYU-rus) lived in Athens between 342 and 270 B.C. He taught that the way to gain happiness was to free the body from pain and free the mind from fear. To avoid pain, Epicurus said that people should avoid all excesses, including those of pleasure. Next, people should accept that death was the end of all existence. Epicurus said there was no life after death and, therefore, nothing to fear.

By the time Epicurus's philosophy reached imperial Rome, the part about avoiding excess had been forgotten. Instead, wealthy Romans used the philosophy to justify pursuing pleasures.

Stoicism A Greek philosopher named Zeno (ZEE-noh) developed a philosophy that had even more influence on Romans than Epicureanism. Zeno gathered his followers on the porch (or *stoa*) near the marketplace in Athens. Hence, his philosophy became known as Stoicism (STOH-ih-SIHZ-uhm). This philosophy was popular in Rome because it encouraged virtue, duty, and endurance.

Zeno (336–263 B.C.) taught that the universe was controlled by a superhuman power, sometimes called the Universal Law, Divine Reason, or simply Supreme Power. The Stoics taught the virtues of duty, reason, and courage. Pain and pleasure were considered unimportant. Stoic ideas supported traditional Roman values. Wealthy families hired Stoic scholars as tutors for their sons. Many of these young men rose to political power as adults, giving the Stoics great influence in politics.

One of the most noted Stoics was the emperor Marcus Aurelius. During the seven hard and lonely years he spent with his armies on the Danube frontier, Marcus Aurelius wrote in the evenings to console himself. His words show his sadness but also his steadfastness.

Ants, loaded and labouring, mice, scared and scampering; puppets jerking on their strings—that is life. In the midst of it all, you must take your stand, good-temperedly and without disdain, yet always aware that a man's worth is no greater than the worth of his ambitions.

Marcus Aurelius's daily jottings were collected into a book called the *Meditations*. This work

Emperors of the Pax Romana

Name	Dates of Rule (A.D.)	Summary of Reign
Julian dynasty—related to family of Julius Caesar		
Tiberius	14–37	A good administrator; improved provincial government and the empire's tax system; later years marked by wholesale treason trials and executions
Caligula	37–41	Mentally disturbed; assassinated after short, brutal reign
Claudius	41–54	Considered slow-witted as a child but became an able, intelligent emperor; added Britannia to empire; set up government departments for accounts, correspondence, and justice
Nero	54–68	Became emperor at 16; devoted to the arts; a good administrator but increasingly vicious in his use of power; responsible for many murders, including that of his own mother; rebuilt Rome after the great fire of A.D. 64; began persecution of Christians; committed suicide
Army emperors		
Galba, Otho, Vitellus	68–69	Succession crisis; three emperors chosen by various factions in the armies
Flavian dynasty		
Vespasian	69–79	Ended civil war of A.D. 69; restored empire's finances; reformed army
Titus	79–81	Opened Colosseum; reign marked by the eruption of Vesuvius that destroyed Pompeii and Herculaneum
Domitian	81–96	Ruled dictatorially but efficiently; later feared treason everywhere and executed many; was assassinated
The Five Good Emperors, or the Adoptive Emperors		
Nerva	96–98	Senator, appointed emperor by senate; began custom of adopting heir
Trajan	98–117	Spanish-born (first emperor from provinces); conquered Dacia (Romania); empire reached its greatest extent during his rule
Hadrian	117–138	Consolidated earlier conquests rather than adding new lands; reorganized bureaucracy and set up postal service; traveled throughout empire
Antoninus Pius	138–161	Uneventful reign marked by public works and expanded programs for education and child welfare; army declined
Marcus Aurelius	161–180	Faced widespread barbarian invasions on Syrian and Danube frontiers; wrote philosophic work, *Meditations;* Pax Romana ended with his death

established his place in literature as one of Rome's great Stoic philosophers.

Stoics believed that human laws, like the Supreme Power itself, should be reasonable and just. Several social reforms during Rome's golden age show Stoic influence. For example, according to a law passed under Hadrian, the pater familias no longer had the power of life and death within the family. New laws also prohibited masters from killing or injuring their slaves.

Latin literature took many forms.

In literature, as in religion, the Romans first looked to the Greeks for inspiration. By the middle years of the republic, however, the Romans had begun to develop an important body of learning of their own. By Augustus's time, there was a group of writers who were able to record the emperor's deeds in glowing and lasting words. As far as Augustus was concerned, however, the skill of the writer was not as important as his patriotism. With patriotic writers, the emperor was generous.

Livy's history One of the most patriotic works sponsored by Augustus was Livy's history of Rome. It covered the years from Rome's founding to the rule of Augustus in 142 Roman-style books.

Livy had a bias typical of many historians. He liked the past better than the present. He thought the heroes of old—Romulus, Scipio, Cato—were more patriotic than Romans of his own time. The old heroes, he said, had been men of honor, courage, discipline, and moral strength. They did their duty toward family, gods, and state. Because of those virtues, Livy explained, they could conquer every foe.

Virgil's epic poem Patriotic virtue was also the theme of the most famous work of Latin literature, the *Aeneid* (uh-NEE-ihd). The poet Virgil devoted ten years of labor to this masterpiece. Often he was unable to write more than a few lines a day. Even then, he was so worried about the poem's flaws that he wanted it destroyed. Luckily, it was saved by Augustus himself.

The *Aeneid* is an epic consciously modeled after the Greek masterpieces of Homer. It traces Roman origins far back before Romulus and Remus to Aeneas, one of the Trojan warriors in Homer's *Iliad*. Reading the *Aeneid*, Augustus perhaps nodded approvingly at these verses:

Remember, Roman, these are your talents:
To rule people by law, and to establish the
ways of peace,
To spare the conquered, and to crush the
haughty.

The silver age of literature Roman literature kept growing and changing during the empire. Historians refer to the 124 years between the deaths of Augustus and Hadrian as the "silver age" of literature. Rome's best writers were still poets and historians, but their work took on a new tone. Criticism replaced patriotism. Praise was replaced by **satire**, writing that mocked society for its foolishness and wickedness. Imagine what Augustus might have thought about these lines from the poet Juvenal:

What should I do in Rome? I am no good
at lying.
If a book's bad, I can't praise it, or go
around ordering copies.
I don't know the stars [astrology]; I can't
hire out as an assassin.

Juvenal lived from about A.D. 60 to 140, during the height of Rome's glory, yet he still found much to satirize.

While Juvenal wrote about the morals of private citizens, the historian Tacitus (TAS-ih-tus) directed his scorn at Roman government. In his major work, the *Annals*, he portrays every emperor from Tiberius to Nero as cruel and corrupted by power. What were the blessings of the Roman peace? "They make a desert and call it peace," accused Tacitus.

Although many of the writers of the silver age made fun of Rome (or worse), they were not banned or sent into exile. By this time, Rome was so secure as capital of the world that it could tolerate criticism. There were moral and spiritual grounds for the writers' charges, but outwardly Rome was thriving.

Majestic buildings adorned cities.

Of the estimated 10,000 cities in the Roman empire, Rome was the most spectacular. The passion for beautifying the capital did not die with Augustus or Nero. Each emperor sought to make his mark on the city. According to one scholar, Rome became "the most spectacular

The Roman Forum became the showplace of the empire, filled with statues and buildings designed to impress the people Rome ruled.

tourist attraction in the ancient world." Visitors came from the provinces to see its 10,000 statues, 700 public pools and basins, 500 fountains, 37 monumental gates, and 36 marble arches.

After seeing Rome, visitors from Gaul and Spain went home and imitated its splendor. They too surrounded themselves with Roman buildings and gardens. Soon, new cities in western Europe looked like miniature Romes. Roman governors gladly supported the construction of Roman-style buildings. They saw it as a way of building allegiance to Rome itself. Unlike the Greeks who used architecture to glorify their gods, the Romans used it to glorify their rule.

The crowning achievement of Roman architecture was the dome. Once the Romans had learned to use concrete, they were able to mold on the ground rounded tops for their buildings. Then, when the walls and columns of a building were in place, the dome could be hoisted into place on top.

This is just how one of the most impressive buildings in Rome, the Pantheon (PAN-thee-ahn), was built. The Pantheon was dedicated to all the gods. Its domed roof rested on a drumlike structure called a rotunda. Light streamed into the Pantheon through a small opening or "eye" in the top of the dome.

148

Roman law united the empire.

Rome's most lasting contribution to later civilizations was its law. Early Roman law, such as the Twelve Tables, was concerned mostly with the rights of Roman citizens themselves. As the empire grew, however, the Romans came to believe that law should apply to all people.

Slowly, Roman judges began to recognize certain standards of justice. These standards were based largely on the teachings of Stoic philosophers. Here are some of the most important principles of Roman law:

• No person could be judged guilty of a crime until after the facts of the case were examined.
• All persons accused of crimes had a right to face their accusers and defend themselves before a judge.
• If there was doubt about a person's guilt, he or she should be judged innocent.
• Any law that seemed unreasonable or grossly unfair could be set aside.

Long after Rome fell to barbarian rule, the principles of Roman law endured. Those principles became the basis for law in many European countries and, later, for places that fell under European influence. The Roman empire spread far, but its legal ideas have spread farther.

Contrasts marked Roman society.

Most Roman citizens probably were far more concerned with the pains and pleasures of daily living than with literature, philosophy, or law. To many Romans, spending a day at the Colosseum was the chief benefit of Roman civilization. By A.D. 250, there were 150 holidays celebrating emperors' birthdays, gods' feast days, and other special occasions. On many of these days, the government provided games, races, or gladiator shows at public expense.

These public pleasures were enjoyed by rich and poor alike. In most other ways, however, the rich and the poor had little in common.

Life at the top At home, wealthy Romans lived extravagantly. They spent large sums of money on fancy houses, statues for their gardens, high-priced slaves, and especially banquets. A food's taste was less important than its rarity and cost. These were some of the dishes placed on the tables of wealthy Romans: as appetizers, tree fungi in fish-fat sauce, jellyfish and eggs; as main course, dormouse with pine kernels, boiled ostrich; and for dessert, fricassee of roses with pastry, parrot-tongue pie.

Guests normally arrived for a banquet in the late afternoon and did not stop eating until midnight. They had knives and spoons but no forks, and they picked up most foods with their hands. After each course, a slave stationed behind each guest provided a bowl of scented water for washing sticky fingers.

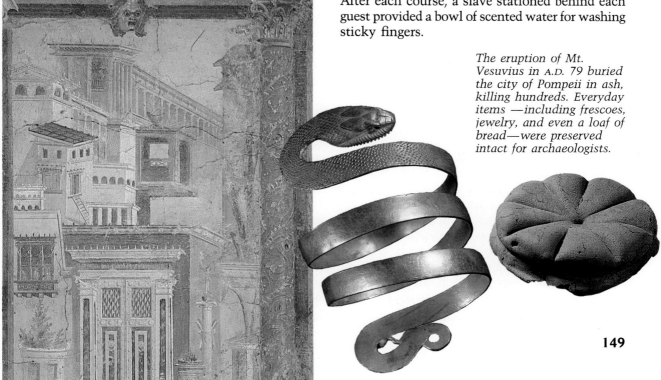

The eruption of Mt. Vesuvius in A.D. 79 buried the city of Pompeii in ash, killing hundreds. Everyday items —including frescoes, jewelry, and even a loaf of bread—were preserved intact for archaeologists.

149

Life at the bottom Most families in Rome never tasted parrot-tongue pie. They were lucky to eat porridge at daybreak, cold sausage at noon, and porridge again for supper. During Rome's golden age, a large share of the city's population was unemployed most of the time. The imperial government supported these people with daily rations of grain, doled out free or far below market cost.

Only a short distance from Rome's elegant temples were the dingy, run-down, rat-infested homes of the poor. Poor families lived in crowded wooden tenements up to seven stories high. Tens of thousands of such buildings filled Rome's slums. The tenements were so poorly built that roofs and ceilings sometimes collapsed, killing those inside. Worst of all, a poor family faced the ever-present danger of fire touched off by a stray ember from someone's little charcoal stove.

Despite these conditions, the poor of Rome were better off than people without work had ever been in other ancient cities. The Roman poor had food and housing. After the collapse of the empire, no government took such care of its poorest citizens for nearly 1,500 years.

Villas in the countryside Most wealthy city dwellers also had country estates, called **villas**. In Italy, these country homes offered an escape from the noise and dirt of Rome itself. Italian villas had libraries, art galleries, swimming pools, and athletic courts. Fountains sparkled in formal gardens, and Greek statues posed on lawns and terraces.

In provinces such as Gaul, North Africa, and Britannia, villas were more than vacation homes. They were the great estates that grew much of the empire's food supply. Peasant farmers lived on the villas and tilled the soil or tended the owner's livestock. The noble owners managed the villa, served as local officials, and amused themselves by hunting.

In later times, villas became increasingly self-sufficient. The people on a villa raised all their own food and made most of the other goods they needed. Many villas were fortified as protection against bandits (or tax collectors).

Section Review 2

Define: (a) Epicureanism, (b) Stoicism, (c) satire, (d) villa

Identify: (a) Epicurus, (b) Zeno, (c) *Meditations*, (d) Livy, (e) Virgil, (f) *Aeneid*, (g) Juvenal, (h) Tacitus, (i) the Pantheon

Daily Life · *The Roman Baths*

For both rich and poor in Rome, the baths were a daily pleasure, something like modern health clubs. Rome alone had 856 baths. The government maintained the 11 largest. For the equivalent of about a quarter-penny, any Roman could be massaged, scrubbed, and soaked in a public bath. Provincial cities built their own baths, imitating Rome.

First, bathers might exercise. Then they went to a hot, dry room to make their bodies sweat. Next came a visit to a hot, steamy room. The final step was a plunge into ice-cold water. Clean and refreshed, bathers wrapped themselves in towels and ambled over the bath's marble floor, between its towering Greek columns, and out among the statues and fountains of the rose garden.

Bathers came to meet friends as well as to wash. The bath built by the Emperor Caracalla (KAR-uh-**KAL**-uh) offered special game rooms for backgammon, chess, and checkers. Out on the immense grounds bordered by trim hedges, men and women strolled, gossiped, and flirted. The serious-minded could browse through the scrolls in the bath's library.

Answer:

1. How were the basic ideas of Stoicism well-suited to Roman traditions? (b) How did Stoicism influence Roman law to become more humane?
2. How did Roman literature change from the time of Augustus to the silver age?
3. (a) Describe some of the differences between the lives of the rich and the poor during the Roman empire. (b) What evidence shows that the Roman government took relatively good care of the poor?

Critical Thinking

4. (a) Restate in your own words the ideas of Roman law given on page 149. (b) Explain why each of these four principles is important to justice today.

Christianity spread through the empire.   3

As the Roman empire spread, Romans came into contact with many religions. In the far-flung parts of the empire, most peoples continued to follow their own religious traditions, even though they were under Roman rule. In Rome itself, cults from many lands took root. The Egyptian goddess Isis was especially popular with Roman women. The Persian warrior god Mithra had a wide following in Rome's army.

By the time of Augustus, Rome's traditional gods—Jupiter, Juno, Mars, and others—had no strong emotional or intellectual appeal to most Romans. Nonetheless, these gods were still important as symbols of loyalty to the Roman state. Roman rulers tolerated many religions, but they also expected Roman subjects to respect traditional Roman gods. This Roman attitude was no problem for the empire's many polytheists, but it was a very great problem indeed for the Jews as monotheists.

Jews came under Roman rule.

Most Jews probably saw the Romans as one of a string of pagan conquerors. After their return to Palestine from Babylon (page 43), the Jews had been ruled by Alexander the Great, by the Ptolemies of Egypt, and by the Seleucids of Persia. In general, the Jews tolerated and were tolerated by these rulers. However, in 168 B.C., the Seleucid king decided to build an altar to the Greek god Zeus in the Jewish temple in Jerusalem. The Jews would not stand for that. Led by Judas Maccabee (MAK-uh-bee), they recaptured and purified the temple in 165 B.C. In 142 B.C., the Jews won their independence.

The entire area of Syria and Palestine fell under Roman influence around 65 B.C. However, the Romans at first allowed the Jewish kingdom to remain independent, at least in name. Jewish kings ruled as representatives of Rome. Some Jews became friendly with the Romans and even went along with their plans to "romanize" Jerusalem. The ruler Herod, for example, was a romanized Jew. His loyalties were divided between Rome and his own people. He was also tolerant of polytheistic faiths. These divided loyalties angered many Jews. Rome finally took over the Jewish kingdom and made it the Roman province of Judaea in A.D. 6.

Jesus taught a new religion.

It was about the time of Rome's takeover that Jesus was born, although the exact year is not known. Jesus was both a Jew and a Roman subject. He is not mentioned in any contemporary Roman historic records. Thus, the story of Jesus' life comes from Christian sources, the Gospels of the New Testament. (*Gospel* is the Greek word for "good news.")

Jesus' life According to the Gospels, Jesus was born in the town of Bethlehem, about five miles south of Jerusalem. He grew up in the village of Nazareth. When he was about 30, Jesus began his ministry. For the next three years, he lived as a wandering prophet and teacher. He recruited 12 followers, or disciples, who accepted his teachings and traveled with him. Jesus touched people with his gentleness and challenged them with his message.

Jesus chose the time of Passover, a Jewish holiday, to visit the temple in Jerusalem. Shortly thereafter, Jesus was arrested and taken to the Roman governor, Pontius Pilate. He was accused of the religious crime of blasphemy. He was also accused of plotting to be king, because his teachings had described the coming of the kingdom

151

of God. For these teachings, he was sentenced to death. On a desolate hill called Calvary outside Jerusalem, Jesus was crucified.

Two days later, the Gospels say that Jesus' follower Mary Magdalene visited his tomb and found his body gone. Over the next 40 days, according to the Gospels, Jesus appeared to his disciples several times. "And it came to pass," concludes the Gospel of Luke, "while he blessed them, he was parted from them, and carried up into heaven."

The teachings of Jesus Among the major beliefs of the Christian faith is the idea of the kingdom of God. Jesus taught that God was preparing a new era in which all who repented of their sins and believed in Jesus as savior would live as God's children. Because Jesus taught that God's kingdom was open to all, regardless of wealth or class, he won many followers among the poor.

Jesus taught that God is love and that his followers should love God above all. After that, God's children should love one another. They should treat others as they wish to be treated themselves. This last teaching has come to be known as the "golden rule."

Apostles spread Jesus' teachings.

Jesus' followers believed he was the messiah (muh-SY-uh), or savior, whom God had promised the Jewish people. (The name Christ comes from the Greek word for messiah, *Christos.*)

The disciples who spread Jesus' teachings are known as the apostles. They were leaders of the earliest Christian church. At first, they preached in Jewish synagogues throughout the Hellenistic lands of Palestine, Syria, Asia Minor, and Egypt. In Jerusalem, they established a small but important church led by the apostle Peter.

The apostle who most profoundly influenced the new Christian religion never knew Jesus in person. This man was known by two names—his Jewish name, Saul, and his Christian name, Paul. At first, Saul thought Christianity should be stamped out. One day while traveling to Damascus in Syria, however, he had a powerful religious experience. He told of seeing a blinding burst of light and hearing the voice of Jesus. From that moment, Saul the Jew became Paul the Christian. The apostle Paul dedicated the rest of his life to spreading the teachings of Jesus.

The peace and cultural unity of the Pax Romana provided an ideal opportunity for the spread of the new religion. As a Roman citizen, Paul traveled freely within the empire. For 13 years (A.D. 45–58), he went from city to city around the eastern Mediterranean winning converts.

Paul had an enormous influence on Christianity. His letters, written to churches with which he worked, form a large part of the New Testament. (These letters are known as the Epistles of Saint Paul.) Paul also declared that Christianity was open equally to anyone, Jew or non-Jew. Without this openness, Christianity might have remained a small Jewish sect rather than becoming a world religion. Finally, through Paul's work, Christian churches were established in every major city in the eastern empire, from Jerusalem to Rome.

Christianity grew slowly but steadily. Christian teachings had strong appeal to the poor and powerless. Women, who were barred from some popular Roman cults, had great influence among Christian groups.

Rome struggled with Judaism and Christianity.

As monotheistic religions, both Christianity and Judaism posed a problem for the Roman empire. Good Roman citizens were expected to worship the emperor as a god. Neither Jews nor Christians were willing to do so.

War against the Jews The Romans went far in trying to keep peace with the Jews. The Roman government promised Jews freedom of worship and excused them from worshiping the emperor.

Despite Roman tolerance of Judaism, however, many Jews remained fiercely opposed to Roman rule. In A.D. 66, a band of Jewish revolutionaries called the Zealots (ZEL-uhts) tried to throw off the Roman yoke. When Roman troops finally put down the rebellion four years later, they burned the Jewish temple. All that remained was a western portion of the wall, which is today the holiest of Jewish shrines. Hundreds of fleeing Jews were captured and crucified. The last stronghold, a fortress near the Dead Sea called Masada (muh-SAH-duh), held out until A.D. 73. Half a million Jews died in that war.

The tiny nation made one more attempt to break free of the Romans. In A.D. 130, the emperor

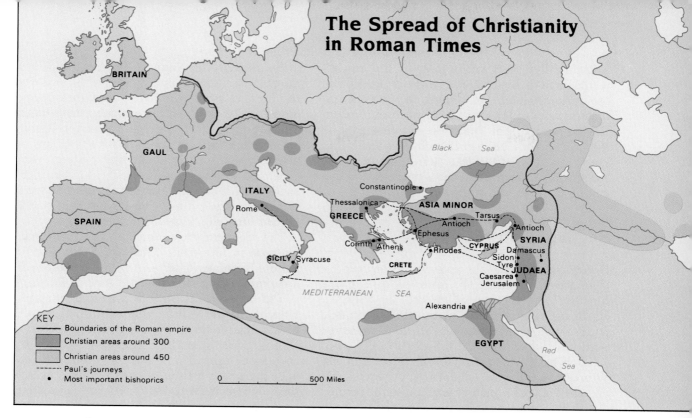

The Spread of Christianity in Roman Times

KEY
— Boundaries of the Roman empire
■ Christian areas around 300
□ Christian areas around 450
- - - Paul's journeys
• Most important bishoprics

0   500 Miles

Map Study

In A.D. 300, was Christianity stronger in the eastern part of the Roman empire or the western part? Name two cities in Greece that Paul visited.

Hadrian ordered that Jerusalem be rebuilt as a Roman colony and that a shrine to Jupiter be built in place of the Jewish temple. The Jews rose in rebellion. In three years of fighting, another half a million Jews died. This war ended the Jewish political state for almost 2,000 years, yet the Jewish religion survived.

Persecution of the Christians As a new religion, Christianity did not win the same respect from Roman rulers as did Judaism. When Christians refused to accept the emperor as a god, Rome struck at them as rebels. In A.D. 64, the year of the great fire in Rome, Nero ordered the first persecution of Christians. According to Christian tradition, the apostles Peter and Paul were killed in Rome on the same day during Nero's rule.

Except for Nero, however, the emperors of the first century did not actively persecute Christians. Later, however, as the Pax Romana began to crumble, the Romans became harsher toward those who would not worship the emperor. Toward the end of the second century, Christians were cruelly persecuted. With Marcus Aurelius's

approval, many Christians were brought before Roman magistrates for trial. Those who gave up their religion and accepted the Roman gods were set free without punishment. Those who held to their faith were tortured and executed in the arena. They were regarded by other Christians as martyrs (people who sacrifice their lives for the sake of a cause or belief).

Religious persecutions showed only the growing weakness of the empire, not its strength. Christianity became a formidable religious force at the very time that Roman power was declining. By A.D. 200, around 10 percent of the people in the Roman empire were Christians.

The Petrine doctrine According to many Christians, Jesus had singled out the disciple Peter as the "rock" on which the Christian church would be built. After preaching in Jerusalem, Peter had traveled to Rome where he had acted as Rome's first **bishop**. A bishop was a church official who set moral standards and supervised the finances of several local churches. Peter died in Rome, a fact that became important to later Christians.

153

Eventually, every major city in the empire would have its own bishop. However, later bishops in Rome claimed to outrank all other bishops because Peter had been the leading apostle. Roman bishops argued that Peter was the first **pope**—the father of the Christian Church. This argument, known as the Petrine (PEE-TRYN) doctrine, was accepted by Christians in the western part of the empire but rejected in the eastern part.

Section Review 3

Define: (a) disciple, (b) messiah, (c) apostle, (d) martyr, (e) bishop, (f) pope
Identify: (a) Jerusalem, (b) Herod, (c) Jesus, (d) Gospels, (e) Pontius Pilate, (f) Paul (Saul), (g) Zealots, (h) Masada, (i) Petrine doctrine
Answer:
1. (a) What attitude did the Roman government take toward most religions? (b) Why did Judaism and Christianity not fit into the empire in the same way other religions did?
2. What religious ideas did Jesus teach?
3. What was Paul's importance for the development of Christianity?
4. (a) How did the existence of the Roman empire help the spread of Christianity? (b) How did the Roman government attack Christianity?

Critical Thinking
5. Rome often persecuted Christians after disasters, such as the great fire in Nero's reign, or in troubled times such as Marcus Aurelius's reign. Why might a government turn against a group in such times?

Rome's empire declined and fell. 4

Historians generally agree that the Roman empire began its decline with the rule of Marcus Aurelius's son, Commodus. Instead of adopting an able successor, Marcus Aurelius made the fateful mistake of choosing his own son to succeed him as emperor. Facing a time of troubles, Rome needed a strong, dedicated leader. Instead, it got the vain, irresponsible Commodus.

In A.D. 180, when Marcus Aurelius died, Commodus was a tall, strapping youth of 19. He loved the thrill of sports and hated the duties of government. To show off his athletic talent, Commodus performed regularly as a gladiator. Friends of his father thought Commodus's showmanship disgraced both himself and the empire. They conspired to assassinate him, but he had them executed. After that, Commodus became a cruel ruler as well as a stupid one. Finally, in A.D. 192, he was strangled in his bath.

The decline of the empire, however, continued for almost 300 years. The end of the Roman empire is usually dated as A.D. 476. In that year, a barbarian king took over the rule of Rome.

The process of decline took place in three stages. First, there was a long time of turmoil known by historians as the "crisis of the third century." During these years, the empire was beset by economic, military, and political problems. Second, there was a time of revival, during which the empire was divided into two parts, an eastern half and a western half. As you will see, this change strengthened the Greek-speaking east but weakened the Latin-speaking west. Third, the western half of the empire was overwhelmed by savage invaders. The eastern empire survived these invasions and existed for 1,000 years after the destruction of the western empire.

Crises weakened the empire.

During the third century (A.D. 200–300), a host of problems confronted the Roman empire. Although it survived, these problems left the empire gravely weakened.

Economic decay During the Pax Romana, trade flowed smoothly over sea routes patrolled by Roman navies and land routes patrolled by Roman armies. Rome's treasuries were enriched by huge amounts of gold and silver that the Roman conquerors collected as plunder. Perhaps most basic and most important of all, the empire's farms grew enough grain to feed the population of the cities. During the crisis of the third century, all three sources of prosperity dried up.

Trade was disrupted on both land and sea. Barbarian raids across the Danube River discouraged merchants from driving their oxcarts over Roman roads. At the same time, bands of pirates began terrorizing Mediterranean sea lanes.

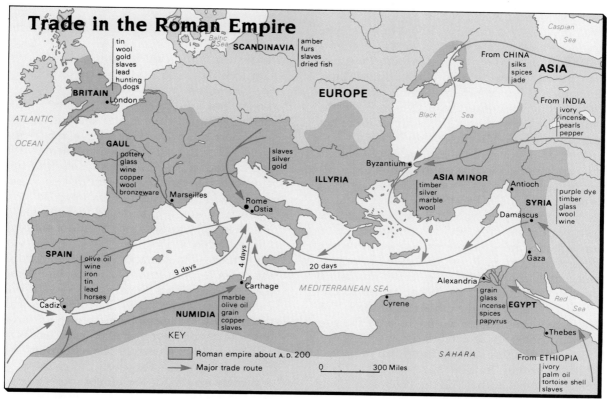

Trade in the Roman Empire

SCANDINAVIA amber / furs / slaves / dried fish

From CHINA silks / spices / jade **ASIA**

From INDIA ivory / incense / pearls / pepper

BRITAIN tin / wool / gold / slaves / lead / hunting dogs
• London

ATLANTIC OCEAN

EUROPE

Baltic Sea

Black Sea

Caspian Sea

GAUL pottery / glass / wine / copper / wool / bronzeware
• Marseilles

slaves / silver / gold

ILLYRIA

Byzantium •

ASIA MINOR timber / silver / marble / wool

Antioch •

SYRIA purple dye / timber / glass / wool / wine

Damascus •

Rome • Ostia •

4 days

9 days

20 days

MEDITERRANEAN SEA

Gaza •

SPAIN olive oil / wine / iron / tin / lead / horses
Cadiz •

Carthage •

Cyrene •

Alexandria •

EGYPT grain / glass / incense / spices / papyrus

Red Sea

NUMIDIA marble / olive oil / grain / copper / slaves

Thebes •

SAHARA

From ETHIOPIA ivory / palm oil / tortoise shell / slaves

KEY
Roman empire about A.D. 200
➝ Major trade route
0 _____ 300 Miles

Map Study

Trade was crucial to Rome's economy. What goods reached Rome from China?
From Scandinavia? How long did a voyage from Alexandria to Rome take?

Rome's gold and silver were drained away to buy luxuries from other lands. Rich Roman families yearned for costly goods from China, India, and Arabia, including spices, perfumes, rubies, pearls, and silk. Rome's small industries produced only wine, cheese, and glass. China, India, and Arabia had little interest in buying such plain goods. Thus, Romans were forced to pay out a fortune in gold and silver every year for the imported luxuries they craved.

Desperate to pay its mounting expenses, the Roman government started minting coins that contained less and less silver. Eventually, Roman coins lost 98 percent of their silver content. As a result, prices shot sky-high. For example, in the second century, a peck of wheat sold for half a denarius. By the end of the third century, the price had risen to 100 denarii. Such an increase in prices is called **inflation.**

Agriculture faced an equally serious crisis. Harvests in Italy and western Europe became increasingly meager. Scholars think that the overworked soil had probably lost much of its earlier fertility.

Military decay The empire's economic troubles were worsened by its growing miltary troubles. Throughout the third century, tribes of northern barbarians called Goths repeatedly overran the legions guarding the Danube frontier. At the same time, Syria and Asia Minor were threatened by Persia. The Persians' proudest victory (and Rome's most humiliating defeat) occurred in A.D. 260 when the Roman emperor Valerian was captured in battle. For the rest of his life, Valerian was forced to crouch down and allow the Persian king to step on him while mounting a horse.

Roman soldiers now fought strictly for money, not for patriotism. To attract recruits into the army, the government promised ever higher cash awards. These costs put an increasing strain on the treasury. Partly to keep costs down, emperors began to recruit troops from the ranks of the barbarians, who would accept lower pay. However, the loyalty of barbarian troops to the empire could hardly be trusted.

Political decay Loyalty was in fact a key problem, perhaps the most serious of all. At one time, Romans cared so deeply about their republic that they willingly sacrificed their lives for it. In the later centuries of the empire, citizens were not actively disloyal, but they were indifferent.

To hold political office had once been considered an honor (as well as an invitation to profit). But times had changed. By the 200's, local officials usually lost money because they were required to pay for costly circuses and baths out of their own pockets. As the empire's prosperity faded, less and less money came in as taxes. However, the government in Rome continued to require each tax district to send in a certain amount. If the local tax collector could not gather up that much, he had to pay the difference himself. Naturally, few people were willing to serve the government under those conditions.

The only groups actively interested in politics were the armies. In a 50-year period (A.D. 218–268), provincial armies and the Praetorian Guard proclaimed 50 generals emperors of Rome. Of these, 27 briefly won the approval of the Roman senate. Seventeen of these men were murdered. Two others were forced to commit suicide.

The empire might very well have collapsed during the crisis of the third century. Remarkably, it survived for another 200 years. The empire was saved by two men who rank among Rome's greatest emperors, Diocletian (DY-oh-KLEE-shuhn) and Constantine (KAHN-stuhn-tyn).

Diocletian reformed the empire.

In A.D. 284, Diocletian, a strong-willed army leader and son of a slave, became the new emperor. With amazing boldness, he tried to restore order in the empire and increase its strength. These were Diocletian's reforms:

1. To beat back the Goths and Persians, Diocletian doubled the size of the Roman armies to 500,000. This secured the boundaries of the empire once again.
2. To build economic stability, Diocletian ordered that all sons had to follow the trade of their fathers. Thus, any movement from farm to city workshop was made illegal.
3. To beat inflation, he used price and wage controls. Costs were fixed for everything from a haircut to a bottle of wine.
4. To restore faith in the ancient gods of Rome, Diocletian ordered a general persecution of the Christians.
5. To increase the prestige of the emperor, Diocletian assumed the manner and costume of a Persian ruler. He wore purple robes embroidered with gold, a crown encrusted with pearls, and scarlet boots. Anyone who approached his throne was required to kneel down and kiss the hem of his robe. He took a new title, *dominus et deus* ("lord and god"), abandoning Augustus's modest title of *princeps* ("first citizen").
6. To improve administration, Diocletian divided the empire into the Greek-speaking east (Greece, Asia Minor, Syria, and Egypt) and the Latin-speaking west (Italy, Gaul, Britannia, and Spain). Because the empire had grown too large and too complex for one ruler, each half was to have its own emperor. The eastern half of the empire included most of the great cities and trade centers of the empire. As a result, the east was far wealthier than the more rural west. Diocletian took the eastern half for himself and named another ruler for the west. Each emperor was supposed to name an assistant ruler who would later succeed him. In this way, Diocletian hoped to solve the succession problem as well.

These reforms were not totally successful. Wages for the new troops added to the already crushing load of taxes. Price controls failed. Christianity continued its rapid growth. Yet during his 21-year reign (A.D. 284–305), Diocletian did stop the decline of the empire. The borders were safe again, and the emperor was once more considered an exalted person. Diocletian retired in 305. He spent his last years peacefully tending his garden. But even while he lived, his plans for the succession failed.

Constantine accepted Christianity.

Civil war broke out immediately after Diocletian retired. By A.D. 311, four rivals were competing for power. Among them was a dashing young commander named Constantine. One of the most critical moments in history occurred

Constantine built this triumphal arch to celebrate his victory over Maxentius.

in A.D. 312 when Constantine marched to the Tiber River to fight his chief rival, Maxentius (mak-SEN-shee-uhs). On the day before the battle, Constantine prayed for divine help. What happened next was reported by a Christian bishop, Eusebius (yoo-SEE-bee-uhs):

And while [Constantine] was thus praying, a most marvelous sign appeared to him from heaven. He said that about noon he saw with his own eyes a cross of light in the heavens, above the sun, and bearing the inscription, "In this sign, conquer."

The next morning, Constantine ordered artisans to put a Christian symbol on his soldiers' shields. Then came the clash between the armies of Constantine and Maxentius. Near the Milvian Bridge, two miles outside Rome, Constantine scored an overwhelming victory. He marched into Rome and became emperor of the western half of the empire. He attributed his victory to the power of the Christian God.

The next year, A.D. 313, Constantine announced an end to the persecution of Christians. From Milan, he granted "both to the Christians and to all men freedom to follow the religion that they choose." By this famous Edict of Milan, Constantine changed Christianity from an outlawed sect into a religion approved by the emperor.

Constantine founded a new capital.

Eventually, Constantine won control of the eastern as well as the western empire. In A.D. 330, he took the momentous step of moving the empire's capital from Rome to the Greek city of Byzantium (bih-ZANT-ee-uhm) in what is now Turkey.

The new capital had four advantages over Rome. First, it stood at a crossroad for trade. Located on a narrow water passageway called the Bosporus (BAHS-puhr-uhs), Byzantium controlled all shipping between the Black Sea and the Mediterranean Sea. The city also dominated the east-west overland trade between Asia Minor and Greece. Second, the city was easy to defend against attack, as it was nearly surrounded by water. Third, the old Rome was a pagan city dedicated to pagan gods. Byzantium was strongly Christian. Finally, Byzantium had the advantage of being in the more prosperous half of the empire, the east.

Thus, the center of empire shifted from west to east. Soon the new capital was protected by massive walls and gleamed with stately buildings. The city even had a new name—Constantinople (KAHN-STANT-uhn-OH-puhl), city of Constantine.

Because of the policies of Diocletian and Constantine, there were now two empires, not one. Because of Constantine's victory at the Milvian Bridge, both empires were Christian.

Barbarians overran the empire.

The third phase of Rome's decline was a century of destruction beginning in A.D. 376 and ending in 476. Many different groups took part in Rome's destruction: Ostrogoths, Visigoths, Franks, Angles, Saxons, Burgundians, Lombards, Vandals. All these groups were semibarbaric peoples who spoke Germanic languages.

Germanic men wore their hair down to their shoulders. They loved to gamble, drink, and fight. They assigned most of the drudgery of farmwork to their sisters, wives, and mothers. The historian Tacitus said they had "blue eyes and reddish hair; great bodies, especially powerful for attack, but not equally patient of hard work." Though the different Germanic groups shared similar ways of life, they hated one another and were frequently at war. Rome often took advantage of this hatred.

When Rome was still strong, the Germanic tribes generally respected the borders guarded by Roman legions. These borders stretched across Europe from the Black Sea to the North Sea. The longest section of the Roman border followed the Danube River. For many years, the Danube marked the dividing line between the barbaric north and the civilized south.

Though fearless fighters, the Germanic tribes were terrified of the Huns, a nomadic people from central Asia. The following exaggerated description by a Germanic historian, Jordanes, shows how the Huns were feared:

> They made their foes flee in horror because their swarthy aspect was fearful, and they had . . . a shapeless lump instead of a head, with pinholes rather than eyes. They are cruel to their children on the very day of their birth. For they cut the cheeks of the males with a sword, so that before they receive the nourishment of milk, they must learn to endure wounds.

When the Huns began to move west, they first attacked the Ostrogoths, the most easterly Germanic tribe. The terrified Ostrogoths fled westward and pressed against their old enemies, the Visigoths. Squeezed off their land, the Visigoths looked for a new home south of the Danube border. Thus began the massive movement of Germanic peoples that eventually destroyed the western half of the Roman empire. In A.D. 378, Visigoths routed a Roman army. This disaster shattered Rome's military reputation.

The Huns kept raiding westward, destroying as they went. Germanic people near the Rhine River—Burgundians, Franks, and Vandals—began to feel the pressure and to move westward also. The Rhine River froze during an especially cold winter in A.D. 406. Bundled in furs, Vandal warriors and their families swarmed across the river ice. They met practically no resistance and so they kept moving westward through the Roman province of Gaul. There were no more than 15,000 Vandal warriors. The population of Gaul was probably 20 million. Yet the Vandals raided the cities of Gaul as if they were defenseless. The empire of the west was now so disorganized that it could not muster even a medium-sized army to stop the barbarians.

Map Study

This map shows the routes of some barbarian groups that invaded the Roman empire. Which group eventually reached North Africa?

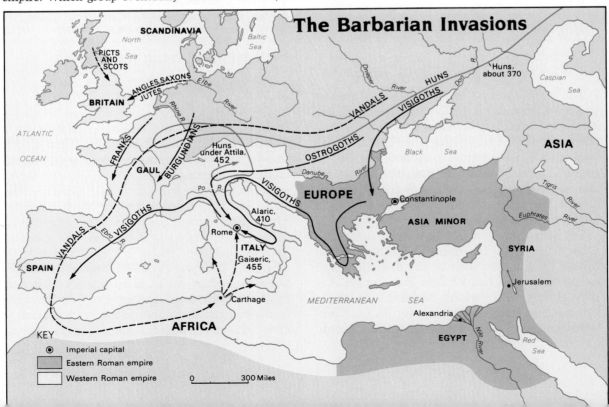

Barbarians sacked Rome.

During the first half of the fifth century, Rome was sacked twice by Germanic armies: first by the Visigoths in A.D. 410, next by the Vandals in A.D. 455.

In 410, Alaric (AL-uh-rik), king of the Visigoths, marched across the Alps toward Rome. Rome still was widely regarded as the center of civilization. The news that Alaric and his army stood outside its walls was shocking. A traitor opened Rome's gates, and thousands of Germans stormed in. They plundered the city for three days.

Rome remained rich enough to act as bait for other looters. In 455, the king of the Vandals from North Africa sailed to Rome in pursuit of more treasure. This ruthless leader, known as Gaiseric (GY-zuh-rik) the Lame, sacked Rome more thoroughly than Alaric had. Thousands of Romans were taken captive and shipped back to North Africa as slaves.

Attila the Hun Meanwhile, the Huns, who indirectly began this mayhem, were still on the rampage. In fact, the Huns seemed more dangerous than ever under their new leader, Attila (AT-uhl-uh). The Germanic writer Jordanes described this terrifying chieftain as a short man with a flat nose and thin, graying beard. "He was haughty in his walk, rolling his eyes hither and thither, so that the power of his proud spirit appeared in the movement of his body."

With his 100,000 soldiers, Attila threatened to conquer the entire empire. In the east, his armies sacked 70 cities. (The Huns failed, however, to scale the high walls of Constantinople.)

In A.D. 452, Attila advanced against Rome. But then the barbarian king was stopped in his tracks by a Christian bishop. The first truly powerful pope of Rome, Leo I, journeyed to Attila's camp near the Po River. No record survives of Leo's words to Attila. Perhaps Leo frightened the Hun by telling of the plague that was then ravishing Italy. Perhaps Attila was simply awed by Leo. Whatever the reason, Attila withdrew his forces.

The last emperor of the west By A.D. 455, the Roman emperor in the west was practically powerless. Germanic tribes now fought one another for possession of the western provinces. Spain belonged to the Visigoths, North Africa to the Vandals. Gaul was overrun by competing tribes: Franks, Burgundians, and Visigoths. Britannia was being invaded by Angles and Saxons. Italy was falling victim to raids by the Ostrogoths.

The last Roman emperor was a 14-year-old boy whose name, Romulus Augustulus, recalled 1,000 years of past glory. In A.D. 476, he lost his throne to a barbarian general named Odoacer (oh-doh-AY-sur). Odoacer sent Romulus Augustulus into exile. After 476, no emperor even pretended to rule Rome and its western provinces. Roman power in the western half of the empire had disappeared.

The eastern half, which came to be called the Byzantine empire, not only survived but flourished for another 1,000 years. Its emperors ruled from Constantinople.

Even though Rome's political power ended in the west, its cultural influence was felt for centuries afterward. Latin remained the language of learning in the west. The Christian Church, governed from Rome by a succession of popes, became the chief civilizing force of western Europe. Civilization, though shaken to its roots by the barbarian terror, did not perish.

Section Review 4

Define: inflation
Identify: (a) Commodus, (b) Diocletian, (c) Constantine, (d) eastern empire, (e) western empire, (f) Battle of Milvian Bridge, (g) Edict of Milan, (h) Constantinople, (i) Germanic peoples, (j) Huns, (k) Alaric, (l) Gaiseric, (m) Attila, (n) Leo I, (o) Romulus Augustulus, (p) Odoacer
Answer:
1. What economic problems did the empire face in the third century?
2. By the third century, how had Rome's army changed since the days of the republic?
3. (a) What important religious change did Constantine bring about in the empire? (b) What political change did he bring about?
4. (a) Why did Germanic tribes invade the empire in the 400's? (b) Why was the empire unable to drive the invaders out?

Critical Thinking
5. (a) List three reasons why Diocletian should be considered a successful emperor. (b) List three reasons why he might be considered a failure.

Summary

1. Augustus's rule began the Pax Romana. Augustus's wise policies began a period of peace that lasted from 27 B.C. to A.D. 180. Despite some unwise or cruel rulers, Roman government worked well under its civil service. The greatest problem was the lack of a clear way of choosing an emperor.

2. Romans extended Greek culture. Romans continued Greek traditions in philosophy, art, and literature. Epicureanism and Stoicism became influential philosophies. Literature moved from patriotic themes, such as Virgil's *Aeneid,* to criticism of Rome. Roman law established basic principles of justice. Although great contrasts in wealth marked Roman society, the poor at least had some care.

3. Christianity spread through the empire. While Judaea was under Roman rule, Jesus began a new religion known as Christianity. Despite early persecution of its followers, Christianity won acceptance.

4. Rome's empire declined and fell. Rome faced many problems in the 200's but partly recovered under Diocletian, who set up reforms and divided the empire into eastern and western halves. Constantine legalized Christianity and moved the capital to Constantinople. During the 400's, barbarians swept into the empire, sacked Rome, and deposed Rome's last emperor.

Reviewing the Facts

1. Define the following terms:
   a. civil service   d. bishop
   b. satire   e. pope
   c. villa   f. inflation
2. Explain the importance of each of the following names, dates, places, or terms:
   a. Pax Romana   j. Paul
   b. Augustus   k. Peter
   c. Marcus Aurelius   l. Zealots
   d. A.D. 180   m. Diocletian
   e. Epicurus   n. Constantine
   f. Zeno   o. Constantinople
   g. Livy   p. Edict of Milan
   h. Virgil   q. A.D. 476
   i. Jesus
3. List four major achievements of Roman civilization during the Pax Romana.
4. (a) What were the main teachings of Christianity? (b) How did the position of Christianity within the Roman empire change between the first and fourth centuries A.D.?
5. How did each of the following factors contribute to the decline of the Roman empire? (a) economic problems (b) the issue of loyalty (c) Germanic invasions

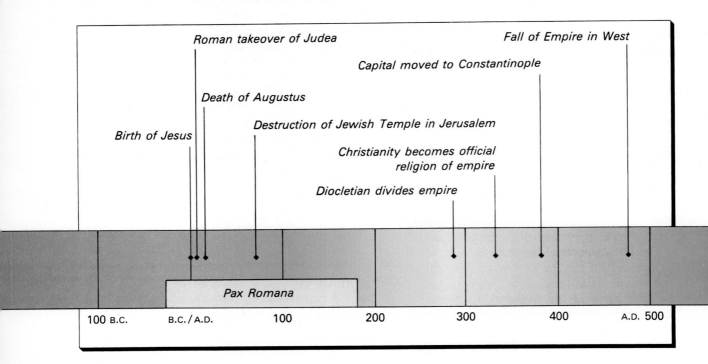

Roman takeover of Judea

Fall of Empire in West

Capital moved to Constantinople

Death of Augustus

Destruction of Jewish Temple in Jerusalem

Birth of Jesus

Christianity becomes official religion of empire

Diocletian divides empire

Pax Romana

100 B.C.   B.C./A.D.   100   200   300   400   A.D. 500

Thinking about History

1. Review the teachings of the philosophers and religious teachers mentioned in this chapter. Discuss several issues on which they might have agreed or disagreed.
2. Conflicts between governments and religious groups have been a frequent theme in history. What conflicts of this type have occurred in modern times? (Look for accounts of such conflicts on news broadcasts or in newspapers and magazines.) In what ways are people trying to resolve these conflicts?
3. The transition of power from one leader to another is a time of crisis for many governments. How was this issue a problem for Rome? How is the problem handled in the United States today? How is it handled in the USSR? Use newspapers or news magazines to find accounts of ways in which new leaders come to power in these and other countries. What are some of the ways government leaders come to office today?
4. Review the quotation from the *Aeneid* on page 147. Do you think these lines are a good description of Rome's achievements? Why or why not?
5. Explain the relationship between Roman law and Stoicism. What parts of our own legal system derive from Roman law?

Writing and Speaking about History

1. Write an introductory paragraph for an essay on the topic, "Augustus's reforms laid the foundation for the Pax Romana." Make sure your paragraph clearly introduces the topic and states the thesis. (See Research Skills Handbook, page 318.)
2. Choose a newspaper editorial to bring into class. Circle the arguments used to support the editor's position. Using the editorial as a model, write an editorial titled, "Rome's Decline: Causes and Consequences."
3. Imagine that you are a tour guide for the Rome Chamber of Commerce in the year A.D. 300. Prepare a talk on the sites and scenes of Roman life for a group of high school historians.

Practicing Skills

1. Use the time line on page 160 to calculate how many years passed between the beginnings of the Pax Romana and the birth of Jesus. (b) How many years passed between the birth of Jesus and the fall of the Roman empire in the West?
2. Approximately 70 to 90 million people lived in the Roman empire at its height. Use an almanac to find modern countries that have a population roughly equal to that of Rome's. Contrast the land area of these nations with that of the Roman empire in A.D. 120.
3. Compare the Roman empire at its height (page 144) with the empire of Alexander the Great (page 116). Describe the boundaries of each empire. Which empire lay mostly in Europe? Which lay mostly in Asia?
4. Use the chart of Roman emperors on page 146 to answer the following questions: (a) What information about each emperor does the chart provide? (b) To what group of emperors did Vespasian belong? (c) Which emperor was not Roman by birth and for what is his reign known?

Investigating History

1. Choose one of the Roman emperors of the Pax Romana from the table on page 146 and write a short report on his life and reign.
2. In A.D. 79, a volcanic eruption destroyed the two Roman towns of Pompeii and Herculaneum. When archaeologists uncovered the towns, they found many details of Roman life perfectly preserved. Look for more information on one of the towns, and report on some of the everyday items found there. What do these items tell you about the ways of life that perished? (See *National Geographic,* May 1984.)
3. The civilization of ancient Rome has had a profound effect on Western civilization. Choose one of the following topics to research: Roman law, Roman architecture, the Latin language. Describe the influence of your topic on modern times.

Decision Making in History

Evaluate the consequences of Emperor Diocletian's decision to divide the Roman empire into two parts. Why do you think Diocletian chose to do this? Can you think of other ways Diocletian might have improved administration?

Research Skills

Giving an Oral Presentation

Many historians address groups. The ability to speak well can help a historian become an active participant in community affairs. Historians need skills in public speaking for a variety of reasons. They may present research findings, introduce other speakers, and nominate people for public office. The goal of any public speaker is always the same: to communicate a message effectively to an audience.

There are three stages to giving an oral presentation: (1) planning, (2) outlining, and (3) delivering. Here are some helpful hints for planning:

1. Decide on the purpose. Is your goal to inform, persuade, or entertain?
2. Evaluate your audience. Who will the listeners be? How much do they already know about the topic? What would they like to learn?
3. Consider how much time you will have to speak. Plan not to say too much or too little. Your audience will appreciate your staying within a time frame.
4. Think about the location from which you will talk.

Like a written report, a speech should be outlined in advance. The outline should include:

1. An introduction of the topic that grabs the attention of the audience and makes listeners want to know more
2. A statement of the thesis, or point of view
3. Several major points to support the thesis
4. A concluding summary that restates the major points

The manner in which a speech is presented is often as important as the content of the speech. Here are some guidelines for effective oral communication:

1. Use notecards to avoid the shuffling of papers.
2. Speak loud enough for a person in the last row to hear clearly.
3. Maintain good eye contact with the entire audience.
4. Show enthusiasm and interest in the topic.
5. Stand up straight and avoid slouching or fidgeting.
6. Use gestures and body movements to emphasize important points.
7. Avoid using expressions such as *well, um,* and *uh* as stalling tactics. Choose silence instead.
8. Practice before a friend or mirror at least once before the actual presentation.
9. Stay within the time allotted for the presentation.

Public speaking was an important part of life in ancient Rome.

Unit Review II

1. Each of the following terms has to do with government. Define the term and then describe the context or contexts in which you studied it in this unit.
   a. democracy
   b. republic
   c. aristocracy
   d. tyrant
   e. consul
   f. senate
   g. assembly
   h. veto
   i. dictator
   j. civil service

2. Match each name in the left column with the correct item in the right column.
   a. Caesar
   b. Socrates
   c. Homer
   d. Augustus
   e. Pericles
   f. Cleopatra
   g. Philip II
   h. Hannibal
   i. Leonidas
   j. Paul

   1. Battle of Zama
   2. Pax Romana
   3. Thermopylae
   4. philosopher
   5. Macedonia
   6. Rubicon
   7. apostle
   8. Delian League
   9. Egypt
   10. *Iliad*

3. Review the maps on pages 116 and 144. Then, tell whether each of the following countries or cities were part of (a) the empire of Alexander the Great in 323 B.C., (b) the Roman Empire in A.D. 120, or (c) both.
   a. Alexandria (in Egypt)
   b. Athens
   c. Carthage
   d. Jerusalem
   e. Persepolis (in Persia)
   f. northwest India
   g. Spain
   h. Gaul

4. In each group of events in a–f, tell which event came *first*.
   a. Golden Age of Athens
      Persian Wars
   b. Diocletian divides the empire.
      Christianity becomes official religion of empire.
   c. Birth of Jesus
      Roman takeover of Judea

   d. Punic Wars
      Roman conquest of Italy
   e. Pax Romana
      Rise of Julius Caesar
   f. Peloponnesian War
      Rise of Alexander the Great

5. Name three ways geography shaped Greek civilization.

6. (a) When did the first civilization arise in Greece? (b) What period in Greek history interrupted civilization?

7. (a) What city-state in Greece was known for its army? (b) What city-state helped develop the democratic form of government?

8. (a) What two groups of people struggled for power in ancient Athens? (b) How did the philosopher Solon resolve the struggle?

9. (a) Show how jealousies among the city-states helped to undermine ancient Greece. (b) Show how the spread of Roman power helped to undermine the Roman republic.

10. (a) What bitter conflict did the people of ancient Rome face in their struggle to achieve a balanced government? (b) How did they resolve it?

11. (a) Describe three ways in which Rome changed after the Punic Wars. (b) How were army leaders able to come to power during this period?

12. (a) Describe the problem of succession that plagued Rome's emperors throughout the history of the empire. (b) How did the Good Emperors temporarily solve this problem?

13. The decline of the Roman empire took place in these three stages. Describe each of the stages.
    a. the crisis of the third century
    b. a time of revival
    c. barbarian invasions

Unit III
The Middle Ages

As the Roman empire broke apart, three regions emerged from the ruins. Western Europe—including Italy, Germany, France, and Britain—went into a decline. The eastern part of the empire—including Greece, Asia Minor, Egypt, and Palestine—became the empire of Constantinople, or the Byzantine empire. A little later, a third power arose—the Muslims. Muslims were followers of Islam, a new religion that first appeared in Arabia during the 600's. Many lands in Southwest Asia, North Africa, and even southern Europe fell under Muslim rule.

In the 500's and early 600's, the Byzantines were clearly the strongest power in the old Roman lands. By the 700's, the Arab Muslims seemed in command. By the year 1000, however, both empires had begun to dwindle under new assaults. At the same time, western Europe began to revive.

The years from about 500 to 1500 are often called the Middle Ages. The term was invented by European historians who saw these years as falling between the glories of classical civilization in Greece and Rome and the great revival of learning in Europe in the 1500's. Yet the years from 500 to 1500 are not merely a bridge between ancient and modern times. During these years, vital new societies emerged around the Mediterrean Sea and in the northern parts of Europe.

Castillo de la Mota, Spain

The Byzantine Empire and the Rise of Islam

After the Muslims captured Jerusalem, they built the Dome of the Rock on the spot where they believed the prophet Muhammad had ascended into heaven.

1. Constantinople ruled an eastern empire.

2. A new faith spread from Arabia.

3. The empires influenced Slavs and Turks.

Inside the gates of Jerusalem, a tall, muscular Arab climbed down from the hump of a white camel. From the camel's back, he took down a dusty prayer rug and carried it up the steps of a magnificent, high-domed church, the Church of the Holy Sepulchre. The Arab's name was Omar. The year was 637.

For about 300 years, Jerusalem had been a Christian city, part of the Byzantine empire. Christians considered the ground enclosed by the Church of the Holy Sepulchre to be the most sacred place on earth. According to tradition, the spot where Jesus had been crucified and the tomb in which he had been buried lay beneath the dome of this church.

Omar, however, was not a Christian. He was a Muslim, one of the first converts to a new religion called Islam (ihs-**LAHM**). He had been a personal friend of Islam's founder, an Arab prophet named Muhammad (moo-**HAM**-uhd).

Omar did not enter the church. Instead, he reverently turned his gaze southeast toward Mecca, the Arab city from which he had come. He knelt on his prayer rug, touching his head to the ground as he prayed toward Mecca. "*Allahu akhbar!*" he cried aloud, meaning "God is most great."

On this day in 637, Omar entered Jerusalem as a conqueror. Some 60,000 Muslim warriors had invaded Palestine to win converts for God —or *Allah*, in the Arabic language. They had defeated the defending Christian armies from Constantinople.

Rising from his prayer rug, Omar asked a Christian priest to show him to the flat stretch of rock where the temple built by the Jewish king Solomon had stood. To Muslims, this plain gray rock was holier than anything else in Jerusalem. Muslims believed that their prophet Muhammad had ascended from this rock into paradise on a golden ladder of light. Omar eagerly followed his guide to the sacred rock, but he found it buried under a mound of garbage and dung. The pious Omar flew into a rage. "Oh, ye men of Greece," he shouted at the Greek-speaking Christians, "ye are the people who shall be slain on this dung-heap."

In the centuries that followed, thousands of Christians and Muslims spilled their blood in wars of religion and conquest. Religious belief can be an immensely powerful force in human affairs. It can inspire great acts of goodness and stunning works of art. It can also drive people to terrible acts against those who hold other beliefs. Both Christians and Muslims claimed theirs was the only true religion. Neither group would allow the other to live in peace.

In this chapter, you will follow the fortunes of two empires, one Christian and the other Muslim. You will see how the Byzantine Christians used their riches to create an artistic masterpiece, the dazzling church of Hagia Sophia in Constantinople. In Jerusalem, the Muslim Arabs erected another architectural masterpiece, the Dome of the Rock, over the very rock on which Christians had dumped garbage. You will see how Christianity spread from Constantinople into Russia and how Islam spread from Arabia as far west as Spain and as far east as India.

Constantinople ruled an eastern empire. 1

Constantinople was founded by Rome's first Christian emperor, Constantine, in 330. He built the city on the site of a Greek seaport known as Byzantium. It was situated at a point where many major trade routes between Asia and Europe came together, as the map on this page shows.

Between the Black Sea and the Aegean Sea lies a much smaller body of water, the Sea of Marmara. Two narrow straits, like natural gateways, control the shipping routes from sea to sea. The gateway between the Aegean Sea and the Sea of Marmara is the Dardanelles. The gateway between the Sea of Marmara and the Black Sea is called the Bosporus. Whoever controls those gates also controls the shipping from much of Asia to the Mediterranean region.

Map Study

What narrow waterway did Constantinople control? Name five routes by which goods reached the city.

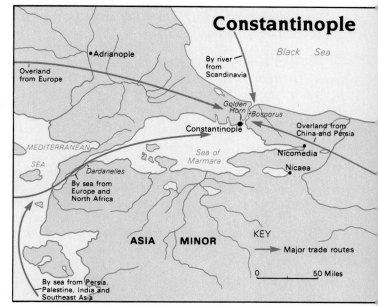

This medieval drawing shows Constantinople's busy harbor, its strong fortifications, its race course, and its great church, Hagia Sophia.

Constantine built his great capital on a peninsula at the southern end of the Bosporus. The city was blessed with a spacious harbor known as the Golden Horn (*horn* because it was shaped like an ox's horn, *golden* because of the wealthy cargoes that floated on its waters).

Constantine liked to call his eastern capital New Rome. Two centuries later, emperors in Constantinople still ruled the eastern part of the old Roman empire. The lands under their control included Greece, Asia Minor, Palestine, Syria, and Egypt. This empire is called the Byzantine empire after the original Greek town on Constantinople's site.

The emperor headed both church and state.

The Byzantine emperors never forgot their Roman heritage. They saw themselves as heirs to the power of Augustus Caesar. To keep up ancient tradition, a senate still met in Constantinople. In truth, however, the power of the emperor was absolute.

Emperors claimed authority from two sources. First, they held the political powers of a Roman ruler. Second, they claimed to rule in Jesus' name

as new apostles. This tradition went back to Constantine, and it gave the Byzantine emperor power similar to that of a pope. Thus, the Byzantine emperor combined political and religious authority in one person.

The Byzantine emperors still considered themselves rightful rulers of all the lands Rome had once held. Even in the 530's and 540's, a hundred years after the plunderings of Visigoths, Vandals, and Huns, one Byzantine emperor tried to reconquer all the western lands that Rome had lost to the barbarians. The name of this ambitious and controversial Byzantine ruler was Justinian (juhs-TIHN-ee-uhn).

Justinian reconquered Roman lands.

Justinian became emperor in 527 and ruled until 565. According to the official court historian, Procopius (proh-KOH-pee-uhs), Justinian was a ruddy-cheeked man of medium height and weight. He never lost his temper and never drank too much wine. He was a conscientious ruler, working from dawn to midnight.

Procopius flattered the emperor in the official histories, but in a *Secret History*, published after Justinian's death, Procopius gave vent to other feelings. Justinian, he wrote, was "deceitful, devious, false, hypocritical, two-faced, cruel, skilled in dissembling his thought, never moved to tears by either joy or pain . . . a liar always."

Whatever the truth may be about Justinian's character, he proved to be an able ruler. He launched three ambitious projects. First, he tried to reconquer Roman lands to the west. Second, he ordered a team of Greek and Latin scholars to compile and simplify the laws. Third, he undertook a massive building program in Constantinople. His works on the city and the laws were of lasting value to civilization. His wars, however, proved to be a waste of men and money.

The campaign to reconquer the Roman empire began successfully. In 533, Justinian sent his best general, Belisarius (BEL-uh-SAIR-ee-uhs), to win back the Vandal kingdom of North Africa. Belisarius broke down the Vandal defenses and rode triumphantly into Carthage. In only a few days, the entire northern coast of Africa beyond Egypt fell under Byzantine rule.

Belisarius's next assignment was to fight the Ostrogoths in Italy. With a tiny army of only

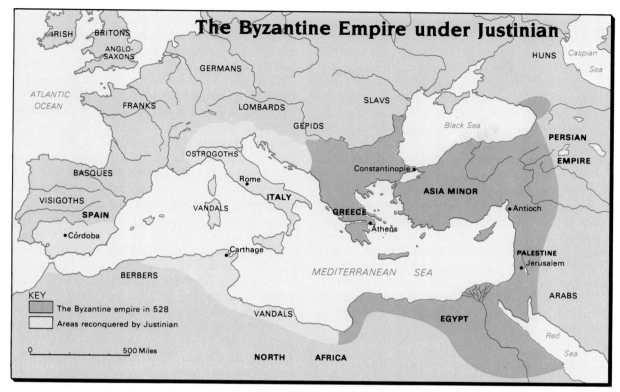

The Byzantine Empire under Justinian

IRISH BRITONS
ANGLO-
SAXONS
GERMANS
ATLANTIC
OCEAN
FRANKS
LOMBARDS
GEPIDS
SLAVS
HUNS
Caspian
Sea
Black Sea
PERSIAN
EMPIRE
OSTROGOTHS
Constantinople •
ASIA MINOR
BASQUES
Rome •
ITALY
• Antioch
VISIGOTHS
SPAIN
VANDALS
GREECE
Athens •
• Córdoba
Carthage •
PALESTINE
Jerusalem •
MEDITERRANEAN SEA
BERBERS
ARABS
KEY
☐ The Byzantine empire in 528
☐ Areas reconquered by Justinian
VANDALS
EGYPT
Red
Sea
0   500 Miles
NORTH   AFRICA

Map Study

Name three major areas that Justinian reconquered. For each area, tell what group or groups his armies had to fight.

8,000 men, the Byzantine general outmaneuvered his barbarian foes. Entering Rome in 536, he received a hero's welcome as the city's liberator. For the first time in 60 years, wrote Procopius, "Rome was again brought under the Romans."

The rejoicing, however, quickly turned to sorrow. The Ostrogoths returned and drove out the Byzantines. The Byzantines struck back. In 18 years of siege and countersiege (535–553), Rome changed hands six times.

When the Byzantines finally won control of the city in 553, the triumph was an empty one. Rome lay in ruins. Fallen statues littered its streets. No water flowed in its magnificent baths. Once home to a million people, Rome's population had dropped to a mere 40,000, nearly half of whom roamed the streets as beggars or looters. The Byzantines, who had come to save Rome, ended by destroying it.

To North Africa and Italy, Justinian added part of Spain as his final conquest. His dream to reunite Roman lands seemed to have succeeded bril-

liantly. After his death, however, all the conquered territory quickly passed back into barbarian hands. Lombards overran Italy. Muslim Arabs swept through North Africa and Spain. Ironically, the destruction of Rome was the one lasting result of Justinian's costly wars.

Justinian ordered a code of laws.

In the long run, Justinian's legal reforms were far more important than his conquests. Between 528 and 534, he assigned a group of legal scholars to an incredible task. They were to codify all Roman laws and legal opinions since the time of Hadrian 400 years earlier! If a law made in Athens in the year 220 contradicted a law made in Alexandria in 350, which law should be followed in Constantinople in 530? This was the kind of perplexing question for which Justinian sought an answer.

The result of his commission's labors was the *Corpus Juris Civilis* (Body of Civil Law), known to later ages as the Code of Justinian. It consisted of four works.

1. *The Codex Justinian* presented nearly 5,000 laws from the Roman empire that Justinian's scholars thought were still useful for Byzantium. The laws were arranged by topic.
2. *The Digest* quoted and summarized the opinions of Rome's greatest legal writers. This massive work had 50 volumes.
3. *The Institutes* was a textbook telling law students how to use the new code.
4. *The Novellae* contained laws made after 534.

Justinian died in 565, but his code lived after him. It was the basis for Byzantine law for the next 900 years. Many centuries later, France and other countries in western Europe turned to Justinian's code as a guide on legal questions concerning justice, property, marriage, and divorce. It was through Justinian's code that western Europe came to know once again the benefits of Roman law.

Constantinople grew in splendor.

While the code was being compiled, Justinian undertook a city building program larger than that of any Roman emperor, including Augustus. When he finished, Constantinople was the wonder of its age. It was known throughout the Eurasian world simply as "The City."

Some 300,000 people made their permanent homes in Constantinople. There were two requirements for citizenship: membership in the Christian church and the ability to speak Greek. The streets, however, were crowded with people from all over the world.

Constantinople was as well protected as any city could be in those dangerous times. Sea walls guarded it from hostile navies. To the west, a moat and three walls blocked the only land route to the city. The outermost wall was just high enough to shield Byzantine archers. The second wall was 27 feet high, and the third was 70 feet high. It is not surprising that Constantinople withstood many foes for more than 1,000 years.

The marketplace The city's main street was the *Mesê* (MEE-zuh), or Middle Way. The tables of merchants lined the Mesê on either side. Some tables were shaded by colorful awnings. Others were set back within colonnaded walkways.

Goods from all over the world found their way here, mostly by ship. Constantinople was noted for its luxury items. There were spices from India; ivory and gold from Africa; honey, timber, and furs from Russia. Cork came from Spain, wine from France, tin and iron from England, and grain and wool from north of the Alps. Bundles of Chinese silk reached the Mesê by camel caravan,

Mosaics were a common Byzantine artform. The one at the left shows Emperor Justinian; above is his wife, Empress Theodora.

a journey of 230 days if all went well. Encouraged by Justinian, two missionaries to China smuggled out a few silkworms and the seeds of mulberry trees. The secret of silk making, guarded by the Chinese for centuries, now belonged to the Byzantines.

The imperial palace The palace was the center of government. Some 20,000 people worked there in the service of the emperor.

In the gardens, peacocks strutted around bubbling fountains. The most impressive fountain was made of gold in the shape of a pineapple. Wine gushed from it into a silver basin filled with pistachio nuts on which a visitor could snack.

In the throne room, a long gold path led from the entrance to the golden throne. Above the throne was a gilded tree with mechanical birds twittering on its branches. Two golden lions stood on either side of the throne, rigged to let forth mock roars. The throne itself was wide enough to seat two persons, a symbol of the emperor's partnership with Jesus. Anyone who approached the throne was expected to lie prone three times, nose down and hands forward. Guests might kiss the emperor's toes or fingertips. The emperor stared ahead, too lordly to speak.

Hagia Sophia Across from the imperial palace stood one of the architectural wonders of the world—the great cathedral called Hagia Sophia (**HAY**-ee-uh soh-**FEE**-uh). It was the greatest monument of Byzantine Christianity, a symbol of the Christian city.

Voice from the Past · A *Question of Courage*

In 532, early in Justinian's reign, a great riot broke out in Constantinople. It began as a fight between the Blues and the Greens, rival teams in the city's popular chariot races. It quickly became a full-scale revolt. The crowd burned much of the city and proclaimed a new emperor. Justinian hid in the palace. With him was his beautiful wife, Theodora, a former actress who had spent her girlhood in the circus. Procopius tells of the debate that went on within the palace while the mob raged through the city:

Now the emperor and his court were deliberating whether it would be better to remain or to flee in the ships. And many opinions were expressed on both sides. And the Empress Theodora also spoke as follows: "As to the belief that a woman should not be daring among men or assert herself boldly, I consider the present crisis does not allow us to debate that. My opinion is that now is a poor time for flight, even though it bring safety. For any man who has seen the light of day will also die, but one who has been an emperor cannot endure to be a fugitive. If now you wish to go, Emperor, nothing prevents you. There is the sea, there are the steps to the boats. But take care that after you are safe, you do not find that you would gladly exchange that safety for death. For my part, I like the old saying that the empire is a fine burial cloth." When the queen had spoken thus, all were filled with boldness and began to consider how they might defend themselves from their enemies.

[Made brave by Theodora's speech, Justinian remained in the city, gave orders for his troops to crush the mob, and restored order.]

1. What two courses of action were the emperor and his court considering?

2. (a) What does Theodora say about whether or not a woman should speak out? (b) What does this statement suggest was the usual opinion about women at the time?

3. (a) What course of action does Theodora support? (b) What does she say about the risk of death? (c) What does she warn the emperor might happen if he flees?

4. How do you interpret the proverb, "The empire is a fine burial cloth"?

One of the greatest wonders of Hagia Sophia was a magnificent table for preparing the Christian ceremony of Communion. For the making of this table, Justinian ordered pearls and sapphires ground into a rich powder and mixed with molten gold and silver. This extravagant mixture was then poured into a mold for the table.

The university Like several other cities in the Roman empire, Constantinople had a university. Its teachers emphasized the arts of writing and speaking well. The professors included ten Latin grammarians, ten Greek grammarians, three orators, two law professors, and several philosophers. (In later years, Latin fell out of use in Constantinople, and only Greek was spoken at the university.) The university served as a training ground for civil servants and imperial administrators.

Scholars in Constantinople copied the greatest works of the ancient writers—Homer, Plato, Archimedes, Euclid, Livy, Virgil, and others. Had the Byzantines not preserved these works, many would have been lost forever.

Education for both men and women was widespread among the upper classes in the Byzantine empire. Only a few women attended the university, but both boys and girls studied at home with tutors. The learned women of Constantinople included writers, philosophers, and at least one doctor.

The Hippodrome Like Rome's Colosseum, the Hippodrome in Constantinople was the site of extravagant and often bloody scenes for public view. The most important sports events were the chariot races, for which the Hippodrome's 60,000 seats were usually filled.

The Church split into two branches.

Just as the Greeks of Athens spent hours debating politics, the Greeks of Constantinople discussed religion. A shoemaker or a rug seller might argue over the nature of God and Jesus. In the marketplace, icons were sold beside fruit and vegetables. (Icons are small art objects that depict Jesus, Mary, or a Christian saint.)

At one point, conflict over icons had weakened and almost destroyed the Byzantine empire. In the 700's, several emperors tried to end the use of icons in churches. The emperors charged that many people prayed to the icons as if they were idols. Riots and bloody fights broke out between

The great dome of Hagia Sophia was a marvel of engineering. The building has been a Christian church, a Muslim mosque, and a museum.

Hagia Sophia's giant dome rose 180 feet from the floor, an amazing engineering feat. Four acres of gold mosaic tiles covered the dome and the surrounding vaults and arches. The floors, walls, and columns gleamed with every imaginable shade of polished marble—red, white, purple, blue, green, and black. Sunlight poured in the dome's 40 windows by day. At night, light blazed from huge silver candelabra hanging on long chains.

172

people who wanted to keep the icons in churches and the icon smashers, or *iconoclasts*.

The pope in Rome took the side of those who supported the icons. He **excommunicated** the Byzantine emperor. (That is, the pope declared that the emperor was outside the church, cut off from all Christians.)

Eventually, the Byzantine church again accepted icons, and the iconoclasts were labeled **heretics**. (A heretic is a person whose ideas are incorrect, in the opinion of the Church.)

The most lasting result of the controversy was an increase in bad feeling between Christians in Rome and Constantinople. Over the centuries, differences had developed between Byzantine Christians and the Christians of western Europe. For example, priests in the eastern empire conducted services in the local languages of their members—Greek, Coptic, Ethiopian, or Russian. Priests in western Europe conducted services only in Latin. Byzantine priests were allowed to marry, but Roman priests could not do so by church law.

Most important, the pope in Rome claimed to be supreme head of the Christian church, independent of any king or emperor. The bishop of Constantinople was known as the **patriarch** (PAY-tree-ARK). He accepted the authority of the Byzantine emperor. The pope in Rome claimed to be the leader of all Christians everywhere. The patriarchs, however, refused to accept the pope as their superior.

The break between Rome and Constantinople became final in 1054. That year, the pope and the patriarch excommunicated each other. The western branch of the Christian Church became known as the Roman Catholic Church. (*Catholic* comes from a Latin word meaning "universal.") The eastern branch became known as the Eastern Orthodox Church. (*Orthodox* comes from two Greek words meaning "correct belief.") Thus, the political break between the eastern and western parts of the old Roman empire became a religious break as well.

Byzantium faced many enemies.

Although Constantinople remained a rich and powerful city for hundreds of years, the Byzantine empire suffered many setbacks and dangers. The history of the empire after 565 was marked by a bewildering series of street riots, religious quarrels, palace intrigues, and foreign dangers. Many times, the empire appeared to be on the verge of collapse. Each time, it fought off its enemies and sprang back to renewed life only to be threatened by another crisis.

The first long crisis began with Justinian's death in 565. Plague swept through the empire, weakening its armies. Meanwhile, the Lombards moved into Italy and won much of the land Justinian had reconquered there. The Avars, a Hun-like people, invaded the Balkan peninsula (Greece and Macedon). To the east, the Persians threatened to pounce on their ancient foes, the Greeks. Then armies of Arabs, inspired by the prophet Muhammad, burst forth from the Arabian desert and threatened the Byzantine empire's very survival.

Section Review 1

Define: (a) law code, (b) icons, (c) iconoclast, (d) excommunicate, (e) heretic, (f) patriarch
Identify: (a) Constantine, (b) Constantinople, (c) Bosporus, (d) Justinian, (e) Procopius, (f) Belisarius, (g) Theodora, (h) Hagia Sophia, (i) Balkan peninsula, (j) Eastern Orthodox Church, (k) Roman Catholic Church
Answer:
1. (a) Why was Constantinople's harbor called the Golden Horn? (b) How did activities on the Mesê support this name?
2. What two sources did Byzantine emperors claim for their power to rule?
3. (a) What were Justinian's military goals? (b) Did he succeed? Explain.
4. (a) What was the value of Justinian's Code when it was written? (b) What was its lasting value?
5. (a) What disagreements arose between the Christian Church of Rome and that of Constantinople? (b) What was the result of those disagreements?

Critical Thinking
6. What factors made Constantinople a great city? (Consider geographic, historic, and cultural influences.)
7. If you were writing a history of the Byzantine empire, how would you rate Justinian as an emperor?

A new faith spread from Arabia. 2

In the mid-600's, Arab victories swept away enormous chunks of the Byzantine empire, including Palestine, Syria, Egypt, North Africa, and Spain. By 650, only Greece and Asia Minor remained to the Byzantines.

The Arabs threatened to take even Constantinople itself. Every year from 673 to 678, their warships lay outside the great sea wall around Constantinople. What saved the Byzantines was a terrifying weapon that no one else possessed— "Greek fire." Greek fire was a mixture of chemicals (probably naphtha, sulphur, and saltpeter) that the Byzantines squirted through copper tubes at enemy ships. The mixture burst into flames on contact with the Arab ships, turning them into deathtraps. It even burned on the surface of the water.

Who were these Arabs who appeared so suddenly and threatened Constantinople so fiercely? Their story begins in the late 500's. The century in which Justinian lived was also the century in which the prophet Muhammad was born in Arabia.

Arab culture arose in the desert.

The Arabian peninsula stretches 1,400 miles north to south along the Red Sea, the sea that separates Arabia from Africa. The peninsula measures 1,250 miles from east to west at its southern edge. To the traveler, its deserts seem to stretch on forever under a blue sky and merciless sun.

The nomads who lived on this desert were called Bedouin (BEHD-oo-ihn). They slept in tents made from camels' hide and drank camel milk. Mounted on camels, Bedouin traveled between widely scattered oases and trading centers. During much of the year, Bedouin routinely raided one another's camps and caravans. However, certain times were considered holy, for making pilgrimages to a sacred shrine in Mecca.

Mecca was the largest of several towns near the western coast of Arabia. A few generations earlier, these town dwellers had themselves been Bedouin, but by the late 500's, they had left the Bedouin life behind. The leading Meccans were wealthy merchants. Travelers to Mecca brought both goods and ideas from the surrounding Roman, Byzantine, and Persian empires.

Before Muhammad, the Bedouins and the townspeople worshiped hundreds of gods and spirits. Spirits called *jinn* were thought to reside in rocks and other natural objects. Mecca was the home of the most sacred of these rocks. The Black Stone of Mecca was (and still is) embedded within the wall of a shrine called the Kaaba (KAH-uh-buh), which in Arabic means "cube." Besides the Black Stone, the Kaaba contained idols representing 360 gods, including one deity called Allah.

This shrine made Mecca an important religious center. Pilgrims flocked to it during the holy months. In this city, around the year 570, Muhammad was born.

Muhammad taught monotheism.

Muhammad was born into a minor branch of a powerful Meccan family. Orphaned at the age of six, the boy was raised by his grandfather and uncle. He received little schooling and probably never learned to read or write. (Even in well-to-do Arabian families, literacy was unusual.) Muhammad became a trader and business manager for Khadya (KAHD-yuh), a wealthy businesswoman 15 years older than he. When Muhammad was 25, he and Khadya married. It was both a good marriage and a good business partnership.

Muhammad had traveled to Syria as Khadya's business agent. There he may have talked with Byzantine Christians and learned about their religion. Communities of Jews were settled in the Arab towns. Both groups were monotheists. A few Arab holy men, known as *hanifs*, had already turned to the worship of one god.

Muhammad took great interest in religion and often spent time alone in prayer and meditation. At the age of 40, Muhammad's life was changed overnight by a vision that came to him while he meditated in a cave outside Mecca. His description was recorded by a follower:

While I was asleep, with a coverlet of silk brocade whereon was some writing, the angel Gabriel appeared to me and said, "Read!" I said, "I do not read." He pressed me with the coverlets so tightly that I thought it was death. Then he let me go, and said, "Read!" ... So I read aloud, and he departed from me at last ... I went forth until, when I was midway on the mountain, I heard a voice from heaven saying, "O Muhammad! Thou art the messenger of God, and I am Gabriel."

Muhammad had other visions in which the angel Gabriel again appeared with messages from Allah (the Arabic word for *God*). Who was Allah? Muhammad believed the messages came from the same God worshiped by Christians and Jews. After much soul searching, Muhammad finally became convinced that he was indeed the last and greatest of the prophets. Khadya and several close friends and relatives were his first followers.

By 613, Muhammad began to preach publicly in Mecca. At first, he had little success. Many Meccans thought his revolutionary ideas were bad for business. They feared that Mecca would lose its position as a pilgrimage center if people accepted Muhammad's beliefs. Some of his followers were stoned in the streets.

The Hegira marked a turning point.

Facing such hostility, Muhammad decided to leave Mecca. In 622, he fled to the town of Medina (muh-DEE-nuh), taking a little band of followers with him. This escape became known as the *Hegira* (hih-JYE-ruh), Arabic for "flight."

The Hegira marked a turning point for Muhammad. In Medina, he attracted many devoted followers. He also won great political influence. Muhammad's new religion became known as *Islam*, which means "surrender to God." Believers became known as *Muslims*, "the surrendering ones." On the Muslim calendar, the year of the Hegira became the year 1, the first year of the Islamic era.

From Medina, Muhammad led raids against Meccan caravans. Later, his armies completely defeated the Meccans. Such victories increased the prestige of Islam. Within ten years, almost all Bedouin had accepted Islam as their faith. In 630, the prophet and 10,000 followers entered Mecca in triumph. Muhammad went to the Kaaba and exultantly declared, "Truth has come and falsehood has vanished." Then, he destroyed the idols in the Kaaba, allowing only the Black Stone to remain. Muhammad died only two years later at the age of 62.

Pilgrims surround the Kaaba in Mecca. The towers in the background are minarets from which muezzins call Muslims to prayer.

The Koran is Islam's holy book.

While Muhammad lived, his followers had listened to his prayers and teachings. The Arabs had a long tradition of oral poetry, and they memorized and recited his words over and over. Muslims who were literate wrote them on scraps of parchment and even on palm leaves. Soon after the prophet's death, a new leader named Abu-Bakr ordered all the words of Muhammad to be gathered into a book. This book is the Koran (koh-RAHN), the holy book of Islam.

The Koran is about the same length as the Christians' New Testament. Its 114 *suras* (chapters) are arranged according to length, not subject. The longest sura comes first, and the shortest comes last.

The Koran was written in Arabic, and only the Arabic version was considered by Muslims to be the true word of God. Only Arabic could be used in worship. Because of this rule, the Arabic language spread widely in the Middle East and North Africa. Wherever Islamic conquerors carried the Koran, Arabic became the language of scholars and poets.

Because their religious art could show no figures of people or animals, Muslims decorated copies of the Koran with fine calligraphy.

The rules of Islam regulated life.

To be a Muslim was both simple and demanding. Muhammad's teachings set forth strict guidelines for right living. Every believer was expected to carry out five duties. These duties were known as the Five Pillars of Islam.

1. *Faith* To become a Muslim, a person had to make a statement of faith: "I testify there is no god but God, and Muhammad is His Prophet."
2. *Prayer* Every day, sleeping Muslims awoke at dawn to the sound of a *muezzin* (myoo-EZ-uhn), or crier, calling them to prayer. Their first morning chore was to purify themselves for prayer. They washed their hands and arms up to the elbow, their feet up to the ankles. They used water if it was available, but the Bedouin of the desert washed themselves with sand. Muslims were required to pray five times daily. Each time, they removed their shoes, turned to face the holy city of Mecca, lay flat on the ground, and recited a formal prayer either silently or in a low voice.

3. *Alms* Muhammad strictly commanded the faithful to give a portion of their wealth as alms to help the needy.
4. *Fasting* For one full month—the holy month of Ramadan (RAM-uh-DAHN)—Muslims were to eat nothing and drink nothing between sunrise and sunset. Only after sunset could families joyfully sit down together for a meal.
5. *Pilgrimage* Once in a lifetime, any Muslim who could afford the journey was expected to make a pilgrimage to Mecca. For many, this involved a grueling journey across mountains, deserts, and seas.

Along with the Five Pillars, the Koran also established other customs, morals, and laws for Islamic society. Believers were not to eat ham or pork. Believers were forbidden to drink wine or other intoxicating beverages. A man was allowed to marry as many as four wives, but only if he could support them all equally well. Marriage with unbelievers was forbidden. Many such rules regulated daily life for Muslims.

Friday afternoon was set aside for communal worship and prayer. Muslims gathered in the local mosque and prayed in unison, facing Mecca. One person led the prayers in the mosque, but he was not a priest in the Christian sense. Unlike many other religions, Islam had no formal priesthood. Women were sometimes prayer leaders for other women, but few women attended services in a mosque. In Islamic society, women and men led very separate lives.

Muhammad taught that there would be a Day of Judgment, at which time those who followed Islam's law would be rewarded. They would be welcomed into paradise, described by the Koran as a fabulous garden. There believers would bask forever, dressed in silk and drinking from rivers of milk and honey. Unbelievers and Muslims who shirked their religious duties faced eternal punishment. On the Day of Judgment, said the Koran, they would be cast into hell to wear shoes of fire, eat filth, and drink boiling water forever.

Islam expanded east and west.

In 732, exactly 100 years after Muhammad's death, Muslim armies from Spain crossed the Pyrenees into southwestern France. There, at the Battle of Tours, they were defeated by a Christian army commanded by the Frankish leader, Charles

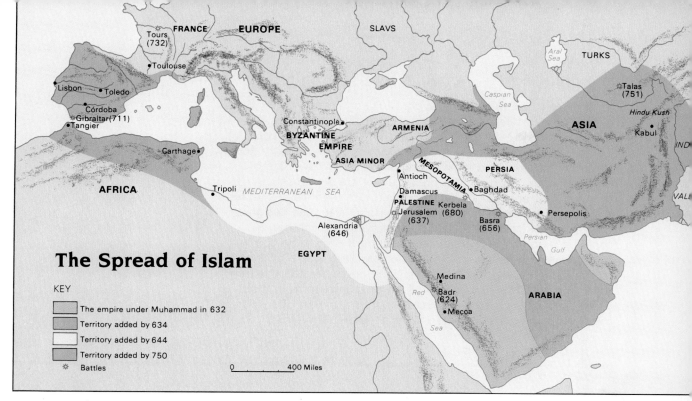

The Spread of Islam

KEY

- The empire under Muhammad in 632
- Territory added by 634
- Territory added by 644
- Territory added by 750
- ❄ Battles

0 _____ 400 Miles

Map Study

By what year had the Muslims won control of each of the following cities?
(a) Mecca (b) Alexandria (c) Tripoli (d) Kabul (e) Toledo (f) Antioch
What was the northernmost battle that Muslim armies fought in Europe?

Martel. As the crow flies, the Muslims were then 2,500 miles from Mecca. Their advance into Europe was stopped at Tours. But consider how far they had already come.

By 732, Muslim Arabs controlled the Iberian peninsula (Spain and Portugal), the land of the Carthaginians (North Africa), the land of the ancient pharaohs (Egypt), the holy land of the Jews and Christians (Palestine), the land of the ancient Babylonians (Mesopotamia), the land of the once great Persian empire, the land of northwestern India, and of course their own vast land, Arabia. They had conquered more territory than the Romans and all in one century.

Reasons for conquest How did they do it, and why? Several factors help explain the blinding speed with which Muslim armies cut down their foes and spread their faith from India to Spain.

First, the Arabs were passionate in their new faith. The Koran taught that wars fought for God were just. A warrior killed in a **jihad** (jih-HAHD), or holy war, was promised immediate entry into paradise. With this belief, Muslims rushed fearlessly into battle.

Second, the arid Arabian peninsula was badly overpopulated in the 600's. Arab armies were filled with warriors eager to move into more bountiful lands. As new converts accepted Islam, they swelled its armies still more.

Third, resistance was weak. The Byzantine and Persian empires had been fighting each other for centuries. Now they were both exhausted.

Results of conquest The Arabs proved tolerant rulers. They offered their subjects three choices: convert to Islam, pay a reasonable tax, or die. The first two choices were by far the most popular.

As Islam spread, Muslim society changed. Muhammad had taught that all Muslims were equal in the eyes of God. However, as Arab armies conquered new lands, people who were not Arabs began to accept Islam. Gradually, Islamic society came to have two classes: an upper class of Arab Muslims and a second class of non-Arab Muslims.

Christians, Jews, and Zoroastrians ranked below both Muslim groups. These groups paid a tax to avoid converting to Islam. (Indeed, their taxes supported the empire.) All three groups formed important communities within the cities of the

177

Daily Life · *Prayer Rugs*

The one piece of art that every Muslim owned was a small, wonderfully patterned carpet called a prayer rug. On this rug the worshiper knelt five times a day to pray. For Persians and Turks, carpet making was both an industry and an art form. A skilled weaver could tie knots at the rate of 900 per hour. Even so, the finest rugs were so densely knotted that an hour's work produced less than three square inches of rug. Ordinary rugs came in many elaborate designs, but prayer rugs followed a particular pattern. Each had a pointed arch in the middle, representing the prayer niche in a mosque. Woven into the border of each rug was a design of flowers, leaves, and vines. Muslims never created pictures of Muhammad or any other human or animal form in their religious art. Such pictures were thought to be an offense to God, who alone can create a living creature. Therefore, weavers used only abstract patterns.

Islamic empire. At least in the early years of the empire, Muslims treated both Jews and Christians with respect because they were also monotheists.

The building of an empire changed Islamic society. No longer was everyone under Muslim rule an Arab or even a believer in Islam. As time went by, the lands under Islamic rule became less a community of believers and more like other empires of history.

Caliphs ruled the Islamic empire.

In Muhammad's last years, he had been a political ruler as well as a religious leader. The leaders who followed him were called **caliphs** (KAY-lihfs), meaning "successors to the prophet." They too had both political and religious power.

The orthodox caliphate (632–661) The first four caliphs were men who had known Muhammad personally, either as friends or relatives. Under their leadership, Islam's wars of conquest were launched. The time in which they ruled is known as the orthodox caliphate.

The first caliph was Abu-Bakr, who ordered the writing of the Koran. The second was Omar, Islam's greatest conqueror. In 636, Syria fell before his fierce Bedouin warriors. We have seen how he entered Jerusalem in 637. By the time of his death in 644, Omar had also won control of Egypt and most of Persia.

Violence plagued the caliphs. Omar was stabbed to death by a Christian slave in 644. The next caliph, Uthman, was murdered by rebel Muslims in 656. Ali, the last of the orthodox caliphs, was also assassinated in 661. These murders sowed the seeds for later civil war and splits within Islam.

The Umayyad caliphate (661–750) With the death of Ali, the office of caliph passed to a new family, the Umayyads (oo-MYE-yads). In their rise to power, however, the Umayyads killed a rival, Husayn, who was Muhammad's grandson. The sin of having killed the prophet's grandson was later to haunt the Umayyad rulers.

The Umayyads continued the wars of conquest. It was under their rule that Arab fleets attacked Constantinople, but their hopes were thwarted by Greek fire. The Umayyad caliphs had much greater success elsewhere. Their armies conquered North Africa and converted the Berber tribes there to Islam. The fierce Berbers then helped the Arabs invade Spain in 711. By 718, Muslim armies had conquered Spain. From Spain, the forces of Islam swept into France but were turned back at Tours in 732. To the east, meanwhile, other Arab armies pushed the borders of the empire out to the Indus River valley. From Asia across Africa into Europe, the Islamic empire stretched over 5,000 miles — about 2,000 miles farther than the distance across the continental United States.

The Umayyads were able rulers and administered their vast empire carefully. However, many Muslims never forgave the death of Husayn. Other Muslims called the luxury of the Umayyad royal court sinful. A rebellion broke out against the Umayyads. In 750, the last Umayyad caliph was killed, and so were 80 other members of the family.

The only survivor of the Umayyad family escaped to Spain. There he established his own separate Islamic kingdom.

The Abbasid caliphate (750–1055) The leader of the revolt against the Umayyads was descended from Abbas, an uncle of Muhammad. The new rulers called themselves the Abbasid (uh-BAS-ihd) dynasty, emphasizing the link to the prophet.

The greatest support for the Abbasids came from Persia. Most Persians had accepted Islam. As converts, however, they were still second-class citizens under the Umayyads. With Persia's own proud history of empire, Persians resented the Arab ruling class. The Abbasids promised a return to the early Islamic idea of equality among believers. Yet going back to the past was impossible. Islam and its followers had changed irrevocably in the years since Muhammad's death.

Religious differences split Islam.

By the time of the Abbasids, Islam was no longer a united religion. The killing of Husayn, which helped cause the fall of the Umayyads, also had religious consequences. Muslims who believed that Husayn had been the rightful caliph became known as Shi'ites (SHEE-ytes). The movement began as a political split, but it became a religious one as well. The Shi'ites were especially strong in what is now Iraq.

Shi'ites denied the authority of the Umayyad caliphs and helped the Abbasids win power. The Abbasids, however, refused to tolerate the Shi'ites and sometimes persecuted them. Over the years, hostility increased between the Shi'ites and the Sunni (or orthodox) Muslims.

Baghdad rivaled Constantinople.

Because Persia was the base of Abbasid strength, the Abbasids moved their capital eastward, closer to the heart of the old Persian empire. On the western bank of the Tigris River, they built the city of Baghdad (BAG-dad), as opulent and glittering as Constantinople. Baghdad became the center of Muslim civilization during its golden age.

The Round City Picture three round walls, one inside the other, encircling a perfectly round city. This was Baghdad. At the very center of the inner circle was the famous Green Dome of the caliph's palace. Four broad avenues thrust into the heart of circular Baghdad, carving the city into four equal quarters. Everything in the round city pointed toward and revolved around the caliph's palace.

Under the Green Dome was a grand throne room. There the caliph awaited his visitors behind an ornate curtain, which was drawn with a flourish. Standing behind the caliph's throne was a grim-faced soldier with a sword always drawn and sharpened. Thus, a visitor who displeased the caliph could be beheaded on the spot.

Wealth from trade Between the middle wall and the palace wall lay Baghdad's main business district. Along the four major avenues, merchants tempted passersby with Arabian perfumes, Syrian glassware, Chinese silks, and Indian silver and rubies. There were also swords from Russia, leather goods from Spain, and slaves from Africa and Scandinavia.

By the year 1000, perhaps 100,000 people lived in Baghdad. Their wealth, like the wealth of Constantinople's citizens, was the result of their city's location. The chief caravan routes from India and China passed through Baghdad. Ships from Arabia and India came to the city too. They sailed from the Persian Gulf up the Tigris River to Baghdad's wharves.

To encourage the flow of trade, Muslim money changers set up banks in cities throughout their far-flung empire. Banks offered letters of credit to merchants. Such a letter of credit was called a *sakk*. A merchant with a sakk from a bank in Baghdad could exchange it for cash at a bank in Mecca or in any other major city within the empire. In Europe, the word *sakk* was pronounced "check." Thus the practice of using checks dates back to the Islamic empire.

Arts and sciences flourished.

Under the Abbasids, the Islamic empire enjoyed a brief but brilliant golden age in arts and sciences. The Islamic empire reached the height of its

Muslim astronomers studied the stars at the royal observatory (left). Below is an Arabic astrolabe.

power and prosperity in the reign of Harun ar-Rashid (hah-**ROON** uh-rah-**SHEED**), who ruled from 786 to 809.

Like Hellenistic civilization, Islamic culture was enriched by many groups. The empire included a rich blend of cultures. Christians, Jews, and Zoroastrians played a large part in the empire's intellectual achievements. Yet the Islamic faith and the Arabic language were the bonds that held the empire together. Arabic became the language of scholarship for all who lived within the empire, much as Latin had been for the Romans and as Greek was for the Byzantines.

Islamic science Science thrived in the Islamic empire as it had in Hellenistic times. Scholars were inspired by ancient Greek sources—the ideas of Aristotle and Plato, the geometry of Euclid, and the medical knowledge of Galen. Manuscripts from many lands were brought back to Baghdad's House of Wisdom, a huge library where scholars translated Greek texts into Arabic. After mastering the Greek sources, Muslim scientists went on to make their own discoveries and inventions.

These were some of their most notable works:

First chemical laboratories The first chemists to work in laboratories were Islamic alchemists (**AL**-kuh-mihsts), who tried to turn ordinary metals into gold. It was an impossible task, but as they worked, alchemists found ways to separate one chemical compound from another.

Treatment of disease The greatest names in Islamic medicine were Rhazes (rah-**ZEES**), and Avicenna (**AV**-ih-**SEN**-uh). Rhazes (850–923) wrote more than 100 treatises on medicine. The most famous of these told doctors how to diagnose smallpox and treat it before the patient's condition became hopeless. Avicenna (980–1037) wrote a five-volume encyclopedia that guided doctors of Europe and Southwest Asia for six centuries.

Footnote to History

The alchemists' name for any distilled substance was *alkuhl,* from which comes our word *alcohol.*

Islamic doctors also excelled in the preparation of medicines.

Use of the astrolabe First used by ancient Greeks, the astrolabe was rediscovered and improved by Islamic astronomers. A sea captain or caravan leader adjusted the pointer on its brass disk to chart the position of a star, which is the most reliable way to find one's position on Earth.

Mathematics One of Islam's many mathematical wizards was named Al-Khwarizmi (al-KWAH-rihz-MEE). He wrote a textbook in the 800's explaining "the art of bringing together unknowns to match a known quantity." He called this technique *al-jabr*. We call it algebra.

Without the concept of zero, higher mathematics is almost impossible. Neither the Greeks nor Romans had a zero in their number system. The Hindus of India first used a number system based on sets of ten and a symbol for zero. The Muslims adopted the system, and from them it spread to western Europe. We therefore speak today of using Arabic numerals.

Islamic literature The science and mathematics of Islam can be appreciated by people of any culture. However, only people who understand Arabic can fully appreciate its literature. The Arabs considered poetry their greatest art. The thousands of poems created during Islam's golden age were meant to be sung and recited aloud in Arabic. Most often, poets sang of war or of romantic love. The goal of the Arab poets was to compress as much meaning and eloquence as possible into very few words.

Among the Islamic writers was the Persian poet and astronomer, Omar Khayyám (kye-AHM). He lived and wrote around 1100, as Islam's golden age was beginning to fade. Omar Khayyám is best known for a collection of four-line poems called the *Rubáiyát* (ROO-be-aht). This famous stanza shows how the poet celebrated the fleeting pleasures of life:

A Book of Verses underneath the Bough,
A Jug of Wine, a Loaf of Bread—and Thou
Beside me singing in the Wilderness—
Oh, Wilderness were Paradise enow!

Islamic writers produced a great variety of literature. For example, the work known in English as *The Arabian Nights* is a collection of folktales that includes the tale of Aladdin's magic lamp and the stories of Sinbad the Sailor. Islamic scholars also filled volumes on history, geography, law, philosophy, and religion. To devout Muslims, of course, the Koran remains the supreme achievement of Islamic literature.

Islamic architecture Throughout their empire, the Muslims built beautiful mosques. The greatest of these buildings stood in Jerusalem. In 691, a caliph ordered a mosque built over the rock from which Muhammad was believed to have ascended into paradise—the rock that Byzantines had once used for a garbage dump. This mosque became known as the Dome of the Rock because its golden dome was its most striking and beautiful feature. The dome stands 70 feet above the sacred rock. Circling around the dome are bands of black inscribed with a swirling golden script. It is the Arabic script with verses from the Koran.

Below the dome, framed by a circle of marble columns, is the sacred rock itself. Muslim worshipers cannot walk on it—not until the Day of Judgment, when they expect saved souls to be brought to this spot and lifted to paradise. Worshipers spread their prayer rugs at the very edge of the walled-off rock and lie down to pray facing, as always, toward Mecca.

Section Review 2

Define: (a) pilgrimage, (b) jihad, (c) caliph, (d) alchemist, (e) astrolabe
Identify: (a) Arabia, (b) Bedouin, (c) Mecca, (d) Kaaba, (e) Muhammad, (f) Allah, (g) Khadya, (h) Medina, (i) Muslims, (j) Islam, (k) Koran, (l) Hegira, (m) Ramadan
Answer:
1. Briefly describe how Muhammad became a religious teacher.
2. Why is the Hegira important to Islam?
3. What are the Five Pillars of Islam?
4. (a) What lands did the Islamic empire control by 732? (b) Give three reasons for the rapid spread of the empire.
5. Name the three groups of leaders who ruled the Islamic empire between 632 and 1055, and briefly describe each period.
6. How did Islam split into Shi'ites and Sunnis?

Critical Thinking
7. How did the Byzantine and Islamic empires both combine political and religious power?

The empires influenced Slavs and Turks. 3

Around the year 800, both the Islamic and the Byzantine empires were strong and stable. The Byzantines had lost much land to the Muslims, but Constantinople still ruled Asia Minor, Greece, and Sicily. At the same time, the giant empire of the Abbasids stretched from Gibraltar to the Indus River valley.

Within both the Byzantine and Islamic empires, the seeds of future trouble had already been sown. Internal divisions weakened the two empires. Enemy attacks eventually destroyed them.

In the meanwhile, the two empires profoundly influenced two groups of invaders—the Slavs and the Turks. The aging Byzantine empire had a powerful cultural impact on the Slavs. Eventually, several Slavic peoples, especially the Russians, adopted the Byzantine form of Christianity. The Turks, on the other hand, became Muslims even while they fought the armies of the Islamic empire.

Byzantine culture influenced the Slavic peoples.

In the 700's, while the Arabs threatened Byzantium from the south, the Slavs struck from the north. The Slavic people were groups of nomads who had migrated into eastern Europe from the plains of Asia. Each group had its own culture, but all spoke related languages. In the 700's and 800's, these groups were perpetually at war with the Byzantines, fighting for possession of the Balkan peninsula and land around the Black Sea.

Conversion of the Slavs While the Slavic rulers coveted Constantinople's wealth and territory, they also admired its civilization. Unlike the Arabs, the Slavs were persuaded to become Christian. Between 850 and 900, Byzantine missionaries began to win Slavic converts. Among the wisest and most statesmanlike of these missionaries was a monk named Cyril (SIHR-uhl). He and other missionaries invented an alphabet for the Slavic languages, so that Slavs could read the Bible in their own tongue. In honor of Cyril, this system of writing is known as the Cyrillic (suh-RIHL-ik) alphabet. It is still used in some Slavic countries.

The Russian kingdom To the north of the Black Sea, a group of Slavs known as Russians lived in the forests south of the Baltic Sea. The story of Russia's origins comes from the *Primary Chronicle*, an account written around 1050 by an anonymous group of Russian monks who included in their story as much legend as fact.

According to this chronicle, the first Russians were a band of hardy hunters from Scandinavia. They migrated south into forestlands occupied by bands of Slavs. The Slavs called these Scandinavians *Rus* (roos). In 862, says the *Primary Chronicle*, the Slavs invited the Rus to become their protectors and rulers. Thus, 862 is the traditional date for the founding of Russia.

The first Russian prince had a decidedly Scandinavian name: Rurik. His capital city, Novgorod (NAHV-guh-rahd), lay far to the north near the border of present-day Finland. Soon, however, Russian princes moved south to Kiev (KEE-yef), a city better placed for shipping furs, amber, slaves, and honey downriver to Constantinople.

From the *Primary Chronicle* comes a charming—and perhaps true—story of how Kievan Russia was converted to Christianity. Princess Olga, who ruled Kiev from 945 to 955, was the first Russian ruler to become a Christian. However, she did not make Christianity the official religion of her kingdom. In 989, the ruler of Kiev was Vladimir (VLAHD-uh-meer), Olga's grandson. He sent envoys to investigate both Roman and Byzantine Christianity. They found the churches of barbaric Germany drab. Soon afterwards, in Constantinople, the envoys visited Hagia Sophia, the magnificent cathedral built by Justinian (page 172). Stunned by the beauty of its golden mosaics, they reported:

> Then we went on to Greece [Byzantium], and the Greeks led us to the buildings where they worship their God, and we knew not whether we were in heaven or on earth. For on earth there is no such splendor or such beauty, and we are at a loss how to describe it. We only know that God dwells there among men.

Vladimir therefore chose to be a Christian in the Byzantine manner, not in the Roman manner. In 989, he commanded his subjects to go to the

Dnieper River for baptism. Thus, Russians looked to Constantinople, not Rome, for religious leadership. This choice would have profound consequences for Russia in years to come, as it cut off the kingdom from western Europe.

The Russian kingdom prospered from its ties to Byzantium. By the year 1000, Kiev had a population of 8,000, making it the equal of Paris, the largest city of western Europe at that time. Kiev's gold-domed churches imitated those of Constantinople. Its mosaics too were much like those found in "The City." The pattern of Russian culture—Slavic in language, Byzantine in style—was established for centuries to come.

The Turks struck from the east.

Between the years 1000 and 1100, both the Byzantine empire and the Islamic empire faced new dangers. Chief among them were the ferocious attacks of a nomadic people from central Asia, the Turks.

The breakup of the Islamic empire The Islamic empire had already lost much of its territory. Spain broke away from the Islamic empire in 756, when the Abbasids came to power. After moving their capital east to Baghdad, the Abbasids lost other parts of their empire in the west—Morocco in 788 and Tunisia in 800. After the death of Harun ar-Rashid in 809, parts of Persia also broke away. Then, in 868, the Abbasids lost control of Egypt.

In 945, a local Persian ruler took over Baghdad and ended the caliph's political power. Although the caliph was still the religious leader of Islam, a **sultan** now held all political power. The power of the Abbasids was broken.

Seljuk Turks In this time of weakness and division, a formidable enemy swept out of Asia. On the flat grasslands between the Black and Caspian seas, nomadic Turks grazed their horses and practiced the art of war. Just as Roman emperors had used barbarians in their armies, caliphs in the 800's used the Turks. Finally, just as Rome fell to the barbarians, Baghdad fell to the Turks.

Large numbers of Turks moved into the Islamic empire around 970. This first group of migrating Turks is known as the Seljuk (SEL-jook) Turks, after the family that led them. By 1000, they had converted to Islam, joining the Sunni branch. Conversion did not stop them, however, from

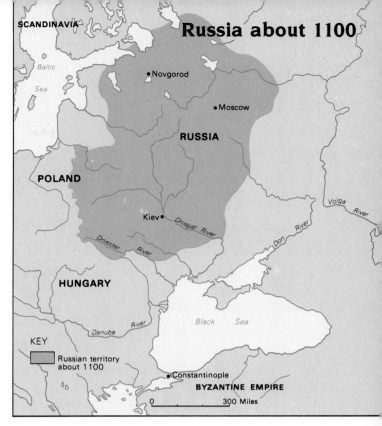

Russia about 1100

Map Study

By what water route would travelers and traders from Kiev have reached Constantinople?

warring with other Muslims. In 1055, they captured Baghdad. Throughout the empire, Turks now replaced Arabs as the ruling class.

Twenty years later, the Seljuk sultans spearheaded a mighty drive against the Byzantine empire. In 1071, at the Battle of Manzikert, the Turks overwhelmed the Byzantines. Within ten years, the Seljuk Turks occupied all of Asia Minor, the eastern heartland of Byzantium. It was a staggering blow to the Byzantines, for even the mighty armies of the Arabs had never come so close to Constantinople by land.

Constantinople fell to the Turks.

After the Battle of Manzikert, the Byzantine empire grew weaker and weaker. Cities in Europe began to take over much of the trade that Constantinople had once controlled.

By 1400, the Byzantine empire was little more than the city of Constantinople itself. All the rest of the empire had fallen to a new branch of Turks, the Ottomans. The Ottoman sultan sent

183

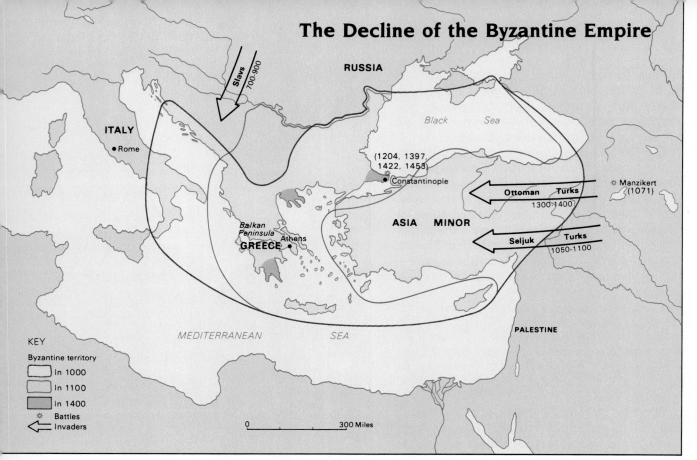

The Decline of the Byzantine Empire

RUSSIA

Slavs 700-900

Black Sea

ITALY
• Rome

(1204, 1397, 1422, 1453)
☼ Constantinople

Ottoman Turks
1300-1400

☼ Manzikert (1071)

Balkan Peninsula
Athens
GREECE •

ASIA MINOR

Seljuk Turks
1050-1100

MEDITERRANEAN SEA

PALESTINE

KEY
Byzantine territory
In 1000
In 1100
In 1400
☼ Battles
Invaders

0 ____ 300 Miles

Map Study
Where was the westernmost boundary of the empire in the year 1000? What territory did the empire control by 1400?

a message to the Byzantine emperor: "Close the gates of the city and rule within it, for I own everything outside the walls." Turkish armies besieged the city in 1397, in 1422, and finally in 1453. By the last siege, the Byzantine soldiers inside the city were outnumbered ten to one by the Turks around their walls.

The last Byzantine emperor, Constantine XI, sent a final plea for peace to the Turkish sultan, 23-year-old Muhammad II. The emperor concluded his letter:

> If [God] should inspire you with a desire for peace, I shall be only too happy. However, I release you from all your oaths and treaties with me, and, closing the gates of my capital, I will defend my people to the last drop of my blood.

In May 1453, the Turks captured the city. Constantine XI died fighting. More than 1100 years after its founding, the empire of Constantinople came to an end.

Section Review 3

Define: sultan,
Identify: (a) Slavs, (b) Cyril, (c) Rus, (d) Kiev, (e) Vladimir, (f) Turks
Answer:
1. How did the invention of the Cyrillic alphabet help convert the Slavs to Christianity?
2. How did the Russian kingdom begin?
3. What were the long-lasting results of Vladimir's choice of Orthodox Christianity?
4. (a) What conquests did the Seljuk Turks make? (b) The Ottoman Turks?

Critical Thinking
5. The Seljuk Turks and the Ottoman Turks came from central Asia, where they had lived as nomads. (a) What advantages might nomads have in fighting against the Byzantine and Islamic empires? (b) What advantages might the empires have had? (c) Why were the nomads successful?

Chapter Review 8

Summary

1. Constantinople ruled an eastern empire. Byzantine emperors claimed both political and religious authority. The most outstanding ruler was Justinian, who tried to restore the glories of the Roman past. He is most noted for his code of laws. After his death, the empire was threatened by revolts, religious quarrels, and invasions. The Roman and Byzantine branches of the Christian Church grew apart and eventually split.

2. A new faith spread from Arabia. Late in the 500's, Muhammad proclaimed the faith of Islam. Gradually, he gained many followers. After his death, Muslim warriors created an empire that spread from Spain in the west to the Indus River valley in the east. Throughout the empire, Muslims followed the same religious duties, which included prayer, fasting, almsgiving, and pilgrimage.

3. The empires influenced Slavs and Turks. By the year 800, both the Byzantine and Islamic empires faced internal and external dangers. The Byzantine empire came under frequent attack from the Slavs, who converted to Christianity, and the Muslims. The Islamic empire was weakened by religious conflict. Baghdad fell to the Seljuk Turks in 1055. Constantinople fell to the Ottoman Turks in 1453.

Reviewing the Facts

1. Define the following terms:
   a. excommunicate   d. jihad
   b. heretic   e. caliph
   c. patriarch   f. sultan
2. Explain the importance of each of the following names, dates, places, or terms:
   a. Constantinople   i. Baghdad
   b. Justinian   j. Slavs
   c. Code of Justinian   k. Kiev
   d. Bedouin   l. Vladimir
   e. Mecca   m. 1054
   f. Muhammad   n. Seljuk Turks
   g. 622   o. Ottoman Turks
   h. Koran   p. 1453
3. Name at least three issues that led to the break between the Roman and Byzantine churches in the year 1054.
4. Explain the importance of each of the following to the development of Islam. (a) Hegira (b) Koran (c) Five Pillars of Islam (d) Shi'ites
5. (a) How did the Umayyad and Abbasid caliphates differ? (b) What were the achievements of each caliphate?
6. (a) How did Byzantine culture influence Slavs? (b) How did the Islamic empire influence Turks?

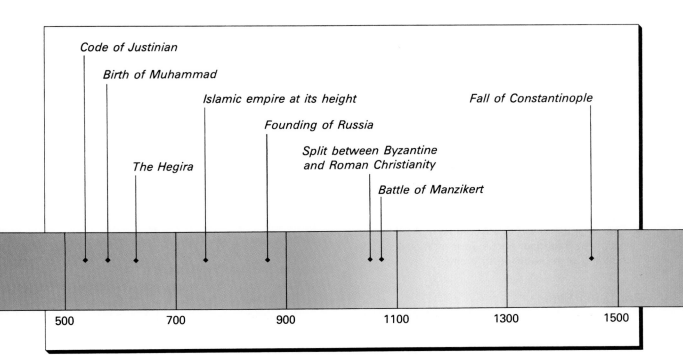

Code of Justinian

Birth of Muhammad

Islamic empire at its height

Founding of Russia

Split between Byzantine and Roman Christianity

Fall of Constantinople

The Hegira

Battle of Manzikert

500   700   900   1100   1300   1500

Thinking about History

1. What place did Christians and Jews have in Muslim society during the Islamic empire? Explain why Muslims tended to show toleration toward those groups but not toward polytheists.
2. Compare Baghdad, Constantinople, and Kiev. What made each a center for trade? Think of other cities about which you have read. Is trade an essential ingredient to city life? Explain.
3. Justinian's code of laws consists of laws drawn up by a government. Islamic law, on the other hand, developed out of religious teachings. What advantages might there be to each type of law? What problems might arise with each?
4. In both the Byzantine and Islamic empires, scholars worked to preserve writings from the past. Why do you think it is important to keep writings from the past? Why would scholars have made copies of books even when they disagreed with their contents?
5. During the rule of Justinian, the imperial palace at Constantinople employed 20,000 people. Today, the executive branch of the United States government employs approximately 2,800,000 people. Why do governments need such large work forces? What kinds of jobs do people working in government do?

Writing and Speaking about History

1. Identify the reasons for the spread of Islam in the 600's and 700's. From this list of reasons, develop a thesis statement about the spread of Islam with the major facts to support it.
2. Write a statement that supports the idea of the jihad from the point of view of a Muslim living in the 600's.
3. Write five questions to be submitted either to Justinian or Omar on the growth and development of an empire. Choose one of the five questions and write an appropriate response.
4. Plan an interview with Justinian and the Abbasid caliph of Baghdad. Focus your interview on the building or remodeling of a city.

Practicing Skills

1. The city of Kiev had a population of about 8,000 people in the year 1000. The city of Baghdad had a population of about 100,000 in the same year. What factors account for the difference?
2. Use an almanac or a statistical abstract to find the current populations of Baghdad and Kiev. How do these figures compare with the ones given above for the year 1000?
3. (a) Use the time line on page 185 to calculate about how many years passed between the birth of Muhammad and the height of the Islamic empire. (b) Compare this figure with the number of years that passed between the founding of the Roman republic and Roman domination in the Mediterranean (page 138).
4. What part of the Byzantine empire under Justinian (page 169) became part of the Islamic empire in 750 (page 177)?
5. Find out what countries are part of the Middle East today. Using a world map as a reference, draw in and label the countries of the Middle East on an outline map of the region. Compare your map to the one of the Islamic empire on page 177. Which countries in the Middle East today were part of the Islamic empire in 750? What countries outside the Middle East were once under Islamic control?

Investigating History

1. Find out about mosaic art, which was used by both the Byzantines and the Muslims. What are some examples of Byzantine and Islamic mosaics? How are mosaics used today?
2. Plan a tour to places of interest in this chapter. For each place, write a short description telling why it is included on the tour, and note some of the things to see (for example, Hagia Sophia in Constantinople, or Baghdad's bazaar). You may want to include a map of the tour to go along with your description.
3. Find out what language is most widely spoken in the Middle East today. In what countries are Hebrew and Persian the major languages? What explanations can you find for these exceptions?

Decision Making in History

What factors probably influenced Justinian's decision to reconquer the western territory of the Roman empire. Given the outcome, do you think he would make the same decision again?

The Early Middle Ages

These chessmen, made of walrus ivory, show the warlike tone of life in Europe during the barbarian invasions of the Early Middle Ages.

1. **New ways of life developed in Europe.**

2. **Charlemagne revived the idea of empire.**

3. **Vikings terrorized Europe.**

4. **Feudalism became the basis for government.**

A huge cauldron of boiling water steamed and bubbled over an outdoor hearth. Two Christian priests stood near it, preparing themselves for a terrible test. The priests had disagreed over a religious issue. They proposed to settle their quarrel by using the ordeal of boiling water. Each priest was expected to plunge his arm into the cauldron and pick up a small ring at the bottom. Afterward, their arms would be inspected, and the one whose burns healed cleanly would be declared the winner.

As a large group of spectators watched in excitement, the first priest boldly thrust his arm into the water and retrieved the ring. His hand and arm were unharmed. When the second priest tried to do the same,

187

he was badly scalded. The first priest was immediately hailed as the victor, even without the usual three-day waiting period to see how the burns healed.

Thousands of trials like this one took place all over western Europe between the years 500 and 1000. These were the years after the German-speaking barbarians destroyed the western half of the Roman empire. Throughout western Europe, Germanic customs replaced the reasoned logic of Roman laws. Trials like the one the priests used were known as trials by ordeal.

There were other kinds of ordeals besides that of boiling water. A person accused of a crime might, for example, be tried by the ordeal of cold water. In this ordeal, the accused person was bound hand and foot with a rope and then thrown into a pond. If the person's body bobbed quickly to the surface, the verdict was guilty. But if the person sank for a count of several seconds, he or she was fished out and pronounced innocent. Another method, called trial by combat, consisted of an armed fight between accuser and accused. If the accuser or the accused was a woman, she could name a warrior to fight for her. The winner was assumed to be telling the truth.

These practices were based on a simple idea. People believed that God would protect the innocent and expose the guilty. Such customs were nothing like the justice of the Romans and the Byzantines, who relied on trained judges and written laws. Trial by ordeal or combat was the rough justice of people who could neither read nor write.

In this chapter on western Europe after the fall of the Roman empire, we will visit no great cities like Constantinople or Baghdad. Europe during these years was too poor and disorganized for such grandeur. For Europeans between 500 and 1000, life was a struggle for survival.

This brutal era is known as the Early Middle Ages or the Early Medieval (meed-ee-EE-vuhl) period. People sometimes call these centuries the Dark Ages, because learning and civilization declined. Yet *Dark Ages* is a negative name and depends on one's point of view. While these times were dark ones for scholars who loved Latin learning, the Early Middle Ages were a glorious time for Germanic kings and warriors.

Civilization did indeed decline, but it did not disappear. During the grim centuries from 500 to 1000, a new kind of society gradually took shape in Europe. It had three roots: (1) the classical heritage from Rome; (2) the beliefs of the Roman Catholic Church; and (3) the customs of the various Germanic tribes. The blending of these elements eventually produced a strong, vital civilization. Before Europe became strong, however, it passed through a long period of weakness, division, poverty, and pain.

New ways of life developed in Europe. 1

By the end of the fifth century, the western half of the Roman empire had fallen to barbarians. The Visigoths held Spain, the Ostrogoths ruled Italy, the Franks controlled Gaul, and the Vandals governed North Africa. Rome's most distant province, Britannia, faced a double peril. Three fierce Germanic tribes—Angles, Saxons, and Jutes—attacked Britannia's eastern shores. At the same time, Celtic peoples—the Picts and Scots—raided Britannia from Ireland and Scotland.

Roman civilization collapsed.

Everywhere Roman civilization was under attack. This account of barbarian attacks was written in Britain around 545 by a chronicler named Gildas the Wise, but it could have been written almost anywhere in Europe:

No sooner have they [the citizens] gone back to their land than the foul hosts of the Picts and Scots land promptly from their coracles [fishing boats] . . . They seize all the northern and outlying part of the country as far as to the wall [a Roman fortification]. Upon this wall stands a timid and unwarlike garrison. The wretched citizens are pulled down from the wall and dashed to the ground by the hooked weapons of their naked foes. What shall I add? The citizens desert the high wall and their towns, and take to a flight more desperate than any before. Again the enemy pursues them, and there is a slaughter more cruel than ever.

The Barbarian Kingdoms about 500

Map Study

Compare this map with the one on page 144. What groups of people moved into the former Roman province of Gaul? What groups lived in the British Isles at this time? What groups bordered the Baltic Sea?

The collapse of trade and towns Constant warfare disrupted trade. Merchants feared pirates on sea and outlaws on land. The collapse of trade was a deathblow to cities in much of Europe.

Towns declined as Roman rule came to an end. Without the empire, there was no need for cities as centers of administration. With little trade, towns were no longer centers for business. Impoverished city dwellers left their decaying cities and drifted out into the countryside to grow their own food. The population of western Europe became overwhelmingly rural.

Loss of literacy and a common language At the same time, learning fell into a decline. The barbarians who invaded the Roman empire could not read or write. Among Roman subjects themselves, the level of learning sank sharply as more and more families left the cities for rural areas. By the year 600, priests were the only Europeans who were literate. Even their Latin was poor by classical standards.

At the height of the Roman empire, scholars from far-off Britannia had spoken the same language as Julius Caesar and Virgil. However, as German-speaking peoples joined the population, Latin began to change. Different dialects developed as new words and phrases became part of everyday speech. By the 800's, French, Spanish, Italian, and other so-called Romance (Roman-based) languages had evolved from Latin.

Personal ties replaced citizenship.

In the years of upheaval between 400 and 600, Germanic kingdoms replaced Roman provinces. The borders of those kingdoms changed constantly with the fortunes of war. The map on page 189 can give only an approximate idea of which group controlled which lands.

More important than shifting boundaries was that the whole idea of government changed. Family ties and personal loyalty, not public government or public law, bound Germanic society together. The Germanic people did not think of themselves as citizens of a state but as members of a family and followers of a particular leader.

Every Frankish, Saxon, or Visigothic chief had a band of warriors who had pledged their loyalty to him. In peacetime, these followers lived in their lord's hall. He gave them food, weapons, and treasure. In battle, warriors fought to the death at their lord's side. It was the greatest disgrace to outlive one's lord.

Although Germanic warriors would willingly die for a leader they knew, they felt no obligation to obey a king who was a stranger to them. And they certainly would not obey some official sent to collect taxes or administer justice in the name of an emperor they had never seen. This stress on personal ties made orderly government for large territories impossible.

Christianity won new followers.

While Roman roads and Roman law crumbled, there was one institution from Roman times that did not break down: the Roman Catholic Church. Throughout the Early Middle Ages, the Church acted as the strongest civilizing force in western Europe.

The work of missionaries Beginning in the 300's and 400's, many Christian missionaries traveled among the Germanic and Celtic groups that bordered the Roman empire. These missionaries risked their lives to spread their beliefs.

Among the most famous and successful was Patrick of Ireland. Patrick was born of Christian parents in Roman Britannia around 400, shortly before the Anglo-Saxon invasions. When he was 16, his village was raided by pagan Celts from Ireland, and he was captured and taken to be a slave. After six years, Patrick escaped from Ireland

to northern Gaul, where he eventually became a bishop. His greatest goal was to convert the Irish to Christianity. In 432, he returned to Ireland as a missionary. Although he was often imprisoned and threatened with death, he established Christian churches throughout the island.

The Franks under Clovis Politics often played an important part in spreading Christianity. In the late 400's, a ruthless Frankish king named Clovis (KLOH-vihs) ruled much of northern Gaul. The Franks were pagans, but Clovis's wife was a Christian who urged her husband to convert.

In 496, Clovis led his warriors into battle against another Germanic army. When the battle began going badly for Clovis, he appealed to the Christian God. "For I have called on my gods," he cried, "but I find they are far from my aid . . . Now I call on Thee. I long to believe in Thee. Only, please deliver me from my enemies." The tide of battle shifted, and the Franks triumphed. Clovis and 3,000 of his warriors asked a bishop to baptize them.

Clovis's conversion was especially welcome to the Roman Church because Catholic bishops wanted his help against other Germanic peoples. The Ostrogoths, Visigoths, and Burgundians were all Christians (and most of them were more civilized than the Franks). However, they were not Catholic Christians. Instead, many Germanic groups had chosen a branch of Christianity known as Arianism (AIR-ee-uh-NIHZ-uhm). The Roman Catholic Church considered Arians heretics. Thus, Clovis's conversion marked the beginning of a special partnership between the Frankish kingdom and the Catholic Church.

By 600, the Roman Catholic Church had succeeded in winning over many of the Germanic peoples who had moved into Rome's former lands. In many places, however, the changeover to Christianity was only on the surface. Some kings even kept two altars, one Christian and one to their earlier pagan gods. Missionaries continued to go out among pagan groups into lands that Rome had never controlled.

Benedict set rules for monasteries.

In the days of the Roman empire, bishops were the most powerful leaders of the Church. Each leading city of the empire had its own bishop. As the population in western Europe shifted away from the cities, however, the Church had to adapt to increasingly rural conditions. One effect was the growth of **monasteries**.

Monasteries were communities in which groups of Christian men or women gave up all their private possessions and lived very simply. They devoted their lives to worship and prayer. Women who followed this way of life were called nuns; they lived in nunneries or convents. Men were called monks and lived in monasteries. Like priests, monks and nuns were expected to live according to the threefold rule of poverty, chastity, and obedience.

The Benedictine Rule A monk named Benedict set a pattern for monastic living. Born about 480 in Italy, Benedict went to school in a ravaged Rome. At the age of 15, he left school and hiked up into the Sabine Hills, seeking solitude. He lived as a hermit in a cave for several years. Hearing of his holiness, a group of monks came to him and persuaded him to be their abbot (monastic leader).

Around 540, Benedict wrote a book describing a strict yet practical set of rules for monastic life. These were some of Benedict's rules:

- Once a monk enters a monastery, he is to remain there for life. Monks should not wander from one monastic house to another.
- Daily life in the monastery should follow a strict schedule. Eight times a day are set aside for prayer and worship.
- Monks should spend seven hours a day at manual labor in kitchen, field, or workshop.
- Two hours a day are reserved for reading the Bible and other Christian books.
- Monks should eat one or two meals daily, depending on the season. They may have a little wine, but no red meat.

Benedict's sister Scholastica (skuh-LAS-tik-uh) became head of a convent in which the same rules were adapted for women. Soon almost all Italian, English, and Frankish monks and nuns were living according to the Benedictine Rule.

Benedict's rules were strict but made some allowance for human frailty. Above all, they provided monks and nuns with a workable system for disciplining their lives.

The achievements of the monasteries In the Early Middle Ages, monastic communities were like islands of stability in a sea of chaos. They

Benedict blesses a monk. Behind them is Monte Cassino, the monastery Benedict founded.

were the best-governed communities anywhere in Europe because they followed an orderly, written body of rules.

Monasteries were also the most educated communities. They operated schools, maintained libraries, and copied books. In the 600's and 700's, the monasteries of Ireland and England were the leading scholarly centers of the day. Above all, the monks of these lands excelled in making beautiful copies of religious writings, decorated with ornate letters and brilliant pictures. Through the work of the monks, at least part of Rome's intellectual heritage was preserved.

Gregory I expanded papal power.

Scattered throughout western Europe, monasteries and convents showed the spreading influence of the Catholic Church. At the head of the Church stood the pope in Rome, at first a bishop like other bishops but gradually becoming the strongest single figure in the Church.

One man who greatly increased the power of the popes was Gregory I. As pope, he wore only a rough monk's robe and humbly called himself "the servant of the servants of God." Yet while Gregory was meek on his own behalf, he was mighty on behalf of the papacy.

Skilled monks at Lindisfarne, England, made this beautiful gospel about the year 700.

Born in 540, Gregory grew up during the awful days when Justinian's Byzantine armies were driving the Ostrogoths from Rome and, in the process, wrecking the city. In 568, a new group of invaders struck at northern Italy. These were the Lombards, a fierce Germanic people. Conditions in Rome had never been worse. Starving Romans foraged for clumps of grass to eat.

Gregory became pope in 590 and soon made the papacy an office of political as well as spiritual power. The Byzantine emperor was too weak to protect Rome, so Gregory dealt directly with the menacing Lombards. In 599, he persuaded them to sign a peace treaty. At the same time, Gregory's palace became the center of Roman government. He used Church revenues to raise armies, repair roads, and relieve the poor. The pope was now acting as the mayor of Rome.

Gregory worked tirelessly to bring new groups into the Church. He sent missionaries to England under the leadership of a monk named Augustine in 596. This mission spread Christianity among the Anglo-Saxon kingdoms there. Gregory also wrote two influential books. One was the *Dialogues*, a collection of simply told religious stories, full of miraculous happenings. Most new Christians in this age could not grasp abstract religious ideas, but they understood Gregory's adventurous accounts of saintly lives. The second book, *Pastoral Care*, advised bishops on carrying out their spiritual duties, especially among new converts.

All that Gregory did as pope—writing books, sending out missionaries, governing Rome—expressed a new view of the world. He ignored the political divisions between kingdoms. In his view, the entire region from Italy to England, from Spain to western Germany was his responsibility as pope. Gregory had a vision of Christendom (KRIS-uhn-duhm), a spiritual kingdom fanning out from Rome to the most distant churches. This idea of a churchly kingdom, ruled by a pope, became a central part of the Middle Ages.

Section Review 1

Define: (a) ordeal, (b) medieval, (c) literacy, (d) monastery, (e) monk, (f) abbot, (g) nun
Identify: (a) Patrick, (b) Clovis, (c) Arianism, (d) Benedict, (e) Scholastica, (f) Gregory I, (g) Lombards, (h) Christendom
Answer:
1. What were the three roots of medieval culture in western Europe?
2. Give two examples of ways civilization in western Europe declined after the fall of Rome.
3. (a) How did Christianity spread during the Early Middle Ages? (b) Why was Clovis's conversion to Christianity important?
4. (a) Describe the way of life followed in a monastery. (b) What part did Benedict play in the development of monasteries? (c) How were monasteries important to the preservation of civilization in this period?
5. What were the achievements of Gregory I?

Critical Thinking
6. (a) How did the Germanic ideas of government differ from the Roman ideas? (b) Which set of ideas is closer to those of our own time? Explain your answer.
7. Would it be correct to say that the idea of Christendom was a replacement for the Roman empire? Why or why not?

Charlemagne revived the idea of empire. 2

After the breakup of the Roman empire, petty kingdoms sprang up all over Europe. For example, England was divided into seven tiny kingdoms, some no larger than the state of Connecticut. By far the largest and strongest of Europe's kingdoms was that of the Franks in what had been the Roman province of Gaul. The foundations for this kingdom were laid by the Franks' first Christian king, Clovis. (As you have probably guessed, the modern name *France* comes from the people of the Franks. *Louis*, the name of 16 later French kings, is a softer-sounding form of Clovis.)

Clovis's descendants lost power.

In 481, when the 15-year-old Clovis became king, the Franks controlled only a small area of flat, marshy land (the present-day Netherlands) on either side of the Rhine River. By the time Clovis died in 511, he ruled most of what is now France.

The Merovingian kings Clovis and his successors are known as the Merovingian (MAIR-oh-VIHN-jee-uhn) dynasty, after a legendary ancestor, Merovech. They were also called "the long-haired kings" because long hair was a symbol of power and authority among the Franks. The Merovingians ruled for about 275 years, but those were not peaceful years.

When a Merovingian king died, his sons treated the kingdom as private property to be divided among themselves. Such divisions weakened the kingdom and often led to civil war as each son tried to seize the whole kingdom. Yet the Merovingians succeeded in keeping the idea of kingship alive.

Mayors of the palace By the year 700, the power of Merovingian kings had dwindled to almost nothing. The most powerful person in the kingdom was not the king but an official known as the *major domo* or mayor of the palace. Officially, a mayor of the palace was in charge of the royal household and estates. Unofficially, he was the power behind the throne. He commanded armies and made policy. In effect, he governed the kingdom in the king's name.

In 714, the position of mayor of the palace was held by Charles, known as *Martel* (the Hammer). Charles Martel was king in all but name. He extended the power of the Franks to the north, south, and east. He even defeated a Muslim raiding party from Spain at the Battle of Tours in 732. (This battle marked the height of Muslim conquests in Europe.) Finally, at his death, Charles Martel passed his power on to his son, Pepin the Short.

Daily Life • Stirrups and Warfare

In Merovingian times, most Frankish warriors were foot soldiers, but during the 700's, warfare changed. The stirrup came into use in Europe. (It may have been invented in India.) As a result, the technology of war changed.

More and more warriors fought on horseback. Without stirrups to brace him, a charging warrior was likely to topple off his own horse. Mounted warriors with stirrups could use heavier armor and weapons. These armored horsemen were known as **knights**. Galloping full tilt at the enemy, a Frankish knight could knock a foot soldier off his feet or an enemy rider off his horse. The horse became essential to a noble warrior. Without a horse, a man was considered a peasant. Gradually, the most important part of an army came to be its mounted knights.

The pope named Pepin king.

Pepin was not content to be the power behind the throne. He wanted to be king in his own right. Pepin wrote a shrewd letter to the pope. Pepin asked, Who should be the rightful ruler of the Franks? Should it be the man who had the title of king but no power? Or should it be the man with the power but no title? The pope answered, "It is better that he who possesses power be called king than he who has none." Thus did Pepin the Short obtain the Church's blessing for seizing the throne.

The pope and the new Frankish king needed each other. Only the Church could give legitimacy to the rule of Pepin and his heirs. At the same time, only a strong king like Pepin could protect the pope from the Lombards, who again threatened Rome. In desperation, Pope Stephen II crossed the Alps in 754 to plead for help. Pepin agreed to fight the Lombards on the pope's behalf. Then occurred an event of immense historic importance. In a dimly lighted chapel, the pope anointed Pepin's head with holy oil and declared him "king by the grace of God."

Pepin was the first king ever to be anointed by a pope. Afterward, it became common for kings in western Europe to be crowned "by the grace of God" in a church ceremony. No longer were kings simply political rulers. They now had some spiritual authority as well.

Pepin soon led an army into Italy and defeated the Lombards in one city after another. In 756, he collected the keys to all the cities he had conquered and gave them to the pope. Thus, the popes became political rulers of scattered Italian lands known as the Papal States.

The Frankish kings and the Roman popes had entered into an informal alliance. It was an unstable alliance, however. Much of the later history of the Middle Ages, as we shall see, was the story of popes struggling to control kings, and vice versa.

Charlemagne extended Frankish power.

Pepin the Short died in 768 and left a greatly strengthened Frankish kingdom to his son, Charles. Charles was in his mid-twenties when he became king and in his early seventies at his death. He was king of the Franks for 46 years (768–814), longer than Augustus Caesar had been emperor of the Romans.

In fact, Charles's reign was a glorious time in the Frankish kingdom, just as Augustus's reign had been for Rome. In Latin, Charles was called *Carolus Magnus*, or Charles the Great. In French, his name became Charlemagne (SHAHR-luh-MAYN). His descendants were known as the Carolingian (KAIR-uh-LIN-jee-uhn) dynasty.

Charlemagne's personality Though his father was Pepin the Short, Charlemagne was gigantic, six feet four inches tall. Charlemagne followed the Frankish custom of wearing a mustache but no beard. His secretary and biographer, a monk named Einhard, wrote this description of him:

> The upper part of his head was round, his eyes were large and lively, nose a little long, hair fair, and face laughing and merry. Thus his appearance was always stately and dignified, whether he was standing or sitting; although his neck was thick and somewhat short, and his belly rather prominent; but the symmetry of the rest of his body concealed these defects.

Charlemagne was a great sportsman. He especially liked to hunt deer on horseback or to plunge into a river and swim great distances. A king in the Middle Ages needed all Charlemagne's great physical strength and energy.

Charlemagne the conqueror In war, the king himself commanded the armies and fought in the front line. Every spring, Charlemagne called together all the great landowners of the kingdom, both nobles and bishops. They met at Charlemagne's capital, Aachen (AH-kuhn), or at another royal residence. Each noble brought his own followers, equipped for battle. This, for example, was one of Charlemagne's orders to his nobles:

> Each horseman is expected to have a shield, lance, sword, dagger, bow, quiver with arrows, and in your carts shall be . . . axes, planes, augers, boards, spades, iron shovels, and other utensils that are necessary in any army. In the wagons shall be supplies for three months, together with arms and clothing for six months.

Summer after summer, Charlemagne led these armies against the enemies that surrounded his

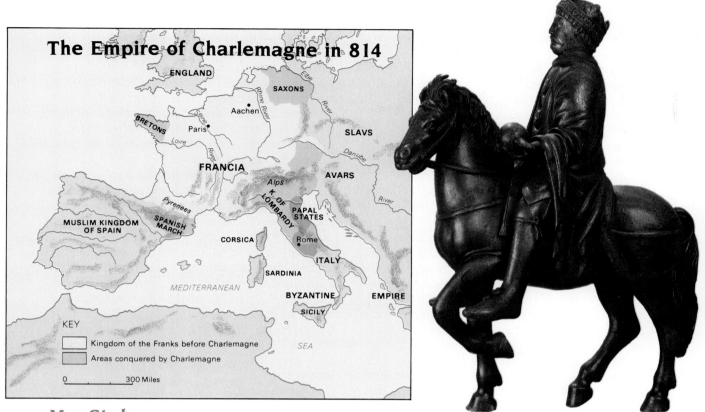

The Empire of Charlemagne in 814

ENGLAND

SAXONS

Aachen •

BRETONS

Paris •

SLAVS

Loire

Rhine River

Elbe

River

Danube

FRANCIA

Seine River

AVARS

Alps

K. OF LOMBARDY

PAPAL STATES

River

Pyrenees

MUSLIM KINGDOM OF SPAIN

SPANISH MARCH

CORSICA

Rome •

ITALY

SARDINIA

MEDITERRANEAN

BYZANTINE

EMPIRE

SICILY

SEA

KEY

Kingdom of the Franks before Charlemagne

Areas conquered by Charlemagne

0   300 Miles

Map Study

Charlemagne, shown at the right, carries an orb as a symbol of imperial power. What enemies threatened his northeastern border?

kingdom. He conquered new lands to both the south and the east.

When a frightened pope again asked for protection against the Lombards, Charlemagne responded. He defeated the Lombards, captured their king, and took over northern Italy in 773.

Five years later, in 778, Charlemagne crossed the Pyrenees Mountains and marched into Muslim Spain. He hoped to win control of northern Spain, but the expedition failed. As the Franks retreated through the mountains, ambushers caught the Frankish rear guard by surprise and slaughtered it. Among the Franks to die was the leader of the guard, Count Roland. This massacre became a Frankish legend, retold in a great epic poem called the Song of Roland.

It was the Franks' eastern frontier, however, where Charlemagne fought his greatest wars. In what is now Yugoslavia and Hungary, an Asian people called the Avars ruled the Slavs. After seven years of brutal warfare, Charlemagne destroyed the Avar kingdom. The Saxons of Ger-

many were even more troublesome. Charlemagne fought them for nearly 30 years before they submitted to his rule and his Christian religion.

Charles did more than encourage missionaries to work among the Saxons and other pagans. He sometimes resorted to baptism by the sword, offering his defeated enemies the choice of becoming Christian or dying on the spot. Not for nothing did Christian chroniclers call him "iron Charles" and "the strong right arm of God."

By the year 800, the Frankish kingdom included two thirds of Italy, all of present-day France, a small part of Spain, and all of German Saxony. It had grown larger than the Byzantine empire. Only a ruler of Charlemagne's energy and ability could hope to govern such an empire.

Charlemagne strengthened his rule.

Like kings both before and after him, Charlemagne needed the help of powerful nobles to govern his kingdom. However, also like other

195

kings, he needed a way to limit the power of those nobles.

Royal officials All of Francia, as the Frankish kingdom was called, was divided into counties. Each county was ruled in the king's name by a powerful landholder called a **count**.

The counts administered justice and raised armies. In theory, the king could dismiss a count at any time. In practice, however, the same count might rule an area for as long as 30 years. Unless the counts were constantly reminded of the loyalty they owed the king, they might quickly become independent rulers.

Wisely, Charlemagne did not trust his counts. He sent out royal agents called *missi dominici* (MIHS-ee doh-MIHN-uh-kee), or "emissaries of the master" to see that counts governed justly and did not abuse their power. Charlemagne also regularly visited every part of his kingdom to judge cases, settle disputes, reward faithful followers, and keep the less loyal in line. By constant watchfulness, he managed to keep his powerful counts under control. (His sons and grandsons, however, were less successful at controlling their nobles.)

The royal estates Much of Charlemagne's power rested on his position as a great landowner. The Carolingian family owned huge estates scattered throughout Francia. Charlemagne and his sons kept a close eye on the management of their lands. This letter, for example, is part of a set of instructions to the overseer of a royal estate.

> *The greatest care must be taken that whatever is prepared by hand—bacon, smoked meat, sausage, partially salted meat, wine, vinegar, mulberry wine, cooked wine, mustard, cheese, butter, malt, beer, mead, honey, wax, flour, all should be prepared with the greatest cleanliness.*
>
> *In each of our estates, the chambers shall be provided with counterpanes, cushions, pillows, bedclothes, coverings for tables and benches.*

Most of a king's wealth came not from taxes but from goods like those listed in that letter— goods produced on the royal estates. These estates supported the royal court and also paid for the daily working of government. A king who allowed his estates to decline would quickly lose his political power too.

Charlemagne revived learning.

Charlemagne's court became the center for a revival in learning. Earlier Germanic kings had shown little interest in learning. Yet Charlemagne understood some Latin and even perhaps a little Greek. He learned to read, and he struggled to learn to write. According to Einhard, he "used to keep tablets and blanks in bed under his pillow that he might accustom his hand to form the letters; however, as he did not begin his efforts [until] late in life, they met with ill success." He was never able to write more than a word or two.

For his court at Aachen, the king recruited the leading European scholars of his day. There was a music teacher from Italy, a poet from Spain, and many others. By far the most influential of these imported scholars was an Englishman named Alcuin (AL-kwihn) of York. Charlemagne also invited Jews to settle in his kingdom because they were literate and could help with administrative work.

For his own numerous sons and daughters and for other children at the court, Charlemagne began a palace school. There students learned to read, write, and do a little arithmetic. Charlemagne himself visited the classes. On at least one occasion, the king's famous temper was aroused, and he pummeled a lazy student for mistakes in grammar.

By Charlemagne's order, monasteries and cathedrals were expected to open schools to train future monks and priests. (Since only boys could enter the priesthood, only boys attended these schools.)

Monasteries increased their libraries. Monks labored to make handwritten copies of rare Latin books. Each copy took many months of toil. As they worked, the monks developed a new style of lettering. Roman books had all been written in capital letters, and there was no spacing between words. To save time, monks began substituting small letters for the Roman capitals. To make the books easier to read, the monks added spaces between the words. Gradually, writers in monasteries perfected a beautiful and readable style of lettering known as Carolingian miniscule (MIHN-ih-skyool). Most of these small letters look almost exactly like the letters printed in a modern book.

The pope made Charlemagne emperor.

By the year 800, Charlemagne was the most powerful king in western Europe. Then he traveled to Rome to help Pope Leo III, who had been attacked by a Roman mob. On Christmas Day in St. Peter's Cathedral, the pope placed a jeweled crown on Charlemagne's head and declared him emperor. The crowd of people in the church (probably coached in advance) shouted, "Hail to Charles the Augustus, crowned by God to be the great and peace-giving emperor of the Romans, life and victory."

What did the title of emperor mean? According to one argument, the title gave Charlemagne new prestige. He could deal as an equal with the Byzantine emperor. The counterargument says Charlemagne gained nothing but trouble from the crowning. The new title added nothing to his power. Moreover, news of the crowning angered the Byzantines and made another enemy on Charlemagne's troubled eastern frontier. After all, in the Byzantine view, the true Roman emperor ruled from Constantinople.

Another theory says that the crowning was the work of the pope and did not please Charlemagne at all. Why would the pope want to make Charlemagne emperor? Perhaps Pope Leo wanted an emperor who would stay in Rome and help govern the unruly city. Perhaps it was a shrewd political move, establishing the pope's power to name an emperor.

Probably Charlemagne's coronation meant different things to different people. Charlemagne and Pope Leo III each had his own motives, which we may never know. However, we do know the long-term consequences of the crowning.

First, the coronation marked another stage in the growing split between the Church of Constantinople and the Church of Rome. After 800, there were two Christian empires, Greek Orthodox in the east and Roman Catholic in the west. Each viewed the other with growing suspicion.

Second, there arose in western Europe a new idea of empire. Later popes repeatedly gave the title "Roman emperor" to one European king or another. In theory, the person entrusted with this title became the protector of all Christendom. The title meant little when held by a weak ruler, but in strong hands it could be a powerful tool.

The Division of the Carolingian Empire, 843

Map Study

The Treaty of Verdun divided Charlemagne's empire among his three grandsons. Which important city lay in Lothair's territory?

Charlemagne's heirs ruled weakly.

When Charlemagne died at his palace in 814, his only surviving son, Louis the Pious, succeeded him as king and emperor. A devoutly religious man, Louis would have made a better monk than a king. As a ruler, he was ineffective. He died in 840.

Louis left three sons: Lothair (loh-THAIR), Charles the Bald, and Louis the German. Like the Merovingian princes, Louis's sons fought one another for the empire. The civil war ended in 843 when the brothers signed a pact called the Treaty of Verdun (vur-DUHN). This document divided Charlemagne's empire into three kingdoms, one for each brother.

Footnote to History

Part of Lothair's central kingdom became known as *Lothair's realm* or *Lotharingia*, a name that was eventually shortened to Lorraine. In the following centuries, as late as World War II, millions of French and German soldiers died in battles over Lorraine.

Charles the Bald's kingdom would eventually become France. Louis the German's kingdom would become Germany. Lothair, the eldest son, kept the title of emperor and took the land between his brothers' kingdoms, including the imperial capitals of Rome and Aachen. His land became a battleground for the future kings of France and Germany.

After the Treaty of Verdun, Carolingian kings became almost as powerless as the long-haired Merovingians had been. Once again, central authority broke down.

At the same time, all of Europe from Ireland to Italy was repeatedly assaulted and plundered by terrible new invasions. From the south, Muslim pirates seized Sicily and raided Italy, even sacking Rome in 846. From the east struck the Magyars, barbarians from central Asia. Like the earlier Huns and Avars, the Magyar warriors terrorized Germany and Italy. And from the north came the most dreaded attackers of all, the Vikings (VY-kingz). Even before Charlemagne's death, the earliest Viking raids struck Europe.

Section Review 2

Define: (a) knight, (b) count, (c) missi dominici, (d) Carolingian miniscule
Identify: (a) Franks, (b) Merovingians, (c) mayor of the palace, (d) Charles Martel, (e) Pepin the Short, (f) Papal States, (g) Charlemagne, (h) Carolingians, (i) Treaty of Verdun
Answer:
1. (a) What practice weakened the power of the Merovingian kings? (b) Into whose hands did their power pass?
2. (a) Explain how the Frankish king and the pope depended on each other. (b) How did kings gain some spiritual authority? (c) How did the pope become a political ruler?
3. (a) Describe how Charlemagne ruled his widespread lands. (b) Why were his own estates important to his government?
4. How did Charlemagne promote learning?
5. (a) What new title did Charlemagne receive from the pope in the year 800? (b) What were the consequences of this event?
6. How did the Treaty of Verdun affect the Frankish kingdom?

7. What groups invaded Europe in the 800's?
Critical Thinking
8. What do you think was Charlemagne's greatest achievement? Give reasons for your answer.

Vikings terrorized Europe. 3

To the monks on Lindisfarne Island near the northeast coast of England, it seemed to be just another peaceful morning when they awoke to perform their daily rituals. But on this morning in 793, a large sailing vessel lay near the shore, barely visible in the mist. Its square sail was striped red and white. Its prow swept upward in a graceful curve like a swan's neck, but at the top was a dragon's head.

As dawn broke, burly warriors jumped from the ship to the island shore, clutching swords and heavy wooden shields. The monks had no weapons. Some were killed at the altar even as they prayed. Others were dragged to the sea and drowned. The monastery was thoroughly ransacked. Golden crucifixes, silver chalices, ivory boxes, and silk and linen tapestries were all piled in the boat. Laughing and shouting, the attackers heaved on their oars. Soon their striped sail disappeared over the horizon.

News of this outrage soon reached the court of Charlemagne. "Never before," wrote Alcuin, "has such a terror appeared in Britain as this that we have just suffered from a pagan race." In 793, the terror was just beginning. From about 800 until the year 1000, the Vikings raided from Ireland to Russia. In many churches, a new prayer became part of the daily worship: "Save us, O God, from the fury of the Northmen."

Footnote to History

In the heat of battle, some Viking warriors lunged against the enemy howling, snarling, and biting their wooden shields in rage. In this state of hyperexcitement, they felt neither fear nor pain. Such warriors, feared even by other Vikings, were known as *berserkrs*, from which comes the modern word for someone in a violent frenzy, *berserk*.

Vikings were skilled seafarers.

The raiders were known by several names: Northmen, Norsemen, and Vikings. Their home lay far to the north in a wintry, rocky, forested region called Scandinavia (SKAN-duh-**NAY**-vee-uh). Today, this region consists of Norway, Sweden, and Denmark.

The people of Scandinavia were Germanic with customs and language similar to those of the Franks, Saxons, and Goths who had earlier invaded Europe. The Scandinavians, however, had had almost no contact with Rome. They were still pagans, worshiping warlike gods. Viking leaders took pride in nicknames like Eric Bloodaxe and Thorfinn Skullsplitter.

The Vikings carried out their raids with terrifying swiftness. They would beach their ships, strike, then quickly shove out to sea again. By the time local troops arrived, the Vikings were long gone.

The Viking warships were the technological marvel of their age. Long, lean, and light, the largest of these ships could hold 300 warriors, who took turns rowing its 72 oars. Most ships were smaller, with crews of 30 to 50 fighters. The prow of each ship swept grandly upward, often ending with the carved head of a sea monster or dragon. Although a ship might weigh 20 tons when fully loaded, it could sail in 3 feet of water. Thus, the Vikings could strike villages and monasteries far inland by rowing up shallow rivers and creeks.

Scandinavians settled far and wide.

Despite their fearsome reputation, it is wrong to think of the Vikings merely as ferocious brutes. They were also wily traders and careful farmers. As explorers, they were unsurpassed. They traveled far beyond western Europe, down rivers into the heart of Russia, to Constantinople, and across the icy waters of the northern Atlantic Ocean.

By the year 900, hundreds of Scandinavian families had made the perilous voyage to the distant island of Iceland. There they built a prosperous settlement.

A Norse queen, Asa, was buried in this Viking ship. Among the Vikings, such burials were a common way to honor a leader. The ship shows the high prow and shallow draft of Viking vessels. At sea, Vikings lashed monster heads like the one below to their ship's prow to frighten away evil spirits. In battle, Viking warriors wore helmets such as the one at the left.

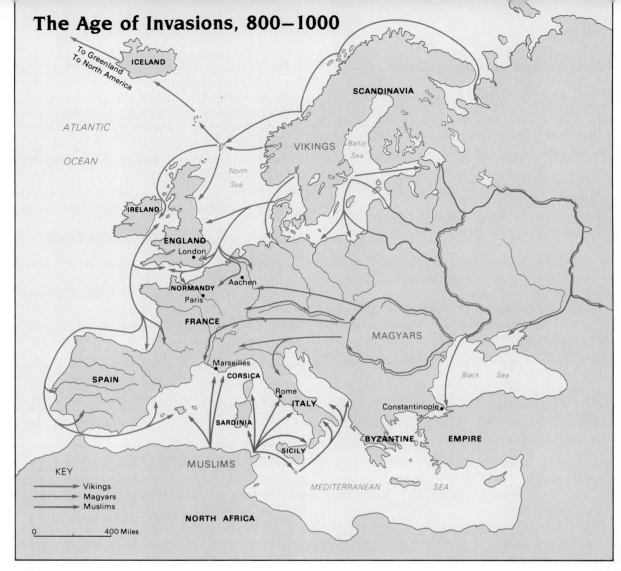

The Age of Invasions, 800–1000

To Greenland
To North America

ICELAND

ATLANTIC

OCEAN

SCANDINAVIA

VIKINGS

Baltic
Sea

North
Sea

IRELAND

ENGLAND
London

NORMANDY   Aachen
Paris

FRANCE

MAGYARS

Black   Sea

Marseilles

CORSICA

SPAIN

Rome

SARDINIA

ITALY

Constantinople

SICILY

BYZANTINE   EMPIRE

MUSLIMS

MEDITERRANEAN   SEA

NORTH AFRICA

KEY

→ Vikings
→ Magyars
→ Muslims

0   400 Miles

Map Study

Of the three great groups of invaders that struck Europe, the Vikings ranged most widely. Name the seas and oceans that they reached. Which group of invaders came overland?

In 982, a red-bearded outlaw named Eric the Red sailed west from Iceland into uncharted Atlantic waters. He came upon an island that was largely buried under a massive sheet of ice. He misnamed the place Greenland. For a while, Norse settlers managed to eke out a living even in that harsh environment. Eventually, however, the settlement was abandoned.

About the year 1000, Eric the Red's son, Leif (leef) Ericson, sailed from Greenland to another unexplored land. This probably was the Canadian island now known as Newfoundland. The Vikings

called it Vinland. There is no question that Leif Ericson reached the Americas before Columbus.

Meanwhile, the Vikings were also settling widely in western Europe. They established their own kingdoms in parts of Ireland and nearly conquered all of England. Only the courage and leadership of the English hero-king, Alfred the Great, finally halted their advance in 886. In northern France, Viking leaders won a rich territory that became known as Normandy.

In all these regions, Viking warriors were the forerunners of Scandinavian settlers. The raiders were followed by whole families of farmers, traders, and artisans whose influence spread widely in much of Europe.

The Viking age ended about 1000.

Around the year 1000, the Viking terror, which had raged for two centuries, slowly receded and died. Why? Three facts help to explain it.

First, Europeans finally worked out a way to respond quickly to raids and small-scale invasions. (The way this system worked will be explained in the next section.)

Second, like so many barbarians before them (including Goths, Franks, and Saxons), the Vikings gradually adopted Christianity. For example, King Guthrum of the Danes agreed to become a Christian as part of his peace treaty with England's King Alfred. As Christians, the Vikings were less inclined to raid monasteries.

Third, after 1000, Europe's climate went through a warming trend that lasted several centuries. That trend explains why Viking settlements on Iceland and Greenland prospered. As farming became easier in Scandinavia, fewer Scandinavians turned to the seafaring life of Viking warriors.

The Vikings were the last great raiders to descend on western Europe. While the eastern lands of the old Roman empire were devastated by the Seljuk Turks, the Ottoman Turks, and other warriors from central Asia, western Europe was at last free of invasions.

Section Review 3

Identify: (a) Vikings, (b) Scandinavia, (c) Iceland, (d) Eric the Red, (e) Greenland, (f) Leif Ericson, (g) Newfoundland
Answer:
1. (a) Where did the Vikings come from? (b) How were they different from the earlier Germanic groups who had invaded Europe?
2. What new lands to the west did the Vikings reach?
3. What factors helped to end the Viking terror?

Critical Thinking
4. Why was it very difficult for kings to defend their territory against Viking raids?

Feudalism became the basis for government. 4

In the late summer of 911, two men who had long been enemies stood face to face near the Seine (sayn) River in what is now France. One man was Rollo, the leader of a Viking army that had been plundering the rich river valley for years. The second man was the almost powerless king of France, known to history as Charles the Simple. Though he bore the title *king*, Charles controlled little of the land that is France today.

The two men had come to make peace. In a formal ceremony, Charles granted Rollo a huge piece of French territory. This part of France became the Northmen's land, or *Normandy*. In return, Rollo placed his hands between the king's hands and swore never to make war against the king again.

As part of the ceremony, Rollo was expected to kneel and kiss the king's foot, but this was more than the proud Viking could stand. "No, by God!" he bellowed. Instead, Rollo ordered one of his henchmen to perform the rite. Charles's foot was hoisted into the air so the tall Viking need not bend his knees. The Viking promptly showed his low opinion of royal dignity by tipping the king onto his back in the dirt. Yet Charles grimly swallowed his pride to win Rollo's oath of loyalty.

Other rulers and warriors in many parts of Europe were making similar agreements. The worst years of the invasions (about 850 to 950) were also the years when a new pattern of life emerged in western Europe. No king or pope dictated this pattern. No brilliant thinker proposed the new system. Instead of one solution, there were hundreds, each depending on local circumstances. Villagers in England responded in one way; villagers in northern Italy responded in another.

Yet overall, the pattern was similar. Everywhere, there was an increasing emphasis on local protection, local government, and local self-sufficiency. This new political system is known as **feudalism** (FYOO-duhl-ihz-uhm). Feudalism was a political and military system based on the holding of land. The control of land was the key to feudalism.

Lords and vassals exchanged vows.

At the heart of the feudal system was an agreement between a **lord** and a **vassal**. When Charles the Simple gave Normandy to Rollo the Viking, Charles became Rollo's lord. When Rollo placed his hands in Charles's and swore loyalty, Rollo became Charles's vassal (a person who receives land from a lord).

The bond between lord and vassal The personal bonds of loyalty that tied a vassal to a lord were the key to the feudal system. The oath sworn between them was the equivalent of today's written contract.

Kneeling, bareheaded, and without his sword, the vassal placed his hands in the hands of his lord. In this humble position, he swore to be the lord's man all the days of his life and to defend the lord against "all men who may live or die." The lord then raised him up and kissed him.

Next came **investiture** (ihn-VEST-ih-choor). In a symbolic gesture, the lord presented the vassal with a stick, a small rod, or a clod of earth. The lord thus transferred into the vassal's hands control of a piece of land. Such a piece of land was known as a **fief** (feef).

Redividing a fief By accepting a fief from Charles the Simple, Rollo became a royal vassal—the vassal of a king. But that grant was not the end of the feudal process. Like other royal fiefs, Normandy was huge. To protect such a fief, the vassal needed a private army.

Since the royal vassal had little money but plenty of land, he could afford to divide his fief into, let us say, 70 smaller estates. Keeping the best land for himself, he would give the other 69 estates as fiefs to 69 warriors who agreed to be his vassals. Thus, the royal vassal himself became the lord of other vassals.

These smaller vassals in turn divided their lands and granted fiefs to warriors of their own. Each local lord used grants of land to attract a personal band of warriors. At the bottom of the scale were the knights, men whose parcels of land were too small to be easily subdivided.

The advantages of this system for defense were clear. Every local lord had a force of knights ready to defend the land against all comers—Vikings, Magyars, Muslims, outlaws, or a neighboring lord. Moreover, lords usually fortified their lands, building strongholds at key places.

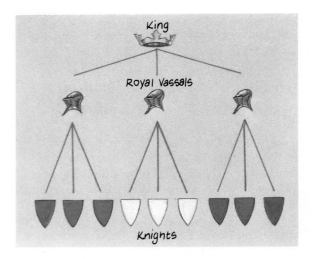

This diagram shows how the feudal system worked in theory. In real life, however, the system became a tangle of conflicting loyalties.

The feudal pyramid In theory, feudal society was a pyramid. At the bottom were many knights, each with a small fief. Above them were their lords, who held larger fiefs. And over all was the king.

In practice, however, the feudal system never worked so clearly. For one thing, an ambitious knight could collect fiefs from several lords by pledging to serve them all. In doing so, he ran a risk. Suppose, as often happened, two of his lords warred with each other. Then the knight would have to choose for whom to fight. His very life might depend on picking the winner. The feudal pyramid often became a complex tangle of conflicting loyalties that both lords and vassals tried to use to their own advantage.

Vassals served in war and peace.

Vassals were required to fight in the lord's army when called. From each of his knights, a lord could demand about 40 days of combat on horseback every year. Weapons, armor, and warhorses were expensive. A vassal needed a certain amount of land so he could afford such gear. Moreover, the skill to use the weapons took training and practice. Gone were the days of citizen-soldiers such as the Greek hoplites or the early Roman legions. Knights in the Middle Ages were specialists in war. Supported by wealth from their fiefs, knights devoted their lives to war.

Women and church leaders as vassals Feudalism was both a military system and a land-holding system. Noblewomen and church leaders often held great estates. Thus, these groups were part of feudalism even though they usually were not warriors.

A noblewoman might inherit a fief from her parents or her husband, or she might control land in the name of her young son. In such cases, a woman fulfilled the feudal duties that went with the land. She sent her vassal knights to war when the lord called. She might also command and defend her castle if her husband was away.

Church leaders too were part of the feudal system. They owed military service just as other vassals did. In the Early Middle Ages, being a churchman was no bar to being a warrior. Fighting bishops such as Turpin of Reims and Odo of Bayeux were famed for their might in battle. In later times, bishops were more likely to send their vassal knights than to go to war themselves.

Peacetime duties Vassals also owed their lords duties in time of peace. When Rollo was given Normandy, he received not only the land with whatever its farms produced but also the right to rule that land. He was expected to hold courts of justice, to charge tolls on the bridges, to collect taxes, and much more. Justice was the lord's largest peacetime reponsibility.

From vassals who were bishops or abbots, a lord was likely to demand governmental and legal services. Being literate, a bishop or abbot could act as the lord's secretary. He could give learned council, keep written records, and write letters for the lord.

In case of financial emergency, lords could ask their vassals for a grant of money. Such a grant was called an **aid**. Traditionally, a lord could call

Voice from the Past · *Feudalism and Marriage*

Lords controlled the marriages of their vassals, both men and women. In the Middle Ages, marriages were an important part of politics. Marriages cemented alliances between families. When a woman married, her husband usually took over her property. Marriage to a wealthy woman might make a vassal even more powerful than his lord. The documents below come from the royal accounting office in England between 1140 and 1282.

- *Ralph son of William owes 100 marks as a fine, to be allowed to marry Margery who was wife of Nicholas Corbet who [held land of the king], and that the same Margery may be allowed to marry him.*
- *Walter de Cancy renders account of £15 to be allowed to marry a wife as he shall choose.*
- *Emma de Normanville and Roheisa and Margaret and Juliana, her sisters, render account of 10 marks for license to marry where they wish.*
- *Roheisa de Doura renders account of £450 to have half of all the lands which belonged to Richard de Lucy, her grandfather . . . and for license to marry where she wishes so long as she does not marry herself to any of the king's enemies.*
- *Alice, countess of Warwick, renders account of £1,000 and 10 palfreys [women's saddle horses] to be allowed to remain a widow as long as she pleases, and not to be forced to marry by the king . . . and to have the custody of her sons.*

1. Which sections show that the lord (in this case, the king) controlled the marriages of both men and women?
2. What right do most of the vassals seem to want?
3. (a) What fact suggests that Margery may have been a wealthy woman?
(b) What was the probable source of her wealth?
4. What two rights is Roheisa de Doura buying from the king?

quo Rexdeda

for aids at three times: (1) when the lord's oldest son was knighted; (2) when the lord's oldest daughter was married; and (3) if the lord was captured in a war and held for ransom. The lord could also travel to a vassal's fief and expect to be housed, wined, and dined for several days.

Historians often describe feudalism as a system in which public power became private. The Roman and Greek idea of public affairs had disappeared. Justice, military power, and political power had all become private possessions. They could be traded among lords or passed down to one's heirs. The duties a person owed were not to a polis or to an empire but to a personal lord.

Manors were the economic side of feudalism.

The great majority of people in the Middle Ages were neither lords nor vassals. Medieval writers said that there were three groups of people: those who fought (the nobles), those who prayed (the men and women of the Church), and those who worked (the peasants). Nobles and church leaders were part of the feudal system. The peasants—horseless, weaponless, and powerless—were outside the political system of feudalism. However, their daily toil lay at the heart of the economic system in the Middle Ages.

The basic economic unit was the **manor**. A manor was a small estate from which a lord's family gained its livelihood. Sometimes a manor was the whole of a fief, sometimes only one part of a fief. If a lord held more than one manor, as was often the case, stewards managed each manor when the lord was absent.

A manor usually covered only a few square miles of land, perhaps with a stream meandering through it. (Fish from streams and ponds were an important source of food.) About one third of the land was cleared for growing grain. Another patch of land was pasture for the peasants' oxen and the lord's horses. The rest was forest.

Self-sufficiency From these meager resources, the laborers on the manor—the peasants—had to produce everything they and the lord needed. Nothing was purchased from outside except salt, iron, and a few unusual objects such as millstones. Everything else—food, fuel, cloth, leather goods, lumber—was produced on the manor. The manor was thus a world unto itself.

Serfs on the land Most peasants were **serfs**. Serfs were not free, but they were not quite slaves either. Unlike slaves, serfs could not be bought, sold, or traded to another lord. Yet serfs could not lawfully leave the manor on which they were born. They were bound to the land. From a different viewpoint, serfs had the right to live on the same manor from birth to death. Although it is hard to understand today, a serf in the Middle Ages may have felt that the right to stay was more important than the freedom to leave.

Free peasants A few peasants enjoyed greater freedom than serfs. They could leave the manor if they wished. These free peasants were not required to do as much work for the lord as the serfs were. Still, one bad harvest or flood could force free peasants to become serfs in exchange for bread and protection. For example, a poor Frankish peasant named William became a serf at the monastery at St. Martin. A monastic document of the eleventh century reads:

> Be it known to all who come after us that a certain man in our service, William, brother of Reginald, born of free parents . . . gave himself up as a serf to St. Martin of Marmoutiers, and he gave not only himself but all his descendants, so that they should forever serve the abbot and monks . . . And in order that this gift might be made more certain and apparent, he put the bell rope round his neck and placed four pennies from his own hand on the altar of St. Martin in recognition of serfdom.

Peasants owed duties on the manor.

All peasants, whether free or serf, were tenants on the lord's manor. They paid dearly for the right to live and grow crops on the lord's land. A typical serf owed the lord the following duties:

- Two or three days' labor every week plowing, planting, and harvesting the lord's own land. (Every sack of grain harvested from this land went to the lord's family.)
- A certain portion of the grain grown on the serf's own land.
- One pig out of every ten pigs raised on the manor, plus the service of slaughtering it.
- As a "gift" at Christmas and Easter, delivery to the lord of so many eggs and chickens.

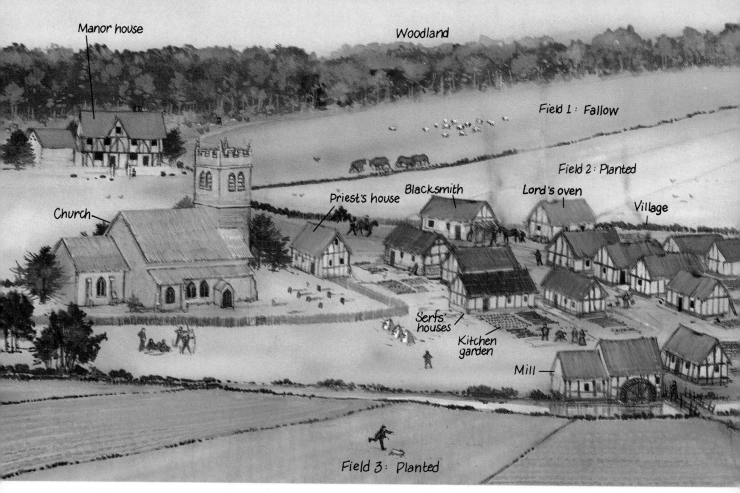

Manor house

Woodland

Field 1: Fallow

Field 2: Planted

Priest's house

Blacksmith

Lord's oven

Village

Church

Serfs' houses

Kitchen garden

Mill

Field 3: Planted

A medieval manor was largely self-sufficient. Its residents raised or made nearly everything they needed for daily life.

- A tax on all grain ground in the lord's mill and all bread baked in the lord's oven. (Any attempt to dodge these charges by baking bread elsewhere was punished as a crime.
- A tax when the serf married. (No marriage could take place without the lord's consent.)

After all these payments to the lord, each peasant's family still owed to the village priest a tithe (church tax), representing one tenth of their income. Together, lord and priest typically collected from each serf six sacks of grain for every ten sacks produced.

Life on a manor was harsh.

Peasant men and women rarely traveled far from their own manor. They could see their entire world at a glance by standing in the center of a plowed field and looking around.

On some manors, the tallest structure on the landscape was a wooden tower set high on a hill and surrounded on four sides by a ditch and a wall. This was the manor's castle, a place of safety for lord and peasant alike whenever Vikings raided or a neighboring lord attacked. (Gigantic stone castles with moats and drawbridges did not exist until later in the Middle Ages.) Not far away was a plain two-story house of rough-hewn timber where the lord's family lived in times of peace.

Across the fields in another direction, one could see the thatch roofs of the peasants' one-room huts in the manor's village. Close by, facing the village well, stood a plain church.

By the stream, the waterwheel of the lord's mill turned slowly and ground the manor's grain into flour. The millwright who built and repaired mills was one of several skilled workers in the

This drawing from the mid-1300's shows peasants stacking sheaves of grain.

village. Another was the blacksmith, who forged the few metal items used on the manor.

For peasant men and women, probably the most familiar sight was the swishing tails of the oxen that they walked behind as they plowed a field. Since few peasants could afford a whole team of oxen, villagers shared their animals. The same team plowed everyone's fields. Land was shared too. Fields were laid out in long, thin strips because the plow was hard to turn. A peasant family might use strips of land scattered in fields all around the village. That way, everyone had a share of both the good land and the bad.

Peasants raised wheat, barley, oats, and rye. Coarse, black bread made from these grains was the main course of many meals. In garden patches, families grew cabbages, onions, beans, and other vegetables. Hens scratched in the dooryards of the houses, more valuable for their eggs than for meat. Half-wild pigs nosed the ground for fallen acorns near the edge of the village woodlands. One slaughtered pig per year might be a peasant family's only source of meat. Honey was used for sweetener. Fruit trees grew apples, pears, cherries, and peaches. Yet after a bad harvest, peasant families lived on the edge of starvation.

In addition to hunger, there was the misery of being chilled to the bone when the winter winds blew. The cold seeped into a peasant's hut through cracks in the log walls. There were no floorboards, only the bare dirt ground. In one corner of the room, in a wooden frame, was a pile of straw crawling with vermin. This was the bed in which the whole family slept, parents and children together. Farm animals (geese, sheep, pigs) were commonly admitted into the hut to increase the general body heat. Though smelly, warming a hut with pig heat was safer than burning a fire in the center of the room and risking that a spark would fly toward the family's straw bed. (A bit of this misery was later relieved by the invention of the chimney.)

Nobles had more to eat and warmer clothing than peasants did. Yet even nobles had little comfort and no protection from sickness or injury.

The years from 500 to 1000 were harsh for Europeans. Change came slowly. When one bad harvest could spell death, people were reluctant to try new ways. Yet, even by 800, changes were taking place that would improve life on the manor. By 1000, Europe was poised for a revival in farming, trade, government, and learning.

Section Review 4

Define: (a) feudalism, (b) lord, (c) vassal, (d) investiture, (e) fief, (f) aid, (g) manor, (h) serf

Answer:

1. (a) What oath did a vassal swear to his or her lord? (b) What did the lord give in return? (c) How did a vassal become the lord of others?
2. (a) What services could a lord demand of vassals in time of war? (b) In peacetime?
3. (a) How did women become lords or vassals? (b) What part did church leaders have in the feudal system?
4. (a) What duties did a serf owe on a manor? (b) How might a free peasant become a serf?

Critical Thinking

5. (a) How was a local community self-sufficient both militarily and economically in the Early Middle Ages? (b) Why was self-sufficiency important in this age?

Chapter Review 9

Summary

1. New ways of life developed in Europe. By the end of the 400's, the Roman empire had been broken into many Germanic kingdoms. Trade collapsed, towns declined, and the level of learning sank. Germanic leaders and customs replaced Roman government and law. Monasteries stood out as centers of orderly life, where learning was kept alive.

2. Charlemagne revived the idea of empire. The Franks had the largest of the Germanic kingdoms. The greatest of the Frankish rulers was Charlemagne, who conquered pagan lands, set up an effective administration, and encouraged learning. After his death, Europe suffered a new wave of invasions.

3. The Vikings terrorized Europe. From 800 to 1000, raiders from Scandinavia threatened much of Europe. They also explored and settled widely. After 1000, the Viking menace declined.

4. Feudalism became the basis for government. Feudalism developed as a form of local protection and government. Vassals pledged loyalty to a lord; in return, the lord gave each vassal a grant of land. Lords and vassals spent most of their lives training for battle and fighting wars. Peasants worked on manors to supply the goods needed to support themselves and the lords.

Reviewing the Facts

1. Define the following terms:
   a. monastery
   b. knight
   c. count
   d. feudalism
   e. lord
   f. vassal
   g. investiture
   h. fief
   i. aid
   j. manor
   k. serf

2. Explain the importance of each of the following names, dates, places, or terms:
   a. Patrick
   b. Clovis
   c. Benedictine Rule
   d. Gregory I
   e. Christendom
   f. Merovingians
   g. Pepin the Short
   h. Charlemagne
   i. missi dominici
   j. Aachen
   k. A.D. 800
   l. Carolingians
   m. Treaty of Verdun
   n. Vikings
   o. Leif Ericson

3. (a) How was learning promoted by Charlemagne? (b) By monasteries?

4. What different methods were used to spread Christianity during the Early Middle Ages?

5. How was Germanic society organized?

6. Explain how the feudal system linked lords and vassals. Include information on investiture, fiefs, and aids.

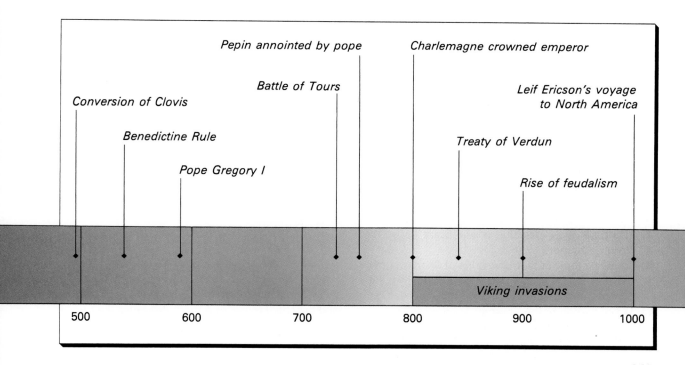

Pepin annointed by pope

Charlemagne crowned emperor

Battle of Tours

Leif Ericson's voyage to North America

Conversion of Clovis

Benedictine Rule

Treaty of Verdun

Pope Gregory I

Rise of feudalism

Viking invasions

| 500 | 600 | 700 | 800 | 900 | 1000 |

7. (a) After 800, what were the titles of the two men who could claim leadership of all Christian Europe? (b) How did these two leaders depend on each other?
8. (a) What part did the manor play in medieval life? (b) Describe the ways land was used on a manor.
9. (a) What obligations did serfs have? (b) What did they get in return?

Thinking about History

1. Benedict's motto was *Laborare est orare* ("To work is to pray"). Explain this idea in your own words. How was Benedict's idea carried out in the daily life of monasteries that followed his rule?
2. Both the stirrup and the Vikings' dragonship were changes in the technology of warfare. How did each affect society? Recall some of the changes in weaponry or tactics that you have studied in earlier chapters. Give an example of another military change that had far-reaching results.
3. Barbarian invasions brought about the fall of Rome. Over the centuries, many groups—including Germans, Huns, Magyars, and Vikings—repeatedly invaded the settled parts of Europe. What caused such groups to invade settled areas? Why was it often difficult for people in settled areas to withstand such attacks? What examples of such warfare have you studied from earlier periods?
4. What people usually gain authority in a society where few people are literate? What group increased its power by having a monopoly on literacy in the Early Middle Ages? How would that fact influence the historic records that are available to us today? Today, some people are described as "functionally illiterate." What does that mean?

Writing and Speaking about History

1. Write a generalization about life on a manor in the year 1000. Use this generalization to develop a thesis statement about manor life.
2. In a paragraph, describe a significant aspect of life on a manor.
3. Prepare a topic outline on the life of Charlemagne. Use the following six headings in your outline. Supply two pieces of information for each heading.
   I. Charlemagne the person
   II. Charlemagne the conquerer

III. Charlemagne the ruler
IV. Charlemagne the landowner
V. Charlemagne and education
VI. Charlemagne and the pope
4. Hold a round-table discussion among Charlemagne, Julius Caesar, and Alexander the Great. Focus the discussion on the benefits and problems of governing a large empire.

Practicing Skills

1. (a) Use the time line on page 207 to decide what event happened about the same time as the beginning of the Viking invasions. (b) What event happened around the end of the invasions?
2. (a) On an outline map of the Roman empire, draw in the boundaries of Charlemagne's empire in the year 814 (page 195). (b) On the same map show the division of Frankish lands after Charlemagne's death.

Investigating History

1. Draw a diagram or make a model of a manor, using the description in the chapter as a guide.
2. Evaluate the medieval diet. What foods provided starches (carbohydrates), proteins, fats, and vitamins? Keep in mind the fact that peasants were usually forbidden to hunt in the lord's forest.
3. The Vikings were as interesting for their explorations, trade, and art as for their raids. Find out about their way of life, including the products they bought and sold, the lands they discovered, and their style of art. Some topics you might include are sagas, ring forts, runes, and the Varangian Guard (in Constantinople).
4. Find out more about Leif Ericson's voyage to North America. What may have happened to his attempt to settle there?
5. King Alfred is the only king whom the English have honored as "the Great." Find out how Alfred rose from being a hunted fugitive to drive back the Great Army of the Danes.

Decision Making in History

Evaluate the consequences of the papal decisions to anoint Pepin and crown Charlemagne. In your opinion, who benefited more from these decisions, the Church or the ruler? Why?

The High Middle Ages

Building a cathedral required both skilled and unskilled workers. In many cases, the work went on for several generations.

1. **Farming improved and trade revived.**

2. **Religious leaders wielded great power.**

3. **Royal governments grew stronger.**

4. **Learning revived and spread.**

5. **Crusaders marched against Islam.**

What was this coming slowly down the dirt road through the wheat fields? Who were these people pulling two-wheeled wagons weighted down with stone blocks? A French abbot watching them knew from their rich robes that these haulers of stone were not peasants but nobles. In 1144, the abbot wrote an account of what he saw outside the town of Chartres (shahrt), southwest of Paris:

Who has ever seen! Who has ever heard tell, in times past, that powerful princes of the world, that men brought up in honor and

209

wealth, that nobles, men and women, have bent their proud and haughty necks to the harness of carts and that, like beasts of burden, they have dragged to the abode of Christ these wagons? . . .

From the stone quarry where the laborers picked up their load, it was a seven-mile trek to the massive structure they were helping to build, the Cathedral of Our Lady of Chartres. The pious workers who dragged the first stones to Chartres never saw the cathedral finished. Few Europeans in the 1100's lived beyond the age of 50. Normally, it took 40 to 60 years to build a cathedral.

In 1180, after two generations of back-breaking labor, the townspeople of Chartres celebrated the dedication of their new cathedral with feasting and bell ringing. Just 14 years later, in 1194, the roof of the great cathedral burst into flame. The work of two generations came tumbling down. Amazingly, the undaunted citizens of Chartres set to work and in just 25 years raised an even more magnificent cathedral, which still stands.

Chartres Cathedral is the symbol of an era. In western Europe, the period from 1000 to 1300 often is known as the Age of Faith. It was an age when hundreds of towering cathedrals were built throughout Europe. Church leaders exerted enormous political and economic influence in Europe. Yet it was not faith alone that built the great cathedrals. The Age of Faith was also a time of increasing material prosperity. In all spheres of life, the High Middle Ages were a time of vigorous growth for European civilization.

Farming improved and trade revived. 1

In the years between 1000 and 1300, dramatic changes were occurring at every level of European society. At the top, new royal families were coming to power. Church leaders were reforming and strengthening the Church. Nobles were creating a glittering society with mock battles and poetry contests. Perhaps the most important changes had begun much earlier at the lowest level of society, with the peasants who worked on the land.

New ways of farming increased food.

A civilization cannot exist without food. Europe's great revival would have been impossible without better ways of farming.

One of the first great improvements in farming had begun in Charlemagne's time. A new, heavier plow slowly came into use. This heavy plow cut deep into the dirt and turned it over. Very gradually, this plow replaced the earlier, lightweight plow that only scratched the top of the ground. With the new plow, farmers could plant crops in the rich, deep soil of Europe's river valleys. This soil produced better harvests, helping peasants get a step ahead in the race with hunger.

Using horsepower For hundreds of years, peasants depended on oxen to pull their plows. Oxen lived on the poorest straw and stubble, so they were easy to keep. However, oxen moved very slowly. Horses needed better food, but a team of horses could plow twice as much land in a day as a team of oxen.

The horse collar and the heavy plow were the newest technology for farming in the Middle Ages.

The problem was that farmers in the Early Middle Ages did not have the right kind of harness to use on horses. Their harness went around the horse's neck. When the horse pulled against its harness, the poor animal was nearly strangled. Sometime before 900, farmers in Europe began using a harness with a collar that fitted across the horse's chest, taking pressure off its neck and windpipe. Over the next two centuries, the new harness was adopted widely in western Europe. As a result, horses gradually replaced oxen for plowing and pulling wagons.

With horses, a farmer could plow more land in a day. As a result, many farmers cleared new fields from the forests. All over England, France, and Germany, axes rang as the great forests that had covered the land began to fall. Along the marshy coastlands of present-day Belgium, peasants built huge seawalls to drain yet more new land. These new fields supplied enough grain to feed a growing population.

The three-field system At the same time, villagers began to organize their land differently. As you have read, peasants in a village shared the land. Each family had a few strips of land scattered around the village fields.

In the Early Middle Ages, peasants usually divided the village's land into two great fields. One field they planted with crops. The other they left to lie fallow for a year. Fallow land was not planted. It was plowed once or twice to keep

In the diagram below, how many acres a year could peasants use to raise crops with the two-field system? With the three-field system?

Planted 300 Acres	Fallow 300 Acres

Two-field System · 600 Acres

Wheat or rye 200 Acres	Barley, peas, oats beans 200 Acres	Fallow 200 Acres

Three-field System · 600 Acres

down weeds, but otherwise it was let alone. Thus, if a village had 600 acres, each year farmers used 300 for raising food. The following year, farmers would plant the land that had been fallow and leave the other field to rest. This way of dividing a village's land was the two-field system.

Around 800, some villages began to organize their land into three great fields instead of two. With the same 600 acres, they used 200 acres for a winter crop of wheat or rye. In spring, they planted another 200 acres with oats, barley, peas, or beans. The remaining 200 acres lay fallow.

Under this new three-field system, farmers could grow crops on two thirds of their land each year, not just on half of it. The result was an immediate increase in food for the village. Moreover, this change gave peasants a healthier diet because peas, beans, and lentils were good sources of vegetable protein.

Like other farming changes, this one spread slowly. Three or four centuries went by before it was in wide use.

Towns grew larger and richer.

Greater amounts of food meant greater numbers of people. Scholars estimate that between 1000 and 1150, the population of western Europe rose by 40 percent, from around 30 million to about 42 million.

As Europe's population increased, people left the countryside to settle in towns. Compared to great cities like Constantinople or Baghdad, European towns were still primitive and tiny. Europe's largest city, Paris, probably had no more than 30,000 people by the year 1200. A typical town in medieval Europe had only about 1,500 to 2,500 people.

Nevertheless, these small communities became a powerful force for change. Townspeople did not fit into the traditional groups of nobles (those who fight), priests (those who pray), and peasants (those who work the land). In effect, townspeople formed a new social class. A walled town was known as a burgh, and the people who made their homes in such towns gradually became known as **burghers**. In France, burgh dwellers became known collectively as the **bourgeoisie** (BOOR-zhwah-ZEE).

Many of Europe's Jews lived in the growing towns. Because Jews were forbidden to hold land,

Medieval shops were often family businesses in which both husbands and wives worked. Here boots, jewelry, and tableware are for sale.

they had never been part of the feudal system. Jews were also barred from many businesses, and so they often did work that Christians could not or would not do. Being literate, Jews sometimes worked as business managers for large landholders. The Church forbade Christians to lend money at interest, yet many people still needed to borrow money. As a result, some Jews became money lenders. From there, it was a short step to all types of banking. When trade began to revive in the later Middle Ages, Jews often were active in long-distance trade. Jewish communities in different cities had the links necessary to arrange credit and transfers of money.

By the High Middle Ages, trade was the very lifeblood of the new towns. Trade and towns grew together. Neither could thrive without the other.

Fairs were centers of trade.

Chartres is a good example of a medieval town. As with any cathedral town, many residents had ties to the Church. Some were priests, monks, or nuns. Others worked for the Church, administering its lands and money. People from the countryside came to town to celebrate religious festivals. Travelers came to the city as pilgrims to honor the holy relics at the cathedral. (A relic was something that people believed had once belonged to Jesus or one of the Christian saints.)

Artisans appeared in the town to meet the needs of all those groups of people. Shoemakers, wheelwrights, candle makers, and others did a lively business in Chartres. At first, these people did not have permanent shops. Instead, they brought their goods to gatherings known as **fairs**.

The local fair Peasants from nearby manors would travel to Chartres on weekly fair days, hauling wagonloads of grain and baskets of hens. Business might take place in the very shadow of the cathedral. Cloth was the most common item offered for sale, but there were also foodstuffs—fish, meat, bacon, salt, honey, oil, butter, cheese, fruit, and wine. Customers could find leather, fur, iron, steel, dyes, knives, sickles, and ropes. Such local fairs met all the needs of daily life for a small community.

No longer was everything produced on a selfsufficient manor. This was a revolutionary change in the economic life of Europe.

The great fairs Four times a year—during religious festivals, when the most pilgrims would be in town—Chartres held great fairs. People came to these fairs from far and wide. Besides buying the wares of local artisans, they could also visit the stalls set up by merchants from as far away as England or Italy.

At great fairs, townsfolk and peasants could taste Russian honey, sample Spanish wine, purchase Flemish cloth, sniff Byzantine perfumes sold by a Venetian, and inspect the handiwork of a local wheelwright. For amusement, people thronged around a pair of jugglers, a strumming minstrel, an acrobat or an animal trainer with a dancing bear.

Guilds controlled crafts and trade.

In a medieval town, even if there were a dozen shoemakers, they all made their shoes the same way and sold them for the same price. Competition was forbidden by the rules of the shoemakers' **guild**. A guild was an association of people who worked at the same occupation.

Merchant guilds The first guilds were formed by merchants. In their hometowns, they erected guild halls where they met to make rules and arrange the details of their business. Members of the merchant guild controlled all the trade in their town. For example, nobody could sell Flemish wool in Chartres except a member of the local merchants' guild.

Craft guilds As towns grew, skilled artisans started another kind of guild, the craft guild. Shoemakers, wheelwrights, glassmakers, wine makers, tailors, grocers, druggists, and others began to meet in their own guild halls. In most crafts, both husbands and wives worked at the family trade. In some guilds, especially cloth making, women were in the majority.

Guild functions Guilds enforced standards of quality. Bakers, for example, were required to sell loaves of bread of a standard size and weight. If a baker cheated a customer with an undersized loaf, his guild might punish him by hanging the loaf around his neck and parading him through the town.

Guilds also fixed the price of everything their members sold. The Church demanded that it be a just price, based on the cost of labor and materials plus a reasonable profit. To make a large profit was thought sinful.

Paying dues to one's guild was a form of insurance. When a member died, the guild paid funeral expenses and also gave some money to support the member's family.

Training new workers The doors of the guild hall were open only to proved masters of the trade. How did someone master a trade? Usually, parents paid a fee to a master to take their child as an **apprentice**. An apprentice lived in the master's home and worked in the shop, which might well be in the same building.

The apprentice worked for the master for 3 to 12 years without pay except for room and board. At the end of this training period, an apprentice went to work for wages as a **journeyman** in the craft. As the final step, a journeyman made an item—whether it was a shoe, a barrel, or a sword—that qualified as a "master piece." Journeymen whose product met guild standards were welcomed into the guild as masters.

Town dwellers won new liberties.

Even a proud master artisan might have begun life as a serf on a manor. Many serfs ran away to town. By the 1100's, according to custom, a serf could become free by living within a town for a year and a day. As the saying went, "Town air makes you free."

At first, feudal lords treated the upstart burghers with contempt. Lords ruthlessly taxed the towns on their lands. Nobles charged fees for everything—the right to hold a fair, the right to use a bridge, or the right to hold a law court.

As time went by, however, burghers worked together to free themselves from the lord or bishop on whose land the town stood. Sometimes they fought for their independence against armies of knights. The greatest weapon the burghers had,

Footnote to History

Many people can trace their last names, or surnames, back to a medieval occupation. Sometimes the name even indicates whether the original worker was a man or a woman. For example, a man who made bread might be surnamed Baker; a woman who did the same job, Baxter. A man who wove cloth was Weaver or Weber; a woman, Webster. Spinning thread was a common job for unmarried women, as the modern use of the word *spinster* implies.

Voice from the Past · *The Hanseatic League*

In the late 1200's, a group of towns in northern Germany began to cooperate in defending their mutual trading interests. This group became known as the Hanseatic (HAN-see-AT-ik) League. From the 1200's to the 1400's, the league had great economic and political power in northern Europe. It had almost complete control over trade in such basic goods as fish, fur, wax, and salt. Here are some of the rules from an agreement made around 1260 among the towns of the league.

Each city shall, to the best of its ability, keep the sea clear of pirates, so that merchants may freely carry on their business.

Whoever is expelled from one city because of a crime shall not be received in another.

If a citizen is seized [by pirates or bandits], he shall not be ransomed, but his sword-belt and knife shall be sent to him [as a threat to his captors]. Any merchant who ransoms him shall lose all his possessions in all the cities [in the league].

If a lord besieges a city, no one shall aid him in any way against the city, unless the besieger is his lord.

If there is war in the country, no city shall on that account injure a citizen from the other cities, either in his person or goods, but shall give him protection.

If any man marries a woman in one city, and another woman from some other city comes and proves that he is her lawful husband, he shall be beheaded.

1. What dangers seem to worry these merchants?
2. What steps do they take to protect themselves from criminals?
3. What reasons might the merchants have given for refusing to ransom someone who had been captured by pirates?
4. What statement shows that the duty a man owed to his lord still outweighed the agreements of the league?

ELVBERG

however, was cash. In exchange for a bag of coins, many lords grudgingly granted towns written charters. Such charters listed the towns' special privileges and tax exemptions. In effect, a town charter bearing the lord's seal was a declaration of independence from the feudal system.

Section Review 1

Define: (a) fallow, (b) two-field system, (c) three-field system, (d) burgher, (e) bourgeoisie, (f) fair, (g) guild, (h) apprentice, (i) journeyman
Identify: (a) Chartres, (b) Age of Faith
Answer:
1. (a) Describe three improvements in farming that took place in the Middle Ages. (b) Explain how each helped to increase the food supply.
2. (a) Why did townspeople make up a new social class? (b) What important tasks did Jews perform in the Middle Ages?
3. (a) Why was it no longer necessary for manors to be self-sufficient? (b) How did people get the daily goods they needed? (c) How did they obtain luxury products such as silk?
4. (a) What was the difference between a merchant guild and a craft guild? (b) What regulations did guilds make?
5. How did townspeople become independent of the feudal system?

Critical Thinking
6. Write a series of cause-and-effect statements for the changes described in this chapter. Try to include as many specific changes as possible. Here is an example: "The heavy plow led to farming rich valley soils. Farming rich valley soils led to increased food production."

Religious leaders wielded great power. 2

During the Early Middle Ages, the Church had acted as the preserver of civilization in many ways. Yet the Church had also suffered in the years between 500 and 1000. Vikings had plundered many monasteries. As a result, the level of learning sank. Many priests could barely read their prayers. Church leaders were sometimes corrupt. Italian nobles controlled the election of popes and sometimes chose men whose morals were questionable. Many bishops and abbots cared more about their position as feudal lords than about their duties as spiritual leaders.

During the years between 1000 and 1300, the state of the Church improved dramatically. Religion spread more widely and deeply in society than before. Thousands of men and women became monks and nuns. At the head of the Church, strong popes challenged the power of emperors and kings.

Monks adopted stricter rules.

One of the first signs of reform in the Church was the founding in 910 of a new French monastery at Cluny (KLOO-nee). Cluny was founded by a nobleman, the Duke of Aquitaine. Unlike many lords, the duke did not try to make Cluny a source of personal wealth and power. Instead, he arranged that the monastery be subject only to the pope, not to any nearby lord or bishop.

The abbots of Cluny held strictly to the Benedictine rule. Soon Cluny's reputation for purity inspired the founding of similar monasteries throughout western Europe. By the year 1000, there were 300 houses under Cluny's leadership. Cluny acted as a headquarters for Church reform.

For many men and women, the Benedictine rule no longer seemed strict enough for a holy life. After the year 1000, new groups of monks and nuns chose to live by even stricter rules. For example, the members of the Cistercian (sihs-TUHR-shuhn) order, founded in 1098, vowed to build their monasteries only in the wilderness. The Cistercians often took the lead in the great movement to clear new farmlands. Their life of hardship won many followers.

Reformers ended abuses.

Reformers hoped to purify the Church by freeing it from control by lords and kings. The first step was to free the papacy from the control of Italian nobles. In 1059, a Church decree declared that all future popes would be chosen at a meeting of leading bishops known as **cardinals**. No longer could the Roman mob, the local nobles, or even the emperor choose a pope.

Reformers were also eager to abolish three conditions that were widespread in the Church of the early Middle Ages. First, they wanted to put an end to the *marriage of priests*. Many village priests married and had families, even though such marriages were against Church rulings.

Second, reformers wanted to stop the buying and selling of Church offices, called *simony* (SYE-muh-nee). Many bishops expected to make a profit from their high position. Every Church office brought with it land and a good income. One greedy bishop wrote: "I have gold and I received the [office of bishop] . . . I ordain a priest and I receive gold. I make a deacon and I receive a heap of silver . . ." Like marriage for priests, simony was against Church law but still was widely practiced.

Lay investiture was the third practice Church reformers wanted to end. Just as vassals received their fiefs in a feudal ceremony, bishops and abbots went through a ceremony to receive their Church offices. In both cases, the ceremony was known as investiture. Who should perform this ceremony for Church officials, a layman (feudal lord or king) or a Church leader? If the ceremony was performed by a layman, it was called lay investiture.

Whoever controlled the ceremony held the real power in naming a bishop. Naturally, kings favored lay investiture. Bishops were powerful nobles, and kings wanted to control them. Naturally too, Church reformers frowned on lay investiture. They said that a bishop should not be the political pawn of any king.

Gregory VII clashed with Henry IV.

In 1073, the foremost leader of the reformers became pope. He took the name of Gregory VII. The new pope quickly carried out the aims of the reform movement. He first ordered all married priests to abandon their wives and children. Then, in 1075, he banned lay investiture.

The young German ruler, Henry IV, flew into a rage. Henry held the title of emperor, passed down since the time of Charlemagne. Henry called a meeting of German bishops, who had all been invested by himself. With their approval, the emperor sent a vicious letter calling Gregory "not pope, but false monk" and ordering him to step down from the papacy.

Gregory replied in the same temper, sending this letter to the German bishops:

> I take from King Henry . . . the government of the whole kingdom of the Germans and the Italians, and I free all Christian people from any oath they have made or shall make to him, and I forbid any to serve the king.

Furthermore, the pope excommunicated Henry.

In this showdown, who would prove the stronger, pope or emperor? Everything hinged on the loyalties of the German bishops and princes. Would they side with their earthly lord or their spiritual lord? They decided to support Pope Gregory. Deserted by his bishops and threatened by rebellious German princes, Henry's position seemed hopeless. The only way to save his throne was to win the pope's forgiveness.

In the middle of winter, 1077, Henry journeyed over the snowy Alps to the Italian town of Canossa (kuh-NAHS-uh). He approached the castle where Pope Gregory was a guest. In Gregory's own words, "He [Henry] presented himself at the gate of the castle, barefoot and clad only in a wretched woolen garment, beseeching us with tears to grant him . . . forgiveness." As pope, Gregory had no choice but to forgive any sinner who came humbly to him. Still, he kept Henry waiting in the snow for three days before ending his excommunication.

This meeting in Canossa was one of the most dramatic confrontations of the Middle Ages, but it solved nothing. It was a master political stroke for Henry, who was free to go home and punish the nobles who had rebelled against him. Yet it was an even greater victory for the pope. He had humiliated the proudest ruler in Europe. The question of investiture was still undecided.

Gregory died in 1085, Henry in 1106. Their successors continued to fight over investiture until 1122. In that year, representatives of the Church and the emperor met in the German city of Worms (vohrms). They reached a compromise known as the *Concordat of Worms*. By its terms, the Church alone would grant a bishop his ring and staff, symbols of Church office. However, the emperor kept the power to grant that bishop the lands that went with his office. Thus, the emperor still had much control over the bishops. (The kings of France and England had reached the same sort of compromise earlier.)

Popes ruled a spiritual empire.

In many ways, the popes who followed Gregory VII exercised greater power than any king or prince. As with Henry IV, a king who quarreled with the pope faced excommunication, which freed all his vassals from their duties to him.

If an excommunicated king or duke continued to disobey, the pope had another weapon—the **interdict**. No Church ceremonies could be performed in the offending ruler's lands. There could be no marriages, no baptisms, no religious services of any sort. In the Age of Faith, fear of the interdict put great pressure on a king to bow to a pope's demands.

Church law and government In the 1100's and 1200's, the Church resembled a kingdom. It was governed by a single ruler (the pope) from a central capital (Rome). A group of advisers, called the papal *Curia*, served as the pope's staff. The Curia supplied him with information, offered advice, and carried out decisions. The pope also had his own diplomats, known as *legates*, who traveled through Europe dealing with bishops and kings.

Outside Rome, the power of the Church was in the hands of bishops. Bishops operated courts of law that rivaled the feudal courts of lords and kings. Bishops' courts ruled on such matters as marriage, divorce, and wills. Thus, all Christians were partly governed by **canon law**, the law of the Church.

The Church was like a kingdom in yet another sense. It collected taxes. Every Christian family was required to give to the Church one tenth of its yearly income as a tithe.

Social services According to canon law, bishops were to use at least one fourth of all tithes to care for the sick and the poor. Orphans, lepers, and beggars received care from Church funds.

Most hospitals in medieval Europe were operated by the Church. Around the year 1200, there were 400 hospitals in England and 12 in Paris alone. No needy person could be turned away.

War against heresy Like other rulers in the Middle Ages, popes thought of themselves as warriors. Time and again, as you will read, they urged Christians to go to war against Muslims. The Church also went to war against enemies closer to home—heretics.

With the widespread interest in religion of the 1100's and 1200's, people seriously pondered religious questions. Not surprisingly, some reached answers that differed from the Church's teachings. Many heresies sprang up in Europe during the 1200's. The Church struck back with all its might. In some cases, whole villages of suspected heretics were slaughtered.

The Inquisition (IN-kwuh-ZISH-uhn) was the leading arm of the Church in the war against heresy. The Inquisition was an organization of experts whose job was to find and judge heretics. Beginning around 1225, popes sent many such experts throughout Europe. These men left no stone unturned in their search for heresy, even accepting rumors and gossip. A person who was suspected of heresy might be questioned for weeks and even tortured. It was almost impossible for a suspect to prove his or her innocence.

Friars preached to the poor.

The Church had another weapon in its fight against heresy. In the early 1200's, wandering **friars** traveled from place to place. By preaching, friars tried to carry the Church's ideas more widely and win heretics back to the Church. Like monks, friars took vows of chastity, poverty, and obedience. Unlike monks, however, friars did not live apart from the world in monasteries. Instead, friars preached to the poor, especially in Europe's rapidly growing towns. Friars owned nothing and lived by begging.

The earliest order of friars were the Dominicans. They took their name from Dominic, a Spanish priest who walked barefoot through southern France preaching against heresy. Because Dominic emphasized the importance of study, many Dominicans were formidable scholars.

A second order of friars was founded by an Italian known as Francis of Assisi (uh-SEE-see). The son of a rich merchant, Francis gave up his wealth and turned to preaching when he was about 20 years old. Francis treated all creatures as if they were his spiritual brothers and sisters. Most famous is the episode in which, according to popular legend, he stopped along the road to preach to a flock of birds. Francis placed much less importance on scholarship than did Dominic.

Caring for the sick and needy was the responsibility of the Church in the Middle Ages. These nuns are treating patients in a French hospital of the 1400's.

Women joined both the Franciscans and the Dominicans, although the Church did not allow them to travel from place to place as preachers. Like the men, these women lived in poverty and worked selflessly to help the poor and sick.

Soon white-robed Dominicans and brown-robed Franciscans were a common sight on the roads of Europe. In this age of reform, friars won wide respect for their poverty and their devout way of life.

Churches rose in a new style.

Although the friars chose to live in poverty, evidence of the Church's wealth could be seen everywhere in the Middle Ages. Between 1000 and 1100, towns in Europe began to build massive stone churches. The huge doors were framed by round arches like the arches on buildings in ancient Rome. The heavy roof pressed down on the thick walls and on two rows of thick pillars within the church. Walls were painted in brilliant colors. This style of architecture was called *Romanesque* (ROH-muh-NEHSK).

Romanesque churches were certainly impressive, but at least one man was not satisfied with them. That man was Suger (soo-ZHAY), abbot of the monastery of Saint Denis (sahn duh-NEE) near Paris. To Suger's eye, Romanesque churches had two great faults. First, they looked heavy and earthbound. Second, their tiny windows set in thick walls let in little light.

In 1137, Suger began to direct the rebuilding of the church at Saint Denis. He wanted the new building to thrust upward as if reaching toward heaven. He wanted light to stream in from all sides, reminding worshipers that God was the light of the world.

Suger's goals—more height and more light—seemed to defy the laws of medieval architecture. To lift a heavy roof higher and higher meant that you had to make the walls supporting it thicker and thicker. But thicker walls meant smaller and fewer windows, hence less light.

For several decades, master builders in France had been experimenting with new techniques. Under Suger's guidance, these ideas came together at Saint Denis. The result was a new style of architecture known as the *Gothic* style. Three new building techniques were the key to Gothic architecture:

1. *Pointed, ribbed vaults* In the new Gothic churches, narrow bands of stone called ribs ran from the roof to the columns below and helped support the roof's weight. The sections of walls between the pillars carried no weight at all. These walls became frames for huge stained-glass windows.
2. *Flying buttresses* Stone roofs pushed not only downward but outward. To support this outward pressure, Gothic builders made braces of beautifully carved stone. These braces slanted up against the outside walls of the cathedral. They were called flying buttresses.
3. *Pointed arches* To emphasize the height of a Gothic church, all the arches rose to points. The highest arch was the vaulted ceiling itself, where all lines came together as if pointing toward heaven.

Soon Gothic cathedrals were rising in many towns of northern France. In 1163, the people of Paris set out to build the tallest church in Christendom. The vaulted ceiling of the Cathedral of Notre Dame (NOH-truh DAHM) eventually rose to 114 feet. Then Chartres, Reims, Amiens, and Beauvais built even higher cathedrals.

The Gothic style spread to other parts of Europe. In all, nearly 500 Gothic churches were built between 1170 and 1270. All were beautiful, but none had windows quite as beautiful as those of Chartres. The stained-glass windows at Chartres illustrated stories from the Bible. As illiterate peasants walked past the 176 windows, they could "read" those stories. The thousands of stone carvings that framed every door in the cathedral showed more Bible stories. Scholars called Chartres "a Bible for the poor."

Section Review 2

Define: (a) cardinal, (b) simony, (c) lay investiture, (d) interdict, (e) legate, (f) canon law, (g) heretic, (h) friar

Identify: (a) Cluny, (b) Cistercian order, (c) Henry IV, (d) Gregory VII, (e) Canossa, (f) Concordat of Worms, (g) Curia, (h) Inquisition, (i) Dominic, (j) Francis of Assisi, (k) Suger, (l) Romanesque, (m) Gothic

Answer:

1. What were the major changes that Church reformers tried to achieve?

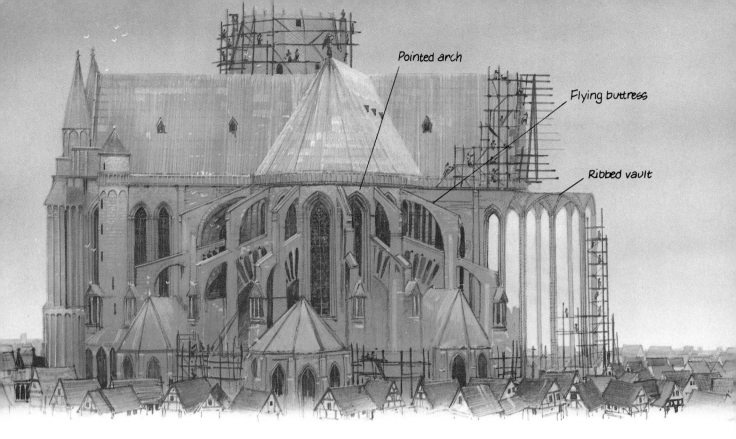

Pointed arch

Flying buttress

Ribbed vault

One of the glories of the cathedral of Chartres is its great rose window (below left). The cathedral of Bourges (below right) in France clearly achieves the twin goals of Gothic architecture, height and light.

2. (a) Why did Henry IV favor lay investiture? (b) Describe the main events in the conflict between Henry IV and Gregory VII.
3. How was the Church similar to a kingdom?
4. (a) In its fight against heresy, how did the Church use the Inquisition? (b) The work of the friars?
5. How was Gothic architecture different from Romanesque architecture?

Critical Thinking
6. Why was the Concordat of Worms a compromise settlement?
7. Suppose you visited a medium-sized town in France around 1250. What evidence might you see in daily life that this was the Age of Faith? List as many examples as you can.

Royal governments grew stronger. 3

In part, Europe owed its prosperity to the coming of more peaceful times. By 1000, the great invasions of Vikings, Magyars, and Muslims had come to an end. Law, order, and peace were slowly gaining ground. By the 1050's, kings, dukes, and counts were winning greater control over their lands, ending petty wars between vassals, driving out nests of bandits, and in general, keeping the peace.

Kings had little more power than other great lords. In the words of the time, the king was "first among equals." Yet, like other lords, kings began to strengthen their control over their own lands. In doing so, they laid the groundwork for the growth of royal power.

Norman conquerors ruled England.

Surprisingly, the king who laid the foundations for royal power in England was not English at all. He was William, Duke of Normandy. Although William was a descendant of Rollo the Viking, by 1050 the Normans were French in language and culture.

The Norman Conquest How did a French duke become king of England? The story began when England's aged King Edward the Confessor died without an heir in January 1066. As Edward's second cousin, William claimed the English crown. William was ambitious, tough, and brave. Yet so was his rival, the English nobleman Harold Godwinson. Harold had been named king by a council of English lords. In the end, perhaps what helped William most was plain luck.

By the summer of 1066, William had gathered an army to invade England. The story of William's invasion is vividly recorded on the famous Bayeux (by-YOO) Tapestry, woven soon after the event. On this piece of linen 231 feet long, the drama unfolds scene by scene. The Norman knights and their horses crowded onto ships. They disembarked on English shores. Then came the battle that changed the course of English history—the Battle of Hastings.

On October 14, 1066, King Harold's English foot soldiers grouped themselves on the top of a small hill. The Norman knights on horseback charged. At the front of the Norman army went Taillefer, the Norman bard, spinning his sword in the air and singing the Song of Roland.

The battle raged from morning till dusk. Several times, the English seemed on the edge of victory. Then, luck stepped in for William. Late in the day, Harold fell dead with an arrow in his eye. The Normans broke through the English lines, and the Battle of Hastings ended in a decisive Norman victory.

William the Conqueror (1066–1087) After his victory, William (now called "the Conqueror") declared all England his personal property. The English lords who had supported Harold lost their lands. William then granted fiefs to about 200 Norman lords who swore oaths of loyalty to him. He also granted lands to the Church, appointing Norman bishops who were his loyal

Footnote to History

As a result of the Norman conquest, French became the language of the upper class in England and remained so for nearly 300 years. About one fourth of the words in modern English are of French origin. In many cases, modern English has two words for the same thing, one French and one English. For example, *flower* comes from a French word, but *blossom* has an English root word.

This scene from the Bayeux Tapestry shows Harold's English footsoldiers forming a shield wall against the mounted Norman knights at Hastings.

vassals. England suddenly had a new ruling class of French-speaking nobles.

William kept about one fifth of England for himself, a powerful base for any king. Thus, William made England the most centralized feudal kingdom in Europe.

Henry II (1154–1189) Thanks to William's harsh but efficient rule, later kings of England had a strong base on which to build. William's great-grandson, Henry II, became king in 1154 and further increased royal power.

Henry's greatest achievement lay in strengthening the royal courts of justice. He sent royal judges to visit every part of England at least once a year. These judges collected taxes, settled lawsuits, and punished crimes. Henry also introduced the use of the **jury** in English courts. A jury in medieval England was a group of local people—usually 12 neighbors—who answered questions about the facts of a case for a royal judge.

Suppose Knight X and Knight Y both claimed a certain piece of land. In earlier times, such a case might have been settled in trial by combat at a lord's court. In Henry's royal court, the judge would call together 12 nearby landholders who were the knights' social equals, or peers. The 12 were sworn to tell the judge what they believed to be true in the case. (The word *jury* comes from the French *juree*, meaning "oath.") Then the judge would decide which knight was in the right. Jury trials became a popular way of settling disputes. Only the king's courts were allowed to conduct them.

As the king's courts gained in importance, the lords' feudal courts declined. Thus, the king of England won power from the nobles.

Over the centuries, case by case, the rulings of England's royal judges formed a unified body of law. Because this law was common to the whole kingdom, it was known as **common law**. Today, the principles of English common law are the basis for law in many English-speaking countries, including the United States.

The Capetian dynasty ruled France.

The kings of France, too, looked for ways of increasing their power. In theory, all French lords were vassals of the French king. In fact, however, after the breakup of Charlemagne's empire, French counts and dukes ruled their lands as if they were independent. By the year 1000, France was divided into about 30 feudal territories.

In 987, the last member of the Carolingian family—Louis the Sluggard—died. To succeed him, France's most powerful nobles chose Hugh Capet (**KAP**-uht), an undistinguished duke from the middle of France. The Capet family ruled only a small territory, but at its heart stood Paris, on a well-protected island in the Seine River. Hugh Capet ruled from 987 to 996. He began the Capetian (kuh-**PEE**-shuhn) dynasty of French kings.

When the French lords chose Hugh Capet, they assumed he would be a weak king. (They had no national loyalties to the region we call France. Such feelings did not exist until centuries later.)

221

What they wanted was someone they could control. Hugh Capet did not disappoint them; neither did his son and grandson. The first three Capetian kings were little more than petty feudal lords.

Though weak rulers, the Capetians survived. The first six Capetians ruled for nearly 200 years (987–1180), an average of 32 years per reign. For many generations, Capetian queens bore healthy sons. Thus, bloody civil wars over the succession were avoided.

Time and geography were on the side of the Capetian kings. Their territory, though small, sat astride important trade routes in northern France. For 200 years, Capetian kings tightened their grip on this strategic area. The power of the French king gradually spread outward from Paris. Eventually, the growth of royal power would unite France.

German kings failed to unite their lands.

After the death of Charlemagne, Germany was the strongest of the kingdoms that arose from the ruins of his empire. Yet in building royal power, the rulers of Germany faced a different set of problems than did the kings of England and France. When the last Carolingian died in 911, the German nobles claimed the right to elect the next king.

Otto the Great (936–973) In 919, the Duke of Saxony, known as Henry the Fowler, was elected king. He ruled until 939, winning several important victories over the Slavs and the Magyars. (One of Henry's distant descendants was the emperor Henry IV, who begged the pope's forgiveness at Canossa.)

Map Study

Which ruler appears to have been more powerful, the king of France or the king of England? What are the two largest empires shown?

The strongest ruler of medieval Germany was Henry's son Otto I, known as Otto the Great. Otto, who became king in 936, consciously copied the policies of his boyhood hero, Charlemagne. He even chose to be crowned king at Charlemagne's old capital, Aachen.

Otto ended the threat of Magyar raids by crushing the Magyars at the Battle of Lechfield in 955. He also set about building up his own power within Germany.

Like other medieval kings, Otto's greatest problem was the power of the nobles within his kingdom. To limit that power, Otto turned for support to the bishops and abbots of the Church. These churchmen were themselves feudal lords with armies of knights at their command.

Otto was able to dominate the Church in Germany by granting fiefs only to loyal bishops and abbots. He made his brother archbishop of Cologne and his son archbishop of Mainz. With armies drawn from Church lands, Otto overpowered the great princes of Germany.

Despite this success, Otto still yearned to be crowned emperor as Charlemagne had been in 800. In 951 and again in 962, he invaded Italy. Italian towns such as Genoa, Pisa, and Venice had grown wealthy from trade with Asia, and they were a powerful bait for the German emperor. During his second invasion, Otto entered Rome to defend the pope from an Italian duke. This time, the pope rewarded Otto with the imperial crown he coveted.

The German-Italian empire created by Otto was known first as the Roman Empire of the German Nation and later as the Holy Roman Empire. It remained the strongest state in Europe until about 1100. In the long run, though, Otto's attempt to revive Charlemagne's empire caused trouble for later German kings. Italian nobles resented German rule. Popes too came to fear the political power of the German kings in Italy. As you have read, Henry IV of Germany nearly lost his crown in a long power struggle with the pope over lay investiture (page 216).

During that struggle, German princes regained much of the power they had lost under Otto. Thus, a later German ruler would have to begin again to build up royal authority. That ruler was Frederick Barbarossa.

Frederick Barbarossa (1152–1190) Seven German princes had the right to elect the German king. By 1152, even these princes realized that Germany needed a strong king to keep the peace. They chose Frederick I. A handsome, golden-haired man and a great warrior, Frederick was the ideal medieval king. His red beard earned him the nickname *Barbarossa* (Italian for "red beard").

Frederick was the first ruler to call his lands the Holy Roman Empire. Yet what he really ruled was not so much an empire as a patchwork of feudal territories. By his own forceful personality and his skill as a soldier, Frederick was able to control the German princes. But whenever he was out of the country, disorder returned.

Frederick did not concentrate on building royal power in Germany. Instead, like Otto the Great, he turned his attention south to the rich cities of Italy. Frederick invaded Italy repeatedly, spreading destruction wherever he went. His brutal tactics led Italian merchants to set aside their differences and unite against him. Also fearful of Frederick, the pope joined with the merchants. Together, Frederick's enemies formed an alliance called the Lombard League.

In 1176, the foot soldiers of the Lombard League faced Frederick's army of mounted knights at the Battle of Legnano (lay-NYAHN-oh). The German knights suffered a smashing defeat. For the first time, foot soldiers defeated feudal knights. The Battle of Legnano showed that towns could wield military as well as economic power. It was an omen for the future.

In 1179, Frederick made peace with the pope and returned to Germany. By that time, however, he had lost his chance to limit the power of the German princes. Their power continued to grow in spite of Frederick's efforts. After he drowned in 1190, his empire was torn to pieces.

Therefore, unlike England and France, Germany did not become a united country during the Middle Ages. There were several reasons why German kings failed to unite their country. First, the system of electing the king weakened Germany. It made the nobles more powerful than the king. Second, German rulers had fewer royal lands to use as a base of power than did the kings of France and England. Third, German kings continued to try to revive Charlemagne's empire by involving themselves in Italian politics. This policy led to wars not only with Italian cities but also with the pope.

Section Review 3

Define: (a) jury, (b) common law
Identify: (a) William the Conqueror,
(b) Harold Godwinson, (c) Battle of Hastings,
(d) Henry II, (e) Hugh Capet, (f) Otto the
Great, (g) Holy Roman Empire, (h) Frederick
Barbarossa, (i) Battle of Legnano
Answer:
1. How did William the Conqueror lay the basis
   for strong central government in England?
2. How did Henry II's royal courts strengthen
   the king's power over the lords?
3. Describe the proceedings at a jury trial in
   medieval England.
4. Give two factors that strengthened the Capetian dynasty.
5. How did German rulers succeed to the throne?
6. (a) How did Otto the Great make the crown
   stronger than the German nobles? (b) What
   problems did Otto's policies create for his
   successors?

Critical Thinking
7. Look at a map of modern Europe. Suppose
   that the descendants of William the Conqueror
   and of Otto I had succeeded in holding the
   lands these two men ruled. How might the
   map of Europe be different today?

Learning revived and spread. 4

As kings grew more powerful, they needed
officials trained in law and record keeping for
their growing governments. At first, most royal
officials came from the Church, because few
others could read or write. By the late 1100's,
however, literacy was spreading to people outside
the Church. Just as Europe's material prosperity
was growing, so was European interest in learning.

Scholars gathered at universities.

At the center of the new growth of learning
stood an institution that was new to Europe—
the university. Athens, Alexandria, Baghdad, and
Constantinople had all had their universities,
but never before had such a center of learning
existed in western Europe. The first universities
in Europe were not ivy-covered buildings on green
campuses. The word *university* originally meant
a group of scholars. People, not buildings, made
up the medieval university.

Universities had arisen at Paris, France, and
Bologna, Italy, by the end of the 1100's. (The
exact dates are uncertain.) Others followed at
Oxford, England, and Salerno, Italy.

Most students came from middle-class families,
not from the nobility. They were the sons of
burghers or well-to-do artisans. (Girls could not
attend.) For most students, the goal was a job
in government or the Church.

Since the university had no buildings, classes
met in rented rooms or in the choir section of
a church. Lucky students sat on a bench. Most
squatted on the straw-covered floor as they tried
to memorize the master's lecture. Because writing
materials were scarce, all exams were oral.

As much as they might love books, few students
could afford to own even one. Because all books
were handwritten, a single book cost the equivalent of $600 or $700. Many students rented
their textbooks, but even this was too costly for
some. Often the only textbook for a course belonged to the teacher who read it aloud, line by
line, and offered his own comments.

To earn a bachelor's degree, students spent 3
to 5 years in school before taking a final exam.
A master's degree required an additional 3 to 4
years (in Paris, as long as 15 years). With such
a degree, however, a scholar could teach anywhere
in Europe. There was no language barrier since
scholars everywhere spoke Latin.

Scholars rediscovered Greek writings.

The revival of learning made Europeans more
interested in the works of ancient scholars. At
the same time, the growth of trade brought Europeans into contact with Muslims and Byzantines. In those empires, the writings of the old
Greek philosophers had survived.

Christian scholars from Europe began visiting
Muslim libraries in Toledo, Spain. There, Jewish
scholars translated Arabic copies of Aristotle and
other Greek writers into Latin. From Constantinople, Europeans brought home Latin translations of Justinian's code of laws. All at once,

Europeans acquired a huge new body of knowledge on science, philosophy, law, and religion.

Christian scholars were excited by the Greek writings but also deeply troubled by them. After all, the ancient Greeks had been pagans. Their knowledge was not based on the Bible but on their own powers of reasoning. Could a Christian scholar use Aristotle's logical approach to truth and still keep faith with the Bible? This was the debate that shook scholars in the 1100's.

Aquinas linked faith and reason.

In the mid-1200's, the scholar Thomas Aquinas (uh-KWYE-nuhs) found no conflict between faith and reason. He believed that the most basic religious truths could be proved by logical argument.

Born in 1225 in Italy, Thomas Aquinas joined the Dominicans when he was about 18 years old. He then went to the University of Paris. After his studies, he stayed to teach there.

Between 1267 and 1273, Aquinas created a scholarly work of colossal scope called the *Summa Theologiae*. In its 21 volumes, he attempted to answer 631 philosophical questions about God and the universe. For each question, he used logic and reason to show the truth of the Church's answer and to refute any other answers. The *Summa Theologiae* was like a cathedral of scholarship. Its stones were reasoned arguments, but it rose from the same foundation as Chartres Cathedral—a foundation of faith.

Poems praised knightly heroes.

Learning was also reviving outside the Church. Most feudal lords cared little about the debate over reason and faith, but they enjoyed the heroic poems known as *chansons de geste* (songs of deeds). Sung to the accompaniment of a lute, each song celebrated a warrior-hero. Unlike learned writings, these poems were not in Latin but in the languages people spoke every day.

One of the earliest and most famous of the heroic poems was the Song of Roland. It praised the courage of the band of French soldiers led by Roland who perished in battle during Charlemagne's reign (page 195). Although the actual battle had been against bandits, the poem transformed it into a battle between a few French

Daily Life · *Medieval Writing Materials*

"Finished, thank God." Medieval students, who sometimes acquired books by renting and then copying them letter by letter, often added these words of relief to their last page. The process of copying a book was indeed a long and painstaking one. It began with the purchase of the paperlike material called parchment or vellum, made from the skin of lambs, calves, or kids. However, a student could not simply sit down with his sheets of vellum and begin to write. The vellum was usually rough when he bought it. The student had to scrape it with a knife or razor, sprinkle it with chalk, and rub it smooth and white with a rough stone. Then, with a ruler and a pointed tool, he drew grooves in the vellum to mark off lines and margins.

The student made his own ink from black soot, charcoal, or bark. His inkwell was a cow's horn set into a round hole in his writing board, and he wrote with the point of a goose feather. He would dip his pen into the ink, write a line, and then, if the weather was damp, dry the ink with the heat from a basin of coals. If he made a mistake, he would scrape it off with a knife and rub the area smooth again with a boar's tooth.

Guests at this wedding banquet in the 1400's ate almost everything with their fingers. For cutting, they used the daggers that they carried all the time. For entertainment, minstrels played from a gallery above the banquet hall.

knights and an overwhelming army of Muslims from Spain. Many an evening, lords and knights heard the familiar tale. They applauded the valor of Roland's friend, Turpin, a warrior-bishop. Surrounded by enemies, Turpin fights on:

Turpin of Reims feels himself overcome,
His body pierced by four spears.
Yet he gets quickly to his feet,
Looks for Roland, runs to him,
And says one thing: "I am not beaten yet.
While life remains, no good knight gives up."

The Song of Roland celebrated courage in battle, but later tales had wider scope. Stories about King Arthur and his knights dealt with battle but also with issues of pride, loyalty, and justice. The story of Tristan and Isolde, like many poems of the period, dealt with ill-fated love.

Poems show how the ideals of noble society were changing. In the early days, little was asked of a knight other than courage in battle and loyalty to his lord. By the High Middle Ages, however, knights were expected to live up to a complex set of ideals. These ideals became known as the code of **chivalry** (SHIH-vuhl-ree).

Knights lived by a code of chivalry.

The word *chivalry* comes from the French word *cheval* (horse) and *chevalier* (horse-riding lord). The code demanded that a knight fight bravely in the defense of three masters: his earthly feudal lord, his heavenly Lord, and his chosen lady. Furthermore, a knight should aid the poor and defend the weak. Few knights actually met these standards. Even so, the ideals of chivalry helped raise European civilization to a new level.

A *knight's education* The education of a young nobleman began at age seven when his parents sent him off to the castle of another lord, possibly a relative. Here he acted as a page, waiting on his hosts and learning manners. In his free hours, he played with fellow pages at fencing, hunting, and chess. Before 1250, pages seldom were taught to read, since this skill was thought unmanly. (Girls learned music and weaving because these were judged to be feminine arts.)

At around the age of 14, the page was raised to the rank of squire. He now waited on a knight of the household, helping him with his armor and weapons. The squire also practiced his own skills with sword and lance on horseback. The squire accompanied the knight on the hunt and in battle.

Becoming a knight A squire became a full-fledged knight when he was about 21 years old. First, to wash away impurities of soul and body, he had an elaborate bath. He spent a day fasting and a night praying in church. Then he knelt before the lord of the manor, who dubbed him a knight by slapping him on the shoulder with the flat of a sword. The new knight was hoisted onto his horse and galloped joyously around the church.

Mock battles for glory After being dubbed a knight, most young men traveled with companions for a year or two. They gained experience fighting in local wars or taking part in mock battles called tournaments.

In a tournament, two armies of knights charged each other, accompanied by the blare of trumpets and the cheers of lords and ladies. As in real war, prisoners captured in the tournament were held for ransom by their captor.

The idea of romantic love arose.

Before 1100, knights seemed interested only in winning the admiration of fellow men. In the Song of Roland and other heroic poems, women played a minor role. Then, in the 1100's, a whole new set of ideals evolved. Under the code of chivalry, a knight's duty to his lady became fully as important as his duty to his lord. Indeed, in many poems, the hero's difficulty resulted from a conflict between the two duties.

Poets called troubadours (**TROO**-buh-DOHRZ) sang the praises of noble ladies and the knights who loved them. Sometimes troubadours sang their own verses in the castles of their lady. Other times they sent roving minstrels to carry their song to court.

Southern France was the homeland of the first troubadours. The most celebrated woman of the age was Eleanor of Aquitaine (1122–1204). Troubadours flocked to her court in the French duchy of Aquitaine. Later, as queen of England, Eleanor was the mother of Richard the Lionheart. Richard himself composed romantic songs and poems. Eleanor's daughter, Marie of Champagne, made love into a subject of study like logic or law. She presided at a famed Court of Love to which troubled lovers brought their grievances.

The role of women changed.

The idea of romantic love placed women on a pedestal where they could be worshiped. Yet women in the High Middle Ages probably had less real power than in earlier years. It is true that Eleanor of Aquitaine ruled England at times for her husband, Henry II, and later for her sons Richard and John. Few other women, however, had such opportunities.

As society became more peaceful and organized, women's roles were increasingly limited to the home and the convent. More and more often, lords passed down their fiefs only to their sons. Women held less property. As royal judges and officials gained power, queens shared less in ruling the land.

Girls from noble families were usually married around the age of 16, often to men in their 30's, 40's, or 50's. (Young men could not marry until they had property of their own, usually after their fathers died.) The girls themselves had little to say in the choice of a husband.

After marriage, a woman had her greatest power and independence while her husband was away at war. After 1100, as you will read in the next section, many knights left home for years to fight in the Crusades. In their absence, women often held power, but usually unofficially.

These women are breaking flax to get fibers to spin into thread and then weave into cloth.

Section Review 4

Define: (a) university, (b) chivalry, (c) page, (d) squire, (e) tournament, (f) troubadour
Identify: (a) Thomas Aquinas, (b) *Summa Theologiae*, (c) Song of Roland, (d) Eleanor of Aquitaine
Answer:
1. Why was learning difficult for students in a medieval university?
2. (a) How did scholars in western Europe become familiar with the writings of the ancient Greeks? (b) What problem did Christian scholars see in these writings? (c) What was the importance of the *Summa Theologiae?*
3. Describe the process by which a young nobleman learned to become a knight.
4. How did the role of women change during the Middle Ages?

Critical Thinking
5. Explain why the ideas of chivalry and romantic love were signs of a less warlike age.

Crusaders marched against Islam. 5

Near Clermont in southern France, a crowd of nobles and churchmen gazed upward at Pope Urban II as he addressed them from a wooden platform. His voice boomed forth:

From the confines of Jerusalem and from Constantinople, a grievous report has gone forth that an accursed race has violently invaded the lands of these Christians, and has depopulated them by pillage and fire.

The year was 1095. The "accursed race" was the Seljuk Turks who had recently stormed Baghdad, taken Jerusalem, and conquered all of Asia Minor from the Byzantine Greeks. The Byzantine emperor, Alexius Comnenus, appealed for assistance against the Turks. In response, the pope called on the knights of Christendom to rescue Jerusalem and the Holy Land (that is, the lands where Jesus had lived) from the Muslim Turks. Urban II's speech—one of the most influential in history—concluded:

Jerusalem is a land fruitful above all others, a paradise of delights. That royal city, situated at the center of the earth, implores you to come to her aid. Undertake this journey eagerly for the remission of your sins, and be assured of the reward of imperishable glory in the Kingdom of Heaven.

A feeling of intense excitement swept through the crowd. "God wills it!" someone shouted. Soon everyone was roaring, "God wills it! God wills it!" Thus began the First Crusade. Over the next two centuries, there were eight official Crusades and countless unofficial ones.

The Crusades had many causes.

In 1096, between 50,000 and 60,000 knights became **crusaders.** A crusader is someone who fights on behalf of a religious cause. The crusaders painted red crosses on their armor and marched eastward on a journey from which few would return. The ambitions of three groups fueled the Crusades.

The pope's goals Urban II, like Gregory VII before him, claimed to be the leader of all Christendom. What better way to show the pope's power than to send an army of knights from all Europe's kingdoms on a holy war?

Urban II also hoped to reunite Byzantine and Roman Christians. The Byzantine empire, though Christian, denied that the pope was the supreme head of the Church. Urban II still hoped to heal this breach. Perhaps a successful Crusade would persuade the Byzantines to unite with Roman Catholics under Urban's banner.

The knights' goals Most knights probably had mixed motives for joining the crusaders' army. Especially in the First Crusade, many were fired by religious zeal. If they died on the Crusade, the pope promised forgiveness for their sins. For other knights, the Crusades were a chance to win glory in battle. Earthly rewards were also tempting. Rich plunder awaited any army strong enough to conquer the cities of the Holy Land.

The merchants' goals Merchants played little part in the early Crusades, but after 1200 their influence grew. Some merchants supported the Crusades with gifts or loans of cash. Others used their ships to transport armies over the sea, often for a hefty fee. The merchants of Pisa, Genoa,

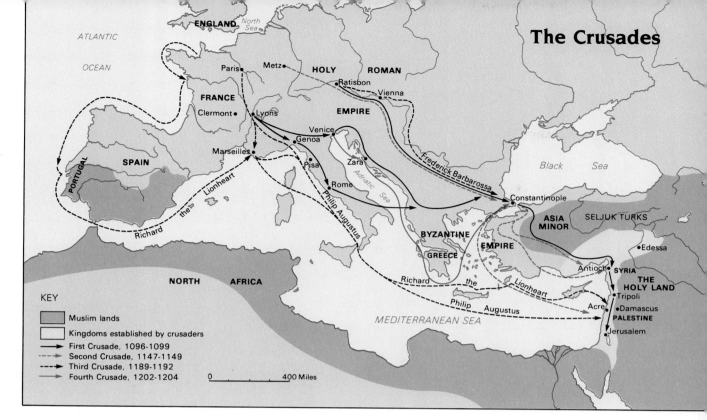

The Crusades

KEY

Muslim lands
Kingdoms established by crusaders
→ First Crusade, 1096-1099
----→ Second Crusade, 1147-1149
- - -→ Third Crusade, 1189-1192
→ Fourth Crusade, 1202-1204

0 ———— 400 Miles

Map Study

Of the three great kings who set out on the Third Crusade, which one took an overland route? Which crusade never reached the Holy Land?

and Venice were eager to win control of key trade routes. For centuries, Muslim traders had ruled the cities of Antioch, Damascus, and Jerusalem. If Christians held those trade centers, more wealth would flow to European merchants.

The First Crusade won Jerusalem.

By early 1097, three huge armies of knights had gathered outside the walls of Constantinople. Most of the crusaders came from France, but there were Germans, Englishmen, Scots, Italians, and Spaniards. They were led by French counts and bishops, not by kings.

The crusaders were well prepared for battle. However, they were woefully unprepared for the trek over the desert to Jerusalem. For two years, they suffered from heat, thirst, hunger, and fever. Yet they somehow mustered enough strength to capture several cities along their route. (Many of their victories were made possible by the fact that the Muslims were fighting among themselves, Arab against Turk.)

Finally, a bedraggled troop of about 12,000 knights (less than one fourth the original army) approached Jerusalem. They besieged the city for a month, sometimes praying and marching barefoot around its walls. Finally, on July 15, 1099, they captured the city.

A dreadful slaughter followed, as Muslim men and women were chased through the streets and murdered. The Jews of the city were rounded up, herded into a temple, and burned to death. One eyewitness reported:

Piles of heads, hands, and feet were to be seen in the streets of the city . . . But these were small matters compared to what happened at the Temple of Solomon [where] men rode in blood up to their knees and bridle reins.

All in all, the crusaders had won a narrow strip of land stretching about 400 miles from Edessa in the north to Jerusalem in the south. Four feudal states were carved out of this territory, each ruled by a French duke or count.

229

Crusaders defended their conquests in the Holy Land by building great castles like Krak des Chevaliers in Syria (above). At left, a wife welcomes her husband home; he wears a cross, the symbol of a crusader.

Later Crusades accomplished little.

The crusaders' states were extremely vulnerable to Muslim counterattack. In 1144, Edessa was reconquered by the Turks. The Second Crusade was organized to recapture the city, but its armies straggled home in defeat.

In 1187, Europeans were shocked by the news that Jerusalem itself had fallen to a Muslim conqueror named Saladin (SAL-uh-dihn). This event touched off appeals by the Church for yet a third Crusade.

The Third Crusade was known as the Kings' Crusade because three of Europe's most powerful monarchs took the cross: the French king Philip Augustus, the German emperor Frederick I (Barbarossa), and the English king Richard I (the Lionheart). Of these three, only Richard won fame. Crossing a river, the 67-year-old Barbarossa fell from his horse and drowned. Philip Augustus caught a fever and went home.

King Richard fought valiantly to regain the Holy Land. In the process, he discovered that his foe, Saladin, could be as chivalrous as himself. Hearing that Richard was ill, Saladin sent his own personal physician and a refreshing gift of snow and peaches. The two leaders came to respect each other and in 1192 agreed to a three-year truce. Jerusalem remained under Muslim control, but Saladin promised that unarmed Christian pilgrims could freely visit the city's holy places.

Crusaders sacked Constantinople.

In 1202, a powerful pope named Innocent III appealed for still another Crusade to rescue Jerusalem from the Muslims. But the knights who took part in this Fourth Crusade never came close to Jerusalem. Instead, they became entangled in Byzantine and Italian politics.

The merchants of Venice were the main culprits in this disaster. They promised to furnish the crusaders with ships and money for their journey to the Holy Land. In exchange, the crusaders were to attack one of Venice's trading rivals—the island of Zara in the Adriatic Sea. The pope protested this diversion but was ignored. The crusaders took Zara. The pope struck back by excommunicating them.

Next, the crusaders moved against Constantinople and the unfriendly Byzantine emperor. The city, split between rival leaders, could not defend itself well. When the crusaders entered the city, they went on a savage spree of looting. They stole the relics from Hagia Sophia and loaded the jewel-studded communion table onto a Venetian ship. (The ship sank and its priceless cargo was never recovered.) The looters set fires that burned much of the city, including libraries with priceless ancient manuscripts. The sack of Constantinople in 1204 ended the Fourth Crusade.

European crusaders controlled Constantinople for 57 years, until the Greeks drove them out in 1261 and restored the Byzantine empire. The breach between the Eastern Orthodox Church and the Roman Catholic Church widened into an ugly and permanent split.

The crusading spirit dwindled.

In the 1200's, Crusades became almost as common as medieval fairs and tournaments. In several later Crusades, armies marched not to the Holy Land but to North Africa. The Fifth Crusade (1218–1221), the Seventh Crusade (1248–1254), and the Eighth Crusade (1270) were all aimed at Islamic cities in Egypt and North Africa. The French king who led the last two Crusades, Louis IX, won wide respect in Europe and was later declared a saint. None of these attempts accomplished much, however.

Of all the later Crusades, the Sixth Crusade (1228–1229) came nearest to success. The Holy Roman emperor, Frederick II, led an army to the Holy Land. There Frederick met with Saladin's nephew and peacefully negotiated a treaty by which Jerusalem was returned to Christian rule. The pope, however, was not pleased. He called the treaty a pact with the devil and excommunicated Frederick.

The Christians' last stronghold in the Holy Land, the city of Acre, fell to the Muslims in 1291. By that time, many Europeans had become cynical about Crusades. Several popes had tried to use them against their religious or political enemies in Europe. For example, Innocent III declared a crusade against the emperor Frederick II.

In the Crusades, all the forces of Europe's revival had come together with explosive energy. The Crusades grew from the forces of religion, feudalism, and chivalry. Yet by 1300, fewer and fewer people were answering the crusading call. People expected their kings to rule wisely at home rather than to set off on knightly adventures. Merchants did not want their flourishing trade interrupted by war. People's loyalty to the idea of Christendom lessened as new loyalties to their own lands of England, France, or Spain grew. The end of the Crusades signaled that the Middle Ages were drawing to a close.

Section Review 5

Define: crusader
Identify: (a) Urban II, (b) Jerusalem, (c) Holy Land, (d) Byzantine empire, (e) Saladin, (f) Richard the Lionheart, (g) Constantinople, (h) Frederick II, (i) Innocent III
Answer:
1. What were the Crusades?
2. What reasons did each of the following have for supporting the Crusades? (a) the pope (b) knights (c) merchants
3. Based on the original goals of the crusaders, which crusade was the most successful?
4. (a) Why was the Third Crusade called the Kings' Crusade? (b) What new view might it have given the crusaders of the Muslims?
5. What happened on the Fourth Crusade?
6. What caused interest in crusading to die down after 1200?

Critical Thinking
7. What factors may have contributed to the crusaders' violence when they reached Jerusalem on the First Crusade?

Footnote to History

In 1212, a German boy named Nicholas convinced many children that they could succeed where armies of knights had failed. Some 20,000 German children set out for Jerusalem believing that the Holy Land would fall to them without a fight. As they crossed the Alps into Italy, many died of hunger. Finally, a bishop persuaded some to go home. Others remained in Italy, where some fell into the hands of dishonest shipowners who sold the young crusaders into slavery in North Africa.

Chapter Review 10

Summary

1. Farming improved and trade revived. Better farming methods made it possible for farmers to grow more food, which brought a population increase in the High Middle Ages. People began to move into towns. Trade expanded, and guilds formed for both merchants and artisans.

2. Religious leaders wielded great power. The great Gothic cathedrals that soared heavenward in many cities were symbols of the Church's power. Yet this power did not go unchallenged. For decades, kings and popes engaged in power struggles.

3. Royal governments grew stronger. England and France developed the basis for strong central governments. Despite the efforts of some strong German rulers, however, Germany did not become united.

4. Learning revived and spread. Europe's first universities developed in the High Middle Ages. Interest in learning grew in part as a result of the rediscovery of ancient Greek writings. Medieval society became more refined as chivalry and romantic love brought changes in knighthood and the view of women.

5. Crusaders marched against Islam. In 1095, the pope called for Christians to go to war to regain the Holy Land. Although the First Crusade captured Jerusalem, later ventures accomplished little.

Reviewing the Facts

1. Define the following terms:
   a. burghers
   b. bourgeoisie
   c. fair
   d. guild
   e. apprentice
   f. journeyman
   g. cardinal
   h. interdict
   i. canon law
   j. friar
   k. jury
   l. common law
   m. chivalry
   n. crusader

2. Explain the importance of each of the following names, dates, places, or terms:
   a. three-field system
   b. Cluny
   c. Canossa
   d. Concordat of Worms
   e. Inquisition
   f. Gothic
   g. William the Conqueror
   h. 1066
   i. Henry II
   j. Hugh Capet
   k. Otto the Great
   l. Frederick Barbarossa
   m. Holy Roman Empire
   n. Thomas Aquinas
   o. Constantinople
   p. Jerusalem
   q. Saladin

3. How did changes in farming lead to an overall change in medieval life?

4. What purposes did guilds serve?

5. Why did the appointment of bishops become the issue in a struggle between kings and popes?

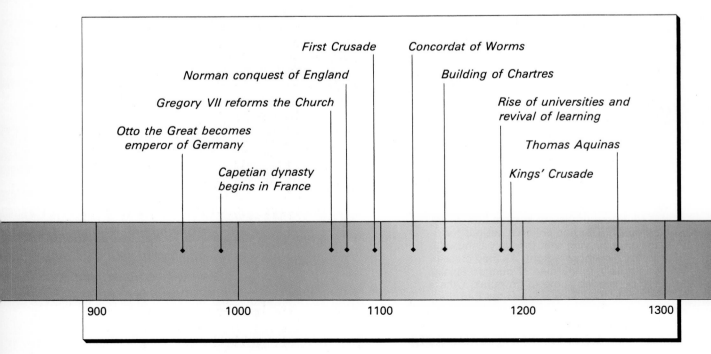

First Crusade

Norman conquest of England

Gregory VII reforms the Church

Otto the Great becomes emperor of Germany

Capetian dynasty begins in France

Concordat of Worms

Building of Chartres

Rise of universities and revival of learning

Thomas Aquinas

Kings' Crusade

900   1000   1100   1200   1300

6. How did the development of Germany differ from that of England and France?
7. (a) Explain how medieval builders solved the problem of supporting the weight of a church roof without using thick walls. (b) What changes did this improvement allow?
8. What debt did universities owe to each of the following? (a) Jewish and Muslim scholars (b) Byzantine scholars (c) monks
9. (a) Why did the Crusades win wide support in Europe? (b) What did they achieve?

Thinking about History

1. The medieval manor was independent and self-sufficient, but towns are interdependent. Explain what this statement means.
2. Guilds set standards for their members' products. How did such rules help to prevent poorly made products? How might this practice be an obstacle to excellence?
3. What factors help to unify a country under one government? Consider what you have read about ancient Egypt, Rome, the Islamic empire, and the medieval kingdoms. Use the following topics as guidelines: (a) geography; (b) language; (c) economic power; and (d) a strong ruler.

Writing and Speaking about History

1. In chart form, compare and contrast the social positions of Egyptian women (page 57), Greek women (pages 103–104), Roman women (page 123), and medieval women (page 203). Which group or groups of women had the most rights? Which had the fewest?
2. Write a 30-word newspaper advertisement for a medieval fair to be held in your home town on October 25, 1250.
3. Hold a panel discussion among the following people. Focus the discussion on the role of each person in the Crusades.

knight	knight's wife
king	queen
child	priest
merchant	serf

Practicing Skills

1. The typical town in medieval Europe in the year 1200 had a population of between 1,500 and 2,000. Locate a town in your area that has a population of about this size. How do you think this town compares with a typical town in the Middle Ages?
2. Compare the illustrations on pages 205 and 212. Use the illustrations to write a thesis statement that tells how the High Middle Ages differed from the Early Middle Ages.
3. Use the time line on page 232 to tell why each of the following dates was significant in the strengthening of royal power.
   a. 962
   b. 987
   c. 1066
4. Label the countries of Europe on an outline map. Compare this map with the one of Europe in 1160 on page 222. Which of the following present-day countries existed as kingdoms in 1160? Which did not exist at all in 1160?
   a. Germany
   b. Spain
   c. France
   d. Italy
   e. England

Investigating History

1. Do a survey of the evolution of armor in the Middle Ages. How did armor change to meet the development of new weapons and methods of warfare during this period?
2. Find books about the cathedrals of the Middle Ages and look for pictures of stained-glass windows. What religious themes are shown? What do the windows tell about occupations in the medieval period?
3. Begin a computer program on the royal families in Europe. Set up one field for the country, one field for the name of the ruler and dates of his or her reign, and one field for important events during that reign.
4. Think of movies or television programs you have seen about the Middle Ages. On the basis of your reading, do you think they were accurate? Explain your answer.

Decision Making in History

Evaluate the decision of Henry IV to ask Pope Gregory for forgiveness. Given the outcome, do you think Henry would make the same decision again?

The Origin of European Nations

There are no pictures of
Joan of Arc that were drawn
during her lifetime. This
picture is one of the earliest.
It appeared in a book called
Lives of Famous Women,
written in 1505, about 75
years after her death.

1. **England and France developed as nations.**

2. **The Church faced a crisis in the 1300's.**

3. **The 1300's brought plague and war.**

4. **New monarchs ruled in western Europe.**

5. **A new empire arose in Russia.**

In April 1429, French peasants peered from their houses and fields
as a small army of perhaps 4,000 soldiers moved across the war-torn
countryside of northern France. Armies were no novelty to these
peasants. France and England had been at war since 1337, and English
armies had tramped all over France. This particular army, however,
was something new. It was French. Its leader was not a hard-bitten
captain but a black-haired, fair-faced peasant girl of 17 who called
herself Joan the Maid. She is known to history as Joan of Arc.

Joan had come to save the French city of Orleans, which the English had been besieging for the past six months. Without help, the city's defenders could not hold out much longer. When Joan reached the threatened city, she sent a message to the English:

You, men of England, who have no right in the kingdom of France, the King of Heaven sends the order through me, Joan the Maid, to return to your own country.

The arrival of this heroic young woman had an electrifying effect on the townspeople of Orleans. They hailed her as champion of all France against the English enemies.

Early in the morning of May 7, 1429, Joan buckled on her white armor. She took up her white linen banner decorated with angels and the lilies of France. The English had built forts blocking the roads into Orleans. Marching against these forts, following Joan's banner into battle, the French army attacked.

You will read later in the chapter whether Joan of Arc and her soldiers won or lost their fight for France. From a historical point of view, the outcome of the battle was less important than its cause. Joan and the men who followed her in 1429 were fighting for a cause that was new to Europe and the world. They were *not* fighting for one feudal lord against another. Unlike the crusaders of an earlier century, they were *not* fighting for Christianity against Muslim enemies. Instead, they were fighting in defense of their homeland, France, against a foreign enemy, England.

Joan of Arc had a feeling of loyalty to a nation—a feeling that we call nationalism. It was a new and powerful force in history. How that feeling of national loyalty arose in France and in England during the 1300's and 1400's is a major theme of this chapter.

In part, the growth of national feeling began with the power struggles of medieval kings from about 1200 to about 1500. These rulers fought against the Church, against powerful lords within their own realms, and against rival kings of other countries.

Slowly, these struggles shattered the power of two great medieval institutions—the Church and feudalism. In their place, we see the beginnings of a powerful new institution—the nation.

By 1500, for the first time, we can speak of nations in the modern sense of the word, not just of feudal kingdoms.

Such a fundamental change took a long time to develop. To see how France and England became separate nations—not just separate kingdoms—we must go back in time 300 years before Joan of Arc put on her white armor. The story begins with the feudal wars of England's King Henry II.

England and France developed as nations. 1

In the late 1100's, France and England were a mixture of interconnected feudal lands. In the early 1200's, however, the two countries began to follow separate paths.

England's king lost his French land.

Henry II, king of England from 1154 to 1189, was also feudal lord of more than half of France. From his great-grandfather, William the Conqueror, Henry had inherited Normandy and other lands in northern France. Henry added to his holdings by marrying Eleanor of Aquitaine, the richest heiress in Europe. She brought him fiefs in southern France. For his French lands, Henry was the vassal of France's Capetian king, Louis VII. However, Henry was a better soldier than Louis and often defeated him.

When Henry and Louis died, the story took a different turn. Henry was succeeded first by his son Richard I, the hero of the Third Crusade. A fearless fighter and skilled general, Richard the Lionheart was able to defend his French lands. When Richard died in 1199 after only ten years as king, he was followed by his younger brother, John, who ruled from 1199 to 1216. John was a complete failure as a military leader; indeed, he won the nickname John Softsword. He soon proved to be no match for the wily king who now wore the French crown, Philip II, known as Philip Augustus.

As a child, Philip had watched his father lose battle after battle to Henry II. When Philip became king in 1180, at the age of 15, he set out to weaken the power of the English kings in France. His greatest triumphs came during John's reign. In 1204, Philip Augustus took Normandy from John. Within two years, he had also won the rest of John's lands in northern France. Only Aquitaine and Gascony in southern France remained loyal to John. By the end of his reign, Philip had tripled the lands under his own direct control. For the first time, a French king was more powerful than any of his vassals. Philip's victories set the stage for England and France to develop as two separate countries.

The barons rebelled against King John.

John's losses in France were just the beginning of his troubles. He soon faced another crisis in England. Some of John's problems stemmed from his own character. According to one historian, John was "selfish, cruel, shameless, cynical, lustful, dishonorable, and utterly false." These character flaws made John's subjects dislike him all the more after his defeats.

In some ways, John's defeats in France proved valuable to England. First, England was gaining an identity as a distinct nation. After John lost Normandy, many lords had to choose whether to hold lands in France or in England. Philip Augustus gave them a year to decide. For those who chose to keep their English lands, England became more important than before. No longer were their interests divided between lands in France and lands in England. Though their ancestors had been Norman, they grew more and more English in customs and loyalty.

John's losses were England's gain for another reason. His unsuccessful wars led directly to the most celebrated document in English history, the Magna Carta.

How did John's wars in France lead to a landmark in English liberty? Wars are always costly. In trying to win back his French lands, John raised taxes to an all-time high. He tried every possible way of squeezing money out of his barons. (The term *barons* includes all the nobles of England who were direct vassals of the king, regardless of their rank. Some were great lords, some were bishops, and a few were simple knights.)

In 1214, John tried again to recover his lands in France. Once again, Philip Augustus defeated him. Soon after John returned to England, his barons revolted. They demanded that John promise to change his ways of governing.

John's situation was hopeless. To keep his crown, he was forced to agree to the barons' terms. Seething with anger, he rode to the appointed meeting place, a broad meadow called Runnymede on the Thames (tehms) River. The barons presented their demands. The date was June 15, 1215, a date that marks a milestone in English history. Four days later, the negotiations between the barons and the king were finished, and John affixed his seal to the document later known as the *Magna Carta* (Great Charter).

The Magna Carta limited royal power.

The English barons were thinking mostly of themselves when they drew up the 63 clauses of the Magna Carta. They wanted to protect themselves from unjust taxes and to safeguard their own feudal rights and privileges. In later years, however, English people of all classes argued that certain clauses in the Magna Carta applied to every citizen.

In the Magna Carta, John made a variety of promises. For example, he agreed to respect the rights and privileges of the city of London. He promised merchants the right to travel freely in and out of England. The most important promises, however, guaranteed what are now considered basic legal rights, both in England and in the United States.

Guarantee of basic rights Clause 12 of the Magna Carta declared that taxes "shall be levied in our kingdom only by the common consent of our kingdom." This clause meant that the king could not arbitrarily demand taxes. He had to have the agreement of his advisers, usually at a meeting of barons called the king's Great Council. In other words, said later generations of English men and women (and eventually, people in the United States), there shall be *no taxation without representation.*

Another important guarantee was stated in Clause 39: "No free man shall be arrested or imprisoned . . . except by the legal judgment of his peers or by the law of the land." In other words, people later claimed, a person had the right to a jury trial and to the protection of the law. (This right to have the law work in known, orderly ways came to be known as *due process of law.*)

The idea of limited monarchy The underlying idea of the Magna Carta was not stated in so many words. It is the idea of limited monarchy. The barons at Runnymede forced their king to recognize limits on his powers. They said that he must follow the established laws and customs of the land. As Winston Churchill, England's great leader of the twentieth century, wrote: "Throughout [Magna Carta] it is implied that here is a law which is above the King and which even he must not break. This [idea] of a supreme

law . . . is the great work of Magna Carta; and this alone justifies the respect in which men have held it."

Parliament became part of English government.

John died in 1216, the year after he signed the Magna Carta. He left a young son, only nine years old, who became Henry III. Henry's long and unhappy reign (1216–1272) was marked by more losses in France and further conflicts with the barons.

For a time, it appeared that the strong foundations of England's royal government laid by William the Conqueror and Henry II would be washed away. Near the end of the 1200's, however, one of England's ablest kings restored royal power. Edward I, the son of Henry III and grandson of John, became king in 1272.

During Edward's long reign (1272–1307), he improved administration and strengthened the royal courts. His laws clarified the division of power between the king and the nobles, usually to the king's advantage.

Edward was able to limit the power of the troublesome barons. One reason for the barons' power had been the king's dependence on them for money. Now times were changing. Edward I was perhaps the first king to realize it. With the growth of towns and trade, it was easier to raise taxes from the middle-class burghers (or *burgesses* as the English called them) than from the upper-class barons.

In the past, people of the towns had been left out of the king's Great Council, the gathering that approved the royal plans for taxes. Only the great barons and bishops were ordinarily summoned to hear the king's requests for more money. Edward I was the first king to see the advantages of including townspeople in the meeting.

The Model Parliament In 1295, Edward I was planning another war to prevent his last remaining French lands from being conquered by the French king. To raise taxes for that war, Edward needed the support of all influential groups—not just the barons but the townspeople as well. Therefore, the king summoned two burgesses from every borough and two knights from every county to a parliament. According to Edward's royal writ,

The Magna Carta

237

Edward I sits above the Model Parliament, with churchmen at the left, barons at the right, and burgesses seated on wool sacks in the center.

the so-called commoners of the kingdom were being summoned because "what affects all should be approved by all." (That is, since taxes affected everyone, all groups should be consulted.)

Thus, in November 1295, knights, burgesses, bishops, and lords met together at Westminster in London to consult with the king. Historians refer to this famous gathering as the *Model Parliament* because its new composition (commoners as well as lords) served as a model for later kings.

Over the next century, from 1300 to 1400, the king called the knights and burgesses whenever a new tax was needed. In Parliament, these two groups gradually formed an assembly of their own called the House of Commons. Nobles and bishops met separately as the House of Lords.

Footnote to History

Because the king's councils involved a lot of talk and discussion, they took their name from the French word *parler* (talk); the meetings became known as *parliaments*.

The strength of Parliament Under Edward I, Parliament was in part a royal tool that weakened the great lords. The knights and burgesses generally sided with the king even when the nobles opposed him. As time went by, however, Parliament became strong enough that, like the Magna Carta, it provided a check on royal power.

England was not the only country to develop something like a parliament. France, as you will read, had a similar group called the Estates General. Spain had an assembly called the Cortes. There were also assemblies in parts of Germany and Italy in the Late Middle Ages. However, England's Parliament proved stronger and longer-lasting than any of the others.

The English Parliament was truly a national assembly. Although its members came from different parts of England, they generally put their loyalty to England ahead of local ties. Their laws applied to the whole country.

Even so, England in 1300 was not yet a true nation. Its kings and barons were bound by the old feudal obligations of lord-to-vassal and vassal-to-lord. As we shall see, it would require 200 years of strife before the feudal order in England finally broke down.

French kings expanded their power.

While England was limiting the power of its kings by the Magna Carta and Parliament, French kings were increasing their power. Early in the 1200's, John's old enemy Philip Augustus did for France what Henry II had already done for England. He gave France a strong central government.

Royal officials called bailiffs (BAY-lifs) were sent out from Paris to every district in Philip's kingdom. These bailiffs presided over the king's courts and collected the king's taxes.

Louis IX France's central government was made even stronger during the reign of Philip's grandson, Louis IX. Louis ruled from 1226 to 1270. He came to the throne as a boy of 12, and in his early years, France was actually ruled by his mother, Blanche of Castile. Blanche carried on the work of Philip Augustus, putting down revolts by the nobles and defeating the English.

When Louis IX began to rule on his own, he showed that his mother had taught him well. Better known as Saint Louis, this immensely pious and popular king had a passion for justice.

So great was his reputation for honor and fairness that even the king of England, a traditional enemy, once appealed to him to settle a dispute.

Louis created a supreme court for France called the Parlement of Paris. This Parlement could overturn the decisions of local courts. The royal courts of France (like those of England) had a double impact: They strengthened the monarchy while weakening feudal ties.

Philip IV and the Estates General In 1302, the king of France was involved in a quarrel with the pope. The French king was Philip IV, a handsome man whose nickname was Philip the Fair. As in England, the French king usually called a meeting of his lords and bishops when he needed support for his policies. To win wider support against the pope, Philip IV decided to include members of the middle class in the meeting.

In France, church leaders were known as the First Estate and great lords as the Second Estate.

The middle-class representatives that Philip invited to the council became known as the Third Estate. The whole meeting was called the Estates General.

The Estates showed the growing power of the townspeople and the middle class as a whole. Like Parliament in its early years, the Estates helped to increase royal power against the nobility. Unlike Parliament, however, the Estates never became an independent force that limited the king's power.

Nation-states began to arise.

By 1300, France and England were slowly taking new shapes, both geographically and politically. Geographically, each country was beginning to reach the borders that it would have, more or less, for the next 600 years. Politically, the kings of each country were becoming more powerful

Voice from the Past · *Chaucer and the English Language*

In 1300, most nobles in England read and wrote not in English but in French. This practice was a holdover from the days of William the Conqueror, when Norman nobles came to England. During the 1300's, however, English became a literary language. The greatest influence on the new status of English was the poet Geoffrey Chaucer (1343–1400). Chaucer's best-known work is *The Canterbury Tales*, poems about a group of pilgrims. Here he describes a young squire traveling with his father, a knight.

With him was his son, a young Squire,
A lover and a fair young bachelor.
His hair was curled as if it had been pressed.
Twenty years of age he was, I guessed . . .
He had already tried his skill in war
In Flanders, Artois, Picardy, and more,
And, for a youth, did well in all those places,
Hoping to stand high in his lady's graces.
His tunic was embroidered with bright flowers,
Red and white, like a meadow after showers.
He liked to sing or play the flute all day.
He was as merry as the month of May.
His coat was short, its sleeves were long and wide.
He sat his horse well and knew how to ride.
He could make songs, write poetry, paint, and dance,
And also joust well with his shield and lance . . .
He was polite and helped whenever he was able,
And carved the roast at his father's table.

1. What clues show that the squire was concerned about his appearance?
2. What were some accomplishments that a young man of the time was evidently supposed to have?
3. Of what accomplishments would his father, an old-fashioned knight, have been proudest?

𝕬𝕟𝕯 𝕒𝕝𝕤 𝕒𝕘𝕣𝕖𝕥𝕖

than the feudal lords beneath them. In both countries, the middle classes—especially the townspeople—were winning a larger share of political power.

Between 1300 and 1500, France and England slowly became a new type of country—a **nation-state**. A nation-state is a group of people who occupy a definite territory and are united under one government. The people of a nation-state are culturally united as well. For example, they generally all speak the same language. Most important, they have a feeling of belonging together and a sense of loyalty to their country.

Section Review 1

Define: (a) baron, (b) limited monarchy, (c) burgess, (d) commoner, (e) bailiff, (f) nation-state
Identify: (a) Henry II, (b) John, (c) Philip Augustus, (d) Magna Carta, (e) Edward I, (f) Model Parliament, (g) Geoffrey Chaucer, (h) Louis IX, (i) Philip IV, (j) Estates General
Answer:
1. Explain why the histories of France and England were tightly interwoven during the Late Middle Ages.
2. (a) Why was John of England called John Softsword? (b) What happened when he tried to increase taxes?
3. (a) List two basic rights that the Magna Carta guaranteed. (b) How did the Magna Carta affect the king's power?
4. (a) How did Edward I change the makeup of England's Parliament? (b) How did the House of Lords and the House of Commons differ?
5. How did each of the following French king's increase royal power? (a) Philip Augustus (b) Louis IX (c) Philip IV

Critical Thinking
6. Why is the Magna Carta called a "landmark of English liberty"?
7. What evidence shows that the power of the middle classes was growing both in France and in England?
8. How did the work of Geoffrey Chaucer show that France and England were becoming two separate countries in the 1300's?

The Church faced a crisis in the 1300's.   2

Feudalism and the Church were the two great forces that shaped society in the Middle Ages. As the Middle Ages drew to a close, feudal loyalties were being replaced by national loyalties. The Church too faced a crisis. At the beginning of the 1300's, the papacy seemed as strong as ever. Soon, however, both pope and Church were in desperate trouble.

Boniface VIII *overreached himself.*

The pope in 1300 was an able but stubborn Italian named Boniface VIII. Boniface well remembered the triumphs of past popes over kings and emperors. He did not realize, however, that these earlier power struggles had weakened the spiritual prestige of the pope. Boniface VIII tried to force the rulers of Europe to obey him as they had obeyed earlier popes.

Already, in 1296, Boniface had issued an official order stating that kings were not to tax the clergy. (Official statements by the pope were called *bulls*.) The bull of 1296 was aimed at the French king Philip IV, who was taxing Church property in France to pay for a war against England. Philip shrugged off the order and continued to tax the Church. Boniface was forced to back down.

A more cautious pope might have taken this setback as a warning. Boniface, however, still believed that the pope was stronger than any king. In 1302, he issued another bull known as *Unam Sanctam*. This bull declared that there were two powers on earth, the temporal (earthly) and the spiritual (heavenly). The spiritual power, he said, was always supreme over temporal power. In short, kings must always obey popes.

Philip merely sneered at this bull. Before Boniface could excommunicate him, the king sent a small army to Italy to kidnap the pope and bring him to France for trial. The pope was taken by surprise when, in September 1303, soldiers burst into his palace at Anagni (ah-NAHN-yee) outside Rome and took him captive. The townspeople of Anagni rescued the pope, but the shock was too much for the elderly Boniface. He died a month later.

Never again would a pope be able to force monarchs to obey him. For more than 100 years (1303–1417), the papacy suffered a serious decline.

The popes moved to Avignon.

Philip the Fair went on boldly to capture the papacy itself. In 1305, he persuaded the College of Cardinals to choose a French archbishop as the new pope, Clement V. In 1309, Clement announced that political violence in Rome threatened his life. Therefore, he was moving to the city of Avignon (AV-een-**YOHN**), right on the borders of France.

Avignon remained the home of the popes for the next 67 years. Yet could a pope rightly rule from any city except Rome? Throughout Europe, Christians were tormented by this question.

Many people concluded that the Avignon popes were mere hirelings of the French kings. The English, the Germans, and the Italians were especially unhappy. They complained that the Church was held captive in Avignon just as, centuries before, the Jews had been held captive in Babylon. Thus, this period in Church history came to be called the "Babylonian captivity."

Visitors to Avignon were shocked by papal extravagance. The pope served dinner on gold and silver plates to guests dressed in costly furs and brocades. He slept on pillows lined with ermine skins. A Spanish churchman wrote, "Whenever I entered the chambers of the churchmen of the papal court, I found brokers and clergy weighing and reckoning the money that lay in heaps before them."

A great schism divided the Church.

The move to Avignon had badly weakened the Church. When reformers finally tried to move the papacy back to Rome, however, the result was even worse.

In 1378, Pope Gregory XI died while visiting Rome. The College of Cardinals then met in Rome to choose a successor. As they deliberated, they could hear a mob outside screaming, "A Roman, a Roman, we want a Roman for a pope, or at least an Italian!" Finally, the cardinals announced to the crowd that an Italian had been chosen: Pope Urban VI. (By his very choice of name, Urban made it clear that he planned to keep the papacy in "the city"—that is, Rome.)

Many cardinals regretted their choice almost immediately. They had not counted on Urban VI's reforming zeal and overbearing personality. After a few months, 13 French cardinals decided to elect another pope. They chose Robert of Geneva, who spoke French. He took the name Clement VII.

Now there were two popes. Each declared the other to be a false pope. Each excommunicated his rival. The French pope moved back to Avignon while the Italian pope remained in Rome. Thus began the split in the Church known as the Great Schism (**SIHZ**-uhm).

Which was the rightful pope? For political reasons, the French supported the pope in Avignon. On the same basis, the English, the Germans, and the Italians favored the Roman pope. In many parts of Europe, two bishops (one loyal to Clement, the other to Urban) claimed to represent the

Daily Life · The Game of Chess

Chess was first played in Asia, perhaps as early as 550 B.C. Spaniards learned the game from the Arabs, who brought it to Spain in the 700's. Around the same time, Italian merchants in the Byzantine empire learned to play chess and took the game home with them. During the Middle Ages, chess became a favorite pastime of nobles in Europe. They changed the names and designs of the chess pieces to resemble the world they knew—a world of kings, queens, bishops, knights, foot soldiers (pawns), and castles (rooks). Thus, when you look at a chess set today, you see a reflection of medieval society.

"true" Church. Churchmen at all levels excommunicated one another. People wondered if they had been baptized or married by a true priest.

After Urban and Clement died, rival groups of cardinals in Rome and Avignon continued to elect two popes. The Great Schism lasted from 1378 to 1417.

Two scholars challenged the Church.

Often, when an old source of authority collapses, new ideas arise. In the late 1300's and early 1400's, the most famous thinkers to respond to the crisis of the Church were two professors. One was an Englishman named John Wycliffe (WIHK-lihf), the other a Bohemian named John Huss.

"Christ was meek," wrote John Wycliffe in one of his many pamphlets. But "the pope sits on his throne and makes lords to kiss his feet." From 1360 to 1382, Wycliffe taught religion at the University of Oxford. His radical ideas were discussed widely throughout England. These were Wycliffe's major ideas:

1. The true head of the Church was Jesus Christ, not the pope.
2. Like Jesus and his disciples, the clergy should own no land or wealth. Poverty was better for the Church than riches.
3. The Bible alone—not the pope—was the final authority for Christian life.

How could an English Christian be guided by the Bible when, as late as 1360, it could be read only in Latin or French? Wycliffe answered by translating the New Testament into English.

Because the popes since 1306 had been French and England was often at war with France, Wycliffe became a kind of English national hero by attacking the pope. When an English archbishop tried to charge him with heresy in 1377, there were riots in the London streets. The archbishop was forced to free Wycliffe. Instead of being burned at the stake, he died peacefully in 1384.

John Huss of Bohemia (now part of Czechoslovakia) was not so lucky. Influenced by Wycliffe's writings, Huss taught that the authority of the Bible was higher than that of the pope. Huss became a spokesman for Czech national feeling as well as for religious reform. He preached his sermons in Czech rather than in Latin. In 1411, Huss was excommunicated.

In 1414, Sigismund, the newly elected emperor of Germany, arranged a Church council to end the Great Schism. He urged Huss to attend and even gave him safe conduct. When Huss arrived at the meeting, however, he was seized and tried as a heretic. In spite of the safe conduct, he was burned at the stake in 1415.

A Church council ended the schism.

The gathering that condemned John Huss was known as the Council of Constance (named for the German city where it met). The council's major task was to end the Great Schism by choosing a new pope.

In 1414, when the Council of Constance began its meetings, there were a total of *three* popes. There was the Avignon pope, the Roman pope, and a third pope elected by an earlier council. With the help of the Holy Roman Emperor, the council forced all three popes to resign. In 1417, the council chose a new pope, Martin V. He made good his claim to being the only pope, thus ending the Great Schism.

Where, Christians wondered, was true religious authority—with the pope, with a Church council, or in the Bible? In a later chapter, we shall see how this confusion led to a violent upheaval in the 1500's known as the Reformation.

Section Review 2

Define: (a) papal bull, (b) schism, (c) excommunicate, (d) heretic
Identify: (a) Boniface VIII, (b) Philip IV, (c) Clement V, (d) Avignon, (e) Urban VI, (f) Great Schism, (g) John Wycliffe, (h) John Huss, (i) Council of Constance
Answer:
1. (a) What power did Boniface claim in *Unam Sanctam?* (b) What actions did Philip IV take in response?
2. Why was the period from 1309 to 1376 called the Babylonian captivity?
3. (a) How did the Great Schism begin? (b) What effects did it have? (c) How did it end?
4. What were Wycliffe's three major teachings?
5. (a) How did Huss inspire national feelings among the Czechs? (b) What happened to Huss?

6. During the earlier part of the Middle Ages, most European Christians had unquestioning faith in the authority of the Church. How did events in the 1300's change this outlook?

The 1300's brought plague and war.

3

A modern historian has called the 1300's "a violent, tormented, bewildered, suffering, and disintegrating age." During the 1300's, Europeans suffered from a series of disasters including crop failures, a terrifying new disease, and a war that dragged on for years.

Artists of the 1300's depicted death as the Grim Reaper, a skeleton on horseback whose scythe cut people down. It was an apt view. Consider what happened to the city of Barcelona in Spain. Famine struck in 1333; then came the plague in 1347, plague again in 1351, and two more years of famine in 1358 and 1359, followed shortly by another two years of plague in 1362 and 1363.

What brought on these catastrophes? Europe's population had been increasing steadily for more than 300 years. Using new methods such as the horse collar and the three-field system, Europeans had begun farming much new land. By 1300, however, almost all the great forests had been cleared and the swamps had been drained. The soil in many places was losing its fertility. Of course, medieval peasants knew nothing about chemical fertilizers. Year by year, the old fields produced smaller crops.

Moreover, a change was taking place in Europe's climate, though Europeans did not know it. From 1000 to 1300, Europe had enjoyed a time when temperatures were warmer than average. Around 1300, that period ended and temperatures dropped. During this "little ice age," as geologists call it, glaciers slowly advanced over Greenland and parts of Scandinavia. Fall frosts came early to the fields of Europe. The shorter growing season meant smaller harvests and a reduced food supply. Hunger paved the way for even grimmer events.

The great plague of 1348, called the Black Death, killed about a third of the people in Europe. In some cities, nine tenths of the population died. Here the people of Tournai (Belgium) bury their dead.

The Black Death struck in 1347.

In 1347, four Genoese ships arrived in Sicily from the Black Sea. Besides trade goods from Asia, the ships brought a dread cargo—a disease that became known as the Black Death. Soon the illness was sweeping through Italy. From Italy, the outbreak followed trade routes to France, Germany, England, and other parts of Europe.

The victims of this terrible plague had a raging fever. Black swellings grew at their necks and joints. The name *Black Death* came from these swellings. Many victims died within 24 hours. No one had any idea what caused this terrifying outbreak, and medieval doctors were helpless against it. (Modern scholars know that fleas from infected rats spread one form of the plague. Thus, the terrible sanitary conditions in Europe's cities were an important cause of the high death rate.)

Death carts loaded with plague victims soon became a common sight in Europe. Whenever plague broke out, people fled in terror. Yet many were already infected and carried the disease with them to new places.

The death rate was appalling. A churchman visiting Avignon in 1348 wrote:

> To put the matter shortly, one half, or more than a half, of the people of Avignon are already dead. Within the walls of the city there are now more than 7,000 houses shut up; in these no one is living, and all who inhabited them have left; the suburbs hardly contain any people at all.

This massive disaster tore medieval society apart. Whole villages disappeared as people either died or fled in fear. Even families were split. Fear of the plague was so great that some parents abandoned their sick children. The Church too failed. Priests were too few (and often too fearful) to give last rites to the dying.

Historians estimate that the plague killed 25 million people—about one third of Europe's population—in the 5 years between 1347 and 1352. The Black Death claimed more lives than any war until the twentieth century. Even more terrible, the plague came back again and again. New outbreaks occurred in 1361, 1369, 1374, 1390, and on into the 1600's. Though never again as severe as the first outbreak, plague became a constant danger.

Peasants rose in revolt.

The decline in population had far-reaching effects. Workers were scarce everywhere. Serfs could demand wages for their work. Thus, landlords could no longer collect their traditional rents and services. As a result, in many places serfdom began to disappear. The manor's economy, based on a fixed labor supply of workers who could not leave, was doomed.

The ruling class fought these changes. Nobles fiercely resisted peasant demands for higher wages. In 1381, peasants in England revolted, burning manors and killing local lords. Similar uprisings took place in France, Italy, and Belgium. In each case, nobles ruthlessly put down the revolts.

Although the peasants did not win the lower taxes or other reforms they wanted, the revolts were important nevertheless. The ideal society of the Middle Ages was gone. No longer was there peace among those who worked, those who prayed, and those who fought.

France and England fought the Hundred Years' War.

War added to the miseries of people in England and France. In 1337 (ten years before the first outbreak of the Black Death), war broke out once more over an English king's claims to land in France. The war lasted, off and on, for 116 years, not ending until 1453. It was called, somewhat inaccurately, the Hundred Years' War. Except for one futile French raid on English shores, the war was fought entirely on French soil.

The Hundred Years' War can be divided into four stages:

1. *1337–1360* Ably led by King Edward III, English forces invaded France. They captured the French king and gained control over much of France.
2. *1361–1396* The French reconquered almost everything the English had won.
3. *1397–1420* The English invaded France again. They conquered the northern half of the country. England's Henry V forced the French king to sign a humiliating treaty.
4. *1421–1453* The French rallied. In 1429, inspired by Joan of Arc, they began a drive that forced the English out of all France, except the western port city of Calais.

New weapons changed warfare.

The Hundred Years' War dealt a deathblow to feudal warfare. During the war, new weapons caused a revolution both in warfare and in society.

The longbow The weapon that gave England its early victories in the war was known as the longbow. Before battle, skilled English bowmen ranged themselves, side by side, along a wide arc. Into the ground they drove long, iron-tipped stakes that pointed outward to impale an enemy's charging horse. As the French attacked, the English bowmen drew their six-foot longbows. Then, as one French chronicler wrote, the sky became so thick with arrows that "it seemed as if it snowed." The arrows were dangerous at a range of 300 yards. They were absolutely fatal within 100 yards.

The result was disaster for the French. Slain and wounded horses tumbled over each other. Thrown on their backs, the French nobles in their heavy armor could not rise. They were as helpless as upside-down turtles. Foot soldiers killed them with long knives. Thus, the finest French cavalry was wiped out. The victors were English foot soldiers, mere commoners.

Such disasters befell the French knights at the Battle of Crécy (1346), the Battle of Poitiers (1356), and the Battle of Agincourt (1415). The age of feudalism, based on the power of warriors on horseback, could not survive long.

The cannon The second weapon that battered down the feudal system was the cannon. The sound of exploding gunpowder was first heard in Europe sometime after 1250. The English fired small cannons at the Battle of Crécy, but these did little more than scare the horses.

After 1400, however, European cannons grew huge and powerful. They could shoot stone balls 20 inches in diameter. In the last years of the Hundred Years' War, both sides used cannons to batter down the walls of each other's castles. Thus, the castle—like the knight's suit of shining armor—became an outdated relic.

National feeling grew in Europe.

Faith in feudalism and in the Church were both shaken by the upheavals of the 1300's. Among the peoples of Europe, they were replaced by a new feeling called **nationalism**.

During the Hundred Years' War, armies began to use cannons against the walls of enemy castles.

Nationalism is a feeling of loyalty to one's own land and people. It is a feeling that cuts across all class lines. During the Hundred Years' War, for example, English barons and peasants alike rejoiced at news of their king's great victories in France. After the Battle of Crécy, a jubilant throng greeted King Edward III when he returned to London. One proud Englishman wrote: "A new sun seemed to have arisen over the people in the perfect peace, in the plenty of all things, and in the glory of such victories."

No longer did people think of the king as simply a feudal lord. Instead, he was seen as a national leader fighting for the glory of the nation-state.

During the third stage of the war, English nationalistic feeling soared when people heard what had happened near the castle of Agincourt in France. In 1415, against 50,000 French troops, England's King Henry V urged his 8,000 soldiers into battle. "Hurrah! Hurrah! Saint George and Merrie England!" shouted the English as they strung their bows. The Battle of Agincourt ended in a stunning English victory.

Five years later, in 1420, Henry V forced the French king, Charles VI, to sign away his kingdom. (Henry was greatly aided by the fact that Charles suffered from periods of insanity.) By the Treaty of Troyes, Charles gave his daughter Katherine to Henry in marriage. Charles also agreed that Henry would inherit the French crown

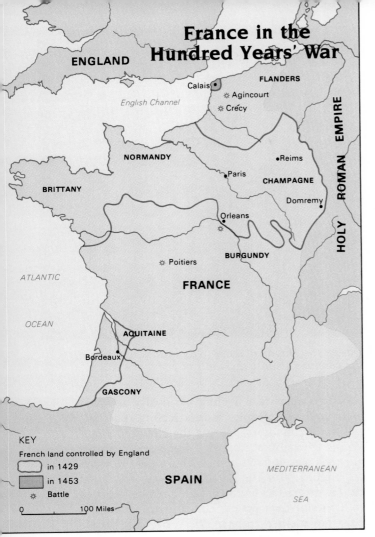

France in the Hundred Years' War

ENGLAND

Calais

Agincourt

Crécy

English Channel

FLANDERS

HOLY ROMAN EMPIRE

NORMANDY

Reims

Paris

CHAMPAGNE

BRITTANY

Domremy

Orleans

Poitiers

BURGUNDY

ATLANTIC

OCEAN

FRANCE

AQUITAINE

Bordeaux

GASCONY

SPAIN

MEDITERRANEAN

SEA

KEY

French land controlled by England

in 1429

in 1453

Battle

0   100 Miles

Map Study

What regions of France did the English control in 1429? What land did they hold in 1453?

when Charles himself died. Thus, it seemed that France and England would become one kingdom.

However, Henry V died in 1422, just before Charles's death. Henry's son, Henry VI, was only nine months old. An English duke ruled northern France in the name of the baby king. Then, in 1429, a French girl felt moved by God to rescue France from its English conquerors. Her name, as you read on page 234, was Joan of Arc.

Joan of Arc turned the tide of war.

Perhaps no one in history accomplished so much in such a short time against such overwhelming odds as did Joan of Arc. In only six months, Joan changed a pathetic prince into a

king, led the French army to victory, and awakened the national spirit of a defeated people.

Yet Joan herself was not surprised by these events. She believed in miracles. She believed that several times, while she was tending her father's sheep, heavenly voices had spoken to her. Her mission, as dictated by those voices, was to drive the English army out of France and give the French crown to France's true king, Charles VI's son.

In February 1429, Joan made a hazardous journey to the court of the prince, Charles the Dauphin (DAW-fuhn). (*Dauphin* was the title given to the eldest son of a French king.) The Treaty of Troyes had robbed Charles of his kingdom. Though the Dauphin still pretended to be king, he lacked both spirit and confidence. He was dumbfounded when a crudely dressed peasant girl entered his court and said to him:

> *God send you long life, gentle Dauphin . . .*
> *I have been sent by God to take you to*
> *Reims to be anointed. Give me soldiers*
> *and I will raise the siege of Orleans, for it*
> *is God's will that the English shall leave*
> *France and return to their own country.*

As you read (page 234), on May 7, 1429, Joan led the French army into battle against the English forts that blocked the roads to Orleans. It was a hard-fought battle for both sides. The air was filled with arrows and the stinking smoke of cannon. Joan stayed always at the thick of the fighting. About noon, the French fought their way close to the main fort and threw up ladders to scale its walls. As Joan climbed swiftly up the first ladder, an English arrow tore into her shoulder. She pulled it out and urged her troops to fight on. The French threw up more ladders, but the English flung them down, throwing French fighters to their deaths. By sunset, the weary French had still not taken the fort. Despairing, their commanders sounded the retreat. The English looked out in victory from the safety of their walls.

Suddenly, Joan and a few soldiers charged back toward the fort. The entire French army stormed after her. This time, there was no stopping the French. They swarmed up their ladders and into the English fort. A mass of English soldiers tried to retreat across the nearby river, but the French set the bridge afire. When the bridge broke, the terrified English, weighed down by heavy armor, drowned in the river beneath.

Over the crackle of the flames and the cries of the dying, the bells of Orleans rang out in joy. The siege of Orleans was broken. Joan of Arc had guided the French onto the path of victory.

After that victory, Joan persuaded Charles to go with her to be crowned king. The route led through enemy territory, and Charles quaked with fear. Yet Joan brought him safely to Reims. At the cathedral on Sunday, July 17, 1429, he was crowned King Charles VII.

Joan had one year of triumph, 1429. Her last two years were years of betrayal and anguish. The English hated her and believed her to be a witch. In 1430, she was captured in battle and turned over to Church authorities to stand trial. Although Charles VII owed his crown to her, he did nothing to rescue her. Condemned as a witch and a heretic, Joan was tied to a stake and burned to death on May 30, 1431. One Englishman, wiser than the rest, cried out, "We are lost. We have burned a saint."

Joan's execution did the English no good. French nationalism did not die. Charles VII overcame his cowardice to become a strong king. By 1453, his troops had won back every part of France except Calais.

Joan of Arc is still revered by the French as their greatest patriot. In 1920, nearly 500 years after her death, the Church retracted its judgment of heresy and declared Joan a saint.

Section Review 3

Define: (a) nationalism, (b) dauphin
Identify: (a) Black Death, (b) Hundred Years' War, (c) Henry V, (d) Battle of Agincourt, (e) Joan of Arc, (f) Orleans, (g) Charles VII
Answer:
1. (a) What was the Black Death? (b) How did trade encourage its spread? (c) What effects did it have on Europe?
2. What was the Hundred Years' War about?
3. (a) What did Joan of Arc believe to be her mission in life? (b) What did she accomplish? (c) How did her life end?
4. (a) What new weapons came into use during the Hundred Years' War? (b) How did each change warfare?

Critical Thinking
5. Why did the Black Death weaken the manorial economy?
6. How did the Hundred Year' War weaken the feudal system?
7. Give evidence that each of the following people was a *national* hero, not just a feudal leader. (a) Henry V (b) Joan of Arc

New monarchs ruled in western Europe. 4

Throughout this chapter, we have seen how the medieval world came apart in the 1300's. Out of that turmoil and pain, however, three strong nation-states of western Europe arose.

France was no longer a patchwork of lands, some attached to the French king, others to the English king. England, stripped of its holdings in France, was now a compact country surrounded by the sea. And, to the south of France, Spain had developed by 1500 as a third nation-state.

New monarchs replaced feudal kings.

Medieval kings had ruled according to feudal custom. To fight wars and govern their kingdoms, they had relied mainly on the support of their vassals. The strong rulers who arose between 1450 and 1500 did not base their power on feudalism (although they certainly used their rights as feudal lords when it suited them). Historians often call these rulers the "new monarchs." The new monarchs had three important new sources of power: control of taxes, a professional army, and professional officials.

Broad taxing power Feudal kings had received most of their income from their own estates and from the feudal aids of their vassals. (Remember that an aid was a grant of money for a specific purpose, such as ransoming the lord from captivity or fighting a war.) The new monarchs demanded every penny of those aids too, but they also received money from other groups. Every class in society—nobility, clergy, townspeople, and peasants—paid some kind of tax to the king.

Professional army Medieval rulers marched to war followed by an army of vassals, who owed military service in exchange for their land. The new monarchs hired soldiers from any class in society. No longer was fighting the specialized work of the nobility, although nobles still commanded most armies. Soldiering became a trade open to all, and professional soldiers were paid from the royal treasury.

Professional officials The new monarchs surrounded themselves with a new class of advisers and officials. Some were nobles, but many were middle-class townspeople. Educated officials from the middle class gave the king loyal service. They were the ruler's natural allies against the haughty and quarrelsome nobles.

Crafty kings strengthened France.

Charles VII, who had won the French throne with Joan of Arc's help, set the French monarchy on the road to recovery. By 1453, he had driven the English out of France, except for the single city of Calais. He set up a royal council, using middle-class men as his officials. He chose his advisers so wisely that he won the nickname "Charles the Well-Served." He also set up the first permanent royal army.

Charles found new sources of money for the royal treasury. Most of his money came from two taxes. One was called the *taille* (TAH-yuh), a tax on land. The other was called the *gabelle* (guh-BEL), a tax on salt. For more than 300 years, these two taxes on basic necessities of life were the main source of money for French kings.

Charles's son became king in 1461. Louis XI was known as "the Spider King." To achieve his ends, Louis resorted to trickery, intimidation, bribery, and espionage. He had spies in almost every noble's court in Europe. A cardinal who once betrayed him was locked up in a small cage for 11 painful years, unable either to stand up or lie down. Nobles who resisted Louis's rule usually were bribed or bullied into submission.

Like his father, Louis wanted to weaken the power of the great lords within France—above all the Duke of Burgundy. Burgundy had long been a thorn in France's side. This mighty dukedom included southeastern France, Flanders, Luxembourg, and other territories. During the Hundred Years' War, the Burgundians often had sided with the English. Louis XI regarded Duke Charles the Bold of Burgundy as his chief enemy.

Perhaps nothing pleased the Spider King more than the news in 1477 that the duke had been killed in battle. By 1482, Louis had added Burgundy to the French state. It was a sizable and critical addition.

Money flowed into Louis's treasury through the taille and the gabelle. Therefore, Louis needed to call together the Estates General only once in his 22-year reign. He did not need its approval for his policies. Thus, Louis passed on to his heirs a monarchy of almost unlimited power. Unlike the kings and queens of England, French rulers after 1500 collected taxes without the consent of their subjects.

The Wars of the Roses split England.

While France was building its strength after the Hundred Years' War, England went through another time of turmoil. The Hundred Years' War was scarcely over when England was split by a civil war beginning in 1455.

Two branches of the royal family claimed the English crown. One branch, headed by the dukes of York, took a white rose as their emblem. The other branch, descended from the dukes of Lancaster, had a red rose as their symbol. Thus, the civil war came to be called the Wars of the Roses. These battles were really a bloody family quarrel.

The wars disrupted the reign of three kings: Henry VI, Edward IV, and Richard III. Finally, Richard III was killed at the Battle of Bosworth Field in 1485. This battle marked the end of the Wars of the Roses and a turning point for England. Richard III often is called England's last medieval king. The man who defeated him set England on a new path.

Henry Tudor made peace in England.

The victor at Bosworth Field was another Henry. By marriage and inheritance, he was connected to both the Lancastrians and the Yorkists. His own family name, however, was Tudor (TOO-duhr). Crowned Henry VII, he began the most renowned dynasty in English history: the Tudor dynasty. (His granddaughter, Elizabeth I, would later become England's greatest queen.)

Henry VII (1485–1509) ruled as a new monarch. His chief ministers were not great lords but members of the middle class. In every part of

Henry Tudor became Henry VII of England, a shrewd and power-hungry new monarch.

his kingdom, he used local landowners as officials called justices of the peace. In doing so, he continued a long tradition of local government that served England well. (As these justices were unpaid, they were no burden on the royal treasury.)

Henry VII made himself as king the richest man in England. Much of his money came from feudal dues, which he collected with truly modern efficiency. Still more money came from "tonnage and poundage," taxes on imported goods. The more trade grew, the more money flowed into Henry's hands. So Henry was eager to encourage trade, and business prospered during his reign. He made treaties with other rulers to open new markets for English merchants.

To safeguard the money he was piling up, Henry VII carefully avoided expensive wars. Thus, he did not need to keep—or pay—a standing army.

Many of England's great nobles had died or fled abroad during the Wars of the Roses. Henry completed the job of destroying their power. He limited their military might by having Parliament outlaw the private armies of paid fighters many lords had kept.

Henry also used the Court of Star Chamber to destroy over-mighty subjects. This court got its name from the starry ceiling in the room where its judges met. The Court of Star Chamber violated most ideas of fairness and justice. It met in secret. People accused of crimes had no right to know what evidence was being used against them. People were tortured so that they would confess. Yet most people in England accepted the Court of Star Chamber because Henry used it to keep peace after years of strife.

It is probably fair to say that Henry was respected but not loved. Unheroic and miserly, he was far from the Middle Ages' idea of a great king. Yet when he died in 1509, England was prosperous and peaceful. The benefits of the new monarchy were plain.

Isabella and Ferdinand strengthened Spain.

As far back as 1063, well before the First Crusade, the pope had urged Christian knights to drive the Muslims (or Moors) out of Spain. This drive became a centuries-long effort known as the *Reconquista* (ray-kahn-KEES-tuh) or reconquest. By the late 1400's, Muslims held only the tiny kingdom of Granada.

Four other kingdoms on the Iberian peninsula were ruled by Christians. The kingdom of Portugal faced the uncharted waters of the Atlantic Ocean. The small kingdom of Navarre sat astride the Pyrenees, bordering France. The large kingdoms of Castile (ka-STEEL) and Aragon (AR-uh-gahn) spanned the neck and midsection of the peninsula. (See the map on page 250.)

A capable and aggressive princess named Isabella was heir to the throne of Castile. Likewise, a determined and crafty prince named Ferdinand was heir to Aragon. Their marriage, in 1469, brought their two kingdoms into close alliance.

The conquest of Granada Beginning in 1482, Ferdinand and Isabella set out to conquer the last Muslim kingdom, Granada. It took ten years, but in 1492, Granada fell to a Christian army. In the final battle, Isabella personally led her army, wearing the red cross of a crusader.

This crusading spirit linked religion closely with Spanish nationalism. To be a "true Spaniard"

The Growth of Spain

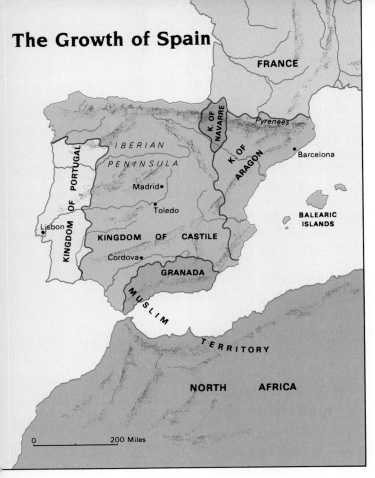

Map Study

What Spanish kingdom nearly surrounded the Muslim territory on the Iberian Peninsula?

came also to mean being a "true Christian." The result was disastrous for Spaniards who were not Christian.

The Inquisition Spain had a long history of religious diversity and tolerance. Since the height of the Islamic empire in the 700's, Muslims, Jews, and Christians had all lived there. The three groups had often lived together in peace. Jews held high positions as bankers, merchants, scholars, physicians, and government officials. Under Ferdinand and Isabella, however, Spain's religious tolerance ended.

As a devout Roman Catholic, Isabella decreed that in a Christian state, there could be only "one king, one law, one faith." She and Ferdinand won permission from the pope to revive the Inquisition, the arm of the Church that had tracked down heretics in the Middle Ages (page 217).

All over Spain, boards of priests met to hear cases of suspected heresy. The primary suspects were Jews and Muslims who had converted to Christianity. Assuming the suspects were guilty, the priests would demand that they confess. If the suspects refused, they often were tortured. Once they confessed, they were burned at the stake. A report by Isabella's secretary shows that 2,000 men and women were executed in this way between 1478 and 1490.

The expulsion of the Jews In the same year as the conquest of Granada (1492), Isabella and Ferdinand began a new campaign against the 200,000 Spanish Jews who openly practiced their religion. They were forced to become Christians or leave the country. The great majority, about 150,000, chose exile.

Jewish families, now homeless, set out from Spain to other lands. The departure of their ships was witnessed by another captain who recorded the event in his diary. That captain was Christopher Columbus, who sailed from the Spanish port of Palos in August 1492.

Columbus was just setting out on a voyage that he hoped would lead to Asia. In fact, his historic voyage took him to the Americas. Some exiled Jews sailed with him. Among them were the expedition's doctor and interpreter. Later, a few Jews became early settlers in the Americas. Most of the exiles, however, went to the Muslim countries of Southwest Asia, including lands that are now Iran, Syria, Israel, and Jordan.

Expelling the Jews and Muslims made Spain a religiously united nation, but it hurt the country economically. Many of Spain's leaders in business and trade had been Muslims or Jews.

After Isabella's death in 1504, Ferdinand seized the part of Navarre south of the Pyrenees. By his death in 1516, Spain had reached its modern borders.

Section Review 4

Define: (a) new monarch, (b) feudal aids, (c) taille, (d) gabelle, (e) tonnage and poundage
Identify: (a) Charles VII, (b) Louis XI, (c) Wars of the Roses, (d) Henry VII, (e) Reconquista, (f) Ferdinand, (g) Isabella
Answer:
1. In general, how did the new monarchs strengthen their powers?
2. List three accomplishments of Charles VII.

3. (a) How did Louis XI win the nickname "the Spider King"? (b) Why did Louis XI and his successors have more power than English rulers of the same period?
4. (a) What part did the middle classes play in Henry VII's government? (b) What methods did Henry use to keep the peace within his kingdom?
5. (a) How did a political marriage begin Spain's development as a nation? (b) How did the position of Spanish Muslims and Jews change in the late 1400's?

Critical Thinking

6. Compare the policies of medieval rulers with the policies of the new monarchs with regard to (a) sources of money, (b) the army, and (c) choosing officials. In each case, explain why the new policies increased royal power.

A *new empire arose in Russia.* 5

At the eastern end of the European continent, in the land known as Russia, another country was taking shape in the 1400's. To understand how Russia developed, you must know something of its geography. The Ural (YOOR-uhl) Mountains divide Europe and Asia. Russians first settled on the European side of the mountains, and the European part of Russia remained its heartland. Later, Russians pushed eastward into the vast wilderness of northern Asia known as Siberia (sye-BIHR-ee-uh).

European Russia is mostly flat. The northern part, near the Baltic Sea, is covered with an immense forest of pine, spruce, and other cone-bearing trees. The southern part is a sweeping, grassy steppe with rich black soil.

The rivers of European Russia seem to twist and turn in every direction. Eventually, they empty into one of four bodies of water—the Caspian Sea, the Black Sea, the Baltic Sea, or the Arctic Ocean. In the warm months, barges floated easily over these broad and abundant rivers. In the freezing Russian winters, horse-drawn sleds glided safely over the thick river ice. Thus, in every season, Russians depended on their rivers for transportation and trade.

The Mongols conquered Russia.

During the 700's and the 800's, groups of people who spoke Slavic languages migrated from Asia into eastern Europe. They fought a series of bitter battles with the Byzantine empire. Yet these Slavs also accepted Eastern Orthodox Christianity along with other Byzantine influences (page 182). In the Early Middle Ages, the group of Slavs who became known as Russians built a rich trading kingdom centering on the city of Kiev.

In the middle 1200's, a fierce group of horsemen from central Asia slashed their way into Russia. These nomads were the Mongols. (You will read more of them in Chapter 12.) In 1240, they completely destroyed Kiev. Its churches were burned, its rich treasures were plundered, and even its tombs were broken open and the bones scattered. By 1241, the Mongols ruled all of Russia. From that time on, Russian history followed a new course.

In some ways, the Mongols actually began the work of uniting Russia. Kievan Russia had been a collection of small, independent kingdoms. The Mongols forced all the kingdoms of Russia to pay them tribute. In each kingdom, a Russian prince ruled under the Mongols and collected tribute for them. As long as a prince was obedient, the Mongols allowed him to rule as he wished. Russian historians call the period of Mongol rule from 1240 to 1480 "the Mongol yoke."

Moscow's princes united Russia.

Moscow, located in the northern forests, suffered less from Mongol raids than did the cities of the steppe such as Kiev. Moscow was first settled in the 1100's. By 1250, it was a primitive hamlet enclosed by a crude log wall. It took the princes of Moscow 240 years (1240–1480) to build a strong and independent state (map, page 252).

Note the location of Moscow near the headwaters of three great rivers: the Volga (VAHL-guh), the Dnieper (NEE-puhr), and the Don. If the ruler of Moscow could gain control of these rivers, he could control nearly all of European Russia.

Moscow began its rise to power under the Mongols. Its prince from 1328 to 1341 was Ivan I. As tax collector for the Mongols, he became known as Ivan Moneybags. He served the Mongols so well that they gave him the title of "Great

Russia and
Eastern Europe
in 1480

SWEDEN
Novgorod
Baltic
North
Sea
Sea
HOLY ROMAN
EMPIRE
Danube River
POLAND
HUNGARY
Kiev
Dnieper River
OTTOMAN
EMPIRE
Istanbul
Black   Sea
TERRITORY CONTROLLED   KHANATE OF
BY   MOSCOW
Moscow
KHANATE OF
THE GOLDEN HORDE
Don River
KHANATE OF
THE CRIMEA
KAZAN
Ural Mts.
Ural River
KIRGHIZ   TURKS
Volga River
KHANATE
OF
ASTRAKHAN
Caspian
Caucasus   Mts.
Sea

KEY
Mongol
territory

0   500 Miles

Map Study

Mongol rulers were known as khans. What areas shown on the map were ruled by Mongols? What power bordered Moscow's lands on the southwest?

Prince." In 1328, the head of the Russian Orthodox Church made Moscow his residence. The Church became a major ally of Moscow's princes.

Ivan and his successors gradually enlarged their kingdom by purchase, war, trickery, and clever marriages. Generation after generation, they plotted to win control of the small states that encircled Moscow. By the 1400's, Moscow had become the strongest of the Russian states under the Mongols.

The prince of Moscow became czar.

The Russian state became a true empire during the 43-year reign of Ivan III (1462–1505). Born in 1440, Ivan was a boy of 13 when Constantinople fell to the Turks in 1453. In 1472, Ivan married the niece of the last Byzantine emperor. At that time, he began calling himself **czar**, the Russian word for *caesar* or *emperor*.

In 1480, Moscow finally freed itself from the Mongol yoke. Ivan III refused to pay the Mongol's their tribute. Rising to the challenge, the Mongol ruler led his army to the banks of the Ugra River. The Russian army stood on the opposite bank. The two armies glowered at each other, neither daring to cross the river. Finally, without shooting

a single arrow, the Russians and the Mongols turned around and marched back home. After this bloodless face-off, Moscow was free of Mongol control.

Ivan wanted to make Moscow a fitting capital for an emperor. The center of the city was a walled citadel or fortress known as the *Kremlin.* Ivan tore down the old triangular wall around the Kremlin and erected a massive new wall 60 feet high and 15 feet thick. Inside, he built a palace for himself, another palace for the head of the Russian Church, and three great churches.

Moscow became the capital of a new and aggressive empire. By the time of his death in 1505, Ivan had tripled the territory under Moscow's control. Ivan III was both the first czar and the first leader of a united Russian nation. Russians call him Ivan the Great.

Ivan IV ruled through terror.

The next important figure in Russian history also had a well-earned nickname: Ivan the Terrible. He came to the throne as Ivan IV in 1533, when he was only three years old. His youth was marked by struggles for power among Russia's nobles. These nobles, themselves often minor princes, were known as **boyars**. Like the feudal lords of western Europe, they held large estates. Just as the feudal lords struggled against the growing power of the kings in England and France, the boyars opposed the growing power of Russia's czars.

Ivan's mother, who acted as regent, died in 1538 when he was eight, probably poisoned by her boyar enemies. For the next eight years, the boyars kept Ivan a virtual prisoner, poorly fed and badly clothed. As a result, Ivan mistrusted and hated the boyars for the rest of his life.

In 1547, when he was 16, Ivan took power into his own hands, having himself crowned czar. He married the beautiful Anastasia, related to an old boyar family, the Romanovs. (You will hear more of this family later.)

The years from 1547 to 1560 are often called Ivan's "good period." He won great victories against the Mongols and destroyed the Mongol khanate on the Volga River. He also gave Russia a code of laws in 1550 and ruled justly. Hoping to increase Russia's trade with Europe, he began a long war to win access to the Baltic Sea.

Ivan IV is probably better remembered for his later "bad period," which began after his beloved Anastasia died in 1560. Little is known about these years because the records were lost in a great fire that swept Moscow. Some historians believe Ivan was insane part of the time. Others say his acts of cruelty were little different from those of other European rulers—for example, the use of the Inquisition by Ferdinand and Isabella in Spain.

Whatever the explanation, Ivan turned brutally against the boyars. He accused them of poisoning his wife. He organized his own police force whose chief duty was to hunt down "traitors" and murder them. The members of this police force were called *oprichniki* (oh-**PREECH**-nihk-ee), or "separate class." They dressed in black and rode black horses with dogs' heads on their saddles as symbols of terror. Thousands of boyars and ordinary people as well died in this reign of terror.

Ivan's uncontrollable rage at last led him to an act that was both the greatest personal tragedy and the greatest political disaster of his reign. In 1581, during a violent quarrel, he killed his older son and heir. Thus, when Ivan himself died in 1584, only his unintelligent younger son remained to succeed him as czar.

Ivan IV built St. Basil's Cathedral in Moscow to celebrate his victories over the Mongols.

Russia at the time of Ivan's death was an isolated and primitive empire. The story of how this empire became a major European power is left to a later chapter.

Section Review 5

Define: (a) czar, (b) boyars, (c) oprichniki
Identify: (a) Ural Mountains, (b) Slavs, (c) Kiev, (d) Ivan I, (e) Kremlin, (f) Ivan IV
Answer:
1. Describe the geography of Russia.
2. (a) When did the Mongols conquer Russia? (b) How did they rule it?
3. (a) What geographic advantages helped Moscow's rise to power? (b) What other factors helped the city?
4. What achievements explain why Ivan III is known as Ivan the Great?
5. (a) What were the accomplishments of Ivan IV? (b) How did he come to be known as Ivan the Terrible?

Critical Thinking
6. (a) How was the czars' situation like that of the new monarchs? (b) How was it different?

253

Chapter Review 11

Summary

1. England and France developed as nations. In England, the signing of the Magna Carta limited royal power. The middle class grew stronger when townspeople were included in Parliament. In France, Philip II won much English-held land and strengthened royal power. Later rulers set up royal courts and included the middle class in the Estates General.

2. The Church faced a crisis in the 1300's. The Babylonian captivity and the Great Schism weakened the authority of the Church. John Wycliffe, John Huss, and their supporters called for changes in the Church.

3. The 1300's brought plague and war. The Black Death killed millions and weakened the manorial economy. The Hundred Years' War further diminished feudal power, as the longbow and cannons doomed armored knights and castles. During the war, national loyalties increased in England and France.

4. New monarchs ruled in western Europe. Rulers in France, England, and Spain found new sources of tax money, hired professional soldiers, and chose middle-class officials. The Tudor dynasty came to power in England. French kings strengthened royal control. In Spain, the Reconquista linked Spanish nationalism with the crusading spirit, ending religious toleration for Jews and Muslims.

5. A new empire arose in Russia. The Mongol invasion destroyed Russia's old Kievan civilization. Beginning in the 1300's, Moscow became the new center of Russian power. Moscow's rulers eventually drove out the Mongols and added to their own territory.

Reviewing the Facts

1. Define the following terms:
   - a. nation-state
   - b. nationalism
   - c. czar
   - d. boyar
2. Explain the importance of each of the following names, dates, places, or terms:
   - a. 1215
   - b. Model Parliament
   - c. Estates General
   - d. Babylonian captivity
   - e. Great Schism
   - f. Council of Constance
   - g. Black Death
   - h. Hundred Years' War
   - i. Joan of Arc
   - j. Wars of the Roses
   - k. Henry VII
   - l. Charles VII
   - m. Ferdinand of Aragon
   - n. Isabella of Castile
   - o. Reconquista
   - p. 1492
   - q. Moscow
   - r. Ivan III
3. (a) How did the Magna Carta come to be signed? (b) Why is it important?
4. (a) What was new about the Model Parliament? (b) When did it first meet?

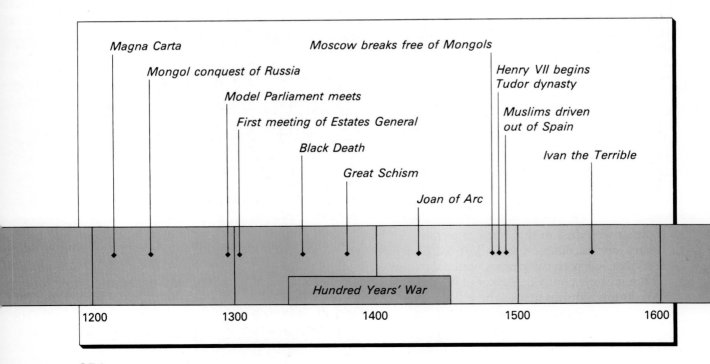

Magna Carta

Mongol conquest of Russia

Model Parliament meets

First meeting of Estates General

Black Death

Great Schism

Joan of Arc

Moscow breaks free of Mongols

Henry VII begins Tudor dynasty

Muslims driven out of Spain

Ivan the Terrible

Hundred Years' War

1200   1300   1400   1500   1600

5. Briefly describe how each of the following kings helped France become a strong nation-state. (a) Philip Augustus (b) Louis IX (c) Charles VII (d) Louis XI
6. (a) How was the Church's authority weakened by the Babylonian captivity? (b) How was the Church's authority weakened once again by the Great Schism?
7. Identify three factors that led to a population drop in the 1300's and explain the part each played in the decline.
8. How did the Hundred Years' War contribute to the rise of nationalism?
9. Briefly describe the new policies that were followed by the monarchs who came to power between 1450 and 1500.
10. How did Russia begin to become a unified empire?

Thinking about History

1. Were the Late Middle Ages in Europe a time of disintegration or a time of growth? Discuss this issue and find evidence in the chapter to support your point of view.
2. Why was the power of English rulers more limited than that of French rulers? Your answer should include information about the Magna Carta, Parliament, Estates General, and taxes.
3. Isabella of Castile said that a country should have "one king, one law, one faith." Choose two of the following and explain why they might or might not agree with that statement. (a) a Roman emperor (b) an Athenian from the time of Pericles (c) a modern citizen of the United States (d) an Egyptian pharaoh
4. Although England, France, Spain, and Russia developed in very different ways, you can find some similarities. In which countries did conflict with a group that could be labeled "outsiders" aid the growth of unity? How did rulers use oppressive means to increase their own power?
5. Joan of Arc, John Wycliffe, and John Huss were all both religious and national figures. How did the Church react to each? Why might Church leaders in the 1300's and 1400's have considered nationalism a threat?

Writing and Speaking about History

1. Make a list of the ways in which the outlook of European peasants changed during the 1300's.

Include information about the plague, the feudal system, the growth of nationalism, and the role of the Church in this time period. Use your list to develop a thesis statement.
2. Use the thesis statement that you developed above to outline an essay on the life of a European peasant in the 1300's. Write an introductory paragraph for the essay. (See Research Skills Handbook, page 318.)
3. Each of the following people was a victim of persecution. Choose one of them to interview. Focus the interview on both the causes and effects of the persecution.
   John Wycliffe
   John Huss
   Joan of Arc
   A Muslim in fifteenth-century Spain
   A Jew in fifteenth-century Spain

Practicing Skills

1. Find the three dates on the time line that relate to Russia. Explain the significance of each date in Russian history.
2. Use the maps on pages 246, 250, and 252 to describe the locations of each of the following cities:
   a. Kiev   d. Calais
   b. Orleans   e. Novgorod
   c. Cordova   f. Toledo

Investigating History

1. Increased trade, which encouraged contacts among different peoples, helped spread the Black Death. Organize a debate on the following issue: A highly contagious disease such as the Black Death would or would not spread even more rapidly today than in the Middle Ages.
2. Research one of the following topics: (a) the history of archery; (b) Welsh castles; (c) the Louvre in Paris; (d) the Order of the Garter in England. For each topic, find out about its origins, important people associated with it throughout its history, and its present-day status.

Decision Making in History

Pretend you are an adviser to King John of England. On what basis will you recommend that he sign the Magna Carta? Should King John stipulate any reservations to the nobles? Why?

Research Skills

Outlining

Notetaking and outlining are closely related. Both are valuable ways to keep track of information you have read. However, outlining is more detailed and formal than notetaking. It involves the following steps:

1. Use roman numerals—I, II, III, and so forth—for the major topics.
2. Number subtopics under each major topic A, B, C, and so forth.
3. Number minor topics under subtopics 1, 2, 3, and so forth.
4. Use lowercase letters—a, b, c, and so forth—to explain minor topics.
5. Place a period after each topic number or letter.
6. Never write a single subtopic, such as an A without a B or a 1 without a 2. When there is material for only one subtopic, include the information in the main topic.
7. Begin each topic farther to the right than the main topic above it.
8. Express all topics as complete sentences.

Here is a sample outline of the fifth section in Chapter 10 of this text (pages 228–231). Notice how it follows the guidelines. Copy the outline on a separate sheet of paper. Complete Sections B, C, D, and E on your own.

D. Crusad
  1.
    a.
    b.
  2.
    a.
    b.
E. The
  1.
    a.
    b.
  2.
    c.

B. The First Crusade won Jerusalem.
  1.
    a.
    b.
  2.
    a.
    b.
C. Later Crusa
  1.
    a.
    b.
  2.
    a.
    b.

V. Crusaders marched against Islam.
  A. The Crusades had many causes.
    1. The pope wanted the Crusades.
      a. Urban II wanted to show his power by sending knights on a holy war.
      b. Urban II also wanted to reunite Byzantine and Roman Christians.
    2. Knights wanted the Crusades.
      a. Many were fired by religious zeal.
      b. Earthly rewards tempted knights.
    3. Merchants wanted the Crusades.
      a. After 1200, the role of merchants in the Crusades grew.
      b. Merchants were eager to win control of key trade routes.

Unit Review III

1. Identify the religion (Islam, Eastern Orthodoxy, or Roman Catholicism) with which each of the following people, places, or things is associated. Describe the significance of each.
   a. friar
   b. Constantinople
   c. Koran
   d. patriarch
   e. canon law
   f. cardinal
   g. Gregory I
   h. Baghdad
   i. Concordat of Worms
   j. caliph
   k. Hagia Sophia
   l. Great Schism

2. Draw a timeline that extends from 500 to 1500. Divide the timeline into 200-year increments. Place the following events on the timeline.
   a. Fall of Constantinople
   b. Beginning of Viking invasions
   c. Birth of Muhammad
   d. Battle of Tours
   e. Treaty of Verdun
   f. Revival of learning
   g. Charlemagne crowned emperor
   h. Norman conquest of England
   i. Magna Carta
   j. War of the Roses

3. Explain the significance to world history of each of the events on your timeline.

4. (a) What was the Code of Justinian? (b) Describe its impact on western Europe.

5. What is the significance of the year 1054 to the Christian Church?

6. (a) Who began the Islamic religion? (b) What are its followers called?

7. What is the significance of 622 to Islam?

8. (a) Who invaded western Europe in the 500's? (b) What happened to Roman civilization as a result of those invasions?

9. (a) How did the Viking invasions contribute to the growth of feudalism? (b) How was feudalism both a system of government and a way of life?

10. Describe at least two factors that led to the gradual decline of feudalism after the year 1000.

11. For each topic listed below, compare life in the Early Middle Ages with life in the High Middle Ages.
    a. farming
    b. trade
    c. royal power
    d. religion
    e. learning

12. (a) What were the Crusades? (b) How did the rise of national loyalties contribute to the decline of the Crusades?

13. Between the years 1000 and 1500, France, Spain, and England developed into strong nation-states. Choose one of these countries and show how royal power increased during these years.

14. How did the rise of royal power bring about a crisis in the Catholic Church during the 1300's?

15. Why did Germany fail to become a unified nation-state during the Middle Ages?

16. (a) Describe the civil war that rocked England in 1455. (b) How was the end of this war a turning point for England?

17. (a) To what family did Henry VII of England belong? (b) How did his reign strengthen the English monarchy?

18. Use the following topics to outline Russian history between the late 800's and the late 1500's.
    a. conversion to Christianity
    b. Mongol Invasion
    c. Moscow
    d. Ivan the Great
    e. Ivan the Terrible

19. How did the Russian monarchy in the late 1500's differ from the monarchies of western Europe around this same time?

Unit IV

An Age of Empires

CHAPTERS

Before 1500, different regions of the world generally developed in isolation. While trade provided some links among Europe, Asia, and Africa, each region maintained its own culture with little outside influence. The peoples of the Western Hemisphere—North and South America—were the most completely separated.

During these years, several dynasties rose and fell in China. At its height, China enjoyed a golden age and had a strong influence over its neighbor, Japan. India too had a golden age in art, science, and literature under the Gupta dynasty. In Africa, trade led to the growth of mighty empires in western regions and prosperous city-states on the eastern coast. In the Americas, the great civilization of the Mayas flowered and then disappeared. In 1500, the empires of the Aztecs and the Incas were at their height.

Around 1500, European ships began to reach ports in Africa, Asia, and the Americas. Their coming heralded a new age of global trade, migrations, and cultural contact.

The Forbidden City, Peking, China

Chapter 12

300 - 1650

Golden Ages in China and Japan

Emperor Yang-ti rides through the imperial gardens with some attendants, while others care for his water lilies.

1. **Two great dynasties ruled China.**

2. **The Mongols conquered a vast empire.**

3. **China chose stability over change.**

4. **Japan developed a unique civilization.**

5. **Japan turned to isolation.**

Day after day, the golden leaves of autumn fluttered lazily to the ground outside the palace of the Chinese emperor Yang-ti. Yet the trees in Yang-ti's garden remained as green as in the summertime. How could this be?

Watchful peasants were seated in the branches of every tree. Each peasant held a basket filled with artificial leaves made of green silk. Whenever a natural leaf fell, a peasant instantly replaced it with a silken leaf.

At the same time, on Yang-ti's huge artificial lake, other peasants paddled boats among the thousands of floating lotus flowers. Blossoms that had withered overnight were plucked off and replaced by delicate petals of white and pink silk. Thus did the ambitious Yang-ti, who ruled China from 605 to 618, try to bring even the seasons under his control.

What was happening elsewhere in the world? In the year 618, the prophet Muhammad was just beginning to preach about Allah. The golden age of Islamic civilization lay 200 years in the future. The golden age of Rome lay 500 years in the past. Nowhere else in the world was there a monarch who could equal the power and wealth of Yang-ti. China in the 600's enjoyed a golden age of political unity and artistic splendor.

This chapter covers 1,300 years in the history of two Asian peoples, the Chinese and the Japanese. From 300 to 1650, both China and Japan passed through ages of extraordinary cultural vitality and richness.

Two great dynasties ruled China.   1

As you read in Chapter 4, the Han dynasty collapsed in A.D. 220. For 350 years, no emperor was strong enough to hold China together. More than 30 local dynasties rose and fell. A Chinese poet wrote, "The land was divided like a melon, or shared like beans."

Under the Shang, the Chou, and the Han, the center of China's civilization had been in the north, in the plains along the Yellow River. After 220, however, barbarians from beyond the Great Wall conquered much of northern China. Chinese nobles moved to the safer south, along the Yangtze River. During this long time of troubles, the south slowly became the new center of Chinese civilization.

The Sui dynasty reunited China.

In the late 500's, a new dynasty united China once again. In 581, Sui Wen-ti took over the north and then conquered the south. He brought China once again under the rule of a strong central government.

The new ruling family called themselves the Sui (sway) dynasty. (Recall the Chinese custom of giving the family name first and then the personal name.) There were only two Sui emperors, Wen-ti and his son, Yang-ti. Their dynasty was short (589–618), but it laid the foundation for the golden age that followed.

The Grand Canal The second Sui ruler, Yang-ti, completed the work of reuniting China. His greatest single accomplishment was the building of the Grand Canal. The canal cut across the center of China, tying together its two great rivers, the Yellow River in the north and the Yangtze River in the south.

The canal helped to unite northern and southern China both politically and economically. From his capital in the north, the emperor demanded obedience and tribute from the people of southern China. Barges carried tons of food from the rich rice fields of the south to the less fertile north.

The digging of this 1,000-mile waterway was a prodigious feat. Tens of thousands of peasant men and women toiled on the project for five years between 605 and 610. Perhaps as many as half the workers died on the job. (Yet more died on Yang-ti's project of rebuilding the Great Wall to keep out raiding Turks.)

The overthrow of the Sui The endless work of building canals, walls, and palaces turned people against the Sui dynasty. Yang-ti ranks as one of the most hated emperors in China's history. Overworked and overtaxed, the peasants rebelled. Rebel armies arose all over China. In 618, his own servants strangled Yang-ti.

T'ai-tsung founded the T'ang dynasty.

A young rebel general soon won the throne. He took the name T'ai-tsung (tye-dzoong), which meant "Grand Ancestor." The dynasty he founded was the T'ang. The T'ang dynasty ruled a united China from 618 to 907, nearly 300 years. T'ai-tsung's brilliant reign (627–649) ushered in a golden age when China was the richest, most powerful country in the world.

T'ai-tsung led armies northwest against the Turks of central Asia and northeast against the Koreans. His soldiers, clad in armor of rhinoceros hide, reconquered the northern and western lands that China had lost since the decline of the Han dynasty. Korea fought off T'ai-tsung's invasion, but it fell to his son in 660. For the next 90 years, Korea was forced to pay tribute to China.

T'ai-tsung remembered the Sui dynasty's mistake of overtaxing peasants. He lowered taxes.

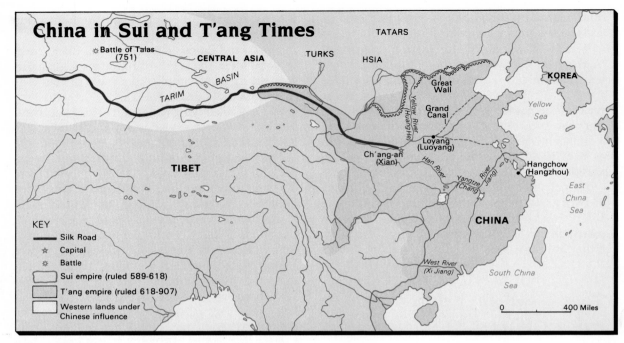

China in Sui and T'ang Times

TATARS

☆ Battle of Talas (751)

CENTRAL ASIA

TURKS

HSIA

Great Wall

KOREA

TARIM BASIN

Yellow Sea

Grand Canal

Yellow River (Huang He)

Loyang (Luoyang)

TIBET

Ch'ang-an (Xian)

Han River

Hangchow (Hangzhou)

East China Sea

Yangtze River (Chang)

CHINA

KEY
— Silk Road
☆ Capital
✸ Battle
▢ Sui empire (ruled 589-618)
▢ T'ang empire (ruled 618-907)
▢ Western lands under Chinese influence

West River (Xi Jiang)

South China Sea

0 ___ 400 Miles

Map Study

Which dynasty controlled a larger area, the Sui or the T'ang? What region was under Chinese influence but was not part of China during this period? Name two regions shown here that were independent of China.

He also took lands from wealthy landlords and gave those lands to peasants.

Wu Chao strengthened T'ang rule.

Another able T'ang ruler was Empress Wu Chao (woo jaow). She became the only woman ever to rule China in her own name.

In 635, when she was 13, the beautiful Wu Chao left her family for T'ai-tsung's court. When T'ai-tsung died in 650, his son succeeded him. The new emperor made Wu Chao his chief wife and empress. After his death in 683, she ruled in her sons' names. Finally, in 690, Wu Chao took the throne herself.

China benefited from the empress's strong leadership. Her armies won victories in Korea. She lowered taxes. She also encouraged the spread of Buddhism in China.

Scholar-officials governed China.

The T'ang dynasty's most important reform was a system for choosing government officials. As early as the first century B.C., the Han emperor

Wu-ti had begun granting government jobs to scholars who passed an examination on the Five Classics of Confucius. Now, 700 years later, the system was revived and expanded.

Candidates for high office had to pass three grueling exams. Any man, from peasant to noble, could take the first exam. (Women could not compete except during Wu Chao's reign.) In theory, even a peasant could rise in government by doing well on the exams. In practice, however, the system favored wealthy men, because only they could afford an education.

The fortunate few who made it through the first test were known as Budding Scholars. They journeyed to their provincial capitals to take a second exam. If successful again, they traveled to the T'ang capital of Ch'ang-an. Here, locked in windowless cells, they spent days of mental torture taking the final exam.

The successful scholar became a member of China's elite class of scholar-officials. He might serve as a teacher or an administrator. In return, he was freed from paying taxes or serving in the army. He could adopt the fashion of growing his fingernails long. (A two-inch fingernail showed clearly that its owner did no manual labor.) Finally, the scholar-official could use his special privileges to gain land and amass a fortune.

China continued to use the examination system for over 1,000 years. The system had its weaknesses. It did not weed out selfish or corrupt officials. Also, training in writing poetry and quoting Confucius was not always helpful in collecting taxes or supervising canal repairs.

With all its faults, however, the system gave China a remarkably intelligent governing class. No longer did a few ruling families control the country. Now talent was more important than high birth in winning power. As a result, many moderately wealthy families shared in China's government. Scholar-officials and their families formed a new class in Chinese society. This class is often described as the **gentry**, a large, well-to-do group of people who rank below nobles but above the common people.

Some scholars struggle with their exams, while others wait outside to learn if they passed.

Ch'ang-an was the T'ang capital.

The capital of T'ang China was Ch'ang-an, a city of about 2 million people. Ch'ang-an's layout showed the Chinese passion for order. Its walls, 18 feet high, formed a rectangle 6 miles long and 5 miles wide. The walls were carefully aligned with the cardinal points of the compass. In each wall were three evenly spaced gates. The streets within the city formed neat, rectangular blocks. The main avenue was almost 500 feet wide, about 5 times wider than New York's Fifth Avenue.

The imperial palace lay within a complex of palaces and beautifully landscaped parks. The stone-paved road that led to the main palace curved in the shape of a dragon's tail.

Booming drums regulated daily life in Ch'ang-an. At daybreak, the police who patrolled the streets beat on their drums to announce the opening of the city gates. At sunset, the markets closed and people scurried home to the beat of drums as the police locked the city gates. Anyone caught on the streets after the evening drums had sounded could be severely punished.

Within the city, more than 200 different trades and professions had their own sections. So did the various groups of foreigners—Jewish traders and shopkeepers, traders from India, musicians and dancers from Burma, Buddhist pilgrims from many lands, and caravan leaders from the deserts.

Shops in Ch'ang-an sold rugs from Persia, glassware from Syria, lapdogs from Samarkand (in central Asia), pine nuts from Korea, peacock feathers from Burma, and ivory and gems from Vietnam. Chinese women took up foreign fashions. Their silk gowns (tight bodice, plunging neckline, winglike shoulderpads) were modeled after Persian styles. Their hair was done up in the elaborate fashion begun by the princesses of Samarkand.

Once, China had been cut off from the rest of the world by oceans, mountains, and deserts. The T'ang emperors did not isolate themselves behind such barriers. Imperial armies guarded the Great Silk Road, which linked China to the west. Merchandise and travelers moved safely across it in both directions. Sea trade connected China to India and Southeast Asia. In fact, China was more open to foreign trade and influence during the T'ang years than at any other time in history.

Drums such as this one regulated the lives of Chinese city dwellers. The booming of the drums announced daybreak and curfew.

Poets captured moments of beauty.

In earlier times, Chinese nobles had enjoyed rural pastimes such as horseback riding and hunting, much as the feudal lords of Europe did. In T'ang times, however, the gentry preferred living in the sophisticated atmosphere of cities. There the scholar-officials enjoyed the pleasures of literature and art.

During the golden years of T'ang China, every educated person was expected to write poems. For the gentry, it was almost a daily habit. "At this age," wrote a Chinese chronicler, "whoever was a gentleman was a poet." (Of course, educated people were still a tiny minority.)

Three qualities marked the Chinese poetry of this period. First, images from nature filled nearly all the poems. Mention of a butterfly's wing or a mountain stream subtly suggested the poet's mood. Second, each poem focused sharply on a single moment. Third, poems were brief, seldom longer than a dozen lines.

Li Po (lee boh) and Tu Fu were the most celebrated poets of the 700's. They were friends, but their poems were quite different. Li Po often wrote about the pleasures of life, whereas Tu Fu praised orderliness and the Confucian virtues.

Tu Fu's masterly touch shows in this poem titled "Welcome Rain One Spring Night":

A good rain knows its season
And comes when spring is here;
On the heels of the wind it slips secretly
into the night;
Silent and soft it moistens everything.

The T'ang dynasty lost power.

By the early 700's, the T'ang dynasty was weakening. Crushing taxes brought hardship to the people but still failed to meet the rising costs of government. In times of famine, peasants fled their villages and ranged the countryside in bandit gangs.

Moreover, the T'ang could not control the vast empire they had built. In 751, Arabs soundly defeated the Chinese on China's western frontier at the Battle of Talas. Central Asia passed out of Chinese control and into Muslim hands.

To the Chinese, these troubles showed that the T'ang dynasty was losing the Mandate of Heaven. In 755, an army general led a revolt against the emperor. Although a new T'ang emperor regained the throne in 766, the T'ang dynasty never recovered its power and prestige. The government lost control over the more distant parts of China. At the same time, the Chinese began to turn away from foreign contacts, so trade declined. Finally in 905, Ch'ang-an was sacked and burned by rebels. In 907, the last T'ang emperor, a child, was murdered.

The Sung ruled a smaller empire.

After the end of the T'ang dynasty in 907, rival warlords divided China into unstable kingdoms. A poet summed up the chaos of these times: "States rose and fell as candles gutter out in the wind."

In 960, an able army leader proclaimed himself Emperor Sung T'ai-tsu (soong tye-dzoo). The Sung dynasty, like the T'ang, lasted about three centuries (960–1279).

Military decline The Sung dynasty was never as strong as either the Han or the T'ang. The Battle of Talas had marked the beginning of 500 years of military decline for China. Sung armies never regained the western lands lost at Talas in

751. More serious, they never regained the northern lands lost to the nomadic Hsia (shee-ah) and Tatars (TAHT-uhrz) during the T'ang decline.

Sung emperors tried to buy peace with their northern enemies. Beginning in 1004, they paid to the Tatar khan (chieftain) 6,250 pounds of silver and 200,000 bolts of silk each year. To appease the Hsia, they sent a yearly "gift" of 4,375 pounds of silver, 150,000 bolts of silk, and 30,000 pounds of tea. This policy worked for over 100 years.

Move to the south In the end, however, bribes failed to stop the barbarians. In 1126, the Tatars galloped as far as the Yellow River and captured the Sung capital of K'ai-feng (kye-fung).

The emperor was taken prisoner, but his family fled south across the Yangtze River to Hangchow (hahng-joh) in southern China. Thus the traditional center of Chinese civilization, the Yellow River valley, was lost to the Tatars. After 1126, the Sung emperors ruled only southern China.

Merchants thrived in Hangchow.

Despite its military troubles, the Sung dynasty was truly a golden age in southern China. Merchants prospered by selling rice, tea, fish, and other wares in the markets of Hangchow.

Unlike the orderly Ch'ang-an, Hangchow was a marvel of noise and confusion. There were no nightly curfews. Wine flowed all night in the city's restaurants. The canals that twisted through every section of Hangchow were choked with barges piled high with cargo. Mules laden with sacks clattered across the "rainbow bridges" that arched over the canals.

Paper money In the busy markets, two kinds of money passed from hand to hand. First, there were copper coins with square holes cut through the center. The standard unit for trading was "a thousand cash," a thousand coins fastened together on a long string. However, these strings of coins were clumsy and burdensome.

Therefore, between the years 1000 and 1100, the Sung government began to print paper money—the first such money in the world. The merchants of Hangchow could leave their strings of metal cash with bankers in exchange for paper bank notes. Each note carried the warning, "Counterfeiters will be beheaded."

Trade in silk and porcelain Merchants from Hangchow sent trade goods south to the Malay

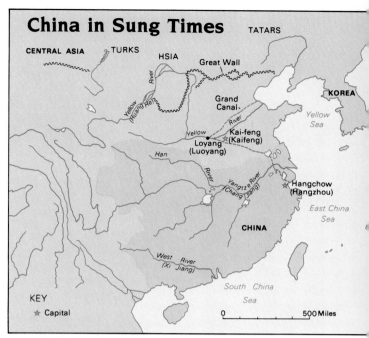

China in Sung Times

Map Study
Compare this map with the one on page 262. What lands has China's emperor lost?

Peninsula and west to India, the Persian Gulf, and even the coast of Africa. Two luxury items were especially easy to trade for a profit in any Asian or African port. One, of course, was Chinese silk. The other was porcelain.

For hundreds of years, the Chinese were the only people who knew the secret formula for combining certain clays and minerals to produce the fine, bone-hard substance called porcelain. Even today, people call such fine cups and dishes "china." The porcelain of Sung times was famous for its delicacy and its subtle colors with such delightful names as plum-colored blue and crushed-strawberry red.

Artists painted beauties of nature.

Like the T'ang period, Sung times were an age of artistic brilliance. The T'ang dynasty was the golden age of the poet. The Sung dynasty was the golden age of painting.

Every well-to-do family had a cherished collection of silk scrolls tucked away in a cabinet. When a scholar wished to escape the hustle and bustle of court life, he could find peace and

265

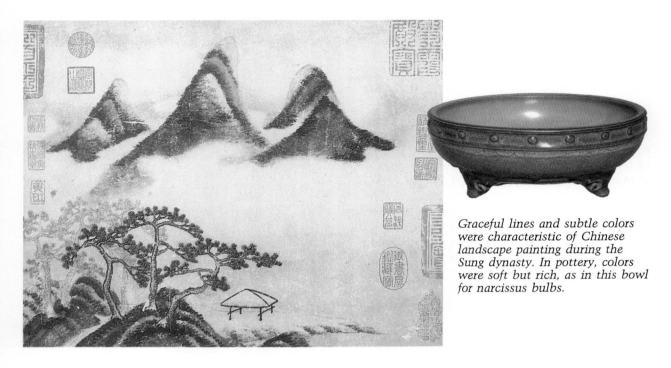

Graceful lines and subtle colors were characteristic of Chinese landscape painting during the Sung dynasty. In pottery, colors were soft but rich, as in this bowl for narcissus bulbs.

comfort by unrolling a scroll to view the beauties of nature. When he had sat long enough with trees, waterfalls, and mountain mists, he rolled up the scroll and returned it to the cabinet.

Sung artists did not use brightly colored paints. Black ink was their favorite paint. Said one Sung artist, "Black is ten colors." Grace of line was at the heart of Sung art.

China led the world in technology.

During the years of the T'ang and the Sung dynasties, no other area of the world was China's equal in skilled workers, science, and technology. Three Chinese inventions—printing, gunpowder, and the compass—were destined to have a revolutionary impact on the rest of the world. All three originated during the T'ang dynasty and were fully developed during the Sung.

Printing The Chinese began to print books around the year 600. Printers first cut a block of wood the size of two book pages. Over the block they pasted a sheet of thin paper on which the text was written. Using the writing on the paper as a guide, they carved around the characters so that they stood out in relief. By brushing ink onto the carved block and pressing it onto blank sheets of paper, a printer could produce a copy

of the original page. In one day, an expert printer could make 2,000 copies.

Sometime in the Sung dynasty, probably in the 1040's, an inventor named Pi Sheng (bee shung) took the next logical step—movable type. He arranged the individual characters on an iron plate coated with sticky resin and tar to hold them in place. Thus, the same characters could be used over and over, instead of carving a new set for each page. (Europeans did not discover how to print books until 1450.)

Magnetic compass The Chinese also learned that a magnetized needle floating in a bowl of water always points north-south. They first used

Footnote to History

Beginning in Sung times, the Chinese considered it beautiful for women to have very tiny feet. Upper-class parents would wrap their daughter's feet in tight bandages when she was about five years old. As the child grew, the wrappings forced her foot to curl painfully until the toes and heel came together. Women whose feet had been bound could hobble only a few steps. For a man, having such a wife was a sign of wealth because she could do little household work.

this device to make sure their houses faced south, as custom required. By 1119, traders from south China had discovered how useful the compass could be for finding directions at sea. Eventually, Arab traders carried the compass to the Mediterranean Sea.

Gunpowder As early as the 600's, fireworks lit up the evening sky over Ch'ang-an during festivals. The Chinese called their thrilling firecrackers "fire trees," "flame flowers," and "peach blossoms."

Sometime after the year 1000, the Chinese experimented with explosive weapons. They made a kind of hand-grenade and shot off small rockets. However, gunpowder remained a minor invention until Europeans learned of it, probably by way of the Arabs and Mongols.

Eventually, the Sung dynasty collapsed. It had already abandoned the northern half of China to the Tatars. In the 1200's, it lost the southern half as well to the Mongols, a warlike people akin to the Tatars. The destructive fury of the Mongols affected much of Asia and Europe.

Section Review 1

Define: (a) gentry, (b) porcelain
Identify: (a) Sui dynasty, (b) Grand Canal, (c) T'ai-tsung, (d) T'ang dynasty, (e) Wu Chao, (f) Ch'ang-an, (g) Great Silk Road, (h) Battle of Talas, (i) Sung T'ai-tsu, (j) Sung dynasty, (k) Hangchow
Answer:
1. (a) What made the Sui dynasty important? (b) Why was it short-lived?
2. (a) How did Chinese officials earn their jobs? (b) What were the good points of this system? (c) The weaknesses?
3. (a) What part did the Tatars and the Hsia play in Chinese history? (b) What was the policy of the Sung toward them?
4. Describe the role of trade in China under the T'ang and Sung dynasties.
5. What political and military changes took place between T'ang and Sung times?
6. Describe three important inventions that the Chinese developed during the T'ang and Sung periods.

Critical Thinking
7. Explain why you agree or disagree with the following statement: "T'ang poetry and Sung painting share some basic values that were important in China."

The Mongols conquered a vast empire. 2

Who were the Mongols? To their enemies, they were "the devil's horsemen"—the ugliest, filthiest barbarians that ever lived. Of course, the Mongols saw themselves differently. In their own view, they were a noble people whose warlike, nomadic way of life was superior to the soft ways of city people. They felt nothing but contempt for the rich civilizations of India, China, and Persia.

Between 1200 and 1350, the Mongols conquered lands from the Pacific Ocean to the Adriatic Sea. Sweeping out of central Asia, they conquered much of the Islamic empire and destroyed Baghdad. They sent their armies westward to Russia, eastward to China, and south to the Himalayas. They ruled the largest unified land empire in history.

The Mongols came from the steppe.

The homeland of the Mongols was a vast grassland north of China's Great Wall. The hardy grasses there supported huge herds of horses, cattle, yaks, and sheep. Except for grass, the land was bare. One could travel for weeks without seeing a single tree. Savage winds swept the plain.

Mongolia lies at the eastern end of an enormous belt of **steppe**, or dry grassland, that stretches all across Asia and into eastern Europe. In this huge region lived a bewildering number of nomadic bands. You have already read some of their names—Huns, Avars, Turks, Tatars.

Whether called Hun, Tatar, or Mongol, the people of the eastern steppe followed basically the same way of life for centuries. They practically lived on horseback, following their huge herds of cattle, sheep, and horses over the steppe. They camped at night in great circular tents made of felt. Mare's milk was the one staple of their diet.

267

The Mongols were fearsome warriors. Mounted on tough war ponies, their armies could cover great distances while living off the land. A Mongol warrior's most important weapon was his bow made of wood, horn, and sinew. Pulling the bow took over 100 pounds of force, and the Mongol archer pulled it while riding at a full gallop. He could hit an enemy over 200 yards away.

Genghis Khan united the Mongols.

For centuries, the Mongols had lived in loosely organized groups. Each group had its own leader, known as a **khan**. Around 1200, however, they suddenly united under the leadership of one of history's greatest conquerors. His name was Temujin (**TEM**-yoo-jin), but he is better known by his title, Genghis (**JENG**-gihs) Khan.

Temujin was born sometime around 1160. The first 20 years of his life were a struggle for survival. When he was 13, his father was murdered and Temujin nearly met the same fate at the hands of a rival Mongol family. However, he survived to become a minor chieftain.

Temujin spent the next 20 years fighting for power on the Mongolian steppe. He defeated his rivals one by one, showing no mercy. (After one victory, he slaughtered every person in the defeated group who was taller than a cart axle. Only the youngest children survived. They were brought up as his followers.)

In 1206, Temujin became the accepted ruler of all the steppe people. He took the title Genghis Khan, meaning "ruler of all between the oceans."

Between 1206 and his death in 1227, Genghis Khan conquered most of Asia.

Several traits lay behind Genghis Khan's stunning success as a conqueror. First, he was a brilliant organizer. He grouped his warriors in armies of 10,000, which in turn were organized into brigades of 1,000. Brigades were broken down into companies of 100, and companies were divided into 10-man platoons. Each group had its own commander. This organization meant that the army could carry out orders swiftly.

Second, Genghis Khan was shrewd as well as warlike. He never plunged recklessly into battle against an unknown enemy. He employed spies brilliantly to find out enemy weaknesses.

Finally, Genghis Khan used cruelty as a weapon. He believed in terrifying his enemies into surrender. If a city refused to open its gates to him, he might kill the entire population when he finally captured the place. The terror that the Mongols spread led many towns to surrender without a fight.

The Mongol empire divided.

Genghis Khan died in 1227, but the Mongol conquest continued. The sons and grandsons of Genghis Khan were responsible for the massacre of untold millions and the destruction of some of Asia's greatest cities. In about a 50-year period (1229–1279), they overthrew the Abbasid dynasty in Persia, burned Baghdad, conquered Kievan Russia, terrorized eastern Europe, and defeated China's Sung dynasty.

Mongol horsemen sharpened their riding skills in swift games of polo. Their small ponies were nimble enough for such games, but they were also hardy enough for long treks across the harsh lands of central Asia.

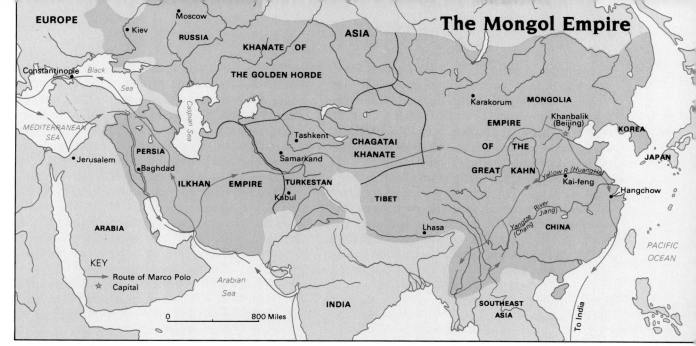

The Mongol Empire

Map Study

Name two cities that Marco Polo visited on his way to China. Which khanate controlled Russia? Persia? Korea?

By 1259, there were four khans, each ruling a different part of the empire. One khan ruled the central steppes of Turkestan. A second held the lands of the fallen Islamic empire in Persia. A third ruled Russia. These three khans owed loyalty to the fourth khan, known as the Great Khan, who ruled China. As time went by, however, each khan became more and more independent.

Kublai Khan ruled China.

The conqueror of Sung China was Genghis Khan's grandson, Kublai (KOO-blye) Khan. He ruled China from 1260 to 1294, taking the Chinese name Yüan for his dynasty. Unlike his barbarian ancestors, Kublai Khan spent almost his entire life within China. Far from the Mongolian steppe, he did not share his ancestors' hatred for civilization. On the contrary, he rather enjoyed living in the luxurious manner of a Chinese emperor. He ruled from a square capital in northern China that he called Khanbalik (City of the Great Khan). Today it is called Peking.

Failure to conquer Japan Kublai Khan tried to extend his rule to Japan. In 1281, the Great Khan sent two fleets carrying a total of 150,000 warriors against Japan. It was the largest seaborne invasion force in history until World War II. The Japanese

warriors fought the invaders to a standstill for 53 days. Suddenly, the sky darkened and a typhoon swept furiously across the Sea of Japan. Mongol ships were upended, swamped, and dashed to bits against the shore. Many Mongols drowned and others were quickly slain by the Japanese. For centuries afterward, the Japanese spoke reverently of the *kamikaze*, or "divine wind" that had saved Japan.

Marco Polo at the Mongol court Though warlike and cruel, the Mongols made the caravan routes across central Asia safe again for trade and travel. Ever since the decline of the T'ang dynasty, robbers and warring tribes had nearly shut down those routes. The Mongol empire put an end to such dangers. For about a century (1250–1350), Mongol armies kept peace across central Asia, just as Roman armies had once done around the Mediterranean Sea.

Footnote to History

In his quiver, a Mongol archer carried long-range arrows, short-range arrows, arrows to pierce armor, arrows to shoot fire into enemy camps, arrows with explosive tips, and even whistling arrows to use as signals.

The most famous European to travel across Asia in these years was an Italian youth from Venice named Marco Polo. He was 17 when he set out from Venice with his father and uncle, who were on their second visit to Khanbalik. In 1275, after three years of travel, the Polos reached the court of Kublai Khan.

The shrewd khan made young Marco Polo a trusted official of the Mongol government. Nearly all the khan's highest officials were foreigners, because he distrusted the Chinese and kept them out of government. Polo served the Great Khan well for 17 years. He traveled across the Yellow and Yangtze rivers and returned with detailed reports of the empire. In 1292, two years before Kublai died, the Polos left China and made the long homeward journey to Venice by sea.

Captured in a war with the rival city of Genoa, Marco Polo had time in prison to tell the full story of his travels and adventures. To his awed listeners, he spoke of China's fabulous cities, its great armies, its fantastic wealth, and the strange things he had seen there. He mentioned the burning of "black stones" (coal) in Chinese homes. (Coal as a fuel was then unknown in Europe.) He told too of a new year's celebration in which the Great Khan received 100,000 white horses as a gift. He described a postal service in which 200,000 horses sped messages on paved roads between 10,000 relay stations. He told all these marvelous tales and more.

A fellow prisoner gathered Marco Polo's stories into a book. It was an instant success in Europe, but most readers did not believe a word of it.

Voice from the Past · *The City of the Great Khan*

After Marco Polo was released from prison in Genoa, he spent the rest of his life quietly in Venice. He died in 1324 at the age of 70. According to legend, he was asked on his deathbed to take back the so-called tall tales in his book. He answered that he had told less than half the wonders he had seen on his travels. Here is his description of Khanbalik.

The new royal city is a perfect square, each of its sides being 6 miles long. The city wall has 12 gates, 3 on each side of the square. The whole city was laid out by line. The streets are so straight that if you stand at one gate, you can see the gate on the other side of the city.

The throngs of inhabitants and the number of houses in Khanbalik are greater than the mind can grasp. The suburbs have even more people than the city itself. Within each suburb, there are many hotels at which merchants can stay.

Everything that is most rare and valuable in the world finds its way to this city. This is particularly true for rich goods from India, such as precious gems, pearls, and spices. From other parts of Cathay [China] itself, at least 1,000 carriages and packhorses loaded with raw silk enter the city each day.

In the center of the city is a great bell, which is rung every night. After the third stroke, no one dares to be found on the streets, except for some emergency. In such necessary cases, the person is required to carry a light. Groups of 30 or 40 guards patrol the streets all night, looking for people who are out of their houses after the great bell has rung.

1. What features show that the city was carefully planned?
2. What evidence shows that Khanbalik was larger than cities in Europe?
3. What statements show that trade was important in Khanbalik's economy?
4. Compare this description to that of Ch'ang-an (page 263). How are the two cities alike?

per que excita

They thought Polo's account was a marvelous collection of tall tales. It was clear to Marco Polo, however, that the civilization he had visited was the greatest in the world.

Section Review 2

Define: (a) nomad, (b) steppe, (c) khan, (d) kamikaze
Identify: (a) Mongols, (b) Genghis Khan, (c) Kublai Khan, (d) Yüan, (e) Marco Polo
Answer:
1. (a) Describe the Mongols' way of life. (b) How did this way of life make them strong warriors?
2. List three factors that helped Genghis Khan conquer an empire.
3. (a) What conquests were made by Genghis Khan? (b) What did his descendants add to the empire? (c) Identify the four areas the khans ruled after 1259.
4. How did the spread of Mongol rule affect trade between Europe and Asia?
5. Name at least three things in China that impressed Marco Polo.

Critical Thinking

6. (a) What evidence is there that the Chinese way of life influenced the Mongol conquerors? (b) What evidence is there that the Mongol rulers partly resisted Chinese influence?

China chose stability over change.

3

After Kublai Khan's death in 1295, Mongol rule weakened. Between 1295 and 1333, seven Mongols schemed and murdered their way to the Dragon Throne. China was beset by famines and revolts. The Yuan dynasty of the Mongols was near its end.

The Ming dynasty brought peace.

The leader who freed China from the Mongols was a commoner named Chu Yuan-chang (joo yoo-ahn-jang). Born into a peasant family in 1328, he was orphaned at the age of 16 and lived as a

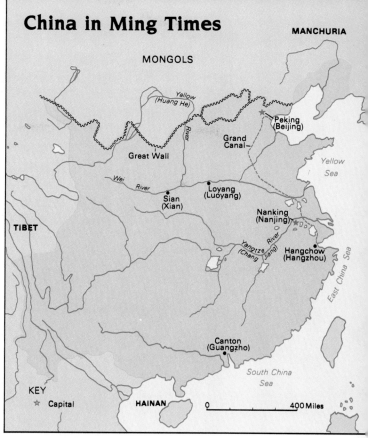

China in Ming Times

Map Study

What evidence shows that the Ming dynasty was more powerful than the Sung (map, page 265)?

beggar. He entered a Buddhist monastery where he learned to read and write. In 1352, Chu joined one of the secret groups resisting the Mongols. He proved to be a brilliant military leader. In 1368, Chu proclaimed himself the emperor of the new Ming (meaning "brilliant") dynasty. For himself, he took the name Ming T'ai-tsu, meaning "Grand Progenitor." By 1382, Ming T'ai-tsu had succeeded in bringing all of China under his rule.

China was divided into two major geographic zones. The southern, rice-growing zone followed the Yangtze River and centered on the seaports along the East China Sea. The northern zone was traditionally considered the true heartland of China. It had been the home of Confucius and of the Han and T'ang emperors. The first Ming emperor, Ming T'ai-tsu, was a southerner. He built his capital at Nanking (which meant "southern capital") on the Yangtze River and ruled there until his death in 1398.

Ming T'ai-tsu's son, Yung-lo, ruled from 1403 to 1424. He decided that he wished to rule from

Ming emperors such as Ch'eng-tsu (below) lived in the Forbidden City. The drawing above shows one of the city's hundreds of courtyards. Because the emperor stood for peace and harmony in China, the plan of the city emphasized balance, order, and symmetry.

the north, and he chose Kublai Khan's city of Khanbalik. Yung-lo gave Khanbalik a new name—Peking ("northern capital").

Peking was laid out in the traditional manner of a Chinese walled city. Gates facing north, south, east, and west pierced a high wall that enclosed the outer city. Broad avenues led from the outer gates to a smaller rectangular wall that surrounded the inner Imperial City. This city within a city was the center of routine government business.

Inside the Imperial City was yet another walled city with pagoda-like towers at its four corners. This was the Forbidden City—forbidden to everyone except the emperor and his court. Most residents of Peking lived and died without ever seeing what lay inside. The 250 acres of the Forbidden City held reception halls, private palaces, libraries, theaters, gardens, and athletic fields. More than 6,000 cooks prepared lavish meals for the 10,000 to 15,000 people who ate at the Court of Imperial Entertainments.

Ming scholars looked to the past.

From earliest times, the Chinese honored the ways of their ancestors. When a new dynasty came to power, its goal was not to bring new ways but to rule according to the good traditions of the past. Thus, China generally progressed by small adjustments, not by great changes.

The Ming emperors brought China's scholar-officials back to power. The Mongol emperors had deliberately excluded the scholar-officials (the gentry) from government. Ming T'ai-tsu restored the examination system (page 262).

Ming T'ai-tsu prized education so much that he opened public elementary schools in many cities. The use of printing made books easier to obtain in China than anywhere else in the world. Few rural children learned to read or write, but China's cities probably had a higher literacy rate than any other civilization in the 1300's.

To preserve the wisdom of the past, the second Ming emperor, Yung-lo, commissioned an encyclopedia of worthy Chinese writings from past ages. More than 2,000 scholars worked on the project for 4 years. When completed in 1408, the *Yung-lo Encyclopedia* filled 11,095 hand-written volumes. (The project was so huge that it was never printed.)

Such works of scholarship were impressive, but they also showed an overwhelming concern with the past. During the Ming dynasty, scholars held rigidly to Confucian ways of thinking. They did not strive for original ideas. Compared to their earlier achievements in science and technology, the Chinese of Ming times made few advances. Gradually, China lost its position of world leadership in those fields.

China limited foreign contacts.

During the first century of the Ming dynasty, from about 1350 to 1450, China was the greatest naval power in the world. In 1433, China's Grand Fleet crossed the Indian Ocean and sailed south along Africa's eastern coast. This immense fleet had over 100 ships manned by 27,500 sailors. Its commander, the 62-year-old Cheng Ho (jehng huh), had made seven such voyages since 1405. The ships of the Grand Fleet carried silks, porcelain, and art objects to exchange for ivory, rhinoceros horns, pearls, and jewels.

Cheng Ho's seventh voyage was the largest naval expedition launched by the Ming dynasty. It was also the last. Later Ming emperors decided such voyages were a waste of money. The Grand Fleet decayed. Even Cheng Ho's records were burned.

China's abandonment of its Grand Fleet marked an important turning point in world history. At the very time that China lost interest in exploration, the European kingdoms of Portugal and Spain began sending ships south around Africa. Eventually, European ships sailed east to Asia and west to the Americas. The story of these voyages is told in Chapter 15.

This turnabout suggests the different paths that western Europe and Asia took beginning in the 1400's. While China was turning inward, western Europe was ready to turn outward. Europeans wanted such Asian products as spices and silks. Christians from Europe also wanted to teach their religion to the people of Asia.

Europeans reached China in the 1500's.

The first Europeans to reach China by sea were the Portuguese. In 1513, a small fleet of Portuguese ships sailed into the South China Sea and anchored near Canton. Eager to make a quick fortune, the Portuguese grew impatient when the Chinese showed little interest in trade. The Portuguese sank Chinese vessels with their cannon. Horrified Ming officials closed their harbors to the "ocean devils" from Europe.

The Portuguese persisted in their efforts to trade for Chinese silk. At last, in 1557, the Chinese allowed them to operate a trading base at Macao (ma-COW). The base lay on an island near Canton and could be closely watched. For the next 200 years, the Chinese forced Europeans to conduct all their trade with China from Macao.

At first, Christian missionaries were more welcome in China than were Portuguese merchants. In 1583, a scholarly young Italian priest named Mateo Ricci (muh-TAY-oh REE-chee) went to China. Ricci learned Chinese and dressed like a scholar-official. Ming officials conceded that Ricci was less barbaric than other "ocean devils." In 1601, Ricci was at last permitted to travel north to Peking. He entered the Forbidden City and presented gifts of tribute to the emperor.

The scholars at court were not impressed with the missionary's gifts, but they were fascinated by two mechanical clocks that Ricci showed them. They were also impressed by his knowledge of astronomy. Because of his knowledge and his respect for Chinese ways, Ricci was accepted as a fellow scholar.

Within the Forbidden City, Ricci wrote in classical Chinese a Christian tract titled *The True Doctrine of God*. It was widely printed in China and helped other Roman Catholic missionaries convert thousands of Chinese. Ricci died in Peking in 1610.

The Ming dynasty collapsed.

By 1600, the Ming had ruled for more than 200 years and the dynasty was weakening. Ming officials were corrupt. The government was out of money, despite crushing taxes. High taxes and bad harvests pushed millions of peasants toward starvation. Many were reduced to a homeless life of begging and banditry. As in the past, they joined secret societies and plotted revolt.

Dangers also threatened from outside China. To the north and east of China lay Manchuria (man-CHOOR-ee-uh). The people of that region were called the Manchus (MAN-chooz). Though the Chinese considered them barbarians, the Manchus had already adopted many Chinese ways. Indeed, they had set up a kingdom modeled after China. By the late 1500's, the Manchus were a threat on China's northern border.

Peasant revolt and Manchu invasion combined to bring down the Ming dynasty. As an army of peasant rebels approached Peking, the last Ming emperor despaired. "I have incurred the wrath of the gods on high," he wrote. "My ministers have deceived me. I am ashamed to meet my ancestors." Setting aside his brush, the emperor hanged himself from a locust tree. Thus, in 1644, the Ming dynasty ended.

A foreign dynasty took power.

Soon after the death of the last Ming emperor, Manchu armies entered China and took over Peking. The Manchu ruler was declared China's new emperor. As the Mongols had done, the Manchus took a Chinese name for their dynasty— the Ch'ing dynasty.

The Manchu conquerors tried to keep themselves separate from the Chinese people. Manchus could hold government positions without taking the civil service examinations. Marriage between Chinese and Manchus was barred. The Manchu rulers forced all Chinese men to braid their hair into a long pigtail as a sign of low status.

In most respects, however, life under the Ch'ing was much the same as life under the Ming. The Ch'ing dynasty ruled for more than two centuries (1644–1912). In Chapter 29, you will see how revolutionary changes began to transform Chinese society under the later Ch'ing rulers.

Section Review 3

Define: literacy
Identify: (a) Ming T'ai-tsu, (b) Ming dynasty, (c) Nanking, (d) Peking, (e) Forbidden City, (f) Cheng Ho, (g) Macao, (h) Mateo Ricci, (i) Manchuria, (j) Ch'ing dynasty
Answer:
1. (a) How did Peking become the capital of China? (b) What was the difference between the Imperial City and the Forbidden City?
2. What factors encouraged learning in Ming China?
3. (a) What evidence indicates that the Chinese lost interest in contacts with other peoples after 1433? (b) Why did they make an exception for Mateo Ricci?
4. What factors, both within China and outside its borders, contributed to the downfall of the Ming dynasty?

Critical Thinking
5. Suggest some reasons why many Chinese rulers thought it important to build a grand capital city for their dynasty.

Japan developed a unique civilization. 4

Japan lies east of China, in the direction of the sunrise. In fact, the name *Japan* comes from the Chinese words *jih pen*, which mean "origin of the sun." The islands of Japan are separated from China by 500 miles of ocean. The nearest part of the Asian mainland is Korea, across 100 miles of water. In their early history, the Japanese were close enough to feel the civilizing influence of China. Yet they were far enough away to be reasonably safe from invasion.

About 3,000 volcanic islands make up the Japanese island group, but many are very tiny. Most of Japan's people have always lived on the four largest islands: Hokkaido (hah-KYE-doh), Honshu (HAHN-shoo), Shikoku (shih-KOH-KOO), and Kyushu (kee-YOO-shoo).

Japan's total land area is about equal to California's. The climate is temperate and the land is wooded. The islands are so mountainous, however, that only one fifth of the land is suitable for farming.

Clans dominated early Japan.

The first historic mention of Japan comes from Chinese writings of about A.D. 300. Archaeological evidence shows that people had lived in the Japanese islands for many centuries before that. However, because the early Japanese had no writing system, they left no historic records of their own.

Japan in the year 300 was not a united country. Instead, each **clan** controlled its own territory. A clan was a group of people who believed they were descended from the same ancestor.

The Yamato emperors The leading clan was the Yamato. The Yamato chiefs came to be called the emperors of Japan. Yet these emperors had no real power over the country as a whole. When rival clans fought for power, the winner gained control of the emperor and then ruled in the emperor's name.

The Shinto religion The Yamato rulers claimed the sun goddess as their ancestor. Other clans worshiped their own nature gods and goddesses. In different parts of Japan, people honored thousands of local gods and spirits. Their varied customs and beliefs eventually combined to form Japan's earliest religion. It was called Shinto (SHIHN-toh), meaning "the way of the gods."

The central idea of Shinto was the worship of nature. The sun goddess was the chief deity, but hundreds of lesser gods and spirits were thought to dwell in nature. Any unusual tree, rock, waterfall, or mountain was considered the home of a *kami*, or nature god.

The Japanese adapted Chinese ideas.

Around the year 500, the Japanese began to have more contact with mainland Asia. They were soon influenced by Chinese ideas and customs, about which they first learned from Korean travelers.

Buddhism in Japan For centuries, Korea had been in close touch with China. During the 500's, many Koreans migrated to Japan, bringing Chinese influences with them. One such group of Korean travelers brought with them a bronze statue of the Buddha. Within 50 years, the new religion had spread widely in Japan. For many centuries, the greatest Japanese scholars and sages lived as Buddhist monks.

The Japanese did not give up their Shinto faith. Shinto and Buddhism comfortably coexisted. Some Buddhist rituals became Shinto rituals, and some Shinto gods were worshiped in Buddhist temples.

Cultural borrowing The most influential convert to Buddhism was Prince Shotoku (shoh-toh-koo). In 607, Prince Shotoku sent a group of scholars to study Chinese civilization firsthand

Map Study

At the narrowest part of the sea, how far is Japan from Korea? From China? What sea lies east of Korea? West of Korea?

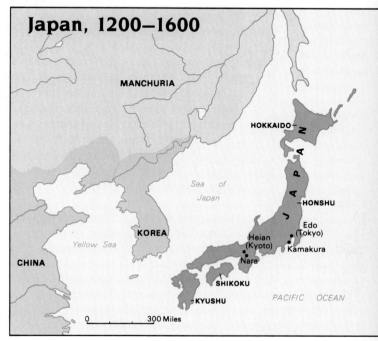

Japan, 1200–1600

For a noble family in Japan, amusements included music, games, and writing poetry or love letters. The screen in the background, with its view of a landscape, shows the Chinese influence on Japanese art.

at Ch'ang-an. These scholars braved the dangers of shipwreck and storm without even a compass to guide them on the 500-mile voyage. Over the next 200 years, while the T'ang dynasty was at its height, the Japanese sent many such groups to learn more of Chinese ways.

The Japanese adopted the Chinese system of writing. Japanese artists painted landscapes in the Chinese manner. The gracefully curved, winglike roofs of Japan's Buddhist pagodas imitated Chinese roofs. The Japanese even followed Chinese styles in the simple arts of everyday living such as cooking, gardening, drinking tea, and hairdressing.

Imperial government For a time, Japan also modeled its government on China's. Prince Shotoku drew up a written plan of government based on the teachings of Confucius. Shotoku and his successors tried to build a strong central government like that of the T'ang rulers. Shotoku also tried to introduce China's examination system in Japan. However, the attempt failed. In Japan, noble birth remained the key to winning a powerful job. Unlike China, Japan continued to be a country where a few great families held power.

In imitation of Ch'ang-an, Japanese builders laid out a magnificent square city on the island of Honshu. This city, called Nara, was the first capital in Japanese history.

The Japanese adapted and changed Chinese ways to suit their own needs. While they learned much, they also retained their own traditions. Then, in the 800's, Japan's ruling family abruptly broke contact with the T'ang court. Japanese leaders felt they had nothing more to learn from China. Japan's own culture was about to come into full flower.

Court society developed at Heian.

Nara was the Japanese capital from 710 to 784, less than a century. In 794, Emperor Kammu built a new capital city called Heian (**HAY**-ahn). Its modern name is Kyoto (kee-**OHT**-oh). Japan's 400-year golden age from 794 to 1185 is known as the Heian age.

"Dwellers among the clouds" Historians estimate that there were about 5 million Japanese in the year 800. Most were farmers and fishers living in tiny villages. Heian itself had a population of about 100,000 of which only 3,000 belonged to the noble class. These families lived so far above the common people that they were called "dwellers among the clouds."

Men and women of noble birth in Heian lived outdoors as much as possible. They gossiped and sipped tea around the fishponds of their beautiful gardens. A Japanese woman seated in her garden was as colorful as the surrounding cherry blossoms. She wore up to 12 silk gowns, one over the other. As the breezes blew, the various colors showed in shifting patterns. If one color of her dress was off by a mere shade, people at court might snicker about it.

Men and women alike used cosmetics heavily. They blackened their teeth because white teeth were considered ugly. They covered their faces with white powder. Women plucked out their eyebrows and painted artificial brows high on their foreheads. Sometimes they gilded their lips. Men used perfumes as a mark of identification.

To be accepted in Heian society, one had to write poetry. To start a romance, a man or woman composed a short poem showing the writer's fine taste and artistry. The poem had to be written on a sheet of colored paper with a shade and texture that perfectly suited the feeling of the poem. The other person replied in the same way. If each person liked the other's poem, the man and woman went on with their flirtation. The slightest blunder with the brush might end the romance.

Leading women authors The best accounts of this elegant society come from the diaries, essays, and novels written by women of the court. The women writers of the Heian court were far more noteworthy than the male writers of the time.

Why? Two reasons have been suggested. First, Japanese women in the Heian Age were held in high esteem, unlike women in China or the Greco-Roman world. Men deferred to their artistic taste and their intellect. Second, Japanese men were bound by custom to use only Chinese characters when they wrote. Women wrote in a simpler script called *kana* that was better suited to the Japanese language. Thus, ideas flowed much more smoothly from a woman's brush.

The leading writer of this period was Lady Murasaki Shikibu (moo-rah-sah-kee shee-kee-boo). Around the year 1000, she wrote *The Tale of Genji*, which has been called the world's first true novel. It tells a long, involved story about the countless loves of its hero, Prince Genji, "the Shining Prince." A modern edition of it fills over 4,000 pages. Japanese scholars have so valued Lady Murasaki's masterpiece that their commentaries on it fill 10,000 volumes.

Feudal lords divided the land.

During the Heian Age, Japan's central government was strong. However, this strength was soon to be challenged by great landowners and clan chiefs who acted more and more as independent local rulers.

Between 1000 and 1200, Japan developed a feudal system much like the one in Europe during the Middle Ages. Each lord surrounded himself

with a bodyguard of loyal warriors. Wars between rival lords became commonplace. Lesser lords pledged to fight for greater lords in exchange for protection. Peasants began to pay taxes to the lords, not to the central government.

The warriors who fought for the lords were called **samurai** (SAM-yuh-RYE), meaning "one who serves." The samurai lived according to a harsh code called *bushido*, which meant "the way of the warrior." A samurai's honor was constantly on the line. He had to prove his absolute courage in battle and absolute loyalty to his lord. Dying an honorable death was judged more important than living a long life.

A samurai's armor was one of the most elaborate costumes ever worn. It consisted of leather shinguards, billowing pantaloons, a kimono, broad thigh guards tied over the pantaloons, metal-cased shoulder guards, a chest protector, an iron collar, a cotton skullcap, an iron facemask, and a visored helmet. The samurai trained himself to get into this outfit in a minute. This armor weighed much less than the chain mail worn by European knights, and it provided good protection in battle.

Shoguns ruled puppet emperors.

By the 1100's, two clans, the Taira (tah-ee-rah) and the Minamoto (mee-nah-moh-toh), had gathered the largest armies of samurai. Up and down the island of Honshu, the armies of the two clans fought murderous battles. Heian was burned several times. After almost 30 years of fighting, the war ended in 1185 with a Minamoto victory.

In 1192, the emperor gave a Minamoto leader named Yoritomo the title of **shogun** (SHOH-guhn). The title meant "supreme general of the emperor's army." In effect, the shogun had the powers of a military dictator. Officials, judges, taxes, armies, roads—all were under his authority.

The emperor still lived in Kyoto, rebuilt on the ruins of Heian. Although the emperor enjoyed great prestige, the real center of power was at the shogun's military headquarters at Kamakura. The 1200's are known in Japanese history as the Kamakura shogunate. The system of central government led by the shoguns lasted in Japan until 1868, nearly 700 years.

Under the early shoguns, the local lords still held great power. Instead of trying to wipe out

In addition to this impressive suit of armor, a samurai wore two razor-sharp swords as symbols of his profession and high rank.

Section Review 4

Define: (a) clan, (b) kami, (c) kana, (d) samurai, (e) bushido, (f) shogun
Identify: (a) Yamato, (b) Shinto, (c) Shotoku, (d) Nara, (e) Heian, (f) Kyoto (g) Murasaki Shikibu, (h) Minamoto, (i) Kamakura
Answer:
1. (a) Where is Japan located? (b) Give a brief geographic description of Japan.
2. (a) Name at least five things the Japanese borrowed from China. (b) What did Shotoku do to make Japan more like China?
3. (a) What was the Heian Age? (b) Briefly describe Heian society.
4. (a) How was Japan's feudal system organized? (b) What were the most important characteristics of the samurai?
5. (a) What powers did the shoguns have? (b) How did the shogunate affect feudalism in Japan?

Critical Thinking
6. Compare Japan's system of government to that of China. (a) Why might a casual observer think the two were similar? (b) What were the fundamental differences?

Japan turned to isolation. 5

A Japanese Buddhist once wrote, "The proud do not last long, but vanish like a spring night's dream. And the mighty ones too will perish, in the end, like dust before the wind." Japan's history from 1300 to 1600 was filled with the rise and fall of proud and mighty lords.

Feudal lords controlled Japan.

After the decline of the Kamakura shoguns, the most powerful of the feudal lords became nearly independent rulers in their own areas. They were known as **daimyo** (DYE-mee-OH), which means "great name." Each daimyo commanded his own army of sword-wielding soldiers. Peasants as well as samurai took up arms. Dangerous bands of lordless samurai roamed the land.

feudalism, the Kamakura shoguns chose to build upon it. They worked with the local lords. A lord who loyally served the shogun was given almost a free hand to rule his own province.

The Kamakura shoguns were strong enough to turn back the two naval invasions sent by the great Mongol ruler Kublai Khan in 1274 and 1281 (page 269). However, the Japanese victory over the Mongols drained the shogun's treasury. Loyal samurai were bitter when the government failed to pay them. The Kamakura shoguns lost prestige and power. Samurai attached themselves more closely to their local lords, who soon fought one another as fiercely as they had fought the Mongols. Civil war shook the land.

The years from 1467 to 1568 were known as the Age of the Country at War. Rival armies repeatedly attacked and burned Kyoto, the imperial capital. The powerless emperors lived in poverty amid the ruins of their city. (One emperor was so poor that, when he died, his burial was delayed for six weeks until money could be scraped up for a funeral.) Disorder spread through the country. At the same time, Japanese pirates terrorized both their own seacoast and the coastal cities of southern China.

Europeans reached Japan.

The first European ships arrived in Japan in 1543, during this time of fighting and disorder. As in China, these first Europeans were Portuguese. Unlike China, Japan had no strong central government to bar or limit contact with Europeans. Thus, some daimyo welcomed the first Portuguese merchants and missionaries. If one daimyo turned against the Europeans, they could always find another daimyo to help them.

The Japanese looked with amusement at the Portuguese sailors, who dressed in button-down jackets and baggy trousers, or pantaloons. The Japanese called the strange-looking newcomers *nampan*, meaning "southern barbarians." As other ships arrived on their coast, the Japanese received the visiting nampan (mainly Portuguese and some Dutch) with courtesy. Japanese merchants eagerly traded silks for guns. For a brief time (around 1600), rich daimyo thought it stylish to wear pantaloons, smoke tobacco, and play cards in the European manner.

From swords to guns The novelty that most intrigued the Japanese were the Europeans' guns. One Japanese writer described his experiment with a musket:

> Set up a small white target on a bank, grip the object [musket] in your hand, compose your body, and closing one eye, apply fire to the hole. The pellet hits the target squarely. The explosion is like lightning and the report like thunder. Bystanders must cover their ears.

Japanese craftsmen quickly learned how to make guns in their own workshops. Power-hungry daimyo began to equip their troops with muskets and bullets.

Catholic missionaries As in China, Catholic missionaries came to China close on the heels of European merchants. The leader of the first Christian mission to Japan later became one of the Church's most beloved saints, Francis Xavier (ZAY-vee-uhr). During Xavier's two years in Japan (1549–1551), he baptized hundreds of converts.

For almost 90 years, Catholic missionaries traveled freely in Japan. With amazement, they noted the Japanese habit of taking daily baths. (In Europe at this time, people rarely washed.) With some shame, the missionaries tried to change their own European table manners because these offended the Japanese. "They are much amazed," wrote one priest, "at our eating with the hands and wiping them on napkins, which then remain covered with food stains, and this causes them disgust."

Strong leaders restored order.

Soon after the Europeans arrived, a series of determined rulers strengthened Japan's central government. In the 1560's, a ruthless daimyo named Oda Nobunaga (oh-dah noh-boo-nah-gah) used firearms to defeat armies ten times larger than his own. He entered Kyoto in triumph in 1573. Nobunaga won and held the area around Kyoto, although he did not control all Japan.

After Nobunaga was assassinated by one of his own generals in 1582, two other ruthless but able men completed the process of uniting Japan. First Nobugnaga's best general, Toyotomi Hideyoshi (toh-yoh-toh-mee hee-deh-yoh-shee), killed the assassin. Then Hideyoshi went on to win control over the shogunate at Kyoto. Many Japanese historians regard him as the greatest of their country's founding fathers. Although he never took the title of shogun, Hideyoshi was in fact the absolute ruler of Japan.

In 1588, Hideyoshi ordered a "sword hunt," in which he commanded all peasants to surrender their swords. Other decrees set up strict barriers between social classes. Hideyoshi himself had risen from common foot soldier to ruler of the country, but he did not intend for others to follow that path. Never again could a peasant or merchant hope to wear the armor of a samurai.

Hideyoshi's armies crushed any daimyo who defied him. He even had ambitions to conquer Ming China. However, his armies were defeated in Korea in 1597. The great Hideyoshi died a year later of natural causes.

The last of Japan's three unifiers was Tokugawa Ieyasu (toh-koo-gah-wah ee-yeh-yah-soo), one of Hideyoshi's strongest supporters. In 1600, Ieyasu defeated his rivals at the Battle of Sekigahara. He assumed the title of shogun in 1603. He then moved Japan's administrative center east to the place where his own support was strongest— the small town of Edo, later named Tokyo.

To keep the daimyo from rebelling, Ieyasu required that they spend at least half their time at his capital. Even when they returned to their own lands, they were forced to leave their families in Edo.

Ieyasu founded the Tokugawa shogunate. On his deathbed in 1616, Ieyasu advised his son and successor, "Take care of the people. Strive to be virtuous. Never neglect to protect the country." For the most part, his advice was well followed. Tokugawa shoguns gave Japan stability until 1868.

Japan's door slammed shut.

By 1600, as many as 300,000 Japanese (out of a population of 20 million) had become Christian. The growing influence of the missionaries worried Japan's leaders. Hideyoshi threatened Christians with banishment. Ieyasu, the Tokugawa shogun, was alarmed by reports that the Spanish had conquered an island in the Philippines. Might these aggressive Europeans soon turn their guns against Japan? Might the missionaries plot with Japanese Christians to overthrow him?

In 1614, Ieyasu banned Christianity in Japan. Over the next 20 years, Tokugawa officials rounded up Christians and subjected them to torture and execution. In 1638, about 36,000 Japanese Christians made a final, desperate stand behind the walls of an old fortress. Their futile defense ended tragically. Only 105 of the Christians came out alive.

The Tokugawa shoguns also banned all European merchants except the Dutch. Just as the Chinese had limited the Europeans to Macao, the Japanese now confined Dutch merchants to the port of Nagasaki. For the next 200 years, Japan remained closed to Europeans. (It did not, however, break off contact with China.)

The Tokugawa policy of isolation from Europe had far-reaching effects on Japan. Gradually, Japan fell behind Europe in science, technology, and military power. On the other hand, isolation gave Japan a long period of peace and stability. During the years of the Tokugawa shogunate, Japanese culture was rich and creative. Buddhist monks developed a unique religious outlook, and artists perfected an exquisite style of painting.

Zen Buddhism stressed meditation.

Buddhism in Japan followed a path of quiet contemplation. *Zen* was the Japanese word for meditation. Though there were other forms of Buddhism in Japan, Zen Buddhism had the greatest influence on Japanese culture.

Zen Buddhists seek spiritual enlightenment through meditation. Strict discipline of mind and body was the Zen path to wisdom. Young monks would sit rigidly for hours, staring straight ahead with unblinking eyes. If they fidgeted or showed signs of losing concentration, a Zen master might

Daily Life · The Tea Ceremony

The Zen spirit appeared in the popular tea ceremony. A small group of close friends gathered in a plain, low-ceilinged room to share tea. The tea was not intended to quench their thirst but to lift their minds. A tea master served them, using the host's tiny tea utensils. The master first poured hot water into a ceramic cup containing green powdered tea. A guest would meditate before and after sipping, then another friend would do likewise. When the cup was finally empty (after at least an hour of sipping), the friends would admire it as a fragile symbol of eternity.

Tranquil Zen gardens are still maintained in Japan today. Sand patterns, carefully chosen rocks, and subtle blends of leaf color and texture are the main features of such a garden.

shout at them and beat them with a stick. Some Zen masters helped their disciples to free themselves from ordinary ways of thinking by asking unanswerable riddles. The master might say, for example, "When both hands are clapped, they make a sound. What is the sound of one hand clapping?"

Art suggested nature.

Japanese paintings, like tea, were made for meditation and spiritual enlightenment. Japanese artists followed the style of painting that arose in China under the Sung dynasty (page 265). Japan's greatest master of the Sung style was a Zen monk named Sesshu (sehs-shoo), who worked during the late 1400's. Sesshu's most famous surviving work is a silk scroll 55 feet long. It shows the four seasons in shades of black, white, and gray. To appreciate this great work, one must roll it open slowly and meditate on the differences between appearances and reality with each passing image of tree and rock.

Nature played a key role both in Japanese art and in Zen meditation. During the 1400's, a small garden of jagged rocks and clipped shrubs became a common feature of the Zen temple. These gardens had symbolic meaning. Instead of seeing merely a gray rock surrounded by raked white pebbles, a Zen meditator might see a lofty mountain peak towering above a vast sea. The garden was always starkly simple. As one gardener-artist of medieval Japan warned, "Take caution not to . . . overcrowd the scenery to make it more interesting. Such an effect often results in a loss of dignity and a feeling of vulgarity."

The artistic traditions that developed during Japan's period of isolation had lasting importance for the country. For 200 years, Japan was able to continue on its own path, with little influence from the outside world.

Section Review 5

Define: (a) daimyo, (b) nampan
Identify: (a) Francis Xavier, (b) Oda Nobunaga, (c) Toyotomi Hideyoshi, (d) Tokugawa Ieyasu, (e) Zen, (f) Sesshu
Answer:
1. Describe the political situation in Japan during the 1400's and 1500's.
2. (a) When did the first Europeans reach Japan? (b) How were they received?
3. What part did each of the following play in unifying Japan? (a) Oda Nobunaga (b) Toyotomi Hideyoshi (c) Tokugawa Ieyasu
4. (a) What was Tokugawa Ieyasu's policy toward the daimyo? (b) Toward Europeans?
5. (a) What policy did later Tokugawa shoguns adopt toward other countries? (b) How did this policy affect Japan?

Critical Thinking
6. (a) How did Japanese policy toward Christianity change between the 1550's and the early 1600's? (b) Give several reasons to explain this change.

Chapter Review 12

Summary

1. Two great dynasties ruled China. After the Sui reunited China in the late 500's, the country experienced a golden age. The T'ang, noted for poetry, expanded the examination system. Printing, the compass, and gunpowder were invented. The Sung dynasty, noted for its art, moved the capital to southern China.

2. The Mongols conquered a vast empire. After Genghis Khan united the nomadic Mongols, they conquered most of Asia. China's ruler, Kublai Khan, encouraged trade and hired non-Chinese officials. Among them was Marco Polo, whose tales increased European interest in Asia.

3. China chose stability over change. The Ming dynasty at first encouraged trade but later limited foreign contacts. Under the Ming, traditional values were stressed. The Manchus, who succeeded the Ming, followed similar policies.

4. Japan developed a unique civilization. From the 500's to the 800's, Japan borrowed heavily from Chinese culture. Japan enjoyed a golden age, especially for literature, during the Heian period. Gradually, powerful landowners built up samurai armies in a feudal system. A shogun replaced the emperor as effective ruler.

5. Japan turned to isolation. Following the Kamakura shoguns, strong local lords called daimyo challenged the authority of the shogun. After a period of disorder, Japan was reunited. Under the Tokugawa shoguns, Japan cut off European contacts and banned Christianity. During this time, Japan fell behind Europe.

Reviewing the Facts

1. Define the following terms:

   a. gentry
   b. steppe
   c. khan
   d. clan
   e. samurai
   f. shogun
   g. daimyo

2. Explain the importance of each of the following names, places, or terms:

   a. Sui
   b. T'ang
   c. Ch'ang-an
   d. Buddhism
   e. Sung
   f. Great Silk Road
   g. Mongolia
   h. Genghis Khan
   i. Kublai Khan
   j. Marco Polo
   k. Khanbalik
   l. Ming
   m. Peking
   n. Ch'ing
   o. Shinto
   p. Heian
   q. *The Tale of Genji*
   r. Francis Xavier
   s. Tokugawa Ieyasu

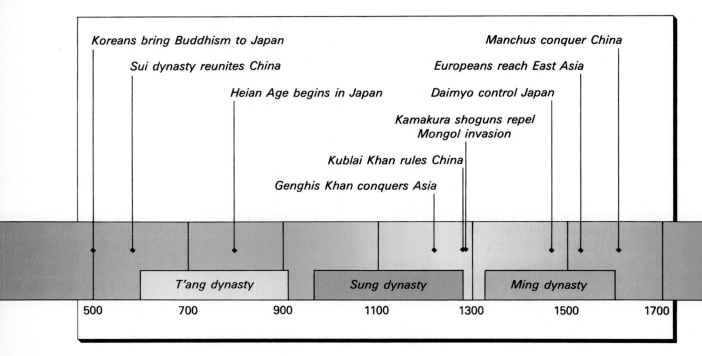

Koreans bring Buddhism to Japan

Sui dynasty reunites China

Heian Age begins in Japan

Manchus conquer China

Europeans reach East Asia

Daimyo control Japan

Kamakura shoguns repel Mongol invasion

Kublai Khan rules China

Genghis Khan conquers Asia

T'ang dynasty

Sung dynasty

Ming dynasty

500   700   900   1100   1300   1500   1700

3. (a) How did a person become a member of the gentry in China? (b) What benefits did that position bring?
4. What major T'ang inventions became important outside China?
5. (a) What caused the Sung to move to southern China? (b) What were the results?
6. (a) What methods did the Mongols use to build an empire? (b) What areas did they conquer?
7. What was China's attitude toward trade and foreign contact in each of the following periods? (a) T'ang (b) Mongol (c) between 1400 and 1433 (d) after 1433
8. Describe Japan's early relations with China.
9. What were the characteristics of the Heian Age?
10. Describe Japanese feudal society in the 1400's.
11. (a) What was the Japanese attitude toward Europeans in the early 1500's? (b) After 1600?

Thinking about History

1. What factors led China to turn away from foreign contact? What reasons did Japan have for its policy of isolation? What countries today place strict limits on trade and foreign contact? What advantages and disadvantages do you see in such a policy?
2. In China, long fingernails and bound feet became fashionable. Why were these styles regarded as signs of wealth and status? What are some modern examples of status symbols?
3. Why did both the Mongols and the Manchus find it necessary to use special customs to keep themselves separate from the Chinese people they ruled? What problems does a minority ruling group face in such a situation?

Writing and Speaking about History

1. Prepare an outline for an essay on this topic: "Chinese civilization during the 1200's was more advanced than European civilization at this time." Write an introductory paragraph for the essay. Then write a topic/transition sentence for each paragraph in the body of the essay. (See Research Skills Handbook, page 318.)
2. As a spy at the T'ang court in the mid-700's, write a report for a rural warlord on the apparent weaknesses of the T'ang dynasty.
3. Prepare a statement to be delivered at an urban planning conference on the features of one of these three cities: Ch'ang-an in the T'ang dynasty, Hangchow in the Sung dynasty, Peking in the Mongol dynasty. Include at least one visual aid in your presentation.

Practicing Skills

1. (a) Use the timeline on page 282 to calculate about how many years passed between the end of the Sung dynasty and the beginning of the Ming dynasty. (b) What happened in China during the intervening years?
2. (a) Using the maps of China on pages 262, 265, 269, and 271, compare the size of each empire. Which empire was the largest? Which empire extended furthest west? Which empire included Korea? (b) What was the capital of each empire?

Investigating History

1. Read some poems written during the T'ang dynasty. A good source is *Translations from the Chinese* by Arthur Waley. Then write a short poem about your favorite landscape, season, or natural object. If you wish, illustrate your poem with a simple line drawing.
2. Much of China's influence on Japan came by way of Korea. Where is Korea located? When was it unified? What did it borrow from China? How did Koreans change Chinese writing, printing, and porcelain?
3. Make a chart comparing events in China and Japan. Show the Chinese dynasties (Sui to Ch'ing) and the comparable dates in Japanese history. Include important dates in each civilization. Then compare your chart with the timelines in Chapters 8–11 and 13 and 14 to find out what was happening elsewhere during these periods of Asian history.
4. In traditional Asia, hand fans were widely used by both women and men, including samurai and scholars. What materials were fans made of? How were they decorated? How were they used by different members of society?

Decision Making in History

As one of Kublai Khan's advisors, what issues will you consider in deciding whether or not to attempt the conquest of Japan? How do you rank the importance of each issue? What will your decision be? Why?

Civilizations of India and Southeast Asia

Although the Taj Mahal was built by a conquering dynasty in the 1600's, it has become a symbol of India. The four outer towers are minarets, from which leaders call Muslims to prayer.

1. **India flourished under the Guptas.**

2. **Mughals ruled India in splendor.**

3. **Kingdoms arose in Southeast Asia.**

Shah Jahan, the ruler of northern India, was one of the wealthiest kings in the world. He was also a heartbroken man. In 1631, after 19 years of marriage, his beloved wife, Mumtaz Mahal (moom-**TAHZ** mah-**HAHL**), had died. She had given her husband 13 children but died giving birth to the fourteenth. The grieving monarch commanded that a tomb be built "as beautiful as she was beautiful."

Those events were the beginning of the romantic story of the Taj Mahal. Fine white marble and jewels were gathered from many parts of Asia and brought to a spot near Agra. For 22 years, 20,000 workers labored on Shah Jahan's last gift to his queen.

The ivory-white beauty of India's greatest monument is difficult to describe. Artists have praised it for its perfect proportions. Visitors have marveled at the way the towering dome and four minarets seem to change colors as the sun moves across the sky. Inside are thousands of carved marble flowers inlaid with tiny sapphires, bloodstones, rubies, and lapis lazuli.

Shah Jahan dreamed of building an identical tomb of black marble for himself nearby. The two tombs were to be linked by a bridge of polished silver, a symbol of the royal couple's love. However, the black tomb was never built. One of Shah Jahan's sons revolted and imprisoned his aged father not far from the Taj Mahal. When the old emperor died in 1666, a mirror was found in his prison room. It was angled so that the dying man could gaze at the reflection of the Taj Mahal. When he died, Shah Jahan was buried in the Taj Mahal next to the bejeweled casket of Mumtaz Mahal.

During their lives, Shah Jahan and Mumtaz Mahal prayed to Allah, the Muslim name for God. In the 1600's, Islam was fairly new to India. The religion of ancient India had been Hinduism (pages 70–72), not Islam. At the point where Chapter 4 ended, with the fall of the Maurya dynasty in 180 B.C., the prophet Muhammad (founder of Islam) had not been born.

In this chapter, we must go a long way back in time to a dynasty of Hindu rulers called the Guptas. These powerful kings lived more than 1,000 years before the building of the Taj Mahal. We will see how Hinduism developed during this early period. Then we will see how Islamic Turks swept in from central Asia, slaughtering Hindus and destroying their temples. These conquerors brought the Muslim religion to India.

In the 1,400 years described in this chapter, there was much violence. However, there was also much splendor and beauty. The marble domes and minarets of the Taj Mahal stand as a monument to the achievements of these years.

India flourished under the Guptas. 1

In India, 500 years of disunity followed the end of the Mauryan dynasty (page 76) in 180 B.C. In northern India, waves of invaders continued to arrive from Persia, Afghanistan, and the plains

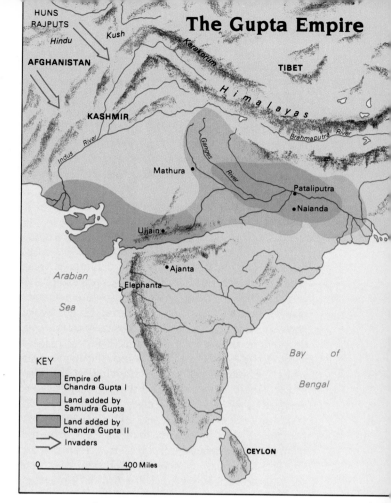

The Gupta Empire

Map Study

What river valley formed the heartland of the early Gupta empire? Under what ruler did the empire reach its greatest size?

of central Asia. These newcomers set up many warring states and kingdoms. Southern India was not affected by those invasions. Politically, the south remained a land apart.

The Gupta dynasty ruled the north.

In A.D. 320, a Hindu prince named Chandra Gupta (CHUHN-druh GOOP-tuh) was crowned king of the upper Ganges valley. (He was no relation to the long-dead Chandragupta Maurya.) The new king was the first in a line of remarkable rulers who brought a golden age to India.

The Gupta dynasty ruled a mighty empire for nearly 150 years (320–467). After the founder of the line, Chandra Gupta I, came Samudra Gupta, called the Poet King. Samudra Gupta extended his kingdom to the mouth of the Ganges River, winning another nickname—"exterminator of all other kings."

The third Gupta ruler, Chandra Gupta II, was both a man of learning and a conqueror. During his reign, the Gupta empire stretched across northern India from sea to sea. For the first time in 500 years, northern India was united under one government.

Indian scholars in Gupta times left few written histories. To a Hindu, the passage of worldly time from past to present was unimportant. Therefore, few Indian scholars bothered to record current events. Instead, Indians celebrated their past in oral accounts called *itihas* (meaning "so it was told"). These oral records were very accurate, but they do not emphasize dates. Thus, modern historians have problems pinpointing when key events in Indian history took place.

Much of what we know about India comes from Chinese monks who traveled to India to study Buddhism in the land where it had begun. Around A.D. 405, the Chinese monk Fa-Hsien traveled widely in India and greatly marveled at the peace and prosperity he saw. He reported that the government supported free hospitals for the sick. He was especially impressed that as a stranger, he could travel freely and without fear.

Science and learning advanced.

Learning thrived during the Gupta period. Young Hindus of the priestly (Brahmin) castes attended school from the age of 9 to 30. The university at Nalanda on the Ganges River was famous throughout Asia and attracted students of philosophy from faraway kingdoms. Gupta scholars made many advances in science. The following list details only a few.

Inoculation Indian doctors were the first to give injections. Cowpox injections helped to stop epidemics of the deadly disease smallpox. In India's free hospitals, inoculation was widely used 1,000 years before Europeans first tried it.

Surgery Indian surgeons were remarkably advanced. They sterilized their cutting tools. They knew how to set broken bones. They repaired injured ears and noses by techniques of plastic surgery.

Number system Hindu mathematicians were the first to use a system of numbers based on

ten. (Muslims of Baghdad adopted the system and passed it along to Europe, so Europeans called these numbers Arabic numerals.) Hindu philosophers understood the concept of zero and wrote it as a number. They also had a symbol for infinity.

Kalidasa wrote great drama.

The greatest literature of India's golden age was drama. Imagine an Indian actor wearing a sparkling, richly embroidered costume and the jeweled crown of a king. Standing beside him is an actress in the plain cotton gown of a poor hermit's daughter. The actress is playing the title role in one of the most famous plays in world literature, *Shakuntala*. The plot involves an unfortunate accident by which the king, though married to Shakuntala, loses all memory of her.

Shakuntala was written by the poet and dramatist Kalidasa (KAH-lih-DAH-suh), whose genius has been compared to Shakespeare's. Unlike Shakespeare, however, Kalidasa wrote no tragedies. There might be moments of sorrow during the play, but all his plays ended happily.

Emotion is the key to Indian drama. Audiences at the Gupta court recognized eight pure emotions known as *rasas*. One scene might make them feel the emotion of laughter, another sadness, a third pride. The other five rasas were love, anger, fear, loathing, and wonder. Then the final scene of a drama swept the audience up in an overpowering emotion that combined all the others.

Huns destroyed the Gupta empire.

The last Gupta rulers faced the same frightening challenge as the last Roman emperors. During the 400's, the Huns rampaged across Asia and Europe. While Attila was terrifying Rome, other Hun chieftains crossed the rocky passes of the Hindu Kush into India. Under constant attack from the Huns, the Gupta empire shrank. The Gupta dynasty disappeared from history during the 600's.

For the people of northern India, the next six centuries (650–1250) were ones of turmoil. First, several proud, warlike tribes from central Asia crossed the Hindu Kush mountains and settled in northwestern India. The local Hindus called this new ruling group Rajputs, a name that meant "sons of kings."

The Rajputs built new kingdoms.

In the 800's and 900's, northern India once again became a land of small kingdoms, ruled by Rajput warrior-kings. Soon after coming to India in the 500's, the Rajputs converted to Hinduism. They claimed membership in Hinduism's second highest caste, the Kshatriyas (or warriors).

Like European knights and Japanese samurai, Rajput men lived by a code of honor and bravery. Women were respected and had some property rights as well. However, both poetry and drama stressed that a woman's highest virtue was devotion to her husband. If her husband died, a faithful wife could show her love by a Hindu rite known as *suttee*. As her husband's body burned on a funeral pyre, she would remain at his side and die honorably in the flames.

An age of great temples By the 800's, three gods had risen to new importance in Hinduism: Brahman the Creator, Shiva the Destroyer, and Vishnu the Preserver. Poems, tales, and songs honored these gods and told of their deeds.

The 800's and 900's were a great age of temple building. Hindus could worship at a temple dedicated to the energetic Shiva, or they might become devotees of Vishnu, a loving god. (The creator-god, Brahman, though greatly honored, was seldom worshiped directly.) Among the great temples were those on the island of Elephanta, off India's west coast. Here, towering sculptures of Hindu gods fill caves that were cut into solid rock.

Decline of Buddhism During the Rajput centuries, Buddhism almost ceased to exist as a separate faith. Indians still worshiped figures of the Buddha, but they now worshiped him in Hindu temples. Hindu priests taught that the gentle Buddha had come to earth as an incarnation of the loving god, Vishnu. Thus, Indian Buddhism slipped quietly back into Hinduism.

Hindus and Muslims met in war.

In the 700's, Hinduism was one of the oldest religions in the world. Islam was the newest. The fierce conflict between Hindu and Muslim that began in this century has been called "probably the bloodiest story in history."

Arab Muslims conquered a major portion of the Indus River valley in 712, just as other Arab armies were conquering Spain. This first Muslim invasion, however, was mild compared to what followed.

In 997, a Turkish chieftain named Mahmud (muh-MOOD) became sultan of a little state in eastern Afghanistan called Ghazni. Mahmud of Ghazni was no barbarian. He loved Persian poetry and the Koran. He also loved gold and silver, and he made a solemn vow to plunder India

The Buddhist temples at Ajanta were hollowed out of granite cliffs between 100 B.C. and A.D. 500. Within the caves, the walls are covered with magnificent paintings.

287

every year. For 17 successive years, Mahmud's troops sacked India's cities and destroyed Hindu temples. They massacred and enslaved thousands. The Rajputs resisted bravely, but their slow-moving war elephants were no match for the lightninglike attacks of the Turkish cavalry. Mahmud of Ghazni died in 1030, leaving behind a legacy of hatred between Hindu and Muslim.

Muslim sultans ruled from Delhi.

About 160 years later, in 1191, another Turkish sultan named Muhammad Ghuri (GOO-ree) rode into India bent on conquest. A desperate stand by the Rajputs defeated him. The next year he returned and took a terrible revenge. His armies conquered city after city. At Nalanda, he destroyed the famous university. Much of northern India was conquered by Turkish armies and ruled by Turkish generals from the city of Delhi.

Thus began what is called the Delhi sultanate. For over 300 years (1200–1526), northern India was ruled by Turkish sultans from their courts in Delhi. These Turkish rulers were Muslims, and they treated the Hindus as a conquered people. Hindu kingdoms survived as independent states only in the Deccan, to the south.

The conquest of the Muslim Turks, though cruel, may have saved India from the Mongols. Although the Mongols raided and threatened India, the Turkish rulers were strong enough to turn them back.

Section Review 1

Define: (a) itihas, (b) caste, (c) inoculation, (d) rasa, (e) suttee, (f) sultan
Identify: (a) Shah Jahan, (b) Mumtaz Mahal, (c) Taj Mahal, (d) Chandra Gupta, (e) Gupta

Voice from the Past · *The Harshest of Sultans*

The most powerful of the Delhi sultans was the harsh Ala-ud-din (ah-LAH-ood-DEEN), who took the throne by murdering his uncle in 1296. A Muslim historian wrote the following account of Ala-ud-din's cruel measures.

The people were pressed and [taxed] and money was exacted from them on every kind of pretext . . . The people became so absorbed in trying to keep themselves alive that rebellion was never mentioned. Next [Ala-ud-din] set up a system of espionage so minute that nothing done, good or bad, was hidden from him . . . Nobles dared not speak aloud even in thousand-columned palaces, but had to communicate by signs. In their own houses, night and day, dread of spies made them tremble . . .

The Hindu was to be [made so poor] as to be unable to keep a horse, wear fine clothes, or enjoy any of life's luxuries. No Hindu could hold up his head . . . "I am an unlettered man," [Ala-ud-din] said, "but I have seen a great deal. Be assured that the Hindus will never become submissive and obedient till they are reduced to poverty. I have therefore given orders that just enough shall be left to them of [grain], milk, and curds, from year to year . . . Although I have not studied the science or the Book, I am a Muslim of the Muslims. To prevent rebellion, in which many perish, I issue such ordinances as I consider to be for the good of the State and the benefit of the people."

1. (a) What measures did the sultan use to prevent the nobles from plotting against him? (b) To prevent the common people from rebelling against him?
2. (a) What was the religion of the sultan? (b) What did he mean by "the Book"?
3. What was his policy toward Hindus?
4. What justification did the sultan give for his policies?

dynasty, (f) Arabic numerals, (g) Kalidasa, (h) Huns (i) Rajputs, (j) Turks

Answer:

1. (a) How did Gupta rule affect northern India? (b) What were some of the key achievements in the arts and sciences under the Guptas?
2. What brought the Gupta empire to an end?
3. (a) In the Rajput kingdoms, what virtues were expected of a man? (b) Of a woman?
4. What changes in religion took place in Rajput times?
5. (a) What was the Delhi sultanate? (b) How did it come into being? (c) What was its effect on the Hindu population?

Critical Thinking

6. Briefly summarize the status of each of the following religions in northern India about the year 1200. (a) Hinduism (b) Buddhism (c) Islam

Mughals ruled India in splendor. 2

The greatest menace to the Delhi sultans came from their own homeland, the steppes of central Asia. Late in the 1300's, a fearsome conqueror rode out over the dusty steppe of Turkestan. He was Timur the Lame, or Tamerlane.

Tamerlane destroyed Delhi.

Tamerlane boasted descent from Genghis Khan, even though he was more Turk than Mongol. He led his forces westward into Persia, northward into Russia, and westward again into Mesopotamia and Asia Minor. From his capital in Samarkand, Tamerlane terrorized all of western Asia. To mark his victories, he erected heaps of human skulls where villages had been.

In 1398, Tamerlane led his armies south through the mountain passes into India. Within a few months, he had taken Delhi itself. Although he was a Muslim, he massacred Muslims and Hindus alike. About 100,000 people were sold into slavery. A witness wrote, "The city was utterly destroyed . . . for two whole months, not a bird moved in the city."

Unlike Genghis Khan, Tamerlane failed to build an empire that outlasted his own life. After his death in 1405, nothing remained of his conquests. Delhi was rebuilt, but the Turkish sultans who ruled there for the next century were weaker than their predecessors. To the west, Rajput princes strengthened their Hindu states. No single ruler was able to dominate India. Wars among the rival states and kingdoms were frequent.

Babur founded the Mughal dynasty.

In 1526, another Turkish-Mongol conqueror from central Asia ended the feeble Delhi sultanate for good. His name was Babur (BAH-buhr), which meant "the tiger." He traced his descent from Genghis Khan on his father's side and from Tamerlane on his mother's side. Babur was a hulking, broad-shouldered, big-bellied man. As his son testified, "He never hit a man whom he did not knock down." He was also a wily politician, a skilled general, and an educated man who wrote an autobiography.

Babur conquered India with cannon and firepower. His troops carried a supply of gunpowder, muskets, and several hefty cannon across the mountain passes from Afghanistan into northern India. Soon Babur captured Delhi and Agra in north-central India. The Delhi sultanate was thus overthrown after 320 years (1206–1526).

The new empire established by Babur came to be known as the Mughal (MOO-gahl) empire. (*Mughal* was another form of the name *Mongol*.) Mughal rule became a byword for wealth and splendor.

Akbar enlarged the Mughal empire.

By far the greatest and most talented of India's Mughal monarchs was Babur's grandson. Though his Muslim name was Muhammad, he was known as Akbar, which means "most great." Akbar was 13 when his father (Babur's son) had a fatal fall down a flight of palace stairs. Akbar ruled the Mughal empire with wisdom and fairness from 1556 to 1605.

Early in his reign, Akbar added new lands to the Mughal empire. Dressed in golden armor and mounted on an elephant, he fought countless battles against tough Rajput challengers. By the end of his reign, the Mughal empire covered almost all of northern India and much of the Deccan.

Like the Delhi sultans, the Mughal rulers were Muslims. However, Hindus in Mughal lands outnumbered Muslims by at least four to one. To unify his empire, Akbar decided that he needed Hindu support. Therefore, after defeating the Rajput princes, he did not seek revenge. Instead, he spared the Rajputs' lives and invited them to help rule. He married a Rajput princess and entrusted Hindus with high government offices. Akbar also removed the special taxes that Hindus had paid their Muslim rulers. His tax system stressed fairness. For example, in years of famine, taxes were dropped.

Akbar's wise policy toward Hindus was based on his personal religious tolerance. In his adult years, he ceased to believe that Islam was the only true faith. What Hindus taught might also be true, he thought. He was interested, too, in the teachings of Christian missionaries.

After learning about all these faiths, Akbar concluded that a new religion could embrace them all. He called his new religion *Din Ilahi* (Divine Faith) and made himself its leader. He made few converts, however, and his religion died with him in 1605.

Splendor disguised a weakening empire.

Under Akbar's successors, the strong empire he had built began to weaken. Later rulers were neither as tolerant nor as skilled in administration as Akbar had been.

A strong queen Akbar's son was named Jahangir (juh-**HAHN**-geer), meaning "world-grasper." He was sadly misnamed, however. Addicted to both wine and opium, he played little part in governing. His reign (1605–1627) might have been an even greater disaster for India if he had not married an able woman.

In 1611, Jahangir married a Persian princess whom he called Nur Jahan ("the light of the world"). Nur Jahan was probably the most powerful woman in India's history before modern times. For many years, she was the true ruler of the empire.

Religious intolerance You have already read about the next Mughal monarch—Shah Jahan, the builder of the Taj Mahal. In his 30-year rule (1628–1658), Shah Jahan was as cruel toward his enemies as he had been loving toward his wife. He was followed by his even more ruthless son, Aurangzeb (**OH**-rung-zeb), who imprisoned his aging father as you have read.

Shah Jahan and especially Aurangzeb turned away from Akbar's policy of treating Hindus and Muslims as equals. Aurangzeb tried to make his empire an Islamic state. In 1669, he ordered the destruction of Hindu temples. He also returned to the policy of taxing non-Muslims more heavily than Muslims. No longer did Hindus serve the empire in high positions. By his intolerance, Aurangzeb weakened his government.

Extremes of wealth and poverty During Shah Jahan's reign, the Mughal empire was at its peak. Its glittering treasures amazed European visitors. For example, at the Red Fort at Agra (one of three royal residences built of red sandstone) the Mughal treasury contained these items:

> 750 pounds of pearls, 275 pounds of emeralds, 5,000 gems from Cathay (China) . . . 200 daggers, 1,000 gold studded saddles with jewels, 2 golden thrones, 3 silver thrones, 100 silver chairs, 5 golden chairs, 200 most precious mirrors . . .

The list goes on and on. And it was said that the treasury at Lahore, the Mughals' third capital, was three times the size of Agra's.

India's poor, however, had few comforts. A European traveler left a description of a poor family's house that was not far from the great treasury of Agra:

> Their houses are built of mud with thatched roofs. Furniture there is little or none except some earthenware pots to hold water and for cooking and two beds . . . Their bed

Footnote to History

Akbar was an intelligent and cultured man who was eager for all kinds of knowledge, but he never learned to read or write. He mastered many fields of knowledge, from science to poetry, through conversation with scholars at his court. Some recent historians suspect he had the learning disability known today as dyslexia, which makes it difficult for a person to perceive letters and words.

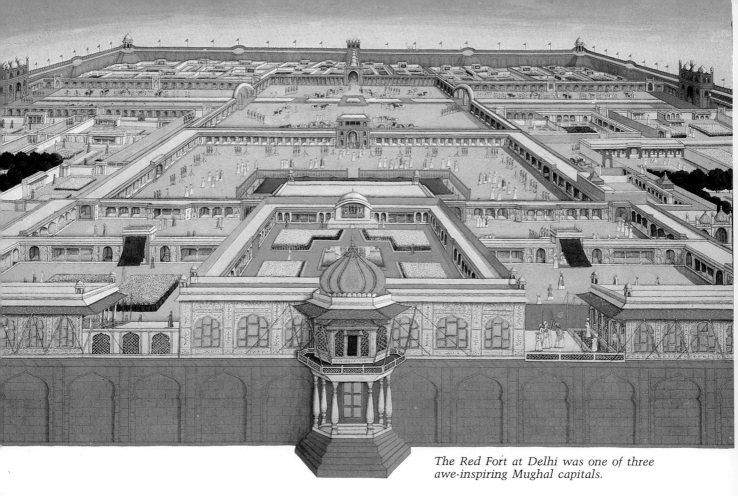

The Red Fort at Delhi was one of three awe-inspiring Mughal capitals.

cloths are scanty, merely a sheet or perhaps two . . . This is sufficient in the hot weather, but the bitter cold nights are miserable indeed . . .

In 1630 (during Shah Jahan's reign), a Dutch merchant visited northern India during one of the region's frequent famines. He wrote, "As the famine increased, men abandoned towns and villages and wandered helplessly . . . wherever you went, you saw nothing but corpses."

Hinduism and Islam were rivals.

All India's earlier conquerors had eventually blended into the Hindu system, but the Muslims did not. Their strong monotheism kept them from being absorbed by the Hindu majority.

Yet Hinduism and Islam did affect each other. For example, Hindus began to dress in the same styles as Muslims. Hindu women in northern India began to veil their faces as Muslim women did. Northern Hindus also adopted the idea of **purdah**. Purdah was a Muslim practice of keeping women in seclusion. Women were not allowed to go out in public or meet socially with any man outside the family.

Some Hindus converted to Islam. Islam's idea of the equality of all believers had a strong appeal to lower-caste Hindus and to untouchables.

A few thinkers tried to blend the ideas of Hinduism and Islam. One such thinker was Nanak, who lived from 1469 to 1539. Nanak became the *guru* (religious teacher) of a new religion. His teachings combined the strict monotheism of Islam with the Hindu idea of a mystical union with God. Followers of Nanak became known as Sikhs (seeks), meaning "disciples."

The Mughal rulers persecuted the Sikhs and killed two of their gurus. As a result, the Sikhs became a community of soldiers, ready to defend themselves or to attack. Many Sikh men took the last name Singh, meaning "lion," while women took the name Kaur, meaning "lioness." When Mughal rule weakened, the Sikhs set up an independent military state in northern India.

291

Europeans reached India's coast.

While Shah Jahan concentrated on building lavish tombs and palaces, Europeans were increasing their influence in Asia. In 1498, a Portuguese captain and adventurer, Vasco da Gama, arrived in India after sailing all the way around Africa. He reached India in 1498. For the first time, powerful newcomers had arrived in India by sea rather than through the mountain passes of the Himalayas to the north.

Da Gama's voyage marked a great turning point in India's history. After 1500, control of the seas around India became the key to controlling India itself. The Mughal rulers, however, took little interest in building warships. In the end, the weakness of their navy proved fatal to both the Mughal empire and the smaller Hindu kingdoms to the south.

The spices Da Gama took back from his voyage sold in Europe for 27 times their cost in India. Obviously, there were fortunes to be made in the Indian Ocean. Portuguese merchants were quick to go after them.

The Portuguese did not try to conquer India or the spice-producing islands south of China (the East Indies). Instead, they set up strong bases at strategic points all along the major Asian sea lanes.

A Portuguese sea captain named Alfonso de Albuquerque (al-buh-KEHR-kay) seized the western Indian port of Goa in 1510. In 1511, his fleet sailed to the East Indies and occupied the strategic port of Malacca (muh-LAK-uh) on the Malay peninsula. (See map on page 293.) In 1515, he captured his last great prize, the Muslim city of Hormuz (hor-MOOZ). It lay at the entrance to the Persian Gulf. From these three bases and the East African city of Zanzibar, the Portuguese dominated the Indian Ocean trade for the remainder of the 1500's. For the time being, however, the Europeans were not a serious threat to the Mughal emperors.

Section Review 2

Define: (a) purdah, (b) guru
Identify: (a) Tamerlane, (b) Babur, (c) Mughal dynasty, (d) Akbar, (e) Aurangzeb, (f) Sikhs, (g) Da Gama
Answer:
1. (a) How was the Delhi sultanate affected by Tamerlane? (b) By Babur?
2. List two major achievements of Akbar.
3. Compare the home of a poor family with the royal residences of the Mughals.
4. What are some customs that Hindus adopted from Muslims?
5. (a) What important change was marked by Da Gama's arrival in India? (b) How did the Portuguese come to control trade in the Indian Ocean?

Daily Life · *Cloths of Many Colors*

Indian farmers raised cotton to make cloth as early as 3000 B.C. By 300 B.C., Indian clothmakers were printing unique designs on their fabrics. Although European merchants at first were dazzled by India's jewels, they soon found that they could make even greater fortunes in the cloth trade. From Indian looms came cloth of many different weights and patterns. In Europe, each type of cloth came to be known by the name of the Indian city or region where it was woven. For example, the fabric madras takes its name from the Indian city Madras, calico from the city Calicut, cashmere from the region Kashmir. *Chintz* comes from a Hindi word whose root means "bright" or "many-colored." Even the word *dungaree* comes from the name of a section of Bombay where sturdy blue denim was woven.

The Brooklyn Museum

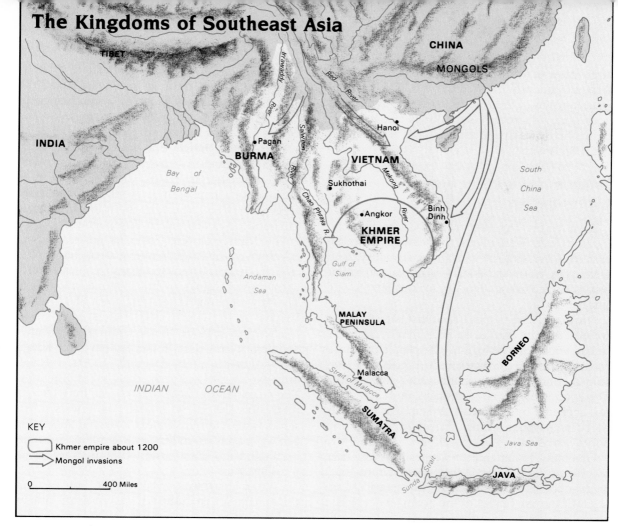

The Kingdoms of Southeast Asia

Map labels: TIBET, CHINA, MONGOLS, INDIA, Hanoi, Pagan, BURMA, VIETNAM, Sukhothai, Bay of Bengal, Angkor, Binh Dinh, South China Sea, KHMER EMPIRE, Andaman Sea, Gulf of Siam, MALAY PENINSULA, BORNEO, Malacca, INDIAN OCEAN, SUMATRA, Strait of Malacca, Java Sea, JAVA, Sunda Strait, Irrawaddy River, Red River, Salween River, Chao Phraya R., Mekong River

KEY
Khmer empire about 1200
Mongol invasions

0   400 Miles

Map Study

What geographic reason helps to explain why Vietnam was more heavily influenced by China than other countries in Southeast Asia?

Critical Thinking

6. (a) What were the critical differences between the beliefs of Hindus and Muslims? (b) What effect did the policies of Akbar, Aurangzeb, and Shah Jahan have on relations between Hindus and Muslims?

Kingdoms arose in Southeast Asia.

3

East of India, across the Bay of Bengal, lies Southeast Asia. It includes the modern countries of Burma, Laos, Kampuchea, Vietnam, Malaysia, Indonesia, Thailand, Singapore, and Brunei.

Many groups settled Southeast Asia.

For thousands of years, many groups of people passed through Southeast Asia on routes linking Asia and the Pacific islands. As a result, the region has a great variety of languages and cultures. Burma alone includes more than 100 different language groups.

Southeast Asia has never been united either politically or culturally. Seas and straits separate the islands. On the mainland peninsula, five great rivers flow from the north and cut valleys to the sea. Between the valleys rise hills and mountains, making travel and communication difficult.

Southeast Asia lies on the most direct sea route between India and China. Throughout Southeast Asia's history, the key to political power has often been control of trade routes and harbors. Pirates frequently infested the seas, and powerful local kings used their fleets to protect merchants from piracy. In return, such kings charged merchants high fees to use their ports or pass through their waterways.

Traders and settlers carried India's culture.

Even before the rise of the Gupta dynasty, Indian traders were plying the seaways of Southeast Asia. Among the goods that attracted them were gold from the Malay peninsula, fragrant woods such as sandalwood, precious jewels, and spices.

During Gupta times, Buddhist missionaries were active in Southeast Asia. Hinduism, too, spread widely in the region. The people of Southeast Asia adopted many Hindu myths and worshiped Hindu gods, especially Shiva and Vishnu. Yet some key ideas of Indian Hinduism were not accepted by Southeast Asians. For example, the caste system never became important in Southeast Asia.

Gradually, Indian influence spread to most areas of culture. Southeast Asian poets wrote long, elegant poems in India's ancient language of Sanskrit. Often the heroes of the poems were Hindu gods or warriors. Southeast Asian rulers built palaces and temples following Indian styles of architecture. They enjoyed Indian musicians and dancers. Some kings even encouraged Brahmins (members of India's highest caste) to come from India to serve as royal officials.

Trade furthered these cultural contacts. In some parts of Southeast Asia, Indian traders and merchants settled permanently. They intermarried with well-to-do local families. Thus, peacefully and without conquering armies, Indian ways of life became deeply rooted in Southeast Asia.

The Khmer empire ruled Kampuchea.

Many kingdoms rose and fell in Southeast Asia's river valleys and deltas and on its islands. None was ever able to unite the entire region, but many of these kingdoms had moments of glory and left monuments of lasting beauty.

A people known as the Khmers (kuh-**MAIRZ**) built the longest-lasting empire of the region.

They came from the northern part of what is now Kampuchea, moving southward along the Mekong River. They established a small kingdom in the late 500's and gradually expanded at the expense of neighboring kingdoms.

The Angkor period The greatest Khmer king was Jayavarman II (JUH-yah-VAHR-muhn), who came to the throne in 802. In his 50-year rule, this mighty conqueror greatly enlarged the Khmer kingdom. By 850, the Khmers' rule had reached the boundaries of modern Kampuchea.

The Khmer empire's time of greatest power is known as the Angkor period, after their capital city of Angkor. This capital was a splendid city with fine buildings of brick, stone, and wood. The Angkor period lasted from about 850 to about 1250.

The most famous and splendid of the Khmer buildings was Angkor Wat, a temple to the Hindu god Vishnu. Built in the early 1100's, the rectangular temple was more than half a mile long. The surrounding moat reflected its nine towers, their roofs shining with gold. The towers themselves were shaped like lotus blossoms, suggesting beauty, fragrance, and the power of life. The temple included a library and living quarters for its priests.

Khmer aristocrats lived in fine houses with tile roofs (not thatched with straw like the homes of commoners). They rode in gold or silver chair-cars or litters, carried on the shoulders of their servants. Other servants attended the nobles, shading them from the sun with golden-handled parasols.

Women had high status in the Khmer empire, as in most parts of Southeast Asia. Women from the lower classes ran market stalls. They sold ivory, feathers, oils, perfumes, and pearls. Upper-class women often were well educated and sometimes served as royal judges. All the king's guards and servants were women, for only women were allowed within the palace.

The decline of the Khmer empire After the splendors of the Angkor period, the Khmer empire began to decline around 1250. It was threatened by the Mongols, who sacked Vietnam's capital of Hanoi in 1257 and conquered Burma in 1287.

The Khmer empire itself never fell to the Mongols. With the Mongols, however, came another group of people—the Thais (tyes) from the borders of China. The Thais established their

Still magnificent even as ruins, the temple complex of Angkor Wat stands on the site of the ancient capital of the Khmer empire. Built in the 1100's, the temples have suffered damage in the many wars that have swept what is now Kampuchea.

own kingdom, which grew stronger as the Khmer grew weaker. In 1430, a Thai army captured Angkor, ending the Khmer empire.

Muslim traders introduced Islam.

During the later years of the Khmer empire, a new influence reached Southeast Asia. Between the 1200's and the 1400's, Muslim traders from Arabia and India brought their religion to the area. Like the Hindu traders before them, the Muslim traders settled in towns and villages along the coasts. Islam became an important religion in the area, along with Hinduism and Buddhism.

Islam spread along the trade routes into the islands of what is now Indonesia. Parts of the Malay peninsula and also such islands as Sumatra and Java became strongholds of Islam.

China dominated Vietnam.

Although China lies just north of Southeast Asia, the Chinese had surprisingly little influence on the region. Only Vietnam fell under China's rule. Vietnam lies on the eastern side of the Southeast Asian peninsula. Around 100 B.C., during the mighty Han dynasty, China took much of Vietnam. Vietnam remained under Chinese influence for 1,000 years.

Although the Vietnamese accepted many Chinese ways, they never thought of themselves as Chinese. They kept their own language and customs, and they frequently rebelled against their Chinese rulers. When China's T'ang dynasty grew weaker, in the early 900's, Vietnam broke away. It became an independent kingdom in 939 and began a long, slow period of expansion.

Vietnam was unique in Southeast Asia, because it was the only country to be heavily influenced by China. All the other countries of Southeast Asia show much stronger links to India.

Section Review 3

Identify: (a) Bay of Bengal, (b) Southeast Asia, (c) Malay peninsula, (d) Khmers, (e) Angkor
Answer:
1. (a) Describe the location of Southeast Asia. (b) What are its major geographic features?
2. Describe the contacts between India and Southeast Asia.
3. (a) What territory was included in the Khmer empire? (b) When did it arise and what years marked its height? (c) What ended the empire?
4. How did Islam reach Southeast Asia?
5. What part did China play in Southeast Asia?

Critical Thinking
6. In Southeast Asia, how did geography influence each of the following? (a) political power (b) foreign contacts

295

Summary

1. India flourished under the Guptas. India experienced 500 years of disunity and invasions before Chandra Gupta reunited the north in A.D. 300. Gupta rule marked a golden age for Hindu India. It was a time of advances in medicine, mathematics, and astronomy as well as outstanding artistic achievements. After the fall of the Gupta empire, small Rajput kingdoms arose. Invasions by Muslim Turks and the harsh rule of the Delhi sultans led to hatred between Hindus and Muslims.

2. Mughals ruled India in splendor. Late in the 1300's, Tamerlane—a fierce conquerer from central Asia—swept over northern India. Devastated by Tamerlane, northern India was next conquered by Babur, who set up the Mughal empire. The wise rule of Akbar kept peace between Hindus and Muslims, but his successors destroyed these gains. The arrival of Europeans further weakened the empire.

3. Kingdoms arose in Southeast Asia. Southeast Asia is noted for its geographic and ethnic diversity. Several kingdoms, among them the Khmer, developed there, but none united the region. Because of its location on key trade routes, Southeast Asia was influenced by both China and India and later attracted European interest.

Reviewing the Facts

1. Define the following term: purdah
2. Explain the importance of each of the following names, places, or terms:
   a. Gupta dynasty
   b. Chandra Gupta I
   c. Kalidasa
   d. Huns
   e. Rajputs
   f. Brahman, Shiva, Vishnu
   g. Turks
   h. Delhi
   i. Tamerlane
   j. Mughal
   k. Akbar
   l. Taj Mahal
   m. Sikhs
   n. Vasco da Gama
   o. Khmers
   p. Angkor Wat
3. What were the major achievements of the Gupta period, politically and culturally?
4. Between the time of the Rajput kingdoms and Mughal rule, what changes took place in each of the following religions in India? (a) Hinduism (b) Buddhism (c) Islam
5. Why is Akbar regarded as a great ruler?
6. (a) Why were Europeans eager to trade with India? (b) How did they gain control of trade without taking over India?
7. How did geography influence the development of Southeast Asia?
8. What foreign countries influenced Southeast Asia?

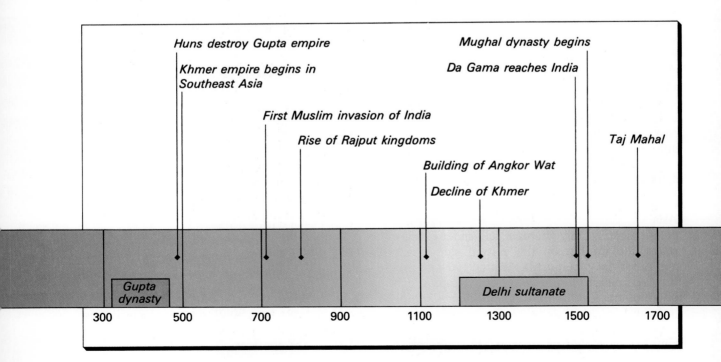

Huns destroy Gupta empire

Khmer empire begins in Southeast Asia

First Muslim invasion of India

Rise of Rajput kingdoms

Mughal dynasty begins

Da Gama reaches India

Building of Angkor Wat

Decline of Khmer

Taj Mahal

Gupta dynasty

Delhi sultanate

300   500   700   900   1100   1300   1500   1700

Thinking about History

1. Trace the changing relations between Hindus and Muslims in India. Include in your answer information about (a) Mahmud of Ghazni, (b) the Delhi sultanate, (c) Akbar, (d) Shah Jahan and Aurangzeb, and (e) Sikhs.
2. How did the role of women in Indian society change from Rajput time to Mughal times? How did the position of women in Southeast Asia differ from that of Indian women?
3. Writers sometimes call Southeast Asia "the crossroads of Asia." Suggest at least three reasons why this is an appropriate name.
4. In the late 1400's and early 1500's, Portuguese merchants reached China (page 273), Japan (page 279), and India (page 292). Compare the way people in each country reacted to the foreigners.
5. Show how each of the following contributed to Indian history and culture. (a) Chandra Gupta I (b) Akbar (c) Hinduism (d) Mughal rulers

Writing and Speaking about History

1. Write a memorandum from Alfonso de Alburquerque to the king of Portugal urging the king to establish control of the major ports on the Indian Ocean.
2. Write a paragraph that summarizes the contributions to Indian civilization made during the Gupta dynasty.
3. Write a paragraph that summarizes the contributions to Indian civilization made during the rule of Akbar.
4. Prepare an *itiha* (oral account) that chronicles one of the following events:
   the discovery of inoculations
   the fall of the Gupta empire to the Huns
   the destruction of Delhi by Tamerlane
   war between Hindus and Muslims
   the building of the Taj Mahal
   the arrival in India of Europeans

Practicing Skills

1. Review the dates on the timeline on page 296. Which three relate to an empire that grew up in the present-day country of Kampuchea? Compare the length of that empire to the amount of time the Gupta dynasty held power in India.
2. On a world map, locate the countries found in Southeast Asia today. Draw them on an outline map of the region. Compare that map to the one on page 293. What kingdoms once controlled each country?
3. Compare and contrast the building of the Taj Mahal and the Great Pyramid at Giza. What methods were used in building each? Would they be built today? Give reasons for your answer.
4. In the late 1400's, Vasco da Gama found that he could sell Indian spices in Europe for 27 times the amount he paid for them. Not all of this money was profit, however. He and other Portuguese spice traders had many expenses. What would they have been?

Investigating History

1. A poet once spoke of India as having gems "rich beyond all measure." Find out about some of India's famous gems such as the Koh-i-noor, Hope, and Orloff diamonds and the Star of India sapphire. Who has owned them in the past and where are they now?
2. Choose one of the following three cities that were important in Indian history: Agra, Delhi, Lahore. Plan a trip to the city that you chose, giving a brief description of famous sites to visit. To go with the description, make a timeline of important events that took place in that city.
3. Even though Indians under the Gupta discovered a way to inoculate people against smallpox, it was not until the 1960's and 1970's that the disease was completely eliminated. Find out who accomplished this feat and how they did it. What was the first year in which no one on Earth had smallpox?
4. Indian legends portray Krishna as a god in human form, with godlike strengths and human failings. Read some of these stories and prepare a summary of one that describes Krishna's childhood. Retell the story to the class.

Decision Making in History

Assume that you are Emperor Akbar. You are thinking about establishing one state religion that would include ideas from the major religions already represented in India. Present arguments for and against such a policy. Then decide what you would do and explain why you made that choice.

Africa and the Americas

More than a thousand years old, these stone temples at Tikal in Guatemala were built during the height of Maya civilization.

1. **Early civilizations arose in Africa.**

2. **African empires thrived on trade.**

3. **Indians developed many ways of life.**

4. **Empires flourished in the Americas.**

High over the rain forest of northern Guatemala, airplane pilots in the 1950's saw the tops of five stone pyramids piercing the canopy of green leaves. The pilots realized that the pyramids had to be tall. The vine-woven treetops were at least 100 feet high. Archaeologists later learned that the towering pyramids were the remains of the ancient city of Tikal (tih-**KAHL**).

Beginning about 200 B.C., Central America's Mayas (**MY**-uhz) built layer upon layer of city on the site of Tikal. At its height around A.D. 750, the city had about 40,000 people. The people who lived around Tikal were good farmers. They also traded from the Gulf of Mexico to the Pacific. By the year 900, however, only a few squatters remained in the decaying city. Archaeologists are still trying to learn more about this once-magnificent city.

Leave the rain forest now and travel in time and space to the steely gray Nubian desert in Africa. Here, too, stand rows of crumbling pyramids, the remains of a lost civilization.

The city here was Meroë (MEHR-uh-WEE). Meroë was the capital of a kingdom called Kush. Its four-century golden age ended about A.D. 150, while Tikal was still new. The people of Meroë, who were known as Kushites, traded with Egypt. They also traded indirectly with Greece, Rome, and India. Some of Meroë's buildings had columns much like those in ancient Rome. The Kushite lion god had four arms and three faces. Some archaeologists think it resembles the Hindu god Shiva. The Kushites also worshiped some of the same gods as the Egyptians.

After Meroë fell, it was forgotten by people in other lands. A Scottish traveler who reported its ruins in the 1700's had trouble convincing Europeans of its existence.

Until 1500, the people of the Americas had almost no contact with Africa, Asia, or Europe. During much of that time, large parts of Africa were also isolated. Our knowledge of early civilizations in Africa and the Americas is limited. In some cases, linguists have not been able to decipher the writings from these cultures. In others, particularly in Africa, knowledge was passed on orally and is just now being written down and analyzed.

Though our knowledge is incomplete, we do know that rich civilizations developed on all three continents—Africa, North America, and South America. This chapter traces the rise and fall of some of those civilizations, spanning thousands of years.

Early civilizations arose in Africa. 1

The lands of North Africa have long been part of the Mediterranean world—the world of the Phoenicians, Greeks, Romans, and later the Arabs. South of Africa's Mediterranean coast, however, the land becomes drier and more barren. Eventually, the landscape becomes an empty waste of sand and gravel. This is the Sahara, the largest desert in the world.

Historically, the Sahara has been a great dividing zone in Africa. The lands south of it followed different patterns of development from the Mediterranean cultures. All the African societies described in this chapter had their centers south of the Sahara, although many traded with lands to the north.

Africa has four major regions.

Africa is the second largest continent. (Only Asia is larger.) Africa covers 11.7 million square miles, giving it about 20 percent of Earth's land surface. Geographers divide Africa into four general regions.

The northern and southern coasts Narrow strips of fertile land border both the northern coast and the southern tip of Africa. In these two areas, rainfall is moderate and temperatures are warm. Summers tend to be hot and dry. Though these areas make up only a small part of the vast continent, they support dense populations.

The deserts Altogether, deserts make up about one third of Africa's land. The largest desert, the Sahara, is roughly the size of the United States. The Sahara is one of the hottest, driest, and most forbidding territories on Earth. *Sahara* come from the Arabic word *sahra*, meaning "desert." It suggests the gasping sound made by parched travelers.

The Sahara was not always a desert. Before 5000 B.C., rain fell regularly there. Herds of elephants and giraffes roamed through fields of tall grass. Over the centuries, many groups of people made their homes on the Saharan plain. Some hunted wild animals and fished in the streams. Later, others grazed herds of domesticated sheep and cattle along rivers. Farmers raised grain. These cultures vanished, however, as the climate grew drier and drier. By 2000 B.C., the Sahara had become the desert it is today.

Because the Sahara is so vast, it has been likened to a waterless ocean. People have used camels, the "ships of the desert," to cross it since about A.D. 400. Travelers follow time-honored routes between **oases**. An oasis is a place where underground water comes to the surface in a spring or well. Marked by tall date palm trees, oases dot the desert like islands in the sea.

The savannas Another third of the continent consists of grassy plains with a few scattered trees. Such plains are called **savannas** (suh-VAN-uhz).

Regions of Africa

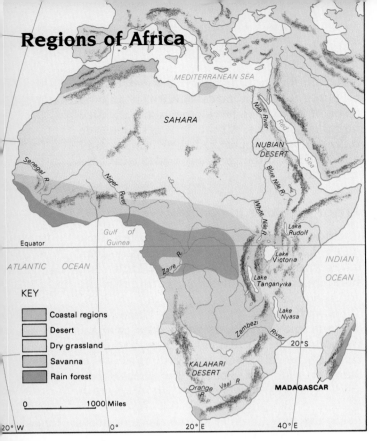

Map Study
What river flows through the rain forest? Into what body of water does the Niger River empty?

Savannas cover much of central Africa, both north and south of the equator.

In the savanna, rainy seasons alternate with dry seasons. When the land is drenched with rain, tall grasses and umbrella-shaped acacia trees come to life. Farming is difficult on the savanna because heavy rains can strip minerals from the soil. Then, when the dry season comes, the ground turns almost as hard and dusty as the desert.

Nevertheless, the savannas have always supported the largest share of Africa's population. In most years, early farmers had enough rainfall to raise their crops of millet (a type of grain) and African rice. On lands close to the desert that were too dry to farm, nomads lived by herding.

The rain forest About one fifth of Africa is rain forest. The forest zone stretches inland from the Atlantic Ocean, straddling the equator. Twisting through the forest are the branches of Africa's second longest river, the Zaire (zah-EER).

Rain falls almost daily in the rain forest. Mahogany and teak trees tower 200 feet above the forest floor. Their leaves form a canopy that blocks sunlight from reaching the forest floor. At ground level in a rain forest, the earth is nearly bare.

In early times, fishing villages grew up along the rivers in the rain forest. Later, farmers raised such root crops as yams. Grains would not grow in the damp climate. Farmers did not keep cattle or other livestock because of a tiny but deadly creature known as the tsetse (SET-see) fly. This blood-sucking insect carries sleeping sickness. The disease may weaken or kill people, and it is absolutely fatal to most livestock.

Societies developed many ways of life.

By the earliest historic times, a wide variety of societies existed in Africa south of the Sahara. Groups differed in their ways of governing themselves, in their family organizations, and in their ways of making a living.

Family ties As in other parts of the world, family organization was central to African society. In many African societies, families were organized in groups called **lineages** (LIHN-ee-ihj-uhz). The members of a lineage believed they were descended from a common ancestor. Besides its living members, a lineage also included past generations (spirits of ancestors) and future generations (children not yet born).

In some African societies, lineage groups took the place of kings or other rulers. For example, a people called the Tiv in what is today Nigeria had no formal government. If a dispute arose among them, it was settled by respected elders from the lineages.

People in a lineage felt strong loyalties to one another. The lineage helped members in times of trouble, negotiated marriages for them, and supported members politically. Members of a lineage also had religious duties.

Religions African religions blended monotheism (belief in one supreme God) and polytheism (belief in many gods). Most African groups honored a large number of gods and spirits. Above these lesser gods was the principal creator of the universe. However, this High God or Supreme Spirit was thought to be too powerful and distant to listen to human appeals.

In daily life, the spirits of departed ancestors were especially important. As part of the lineage, they were the guardians of traditions, values, and laws. Most families believed that the spirits could either make trouble or bring good fortune, depending on how well their living relatives honored them. Thus, the lineage was a religious group as well as a social and political unit.

At least one member of a village was trained in the magic art of communicating with both good and evil spirits. This important person, known as the *diviner*, called on the spirits for aid whenever there was an illness or village crisis. The diviner also tried to cure sickness or anger within the village by religious rituals.

After North Africa became part of the Islamic empire, traders brought the Muslim religion to many parts of Africa south of the Sahara. Even in places where Islam became strong, however, African religious traditions often survived too.

The arts flourished in many forms.

The arts linked religion, politics, and everyday life. Some types of art honored the king or the spirits of ancestors. Other forms of art included music for daily life or everyday objects made with fine craftsmanship.

Sculpture Artists in the rain-forest kingdoms used the beautifully grained woods that grew there to create works of art. The long tradition of metalworking in Africa likewise led to striking sculpture in gold and bronze. Most wooden sculptures from ancient times have crumbled to dust, victims of dampness or hungry insects. Ants could not devour bronze or gold, however, so some of these marvelous works have survived.

Some of the most famous African sculptures were created by the Yoruba (YOR-uh-buh), a group of people in the rain forest of what is now Nigeria. Two successive groups of Yoruba people made fine bronze sculptures between 1100 and 1600 (Europe's late Middle Ages). One group governed a forest kingdom called Ife (EE-fay). The bronze heads of Ife were wonderfully natural and lifelike. As Ife declined, a second Yoruba group formed the state of Benin (buh-NEEN). Metalworkers in Benin made a series of bronze plaques that hung in the palace of their *oba* (king). The plaques showed people commonly seen at the royal court: acrobats, warriors, royal sentries, drummers, and others.

Music and dance Many kinds of African music had very complex rhythms. For example, several drummers might play together, each following a different rhythm. Such music is called *polyrhythmic* (having many rhythms).

Music often accompanied dance. In many societies, dancers wore masks to honor spirits or family ancestors. Thus, the art of the carved masks, the music of the drums, and the dancing of the villagers shared a common religious purpose. They bound a community together and enabled it to pass its heritage on through the centuries.

Oral history Most African languages had no writing systems. Instead, each group handed down its history and laws by word of mouth.

In many West African societies, specially trained people known as *griots* (GREE-ohz) were the record keepers. Griots memorized the great deeds of past kings, family histories, and important events in their village. Young griots studied with older ones so that knowledge of the past was handed down accurately. Even after Arab traders brought Arabic writing to sub-Saharan Africa, griots remained the historians of their people.

A sculptor at the royal court of Benin in what is now Nigeria created this bronze figure. The man is wearing a leopard skin and blowing a horn. It was made about 1600.

301

Section Review 1

Define: (a) oasis, (b) savanna, (c) lineage, (d) monotheism, (e) polytheism, (f) diviner, (g) griot

Identify: (a) Sahara, (b) Zaire River

Answer:

1. What are the four general geographic regions of Africa?
2. (a) How did people make a living on the savannas? (b) In the rain forest?
3. What functions did the lineage perform in African society?
4. How did African religions embrace polytheism and monotheism?
5. How did many West African societies keep records?

Critical Thinking

6. How did the lineage system ensure that society's values would be upheld?

African empires thrived on trade. 2

Many powerful states arose in Africa before 1500. The states of eastern Africa date as far back as ancient Egypt. Among them was the kingdom of Kush, with its capital at Meroë. Other African states arose in the savanna and the forests of western Africa.

Kush was an ironworking center.

The first group of people to build cities in sub-Saharan Africa were the Kushites. They lived south of Egypt along the Nile River. The great ruins of Meroë are the remains of their work.

Egypt dominated Kush from about 2000 to 1000 B.C. Egyptian armies raided and even occupied Kush for a brief period. More important, the people of Kush learned about Egyptian civilization through trade. The Kushites adopted the Egyptian idea of a god-king. They wrote with Egyptian hieroglyphics and built pyramids.

In 751 B.C., a Kushite king named Piankhi (**PYANG**-kih) led an army down the Nile and conquered Egypt. Piankhi and his descendants became

Egypt's Twenty-fifth Dynasty. After a century of power, Assyrians drove the Kushite rulers out of Egypt around 650 B.C. The Assyrians never conquered Kush itself, however.

The Kushites had long known the use of iron. After facing the iron weapons of the Assyrians, the Kushites began to make more use of the metal. The mining and smelting of iron soon became the base of Kush's economy. Around 590 B.C., the Kushites moved their capital south to Meroë to be near supplies of iron ore. There Kush enjoyed a golden age from 250 B.C. to A.D. 150.

The ironworkers of Meroë were so busy that their slag heaps encircled the city. Traders took donkeyloads of iron ingots, tools, and spearheads from Kushite foundries to the Red Sea. There the Kushites exchanged iron goods for luxuries from India and Arabia, including jewelry, glass bottles, fine cotton cloth, and lamps of bronze and silver.

The kingdom of Kush began to decline around A.D. 150. Finally, around A.D. 325, an Ethiopian king from the city of Axum destroyed the city.

Christian kings ruled in Ethiopia.

Meroë's conquerors lived about 400 miles to the southeast in what is now Ethiopia. In ancient times, Axum was the capital of this rugged country of high plateaus.

Axum's King Ezana celebrated his triumph over the Kushites with this inscription carved on a tall stone pillar:

> Meanwhile I burnt their towns, [both] those built of brick and those built of reeds, and my soldiers carried off their food, as well as copper, iron, and brass; they destroyed the statues in their temples as well as their storehouses for food, and their cotton trees, casting them in the river Sida [the Nile].

By A.D. 300, Axum had grown rich and powerful by controlling trade between the African interior and the Red Sea. Persian and Arab merchants sailed to the Ethiopian port of Adulis. Here they exchanged their wares for gold, ivory, and spices.

Byzantine Greeks also traded with Axum. They were astonished at the splendor of the Ethiopian royal court. One Byzantine visitor to Axum described the king riding through the streets of his

302

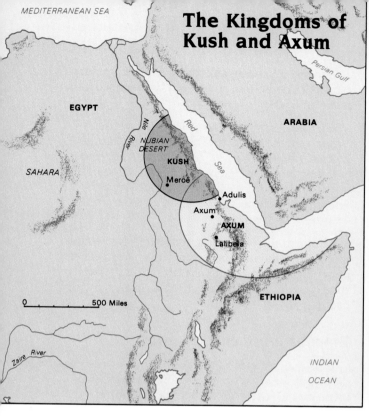

The Kingdoms of Kush and Axum

MEDITERRANEAN SEA

EGYPT

SAHARA

NUBIAN DESERT

KUSH

Meroë

Adulis

Axum

AXUM

Lalibela

ETHIOPIA

Red Sea

Nile River

ARABIA

Persian Gulf

Zaire River

INDIAN OCEAN

0 — 500 Miles

Map Study

Ethiopia's famous rock churches (right) are near the town of Lalibela, named for the king who built them. On what sea did Axum's major port lie?

capital in a four-wheeled, gold-plated chariot pulled by four elephants. The linen garment around the king's waist glittered with beautiful gold embroidery.

King Ezana became a Christian in A.D. 324, shortly before he destroyed Meroë. Ethiopia's rulers remained Christian through the centuries. When Islamic armies swept through Egypt in the 600's, Ethiopia remained independent.

During Europe's Early Middle Ages (500–1000), Ethiopia's kings lost contact with Christian lands to the north. Then, in 1520, a Portuguese explorer named Francisco Alvares journeyed into the Ethiopian highlands. He was amazed to find Christians worshiping in handsomely decorated churches. Built around 1200, many of the churches had been hollowed out of solid rock at the command of a devout king named Lalibela (LAH-lee-BAY-luh). Instead of towering skyward, each church was carved into bedrock below ground. Worshipers reached the church door by climbing down a flight of stairs about 30 to 40 feet deep.

Coastal cities traded with Asia.

Trade was vital to the growth of cities on the East African coast of present-day Kenya and Tanzania. Today, beachcombers in Tanzania find multicolored chips of pottery in the sand. These are fragments of Chinese porcelain that was traded centuries ago in East Africa.

From 1100 to 1500, there were more than 35 African city-states strung out over a coastal strip 1,000 miles long. These cities bore lovely sounding names: Malindi (muh-LIHN-dee), Mombasa (mahm-BAHS-uh), and Zanzibar (ZAN-zuh-bahr).

The ancestors of the people who lived in these cities had migrated to the East African coast during the 700's. Most came from inland Africa and spoke languages from the Bantu language family. Other settlers on the coast were Arab Muslims who fled their homeland to escape political enemies.

The two peoples, Bantu and Arab, intermarried, and their cultures fused. Their language was mostly Bantu but later gained many Arabic words.

303

Islam became the major religion of the cities on Africa's eastern coast. This new culture came to be known as *Swahili* (swah-**HEE**-lee), from an Arabic term meaning "people of the coast."

Most of the Swahili people lived by farming, fishing, and trading. They built small houses with walls of smoothed, sun-dried mud. Such houses clustered in villages all along the coast.

At the best harbors, large towns grew up. The tiny homes of the common people formed a ring around the stone buildings of the central town. The beauty of these central towns, where the oldest and richest trading families lived, impressed all who visited them. A Portuguese traveler in the early 1500's described Mombasa as having high, handsome houses of white-washed stone. He noted that the women wore silks and gold.

At Swahili ports, trading vessels regularly arrived from Arabia, India, and China. The most common ships in a Swahili harbor were triangular-sailed Arab vessels called *dhows* (dowz). For centuries, the Arabs acted as the chief middlemen in the Indian Ocean. They brought Asian luxuries to Africa and African luxuries to Asia. In the marketplaces of Kilwa, Mombasa, and Zanzibar, Arab merchants exchanged porcelain bowls and vases from China, jewels and cotton cloth from India, and African ivory, gold, tortoise shells, and rhinoceros horns.

The African gold and ivory in Swahili markets came from the interior. Gold mines, for example, were located 300 miles inland near a great African city called Zimbabwe (zihm-**BAHB**-way). This city, whose stone ruins still rise grandly over the southern savanna, was once the capital of an inland kingdom.

The kings of Zimbabwe and the sultans of the coastal cities enjoyed power and wealth for many centuries. Then their lives were violently upset by the coming of the Portuguese.

The Portuguese reached East Africa.

Portuguese explorers first arrived in the early 1500's, sailing north along Africa's east coast on their way to India. The Portuguese were eager for Asian wealth. They were also old enemies of the Muslims, who controlled trade in eastern Africa. The Portuguese came with cannons, a weapon previously unknown to the peoples of East Africa.

One by one, the Swahili cities fell to Portuguese attacks. The sultan of Mombasa described this scene in 1505:

> He [the Portuguese] raged in our town with such might and terror that no one, neither man nor woman, neither the old nor the young, nor even the children however small was spared to live . . . The stench from the corpses is so overpowering that I dare not enter the town.

Although the Portuguese conquered the Swahili towns, they did not succeed in ruling them. Their heavy taxes and frequent wars with the Arabs ruined trade. The coastal cities went into a long decline.

Empires arose on the savannas.

While city-states were flourishing in eastern Africa, other kingdoms were developing in western Africa. They arose in the savannas, the sweeping grasslands between the Sahara and the tropical rain forests. Three empires—Ghana, Mali, and Songhai—rose to power there between A.D. 300 and 1600.

The wealth of the savanna empires was based on two precious substances: gold and salt. The gold came from a forest region south of the savanna between the Niger (**NYE**-juhr) and Senegal (**SEHN**-ih-**GAHL**) rivers. Miners dug gold from shafts up to 100 feet deep or sifted it from river sands. Until about 1350, at least two thirds of the world's supply of gold came from West Africa.

Despite this wealth in gold, however, the savanna and the forest were poor in salt, and salt is essential to the human diet. The Sahara, on the other hand, was rich in salt. Deep in the desert lay a salt-mining village called Taghaza. Salt was so common there that miners used slabs of it to build huts. Arab and Berber traders carried Taghaza's salt across the Sahara by camel caravan.

After a frightful six-month journey, these traders reached the market towns of the savanna. Meanwhile, other traders brought gold north from the forest region. The two sets of merchants met in Jenné (je-**NAY**), Timbuktu (**TIM**-buhk-**TOO**), and other trade centers. There they exchanged goods under the watchful eye of the tax collector. Kings taxed this trade heavily. In return, royal guards kept peace in the markets. Royal officials made

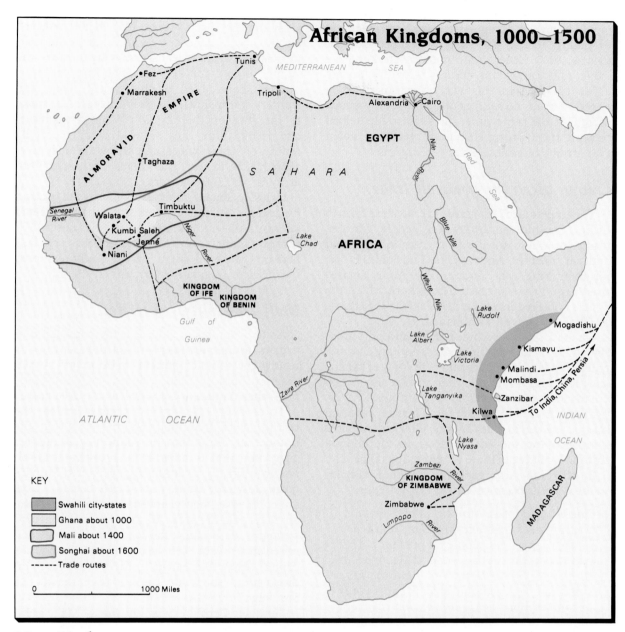

African Kingdoms, 1000–1500

MEDITERRANEAN   SEA

Tunis
Fez
Marrakesh
ALMORAVID   EMPIRE
Tripoli
Alexandria • Cairo
EGYPT
Taghaza
S A H A R A
Nile River
Red Sea
Senegal River
Walata
Timbuktu
Kumbi Saleh
Jenné
Niani
Niger River
Lake Chad
AFRICA
Blue Nile
KINGDOM OF IFE
KINGDOM OF BENIN
Gulf of Guinea
White Nile
Lake Rudolf
Mogadishu
Lake Albert
Lake Victoria
Kismayu
Malindi
Mombasa
Zaire River
Zanzibar
Lake Tanganyika
Kilwa
To India, China, Persia
ATLANTIC   OCEAN
INDIAN OCEAN
Lake Nyasa
Zambezi River
KINGDOM OF ZIMBABWE
MADAGASCAR
Zimbabwe
Limpopo River

KEY
Swahili city-states
Ghana about 1000
Mali about 1400
Songhai about 1600
------ Trade routes

0   1000 Miles

Map Study

Which savanna empire reached Africa's west coast? What towns would a caravan go through on the shortest route from Tunis to Niani?

sure that all traders weighed goods fairly and did business according to law.

Some traders took part in a fascinating exchange called the silent trade. At a spot near the Niger River, Arab traders would pile their slabs of salt in neat rows. Pounding on drums, they would invite the gold merchants to trade. Then the Arabs would mount their camels and ride off a few miles. The gold merchants would arrive, look over the piles of salt, leave some of their gold, and withdraw into hiding. Next the Arabs would return and decide whether enough gold had been offered for their salt. If so, they would take the gold and leave the salt. If not, they would beat their drums, suggesting a second round of trading. Thus, the traders swapped salt for gold without either group meeting the other.

No one knows for certain why the traders chose to work in this way. Most likely they hoped to keep the sources of their precious goods secret. At the same time, the silent trade helped prevent the fighting that may break out when two groups of strangers try to bargain.

Ghana taxed the gold-salt trade.

The trade routes lay across the savanna farmed by the Soninke (soh-NIHN-keh) people. The Soninke king demanded a heavy tax in both gold and salt from the Arab traders. The Soninke title for their king was *Ghana*. The Arabs applied this name to the entire territory from which the Ghana collected taxes. By the year 700, the empire of Ghana was well established.

Ghana's ruler demanded taxes and gifts from the chiefs of surrounding lands. As long as those chiefs made their payments, the king of Ghana left them in peace to rule their own people. When Ghana had a strong king, it controlled a wide territory. If the king was weak, Ghana's kingdom shrank. For much of its history, Ghana dominated a region about the size of Texas. Its capital city, Kumbi Saleh, was home to about 30,000 people.

In 1076, an Arab geographer named al-Bakri wrote a description of Ghana's royal court:

The king adorns himself like a woman, wearing necklaces and bracelets, and when he sits before the people he puts on a high cap decorated with gold and wrapped in turbans of fine cotton . . . Behind the king stand ten pages holding shields and swords decorated with gold, and on his right are the sons of the vassal kings of his country wearing splendid garments and their hair plaited with gold.

Gold nuggets and slabs of salt (collected as taxes) were stashed away in the royal palace.

Footnote to History

One gold nugget belonging to the ruler of Ghana weighed 30 pounds, and he tethered his horse to it.

Only the king had the right to own gold nuggets, although gold dust freely circulated in the marketplace. By this means, the king limited the supply of gold and kept its price from falling.

The Ghana acted as chief priest, judge, and military commander. His people believed he spoke to the gods on their behalf. When his subjects approached him, they showed their respect by falling on their knees and throwing dust over their heads. In war, the Ghana could gather an army of 200,000 warriors.

In 1076, Ghana's northern borders were overrun by zealous Muslim Berbers from the Almoravid (al-MOHR-uh-vihd) kingdom to the north. Although Ghana's armies eventually drove the Berbers out, the gold-salt trade was badly disrupted by the war. Ghana never regained its power.

Mali won control of trade.

As old supplies of gold near the coast ran out, miners found new deposits farther east. As a result, the most important trade routes shifted eastward too. By 1200, a different group of people—the Mandingo—controlled the gold trade.

To this day, Mandingo legends celebrate the rise to power of Sundiata (suhn-dee-AH-tuh), the founder of the empire of Mali. The Mandingo griots say that Sundiata's 11 brothers were all put to death by a ruthless king named Sumanguru. Sundiata alone was spared because, as a child, he was sickly and seemed likely to die anyway. As he grew to manhood, he gained strength. He became the leader of a village and raised an army. In 1235, he destroyed Sumanguru's capital. After that battle, in the words of a Mandingo griot, "the world knew no other master but Sundiata."

Sundiata's empire was known as Mali (again not to be confused with the modern country of the same name). Its capital was the city of Niani. Like Ghana, Mali collected taxes from many local chiefs who were otherwise independent.

The influence of Islam in the savanna region was growing. Muslim traders and officials held high positions in Mali as they had in Ghana. Yet most people worshiped traditional African gods. Many people who converted to Islam still kept some of their old ways.

Influenced by Arab traders, some of Mali's kings became Muslims. The most famous of these was

The first European map of western Africa, drawn in 1375, showed Mansa Musa (lower right) holding a giant nugget of gold. An African goldsmith of the Baule people made the pendant mask at the upper left.

Mansa Musa (MAHN-suh MOO-suh), Sundiata's grandnephew. Mansa Musa ruled Mali from 1307 to 1332. He set out from Timbuktu on a remarkable pilgrimage to Mecca in 1324. According to one report, his caravan consisted of 60,000 people. In front of Mansa Musa went a troop of 500 slaves, each carrying a 6-pound staff of gold. Piled on the backs of 80 camels were 12 tons of gold. Mansa Musa's pilgrimage was the talk of the Muslim world.

Songhai conquered Mali.

By the late 1300's, Mali's empire was weakening. Once more, the trade routes were shifting eastward as old mines ran out of gold and new mines were discovered. Between 1350 and 1450, the Songhai (SONG-hye) people replaced the Mandingo as controllers of trade. The Songhai farming, fishing, and trading villages lay along the banks of the middle Niger.

The Songhai had two extraordinary kings. One was a ruthless conqueror named Sunni Ali. The other was an excellent administrator whose name was Askia Muhammad.

"Always conqueror, never conquered"—thus did an Arab writer describe Sunni Ali, founder of the Songhai empire. First he attacked and sacked the Malian cities of Timbuktu and Jenne. Then he extended his control over the surrounding savanna and into the rain forest.

After Sunni Ali's death, one of his generals seized power. The new king, Askia Muhammad, divided his huge empire into provinces ruled by governors. He set up an efficient tax system and chose able officials. Under his rule, the Songhai empire was prosperous and well governed.

Timbuktu was among the cities that flourished at this time. A famous university there attracted Muslim scholars from as far as Tangiers. One visitor wrote:

Here are a great store of doctors, judges, priests, and other learned men that are bountifully maintained at the king's cost and charges. And hither are brought diverse manuscripts of written books out of Barbary

Voice from the Past · *Ibn Battuta's Travel in Africa*

One of the greatest travelers in history was an Arab named Ibn Battuta (IHB-uhn bat-TOO-tah). Born in 1304 in Morocco, Ibn Battuta spent his entire adult life traveling through Muslim lands. He visited Mecca and Baghdad, Mombasa, and Kilwa. He traveled to India, Southeast Asia, and China. In 1352, this world traveler made the rugged trip across the Sahara to the savanna kingdoms. Here he found a number of things that surprised him.

My stay in Walata lasted about 50 days ... It is an excessively hot place and has only a few small date palms ... The women are treated with more respect than the men, an amazing state of affairs. A man's heirs are his sister's sons, not his own sons. I have never seen such a custom anywhere else in the world except among the Indians of Malabar. But the Indians are heathens, while the people of Walata are Muslims, most careful about making their prayers, studying books of law, and memorizing the Koran. Yet their women show no shyness before men and do not veil themselves, though they go to prayers faithfully ...

[Ibn Battuta then went on from Walata to Mali and described the people there.]

They are seldom unjust and have a greater hatred of injustice than any other people ... There is complete security in their country. Neither the traveler nor the man who stays at home has anything to fear from robbers or men of violence.

1. What did Ibn Battuta find most surprising about the customs in Walata?
2. (a) List the customs in Walata and Mali that Ibn Battuta seemed to admire.
(b) What did he think of their practice of Islam?
3. From Ibn Battuta's reactions, what can you deduce about the way women lived in other Muslim countries he had visited?

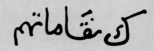

(northern Africa), which are sold for more money than any other merchandise.

Despite its wealth and learning, however, the Songhai empire lacked gunpowder and cannon. In 1591, a Moroccan sultan named El Mansur led an army of about 4,000 men over the Sahara. Most of the invaders collapsed and died as they hauled their heavy guns across the desert. The 1,000 survivors used their cannon to destroy 27,000 Songhai warriors armed only with swords and spears. Thus ended the great savanna empire of Songhai.

Section Review 2

Identify: (a) Kush, (b) Ethiopia, (c) Swahili, (d) Ghana, (e) Mali, (f) Songhai, (g) Soninke, (h) Mandingo, (i) Sundiata, (j) Mansa Musa, (k) Sunni Ali

Answer:
1. How did Kush's relations with Egypt change over the years?
2. (a) How did Axum become a powerful city? (b) What set Ethiopia apart from other African kingdoms?
3. Describe Swahili trade.
4. What effect did the Portuguese have on East Africa?
5. How did Ghana, Mali, and Songhai profit from trade?
6. What factor brought about the downfall of Songhai?

Critical Thinking
7. The use of new technology plays a large part in history. Show how the Kushites, the Portuguese, and the Moroccans used new technology to their advantage.
8. Describe some of the effects of trade on African society.

Indians developed many ways of life.

3

Medieval Europeans were dimly aware of Africa south of the Sahara. However, they were totally unaware that two giant continents lay west of the Atlantic Ocean.

The Americas have many environments.

Together, the American continents stretch more than 9,000 miles from north to south. North America includes all the land north of the Isthmus of Panama. Thus, Mexico and Central America are part of North America. So are the islands in the Caribbean Sea. South America includes all the land south of the isthmus.

North America has almost every kind of land and climate. There is tundra in the far north—a frozen, treeless land where only moss and stunted bushes grow. In contrast, rain forest covers much of the Isthmus of Panama. Between these two extremes lie thousands of square miles of mountains, plains, and plateaus.

South America is much smaller and lies farther east than North America. Both continents have mountains in the west. However, the Andes of South America are higher and narrower than the Rocky Mountains and the Sierra Nevada of western North America. The Andes are the world's longest mountain chain.

Both continents have great river systems. In North America, the Mississippi and its tributaries drain the central plains. Through South America flows the Amazon River, which carries more water than any other river in the world—more than the Mississippi, Yangtze, and Nile rivers combined.

The first Americans came from Asia.

Most scientists believe that the first human beings to settle in the Americas came during the last Ice Age, between 20,000 and 40,000 years ago. During that period, great ice sheets covered much of northern Europe, Asia, and North America. So much water was locked in the ice sheets that the level of the oceans dropped. The

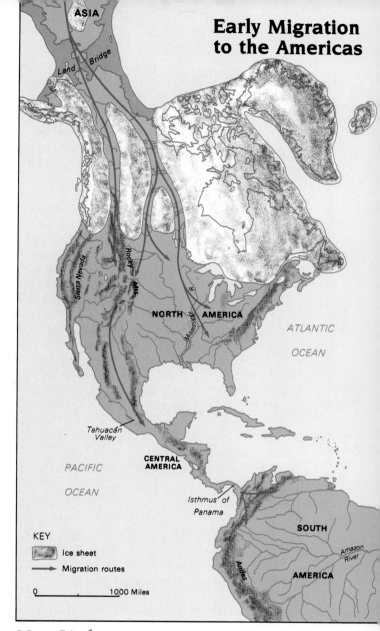

Early Migration to the Americas

Map Study

What narrow bridge of land links North and South America?

low sea levels uncovered land that formed a bridge between Asia and North America.

Bands of Paleolithic hunters and gatherers wandered across this land bridge from Asia. Without knowing it, they became the first Americans. Today, they are usually called Indians. (The name *Indian* came into use, as you will read later, after Christopher Columbus reached the Americas in 1492 and mistakenly thought he was near some islands in Asia, the Indies.)

This pottery figurine from ancient Mexico shows a woman grinding corn on a stone slab called a metate. Her child reaches under her arm to take one of the tortillas she has made.

The two continents offered plenty of living space. Groups of Indians fanned out over mountains, woodlands, plains, deserts, and rain forests. They adapted to the demands of each environment. About 7000 B.C., a band of Indians reached the most distant tip of South America. By that time, the land bridge to Asia had sunk under Arctic waters.

Farmers learned to raise corn.

The first people to reach the Americas lived by hunting game and gathering wild foods. Their descendants, however, discovered a new way of life. Like the people of ancient Egypt and Southwest Asia, the Indians learned to farm.

America's earliest farmers lived in the Tehuacán (TAY-wuh-KAHN) Valley, about 150 miles southeast of modern Mexico City. Around 5000 B.C., Indians there raised avocados, squash, beans, and chili peppers. Gradually, they added another crop—corn, or maize.

Corn became the most important crop in the Americas. Over the centuries, corn growing spread to most parts of the two continents. The people of Mexico and Central America revered corn as "the food of the gods."

Corn gave Indian farmers a stable food supply. They began to build permanent villages. Even farmers, however, continued to use wild foods for part of their diet. Many groups chose not to farm. They continued to hunt and gather.

Many cultures developed in North America.

Many Indian groups lived in the present-day lands of the United States and Canada. Each group had its own language, customs, and way of life. Along the northern Pacific coast, some groups fished for salmon, hunted for seals, and carved tall totem poles from giant evergreen trees. Along the Atlantic coast, Indian peoples farmed, hunted deer and rabbits, and made canoes of birchbark. The languages of the Indians were as varied as their ways of life. There were about 30 languages, with perhaps 2,000 dialects, spoken by Indian peoples.

The Hopewell of the eastern woodlands In the well-watered woodlands of what is now the eastern United States, Indians lived by a combination of farming, hunting, fishing, and gathering wild foods. One group, known to archaeologists as the Hopewell culture, lived in southern Ohio. They flourished from about 100 B.C. to A.D. 300. Family groups of 30 to 40 people lived together in large, rectangular houses made of bent saplings covered with bark, skins, or grass mats. They raised corn, squash, and tobacco.

The Hopewell people traded widely to get the beautiful, glossy green and black stones they used for beads and spear points. They also valued items from the seacoast—seashells, turtle shells, and shark teeth. They worked copper to make jewelry and shaped clay into fine pottery.

The spectacular achievements of the Hopewell can still be seen today—great cone-shaped burial mounds that rise 30 or 40 feet high. These Indians also made other great earthworks in geometric shapes. The scope of their public projects show that Hopewell society was organized with strong leaders. The quality of Hopewell crafts suggests that they had many specialized workers.

The Hohokam of the Southwest In the dry southwestern part of what is now the United States, Indians followed a very different way of life from that of the woodlands. One group of Indians who lived in the Southwest was named

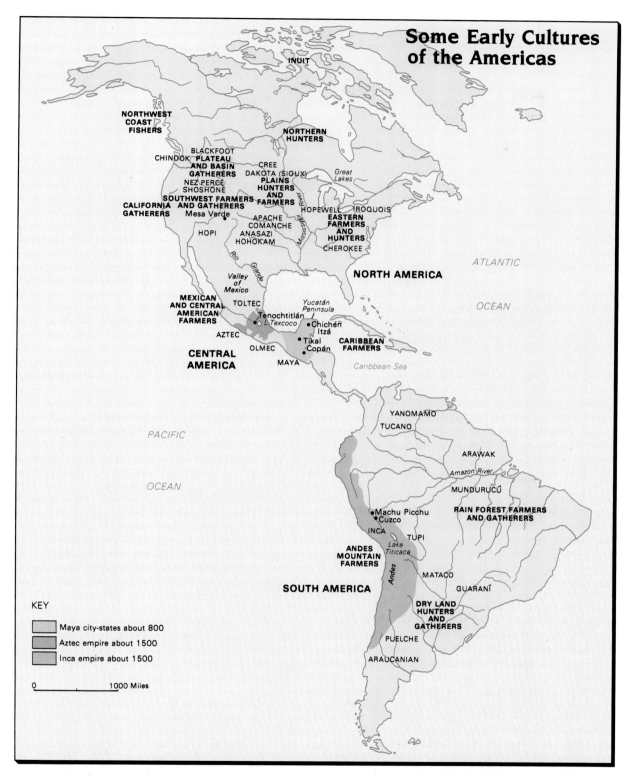

Some Early Cultures of the Americas

INUIT

NORTHWEST COAST FISHERS

NORTHERN HUNTERS

BLACKFOOT
CHINOOK PLATEAU AND BASIN GATHERERS
CREE
DAKOTA (SIOUX)
NEZ PERCÉ
SHOSHONE
PLAINS HUNTERS AND FARMERS
SOUTHWEST FARMERS AND GATHERERS
HOPEWELL
IROQUOIS
CALIFORNIA GATHERERS
Mesa Verde
EASTERN FARMERS AND HUNTERS
HOPI
APACHE
COMANCHE
ANASAZI
HOHOKAM
CHEROKEE

Great Lakes

Mississippi River

ATLANTIC

NORTH AMERICA

OCEAN

Valley of Mexico

Rio Grande

MEXICAN AND CENTRAL AMERICAN FARMERS
TOLTEC
Tenochtitlán
L. Texcoco
Yucatán Peninsula
Chichén Itzá
AZTEC
OLMEC
Tikal
Copán
MAYA
CARIBBEAN FARMERS

CENTRAL AMERICA

Caribbean Sea

YANOMAMO
TUCANO

ARAWAK

Amazon River

PACIFIC

MUNDURUCÚ

OCEAN

Machu Picchu
Cuzco
INCA
TUPI
Lake Titicaca
RAIN FOREST FARMERS AND GATHERERS

ANDES MOUNTAIN FARMERS
Andes
MATACO
GUARANÍ

SOUTH AMERICA

DRY LAND HUNTERS AND GATHERERS

PUELCHE

ARAUCANIAN

KEY

Maya city-states about 800

Aztec empire about 1500

Inca empire about 1500

0   1000 Miles

Map Study

Which of the three major Indian empires described in this chapter was the largest? In what areas of the Americas did Indians get most of their food by a combination of hunting and farming?

311

This giant earth mound in the shape of a serpent lies in the Ohio River valley. It was built more than 2,000 years ago by a group of woodland Indians that scholars call the Adena. The Hopewell lived later in the same geographic area.

the Hohokam (ho-**HO**-kahm). The name *Hohokam* means "those who have vanished" in the language of the Pima Indians, modern descendants of the Hohokam.

The Hohokam culture arose about 100 B.C. between the Gila (**HEE**-luh) and the Salt rivers in what is now Arizona. The Hohokam triumphed over their harsh desert environment. They built dams on the rivers and dug irrigation canals up to 25 miles long. With these irrigation canals, they were able to bring water to their fields of corn and cotton.

The Hohokam people seem to have lived in peace, for their villages show little provision for defense. A Hohokam house began with a pit dug in the dry, firm ground. Above the pit, the builders raised a structure of branches and brush. Besides such houses, a Hohokam village also had a ball court. Players used rubber balls imported from Central America.

The Hohokam developed many skills. They made fine red-and-tan pottery and wove cloth from the cotton that they grew. They used turquoise and shells to make jewelry.

The Hopewell and Hohokam societies were only two of the hundreds of Indian groups in the northern part of North America. The map on page 311 shows where some of the other groups lived by 1500. Yet such a map can only suggest what territory each group occupied, because many groups traveled widely. Related groups might live far apart.

Section Review 3

Define: (a) tundra, (b) isthmus
Identify: (a) Tehuacán Valley, (b) Indians, (c) Hopewell, (d) Hohokam
Answer:
1. How do most scientists believe that the first humans reached the Americas?
2. When and where did farming begin in the Americas?
3. (a) What kind of houses did the Hopewell build? (b) What can be inferred about Hopewell society from their burial mounds?
4. How did the Hohokam grow food?

Critical Thinking
5. What characteristics did the Hopewell and Hohokam societies share, in spite of the great differences in their environments?

Empires flourished in the Americas.   4

By A.D. 1500, only about 1 million Indians lived in what is now Canada and the United States. The lands farther south were much more heavily settled. Population figures vary widely, but recent scholars estimate that between 50 and 60 million Indians lived in Mexico, Central America, and South America by 1500.

The Olmecs lived in Mexico.

The first major American civilization seems to have arisen in the swampy lowlands of Mexico's Gulf Coast around 1200 B.C. The creators of this civilization were the Olmecs.

By slashing and burning the trees of the dense rain forest, the Olmecs cleared enough land for farming. Yet the forest was never far away. Late at night, the Olmecs doubtless heard the howls of the wild jaguar, a spotted cat that still lives in the area. The Olmecs carved stone figures that were half jaguar and half human, suggesting that they worshiped the jaguar's spirit. Among their many achievements, the Olmecs produced fine pottery, invented a system of writing, and developed a calendar. Ceremonial ballgames, which were important to nearly all later Indian societies in the region, began with the Olmecs.

The Olmec civilization flourished for about 800 years. It perished around 400 B.C. Our knowledge of the Olmecs is limited. However, later civilizations of Mexico and Central America clearly show the influence of the Olmecs.

The Mayas built great cities.

Around 500 B.C., the Mayas began to create their civilization in the southern Gulf Coast region and present-day Guatemala. In the insect-infested rain forest, the Mayas built a brilliant civilization. Historians call the years from 500 B.C. to A.D. 250 the Formative Period of Maya civilization. The Mayas reached their height during their Classic Period, from A.D. 250 to 900.

Slashing trees with stone tools, the Mayas cleared the rain forest to grow corn. Although they had no wheeled vehicles and no beasts of burden such as horses or oxen, they moved great pieces of stone to build their temples. They had no iron tools, yet they shaped their stone blocks so skillfully that their pyramids still stand.

The pyramids were the center of Maya religious ceremonies. Around them, cities grew up where priests, government officials, some merchants, and artisans lived. Peasant farmers probably lived outside the cities in thatched huts. The farmers came to town for religious events and to visit the market.

Like the ancient Greeks and Phoenicians, the Mayas built city-states. The ruins of at least 80 have been found. Each city-state had a hereditary ruler, nobles, and priests. Four or five of the most powerful city-states dominated their smaller neighbors.

Tikal Tikal was the largest Maya city. In its heyday, five pyramid-temples towered over its plazas and avenues. The tallest, the Temple of the Giant Jaguar, was as high as a 20-story building. A flight of stairs led up one side of each pyramid to a small temple at the top. Intricately carved panels over the temple entrances were painted bright red, blue, and orange. The priests who climbed to these temples offered sacrifices of corn, cocoa beans, and an occasional monkey to the gods.

The calendar Maya priests also measured the nightly movements of the moon and stars. Keeping track of time was crucial to the Maya priests. The calendar allowed them to predict what their

Daily Life · *Ball Games of the Mayas*

In Tikal's sports plaza, priests and others attended ball games. The games were something like a combination of modern basketball, soccer, jai alai, and volleyball. The ball court was a narrow alley flanked by two high walls. Players used a solid ball made from the sap of Yucatan rubber trees. Using only their hips, knees, and forearms, players on two teams passed the ball up and down the court, trying to put the ball through one of the stone rings on each wall. Because the ball weighed about five pounds, players protected themselves with helmets, gloves, knee pads, and broad belts.

heavenly gods (sun, moon, planets) would be doing from day to day. It also foretold dramatic events, such as eclipses of the sun.

The Maya calendar was both accurate and complex. The Mayas kept track of time on three different calendars. They measured the solar year to 365 days, very close to our own. They also counted a sacred year of 260 days. Third, they kept track of what was called the Long Count, in which a full cycle lasted about 400 years. After 13 such cycles, the Mayas believed, the world would be destroyed and created again.

Clearly, the Mayas were skilled mathematicians. As early as 300 B.C., they discovered the concept of zero, an idea unknown to Greeks and Romans. For numbers, the Mayas used a system of dots and bars. Five dots were equal to one bar. A shell symbol represented zero.

New cultures replaced the old.

Most Maya cities declined after the year 700. By 900, Maya civilization had collapsed. No one knows exactly why. Some scholars believe that peasants revolted against the ruling class. At the same time, invaders from the north disrupted the fragile economy of all of Mexico and Central America. Crop failure and famine may also have played a part in the Maya decline.

North of the fertile Valley of Mexico lay a dry and barren plain of scrubby grasses and cactus, a semi-desert. For centuries, this area was the homeland of warlike peoples, including the Chichimecs, the Toltecs, and the Aztecs. These groups were like the Huns and Mongols of Asia. They raided the richer, more settled civilizations whenever they could.

Between 900 and 1300, successive waves of northern warriors swept into the Valley of Mexico. One of these groups, the Toltecs, established an empire. The Toltecs learned to build pyramids and ball courts in the style of their more civilized

Footnote to History

The wealthiest Mayas showed off their high status by nibbling cocoa beans. These tasty, chocolate-flavored beans served as a common medium of exchange in Tikal's marketplace. Thus, to eat them was like eating money.

predecessors. They dominated the Valley of Mexico for 200 years. Around 1160, their capital of Tula was destroyed by new invaders.

The Aztecs built an empire.

Among the invaders was a fierce and desperately poor band of barbarians. These invaders were known by two names: Mexicas and Aztecs.

According to their own legends, the Aztecs came from a northern land called Aztlan. Migrating to the Valley of Mexico, they wandered until their god of war showed them where to build a city. "Look for an eagle perched on a cactus and holding a snake," said the god.

The Aztec priests stood on the shore of a great salt lake, Lake Texcoco (tehs-KOH-koh), and looked out over the water. They saw the eagle with a snake wriggling in its beak. The cactus on which the bird perched grew on one of Lake Texcoco's islands. (The eagle, snake, and cactus appear today on Mexico's flag.)

Tenochtitlán The Aztecs settled on the island, probably about 1325. Their island city was called Tenochtitlán (tay-NOCH-tee-TLAHN), which meant "Place of the Prickly-Pear Cactus." As the Aztecs gained power and wealth, Tenochtitlán became one of the most magnificent cities in the world.

Scholars guess that about 300,000 Aztecs may have lived in Tenochtitlán in 1500. (That figure would make the Aztec city five times larger than London at the same time.) People traveled to and from the lake city over three long causeways. Within the city, the quickest way to get from one's home to the Great Temple was to paddle a boat up one of the major canals that crisscrossed the island. The royal palace boasted wonderful gardens, fountains, baths, and a well-stocked zoo.

Human sacrifice The legendary god that led the Aztecs to their city was also the god of the sun. Aztec priests believed it was their sacred duty to feed human hearts to him. The Aztecs thought that the sun's life-giving light could flicker out at any time. They believed the sun could burn brightly only as long as they fed its god human blood. The Aztecs fought their wars in the Valley of Mexico in part to get victims for sacrifice.

After some 200 years of nearly constant war, the Aztecs triumphed over almost all their neighbors. By the year 1500, the Aztec king was

This Aztec drawing shows Tenochtitlán beneath the legendary eagle on the cactus.

taking tribute in gold, silver, fine cloth, feathers, cocoa beans, and furs from an immense area. Perhaps as many as 11 million Indians were subjects of the Aztec ruler. Yet within a few years, the mighty Aztec empire would come to an end, as you will read in Chapter 17.

The Incas built an empire in Peru.

Some 2,800 miles south of the Aztec capital was an even larger empire. The Incas built their capital of Cuzco high in the Andes in what is now Peru. Separated by immense geographic barriers, the Aztecs and the Incas probably never knew of each other. Yet the rise of the two empires was similar.

Civilization in the high valleys of Peru was already at least 1,000 years old when the Incas started their climb to power around the year 1200. The Incas had learned from earlier peoples how to build fortress walls using gigantic blocks of stone. Inca stonemasons had no mortar, but they cut the stones so carefully that many of their walls still stand, despite earthquakes.

Like earlier Peruvians, the Incas grew corn at elevations up to 11,000 feet. On even higher lands, they planted potatoes on terraced fields.

Like the Aztecs, the Incas worshiped the sun as their main god. Inca princes proudly called themselves "Sons of the Sun."

The Incas were excellent adminstrators, even though they never developed a system of writing. They kept records by tying knots in a bundle of strings, a device called a *quipu* (KEY-poo). The position of the knots indicated payment to the government of so many baskets of corn, so many bags of gold, and so on.

A 10,000-mile network of stone highways held the Inca empire together. Swift runners used these highways to carry the commands of the Inca ruler to all his officials. After memorizing a message from the emperor, a courier from Cuzco would run to a relay station. Here a second courier would jog alongside the first. After learning the message, the second runner carried it to the next relay point. Inca messages traveled this way at the brisk rate of 140 miles a day.

For the Incas as for the Aztecs, the 1400's were a time of conquest. By 1493, their empire stretched about 2,500 miles from present-day Ecuador to the middle of Chile. The Inca ruler had the power of life and death over his 6 million subjects. Soon, as you will read in Chapter 17, the 200-year-old empire would fall. Its defeat by Europeans came as a total surprise.

Section Review 4

Define: (a) city-state, (b) quipu
Identify: (a) Olmecs, (b) Mayas, (c) Aztecs, (d) Tenochtitlán, (e) Incas
Answer:
1. Where did the first major American civilizations begin?
2. (a) How was the Maya society organized? (b) What shows that the Mayas were skilled mathematicians?
3. How did the Aztec empire begin?
4. How did the Inca rulers control their empire?
5. Describe the architectural achievements of the Mayas, Aztecs, and Incas.

Critical Thinking

6. Why do you think so little is known about the Mayas when a great deal is known about some people who lived during the same centuries in other parts of the world?

Chapter Review 14

Summary

1. Early civilizations arose in Africa. Sub-Saharan Africa has four geographic regions: the northern and southern coasts; the deserts; the savannas; and the rain forest. A variety of societies developed in those regions. In many groups, lineages were central to both family organization and religion. Art and music expressed the values of these societies.

2. African empires thrived on trade. The Kushites built the first cities south of the Sahara. Meroë was conquered by Ethiopia, a Christian kingdom. In cities along the eastern coast of Africa, the Swahili culture arose. In the 1500's, the Portuguese destroyed the Swahili cities. In western Africa, the empires of Ghana, Mali, and Songhai developed on the savanna.

3. Indians developed many ways of life. Most scientists believe that the first Americans came from Asia by crossing a land-bridge about 20,000 to 40,000 years ago. Groups of Indians spread out over North and South America, creating many different ways of life. Corn became the basic crop of many farming groups, while other groups continued to hunt and gather food.

4. Empires flourished in the Americas. The largest Indian civilizations developed in Mexico and in Central and South America. The Mayas are known for their huge stone pyramids and accurate calendar. The Aztecs built an empire in the Valley of Mexico. The Incas ruled an empire in Peru, uniting it by skilled administration and good roads.

Reviewing the Facts

1. Define the following terms:
   a. oasis
   b. savanna
   c. lineage
2. Explain the importance of each of the following names, places, or terms:

   a. Sahara
   b. Yoruba
   c. griots
   d. Kushites
   e. Ethiopia
   f. Ghana
   g. Mali
   h. Songhai
   i. Mansa Musa
   j. Tehuacán Valley
   k. Hopewell
   l. Hohokam
   m. Olmecs
   n. Mayas
   o. Aztecs
   p. Tenochtitlán
   q. Incas

3. Describe the climate and vegetation of Africa's major geographic regions.
4. (a) Who were included in a lineage? (b) How did the lineage system help to organize society?
5. What was the basis for Kush's prosperity?

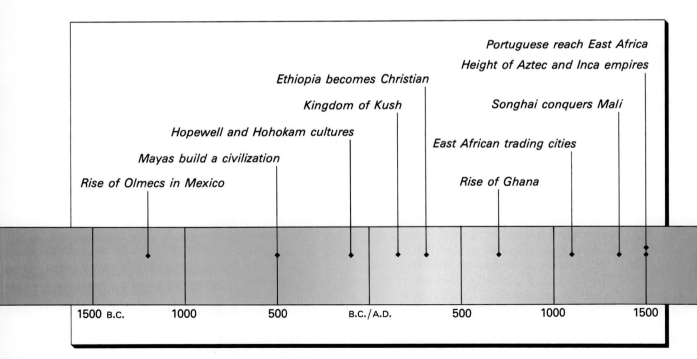

Rise of Olmecs in Mexico

Mayas build a civilization

Hopewell and Hohokam cultures

Kingdom of Kush

Ethiopia becomes Christian

Rise of Ghana

East African trading cities

Songhai conquers Mali

Height of Aztec and Inca empires

Portuguese reach East Africa

| 1500 B.C. | 1000 | 500 | B.C./A.D. | 500 | 1000 | 1500 |

6. (a) Describe the location of the kingdom of Axum. (b) How did this kingdom obtain its wealth? (c) How was Ethiopia unique among African kingdoms?
7. What was the importance of trade in the following areas? (a) the Swahili coastal cities (b) the western savanna kingdoms
8. Compare the ways of life of the Hopewell and the Hohokam.
9. Where and when did each of the following civilizations begin? (a) Olmec (b) Maya (c) Aztec (d) Inca
10. Briefly describe the culture of the Mayas, Aztecs, and Incas.

Thinking about History
1. The griots were oral historians. What are some other examples of oral history? What is the place of oral history today?
2. What were some lasting effects of African trade?
3. Choose two of the societies described in this chapter and explain how each adapted to its geographic environment. Try to pick contrasting examples.

Writing and Speaking about History
1. Write a generalization about each of the following empires. Support each generalization with two pieces of evidence. (See Research Skills Handbook, page 2.)
   a. Kush   d. Inca
   b. Axum   e. Aztec
   c. Mali
2. You are a newspaper reporter who travels back through time. In the woodlands of the place that would one day become the state of Ohio, you discover a Hopewell Indian settlement. Write the headline for the story you will write when you return to the present.
3. Conduct an interview with an Aztec or Inca leader. Topics to be discussed should include:
   the expansion of an empire
   ways to unify an empire
   the role of religion in society

Practicing Skills
1. Review the timeline on page 316. (a) Which events refer to African history? (b) Which events happened in the Americas?

2. Compare the timelines on pages 282, 296, and 316. Describe what was happening in each of the following places around the year 1500. (a) Central America (b) East Africa (c) India (d) China
3. Make a chart like the one below. Use a current almanac to find information to complete the chart.

	Population	Land Area (sq. mi.)	Percent of Earth's Surface
Africa			
North America			
South America			

4. Write a series of four entries in your diary describing various geographic conditions you encounter on a trip from the Bering Sea to the southern tip of South America. Trace your journey on a map.

Investigating History
1. In Alex Haley's book *Roots,* find his account of a present-day griot. Report to the class on the griot's work.
2. Find out what Indian groups lived in your area. What kinds of shelters did they build? What foods did they live on? What language did they speak? How was their society organized?
3. Over the years, African music has influenced both jazz and rock and roll. Make an audio presentation of African music, perhaps with records or tapes from the library. Show pictures to the class of some of the instruments used.
4. Research one of the following topics to present to the class: the kingdom of Prester John; the discovery of Machu Picchu; the city of Chichén Itzá; the legend of Quetzalcoatl.

Decision Making in History
1. In about 324 A.D., King Ezana of Axum decided to destroy the kingdom of Kush. Why do you think he made this decision? What could he have done instead?
2. Suppose Inca and Aztec leaders had known well in advance that Europeans were going to invade their territories. What could they have done to prevent the conquest of their lands?

Research Skills

Writing a Historical Essay

As a student historian, you may write several essays during the school year. Often a teacher will assign a broad topic for an essay, such as the accomplishments of the Guptas or Japanese society during the Heian Age. Your job will then be to:

1. Formulate a thesis that focuses on one aspect of the topic.
2. List the main ideas you will use to support your thesis.
3. Organize the thesis and the main points into an outline of the essay, as shown below.

- The introductory paragraph briefly states the thesis and the main ideas that support it.
- Each developmental paragraph in the essay discusses one of the main ideas mentioned in the introduction.
- Each developmental paragraph begins with a topic sentence that states the main idea and provides a transition from the preceding paragraph.
- Subsequent sentences in the developmental paragraph develop the main idea. Connecting words such as *in addition, most important, furthermore, next,* and *then* provide a transition from one sentence to the next.
- The concluding paragraph restates the thesis and summarizes the main ideas.

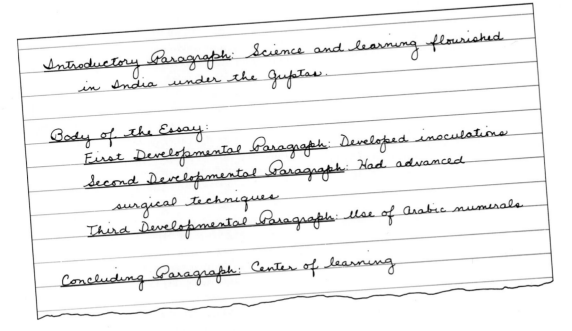

Introductory Paragraph: Science and learning flourished in India under the Guptas.

Body of the Essay:
First Developmental Paragraph: Developed inoculations
Second Developmental Paragraph: Had advanced surgical techniques
Third Developmental Paragraph: Use of Arabic numerals

Concluding Paragraph: Center of learning

Unit Review IV

1. With what civilization is each of the following people associated? What role did that person play in the civilization?
   a. Kublai Khan
   b. Tokugawa Ieyasu
   c. Sesshu
   d. Chandra Gupta I
   e. Akbar
   f. King Ezana
   g. Mansa Musa

2. Match the term in the first column with the correct definition in the second.
   a. dynasty
   b. clan
   c. caste
   d. gentry
   e. samurai

   1. people descended from the same ancestors
   2. series of rulers from the same family
   3. a large, wealthy group of people who rank below nobles
   4. a Japanese warrior
   5. a Hindi birth group

3. Describe the location of each of the following cities. Why was each city important?
   a. Peking
   b. Heian
   c. Ch'ang-an
   d. Axum
   e. Timbuktu
   f. Mombasa
   g. Tikal
   h. Tenochtitlán

4. Describe the examination system that was revived during the T'ang dynasty in China.

5. (a) Who were the Mongols? (b) What lands did they conquer between 1200 and 1350?

6. (a) How did Buddhism reach Japan? (b) What institutions did Japan borrow from China and then later adapt?

7. (a) What was Japan's golden age called? (b) Describe Japanese society during this age.

8. Describe the system of feudalism that grew up in Japan between 1000 and 1200.

9. (a) List three accomplishments of Gupta India. (b) What brought about the fall of that empire in the 400's?

10. (a) How were the men of Rajput India similar to European knights and Japanese samurai? (b) What happened to Buddhism and Hinduism in India during the Rajput centuries?

11. (a) What two groups of people entered into fierce conflict in India beginning in the 700's? (b) How did the beliefs of these people differ?

12. (a) How has the location of Southeast Asia impacted life there? (b) What present-day countries make up Southeast Asia?

13. (a) Describe the four general geographic regions found in Africa. (b) Which of these four regions has always supported the largest share of Africa's population?

14. (a) What group of people first built cities in sub-Saharan Africa? (b) Who conquered them?

15. (a) Describe the city-states that thrived in East Africa between 1100 and 1500. (b) With whom did these cities trade?

16. (a) What kingdoms arose in the savannas of western Africa? (b) In what type of trade did these kingdoms engage?

17. (a) When do scientists believe the first human settlers arrived in the Americas? (b) How did these settlers get the name *Indians*?

18. (a) Where did America's first farmers live? (b) What was their most important crop?

19. (a) In what part of the Americas did the Maya civilization arise? (b) Describe two features of that civilization.

20. (a) When did the Aztecs settle in Mexico? (b) Why did they conquer their neighbors?

21. (a) What empire in South America flourished at about the same time as the Aztec? (b) Describe the architectural achievements of that empire.

Unit V

The Spread of New Ideas

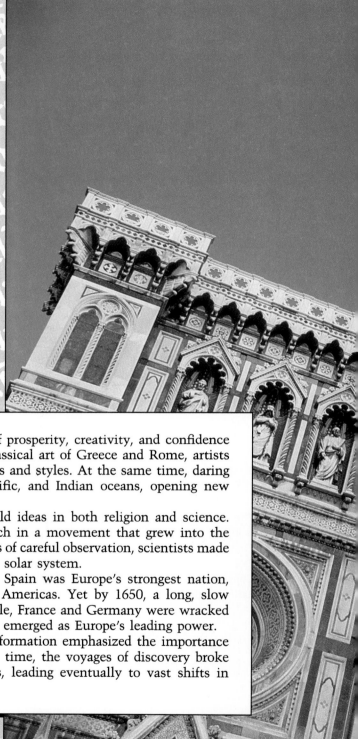

CHAPTERS

During this era, Europe entered a new age of prosperity, creativity, and confidence known as the Renaissance. Inspired by the classical art of Greece and Rome, artists and writers experimented with new techniques and styles. At the same time, daring European explorers crossed the Atlantic, Pacific, and Indian oceans, opening new seaways to European trade.

The new era brought challenges to long-held ideas in both religion and science. Martin Luther broke with the Catholic Church in a movement that grew into the Protestant Reformation. Adopting new methods of careful observation, scientists made startling discoveries about Earth's place in the solar system.

Politically, the age was turbulent. In 1550, Spain was Europe's strongest nation, ruling an empire that included much of the Americas. Yet by 1650, a long, slow decline had begun in Spanish power. Meanwhile, France and Germany were wracked by civil and religious wars. Eventually, France emerged as Europe's leading power.

The heritage of the Renaissance and the Reformation emphasized the importance of the individual mind and soul. At the same time, the voyages of discovery broke down the isolation among world civilizations, leading eventually to vast shifts in food crops, livestock, and human settlement.

Cathedral of Santa Maria de Fiore, Florence, Italy

The Renaissance and Exploration

Renaissance Florence lay on the Arno River. It was a city of about 100,000 people. Notice the various styles of architecture in the palaces and churches. (The artist has shown himself, or another painter, drawing the city from a hilltop.)

1. **The Renaissance began in northern Italy.**
2. **Florence led the way in arts.**
3. **Three artistic giants ruled the Renaissance.**
4. **Explorers opened new sea routes.**

An intriguing idea darted into the mind of Leonardo da Vinci (LAY-uh-NAHR-doh duh VEEN-chee). Eagerly he flipped open his notebook and wrote this message to himself: "Dissect the bat, study it carefully, and on this model construct the machine."

The machine that Leonardo imagined had huge, batlike wings measuring 80 feet from tip to tip. Below the wings, he imagined a person standing on a wooden framework and pedaling furiously. By ropes and pulleys, the pedals would make the wings flap. With this device, thought Leonardo, a person could fly.

322

The flying machine was only one idea among hundreds that excited Leonardo. Looking through his notebooks (5,700 pages of which have survived), we can track Leonardo's lifelong quest for knowledge. He wanted to know the physical universe inside and out—how it worked and how its hidden laws could be mastered by the human mind.

On one page are drawings of the muscles and tendons of a man's arm as it swings forward. On another page, Leonardo made a rough sketch of a falling man clinging to a tent-shaped cloth. A note next to it explains its purpose:

If a man has a tent made of linen of which the [openings] have all been stopped up . . . he will be able to throw himself down from any height without injury.

Here, in other words, is the first design for a parachute.

Leonardo knew he was a genius. In 1482, he wrote a letter offering his services to the duke of Milan in northern Italy. Leonardo assured the duke that there was no better weapons designer, military engineer, painter, or architect than himself. He concluded, "I commend myself to Your Excellency with all possible humility."

Another Italian of this time, Christopher Columbus, had fewer ideas than Leonardo. However, he believed in his one great idea as firmly as Leonardo believed in parachutes and flying machines. Columbus thought he could reach Asia by sailing west across the Atlantic Ocean. He

This sketch from one of the Leonardo da Vinci's notebooks shows an idea for a flying machine.

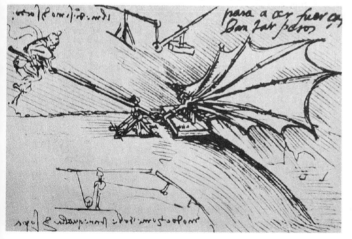

was looking for a patron to pay for his voyage at the very time that Leonardo was trying to interest the duke of Milan in new ideas for bridges and armored vehicles.

Columbus (born in 1451) and Leonardo (born in 1452) were only two of many individuals whose genius and daring made the years from 1300 to 1600 a golden age. They lived during the time we call the Renaissance (REN-uh-SAHNTS). The word means "rebirth."

What was being reborn? The educated men and women of Italy hoped to bring back to life the classical culture of Greece and Rome. Yet bringing back a past golden age is never possible. In striving to revive the past, the people of the Renaissance in fact created something new.

The Renaissance was a time of great intellectual and artistic creativity. Above all, people of the Renaissance had a new view of themselves and their world.

The Renaissance began in northern Italy. 1

Like other great changes in history, the Renaissance did not replace the Middle Ages overnight. Nor did the change take place at the same time everywhere in Europe. The Renaissance began in Italy around 1300. Later, its new styles of art, writing, and thought spread northward to the Netherlands, France, Germany, and England.

It is important to remember that early writers and artists of the Renaissance were creating their masterpieces in Italy while France and England were still locked in the Hundred Years' War. The bustling cities of northern Italy seem to be in a different world from the feudal villages of northern Europe, but both existed at the same time.

Italy offered new opportunities.

The Renaissance began in the city-states of northern Italy, especially Florence. The region of Italy that lies north of Rome and south of the Alps was different from the rest of Europe in two ways.

Urban centers First, northern Italy was a highly urban region. By 1350, three cities there had

Renaissance Italy

Map Study

What sea did Venice control? Who ruled Rome and the surrounding territory? What states bordered Genoa?

populations of about 100,000, a huge figure by medieval standards. Two of those cities—Genoa in the west and Venice in the east—were major seaports whose merchants dominated the rich Mediterranean trade. The third city, Florence, was located inland on the Arno River. Its thriving economy was based on the making of fine woolens, leathers, and silks.

Aside from those three large cities, northern Italy had a number of other good-sized towns, as the map on this page shows. Thus, northern Italy was urban while the rest of Europe was still mostly rural. (The Black Death of 1348 struck Italy's cities hard, but they recovered quickly.)

The power of merchants Second, northern Italy was a merchant's region. In these cities, wealthy merchants dominated politics and society as well as business. You have read how the Lombard League defeated the Holy Roman Emperor, Frederick Barbarossa, in 1176 at the Battle of Legnano (page 223). After that defeat, the Holy Roman emperors had little control over Italy's cities.

The popes had left Rome for Avignon and were later weakened by the Great Schism. They could not dominate Italy's cities either.

Milan, Genoa, Florence, Venice, and the other independent city-states ran their own affairs. Each collected taxes and supported an army. Within these cities, merchants were the wealthiest and most powerful class.

Unlike feudal nobles, merchants did not inherit their social rank. Success in business depended mostly on the merchant's own wits. As a result, successful merchants took pride in their achievements. They believed they were great because of their merit as individuals. The theme of individual achievement is an important one in the Renaissance, as you will see.

Just as these merchants competed with one another in business, they also competed as patrons, or sponsors, of the arts. A Florentine merchant was as proud of spotting a promising young painter as of making a profitable deal in silks. Throughout northern Italy, wealthy families spent their money lavishly for the glory of helping artists create works of genius.

Such was the setting for the Renaissance. Like the blossoming of a flower, the Renaissance first showed itself as a lovely bud in the 1300's. Three of the earliest geniuses in this golden age were a painter, a poet, and a letter writer.

Giotto painted lifelike figures.

Giotto di Bondone (JOHT-oh dee bohn-DOH-nay) was 38 years old when, in 1304, he carried his paints and brushes into a small, empty building in Padua, Italy. The building, called the Arena Chapel, was owned by a wealthy merchant who had commissioned Giotto to decorate it with scenes from the Bible. Giotto dabbed his brush in pigment and applied his first masterly stroke to the wet plaster. (The technique of painting on wet plaster was known as *fresco* painting.)

Most painters of the time would have covered the walls with flat, stiff-looking figures like those painted throughout the Middle Ages. Giotto had a different style. He painted human figures that looked real and lifelike, with bodies and faces that seemed fully rounded. When Giotto painted on a flat wall, he created an illusion of depth. The people in his paintings all seemed to be interacting with one another. Their faces showed realistic emotions. Giotto's acclaimed frescoes began a revolution in art.

Dante wrote *The Divine Comedy.*

Dante Alighieri (DAHN-tay AH-lee-GYAY-ree) was to the world of poetry what Giotto was to the world of painting. Dante was born in Florence in 1265, only a year before Giotto's birth. At the age of 9, Dante met an 8-year-old girl, Beatrice Portinari. Although he did not see her again for 10 years, she became his spiritual ideal. "From that time forward," he wrote later, "love quite governed my soul." He continued his spiritual love for her from afar, although he rarely saw or spoke to her. She died in 1290, at just 24 years old. Yet Dante worshiped her memory until his own death in 1321. For Dante, Beatrice was his muse—that is, the guiding genius of his writing. In his poems, he spoke of her as a kind of goddess.

Dante's most famous work was *The Divine Comedy.* (In this sense, *comedy* refers to a literary work with a joyous ending.) This long poem has three parts. In the first part, Dante imagines that the ancient Roman poet Virgil is guiding him on a tour of "the inferno" (hell). In the second part, Dante and Virgil visit a zone called purgatory, which lies between hell and heaven. Finally, in the third part, Dante is guided through paradise by the famous medieval monk, St. Bernard. Eventually, he meets Beatrice there.

Dante filled his poem with real people. He called dead friends and enemies by name and told of their earthly adventures. *The Divine Comedy* is full of comments on the political events of Dante's time. He showed a keen interest in human personalities.

Dante's masterpiece showed both the religious ideas of the Middle Ages and the worldly concerns of the Renaissance. *The Divine Comedy* was a kind of philosophic bridge between Europe's past and its future.

At a time when other serious poets wrote in Latin, Dante wrote *The Divine Comedy* in the **vernacular**, or everyday language of his homeland. By his work, Dante gave the Italian language new prestige, and he is sometimes called the creator of modern Italian. His example encouraged other poets to write in their own vernacular languages, as England's Geoffrey Chaucer did later in the 1300's (page 239).

Petrarch wrote poems and letters.

Another Italian poet, Francesco Petrarch (PEE-trahrk), was born in 1304, the year that Giotto began work on the Arena Chapel. Petrarch wrote both in Italian and in Latin. In Italian, he wrote beautiful sonnets in honor of a mysterious woman named Laura, who was his muse and spiritual ideal as Beatrice had been Dante's. (Little is known of Laura except that she died of the plague in 1348.) In classical Latin, he wrote letters to his many influential friends.

In Petrarch's letters, he imitated the graceful style of his favorite classical author, Cicero, the ancient Roman senator. Petrarch's writing showed a new idea of beauty. Instead of the complexity of medieval poetry, Petrarch strove for the classical virtues of simplicity and purity. If Dante's works were a bridge between the Middle Ages and the Renaissance, Petrarch had crossed that bridge and stood fully within the new age.

New values shaped the Renaissance.

No age or time breaks completely with the past. Yet the men and women of the Renaissance came to have a new outlook on life. Here are some of the characteristics that set the Renaissance apart from the Middle Ages.

Celebration of the individual Artists in the Middle Ages did their work skillfully. In general, however, they did not win fame as individuals. The glassmakers, stonecutters, and wood-carvers of the great cathedrals worked for the glory of God, not for personal glory. Even the author of the *Song of Roland* is unknown.

By the 1300's, however, artists and writers in northern Italy were eager to be known and remembered as individuals. From this time on, we know the names of people who created works of art. Fame was the final reward for superior talent.

Two new art forms show this interest in individual fame: portrait painting and autobiography. Wealthy patrons wanted their faces recorded for all time. Artists often painted self-portraits too. Autobiographies were the written equivalents of self-portraits. People believed that their own lives were interesting and important not just to themselves but to others. They wished to share their lives with the world.

Admiration for the classical culture of Greece shows in this Renaissance painting, "The School of Athens." Under the central arch, Plato talks with his pupil Aristotle. They are surrounded by important figures from both ancient and Renaissance times. (This work is by Raphael, who is discussed on page 334.)

Love of classical learning Renaissance scholars despised the art and literature of the Middle Ages. Since the fall of Rome in 476, they said, the people of Europe had lived in darkness and ignorance. Even the beautiful Gothic cathedrals were dismissed as the work of barbarians. Admiring only Greek and Roman art, a Renaissance artist once cried, "Cursed be the man who invented this wretched Gothic architecture!" Petrarch summed up the Renaissance attitude by calling the medieval years "the Dark Ages."

Petrarch and other Renaissance scholars loved the writings of ancient Greece and Rome. Scholars who studied classical texts were called **humanists**, from the Latin word *humanitas*. According to Cicero, humanitas meant the learning that every educated, civilized person should have. Petrarch himself is considered the first humanist. He and his followers were the cultural leaders of the Renaissance. Under their influence, all painting, sculpture, and architecture carried on the traditions of ancient Greece and Rome.

Enjoyment of worldly pleasures In Renaissance Italy, almost everyone with money openly enjoyed material luxuries, fine music, tasty foods, and beautiful surroundings. For example, clothing itself became almost a work of art. Women's gowns were sometimes so encrusted with pearls or golden beads that the fabric underneath was nearly hidden. Men wore colorful stockings, fancy jackets called doublets, and plumed hats. Both men and women perfumed their clothing and hair.

This enjoyment of worldly goods showed a new attitude. In the Middle Ages, devoutly religious people had proved their piety by wearing poor, rough clothing and living on the plainest foods. Renaissance humanists suggested that a person might love and enjoy life without offending God. Most historians agree that Renaissance art and literature show a growing interest in earthly and human subjects.

Ideals differed for men and women.

For Renaissance thinkers, the ideal individual strove to master almost every art. Those who excelled in many fields were admiringly known as "universal men." Later ages called such people "Renaissance men."

A book called *The Courtier* became widely popular because it told young people how to become an accomplished person whom everyone would admire. Its author was Baldassare Castiglione (KAHS-tee-LYOH-nay).

The ideal man A young man, said Castiglione, should be well educated in the Greek and Latin classics. He should be charming, polite, and witty. He should be able to dance, write poetry, sing, and play music. In addition, he should be physically graceful and strong, a skilled rider, wrestler, and swordsman.

Renaissance men tried to live up to this ideal. In his autobiography, Leon Battista Alberti (1404–1472) boasted of his many skills. Here, in the third person, is Alberti's description of his accomplishments and interests:

> He played ball, hurled the javelin, ran, leaped, wrestled, and above all delighted in climbing steep mountains . . . As a youth, he excelled in warlike games. With his feet together, he could leap over the shoulders of men standing by . . . He delighted in the organ and was considered an expert among the leading musicians.

In addition, Alberti designed and built several churches and made a scientific study of perspective. Alberti summed up the spirit of his times when he wrote, "Man can do anything if he will."

The ideal woman Upper-class women of the Renaissance were as well educated as the men. According to *The Courtier*, women too were expected to know the classics, to write well, to paint, to make music, to dance, and to be charming. Yet they were not expected to seek fame as men did. Like Beatrice and Laura, they were expected to inspire poetry and art but rarely to create it.

The most honored woman of the Renaissance in northern Italy was probably Isabella d'Este. Born into the ruling family of the city-state of Ferrara, she married the ruler of another city-state, Mantua. Her art collection was famous throughout Europe. She brought many of the greatest Renaissance artists, including Leonardo da Vinci, to the court of Mantua. She was also skilled in politics. She defended Mantua when her husband was taken captive in war and won his release.

Isabella d'Este and a few other women such as Caterina Sforza (who ruled Milan from about 1488 to 1500) exercised real political power. For the most part, however, women were expected to create a charming court and home but not to take part in public life. Although upper-class women of the Renaissance were far better educated than the women of the Middle Ages, most Renaissance women had less political, economic, and social influence than medieval women.

Renaissance individualism shows in these realistic portraits. The Duke of Urbino, who fought his way to a dukedom by his military skill, suffered a broken nose in battle. His wife, Battista Sforza, came from the ruling family of Milan. Behind them lies their duchy.

Section Review 1

Define: (a) Renaissance, (b) fresco,
(c) vernacular, (d) humanist
Identify: (a) Leonardo da Vinci, (b) Giotto di
Bondone, (c) Dante Alighieri, (d) *The Divine
Comedy*, (e) Francesco Petrarch, (f) *The
Courtier*, (g) Isabella d'Este
Answer:
1. What conditions in northern Italy encouraged
   the beginning of the Renaissance?
2. How did Giotto revolutionize painting?
3. (a) What are the topics of the three major
   parts of *The Divine Comedy*? (b) In what
   two ways did Dante change the writing of
   poetry?
4. How did Petrarch draw on the classics in his
   writings?
5. What new art forms showed the Renaissance
   interest in the individual?
6. List three characteristics of the Renaissance.
7. (a) What was the Renaissance ideal for a young
   man? (b) For a young woman?

Critical Thinking

8. The wealth of northern Italy was important
   in fostering the many artists of the Renaissance. How were money and art related?
9. Which of the characteristics of the Renaissance
   do you consider most revolutionary? Explain
   your answer.

Florence led the way in arts.   2

The Renaissance burst into full flower in the
1400's. This century was called the *Quattrocento*
(kwah-troh-CHEN-toh) in Italian. During the
Quattrocento, dozens of the most talented painters
and sculptors in history competed for fame in
the thriving cities of northern Italy. In the forefront
of artistic developments was Florence, the City
of Flowers.

Cloth and banking enriched Florence.

The golden age of Florence was based on the
golden florins (the city's coin) of its merchants
and bankers. Florentines made their wealth chiefly
through two industries—textiles and banking.

In 1338, one Florentine writer boasted that 200
workshops in Florence produced more than 70,000
pieces of cloth. Merchants in the various cloth
guilds employed 30,000 Florentines, one third
the city's population. As a result of the general
prosperity, Florentines were well fed, consuming
110,000 sheep, goats, and pigs and 70,000 casks
of wine in a year.

The riches gathered by the cloth guilds gave
Florence a second major industry, banking. By
1300, wool merchants routinely deposited their
gold coins in Florentine banking houses.

Florentine bankers grew rich loaning their de-
positers' money to borrowers. By the 1300's,
Florence was the financial center of Europe. From
London to Rome, merchants figured their losses
or gains in terms of one coin: the florin. Kings,
princes, nobles, and merchants throughout Europe
depended on loans from Florence's banks. At
times during the Hundred Years' War, both French
and English armies were paid with loans from
Florentine bankers.

Among Florence's leading merchants, the pursuit of wealth and the scramble for political power
went hand in hand. Florentines boasted that they
had a republican form of government like that
of ancient Rome. In theory, any citizen who
belonged to one of the city's 21 guilds could hold
office. However, membership in the guilds was
tightly restricted. As a result, only about 3,500
men were eligible to vote—about 3 percent of
the total population. Among these citizens, the
competition for office never ceased.

Although ruled by a wealthy elite, Florence
had a democratic social atmosphere. Visitors in
Florence were amazed to hear a lowly journeyman
address a leading citizen by his first name.

The Medici ruled Florence.

As the golden age of the Quattrocento began,
Florence came under the political rule of one
powerful family, the Medici (MEHD-uh-chee). The
Medici had made a fortune in trade and banking.

Cosimo (KOH-see-moh) de Medici was the
wealthiest man of his time. In 1434, he won
control of the government of Florence. He did
not seek political office for himself, realizing
that he could rule more effectively behind the

scenes. He made sure, however, that all eight members of the city council were loyal to him. The lower classes of the city loved him because he championed popular causes. For 30 years, Cosimo de Medici was virtually dictator of the city of Florence.

Like Pericles of ancient Athens, Cosimo took pleasure in beautifying the city he ruled. From his personal fortune, he spent 400,000 florins on artistic and scholarly projects. He paid off the staggering debts of a bankrupt friend and took in exchange the friend's collection of 800 books by classical authors. To house this rare collection, he built the first free public library in western Europe.

Cosimo de Medici died in 1464, but his family remained in control of Florence. After a brief rule by Cosimo's sickly son, power passed in 1469 to Cosimo's 21-year-old grandson, Lorenzo. He soon became known as Lorenzo the Magnificent. Lorenzo ruled with absolute power, yet he kept up the appearances of a republican government. He held the goodwill of the common people with balls, festivals, carnivals, and celebrations of all sorts. Like his grandfather, Lorenzo continued the tradition of beautifying his city.

Artists beautified Florence.

Florence entered its golden age through a set of gleaming metal doors. In 1401, the wool manufacturers' guild wanted an artist to create new doors for the Baptistry of the local cathedral, an old eight-sided building. The guild held a contest, inviting Florence's most promising artists to submit designs for the doors. With great fanfare, the judges announced the winner. The guild had bestowed the honor upon a 23-year-old goldsmith named Lorenzo Ghiberti (gee-**BEHR**-tee).

Ghiberti spent the next 50 years creating two pairs of bronze doors for the Baptistry. At a time

Footnote to History

Every year, in his country villa, Lorenzo invited the finest scholars of Italy to a banquet in honor of Plato's birthday. While sipping wine and listening to music, they tried to equal the intellectual discussions of the ancient Athenians.

when 200 florins was a princely sum, the wool merchants and the city council spent 22,000 florins on the first pair alone. The new doors were so magnificent that the artist Michelangelo later likened them to the gates of paradise.

The finished doors were divided into panels, each showing a scene from the Bible. Each scene looked like a deep stage with the background trees and buildings far behind the people in the foreground. Yet the sculptured metal is only four inches deep at most. Ghiberti died in 1455, just three years after completing the doors.

Meanwhile, an architect named Brunelleschi (BROO-nuh-**LAYS**-kee) was working on the Cathedral of Florence, directly across the street from the Baptistry. Brunelleschi had been one of the losers in the contest to make the Baptistry doors. By 1420, however, his genius was recognized. Brunelleschi proposed to cap the cathedral with a gigantic dome. Such a dome had not been built in Europe since Roman times. Between 1420 and 1436, admiring Florentines watched his dome rise slowly. When it was completed, the cross at its top stood 370 feet above street level. It was twice as high as the famous dome of Constantinople's Hagia Sophia.

Donatello revolutionized sculpture.

Florence was also home to a host of younger artists. The most talented was a 17-year-old sculptor named Donatello (DAHN-uh-**TEHL**-oh). He came to work in Ghiberti's workshop just after 1400.

Donatello (1386–1466) left Ghiberti's workshop and journeyed to Rome to study its ancient ruins. When he returned to Florence, he was eager to make free-standing statues like those of the ancient Greeks and Romans. He rejected the style of medieval stonecutters, who usually carved only the front of their human figures. The back side merged into a cathedral's walls. Above everything else, Donatello wanted his figures to seem real and alive.

Like the ancient Greeks, Donatello wanted to show the strength and grace of the human form. In his statue "David," Donatello was the first European sculptor since ancient times to make a large, free-standing human figure in the nude. He was also famous for his heroic statues of men on horseback.

A diagram shows how perspective works in this fresco by Masaccio. Lines come together at a vanishing point near the center. The horizontal line running through the vanishing point shows the eye level of the viewer.

Masaccio developed perspective.

To Ghiberti, Brunelleschi, and Donatello, we must add the name of a fourth genius of Florence's golden age: Masaccio (mah-ZAHT-choh). Last of the four to be born (1401), Masaccio was also the first to die (1428). Yet in his 27 years, he changed painting as profoundly as Donatello changed sculpture.

One hundred years earlier, Giotto had started a revolution in the arts by giving a sense of depth and roundness to his paintings. Masaccio carried the revolution a step farther by using a technique called perspective.

Commissioned in 1425 to decorate a chapel in Florence, Masaccio used his new technique in a fresco called "The Healing of the Cripple and the Resurrection of Tabitha" (above). The picture shows two events in the life of the apostle Peter. Buildings stand at each side of the picture. Their upper stories slant downward, and the ground level slants up. People in the foreground look much larger than those in the distance. The slanting lines of the buildings and the relative

sizes of human figures give the scene an illusion of depth.

Masaccio realized that objects look smaller the farther they are from the viewer. He also realized that parallel lines, like the edges of a road, seem to come together in the distance. These are the principles of perspective. As a result of his new ideas, Masaccio has been called the "father of modern painting."

Machiavelli wrote about politics.

The golden age of Florence lasted nearly a century. Lorenzo the Magnificent died in 1492. Then, just two years later, a shocking event shattered the self-confidence of the Florentines. In 1494, King Charles VIII of France led an army across the Alps into northern Italy. His main goal was to claim Naples in the south, but his invasion route led past Florence, which he attacked.

Piero de Medici (son of Lorenzo) surrendered without a fight. Outraged by their ruler's weakness, a mob of Florentines stormed the Medici palace and drove Piero into exile.

For the next two generations, Florence and other Italian cities suffered from war and political upheavals. Spain's King Ferdinand of Aragon contested the French king's claim to Naples. In the early 1500's, French and Spanish armies attacked all along the Italian peninsula. All the great Italian cities—Florence, Milan, Venice, Rome—were forced to ally themselves with one foreign power or the other. Diplomacy and war became the keys to survival.

One result of the turmoil was a provocative book called *The Prince*. Its author, Niccolò Machiavelli (MAH-kyah-VEHL-ee), was bitter about the invasion of Italy by foreigners. Born in Florence in 1469, Machiavelli spent his youth under the rule of Lorenzo the Magnificent. As an adult, he saw the golden age begin to crumble. He served his city as a diplomat to many courts, where he observed dukes and kings. He tried to understand why one ruler succeeded while another failed.

In 1513, Machiavelli wrote a book of advice to rulers. *The Prince* is a book about power. How can a ruler gain power and keep it despite his enemies? asked Machiavelli. In answering this question, he began with the idea that most people are selfish, fickle, and corrupt. To succeed in such a wicked world, Machiavelli said, a prince must be strong as a lion and shrewd as a fox:

> . . . *for the lion cannot protect himself from traps, and the fox cannot defend himself from wolves. One must therefore be a fox to recognize traps, and a lion to fight wolves.*

Machiavelli said that a prince might have to trick his enemies and even his own people for the good of the state. His ideal ruler was the crafty Spanish king, Ferdinand of Aragon. When the king of France complained that Ferdinand had deceived him twice, Ferdinand boasted, "He lies, the drunkard. I have deceived him more than ten times!"

In *The Prince*, Machiavelli was not concerned with what was morally right but with what was politically effective. He believed that, in politics, the end justifies the means. According to *The Prince*, even immoral acts were justified if they served the interests of the state. Thus, although Machiavelli was himself an upright, honest, and religious man, his name has come to stand for trickery and double dealing.

Voice from the Past · *The Dangers of Flattery*

In *The Prince*, Machiavelli advised rulers that they must always *seem* to be honest, merciful, and true to their word, even if they were not always so. However, he warned princes that they must beware of people who tried to flatter them.

I must not leave out . . . a mistake that is hard for princes to avoid . . . And this is with regard to flatterers, of which courts are full . . . There is no other way of guarding oneself against flattery except by letting men understand that they will not offend you by speaking the truth. But when everyone can tell you the truth, you lose people's respect. A prudent prince must therefore take a third course, by choosing for his council wise men and by giving them alone full liberty to speak the truth to him. And they may speak the truth only of those things that he asks, so he must ask them about everything . . . A prince, therefore, should always take advice, but only when he wishes, not when others wish . . . He ought to be a great asker and a patient hearer of the truth . . . Indeed, if he finds out that anyone has hesitated to tell him the truth, he should be angry.

1. (a) Why might a prince's court be full of flatterers? (b) Why would flatterers be dangerous to a prince?
2. How does Machiavelli say a prince can avoid being fooled by flatterers?
3. Why must a prince be "a great asker"?
4. Why might it be difficult for a prince to follow Machiavelli's advice?

Eloque re ergo

Section Review 2

Define: Quattrocento
Identify: (a) Cosimo de Medici, (b) Lorenzo de Medici, (c) Ghiberti, (d) Brunelleschi, (e) Donatello, (f) Masaccio, (g) Machiavelli
Answer
1. What were the main businesses of Renaissance Florence?
2. (a) Describe the government of Florence. (b) How did Cosimo de Medici control the city for 30 years?
3. (a) What were Donatello's goals in sculpture? (b) How did he accomplish these goals?
4. What contributions did Masaccio make to painting?
5. (a) What was Machiavelli's view of human nature? (b) Describe the advice he gave to rulers.
6. What political events threatened the Italian city-states in the 1500's?

Critical Thinking
7. In many ways, the achievements of the Renaissance were linked to civic pride. Explain how this statement applies to Florence during the Quattrocento.

Three artistic giants ruled the Renaissance. 3

In 1513, while Machiavelli was writing *The Prince*, Leonardo da Vinci took regular walks in the pope's garden in Rome. Leonardo was an old man now with a flowing white beard. Though born in Florence, he had spent his most productive years as a painter in Milan. Now, in his last years, Leonardo sought the favor of the pope. After the death of Lorenzo de Medici, the popes became the foremost patrons of art.

In Rome, during the early 1500's, Renaissance art reached new grandeur. This period is known as the High Renaissance. Three artists lifted Renaissance art to unsurpassed brilliance. The three were Leonardo, Raphael Santi (RAF-ay-el SAHN-tee), and Michelangelo Buonarroti (MYE-kel-AN-juh-loh BWOH-nahr-ROH-tee).

Popes supported the arts.

In the Middle Ages, Rome had fallen into a sad state of disrepair. Goats grazed among the ruins of ancient palaces. The Forum, where great orators had once spoken, became a pig market. When the Babylonian captivity and the Great Schism (page 241) were over, however, Rome began to recover. In the mid-1400's, Renaissance popes were determined to beautify the city.

In their tastes and ambitions, these Renaissance popes were much like the Medici and other Italian princes of their time. They loved fine foods and fine wines as well as fine arts. Pope Nicholas V, for example, spent vast sums collecting classical texts for the Vatican library.

One Renaissance pope in particular stands out. Julius II, who was pope from 1503 to 1513, loved art and power in equal measure. He longed for Rome again to become, in Livy's phrase, "the capital of the world." To glorify his city, Julius enlisted Italy's greatest artists including a brilliant Florentine named Michelangelo.

Michelangelo excelled in many arts.

Born in 1475, Michelangelo was apprenticed at the age of 13 to a painter. Soon, however, Michelangelo turned from painting to sculpture. He quickly surpassed his famous predecessor,

Michelangelo's many-sided genius shows in his "Pieta" (far left), "David," (left) and the Sistine Chapel (above). Recently, 400 years of grime was cleaned from the chapel ceiling to reveal the original beauty of Michelangelo's colors.

Donatello. In 1498, he was commissioned by a Roman cardinal to create "a Virgin Mary clothed, with the dead Christ in her arms, of the size of a proper man, for the price of 450 golden ducats of the papal mint." The result was a marble sculpture known as the "Pieta" (pee-ay-**TAH**).

In 1504, another masterpiece by Michelangelo was hoisted onto a pedestal in a public square in Florence. His white marble statue of David, the Biblical warrior and king, stood 16 feet tall. It showed a strong young athlete whose muscles rippled with power. Even more awesome than the body was the face, which seemed to radiate strength and vigor. Better than any other single work of art, Michelangelo's mighty statue of David summed up the Renaissance belief in human dignity and greatness.

In 1505, Pope Julius II invited the 30-year-old Michelangelo to Rome. Despite quarrels between the two high-tempered men, Michelangelo did some of his best work for Julius. When the pope wanted him to paint the ceiling of the Sistine (sihs-**TEEN**) Chapel, Michelangelo grumbled that he was a sculptor, not a painter. Finally, however, he agreed to undertake the task.

Every day for four years (1508–1512), Michelangelo climbed the scaffolding in the Sistine Chapel about 65 feet above the floor. Lying flat on his back, he covered the ceiling with more than 300 massive human figures. It was messy, tiring work. Michelangelo, who also wrote poetry, vividly described his daily agony:

My stomach is thrust towards my chin,
My beard curls up, towards the sky,
My head leans right over onto my back,
My chest is like that of an old shrew,
The brush endlessly dripping onto my face
Has coated it with a multi-colored paving.

Yet even as paint trickled into his eyes, Michelangelo never lost sight of his grand design. Toward the center of the ceiling, he painted the scene that was to command the viewer's attention. This scene showed God reaching out to infuse spirit into Adam, the first man.

Within his own lifetime, Michelangelo was recognized as a universal genius. He worked as sculptor, painter, and architect. (His poetry did not come to light until after his death.) In his last years, he designed a huge dome for the new St. Peter's Cathedral. A younger artist called him "the divine Michelangelo" and wrote, "The world has many kings, but only one Michelangelo." Michelangelo died in 1564. He was 89.

Raphael perfected painting.

In 1508, the same year Michelangelo began painting the chapel ceiling, a young artist named Raphael started painting the walls of Julius II's private library. It was a short walk from library to chapel. Raphael, always eager to learn from older artists, often dropped in on Michelangelo.

The pope's library held both Christian and classical works. Raphael's assignment was to celebrate this knowledge and show its underlying unity.

Gradually, Raphael transformed the library into a kind of Renaissance hall of fame. On one wall, in a painting called "The School of Athens," were the white-bearded Plato and the black-bearded Aristotle in deep discussion. Around them were groups of listeners, including the greatest figures of both classical and Renaissance times. Among them, the pope certainly would have recognized the face of young Raphael and the brooding figure of Michelangelo. Another wall, dedicated to poetry and music, showed Homer and Dante.

Besides artistic genius, Raphael was blessed with a pleasant personality. His easy temper made him the favorite painter of Julius II's successor, Pope Leo X (a son of Lorenzo de Medici). For his patrons, Raphael painted dozens of lovely madonnas and flattering portraits. His death in 1520, when he was only 37, plunged the papal court into sadness.

Leonardo was both scientist and artist.

When Leonardo da Vinci came to Rome in 1513, he was 61. The aging artist, curious as ever, still filled his notebooks with inventions and new observations. As a painter, however, his best years lay behind him. In Milan, while he was experimenting with bicycles, hydraulics, masonry, and countless other things, he produced one of the most famous paintings in history.

Leonardo's fascination with the human personality shows in the "Mona Lisa," completed in 1506. It was a portrait of a Florentine woman, probably Lisa Gheradini del Giocando. Though only 24, she had been married 3 times. The picture fascinates viewers because the woman's face seems to change expression. Is she smiling in

Leonardo da Vinci's "Mona Lisa"

welcome or smirking in disdain? Are her eyes friendly or cold? One scholar has called this painting "the first distinctly psychological portrait of the Renaissance."

Section Review 3

Identify: (a) Raphael, (b) Michelangelo, (c) Pope Julius II

Answer

1. (a) What was the condition of Rome in the early 1400's? (b) Who took on the task of beautifying the city?
2. Name three major works of Michelangelo and briefly describe each one.
3. What was Raphael's task in the work he did for the library of Julius II?
4. Why is the "Mona Lisa" a significant painting?

Critical Thinking

5. Why is it common for powerful rulers to begin massive projects in building and the arts?
6. Which of the three artists discussed in this section do you consider the greatest? Explain your answer.

Explorers opened new sea routes. 4

You have seen how Renaissance artists looked at human life in a new way. Running parallel with this human discovery was the geographic discovery of lands beyond Europe.

During Leonardo's lifetime (1452–1519), Europeans greatly expanded their knowledge of the world. Portuguese sea captains charted the entire coast of Africa. Europeans crossed the Atlantic Ocean and reached two vast continents—the Americas—of which they had known nothing. In 1519, the year of Leonardo's death, five ships sailed from Spain. One of those ships eventually made its way completely around the world.

Was it just coincidence that great explorers lived during the same period as the great artists of the High Renaissance? No, like the artists, the explorers were confident, ambitious, and eager for individual glory. In short, they shared many values of the Renaissance.

New ideas made exploration possible.

In the late 1200's, a Venetian named Marco Polo had written a book about his adventurous travels to the court of Kublai Khan in China (page 269). Two centuries later, an Italian sea captain named Christopher Columbus read Marco Polo's book. Columbus resolved to reach Cipangu (Polo's name for Japan) by sailing west across the Atlantic.

Why did 200 years go by before someone took up the challenge of finding a new route to Asia? By the late 1400's, Europe had changed in a number of ways since Marco Polo's time.

Economic need As merchants from the Italian seaport of Venice, Marco Polo's family had no need to discover a new trade route to Asia. The old route was good enough for them. During the Middle Ages, Venice and Genoa controlled the only practical route by which Asian goods reached Europe. For centuries, Arab and Turkish caravans had carried Chinese silks and Indian spices overland to the bazaars of Antioch and Alexandria. There Italian merchants bought the goods and carried them west to Europe. Every time the Asian goods changed hands, their price went up.

By the 1400's, the "new monarchs" of France, England, Spain, and Portugal wanted a share of this profitable trade. They wanted routes that they themselves could control. (Many of these rulers were also heavily in debt to Italian bankers.) Thus, the rulers of many European countries began to seek new routes to Asia.

Technological skills In the 1200's, it would have been nearly impossible for a European sea captain to cross 3,000 miles of open water and find the way home again. Medieval ships and navigational tools were adequate for the sheltered waters of the Mediterranean Sea, but they were hopelessly inadequate for the Atlantic Ocean.

In the 1400's, however, shipbuilders designed a new vessel called a **caravel**. The caravel had triangular sails for tacking into the wind. It had square sails for running before the wind. Its carefully designed hull could ride out an ocean storm.

Two other inventions were critical for crossing the Atlantic Ocean—the compass and the astrolabe. Muslim mathematicians and instrument makers had perfected both (page 181). Italian sailors knew of the magnetic compass as early as 1200, but it became more useful as Europeans made more charts of coastlines and currents. The astrolabe was a brass circle with carefully adjusted concentric rings marked off in degrees. Using these rings to sight the stars, a sea captain could tell how far north or south of the equator he was. Without the astrolabe, Columbus would almost certainly have been lost at sea.

Geographic knowledge In 1410, a humanist translated a manuscript dating from about A.D. 150. Written by the Greek geographer Ptolemy (TAHL-uh-mee), the work described Africa, Asia, and Europe. Scholars of the 1400's believed that these three were Earth's only continents. Ptolemy also said that Earth is a sphere. By the 1400's, most educated Europeans accepted that idea too.

Based on Ptolemy's writings, Renaissance mapmakers figured that about 3,000 miles of Atlantic Ocean lay between Europe and China. They were wrong. The actual distance was closer to 11,000 miles, including the Atlantic Ocean, the American continents, and the Pacific Ocean.

Columbus believed the writings of Ptolemy and the estimates of the mapmakers. He thought a skillful navigator such as himself could sail straight across the western ocean and return in a few months with a rich cargo of spices.

Voyages of Discovery

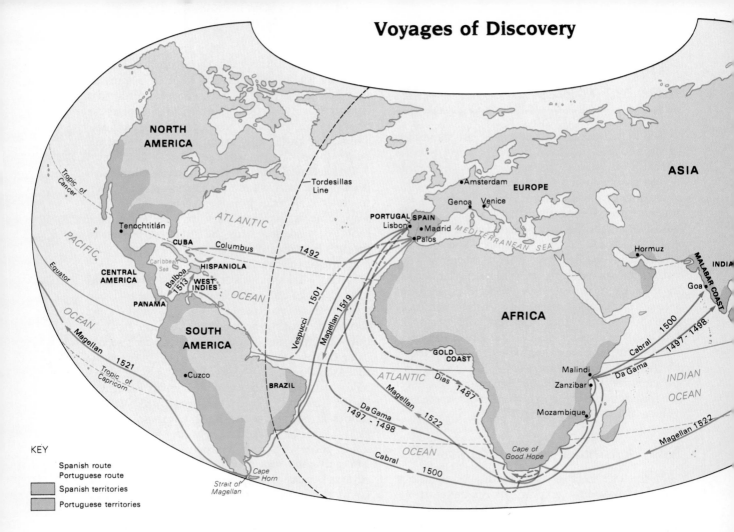

KEY

Spanish route
Portuguese route

Spanish territories

Portuguese territories

Remember the cocky statement by Alberti, "Man can do anything if he will." Columbus had the Renaissance spirit of self-confidence and its passion for fame. He and Europe's other explorers needed all their confidence to face the dangers of the sea.

The Portuguese explored Africa.

The Portuguese took the lead in exploration. For several centuries, they had been sailing and fishing farther and farther south along Africa's west coast.

Henry the Navigator The man who began the great age of exploration never sailed into unknown waters himself. Like the patrons who supported Renaissance artists, Portugal's Prince Henry the Navigator organized and paid for voyages.

Henry, third son of a Portuguese king, devoted his life to sending ships south along the west coast of Africa. At first, his goal was to find gold. Legend said that a "river of gold" lay south of the Sahara, the vast desert that divides northern Africa from southern Africa. In the 1440's, Henry's ships passed one cape after another. Soon he began to think of Asian spices. He began to hope that a Portuguese caravel might sail around Africa to Asia. He never saw it happen, however. Prince Henry died in 1460.

Bartholomeu Dias and Vasco da Gama In 1488, a Portuguese captain named Bartholomeu Dias (DEE-ahsh) finally reached the southernmost tip of Africa. His ships were so battered by storms that Dias named the spot the Cape of Torment. King John II of Portugal, however, was so pleased at the thought of his ships rounding Africa and sailing to Asia that he renamed it the Cape of Good Hope.

Then, in 1497, four Portuguese ships sailed around the Cape of Good Hope. Commanded by

Map Study

What explorers rounded the Cape of Good Hope going east? Going west? Many of the ships on those voyages were caravels such as those shown above. What sea did Columbus (top) reach?

a tough and able captain, Vasco da Gama, the ships traveled north along Africa's east coast as far as Zanzibar. From there, Da Gama steered boldly eastward with the monsoon winds across the open Indian Ocean. Finally, the ships arrived at the Malabar Coast of India on May 20, 1498.

As the Portuguese sailors wearily stepped ashore, they were met by Arab merchants. "May the devil take you!" the Arabs exclaimed menacingly. "What brought you here?" The Arabs had long controlled India's spice trade. They rightly saw the Europeans as a threat.

Although the Indian merchants thought the Europeans' trade goods were of poor quality, the Portuguese were able to load their ships with pepper and cinnamon. They then set sail on the long voyage home. Only 54 of the original 170 sailors returned to Portugal two years later in 1499. The spices they brought back sold for 60 times the cost of the entire expedition.

Columbus reached the Americas.

While Dias and Da Gama were charting the route around Africa, Christopher Columbus made three voyages across the Atlantic Ocean. He claimed that the land he reached there was part of Asia. But had he truly found a shorter way to Asia than Da Gama's?

Columbus's first Atlantic crossing was in 1492, and it was by far his happiest voyage. King Ferdinand and Queen Isabella of Spain gave him three ships. On the morning of August 3, Columbus set sail from Palos, Spain. He had a crew of 90 men and boys on the *Santa Maria* (his flagship) and two smaller ships, the *Niña* and the *Pinta*. Strong winds briskly drove the little fleet westward. Weeks passed with no sight of land. The crew was growing impatient. On October 9, Columbus promised his fearful crew that he would turn back unless they sighted land in the next three days.

On October 12, two hours after midnight, a lookout on the *Pinta* saw in the distance what seemed to be a white cliff shining in the moonlight. They had reached land at last. Columbus believed he had reached the East Indies, near Japan and China. Therefore, he called the people he met "Indians." In fact, he was nowhere near Asia. He had reached the Bahamas.

337

When Columbus returned to Spain in 1493, Isabella and Ferdinand gave him a hero's welcome and the title Admiral of the Ocean Sea. They promised him a larger fleet for his next trip.

The thrill of discovery soon wore off. Columbus crossed the Atlantic three more times (in 1493, 1498, and 1502). He explored all the major islands of the Caribbean—Cuba, Hispaniola, Jamaica, and Puerto Rico. On his fourth voyage, he explored the coast of Central America. Nowhere did he find the fabulous civilization described by Marco Polo.

The hurricanes and hardships of his fourth voyage nearly killed Columbus. He returned to Spain white-haired and arthritic. He died in 1506, insisting to the bitter end that the lands he had explored were Asia.

Other explorers reached the Americas.

Columbus's mistake was soon corrected. A Florentine merchant named Amerigo Vespucci (AHM-uh-REE-goh veh-SPYOO-chee) crossed the ocean in 1499 and 1501. In his letters, he described the coastline of the land we know as Brazil. This was not Asia, he wrote, but a newly discovered continent.

One of Vespucci's letters fell into the hands of a German publisher, Martin Waldseemüller (VAHLT-zay-MOO-luhr). In 1507, Waldseemüller published a new map of the world, showing a great blob of land west of the Atlantic. He labeled this land *America* to honor Amerigo Vespucci.

If this was indeed a new continent, how big was it? How far was it from Asia? Was there a way either through it or around it? For a Renaissance explorer, these were urgent questions.

In 1513, a Spaniard named Vasco Nuñez de Balboa slashed through the rain forests of Panama. He climbed over a hill and beheld a vast ocean. Dressed in full armor, Balboa plunged into the water up to his knees and claimed the entire ocean for Spain. Balboa had reached what is now called the Pacific Ocean.

Portugal claimed Brazil.

When Columbus first reached the Americas, it was not clear what lands he had found. The king of Portugal suspected that the Spanish might be taking over some lands that Portuguese sailors had reached first. Soon rivalry between Spain and Portugal reached a dangerous level.

In 1493, to keep peace, Pope Alexander VI ruled that Spain and Portugal might divide the

Daily Life · The Spices of Life

"Take ginger, clove, and a little pepper, and crush together." So began a French recipe from 1393 for making a "black pudding." Indeed, without these spices, the pudding would have been little more than tasteless mush. Europeans craved spices partly because their food would have been so monotonous otherwise. In summer, most people depended on foods that were raised locally. In winter, they had only what could be dried or pickled for storage.

The poor flavored their foods with herbs from their own dooryard gardens: garlic, thyme, marjoram, bay leaf, and savory. The rich bought spices from distant lands: cinnamon, nutmeg, ginger, turmeric, cardamom, clove, mace, saffron, and—above all—pepper. Besides flavoring everything from meat to preserved fruit, spices often were mixed as medicines too. During the 1600's, thanks to the voyages of explorers, spices reached Europe in larger quantities, and prices fell. Soon pepper and other spices could be found in most kitchens.

so-called "Indies" between themselves. He ordered a line drawn from north to south through the Atlantic Ocean. This line was known as the Line of Demarcation. All newly discovered lands east of that line would be Portugal's. All such lands west of that line would be Spain's.

In 1494, the Portuguese persuaded the Spanish to move the line a few degrees farther west. Their agreement of 1494 was called the Treaty of Tordesillas (tor-duh-SEE-yahs). Explorers later found that the line cut across South America near the mouth of the Amazon River. Since the mouth of the Amazon lay east of the line, Portugal claimed that river and the lands around it. Here lay Portugal's only share of the Americas.

In 1500, a second event strengthened Portugal's claims. A Portuguese sea captain named Pedro Alvares Cabral explored the forest along the mouth of the Amazon River. Cabral's men cut down a tree and found its wood was as red as a glowing coal from a charcoal brazier. They called it "brazil" wood from the Portuguese word for a brazier—hence the name of the country that Portugal later colonized.

Magellan's crew rounded the globe.

In 1519, a Portuguese nobleman named Ferdinand Magellan (muh-JEHL-uhn) decided he could reach Asia by sailing around the southern tip of the new continent. The king of Spain agreed to pay for the voyage. He gave Magellan five old ships that were barely seaworthy.

With 230 men aboard, Magellan's ships sailed in September 1519. For three years, nothing was heard from them, and they were given up for lost. Then, in September 1522, a lone ship with tattered sails limped into a harbor in Spain. The 18 men who staggered ashore were the only survivors of Magellan's crew. All the others had died of hunger, cold, disease, or shipwreck.

As planned, Magellan had crossed the Atlantic and led his fleet south along the South American coast. One ship had capsized in a storm. The crew of another had mutinied. Three ships remained. In August 1520, Magellan reached a strait near the southern tip of South America. Vicious winds and jagged rocks made passage difficult. Somehow, after 38 days of struggling, the three ships reached the other side safely. This strait is now called the Strait of Magellan.

Magellan explored the western coast of South America. Then he headed out into the Pacific Ocean in search of Asia. Little did he realize that the Pacific was almost three times wider than the Atlantic. (It is 9,300 miles from Panama to the Philippine islands.) After three months, the sailors were so short of food that they ate rats, leather, and sawdust. Many died of hunger or of diseases brought on by malnutrition.

Finally, they reached the Philippines. Here was Asia at last. Unfortunately, Magellan joined in a war between local groups. He was killed by a poisoned arrow. One of the Spanish ships was destroyed there too.

The remaining crew members set out for home in the last two ships. One was captured by the Portuguese while sailing toward India. That left only one ship and a sickly crew to sail home around Africa.

In 1522, as the survivors recounted their three-year adventure, it became clear what they had achieved. They had sailed around the world. They had proved that the Americas were separate continents that lay thousands of miles from Asia. Perhaps most important, they had learned that the world was much larger than any European had thought.

To the Europeans, this world seemed ready to be conquered by ambitious men. Renaissance sea captains had demonstrated in their own way that "man can do anything if he will." Spaniards made themselves rulers of the lands once held by the Aztecs and the Incas. First Spain and later Portugal, France, and England built great colonial empires in the Americas.

Worldwide contact brought hazards and benefits.

In the early 1500's, for the first time in history, all the continents around the Atlantic came in regular contact with one another. Sea lanes now connected Europe, Africa, North America, and South America. This development brought change on both sides of the Atlantic. In Europe, the changes were generally welcomed. For the peoples of the Americas and later the people of Africa, life was brutally disrupted.

Epidemics Before the Spanish came, the deadly germs of smallpox, measles, and influenza were unknown in the Americas. The Indians did not have the immunities that Europeans had developed through long contact with those diseases. Columbus's voyages ended the Americas' isolation. Suddenly, Indians were exposed to germs carried by European explorers and colonizers.

Deadly epidemics swept over the Caribbean islands. Smallpox wiped out whole villages in a matter of months. Hispaniola had an estimated population of 250,000 Indians in 1492. Twenty years later, the population had fallen to 60,000. Just 50 years after that, Spaniards on Hispaniola counted only 500 Indians. Smallpox spread to Mexico where it helped destroy the Aztec empire. In the first century of Spanish rule (1500–1600), Indians in Central and South America sickened and died by the millions. By 1650, the population of central Mexico had declined by 85 percent.

The impact of corn and potatoes European ships also carried a great number of beneficial goods across the Atlantic. Before Columbus's voyages, people in the Americas had never seen horses, cows, chickens, pigs, sheep, goats, donkeys, or oxen. In the 1500's, these farm animals came to the Americas with European settlers.

Spanish colonists also brought a wide variety of new plants to the Americas, including wheat, barley, rye, oats, rice, oranges, apples, bananas, apricots, peaches, pears, coffee, sugarcane, and olive trees.

Crossing the Atlantic in the other direction were plants that Europeans, Asians, and Africans had never before used. Among those plants were corn (or maize), manioc (or tapioca), potatoes, tomatoes, kidney beans, lima beans, squash, avocados, pineapples, melon, tobacco, quinine, and cacao (for chocolate).

In time, the potato—a staple of the Inca diet—was transported in European ships to almost every part of the Eastern Hemisphere. Both in Asia and in Africa, it became a tremendously important food. In Europe, crops of potatoes and corn yielded more calories per acre than the traditional crops of wheat, barley, or rye.

This revolution in the world's food supply eventually enriched the diets of people the world over. History books often dwell too much on the rise and fall of empires. The planting of the first white potato in Ireland and the first sweet potato in China probably changed more lives than the deeds of a hundred kings.

The slave trade began in the 1500's.

The settlement of the Americas affected Africa in an unexpected way. Ever since the time of Prince Henry the Navigator, trade between Europeans and Africans had been increasing. In western Africa, the powerful kings who ruled the forest kingdoms controlled trade with the Europeans for a time. The African rulers refused to allow Europeans to travel inland. Instead, the Portuguese traders paid rent to the Africans for small posts near the coast.

To maximize their profits, slave traders loaded their ships with as many captives as possible. The diagram below shows how a ship was filled. Under such inhuman conditions, many people died during the voyage.

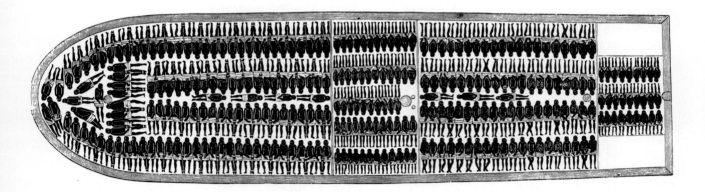

Nonetheless, European influence had far-reaching effects. Some African rulers traded for guns, which they used to expand their power over their neighbors. In this way, kingdoms arose that depended on a steady supply of guns and gunpowder from Europe. In exchange, more and more European traders wanted slaves. The effects of the slave trade were devastating to some African societies.

In 1441, while exploring the West African coast for Prince Henry the Navigator, a sea captain returned to Portugal with 12 slaves. The unfortunate Africans were readily sold to Portuguese nobles for use on their estates. This was the beginning of the Atlantic slave trade.

The growth of the slave trade was linked closely to the growth of European colonies in the Americas. Europeans began gold mines, silver mines, and plantations to raise sugar and other crops. Who was to work on these enterprises? European immigrants were too proud and too few to do the heavy work themselves. After the great epidemics, there were not enough Indian workers either. The solution seemed to be captives from Africa.

Ships with chained men and women aboard were soon a regular sight in the harbors of Cuba, Hispaniola, and the Bahamas during the 1500's. By 1540, about 10,000 Africans each year became slaves in the Americas. The slave trade peaked in the 1700's. In that century, between 6 and 7 million Africans were shipped to the Americas as slaves. European trade in African slaves continued for 400 years before it finally came to an end in Brazil in 1870.

The human cost of the slave trade was terrible. Besides the approximately 10 million Africans who reached the slave markets, millions of others died in the hands of their captors.

Usually, a person captured for the slave trade was first made prisoner by other Africans. Some powerful African groups made a business of raiding inland villages and marching their captives to the coast for trade. The march was brutal, and many died along the way. At trading stations along the coast, the survivors were sold to European sea captains for rum, guns, and gunpowder. Many more captives died in the crowded, stinking holds of the slave ships. Modern historians estimate that for every two Africans sold in the Americas, at least one died on the way.

Europe's power touched many lands.

The Age of Exploration marks the beginning of a period when Europe dominated much of the world. That period lasted more than 400 years, from the 1500's to the 1900's.

The people of Europe had gained political mastery over two huge continents, North and South America. Europeans were also the undisputed masters of the ocean routes across the Atlantic. Africa, the Americas, and Europe were now bound together by new economic and political ties. Until the mid-1900's, Europe controlled those ties for its own advantage.

Section Review 4

Define: caravel
Identify: (a) Columbus, (b) Henry the Navigator, (c) Dias, (d) Da Gama, (e) Vespucci, (f) Balboa, (g) Line of Demarcation, (h) Magellan
Answer
1. What is the link between Marco Polo and Columbus?
2. (a) Describe the route of trade goods from Asia to Europe in the late Middle Ages. (b) Why did the monarchs of France, Spain, Portugal, and England want to find new routes to Asia?
3. What technological improvements made long sea voyages possible in the 1400's?
4. (a) What was the goal of Prince Henry the Navigator? (b) Who achieved that goal?
5. (a) What was Columbus's goal in 1492? (b) Why did later voyages disappoint him?
6. What two events enabled Portugal to claim Brazil?
7. What was the significance of Ferdinand Magellan's voyage?
8. (a) What were the major results of exploration and colonization for Europe? (b) What changes took place in the Americas as a result of European exploration and settlement?
9. (a) How did the African slave trade begin? (b) Why did the slave trade increase with the growth of European colonies in the Americas?

Critical Thinking
10. How did Columbus exemplify the spirit of the Renaissance?

341

Summary

1. The Renaissance began in northern Italy. Northern Italy was a highly urban region. Merchants dominated the cities and competed as patrons of the arts. Painting and poetry changed greatly owing to the work of early Renaissance artists. Some of the characteristics of the Renaissance were a celebration of the individual, a love of classical learning, and an enjoyment of worldly pleasures.

2. Florence led the way in arts. During the 1400's, or Quattrocento, Florence was a wealthy city with a thriving textile industry and a strong banking business. Florence was under the control of the Medici family for most of the 1400's, although the city continued to call itself a republic. Such artists as Ghiberti, Brunelleschi, Donatello, and Masaccio beautified the city with their work. After the death of Lorenzo de Medici, while Florence was in a period of turmoil, Machiavelli wrote a book of advice to rulers called *The Prince*.

3. Three artistic giants ruled the Renaissance. Leonardo da Vinci, Raphael Santi, and Michelangelo Buonarroti were the leading artists of the High Renaissance. Pope Julius II commissioned Michelangelo and Raphael to glorify the Vatican.

4. Explorers opened new sea routes. During the late 1400's, rulers of many European nations were eager to find new trade routes to Asia. Advances in shipbuilding and navigation made possible long ocean voyages. The Portuguese explored the African coast and reached India by sailing around Africa. In 1492, Columbus reached the Americas while trying to sail to Asia across the Atlantic Ocean. Other explorers quickly followed him. The pope divided the newly discovered lands between Spain and Portugal. In 1519, Magellan began a voyage around the world that was completed by some of his crew in 1522. Huge numbers of Indians died from diseases brought by the Europeans. New food crops were introduced to both the Americas and Europe. The slave trade began in the 1500's and grew with the demand for slaves in the Americas.

Reviewing the Facts

1. Define the following terms:
   a. vernacular   b. humanist   c. caravel
2. Explain the importance of each of the following names, dates, places, or terms:
   a. Leonardo da Vinci   f. Isabella d'Este
   b. Giotto   g. Quattrocento
   c. Dante   h. Florence
   d. Petrarch   i. Cosimo de Medici
   e. *The Courtier*   j. Lorenzo de Medici

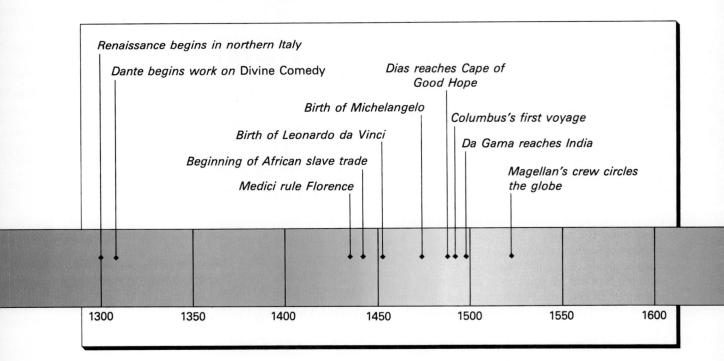

Renaissance begins in northern Italy

Dante begins work on Divine Comedy

Dias reaches Cape of Good Hope

Birth of Michelangelo

Birth of Leonardo da Vinci

Columbus's first voyage

Beginning of African slave trade

Da Gama reaches India

Medici rule Florence

Magellan's crew circles the globe

| 1300 | 1350 | 1400 | 1450 | 1500 | 1550 | 1600 |

k. Donatello
l. Masaccio
m. *The Prince*
n. Sistine Chapel
o. Raphael
p. Henry the Navigator
q. 1488
r. 1492
s. Amerigo Vespucci
t. Line of Demarcation
u. Magellan

3. (a) What was the Renaissance? (b) Where did it begin?
4. Briefly describe one work created by each of the following artists. (a) Giotto (b) Donatello (c) Dante (d) Masaccio
5. How did the works of Michelangelo reflect the spirit of the Renaissance?
6. How did the Renaissance emphasis on the individual affect each of the following groups? (a) Italian merchants (b) artists and writers (c) explorers
7. (a) Why were many European monarchs eager to find new trade routes to Asia in the 1400's? (b) Describe the two different routes explorers eventually found.
8. (a) What was Columbus's great achievement? (b) What was his mistake? (c) Why were the Americas named for Amerigo Vespucci?
9. How did Brazil become a Portuguese possession?
10. (a) What was Magellan's goal? (b) What did his voyage prove?
11. What changes did European exploration and settlement bring to each of the following continents? (a) Europe (b) the Americas (c) Africa

Thinking about History

1. The men and women of the Renaissance strove for a rebirth of the classical culture of Greece and Rome. Compare the sculpture and architecture of the Renaissance to those of the Classical Age.
2. Compare the golden age of Florence to the golden age of Athens. In your answer, include information on government, public works, and the arts.
3. Why does Renaissance art appeal to people today?
4. (a) What rulers have you studied who would fit Machiavelli's definition of a good leader? (b) Choose one such leader and tell which of his or her actions Machiavelli would have praised.
5. Columbus discovered the Americas by mistake and never acknowledged that he had not reached Asia. Does he deserve his status as a great hero? Why or why not?

Writing and Speaking about History

1. Write a thesis statement that explains why the Renaissance developed in northern Italy. Then prepare an outline for an essay based on your thesis. Write the introductory and concluding paragraphs of your essay. (See Research Skills Handbook, page 318.)
2. Suppose the artists and literary people mentioned in this chapter are competing for an international artist-of-year award. Prepare a nominating speech for the artist you feel is most deserving.

Practicing Skills

1. Review the timeline on page 342. (a) List the four voyages of exploration and their dates. (b) What are the dates for the births of two Renaissance artists? (c) About how many years passed between the start of the Renaissance and the birth of these artists?
2. In Columbus's time, sailors knew how to measure latitude but not longitude. On a world map that has longitude and latitude lines, find the approximate longitude and latitude of India and the West Indies. Why did Columbus think the West Indies were islands near India?
3. The Renaissance saw the triumph of the individual in various fields of activity. How does the art in this chapter reflect this statement?

Investigating History

1. The history of the city-states of Renaissance Italy is filled with colorful characters and devious villains. Prepare a report on one of the following topics: (a) Bartolomeo Colleoni, (b) Francesco Sforza, (c) the Borgia family, (d) Francesco Foscari.
2. Using books from the library, find several examples of the works of one of the following artists: (a) Piero della Francesca, (b) Botticelli, (c) Fra Angelico, (d) Fra Lippo Lippi, (e) Titian, (f) Tintoretto. Write a brief account of the artist's life and significance. Include a description of the artist's style.

Decision Making in History

Assume that you are Christopher Columbus evaluating the possibility of sailing west to the Spice Islands. What arguments could be made both for and against the venture? Given the context of the times, what would your decision have been?

The Reformation and the Scientific Revolution

This painting is a symbolic picture of Luther and his supporters. Using a giant quill, they are writing their demands for religious reform on the door of All Saints Church in the German town of Wittenberg.

1. **Martin Luther began a religious revolt.**

2. **Protestantism spread in northern Europe.**

3. **The Catholic Church made changes.**

4. **Scientists challenged old assumptions.**

Sweat glistened on the brow of a black-robed friar, Martin Luther. Torches lit the great hall in which he stood. Jammed together, craning their necks to see Luther, were the princes and bishops of Germany. They were members of the Imperial Diet (or assembly) of the Holy Roman Empire. At the head of the diet was the newly elected Emperor Charles V. The 21-year-old emperor stared grimly from his throne at the 37-year-old friar.

It was early evening on April 18, 1521. The setting was the town of Worms (vawrms) in Germany. Though they did not know it, the dignitaries who packed the hall were witnesses to a great turning point in European history.

About 20 books were stacked on a table near Luther. Europeans from London to Rome knew of the radical ideas these books contained. In them, Luther accused bishops, archbishops, and the pope of straying dangerously far from the teachings of Jesus. Throughout Germany, Luther's books sold out as fast as they were printed. The German people regarded Luther as a national hero. The Church considered him a dangerous heretic.

At the Diet of Worms, Luther and his ideas were on trial. A Church official named Eck pointed at the stack of books. Were these Luther's work? he asked. "Yes," said Luther. Would Luther take back the heretical ideas in these books? Luther's reply rang through the hall:

> Unless I am convinced by Scripture and plain reason . . . my conscience is captive to the Word of God. I cannot and I will not recant [take back] anything, for to go against conscience is neither right nor safe. Here I stand. I cannot do otherwise. God help me. Amen.

Luther's defiant words led to a revolutionary change in the Christian religion. Many Europeans stopped accepting the pope as the head of a united Church. In this chapter, you will read about the split between the Catholic Church and a new group of Christians called Protestants.

Religious leaders such as Martin Luther were not the only ones to challenge the Catholic Church's authority in the 1500's and 1600's. Scientific thinkers too began to question traditional ideas. This challenge led to a new way of thinking called the scientific revolution.

Comparing these two revolutions, we could say that Protestantism changed the way many Christians thought of God, heaven, and the soul. The scientific revolution changed the way Europeans thought about Earth and the universe.

Martin Luther began a religious revolt. 1

Martin Luther's dramatic stand at Worms grew out of a long history of protest within the Church. Leaders such as Wycliffe (page 242) and Hus (page 242) were part of that history. By 1500, many forces had weakened the power of the Catholic Church. The most important of these forces were the new ideas of the Renaissance and the new technology of the printing press. The greatest

changes took place between 1517 and 1555. Thus, the new religious movement began during the last years of the High Renaissance in Italy.

The Catholic Church faced problems.

The Renaissance popes who ruled Rome from 1447 to 1534 patronized the arts, collected ancient manuscripts, and vigorously defended the Papal States from French and Italian armies. These worldly concerns left the popes little time for spiritual duties. It was a serious failing. One Renaissance pope, Pius II (1458–1464), wrote:

> People say that we live for pleasure, gather wealth, bear ourselves arrogantly, ride on fat mules and handsome palfreys [horses] . . . And there is some truth in their words: many among the cardinals and other officials of our court do lead this kind of life. If the truth be confessed, the luxury and pomp of our court is too great.

There were abuses among the lower clergy as well. Many priests and monks were so poorly educated that they could scarcely read. Some village priests had semi-official wives. How could such a pope as Alexander VI (1492–1503) condemn them? He publicly acknowledged his own five children, born before he became pope.

Many people were devoutly religious.

People had come to expect higher standards of conduct from priests and church leaders. During the 1400's and early 1500's, groups of Christians throughout Europe set increasingly strict standards for their own lives. In the Netherlands, for example, a group called the Brethren of the Common Life attracted many men and women. They lived very simply while helping the poor, the hungry, and the sick. Such groups spread to Germany, France, and Italy.

Likewise, Europeans in the 1500's expected a higher level of learning from priests. In the Middle Ages, when few people were literate, a priest who could read even a little was respected. During the Renaissance, however, learning spread more widely in society. By 1500, well-educated people sneered at the priest who was a poor reader.

Two groups of people led the demand for reform and for higher standards of religion. One group included popular religious leaders who roused the people with fiery sermons. The other group consisted of Renaissance writers who became known as Christian humanists.

Savonarola An Italian friar named Girolamo Savonarola (jih-**ROHL**-uh-moh SAV-uh-nuh-**ROH**-luh) came to Florence to preach in 1490. In eloquent sermons, he called for reform of the Church. Florentines flocked to hear him. In 1494, he helped overthrow Florence's ruler, Piero de Medici. From 1494 until 1498, Savonarola virtually controlled Florence.

In 1497, Savonarola demanded that the people of Florence gather their personal "vanities" and burn them in a giant bonfire. People threw wigs, velvet gowns, and even rare manuscripts and paintings into the flames. Only a year later, however, Florentines turned against Savonarola. Before a jeering mob, a hangman executed him.

The case of Savonarola showed how easily a leader could turn people's religious passions in revolutionary directions. Yet more moderate voices also called for change. Popular books by humanist authors called attention to corruption in the Church and the need for reform.

Erasmus and More Around 1475, Renaissance ideas began to spread beyond Italy to northern Europe. This development is often called the Renaissance of the North. Scholars in northern Europe valued the Greek and Roman classics just as much as Italian humanists did. However, northern scholars showed more interest in religion. Thus, the leaders of the northern Renaissance are often called Christian humanists.

The best known of the Christian humanists were Thomas More of England and Desiderius Erasmus (DEZ-uh-**DAIR**-ee-uhs ih-**RAZ**-muhs) of Holland. The two were close friends.

Born in Rotterdam, Erasmus (1466–1536) was honored by princes, kings, and cardinals for his brilliant writings. In 1509, while he was a guest in More's house, Erasmus wrote his most famous work, *In Praise of Folly*. This short book poked fun at greedy merchants, heartsick lovers, quarrelsome scholars, and pompous priests. Erasmus's most stinging barbs were aimed at the clergy.

Voice from the Past · *Gold and Silver in Utopia*

In *Utopia*, Sir Thomas More described a society in which everyone had enough food, clothing, and possessions for a comfortable life. No one had more than necessary or sought wealth for its own sake.

Silver and gold get no more respect from anyone than their intrinsic value deserves—which is obviously far less than that of iron . . . [The author then describes the Utopians' way of making sure that people do not prize precious metals or jewels too much.] According to this system, plates and drinking vessels, though beautifully designed, are made of quite cheap stuff like glass or earthenware. But silver and gold are the normal materials . . . for the humblest items of household equipment, such as chamber-pots. They also use chains of solid gold to immobilize slaves. And anyone who commits a really shameful crime is forced to go about with gold rings on his ears and fingers, a gold necklace round his neck, and a crown of gold on his head . . .

It's much the same with jewels . . . If they happen to come across one, they pick it up and polish it for some toddler to wear. At first, children are terribly proud of such jewelry—until they are old enough to notice that it's only worn in the nursery. Then . . . they give it up.

1. What reasons do you think a Utopian could give for thinking that iron was more valuable than gold or silver?
2. How did the Utopians use psychological methods to keep people from valuing gold and jewels?
3. *Utopia* is a satire, a form of literature that makes fun of foolishness or wickedness. What forms of foolishness or wickedness in European society is More mocking in this passage?

glass

This drawing of a printing shop in the 1500's shows the steps in the printing process. At the left, handwritten copy is taped to the wall. Workers take letters from type cases to make up a page. Another person (center, rear) inks a page of type that has been set. At the right, a man pulls the handle of the press that prints the sheets. A young apprentice (front) carries away the freshly printed pages to dry.

For example, he wrote, "One of their chief beliefs is that to be illiterate is to be of a high state of sanctity [holiness], and so they make sure they are not able to read."

How might a truly good society be organized? In 1516, Thomas More tried to answer this question in a book called *Utopia*. It told about a peace-loving people who lived in the imaginary land of Utopia, a Greek word meaning "nowhere." Utopia was a nearly perfect society based on reason and mercy. Greed, corruption, war, and crime had been weeded out.

Thousands of Europeans read the works of More and Erasmus. The reason that these authors could command such a wide audience was a remarkable technological breakthrough—the printing press.

The printing press spread new ideas.

The impact of the printing press on European society was revolutionary. It might be compared to the combined impact of television and the computer in recent times.

The first Europeans to use movable type were some printers in Mainz (mynts), Germany, between 1440 and 1450. The most famous of them was Johann Gutenberg (GOOT-uhn-burg), who printed a Bible around 1455. This Bible was the first full-size book printed with movable type.

Printing spread quickly to other cities in Europe. Print shops opened in Rome (1467), Venice (1469), and Paris (1470). By 1500, presses in about 250 cities had printed between 9 and 10 million books. For the first time, books were cheap enough that many Europeans could buy them.

How did printing prepare the way for a religious revolution? First, many writers criticized the corruption of the Renaissance popes. Erasmus, for example, wrote a savage satire about Pope Julius II.

Second, printed books on religion encouraged popular piety. Many printed books were illustrated with woodcuts and engravings. In Germany, an artist named Albrecht Dürer (DYOOR-uhr) drew Jesus and other biblical figures as if they lived in a German town. His beautiful pictures deeply stirred people's religious feelings.

Third, the printing press made the Bible available to all Christians who could read. When books were scarce, most Christians had depended completely on priests to interpret the Bible. After the Bible was printed, people could read it for themselves. Some, like Luther, interpreted what they read differently from the Church.

Footnote to History

Europeans had already learned from the Arabs how to make paper from old, shredded rags. Rag paper was much cheaper than parchment (made from sheepskin) or vellum (made from calfskin). Before the use of paper, a bookmaker had needed about 25 sheepskins to make a 200-page book.

Fourth, with the printing press, new ideas spread more quickly than ever before. Remember the stack of books for which Luther stood trial at the Diet of Worms. The ideas in them were similar to earlier writings of John Wycliffe and John Huss. Luther's books caused a revolution partly because so many people read them in a short time. With the printing press to spread a writer's ideas, the pen could indeed be mightier than the sword.

Luther challenged the Church.

All his life (1483–1546), Martin Luther wished only to be an obedient, God-fearing Christian. He did not set out to lead a religious revolution. What led this strongly religious man to defy the pope and Church traditions?

Luther's background The son of a copper miner, Luther was born in a tiny town in the German region of Saxony. As a child, he felt guilty and fearful much of the time. His father's bursts of anger terrified him. The stern teachings of local priests deeply impressed Luther.

When Luther was 21, he narrowly escaped death. During a storm, a great bolt of lightning struck near him, knocking him down. Afraid for his life, Luther cried, "Saint Anne, help me! I will become a monk." Luther's father, who wanted his son to be a lawyer, was furious.

As a monk, Luther tried desperately to win peace of mind. He confessed his sins at great length. He fasted regularly. He slept without a blanket until he nearly froze. Nevertheless, he still felt sinful, lost, and rejected by God.

Sometime between 1512 and 1515, Luther was alone in his study puzzling over a phrase in the Bible: "The just shall live by faith." In a flash, Luther thought he understood. Praying and fasting were not the keys to salvation. Instead, a strong faith in God was all that mattered. He wrote later, "Thereupon I felt myself to be reborn and to have gone through open doors into paradise."

The 95 theses Martin Luther might have lived quietly after finding peace. In 1517, however, something occurred that made him take a public stand. Like many other citizens of Wittenberg, he was offended by the deeds of a friar named Johann Tetzel. Tetzel was raising money in nearby towns to rebuild St. Peter's Cathedral in Rome by selling letters of indulgence.

This portrait of Martin Luther, drawn by one of his friends, shows him thoughtful and serious.

Indulgences were pardons from the Church for certain sins. Strictly speaking, an indulgence could free a sinner only from the penance a priest had set, such as saying a certain number of prayers. The sinner would still have to pay the penalty set by God. Unfortunately, Tetzel was overeager to collect money. He gave people the impression that they could buy their way into heaven.

Luther was deeply troubled by Tetzel's tactics. On October 31, 1517, he took up his pen and wrote 95 theses (formal statements) attacking the "pardon-merchants." He posted his theses on the door of the castle church in Wittenberg and invited fellow scholars to debate him. Excited by the challenge, someone copied Luther's words and took them to a printer. Within six months, Luther's name was known all over Germany. The religious crisis later known as the Reformation had begun.

The pope tried to silence Luther.

Soon Luther went far beyond criticizing indulgences. He wanted a full reform of the Church. Luther's teachings rested on three main ideas:

1. *Salvation by faith alone* In Luther's view, people could not win salvation by their own efforts—what the Catholic Church called "good works." Faith in God was the only way to salvation.
2. *The Bible as the only authority for Christian life* All Church teachings, said Luther, should be clearly based on the words of the Bible. The pope, he said, was a false authority. (The Catholic Church accepted both the Bible and Church traditions as authorities.)
3. *The priesthood of all believers* According to Luther, each person had a relationship with God and all people with faith were equal. Therefore, people did not need priests to interpret the Bible.

On June 15, 1520, Pope Leo X issued a bull (an official statement) threatening Luther with excommunication unless he recanted. Luther did not take back a word. Instead, his students at Wittenberg gathered around a bonfire and cheered as he threw the bull into the flames. Leo answered by excommunicating Luther.

Charles V opposed Luther.

The pope seemed powerless to touch Luther. However, the young Holy Roman Emperor, Charles V, had greater authority in Germany. We have seen how Charles summoned Luther to Worms in 1521 to stand trial. Charles promised Luther safety from arrest while at Worms. Would Luther back down at last? As you have read, he did not.

Luther made his famous speech on Thursday, April 18. The next day, Charles replied: "A single friar who goes counter to all Christianity for a thousand years must be wrong . . . I will proceed against him as a notorious heretic." On May 26, Charles issued an imperial order, the Edict of Worms. It declared Luther an outlaw and heretic. According to this edict, no one in the empire was to give Luther food or shelter. All his books were to be burned. Legally, there was no place in Germany for Luther to hide.

However, Luther lived comfortably in Germany for almost 25 years after his trial at Worms. Charles V, the most powerful ruler in Europe, could neither capture Luther nor stamp out his ideas. What accounts for this extraordinary failure?

First, Charles's huge empire was simply too much for him to govern effectively. Charles belonged to a family called the Hapsburgs, who had risen to power in Austria. After the 1400's, most Holy Roman emperors were chosen from the Hapsburg family. By a series of careful marriages, the Hapsburgs won more and more lands. In 1521, their holdings included not only Austria and lands in Germany but also the Netherlands, parts of Italy, Spain, and Spain's empire in the Americas.

Charles had another problem. The German people, although divided politically, had a strong national spirit, and they resented sending German money to Rome. Luther's attacks on the pope's "greed" were popular with many Germans. An Italian churchman visiting Germany in 1521 wrote, "Nine tenths of the people are shouting 'Luther!' And the other tenth shouts 'Down with Rome!'"

Luther's ideas spread in Germany.

For almost a year after the Diet of Worms, Luther shut himself away in a castle owned by Prince Frederick the Wise of Saxony. While there, Luther translated the New Testament into German. Now even Germans who did not know Latin could read the Bible.

Luther returned to Wittenberg in 1522. There he discovered that many of his ideas were already being put into practice. Town priests had given up their colorful robes. They dressed in ordinary clothes and called themselves ministers. They led services in German instead of in Latin. Some ministers had married, because Luther taught that the clergy should be free to wed.

Luther and his followers had taken the long step from wanting reform within the Catholic Church to becoming a separate religious group. They became known as Lutherans.

The revolt against the papacy became much broader. In 1524, German peasants, excited by reformers' talk of Christian freedom, demanded an end to their economic and political bondage. Serfdom, they cried, must be abolished. Bands

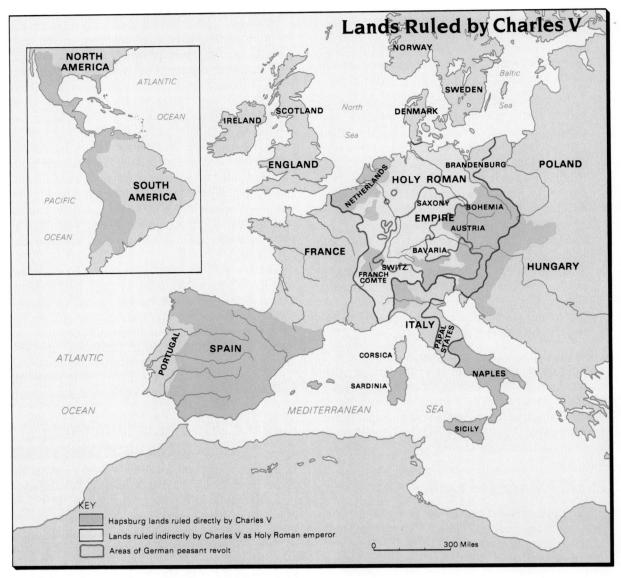

Lands Ruled by Charles V

KEY

- Hapsburg lands ruled directly by Charles V
- Lands ruled indirectly by Charles V as Holy Roman emperor
- Areas of German peasant revolt

0   300 Miles

Map Study

On what three continents did Charles V control lands? Name three European areas of which Charles was the ruler.

of angry peasants went about the countryside raiding monasteries, pillaging, and burning.

Luther was horrified by the peasants' revolt. He insisted that he wanted only peaceful reform, not violence and lawlessness. To the German princes, he wrote a savage letter urging them to show the peasants no mercy.

With brutal thoroughness, the princes' armies crushed the peasant revolt of 1524–1525. Perhaps 100,000 people were massacred. The lower classes

felt betrayed by Luther, and many turned away from his religious leadership.

After 1525, the success of Lutheranism depended increasingly on the support of German princes. Some princes liked Luther's ideas for selfish reasons. They saw his teachings as a good excuse to seize Church property. Other princes, however, genuinely shared Luther's beliefs.

In 1529, princes loyal to the pope agreed to join forces against Luther's ideas. Princes who supported Luther signed a protest against that agreement. From that time on, these protesting princes came to be known as Protestants.

Eventually, the term *Protestant* was used for many Christians who turned away from the papacy and the Catholic Church. Their movement was commonly known as the Protestant Reformation.

Section Review 1

Define: (a) heretic, (b) excommunicate, (c) indulgence, (d) minister
Identify: (a) Martin Luther, (b) Diet of Worms, (c) Savonarola, (d) Erasmus, (e) Thomas More, (f) *Utopia*, (g) Gutenberg (h) Charles V, (i) Hapsburg family
Answer:
1. What criticisms were made of many popes and lower clergy during the 1400's and 1500's?
2. Identify four ways in which the printing press prepared the way for the Reformation.
3. (a) What events led Luther to take a stand against the Church? (b) Summarize his three main ideas.
4. (a) What was the Edict of Worms? (b) Why was it unsuccessful?
5. (a) To whom was the term *Protestant* first applied? (b) What broader meaning did the term acquire?

Critical Thinking
6. Politics and religion were closely intertwined in the 1500's. How did each of the following political factors affect the spread of Luther's ideas? (a) the size of the Holy Roman Empire (b) German nationalism (c) the ambition of the German princes
7. Would you define Luther as a revolutionary? Why or why not?

Protestantism spread in northern Europe. 2

Martin Luther continued to write pamphlets and deliver sermons until his death in 1546. As time passed, however, the Protestant Reformation depended less and less on his leadership. Other reformers were also clamoring for change. Among them were John Calvin of France and John Knox of Scotland. Soon the Catholic Church was being challenged in many parts of Europe, especially in England.

Henry VIII *broke with the pope.*

When Henry VIII became king of England in 1509, he was 18 years old. He was the son of the "new monarch" Henry VII (page 248). Young Henry was handsome, strong, and intelligent. He loved tennis, classical literature, music, and food.

In religion, Henry VIII was a devout Catholic. He detested Luther. In 1521, Henry wrote a pamphlet calling Luther "a great limb of the Devil" and many other such names. Impressed by Henry's loyalty, the pope gave him a special title, "Defender of the Faith."

Yet political needs soon proved more important to Henry than religious loyalty. Henry was only the second king of the Tudor family, and he was anxious about the future of his line. Henry and his wife, Catherine of Aragon, had only one child—a daughter named Mary, born in 1516. Their five other babies, including three boys, had died in infancy. Henry feared that another civil war like the Wars of the Roses (page 248) would occur unless he had a male child to inherit his crown.

By 1527, Henry was convinced that Catherine would have no more children. He wanted a new queen to give him a son. He had already picked her out: a dark-eyed 20-year-old named Anne Boleyn (boo-**LIHN**).

How could Henry legally end his marriage to Catherine? Church law did not allow divorce, but the pope might set aside Henry's marriage by saying that it had never been legal in the first place. Such matters were often arranged.

In 1527, the king asked the pope to end the marriage. Unfortunately, 1527 was a very bad year to ask the pope for a favor. Pope Clement VII had taken the losing side in a war against Holy Roman Emperor Charles V. Charles's armies swept into Rome in 1527 and held the pope prisoner in the Vatican. Henry's unwanted wife, Catherine of Aragon, was the emperor's aunt. Charles would not allow his prisoner, the pope, to end his aunt's marriage. The pope turned down Henry's request.

Henry VIII, the second Tudor king of England, broke with the Roman Catholic Church in 1534.

The king sought Parliament's help.

Henry soon looked for more radical answers to his marriage problem. In 1529, he called Parliament and asked it to pass a group of laws that stripped away the pope's power in England. This Parliament is known as the Reformation Parliament. It met whenever the king summoned it for seven years (1529–1536).

Parliament soon legalized Henry's divorce from Catherine. In January 1533, Henry married Anne. Parliament passed a law stating that the king was not responsible "to any foreign princes or potentates of the world." (In other words, the pope was not to interfere with the king's divorce and remarriage.)

After being crowned queen in May, Anne gave birth to Henry's child in September. Imagine the king's frustration when he learned that the child was a girl. (Little did he realize that this daughter, Elizabeth, would be the greatest Tudor monarch of all.)

In 1534, Henry's break with the pope was made complete when Parliament voted to approve the Act of Supremacy. This act declared, "The king's majesty justly and rightly is and ought to be . . . the only supreme head in earth of the Church of England."

The English king, not the Roman pope, was now the official head of England's Church. Henceforth the king's agents collected all Church moneys. All priests and bishops were subject to the king's appointment and approval. Thus began the church that is called the Church of England.

The acts of the Reformation Parliament strengthened both the king and Parliament itself. The king won control of the Church of England. At the same time, Parliament gained power. Never before had a ruler asked Parliament to act on such fundamental questions.

Henry VIII *enforced his changes.*

Only a few people in England proved more loyal to the pope than to the king. The most famous of them was Thomas More. He refused to take an oath supporting the Act of Supremacy. For this refusal, Henry VIII ordered More beheaded. At his execution, More forgave his executioner and asked spectators to pray for the king. He said, "I die the king's good servant, but God's first." His death shocked people all over Europe.

The closing of the monasteries Soon after making himself supreme head of the Church of England, Henry made another sweeping change in religion. He closed all English monasteries and seized their wealth and lands. The monasteries had owned almost one third of the land in England, so this act vastly increased royal power and enriched Henry's treasury.

To raise money, Henry sold much of the land he had seized to nobles and to members of England's rising middle class. Suddenly there were many English landowners who stood to lose property if England returned to the Catholic Church. This group formed a solid base of support for the Protestant Reformation in England.

In most other ways, Henry remained more Catholic than Protestant. He insisted that English priests make no changes in Catholic rituals and doctrines.

Henry's later marriages Meanwhile, Anne Boleyn had fallen rapidly out of favor with the king. Henry ordered her imprisoned in the Tower of London and later beheaded in 1536.

Within a month of Anne's death, Henry VIII married a third time. His new wife, Jane Seymour, lived just long enough to fulfill his dearest wish. On October 12, 1537, she bore a son, Edward. Then she died 12 days later.

Henry VIII married three more times. To win an alliance with Germany's Lutheran princes, he arranged to marry Anne of Cleves, a German princess he had never met. After only a few months, he had that marriage set aside. The king's fifth wife, Catherine Howard, was young and beautiful but foolish. She was executed on charges of adultery after less than a year as queen. In 1543, he married Catherine Parr. A mature woman, she loyally cared for Henry, who was now so fat and ill that he could hardly move, until his death in 1547.

Henry's children After Henry's death, all three of his children eventually inherited the throne. Edward VI was the first to rule. As he was a staunch Protestant, the Protestants gained power during his reign. Edward's half-sister Mary ruled England next. She was a Catholic who returned the English Church to the rule of the pope. England's next ruler was Anne Boleyn's red-headed daughter, Elizabeth. Elizabeth I returned her kingdom to Protestantism.

Women influenced the Reformation.

Mary and Elizabeth Tudor could force their religious ideas on their subjects because they were queens. However, many other women also played prominent roles in the Reformation.

Some women of the nobility protected Protestant leaders who lived and taught within their lands. In France, one of the most influential Protestants was Marguerite of Navarre, the sister of King Francis I. Besides protecting several Protestant preachers, she passed her Protestant ideals on to her descendants. Her grandson, Henry of Navarre, later became Henry IV of France.

Educated women wrote treatises on religious issues that were widely read. Margaret More, daughter of Sir Thomas More, was a recognized

Marguerite of Navarre, sister of France's king, protected French Protestants.

scholar. Likewise, Catherine Parr, the last wife of Henry VIII, wrote a book that discussed such questions as justification by faith.

Protestant ideas also spread widely among middle-class women. Protestantism appealed to the middle classes—both men and women—partly because preachers spoke in the vernacular, not in Latin. In addition, nationalist feelings against Rome were as strong among women as among men in Germany, England, and the Netherlands.

Women, like men, often suffered for their religious views. In the bitter struggles over religion, many women died for their beliefs.

Women's influence on the Protestant movement was greatest in the early years, between 1519 and 1580. As the Protestant religion became more firmly established, its organization became more formal. There were fewer opportunities for women to act as leaders. Women once again found themselves in the background.

Calvin formalized Protestant ideas.

The Church of England remained close to the Catholic Church in many of its doctrines and ceremonies. Meanwhile, other forms of Protestantism were developing elsewhere in Europe.

When Luther stood trial at Worms, John Calvin was a boy of 12 in Noyon (nwah-YOH), France. No one could have guessed that this shy, studious child would in some ways have even greater influence than Luther. Luther had sparked the religious revolution. A generation later, Calvin gave order to the new faith.

Calvin studied law and philosophy at the University of Paris. Early in the 1530's, he came under the influence of French followers of Luther. When King Francis I ordered these Protestants arrested, Calvin fled. Eventually, he made his way to Switzerland.

In 1536, Calvin published a book called the *Institutes of the Christian Religion*. This work set forth a systematic Protestant philosophy. The first edition of the *Institutes* was completely sold out in a year.

Calvin taught that men and women are by nature sinful. By God's grace, however, a very few people will be saved from sin. Calvin called these few the "elect." Because God is all-knowing, Calvin said, He has known since the beginning of time who will be saved. Calvin's doctrine is called **predestination**.

Calvin said that the duty of the elect is to rule society so as to glorify God. Therefore, he taught, the church should dominate the state. Calvin hoped for a **theocracy**, a government controlled by church leaders. This idea was a major difference between Calvinism and Lutheranism, for Luther preached obedience to earthly rulers. Calvin's ideas gave more support for revolt against an "ungodly" ruler, an idea that later influenced events in Scotland and several other countries.

Calvin did more than write about his ideas. He actually set up the kind of theocracy he had described in his book. In 1541, Protestants in the French-speaking city of Geneva, Switzerland, asked Calvin to lead their community. When Calvin arrived there in the 1540's, Geneva was a self-governing city of about 20,000 people.

To many Protestants, Geneva under Calvin's rule became a "city of saints." Calvin and his followers regulated the lives of everybody who lived in the city. Everyone in Geneva attended classes in religion. No one wore brightly colored clothing or played cards. No one could argue in defense of the pope. No one could visit a public inn after nine o'clock at night. For breaking such rules, a person might be imprisoned, excommunicated, or banished from the city. Moreover, in Protestant Geneva as in Catholic Rome, anyone who preached a different set of doctrines might be burned at the stake.

Knox led the Scottish Reformation.

Protestants from everywhere in Europe came to Geneva to see how a sober, purified city was organized. Among the admiring visitors was a preacher from Scotland named John Knox. When he returned to Scotland in 1559, Knox put Calvin's ideas on church organization to work in Scottish towns. Each community church was governed by a small group of laymen called elders or presbyters (PREHZ-buh-tuhrs). From this organization, followers of Knox became known as Presbyterians.

In 1567, Protestant nobles led by Knox overthrew the Catholic queen of Scotland, Mary Stuart, in a nearly bloodless revolt. They put her one-year-old son, James VI, on the throne. Real power, however, was in the hands of the Protestant nobles. They created a national church and made Calvinism Scotland's official religion.

Protestant churches spread widely.

Elsewhere in Europe, the Calvinist form of church organization was widely adopted by Swiss, French, and Dutch reformers. Except for Scotland, no other kingdom officially converted to Calvinist belief. However, as the map on page 355 shows, communities of Calvinist Protestants were to be found from England to Italy.

In Sweden, Norway, and Denmark, Lutheranism became the official religion. Denmark had ruled both Sweden and Norway until 1523. In that year, Sweden revolted against the Danish king. The leader of the Swedish independence movement, Gustavus Vasa, became Sweden's new king. He soon ended papal power in Sweden and seized Church lands. Norway remained under Danish control and became Lutheran when Denmark made Lutheranism the official religion of the country in 1536.

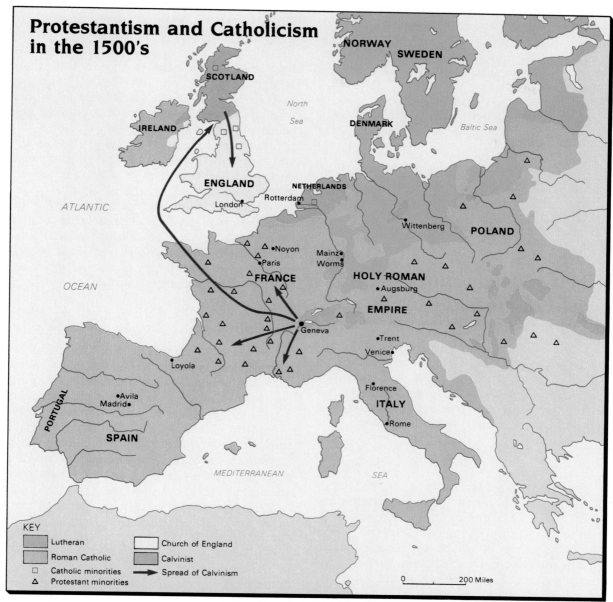

Protestantism and Catholicism in the 1500's

NORWAY
SWEDEN
SCOTLAND
IRELAND
North Sea
DENMARK
Baltic Sea
ENGLAND
NETHERLANDS
London
Rotterdam
ATLANTIC
Wittenberg
POLAND
OCEAN
•Noyon
Mainz•
•Paris
Worms
FRANCE
HOLY ROMAN
•Augsburg
EMPIRE
Geneva
•Trent
Venice•
Loyola
Florence•
•Avila
ITALY
Madrid•
•Rome
PORTUGAL
SPAIN
MEDITERRANEAN
SEA

KEY
Lutheran
Church of England
Roman Catholic
Calvinist
☐ Catholic minorities
➔ Spread of Calvinism
△ Protestant minorities
0 ___ 200 Miles

Map Study

Where was Protestantism stronger, in northern Europe or in southern Europe?
Where was the center of the Calvinist movement?

Section Review 2

Define: (a) elect, (b) predestination, (c) theocracy, (d) presbyters
Identify: (a) Henry VIII, (b) Catherine of Aragon, (c) Anne Boleyn, (d) Reformation Parliament, (e) Edward VI, (f) Mary Tudor, (g) Elizabeth I, (h) John Calvin, (i) John Knox

Answer:
1. Why did Henry VIII of England want to end his first marriage?
2. What part did Parliament play in the English Reformation?
3. (a) What changes did Henry make in the English Church? (b) What changes did each of his children make when they succeeded him?

4. (a) Briefly describe Calvin's idea of the elect and their place in society. (b) How were Calvin's political ideas different from Luther's?
5. How did Calvinism become the official religion of Scotland?
6. Where in Europe did Lutheranism become the official religion?

Critical Thinking

7. (a) What did Thomas More mean by his statement, "I die the king's good servant, but God's first"? (b) How does this statement show the dilemma that many people faced in the 1500's?

The Catholic Church made changes. 3

While Protestants won many followers, millions of Catholics held fast to their traditional beliefs. Catholics in the 1500's had their own religious reformers. One great champion of Catholic reform was Ignatius (ig-**NAY**-shus) of Loyola, later canonized as Saint Ignatius.

Ignatius began the Jesuits.

Born in 1491, Ignatius grew up in his father's castle in Loyola in eastern Spain. The great turning point in his life came in 1521 when he was in the Spanish army fighting the French. A cannonball shattered his right leg, leaving him an invalid for months. During his recovery, Ignatius thought about his past sinfulness and the events of the life of Jesus. His daily devotions seemed to cleanse his soul. In 1522, he began writing a book. Titled *Spiritual Exercises*, his book laid out a day-by-day plan of meditation, prayer, and study.

Over the next 18 years, Ignatius gathered a band of followers. Eventually, he won the support of Pope Paul III. In 1540, the pope made Ignatius's company a new monastic order called the Society of Jesus. Those who later joined the order were commonly called Jesuits (**JEHZ**-uh-wuhts).

What made the Jesuits unique was their emphasis on absolute discipline and obedience. They were like a spiritual army. These disciplined Catholics were willing to go anywhere in the world in the service of the pope.

The Jesuits concentrated on three activities. First, they founded superb schools throughout Europe. Jesuit teachers were rigorously trained in both classical studies and theology. Priests who attended the Jesuit schools were far better educated than many other priests.

The second mission of the Jesuits was to convert non-Christians to Catholicism. Jesuit missionaries risked their lives preaching Christianity in the Americas, Africa, and Asia.

The Jesuits' third goal was to prevent Protestantism from spreading. The zeal of the Jesuits overcame the drift toward Protestantism in Poland and southern Germany (Bavaria). These regions today are overwhelmingly Roman Catholic because of the work of the Jesuits.

Reforming popes led the Church.

Two popes of the 1500's, Paul III and Paul IV, took the lead in reforming the Catholic Church. They had two goals. One was to strengthen and purify the Catholic Church for its own sake. Their other goal was to combat Protestantism.

Pope Paul III (1534–1549) took three important steps in reforming the Catholic Church. First, he directed a council of cardinals to make a thorough investigation of simony, indulgence selling, and other abuses within the Church. Second, he approved the Jesuit order. Third and most important, he decided to call a great council of Church leaders.

In 1545, Catholic bishops and cardinals met in the town of Trent in northern Italy. After much heated discussion, they agreed on the following doctrines:

1. The pope's interpretation of the Bible was final. Any Christian who substituted his or her own interpretation was a heretic.
2. Christians were not saved by faith alone, as Luther argued. They were saved by faith *and* by good works.
3. The Bible and Church tradition shared equal authority for guiding a Christian's life.
4. Indulgences, pilgrimages, and venerations of holy relics were all valid expressions of Christian piety. (But the false selling of indulgences was banned.)

The picture above shows the interior of a Protestant church with the minister at the pulpit. At the right is a ceremony in a Roman Catholic church. Bishops are gathered in front of the pope. What differences do the pictures show between the two styles of worship?

Another reforming pope, Paul IV (1555–1559), vigorously carried out the council's decrees. In 1559, he drew up a list of books that he considered dangerous to the Catholic faith. This list was known as the *Index of Forbidden Books.* Catholic bishops throughout Europe were ordered to gather up the offensive books (including Protestant Bibles) and burn them in great bonfires. In Venice alone, 10,000 books were burned in one day.

Historians have given two different names to this wave of reform in the Catholic Church. Protestant historians have generally called it the Counter-Reformation. They argued that its goal was to stamp out Protestantism. Catholic historians usually called this period the Catholic Reformation. They stressed the sincere desire of popes, cardinals, nuns, and monks to end Church corruption.

Religion divided Europe.

While the popes tried religious measures to strengthen the Church and crush Protestantism, Holy Roman Emperor Charles V turned to military measures. In 1544, Charles finally felt safe enough from his French and Turkish enemies to take up arms against the Protestant princes of Germany.

These Protestant rulers had joined together in a defensive group called the Schmalkaldic (shmahl-KAHLD-ik) League. In 1547, Charles's troops met the Schmalkaldic princes in battle and badly trounced them. However, the Catholic princes of Germany refused to join Charles in his war against Protestantism.

Weary of fighting, Charles ordered all German princes, both Protestant and Catholic, to assemble for an Imperial Diet in the city of Augsburg. At that meeting, the princes agreed that the religion of each German state was to be decided by its ruler. This famous religious settlement, signed in 1555, was known as the Peace of Augsburg.

By the terms of the Peace of Augsburg, German princes could choose either Lutheranism or Catholicism. Calvinism and other forms of Protestantism were outlawed.

From the point of view of Charles V, the Peace of Augsburg was not a happy settlement. After all, it led to religious division, not unity. All his life, Charles V had been deeply attached to the great institutions of the Middle Ages—feudalism, chivalry, and the Catholic Church. As Holy Roman emperor, he had hoped to preserve these institutions. However, the forces of historical change were too powerful for him to stop.

Charles was sick of troubles. He was eager to give up his crown, which had brought him little but grief. To his son, Philip II, he gave Spain, parts of Italy, the Netherlands, and Spain's holdings in the Americas. He turned over the Holy Roman Empire to his brother, Ferdinand. Then Charles V, once ruler of the largest empire in the world, retired to a monastery in Spain. He died there in 1558.

Section Review 3

Identify: (a) Ignatius Loyola, (b) Society of Jesus, (c) Council of Trent, (d) Index of Forbidden Books, (e) Peace of Augsburg
Answer:
1. (a) Who were the Jesuits? (b) What were their goals and achievements?
2. How did each of these popes strengthen the Catholic Church? (a) Paul III (b) Paul IV
3. What conclusions did the Council of Trent reach?
4. How did the Peace of Augsburg affect the states of Germany?

Critical Thinking
5. (a) What are the two names for this period of reform in the Catholic Church? (b) How do these two names show different attitudes on the part of historians? (c) Why might such differences arise?

Scientists challenged old assumptions. 4

The other revolution that began in the early 1500's developed more slowly and quietly than the Reformation. In fact, this revolution in scientific thinking was so gradual that it went nearly unnoticed for about 100 years. Eventually, however, the new scientific ways of thinking profoundly changed the whole world.

Before 1500, scholars generally decided what was true or false by quoting an ancient Greek or Roman author. For example, medieval scholars assumed that whatever Aristotle said about the natural universe was true unless the Bible said otherwise. Few European scholars tested Aristotle's ideas by looking at nature for themselves.

In the late 1500's, however, a few scholars published works that challenged the ideas of the ancient thinkers. A profound change in European thought was beginning. Historians call it the Scientific Revolution.

Copernicus and Kepler studied the solar system.

Among the first of the ancient theories to be challenged in the Scientific Revolution were the ideas of the astronomer Ptolemy (TAHL-uh-mee). About A.D. 150, during Roman times, Ptolemy wrote that Earth was the center of the universe. Ptolemy said that the sun, the moon, the stars, and five planets—Mercury, Venus, Mars, Jupiter, and Saturn—all circled around Earth. Scholars accepted Ptolemy's ideas for 1,400 years.

In 1543, a Polish scholar known by the Latin name of Nicolaus Copernicus (koh-PUHR-nih-kuhs) published a book challenging Ptolemy's theory. Copernicus's book was called *On the Revolutions of the Heavenly Bodies.* It argued that Earth and the other planets moved around the sun. Furthermore, said Copernicus, Earth was constantly spinning or rotating, which explained why the sun appeared to rise and set each day.

At first, Copernicus's book caused little excitement. Only a few scholars knew about it, and most of them did not agree with him. Copernicus himself wrote no more. Born in 1473, he had not published his book until he was on his deathbed. Furthermore, his arguments were based strictly on logic and geometry, not on direct observation.

Early in the 1600's, a German named Johannes Kepler (1571–1630) made careful observations of Mars and other planets. His data showed that Copernicus's ideas were right. Kepler concluded that Earth did in fact move around the sun, and so did the other planets.

Kepler worked out a series of mathematical equations that described how each of the planets moved around the sun. His three principal equations are known as Kepler's laws of planetary motion.

Galileo used a telescope.

In 1610, an Italian scientist named Galileo Galilei (GAL-uh-**LEE**-oh GAL-uh-**LAY**-ee) published a little book called *Starry Messenger*. This book began a controversy that went on for years.

European scholars had long believed that the universe was made of two totally different substances. Earth, they thought, was made of impure material that changed and decayed with time. They thought that the moon and the stars, on the other hand, were made of a pure, eternal substance that was smooth and perfect.

Galileo's observations of the heavens Galileo argued in his book that the moon was not smooth at all. It had mountains and plains on it just as Earth did. Moreover, Galileo said that the sun was not a perfect ball of heavenly light. Instead, it had many dark spots on it.

How did Galileo know? He had seen the sunspots and moon mountains while gazing through a telescope. The telescope was not entirely Galileo's invention. A Dutch lensmaker was the first to make an instrument to enlarge far-off objects. However, Galileo was the first astronomer to study the night sky through a telescope. Nobody else had ever seen the moon and planets as Galileo saw them through his telescope. Enlarged, they looked more Earthlike than heavenly. Galileo's observations, like those of Kepler, strongly supported the Copernican theory of a sun-centered solar system.

Galileo's experiments in physics Besides his important work in astronomy, Galileo started a whole new field of scientific investigation. This was the modern science of dynamics, which studies matter in motion.

As a youth of 18, Galileo watched the movements of a cathedral's chandelier as it swung back and forth on its chain. Aristotle had said that a pendulum swings more slowly as it approaches its resting point. Galileo tested this idea and found it wrong. Feeling his pulse to keep time, he found that each swing of the pendulum took exactly the same amount of time, from the first long sweep to the last tiny quiver.

Galileo performed other experiments in this careful way. For days, he rolled balls down a slope and measured the speed at which they moved. His data led him to conclude that a falling object accelerates at a fixed and predictable rate.

Galileo used this telescope to observe the moon. His drawings showed that the moon's surface is rough, not smooth as others thought.

Scientists used precise tools.

During the Scientific Revolution, scholars developed ways to make precise, reliable observations. Galileo's telescope was only one of the important instruments that aided science during the early 1600's. Other scientists and artisans developed more such tools.

Microscope The first microscope was invented by a Dutch maker of eyeglasses, Zacharias Janssen (**YAHN**-sen) in 1590. In the 1650's, Anton van Leeuwenhoek (**LAY**-vuhn-HOOK) used a microscope to observe bacteria swimming in his own saliva. He also described red blood cells.

Thermometer Galileo made the first thermometer in 1603, using alcohol for measuring temperatures. A German physicist named Gabriel Fahrenheit (**FAHR**-uhn-hyte) made the first thermometer using mercury. Fahrenheit's thermometer showed water freezing at 32° and boiling at 212°. A Swedish astronomer named Anders Celsius (**SEL**-see-uhs) created another scale for the mercury thermometer. Celsius's scale showed freezing at 0° and boiling at 100°.

Barometer One of Galileo's students developed the first mercury barometer, a tool for measuring atmospheric pressure and predicting weather. Evangelista Torricelli (TOR-uh-**CHEL**-ee) made this advance in 1655.

Daily Life · *Pendulums and Clocks*

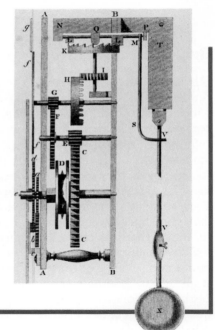

Since Greek times, people had marked the passing hours with water clocks—clocks in which water dripped at a steady rate from one container into another. In winter, however, these water clocks froze. In the 1200's and 1300's, European inventors worked on clocks that were driven by weights. In the 1400's, they turned to spring-driven clocks. Yet none of these timepieces was very accurate.

When Galileo saw that a pendulum always took the same amount of time, the way was open to a new method of measuring time. In 1656, a Dutch astronomer, Christian Huygens (HYE-guhnz), built a clock using a pendulum. It was more accurate than earlier ways of measuring time. Pendulum clocks were not surpassed in accuracy until the use of electricity.

New ideas caused conflict.

Rarely are new ideas accepted right away. In fact, they are more likely to be treated at first with deep suspicion. Many early scientists found themselves in conflict with the Catholic Church. By far the best known of these conflicts was the case of Galileo. As you have read, Galileo's observations convinced him that Copernicus was right. Yet, after a Church ruling banned Copernicus's ideas in 1616, Galileo was not free to say so.

Galileo thought he had a solution. In 1632, he wrote a book presenting the ideas of *both* Copernicus and Ptolemy. He himself, he said, was neutral. Yet Church officials saw clearly that Galileo gave all the strongest arguments to the Copernican theory. In fact, he seemed to be mocking the Church-approved ideas of Ptolemy.

Jesuit leaders charged that Galileo's ideas threatened to do the Church more harm "than Luther and Calvin put together." The pope decided to suppress the opinions of this famous scientist. Therefore, in 1633, the aged Galileo was called to Rome to stand trial.

Under the threat of torture, Galileo knelt before the cardinals and read aloud a signed confession. In it, he called the ideas of Copernicus "a false opinion." He said, "I abjure, curse, and detest the aforesaid errors and heresies."

Galileo was never again a free man. He was allowed to return to his home near Florence, but he was kept under house arrest until he died in 1642. Nevertheless, the revolution that Galileo helped to start could not be stopped.

Section Review 4

Define: Scientific Revolution
Identify: (a) Ptolemy, (b) Copernicus, (c) Kepler, (d) Galileo, (e) Leeuwenhoek, (f) Fahrenheit, (g) Celsius, (h) Torricelli
Answer:
1. (a) According to Ptolemy, what was Earth's position in the universe? (b) How did Copernicus's view differ? (c) Which theory did Kepler's observations support?
2. What revolutionary conclusion about the sun and moon did Galileo reach by gazing at the heavens through a telescope?
3. List four new instruments that came into use during the Scientific Revolution. After each, write its purpose.
4. (a) How did Galileo arouse the Church's anger? (b) What was the result?

Critical Thinking
6. (a) How did Galileo, Kepler, and other scientists of this period try to determine scientific truth? (b) How was this method different from that used by medieval thinkers? (c) Give an example of how each method might be used in everyday life today.

360

Chapter Review 16

Summary

1. Martin Luther began a religious revolt. The early 1500's brought two kinds of revolution—one in religion, the other in science. The Protestant Reformation, which split Europe into Catholic and Protestant states, began with Martin Luther's criticism of the selling of indulgences. Luther was later excommunicated and outlawed for teaching ideas that conflicted with Church doctrine. He gained the support of many Germans, however, and the new technology of the printing press spread his ideas throughout Europe.

2. Protestantism spread in northern Europe. Several countries turned to Protestantism. Henry VIII of England broke with the Catholic Church when the pope would not set aside his first marriage. John Calvin set forth a systematic Protestant theology based on the doctrine of predestination. One of his followers, John Knox, led a revolt that made Calvinism the official religion of Scotland.

3. The Catholic Church made changes. At the same time, the Catholic Church experienced reforms. Ignatius of Loyola formed the Society of Jesus to serve the pope. Pope Paul III called the Council of Trent, which reaffirmed Church doctrine. Paul IV enforced the new decrees and drew up a list of books believed dangerous to the Catholic faith.

4. Scientists challenged old assumptions. In the Scientific Revolution, scientists broke with the ancient teachings of Ptolemy. Knowledge of the universe increased. Copernicus proclaimed that Earth moved around the sun. The observations of Kepler and Galileo supported his theory.

Reviewing the Facts

1. Define the following terms:
   a. theocracy
   b. predestination
2. Explain the importance of each of the following names, places, or terms:
   a. Savonarola
   b. Erasmus
   c. More
   d. *Utopia*
   e. Gutenberg
   f. Dürer
   g. Luther
   h. Charles V
   i. Diet of Worms
   j. Henry VIII
   k. Catherine of Aragon
   l. Reformation Parliament
   m. Mary Tudor
   n. Calvin
   o. elect
   p. Geneva
   q. Knox
   r. Ignatius
   s. *Index of Forbidden Books*
   t. Peace of Augsburg
   u. Copernicus
   v. Kepler
   w. Galileo

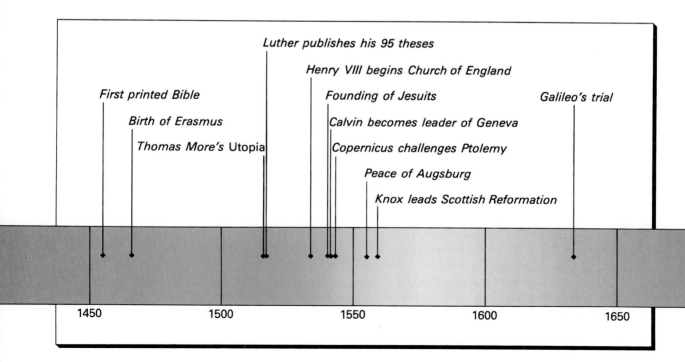

First printed Bible

Birth of Erasmus

Thomas More's Utopia

Luther publishes his 95 theses

Henry VIII begins Church of England

Founding of Jesuits

Calvin becomes leader of Geneva

Copernicus challenges Ptolemy

Peace of Augsburg

Knox leads Scottish Reformation

Galileo's trial

1450   1500   1550   1600   1650

3. Why were some people unhappy with the Catholic Church in the 1400's and early 1500's?

4. (a) When did the printing press first come into use? (b) How did it affect attitudes toward the Church in the 1500's?

5. Briefly describe the controversy that arose over indulgences.

6. How did Luther come to be outlawed? (Include information on Leo X, Charles V, and the Edict of Worms in your answer.)

7. (a) What was the peasant revolt of 1524? (b) What were its results?

8. (a) Why did Henry VIII want to set aside his marriage to Catherine of Aragon? (b) What made him challenge the Church?

9. (a) How did Henry strengthen Protestantism in England through the Act of Supremacy? (b) By his policy toward monasteries? (c) How did the religious outlooks of his children vary?

10. What was Calvin's view on salvation?

11. How was Geneva an example of Calvinist ideas?

12. How did Calvinism become established in Scotland in the 1500's?

13. (a) Who were the Jesuits? (b) In what ways did they serve the Catholic Church?

14. How did Protestants and Catholics (as expressed by the Council of Trent) differ on the following matters? (a) salvation (b) interpretation of the Bible (c) final religious authority

15. (a) What was Ptolemy's view of the universe? (b) How was that view contradicted by Copernicus, Kepler, and Galileo?

16. (a) Why was Galileo put on trial by the Church? (b) What were the results of the trial?

Thinking about History

1. During the period covered by this chapter, both Luther and Galileo were brought to trial. In what ways were their trials similar? How did the results of the two trials differ? Why do you think the two men had different fates?

2. The United States Constitution provides for the separation of Church and State. How was this idea different from the settlement reached in the Peace of Augsburg and the Act of Supremacy?

3. Within about 100 years from the invention of the printing press, the Catholic Church established the *Index of Forbidden Books.* How might these two events have been related?

Writing and Speaking about History

1. The leaders of the Protestant Reformation were doing more than protesting practices of which they disapproved. They were also advocating for practices in which they believed. Write an essay discussing both these aspects of the Reformation.

2. During the Protestant Reformation, many people died for their religious beliefs. Yet, Galileo, a scientist, chose not to perish for his revolutionary ideas. Conduct an interview with Galileo in which you discuss his decision to recant his beliefs.

Practicing Skills

1. Make a timeline (from 1480 to 1550 in ten-year increments) that traces the significant events in Luther's life.

2. Use an almanac to find the proportion of Catholics and Protestants living in the following countries today:
   a. Poland   d. Switzerland
   b. France   e. Sweden
   c. West Germany
   How do these statistics compare with the map on page 355?

Investigating History

1. Report on the life of one of the following people: Girolamo Savonarola, Thomas More, Catherine Parr, John Knox, Mary Tudor.

2. Prepare a bulletin board display showing drawings or pictures of the modern descendants of inventions developed during the Scientific Revolution (telescope, microscope, thermometer, barometer). Include captions describing the uses of each.

3. In *Utopia,* Thomas More described what he considered a perfect society. Since that time, a number of groups have tried to build their own versions of Utopia. Use an encyclopedia to find out about Utopian societies. What are some famous ones?

Decision Making in History

Evaluate the decision of Charles V to sign the Peace of Augsburg. Take into account his devotion to the Catholic Church as well as the political and economic forces that threatened his empire. What other choices did he have? Do you think he made the right decision?

The Spanish Empire and Shifts in European Power

1. Spain built an overseas empire.

2. Spain was a Catholic bulwark.

3. The Netherlands won independence.

4. France's crown changed hands.

5. Religious wars split Germany.

In full royal splendor, the Aztec ruler Montezuma greeted the Spanish explorer Cortés and his translator, Doña Marina. According to tradition, the Aztec ruler's feet could not touch the ground, and his subjects could not look directly at his face.

For several months, messengers had been bringing frightening reports to Montezuma, emperor of the Aztecs, in his capital city of Tenochtitlán in the Valley of Mexico. The reports told of white-skinned, bearded men arriving at the coast in winged towers. Were these strangers merely men from distant lands? Or was their leader, as Montezuma feared, the ancient ruler-god of the Aztecs, Quetzalcoatl (ket-suhl-KWAH-tuhl), returning to claim the Aztec kingdom?

In fact, the strangers were a small force of Spaniards under the leadership of Hernán Cortés (air-NAHN kor-TEHZ). Cortés had sailed in March 1519 from the Spanish settlement on Cuba with about 600

363

Spaniards, 11 ships, 16 horses, and a few brass cannon. His goal was to explore and colonize the North American mainland. Without knowing it, Cortés's little group of Spaniards was approaching the vast Aztec empire with its 11 million people (pages 314–315).

Montezuma soon sent his own ambassadors to see these newcomers. Whether they were gods or men, he hoped rich gifts would persuade them to go away. Aztec ambassadors presented Cortés with ornaments of gold and turquoise. The most impressive presents, in the eyes of the gold-hungry Spaniards, were two discs as big as the wheels of a cart. One, made of gold, represented the sun. The other, of silver, represented the moon.

Far from persuading Cortés to leave, the sight of so much gold and silver only stiffened his determination to win more. So that none of his men could sail home with the treasure, he ordered all his ships sunk.

For the Spaniards, it was now conquer or die. If they failed, they might be carried up the steps of an Aztec temple and sacrificed to the sun god. Torn between hope and terror, Cortés's small force set off on the 250-mile march to Tenochtitlán. Never in history had so small an army planned to topple so great an empire.

As you will see in this chapter, Cortés's actions in the spring of 1519 had far-reaching results. His handful of Spaniards destroyed the Aztec empire, and this conquest laid the foundation for an empire that made Spain the richest power in Europe.

Spain quickly put its great wealth at the service of Catholicism in the religious wars that shook Europe throughout the 1500's and 1600's. There was little peace between Catholics and Protestants in those years. Armies from Catholic Spain fought for 80 years against Protestants in the Netherlands. France was torn apart by assassinations, massacres, and civil wars—often fueled by religious hatred. In Germany, Protestants and Catholics fought one of the most destructive wars in European history, the Thirty Years' War (1618–1648).

The period of time covered in this chapter was a time of violence. However, it was also a time of great creativity. Dutch and Spanish artists produced some of the greatest treasures of European art. Literature too flourished, especially in Spain and France.

Spain built an overseas empire. 1

In the 1490's, Christopher Columbus (page 337) founded the earliest Spanish settlements in the Americas on the islands of Hispaniola and Cuba. Within a generation, Spain's lands in the Americas grew to a great empire. Sailing out from the islands, daring Spanish fortune hunters called **conquistadors** (kohn-KEES-tuh-dohrs) searched the Americas for gold and precious gems. Hernán Cortés was one of the earliest, and most successful, of these conquistadors.

Cortés conquered the Aztecs.

After Cortés's fateful decision to sink his ships, he was committed to war against the Aztecs. The Spaniards were overwhelmingly outnumbered, but they did have several advantages. They were equipped with weapons the Aztecs had never seen. There were horses, steel swords and armor, crossbows, and light artillery.

Cortés also had another advantage. Traveling with him was a young Indian woman who had been given to him as a slave when his group first landed. Her name was Malinche, and she spoke the Aztec language and several others. She learned Spanish rapidly. The Spaniards gave her a Christian name, Marina.

Doña (Lady) Marina soon became Cortés's invaluable aide. She explained that the Aztecs were hated and feared by most of the Indians they ruled. She helped him win allies among these Indians. Later, she played on Montezuma's fears to keep him from taking a strong stand against the Spaniards.

On November 8, 1519, Cortés reached Tenochtitlán. Montezuma invited the Spaniards into the city as his honored guests. Much impressed with the place, Cortés would later call Tenochtitlán "the most beautiful city in the world."

Why did Montezuma let the Spaniards enter his capital? He still feared that Cortés might be Quetzalcoatl, a light-skinned god who had once ruled the lands around Lake Texcoco. One day he had vanished mysteriously, but he vowed to return and claim his kingdom. As fate would have it, Cortés arrived in exactly the same year

Quetzalcoatl was expected to return. As the legend had foretold, Cortés came in "white-winged ships" from across the eastern sea. Thus, Montezuma feared Cortés as a god. His fear led to the fall of the Aztec empire.

After several days of sight-seeing in Tenochtitlán, the Spaniards boldly took Montezuma prisoner and kept him in their quarters. Despite his apparent success, however, Cortés was still in an explosive situation. While he was out of the city, one of his lieutenants interfered with an Aztec religious ceremony. An uprising broke out against the Spaniards.

When Cortés returned, he and Marina forced Montezuma to go out on the roof of the Spanish barracks to calm the crowd. The Aztecs flung stones at their former ruler, now the puppet of Cortés. Soon after, word came that Montezuma was dead. The Spaniards said he had been killed by a stone from the mob. Not surprisingly, the Aztecs believed the Spanish had killed him. The Spaniards were now surrounded by thousands of Aztecs demanding their blood.

On the night of June 30, 1520, the Spaniards tried to sneak out of the city, but a guard spotted them. The Aztecs swarmed out to attack the hated foreigners. Many Spaniards, slowed by the loot they carried, were either clubbed to death or carried away for sacrifice. Among those who escaped were Cortés and Doña Marina.

The Aztecs might have pursued Cortés and destroyed his small force, but another disaster befell the Aztecs just then. The morning after Cortés's flight, smallpox broke out in the city. This terrible disease, brought by the Spaniards, killed many Aztec leaders (page 340). Partly for that reason, the Aztecs failed to follow the fleeing Spaniards and wipe them out.

A year later, in 1521, Cortés returned. This time he had with him a huge army of Aztec-hating Indians. Trapped in their island city, the Aztecs refused to surrender. Cortés's army had to fight its way into the city, block by block. After an 85-day siege, Tenochtitlán lay in ruins. When it was rebuilt, it was as a Spanish capital for an empire called New Spain.

Voice from the Past · *An Aztec Poem*

An anonymous Indian poet voiced the grief that the Aztecs felt for the ruin of their once beautiful capital, Tenochtitlán.

Broken spears lie in the roads;
we have torn our hair in our grief.
The houses are roofless now, and their walls
are red with blood.

Worms are swarming in the streets and plazas,
and the walls are splattered with gore.
The water has turned red, as if it were dyed,
and when we drink it,
it has the taste of brine.

We have pounded our hands in despair
against the adobe walls,
for our inheritance, our city, is lost and dead.
The shields of our warriors were its defense,
but they could not save it.

We have chewed dry twigs and salt grasses . . .
we have eaten lizards, rats, and worms . . .
Gold, jade, rich clothes, quetzal feathers—
everything that once was precious
was now considered worthless.

1. The poet tells a whole story in the first stanza. What information can you deduce from reading just four lines?
2. During the siege, the city's defenders had no way of bringing food into the city. What were the consequences?
3. (a) Which parts of this poem might apply to the fall of Troy, Carthage, or another great city? (b) What details are specific to Tenochtitlán?

High in the Andes lie the ruins of the great Inca city Machu Picchu. Though the Spaniards searched for it, no outsider found it until 1911.

Pizarro conquered the Incas.

Cortés was only one of many Spanish adventurers who hoped to win a large fortune in the Americas. Another was Francisco Pizarro (puh-**ZAHR**-oh). A gray-bearded man of 62, Pizarro landed on the coast of Peru in 1532 with about 200 soldiers. The Spaniards panted up the western slopes of the Andes and followed the Inca road to the city of Cajamarca (kah-huh-**MAHR**-kuh). They found the city deserted.

The Inca ruler, Atahualpa (AHT-uh-**WAHL**-puh), and his army were camped close by. Atahualpa had won the throne after a bitter war with his brother. The war between the two brothers severely weakened the Inca empire. Even so, Atahualpa had 30,000 men to fight Pizarro's small troop. Pizarro, on the other hand, had horses and superior weapons.

Through a messenger, Pizarro invited Atahualpa to Cajamarca for a friendly visit. The Inca ruler agreed. Meanwhile, the Spaniards hid themselves and their horses in the narrow alleys of the city. They waited in silence as Atahualpa was carried into the city on a gold litter. He was accompanied by a guard of between 5,000 and 6,000 men. The guards were not armed.

A Spanish priest greeted Atahualpa. Suddenly a shot rang out. From all directions, the Spaniards charged their startled visitors. Not one Spaniard died, but the slaughter of Inca guards was dreadful. Most important, Atahualpa was taken prisoner. Since only the emperor could lead the Inca army, no one could rescue him. The emperor's absolute power was his empire's fatal flaw.

Atahualpa offered a huge ransom for his release. He promised to fill a large room with gold and another with silver. Pizarro agreed to free the Inca when the ransom was paid. Soon the rooms were filled as promised. Pizarro melted down the finely crafted objects into gold and silver bricks. Then, breaking his promise, he ordered Atahualpa strangled to death.

A few months later in 1533, Pizarro's horses clattered down the streets of Cuzco (**KOOZ**-koh), the Inca capital. The Spaniards were now rulers of Peru, and Pizarro was rich beyond measure. However, the Spaniards began to fight among themselves. In 1541, a group of Pizarro's old comrades broke into his home and killed him.

Spaniards explored widely.

Emboldened by the riches of Cortés and Pizarro, other soldier-adventurers set out in search of more treasures. Hernando de Soto sailed north from Cuba in 1539. He landed on the Florida coast and marched inland as far as the Mississippi River. He claimed the river and the land along it for Spain. Having fought with Pizarro, he dreamed of conquering another glittering empire. Instead, he died of sickness in 1547, and his soldiers dropped his body into the Mississippi.

Another Spaniard, Francisco Coronado, crossed the Rio Grande in 1540. He explored as far north as the plains of Kansas. One of his captains discovered the spectacular beauty of the Grand Canyon. Yet like De Soto, Coronado found no gold. He returned to Mexico bitterly disappointed.

Meanwhile, far to the south, a man and a woman extended Spain's conquests in the Andes Mountains. In 1540, Pedro de Valdivia (vahl-DEE-vyah) and Ines Suarez (IH-nehz SWAH-rayth) led a small army south from Spain's strongholds in Peru. They marched along the coastal desert of what is now Chile. In 1541, they founded the city of Santiago, Chile's modern capital. Between 1540 and 1547, they rode and fought together, conquering much of Chile for Spain.

By 1550, Spanish territory reached all the way from present-day Kansas to Chile. Spain's American lands were larger than the empires of Alexander the Great or Julius Caesar. This was also the first empire in history that was separated from its capital by an immense ocean. Its ruler was Spain's Charles I, who also held the title of Holy Roman Emperor as Charles V.

Colonists enslaved the Indians.

The king of Spain claimed absolute power over his American lands. He entrusted the power to make laws for these lands to a group of officials called the Council of the Indies. The council met in Spain and sent its laws to two capitals in the Americas. One capital was Mexico City, which the Spanish had built over the ruins of Tenochtitlán. The other capital was Lima, Peru. Pizarro founded Lima in 1535 and made it the capital of Peru because communication with Spain was easier from the coastal Lima than from the inland Cuzco.

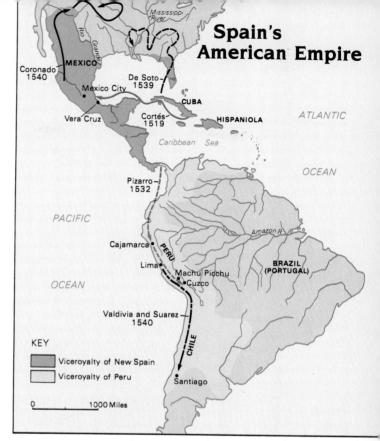

Spain's American Empire

Map Study

What viceroyalty included the former land of the Aztecs? Which Spanish explorer traveled farthest north? When did Pizarro go to Peru?

In both Mexico City and Lima was a royal agent called a **viceroy.** The viceroy in Mexico City ruled Spain's North American territory, called New Spain. The viceroy in Lima ruled Spain's South American lands, called Peru. Viceroys were noblemen born in Spain. No Spaniard born in the Americas could hope to reach such high office.

The viceroy's authority did not matter much to the average Aztec, Inca, or Maya. For the conquered Indians, the only rulers who mattered were the ruthless conquistadors who seized their villages. The Council of the Indies granted to certain settlers a privilege called an *encomienda* (EHN-koh-mee-EHN-duh). The holder of an encomienda became master of a particular area. He could force Indians in his lands to work long hours in his cornfields, sugar plantations, or silver mines. In effect, the Spaniards treated the Indians as slaves. Abuse in Spanish silver mines killed thousands of Indians.

367

Section Review 1

Define: (a) conquistador, (b) viceroy, (c) encomienda

Identify: (a) Montezuma, (b) Tenochtitlán, (c) Cortés, (d) Doña Marina, (e) New Spain, (f) Pizarro, (g) Atahualpa, (h) De Soto, (i) Coronado, (j) Valdivia, (k) Suarez

Answer:

1. (a) What was the legend of Quetzalcoatl? (b) How did it help Cortés?
2. How did Cortés finally conquer Tenochtitlán?
3. Why was the conquest of the Incas relatively easy after the capture of Atahualpa?
4. (a) How was Spain's American empire governed? (b) What qualified a person to become a viceroy?
5. (a) What types of economic enterprises did Spanish settlers establish in the Americas? (b) What workers did they use there?

Critical Thinking

6. List five factors that contributed to Cortés's success and explain how each one helped him. Be sure to consider political and social factors as well as military ones.

Spain was a Catholic bulwark.

2

The riches of Spain's new empire were fabulous. By 1600, the amount of gold taken from American mines and shipped to Spain was estimated at 750,000 pounds. American silver mines yielded even greater treasure. Between 1550 and 1650, roughly 16,000 *tons* of silver bullion (metal bars) were unloaded from Spanish galleons and carted over Spanish roads. Between a fifth and a fourth of every shipload of treasure went to the king of Spain as his royal share. With the vast wealth of its American territories, Spain began to play a commanding role in Europe.

Philip II *ruled an empire.*

In 1556, Charles V divided his empire, giving Spain to his shy and serious son, Philip II, who ruled from 1556 to 1598. Under Philip's rule, Spain became the staunchest supporter of Catholicism and the most dangerous enemy of Protestantism.

Europe was entering a time of violent conflict over religion. In 1559, Spain and France signed a treaty ending the long series of wars they had fought over lands in Italy. Thereafter, for nearly 100 years, most of the wars in Europe were fought over religion.

Philip's inheritance from Charles V included more than Spain and its American colonies. He also ruled the duchy of Milan in northern Italy, the kingdom of Naples in southern Italy, the territory called Franche-Comté on France's eastern border, and all 17 provinces that made up the Netherlands.

Toward the middle of Philip's reign, another great prize fell into his hands. In 1580, the king of Portugal died without an heir. Philip quickly seized the small but important Portuguese kingdom. Counting Portuguese strongholds in Africa, India, and the East Indies, he now had an empire that circled the globe.

Spain's wealth and its power grew together. Minted into coins, Spain's gold and silver supported an army of about 50,000 soldiers. Through the late 1500's, Spain had by far the largest and best-equipped army in Europe. Looking at Spain's awesome military machine, people said, "When Spain moves, the whole world trembles."

The nerve center of the Spanish empire was Philip's palace, the Escorial (es-**KOHR**-ee-uhl). All the roads and ship lanes in Spain's far-flung empire led ultimately to its massive, gray stone walls about 26 miles northwest of Madrid, the capital. The Escorial's outer gates were so huge that the keys to open them weighed half a ton. Within the gigantic walls, there were 86 staircases to climb, 1,200 doors to open, and 84 miles of corridors to explore.

In a small, candle-lit room within the Escorial, Philip II worked far into the night. The most powerful ruler in Europe, he was also the hardest working. He demanded reports, reports, and more reports from his chief advisers. Then, in his tiny office, he would agonize over decisions. Much of the time, he could not bring himself to choose one policy over another. At such times, the government of Spain ground nearly to a halt. Yet Philip would not allow anyone to help him. Deeply suspicious, he trusted no one for long.

The Spanish architects who planned the Escorial (above) were influenced by the buildings of Renaissance Italy. Yet they created a much plainer, sterner palace, well suited to the character of Spain's Philip II (right). Philip's preference for severe black clothes set a style for men in Europe.

As his own court historian wrote, "His smile and his dagger were very close."

The Escorial was more than a palace. It was also a monastery. From his bedroom, Philip II could slide open a hidden window that allowed him to watch the monks' church services. There, in private, he took part in their prayers.

The two functions of the Escorial—palace and monastery—show clearly the character of Philip II. Throughout his reign, he doggedly sought to strengthen both his monarchy and the Catholic Church.

Spain battled for Catholicism.

Philip II was eager to see Catholicism triumph over its religious rivals, the Muslim Ottoman Turks and the Protestants. Against the Ottomans, Philip achieved a stunning victory. However, Philip's struggles against Protestantism caused him only frustration.

War against the Ottoman Turks In 1571, the pope called on all Catholic princes to take up arms against the mounting power of the Ottoman empire. Philip responded like a true crusader. Huge Spanish galleons joined Venetian ships in the Mediterranean Sea and rowed toward the coast of Greece.

On October 7, 1571, near the Greek seaport of Lepanto (lih-**PAN**-toh), 200 Spanish-Venetian ships met the Ottoman fleet of 300 ships in a ferocious battle. Philip II's half-brother, Don John of Austria, commanded the Christian forces. His ships slammed into the Turkish galleys. Then the Spaniards and Venetians swarmed aboard and slaughtered the foe with sword and musket. The Battle of Lepanto crushed the Ottoman navy. It was a major victory for Christendom.

War against Protestant forces As the champion of Catholicism, Philip wanted first and foremost to crush Protestantism in his own lands. He also worked constantly to weaken or overthrow Protestant rulers throughout Europe.

No other place on the map of Europe gave Philip as much trouble as a tiny corner of his own empire, the Netherlands. Later in this chapter, you will read how the Dutch rose in revolt against Philip (page 372). In his efforts to crush

369

the revolt, Philip spent a fortune in Spanish gold to no avail.

After the Dutch, Philip's greatest Protestant enemy was Elizabeth I of England. Philip had once been married to Elizabeth's Catholic sister, Mary (page 353). After Mary's death in 1558, he hoped to keep England as an ally and a Catholic country. For a while, he even hoped to marry Elizabeth. Gradually, however, Elizabeth showed that she intended to keep England Protestant and that she did not intend to repeat her sister's mistake of marrying an unpopular foreign king. Later, Elizabeth openly assisted the Dutch rebels with money and troops. She also encouraged English sea captains to raid Spanish treasure ships for gold.

In 1588, Philip struck at England. He assembled a fleet of 130 ships with 31,000 men. This fleet was known as the Armada (ahr-MAHD-uh). Philip had high hopes for his mighty Armada, but the skilled English sea captains destroyed it. For England, the victory was the high point of the Elizabethan age (Chapter 18).

Spain had a golden age in art and literature.

Despite these military setbacks, Spain remained a mighty nation. Philip's reign marked the beginning of a golden age for Spanish culture.

El Greco and Velázquez   The works of two great artists showed both the pride and the piety of Spain during its golden age. The first of these artists was El Greco (GREH-koh). The second was Diego Velázquez (vay-LAHTH-kayth).

El Greco (1541–1614) was not a Spaniard by birth but a Greek from the island of Crete. His real name was Kyriakos Theotokopoulos, but the Spanish gave him the name El Greco, which means "the Greek." His major works were all painted in Spain.

El Greco painted Catholic saints and martyrs as huge, long-limbed figures. The backgrounds of his paintings were usually a mass of swirling gray clouds. The use of deep, vibrant colors heightened the drama and religious intensity of El Greco's paintings.

El Greco's saintly figures showed the strength of the Catholic faith in Spain. The paintings of Velázquez (1599–1660) showed the pride of Spain's royal family. Velázquez was best known for his

The dramatic sky in this painting of Saint Bernardino is typical of El Greco's work.

portraits of Spanish kings and princes mounted on rearing stallions.

Cervantes   In 1605, an unsuccessful Spanish playwright named Miguel de Cervantes (suhr-VAN-teez) published a book that many critics call the first modern European novel. The book was named for its main character, Don Quixote (kee-HOH-tee) of La Mancha. In his own life, Cervantes had had his ups and downs. He had been wounded in the Battle of Lepanto and jailed for debt. He worked for a time as a tax collector. These varied experiences seem to have made Cervantes tolerant of humankind.

Don Quixote de la Mancha was a gentle satire of chivalry. Don Quixote was a Spaniard of noble birth and noble mind who went a little crazy after reading too many books about heroic knights. Hoping to "right every manner of wrong," he rode forth in a suit of rusty armor, mounted on a feeble nag. At his side, through all his adventures, was a stout and comical little squire named Sancho Panza.

Because of his romantic ideals, Don Quixote never saw things as they were. He saw a common tavern by the road as a grand castle. To him, a windmill became a hostile giant to be challenged and fought. Of course, Don Quixote's wild notions caused no end of trouble. Strangers laughed at his chivalric speeches, knocked him off his horse, and left him in the mud.

Sancho Panza, more sensible than his master, objected to everything the foolish knight proposed, but Don Quixote never listened. This bit of dialogue was typical:

> *"What the devil kind of vengeance are we going to take," asked Sancho, "seeing there are more than twenty of them and not more than two of us, or maybe only one and a half?"*
> *"I," replied Don Quixote, "am worth a hundred."*

So saying, the knight charged to the attack, only to receive another beating.

Don Quixote's misadventures made it clear that the age of knights in shining armor had passed. By 1600, chivalry seemed outdated and somewhat foolish to Cervantes's readers, even though its ideals still had some sentimental appeal, especially to kings and queens.

Spain's economy weakened.

With a prayer on his lips, Philip II died in his palace bed in 1598 after a reign of 42 years. His successors were weaker kings, notable mostly because Velázquez painted their portraits.

In the next 50 years, Spain's golden age gradually lost its glitter. By 1650, the Spanish economy was in a dreadful state. The king was hopelessly in debt to foreign creditors. In every Spanish town, prices soared wildly.

Strangely, Spain's great wealth in the 1500's was the direct cause of its poverty later. Boatloads of gold and silver from the Americas flooded Spain—and later the rest of Europe—with precious metals. As a result, the value of gold and silver dropped, and prices doubled and redoubled. Such an upward spiral of prices is called **inflation**.

Spain was most seriously affected by these skyrocketing prices. Spaniards found that they could neither eat gold nor hammer it into shoes.

Unlike many other parts of Europe, Spain never had a large middle class. The most powerful group in Spanish society was still the great feudal landholders. No class of burghers or bourgeoisie won political influence in Spain as such groups did in England and France.

Spain's methods of manufacturing were also old-fashioned. The guilds that had grown up in the Middle Ages still dominated business. These guilds did not produce enough manufactured goods for Spain's use. Instead, Spaniards imported much of what they needed from the Netherlands, France, and England. Thus, Spanish gold and silver tended to flow right out of Madrid into the pockets of Spain's worst enemies—the hard-working, hard-bargaining Dutch burghers of Amsterdam.

Section Review 2

Define: inflation
Identify: (a) Philip II, (b) Escorial, (c) Battle of Lepanto, (d) the Armada, (e) El Greco, (f) Velázquez, (g) Cervantes, (h) Don Quixote
Answer:
1. (a) What lands did Philip II inherit? (b) What lands did he add to his empire?
2. What made Spain's government inefficient?
3. What were Philip's two goals?
4. (a) What action did Philip take toward the Ottoman empire? (b) What Protestant lands caused difficulties for Spain?
5. How did Spain's wealth from the Americas weaken its economy?

Critical Thinking
6. Cervantes, El Greco, and Velázquez present very different outlooks on life. What might Philip II have thought of the works of each man, if he had known of them? (Only El Greco's works were actually produced during Philip's lifetime.)

The Netherlands won independence. 3

Of Spain's many enemies in the late 1500's, the most stubborn (and successful) were the people who lived in the low marshlands between northern Germany and northern France. Today, this region is divided into two nations, Belgium to the south and the Netherlands to the north. In the 1500's, the whole region was known as the Netherlands, or the Low Countries. The northerners, known as the Dutch, took the lead in the battle with Spain.

It is not surprising that the Dutch rebelled against Spanish rule in the late 1500's. In culture, customs, and religion, the Dutch were strongly at odds with Spain and its ruler, Philip II. Broadly speaking, Spain still held to the great institutions of the Middle Ages: the Catholic Church, the feudal system of landholding, and the guild system for producing goods. The Netherlands, on the other hand, had many Protestant congregations. The feudal system had little influence on the busy towns of the Netherlands. Moreover, as Spain's economy faltered, the Dutch were taking the lead in new ways of doing business.

The Dutch revolted against Spain.

The Netherlands had long been part of the Holy Roman Empire. When Charles V divided his lands, he gave the Netherlands to Philip II along with Spain. Thus, the only link between the two lands was that they shared a ruler.

Spain, as you have read, was a thoroughly Catholic country. In the Netherlands, about one third of the people were Calvinists. Although they were a minority, the Calvinists were a strong, tightly knit group that included many powerful nobles and wealthy merchants.

In 1559, Philip II sent his sister Margaret to govern the Netherlands with the twin goals of stamping out Protestantism and raising taxes. These policies soon antagonized many Dutch.

In 1566, mobs of angry Calvinists rampaged through Catholic churches in many parts of the Netherlands. Calling themselves the Sea Beggars, they smashed windows, burned books, destroyed altars, and ruined all the rich ornaments.

In response, Philip II sent 20,000 soldiers under the Spanish Duke of Alva to destroy Protestantism in the Netherlands. The duke's troops broke into Dutch homes and carried off suspected heretics. On a single day in 1568, Alva executed 1,500 people. Between 1568 and 1578, the Netherlands flamed as war raged between Catholics and Protestants, Dutch and Spaniards.

The greatest leader of the revolt against Spain was Prince William of Orange. (He was also known as William the Silent for his remarkable ability to keep his plans secret.) Born a Lutheran but raised a Catholic, William's motives for fighting the Spaniards were political, not religious. He hated to see his country ruled by foreigners and wanted to free the Netherlands from Spain.

At first, William and the Dutch lost battle after battle, town after town to the Spaniards. Then, at the town of Alkmaar, the Dutch took a desperate step. Their lands were called the Low Countries because much of the land was actually below sea level. Only great dikes kept the seawater from flooding over the fields. To drive out the Spanish, the Dutch opened the floodgates, covering the land around Alkmaar with water. Thereafter, the Dutch took this terrible step several times, destroying their countryside to save their towns from Spain.

By 1579, the Dutch were in control of the northern part of the Netherlands. Seven provinces, led by the province of Holland, united and declared themselves independent of Spain in 1581. This country became the United Provinces of the Netherlands.

Meanwhile, the southern part of the Netherlands (which is modern-day Belgium) remained under Spanish control. The majority of people in this region were Catholics, and their language was closer to French than to German.

William the Silent hoped to establish a country where both Protestantism and Catholicism were tolerated. Few people, however, were ready to accept this idea. William himself was murdered in 1584 by a fanatic. Today, Dutch Catholics and Protestants alike honor him as the "father of his country."

Gradually, the idea of religious toleration did take root in the Netherlands. Somehow the Dutch managed to overcome the religious hatreds stirred up by their war for independence. In the 1600's, the United Provinces was the one country in

Europe that accepted people of almost all faiths. Jews, unable to practice their religion in most parts of Europe, found a haven in Amsterdam and other Dutch cities. Scholars from many parts of Europe also came to live in the United Provinces or sent their books there to be published. For the times, this kind of religious toleration was rare.

The Dutch established a republic.

Another distinctive feature of the United Provinces of the Netherlands was its government. Unlike most states of Europe, the United Provinces was not a kingdom but a republic. Each province had an elected governor called a *stadtholder*. The power of this official depended on the active support of the province's leading merchants and landholders.

Each of the seven provinces sent delegations to a legislative body called the States General. These lawmakers had few powers because each province jealously guarded its independence. Nevertheless, members of the States General were so proud of themselves that they insisted on being called "Their High Mightinesses."

The Dutch built a trading empire.

While Spain lived on the gold and silver from its colonies, a new economic system was thriving in the Netherlands. The Dutch took the lead in the development of a new way of organizing business, a system that later came to be called **capitalism**.

Capitalism and the commercial revolution What were the features of this new economic system? Capitalists were people who invested large sums of money (or *capital*) in business ventures. Their goal was to make enough money to pay all the costs of the venture plus some additional money (or *profit*).

A capitalist who made a profit on a trading expedition did not spend all the money on luxury items. Instead, the successful capitalist reinvested the profit in another, probably larger, venture. Of course, there was always the risk of failure. Capitalists risked losing not only the chance for profit but all the capital they had accumulated as well. During the 1660's, however, the hope of profit kept the Dutch economy booming.

This painting by Vermeer shows the three-story houses that were common in Dutch towns. The top floor often served as the owner's warehouse.

The merchants of Amsterdam traded in many goods. They bought surplus grain in Poland and crammed it into their warehouses. Then, they waited for news of poor harvests in southern Europe so they could ship the grain south while prices were highest. Tons of smoked and pickled herring also found a ready market. Western Europe was short of timber, a fact that Dutch merchants were quick to exploit. They shipped great quantities of Scandinavian lumber to Spain, France, Italy, and England, all in ships owned by Dutch capitalists.

The Dutch had the largest fleet of ships in the entire world—10,000 ships in 1600. Even merchants of other countries often sent their cargoes in Dutch ships and, of course, paid dearly for it.

Banking As the trade routes of the Atlantic became more important than those of the Mediterranean, the Dutch replaced the Italians as the bankers of Europe. Soon after its founding in 1609, the Amsterdam Exchange Bank won a reputation as the safest, soundest bank in Europe.

Princes and merchants from many countries deposited money there. They also borrowed from the Dutch banks, and the interest on such loans enriched Amsterdam's bankers.

The Dutch East Indies Company Probably the most ambitious Dutch enterprise was the trade in Asian spices. The spice trade was dangerous because Portugal controlled the shipping routes of the Indian Ocean. To break Portugal's hold on the trade, the Dutch needed a large fleet with heavy guns, an army of soldiers, and tons of supplies.

The capital for such a venture was too much for any one merchant. Therefore, in 1602, 17 of Amsterdam's wealthiest men pooled their money to form a trading firm called the Dutch East Indies Company. The Dutch government gave the company power to make war, coin money, and rule colonies as if it were a sovereign state.

Within 20 years, the fleets of the aggressive Dutch company had secured strong bases on the islands of Java and Ceylon. Shiploads of Asian pepper, cloves, and nutmeg were hoisted into company warehouses where they sat until prices shot up to a properly high level. Then the goods were sold, and the company directors shared the profits in proportion to the size of their original investment.

Dutch merchants took the lead in their capitalist approach to trade, but merchants in other nations soon followed. During the late 1500's, French and English merchants also expanded their markets and invested profits in bold enterprises. So important were these changes to the future growth of Europe that historians have called them the Commercial Revolution.

Amsterdam became a great city.

Holland was the wealthiest Dutch province, and Amsterdam was Holland's largest, most flourishing city. In fact, by 1650, Amsterdam had become the financial and commercial center of Europe, far surpassing the Italian cities of Venice and Florence.

Amsterdam's growth through the early 1600's was spectacular. In 1610, there were 50,000 people living in Amsterdam. Only 10 years later, the population had doubled to 100,000. By 1660, the figure had swollen to 200,000. This phenomenal growth was due partly to Amsterdam's location on a sheltered bay, the Zuider (ZYE-duhr) Zee. However, human skill did far more than geography to account for Amsterdam's wealth.

Hoping to boost their city's commerce, a group of Dutch engineers designed a remarkable network of canals. The plan was approved in 1610 and completed in 1663. Three 80-foot-wide semicircular canals ran from the Zuider Zee into the heart of the fan-shaped city. A web of 600 smaller canals fed into the larger ones so that every dwelling in the city could be reached by water.

The Dutch merchants even designed their houses so that they could move merchandise efficiently. The top floor of each three-story house usually served as the owner's warehouse. It was equipped with a hoisting beam that jutted out over the water. When a barge tied up below, the merchant could lower a hook from the hoisting beam and thus quickly gather in a shipment of wheat, beer, or herring.

Imagine that it is a winter morning in the 1630's. Let us take an early stroll along a narrow

Daily Life · *Tulips and Trade*

Amsterdam in the 1600's was a hotbed of financial speculation. People bought and sold goods of all sorts in hopes of making a profit. In the mid-1630's, a new money-making craze swept the city—tulip bulbs. Everyone in Amsterdam, it seemed, had gone mad over exotic strains of tulips imported from Turkey. It was common for a single tulip bulb to be bought and sold ten times in one day, always for a profit. A wealthy Dutchman once traded his mansion for three tulip bulbs and considered it a bargain!

Rembrandt van Rijn's dramatic painting, "The Night Watch," shows the civic leaders of Amsterdam keeping guard over their city.

lane beside one of Amsterdam's canals. In the soft light of dawn, the milk pails of a milkman clank loudly. Moments later, the neighborhood baker drags a cart along the lane and calls out to the homeowners opening their shutters, "Hot white bread! Rye bread rolls! Barley biscuits!"

In the frosty air, as Dutch neighbors greet one another across the canal, their bodies seem oddly round and bulky. To keep warm, they bundle up in layer upon layer of woolen clothing. Men wear seven or eight waistcoats and pairs of trousers. Women pile on layer after layer of petticoats.

In one of the narrow houses, a family is taking the first meal of the day. The family members begin with a solemn Calvinist prayer before settling down to a standard Dutch breakfast: bread, cheese, butter, and beer. When finished, all stand to pray again. In the course of the long day, they look forward to three more meals. For the main feast at midday, a prosperous family will set out plates of herring, almonds, fruits, and a rice pudding dessert. The poor usually make do with four meals of cheese, bread, broth, and many tankards of beer.

Dutch artists developed a new style.

During the 1600's, Amsterdam became what Florence had been during the 1400's. It boasted not only the best banks but also the best artists in Europe.

The greatest Dutch artist of the period was Rembrandt van Rijn (REHM-brant vahn ryne), who lived from 1606 to 1669. Rembrandt's paintings realistically captured moments of drama. In 1632, a wealthy physician commissioned Rembrandt to paint a group portrait. The artist showed the distinguished doctor standing over the corpse of an executed criminal, lecturing a group of fellow surgeons. Rembrandt's most famous group painting, "The Night Watch," showed his mastery of light and shadow.

Dozens of other artists worked in Amsterdam. The older master Franz Hals (1580–1666) painted brighter and less somber works than Rembrandt. His merry spirit showed itself in the vigorous faces of the people he painted.

The Dutch often chose domestic, indoor settings for their portraits. They apparently enjoyed

Both this painting and the one on page 373 are by Dutch artist Jan Vermeer. How are the two pictures similar in style and content?

seeing themselves doing chores in their homes and workshops. For example, the young artist Jan Vermeer (1632–1675) became famous for his paintings of middle-aged women doing such tasks as pouring milk and sewing. In his paintings, light from an open window seemed to flood the room.

Dutch art showed more interest in groups than in heroic individuals such as Michelangelo's "David" or Velázquez's Spanish monarchs. Frequently, Dutch artists painted group portraits of people—families, civic leaders, military units. As many as 40 people may appear in one painting. Taken as a whole, Dutch art revealed the prosperity, the civic spirit, and the values of a new age in Europe.

Section Review 3

Define: (a) republic, (b) capitalism, (c) capital, (d) profit, (e) Commercial Revolution
Identify: (a) the Netherlands, (b) Sea Beggars,
(c) William of Orange (the Silent), (d) stadtholder, (e) Dutch East Indies Company, (f) Amsterdam, (g) Rembrandt
Answer:
1. (a) List three ways in which the Netherlands differed from Spain. (b) How did the Netherlands become a part of Spain?
2. (a) What policies did Philip's sister Margaret and the Duke of Alva follow in the Netherlands? (b) What were the results?
3. (a) What was William the Silent's political goal? (b) His religious goal? (c) What did he achieve?
4. How were the Dutch able to stop the Spaniards at Alkmaar?
5. (a) What part of the Netherlands declared itself independent of Spain in 1581? (b) What happened to the rest of the Netherlands?
6. (a) Describe the government of the Netherlands. (b) Briefly describe the way businesses in the Netherlands were organized.
7. (a) Why was the Dutch East Indies Company formed? (b) What help did the Dutch government give the company?

Critical Thinking
8. How was the United Provinces of the Netherlands unusual for its time in both politics and religion?

France's crown changed hands.   4

In 1559, France's future looked bleak. Its long series of wars with Spain for control of Italy had come to an end, with Spain the clear winner. France was exhausted by the wars. Moreover, the French king, Henry II, was severely injured in a jousting tournament and died from his wounds in 1559. Henry II had been a member of the Valois (va-LWAH) dynasty, the family that had ruled France since 1328.

Not content with defeating France, Philip II worked for the rest of the 1500's to weaken the French monarchy. His efforts helped bring about the downfall of the Valois. Yet, by destroying the Valois, Philip II unwittingly helped bring to power a strong new king, Henry IV.

Catherine de Medici ruled France.

Henry II left four young sons, all of whom were incompetent. All had short lives, so that three of Henry's boys briefly wore the French crown. Their strong-willed mother, Catherine de Medici, really ruled France in their name.

Catherine came to power at a time when France was deeply divided over religion. Calvinist ministers had made thousands of converts in France. French followers of Calvinism were known as Huguenots (HYOO-guh-nahts). By 1559, about one sixth of France's population was Calvinist.

Most of the major towns and cities in France were divided between Catholics and Huguenots. Intense hatred between the two groups frequently led to violence. Groups attacked each other's churches. Thousands of people were tortured, burned, or beaten to death for their beliefs.

Two ambitious French families further inflamed these religious hatreds. On one side was the House of Bourbon (BOOR-buhn), a family of French nobles who had become Protestants. On the other side was the House of Guise (geez), a noble family who staunchly championed Catholicism. The Bourbon and the Guise families hated each other, and each hoped to overthrow the Valois monarchy and start a dynasty of its own. Between 1562 and 1589, there were nine civil wars between Bourbons and Guises, Huguenots and Catholics.

The worst outbreak of fury began in Paris on August 24, 1572—the date known on the Catholic calendar as St. Bartholomew's Day. With the first light of dawn, Catholic mobs in Paris hunted for Protestant neighbors, dragged them from bed, and murdered them. The massacres spread to other cities and went on for over a month. About 12,000 Huguenots were killed.

The queen mother herself, Catherine de Medici, was largely to blame for the massacre. Catherine was Catholic, but her motives were not religious. Politics concerned her far more than religion. In 1572, she feared she was losing her influence over her weak son, King Charles IX. The Admiral de Coligny (koh-lee-NYEE), a Protestant noble, had become the king's closest adviser. To keep her position as the power behind the throne, she arranged for Coligny to be killed.

At first, the weak king objected to his mother's scheme. Finally, however, he yielded to her browbeating. He shouted in a fit of temper, "I consent. But then you must kill all the Huguenots in France so that none shall be left to reproach me. Kill them all! Kill them all." With Catherine's complete approval, the St. Bartholomew's Day massacre of the Huguenots began. On the same day, a hired killer assassinated Coligny.

The Valois dynasty ended.

After the St. Bartholomew's Day massacre, French politics became even more violent and confused. In 1574, Charles IX died of tuberculosis. His younger brother, Henry III, was destined to be the last Valois king of France. Though Henry reigned for 15 years, he did not rule. Nobody ruled France in these years of civil war.

Just as some German nobles supported Lutheranism to weaken the emperor, some French nobles became Protestants to weaken their Catholic king. Among the upper classes, religion and politics were closely linked.

For a while, it appeared that the Guise family might triumph and place their Catholic duke on the throne. Catholics both inside and outside France rallied around the Guise banner. Spain's Philip II supported the Catholic cause by sending Spanish armies into France. His French ally, the Duke of Guise, marched triumphantly into Paris.

Many French people—Catholics as well as Protestants—were outraged. Had France fought Spain for years only to have Spain handpick France's king? Nationalism began to outweigh religion for some French Catholic leaders. These leaders, known as the *politiques* (poh-lih-TEEKS), wanted peace for France. They wanted a king strong enough to stop the wars that were tearing France apart. The politiques worked for religious toleration and a strong monarchy.

In 1589, Catherine de Medici died. Shortly afterward, King Henry III ordered nine of his soldiers to murder the Catholic Duke of Guise. In revenge, a Dominican friar stabbed the king to death.

Henry IV brought peace.

The heir to the French throne was Prince Henry of Navarre. He was descended from the popular medieval king, Saint Louis (Louis IX). Henry was robust, athletic, and handsome. He soon showed himself to be decisive, fearless in battle, and a clever politician as well. He was the leader of the House of Bourbon and therefore a Huguenot. With the support of both the Protestants and the Catholic politiques, he became the first Bourbon king of France, Henry IV. Yet it took him nine more years of fighting to secure his crown.

Many Catholics, including the people of Paris, still opposed Henry. For the sake of his war-weary country, Henry chose to give up his religion. In 1593, he became a Catholic. Shortly afterward, the Catholics of Paris warmly welcomed him as their king. Explaining his religious turnabout, Henry IV is sometimes quoted as saying: "Paris is well worth a Mass."

In 1598, Henry took another giant step toward healing France's wounds. He declared that the Huguenots could henceforth worship in peace. In every district, Huguenots could set up at least one house of worship. Paris was the only large French city where Protestant worship was strictly banned. This declaration of religious toleration was known as the Edict of Nantes.

Henry devoted the rest of his reign to rebuilding France and restoring its prosperity. "I hope to make France so prosperous," he said, "that every peasant will have chicken in the pot on Sunday." Although chicken dinners remained beyond the reach of most peasants, no other French king had cared so much for the welfare of the common people. Aided by an able finance minister, the Duke of Sully, Henry restored the French monarchy to a strong position. Spanish armies no longer invaded French soil. After a generation of war, most French people welcomed Henry's peace.

Some people, however, hated the compromising spirit of their Bourbon king. In 1610, one such fanatic leaped into the royal carriage and stabbed Henry to death.

Cardinal Richelieu controlled France.

Henry's nine-year-old son, Louis XIII, became the second Bourbon monarch. Louis reigned from 1610 to 1643. Even after he became an adult, Louis XIII lacked the ability and strength of his father. However, he at least had the good sense to turn over the business of government to someone more gifted than himself.

In 1624, Louis appointed a Catholic cardinal named Richelieu (RISH-uh-loo) to be his chief

Richelieu was the power behind the French throne from 1624 to 1642. A shadowy figure, he was sometimes called "the gray eminence."

minister. Richelieu became virtual ruler of France. No statesman in Europe could match the iron will and cunning mind of this lean-faced, hawk-nosed cardinal.

The wily Richelieu devoted himself to two goals: increasing the power of the Bourbon monarchy and making France the strongest state in Europe. He saw three dangers to the French state: (1) the independence of the Huguenot cities, (2) the power of the French nobility, and (3) the

Footnote to History

Richelieu, plagued by ill health, often shunned the hectic social life of the royal court. He retreated to the peace and quiet of his own household and the companionship of his 14 cats.

encircling armies of the Hapsburgs. He fought relentlessly against all three.

First, Cardinal Richelieu feared a provision in the Edict of Nantes that gave Huguenots the right to fortify their cities. A walled city could defy the king. Indeed, several Huguenot cities had already rebelled, including the stronghold of La Rochelle. In 1627, royal troops besieged La Rochelle and starved it into submission. The loss of La Rochelle and other walled cities was a major setback for French Protestantism. Huguenots continued to worship freely while Richelieu lived, but later even this privilege was revoked.

The French nobles were the next group to lose their privileges under Richelieu. Many were ordered to take down their fortified castles. Richelieu's spies reported those who resisted or plotted against the king. In addition, Richelieu strengthened the powers of government agents to collect taxes and administer justice. These officials, called *intendants*, came from the ranks of the French middle class. They were staunchly loyal to the crown. Thus, the French ruler no longer needed the military and political services of the nobility. For the next 100 years, Bourbon kings would rule France as absolute monarchs, and no nobles would be strong enough to resist.

Richelieu triumphed over the Spanish and Austrian Hapsburgs as well. His successes formed part of the story of the Thirty Years' War (pages 380–381).

French thinkers questioned authority.

As France regained its political power, a new French intellectual movement began as well. The leading French thinkers of the 1500's witnessed France's religious wars with horror. What they saw turned some of them into skeptics (doubters) about the doctrines of all religions. To doubt old ideas, they thought, was the first step toward finding truth. The work of three French writers—François Rabelais (RAB-uh-**LAY**), Michel de Montaigne (mahn-**TAYN**), and René Descartes (day-**KART**)—marked another sharp break from the ideas of the Middle Ages.

Rabelais (1483–1553) François Rabelais was a monk who loved to laugh at human folly. He fled the monastery to pursue a career in medicine. Between 1532 and 1535, he published two satires on European society, *Gargantua* and *Pantagruel*. The comic heroes of these books were keen-witted giants with immense appetites for food and fun. Rabelais ridiculed everything that restricted the human spirit. People, he wrote, should live by one rule: "Do as you wish."

Montaigne (1533–1592) A later writer and thinker, Michel de Montaigne lived during the worst years of the French religious wars. Early in his life, the death of a dear friend caused him overwhelming grief. He shut himself away in his private library and thought deeply about life's meaning.

Montaigne set forth his thoughts in a new form of literature, the essay. An essay is a short written work on a single topic. It usually expresses the personal views of the writer. In his essays, Montaigne told about himself, his lost friend, the meaning of friendship, the books that he loved, the doctors that he shunned, and many other topics.

In the first edition of his *Essays* (published in 1580), Montaigne warned readers that his subject goes no deeper than himself:

> *This is an honest book, reader . . . I want to be seen here in my simple, natural, ordinary fashion, without pose or artifice; for it is myself that I portray. My defects will here be read to the life . . .*

In fact, Montaigne's essays showed him to have more virtues than defects. An admirer once called him "the wisest Frenchman that ever lived."

Descartes (1596–1650) The third important French writer and thinker of this age was René Descartes. Descartes was both a mathematician and a philosopher. In his mathematical writings, he developed the basic ideas of analytic geometry. He also studied optics, astronomy, and natural philosophy in its connections with what is now called psychology.

Descartes is considered the founder of modern philosophy. His most famous work was his *Discourse on Method*, which he wrote as a guide for "seeking truth in the sciences." Descartes believed nothing should be accepted on faith. Everything should be doubted until proved by reason. How could he prove his own existence? Descartes knew himself to be thinking, doubting. The one thing each person knows for certain, wrote Descartes, is, "I think, therefore I am."

Section Review 4

Define: (a) politiques, (b) intendants, (c) essay
Identify: (a) Valois, (b) Catherine de Medici, (c) Huguenots, (d) Henry IV, (e) Edict of Nantes, (f) Richelieu, (g) Rabelais, (h) Montaigne, (i) Descartes

Answer:

1. (a) What political problems did France face in 1559? (b) How did religion divide the French people?
2. (a) What two noble families wanted to overthrow the Valois? (b) What was the religion of each?
3. (a) How did Catherine de Medici use religious hatreds to maintain her political power? (b) What role did she play in the St. Bartholomew's Day massacre?
4. What were the goals of the politiques?
5. (a) Why did Henry IV change his religion? (b) What did he do to establish religious toleration in France?
6. (a) What were Richelieu's two goals? (b) Why did he fear the Huguenot cities? (c) How did he weaken the French nobles?

Critical Thinking

7. Henry IV defined his own religion this way: "Those who follow their consciences are of my religion, and I am of the religion of those who are brave and good." Why was this a wise political statement for him to make as France's king?
8. Explain why Richelieu is generally considered a politique, even though he was a cardinal in the Catholic Church.

Religious wars split Germany. 5

For a time, the German princes and electors had settled their religious differences by the Peace of Augsburg in 1555 (page 357). They had agreed that the churches in Germany could be either Lutheran or Catholic, but not Calvinist. Furthermore, the prince of every state was to decide the religion of that state.

The Catholic and Lutheran princes of Germany watched each other warily. As tension mounted, the Lutherans joined together in the Protestant Union in 1608. The next year, Catholic princes formed the Catholic League. It would take only a spark to start a war.

Germans fought the Thirty Years' War (1618–1648).

The spark came in 1618. A Protestant mob rioted in the streets of Prague in the Czech kingdom of Bohemia. These Czechs were angry that their king, Ferdinand II, was both a foreigner—a German-speaking Austrian—and an ardent Catholic. Ferdinand was also a leader of the Hapsburg family. (He was a nephew of Charles V, a cousin of Philip II.) In 1619, he became Holy Roman Emperor.

As an Austrian, Ferdinand II aroused the Czechs' national hatred. As a Catholic, he menaced the religious freedom of the Lutheran princes of Germany. As a Hapsburg, he posed a threat to the Bourbon kings of France. Ferdinand's many enemies soon united against him.

In 1618, Ferdinand sent an army into Bohemia to put down the Protestant revolt. Several German Protestant princes took this chance to challenge their Catholic emperor.

Thus began the struggle known as the Thirty Years' War. This war was as confusing as it was vicious. To simplify it, we can divide the Thirty Years' War into two major phases: the phase of Hapsburg triumphs and the phase of Hapsburg defeats.

Between 1618 and 1630, Hapsburg armies from Austria and Spain crushed the troops hired by the Protestant princes. The Czech uprising also failed, and its leaders were executed. In 1625, the king of Denmark entered the war on the Protestant side. On the Catholic side, Ferdinand II hired a ruthless soldier of fortune, Albrecht von Wallenstein. Wallenstein raised an army of 125,000 men. He paid them by allowing them to plunder German villages. Wallenstein's huge armies destroyed everything in their path. By 1629, the Protestant cause in Germany looked weak indeed.

Then the tide of war suddenly shifted as the Protestants found a new leader. In 1630, a tall Swedish king named Gustavus Adolphus landed on the north coast of Germany. With him was a tough, tightly disciplined army of 13,000 men. For two years (1630–1632), Protestant princes rallied around his banner. Gustavus Adolphus outmaneuvered the Hapsburg armies and drove them out of northern Germany. Then Gustavus Adolphus was killed in battle in November 1632. Wallenstein died soon after, murdered by his own officers.

The remaining years of the German war were dominated by Cardinal Richelieu, the power behind the French throne. Richelieu cared nothing that the Hapsburgs were Catholic as he was. He loved France and feared the Hapsburgs, so he brought France into the war on the Protestant side. In 1635, he sent French troops into Germany to join Swedish and German Protestants.

The war dragged on for 13 more years. It left Germany ravaged. The German population sank from 20 million to 13.5 million. Only a small share of these died in battle. Many died of hunger, as armies burned and destroyed the crops. Others died of such diseases as plague, dysentery, and typhus that spread from army camps to the people nearby. Still others simply fled. Whole villages disappeared. Many peasants were forced back into serfdom after marauding armies destroyed their homes. Both trade and agriculture were in a shambles. Germany's economy was ruined.

The Treaty of Westphalia ended the war.

Gradually, the French and their Protestant allies wore down the Austrian Hapsburgs and their Spanish allies. In 1648, Ferdinand II's son (the new Holy Roman Emperor) agreed to a peace treaty that heavily favored his Swedish, French, and Protestant enemies.

The Thirty Years' War ended with the Treaty of Westphalia. These were its major terms:

1. France took Alsace, a fertile strip of land along the west bank of the Rhine River.
2. Sweden took a piece of northern Germany on the North Sea and another piece on the Baltic Sea.
3. The princes of Germany won almost total independence from the Holy Roman Empire. Each German state could sign treaties and go to war without the approval of the emperor.

4. Calvinism gained equal privileges with Lutheranism and Catholicism. A Calvinist prince in Germany could now dictate the religion of his state.
5. The Dutch Republic (or United Provinces) won recognition as an independent state.

The long-term consequences of the treaty were more important than its terms. In effect, Germany lost what little unity it once had. Its 300 states became virtually independent. The Holy Roman Empire, which had earlier held the German princes together, survived only in name.

As the big losers of the Thirty Years' War, the Hapsburg states of Austria and Spain declined in power. As the major winner of the war, France emerged as Europe's strongest state.

Another European nation, England, was fortunate to stay out of the ruinous Thirty Years' War. However, England was going through serious religious and political troubles of its own. England's troubles as well as its growing strength will be described in the next chapter.

Section Review 5

Identify: (a) Ferdinand II, (b) Bohemia, (c) Thirty Years' War, (d) Wallenstein, (e) Gustavus Adolphus, (f) Treaty of Westphalia
Answer:
1. (a) Why did the Protestants of Bohemia riot in 1618? (b) What happened when Ferdinand II tried to put down the revolt?
2. What was the turning point in the Thirty Years' War?
3. Why did France, a Catholic kingdom, join the Protestant side?
4. (a) What were the economic and social effects of the Thirty Years' War on Germany? (b) What was the political effect on German unity?
5. What did each of the following gain from the war? (a) France (b) Sweden (c) Dutch Republic (d) German Calvinists
6. (a) Which powers were the major losers in the war? (b) Which was the major winner?

Critical Thinking
7. Give evidence to support the following statement: The Thirty Years' War was more a political conflict than a religious one.

Chapter Review 17

Summary

1. Spain built an overseas empire. Early in the 1500's, Spain began building a vast empire in the Americas. Cortés conquered the Aztecs of Mexico, and Pizarro defeated the Incas of Peru. Explorations by others extended Spain's empire from what is now Kansas to Chile. Spain prospered, and its art and literature flourished.

2. Spain was a Catholic bulwark. At the center of Spain's empire was its emperor, Philip II, who ruled his lands absolutely. Determined to support Catholicism, Philip played a large part in the defeat of the Ottomans at Lepanto. His attempt to invade England with the Armada failed. He also failed to put down a revolt against Spanish rule in the Netherlands. Spain's prosperity, based only on gold and silver from its empire, soon collapsed.

3. The Netherlands won independence. Successful in their revolt against Spain, the Netherlands had a thriving trade and a capitalist economy. The Dutch established a republic in which many religious viewpoints were accepted. The artists of the Netherlands reflected its prosperity and civic spirit.

4. France's crown changed hands. After 1559, France was mired in a series of wars between Catholics and Huguenots as well as a power struggle between the reigning Valois kings and the competing houses of Bourbon and Guise. The civil war ended when Henry IV won the throne, changed his religion to Catholicism, and passed laws granting toleration to both Catholics and Huguenots. The skillful governing of Richelieu, minister to Louis XIII, made the French monarch an absolute ruler. During this era, French thinkers developed new literary forms and laid the basis for modern philosophy.

5. Religious wars split Germany. Germany became more disunited when conflicts between Catholics and Protestants led to the Thirty Years' War. The war caused great suffering in Germany, led to the decline of Hapsburg Spain and Austria, and left France the strongest state in Europe.

Reviewing the Facts

1. Define the following terms:
   a. conquistador
   c. inflation
   b. viceroy
   d. capitalism
2. Explain the importance of each of the following names, dates, places, or terms:
   a. Cortés
   e. Lepanto
   b. Pizarro
   f. Armada
   c. encomienda
   g. Cervantes
   d. Philip II
   h. El Greco

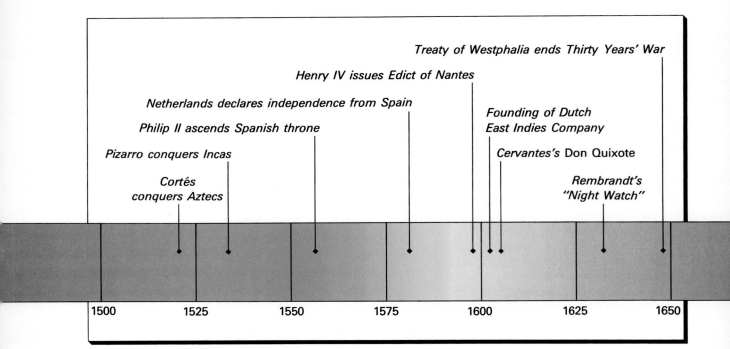

Treaty of Westphalia ends Thirty Years' War

Henry IV issues Edict of Nantes

Netherlands declares independence from Spain

Philip II ascends Spanish throne

Founding of Dutch East Indies Company

Pizarro conquers Incas

Cervantes's Don Quixote

Cortés conquers Aztecs

Rembrandt's "Night Watch"

| 1500 | 1525 | 1550 | 1575 | 1600 | 1625 | 1650 |

i. William the Silent
j. Rembrandt
k. Huguenot
l. Catherine de Medici
m. politique
n. Henry IV
o. Edict of Nantes
p. Richelieu

q. intendant
r. Rabelais
s. Montaigne
t. Descartes
u. 1618–1648
v. Hapsburg
w. Treaty of Westphalia

3. (a) What advantages did the Spaniards have in the conquest of the Aztecs? (b) How did Pizarro conquer the Incas?

4. (a) Into what two areas was Spain's American empire divided? (b) What was the Council of the Indies?

5. (a) What was the outcome of Spain's attack on the Ottoman empire? (b) Of the Spanish Armada? (c) Of Spain's war in the Netherlands?

6. (a) What was the source of Spain's wealth in the mid-1500's? (b) What economic problems did the country face by 1650?

7. What was the Commercial Revolution?

8. How did the Dutch win part of the profitable spice trade?

9. How were religion and politics linked in France's civil wars?

10. (a) What new French dynasty began with Henry IV? (b) How did Henry gain the support of French Catholics? (c) What steps did he take to reunite and strengthen France?

11. (a) How did the Thirty Years' War begin? (b) What were the results of the war?

12. (a) In 1559, what nation was the most powerful in Europe? (b) By 1650, what nation was the most powerful?

Thinking about History

1. A phrase often used to explain the conquistadors' reasons for sailing to the Americas is, "gold, glory, and God." What does this phrase mean? How well does it describe the conquistadors?

2. This chapter described wars between Spain and England, between Spain and the Netherlands, within France, and within Germany. Why is it difficult to say whether these wars were "really" about politics or "really" about religion?

Writing and Speaking about History

1. In chart form, compare the Dutch revolt against Spain with the Thirty Years' War in Germany. For each war, list the dates, reasons, chief protagonists, and outcome.

2. Using some or all of the categories in the preceding chart, write a compare/contrast essay on the topic. (See Research Skills Handbook, page 384.)

3. Assume that you are a Spanish explorer about to appear before the king of Spain. Prepare a speech in which you argue for the colonization of an area you have explored. Describe the area and its advantages to Spain.

Practicing Skills

1. Review the timeline on page 382. (a) What three events on the timeline have to do with religious conflict or the resolution of religious conflict? (b) What is the date of each event?

2. By 1600, the amount of gold taken from the Americas by Spain was estimated at 750,000 pounds. The amount of silver was even greater—16,000 tons of bullion by 1650. Find out what the current value of silver and gold is. How much would Spain's treasure be worth today? Find out whether that treasure was worth more or less in the 1600's.

Investigating History

1. Among the many changes the Spaniards brought to the Americas, one of the most dramatic was their introduction of the horse. Prepare a report on how the arrival of horses changed the culture of the Plains Indians of North America.

2. Investigate the works of one of these artists: Rembrandt, Velázquez, Hals, Vermeer, El Greco. Choose one painting that you particularly like and explain why it appeals to you.

3. Under the Treaty of Westphalia, France took a region called Alsace from Germany. Look up Alsace in an encyclopedia. (It is sometimes referred to as Alsace-Lorraine.) How long have France and Germany been struggling for control of this region? At what key points has it changed hands?

Decision Making in History

Evaluate the circumstances that led to Cortés's victory over Montezuma. Which circumstances were in Cortés's favor? Which circumstances were in Montezuma's favor? Of the events that took place, which one do you feel was most influential in deciding the outcome?

383

Research Skills

Comparing and Contrasting

As a historian, you are familiar with at least two civilizations—the one or ones from the past that you are studying and the one from the present in which you live. It is natural, as you read, to notice similarities and differences between a past civilization and your own. When you look for likenesses between two subjects, you are comparing them. When you look for differences, you are contrasting them.

Comparisons and contrasts between two events, people, or civilizations can make a good basis for an essay. Your first step in writing such an essay is to choose categories that are common to both topics. You can use those categories to compare the two topics in chart form. For example, here is a chart that you might complete in comparing the golden age of Florence to the golden age of Athens:

	Florence	Athens
Government		
Public works		
Art and literature		

"Discus Thrower" (classical)

Such a chart helps you formulate the thesis statement for your essay. The thesis is stated in the introductory paragraph of the essay and restated in the conclusion. The remaining paragraphs develop the thesis statement.

There are two main ways in which you can organize the developmental paragraphs. The first method is the point-by-point method. The second is the whole-to-whole method.

1. In the point-by-point method, you move back and forth between the two topics. For example, you might describe government in Florence and government in Athens followed by public works in Florence and public works in Athens.

2. The whole-to-whole method deals with one topic at a time. In this arrangement, you would discuss government, public works, and art in Athens and then proceed to the same categories for Florence.

In choosing a method, consider which will better serve your purpose. Will the information be clearer if you present a general view of each topic separately? Or will the likenesses and differences be more pronounced if aspects of each topic are presented side by side?

"Pieta" (Renaissance)

In comparing classical art with Renaissance art, you might point out the difference in subject matter.

Unit Review V

1. Put each set of terms below in one of the following categories: the Renaissance, the Reformation, the Age of Exploration. Then define each term.
   a. viceroy; conquistador
   b. theocracy; predestination
   c. vernacular; humanist
   d. capitalism; commercial revolution

2. Tell whether each of the following people was a religious leader, an explorer, or a Renaissance artist. Then describe a major contribution of each person.
   a. Leonardo
   b. Luther
   c. Loyola
   d. Calvin
   e. Cortés
   f. Magellan
   g. Raphael
   h. Knox
   i. Michelangelo
   j. Pizarro
   k. Cervantes
   l. Vespucci

3. (a) What years does the Renaissance encompass? (b) What were its main characteristics?

4. (a) Where did the Renaissance begin? (b) In what way was this region different from the rest of Europe?

5. (a) How did Giotto's frescoes begin a revolution in art? (b) How did Dante's *The Divine Comedy* revolutionize poetry?

6. (a) What city in northern Italy led the way in arts? (b) What powerful family ruled this city in the 1400's?

7. (a) In what way was the geographic discovery of new lands related to the Renaissance? (b) Describe the economic motivations that spurred exploration on.

8. What was Columbus's mistake?

9. (a) How did Brazil become a Portuguese possession? (b) What feat did Magellan's crew accomplish?

10. Describe three results of exploration.

11. (a) How did many Catholics feel about abuses within the Church during the 1400's and early 1500's? (b) Describe the impact of the printing press on religion.

12. (a) Explain the origin of the term *Lutheran*. (b) Of the term *Protestant*.

13. (a) Why did Henry VIII break from the Catholic Church? (b) How did his actions strengthen the English monarchy?

14. (a) How do Calvinism and Lutheranism differ? (b) How did Calvinism become the official religion of Scotland?

15. Describe the work of at least two people who reformed the Catholic Church in the 1500's.

16. Describe the contribution of each of the following to the Scientific Revolution. (a) Copernicus (b) Kepler (c) Galileo

17. (a) What was the source of Spain's wealth in the mid-1500's? (b) What was the cause of its eventual economic downfall?

18. (a) What three religious rivals did Spain war against in the 1500's? (b) What was the outcome of each war?

19. (a) Who were the opponents in the civil wars that rocked France in the mid-1500's? (b) How did Catherine de Medici use religious hatreds for her own purposes?

20. (a) Who was Cardinal Richelieu? (b) What were his two goals?

21. Explain how each of the following impacted religion during the 1500's and 1600's.
    a. Act of Supremacy
    b. Council of Trent
    c. Peace of Augsburg
    d. Edict of Nantes
    e. Treaty of Westphalia

Unit VI

The Transition to Modern Times

The question of government was crucial in this era. While the power of kings and queens reached new heights, that power also faced new challenges. Both in Europe and the Americas, people asked, What is the rightful basis for government? Is it the word of a monarch or the will of the people?

In France, Russia, Austria, and Prussia, rulers held unchallenged control. In contrast, English monarchs found their actions limited by the growing political strength of Parliament. The struggle between king and Parliament led to new political theories. While some philosophers supported the idea of a strong monarch, others argued that citizens had the right to rebel against unjust governments.

This debate became part of a movement known as the Enlightenment. The leading thinkers of the Enlightenment believed that human reason was the key to a better world. The use of reason, they said, would lead to a golden age of progress and liberty.

In the name of liberty, people in both America and France overthrew their monarchs in the late 1700's. Americans successfully established a republic with a Constitution based on Enlightenment ideals. However, the French soon found themselves under the tyranny of a new ruler, Napoleon.

Linderhof Castle, Bayern, West Germany

England: Tudor Queen and Stuart Kings

Queen Elizabeth sits in triumph, her hand on the globe. The ships shown in the background symbolize the English victory over the Armada.

1. **Elizabeth I faced many challenges.**

2. **Elizabethan England was a golden age.**

3. **England had a civil war.**

4. **Parliament won political power.**

As she rode through the ranks of the cheering soldiers, Elizabeth Tudor planned her speech to stir their fighting spirit. As queen of England, she was their leader, and she bore the fearful responsibility for the crisis that threatened all England.

On this day in August 1588, the Spanish fleet that Philip II called his Invincible Armada was somewhere off the English coast. Everyone knew that the Armada was coming to invade England, but nobody knew when or where it would strike.

An English army of 10,000 men was camped along the Thames River 20 miles east of London to defend their country from the invaders.

Now the queen herself was in the camp, and the soldiers were wildly excited to see their high-spirited, beloved sovereign seated proudly on her white horse. For this special occasion, Elizabeth wore her brightest red wig adorned with two white plumes that were easy for all to see above the soldiers' long pikes.

From her horse, the queen called to her troops, "My loving people!" They stopped their shouts and listened to her words.

My loving people ... Let tyrants fear! I have always so behaved myself that, under God, I have placed my chiefest strength and safeguard in the loyal hearts and good will of my subjects. Therefore, I am come amongst you ... being resolved, in the midst and heat of battle, to live or die amongst you all—to lay down for my God, and for my kingdom, and for my people, my honor and my blood even in the dust! I know I have the body of a weak and feeble woman, but I have the heart and [courage] of a king, and a king of England too, and think foul scorn that ... any prince of Europe should dare to invade the borders of my realm.

As you will read in this chapter, Elizabeth's navy had already destroyed the Spanish Armada, even as she spoke. This stirring victory raised English pride in their nation and their queen to new heights.

Elizabeth I was the last and greatest of the Tudor dynasty. She ruled England for 46 years, from 1558 to 1603. During her reign, daring English captains roamed the seas in search of treasure. English writers, scholars, and poets produced great works of art.

Yet, for all of its glory, the Elizabethan Age was not without troubles. In fact, political and religious conflicts raged frequently. By the end of Elizabeth's reign, England was on the brink of a great crisis. The central question was, Who would rule England—Parliament or the monarch? To answer that question, much English blood was spilled.

This chapter traces English history from Elizabeth's golden age through the troubled reigns of the Stuart kings. Finally, a revolution led to the beginning of a new era with a new philosophy of government.

Elizabeth I faced many challenges. 1

The 25-year-old Elizabeth came to the throne in 1558 at the death of her half-sister, Mary Tudor. Elizabeth was the third of Henry VIII's children to rule England. Like her father, Elizabeth had a fierce temper and a robust nature. Athletic as a girl, she showed amazing energy and strength into her old age.

One courtier who observed Elizabeth closely concluded that she was "more than a man, and (in truth) sometimes less than a woman." At times, she was quite crude. She would spit on the floor and swear in an astonishing manner. When her temper boiled over, she sometimes cuffed an offending courtier with a sharp blow to the head.

The other side of Elizabeth's character was graceful, witty, and refined. Her wardrobe included 2,000 velvet and jewel-encrusted gowns. She composed poetry and strummed a lute. She boasted of being as well-read in the classics as any prince in Europe. She had a scholar's command of Greek and Latin and spoke fluently in French, Italian, and Spanish. Her mind was remarkably quick, and nothing escaped her keen, penetrating eyes. One observer wrote of her:

All her faculties were in motion, and every motion seemed a well-guided action; her eyes were set upon one, her ears listened to another, her judgment ran upon a third, to a fourth she addressed her speech.

Elizabeth understood all too well the widespread prejudice against a woman ruler. All during her reign, Parliament urged her to marry a suitable man, either foreigner or Englishman. Yet she always resisted these pressures for the good of England and the preservation of her own power. Though she had many suitors, she remained unmarried until her death. She was nicknamed the "Virgin Queen."

This gifted queen needed all her intelligence and energy to guide England safely through the troubles of the late 1500's. These troubles came from four directions at once: religious conflicts, a rival queen, Spanish ambitions, and financial difficulties.

Religious issues divided England.

Elizabeth inherited the religious problem from her father, King Henry VIII. Henry had broken with the papacy in 1534 (page 351). In that year, he had persuaded Parliament to enact a law that made him, not the pope, head of the Church of England.

Since then, royal policy on religion had changed directions several times. Protestantism gained strength under Elizabeth's young half-brother, Edward VI (1547–1553). Then, her half-sister, Mary Tudor (1553–1558), made every effort to return the country to Catholicism. At first, no one knew which religion Elizabeth would choose. After all, she had been Protestant when Edward ruled and Catholic during Mary's reign.

When Elizabeth came to power, she knew she could not hope to satisfy either the extreme Catholics or the extreme Protestants. She decided, therefore, to establish a state church that moderate Catholics and moderate Protestants might both accept, however grudgingly.

In 1559, the first Parliament of Elizabeth's reign granted her request for two religious laws. The first, the Act of Uniformity, set up a national church much like the one under Henry VIII. This was to be the only legal church in England. People were required to attend its services or pay a fine. The second law, a new Act of Supremacy, declared Elizabeth the Supreme Governor of England's institutions, its church as well as its state.

As a concession to Protestants, priests in the Church of England were allowed to marry and to deliver sermons in English, not Latin. As a concession to Catholics, the Church of England kept all the trappings of a formal priesthood such as rich robes and golden crucifixes. To avoid controversy over doctrine, the wording of the queen's Book of Common Prayer was intentionally vague.

What mattered most to Elizabeth was not the religious beliefs of her subjects but their loyalty and obedience. She wanted no religious wars in England. It was not her intention, she said, "to pry windows into men's souls." Even so, during her long reign, Elizabeth ordered several dozen people burned at the stake for openly defying the official religion.

Catholics were unhappy with the Protestant aspects of the new Church of England. Still, it was more than ten years before the pope took action against Elizabeth by excommunicating her. That he waited so long was partly a tribute to the moderation of Elizabeth's policies.

Mary Stuart plotted against Elizabeth.

Outside England, devout Catholics looked for a champion to overthrow the Protestant queen. They found such a champion in Mary Stuart, Queen of Scots, Elizabeth's Catholic cousin.

In the 1560's, England and Scotland were separate kingdoms ruled by female cousins, Elizabeth Tudor in England and Mary Stuart in Scotland. As the great-granddaughter of England's Henry VII, Mary Stuart had a good claim to the English throne. She hoped some day to be England's queen as well as Scotland's.

French, Spanish, and Irish Catholics, and even the pope himself actively supported Mary in her quest to unseat Elizabeth. In fact, Mary received more support from these outsiders than she did from her own Scottish subjects. The Scots were fast converting to the Presbyterian creed preached by John Knox (page 354).

In 1567, an army of Scottish Presbyterians rose in revolt against Mary. To escape, Mary was forced to flee south to England. She thus placed herself at Elizabeth's mercy. For 20 years, Mary lived as part guest and part prisoner at an English estate set aside for her use.

Even as a prisoner, Mary could not rid herself of the itch for power. She foolishly became the center of some Catholic plots to overthrow Elizabeth. Finally, English spies intercepted a message from Mary agreeing to a scheme for murdering Elizabeth. The letter sealed her fate.

Elizabeth ordered Mary beheaded in 1587. Mary went to her death in a robe of black satin and a bodice of crimson velvet. English Protestants lit bonfires of celebration when they heard that the ax had fallen. Elizabeth, however, wept at the thought of having shed the blood of a cousin and fellow queen.

Philip of Spain threatened England.

When Mary Queen of Scots died, Philip II of Spain also grieved but for a different reason. He had been one of Mary's strongest supporters in her bid for the throne. With Mary's death, relations between England and Spain reached their lowest point.

The marriage question When Elizabeth first came to the throne in 1558, Philip II had seemed to be her ally. In those days, Philip had been more concerned with the power of Catholic France than with the threat of Protestant England. Moreover, he had been Elizabeth's brother-in-law, the husband of Mary Tudor. After Mary's death, Philip let it be known that he hoped to marry Elizabeth.

Elizabeth deliberately kept Philip (and dozens of other suitors) waiting. In fact, Elizabeth never had any intention of marrying Philip. She charmed, dazzled, and raised hopes in first one king or prince and then another. She used the hopes of a marriage to win diplomatic advantages with many European countries. Eventually, it became clear to all that the strong-willed sovereign would not marry anyone.

Drake and the sea dogs After Elizabeth turned down Philip as a husband, relations between England and Spain grew cool. By the 1570's, the two countries were enemies.

While still pretending friendship for Philip, Elizabeth secretly encouraged English adventurers to attack Spanish treasure fleets. These fleets sailed regularly from the Americas to Spain with rich cargoes of gold and silver. The bold English captains who raided them were known as "sea dogs." To the Spanish, they were simply pirates.

The greatest of the sea dogs was Francis Drake. On his most daring expedition (1577–1580), Drake raided Spanish ships in the Caribbean and along the eastern coast of South America. Then he did what no English captain had done before. He sailed through the Strait of Magellan around the tip of South America and captured Spanish treasure along the coast of Chile and Peru as well. From there, Drake sailed as far north as San Francisco Bay, crossed the Pacific Ocean, and returned triumphantly home with stolen prizes valued at 600,000 pounds. (This sum was more than twice the *yearly* revenue of the English crown.)

Drake thus became the first person since Magellan's crew to sail around the world. Instead of apologizing to Spain for his piracies, Queen Elizabeth knighted him aboard his ship, the *Golden Hind.*

The Armada In the 1580's, Elizabeth further angered Philip by aiding Dutch Protestants in their revolt against Catholic Spain (page 369). Elizabeth's decision to execute Mary Queen of Scots was the final straw, provoking Philip to wage war against England.

In 1588, Philip struck. He assembled a fleet of 130 ships with more than 31,000 men. This Invincible Armada, as Philip called it, sailed for

Daily Life · *Knives, Forks, and Spoons*

Queen Elizabeth ate most of her food with her fingers, as did everyone else in her day. In general, the only piece of tableware was a knife. When dinner was served, diners pulled out their knives (which they had brought with them) and began to eat. For example, meat was passed on a large platter. Each guest cut off a piece and put it on a slice of bread to hold. Spoons rarely appeared on the table, although cooks and kitchen help used them for stirring. People simply drank their soup.

During the 1500's, people began to use both spoons and forks. As with knives, guests usually brought their own. The use of forks began in Italy and spread slowly northward. In England, household records show that a few people owned forks by the mid-1600's. Not until 1750 could you regularly expect to find a fork at your place when you sat down to eat.

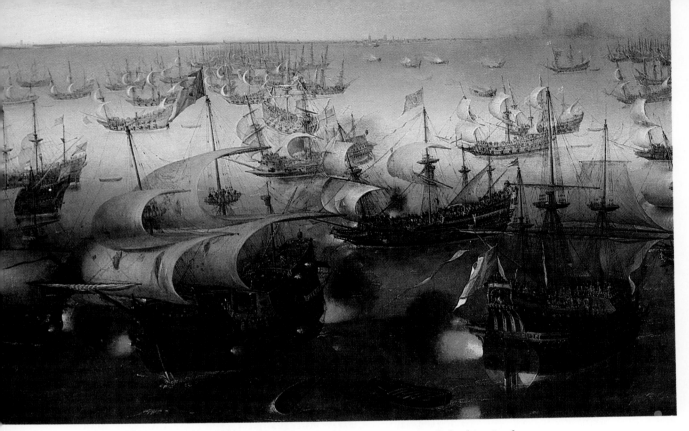

A Spanish ship from the Armada (left) turns its guns on an English ship. In the distance, five English fireships drift toward the Spanish fleet.

England. In late July, it boldly entered the English Channel.

Warily keeping their distance, the English captains—including Sir Francis Drake—set fire to a few of their own ships. Winds and currents carried the burning ships into the closed ranks of the Armada. To avoid these blazing hazards, the Spanish broke up their tight formation.

Now the smaller, faster English ships with their better guns began pounding the giant Spanish ships. As guns boomed and masts broke, a furious storm came up and scattered the damaged Armada. The Spanish commander decided to give up the invasion and run for home. However, more storms wrecked many of his ships. Barely half the Invincible Armada made it back to Spain.

Elizabeth had financial problems.

Another problem for Elizabeth was money. The yearly income of the English ruler was about 200,000 pounds. This was a meager sum indeed compared to the tons of gold collected by her rival, Philip II. The House of Commons always balked at a ruler's request for new taxes. How then was the queen to find enough money for the costly business of defending her country?

Elizabeth was, first of all, extremely tight-fisted. Soldiers in her army had cause to grumble about their poor wages and lack of supplies. The queen was always generous with her compliments but stingy with her cash.

Much of Spain's wealth came, as the English knew well, from its American colonies. England had played little part in the early voyages of exploration. In the late 1500's, however, the English began to think about building an American empire of their own.

Who had the funds to support such a venture? Certainly the queen did not, nor did a single merchant or even a partnership of merchants. Instead, English business leaders set up a special organization to attract capital from many people. It was known as the **joint-stock company**.

Investors in a joint-stock company bought shares of ownership. If the company went bankrupt, its owners lost the money they had invested. If the company prospered, the investors' shares of ownership entitled them to collect a proportional share of the profits. (Drake's voyage around the world in 1577 was a joint-stock enterprise that returned a 4,600 percent profit to its stockholders.) The joint-stock company was a sign that the Commercial Revolution (page 373) that began in the Netherlands had spread to England.

In 1589, a London merchant named Sir Thomas Smyth began to organize a company to settle the part of North America known as Virginia (named in honor of the Virgin Queen). The continuing threat of war with Spain, however, delayed such plans. Not until after Elizabeth's death did the English found permanent colonies in North America.

The most successful of England's joint-stock companies received its charter from the queen in 1600. Known as the English East India Company, its ambitious goal was to carve out a share of the rich East Indies spice trade.

Among the company's 101 owners were a London ironmonger, a vintner, and a leather seller, each of whom invested 200 pounds in the venture. They and their fellow owners waited through three suspenseful years before the company's four ships returned from the East Indies. As hoped, the ships carried tons of pepper, cloves, and other spices. In its first 21 years of business, the East India Company increased its capital 50 times over. Its owners became rich beyond their wildest imaginings.

While such ventures did not enrich the queen directly, they strengthened England economically. Moreover, the deeds of the sea dogs and the merchants weakened Spain at minimum cost to Elizabeth. Nonetheless, the queen's constant need for money would carry over into the next reign and lead to bitter conflict between the monarch and Parliament.

Parliament began to assert itself.

Toward the end of Elizabeth's reign, conflicts between Elizabeth and Parliament arose more and more often. Her religious compromise, which had kept peace for so many years, was no longer satisfactory. The people who objected most strongly were Puritans—men and women who wished to purify the Church of England of practices that they thought were too close to Catholicism. Puritans hated to see gold crucifixes at the altar and bishops dressed in richly ornamented robes.

The Puritans were a minority in the English population, but they were active in politics. When Parliament met, they formed a strong group in the lower house, the House of Commons. Puritan members of Parliament were outspoken in their demands for changes in the Church of England. Their bold speeches and petitions sent the queen into a towering rage. The rituals and organization of the church, she said, were her business. She wanted no suggestions about it from Commons.

Puritans were not the only outspoken members of Parliament. Others in Commons also wanted to be heard. Elizabeth, however, would have none of it. Instead, she left her successor, James I, a legacy of doubt and resentment. The question of who would rule England was yet to be resolved.

Section Review 1

Define: joint-stock company
Identify: (a) Elizabeth I, (b) Act of Uniformity, (c) Act of Supremacy, (d) Mary Stuart, (e) Philip II, (f) Francis Drake, (g) Armada, (h) Virginia, (i) English East India Company, (j) Puritan
Answer:
1. (a) Describe the religious problem that Elizabeth inherited from her father. (b) How did Elizabeth deal with the problem at the beginning of her reign?
2. (a) What threat did Mary Stuart pose to Elizabeth? (b) How did Elizabeth deal with that threat?
3. How did each of the following contribute to worsening relations between England and Spain? (a) English sea dogs (b) Dutch Protestants (c) Mary Stuart
4. What solution helped Elizabeth ease England's financial problems?
5. (a) Why did some members of Parliament begin demanding changes in policy? (b) How did Elizabeth respond?

Critical Thinking
6. Despite the advice of her councilors, Elizabeth chose never to marry. From a political point of view, do you think her decision strengthened or weakened her position as queen? Why?

Church spires formed the skyline of Elizabethan London. The grandest was St. Paul's, the large building at the top left. The Globe Theater and the Bear

Elizabethan England was a golden age.

2

For England, the defeat of the Armada produced a burst of pride and self-confidence. The late 1500's became a golden age economically, politically, and culturally. The center of this age was England's greatest city, London.

London was a bustling city.

In 1588, the year of the Spanish Armada, London was the most populous city in Europe. There were probably 200,000 Londoners who celebrated Sir Francis Drake's exploits. More than most cities at the time, London was densely populated and hummed with activity. Its medieval walls enclosed a space of only one square mile. Within that square mile, houses were so close together that neighbors could reach out their second-story windows and shake hands across the narrow streets.

Velvet-clad merchants dominated the commercial life of the city. However, they daily rubbed elbows with swarming masses of ragged poor.

Standing in the doorways of their little shops, sellers of odds and ends would yell at a well-dressed man or woman: "What do you lack?"

That was a standard cry heard by everyone throughout the city.

Another constant sound was the roar of the Thames River as it rushed through the great stone arches of London Bridge. This famous bridge spanned the river for 350 yards at one of its roughest parts. "The bridge at London," wrote one Englishman, "is worthily to be numbered among the miracles of the world."

The crowds passing over the bridge heard the water below but could not see it. Blocking their view were rows of shops and houses built right on top of the bridge. Like every other part of London, the bridge was a place of commerce.

The character of the city during its golden years was at once elegant and raw. We can best see this by observing a few of the many ways Londoners earned a living.

Boaters Because the streets of London were clogged with carts and crowds, the fastest way through the city was the Thames. Boaters waited along each bank of the Thames to offer rides, much as taxi drivers do today. Passengers in a hurry might order the boater to take a chance and shoot the rapids under London Bridge. More prudent souls heeded the old proverb: "London Bridge was made for wise men to walk over and fools to go under."

Water carriers In the days before pipes and plumbing, water carriers were a common sight

Garden, octagonal buildings, stood on the south side of the Thames. Above the gate to London Bridge, traitors' heads were displayed on pikes.

on city streets. Of course, only the well-to-do could afford to hire water carriers or "cogs" to bring fresh water to their homes. The poor went out to the city wells and the river to carry home their own water.

Because even the homes of the wealthy lacked plumbing, buckets were stashed in dark, closetlike rooms to collect human waste. Though there was a law against it, the buckets were usually emptied out the front door. A more sanitary contrivance, the flush toilet, was invented in 1596, but only the queen and a few others had such a luxury.

Cappers Those who followed the hat-making trade were popularly known as cappers. To keep cappers in business, the government of London passed a law in 1571 requiring that everyone over seven years of age wear a hat on Sundays and other holidays. The law was designed to prevent masses of idle cappers from rioting.

Barbers The barbers of London did a nice business catering to English gentlemen. The style of a Londoner's hair and beard received as much attention as his brightly colored doublets, stockings, hats, gloves, and knee-breeches. A writer of the period has left us this picture of the beard-trimmer's art:

And therefore if a man have a lean and straight face, a Marquess Otto's cut will make it broad and large; if it be platterlike,

a long, slender beard will make it seem the narrower; if he be weaselbeaked, then much hair left on the cheeks will make the owner look big like a bowdled hen and so grim as a goose.

Rogues and vagabonds Lacking an honest trade, many young Londoners fell into a life of crime. Lurking everywhere on London's streets were the coneycatcher, the nip, the foist, the wild rogue, the ruffler, and the angler. These were just some of the nicknames for the city's horde of petty criminals. Each name indicated a special branch of thievery.

The angler, for example, literally fished for stolen goods. Attaching a hook to the end of a long pole, the thief would stick the pole through a victim's window and then pull out whatever it caught. One angler was said to have stripped the bedclothes right from under the nose of a snoring man.

Jailers and executioners The many criminals of London gave employment to jailers and executioners. Petty thieves, for example, were normally punished by painful mutilation. A judge might tell the jailer either to cut off the thief's right ear or to brand it with a red-hot iron. Executioners also had much to do, because there were 200 crimes in Elizabethan England that were punishable by death. Some 800 English citizens were hanged every year.

Shakespeare wrote drama and poetry.

Nowhere in England could one see a greater variety of people—both high and low—than in London. Watching this pageant of human life was a man who became a master at revealing human nature in all its forms: the good and the evil, the wise and the foolish, the gentle and the terrible. No one better symbolizes England's golden age of literature than the poet and dramatist William Shakespeare. Many people regard him as the greatest writer of all time.

William Shakespeare was born in 1564 in Stratford-upon-Avon, a small town about 75 miles northwest of London. He spent an unremarkable childhood in this little town, attending grammar school with other boys and taking part in some of the town's lively fairs and pageants. At the age of 18, Will married Anne Hathaway. Records show that by 1592 he and Anne and their three children were living in London. It was in London that Shakespeare displayed his great genius both as a poet and a playwright.

It is difficult to define Shakespeare's genius. To some, it lies in his remarkable understanding of human nature. William Shakespeare revealed the souls of men and women brilliantly in scenes of dramatic conflict. However, Shakespeare was more than a skilled observer of human nature. He was also a poet who understood the sound and weight of every word. These lines from the tragedy *Macbeth* show Macbeth's despair:

Tomorrow and tomorrow and tomorrow
Creeps in this petty pace from day to day
To the last syllable of recorded time
And all our yesterdays have lighted fools
the way to dusty death.

The theater was popular in London.

English people enjoyed plays and drama long before William Shakespeare. As early as the Middle Ages, companies of actors traveled from town to town, performing in the courtyards of inns. The inn's guests watched from upper windows, either hooting or applauding the performance.

There were no fixed stages or theaters until 1576. In that year, an enterprising actor named James Burbage built the first permanent playhouse just outside the walls of London. He called it simply "The Theater." Londoners quickly got

William Shakespeare (1564–1616) wrote 38 plays, including Hamlet, Othello, *and* Romeo and Juliet.

into the habit of packing the house every afternoon. (Evening shows were impossible because audiences could not see actors by moonlight.)

The number of theaters in England grew rapidly. In 1599, Richard and Cuthbert Burbage (sons of James) built the Globe Theater about half a mile from London Bridge. The Globe soon became home to a company of actors, one of whom was Shakespeare.

Shakespeare's most famous plays were first performed at the Globe. As in other theaters of the day, the audience sat around a central yard that was open to the sky. A wooden platform or stage jutted out into this yard, and a curtain

Footnote to History

Shakespeare invented new words and used old words in new ways. Among the more than 1,700 words that he was first to use are *bump, courtship, critic, dwindle, gnarled, hurry, lonely, majestic,* and *road.* It is hard to imagine English without them!

This drawing shows the stage areas and seating galleries of the Globe Theater. No picture exists of the original Globe, which burned in 1613.

was placed at the back of it (not in front as in modern theaters). Actors performed scenes in three places: on the main stage, in a space behind the drawn curtain, and on a balcony above the stage. Thus, as one scene ended on the balcony, the next could begin immediately on the main stage. There was no painted scenery, but actors used a great variety of props, including swords, cannon, cages, live animals, and artificial heads.

The Globe seated about 2,300 people. For a penny, one could sit or stand on the ground itself as a so-called groundling. For two or three pennies, one was admitted to the sheltered galleries three stories high that encircled the yard. Those who came to the theater to show off their fine clothes and good looks could be seated on the stage itself. Of course, such seats cost more.

Shakespeare's plays were written during the reigns of two English monarchs, Elizabeth I and her successor, James I. Shakespeare died in 1616. His friend and fellow playwright, Ben Jonson, said of him: "He was not of an age, but for all time."

Section Review 2

Identify: (a) London, (b) William Shakespeare, (c) James Burbage, (d) Globe Theater
Answer:
1. How do do each of the following livelihoods reflect the character of London during the mid-1500's? (a) boater (b) water carrier (c) capper (d) barber (e) rogue (f) jailer

2. Why do many scholars consider William Shakespeare the greatest English writer of all time?
3. Describe the stage and seating arrangements of an Elizabethan theater.

Critical Thinking
4. What did Ben Jonson mean when he wrote, "He [Shakespeare] was not of an age, but for all time"?

England had a civil war.

3

On a cold day in March 1603, the reign of Queen Elizabeth I quietly came to an end. Elizabeth was dead at the age of 69. Never having married, she left no child to inherit her throne. The Tudor dynasty died with her.

Elizabeth's nearest relative was her Scottish cousin, James Stuart. James was the only son of Mary Stuart, whom Elizabeth had executed for treason 16 years earlier. James Stuart was already King James VI of Scotland when Elizabeth died. In 1603, he became King James I of England as well. Although England and Scotland remained separate countries for another 100 years, they now shared the same king.

James I clashed with Parliament.

With the throne, James inherited all the unsettled problems of Elizabeth's reign. Key among these was the question of how much say Parliament would have in governing England.

As king, James believed he had absolute authority to govern England as he saw fit. Royal authority, James declared, came directly from God, and kings were answerable only to God, not to the people or Parliament. This theory that royal power came from God is called the **divine right** of kings.

Elizabeth too had believed in her divine right to rule, but Elizabeth had had more tact than James. Often, she flattered Parliament in an attempt to get her way. James had no such tact. In addition, Parliament was growing impatient. It was an explosive combination.

Quarrels with Parliament James's worst struggles with Parliament revolved around money. Despite Elizabeth's frugal habits, she had left behind a sizable debt. James needed money, and Parliament had no desire to give it to him. James's manner with Parliament did not help. He felt it was beneath his dignity to bargain over money.

Puritan members of Parliament were especially offended by their new Stuart king. They complained that the Church of England was too Catholic. They urged James to make major changes in church rituals. The king angrily refused. Like Elizabeth, he insisted that the Church was strictly the ruler's business, not Parliament's.

The King James Bible Indeed, James was very interested in religion, and scholarship was his great strength. It bothered him that although there were many translations of the Bible, none was fully satisfying. Therefore, he gave to several committees of Bible scholars the task of creating a single authoritative text. The new version of the Bible was first printed in 1611. As befits a book produced in the age of Shakespeare, the King James Bible is noted for the elegance and power of its language. The King James Bible is still read by millions of English-speaking Protestants throughout the world.

The English founded American colonies.

Another achievement of James's troubled reign was the founding of the first permanent English colonies in North America. In 1604, James concluded a peace treaty with Spain. As a result, English joint-stock companies could go ahead with their plans for colonies without fearing that the Spanish would attack their settlements.

James granted a charter to the Virginia Company in 1606. The first English settlers arrived in Virginia in 1607 and named their community Jamestown in honor of their king. The colony was a disaster for these newcomers. Four out of every five died of hunger, disease, or Indian attacks.

Jamestown was also a financial disaster for its English backers. Far from winning profits, the company's organizers had to put more and more money into the venture to keep the colony going. In 1624, the London investors finally gave up. They turned over Virginia to the king's rule.

Pocahontas, an Indian princess, married a Jamestown settler. She is shown here, aged 21, in English dress while visiting London in 1616.

Nonetheless, the colonists in North America did not give up. Despite untold sufferings, they had gained a foothold in their new land. Other English settlers soon followed. Settlements began at Plymouth and Boston in Massachusetts.

By the end of Stuart times, England controlled much of the Atlantic coast of what is now the United States. English explorers had also claimed much of Canada. A rival power, France, was also building its power in North America. These developments set the stage for later conflicts between France and England.

The policies of Charles I led to war.

In 1625, James I died. His son, Charles I, became the second Stuart king to rule England. He inherited his father's problems with Parliament and made them even worse.

Charles was a firm believer in the divine right of kings. He had courage and intelligence. Like his father, however, he had too much pride and not enough common sense. Also like his father, he was always in need of money. As a result, the king and Parliament clashed constantly.

In 1626, a costly war with Spain forced Charles to go to Parliament for money. When Parliament refused to grant him the needed funds, Charles responded by dismissing it. The following year, the country became involved with a war with France as well as Spain. To pay for the war, Charles demanded forced loans from knights and nobles. He promptly imprisoned those who refused to pay. He also quartered troops in private homes at the homeowners' expense.

By 1628, financial needs forced the king to call Parliament again. Parliament, however, had had enough. It refused to grant Charles any money unless he signed a document that was known as the Petition of Right. In this document, the king made the following concessions:

1. He would not imprison subjects without due cause.
2. He would not force loans or levy taxes without the consent of Parliament.
3. He would not house soldiers in private homes without the owner's consent.
4. He would not impose martial law in peacetime.

The next year, weary of dealing with Parliament, Charles dissolved it. For the next 11 years, from 1629 to 1640, he refused to call Parliament at all. During these years, the king resorted to all kinds of fees and fines on the English people to raise money. His unpopularity grew greater every year.

England reached the brink of war.

Although Charles's taxation policies enraged the English people, it was his religious policies that eventually cost him his head. During his reign, thousands of Puritans fled England to escape persecution. Worse still, Charles chose William Laud to be archbishop and lead the Church of England. In truth, Laud was a staunch Protestant. However, his love of ceremonies and rich robes was so great that many Puritans thought he might be a secret Catholic.

In 1639, Laud foolishly decided to force Charles's Presbyterian subjects in Scotland to follow the Church of England's style of worship. To defend their religion, the Scots gathered a huge army and threatened to invade England.

Charles needed money to meet this danger —money he could get only from Parliament.

Between gritted teeth, he called a new Parliament. It turned out to be a mistake for the king.

Throughout the autumn of 1641, Parliament passed laws to limit the king's power. Charles was furious. In January 1642, he decided to take drastic action. Accompanied by 400 swordsmen, he strode into the House of Commons and demanded the arrest of five of its leaders. Alerted ahead of time, the men had escaped and were hiding in London. "I see that the birds are flown," said the embarrassed king as he stomped from the House.

News of the king's action angered Londoners. A mob raged outside Charles's palace. The city was now too dangerous for the king. He abandoned it and raised an army in lands in the north where people were still loyal to him.

Cavaliers and Roundheads fought a civil war.

The king's flight to the north in 1642 marked the beginning of the English civil war. Two groups of English people squared off to fight.

Those who remained loyal to King Charles were known as Royalists or *Cavaliers.* (The term was an insult because it was linked to the Spanish *cavaliero,* suggesting that a person was a Spanish sympathizer.) In general, the Cavaliers included English nobles and church officials.

On the other side were the Puritan townspeople and merchants who supported Parliament. Puritans cropped their hair short over their ears, instead of wearing it long and curled as the fashionable Cavaliers did. For this reason, Cavaliers mockingly called the Puritans *Roundheads.*

A Roundhead soldier summed up the issues this way:

The question in dispute between the King's party and us was whether the King should govern as a god by his will, and the nation be governed by force like beasts; or whether the people should be governed by laws made by themselves and live under a Government derived from their own consent.

At first, the Cavaliers held the advantage, controlling about three fourths of the country. They also had most of England's experienced military leaders. However, Parliament had great financial resources on which to draw. All the Puritans needed was a general who could win, and by 1644, they had found a military genius—Oliver Cromwell.

Cromwell was a country gentleman who had served in the House of Commons. Now he organized an army of zealous Protestants and inspired each soldier with the thought that God favored the Roundheads. "Truly," said Cromwell to his troops, "I think he that prays best will fight best." His military machine was called the New Model Army.

At first, most English people went on with their lives, untouched by the civil war. As the war dragged on, however, more and more villages were destroyed, more crops were ruined, and more hatreds were aroused. By the end of the war, 100,000 people had died in battle. The hatreds and the sufferings of the war had made people on both sides much more radical in their ideas than they had been at the beginning.

In 1646, Cromwell's New Model Army defeated the king's forces. Charles himself was a prisoner in Scotland. It seemed that Parliament had won, but the fighting was not over.

In 1647, Parliament tried to dissolve the New Model Army, but the army refused to obey. The army and its leaders were much more strongly Puritan and much more radical politically than members of Parliament. The army did not intend to give up control of the country.

In desperation, some members of Parliament joined forces with the king. Cromwell defeated them and captured Charles in August 1648. Then, Cromwell and his army marched into London and surrounded Parliament. Army leaders ordered the expulsion of 143 members of the House of Commons.

In 1649, Cromwell and the Puritans brought Charles to trial for treason. The king listened as the sentence of death was read aloud. Parliament's makeshift court declared, "Charles Stuart, as tyrant, traitor, murderer, and public enemy to the good people of this nation, shall be put to death by the severing of his head from his body."

The execution was set for Sunday, January 30, 1649. It was a cold day. As Charles was dressing, he asked his attendant to bring him an extra shirt to wear. He did not wish to tremble from the cold, he said, and have people think he was afraid. He went calmly to the place of execution,

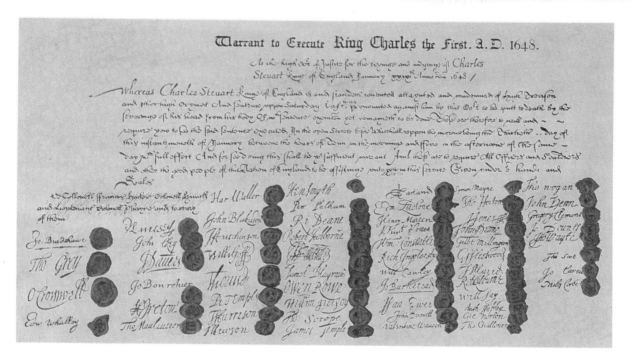

Charles I's death warrant, signed by 59 Puritans, accused him of treason.

laid his head on the block, and himself gave the signal to the headsman.

The execution of Charles was revolutionary. Kings had often been overthrown, killed in battle, assassinated, or put to death in secret. Never before, however, had a monarch faced a public trial and an official execution.

Cromwell ruled as military dictator.

With the king gone, Oliver Cromwell now held the reins of power. Of Parliament's original members, only a few remained. They had lost the respect of the nation and the army. In 1653, Cromwell announced to them, "You are no Parliament, I say you are no Parliament, and I will put an end to your sitting." His soldiers then drove the members out of the building.

To set up a new government, in 1653 Cromwell drafted a constitution, the first written constitution of a major European nation. This constitution set up a republic in which Cromwell ruled England as Lord Protector. In fact, his protectorate was little more than a military dictatorship, thinly disguised by talk of English liberty.

Now that the Puritans were in power, they set about reforming English society. Puritan laws shut down theaters and forbade sporting events. Under Cromwell, merrymaking and amusement became illegal. Many English people bitterly resented the Puritan dictatorship.

The conquest of Ireland Harsh as Cromwell's policies were in England, they were far harsher in Ireland. The island of Ireland had fallen under English rule during the reign of Henry VIII, but the Irish rebelled frequently against their English overlords. Elizabeth, James, and Charles each faced the problem of putting down Irish revolts.

After Charles was beheaded, the Irish rose again. In August 1649, Cromwell himself landed on Irish shores with a Protestant army. The English laid siege to the town of Drogheda. When it fell, Cromwell's army put all of its 9,000 inhabitants to the sword. They took special satisfaction in killing the town's Catholic priests and friars.

The Irish suffered more than a single massacre. Their lands and homes were taken from them and given to English soldiers as spoils of conquest. Several counties were set aside as strictly English property, and all Irish families who lived there were driven out. The general misery and homelessness took a frightful toll. One scholar estimates that 616,000 Irish, nearly half the island's population, perished from famine and plague between 1641 and 1652.

The death of Cromwell Oliver Cromwell ruled until his death in 1658. Next, his son Richard briefly held the title of Lord Protector. However,

401

Richard did not command the same respect as his father. His enemies laughed at him behind his back, calling him "Tumbledown Dick." The army deserted him. The English people, even many Puritans, yearned for the days when their government was headed by a king.

Section Review 3

Define: divine right
Identify: (a) James I, (b) King James Bible, (c) Jamestown, (d) Charles I, (e) Petition of Right, (f) William Laud, (g) Cavalier, (h) Roundhead, (i) Oliver Cromwell, (j) New Model Army
Answer:
1. (a) Why did James I clash with Parliament? (b) Name two things that he achieved during his reign despite such clashes.
2. (a) Why did Charles I clash with Parliament? (b) Why did he agree to sign the Petition of Right?
3. (a) What action of Archbishop Laud led to a confrontation between the king and Parliament? (b) What event marked the beginning of civil war?
4. (a) What two groups opposed each other during the war? (b) Over what issue did they fight?
5. (a) Who took control of England after the king's death? (b) Describe life for the English and Irish under his rule.

Critical Thinking
6. How do you think the death of Charles I affected other European monarchs who believed as he did in the divine right of kings? What advice would you give those monarchs?

Parliament won political power. 4

In 1659, an army general named George Monck decided the time had come for the English people to restore the monarchy. He marched into London and recalled Parliament. To no one's surprise, Parliament promptly voted to bring back a Stuart to rule England.

Charles II *restored the monarchy.*

Parliament invited Prince Charles Stuart, the elder son of Charles I, to return from exile. On a fine day in May 1660, Prince Charles sailed up the Thames. The crowds in London welcomed him with joyous shouts. Church bells rang throughout the realm. On this jubilant note, the reign of King Charles II began. Because he restored the monarchy, the period of his rule (1660–1685) is known as the Restoration.

Charles restored more than the monarchy. He also restored the theater, sporting events, dancing, and merrymaking in general. Life at Charles's court was elegant, colorful, and scandalous. It was not long before people were calling their new king "the merry monarch."

Drama and poetry Theater and the arts flourished during the Restoration. Not surprisingly, comedy dominated the stage. High society flocked to see amusing plays that poked fun at the manners and morals of the times. For the first time, women appeared on the English stage to play female roles. (In Shakespeare's time, beardless boys had played women's parts.)

The greatest writer of the period, however, was not a dramatist but a poet. John Milton, aged and blind, was a devout Puritan. He had worn out his eyesight writing propaganda for Cromwell. He took no joy in the Restoration, but his greatest poem, *Paradise Lost,* was published under Charles II. It was a work of Christian philosophy, an attempt to explain why life's suffering and pain are justified in God.

A *moderate ruler* Although Charles restored the monarchy, he did not try to restore the idea of the divine right of kings. Unlike his father and grandfather, Charles II had the good sense not to push himself or others too hard.

In religion, as in other things, Charles tried to steer a middle path. He wanted to give both Puritans and Roman Catholics some measure of religious freedom. In this, however, he met with firm opposition from Parliament. The Church of England remained the only legal religion.

The passage of habeas corpus Although England did not have religious freedom, the English people did win another important guarantee of freedom during Charles's reign. In 1679, Parliament passed a law known as habeas corpus. (*Habeas corpus* is a Latin term that means "you have the body.") This law gave every prisoner the right to obtain a writ or document ordering that the prisoner be brought before a judge. The judge could then decide whether the prisoner should be brought to trial or set free.

The Habeas Corpus Act meant it was no longer possible for the king or queen to put someone in jail simply for opposing the ruler. It also made it impossible for the monarch to hold someone in jail indefinitely without a trial. Today habeas corpus remains one of the most important guarantees of personal freedom in both the United States and England.

Problems over religion and money Although Charles had learned many lessons from his Stuart predecessors, in the end the very issues that ruined his father and grandfather returned to haunt him. Those issues were, of course, religion and money.

Charles had had Catholic leanings for many years. In addition, he was unable to live on the money that Parliament provided him. In secret, he turned to the Catholic and wealthy king of France, Louis XIV. Charles and Louis entered into a secret agreement. Louis promised to give Charles a lump sum of money every year. In return, Charles agreed to become a Catholic at some time in the future.

Although the people of England did not know of the agreement, they did know that their king was sympathetic to Catholicism. They also knew

Voice from the Past · *The London Fire*

On the night of Sunday, September 2, 1666, a disastrous fire broke out in London. It began in a baker's shop and raged for 3 days, destroying more than 13,000 houses and leaving 100,000 Londoners homeless. The following account comes from the diary of Samuel Pepys (peeps), a royal official.

Jane [woke] us . . . about three in the morning to tell of a great fire they saw in the City . . . [Pepys soon goes down to see for himself.] Everybody endeavoring to remove their goods, and flinging into the river . . . poor people staying in their houses as long as till the very fire touched them, and then running into boats . . . Having stayed, and in an hour's time seen the fire rage every way, and nobody, to my sight, trying to quench it, but to remove their goods, and leave all to the fire . . . So I was called for and did tell the King . . . that unless his Majesty did command houses to be pulled down nothing could stop the fire . . . [Carrying the King's command, Pepys finds London's Lord Mayor.] At last met my Lord Mayor in Canning-Street, like a man spent, with a handkercher about his neck. To the King's command he cried, like a fainting woman, "Lord! What can I do? I am spent. People will not obey me. I have been pulling down houses, but the fire overtakes us faster than we can do it" . . .

As it grew darker, [the fire] appeared more and more, and in corners and upon steeples, and between churches and houses, as far as we could see up the hill of the City, in a most horrid malicious bloody flame . . . it made me weep to see it. The churches, houses, and all on fire and flaming at once; and a horrid noise the flames made, and the crackling of houses at their ruin.

1. How did Londoners try to save their possessions?
2. (a) What step did Pepys recommend for stopping the fire? (b) How would this step have halted the fire?
3. What two reasons did the Lord Mayor give for his inability to stop the fire?
4. What service that almost every town has today was evidently lacking in London in the 1600's?

Pepys

After the great fire of London, St. Paul's Cathedral and many other churches were rebuilt by the noted architect, Sir Christopher Wren.

that he had no legitimate child to inherit the kingdom. Therefore, when Charles died, the throne of England would pass to his brother, James, who was openly Catholic.

Political parties developed.

The debate in Parliament over James's succession was fierce. Those who opposed James formed a group dedicated to keeping him off the throne. Those who defended both the king and his Catholic brother formed another group.

Each group invented a scornful label for the other. James's opponents were labeled "Whigs" (a Scottish word for assassins). His supporters were mockingly called "Tories" (the nickname for Irish bandits). These two groups were the ancestors of England's first political parties.

Long after the deaths of Charles and James, members of Parliament continued to identify with either Whigs or Tories. The two-party political system in both the United States and England today has its roots in this conflict.

404

James II *lost his throne.*

In 1685, Charles II died, and James II became king of England. Like his father, Charles I, James asserted his divine right to rule without Parliament's consent.

At first, the Tories in Parliament supported James. Soon, however, he antagonized even his firmest friends by appointing several Catholics to high office. This action openly violated the laws passed earlier by the Restoration Parliament. Tories as well as Whigs protested. James responded by dissolving his first Parliament and never calling another.

Three other events excited the fears of English Protestants. First, in 1687, James announced that government posts would be open to Catholics as well as Protestants. Second, James stationed 13,000 soldiers just outside London. Many Londoners feared that he was preparing to force England to accept Catholicism as the state religion. Third and most disturbing, James announced in 1688 that his second wife had given birth to a son. English Protestants were terrified at the prospect of a line of Catholic kings.

The infant prince was not James's only possible heir, however. James's first wife had been a Protestant. She had raised their eldest daughter, Mary, as a Protestant. Now an adult, Mary was the wife of William of Orange, a powerful Protestant prince of the Netherlands.

Whigs and Tories seized on a bold plan. They invited William and Mary to overthrow James II for the sake of Protestanism. William and Mary accepted the challenge.

William landed on English shores in November 1688 and led his army north to London. Nobody tried to stop him. The general of the English army, John Churchill, deserted James and joined William. Without any troops to fight for him, James sailed for France where he remained in exile until his death. Compared to Cromwell's civil war, this revolution was peaceful. The English still celebrate it as the Bloodless Revolution or the Glorious Revolution.

The English won a Bill of Rights.

In 1689, Parliament asked William and Mary to rule England as joint sovereigns. At their coronation, they solemnly vowed "to govern the people of this kingdom of England . . . according to the statutes in Parliament agreed on and the laws and customs of the same." This oath shows the significance of the Glorious Revolution. William and Mary recognized Parliament as the leading partner in ruling England.

To make clear the limits of royal power, in 1689 Parliament drafted a Bill of Rights. This document listed many things that a ruler could *not* do. These were the major prohibitions:

- No suspending of Parliament's laws
- No levying of taxes without a specific grant from Parliament
- No interfering with a member's freedom of speech in Parliament
- No penalty for a citizen who petitions the king about grievances
- No standing army to be kept in time of peace
- No posting of excessive bail in royal courts

William and Mary officially consented to these limits on their power.

Political ideas grew from conflict.

Did the English people have a right to rebel against Charles I in 1642 and against James II in 1688? Could a ruler lawfully be overthrown by his subjects?

The revolutionary events of the 1600's challenged two English philosophers to think about these questions. No, said Thomas Hobbes, there was no such thing as a right to rebel. Yes, said John Locke, people oppressed by their government had every right to rebel against it.

Thomas Hobbes wrote his most famous work, *Leviathan* (lih-VYE-uh-thuhn), in 1651, two years after the beheading of Charles I. The horrors of civil war convinced him that all humans were naturally wicked. Left to themselves, he thought, people would give free rein to their evil ways. Governments were created, said Hobbes, to protect people from their own selfishness. The best government was one that had the awesome power of a leviathan (sea monster). Since the chief purpose of government was to stop society from falling into disorder, Hobbes reasoned, an absolute monarchy was best.

John Locke held a different, more positive, view of human nature. He believed that people had the gift of reason. As reasonable beings, they had the natural ability to govern their own affairs and to look after the welfare of society.

Governments were formed, said Locke, to protect three basic human rights: the right to life, the right to liberty, and the right to property. These rights were absolute, belonging to all people everywhere as their birthright. What was government? It was a contract in which the rulers promised to safeguard people's natural rights. If any government abused these rights instead of protecting them, said Locke, then the people were justified in rebelling.

Locke's ideas were published in 1690, only two years after the Glorious Revolution. His two *Treatises on Government* served to justify the overthrow of James II.

Locke's theories had immense importance for future revolutionaries. Less than 100 years later, on the other side of the Atlantic Ocean, a young lawyer named Thomas Jefferson would use Locke's ideas to justify the rebellion of 13 American colonies against their English king, as you will read in a later chapter.

Section Review 4

Identify: (a) Charles II, (b) Restoration, (c) John Milton, (d) habeas corpus, (e) Tory, (f) Whig, (g) James II, (h) William and Mary, (i) Glorious Revolution, (j) Bill of Rights, (k) Thomas Hobbes, (l) John Locke

Answer:
1. Besides the monarchy, what else was restored in the Restoration?
2. (a) In what way was Charles II a moderate leader? (b) How did religion and money cause problems for him toward the end of his reign?
3. How did the succession of James II lead to the development of political parties?
4. (a) Why did Parliament invite William and Mary to rule England in 1588? (b) Name three ways the Bill of Rights limited royal power.

Critical Thinking
5. Explain why habeas corpus was an important landmark for personal freedom.
6. Hobbe's *Leviathan* was written two years after Charles I was beheaded. Locke's *Treatises on Government* was written two years after the Glorious Revolution. How was each work influenced by events of the time?

Chapter Review 18

Summary

1. Elizabeth I faced many challenges. The last of the Tudor rulers, Elizabeth I was a gifted queen who guided England through the troubles of the 1500's. These included religious conflicts between Catholics and Protestants; a plot against her life by her Scottish cousin, Mary Stuart; the threat of Philip II's Invincible Armada; and severe financial difficulties. Toward the end of her reign, Parliament began demanding rights that Elizabeth was not prepared to grant.

2. Elizabethan England was a golden age. Under Elizabeth I, England had a golden age. The center of this golden age was London, the most populous city in Europe. Elizabethan London bustled with trade and was filled with people from every class, from the well-to-do to criminals. This human pageant was brilliantly captured by William Shakespeare, whom many regard as the greatest writer of all time.

3. England had a civil war. Elizabeth's cousin, James Stuart, King of Scotland, succeeded her at her death in 1603. His reign is remembered for the King James Bible, the establishment of the first English colony in the Americas, and bitter quarrels with Parliament over money and religion. His son, Charles I, had even more difficulty with Parliament. Eventually, those difficulties led to a civil war in which Puritan members of Parliament fought the king's supporters. Oliver Cromwell led the Puritans to victory. After the beheading of the king, Cromwell established a severe military dictatorship.

4. Parliament won political power. In 1660, Charles II, son of Charles I, was recalled from exile to restore the monarchy. Although Charles II followed moderate policies and saw the passage of habeas corpus, his death sparked hostilities over the Catholic religion of his successor, James II. Eventually, James's harsh policies and staunch Catholicism led to a Glorious Revolution, in which Parliament forced James II off the throne and invited James's Protestant daughter, Mary, and her Dutch husband, William, to rule England. In 1588, William and Mary signed the Bill of Rights, which limited royal power and recognized Parliament as the real ruler of England.

Reviewing the Facts

1. Define the following terms:
   a. joint-stock company   b. divine right
2. Explain the importance of each of the following names, dates, places, or terms:
   a. Elizabeth I   d. Philip II
   b. Puritan   e. Francis Drake
   c. Mary Stuart   f. Invincible Armada

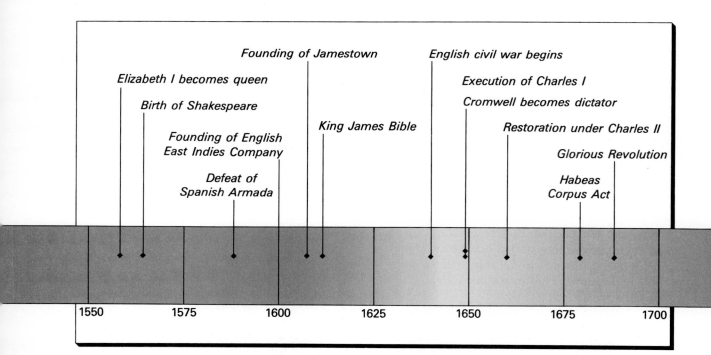

Elizabeth I becomes queen

Birth of Shakespeare

Founding of English East Indies Company

Defeat of Spanish Armada

Founding of Jamestown

King James Bible

English civil war begins

Execution of Charles I

Cromwell becomes dictator

Restoration under Charles II

Glorious Revolution

Habeas Corpus Act

1550   1575   1600   1625   1650   1675   1700

g. London
h. William Shakespeare
i. Globe Theater
j. James I
k. Charles I
l. Petition of Right
m. Cavalier
n. Roundhead
o. Oliver Cromwell
p. Charles II
q. habeas corpus
r. Whig
s. Tory
t. 1688
u. Bill of Rights

3. (a) Describe four obstacles that Elizabeth faced during her reign. (b) How did religious conflict affect three of them?

4. (a) How was the vitality of Elizabeth's reign reflected in the city of London? (b) How do the writings of William Shakespeare symbolize the golden age of English literature?

5. (a) What unresolved problem did James I inherit when he came to the throne? (b) How did his behavior make matters worse?

6. Describe the sequence of events that led to the English civil war, using the following topics. (a) divine right (b) war with Spain (c) forced loans (d) Petition of Right (e) Archbishop Laud (f) the visit of Charles I to Parliament

7. What social changes took place in England during the protectorate of Oliver Cromwell and after the Restoration?

8. Describe the sequence of events that led to the Glorious Revolution, using the following topics. (a) divine right (b) James's policy of toleration (c) James's army of 13,000 (d) the birth of James's son

9. (a) Why did Hobbes oppose the civil war? (b) Why did Locke support the Glorious Revolution?

Thinking about History

1. The text quotes Elizabeth I as saying, "I have placed my chiefest strength and safeguard in the loyal hearts and good will of my subjects." How did her reign confirm her statement?

2. It has been said that whoever controls the purse strings controls the government. (a) How was this true in Stuart England? (b) Why is legislative control of finances crucial in a democracy?

3. Describe how the Puritan role in English politics expanded from Elizabethan England to the reign of Charles I.

4. Explain why the English civil war can be called a contest between ideas of divine right and government by the people. Which prevailed? Why?

Writing and Speaking about History

1. Use the information on pages 398–402 to outline England's civil war. (See Research Skills Handbook, page 256.)

2. (a) As personal advisor to Philip II, write a marriage proposal to Elizabeth I outlining the political and economic advantages of such a union. (b) As a personal advisor to Elizabeth I, write a reply declining the proposal.

3. Standing in the doorways of their shops, a group of London merchants are discussing life in England in the 1500's. What might they say about their country during this time?

Practicing Skills

1. Review the timeline on page 406. (a) Which events took place during the reign of Elizabeth I? (b) Which events took place during the reign of James I? (c) About how many years passed between the Restoration and the Glorious Revolution?

2. In 1588, the mighty Spanish Armada contained 130 ships and more than 31,000 men. Use an almanac to find out how many attack ships and navy personnel the United States has today. Compare the two sets of figures. To what conclusion do you come?

Investigating History

1. Shakespeare wrote several plays about historic figures, among them *Julius Caesar, Anthony and Cleopatra, Henry V,* and *Richard III.* Read passages from one of these plays and look for ways in which the playwright reveals different aspects of human nature.

2. Charles II took a great interest in the world around him. This was reflected in his founding of the Royal Society. Find out about the Royal Society. What activities did it promote? Who were some of its members?

3. The Great Fire provided an unequaled opportunity to redesign London. The leading architect of the new London was Christoper Wren. Find out about his work.

Decision Making in History

As an advisor to Oliver Cromwell in 1649, you must recommend a course of action on what to do with Charles I. What will you recommend and why?

Europe in the Age of the Absolute Monarchs

Louis XIV's grand palace at Versailles was a monument of beauty and splendor. It also stood at a safe distance from the dangerous mobs of Paris.

1. **The Sun King ruled France.**

2. **Peter the Great changed Russia.**

3. **Austria and Prussia rose to power.**

"Sire, it is time."

In the privacy of his bedroom, the French king awoke, as he always awoke, to the whispered announcement of his chief valet. It was 7:30 A.M. at the royal palace of Versailles (vair-SYE), 11 miles southwest of Paris. From this moment until midnight, King Louis XIV understood that his every move would be watched and commented on a thousand times by the courtiers who lived at Versailles.

Louis had trained them all to depend on his little favors. A kingly nod to one courtier, a glance at another, a kind word to a third were treasured by the French nobles. Now, outside the curtains of his canopy bed, the 100 nobles on whom he had conferred his greatest favors were waiting. Every morning, these 100 privileged ones were permitted to enter the royal bedchamber and help the great king dress for the day.

First, the four highest-ranking nobles would approach the bed. Only one of these four was judged worthy enough to draw the curtain of the king's bed. For the next two hours, different groups of honored courtiers would file into the room to aid the king as he dressed. One noble would receive the king's discarded nightcap from the royal hand. Another would present Louis with his royal slippers. A third and a fourth would hold the two sleeves of Louis's nightdress as he stepped out of it.

Meanwhile, outside the king's bedchamber, thousands of lesser nobles would station themselves in palace halls. They hoped the king might see them as he passed and perhaps favor them with a nod or a look.

At 10 A.M. on the dot, Louis would be carried in a sedan chair into his chapel to attend the Catholic mass. Hundreds of nobles stood ready to greet him there and bow toward him just as he bowed toward the holy altar. It was as if the king, not God, was the true object of their worship.

For French nobles, success or failure in life depended on winning Louis's favorable attentions. A single blunder at court might doom their hopes of advancement. Thus, they were careful to follow the intricate rules of etiquette laid down by their demanding king. For example, whenever they met a procession of servants carrying the king's dinner, they were required to doff their hats and bow low. Knocking on someone's door was considered rude. The proper way to announce one's presence was to scratch lightly at the door with the little finger of the left hand.

Louis XIV, who ruled France from 1643 to 1715, was the most powerful monarch in French history. He was an **absolute monarch**, a ruler with unlimited power. Unlike England's ruler, Louis did not share his power with a parliament. In Louis's view, he and the nation were one and the same. He reportedly boasted, *"L'état, c'est moi,"* meaning "I am the state."

Although Louis XIV was the most powerful monarch of his time, he was by no means the only absolute ruler. Of all the major nations of Europe, only England (as you have seen) and the Dutch Netherlands resisted absolute rule. Elsewhere in Europe—France, Russia, Prussia, and Austria—powerful rulers dominated their lands. This chapter looks at Europe during the brief age (1648–1763) of absolute monarchs.

The Sun King ruled France. 1

Just as the sun is the center of the solar system, Louis was the center of France's government. Just as the sun dazzles people's eyes, so Louis dazzled France (and indeed all of Europe). "The Sun King" was the flattering description Louis liked best.

Louis XIV was the third king of the Bourbon dynasty. His father, Louis XIII, had been a weak ruler who left government in the hands of the powerful Cardinal Richelieu (page 378). Richelieu died in 1642, followed six months later by Louis XIII in 1643.

The heir to the throne, little Louis XIV, was only five years old. Although technically he became king in 1643, real power rested in the hands of his mother, Anne, and her prime minister, the ruthless Cardinal Jules Mazarin (MA-za-RAN).

Violence marred Louis's childhood.

Like Richelieu, Mazarin worked steadily to increase France's power. Mazarin's greatest triumph came in 1648 when he represented France at the peace conference after the Thirty Years' War. The terms of the Treaty of Westphalia (page 381) made France the strongest nation in Europe.

Although France was at the peak of its power, its king was still a frightened, lonely ten-year-old boy. In fact, the young Louis XIV had much to fear. Many people in France hated Mazarin and his harsh policies. In 1648, this hatred broke out in a revolt led by nobles who feared that Mazarin was stripping away their powers and privileges. A series of terrifying riots began in Paris and spread to the countryside. These violent outbreaks were called the *Fronde*. (*Fronde* meant "slingshot" and was a scornful term suggesting that the rebels were naughty children.) The riots and revolts continued for five years.

During the years of rioting, Louis's life was often in danger. In 1651, a group of rebels broke into the royal palace in Paris and roughly demanded to see the 13-year-old king. The terrified queen mother led them to the chamber where they found Louis sleeping—or rather, pretending to sleep. Satisfied that the king had not escaped

Paris, the rebels stomped out. Ever after, the king hated Paris. His later move to Versailles was partly caused by bitter memories of Paris.

In the end, the Fronde rebellion failed because its leaders distrusted one another even more than they distrusted Mazarin. Peasants and townspeople grew weary of disorder and fighting. For many years afterward, the people of France accepted the oppressive laws of an absolute king, because they were convinced that the alternative, rebellion, was even worse.

Louis ruled in grand style.

In 1661, Cardinal Mazarin died. Louis XIV, now 23, was glad to be rid of him. The king wished to rule France himself, to be king in fact as well as name. For the next 54 years, from 1661 to 1715, Louis dominated France.

Louis was indeed an impressive figure. Although he stood only 5 feet 5 inches tall, many people who saw him commented on his imposing height. His erect and dignified posture made him appear tall. (It also helped that he wore high-heeled shoes.)

Louis had very strong likes and dislikes. He hated cities but loved to travel through France's countryside. Because he hated delays, the people who traveled with him were at his mercy. Louis allowed no stopping except for his own comfort.

As king, Louis lived in a grand style. Eating was one of his chief pleasures. Nearly 500 cooks, waiters, and other servants worked day and night to satisfy his tastes. An observer claimed that the king once consumed four plates of soup, a whole pheasant, a partridge in garlic-flavored sauce, two thick slices of ham, a salad, a plate of pastries, fruit, and hard-boiled eggs in a single sitting!

The form of service was as important to Louis as the food itself. For example, three cupbearers busied themselves for eight minutes in the ritual of refilling the royal wineglass.

Colbert improved France's economy.

To Louis, all the pomp and ceremony of his court glorified France as well as himself. He wanted to make France the leader of Europe. As king, he devoted himself to helping France attain economic, political, and cultural brilliance.

Early in Louis's reign, France made impressive gains as an economic power, thanks largely to the efforts of a humorless Frenchman with scowling black eyebrows named Jean Baptiste Colbert (kohl-BAIR). Colbert was Louis's minister of finance.

Like other economists of his time, Colbert believed that a country's economic strength rested on its supply of gold and silver. The best way for a country to get gold and silver was to export more manufactured goods than it imported. This policy of favoring exports over imports is known as **mercantilism** (MUHR-kuhn-TEE-lihz-uhm).

In the 1700's, mercantilism was a kind of competitive game played by the rival countries of Europe. The winner of the game was the country that succeeded in keeping the most gold and silver in its treasury.

Suppose that France sold more goods to the Netherlands than the Netherlands sold to France in return. Then the Netherlands would be forced to pay its debt to France with gold and silver. Winners of this export-import competition were said to have a favorable **balance of trade**. Losers had an unfavorable balance.

In 1665, when Colbert became Louis's minister of finance, France was one of the big losers in the mercantilist game. Its textile, shipbuilding, and mining industries were weak. As a result, the French imported more goods than they exported. Each year, France paid out precious gold from its treasury to other countries.

For nearly 20 years, Colbert worked 10 to 15 hours a day to build up France's economy. To expand French industries such as glassmaking and weaving, he gave investors subsidies and tax benefits. To improve trade within France, he encouraged the building of new canals and roads. To protect French shipping, he added more than 100 warships to Louis's navy. Colbert encouraged skilled workers from other countries to settle in France.

Colbert also put high **tariffs** on imports. A tariff is a tax on goods arriving in a country. By raising the price of goods from other countries, tariffs discourage people from buying foreign products.

Many of France's skilled workers and business leaders were Huguenots (French Protestants). They took a leading role in commerce, banking, and industry—all the economic activities that Colbert had encouraged. Both France and the Huguenots prospered from Colbert's policies.

Sadly, a single mistake by Louis undid much of Colbert's work soon after the minister's death in 1683. Louis, a devout Catholic, revoked the Edict of Nantes (page 378). For almost 100 years, the Edict of Nantes had protected the religious freedom of the Huguenots. Suddenly, Huguenots could no longer attend their own churches or schools. Instead, they could be imprisoned as enemies of the state.

Louis paid a high price for his religious intolerance. To escape persecution, 200,000 Huguenots fled France. Thus, the country lost many of its skilled workers and business leaders. The mercantilists of rival countries gloated over Louis's economic blunder.

The French court set styles.

Louis was more successful in his cultural goals. During Louis's reign and long after his death, the French practically dictated the artistic tastes and fashions of Europe, extending eastward even into Russia. Every ruler in Europe, from great kings to petty dukes, tried to imitate Louis's life style, especially his grand palace at Versailles.

In 1661, as one of his first decisions after Mazarin's death, Louis ordered his royal country house at Versailles to be enlarged on a colossal scale. For years, thousands of marble blocks littered the grounds as Louis and his architects rode about directing workers to place a statue here or there.

Louis officially moved his court from Paris to Versailles in 1682. However, the palace was far from complete. Nobles living at Versailles seldom had any rest from the incessant banging of the stonemasons' hammers. In 1685, for example, the palace grounds swarmed with 46,000 workers busily building the Sun King's dream palace.

Footnote to History

When Louis built his Hall of Mirrors, the only mirror-makers in Europe lived in Venice. The Venetian rulers jealously guarded this profitable business. Colbert sent spies to Venice to lure mirror-makers to France with the secrets of their trade. The result was a valuable new French industry.

The gold fleurs-de-lis that adorn Louis XIV's cape in this portrait were the emblem of the Bourbon dynasty. The high heels on his shoes made him appear taller.

The most dazzling of all the rooms was the Hall of Mirrors. Along one wall of this room, 17 towering windows gave a splendid view of the palace gardens. Light from these windows flooded the room and reflected the gardens in 17 huge, gold-framed mirrors on the opposite wall. In the Hall of Mirrors, Louis entertained foreign princes. Here his daughters' wedding guests danced by the light of thousands of candles that sparkled and reflected in the windows and mirrors.

Although a courtier's life at Versailles was glamorous, it was far from comfortable. Nobles from all over France flocked to Versailles to seek favors from the king. About 1,000 nobles and their 4,000 servants crowded into the palace's 226 rooms. Even the best rooms were cramped and uncomfortable. Smells from the outdoor latrines seeped through the windows—in the few

Parquet floors, marble walls, and gilded wood gleamed in the Hall of Mirrors where Louis XIV held his most lavish receptions.

rooms that had windows. Many lower-ranking nobles settled for windowless, closetlike cubicles. In the summer, they roasted in these stifling quarters; in the winter, they froze.

Yet thousands of French nobles gladly endured discomfort to share the glamour of Louis's court with its spectacular entertainments. One famous party in July 1689 lasted all day and night. After feasting and dancing to the music of the royal orchestra, awed onlookers watched as fireworks rocketed into the night sky. Some of the rockets twisted and turned to write the royal monogram, double L's, in fiery letters against the darkness.

France led Europe in the arts.

For his entertainment, Louis XIV demanded good music. At times, he could be heard humming the operas composed by the chief musician at his court, Jean Baptiste Lully (loo-**LEE**). Italian composers had written the first European operas around 1600. Now, thanks to Louis, operas became popular throughout Europe. They combined music, dance, and drama with the opportunity for spectacular costumes and special stage effects.

Comedies and tragedies Another of the king's favorite entertainers was comic actor and playwright Jean Baptiste Poquelin, better known by his stage name, Molière (moh-**LYAIR**). Molière lived from 1622 to 1673. This witty dramatist wrote some of the funniest and most popular plays in French literature: *Tartuffe, The Miser, the Misanthrope, The School for Wives.* Each play is a biting satire on French society.

While comedy was Molière's specialty, tragedy was the specialty of his two friends and fellow dramatists, Pierre Corneille (cor-**NAY**) and Jean Baptiste Racine (rah-**SEEN**). These authors modeled their tragedies on the works of the ancient Greek playwrights Aeschylus and Sophocles (page 109), whom they greatly admired.

Like the classical Greek dramatists, the French playwrights always observed the "three unities" of classic drama. First, all action was related to a single plot; there were no subplots. Second, all the action took place in a single setting. Third, all the action took place in a single day. (These strict rules made French tragic dramas very different from the English tragedies of Shakespeare, whose work was not admired at the French court.)

Royal patronage Louis XIV was the principal patron of these artists. Not since Augustus of Rome had there been a monarch who aided the arts as much as Louis. He treated Racine, for example, as one of his favorite courtiers and gave him a generous pension for life. He brought hundreds of pieces of Renaissance sculpture from Italy to exhibit in his Versailles gardens. The "Mona Lisa" by Leonardo da Vinci was one of the smaller paintings that hung in his bedroom.

All of Versailles was a monument to the king's classical tastes in art. The buildings and grounds of the palace gave an impression of perfect balance, elegance, and classical grandeur. The chief purpose of art was no longer to glorify God, as it had been in the Age of Faith. Now the purpose of art was to glorify the king.

Louis fought costly wars.

By any measure, France was the most powerful country in Europe. In 1660, France had about 20 million people—4 times as many as Spain or England and 10 times as many as the Dutch republic. The French army, numbering 100,000 in peacetime and as many as 400,000 in wartime, was far ahead of other nations' armies in size, training, and weaponry.

By comparison, all of France's rivals were in decline or disorder. England was still recovering from its civil war. Spain continued its long decline. The Thirty Years' War had left most of Germany devastated.

Despite France's strength, however, Louis XIV failed in many of his military goals. Between 1667 and 1713, Louis fought a series of wars to expand France's boundaries to the Rhine River and to the Alps. Rather than bringing glory to France, these wars brought the country to the brink of bankruptcy.

Alone, no other country was a match for France. However, by joining together, weaker countries could equal or even exceed French power. This defensive strategy is known as a **balance of power**. In such a balance, no one country or group of countries can dominate others. Many smaller countries banded together to stop France's aggression.

Three times in 30 years (1667–1697), Louis sent French armies into the Netherlands to try to extend his borders to the Rhine River. Each

time, he was stopped. At various times, England, Sweden, the Netherlands, Spain, Austria, and several German states joined forces against Louis. By the time the third war ended in stalemate in 1697, Louis had almost emptied the French treasury. His only important gain had been the German province of Alsace.

In 1700, the balance of power was once again threatened when the childless king of Spain, Charles II, died. On his deathbed, Charles bequeathed the Spanish throne and the huge Spanish empire to Louis's 17-year-old grandson, Philip. The two greatest powers in Europe, enemies for so long, were now linked by bonds of blood.

Smaller countries felt threatened by this sudden increase in the power of the Bourbon dynasty. In 1701, England, Austria, the Dutch republic, Denmark, Portugal, several German states, and the Italian duchy of Savoy all joined together against France and Spain. They fought a long and painful struggle known as the War of the Spanish Succession.

The War of the Spanish Succession was a disaster for Louis. Several times he sued for peace. Each time, negotiations broke down because Louis insisted that his grandson must keep the Spanish throne. The costly war dragged on for 13 years.

At last, in 1713, a peace treaty was signed in the Dutch city of Utrecht. In the Treaty of Utrecht, France and Spain managed to win only two points. First, Louis's grandson, Philip V, was allowed to remain king of Spain as long as the thrones of France and Spain were not united. Second, France kept the disputed territory of Alsace. On all other matters, France and Spain were the losers.

Great Britain,* on the other hand, was one of the victors in the war. From Spain, Britain took an important fortress at the southern tip of Spain known as the Rock of Gibraltar. This fortress gave Britain control of the strategic gateway to the Mediterranean Sea. (The British still hold Gibraltar today.) From France, Great Britain won several colonies in North America, including Nova Scotia, Newfoundland, and the Hudson Bay territory.

The Austrian Hapsburgs, also victors in the war, gained the Spanish Netherlands (what is

*In 1707, the kingdoms of England and Scotland were united by law. After that date, the kingdom was called Great Britain.

now Belgium). They also took over Spain's Italian lands, including Sardinia, Naples, and Milan.

Two smaller states on the winning side gained power and prestige. The German state of Prussia and the Italian duchy of Savoy were both recognized as kingdoms. These ambitious kingdoms later proved important in the development of Germany and Italy as nations.

The Treaty of Utrecht set up a new balance of power in Europe. On one side stood France and Spain, weakened but still imposing, both ruled by Bourbon kings. On the other side were the combined forces of Britain, Austria, and the Netherlands. The balance, however, was delicate. Any shift in power could tip Europe into a war.

Louis XIV's reign came to a sad end.

The War of the Spanish Succession left France near ruin, and Louis's last years were more sad than glorious. He still went through the same daily rituals at Versailles. In his old age, however, he was sorry for the great suffering his wars and high taxes had caused the people of France. Louis had suffered personal losses too. His only legitimate son died in 1711, and his favorite grandson died a year later.

In 1715, the saddened Sun King, now 77, developed gangrene in one leg. Gracious to the end, he said farewell to his wife, his courtiers, and his weeping servants. Then he called to his bed his five-year-old great-grandson, the future Louis XV. "My child," said the dying king, "do not imitate me in the taste that I have had for building or for war. Try, on the contrary, to be at peace with your neighbors ... Try to comfort your people, which unhappily I have not done."

Section Review 1

Define: (a) absolute monarch,
(b) mercantilism, (c) balance of trade,
(d) tariff, (e) balance of power
Identify: (a) Louis XIV, (b) Jules Mazarin,
(c) Jean Baptiste Colbert, (d) Versailles,
(e) Molière, (f) Corneille, (g) Racine
Answer:
1. (a) What was the Fronde? (b) How did it affect Louis XIV? (c) How did it make the people of France feel about absolute rule?

2. Why was "the Sun King" a fitting title for Louis XIV?
3. (a) What did Colbert do to improve France's economy? (b) How were his achievements undermined by Louis XIV?
4. (a) How did Louis XIV promote culture in France? (b) What purpose did art serve during his reign?
5. (a) What was the War of the Spanish Succession? (b) How did the Treaty of Utrecht affect each of the countries involved in the war?

Critical Thinking
6. Under Louis XIV, France succeeded in dominating Europe culturally but failed to dominate it militarily. Suggest some reasons for both its success and its failure.

Peter the Great changed Russia. 2

Like the king of France, the czar of Russia was an absolute ruler. In 1682, the year that Louis moved his court to Versailles, Peter Romanov became Czar Peter I. The log houses and onion-domed churches of Moscow, capital of Russia, were very different from the elegant corridors of Versailles. Yet in many ways, Peter I was like the Sun King.

Like Louis, Peter I came to the throne as a child. Also like Louis, Peter had a boyhood filled with violence, as older people used him in a struggle for power. Later, when Peter held power in his own hands, he avenged himself on his enemies, torturing them without mercy.

In some ways, Peter Romanov grew up to be a bullying brute. However, he was also a brilliant and able czar. His impact on Russian culture was probably even greater than the impact of Louis XIV on French culture. Peter I, called Peter the Great, made Russia a major European power for the first time.

Russia was isolated from Europe.

Peter I was neither the first czar to rule Russia nor the first to earn the title of "great." Both distinctions had gone in the 1400's to Ivan III (page 252). In 1480, Ivan had freed Moscow from the Mongol overlords who ruled Russia. Ivan took the title of czar (emperor) and began to widen Moscow's rule.

The rise of the Romanovs Peter's family, the Romanovs, came to power in a time of troubles during the early 1600's. After the death of Ivan IV (Ivan the Terrible; page 253) in 1684, Russia was torn by power struggles among the nobles, or boyars.

In 1613, representatives from 50 Russian cities met to choose the next czar. Their choice was Michael Romanov, grandnephew of Ivan the Terrible. Thus began the Romanov dynasty, which was destined to rule the Russian empire for 300 years (1613–1917).

A land of boyars and serfs When the Romanov family came to power, Russian society was still dominated by the great, landowning families of the nobility, the boyars. Their vast estates were worked by serfs.

Serfdom in Russia lasted much longer than it did in western Europe. In France, England, and other parts of western Europe, serfdom developed in the late days of the Roman empire and began to weaken in the late 1300's and 1400's. In Russia, however, serfdom developed much later and continued to thrive into the late 1700's.

Serfdom in Russia was not much different from slavery. When a landowner sold a piece of land, the serfs were sold with it. Landowners could give serfs away as presents or to pay debts. It was against the law for serfs to run away from their owners.

An isolated land When Peter I came to the throne in 1682, most Russian boyars knew little of western Europe. In the Middle Ages, Russia had looked to Constantinople, not to Rome, for leadership. During most of the Renaissance, Russia was under the rule of the Mongols and remained cut off from western Europe. Thus, the ideas of the Renaissance, the Age of Exploration, and the Scientific Revolution had scarcely touched Russia.

Geographic barriers also kept Russia closed in on itself. Its only seaport was Archangel on the White Sea, which was choked with ice much of the year.

Religious differences widened the gap between western Europeans and Russians. The Russians had adopted the Byzantine, or Eastern Orthodox, branch of Christianity. Western Europeans were

Peter the Great planned to make Russia a westernized nation and a naval power.

mostly Roman Catholics or Protestants, and the Russians shunned them as heretics. The few travelers from western Europe who reached Moscow were mostly Germans, and they stayed in the so-called German quarter of the city.

Peter dreamed of modernizing Russia.

In the 1670's and 1680's, people in the German quarter often saw the young Peter Romanov striding on long legs through their part of town. He was fascinated by the modern tools and machines in the foreigners' shops. Above all, he had a passion for ships and the sea.

Peter's love of ships was more than a boyhood fancy. The young czar believed that Russia's future depended on having a warm-water port. Only then could Russia compete with the more modern nations of western Europe.

After his troubled childhood, Peter I finally took full power in his own name in 1696, when he was 24 years old. He had the mind of a genius, the body of a giant, and the ferocious temper of a bear. One could not help but look up to Peter, who stood about 6 feet 8 inches tall.

Peter I came to the throne determined to modernize Russia. In 1698, at the age of 25, he went with 200 servants and 55 nobles on an overland journey to western Europe to learn about European customs. Never before had a czar traveled among western heretics.

On his journey, Peter insisted on keeping his identity a secret. He went to the Netherlands in the plain clothes of an ordinary worker. Pretending to be just another shipyard worker, he rose at dawn every morning and carried his own sack of carpenter's tools to the worksite. Nobody was fooled. A Russian giant in a Dutch seaport was a conspicuous sight. Yet if a fellow worker addressed him as "Your Majesty" or "Sire," he would not answer. No, he was just plain "Carpenter Peter," and for four months in Amsterdam, the czar insisted that everyone honor his disguise.

Traveling to England to see more ships, Peter presented himself to the king, toured London, and brushed off the gaping crowds that dogged his footsteps. An English gentleman who loaned Peter his house returned to find that the czar and his friends had played wild games with his property. Among other acts of destruction, they had thrown things at his paintings and flattened the hedges in his garden with a wheelbarrow.

Peter made many changes in Russia.

Peter admired everything that he saw in Europe—its ships, its industries, its cities, its elegant music, its fashions in clothing, even the way men shaved their faces. What would it take to make Moscow more like the countries of western Europe? Gentle persuasion would not do it. What was needed, in Peter's view, was to hammer Russia into a modern mold. "For you know yourself," said Peter to an official, "that, though a thing be good and necessary, our people will not do it unless forced to." Few rulers in history have attempted reforms as sweeping as Peter's.

The status of women Until 1700, Russian women followed the Byzantine custom of secluding themselves at home and veiling their faces in public. Peter set a new fashion by inviting noblewomen to social gatherings. Moreover, he demanded that they come without veils. The czar also decreed that parents could no longer marry off their daughters and sons unless the young people agreed to the match.

The Russian calendar Though Russian Orthodox priests opposed the change, Peter forced his people to give up their old calendar. No longer would Russians celebrate the new year on September 1. Henceforth, said Peter, Russians would follow the European custom of starting their year on January 1. In addition, Russians would date each year from the birth of Jesus, not from the

Daily Life · *The Barber King*

Surprisingly enough, the first thing Peter reformed when he returned to the Kremlin was not the army or industries but beards. To Peter, the Russian custom of wearing beards symbolized everything that was backward about his country. When his nobles fell on their knees to welcome him home, the czar raised them up, whipped out a long European razor, and commanded them to hold still while he shaved off their beards. The boyars were horrified. Russian men of the time treasured their beards as symbols of manhood and Christianity. Yet Peter decreed that all Russian nobles must shave off their beards. To make sure his decree was obeyed, he posted barbers at Moscow's gates. Noblemen who wished to keep their beards had to pay a beard tax every year and hang a metal tag from their necks to prove that they had indeed paid it.

creation of the world as their old calendar had done. Thus, the czar's decree changed the Russian year 7208 into the European year of A.D. 1700.

Agriculture From Europe, Peter brought back specimens of potatoes and encouraged landowners to grow the new crop. Potatoes became a staple food in Russia because they grew well in its cold climate.

Factories and mines To strengthen Russia's economy, Peter adopted the mercantilist ideas fashionable in Europe. He encouraged exports and discouraged imports. As a good mercantilist, Peter favored factories and subsidized their growth. Peter's factories were really more like centralized workshops, with perhaps a few machines run by hand. Still, when he came to the throne, Russia had only 13 such factories, and by the time of his death, there were about 200.

Peter also aided Russia's iron industry. With rich deposits of iron ore and large forests that supplied charcoal for smelting the ore, Russia soon was selling iron to other countries.

Newspapers Even literate Russians knew little of events outside their own country. To combat this ignorance, Peter started Russia's first newspaper and edited its first issue himself.

Peter I was an absolute ruler.

Like Louis XIV, Peter I of Russia was an absolute monarch. Many of the changes he made in his country were for the sake of increasing his own power.

For example, Patriarch Hadrian, the head of the Russian Orthodox Church, died in 1700. For more than 20 years, Peter neglected to appoint another patriarch. Then, in 1721, he abolished the office of patriarch altogether. In its place, he set up a group of high priests called the Holy Synod. At its head was Peter himself. The Russian church was now the czar's church, much as the English church had been made into the king's church by Henry VIII (page 351).

Peter also reduced the power of the great landowners, the boyars. He rarely gave high posts in government to the most powerful boyar families. Instead, Peter recruited able men from lower-ranking families, promoted them to positions of authority, and rewarded them with grants of land. Because these men owed everything to the czar, they were loyal to him.

When Peter first came to power, the Russian army was made up of cavalry (soldiers on horseback) who fought with sabers. They served only on a part-time basis. The armies of western Europe, on the other hand, were made up of highly trained infantry (foot soldiers) who marched forward while firing a constant barrage of bullets. These expert marksmen were full-time, professional soldiers.

To modernize his army, Peter hired European officers who drilled his soldiers in European tactics with European weapons. Russian soldiers no longer served on a part-time basis. Instead, as in western Europe, being a soldier became a lifetime job. By the time of Peter's death, the Russian army numbered 200,000 men. To pay for this huge army, Peter laid heavy taxes on nearly everyone in Russia.

Peter expanded Russia's empire.

Peter used his huge army to crush peasant revolts within Russia. He also turned it against neighboring countries to satisfy his greatest ambition—winning a warm-water seaport for Russia. He wanted, as he put it, a "window on the sea."

Peter believed that Russia needed a good navigable strip of coastline both on the Baltic Sea to the northwest and on the Black Sea to the south. The Swedes held the Baltic coast. The Ottoman Turks and their Tatar vassals held the Black Sea.

To win a warm-water port, Peter's first goal was to take Azov on the Black Sea from the Turks. His earliest campaign in 1695 failed badly. Undaunted, he saw that he needed warships. He helped build one with his own hands and besieged Azov again in 1696. This time the city fell to the Russians, though the Turks regained it several years later.

Peter then turned north to fight for a piece of the Baltic coast. His war against the Swedes, known as the Great Northern War, lasted 21 years (1700–1721).

At first, this war too went badly for the Russians. Early in the war, the Swedish King Charles XII scored a brilliant victory against the Russians. Then, in 1708, the Swedes suddenly invaded the Ukraine, a region on Russia's southwestern border. At first, Peter did not oppose the invaders. Instead, he left the Swedes to be starved and demoralized

Although St. Petersburg lay farther north than Moscow, the new city's location on the coast gave it a somewhat milder climate than the old capital.

by Russia's most potent weapon, the winter cold. In the spring of 1709, Peter's army set upon the weakened, frostbitten Swedes and annihilated them at the Battle of Poltava.

The remaining 12 years of the Great Northern War went well for Peter. Sweden's Charles XII died in battle in 1719, and Peter successfully invaded both Finland and Sweden. The treaty of peace, signed in 1721, finally gave Russia a broad belt of land on the Baltic Sea.

Peter built a new capital.

Actually, Peter had secured his "window on the sea" many years before Sweden officially surrendered it. In 1703, he began building a new city on Swedish lands occupied by Russian troops.

The site for this city was a low-lying swamp at the mouth of the Neva River. The climate was damp and unhealthful, and the drinking water caused dozens of diseases. On the whole, the location was fine for wolves and wild ducks but terrible for people. To Peter, however, the location seemed ideal because ships could sail down the Neva into the Baltic and on to western Europe. Here at last, as Peter said, "a great window for Russia to look out at Europe" could be built. He called it St. Petersburg after his patron saint.

To build a city on this desolate swamp was no easy matter. Every summer, the czar's officials forced thousands of luckless serfs to leave home and trudge to the work camps on the Neva River. They had only the crudest tools and a few wheelbarrows. Workers lugged soil and stones across the swamp to make the city's foundations. Thousands of people perished from the terrible working conditions and rampant diseases. Estimates of the dead range from 25,000 to 100,000. St. Petersburg well deserved to be called "a city built on bones." Peter himself shared some of the hardships. He lived at the building site in a house that was little more than a log cabin.

In 1712, the czar proclaimed St. Petersburg his new capital. Russian nobles groaned when Peter ordered them to leave the comforts of Moscow and settle in St. Petersburg. Peter, however, was delighted with his new capital. "Truly," he wrote, "we live here in heaven."

418

In the fall of 1724, Peter was with his army along the Gulf of Finland. A ship ran aground, and the soldiers on it were about to drown. The 52-year-old czar plunged into the icy water to help, heedless of his own safety. He caught a cold that grew worse through the winter, and he died early in 1725. Near his death, he said, "I hope God will forgive me my many sins because of the good I have tried to do for my people."

For better or for worse, Peter the Great had tried to transform the culture and government of Russia. To an amazing extent, he had succeeded. By the time of his death, Russia was a power to be reckoned with in Europe.

Section Review 2

Define: (a) boyar, (b) serf
Identify: (a) Peter the Great, (b) Russian Orthodox Church, (c) St. Petersburg
Answer:
1. (a) When did the Romanovs come to power? (b) Describe Russian society under the early Romanovs.
2. (a) Why had Russia been cut off from western Europe? (b) What was Peter's goal for his country?
3. (a) Describe three reforms that Peter made for the sake of modernizing Russia. (b) Describe three reforms he made for the sake of his own power.
4. (a) Why was the Great Northern War fought? (b) What was its outcome?

Critical Thinking
5. (a) What cultural obstacles did Peter I face in his attempt to make Russia more like the countries of western Europe? (b) Why are rulers usually more successful in making political and military changes than social changes?

Austria and Prussia rose to power.

3

Between France in the west and Russia in the east lay the rolling plains of eastern Europe. The major powers of the region were the Holy Roman Empire, the kingdom of Poland, and the Ottoman empire. Unlike France and Russia, which were highly centralized monarchies, the three powers of eastern Europe were not well organized.

Weak empires ruled eastern Europe.

Geographically, eastern Europe is a sweeping plain that extends from the Elbe River in what is now Germany to the Ural Mountains in Russia. The lack of mountains or other natural frontiers left this region open to constant warfare, migration, and shifting boundaries. Rulers in eastern Europe had trouble establishing firm borders.

Socially, eastern Europe followed a different path of development from western Europe. During the late Middle Ages, serfs in western Europe slowly won freedom, and the middle-class townspeople gained power. In eastern Europe, the landowning aristocracy gained more and more control over their serfs. By 1700, Polish landowners could demand as much as five days' work a week from their serfs, leaving the serfs only two days to grow their own food. There was a great gap between the aristocracy and the serfs, with few middle-class merchants or free artisans between the two extremes.

Politically, eastern Europe fell under the rule of the Holy Roman emperor, the Ottoman emperor, and the king of Poland. Each of these rulers had more power in theory than in fact.

Poland On the map on page 420, the kingdom of Poland appears to be a large, united country. However, the king of Poland was elected by the Polish nobility, who allowed him practically no power. Poland's king had little income, no law courts, no officials, and no standing army. Usually, the nobles chose a foreigner as their king because they were too jealous of one another's power to choose someone from their own ranks.

The Ottoman empire The sultan of the Ottoman empire still exercised some power. He collected taxes and had a large standing army. The greatest of the sultans, Sulieman the Magnificent, had conquered Hungary and threatened Vienna. Since his death in 1566, however, the mighty empire had been steadily declining. The government in Istanbul (once Constantinople) was corrupt, and the large army was poorly equipped.

The Holy Roman Empire The Holy Roman Empire in the early 1700's was little more than

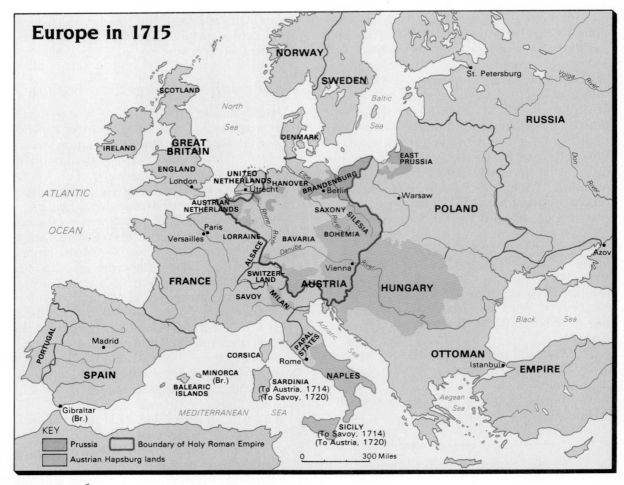

Europe in 1715

NORWAY
SWEDEN
SCOTLAND
North Sea
Baltic Sea
St. Petersburg
Volga River
RUSSIA
IRELAND
GREAT BRITAIN
DENMARK
EAST PRUSSIA
ENGLAND
London
UNITED NETHERLANDS
Utrecht
HANOVER
BRANDENBURG
Berlin
Elbe
Warsaw
Don River
ATLANTIC
OCEAN
AUSTRIAN NETHERLANDS
Rhine River
SAXONY
SILESIA
POLAND
Paris
Versailles
LORRAINE
BOHEMIA
Oder River
ALSACE
BAVARIA
Danube
Azov
SWITZER-LAND
Vienna
River
FRANCE
SAVOY
MILAN
AUSTRIA
HUNGARY
Black Sea
PORTUGAL
Madrid
CORSICA
PAPAL STATES
Rome
Adriatic Sea
OTTOMAN
Istanbul
EMPIRE
SPAIN
MINORCA (Br.)
BALEARIC ISLANDS
SARDINIA (To Austria, 1714) (To Savoy, 1720)
NAPLES
Aegean Sea
Gibraltar (Br.)
MEDITERRANEAN SEA
SICILY (To Savoy, 1714) (To Austria, 1720)

KEY
Prussia   Boundary of Holy Roman Empire
Austrian Hapsburg lands
0   300 Miles

Map Study

What mainland regions of Italy did the Hapsburgs hold? What regions made up their largest single piece of territory? Why was Gibraltar a key point?

a name. In fact, after the Thirty Years' War, it consisted of about 300 states, each of which jealously guarded its rights and liberties.

In short, eastern Europe was a region of old, weakening empires and kingdoms. Historians call this situation a power vacuum. Such weakness tempts ambitious leaders to move into the area to fill the power vacuum.

In the late 1600's, two German-speaking families were eager to take advantage of eastern Europe's power vacuum. One was the Hohenzollern (HOH-ehn-TSAHL-uhrn) family of north Germany; the other was the Hapsburg family of Austria. Their ambitions threatened to upset Europe's delicate balance of power.

Austria regained power in the 1700's.

Even after the terrible losses in the Thirty Years' War, Austria still remained the most powerful and important state within the empire. Its ruling family, the Hapsburgs, was one of the oldest and most distinguished dynasties in Europe. As far back as the 1400's, most of the Holy Roman emperors were Hapsburgs.

The Hapsburg ruler in 1713 was Charles VI. Austria had just won much territory in the War of the Spanish Succession (page 413). Despite this victory, however, Charles's empire was not an easy one to rule. It had three main parts. First, there was the dukedom of Austria on the middle stretches of the Danube River. Second, to the west, there was the kingdom of Bohemia. Third, to the east, lay the kingdom of Hungary. In addition, there were other German states and scattered lands in Italy.

Nothing about this patchwork empire was either natural or logical. Within its border existed a diverse assortment of peoples—Czechs, Hungarians, Croatians, Italians, and Germans. What held the empire together, generation after generation, was the fact that the Austrian, Hungarian, and Bohemian crowns were all worn by the same ruler, a Hapsburg.

How could the Hapsburgs make sure that they never lost claim to the lands that formed their empire? Charles VI spent his entire reign (1711–1740) working out an answer to this problem. By endless arm twisting, he persuaded the other rulers of Europe to sign an agreement known as the Pragmatic Sanction. By its terms, all the countries recognized Charles's only child as the heir to all his Hapsburg territories. That heir was a young woman named Maria Theresa.

In theory, the Pragmatic Sanction guaranteed Maria Theresa a peaceful reign. Instead, she faced years of war. Her main enemy was Prussia, a new state to the north of Austria. Like Austria, Prussia rose to power in the late 1600's. Soon Prussia's ruling family, the Hohenzollerns, challenged Maria Theresa and the Hapsburgs.

The Hohenzollerns ruled Prussia.

Like the Hapsburgs of Austria, the Hohenzollerns built up their state from a number of scattered holdings. At first, the small duchy of East Prussia in northern Poland was of little importance to the Hohenzollerns. Their most valued possession was a small state in the Holy Roman Empire called Brandenburg.

Brandenburg was never very powerful, but in the middle 1600's it enjoyed one distinction. Its ruling prince held the cherished title of elector. He was one of the seven electors who chose the Holy Roman emperor.

Maria Theresa (1717–1780) became ruler of the Hapsburg lands in 1740, when she was 23 years old. Although she lost Silesia and later Naples, she strengthened Austria by reforming administration and finance. Her father, her husband, and her son were all Holy Roman emperors. She was denied the title because she was a woman, but she was generally called empress anyway.

421

In 1640, a 20-year-old Hohenzollern named Frederick William inherited the title Elector of Brandenburg. Frederick William, later called the Great Elector, had the unhappy experience of seeing Brandenburg overrun by rival armies during the Thirty Years' War. His capital, Berlin, was so badly devastated that its population fell from 14,000 to 6,000.

Frederick William, a tall and muscular man with piercing blue eyes, concluded that there was only one way to safety. Brandenburg, he decided, must have a strong standing army. At first, with his almost empty treasury, he could equip and feed only about 8,000 men. Yet even this small force gave him some leverage in dealing with other states.

With a keen eye for his own advantage, the Great Elector made alliances with the French, the Swedes, the Dutch, and the Poles. He offered the services of his army to any power that paid him well and granted him a little slice of territory. In some wars, he got money from Louis XIV, and in other wars, from Louis's enemies. So well did Frederick William play the diplomatic game that his armies rarely went into battle. Thus, he saved a great deal of money, which he used to build a larger army. The larger army, of course, allowed him to strike even better bargains.

The Prussian army grew in strength.

The three Hohenzollerns who followed the Great Elector were all named Frederick or Frederick William. They all followed his formula for success: Build a bigger and better army.

Frederick I The Great Elector's son was the first Hohenzollern to call himself a king. By the Treaty of Utrecht in 1713, his duchy of East Prussia (which lay outside the Holy Roman Empire) was recognized as a kingdom. Thereafter, all the Hohenzollern territories, including Brandenburg, were grouped under the name Prussia. To live like a true king, Frederick I built ornate country palaces in imitation of Versailles.

Frederick William I Frederick I's son and successor, Frederick William I, was a harsh and mentally unbalanced character who loved only his army. In his 27-year reign (1713–1740), he refused to spend money on anything but his soldiers. He dressed in an army uniform and prowled the streets of Berlin, barking out commands to

soldiers and civilians alike. The Sergeant-King, as he was called, had a vicious temper. When displeased, he would fly into a rage and clobber the offending person with his walking stick.

Frederick William's obsession with his army had a lasting effect on Prussia. He more than doubled the size of the army, from 40,000 to 85,000 soldiers. He promoted his officers only from Prussia's landowning nobility, called the *junkers* (YUNK-uhrs). These army officers were far superior in social status and power to any civilian. Thus, more than any other country in Europe, Prussia became a military society. In fact, as a foreigner said, "Prussia is not a state that possesses an army, but an army that possesses a state."

Frederick II (the Great) The Sergeant-King worried that his son, another Frederick, might turn out badly because he enjoyed too many nonmilitary interests—music, philosophy, and literature. The scholarly young prince hated his father and tried to run away to France, but he and a companion were caught. As punishment, the furious father ordered Frederick, age 18, to witness the beheading of his friend. Despite such bitter quarrels, however, Frederick II followed many of his father's policies when he came to the throne in 1740.

Frederick II invaded Hapsburg lands.

In 1740, the same year that Frederick II became king of Prussia, Austria's Maria Theresa succeeded her father as the Hapsburg monarch. The newly crowned Prussian king scorned the Pragmatic Sanction, which his father had signed. Frederick wanted Austria's iron-rich land of Silesia. He assumed that, being a woman, Maria Theresa would lack the forcefulness to defend her lands.

The Prussian army invaded and occupied Silesia in December 1740. Thus began the War of the Austrian Succession. Following Prussia's lead, other countries leaped to take advantage of Maria Theresa's supposed weakness. France, Spain, and the German state of Bavaria all sent armies across Austria's western border.

Austria's young queen reacted quickly. She had recently given birth to her first son, but nonetheless she made a dashing journey across Austria to her Hungarian lands. There, Maria Theresa appeared in person before an assembly

As a boy, Frederick II of Prussia hated the army. After he became king, however, he valued the power his army gave him. Prussian troops were the best armed and best drilled in Europe.

of Hungarian nobles, who were not especially friendly to their Hapsburg rulers. Holding the infant prince, she delivered a stirring speech that instantly won over the assembly. The Hungarians pledged to give her an army of 100,000 men.

Maria Theresa also got help from Great Britain. Britain entered the war to fight its archrival France, which was allied with Prussia. With Great Britain, Russia, and the Dutch Netherlands on her side, Maria Theresa managed to stop Prussia and its allies from swallowing Austria and her other lands. She was not able, however, to turn the Prussian fighting machine out of Silesia. In 1748, at the Treaty of Aix-la-Chapelle, Austria lost Silesia.

Maria Theresa resolved to regain Silesia. Her determination to strike back at Frederick led to both a "diplomatic revolution" and a second Austrian-Prussian war.

Alliances shifted in Europe.

For more than 200 years, the Bourbon kings of France had been the chief enemies of the Austrian Hapsburgs. But was France still a threat to Austria? No, decided Maria Theresa's foreign minister, Count Kaunitz (KOW-nits). Austria's chief foe was now Prussia. Recognizing this, Kaunitz worked tirelessly to make France an ally. Aware of Austria's shrewd maneuvering, Britain decided its wisest move was to make an alliance with Prussia. After all, Britain had Europe's strongest navy and Prussia the strongest army. Together, they should be unbeatable.

By 1756, a so-called diplomatic revolution had taken place. Austria, France, and Russia were now allied against Britain and Prussia. With powerful enemies on three sides, Prussia's Frederick II decided to strike first.

Once again, Prussia and Austria were at war. This time, almost every country in Europe took part. In Europe, the war was known as the Seven Years' War (1756–1763). In North America, where France and Great Britain battled for colonies, it was known as the French and Indian War. Even Asia was involved, for there too France and Britain were rivals for colonies. Many historians refer to this war as the first true world war.

In 1763, the war on three continents ended with the signing of the Peace of Paris. Maria

Voice from the Past · *A Call to Arms*

The year was 1741. Maria Theresa had lost Silesia. Prague, the capital of Bohemia, had also fallen. The future looked grim, as this letter from the queen to her chancellor, Prince Kinsky, reveals.

So Prague is lost, and perhaps even worse will follow unless we can secure three months' supplies. It is out of the question for Austria to supply them, and it is even doubtful if Hungary will be able to do so.

Here then, Kinsky, we find ourselves at the sticking point where only courage can save the country [Bohemia] and the Queen, for without the country I should indeed be a poor princess. My own resolve is taken: to stake everything, win or lose, on saving Bohemia; and it is with this in view that you should work and lay your plans. It may involve destruction and desolation that 20 years will be insufficient to restore, but I must hold the country and the soil, and for this all my armies, all the Hungarians shall die before I surrender an inch . . . You will say that I am cruel; that is true. But I know that all the cruelties I commit today to hold the country I shall one day be in a position to make good a hundred-fold. And this I shall do. But for the present I close my heart to pity . . .

Maria Theresia

1. Maria Theresa refers to Austria, Bohemia, and Hungary in this letter. How are the three countries connected?
2. (a) What is Maria Theresa's resolve? (b) What alternative, if any, does she have?
3. (a) How do the sentiments expressed by Maria Theresa compare with those of Elizabeth I at the time of the Armada? (page 389) (b) What traits do these women share?

Theresa gained nothing from the war. Silesia remained in Prussian hands. The chief loser was France, which surrendered all of Canada to Britain.

Of the five major powers that fought the Seven Years' War, only one emerged with a major prize. This was Britain, the only country of the five whose king was *not* an absolute monarch. In the next chapter, we will see how new ideas began to replace absolutism in Europe.

Section Review 3

Define: junker
Identify: (a) Holy Roman Empire, (b) Hapsburg, (c) Hohenzollern, (d) Pragmatic Sanction, (e) Great Elector, (f) Frederick I, (g) Frederick William I, (h) Frederick the Great, (i) Maria Theresa
Answer:
1. (a) Describe the geography of eastern Europe. (b) How did the region's geography make it difficult for strong states to develop there?
2. (a) Identify the three main parts of the Austrian Hapsburg empire in 1713. (b) How did Charles VI try to keep the title to these lands for his daughter?
3. How did Frederick William build up the power of Brandenburg after the Thirty Years' War?
4. (a) What distinguished Frederick I from earlier Hohenzollern rulers? (b) What happened to the Hohenzollern territories during his reign?
5. (a) Why was the War of the Austrian Succession fought? (b) Describe the diplomatic revolution that took place after the war.
6. (a) Why was the Seven Years' War fought? (b) What country was the chief loser in the war? (c) Who emerged as the winner?

Critical Thinking
7. One observer of Prussia in the 1700's commented, "Prussia is not a state that possesses an army, but an army that possesses a state." Explain what this statement means.
8. Maria Theresa ruled a very large empire. Did the size of her empire add to or diminish its strength? Explain your answer.

424

Chapter Review 19

Summary

1. The Sun King ruled France. Louis XIV of France became king in 1643 at the age of five. For the next 17 years, real power rested in the hands of his minister, Cardinal Jules Mazarin. After Mazarin's death, Louis became the most powerful monarch in French history.

During his reign, Louis succeeded in some areas and failed in others. He wisely chose Jean Baptiste Colbert as his minister of finance but foolishly undid much of Colbert's work by forcing thousands of Huguenots out of France. As king, he patronized the arts and made France the cultural center of Europe. He also tried to expand France's power through wars but witnessed the defeat of his armies time and time again. Louis died regretting the costliness of his court and his wars.

2. Peter the Great changed Russia. Peter I of Russia came to the throne in 1682. At the time he came to power, Russia was a backward, isolated nation. Peter set out to win a warm-water port for Russia and modernize his country.

Like Louis XIV of France, Peter was an absolute ruler. During his reign, he made sweeping reforms that both modernized Russia and increased his own power. Peter also extended his country's borders. He won from Sweden a broad belt of coast on the Baltic Sea. There he built St. Petersburg, the new capital of Russia.

3. Austria and Prussia rose to power. Both Austria and Prussia lay on the sweeping plains of eastern Europe. Prussia was the creation of the Hohenzollern rulers of Brandenburg, who had extended their power by offering their armies' services in exchange for land. Austria, the most powerful state in the Holy Roman Empire, was ruled by the Hapsburgs. In 1740, the ruler of Prussia, Frederick the Great, invaded Silesia, a territory of Austria. One war followed another as the Hapsburg queen Maria Theresa tried to block Prussia's advances. The other countries of Europe, trying to protect the delicate balance of power, took part as well. In the end, a war was fought on three continents. Maria Theresa lost Silesia while her ally France surrendered much of its overseas empire to Prussia's ally, Great Britain.

Reviewing the Facts

1. Define the following terms:
   a. absolute monarch
   b. mercantilism
   c. tariff
   d. balance of trade
   e. balance of power

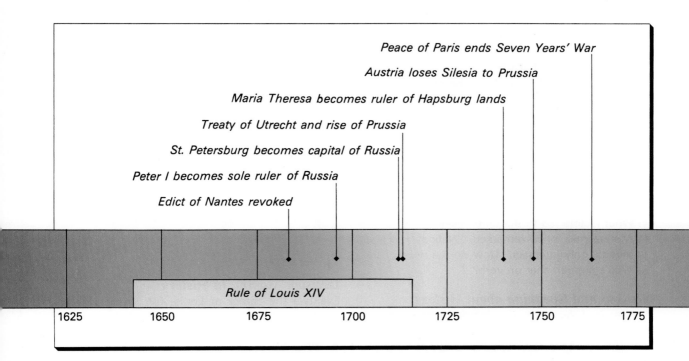

Peace of Paris ends Seven Years' War

Austria loses Silesia to Prussia

Maria Theresa becomes ruler of Hapsburg lands

Treaty of Utrecht and rise of Prussia

St. Petersburg becomes capital of Russia

Peter I becomes sole ruler of Russia

Edict of Nantes revoked

Rule of Louis XIV

| 1625 | 1650 | 1675 | 1700 | 1725 | 1750 | 1775 |

2. Explain the importance of each of the following names, places, or terms:
   a. Versailles
   b. Louis XIV
   c. Cardinal Mazarin
   d. Fronde
   e. Jean Colbert
   f. Molière
   g. War of the Spanish Succession
   h. Treaty of Utrecht
   i. Peter I
   j. Charles XII
   k. St. Petersburg
   l. Hohenzollern
   m. Hapsburg
   n. Maria Theresa
   o. Prussia
   p. Seven Years' War
   q. Peace of Paris
3. (a) Name the powerful rulers that dominated France, Russia, Prussia, and Austria in the middle 1700's. (b) What term accurately describes them?
4. (a) Describe two of Louis XIV's accomplishments as king. (b) Describe two of his failures.
5. (a) Describe Russia when Peter I came to the throne. (b) What two goals did Peter have for Russia? (c) What did he do to accomplish each goal?
6. (a) Describe the geography of eastern Europe. (b) Why was it often invaded?
7. (a) Explain how Austria became a strong power. (b) Why were its lands difficult to rule?
8. (a) Explain how Prussia became a great power. (b) Why did it become a military state?
9. (a) What countries fought in the War of the Austrian Succession? (b) Why did the opponents switch sides after the war?

Thinking about History

1. (a) How was the noble class a problem for rulers in both France and Russia? (b) How were Louis XIV's methods of dominating his nobles different from Peter the Great's methods?
2. In what way was the repeal of the Edict of Nantes similar to the expulsion of Muslims and Jews from Spain in 1492?
3. Compare the French attitude toward Louis XIV with the English attitude toward the Stuart kings. What factors led to the differences?
4. A statesman once remarked, "Nations have no friends, only interests." How do the wars of the 1700's support that proverb?

Writing and Speaking about History

The research paper begins with the process of narrowing down a topic. For example, this chapter deals with the broad topic: *Europe in the Age of Absolute*

Monarchs. Within this topic, a historian might find these general topics of interest:
   France under Louis XIV
   Russia under Peter the Great
   Prussia under the Great Elector
(a) For each of these general topics, suggest a problem or question to research. (b) Choose one of these problems, and identify a specific topic for a research paper. (See Research Skills Handbook, page 468.)

Practicing Skills

1. Using the timeline on page 425, name two events that took place in Russia during the time that Louis XIV ruled France.
2. How does the art on pages 408, 411, and 412 reflect the splendor of France during the Age of Louis XIV?
3. When Louis XIV revoked the Edict of Nantes, 200,000 Huguenots fled France. Assuming the total population of France at this time was about 19,500,000, what percentage of the population was lost in this exodus?

Investigating History

1. Since the time of Louis XIV, French fashions have greatly influenced the way people dress. Find information about the style of dress at the court of Louis XIV. Prepare a display of the clothes noblemen and noblewomen wore.
2. The French national theater, a repertory theater, had its beginnings with a group of Molière's actors. What is a repertory theater? Find out which other countries have national theaters.
3. Governments frequently move their capital cities for political or economic reasons. For a modern example, find out why Brazil's capital was moved from Rio de Janeiro to Brasília. What are the advantages and disadvantages of such a move?
4. Research one of the following topics: (a) samovar, (b) Palekh miniatures, (c) Cossacks, (d) Siberia, (e) crown sable, (f) balalaika. Describe its importance to the economy or culture of Russia.

Decision Making in History

Evaluate the career of Louis XIV. What were his greatest accomplishments? What were his greatest failures? As his advisor, what would you tell him to do differently?

Enlightenment in Europe, Revolution in America

1. **European thinkers expressed new ideas.**

2. **Writers advocated liberty and reason.**

3. **Enlightened despots sought progress.**

4. **Britain developed new forms of leadership.**

5. **Americans created a republic.**

As the most famous writer of his day, Voltaire (leaning forward at left) was an honored guest at courts throughout Europe. Here, dining at the Prussian palace, he carried on an earnest discussion with Frederick II.

It was a sad and shocking tale that the young man told, and the old Frenchman who listened to it was deeply moved. The young man was Donat Calas, a youth whose family had been forced to flee in poverty and disgrace from the French city of Toulouse. His hearer was Voltaire (vohl-**TAIR**), whose name was famous throughout Europe for his brilliant letters, pamphlets, plays, and satires.

Donat Calas told how, in 1761, his older brother Marc had been found hanged from the rafters of the family linen shop. Neighbors quickly accused the boy's father, Jean Calas, of killing his son.

The story of murder was all lies, said Donat Calas. He explained that Jean Calas was a Huguenot, hated as a heretic by the Catholic citizens of Toulouse. Because they thought his religion was evil, they

427

believed he would act in evil ways. Young Marc had planned to become a Catholic, said the neighbors, and so his father killed him.

The neighbors told this story in court, and the judges of Toulouse believed them. Jean Calas was tortured and then executed. The judges ordered all his property to be confiscated. The surviving members of the Calas family, including Donat, were driven from their home and fled to Switzerland.

Donat Calas wept as he described the misfortunes of his family. Of course, he repeated, his father was innocent. What had really happened was obvious, Donat concluded. His moody and unhappy brother Marc had taken his own life. Jean Calas was executed only because of prejudice against the Huguenots.

Donat Calas had indeed found a sympathetic listener. Few people hated injustice and prejudice more than Voltaire. Now 68 years old, Voltaire had written thousands of letters and pamphlets denouncing intolerance and bigotry of all kinds.

Voltaire had hundreds of influential friends in Europe. From his country estate near Geneva, Voltaire sent forth a barrage of letters about the execution of Jean Calas. Friends rallied to the cause and wrote letters of their own.

French officials felt the sting of Voltaire's pen. In 1765, three years after the execution of Jean Calas, King Louis XV's council overruled the Toulouse judges and declared Calas innocent of murder. His family could return to Toulouse, reclaim their property, and collect a huge payment for the wrongs done to them.

Voltaire wept for joy at the news. In a long, happy letter to a friend, he exclaimed, "What great victories reason is winning among us!" Note that he did not take credit for the victory himself. No, the true victor in the struggle for justice was a higher power that he called reason.

Voltaire and his scholarly friends honored reason as if it were a kind of divine force. They hoped that, through the power of reason, society would make steady progress toward liberty and justice. In a society ruled by reason, they thought, injustice would disappear.

In this chapter, we will say more about Voltaire and his fellow thinkers. The period of their greatest influence was known as the Age of Enlightenment and spanned the middle years of the eighteenth century (roughly 1720–1790).

In the English colonies of North America, the ideals of the Enlightenment played a large part in sparking a revolution against Great Britain. These ideals of liberty and reason helped to shape the government of the new country created by that revolution—the United States of America.

European thinkers expressed new ideas. 1

The Age of Enlightenment brought together the ideas of the Renaissance and the Scientific Revolution. Remember that Renaissance artists and writers adopted a secular outlook on life instead of the more spiritual outlook of the Middle Ages. They were also among the first Europeans to look critically at society in an effort to improve it. These new attitudes found their way into the Enlightenment.

Now recall the ideas of the Scientific Revolution. Copernicus, Kepler, and Galileo showed that the idea of an Earth-centered universe was wrong. Descartes had created a scientific philosophy for seeking truth. Everything had to be tested by the standard of reason. This idea too was basic to the Enlightenment.

Newton discovered the law of gravity.

In the history of ideas, as in other kinds of history, beginnings are seldom clearly marked. Isaac Newton may be called either the last and greatest figure of the Scientific Revolution or the first figure of the Enlightenment. Newton recognized what he owed to such earlier thinkers as Galileo and Kepler when he said, "If I have seen farther than others, it is because I have stood on the shoulders of giants."

Isaac Newton was born in England in 1642, while conflict was raging between the king and Parliament. Newton studied at Cambridge University and became a professor there. By the time he was 24 years old, he was certain that all physical objects (stones, birds, planets, stars) were affected equally by the same forces. However, he could not yet prove his ideas mathematically, and it was more than 20 years before he published these ideas.

In 1609, the astronomer Kepler had worked out laws for a planet's motion around the sun (page 358). Galileo had studied the motion of pendulums and the acceleration of balls rolling down a slope (page 359). Newton's great achievement was to discover that the same force ruled the motions of the planets, the rolling balls, the pendulum, and all matter on Earth and in outer space. He disproved the idea that one set of physical laws governed Earth and another set governed the rest of the universe.

All objects attract one another, said Newton. He called this attraction "gravitation." The attraction varies both with the mass of the objects and with the distance between them. In 1687, Newton at last published his fully developed theories in a book titled *Mathematical Principles of Natural Philosophy*. In a single sentence, he summarized the workings of the universe:

Every particle of the universe attracts every other particle with a force varying inversely as the square of the distance between them and directly proportional to the square of their masses.

European scientists who read Newton's work were overwhelmed by its brilliance. Newton's laws became the starting point for investigating everything in nature.

The philosophes advocated reason.

In the early 1700's, a group of thinkers set forth the idea that people could apply reason to all aspects of life just as Newton had applied reason to science. These thinkers were known as **philosophes** (FEE-luh-sohfs). At the heart of their philosophy were five ideas:

1. *Reason* Enlightened thinkers such as Voltaire regarded reason as a sort of divine force, as we have seen. Reason, they said, was the absence of intolerance, bigotry, or prejudice in one's thinking.
2. *Nature* The philosophes referred to nature frequently. To them, what was natural was also good and reasonable. They believed that there were natural laws of economics and politics just as there were natural laws of motion.
3. *Happiness* A person who lived by nature's laws would find happiness, the philosophes

said. They were impatient with the medieval notion that people should accept misery in this world to find joy in the hereafter. The philosophes wanted well-being on Earth, and they believed it was possible.
4. *Progress* The philosophes were the first Europeans to believe in progress for society. Now that people used a scientific approach, they believed, society and humankind could be perfected.
5. *Liberty* The philosophes envied the liberties that the English people had won in their Glorious Revolution and Bill of Rights (page 404). In France, there were many restrictions on speech, religion, trade, and personal travel. Through reason, the philosophes believed, society could be set free.

Voltaire combated prejudice.

Thousands of Europeans in the 1700's shared these five ideas and thought of themselves as enlightened. None, however, was as widely admired (or as widely hated) as a Frenchman who called himself by an invented name, Voltaire.

Voltaire's real name was François Marie Arouet (AH-rweh). Born in Paris in 1694, he nearly died in infancy. He remained frail all his life and complained of almost every ailment: smallpox, fever, gout, a chronic itch, coughing fits, partial deafness and blindness, lost teeth, dropsy, paralysis, and grippe. He often ended his letters to friends by saying that he expected to die soon. Yet he did not put down his pen until death finally took him at the age of 84.

As a young writer, he adopted the name Voltaire, possibly because Arouet sounded too close to the French word for king. Voltaire's sharp tongue made him enemies at the French court, and twice King Louis XV had him jailed in a Parisian prison called the Bastille (ba-STEEL). All his life, therefore, Voltaire held a grudge against the French monarchy.

After one stay in prison, Voltaire was exiled to England for two years. While there, he read the works of John Locke, with their emphasis on reason and the natural rights of all human beings (page 405).

Voltaire came to admire the English government much more than his own. After he returned to Paris, much of his work mocked the laws and customs of France and even dared to raise doubts about the Christian religion. The French king and France's Catholic bishops were outraged. In 1734, fearing another unpleasant stay in the Bastille, Voltaire fled from Paris to a spot near the French border.

In his later years, Voltaire was less a French citizen than a citizen of the world. He moved to Switzerland, seeking freedom to write and publish his works. There, in 1758, Voltaire wrote his most famous work, *Candide*, a short, satiric novel that he dashed off in three days. Voltaire spent his last years living with his niece in the little Swiss village of Ferney.

From his study overlooking a lovely garden, Voltaire used his quill pen as if it were a deadly weapon in a thinkers' war against humanity's worst enemies—prejudice, superstition, and intolerance. Such attitudes were, he said, *l'infame*—infamous or shameful things. He often ended his letters with a fighting slogan, *"Écrasez l'infame!"* (ay-crah-zay lahn-fam). The phrase meant "Crush the infamous thing!" Soon it was the battle cry of every enlightened thinker in Europe.

Salons were intellectual centers.

In the 1700's, Paris was the cultural and intellectual capital of Europe. There, it was the fashion among wealthy hostesses to invite the best poets, the keenest wits, and the most charming conversationalists to their mansions for refined conversation.

Such social gatherings were known as *salons*. One guest might be invited to read a poem or play a piece on the flute or harpsichord. The other guests would comment on the performance, showing off their good taste and broad understanding. The women who organized the salons were, in effect, the drama and music critics of their age.

The most influential of the salon hostesses in Voltaire's time was Marie Thérèse Geoffrin (zhoh-**FRAHN**). In her autobiography, Madame Geoffrin explained how her tastes and education were shaped early in life by her grandmother:

She taught me to think, and made me reason; she taught me to know men, and made me say what I thought of them, and told

Mme Geoffrin (third from right in front) hosts a salon at which an actor reads from a play. Enlightenment culture was limited to the wealthy class.

me how she herself judged them ... She could not endure the elegancies that dancing masters teach; she only desired me to have the grace that nature gives to a well-formed person.

Every Monday the great artists of Paris assembled in the Geoffrins' drawing room. Every Wednesday, the foremost writers and scientists dined at her elegant table. Her husband, a much older man, sat politely through these dinners and rarely spoke.

Diderot planned an encyclopedia.

Marie Thérèse Geoffrin also sponsored one of the most ambitious intellectual projects of the Enlightenment. The philosophe Denis Diderot (dee-**DROH**) imagined a set of large books to which all the leading scholars of Europe would contribute articles and essays. This *Encyclopedia,* as he called it, would bring together all the most current and enlightened thinking about technology, science, mathematics, music, art, medicine, government, law, geography, and more. Madame Geoffrin was so fond of the project that she contributed nearly half the total cost. Other hostesses also gave money to the effort. The first volume of the set was published in 1751 and distributed to 1,431 subscribers.

In a dingy attic room in Paris, Diderot labored for 20 years to complete the project. His seventh volume provoked the French king, Louis XV. Therefore, government censors banned further volumes. Fearing arrest, some leading philosophes withdrew from the project and urged Diderot to quit. Diderot pressed on, however, and found ways around the ban on publishing. The last volume under his editorship, number 28, was finally printed in 1772.

The popularity of the *Encyclopedia* soon spread to French-reading buyers all over Europe. It also inspired English and Scottish writers to produce their own *Encyclopedia Britannica* in the 1770's.

Scientific knowledge advanced.

In the 1700's, it was fashionable for wealthy families to display scientific instruments in their homes. They invited their guests to observe the planets through a telescope or an insect's wing under a microscope. Most educated men and women only dabbled at science. A few, however, pursued their observations and experiments seriously and made breakthroughs in every branch of scientific inquiry.

The discovery of oxygen Before the Enlightenment, no one knew that air was made up of a mixture of gases (mostly oxygen, nitrogen, and carbon dioxide). Then, in 1774, an English minister and scientist named Joseph Priestley separated one pure gas from air. He noticed how good he felt after breathing this special air and watched how alert two mice were while breathing it. Wrote Priestley, "Who can tell but that, in time, this pure air may become a fashionable article of luxury? Hitherto only two mice and I have had the privilege of breathing it."

Meanwhile, in France, during the 1770's, Antoine Lavoisier (lah-vwah-**ZYAY**) was performing similar experiments. In 1779, Lavoisier named the newly discovered gas oxygen.

Electricity Electricity mystified the scientific thinkers of the 1700's. Why, they wondered, did electric sparks sometimes jump between objects and give people a shock? In the British colony of Pennsylvania, a printer named Benjamin Franklin thought there might be a connection between a lightning bolt in a thunderstorm and the puzzling little electric sparks.

To test his theory, Franklin performed one of the most famous—and dangerous—experiments in the history of science. In 1752, he sent up a kite during a thunderstorm. At the end of the kite string was an iron key. A bolt of lightning struck the kite, and in a flash, the key emitted an electric spark. Wrote Franklin:

When the rain has wet the kite twine so that it can conduct the electric fire freely, you will find it stream out plentifully from the key at the approach of your knuckle.

Enthralled by Franklin's experiment, a number of Europeans tried to repeat it, and several were killed instantly by the shock.

Geography Two centuries after the voyages of Columbus and Magellan, vast stretches of the Pacific Ocean were still unknown to Europeans. In 1768, the English navigator and mapmaker James Cook set out on the first of three voyages to explore and chart the South Pacific.

Cook was not in search of gold, as Dias, Da Gama, and Columbus had been. Instead, Cook's

Daily Life · A Defense against Smallpox

In the 1600's and 1700's, few words conjured up as much dread as smallpox. An infectious disease, it struck 60 of every 100 people. Of those 60, at least 20 died, and another 20 were horribly disfigured by scars.

Then, in the early 1700's, Lady Mary Wortley Montagu made an amazing observation. While traveling in Turkey, she saw that mothers there deliberately infected their young children with smallpox by breaking the skin and applying some liquid taken from the sore of a victim. (Such a process is called inoculation.) Children who were inoculated caught smallpox, but they had a good chance of getting only a mild case that protected them from ever having the disease again. Lady Montagu bravely had her son inoculated. She then returned to Britain and spread news of the procedure. By the middle 1700's, inoculation, although still dangerous, was being used all over Europe.

In 1796, British physician Edward Jenner discovered that an inoculation with the less dangerous disease cowpox (taken from a cow) gave permanent protection from smallpox for humans. Because cowpox was a much milder disease, the risks for this form of inoculation were much lower. Jenner used cowpox to produce the world's first vaccination.

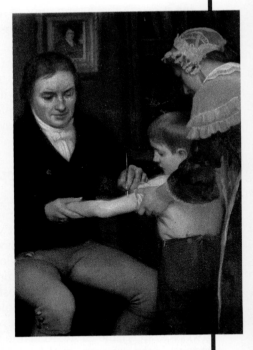

voyages were scientific expeditions. They were sponsored by the Royal Society of London, a group founded in the mid-1600's to encourage the growth of scientific knowledge. Astronomers, artists, and a botanist went with Cook to gather information about distant parts of the world.

Captain Cook became the first European to reach and chart the east coast of Australia and the islands of Tahiti, New Zealand, and Hawaii. He died in 1779 during a fight with the Hawaiian islanders.

New forms dominated music.

Educated men and women of the Enlightenment were as interested in music as in literature and science. This age produced some of Europe's most brilliant musicians.

The baroque period Music of the late 1600's and early 1700's is called *baroque*, which in French means "odd." The term was first used for art that was more ornate than the art of the Renaissance. Baroque music is noted for its drama and complexity.

Two musical techniques, the fugue and counterpoint, reached their height in baroque music. In a fugue, the composer repeats a single melody, or two or three melodies, with slight variations on different musical instruments. We may hear the theme first on a horn, then on a violin, and later on a cello.

Counterpoint is the weaving of two or more melodies together. Probably the plainest example of counterpoint is a simple tune—"Three Blind Mice," for example—sung in rounds. Musicians in the 1700's created very intricate counterpoint.

Baroque music reached its height in the early 1700's. The greatest of the baroque composers were Johann Sebastian Bach (1685–1750) and George Frederick Handel (1685–1759).

The classical period By the time Bach and Handel died in the mid-1700's, the age of baroque music was passing. New composers wrote less ornate works. Unity, clarity, and balance became more important than the intricate patterns of baroque music. New forms, such as the symphony, the concerto, and the sonata, came to dominate music.

The period from 1750 to 1820 is known as the classical period in European music. Its most noted composers were Joseph Haydn (HYE-d'n), Wolfgang Amadeus Mozart (MOH-tsahrt), and Ludwig van Beethoven (BAY-TOH-vuhn).

Haydn, born in 1732, was not the first European to write full symphonies for strings and woodwinds. However, his compositions were so superior to earlier works that he is honored today as the "father of the symphony."

Mozart was a child prodigy who began composing music at the age of five and performed for Britain's King George III at the age of eight. At 12, he wrote his first opera. Mozart's operas baffled audiences with their originality and brilliance. His great operas—*The Marriage of Figaro*, *Don Giovanni*, and *The Magic Flute*—are widely performed today. In 1791, at the age of 35, Mozart died in poverty.

Beethoven (1770–1827) is considered by many to have been the greatest European composer of all time. While his earlier works were in the same classical style as Mozart's, the music of Beethoven's later years began new trends, which carried music on into the Age of Romanticism (Chapter 23).

Section Review 1

Define: (a) philosophe, (b) salon
Identify: (a) Age of Enlightenment, (b) Newton, (c) Voltaire, (d) Marie Thérèse Geoffrin, (e) Diderot, (f) *Encyclopedia*, (g) Priestley, (h) Lavoisier, (i) Franklin, (j) Cook, (k) baroque, (l) Bach, (m) Handel, (n) Haydn, (o) Mozart, (p) Beethoven
Answer:
1. Describe the five ideas that were at the heart of the Enlightenment.
2. (a) Describe an evening in a Parisian salon. (b) What role did French women play in these salons?
3. (a) What was the purpose of the *Encyclopedia*? (b) What British work did it inspire?
4. (a) Describe three scientific accomplishments of the Englightenment. (b) Describe the two periods of music that flourished during the Enlightenment.

Critical Thinking
5. "If I have seen farther than others," said Newton, "it is because I have stood on the shoulders of giants." Who were the giants to whom Newton was referring? Could this be said of any scientific accomplishment? Explain.

Wolfgang Amadeus Mozart, 7 years old, and his sister Maria Ann, 12, toured the capitals of Europe giving recitals with their father.

Writers advocated liberty and reason. 2

Diderot once wrote, "I am a good citizen, and everything that concerns the welfare of society and the life of my fellow men is very interesting to me." The Age of Enlightenment was a time for thinking about the welfare of society, the freedom of the individual, and the happiness of humanity. In the opinion of the philosophes, these three ideals were almost identical. People could only be truly happy, they said, in a good society that allowed economic, religious, and political liberty.

The champion of economic liberty was a Scottish professor named Adam Smith. The champions of political liberty were a French aristocrat named Montesquieu (MOHN-tes-KYOO) and a Swiss commoner named Rousseau (roo-SOH). All three claimed to have discovered the "natural laws" by which society works.

Adam Smith supported free trade.

As a professor at the University of Edinburgh, Adam Smith (1723–1790) devoted almost every waking hour to philosophic questions. Often, he was so busy with his own thoughts that he dressed in rumpled, mismatched outfits.

In Diderot's *Encyclopedia*, Smith read the ideas of French economic theorists who called themselves "physiocrats." The physiocrats argued that the old mercantilist ideas about wealth were wrong. Did nations become wealthier by placing heavy tariffs on foreign goods? No, said the physiocrats. All such governmental regulations actually interfered with the production of wealth.

Instead, said the physiocrats, the government should give merchants a free hand to produce and sell their goods openly in the world market. The economy would prosper by itself if the government left it alone. The French phrase for "leave alone" was *laissez faire* (LAY-zay FAIR).

Adam Smith defended the idea of a free economy in his book *The Wealth of Nations*, published in 1776. He argued that a free economy could produce far more wealth than an economy regulated by governmental laws. His arguments rested on three so-called natural laws of economics.

The law of self-interest People act for selfish reasons, said Smith. They work for their own good, not for their neighbor's good. For example, bakers do not bake bread out of concern for hunger. Bakers bake bread to make money. Their motives are selfish. In his second and third laws, Smith explained how both the buyer and the seller gain from the other's selfish motives.

The law of competition In a free market, every baker competes with other bakers. To stay in business, each baker must try to make bread more efficiently and sell it at a lower price than rival bakers can. In other words, competition forces people to make a better product. Thus, competition among selfish individuals leads naturally to economic progress for all.

The law of supply and demand What happens if bakers make more bread than people want to buy? In other words, what happens when the supply of bread exceeds the demand for it? In that case, said Smith, bakers would have to lower their prices to attract more customers. The low price would drive the least efficient bakers out of business. This process would continue until there were just enough bakers to meet their customers' demand for bread.

According to Smith, in a society where these natural laws were free to operate, plenty of goods would be produced at the lowest possible price. On the other hand, if the government interfered in the economy, none of the natural laws could operate. Economic liberty, said Smith, was essential to economic progress.

Montesquieu advocated separation of powers.

A French nobleman, the Baron de Montesquieu (1689–1755), devoted himself to the study of political liberty. For years, he studied the history of ancient Rome. He concluded that Rome's collapse was directly related to its loss of political liberties.

Montesquieu believed that Britain was the best-governed country of his own day. Here was a government, he thought, in which power was balanced among three groups of officials. The British king and his ministers held **executive** power. They carried out the laws of the state. The members of Parliament held **legislative** or law-making power. The judges of the English courts held **judicial** power. They interpreted the laws to see how each applied to a specific case. Montesquieu called this division of power into three branches **separation of powers**.

Although Montesquieu oversimplified the British system, it gave him the idea for his most famous book, *On the Spirit of Laws*. Published in 1748, it contained such maxims on government as these:

- When the legislative and executive powers are united in the same person . . . there can be no liberty.
- Again, there is no liberty if the judiciary power be not separated from the legislative and executive [power].
- Power should be a check to power.

434

(This last statement meant that each branch of government would limit the power of the other two branches. Thus, no branch could become a threat to liberty.)

Montesquieu's book was admired by political leaders in the British colonies of North America. His ideas about separation of powers became the basis for the United States Constitution.

Rousseau championed freedom.

The third great champion of liberty during the Enlightenment was a strange figure indeed. His name was Jean Jacques Rousseau.

Rousseau (1712–1778) was born in the Swiss city of Geneva, the son of a watchmaker. When he was 13 years old, he was apprenticed to an engraver, a harsh and unkind man. After three unpleasant years, Rousseau fled to Italy. Thereafter, he worked at many jobs, including music teacher, tutor, and secretary.

Eventually, Rousseau made his way to Paris and won recognition as a writer of essays. Diderot and other Enlightenment leaders tried to befriend him. Yet Rousseau felt out of place in the elegant salons of Paris. He much preferred walking in the woods. Sooner or later, Rousseau quarreled

Jean Jacques Rousseau

with almost everyone. At times in his later years, he was undoubtedly insane. Nonetheless, his ideas about government were brilliant.

Rousseau's best known book on government was *The Social Contract*, published in 1762. The book begins with the declaration, "Man is born free, yet everywhere he is in chains." In other words, liberty was every person's natural birthright, and yet most people were oppressed.

How did this unnatural state of things come about? In brief, this was Rousseau's answer: In the earliest times, people had lived as free and equal individuals in a primitive "state of nature." As people became civilized, however, the strongest among them forced everyone else to obey unjust laws. Thus, freedom and equality were destroyed.

Like Locke, Rousseau argued that the only legitimate government was one that ruled with the consent of its people. However, Rousseau believed in a much broader democracy than Locke had advocated. The people, not monarchs or aristocrats, should be sovereign (dominant), said Rousseau. He believed that liberty and justice would thrive in a state where the "general will" of the people was all-powerful.

Section Review 2

Define: (a) executive, (b) legislative, (c) judicial, (d) separation of powers
Identify: (a) physiocrat, (b) laissez faire, (c) Adam Smith, (d) Montesquieu, (e) Rousseau
Answer:
1. (a) How did the philosophes feel about economic, religious, and political liberty? (b) Who was the greatest champion of economic liberty? (c) Who were the leading champions of political liberty?
2. What were Adam Smith's three natural laws of economics?
3. (a) What did Montesquieu believe led to the fall of Rome? (b) What did he admire about the government of Great Britain?
4. (a) What was Rousseau's view on government? (b) How did it differ from Locke's?

Critical Thinking
5. (a) What did Montesquieu mean when he said, "Power should be a check to power?" (b) How did his viewpoint reflect enlightened ideas?

435

Enlightened despots sought progress. 3

What did the kings and queens of Europe think about the ideas of the philosophes? The French king, Louis XV (1715–1774), liked to be entertained but not enlightened. He was openly hostile to the philosophes and often ordered their writings censored.

Other monarchs, however, were enchanted by the new ideas about reason and progress. Several rulers conducted scientific experiments, played musical instruments, dabbled at poetry, read books of philosophy, and corresponded with Voltaire. They were what historians call **enlightened despots**. A despot is an absolute ruler, one who controls all the powers of government. Enlightened despots, therefore, were absolute rulers who supposedly used their great power for the good of the people they ruled.

The philosophes were willing to consider a ruler enlightened if he or she (1) favored religious tolerance, (2) made economic and legal reforms, and (3) could justify his or her reign by its usefulness to society rather than by divine right. In the 1700's, Frederick II of Prussia and Catherine II of Russia were the foremost of Europe's enlightened despots.

Frederick II made reforms in Prussia.

Frederick II was the young Prussian king who invaded Austria in 1740 and began the War of the Austrian Succession (page 422). Born in 1712, Frederick ruled Prussia from 1740 to 1786 during the Enlightenment. He is known as Frederick the Great.

Frederick was brilliant. He had a keen ear for music and a passion for witty conversation. He always carried his flute with him, even on military campaigns. He wrote long, flattering letters to his intellectual hero, Voltaire. Voltaire, who loved to be flattered, answered Frederick's letters with flowery phrases of his own.

Frederick invited Voltaire to come to Prussia so that they might talk of philosophy. Voltaire consented, and for three years (1750–1753) he lived in Frederick's palace at Potsdam. At first, the two men seemed like ideal companions. Both were witty. Both cared nothing for appearances and dressed in shabby, rumpled clothes. Each friend paid the other elegant compliments.

Before long, however, the king and the philosophe got on each other's nerves. Voltaire disliked editing Frederick's mediocre poetry. Frederick suspected Voltaire of some shady business dealings. Eventually, Voltaire tried to sneak out of Potsdam, but Prussian soldiers captured him and made him spend the night in jail. Both men were now thoroughly angry. Returning to France, Voltaire described the Prussian king as "a nasty monkey, perfidious friend, wretched poet." Frederick returned the abuse, calling Voltaire a "miser, dirty rogue, coward."

Was Frederick truly an enlightened ruler? His opinions were generally liberal and humane, but his deeds were not always so. He granted religious freedom to Catholics and Protestants, but he discriminated against Polish and Prussian Jews. He reduced but did not abolish the use of torture in his kingdom. He allowed freedom of the press. He admitted that serfdom was wrong. Yet he did nothing to end it because he needed the support of landowners.

Perhaps Frederick's most important contribution was his attitude toward being king. He called himself "the first servant of the state." From the beginning of his reign, he made it clear that his goal was to serve and strengthen his country. This attitude was clearly one that appealed to the philosophes.

Catherine the Great ruled Russia.

Catherine II of Russia was another monarch who wrote letters to Voltaire and claimed to rule by enlightened principles. Voltaire, in turn, flattered Catherine, calling her "the star of the north," "benefactress of Europe," "first person in the universe."

Catherine was born in 1729, the daughter of an unimportant German prince. At 15, she was sent to the distant Russian court at St. Petersburg to be married to the Grand Duke Peter, heir to the Russian throne.

Peter the Great's daughter, Elizabeth, was the ruler of Russia when Catherine arrived. The Grand Duke, whom Catherine was to wed, was her nephew. Peter was mentally unstable. His chief pleasures were playing with toy soldiers and torturing dogs and cats.

Catherine soon saw that Peter's weakness and cruelty gave her an opportunity to seize power. She made important friends among Russia's army officers, and she became known as the most intelligent and well-informed person at court. In 1762, only months after her husband became czar as Peter III, Catherine had him arrested and imprisoned. Soon afterward, Peter conveniently died in prison, probably by murder. In September 1762, Catherine was crowned Catherine II of Russia, beginning a reign that lasted 34 years.

Though Russia was not her native land, Catherine II dedicated herself totally to the country's welfare. In 1767, she called a large convention of nobles, free peasants, and townspeople to frame a constitution for Russia. To guide them, she wrote a brilliant essay suggesting many reforms. She wanted to stop capital punishment, end the use of torture, and abolish serfdom. Unfortunately, the delegates to the convention debated and quarreled for months. Finally, Catherine lost patience and dismissed them. Though they had accomplished nothing, Catherine had tried to listen to the wishes of the common people.

Even without a constitution, Catherine put several of her enlightened ideas into effect. She limited the use of torture (but kept the death penalty). She allowed greater religious freedom to Roman Catholics and Jews. She encouraged education.

Catherine honored the great writers of the Enlightenment. (She herself wrote a large number of plays, fairy tales, and satiric essays.) Learning that Diderot desperately needed money, she wrote to him offering to buy his personal library for any price he named. He suggested a figure. She paid him twice what he asked and allowed him to keep the books during his lifetime.

In spite of her sympathy for enlightened ideas, however, Catherine did little to improve the life of the peasants in her empire. A great turning point in her plans for reform came in 1773. In that year, there was a massive uprising of Russian serfs, soldiers, and escaped prisoners. The leader of the rebellion was a soldier named Pugachev, who claimed to be the dead Peter III. As in the peasant revolts of western Europe in the 1300's, serfs burned manor houses and murdered landowners. When Pugachev promised to end serfdom, the revolt spread like wildfire. His mobs threatened Moscow itself.

As wife of the heir to the throne, Catherine (shown here at 19) had the title Grand Duchess.

With great brutality, Catherine's army crushed the rebellion. Her soldiers destroyed whole villages. The roads of Russia were lined with gallows for hanging rebels. Pugachev was brought in an iron cage to Moscow and was executed.

After the revolt, Catherine saw that she could not keep her throne without the nobles' support. She dropped her plans for ending serfdom and gave the Russian nobles absolute control over their serfs. Thus, under the "enlightened despot" Catherine, Russian serfs lost their last traces of freedom. By the end of her reign, nearly 95 percent of Russia's people toiled as serfs for all-powerful landlords.

Catherine expanded Russia's lands.

Like Frederick II, Catherine ignored the philosophes' arguments against war. She waged war relentlessly against Russia's southern neighbor, the Ottoman Turks.

437

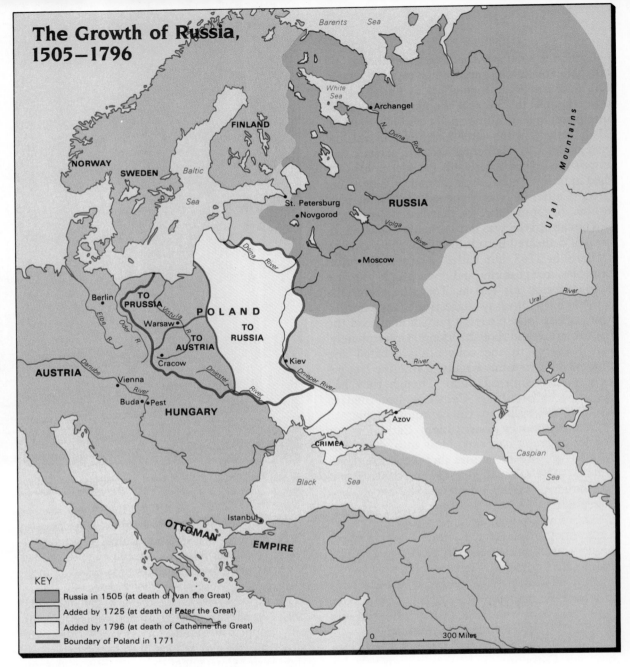

The Growth of Russia, 1505–1796

KEY
- Russia in 1505 (at death of Ivan the Great)
- Added by 1725 (at death of Peter the Great)
- Added by 1796 (at death of Catherine the Great)
- Boundary of Poland in 1771

0   300 Miles

Map Study

What port did Russia have on the White Sea? On the Baltic? Along what seas did Catherine II win land? What three countries divided Polish lands?

Just as Peter the Great had fought for years to win a port on the Baltic Sea, Catherine was determined to win access to the Black Sea. In 1783, her armies won the Crimean Peninsula on the Black Sea. This victory brought Russia a giant step closer to Catherine's goal of reaching the Mediterranean Sea.

Catherine's conquests of Turkish territory threatened the delicate balance of power that existed in eastern Europe. Prussia's Frederick the Great and Austria's Maria Theresa both feared that Russian armies might grab the strategic straits leading to the Mediterranean Sea, the Bosporus, and the Dardanelles.

438

The partition of Poland It was a dangerous situation until Frederick suggested a scheme that satisfied all three countries—Austria, Prussia, and Russia. Frederick proposed that the three powerful countries should take chunks of territory from the weak kingdom of Poland, rather than fight a costly war over Turkish lands.

Catherine and Maria Theresa agreed to Frederick's plan. In 1772, Austria, Russia, and Prussia each took a generous slice of Poland and sent troops to occupy it. Poland's wishes in the matter were ignored. This flagrant land grab was known as the First Partition of Poland.

There were two later partitions, both suggested by Catherine. In 1793, Russia and Prussia took more of Poland's land. Two years later, in 1795, the three greedy neighbors took the rest. On a map of Europe, Poland no longer existed. It did not appear again as an independent country until after World War I.

Catherine's achievement Catherine was the only monarch who lived long enough to participate in all three partitions of Poland. By war and diplomacy, she had vastly enlarged the Russian empire, adding 200,000 square miles of Turkish and Polish lands.

At the end of her remarkable reign (1762–1796), Catherine the Great wrote the epitaph for her own tomb: "Enthroned in Russia, she desired nothing but the best for her country and tried to procure for her subjects happiness, liberty, and wealth. She forgave easily and hated no one." She exaggerated only a little.

Section Review 3

Define: enlightened despot
Identify: (a) Frederick II, (b) Catherine II
Answer:
1. According to the beliefs of the philosophes, what did a ruler have to do in order to earn the title *enlightened?*
2. (a) In the 1700's, what despots were the foremost of Europe's enlightened rulers? (b) In what respect did each try to be an enlightened ruler? (c) In what respect did each fail?
3. (a) How did Catherine the Great expand Russian lands? (b) Why did this concern Prussia and Austria? (c) What solution did Frederick II propose?

Critical Thinking
4. What did Frederick II mean when he called himself the "first servant of the state?" Was he? Explain.
5. Was the partition of Poland in accord with the principles of the Enlightenment? Why or why not?

Britain developed new forms of leadership. 4

The philosophes looked on England's government as the most progressive in Europe. England's ruler was no despot, not even an enlightened one. The Glorious Revolution of 1688 had given England a **constitutional monarchy**. The power of the ruler was limited by law.

Even while the English monarch's power was being limited at home, the power of the English nation was spreading overseas. During the 1600's and 1700's, England won colonies in many parts of the world, including North America and India. Indeed, after 1707 (when the kingdoms of England and Scotland were officially joined), the country even had an impressive new name—Great Britain. To rule this far-flung empire, Britain's monarch and Parliament developed new ways of working together.

Britain was a limited democracy.

After 1688, no British monarch could rule without the consent of Parliament. At the same time, Parliament could not rule without the consent of the monarch. Thus, there was danger of a stalemate if the crown and Parliament disagreed.

During the 1700's, that problem was gradually solved by the development of an executive committee called the **cabinet**. This committee acted in the ruler's name but in reality represented the majority party of the House of Commons. Only temporary and makeshift at first, the cabinet eventually became one of Britain's most durable institutions.

The development of the cabinet Under William and Mary, the cabinet was nothing more than a group of the monarchs' most influential ministers. Like earlier rulers, William III, who was far more involved in governing than his wife, appointed and dismissed ministers at will. They were, after all, his servants.

However, because William needed Parliament's support, he began thinking about the political connections of his cabinet ministers. Since the Whigs then held a majority of seats in the House of Commons, William decided that his cabinet ministers should also be Whigs. By choosing Whigs, the king hoped to assure himself a majority vote in Parliament. Thus, for the first time, the cabinet ministers acted as links between the king and the majority in Parliament.

The rise of the prime minister Over the years, one minister began to dominate the cabinet. This trend became clear during the reign of a new dynasty, the Hanoverians (HAN-oh-**VAIR**-ee-uhns).

In 1714, the last of the Stuart rulers, Queen Anne, died. The British crown passed to a distant relative from the little German state of Hanover. This German prince became George I of England, even though he spoke no English and cared more about Hanover than about England. George I ruled Britain from 1714 to 1727.

Partly because George I and his son George II knew as little of English politics as they did of the English language, they relied heavily on their ministers. In particular, both relied on the shrewd Sir Robert Walpole.

Walpole began his career as a Whig member of the House of Commons in 1702. He was re-elected again and again for almost 40 years. By hook and by crook, he rose to a position of party leadership. In 1721, George I made him a cabinet minister by appointing him to the powerful post of First Lord of the Treasury.

Walpole soon dominated both the other ministers in the cabinet and the Whig members of Parliament. He also managed to keep on the good side of both George I and George II. For 20 years (1721–1741), he was the unofficial ruler of Great Britain.

Walpole set the basic pattern of British politics in modern times. The king's cabinet became the center of power and policymaking. The leader of the majority party in Parliament headed the cabinet as the **prime minister**. Walpole was the first person to act like a modern prime minister, although he did not use the title.

Limited democracy The British form of government was considered ideal by the thinkers of the Enlightenment, but it was far from a democracy. A small, wealthy group of citizens elected the members of the House of Commons.

In Walpole's time, only about 5 percent of the British population had the right to vote. Voting was limited to men who owned at least 40 shillings' worth of land. No women could vote. The upper classes—town merchants and country nobles—ran the government.

Britain built a worldwide empire.

Because wealthy merchants and aristocrats dominated the British government, British policies catered to their interests. To a British mercantilist, colonies were the key to prosperity. Thus, much of Britain's energy in the 1700's was directed toward winning and controlling colonies.

When the Seven Years' War (page 423) ended in 1763, Great Britain stood as the strongest colonial and naval power in Europe—indeed, in the world. As one proud Englishman wrote, "I shall burn my Greek and Latin books. They are the histories of little people. We subdue the globe."

In Asia, the French had been driven from the east coast of India, and Britain soon began extending its hold on the Indian subcontinent. In North America, Britain controlled all the territory east of the Mississippi River.

The most valuable part of Britain's North American empire was also the smallest part. Some tiny islands in the Caribbean Sea—Jamaica, St. Kitts, Barbados, and others—formed the British West Indies. In the 1700's, planters on these islands shipped about 250 million pounds of sugar to London every year. The sugar trade was a major source of British prosperity.

Far to the north of these islands lay Canada, which Britain had won from France during the war. Canada was by far the largest part of the British empire. It was rich in furs and timber, and these raw materials attracted the interest of British mercantilists. However, most of Canada was a sparsely populated wilderness.

Between Canada and the Caribbean lay 13 British colonies along the Atlantic seaboard. Virginia, founded early in the 1600's (page 398), was the oldest of these colonies. By 1750, there were hundreds of small settlements strung along the Atlantic coast. At the same time, hardy families of farmers and fur trappers were eager to push into the thick forests of the Appalachian Mountains.

When George III became king of Great Britain in 1760, his Atlantic coastal colonies were growing by leaps and bounds. Their combined population went from 275,000 in 1700 to 1,850,000 in 1765, a sevenfold increase.

Britain wanted profitable colonies.

According to the mercantilists, colonies existed for only one reason—to enrich the mother country. To make sure that the North American colonies fulfilled their purpose, Britain tried to keep tight control over all the economic activities of the colonists.

The Navigation Acts of 1660 and 1663 were good examples of mercantilist policy. Among other provisions, these laws said that colonists could not sell their most valuable products to any country except Britain. Virginia tobacco farmers, for example, were not free to learn whether French or Dutch merchants would offer a higher price for their valuable crop than British merchants. Colonists could not buy French or Dutch goods without paying high taxes on them.

In addition, colonists were expected to buy British manufactures. No ironware—not even a single nail—could be manufactured legally in the British colonies. Colonists had to buy all such products from Britain.

These restrictions and many others limited what colonists could legally buy, make, sell, and ship. Of course, colonists might still buy foreign goods, make nails, or sell tobacco abroad illegally. Colonial merchants became expert at smuggling. In practice, Britain found enforcing the Navigation Acts was almost impossible.

Britain imposed new taxes.

After the Seven Years' War ended in 1763, George III and his ministers decided that the time had come to deal firmly with the 13 colonies. Great Britain had run up a huge debt in the war against France. During the war, the British government had taxed people in Britain to pay the soldiers. Because American colonists benefited from Britain's victory, the king and his ministers expected the colonists to help pay the costs of the war.

British North America, 1763

KEY
- British territory before 1763
- Acquired from France
- Acquired from Spain

0   800 Miles

Map Study

Where were Britain's largest holdings in North America before 1763? What country controlled the lands west of the Mississippi River?

American colonists had never paid taxes directly to the British government before. In 1765, Parliament passed a controversial law called the Stamp Act. According to this law, colonists had to pay a tax to have an official stamp put on wills, deeds, and other legal documents. Newspapers and other printed material had to be stamped too, as did playing cards.

American colonists were outraged. Colonial lawyers argued that the stamp tax violated colonists' natural rights. In Britain, citizens consented to taxes through their representatives in Parliament. Because the colonists had no representatives in Parliament, Parliament could not tax them.

In Boston and other American cities, colonists rioted against the Stamp Act. "No taxation without representation!" became their battle cry. The protests became so fierce that Parliament gave up and repealed the Stamp Act in 1766.

Although the Stamp Act was dead, the basic conflicts between Britain and the 13 colonies remained. Did the colonies exist to enrich Britain, or were colonists entitled to trade for their own profit? The ideas of the physiocrats (and later Adam Smith) seemed to support the colonists. Did colonists have the same political rights to representative government that people in Britain had? The colonists soon began to use arguments from Locke and other enlightened thinkers to prove that they did have such rights. Only 10 years after the repeal of the Stamp Act, these issues led the colonies to declare their independence from Great Britain.

Section Review 4

Define: (a) constitutional monarchy, (b) cabinet, (c) prime minister
Identify: (a) George I, (b) Robert Walpole, (c) George III, (d) the Navigation Acts, (e) the Stamp Act
Answer:
1. Why did the philosophes regard Britain's government as the most progressive in Europe?
2. (a) Why was there danger of stalemate in the British government if the crown and Parliament did not agree? (b) What solution to this problem emerged over time?
3. What pattern of British politics did Walpole establish?
4. (a) In what area did Great Britain concentrate much of its energies during the 1700's? (b) Why?
5. (a) Describe the British empire in 1763. (b) What steps did Britain take to keep economic control over that empire?
6. (a) Why did the end of the Seven Years' War mark a shift in British policy toward the colonies? (b) How did the colonists react?
7. (a) Describe the basic conflict that existed between Great Britain and the colonies in 1776. (b) Whose ideas supported the rights of the colonists?

Critical Thinking
8. The British government felt that the Stamp Act was justifiable. The colonists strongly disagreed. In your opinion, who was correct? Support your point of view.
9. Why is it said that the British monarch "reigns but does not rule"? Support your answer with evidence from the chapter.

Americans created a republic.   5

In July 1776, a group of colonial Americans signed their names to a large piece of parchment titled *A Declaration.* Soon to be known as the Declaration of Independence, the document was firmly based on the ideas of John Locke and the Enlightenment.

Locke had said clearly that people had the right to rebel against an unjust ruler, as the English had done in the Glorious Revolution of 1688 (page 405). Now, in 1776, Americans justified their revolution by a long list of George III's abuses.

The prime author of the Declaration of Independence, Thomas Jefferson, summed up many of the ideas of the Enlightenment near the beginning of the document:

> We hold these truths to be self-evident, that all men are created equal, that they are endowed by their Creator with certain unalienable rights, that among these are life, liberty, and the pursuit of happiness.

The document ended by breaking the ties between the colonies and Britain. The colonies, said the Declaration of Independence, "are absolved from all allegiance to the British Crown."

From George III's point of view, the signers of this declaration were committing treason. From the American point of view, the colonists were justified in rebelling against a tyrant who had broken the social contract.

Growing hostility led to war.

In 1765, the year colonists rioted against the Stamp Act, most Americans still thought of themselves as loyal subjects of the British king. They had no thoughts either of revolution or of independence. Yet by 1776, many Americans were willing to risk their lives to break free of Britain.

Between 1765 and 1776, one event after another steadily led toward war. Colonial leaders who were eager for independence, such as Boston's Samuel Adams, encouraged conflict. At the same time, George III and his ministers antagonized many moderate colonists by their harsh stands.

In 1773, to protest an import tax on tea, Sam Adams organized a raid against three British ships in Boston harbor. The American raiders dumped 342 chests of tea into the water.

George III, infuriated by the Boston Tea Party, ordered the British navy to close the port of Boston. More British troops moved in to occupy the rebellious city.

In September 1774, representatives from every colony except Georgia gathered in Philadelphia. This First Continental Congress, as it was called, protested the treatment of Boston. The group decided to send a list of complaints to the king. When the king paid little attention to their demands, all 13 colonies sent delegates to a Second Continental Congress in 1775.

Early on April 19, 1775, British soldiers and American militiamen had an open confrontation on the village green in Lexington, Massachusetts. From there, the fighting spread to nearby Concord. By day's end, Americans had killed 73 British soldiers, and 49 American militiamen had been killed in return.

By the time the news of the fighting reached the other colonies, the Second Continental Congress was meeting in Philadelphia. Its members voted to raise an army under the command of a Virginian named George Washington. The American Revolution had begun.

Americans won their independence.

At first, the odds seemed heavily weighted against Washington's ragtag, poorly trained army. The revolutionaries were challenging what was then the largest empire in the world. Opposing them were about 50,000 well-drilled, well-equipped professional soldiers. Added to these numbers were the 52,000 Americans who fought on the British side. (It is estimated that only one third of the American colonists actively supported the revolution while another third opposed it. The rest tried to remain uninvolved and waited to see which side would win.)

In the end, however, the Americans won their war for independence. Five factors help to explain their remarkable victory.

First, the Americans' motivation for fighting was much stronger than that of the British. The troops in Washington's army were defending their homeland. The British soldiers, on the other hand, were fighting mostly for money.

Second, Americans skillfully used hit-and-run tactics, shooting from behind trees and rocks.

Voice from the Past · *Toleration in Virginia*

Few people expressed the ideals of the Enlightenment better than Thomas Jefferson—writer, legislator, diplomat, president, scientist, farmer, inventor, and fierce advocate of freedom. Below is an excerpt from his bill for religious freedom passed by the Virginia General Assembly in 1786.

Sect. II. We the General Assembly of Virginia do enact that no man shall be compelled to frequent or support any religious worship, place, or ministry whatsoever, nor shall be enforced, restrained, molested, or burdened in his body or goods, nor shall otherwise suffer, on account of his religious opinions or beliefs; but that all men shall be free to profess, and by argument to maintain, their opinions in matters of religion, and that the same shall in no wise diminish, enlarge, or affect their civil capabilities.

1. What does this bill propose?
2. (a) How do the proposals in the bill reflect enlightened thinking? (b) Why was the bill a landmark for religious freedom?

Th Jefferson

Besides writing the Declaration of Independence and serving as the third president of the United States, Thomas Jefferson was interested in literature, architecture, farming, and natural history. He designed his own home, Monticello (above), with classical proportions and balance. He was also an inventor. Among his inventions was a device (right) for copying a letter even as he wrote it.

The British, trained to fight in closed ranks, were harrassed and confused by the Indian-style tactics of American sharpshooters. The red British uniforms made clear targets.

Third, time itself was on the side of the Americans. The British could win battle after battle, as they did, and still lose the war. Fighting an overseas war, 3,000 miles from London, was terribly expensive. After a few years, tax-weary British citizens clamored for peace.

Fourth, the British generals were mediocre, whereas the American leader, Washington, was one of history's great men. When all seemed lost early in the war, he managed to inspire his demoralized troops to stay with him through yet one more winter and to fight one more spring campaign. His tenacity and courage kept American hopes alive.

Fifth and possibly most important, the Americans did not fight alone. In 1778, their envoy in Paris, Benjamin Franklin, persuaded France to enter the war on the American side. As an absolute monarch, Louis XVI of France had little sympathy for the ideals of the American Revolution. However, he was eager to weaken France's rival, Britain. Spain too declared war on Britain, as did several German states.

French entry into the war proved decisive. In 1781, a combined force of about 9,500 Americans and 7,800 French trapped a British army commanded by Lord Cornwallis near Yorktown, Virginia. Unable either to escape or to get supplies, Cornwallis surrendered. When this news reached London, George III's prime minister threw up his hands and exclaimed, "It is all over!" Indeed it was.

In Paris in 1783, three American diplomats led by Benjamin Franklin signed a treaty with the British that ended the war. By this treaty, Great Britain agreed to recognize the United States as an independent nation. The treaty set the western boundary of the new nation at the Mississippi River. Britain kept Canada and gave back Florida to its earlier owner, Spain.

Americans approved the Constitution.

For the recently formed nation of the United States, the first five years after the Treaty of Paris were a time of acute financial worry and political quarrels. The 13 states formed a loose confederation, but the country had no effective central government.

In 1787, Washington, Franklin, and other leaders met in Philadelphia to draw up a new plan of government. Their plan, called the Constitution of the United States, was approved by state conventions in 1788. It went into effect in March 1789, when Washington took the oath of office as the first president.

The writers of the United States Constitution took the political theories of the Enlightenment and skillfully turned them into a working government. Adapting the ideas of Montesquieu, they divided the government into three separate branches: President, Congress, and Supreme Court. Each branch could check the power of the other. Adapting the ideas of Locke, the authors of the Constitution tried to ensure that the laws of Congress would always reflect "the consent of the governed."

The Constitution set up a **federal** form of government. That is, power was divided between the national government and the governments of the separate states. This federal plan of government, a novelty in Washington's time, proved remarkably flexible and durable.

Nothing sums up the spirit of the Enlightenment better than the first sentence of the United States Constitution. The famous preamble makes a commitment to reason and to belief in human progress.

We the People of the United States, in order to form a more perfect Union, establish justice, insure domestic tranquility, provide for the common defense, promote the general welfare, and secure the blessings of liberty to ourselves and our posterity, do ordain and establish this Constitution for the United States of America.

Had he lived only nine years more, Voltaire might have read these enlightened words and smiled in approval.

Section Review 5

Define: federal
Identify: (a) Declaration of Independence, (b) Thomas Jefferson, (c) Boston Tea Party, (d) Continental Congress, (e) George Washington, (f) United States Constitution
Answer:
1. (a) How did George III feel about the signers of the Declaration of Independence? (b) How did the signers feel about their actions?
2. Between 1765 and 1776, the attitude of Americans toward revolution changed dramatically. Describe three events that contributed to this change of feeling.
3. (a) Describe the five factors that contributed to American victory in their war for independence. (b) What help did Benjamin Franklin secure for the revolutionaries?
4. How did the writers of the United States Constitution adapt the political theories of the Enlightenment?

Critical Thinking
5. How does the opening statement from the Declaration of Independence (page 442) reflect enlightened thinking?

Chapter Review 20

Summary

1. European thinkers expressed new ideas. Much of the eighteenth century was governed by the spirit of the Enlightenment, a time when thinkers and writers, known as philosophes, valued reason above all else. Voltaire, a leading philosophe, dedicated his life to fighting prejudices. Scientific discoveries, exploration, and great music were all offshoots of the Enlightenment.

2. Writers advocated liberty and reason. Enlightened thinkers believed that their goals of social welfare, individual freedom, and the happiness of humanity could be reached through greater economic and political freedom. Adam Smith called for an economy free of government interference. Montesquieu urged that political abuses could be curbed by a separation of power in government. Rousseau went even further, calling for a state in which the people were sovereign.

3. Enlightened despots sought progress. Several eighteenth-century rulers were known as enlightened despots. They were absolute rulers who supposedly used their great power for the good of the people they ruled. Enlightened despots included Frederick II of Prussia and Catherine II of Russia. Although each had enlightened ideas, their deeds did not always reflect these.

4. Britain developed new forms of leadership. By the late 1600's, Great Britain was a constitutional monarchy in which the power of the ruler was limited by law. In the 1700's, a cabinet and prime minister developed, both of which helped prevent a stalemate between the monarch and Parliament. However, Britain was not a full democracy, as only men of wealth could vote.

By 1763, Great Britain was the strongest colonial power in the world. Colonists in the Americas, however, were growing increasingly resentful of Britain's mercantilist policies.

5. Americans created a republic. Between 1765 and 1776, a series of hostile events led to the breaking of ties between Great Britain and its 13 American colonies. On July 4, 1776, a group of American colonists formally broke those ties with the signing of the Declaration of Independence. A war for independence followed in which the American colonists were victorious. A peace treaty signed in 1783 recognized the United States of America as a separate nation. Five years later, the United States Constitution, based on the ideas of Locke and Montesquieu, established a federal form of government. Its commitment to reason and its beliefs in human progress were clear statements of enlightened ideals.

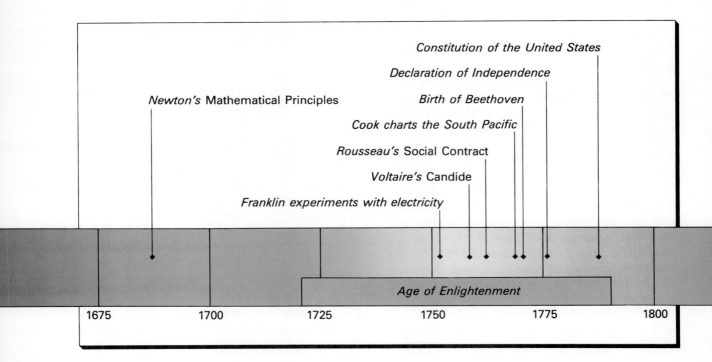

Constitution of the United States

Declaration of Independence

Newton's Mathematical Principles

Birth of Beethoven

Cook charts the South Pacific

Rousseau's Social Contract

Voltaire's Candide

Franklin experiments with electricity

Age of Enlightenment

1675   1700   1725   1750   1775   1800

Reviewing the Facts

1. Define the following terms:
   a. philosophe
   b. executive
   c. legislative
   d. judicial
   e. separation of powers
   f. enlightened despot
   g. constitutional monarchy
   h. cabinet
   i. prime minister
   j. federal

2. Explain the importance of each of the following names, places, or terms:
   a. Age of Enlightenment
   b. Newton
   c. Voltaire
   d. Diderot
   e. Franklin
   f. Cook
   g. Bach
   h. Haydn
   i. Mozart
   j. Beethoven
   k. Smith
   l. Montesquieu
   m. Rousseau
   n. Catherine II
   o. Declaration of Independence
   p. Washington

3. (a) Who was Jean Calas? (b) How did Voltaire's defense of Calas reflect enlightened ideals?

4. (a) Briefly describe the ideas that characterized the Enlightenment. (b) How did salons promote these ideas? (c) How did Diderot's *Encyclopedia* reflect these ideas?

5. What advances were made during the Enlightenment in the fields of science and geography?

6. (a) How did baroque music differ from classical music? (b) Name composers of each.

7. How did Adam Smith believe each of the following contributed to economic prosperity? (a) self-interest (b) competition (c) supply and demand

8. (a) List the reforms made by Frederick II and Catherine II. (b) What prevented each of these rulers from being truly enlightened?

9. Describe the partitions of Poland.

10. Describe the issues that separated Britain and its American colonies by the mid-1770's.

11. How did the American colonists put the ideas of John Locke into action?

12. What enlightened ideas were expressed in the Constitution of the United States?

Thinking about History

1. The French government censored Diderot's *Encyclopedia*. Why have governments in many parts of the world censored books?

2. How did the Renaissance (Chapter 15), the Reformation (Chapter 16), and the Scientific Revolution (Chapter 16) each contribute to the Enlightenment?

3. Enlightened thinkers believed that happiness depended on political, economic, and religious freedom. How well were these goals met during the eighteenth century in Europe?

4. What social level of society took part in the Enlightenment? Support your answer with evidence from the chapter.

Writing and Speaking about History

1. Choose one of the following topics as the broad area of interest for a research paper.
   Enlightenment
   British empire
   American Revolution
   Narrow down the topic until you have developed a working thesis.

2. Prepare a brief speech (one or two minutes) nominating a person from this chapter for a Nobel Peace Prize.

Practicing Skills

1. Make a chart that summarizes English limitations on absolute rule. Include these topics (with dates) in your chart.
   a. Magna Carta
   b. Model Parliament
   c. Petition of Right
   d. Habeas Corpus
   e. Bill of Rights
   f. Cabinet
   g. Prime Minister

2. Trace the American Revolution on a timeline. Extend the timeline from 1765 to 1790 in five-year increments.

Investigating History

1. Make a diagram showing how Montesquieu's idea of the separation of powers is practiced in the United States.

2. Prepare a program for an eighteenth-century salon featuring one or more of the writers and musicians in this chapter. Make a list of eighteenth-century guests to invite.

3. Prepare an audio demonstration contrasting baroque and classical music.

Decision Making in History

Evaluate the pros and cons of the American Revolution. What did the colonists stand to gain by declaring their independence from Great Britain? What did they stand to lose?

The French Revolution and Napoleon

Rebellious Parisians and soldiers dragged cannons toward the Bastille on July 14, 1789. The fall of the Bastille marked the beginning of the French Revolution.

1. **The French monarchy faced a crisis.**
2. **Revolution brought reform and terror.**
3. **Napoleon conquered much of Europe.**
4. **Napoleon's empire collapsed.**

Beneath the towering gray walls of an old fortress, a shouting mob of Parisians brandished their stolen muskets. They had been rioting for several hours on this gray and misty day, July 14, 1789. The muskets in their hands and the ammunition in their pockets had been taken that morning from a military hospital on the other side of Paris. Now they were clamoring at the gates of the fortress called the Bastille.

Built in the Middle Ages, the Bastille served in the 1700's as a jail for political prisoners. It was guarded by 114 soldiers loyal to the French king. Their aristocratic commander, the Marquis de Launay (mahr-KEE duh loh-NAY), firmly refused to turn over the fortress and its 20,000 pounds of gunpowder to the mob. After several tense hours of waiting, he gave the order to fire. Cannons thundered from the battlements.

Some of the rioters were killed, and hundreds of others quickly took cover. They loaded their stolen weapons. It was a battle now between the soldiers' heavy cannons and the civilians' light muskets, and the civilians were taking a beating.

However, other soldiers in Paris sympathized with the mob. A few blocks from the Bastille, an ex-officer in the French Guard pleaded with his comrades:

> Brave guards, can't you hear the cannons? ... That villain De Launay is murdering our brothers, our parents, our wives and children who are gathered unarmed around the Bastille. Will you allow them to be massacred? ... Will you not march on the Bastille?

Tears streamed down the man's face as he spoke. Moved to fury by his speech, 60 soldiers followed him to the Bastille dragging 4 cannons with them. Facing these heavy guns, the Marquis de Launay had no choice but to surrender.

It was a moment of triumph for the working people of Paris, a moment of stark terror for the marquis and his men. The mob dragged the captive soldiers through the narrow lanes of the city. "Stones were thrown at me," said one soldier, "and women gnashed their teeth and brandished their fists at me." That soldier survived the fury of the mob, but De Launay and others were hacked to death.

Meanwhile, in his palace at Versailles, France's King Louis XVI was peacefully asleep. Awakened by a duke, he heard the horrifying news of the fall of the Bastille. "Why, this is a revolt!" exclaimed the king. "No sire," the duke replied. "It is a revolution."

It was indeed a revolution that confronted Louis in the summer of 1789. Historians generally divide this revolution into four stages. First, there was a relatively moderate stage (1789–1792) in which the leaders wrote a constitution and a bill of human rights. Second came a radical and bloody stage (1793–1794) called the Reign of Terror. Third, there was a period of reaction against the violence of the revolution (1794–1799). In the fourth and final stage (1799–1815), an ambitious young general named Napoleon Bonaparte made himself France's dictator and later its emperor.

In this story of violent change and upheaval, the storming of the Bastille was only one episode. Yet it was a crucial one, as we shall see.

The French monarchy faced a crisis. 1

Why did millions of French people suddenly revolt against institutions that their ancestors had accepted for hundreds of years? Ways of life that once served people well can become rigid over time. New conditions change the way people see their world. What seems reasonable in one age may later seem hateful and unnecessary.

By the 1770's, the old institutions of monarchy and feudalism no longer worked for France. As a group, these institutions were known as the Old Regime.

The Old Regime had three estates.

Since the Middle Ages, the people of France had been divided into three large social classes or **estates.** The Roman Catholic clergy formed the First Estate. The nobles made up the Second Estate. The commoners were the Third Estate. In the 1300's, these three groups had begun meeting as the Estates General (page 239), a French institution much like the early English Parliament.

The Old Regime worked well for the members of the First Estate and the Second Estate. They enjoyed wealth and special privileges under law. The Third Estate, however, had many reasons for dissatisfaction.

The First Estate The Catholic Church held about 10 percent of all the land in France. The highest officials of the French Church—the archbishops, bishops, and abbots—were enormously wealthy. Parish priests, on the other hand, were nearly as poor as the peasants to whom they preached.

French clergy paid no direct taxes to the royal government. Instead, they gave the government a "free gift" of about 2 percent of their income.

The Second Estate Although nobles made up less than 2 percent of France's population, they owned about 20 percent of the land. They also held all the highest offices in the church, the army, the government, and the courts of law. For centuries, the people of this estate had enjoyed the privilege of paying no taxes. Their refusal to pay taxes was one cause for revolution.

The Third Estate About 98 percent of France's people belonged to the Third Estate. There were actually three groups in the Third Estate: (1) a city-dwelling middle class called the **bourgeoisie** (boor-zhwah-ZEE), (2) urban lower classes, and (3) peasant farmers. Although these three groups belonged to the same political classification, they were very different economically.

The bourgeoisie had been growing slowly in numbers and power since the Middle Ages. By profession, its members were lawyers, doctors, manufacturers, bankers, merchants, and shop-keepers. Many were well educated and believed strongly in the Enlightenment ideals of liberty and equality. Some of the bourgeoisie were as rich as nobles. Like nobles, wealthy middle-class men dressed in powdered wigs, fine waistcoats, and tight-fitting knee breeches called *culottes* with silk stockings below the knee. Yet the law treated them as peasants. Members of the bourgeoisie yearned for social status and political power equal to their wealth.

The workers of France's cities—butchers, brewers, weavers, tanners, peddlers, cooks, servants, and others—formed a second group within the Third Estate. They were poorer than the bourgeoisie, and their poverty showed in their clothing. Unlike the nobles and the bourgeoisie, poor men wore shirts and loose-fitting trousers that came down to their ankles. As a class, these urban workers were called *sans-culottes* (those who are without knee breeches).

The poor people of France's cities often went hungry. Most of Paris's poor people ate three pounds of bread a day and very little else. If the cost of bread rose, hungry mobs attacked carts of grain and bread to steal what they needed. In 1788, grain harvests were small. The price of bread doubled. Thus, the sans-culottes were in a dangerous mood in the spring of 1789.

The largest group within the Third Estate were the peasants. They made up more than four fifths of France's 26 million people. As a rule, French peasants in the 1700's lived better than peasants elsewhere in Europe. Even so, they lost about half their income in taxes. They paid feudal dues to the nobles, tithes to the church, and royal taxes to the king's agent.

Besides taxes in money, peasants owed the *corvée*. The corvée was a form of tax that was paid with work rather than money. Every year, the law required the peasants to work without pay on government roads for a certain number of days.

Thus, the bourgeoisie, the sans-culottes of the cities, and the peasants of the countryside all had reasons to hate the Old Regime. The French Revolution was partly the outcome of these resentments from the lower classes. It was also the result of weak leadership at the top.

Louis XVI was a weak ruler.

Louis XVI, who became king in 1774, was good-hearted and generous. However, he was not a strong leader. He was indecisive and allowed matters to drift.

Louis and his wife, Marie Antoinette, were a devoted couple. They married when he was 15 years old and she was 14. Marie Antoinette was pretty, light-hearted, and charming. However, she was unpopular from the day she set foot in France because she came from the royal family of Austria, France's longtime enemy. The queen made herself even more unpopular by her habit of buying expensive gowns and jewels while the poor went hungry and the government treasury was empty.

Louis's government was deeply in debt. Part of the debt arose because Louis had borrowed heavily to help the American revolutionaries in their war against Great Britain. Britain was France's chief rival, and Louis had seized the chance to strike at the British.

Louis's ministers hoped to avoid bankruptcy by taxing the nobles. The nobles, however, refused to pay taxes unless the king called a meeting of the Estates General, which had not met since 1614. Reluctantly, Louis called a meeting of the estates at Versailles on May 1, 1789. As it proved, his order was nothing less than an invitation to revolution.

The National Assembly took power.

The First and Second estates (clergy and nobles) had dominated the Estates General in the Middle Ages. They still expected to do so in 1789. Under

On June 20, 1789, the king locked the Third Estate out of its meeting hall. Furious, members met at an indoor tennis court nearby, where they vowed to stand fast until a constitution was established.

the estates' medieval rules, each estate was to meet in its own hall and vote either for or against a given proposal. In the final decision, each estate was to have one vote. Thus, the First and Second estates could always outvote the Third Estate two to one.

In 1789, the Third Estate demanded that all three estates meet together. The votes of all members would count equally. The 610 members of the Third Estate would thus outnumber the 591 members of the combined First and Second estates.

Siding with the nobles, the king ordered the estates to follow the old rules. The representatives of the Third Estate, however, became more and more determined to wield power. The leading spokesman for their viewpoint was a clergyman sympathetic to their cause, the Abbé Sieyès (ah-**BAY** syay-**YAS**). In a bold pamphlet, he had written, "What is the Third Estate? Everything. What has it been up to now in the political order? Nothing. What does it demand? To become something herein."

On June 16, the Abbé Sieyès rose to address an excited gathering of bourgeois deputies. He suggested that the Third Estate change its name to the National Assembly. He called on the new assembly to pass laws and reforms in the name of the French people.

After a long night of excited debate, the deputies of the Third Estate agreed to Sieyès's idea by an overwhelming majority. The vote of June 17, 1789, created the National Assembly. In effect, the deputies proclaimed an end to absolute monarchy and the beginning of representative government. This vote was the first deliberate act of revolution.

Parisians stormed the Bastille.

In this crisis, Louis XVI acted indecisively. He tried to make peace with the Third Estate by yielding to their demands. He ordered the nobles and clergy to meet as one law-making body with the Third Estate (now the National Assembly). At the same time, the king sent orders for his mercenary army of Swiss guards to march toward Paris. He called on these Swiss troops because he could no longer trust the loyalty of French soldiers. The bourgeois deputies feared, with good

A Parisian woman (left) and Marie Antoinette symbolized two different classes.

reason, that the troops were coming to break up the National Assembly.

In Paris, mobs were already rioting over the high price of bread. The riots reached their peak in the storming of the Bastille. What the mob wanted was the Bastille's supply of gunpowder to defend Paris and the National Assembly against the king's foreign troops.

The fall of the Bastille was important for several reasons. Militarily, it forced Louis to give up his plan of bringing his foreign troops into the city. Politically, it reduced the king's power and saved the National Assembly. With this victory, Parisians took the lead in the revolution.

Perhaps most important, the fall of the Bastille became a great symbolic act of revolution in the minds of French people. Ever since 1789, they have celebrated July 14 as a national holiday similar to the United States' Fourth of July.

The Great Fear swept France.

Before long, rebellion was spreading from Paris into the countryside. From one village to the next, wild rumors circulated about a plot against the common people. People said that nobles were hiring brigands to terrorize the peasants.

A wave of panic, called the Great Fear, swept France. Peasants banded together and hid in forests and caves. When they met no enemy brigands, they became brigands themselves. Waving pitchforks and torches, they broke into nobles' manor houses. Once inside, they tore up the old legal papers that bound them to pay feudal dues. Then they burned the manor houses as well.

In October 1789, thousands of Parisian women rioted over the rising price of bread. Their anger quickly turned against the king and queen. Why was the royal couple living in luxury at Versailles while the people starved? The women demanded that Louis and Marie Antoinette come to Paris where they could be guarded.

Seizing knives and axes, the women marched on Versailles. They broke into the palace, ransacked the queen's apartments, and killed three guards. Finally, the king appeared on a balcony and told the angry mob below, "My friends, I will go to Paris with my wife and children." Never again would Louis and his family see the beautiful palace at Versailles.

Section Review 1

Define: (a) estates, (b) bourgeoisie, (c) sans-culottes, (d) corvée

Identify: (a) July 14, 1789, (b) Bastille, (c) Louis XVI, (d) Old Regime, (e) Estates General, (f) Marie Antoinette, (g) National Assembly, (h) Great Fear

Answer:

1. (a) What were the three estates in France? (b) What part did each play in French society and government?
2. (a) Briefly describe each of the groups that made up the Third Estate. (b) Why was each dissatisfied with the Old Regime?
3. How did the characters of King Louis XVI and Queen Marie Antoinette add to the crisis that France faced?
4. Why did the king need to call a meeting of the Estates General?
5. (a) What was the voting system in the Estates General before 1789? (b) How did the Third Estate wish to change this system? (c) How did Louis react? (d) What was the result?
6. (a) Why was the fall of the Bastille important militarily? (b) Politically? (c) Symbolically?
7. What happened during the Great Fear?

Critical Thinking

8. At first, Louis XVI called the fall of the Bastille "a revolt," but he was told it was "a revolution." What is the difference?

Revolution brought reform and terror.

2

The night of August 4, 1789, was one of the most astonishing nights in the history of France. In a matter of hours, the National Assembly swept away the ancient privileges of the nobility and the clergy.

One by one, the nobles in the assembly gave impassioned speeches declaring their love of liberty and equality. The nobles who made these grand speeches were moved by fear as well as idealism. The Great Fear was at its height, and peasant bands were terrorizing the countryside.

The Assembly adopted many reforms.

The emotional speeches went on through the night. By morning, the National Assembly had voted to end feudalism, serfdom, church tithes, and the special privileges of nobles and clergy. The Old Regime was dead. "Liberty, Equality, Fraternity" became the slogan of the revolution.

The Rights of Man Three weeks later, on August 27, 1789, the National Assembly adopted a set of revolutionary ideas called *A Declaration of the Rights of Man and of the Citizen*. The first article of the document declared, "Men are born and remain free and equal in rights." The second article stated:

The aim of all political association is the preservation of the natural ... rights of man. These rights are liberty, property, security, and resistance to oppression.

Other articles of the famous document guaranteed citizens equal justice, freedom of speech, and freedom of religion.

A limited monarchy For two years, the National Assembly argued over a new constitution for France. By 1791, they had made huge changes in France's government and society.

The National Assembly created a limited, constitutional monarchy somewhat like the British government. An elected assembly held the law-making power. Although the monarchy lost its absolute powers, the king and his ministers still held the executive power to enforce laws.

Departments The National Assembly abolished France's traditional provinces, which had existed since the Middle Ages. Instead, the assembly divided France into 83 districts called departments. A council of officials elected by the local citizens administered each department.

A state-controlled church The Catholic Church lost both its lands and its political independence. The government took over church lands. The assembly also ruled that church officials and priests were to be elected by property owners and paid as state officials. This law alarmed millions of devout French peasants, who rallied to the support of their parish priests.

These changes in the Catholic Church drove a wedge between the peasants and the bourgeoisie. From this time on, the peasants often opposed further revolutionary changes.

The king reluctantly approved the constitution and the Declaration of the Rights of Man. Then, in June 1791, Louis and his family tried to escape from France to the Austrian Netherlands. Just as they neared the French border, however, a postmaster recognized the king from his portrait on some paper money. The royal family returned to Paris under guard. As a result of this attempted escape, Louis XVI discredited both himself and the plan for constitutional monarchy. His action increased the influence of his radical enemies and sealed his own doom.

In September 1791, having completed its new constitution, the National Assembly stepped down from power. It was followed by a newly elected group called the Legislative Assembly.

France was split by factions.

Despite the new government, the old problems remained. Angry cries for more liberty, more equality, and more bread soon caused the leaders of the revolution to turn against one another.

The Legislative Assembly split into three general groups. Each group tended to sit together in its own part of the meeting hall. On the benches to the right sat the conservatives, those who opposed more changes in government. In general, they trusted the king and upheld the idea of limited monarchy. On the left side of the hall sat the radicals, those who clamored for more sweeping changes. They hated the king and wanted to set up a republic in which the common people had full power. In the center sat the moderates. They wanted some further reforms but not as many as the radicals demanded.

To this day, radical politicians are commonly described as being "on the left," and conservative politicians are said to be "on the right." Moderates are called "centrists." These terms began with the French Revolution.

Outside the government, there were far more extreme groups, both on the right and on the left. People on the extreme right hoped to undo the revolution and restore the Old Regime. Among this group were the emigrés (EHM-uh-grayz) —nobles who had fled during the peasant uprisings. They lived abroad and plotted against the revolution. On the extreme left were the sans-culottes of Paris. Their radical leaders set

Voice from the Past · *The Rights of Woman*

In 1791, a woman revolutionary named Olympe de Gouges (goozh) demanded the same rights for French women that French men were demanding for themselves. Here is part of her "Declaration of the Rights of Woman."

Woman is born free and lives equal to man in her rights. Social distinctions can be based only on the common utility . . .

The law must be the expression of the general will; all female and male citizens must contribute either personally or through their representatives to its formation; it must be the same for all: male and female citizens, being equal in the eyes of the law, must be equally admitted to all honors, positions, and public employment according to their capacity and without other distinctions besides those of their virtues and talents . . .

No one is to be [persecuted] for basic opinions; woman has the right to mount the scaffold; she must equally have the right to mount the rostrum [a public speaking platform].

1. What legal rights does De Gouges ask for women?
2. What political positions does she say should be open to women?
3. (a) What is implied by "the right to mount the scaffold"? (b) By "the right to mount the rostrum"?

les femmes

up a new city government with representatives from each of Paris's 48 sections. This powerful city council, known as the Paris Commune, became a dominant force in the revolution.

France went to war with Austria.

France faced not only a revolution at home but also a disastrous foreign war. The ruler of Austria, Marie Antoinette's brother, threatened to attack France.

French radicals were delighted at the idea of war with Austria. They hoped that the war would give them a chance to spread their revolution to all the peoples of Europe. On April 20, 1792, the Legislative Assembly declared war on Austria. Soon Prussia joined Austria against France.

The war began badly for the poorly equipped French armies. By the summer of 1792, enemy armies were advancing toward Paris.

On July 25, the Prussian commander threatened to destroy Paris if the revolutionaries harmed any member of the royal family. This rash statement provoked the fury of the mob. On August 10, about 70,000 men and women surged into the palace in Paris where the royal couple was staying. The king's Swiss guard of 900 men fought desperately to defend Louis. The mob brutally massacred them and swarmed through the palace. Louis and Marie Antoinette were imprisoned in a stone tower.

Under the threat of the Parisian radicals, the Legislative Assembly gave up the idea of a limited monarchy. The lawmakers set aside the Constitution of 1791 and declared the king deposed. The assembly then ended its own existence by calling for the election of a new legislature.

The new governing body, elected in September, was called the National Convention. Just as the new government took office, France had a stroke of luck. A French army managed to defeat the Austrians and Prussians. For the moment, France was out of danger from abroad.

The radicals executed Louis XVI.

During the desperate summer of 1792, the leaders of the frenzied mobs on the streets had more real power than any governmental assembly. Although the mobs were poor, their leaders came from the bourgeoisie.

Both men and women of the middle class joined political clubs. The most radical of these clubs in 1792 was the Jacobin (JAK-uh-buhn) Club, where violent speechmaking was the order of the day. Its members wanted to remove the king and establish a republic.

One of the frequent speakers before the Jacobin Club was Georges Danton (dahn-TOHN), a leader of the Paris Commune. Fearless and devoted to the rights of Paris's poor, Danton used his talent for speechmaking to win political leadership.

Another prominent radical leader was Jean Paul Marat (muh-RAH). The very opposite of the strong, bull-like Danton, Marat was a thin, high-strung, sickly man who had hoped to win fame for his scientific research. After the revolution broke out, he edited a radical newspaper called *The Friend of the People*. His fiery editorials called for "five or six hundred heads cut off" to rid France of the enemies of the revolution.

By August 1792, Danton and Marat were two of the most powerful of the radical leaders. Together with the Paris mob, these men set the revolution on a new and more violent path.

The National Convention met in Paris on September 21. It quickly abolished the monarchy. Next, the assembly declared France a republic. Every adult male citizen had the right to vote and hold office. Women could not vote, however, despite the important part they had already played in the revolution.

Louis XVI was king no longer. Under the new republic, he was just a common citizen and prisoner. What was to be done with this dangerous citizen? The delegates to the National Convention tried him for treason and found him guilty.

The radicals demanded that Louis be condemned to death. They won by a single vote. On the morning of January 21, 1793, the ex-king walked with calm dignity up the steps of the scaffold to be beheaded by a machine called the guillotine (GIHL-uh-TEEN). Thousands died by the guillotine during the French Revolution.

France created a citizen-army.

The new republic's first problem was the hostile armies of Austria and Prussia. In the fall of 1792, Britain, Spain, and Portugal joined Prussia and Austria in an alliance known as the First Coalition. (A **coalition** is a temporary alliance between

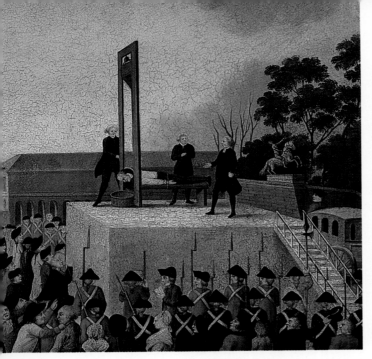

The guillotine was invented by a doctor as a more humane form of execution than the ax.

groups who are usually on different sides.) In the face of so many enemies, France suffered a string of defeats.

The Jacobin leaders took extreme steps to meet the new danger. In February 1793, the convention drafted into the army 300,000 men between the ages of 18 and 40. By 1794, this number had grown to 800,000. Women too asked for the right to form regiments to defend France. The government never granted their request. However, a number of women fought beside men in France's armies during the revolution.

Most armies in Europe were made up of mercenaries, but the new French army was a people's army of loyal patriots. Led by dedicated officers, the French scored victory after victory.

Robespierre began the Terror.

Foreign armies were not the only enemies of the French Republic. The Jacobins had thousands of enemies within France itself—peasants who were horrified by the beheading of the king, priests who would not accept control by the government, and rival leaders who were stirring up rebellion in the provinces.

As dozens of leaders struggled for power, one man slowly gathered control into his own hands. His name was Maximilien Robespierre (ROHBZ-pihr).

Robespierre was one of the few members of the Jacobin Club who did not dress like a revolutionary. He wore a powdered wig in the old style, knee breeches, and stockings. Nicknamed "the Incorruptible," Robespierre never enriched himself at the public expense, unlike many of the men around him. In his fanaticism, however, Robespierre was merciless. His period in power is fittingly known as the Reign of Terror.

Robespierre and his supporters set out to build a Republic of Virtue. They tried to wipe out every trace of France's past monarchy and nobility. Many families named Leroy (king), for instance, changed their names to something less political. (Even if they did not support the monarchy, it was safer to take a new name.) Decks of cards no longer had kings, queens, and jacks. Instead, they had cards called liberties, equalities, and fraternities.

Firm believers in reason, the radicals wanted to make the calendar scientific. They divided the year into 12 months of 30 days and gave each month a new, "reasonable" name. October, for instance, was renamed Brumaire, or Fog Month. The new calendar had no Sundays because the radicals considered religion old-fashioned and dangerous. The Paris Commune closed all churches in the city. Towns all over France soon did the same.

In the summer of 1793, Robespierre formed the Committee of Public Safety. As head of the committee, Robespierre decided who should be judged an enemy of the republic. Those he accused were often tried in the morning and guillotined that very afternoon. From July 1793 to July 1794, he governed France nearly as a dictator.

The widowed queen, Marie Antoinette, was the most famous victim of the Terror. Calm and dignified, she rode in the death cart past jeering crowds. On the scaffold, she accidently stepped on her executioner's foot. "Monsieur," she apologized, "I beg your pardon. I did not do it on purpose." These were her last words.

However, the so-called enemies of the republic who most troubled Robespierre were not monarchists like Marie Antoinette. They were fellow revolutionaries who challenged his leadership. In October 1793, many of the leaders who had first helped set up the republic were executed. Their only crime was that they were less radical than Robespierre.

By the beginning of 1794, even Danton found himself in danger. (Marat had already been stabbed to death by a young woman from another political faction.) Danton's former friends in the National Assembly, afraid to defend him, joined in condemning him to death. On the scaffold, he told the executioner, "Don't forget to show my head to the people. It's well worth seeing."

Besides leading political figures, thousands of obscure people were sent to death on the flimsiest of charges. An 18-year-old youth was guillotined for sawing down a tree that had been planted as a symbol of liberty. A tavern keeper died because he had sold sour wine "to the defenders of the country."

During the Terror, at least 3,000 people were executed in Paris. Some historians believe as many as 40,000 were killed all together. Fully 80 percent were peasants, sans-culottes, or bourgeoisie—common people for whom the revolution had supposedly been fought.

Robespierre fell from power.

By July 1794, members of the National Convention knew that none of them was safe from Robespierre. To save themselves, they turned on him. A group of conspirators demanded his arrest, shouting "Down with the tyrant!" Robespierre tried to speak in his own defense, but delegates to both left and right shouted him down. Within two days, the revolution's last powerful leader went to the guillotine.

With Robespierre's execution, the radical phase of the French Revolution ended. Robespierre died on July 28, 1794. On the new revolutionary calendar, July was called *Thermidor* from the French word for "heat." Hence, the revolt against Robespierre is called the *Thermidorian reaction.*

Moderates ruled in the Directory.

Public opinion in France now shifted dramatically to the right. People of all classes were sick of the Terror. They were also sick of the skyrocketing prices for bread, salt, and other necessities of life.

In 1795, moderate leaders of the National Convention drafted a new constitution. This new plan of government put power firmly in the hands of the upper bourgeoisie. This constitution, the third since 1789, called for a two-house legislature and an executive body of five men known as the Directory.

The five directors were moderates, not revolutionary idealists. Some of them freely enriched themselves at the public's expense. Despite their corruption, however, they gave their troubled country a period of order.

The Directory also found the right general to command France's armies. With a string of astounding victories, this general crushed France's foes. The name of this supremely talented young man was Napoleon Bonaparte.

Section Review 2

Define: (a) emigrés, (b) guillotine, (c) coalition
Identify: (a) *Declaration of the Rights of Man and of the Citizen*, (b) Legislative Assembly, (c) Paris Commune, (d) Jacobin Club, (e) Danton, (f) Marat, (g) Robespierre, (h) Committee of Public Safety, (i) Reign of Terror, (j) Directory
Answer:
1. What rights were proclaimed in *A Declaration of the Rights of Man?*
2. (a) What reforms did the National Assembly make in France's government? (b) In the Catholic Church?
3. What was the result of the royal family's attempt to escape France?
4. (a) What were the basic political divisions within the Legislative Assembly? (b) How did seating arrangements there affect the labels given to political groups?
5. (a) How did the limited monarchy come to an end? (b) What was the fate of Louis XVI?
6. After 1793, how did the French army differ from the armies of its enemies?
7. (a) Briefly describe the Reign of Terror. (b) How did it end?
8. What political outlook did the Directory represent?

Critical Thinking
9. There is a saying, "Revolutions devour their own children." (a) What evidence from the French Revolution supports that proverb? (b) Why might revolutions in general have such an effect?

Napoleon conquered much of Europe. 3

Napoleon was a small man (five feet six inches tall) who cast a long shadow over the history of modern times. As a military genius, he ranks with Alexander the Great of Macedonia, Hannibal of Carthage, and Julius Caesar of Rome. In only four years (1795–1799), Napoleon rose from obscurity to mastery of France.

Napoleon rose through the army.

Napoleon Bonaparte was born in 1769 on the island of Corsica in the Mediterranean Sea. In that same year, French troops invaded Corsica and crushed a movement for Corsican independence. "I was born," wrote Bonaparte later, "when my country was dying."

When Bonaparte was ten years old, his parents sent him to a military school outside Paris where his French schoolmates snubbed him as a foreigner. Cut off from other students, Bonaparte devoted himself to mastering military tactics. In 1785, when he was 16, he finished school and became a lieutenant in the artillery. When the revolution broke out, he joined the army of the new government.

In October 1795, fate handed the young officer a chance for glory. An army of royalists threatened the palace where the National Convention was meeting, and a government official told Bonaparte to defend the palace. Bonaparte and his gunners greeted the thousands of royalists with a deadly cannonade. Within minutes, the attackers fled in panic and confusion. Napoleon Bonaparte was the hero of the hour. He was hailed throughout Paris as the savior of the French Republic.

In 1796, the Directory appointed Bonaparte to command a French army against Austria and the Kingdom of Sardinia. Crossing the Alps, the young general swept into Italy and won a series of remarkable victories. The French marched into Milan and made it the capital of a new Italian republic dominated by France.

Though Bonaparte posed as the liberator of northern Italy, he was in fact its conqueror. After a year of triumphant campaigning (1796–1797), Bonaparte was the most famous general in Europe.

Napoleon seized power in France.

Watching the early disorders of the French Revolution, a British statesman made this astute prediction:

> In the weakness of authority . . . some popular general shall draw the eyes of all men upon himself. Armies will obey him on his personal account . . . The person who really commands the army is your master.

In 1799, the prediction came true.

By 1799, the Directory had lost the confidence of the French people. They were accused of corruption. In several elections, voters rejected the Directory's candidates. Only the directors' control of the army kept them in power.

Bonaparte decided that the time had come to seize political power. On November 9, 1799, he ordered 500 of his troops to occupy one chamber of the national legislature and drive out its elected members. The second chamber of the legislature, terrified by this show of force, voted to end the Directory. The chamber turned over power to three officials known as consuls. Bonaparte was one of the three.

Soon Bonaparte assumed dictatorial powers as the First Consul of the French Republic. Such a seizure of power is known as a **coup** from the French phrase *coup d'état* (koo day-TAH) or "stroke of state."

A Second Coalition attacked France.

At the time of Bonaparte's coup, France was still at war. Bonaparte's Italian campaign of 1796–1797 had forced Austria and Prussia to make peace, thus ending the First Coalition. The British navy, however, continued its damaging attacks against French shipping. In 1799, British diplomats arranged a Second Coalition of anti-French powers. The Second Coalition consisted chiefly of Britain, Austria, and Russia.

Once again, Napoleon rode out from Paris at the head of his troops. Once again, he led a huge French army over treacherous Alpine passes into northern Italy. Once again, he was victorious. The Austrians were forced to accept his peace terms. The Russians also made peace.

The British fought on, but in 1802, they agreed to Bonaparte's conciliatory peace terms. The

British and the French signed a peace treaty at Amiens (ahm-**YAN**) in March 1802. For the first time in ten years, Europe was at peace. Sadly, however, this peace did not last long.

Napoleon became emperor.

At first, Bonaparte pretended to be the constitutionally chosen leader of a free republic. In 1800, he and his two fellow consuls asked the French people to approve a new constitution, the fourth in eight years. They held a **plebiscite** (**PLEHB**-uh-syte), an election in which all citizens vote yes or no on an issue.

In the plebiscite of 1800, the French showed how desperate they were for strong leadership. They voted overwhelmingly for Bonaparte's constitution, which gave all real power to Bonaparte himself as the First Consul.

Bonaparte saw that he could take as much power as he wanted. In 1802, yet another plebiscite made him consul for life. French voters approved the change by a staggering majority (3,568,885 voting yes and only 8,374 voting no).

Two years later, in 1804, Bonaparte decided to make himself emperor. Again, the French voters agreed to his decision. Dressed in a splendid robe of purple velvet, Napoleon walked down the long aisle of Notre Dame Cathedral in Paris on December 2, 1804. The pope waited for him with a glittering crown. As thousands watched, the new emperor took the crown from the pope's hands and placed it on his own head.

Napoleon restored order.

At his coronation, Napoleon Bonaparte became Emperor Napoleon I. The French Republic was dead. In its place stood an absolute monarchy known as the French empire. Yet Napoleon did not try to return France to the days of Louis XIV. He kept many of the changes that had come with the revolution.

Economic order Napoleon managed to slow inflation by balancing the government's budget and setting up a national bank. The sans-culottes of Paris were finally able to buy bread.

Social order Noble emigrés returned to France by the thousands. Napoleon welcomed them as long as they behaved themselves politically. The bourgeoisie were also well pleased with Napoleon

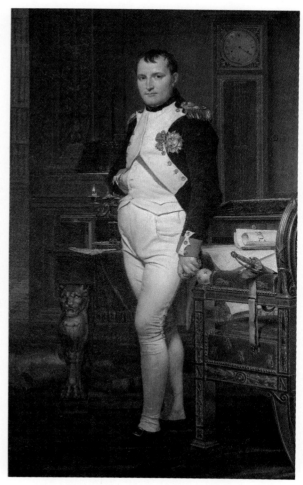

Napoleon (1769–1821) rose through the army to become emperor of France. His loyal troops affectionately nicknamed him "the little corporal."

because he promoted officials according to merit, not according to noble family.

Religious order Both the clergy and the peasants wanted to restore the Catholic Church's position in France. In 1801, Napoleon signed a *concordat* (agreement) with Pope Pius VII. It spelled out a new relationship between church and state.

Napoleon agreed to recognize Catholicism as the faith of "the great majority of Frenchmen." The French government would appoint Catholic bishops, but those bishops could appoint parish priests without government interference. Everyone in France was free to worship as he or she wished.

For his part, the pope stopped trying to win back the lands that the revolutionary government had taken from the church. He also accepted Napoleon's policy of toleration for Protestants and Jews. This religious settlement of 1801 gave Catholics a favored position in France but not absolute dominance.

Legal order Napoleon thought his greatest work was his comprehensive code of laws known as the Napoleonic Code. Drafted by French jurists between 1801 and 1804, the new code gave the country a single set of laws.

In some ways, the Napoleonic Code grew out of the principles of liberty and equality of the French Revolution. It abolished the three estates of the Old Regime and granted equal rights before the law to people of all classes.

In other ways, the code limited liberty. Napoleon had even more power to censor newspapers than the king had had under the Old Regime. The code took away some rights that women had won during the revolution, such as the right to hold property. The new laws also restored slavery in the French colonies of the Caribbean, which had been abolished by the revolution.

The laws of the new code applied equally to all French citizens except one: Napoleon himself. He asserted his right, as emperor, to stand above the law. As he said, "If there are problems with a government that is too strong, there are many more with a government that is too weak. Things don't work unless you break the law every day."

Napoleon extended France's power.

Napoleon was not content to be simply master of France. Eager to extend his power, he took over part of Italy, set up a puppet government in Switzerland, and threatened Great Britain. In response, the British declared war in 1803. The Peace of Amiens had lasted only a year.

In 1805, Britain persuaded Russia, Austria, Sweden, and Prussia to join the Third Coalition against France. Napoleon met this challenge with his usual boldness. He believed that he was a "man of destiny" who could do no wrong. He wanted to "modernize" all Europe—that is, to force all of Europe to accept his idea of modernization. Between 1805 and 1807, in a series of brilliant battles, he nearly succeeded.

The Battle of Ulm (October 1805) Invading the Austrian empire, the French army caught 50,000 Austrians in a deadly trap and forced them to surrender. Napoleon entered Vienna in triumph.

The Battle of Austerlitz (December 1805) On the first anniversary of his coronation as emperor, Napoleon won his greatest victory at Austerlitz (AW-stuhr-lits). Commanding 73,000 French troops, he smashed an army of 87,000 Russians and Austrians, took 20,000 prisoners, left 15,000 enemy dead on the field, and forced the Austrian emperor to make peace.

The Battle of Jena (October 1806) Moving north against Prussia, Napoleon and his troops won another devastating victory at Jena (YAY-nuh), wounding or killing 27,000 and taking 18,000 prisoners. As a result of this battle, French troops occupied Berlin.

The Battle of Friedland (June 1807) Advancing eastward into the Prussian part of Poland, Napoleon wiped out a large Russian army. Czar Alexander I, grandson of Catherine the Great, met with Napoleon on a raft moored in the middle of a Polish stream. Here the two rulers agreed to divide Europe between them. In this treaty, called the Peace of Tilsit, the czar agreed to allow France to dominate Europe as far east as Poland. In return, Napoleon gave Alexander a free hand to attack the Ottoman empire.

The Battle of Trafalgar (October 1805) In his war against the Third Coalition, Napoleon lost only one major battle, the Battle of Trafalgar (truh-FAL-guhr). However, this great sea battle was probably more important than all Napoleon's victories on land.

The Battle of Trafalgar took place in 1805 off the southern coast of Spain. The commander of the British fleet was Admiral Horatio Nelson, as brilliant in warfare at sea as Napoleon was on land. With 27 ships, Nelson attacked a 33-ship French fleet. In the middle of the furious battle, Nelson was struck in the back by a French shell. As he lay dying aboard his flagship, Nelson heard the welcome news of British victory. "Now I am satisfied," murmured the admiral. "Thank God, I have done my duty."

The destruction of the French fleet at Trafalgar forced Napoleon to give up his plan to invade Britain. Across the barrier of the English Channel, Great Britain remained a strong enemy able to challenge his power. Eventually, Napoleon's extravagant efforts to crush Britain led to his own undoing.

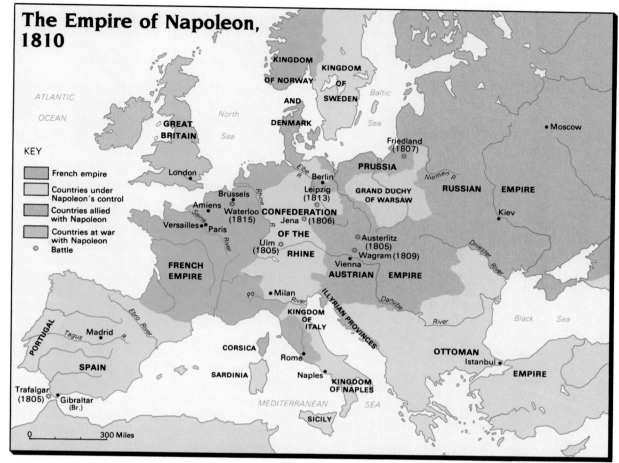

The Empire of Napoleon, 1810

KINGDOM OF NORWAY AND DENMARK

KINGDOM OF SWEDEN

ATLANTIC OCEAN

GREAT BRITAIN

North Sea

Baltic Sea

Moscow

KEY
- French empire
- Countries under Napoleon's control
- Countries allied with Napoleon
- Countries at war with Napoleon
- ✿ Battle

London

Brussels

Amiens

Waterloo (1815)

Versailles • Paris

Seine

Rhine

Elbe R.

Berlin

Leipzig (1813)

PRUSSIA

Friedland (1807)

Niemen R.

GRAND DUCHY OF WARSAW

RUSSIAN EMPIRE

Kiev

CONFEDERATION

Jena ✿ (1806)

OF THE

Ulm ✿ (1805)

RHINE

FRENCH EMPIRE

River

Austerlitz ✿ (1805)

Wagram (1809)

Vienna

AUSTRIAN EMPIRE

Dniester River

Po

• Milan

River

ILLYRIAN PROVINCES

Danube

River

Black Sea

KINGDOM OF ITALY

PORTUGAL

Tagus R.

Madrid

Ebro River

SPAIN

CORSICA

Rome •

OTTOMAN

Istanbul •

EMPIRE

SARDINIA

Naples •

KINGDOM OF NAPLES

Trafalgar ✿ (1805)

Gibraltar (Br.)

MEDITERRANEAN SEA

SICILY

0 _____ 300 Miles

Map Study

In 1810, what was the only country still fighting Napoleon? What countries were allied with him? What made Prussia's position dangerous?

Napoleon dominated Europe.

Through the first decade of the new century (1800–1810), Napoleon built Europe's greatest empire since Roman times. His victories over the Third Coalition gave him mastery over most of Europe. The only major European countries outside Napoleon's power were Britain, the Ottoman empire, Russia, and Sweden.

The map above shows the extent of Napoleon's power. The lands and kingdoms he dominated fell into three main categories.

First, there were the lands that Napoleon annexed directly to France. These territories included the Dutch republic and a number of Italian states.

Second, there were lands that remained independent in name but were in fact controlled by Napoleon. These included Spain, the Grand Duchy of Warsaw, and several German-speaking kingdoms in central Europe. (Napoleon ended the Holy Roman Empire once and for all by forcing the last emperor to step down.) This group of countries kept their traditional capitals rather than being governed from Paris. However, the rulers of these countries were nothing more than Napoleon's puppets. Three of them were his own brothers.

In a third category, the powerful countries of Russia, Prussia, and Austria were loosely attached to Napoleon's empire through treaties of alliance. Their chief duty as allies was to support Napoleon in his campaign to crush Britain.

The French empire was huge, but it was also unstable. At its largest, it held together for only

461

five years (1807–1812). Then it quickly fell to pieces. Its sudden collapse was caused in part by Napoleon himself.

Section Review 3

Define: (a) coup, (b) plebiscite, (c) concordat
Identify: (a) Napoleon Bonaparte,
(b) Napoleonic Code, (c) Austerlitz,
(d) Horatio Nelson, (e) Trafalgar
Answer:
1. How did the National Convention and the Directory both help Napoleon rise to power?
2. How did Napoleon seize power?
3. How did Napoleon expand his power through plebiscites?
4. (a) What policy did Napoleon adopt toward the emigrés? (b) What actions won him the support of the bourgeoisie? (c) What agreement did he make with the Catholic Church?
5. (a) How did the Napoleonic Code carry out the ideas of the French Revolution? (b) How did it limit liberty?
6. What major powers did Napoleon defeat or force into alliance with France?
7. Into what three categories were the lands that Napoleon conquered divided? Give specific examples of each.

Critical Thinking
8. Napoleon claimed to be a freely elected leader. (a) What facts support his claim? (b) What facts do not?

Napoleon's empire collapsed.

4

"I love power," said Napoleon, "as a musician loves his violin." It was the drive for power that had raised Napoleon to great heights. Now that same love of power led to his doom. He made three disastrous misjudgments.

Napoleon set up the Continental System.

Napoleon's first misjudgment was to try to cut off all trade with Britain. In 1806, he declared that no state under his control could import British goods. In effect, this policy meant that all ports on the European continent were closed to British shipping. Napoleon's navy set up a blockade to keep British ships from reaching Europe.

Napoleon called his policy the Continental System because it was supposed to make Europe more self-sufficient. His goal was to destroy Britain's commercial and industrial economy.

Unfortunately for Napoleon, his blockade was not nearly tight enough. Smugglers from Spain to Denmark managed to bring in cargo from Britain. British trade, though weakened, was not destroyed.

Indeed, Britain responded with its own blockade. The British navy stopped ships bound for the continent and forced them to sail to a British

Daily Life · Canned Food

Napoleon knew the importance of food in war. He is supposed to have said, "An army marches on its stomach." The emperor offered a prize to anyone who could find a new way to preserve food for long marches. In 1809, a French candy maker named Nicolas Appert discovered that he could keep food from spoiling by putting it in a sealed container and heating it to a high temperature.

Until the late 1800's, eating canned food remained a risky business. Early canners often failed to heat the food enough to kill all bacteria. Yet another problem was opening the cans. Before the invention of the can opener in about 1870, directions on some cans told hungry customers to use a hammer and chisel.

Spanish artist Francisco Goya (1746–1828) saw the horrors of his country's war against Napoleon. This scene shows French troops shooting Spanish rebels.

port to be searched and taxed. Because the British had a stronger navy, they were better able than the French to make their blockade work.

The British navy regularly stopped the ships of neutral countries, including merchant vessels of the United States. Americans were so angered by these actions that the United States Congress declared war against Britain in 1812. The War of 1812, which ended in a draw, was only a minor inconvenience for Britain in its struggle with Napoleon.

The Continental System hurt Napoleon more than it hurt his enemies. It weakened the economies of France, Germany, and the other lands under Napoleon.

Guerrillas fought the French in Spain.

In 1808, Napoleon's ambition led to a second costly mistake. He planned to make his brother Joseph king of Spain. This move outraged the national feelings of the Spanish people.

For five years (1808–1813), bands of Spanish peasant fighters known as **guerrillas** struck at French armies in Spain. (*Guerrilla* is a Spanish

word meaning "little war.") The guerrillas were not a regular army that Napoleon could meet in battle. Instead, they were ordinary peasants who ambushed French troops and then fled into hiding. The British added to French troubles in Spain by sending troops to aid the rebels.

Napoleon lost about 300,000 men during this Peninsular War (so called because Spain lies on the Iberian Peninsula). The men and money Napoleon wasted in Spain fatally weakened the French empire.

In Spain and elsewhere, nationalism was becoming a powerful weapon against Napoleon. People who at first had welcomed the French as their liberators now felt they were being abused by a foreign conqueror. Like the Spanish guerrillas, Germans and Italians and other conquered peoples turned against the French.

Napoleon invaded Russia.

In 1812, Napoleon's thirst for power led to his most disastrous mistake of all. Because Czar Alexander I refused to stop selling grain to Britain, Napoleon decided to invade Russia.

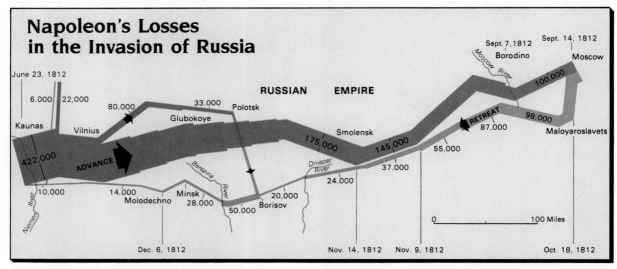

Napoleon's Losses in the Invasion of Russia

June 23, 1812 — Kaunas — 422,000 — ADVANCE

6,000 | 22,000 — Vilnius

80,000 — Glubokoye

33,000 — Polotsk

RUSSIAN EMPIRE

Sept. 7, 1812 — Borodino — Moscow River

Sept. 14, 1812 — Moscow

100,000

RETREAT — 98,000 — 87,000

Maloyaroslavets

175,000 — Smolensk — 145,000 — 55,000

Dnieper River — 24,000 — 37,000

10,000

Niemen River

14,000 — Molodechno — Minsk — 28,000 — Berezina River — 50,000 — Borisov — 20,000

0 — 100 Miles

Dec. 6, 1812 — Nov. 14, 1812 — Nov. 9, 1812 — Oct. 18, 1812

This combination map and graph shows Napoleon's invasion of Russia. The Niemen River marked the Russian border. How many men did Napoleon have when he entered Russia in June, 1812? When he left in December?

In June 1812, Napoleon's army of more than 400,000 men took its first steps on the road to disaster. Many of these troops were not French. The emperor had drafted soldiers from all over Europe, and they felt little loyalty to Napoleon.

The Grand Army, as Napoleon called his forces, marched into Russia, but no Russian army came out to meet it. Instead, Czar Alexander pulled back his troops, refusing to be trapped in an uneven battle. As the Russians retreated toward Moscow, they burned grain fields and slaughtered livestock rather than leave them for the French. This "scorched-earth policy" of the Russians greatly weakened Napoleon's army. Desperate soldiers deserted the French army to search for scraps of food.

When Napoleon finally entered Moscow on September 14, he found the city in flames. Alexander destroyed Moscow rather than surrender it to the French. Napoleon stayed in the ruined city for five weeks, expecting the czar to make a peace offer, but that offer never came. By then, it was the middle of October, too late to advance farther and perhaps too late even to retreat.

Grimly, Napoleon ordered his starving army to turn back. As the snows began to fall in early November, Russian raiders mercilessly attacked Napoleon's ragged, retreating army. With freezing fingers, a French officer wrote a hurried message to his wife: "The Army marches covered in great

snowflakes . . . It is a mob without purpose, famished, fevered."

Soldiers staggered through the snow and dropped in their tracks from wounds, exhaustion, hunger, and cold. The temperature fell to 35° below zero. Finally, in the middle of December, the last survivors crossed the border out of Russia. Of his Grand Army, Napoleon had only 10,000 soldiers who were fit to fight.

A *coalition defeated Napoleon.*

Napoleon's enemies were quick to take advantage of his weakness. Britain, Russia, Prussia, Austria, and Sweden joined forces against him in the Grand Alliance.

In only a few months, Napoleon managed to raise another army. He faced his enemies outside the German city of Leipzig (LYPE-sihg) in October 1813. At this crucial point, Napoleon's brilliance failed him. He lost the Battle of Leipzig (also known as the Battle of Nations), and his army was cut to pieces.

Napoleon's empire crumbled quickly. By January 1814, armies of Austrians, Russians, and Prussians were pushing steadily toward Paris. In March, the Russian czar and the Prussian king led their troops in a triumphant parade through the French capital. Napoleon wanted to fight on, but his generals refused.

In April 1814, the defeated emperor gave up his throne and accepted the terms of surrender drawn up by Alexander I. The victors gave Napoleon a small pension and exiled him to Elba, a tiny island off the Italian coast. The allies expected Napoleon to cause no further trouble. They were wrong. Napoleon had one last battle to fight, the Battle of Waterloo.

Napoleon returned briefly.

As Napoleon arrived in Elba, a Bourbon king arrived in Paris to rule France. It was Louis XVIII, brother of the guillotined king. (The young prince, Louis XVII, had died in prison.) However, the new king was chased from Paris only nine months after his return.

Napoleon escaped from Elba and, on March 1, 1815, landed in France. In a proclamation, he urged the French to rally to his cause. "Victory will march at full speed," he said. "You will be the liberators of your country."

Thousands of French people welcomed Napoleon back. The ranks of his army swelled with volunteers as it approached Paris. Within days, Napoleon was again emperor of France. Louis XVIII fled to the border.

The countries of the Grand Alliance quickly marshaled their armies. The British army, led by the Duke of Wellington, prepared for battle near the village of Waterloo in Belgium.

On June 18, 1815, Napoleon attacked. The British army defended its ground all day. Late in the afternoon, the Prussian army arrived. Together, the British and Prussians launched an attack against the French. Napoleon's exhausted troops gave way. The British and Prussians chased them from the field.

Thus ended Napoleon's last bid for power, called the Hundred Days. Taking no chances this time, the British shipped the prisoner Napoleon to St.

Footnote to History

Not surprisingly, Napoleon found his life on Elba boring, frustrating, and humiliating. His quick wit turned his frustration into a *palindrome*, a word or phrase that reads the same both forward and backward: "Able was I ere I saw Elba."

Helena, a remote island in the South Atlantic. Here Napoleon lived in lonely exile for six years, writing his memoirs. He died in 1821 of a stomach ailment, perhaps cancer. A short time before his death, he attempted to justify all he had done during his life:

Such work as mine is not done twice in a century. I have saved the Revolution as it lay dying. I have cleansed it of its crimes, and have held it up to the people shining with fame. I have inspired France and Europe with new ideas that will never be forgotten.

Without doubt, Napoleon was a military genius and a brilliant administrator. Yet all his victories must be measured against the millions of lives that were lost in his wars. Of his many achievements, only his law code and some of his reforms in France's government proved lasting—and they were not won on the battlefield. A later French statesman and writer, Alexis de Tocqueville, summed up Napoleon's character by saying, "He was as great as a man can be without virtue."

Section Review 4

Define: guerrilla
Identify: (a) Continental System, (b) Peninsular War, (c) scorched-earth policy, (d) Grand Alliance, (e) the Hundred Days, (f) Waterloo
Answer:
1. List Napoleon's three misjudgments.
2. (a) How did Napoleon try to weaken Britain? (b) What were the results?
3. How did the Peninsular War weaken France?
4. Briefly describe Napoleon's invasion of Russia.
5. How did Napoleon fall from power in 1814?
6. (a) What was the reaction to Napoleon's return in France? (b) In the countries of the Grand Alliance?
7. (a) How was Napoleon finally defeated? (b) What happened to him afterward?

Critical Thinking
8. Reread the quotation from Napoleon above on this page. Evaluate his claims that he saved the French Revolution and inspired Europe with new ideas.

Summary

1. The French monarchy faced a crisis. Under the Old Regime, French society was divided into three estates. The First and Second estates had both political power and special privileges. The Third Estate—the majority of the people—had a wide variety of grievances against the Old Regime. When Louis XVI called a meeting of the Estates General in 1789, the Third Estate proclaimed a constitutional monarchy. The Paris mob stormed the Bastille.

2. Revolution brought reform and terror. By 1791, the National Assembly had proclaimed the equality of all men, reformed the government, and weakened the Church. In 1793, radicals won power, declared a republic, and executed Louis XVI. Their citizen-army defeated a coalition of enemies. Led by Robespierre, the radicals condemned thousands to death as enemies of the republic during the Reign of Terror. In 1795, the radicals were overthrown by the more moderate Directory.

3. Napoleon conquered much of Europe. General Napoleon Bonaparte overthrew the Directory in 1799. In 1804, he made himself emperor. He brought stability to France and set up a single legal system under the Napoleonic Code. Napoleon expanded his control over most of Europe.

4. Napoleon's empire collapsed. Napoleon's Continental System weakened European economies. A guerrilla war in Spain drained money and men from France's army. Napoleon's invasion of Russia ended in a disastrous retreat. In 1814, Napoleon was defeated by an alliance of powers. Although he returned briefly in 1815, he met his final defeat at Waterloo.

Reviewing the Facts

1. Define the following terms:
   - a. bourgeoisie
   - b. coalition
   - c. coup
   - d. plebiscite
   - e. guerrilla

2. Explain the importance of each of the following names, dates, places, or terms:
   - a. July 14, 1789
   - b. Louis XVI
   - c. Old Regime
   - d. estates
   - e. sans-culottes
   - f. Marie Antoinette
   - g. Great Fear
   - h. emigrés
   - i. Jacobin Club
   - j. guillotine
   - k. Robespierre
   - l. Reign of Terror
   - m. Bonaparte
   - n. Continental System
   - o. Waterloo

3. What were the four stages of the French Revolution, from 1789 to 1815?

4. Describe French society under the Old Regime.

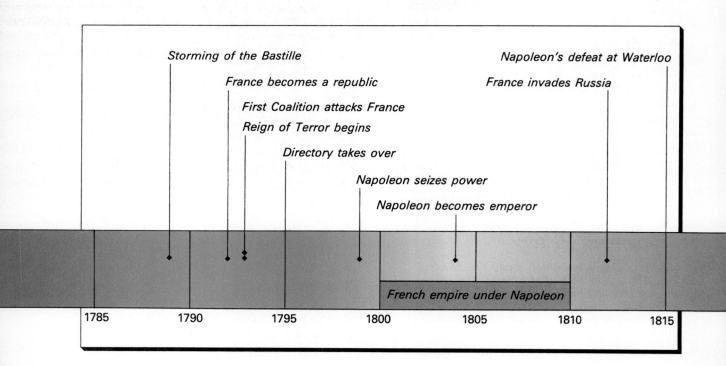

Storming of the Bastille

France becomes a republic

First Coalition attacks France

Reign of Terror begins

Directory takes over

Napoleon seizes power

Napoleon becomes emperor

Napoleon's defeat at Waterloo

France invades Russia

French empire under Napoleon

1785   1790   1795   1800   1805   1810   1815

5. What causes for discontent did each of the following groups have? (a) bourgeoisie (b) urban poor (c) peasants
6. (a) Why was Louis XVI forced to call a meeting of the Estates General in 1789? (b) What was the result?
7. Why is the fall of the Bastille celebrated as a national holiday in France?
8. What form of government did the National Assembly set up?
9. What Enlightenment ideas were expressed in *A Declaration of the Rights of Man?*
10. (a) Explain how the revolution steadily grew more violent. (b) What form of government did the Jacobin National Convention establish? (c) Briefly describe the Reign of Terror.
11. Trace the steps by which Napoleon rose to power.
12. (a) Explain how Napoleon built an empire in Europe, describing the three categories into which the empire was divided. (b) What were Napoleon's major achievements within France?
13. (a) What three major misjudgments led to Napoleon's downfall? (b) What happened when Napoleon invaded Russia?
14. What events ended Napoleon's career?

Thinking about History

1. Compare the quotations from *A Declaration of the Rights of Man and of the Citizen* (page 453) with the beginning of the Declaration of Independence (page 442) and Rousseau's *Social Contract* (page 435). In what ways are their ideas similar? How do they differ?
2. The Abbé Sièyes suggested that the meeting of the Third Estate be renamed the National Assembly. Why was this a revolutionary suggestion?
3. (a) Why was the drafting of French men from every social class into the army a revolutionary approach? (b) How did it promote nationalism?
4. (a) Which groups in France benefited from the changes during the revolution? (b) Which groups did not? Explain.

Writing and Speaking about History

1. As a French newspaper reporter during the 1790's, write a headline and lead paragraph for a story on *two* of the following topics:
   National Assembly
   Legislative Assembly
   National Convention
   Reign of Terror
   Directory
2. Prepare a brief speech in which you accuse Napoleon Bonaparte of actions detrimental to the interests of the French people.

Practicing Skills

1. The French Revolution can be divided into four time periods:
   The Old Regime, before 1789
   The National Assembly, 1789–1791
   The Legislative Assembly, 1791–1795
   The Directory and Napoleon, 1795–1799
   Match each item below with the correct period above.
   a. execution of Louis XVI
   b. Committee of Public Safety
   c. storming of the Bastille
   d. Battle of Jena
   e. Declaration of the Rights of Man
2. Use the map on page 464 to summarize Napoleon's invasion of and retreat from Russia. In your summary, include dates, place names, and significant losses.

Investigating History

1. Draw a cartoon on one of the following themes related to the Old Regime: (a) unequal votes in the Estates General; (b) unjust taxation policies; (c) the extravagance of Marie Antoinette; (d) the social and political position of the bourgeoisie.
2. Debate: The French Revolution was not necessary; the Old Regime could have been changed by gradual reforms.
3. People in many countries reacted to the French Revolution. Compare the reactions of Edmund Burke in *Reflections on the Revolution in France,* Thomas Paine in *The Rights of Man,* and Mary Wollstonecraft in *A Vindication of the Rights of Man* and *A Vindication of the Rights of Woman.* What similarities and differences do you see?

Decision Making in History

The presence of Louis XVI and his family created an awkward situation for the Legislative Assembly. Besides execution, what other course of action might the Assembly have followed? What suggestion would you have made?

Research Skills

The Research Paper: Choosing the Topic

The historical essay and the research paper have much in common. In both, you gather information and then form a conclusion or thesis based on that information. There is, however, one important distinction. In a historical essay, you support your thesis by the facts you choose and by the way you organize them. In the research paper, you support your thesis with information collected from primary and secondary sources. It is possible to write a historical essay on the basis of your readings in this text. For the research paper, however, you must go beyond this text to many different sources.

There are several stages to writing a research paper. In the first stage, you pick your topic. This stage is quite important because the topic must be one that will hold your interest throughout the research process. Here are some hints for choosing a topic:

1. First, choose a broad area of interest that appeals to you. For example, from Unit VI, you might pick Elizabethan England, the Enlightenment, or the French Revolution.

2. Next, find a subject within that broad area that stirs your curiosity. For example, Elizabethan England has many colorful characters whose lives would furnish good topics for a research paper. William Shakespeare is one; Mary Queen of Scots, Sir Francis Drake, and even Elizabeth herself are others.

3. Once you have found a subject, you must identify a specific topic to research. Often the specific topic poses a question, such as "Did Elizabeth's decision not to marry weaken or strengthen her reign?" Another possibility is "Did Elizabeth's religious settlements cause more problems than they solved?" If you are having trouble identifying a specific topic, do some reading in the library.

4. Once you have chosen a specific topic, develop a tentative answer to the problem. Historians call this tentative answer the working thesis. A working thesis does not become a final thesis until you have done some reading and collected some notes. In other words, your working thesis is like a scientist's hypothesis—it must be tested. If, during the course of the research, you find that the working thesis is incorrect or cannot be supported by evidence, then you must alter it to suit your findings.

You might choose a specific topic about Elizabeth I as the subject of your research paper.

Unit Review VI

1. Identify each person listed below. Include dates. Then describe the relationship between the people in each group.
   a. Elizabeth I; Philip II
   b. Oliver Cromwell; Charles I
   c. James II; William of Orange
   d. Louis XIV; Cardinal Mazarin
   e. Peter I; Charles XII
   f. Maria Theresa; Frederick II
   g. Catherine II; Voltaire
   h. George III; Thomas Jefferson
   i. Robespierre; Louis XVI

2. Match the book, document, play, or opera in the left column with the correct author in the right column.

1. Pragmatic Sanction	a. Newton
2. *Macbeth*	b. Mozart
3. *Mathematical Principles*	c. Rousseau
4. *Candide*	d. Adam Smith
5. *The Miser*	e. Montesquieu
6. *The Wealth of Nations*	f. Voltaire
7. *On the Spirit of Laws*	g. Shakespeare
8. *The Social Contract*	h. Charles VI
9. *The Marriage of Figaro*	i. Molière
10. *Paradise Lost*	j. John Milton

3. Describe the difference between each set of terms:
   a. balance of power; balance of trade
   b. divine right of kings; constitutional monarchy
   c. Roundheads; Cavaliers
   d. radicals; conservatives

4. Tell whether in 1715 (page 420) each of the following places was (a) part of the Holy Roman Empire, (b) part of the Austrian Hapsburg lands, (c) both, or (d) neither.
   a. Hungary
   b. Spain
   c. Prussia
   d. Naples
   e. Saxony
   f. Switzerland

5. What was the status of the places in Number 4 in the Empire of Napoleon (page 461)?

6. (a) What religious issues divided England during the reign of Elizabeth I? (b) Describe the issue that tore England apart in the years after her reign?

7. (a) What English king was responsible for the first permanent English settlement in the Americas? (b) Where was this settlement and what was it called?

8. (a) In what way were Louis XIV of France and Peter I of Russia alike? (b) Describe one way in which each ruler showed his power.

9. (a) Describe the diplomatic revolution that had taken place in Europe by 1756. (b) How did the countries involved fare in the war that followed?

10. (a) When did the Enlightenment take place? (b) From what ideas and attitudes did it spring?

11. Name and describe the work of two scientific thinkers who lived during the Enlightenment.

12. Describe the theories of government held by each of the following men:
    a. Thomas Hobbes
    b. John Locke
    c. Montesquieu
    d. Rousseau

13. (a) From what movement in Europe did the American Revolution gain strength? (b) How did the Stamp Act add fuel to the fire?

14. (a) What were the four stages of the French Revolution? (b) In which stage did the storming of the Bastille take place? (c) In which stage was Louis XVI executed?

15. (a) How and when did Napoleon Bonaparte come to power? (b) How did he help the French people? (c) What ideal of the French Revolution did Napoleon destroy?

Unit VII
The Age of European Dominance

CHAPTERS

In the late 1700's, a massive economic shift began in Europe. This great change, known as the Industrial Revolution, gradually transformed how people worked, what they wore, where they lived, and how they traveled. Machine power replaced muscle power. Factories replaced farms as the basis for wealth.

While industrialization changed Europe's economy, a new movement known as nationalism revolutionized the European political scene. New countries were formed from collections of ancient kingdoms and duchies. Governments grew more powerful and organized.

Partly as a result of these economic and political changes, Europe won a new position of leadership in the world. By the late 1800's, much of the world was under European rule. Europe stood at a pinnacle of power and prosperity.

Bridge across the Rhine River to Cologne Cathedral, West Germany

The Industrial Revolution

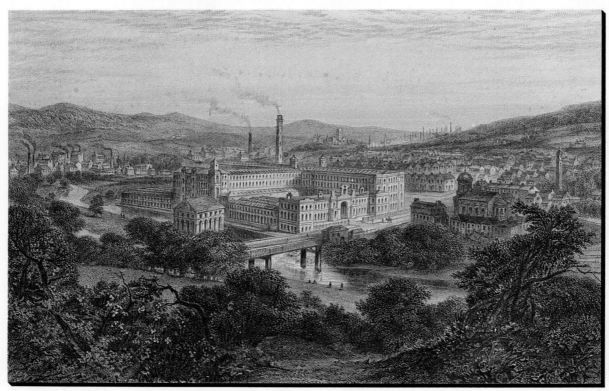

In many parts of Great Britain, industrial towns sprang up almost overnight around 1800. Smoke rising from the factories came to symbolize both plentiful jobs and unhealthy working conditions—some of the pluses and minuses of industrialism.

1. Many factors aided industrial growth.

2. Britain led in the rise of industry.

3. Industry grew and spread to new lands.

4. Industry changed ways of life.

One day in 1828, a British businessman named Joseph Pease stood clutching his hat and eyeing a windswept marshland near the mouth of the River Tees in northeastern England. The only other sign of human life was a scattering of farmhouses where fewer than 40 people lived. This was the small village of Middlesbrough, England.

Pease was one of a group of businessmen who planned to create a coal port and industrial city on the spot. That evening, he wrote in his diary that he could picture "a coming day when the bare fields ... will be covered with a busy multitude, and numerous vessels crowding to these banks denote the busy seaport." That day was not long in coming.

By 1840, only 12 years later, Middlesbrough had been transformed from a sleepy farming village into a bustling seaport that exported 1.5 million tons of coal a year. Its population had mushroomed from

40 to 4,000. Thirty years later, in 1870, the population had grown to 40,000.

Such transformations took place in many parts of England during the period known as the Industrial Revolution. This was a different kind of revolution from the political revolutions that changed the governments of the United States and France. The Industrial Revolution was a series of dramatic changes not in the way a country was governed but in the way work was done.

Before the Industrial Revolution, most work was done by hand. People planted crops, wove cloth, and made shoes all by hand. Then, beginning in the middle 1700's, people began to use machines to do more and more jobs. No longer was muscle power (whether of people, oxen, or horses) the main way to get work done. Waterpower, once used only to run tiny grain mills, came into use for all kinds of machinery. By 1800, steam power was replacing waterpower. In hundreds of factories, steam engines chugged away, turning wheels, pumping water, and driving the great forge hammers in iron mills.

In the 80 years between 1760 and 1840 in Great Britain, one invention led to another with a swiftness for which there is no parallel in history. The average British person born in 1760 saw more changes in his or her lifetime than ten generations of ancestors had seen in theirs.

Though the Industrial Revolution began in Britain, its effects soon spread outward. Eventually, it touched the lives of people worldwide.

Like all great changes, the Industrial Revolution had both good and bad results. Some of its changes led to healthier, more comfortable, and more productive lives for people. Sometimes, however, industrialization caused immense suffering. In this chapter, we will see what a mixed blessing the Industrial Revolution was in the land of its birth, Great Britain.

Many factors aided industrial growth.   1

The Industrial Revolution began in the middle 1700's in the lowland parts of eastern England and southern Scotland. Why industry arose in England at that particular time involves many factors—from England's geographic advantages to the resourcefulness of the British people. Let us look at some of these factors.

Changes in farming led the way.

The Industrial Revolution might not have taken place without the dramatic improvements in farming that began in the early 1700's. This agricultural revolution started sooner than the Industrial Revolution. Then, once industrialization began, the two revolutions went hand in hand.

The enclosure movement By 1700, small farms were disappearing in Great Britain. Wealthy landowners were buying up much of the land that village farmers had once worked. Then the landowners rented fields to families of tenant farmers who worked the land. This process was called **enclosure**, because the new owner sometimes put up a fence or hedge around his land.

The villagers who shared common fields generally kept on with traditional ways of farming. It was difficult to persuade everyone in the village to try a new method. A landowner with a large estate, however, was free to experiment.

In the 1700's, many of these wealthy landowners began to look for ways to increase the size of their harvests. Influenced by the ideas of the Scientific Revolution and the Enlightenment, they applied a scientific approach to their farms. They kept careful records of the methods they used on their land. With such records, they could compare one year's harvest with the next. They also exchanged ideas with one another about land use and crops.

Jethro Tull was one of the first of these scientific farmers. He saw that the usual way of sowing seed by scattering it across the ground was wasteful. Many of the seeds failed to take root. He solved this problem with an invention called the seed drill in 1721. The seed drill allowed farmers to sow seeds in well-spaced rows at specific depths. A larger share of the seed germinated, boosting crop yields.

Crop rotation The most revolutionary discovery of these scientific farmers was a new system of **crop rotation**. For centuries, the chief way to keep a field fertile had been to let it lie fallow every two or three years. This practice arose in the Middle Ages with the two-field and three-field systems on medieval manors (page 211). As

These surveyors are measuring a field so that the landlord can enclose it. The drawing decorates a map of Bedfordshire in southeastern England.

a result, at least a third of the country in any one year was producing nothing but weeds.

After much experimenting, the gentleman farmer Viscount Charles Townshend found that it was not necessary to let the land lie fallow. The secret, he told people, was to rotate crops. One year, a farmer might plant a field with wheat or barley, which tended to wear out the soil. The next year, the farmer could plant turnips or clover, which restored the soil. Not surprisingly, the viscount was nicknamed Turnip Townshend in honor of his favorite crop.

Improved livestock Thanks to the efforts of other farmers, raising livestock also became more productive. For example, in the 1700's, Robert Bakewell began trying to raise larger sheep to provide more meat and wool. By allowing only the best animals to breed, he increased the weight of his sheep and also greatly improved the taste of the mutton.

As more and more farmers followed his lead, farm animals increased dramatically in size and quality. In 1700, the average weight of a steer sold for slaughter was 370 pounds. By 1786, that weight had more than doubled to 840 pounds. The average weight for sheep rose from 28 to 100 pounds over the same period.

Effects on population Scientific farming had a twofold effect. Better livestock and rising crop production meant more food. Fewer people went hungry, and nutrition improved.

On the other hand, the enclosure movement forced many small farmers off the land. Many lost fields that their families had worked for centuries. Some simply left Great Britain and moved to the British colonies in North America. Others crowded into British cities looking for work. They became the labor force for the jobs in manufacturing that were becoming available.

A *rise in population helped industry.*

Mystery still surrounds another change that played a part in the Industrial Revolution. During the 1700's, the population of Europe began to increase more rapidly than at any earlier time. No one knows exactly why.

Since the great plagues of the Middle Ages (page 244), Europe's population had been growing but only very slowly. Although there are no complete statistics for the time, historians estimate that the population of western Europe in 1750 was around 140 million. That was roughly twice what it had been in 1350.

In the 100 years from 1750 to 1850, the numbers increased at a phenomenal rate. By 1850, there were about 266 million Europeans. It had taken 400 years from 1350 for the European population to double. Then it nearly doubled again in just a century.

Historians have long debated the causes of this population explosion. Some point to new farming methods that increased food supplies and improved health. Others point to medical advances such as Edward Jenner's discovery of a smallpox vaccine in 1796. Still others suggest that larger food supplies and better living conditions meant that people lived longer and married younger. These young couples soon had children, shortening the time span between generations.

Whatever the causes of this population explosion, it was not evenly spread throughout Europe. The populations of Prussia and Russia, for example, grew more quickly than those of France and Italy. England's population grew fastest of all. Between 1750 and 1850, it tripled, from 6 million to 18 million.

Was the population explosion a direct cause of the Industrial Revolution? Probably not. After all, the population also rose rapidly in nearby Ireland, where little industrial development took place. Nevertheless, rapid population growth certainly helped quicken industrial progress. With more people, there was an increasing demand for food and other goods. At the same time, population growth supplied the extra workers that the new factories and businesses needed to meet the rising demand for manufactured goods.

Great Britain had many advantages.

In 1700, Great Britain was neither the largest country in Europe nor the smallest. It was, however, rich in all the factors needed for industry.

Abundant natural resources The Industrial Revolution depended on three important natural resources. Two of these were waterpower and coal, which supplied the energy for the new machines. The third was iron ore, used for machines, tools, and buildings. Great Britain was rich in all three.

A favorable geography Geography also gave Great Britain an advantage over other countries. An island nation with many fine harbors, its fleet of more than 6,000 merchant ships sailed to almost every part of the globe. This overseas trade gave Britain access to raw materials and markets. Both were essential to industrial growth. Trade also gave Britain a wealthy class of shipowners and merchants who had money to spare for new projects at home.

A favorable climate for new ideas In the 1700's, British people in many walks of life were interested in science and technology. The Royal Society, founded in London in 1660, had become a world-famous "club" for the exchange of scientific ideas and practical inventions. Smaller clubs sprang up in other parts of the country. In Birmingham, for example, there was a scientific group known as the Lunar Society. Its members (who cheerfully called themselves Lunatics) met about once a month at the full moon.

New ideas were not only encouraged but also rewarded. Business people were willing to invest in the manufacture of new inventions. In fact, the business person and the inventor were often the same person.

A good banking system By the 1700's, Great Britain had the most highly developed banking system in Europe. Making loans was by far the most important service of British banks. By lending money at reasonable interest rates, banks encouraged business people to invest in better machinery, build new factories, and expand their operations.

Political stability Although Britain took part in many wars during the 1700's, none was fought on British soil. For ordinary people, it was a century of peace. This freedom from war and bloodshed gave Britain a tremendous advantage over its European neighbors. British business people did not have to worry about a hostile army destroying their property.

At the same time, the British government favored economic growth. Merchants and business people had considerable influence in Parliament. The government supported laws that encouraged new investment both at home and abroad.

Section Review 1

Define: (a) enclosure, (b) crop rotation
Identify: (a) Tull, (b) seed drill, (c) Townshend, (d) Bakewell, (e) Royal Society
Answer:
1. (a) What was the Industrial Revolution? (b) When did it take place? (c) How did it differ from other revolutions?
2. (a) How did the enclosure movement help scientific farming? (b) What effect did scientific farming have on the labor force? (c) How did a rise in population help the Industrial Revolution?
3. Describe the five factors that contributed to industrialization in Great Britain.

Critical Thinking
4. In what way was Middlesbrough a symbol of the Industrial Revolution in England during the 1800's?
5. Was the revolution in agriculture necessary to the Industrial Revolution? Explain.

Britain led in the rise of industry. 2

In the middle 1700's, the situation in Britain was ripe for the development of industry. The country had a good food supply, a large work force, and plenty of people with money to invest.

All the forces that had been slowly building suddenly came together in a giant burst of inventiveness. The changes appeared first in the textile industry.

Inventions revolutionized the textile industry.

Britain had long been one of the leading sheep-raising areas in the world. Raw wool and wool cloth had been Britain's major trade goods as far back as the Middle Ages. All this cloth was produced by hand. Spinners and weavers (mainly women) worked in their own homes, using spinning wheels and hand looms.

British clothmakers produced other fabrics as well as wool. Linen, a cloth woven from the fiber of the flax plant, was popular for lighter-weight clothing. Even more popular was cotton, which was also light but more durable and easier to care for than linen.

Working by hand at their wheels and looms, spinners and weavers could not keep up with the demand for cloth, especially cotton. Since they could not make as much cotton cloth as people wanted to buy, its cost remained relatively high. Cloth merchants saw that they could make greater profits if they found a way to speed up the work of spinning and weaving.

One invention led to another.

By 1800, six major inventions had totally transformed the cotton industry. The first invention came in 1733, when a watchmaker named John Kay made a shuttle that moved back and forth on wheels. The flying shuttle, as it was called, was little more than a boat-shaped piece of wood to which yarn was attached. Yet it allowed a weaver to work twice as fast.

Now weavers were working so quickly that spinners could not keep up. A prize was offered to anyone who could produce a better spinning machine. The prize went to a textile worker named James Hargreaves.

In 1764, Hargeaves invented a new spinning wheel. He called it the spinning jenny in honor of his wife. This simple machine allowed one spinner to work six or eight threads at a time. Later models could spin as many as 80 threads at once.

Both the flying shuttle and the spinning jenny were hand-operated machines. Richard Arkwright's water-frame, invented in 1768, brought a new breakthrough. The water-frame used the waterpower from fast-flowing streams to drive spinning wheels.

In 1779, Samuel Crompton combined features of the spinning jenny and the water-frame to produce the spinning mule. (It was so named because, just as a mule is the offspring of a horse and a donkey, this machine was the offspring of two inventions.) The mule made thread that was stronger, finer, and more even than earlier spinning machines.

The water-frame and the spinning mule were too large and expensive for people to use at home. Spinning and weaving slowly stopped being work that families did together in their homes. Instead, wealthy textile merchants set up several of the new machines in large buildings called **factories**. At first, the new factories needed waterpower, so they were built near a stream or waterfall.

With so many new machines for turning out thread, the weavers soon fell behind in their jobs. In 1785, a new invention promised to restore the balance by speeding up weaving. This was Edmund Cartwright's power loom, run by waterpower. Early power looms were inefficient, but steady improvements meant that by 1813 more than 2,000 were in use. By 1833, there were more than 100,000, most of them in large factories where they rattled away under the same roof as spinning machines. By the late 1700's, both spinners and weavers were working so fast that cotton growers could not keep up with them.

Much of England's cotton came from the southern part of the United States. In Virginia, Georgia, North Carolina, and South Carolina, farmers raised cotton on large plantations worked by slaves. One of the most time-consuming jobs on the plantation was removing the seeds from the raw cotton. In 1793, American educator Eli Whitney invented a machine to do this tedious chore. His cotton gin made it possible for slaves to pick and clean ten times as much cotton daily as they had before.

Whitney's invention spurred a dramatic increase in American cotton production: from 9,000 bales in 1791 to 987,000 in 1831. Now there was enough raw cotton to keep the factories of Britain humming.

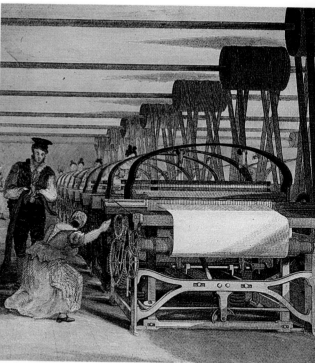

During the Industrial Revolution, jobs such as spinning and weaving gradually moved out of home workshops (left) and into factories with large, power-driven machines (right).

Thanks to continuous technological improvements in spinning and weaving, however, English merchants used all this cotton and still called for more. The output of cotton cloth from British factories rose from 40 million yards in 1785 to more than 2 billion yards in 1850—a staggering 5,000 percent increase.

Watt improved the steam engine.

The early power looms and spinning machines had one large drawback. They ran on waterpower, and so every factory that used them had to be near rushing water. Such places were often far from raw materials, workers, or markets. Therefore, many factory owners were eager for a new source of power. They found it in steam.

As early as 1705, coal miners were using steam-powered pumps to remove water from deep mine shafts. However, this early steam engine, called the Newcomen engine after its inventor, worked very slowly. It also took great quantities of fuel, making it expensive to run.

In 1763, the problem came to the attention of James Watt. Watt was a mathematical instrument maker at the University of Glasgow in Scotland. He helped science professors make the equipment they used in their experiments. Watt pondered the problem for two years. Then, one day in the spring of 1765, as he was strolling along the Glasgow Green, a solution suddenly came to him. Watt saw how to make the steam engine work much faster and more efficiently while burning less fuel.

In the 1770's, Watt went into partnership with a farsighted businessman named Matthew Boulton. Watt and Boulton were both **entrepreneurs** (AHN-truh-pruh-NUHRZ). An entrepreneur is a person who organizes, manages, and takes on the risks of a business.

With Boulton's financial backing, Watt continued to make better and better engines. By 1800, almost 500 steam engines were huffing and puffing in various British factories. James Watt, once a modestly paid craftsman, had become a millionaire.

477

Watt's improvements made the steam engine much more practical for use in industry. For the first time in history, people had a source of power that could be used anywhere and anytime.

Section Review 2

Define:(a) factory, (b) entrepreneur
Identify: (a) John Kay, (b) James Hargreaves, (c) Richard Arkwright, (d) Samuel Crompton, (e) Edmund Cartwright, (f) Eli Whitney, (g) cotton gin, (h) James Watt
Answer:
1. (a) What British industry did the first inventions of the Industrial Revolution affect? (b) Why were merchants in this industry looking for ways to speed up production?
2. (a) Name the six inventions that transformed the cotton industry. (b) How did each of these inventions lead to another?
3. (a) What drawback did early power looms and spinning machines have? (b) How did the invention of the steam engine solve this problem?

Critical Thinking
4. The steam engine has been called the greatest invention of the Industrial Revolution. Do you agree or disagree? Explain.
5. Could the Industrial Revolution have taken place without entrepreneurs? Why or why not? What role do entrepreneurs play in business today?

Industry grew and spread to new lands.   3

In 1800, a businessman could walk through his mill and look with pride at the latest model of the Watt steam engine. He could see the power looms and other machines to which it was connected by drive shafts and belts. Yet most of these mechanical wonders had been delivered to the factory by horse-drawn cart. When the businessman finished his inspection, he rode home in a horse-drawn carriage over mud-rutted roads that dated back to the Middle Ages. Great changes, however, were on the way.

Engineers built roads and canals.

Before the Industrial Revolution, the cheapest and most reliable way to travel in England was by water. Besides its good harbors, England also had many navigable rivers. Barges laden with coal, iron, bricks, and other goods floated up and down the rivers of England. Since a barge drawn by horse could carry a far greater load than a cart pulled by the same horse, water transportation was much cheaper than land transportation.

Yet water transportation had a major drawback. There was only one way to take goods across the stretches of land that lay between rivers. Workers had to unload the boats, put the goods into wagons, drive the wagons to the next river, and move the cargo again onto boats.

To solve this problem, the British built a network of canals. (A canal is a human-made waterway.) In the late 1700's and early 1800's, British workers built more than 4,000 miles of inland waterways. The new canals slashed the cost of transportation. Now coal and other raw materials could be carried by water to more places in Britain.

British roads also improved. John Macadam, a Scottish engineer, was largely responsible for the better roads. Working in the early 1800's, he built roadbeds with a layer of large stones for drainage. Over that bed, he put a carefully smoothed layer of crushed rock. Roads with the "macadam" surface were not nearly so muddy or dusty as the old ones. Heavy wagons could travel over them even in rainy weather without sinking to their axles in mud.

The Railway Age began.

The biggest change in transportation came with the use of steam power. Just as the steam engine itself was a key breakthrough in the late 1700's, the steam engine on wheels gave a tremendous boost to English industry after 1820. This invention is better known, of course, as the railroad locomotive. The railroad revolutionized transportation first in England and later in many parts of the world.

The idea of running wagons on iron tracks was not new. For centuries, horses had pulled carts of iron and coal along railway tracks in and around mines. Before 1800, however, no one succeeded in using steam power to run such a cart.

The Industrial Revolution in Cotton, Coal, and Pig Iron

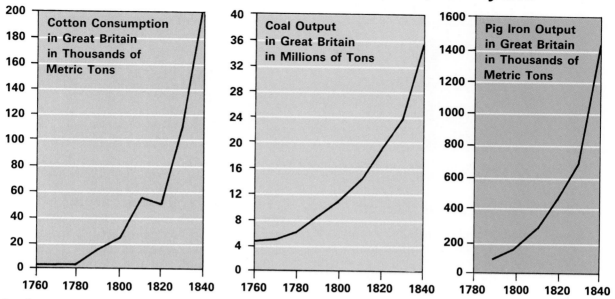

In what 20-year period did the use of cotton first show an increase? About how much pig iron did Britain produce in 1800? In 1820?

These vehicles needed smaller, more powerful engines than the ones that Watt was producing for factory use.

In 1804, an English engineer named Richard Trevithick made an engine that was both small and powerful. In fact, it ran at such high pressures that Watt and others expected it to blow up. Trevithick claimed his engine could pull a cart along a set of rails. A mine owner in Wales bet Trevithick the equivalent of several thousand dollars that such a feat was impossible. Trevithick won the bet by running his locomotive over ten miles of track, hauling ten tons of iron as well. "The public until now called me a scheming fellow," wrote Trevithick at the time, "but now their tone is much altered."

Other British engineers soon built improved versions of Trevithick's locomotive. By 1820, several hundred such vehicles were in operation in and around British mines. One of these early railroad engineers was George Stephenson, who gained a solid reputation by building some 20 engines for mine operators in northern England.

In 1821, Stephenson began work on the world's first railroad line. It was to run 27 miles from the Yorkshire coalfields to the port of Stockton on the North Sea. In 1825, the railroad opened,

using four locomotives that Stephenson had designed and built.

News of this success quickly spread throughout Britain. The entrepreneurs of northern England were especially interested. They wanted a railroad line to connect the port of Liverpool on the northwestern coast of England with the inland city of Manchester, the heart of the spinning and weaving industry. The track was laid, and in 1829, trials were held to choose the best locomotive for use on the new line.

Five engines entered the competition, but none could compare with the Rocket, designed by Stephenson and his son. With smoke pouring from its tall smokestack and its two pistons pumping to and fro as they drove the front wheels, the Rocket hauled a 13-ton load at an unheard-of speed—more than 24 miles per hour!

Footnote to History

In 1745, it took two weeks to travel from London to Edinburgh, a distance of 330 miles. By 1796, better roads cut the traveling time to two and a half days. In 1830, a passenger on a coach could make the trip in 36 hours.

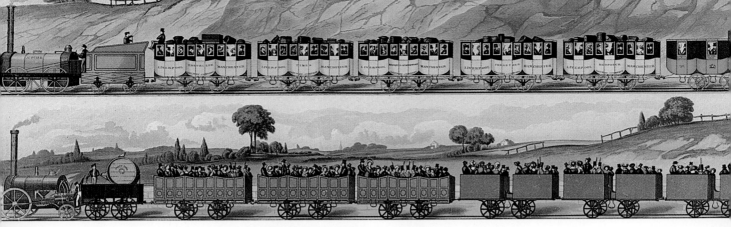

First-class passengers on the Liverpool-Manchester Railway rode in covered carriages (top). Second- and third-class passengers rode in open cars.

Railroads spread across England.

The Liverpool-Manchester Railway opened officially in 1830. It was an immediate success. Thousands of passengers traveled between the two cities every day on a dozen separate trains. Freight trains soon carried more goods back and forth along this route than canals and road coaches combined.

Confident that there were great profits to be made in railroads, British business people began building new lines all over the country. Hundreds of different railroads opened during the 1830's and 1840's. Soon such lines linked nearly all the major cities and towns of Britain. In 1850, only 25 years after the first line had been built, Great Britain had 16,200 miles of railroad track.

Perhaps the only business people who did not welcome the Railroad Age were the owners of canals and freight wagon lines. The "iron horse" soon drove many of them out of business.

Not everything went smoothly on these early railroads, of course. Breakdowns, accidents, and delays were frequent. At first, most passengers traveled in open cars where they were exposed to rain, wind, and the black clouds of soot that poured from the engine smokestack. Despite such drawbacks, however, railroads offered faster and more reliable transportation than anything known in earlier times.

Railroads had far-reaching effects.

No other industrial development had a greater effect on life in Great Britain than the railroads. In fact, the invention and perfection of the locomotive had at least four major effects.

First, railroads encouraged further industrial growth by giving manufacturers a fast, cheap way to transport both raw materials and finished products. Moreover, entrepreneurs could now build factories in many more locations. They no longer needed to be close to supplies of raw materials. Trains could deliver such supplies wherever there were tracks.

Second, the railroad boom provided millions of new jobs. Thousands of people did the backbreaking work of leveling hills, laying track, digging tunnels, and building bridges. Railroads used so much coal and iron that they boosted the demand for workers in those two industries as well. One mile of railroad track, for example, required 300 tons of iron.

Third, railroads gave a further boost to progress in agriculture. Now farmers could send milk and fruit to market in distant cities. In the same way, trains opened new markets for the fishing industry. Fresh fish could now be sold daily even in cities far from the sea.

Last but not least, railroads had enormous influence on the attitudes that ordinary people had about travel. Until this time, most people had thought of travel as something one did only when it was absolutely necessary. By offering quick and reasonably cheap transportation, railroads completely changed this view. Country people, for example, were now more willing to take jobs in distant cities, because they knew they could make regular visits home. At the same time, railroads began to open up a new world of travel for enjoyment. The spread of the railroads through Britain led directly to the growth of such popular seaside resorts as Brighton (south of London) and Blackpool (on the northwestern coast).

Industrialization spread to other countries.

For many years, the Industrial Revolution was limited mostly to the country of its birth, Great Britain. The reason was simple: Britain wanted to keep the secrets of industrialization to itself. Until 1825, it was against the law for engineers, mechanics, and toolmakers to leave the country. Until 1843, it was against the law for anyone in Britain to sell the new machines to people in other countries. Despite such laws, however, the ideas of the Industrial Revolution did spread beyond Britain.

The spread to the United States In 1789, a young British mill worker named Samuel Slater disguised himself as a farmer and boarded a ship headed for the United States. There he built a spinning machine from memory. The next year, a Rhode Island businessman named Moses Brown began work on a factory to house Slater's machines. In 1793, this factory—the first one in the United States—opened for business in Pawtucket, Rhode Island.

Early factories in the United States made only thread. The thread was then given to weavers who worked in their homes. Later, mills combined the spinning of thread with the weaving of cloth. The number of mills grew slowly at first and then more rapidly. By 1850, they had spread over much of the northeastern United States.

The spread to Europe Industry made little headway on the European continent before 1815. The French Revolution and the Napoleonic wars disrupted business all over Europe. By the time peace returned, Britain had a commanding lead.

Goods from Britain's factories flooded European markets. British woolens and cottons were much cheaper than anything textile workers in Europe could make by hand. As a result, many European spinners and weavers found themselves out of work. The countries along the North Sea coast were especially hard hit.

Belgium was one of the first countries in Europe to respond to the British challenge. Like Britain, Belgium had good supplies of coal and fine waterways for transportation. At first, the know-how to build industrial machines in Belgium

Voice from the Past · *A Girl in the Mills*

In 1823, a New England businessman named Francis Lowell built a model factory town at Lowell, Massachusetts. His idea was to hire young women from farming villages. He offered safe, attractive living quarters and opportunities for education as well as jobs. At the age of 13, Lucy Larcom became a mill girl. Years later, she described her life at Lowell.

That children should be set to toil for their daily bread is always a pity; but in the case of my little workmates and myself there were imperative reasons, and we were not too young to understand them. And the regret with which those who loved us best consented to such an arrangement only made us more anxious to show that we really were capable of doing something for them and for ourselves. The novelty of trying to "earn our own living" took our childhood fancy; the work given us was light, and for a few weeks it seemed like beginning a new game with a new set of playmates. Replacing the full spools of bobbins with empty ones on spinning frames was the usual employment given to children. It was a process which required quickness but left unoccupied intervals . . . during which we were frequently allowed to run home.

1. (a) Why did Lucy and other mill girls probably go to work? (b) Why was the idea of young women earning their living a novel one for its time?

2. How did the mill girls feel about their work?

3. In time, Lowell followed the grim path of factory towns in Britain. Describe how Lucy's account differs from the one given by Samuel Coulson on page 485.

The Industrial Revolution in Great Britain, 1850

ATLANTIC OCEAN

SCOTLAND

North Sea

Glasgow
New Lanark
Edinburgh
Firth of Forth
Firth of Clyde
IRON
SHIPBUILDING

Carlisle

Newcastle
Sunderland
Durham
IRON
LEAD
Pennine Chain
COTTONS

IRELAND

Irish Sea

Preston   Halifax   Leeds   York
Liverpool   Manchester   WOOLENS   Hull
Sheffield
METAL GOODS

POTTERY

The Wash

Wolverhampton
Birmingham
IRON
COTTONS
Norwich

WALES

ENGLAND

ATLANTIC OCEAN

Bristol Channel
Cardiff
Bristol
Bath
Thames River
London

COPPER
Plymouth

Southampton

English Channel

0   50 Miles

FRANCE

KEY
- Major industrial areas
- Coal fields
- ✗ Iron ore fields
- --- Major canals
- — Major railways

Map Study
The industrial area in central England is known as the Midlands. What goods were produced there?

came from British workers who left England illegally. In 1799, a British carpenter named William Cockerill began building cotton-spinning machines in Belgium while it was still under French rule. Later, Cockerill's sons opened factories that turned out steam engines, locomotives, and other machinery.

Soon, industrialized "islands" began to dot the European landscape. Among these areas were the coal-rich Ruhr Valley in northwestern Germany and the Po Valley in northern Italy. Cities such as Milan, Frankfurt, and Lyons expanded rapidly on the continent during the middle 1800's.

Britain led the world in industry.

Despite such growth, no other European country came close to rivaling Britain as an industrial power before 1850. In 1850, Britain still produced most of the world's iron and coal. British factories and mills accounted for 70 percent of Europe's cotton cloth production.

Yet another measure of British dominance was railroad development. With 9,797 miles of track in operation in 1850, Britain had more railroad lines than France, Russia, Austria, and all the German and Italian states combined. With its highly developed industrial economy and splendid merchant fleet, Britain made foreign trade a major feature of its economy. During the 1840's, the value of British exports increased at an amazing rate. Little wonder that the country earned the title of "workshop of the world."

Section Review 3

Identify: (a) John Macadam, (b) Richard Trevithick, (c) George Stephenson, (d) Samuel Slater, (e) Moses Brown, (f) William Cockerill
Answer:
1. (a) Name two ways goods were transported before the Industrial Revolution. (b) How was each method improved during the Industrial Revolution?
2. (a) What new invention revolutionized transportation? (b) What role did Trevithick play in this new invention? (c) What role did Stephenson play?
3. How did railroads affect each of the following? (a) the growth of industry (b) employment (c) agriculture
4. (a) What did Britain do to prevent the spread of industrialization? (b) How did the ideas of the Industrial Revolution spread to the United States? (c) How did they spread to Europe?

Critical Thinking
5. How was improved transportation both a cause and an effect of the Industrial Revolution?

Industry changed ways of life. 4

As the pace of industrialization quickened, life changed in many ways. By the 1800's, more people could afford to heat their homes with coal from Wales and to dine on Scottish beef. They had more clothing too, much of it from cloth made on power looms in Manchester or Liverpool. Industrialization affected every part of life.

More people lived in cities.

Perhaps the most obvious change brought about by the Industrial Revolution was in where people lived. For centuries, most Europeans had lived in rural areas. A much smaller share had lived in towns and cities. Now that balance began to shift toward the cities.

The growth of the factory system brought people flocking into cities and towns. Between 1800 and 1850, the number of European cities with more than 100,000 inhabitants rose from 22 to 47. Most of Europe's urban areas at least doubled in population during this period. Some, such as Glasgow and Berlin, tripled or even quadrupled in size.

Factories tended to develop in clusters because entrepreneurs built near sources of power. Major new industrial centers sprang up between the coal-rich area of southern Wales and the Clyde River valley in Scotland (map, page 482). The biggest of these centers developed in England, from the Midlands north along the Pennines and on the northwest and northeast coasts.

London, of course, remained the most important city in Great Britain. Among other things, it was Europe's largest city (twice as populous as Paris, its nearest rival) and was growing larger all the time. This population gave London a vast labor pool for industry. Though lacking nearby sources of raw materials, London thus shared in Britain's industrial growth.

However, new cities were challenging London's leadership. Perhaps the most famous of the new industrial cities was Manchester, which along with the port of Liverpool formed the hub of Britain's cotton industry. "What Manchester thinks today, London thinks tomorrow," declared the city's proud entrepreneurs.

Problems arose as cities grew.

The pride of Manchester's business leaders was typical of their go-ahead spirit. Yet Manchester was also typical of the new industrial cities in other ways. These cities grew so quickly that little thought or planning was given to housing, sanitation, or education for the people who poured in from the countryside to seek jobs. Let us look at life in Manchester in the early 1800's.

It is 5 A.M. on a chilly fall day in 1840. Men, women, and even small children are spilling out of the city's courtyards and alleys to make their way on foot to the cotton mills. Some have already had a cup of tea and a plate of oatmeal, but others

Which town was largest in 1685? In 1881? From information in the text and on the map (page 482), what geographic feature helped the latter?

The Growth of Seven British Cities	1685	1760	1881
Liverpool	4,000	35,000	555,425
Manchester	6,000	45,000	393,676
Birmingham	4,000	30,000	400,757
Leeds	7,000	(not known)	309,126
Sheffield	4,000	20,000	284,410
Bristol	29,000	100,000	206,503
Nottingham	8,000	17,000	111,631

Manchester

1665	1760	1881
6,000	45,000	393,676

will wait until the 8 A.M. break for tea and a piece of bread. The sky is dark, but gas lamps gleam along the alleys, where taverns are already open for business.

Although many of the brick buildings along the streets are new, they are blackened by the smoke and soot that hang over the city all the time. Manchester sprawls alongside the Pennine Hills, which are capped by bare, windswept moors. However, smoke from the clusters of cotton mills that ring the city blot out any glimpse of these open spaces.

Most of the streets are unpaved and have no drains. The larger streets are cleaned from time to time, but the alleys are not. These streets collect heaps of filth and excrement. In courtyards, some of the workers keep pigs that root as best as they can among the garbage. The stench that rises from these areas is almost unbearable.

The smell in other parts of the city is little better. Gasworks, bone works, breweries, and tanneries add their various odors to the smoky air. The city's main river, the Irwell, is filled with so much waste that, in the words of one visitor, it is "considerably less a river than a flood of liquid manure."

In 1760, Manchester had been a market town with a population of around 30,000. It became the center for the expanding British cotton industry for two reasons. First, Manchester was close to the port of Liverpool, where most of the raw cotton from the United States entered Great Britain. Second, the town had abundant sources of power. Streams tumbling down from the nearby Pennines supplied waterpower, and nearby coalfields offered fuel for steam power.

By 1800, there were more than 50 cotton mills in Manchester. By 1830, there were 130. By 1850, Manchester was home to some 300,000 people, 10 times the number that had lived there a century earlier.

This tremendous growth brought great wealth to Manchester—and also enormous social problems. The city was built almost overnight, without plans, without any kind of sanitary codes or building controls. Not until the 1830's did the city have a municipal government to keep order. Before then, Manchester was little more than "a huge overgrown village," as one observer said.

Not all quarters of the city were miserable, of course. Well-to-do merchants and factory owners made their homes in Alderley Edge, a pleasant suburb on the east of the city. For the working people of Manchester, however, Alderley Edge must have seemed light-years away. One person wrote:

> The dwellings of the poor in the back streets and alleys are as woeful as they are degrading. The amount of room occupied by many families is miserably small; great numbers have only one bedroom for the whole family.

Not surprisingly, sickness was rampant. Cholera epidemics regularly swept through the slums of Manchester and other industrial cities. A British government study in 1842 showed that the average lifespan for working-class people in Manchester was 17 years, as compared to 38 years in a nearby rural area.

By the 1840's, changes were in sight. Streets were being paved and drains installed. The city's first three parks were created. Yet many of the grim conditions spawned by rapid industrial expansion would linger for a long time.

Manchester was indeed a city of contrasts. "From this foul drain, the greatest stream of human industry flows out to fertilize the whole world," wrote the French journalist Alexis de Tocqueville after visiting Manchester in 1835.

The Industrial Revolution changed working conditions.

Faced with such living conditions, why did people continue to pour into Britain's cities from the countryside? One reason was that life was harsh in the country too. The cities at least offered plenty of jobs. Moreover, a factory worker could hope for regular wages, rain or shine. In contrast, a spell of bad weather could wipe out a farmer's whole crop.

Families in the the country were used to working from dawn to dusk. Parents expected their children to work long and hard as well. The family worked as a unit, both at farm tasks and at home industries such as spinning and weaving. When such a family moved to town, however, they found that working conditions were different.

In the city, work hours depended on the factory bell or whistle, not on the season or the weather. Factory owners wanted to keep their machines

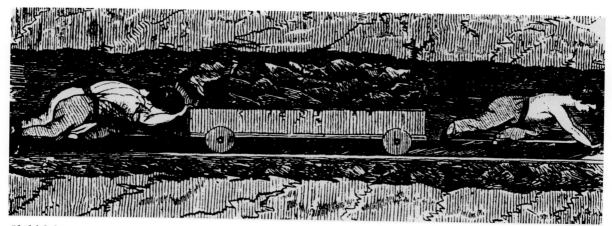

Child labor was one of the most shocking abuses of the early Industrial Revolution. Perhaps the worst conditions were in the mines, where boys and girls dragged cartloads of coal through dark, cramped passages.

running for as many hours a day as possible. As a result, the average worker spent 14 hours a day at the job, 6 days a week. Instead of changing with the seasons, the work was the same week after week, year after year. Workers could not change their pace; they had to keep up with the machines.

Industry also posed new dangers in work. Factories were seldom well-lit or clean. Machines injured workers in countless different ways—a boiler might explode or a drive belt might catch an arm. The most dangerous conditions of all were found in the coal mines, where frequent accidents, damp conditions, and the constant breathing of coal dust combined to make the average miner's life span ten years shorter than that of other workers.

Children suffered in mills and mines.

In the factories as on the farms, whole families worked. Again, however, there were important differences. In the country, children worked side by side with their parents. In factories, family members often worked separately. In such cases, young children were at the mercy of impersonal overseers. During the early 1800's, children as young as six or seven years worked long hours in factories and mines.

Children were especially useful in the mines, where small size was a great advantage in moving about in narrow shafts and tunnels. Many were employed as "trappers," whose job was to keep the ventilation shafts in the mines clear. "It is a most painful thing to contemplate the dull, dungeon-like life these little creatures are doomed to spend," noted one mine visitor, "a life for the most part passed in solitude, damp, and darkness."

Orphan children faced the worst plight. Factory owners employed large numbers of these children in return for room and board. The child workers were seldom fed properly. Their lodgings might be nothing more than piles of straw beside the machines at which they worked 12 or 14 hours a day.

In 1831, Parliament set up a committee to investigate abuses of child labor. A worker named Samuel Coulson told the committee that in busy times, his small daughters started work at 3 A.M. and ended at 10:30 P.M. What rest periods did they have during those 19 hours? "Breakfast a quarter of an hour, and dinner half an hour, and drinking a quarter of an hour."

As a result of this committee's findings, Parliament passed the Factory Act of 1833. The new law made it illegal to hire children under 9 years old. Children from the ages of 9 to 13 were not to work more than 8 hours a day. Young people from 14 to 18 could not be required to work more than 12 hours. In 1842, the Mines Act placed similar limits on the work of children in mining.

While such acts limited the worst abuses, children continued to do exhausting work, often under unhealthy or dangerous conditions. They worked because the money they earned was essential to their families. In 1825, a whole family—husband, wife, and three children—could earn about one British pound a week if they all worked in the mines. How much did the family need to live in any kind of comfort? One writer at the time estimated two pounds. Trapped by poverty, many parents could hardly consider allowing their children *not* to work.

The middle class expanded.

Although poverty gripped the lower class, wealth was spreading among other people in Britain. The Industrial Revolution brought enormous amounts of money into the country. Most of this wealth went into the pockets of factory owners, shippers, and merchants. These people made up a growing middle class.

This new middle class greatly changed the social structure of Great Britain. In the past, landowners and aristocrats occupied the top position in British society. They had the most wealth and the most power. Now, some factory owners and merchants were wealthier than the landowners and aristocrats. In an effort to be like the upper class, the newly rich families bought large estates and lived in high style.

Despite such attempts, there were still important social distinctions between the two classes. Landowners looked down on those who had made their fortunes in the "vulgar" business world. Not until late in the 1800's were rich entrepreneurs considered the social equals of the lords of the countryside.

Gradually, a middle class that was neither rich nor poor began to emerge. This group included an upper middle class of government employees, doctors, lawyers, and those who held management positions in factories, mines and shops. There was also a lower middle class made up of factory overseers and such skilled workers as toolmakers, mechanical drafters, and printers. These people earned incomes that gave them a comfortable standard of living.

Class tensions arose.

In the 1840's, a young German writer named Friedrich Engels went to Manchester, where his family owned a cotton business. Like many other visitors, Engels was appalled by the city's slums. One day, he discussed the subject with a middle-class gentleman as they walked the filthy streets. "I declared that I had never seen so badly built a town in my life," Engels later recalled. "He [the gentleman] listened patiently. At the corner of the street, as we parted company, he remarked: 'And yet there is a great deal of money made here. Good morning, sir!'"

Laissez-faire government Engel's companion cared little for the problems of Manchester's workers. Like many British business leaders of the 1800's, the gentleman believed that the gap between rich and poor was a natural one, an inevitable result of progress. The duties of government, as he saw them, were to wage war abroad and uphold law and order at home. He expected the government to take a hands-off attitude toward economic and social conditions.

This policy, known as laissez-faire, had been set forth by Adam Smith in the late 1700's (page 434). Now, in the 1800's, this idea was popular

Daily Life · A City Police Force

Crime flourished in the fast-growing industrial cities. In 1829, Sir Robert Peel, a British statesman, organized the first modern police force in the world. These London policemen wore blue uniforms, carried rattles to call for help, and brandished billy clubs. Other cities soon copied the idea of a municipal police force. The result was an immediate drop in the crime rate.

Londoners coined the term *bobbies* for these policemen (after Sir Robert's nickname). British police officers are still known as bobbies today.

among the upper and upper middle classes. These groups controlled the British Parliament. In the early 1800's, only men who owned a substantial amount of property could vote. Working people could neither vote nor hold office. Moreover, most members of Parliament came from rural parts of the country. Such bustling cities as Manchester, Leeds, Birmingham, and Sheffield had no representatives at all in Parliament.

Sometimes, workers turned violent in their demands for reform. Between 1815 and 1819, mob demonstrations and riots were common in Manchester and other industrial cities.

The government used violence as well. At one meeting in 1819, about 50,000 people gathered at St. Peter's Fields outside Manchester to hear speeches about reform. Although the gathering was peaceful, city officials panicked and ordered soldiers to break up the crowd. The troops charged with their sabers in hand, killing 11 and injuring hundreds. People all over Britain were shocked that these soldiers, who had last fought at Waterloo, were used against English people.

The beginning of unions Although workers could not vote, they found other ways of bringing pressure for reforms. Many workers joined together in groups called **unions**. A union spoke for all the workers in a particular trade. Unions bargained for better working conditions and higher wages. If factory owners refused these demands, union members could strike, or refuse to work.

The first workers to form unions were those whose special skills gave them extra bargaining power. Carpenters and spinners, for example, were in a far better position to strike than unskilled workers, who could easily be replaced. Thus, early unions helped the lower middle class more than the poorest workers.

The labor union movement was a slow and painful process. For many years, the British government denied the workers' right to form unions. Instead, union members were thrown in jail or fired. Although unions were not legally recognized for many years, they were tolerated after 1825.

Continuing tensions Because England was the first country to industrialize, social problems were the worst there. When the Industrial Revolution reached Belgium, Germany, and other parts of Europe, those countries learned from Britain's mistakes. By 1850, conditions for workers all over Europe gradually were improving.

Yet class tensions and factory abuses remained a major problem for every country that experienced the Industrial Revolution. Speaking in 1848, the French reformer and writer Alexis de Tocqueville gave a warning:

Consider what is happening among the working classes . . . Do you not see spreading among them, little by little, opinions and ideas that aim not to overturn such and such a ministry, or such laws, or such a government, but society itself, to shake it to the foundations upon which it now rests? Do you not see how, little by little, it comes to be said among them that all those placed above them are incapable and unworthy of governing them, that the division of wealth as it has happened in the world up to now is unjust?

De Tocqueville paused, then continued, "Gentlemen, I believe that at this very hour we are sleeping on a volcano." The years to come would prove how right De Tocqueville was.

Section Review 4

Define: union
Identify: (a) Factory Act of 1833, (b) Mines Act of 1842, (c) laissez-faire government
Answer:
1. (a) Why did people flock into British cities and towns during the Industrial Revolution? (b) What problems arose as cities grew?
2. (a) Compare work in the country with city work. (b) What part did children play in factory work?
3. (a) What social class expanded as a result of industrialization? (b) How did landowners and aristocrats react to this growing class?
4. (a) Describe the class tensions that existed in industrialized nations by the mid-1800's. (b) How did laissez-faire governments contribute to this tension?
5. (a) Why did workers join together in unions? (b) How did the British government react?

Critical Thinking
6. The Industrial Revolution has been described as a mixed blessing. Do you agree or disagree? Support your answer with information from the chapter.

Chapter Review 22

Summary

1. Many factors aided industrial growth. Beginning in the late 1700's, the Industrial Revolution — a time of dramatic changes in the way work was done — transformed life in Great Britain. Many factors aided industrialization. These included new methods of farming that improved diets, a population explosion that created a large labor force, abundant mineral resources, a favorable geographic location for trade, a highly developed banking system, a favorable climate for new ideas, and political stability.

2. Britain led in the rise of industry. Industrialization occurred first in the British textile industry. New inventions speeded up weaving and spinning and led to the development of factories. The invention of a steam engine made it possible to locate factories near resources and markets.

3. Industry grew and spread to new lands. As industrialization sped up, businesses needed improved methods of transporting raw materials and finished products. Beginning in the late 1700's, Great Britain experienced a transportation revolution. Advances in transportation included a network of canals, improved roads, and the development of the railroad locomotive. Railroads spurred travel, promoted industry and agriculture, and provided jobs. Soon, de-spite British efforts to keep the secrets of industrialization to themselves, the Industrial Revolution spread to the United States and part of western Europe.

4. Industry changed ways of life. In the 1800's, industrialization affected every part of life in Great Britain. One of the most obvious changes was the growth of cities as people flocked to factories in search of work. Poor city planning, however, created inadequate housing and sanitation, pollution, frequent epidemics, and increased crime. Urban families had to adapt to new patterns of work, many of which threatened their health and the family unit. Working children suffered from abuses until Parliament passed laws to protect them. Some workers sought reforms by organizing unions, but laissez-faire attitudes and a lack of political power impeded progress. Industrialization also led to an expanded middle class that heightened tensions between rich and poor.

Reviewing the Facts

1. Define the following terms:
   a. enclosure
   b. crop rotation
   c. factory
   d. entrepreneur
   e. union

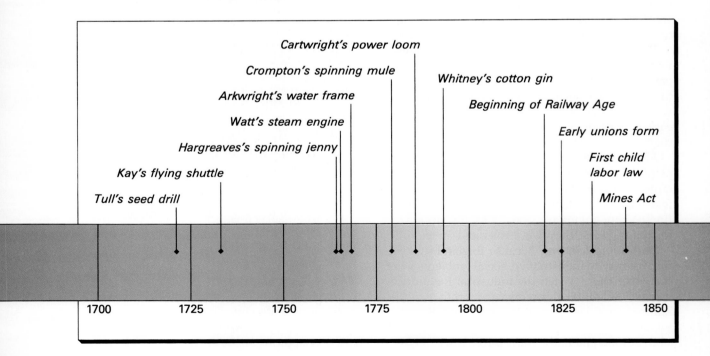

Cartwright's power loom

Crompton's spinning mule

Arkwright's water frame

Watt's steam engine

Hargreaves's spinning jenny

Kay's flying shuttle

Tull's seed drill

Whitney's cotton gin

Beginning of Railway Age

Early unions form

First child labor law

Mines Act

1700   1725   1750   1775   1800   1825   1850

2. Explain the importance of each of the following names, places, or terms:
   a. Industrial Revolution
   b. scientific farming
   c. Jethro Tull
   d. Charles Townshend
   e. Robert Bakewell
   f. John Kay
   g. spinning jenny
   h. water-frame
   i. spinning mule
   j. power loom
   k. Eli Whitney
   l. Newcomen engine
   m. James Watt
   n. canal system
   o. macadam surface
   p. Richard Trevithick
   q. George Stephenson
   r. Samuel Slater
   s. Pawtucket, Rhode Island
   t. Manchester, England
   u. Factory Act of 1833

3. Explain how each of the following aided industrialization in Great Britain. (a) scientific farming (b) enclosure movement (c) population increase (d) geography (e) resources (f) British attitudes

4. Show how one invention led to another in the British cotton industry.

5. (a) What effect did the cotton gin have on British factories? (b) What effect did the steam engine have on industrialization?

6. (a) Why did the Industrial Revolution require better methods of transportation? (b) Name and describe three transportation advances. (c) Which of these had the greatest effect on British industry?

7. (a) What factors led to the rise of industrial centers such as Manchester? (b) What problems did such centers face? (c) Why did these centers attract people despite such problems?

8. (a) How did the expansion of the middle class affect class tensions? (b) What attitude toward the poor did the British government adopt? (c) How did workers try to bring about reform?

Thinking about History

1. One way to measure a country's level of industrialization is to look at its iron and steel output. Why are these materials considered a good indication of an industrialized nation?

2. In the early 1800's, Britain's Parliament passed laws to end the slave trade and abolish slavery in British colonies. How did industrial needs conflict with antislavery policies?

3. Before the Industrial Revolution, textile workers were trained artisans, respected for their specialized skills. How did the Industrial Revolution change their status?

Writing and Speaking about History

1. Write a paragraph about some of the ways life changed after the Industrial Revolution. Choose one of the topics from pages 483–487 of the text for your paragraph.

2. The steam engine has been called the greatest invention of the Industrial Revolution. Conduct an interview with James Watt in which you discuss the significance of this invention.

Practicing Skills

1. Place the following events from this chapter in the correct chronologic order:
   a. Watt's steam engine
   b. Enclosure movement
   c. First factory in United States
   d. First run of Stephenson's rocket
   e. Kay's flying shuttle
   f. First child labor law

2. Review the map on page 482. (a) How many major industrial areas did Britain have in 1850? (b) What resources did each of these areas possess? (c) What industrial city lay on the Thames River?

3. List ten descriptors you might use to aid in the search for appropriate bibliographic sources for this research topic: "Industrialization changed ways of life in Britain." (See Research Skills Handbook, page 578.)

Investigating History

1. Find out more about advances that resulted from scientific farming. Compare medieval farming methods with these new techniques.

2. To better understand conditions in an industrial city, read *Hard Times* by Charles Dickens. Choose illustrative passages to read to the class.

3. Prepare a data base file on important inventions. Set up a field for each of the following categories: type of invention, description of invention, date, inventor, significance. Update your file as you read forthcoming chapters.

Decision Making in History

Assume that as a British businessman in 1820 you have the opportunity to invest in a railroad company. Before you do so, however, you must determine the potential risks and benefits. What geographic, economic, and political factors will you consider before you invest?

Chapter 23

Restoration, Romanticism, and Revolution

During the winter of 1814–1815, most of the crowned heads of Europe came to Vienna. There, rulers and diplomats tried to undo the changes that the French Revolution and the Napoleonic wars had set in motion.

1. European leaders sought stability.

2. New ideals affected politics and art.

3. Latin America won independence.

4. Reform and revolution swept Europe.

The first leaves were beginning to fall from the trees in Vienna, capital of the Austrian empire, as distinguished visitors began to arrive in September 1814. Never before had any city seen such a gathering of European royalty. They came from every corner of the continent— emperors and empresses, kings and queens, princes and princesses, grand dukes and grand duchesses, and hundreds of other lords and ladies. They came to attend a special meeting that promised to be the most glittering social event of their lifetime. With them came thousands of advisers and servants—foreign ministers, secretaries, ladies-in-waiting, and so on.

The Congress of Vienna had been called by four of the Great Powers— Austria, Great Britain, Prussia, and Russia—to celebrate and confirm their victory over the fifth, France. (A Great Power was a country that could shape international events.) After nine years of almost constant war, the allied powers had finally defeated Napoleon, exiling him to the Mediterranean island of Elba. Now the victorious leaders gathered to restore the boundaries of Europe as they had existed before Napoleon's conquests.

Francis I, emperor of Austria, was host for the conference. He spared no expense in entertaining his guests. The royal visitors were treated to what seemed like a never-ending series of balls, parades, fireworks, horse shows, dances, theatrical performances, and concerts. On November 29, an enthusiastic crowd assembled to hear Vienna's most prominent composer, Ludwig von Beethoven (BAY-toh-vuhn) conduct his Seventh Symphony. Of course, there were always parties. "Nothing but visits and return visits," wrote one tired archduke. "Eating, fireworks, public illuminations. For eight or ten days, I haven't been able to work at all. What a life!"

In spite of appearances, some very important business took place in Vienna. The rulers and ministers who gathered there redrew the map of Europe. Their so-called Vienna Settlement lasted about 40 years. During that period (1815–1853), there were no wars among the Great Powers.

The delegates at Vienna hoped to restore the old order. In effect, they wanted to turn back the clock to the time before the French Revolution. In this chapter, we shall look at attempts to preserve the old political and social order. We shall also see the forces that made it impossible for such attempts to succeed.

European leaders sought stability.

1

While hundreds of aristocrats attended glittering parties, the real business of the Congress of Vienna went on behind closed doors. Most of the decisions made at Vienna during the winter of 1814–1815 were made in secret among representatives of the five Great Powers.

The rulers of three of these countries—King Frederick William III of Prussia, Czar Alexander I of Russia, and, of course, Emperor Francis I of Austria—were present at Vienna. However, none of these men was as influential as the suave and polished chief minister of Austria, Prince Klemens von Metternich (MEHT-uhr-nihk).

Metternich dominated the Congress.

Metternich (1773–1859) was a tall, handsome man whose charm worked equally well with his fellow diplomats and with the elegant ladies of Vienna. He was not Austrian by birth; his family had estates in what is now West Germany. Like many European aristocrats, he considered French his first language, though he spoke four others fluently. Metternich thought of himself as a European, not as a citizen of any single country. "Europe has for a long time held for me the significance of a fatherland," he once said.

Early in his career, Metternich linked himself to the Hapsburgs, the rulers of Austria. He rose rapidly through the diplomatic ranks. In 1809, at the age of 36, he became Austria's foreign minister and held that office for the next 39 years, until 1848. Because of his immense influence on European politics, these years are often called the Age of Metternich.

Metternich dominated the Congress of Vienna.

Metternich disliked and distrusted the democratic ideals of the French Revolution. Like most other European aristocrats, he was convinced that Napoleon's warlike dictatorship was the natural result of experiments with democracy. Metternich believed in the value of keeping things as they were. "The first and greatest concern for the immense majority of every nation," he said, "is the stability of laws—never their change."

Metternich had three goals at the Congress of Vienna. First, he wanted to strengthen the countries that surrounded France to prevent future French aggression. Second, he wanted to restore a balance of power, so that no country was a threat to others. Third, he wanted to restore the royal families to the thrones they had held before Napoleon's conquests.

The Congress restored the old order.

Originally, the Congress of Vienna was scheduled to last for four weeks. Instead, it went on for nine months, until June 1815. One reason for the delay was Napoleon's escape from Elba in the spring of 1815. His last, desperate attempt to regain power in France ended in defeat at Waterloo in June 1815 (page 465). After this interruption, the Congress went on with its work. On the whole, the agreements that the diplomats made at Vienna followed Metternich's plans.

The encirclement of France To keep France from renewing its drive for power, the Congress made the countries around France stronger.

- The Austrian Netherlands was united with the Dutch Republic to form a single Kingdom of the Netherlands.
- A group of 39 German states were loosely joined into a newly created German Confederation, dominated by Austria.
- The Congress recognized Switzerland as an independent and neutral nation.
- The Kingdom of Sardinia in Italy was strengthened by the addition of Piedmont and Genoa.

The balance of power Although the leaders of Europe wanted to weaken France, they did not want to go too far. If they destroyed France, they would destroy the balance of power as well. Then a new country might become so strong that it threatened them all. Thus, the victorious powers were surprisingly easy on the defeated France.

France was required to give up all the territories Napoleon had taken. France itself, however, remained intact, keeping roughly the same boundaries it had had in 1790. France also kept most of its overseas possessions, its army, and an independent government. As a result, France remained a major European power.

The winning powers, however, took some prizes for themselves. Austria won the Italian territories of Venetia and Lombardy. Russia took over most of Poland. Prussia gained land in the Rhine valley of western Germany. Britain got a host of small but valuable territories for its overseas empire. Furthermore, the balance of power brought the peace and security needed for Britain's overseas trade to grow and flourish.

Legitimacy The Great Powers agreed that, as far as possible, those rulers whom Napoleon had driven from their thrones should be restored to power. This idea was called the principle of legitimacy. In France, Louis XVIII returned as king. On the French flag, the Bourbon fleur-de-lis replaced the Tricolor of the revolution.

The Congress also restored the Bourbon rulers in Spain and in the Italian Kingdom of the Two Sicilies. Hapsburg princes came back to rule several states in northern Italy. Many (though not all) of the former rulers of the German states of central Europe also regained their thrones.

The Congress of Vienna was a political triumph in many ways. Its settlements were fair enough that no country was left bearing a grudge. Thus, the Congress did not sow the seeds of future wars. In that sense, it was more successful than many other peace meetings in history. Not until 1853 were any of the five Great Powers involved in wars against one another.

New political philosophies arose.

Despite their efforts to undo the French Revolution, the leaders at the Congress of Vienna could not turn back the clock. That revolution had given Europe its first experiment in democratic government. Although the experiment failed, it set new political ideas in motion.

The major political divisions of the early 1800's had their roots in the French Revolution. The political labels of *conservative, liberal,* and *radical* grew from attitudes toward that revolution.

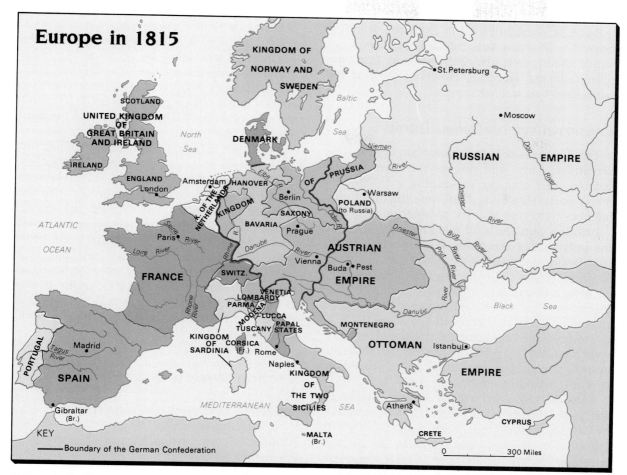

Europe in 1815

KINGDOM OF NORWAY AND SWEDEN

•St.Petersburg

•Moscow

SCOTLAND

UNITED KINGDOM OF GREAT BRITAIN AND IRELAND

North Sea

Baltic Sea

RUSSIAN EMPIRE

IRELAND

ENGLAND

London•

Amsterdam•

DENMARK

Elbe

HANOVER

OF

PRUSSIA

Berlin•

•Warsaw

POLAND (to Russia)

ATLANTIC OCEAN

K. OF THE NETHERLANDS

KINGDOM

SAXONY

Oder R.

BAVARIA

Prague•

Seine River

Paris•

Rhine R.

Danube

River

AUSTRIAN

Dniester

Bug River

River

FRANCE

Loire River

SWITZ.

Vienna•

Buda•

•Pest

EMPIRE

River

Rhone River

LOMBARDY

VENETIA

PARMA

MODENA

LUCCA

Danube

Black Sea

PORTUGAL

Madrid•

Tagus River

KINGDOM OF SARDINIA

CORSICA (Fr.)

TUSCANY

PAPAL STATES

Rome•

MONTENEGRO

OTTOMAN

Istanbul•

SPAIN

Naples•

KINGDOM OF THE TWO SICILIES

EMPIRE

Gibraltar (Br.)

MEDITERRANEAN

SEA

Athens•

CYPRUS

MALTA (Br.)

CRETE

KEY

——— Boundary of the German Confederation

0   300 Miles

Map Study

Compare this map with the one on page 461. What parts of its empire did France lose? What replaced the Confederation of the Rhine?

Conservatism Conservatives argued that the revolution had accomplished nothing but harm. Their goal was to protect, or conserve, traditional forms of government. Some moderate conservatives, mostly in Great Britain, believed in constitutional monarchy. More extreme conservatives believed that absolute monarchy was the best form of government. Metternich was a classic conservative, as were most of the other European leaders at the Congress. Conservatives drew their greatest support from wealthy landowners and nobles who had been satisfied with the old order and were happy to see it restored.

Liberalism Liberals approved of the early reforms of the French Revolution but hated the later violence during the Reign of Terror. Liberals wanted more power given to elected parliaments,

but few favored democracy. Most wanted limited parliaments for which only those who were educated and owned property could vote. Liberals, in fact, feared the "mob" as much as conservatives did. Liberalism appealed mainly to the upper bourgeoisie, business leaders, and merchants. Such people were barred from politics in some countries because they were not of noble birth, no matter how rich they had become.

Radicalism The word *radical* was used at this time to describe supporters of democratic government. Many radicals justified even the Reign of Terror as necessary to make France a true democracy. Radicals believed that the ideals of the French Revolution should be put into practice by governments everywhere. Radicals favored drastic and, if necessary, violent change.

493

Radicals sometimes came from the working class. The Parisian sans-culottes are a good example. Radicalism also drew support from intellectuals and students. However, support for radicalism was not widespread.

Conservatives controlled Europe.

The Congress of Vienna was a victory for conservatives. Kings and princes were restored in country after country, in keeping with Metternich's goals. However, there were important differences from one country to another.

Britain's constitutional monarchy Britain was the only one of the Great Powers with a true constitutional monarchy. Parliament actually had far more power than the ruler. Yet Britain was far from a democracy. Most members of Parliament were wealthy landowners. They were elected by a tiny fraction of the population. Only men who owned a substantial amount of property were qualified to vote. Nevertheless, Britain's form of government was much more open than anything found in eastern Europe.

Absolute rulers in eastern Europe Generally speaking, governments were more conservative in eastern Europe than they were in western Europe. The rulers of Russia, Prussia, and Austria were absolute monarchs. Late in 1815, the rulers of those three countries drew up an agreement called the Holy Alliance. In this agreement against liberalism, Czar Alexander I, Emperor Francis I, and King Frederick William III promised to help one another if any of them were threatened by reformers or revolutionaries.

Tension in France Among the Great Powers, France's position was unique. The old Bourbon dynasty ruled once more, but an elected Chamber of Deputies shared some power with Louis XVIII. This parliament was even less democratic than Britain's. Only about one of every 300 French men (and no French women at all) had the right to vote.

France after 1815 was deeply divided politically. Conservatives were happy with the Bourbon restoration and determined to make it last. Liberals wanted the king to share more power with the Chamber of Deputies and to grant the middle class the right to vote. Many people in the lower class, especially in Paris, remained committed to the ideals of liberty, equality, and fraternity. They were determined to overthrow the Bourbons and make France a republic once again. It was an explosive mixture of ideas and factions that would contribute directly to revolutions in 1830 and again in 1848.

Section Review 1

Define: (a) legitimacy, (b) conservative, (c) liberal, (d) radical
Identify: (a) Congress of Vienna, (b) Great Power, (c) Metternich, (d) German Confederation, (e) Holy Alliance, (f) Louis XVIII
Answer:
1. What was the purpose for which the Congress of Vienna met?
2. Which countries were the Great Powers of Europe?

Daily Life · City of Waltzes

A princely visitor to Vienna in 1815 remarked, "The congress doesn't march—it dances." Indeed it did, to lilting tunes in three-quarter time, written for the new dance that was sweeping Vienna, the waltz. The aristocratic visitors found the waltz far more exciting than the formal minuet that they had danced for years. Adapted from a country dance, the waltz appealed to dancers of all social classes. The word *waltz* came from the German word for "revolving." Partners whirled across the floor with their arms wrapped around each other in a way that many people thought indecent for public view.

3. What were Metternich's three goals at the Congress of Vienna?
4. (a) What were the results of the congress for France? (b) For the small states around France? (c) For the German states?
5. (a) In general, what were the political ideas of conservatives? (b) Liberals? (c) Radicals?
6. How was the British government different from governments in the rest of Europe?
7. How was the Congress of Vienna a triumph for conservatism?

Critical Thinking

8. (a) What are the factors that make a peace conference successful? (b) By those standards, was the Congress of Vienna a success? (c) What trends or movements did the congress fail to recognize?

New ideals affected politics and art. 2

Liberals, conservatives, and radicals debated the roles of kings, parliaments, and people in government. Meanwhile, two new movements were arising that blurred the lines between these political theories. One of the new movements was nationalism. The other was romanticism.

Nationalism was a force for change.

Nationalism is the belief that a person's greatest loyalty should be to a nation-state. In the years after 1800, this belief fired the hearts of millions of Europeans and reshaped the map of Europe.

To understand nationalism, let us review the meaning of the word *nation*. A group of people who share similar traditions, history, and language make up a nation. Usually, they live in the same geographic area as well. If such a group is united under its own government, it is known as a **nation-state.** For nationalists of all groups, forming such a nation-state became the goal of their lives.

In 1815, there were very few nation-states in Europe. A quick glance at the map shows no countries called Italy, Germany, Greece, Hungary, or Poland. Only France and Spain qualified as nation-states. England, like France, had developed as a nation during the late Middle Ages (page 239). However, England was now part of Great Britain, along with Ireland and Scotland. Many Irish and Scots definitely did not think of themselves as part of an English nation.

Modern nationalism was born during the French Revolution. The leaders of the revolution stressed the equality of all French people. Overjoyed at the chance to govern themselves, the French felt a burst of national pride. "Our life, our goods, and our talents do not belong to us," cried one French army volunteer. "It is to the nation, to France, [that] everything belongs." This national pride was an important factor in Napoleon's remarkable victories.

Ironically, France's military success sowed the seeds of its own downfall, because nationalism grew quickly too among the people France conquered (page 463). Fired by national pride, Spaniards, Italians, and Germans rebelled against their French conquerors.

The downfall of Napoleon did not lead immediately to the creation of new nation-states in Europe. In 1815, many national groups were ruled by larger, more powerful states. Most Poles, for example, lived under Russian rule. Hungarians and many Slavs lived under Austrian rule.

As nationalism spread, such groups became more and more unhappy with their situation. They formed nationalist societies, often meeting in secret. These societies published books and newspapers that stressed each group's unique character and the glories of its past.

Greece won its independence.

The first new nation-state to win its freedom was Greece. For centuries, Greece had been part of the Ottoman empire, which controlled most of southeastern Europe. As nationalism spread across Europe, the Greeks were among the first to be affected. Greek nationalists demanded that Greece take its place among the nation-states of Europe. A major revolt against Ottoman rule broke out in 1821.

The Greek war for independence was a difficult struggle. However, the Greeks had two great advantages that other rebellious groups such as the Poles and the Irish did not. First, the Ottoman army was much weaker than the Russian or the British armies. Second, the cause of Greek

Lord Byron, a leading romantic poet, posed for this portrait dressed as a Greek nationalist.

independence was popular with many Europeans whose education had given them tremendous respect for ancient Greek culture. "Fair Greece! Sad relic of departed worth!" lamented Lord Byron, a British poet. "Immortal, though no more; though fallen, great!" Byron went to Greece as a volunteer soldier and died there in 1824.

Eventually, the Great Powers took the side of the Greeks. In 1827, a joint British, French, and Russian fleet destroyed an Ottoman fleet at the Battle of Navarino. In 1830, a treaty granted Greece full independence. This success encouraged other nationalities to seek independence.

Mazzini sparked Italian nationalism.

The situation in Italy was much more complicated than that in Greece. Italy was divided into many different states. Some parts were ruled by Austria. Others were fiercely independent, in the traditions of the Renaissance city-states. Part of Italy was ruled by the pope. Unity was the great ambition of Italian nationalists.

Modern Italian nationalism began with Napoleon. In 1805, he combined the many separate Italian states into a single French-controlled Kingdom of Italy. The Congress of Vienna restored most of the old divisions. Yet the idea of a united Italy survived.

Among Italy's early nationalists was Giuseppe Mazzini (maht-TSEE-nee). "A people destined to achieve great things," argued Mazzini, "must one day or other form a nation-state. Italy therefore will be one. Her geographical conditions, her language, her literature, and the desires of her people all point to this aim."

In 1831, the 26-year-old Mazzini formed a nationalist group called Young Italy, which no one older than 40 was allowed to join. At its peak during the 1830's, Young Italy claimed 60,000 members. Most were of middle-class backgrounds. Unfortunately for Mazzini, the idea of nationalism won little support from the Italian masses. Deep cultural differences divided northern and southern Italy. An urban worker in Milan had little in common with a peasant farmer in Sicily.

Austria proved an even bigger obstacle to Italian unity. The Austrian emperor ruled Lombardy and Venetia in northern Italy. Several of his Hapsburg relatives ruled other Italian states. Metternich saw Italian nationalism as a serious threat to Austria, so he made every effort to suppress such groups as Young Italy. Austrian officials arrested Mazzini many times.

In Italy, as in other European countries, nationalism was closely connected to liberalism. Both ideas appealed to people who were educated and eager to govern their countries. In most cases, both nationalists and liberals came from the middle class. Teachers, lawyers, and business people often led the struggle for more liberal government and the formation of nation-states.

Germany was disunited.

As in Italy, there was tremendous interest in nationalism in the German states during the early 1800's. However, unity seemed far away in 1815. The area where most Germans lived was divided into 39 separate countries. The Congress of Vienna had set up a loose union known as the German Confederation.

Every year, each German state sent representatives to Frankfurt to attend a Federal Diet. The diet was a kind of all-German parliament that discussed the problems of member states. The

German Federal Diet was almost powerless. It had no all-German army to enforce its decisions. It could make no laws unless all 39 states approved. Such agreement was almost impossible because the two largest states—Austria and Prussia—rarely agreed on anything.

Nevertheless, the German Confederation was an important first step toward a German nation. The Federal Diet became a rallying point for liberals and nationalists who wanted unity.

The largest and most powerful member of the German Confederation in 1815 was the Austrian empire. Its Hapsburg emperors ruled peoples of a dozen different nationalities.

The dominant national group within the empire was German. The Hapsburgs themselves were German. So were most of the empire's political and military leaders. Most Germans in the empire lived in and around the city of Vienna. Elsewhere in the empire, there were millions of Hungarians, Czechs, Serbs, Poles, Italians, Romanians, and other peoples.

Metternich was well aware that nationalism posed an enormous threat to the Austrian empire. Throughout his long tenure as Austrian foreign minister, he used censorship and arrests to stop the spread of nationalist ideas. While such tactics slowed nationalism, they did not wipe it out. The result was a constant buildup of pressure as the various peoples moved closer and closer to rebellion against the Hapsburgs.

Romanticism rejected reason.

Nationalism was strongly linked to a second great intellectual movement that began around 1800. That second movement was romanticism. Romanticism affected literature, art, and music, but it also touched politics. Many romantics were also nationalists. Lord Byron, who died fighting for Greek freedom, was a leading romantic poet.

Romanticism was a reaction against the Enlightenment. It was a reaction against the orderly, rational approach of writers such as Voltaire and musicians such as Mozart.

Romanticism was marked by four distinctive characteristics. One was its heavy emphasis on emotion and passion. The romantics stressed feeling over thinking. As the German novelist Johann Wolfgang von Goethe wrote, "What I know, anyone can know, but my heart is my own, peculiar to itself."

Voice from the Past · Poetry and Patriotism

Britain's most popular romantic novelist and poet was Sir Walter Scott (1771–1832). Many of Scott's writings told heroic stories of the Middle Ages. This poem shows the link between romanticism and nationalism.

Breathes there a man with soul so dead,
Who never to himself hath said,
 'This is my own, my native land!'
Whose heart hath ne'er within him burn'd
As home his footsteps he hath turn'd
 From wandering on a foreign strand?
If such there breathe, go, mark him well;
For him no Minstrel raptures swell;
High though his titles, proud his name,
Boundless his wealth as wish can claim;
Despite those titles, power, and pelf,
The wretch, concentred all in self,
Living, shall forfeit fair renown,
And, doubly dying, shall go down
To the vile dust from whence he sprung,
Unwept, unhonor'd, and unsung.

1. According to Scott, what sort of man is dead in his soul?
2. What do you think the phrase "concentred all in self" means?
3. (a) What is the fate of such a person in life? (b) In death?

Romantic painters emphasized dramatic aspects of nature and the human soul (right). Among the leading figures of romanticism were George Sand (top), Beethoven (bottom), and Mary Shelley (center), author of Frankenstein.

A second characteristic of romanticism was its emphasis on the individual. Romantics celebrated individuals, especially heroic rebels. Romantic writers and artists glorified such legendary heroes as the English King Arthur and also such powerful historic figures as Napoleon. It mattered little whether the hero was a revolutionary or a king. It was heroic action that counted.

A third feature of romanticism was its celebration of nature. France's leading romantic novelist, Amandine Aurore Dupin, lovingly described the French countryside and rustic life. (To win a wider audience for her novels, Dupin took the male pen name George Sand.) British writer Emily Brontë made the windswept moors of northern England the setting for her powerful romantic novel, *Wuthering Heights.*

Last but not least, romanticism glorified the past. Romantics yearned for "the good old days," a past that seemed more noble than anything the modern age had to offer. They looked back longingly to a preindustrial age. The deeds of past kings, knights, and outlaws seemed more worthy of song and story than those of factory owners and railway engineers.

Romanticism touched many arts.

Similar ideas—the emphasis on emotion, individual expression, nature, and the glories of the past—affected all the arts. Painting and music as well as literature followed the romantic path.

Romanticism in music In music, Ludwig van Beethoven was a key figure. In his early years, he wrote music in the classical manner (page

Footnote to History

Beethoven never heard his Ninth Symphony. During his last years, he was completely deaf. When he finished conducting the first performance of the Ninth, the audience burst into thunderous applause. Beethoven, facing the orchestra, heard nothing. Only when a singer turned him around did he realize that he was being given a standing ovation.

433). In his later symphonies and concertos, however, Beethoven turned away from the tightly controlled compositions he had written in the 1700's. His ninth and last symphony is an overwhelmingly emotional celebration of freedom, dignity, and spiritual triumph. Later romantic composers such as Robert Schumann and Felix Mendelssohn similarly appealed to the hearts and souls of their listeners.

Romanticism in painting Emotion dominated the work of painters as well. Some painters, such as the English painter Joseph Turner and the German Caspar David Friedrich, used landscape scenes to convey moods. Other artists, including France's Eugene Delacroix, painted dramatic scenes from history to arouse the emotions of the viewer.

Romanticism fueled nationalism.

Many romantics were also whole-hearted nationalists. The celebration of past glories appealed to both romantics and nationalists. So did the strong emotions aroused by nationalism.

Writers collected the ballads and folktales of their national group. Such stories, said romantic nationalists, expressed the time-honored spirit of their people. In Germany, for example, the Grimm brothers gathered a collection of fairy tales, which they published in 1812.

In art, romantics often showed their country as a human figure. The French painter Delacroix, for example, portrayed France as a beautiful woman in such works as "Liberty Leading the People" and "Liberty on the Barricades."

Section Review 2

Define: (a) nationalism, (b) nation-state, (c) romanticism
Identify: (a) Battle of Navarino, (b) Byron, (c) Mazzini, (d) Young Italy, (e) George Sand, (f) Beethoven, (g) Scott
Answer:
1. (a) What are the common characteristics of a nation? (b) Which countries in Europe were nation-states in 1815?
2. Explain how the French Revolution brought about the beginning of modern nationalism.
3. How did Greece become a nation?

4. What were some of the obstacles to Italian unification?
5. Why was the German Federal Diet weak?
6. Why was nationalism a threat to Austria?
7. Name four characteristics of romanticism and give an example of each.

Critical Thinking
8. Reread the quotation by Mazzini on page 496. (a) What four factors does he list as developing Italian nationalism? (b) How would each of those factors help Italy become a nation-state?

Latin America won independence. 3

Just as nationalism became a major force in Europe during the early 1800's, it also became important in the Western Hemisphere. As you know, 13 of Britain's North American colonies became independent in the late 1700's, forming the United States of America (page 443). Between 1800 and 1825, similar wars for independence were fought in the region called Latin America.

The term *Latin America* applies to the lands south of the United States where Spanish, Portuguese, and French are spoken. All these languages developed from Latin. The region includes Mexico, Central America, South America, and the islands of the Caribbean.

Several events outside Latin America helped to spark the drive for independence. The ideals of the Enlightenment spread to the educated people of Latin America. When the French Revolution broke out, many Latin Americans applauded its early reforms, if not its later violence. The American Revolution showed that determined rebels could defeat a European government. Finally, Napoleon's conquests in Europe set off a wave of nationalism that affected Latin Americans as well as Europeans.

Latin American society was divided.

On the surface, the Latin American revolutions of the early 1800's appear similar to the American Revolution. In every case, revolutionaries overthrew a government controlled by a European country. The leaders of the revolution then set up a new national government.

However, there were important differences between conditions in Latin America and in the United States. In Latin America, colonial society was sharply divided into classes based on birth. Struggles among these classes played an important part in the revolutions.

At the top of Latin American society were the *peninsulars*, people who had been born in Spain or Portugal. They held the most important positions in colonial government and in the Roman Catholic Church.

Creoles (**KREE**-ohls) ranked next after the peninsulars. Creoles were people who were born in Latin America but whose ancestors came from Europe. This class included many wealthy landowners and lesser government officials.

The peninsulars and the creoles formed an aristocracy in Latin American society. Together, they made up less than one fifth of the population. Below them ranked the common people who had few political rights and little share in the region's wealth.

The common people included mestizos (meh-**STEE**-zohs), mulattoes (myoo-**LAT**-ohs), blacks, and Indians. Mestizos were people of mixed European and Indian ancestry. Mulattoes were of European and African ancestry. Some mestizos and mulattoes owned small farms or businesses. Most rented small farms from landlords. Most blacks worked as slaves on large plantations, although there were free blacks in many Latin American towns. Lowest ranking of all were the millions of Indians. They were legally free, but they were usually treated no better than slaves.

Slaves revolted in Haiti.

The first Latin American country to free itself from European rule was the French colony on the island of Hispaniola in the Caribbean Sea. Slaves and free mulattoes there rose in revolt against France in 1791.

In 1794, the revolutionaries found a skilled general in an ex-slave, Toussaint L'Ouverture (too-**SAHN LOO**-vuhr-TYOOR). Toussaint (1743–1803) drove the French forces from the island. Then, in 1802, he attended a peace meeting where he was treacherously taken prisoner. He was then sent to France, where he died in prison. However,

the French could not retake the island. Black revolutionary leaders set up the independent country of Haiti in 1804.

Creoles wanted independence.

Elsewhere in Latin America, creoles took the lead in battles for independence. The creoles had a number of long-standing grievances against Spain. Peninsulars held almost all the high government offices in Spain's Latin American lands. Of the 170 viceroys who held office between 1492 and 1810, for example, only 4 were creoles.

Spain also kept tight control over the economy of its colonies. Merchants in Spanish colonies could trade only with Spain. They could send their goods only on Spanish ships. The valuable mines of Mexico and Peru were under direct Spanish control, which the creoles resented.

The direct cause of the Latin American revolts, however, was Napoleon's conquest of Spain in 1808. Napoleon made his brother Joseph king of Spain (page 463). Many creoles might have remained loyal to a Spanish king, but they felt no loyalty at all to a Frenchman placed on the Spanish throne by force.

Toussaint L'Ouverture

Fighting broke out in 1810 in several parts of Latin America. The wars for independence were complicated and confusing. Loyalties were divided. The viceroys and their armies remained loyal to Spain, as did some creoles. Indians and mestizos fought on both sides, often forced into armies against their will.

Bolívar and San Martín led the struggle.

The South American wars of independence produced two brilliant generals whose leadership was largely responsible for the success of the rebels. One was Simón Bolívar (see-MOHN buh-LEE-vahr). The other was the Argentinian José San Martín (hoh-SAY san mahr-TEEN).

Bolívar in the north Simón Bolívar (1783–1830) was a wealthy Venezuelan creole. He had traveled in Europe and read the works of Voltaire, Rousseau, and Montesquieu, even though they were banned in Latin America. Bolívar was both romantic and practical, a writer and a fighter, handsome and brilliant. He won admiration from friend and foe alike. Above all, he was tireless in the struggle for independence.

Bolívar's native Venezuela declared its independence from Spain in 1811. However, the struggle seesawed back and forth. The revolutionaries suffered many defeats, and Bolívar was twice forced into exile.

The turning point came in 1819. Bolívar built up an army from many sources. He promised to end slavery, winning many black volunteers. Other volunteers came from Europe. In January 1819, Bolívar led his 2,500 soldiers on a daring march through the towering Andes into what is now Colombia. Coming from this unexpected direction, he took the Spanish army completely by surprise in Bogotá and defeated them.

Bolívar went on to free Venezuela in 1821. Next, he marched south into Ecuador. In the coastal city of Guayaquil, he met with the other great hero of the independence movement, San Martín.

San Martín in the south When the wars for independence broke out in Latin America, José San Martín (1778–1850) was in Spain fighting Napoleon. Hearing of the revolt in his homeland, Argentina, he returned at once. Soon he commanded a creole army there. While Bolívar was

Simón Bolívar

freeing the northern part of South America, San Martín freed the south.

Argentina declared its independence in 1816. However, the new country was not safe as long as Spanish forces had strongholds in nearby Chile and Peru. Thus, in 1817, San Martín led an army on a grueling march across the Andes to Chile. There he won several decisive victories and freed the country.

Next, San Martín took his army north by sea to Lima, Peru, in 1821. The Spanish army retreated into the mountains of Peru. To drive them out, San Martín needed a much larger force. Otherwise, the Spaniards would remain a threat to all of independent South America. This was the problem that faced San Martín and Bolívar when they met at Guayaquil.

The Spanish were finally defeated.

Mystery has long surrounded the meeting between these two great generals. They differed in many ways. San Martín was a less dashing and romantic leader than Bolívar. San Martín wanted

Latin America about 1830

UNITED STATES

TEXAS

Rio Grande

MEXICO
Dolores
Mexico City

Gulf of Mexico

CUBA
JAMAICA
HAITI
PUERTO RICO
SANTO DOMINGO

BRITISH HONDURAS
HONDURAS

Caribbean Sea

GUATEMALA
EL SALVADOR
NICARAGUA
COSTA RICA
PANAMA

ATLANTIC OCEAN

Caracas
VENEZUELA
Boyacá
Carabobo (1821)
(1819) GREAT COLOMBIA
Bogotá
COLOMBIA

TRINIDAD

Orinoco River

BRITISH GUIANA
DUTCH GUIANA
FRENCH GUIANA

KEY
Independent countries
Spanish colonies
French colonies
British colonies
Dutch colonies
→ San Martín
→ Bolívar
✳ Battle

PACIFIC OCEAN

GALÁPAGOS ISLANDS

UNITED PROVINCES OF CENTRAL AMERICA

Pichincha (1821)
Guayaquil
Quito
ECUADOR

Rio Negro

Amazon River

EMPIRE OF BRAZIL

PERU
Lima

Ayacucho (1824)

La Paz
Sucre
BOLIVIA

São Francisco River

River

Paraguay R

PARAGUAY
Asunción

Rio de Janeiro

Latin America in 1800

UNITED STATES

ATLANTIC OCEAN

VICEROYALTY OF SANTO DOMINGO

Havana

VICEROYALTY OF NEW SPAIN
Mexico City
NEW SPAIN

PACIFIC OCEAN

VICEROYALTY OF NEW GRANADA
Bogotá

GUIANAS

VICEROYALTY OF BRAZIL

Lima
VICEROYALTY OF PERU

VICE-ROYALTY OF LA PLATA

Rio de Janeiro

Buenos Aires

ATLANTIC OCEAN

KEY
Spanish colonies
Portuguese colonies
French colonies
British colonies
Dutch colonies

0   1000 Miles

CHILE
Chacabuco (1817)
Mendoza
Santiago
Maipú (1818)

Andes Mountains

ARGENTINA

Paraná River

Uruguay River

URUGUAY
Montevideo
Buenos Aires
Rio de la Plata

PATAGONIA
Conquered by Argentina 1878-1879

ATLANTIC OCEAN

FALKLAND ISLANDS

Strait of Magellan
Cape Horn

0   1000 Miles

Map Study

By 1830, in what region were most of the lands that were still colonies? In what country did Bolívar and San Martín meet?

the newly independent countries of South America governed as monarchies. In contrast, Bolívar hoped to establish republics that would be dominated by the creoles. Nonetheless, both knew that the first step was to defeat the Spanish.

Although no one knows what the two leaders said to each other, the results were dramatic. San Martín left his army for Bolívar to command and returned to Argentina. Some historians think San Martín left in anger after a quarrel with Bolívar. Others say San Martín deliberately stepped aside in favor of Bolívar, so that the independence movement could unite behind a single leader. Whatever his reasons, San Martín soon sailed for Europe, where he died almost forgotten in 1850. Only later was he recognized as a true Argentinian hero.

Bolívar followed the Spaniards into the heights of the Andes. His forces defeated the Spanish army at the Battle of Ayacucho on December 9, 1824. This was the last major battle of the war for independence. South America was free of Spanish rule.

Brazil freed itself peacefully.

Meanwhile, Brazil won its independence peacefully. In 1807, Napoleon invaded Portugal. As his armies neared Lisbon, the Portuguese royal family fled to Brazil. After Napoleon's defeat, the king of Portugal returned to Europe. However, he left his son, Dom Pedro, as regent of Brazil.

When Brazilians demanded their independence in 1822, Dom Pedro agreed. He defied the Portuguese government's command to sail for Lisbon. On September 7, 1822, he issued the call, "Independence or death!" Brazilians celebrate this day as their national independence day.

In December 1822, Dom Pedro was named emperor. Brazil, South America's largest country, became South America's only monarchy.

Mexicans struggled for freedom.

In most Latin American countries, revolution began in the cities, but in Mexico, it began in the countryside. Only in Mexico did Indians and mestizos take a leading part in the struggle for independence.

The first outbreak of the Mexican revolution came in 1810. A group of creoles plotted a revolt, but the government learned of their plans. One of the leaders was Father Miguel Hidalgo (ee-THAHL-goh), a priest in the small mountain village of Dolores. Hidalgo was a poor but well-educated man, steeped in the ideals of the French Revolution. On September 16, 1810, he called on the Indian peasants of his parish to rebel against their Spanish masters. "My children," he asked them, "will you be free? Will you make the effort to recover from the hated Spaniards the lands stolen from your forefathers 300 years ago?"

Hidalgo's Indians began a 200-mile march toward Mexico City. Armed with sickles, stones, and clubs, this unruly army moved southward, picking up thousands of new recruits and weapons along the way. Creole landlords fled for their lives. Soon Hidalgo had a force of 60,000 men behind him. He declared an end to slavery and called for other reforms.

At Mexico City, however, the main Spanish army and the creoles joined forces against Hidalgo's army. Hidalgo was betrayed by one of his officers, captured, and executed.

The rebels found another strong leader in José María Morelos (moh-RAY-lohs). Morelos was a farm worker turned priest who had fought beside Father Hidalgo. He proved a far better general than Hidalgo had been. By 1813, Morelos's army controlled all of Mexico except for the largest cities. A Mexican congress, called by Morelos, declared Mexico an independent republic in 1813. Morelos wanted to set up a democratic government, tax the wealthy, and distribute lands to the peasants.

Many creoles supported the idea of independence, but they were not willing to accept Morelos's social reforms. A creole officer, Augustín de Iturbide (EE-toor-BEE-thay), captured and executed Morelos in 1815. A few scattered groups of rebels fought on as guerrillas.

Suddenly, events took a new turn. In 1820, a revolution in Spain put a new group in power. Mexico's creoles feared that this Spanish government would take away their privileges. At once, the creoles united in support of independence. The very man who had killed Morelos, Iturbide, made peace with the last guerrilla leader. Then Iturbide proclaimed Mexico independent in 1821. Iturbide later made himself emperor, but he was soon ousted. When he tried to return to power in 1824, he was shot.

Caudillos dominated governments.

By 1830, Latin America was home to 16 independent countries, but the citizens of these new countries had few political freedoms. All the countries were dominated by a small group of wealthy creole aristocrats. "Independence," said Bolívar shortly before his death in 1830, "is the sole benefit we have gained, at the sacrifice of all others . . . He who serves a revolution plows the sea."

Army leaders had come to power during the long struggle with Spain, and they continued to control Latin America after independence. By 1830, nearly all the countries of Latin America were run by **caudillos** (kow-THEE-yohs). Caudillos were political strongmen, usually army officers, who ruled as dictators. Many caudillos cared only for their own power and wealth. They did little to improve the lives of the common people. Changes of government most often took place at bayonet-point, as one caudillo was forced to give way to another.

Foreign interests dominated Latin America's economies.

In one way, Latin America was luckier than other nonindustrial parts of the world. Despite the political confusion, Latin America was never again carved into colonies as Africa and Asia were in the late 1800's. Having won independence, Latin America succeeded in keeping it.

The Monroe Doctrine Spain did not give up hope of winning back its former colonies. France too saw a chance to take over land in Latin America. Both Britain and the United States, however, were determined not to allow such a development.

In 1823, President James Monroe of the United States announced, "the American continents . . . are henceforth not to be considered as subjects for future colonization by any European powers." This statement is known as the Monroe Doctrine. Alone, the United States was not strong enough to enforce the Monroe Doctrine. However, Great Britain also wanted to protect Latin American independence.

British and American economic interests Britain had no political ambitions in Latin America, but it did have large economic interests. During the wars for independence, many Latin American countries began trading with Britain rather than with Spain. British banks and businesses invested heavily in South America, especially in Argentina and Brazil.

Britain's only real economic rival in Latin America was the United States. However, most United States' exports in the early 1800's came from the farm rather than the factory. Thus, there was little direct competition between the United States and Great Britain. Both countries were happy with the economic advantages they gained by Latin American independence.

Section Review 3

Define: (a) Latin America, (b) peninsulars, (c) creoles, (d) mestizos, (e) mulattoes, (f) caudillo
Identify: (a) Toussaint L'Ouverture, (b) Bolívar, (c) San Martín, (d) Battle of Ayacucho, (e) Dom Pedro, (f) Hidalgo, (g) Morelos, (h) Iturbide, (i) Monroe Doctrine
Answer:
1. Describe the divisions in Latin American society under Spanish rule.
2. How did Haiti gain independence?
3. (a) What economic and political grievances did the creoles have? (b) What was the direct cause of revolt in Latin America?
4. (a) How was independence achieved in northern South America? (b) In southern South America?
5. How did Brazil become independent?
6. How did the Mexican revolt differ from revolts in other Spanish colonies?
7. What groups dominated Latin America after independence?
8. Why was the Monroe Doctrine drawn up?

Critical Thinking
9. Historians have often debated the importance of individual leaders in history. (a) Would the Latin American revolts have taken place without Toussaint, Bolívar, San Martín, and Hidalgo? Explain your answer. (b) Which, if any, of the revolts would have succeeded without these leaders?
10. What did Bolívar mean when he said, "He who serves a revolution plows the sea"?

Reform and revolution swept Europe. 4

As we have seen, new ideas had widespread impact in Europe during the early 1800's. Nationalism and romanticism roused people's emotions. Liberalism gained ground with the growth of the middle class in western Europe. Members of this class were eager to have greater political power. They won large gains in Great Britain and France, but they failed, for the time being, in most other parts of Europe.

France overthrew its Bourbon king.

In 1830, a short and almost bloodless revolution ended the rule of France's Charles X. Charles, the last Bourbon king of France, brought on the revolution by his own stupidity. He ignored both middle-class liberals and Parisian radicals and tried to rule as an absolute monarch. He had nothing but contempt for the idea of a limited monarchy such as the one in Britain. "I would rather be a woodcutter," he once said, "than be the king of England."

Charles sparked the revolution by trying to take away what few powers France's Chamber of Deputies held. Riots broke out in Paris as liberals and radicals joined together to rid the country of this impossible king. Charles fled as an exile to Great Britain.

Within a few days, a group of liberal leaders offered the French crown to Charles's cousin, Louis Philippe, who was sympathetic to liberal reforms. Louis Philippe accepted, promising to rule as a "citizen king" who would share power with the Chamber of Deputies. France enjoyed almost two decades of peace and stability before another revolution broke out in 1848.

Britain's middle class won the vote.

Peaceful debate in the British Parliament, not armed revolution, won the most important liberal victory of these years. After a decade of pressure from factory owners and merchants, Parliament passed the Reform Bill of 1832.

The Reform Bill of 1832 set up new districts for electing members of Parliament. Many of the old districts had existed for hundreds of years. Some had been medieval villages but were now empty fields. Yet the owner of that field could elect a member of Parliament. In contrast, new cities such as Manchester and Sheffield had no representatives because those cities had grown up after the districts were formed. The reform bill put an end to such injustices. For the first time, the thriving new industrial cities had representation in Parliament.

The reform bill also gave more men the right to vote. Before 1832, only men who owned a substantial amount of property could vote. After 1832, men who paid a certain amount of rent could also vote. (Around the same time, Catholic men also won the right to vote.)

The Reform Bill of 1832 doubled the number of British voters. Nearly all middle-class men could now take part in elections. Still, this was less than 20 percent of the men in Great Britain.

The working class had little power.

Although Britain had the most liberal government in Europe, working class people still had no political influence. Daniel O'Connell, an Irish nationalist and liberal leader of this time, was asked to explain a political issue to some roadworkers. "Whatever happens," O'Connell told them, "you will still be breaking stones." Nevertheless, the working class was beginning to demand some say in politics.

As the Industrial Revolution progressed, working conditions improved a little. Workers' wages were rising, and ordinary people were better fed and better clothed. Life was no longer a grim struggle to survive. Workers began to organize.

By the 1840's, the Industrial Revolution was sweeping across the continent. It particularly affected the Ruhr and Rhine valleys in western Germany and the Po valley in northern Italy. Factories sprang up in cities such as Frankfurt, Cologne, and Milan. Radical political organizers in these cities were determined that the working-class voice would be heard.

1848 was a year of revolutions.

By 1848, working-class radicals and middle-class liberals in Europe were convinced that the Metternich system—the political agreements of

In 1848, revolts shook many European capitals. Here, troops fire on protestors in Vienna.

the Congress of Vienna—had long outlived its usefulness. Nationalists believed the time had come to sweep away old-fashioned empires and replace them with nation-states.

With such widespread discontent, it was only a matter of time before a violent outburst occurred. The explosion came in 1848. In January of that year, there was a revolution in the Kingdom of the Two Sicilies. Over the next 4 months, almost 50 similar revolts rocked Europe. "What remains standing in Europe?" asked Czar Nicholas I of Russia in April. His empire and Britain were the only major countries not touched by revolt.

The revolts meant different things in different places. In France, the revolutionaries planned to establish a democratic government. In Hungary, they wanted to throw off Austrian rule and set up a Hungarian nation-state. In the German states, rebels hoped for a united Germany.

At first, the revolutions caught Europe's rulers by surprise. Many monarchs granted concessions to the rebels. Even Prussia's King Frederick William IV agreed to the election of a democratic parliament. He also agreed to support an all-German parliament that would meet in Frankfurt. Hungary and several states in northern Italy won temporary freedom from Austria.

The Austrian empire seemed to be falling apart. After 30 years as Europe's most powerful political figure, Metternich resigned. As he left Vienna for exile in Britain, he told a friend, "Everything is finished."

Everything was not finished, however. As spring turned to summer, the revolutionaries seemed to run out of steam. The rebels shared the common aim of overthrowing the conservative order, but they disagreed strongly over what to do next. Meanwhile, the rulers regained their courage. With the strength of their armies behind them, they began a counterrevolution. German princes called their representatives home from Frankfurt, and the all-German parliament vanished almost as suddenly as it had appeared. Elsewhere, Austrian armies crushed the rebels in northern Italy and put down the revolt in Hungary. By 1849, Europe had practically returned to its pre-1848 status.

On the surface, therefore, the revolutions of 1848 brought about little reform. However, the forces of change had not been destroyed, only contained. The demands for independence and an end to the old empires would be heard again and again.

France again overthrew its king.

Radicals were involved in many of the 1848 revolts, but only in France was the demand for democratic government the main point of revolution. Only in France—particularly in Paris—were radicals the moving force behind revolution.

During the late 1840's, King Louis Philippe turned a deaf ear to demands that the Chamber of Deputies be made more democratic. "Get rich by work, and you will have the vote," his chief minister scornfully told the working classes.

Paris rose up against the king in February 1848. Louis Philippe's government collapsed almost overnight. It was replaced by a temporary government led by Alphonse de Lamartine (lahm-ahr-TEEN), one of France's leading romantic poets. "Down with royalty!" shouted the Paris mob.

Lamartine and his colleagues declared France a republic once more.

Things went sour for the new republican government almost from the start. A quarrel split the radicals into factions. One side, led by Lamartine, wanted only political reform. The other, led by Louis Blanc, wanted economic reform as well. Blanc's group demanded that the government set up national workshops to make jobs for the unemployed. Such workshops were indeed set up in Paris, but Lamartine's government soon closed them. This order led to bloody street battles in Paris. More than 10,000 workers were killed before the government subdued the rebels.

A new Napoleon came to power.

The violence turned France against the radicals toward a more moderate, liberal government. The new constitution drawn up later in 1848 called for a parliament and a strong president elected by the people.

France held a presidential election in December 1848, and the winner was none other than Louis Napoleon Bonaparte. Nephew of the great emperor, Louis Napoleon lacked his uncle's intelligence and strength of character. However, he had a name that French voters linked with past glories. "How could I help voting for this gentleman," said one old man in 1851, "I whose nose was frozen at Moscow?"

Louis Napoleon won widespread support from the peasants, who resented the dominance of Paris in French politics and wanted peace and order. Nationalists saw in him a man who could unite all of the country's political factions. Thus, a second Bonaparte came to power swearing to "remain faithful to the democratic Republic and to defend the Constitution."

Like his uncle, Louis Napoleon soon broke that oath. In December 1851, he dissolved the French parliament and declared himself sole ruler of France. Remarkably, an election held later that month (in which all French men had the right to vote) approved his deed by an overwhelming 92 percent. Adopting his uncle's constitution, Louis Napoleon then took the title Emperor Napoleon III.

Why did the French people accept this coup? Louis himself gave perhaps the best explanation: "The Empire means peace. It means peace because France wishes it, and when France is satisfied, the world is quiescent [quiet]."

From his exile in London, the 78-year-old Metternich was puzzled by events in France. Louis Napoleon's success seemed to break all the political rules that Metternich knew. How could a conservative, absolutist monarch come to power in a democratic election? It seemed impossible. Said Metternich:

He must choose between grasping the reins of government either as heir of Napoleon the First or as one elected by universal suffrage. He will destroy himself upon this contradiction.

Time proved Metternich wrong. Napoleon III governed France for the next 20 years.

The times had changed. The rules of politics were changing too. Over the next century, other absolute rulers would come to power through the ballot box. As we shall see, democracy proved to be a form of government that could destroy itself.

Section Review 4

Define: (a) counterrevolution, (b) coup
Identify: (a) Charles X, (b) Louis Philippe, (c) Reform Bill of 1832, (d) 1848, (e) Lamartine, (f) Blanc, (g) Louis Napoleon
Answer:
1. (a) What brought on the French revolt of 1830? (b) What were its results?
2. Explain two ways that the Reform Bill of 1832 broadened the right to vote in Great Britain.
3. What goals did the revolutionaries of 1848 have in each of the following places? (a) France (b) Hungary (c) the German states
4. (a) What did the revolutions of 1848 achieve at first? (b) What happened in the counterrevolution?
5. (a) How did Louis Philippe fall from power? (b) What problems did the new French government face?
6. How did Louis Napoleon become emperor?

Critical Thinking
7. (a) What contradiction did Metternich think would lead to Napoleon III's downfall? (b) Could a leader follow such a path to power today? Explain your answer.

Summary

1. European leaders sought stability. In 1815, representatives from Europe met in Vienna to make a peace settlement. Led by Metternich, they restored former monarchies, blocked France from expanding, and established a balance of power. Many parts of the settlement were opposed by middle-class liberals and by radicals.

2. New ideals affected politics and art. After 1815, European politics were heavily influenced by nationalism, particularly in countries that were divided or ruled by foreign powers. Nationalism was closely linked to romanticism, which glorified emotion, nature, heroic individuals, and the past.

3. Latin America won independence. The early 1800's saw a series of wars for independence throughout Latin America. In Haiti, slaves revolted against France and set up an independent country. Bolívar and San Martín led independence movements in South America. In Mexico, Indians and mestizos played a large part in the war for independence. Brazil won independence peacefully. Although free, Latin American countries were still dominated by a small wealthy class. Many countries fell under military rule. Independence was aided by the Monroe Doctrine.

4. Reform and revolution swept Europe. In Britain, reforms expanded voting rights. Elsewhere in Europe, however, nationalism and the desire for reform led to revolt. France overthrew one king in 1830 but remained a monarchy. In 1848, a wave of revolts swept Europe but were soon put down. Radical demands for reform in France led to the establishment of a republic, but violence soon turned people against the new government.

Reviewing the Facts

1. Define the following terms:
   a. nation-state
   b. caudillo
2. Explain the importance of each of the following names, dates, places, or terms:

   a. Congress of Vienna
   b. 1815
   c. Metternich
   d. conservative
   e. liberal
   f. radical
   g. nationalism
   h. Mazzini
   i. German Confederation
   j. romanticism
   k. L'Ouverture
   l. Bolívar
   m. San Martín
   n. Battle of Ayacucho
   o. Dom Pedro
   p. Hidalgo
   q. Morelos
   r. Monroe Doctrine
   s. Reform Bill of 1832
   t. 1848
   u. Louis Napoleon

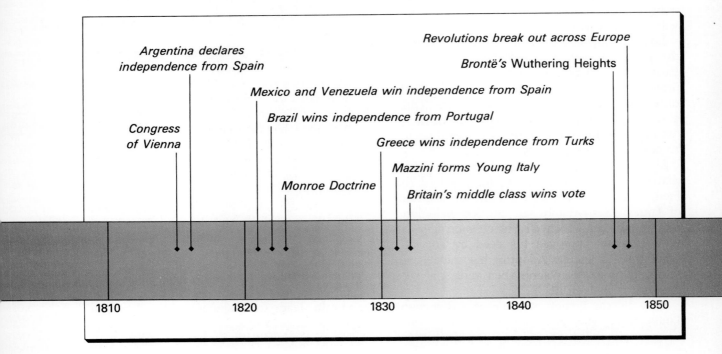

Argentina declares independence from Spain

Revolutions break out across Europe

Brontë's *Wuthering Heights*

Mexico and Venezuela win independence from Spain

Congress of Vienna

Brazil wins independence from Portugal

Greece wins independence from Turks

Mazzini forms *Young Italy*

Monroe Doctrine

Britain's middle class wins vote

1810   1820   1830   1840   1850

3. (a) What were Metternich's goals at the Congress of Vienna? (b) How was each met?
4. (a) How did Britain's government differ from governments in eastern Europe? (b) How was France's government different from both?
5. Describe characteristics of a nation-state.
6. (a) How were nationalist goals achieved in Greece? (b) How were they blocked in Italy and the German states?
7. Describe four characteristics of romanticism.
8. (a) What was the first Latin American country to become independent? (b) How did it do so?
9. (a) What group took the lead in demanding independence in most of Latin America? (b) Why?
10. (a) Describe Bolívar's achievements in South America. (b) Describe San Martín's.
11. How did Brazil become independent?
12. (a) Briefly describe the war for independence in Mexico. (b) How did it differ from revolts in South America?
13. (a) What stand did the United States take in the Monroe Doctrine? (b) Why did both the United States and Great Britain support this doctrine?
14. What were the effects of the Reform Bill of 1832 in Great Britain?
15. What was the result of the French revolt of 1830?
16. How did the events of 1848 help Louis Napoleon win power?

Thinking about History

1. Metternich said, "The first and greatest concern for the immense majority of any nation is the stability of laws — never their change." How might the following leaders have reacted to this statement: an Egyptian pharaoh; Socrates; Octavian (Augustus); Tokugawa Ieyasu of Japan; Elizabeth I of England; Oliver Cromwell; Philip II of Spain; Louis XIV of France; Peter I of Russia; Catherine II of Russia.
2. Explain how the Industrial Revolution and the French Revolution helped the middle class become a power in politics.
3. One of Bolívar's dreams was a united Latin America. Compare the characteristics of a nation-state to the independent Latin American countries. Why did Bolívar's dream fail to come true?

Writing and Speaking about History

1. Write a paragraph that supports this thesis: "The

Congress of Vienna restored the Old Order."
2. Write a feature story in which you discuss the role of Simón Bolívar and José San Martín in liberating South America.
3. As President James Monroe, you are preparing your annual state of the union message. In your speech, you wish to focus on your reasons for issuing the Monroe Doctrine. What will you say?

Practicing Skills

1. Prepare a bibliography card on this textbook as if it were the source for a research paper. (See Research Skills Handbook, page 578.)
2. As the researcher for a paper titled "The Congress of Vienna was a political triumph," prepare five information note cards from pages 491 through 494 of the text.
3. Compare the map of Latin America in 1800 (page 502) with a present-day map of the region. (a) What present-day country or countries lie in the region that was once under Dutch control? (b) Under Portuguese control? (c) Under French control?
4. Review the timeline on page 508. (a) Which events on the timeline have to do with independence movements in Latin America? (b) With nationalistic movements in Europe?

Investigating History

1. The work of many great musicians spanned the period from 1800 to 1848. Among them were Ludwig von Beethoven, Johann Strauss, Frederic Chopin, Franz Liszt, Giuseppe Verdi, Robert Schumann, and Felix Mendelssohn. Research the life of two of these composers. How was each influenced by events of the period?
2. In addition to the national leaders mentioned in the chapter, many other Latin Americans contributed to the independence movement. Among them were Francisco Miranda, Jean Jacques Dessalines, Bernardo O'Higgins, and Antonio José de Sucre. Research the life of one of these men. What part did he play in the struggle for independence?

Decision Making in History

As a close friend to Mazzini, you have been requested to prepare a briefing on the pros and cons of Italian unification. What obstacles do you see? What courses of action do you recommend?

Economic Expansion and Nationalism

The skill of Britain's ironworkers and engineers showed in the towering iron framework of the Crystal Palace. This building housed the Great Exhibition of 1851, a display of inventions and products from around the world.

1. **Industrialism created a global economy.**

2. **Working people gained more influence.**

3. **Italy and Germany formed nations.**

4. **The United States spread westward.**

It was May 1, 1851—a date thousands of British people had been eagerly awaiting for months. By noon, more than 500,000 people had gathered in London's Hyde Park to witness the opening of the Great Exhibition. On display were arts, crafts, and inventions from all over the world. This exhibit was, in many ways, the first world's fair.

The 25,000 people lucky enough to have tickets for the opening ceremonies were crammed inside the Crystal Palace. This remarkable building had been designed especially for the exhibition. It looked like a gigantic greenhouse. More than 1 million square feet of glass on a framework of bare iron formed its walls and roof. The main hall was as long as six football fields and high enough to house several fully grown elm trees.

Promptly at noon, a flourish of trumpets announced the arrival of Queen Victoria and the royal family. Although the queen's political power was limited, her symbolic importance as head of the British empire was immense. During her long reign (1837–1901), Victoria skillfully used ceremonial occasions such as this exhibition to foster national spirit.

Prince Albert, Victoria's German-born husband, stood proudly by her side. He was an intelligent, energetic man who was fiercely devoted to his adopted country. The Great Exhibition had been his idea, a way of showing the world the awesome power of the British empire. It would also, Albert said, "give us a living picture of the point of development at which the whole of mankind has arrived."

Visitors to the Great Exhibition exclaimed over stuffed elephants from India, fine lace from Spain, diamonds from the Netherlands, cigars from Cuba, perfumes from Turkey, cannons from Germany, birchbark canoes from Canada, and porcelain from China and France.

Exhibit after exhibit showed the strength of British industry. Among the wonders on display were a printing press that could turn out 5,000 newspapers per hour and a locomotive engine that could pull a train at 60 miles per hour. While the Great Exhibition celebrated the height of civilization to which the "whole of mankind" had risen, it left no doubt as to which country was in the lead. More than half the exhibits came from Great Britain and its territories.

Many of the 6 million visitors felt that the Great Exhibition marked the dawn of a new age of progress. Indeed, the years after the Great Exhibition were a period of tremendous economic growth. Perhaps the most striking advances during this time were in travel and communications. Railroads, steamships, and the telegraph made the world seem smaller than ever before. News, goods, and people traveled faster.

People responded to the spread of industrialism in a variety of ways. Some groups demanded a new division of wealth, with equal shares for all. Others believed that the path to a better future lay in building strong nation-states. In Europe, nationalism led to the birth of two new nation-states, Germany and Italy. In North America, the United States added new lands and grew to be an industrial power.

Industrialism created a global economy. 1

The people who visited the Great Exhibition of 1851 lived in a world that their grandparents could not have imagined. It was a world of booming factories, speeding trains, and mile-long bridges. Above all, it was a world of change.

The pace of industrialization continued to quicken. In 1858, a German economist wrote, "Railroads and machine shops, coal mines and iron foundries, spinneries and rolling mills seem to spring up out of the ground, and smokestacks sprout from the earth like mushrooms." Between 1850 and 1875, coal production in Germany grew from 6 million tons to 35 million tons per year. During the same years, the total world output of coal nearly tripled. The world output of iron increased fourfold.

Because factory-made goods cost less than handmade items, mass-produced items found their way into every home. Thus, the demand for manufactured goods skyrocketed along with the supply of such goods.

Finally, the great boom brought a tremendous increase in world trade. Between 1850 and 1870, the value of goods bought and sold among countries increased by a staggering 260 percent. In other words, world trade more than tripled during these 20 years. Trade increased more rapidly during this period than at any other time in history.

Steam revolutionized transportation.

By 1850, the same changes that had swept Great Britain in the early 1800's were happening on a global scale. Leading the way were advances in transportation and communication.

The growth of railroads The late 1800's were a golden age for railroad builders. They laid thousands of miles of new track every year, spanning rivers with iron bridges and carving tunnels through mountains. Between 1850 and 1880, the length of railroad track in the world grew from 23,600 miles to 228,400 miles—almost the distance from Earth to the moon!

Although most railroad building took place in Europe and North America, the "iron horse" soon reached every inhabited continent. By 1875, even

Riverboats used steam power to turn huge paddle wheels at the side or rear. Sometimes the boats stoked their engines to race along the Mississippi.

such nonindustrial countries as Brazil and Egypt had more than 1,000 miles of track. Swashbuckling railroad tycoons such as the Englishman Thomas Brassey became giants of industry. At one time, Brassey employed 80,000 workers and was building railroads on 5 continents.

Railroads boosted trade and industry wherever they spread. The iron and coal industries grew to meet the railroads' endless need for tracks, trains, and fuel. Other industries flourished as railroads brought them raw materials and carried their finished products to market.

Steamships Meanwhile, similar changes were taking place with water transportation. In 1807, an American named Robert Fulton designed the first practical steamboat. By the 1840's, more than 500 steamboats were chugging up and down the Mississippi River.

For ocean crossings, the changeover from wind power to steam power was slow. Early steamships needed to stop for fuel too often to make ocean travel practical. In 1850, only 5 percent of all oceangoing ships used steam power. By 1870, however, that figure had grown to 40 percent.

Breakthroughs in transportation Two celebrations in 1869 highlighted the dramatic advances in transportation. One took place in the United States and the other in Egypt.

On May 10, a crowd gathered in a lonely part of Utah to celebrate the opening of the first transcontinental railroad. At Promontory Point, a work crew laying track from the east met the crew laying track from the west. Amid cheers and brass bands, officials hammered a golden spike to mark the meeting place. On the new railroad, travelers could journey from Boston to San Francisco in less than a week.

Six months later, on November 17, a parade of 69 ships sailed out of the harbor of Port Said, Egypt. Led by the yacht of France's Empress Eugenie, the ships sailed southward through the just-completed Suez Canal. This 100-mile canal, planned by French businessman Ferdinand de

Footnote to History

In 1872, French writer Jules Verne published a novel called *Around the World in Eighty Days.* Just 20 years earlier, the journey would have taken about 11 months. Real-life travelers would not have shared all the adventures of Verne's hero, who fought off an Indian attack in the United States and rescued a princess in India. However, travelers *could* have made the trip in the same time. The novel was based on actual railroad and steamship schedules.

Lesseps, linked the Mediterranean and Red seas. No longer did ships from Europe have to go around Africa to reach Asia. The canal shortened the travel time between Europe and India by at least one month.

The telegraph speeded communication.

Trains and steamships carried letters, newspapers, and other kinds of information. However, by the mid-1800's, the field of communications was already far ahead of transportation in terms of speed. The telegraph could send information at the speed of electricity.

Electricity had fascinated the scientists in the Age of Enlightenment (page 431). During the 1840's, several inventors made telegraph systems using wires that carried low-voltage currents. The most successful telegraph was invented by an American artist, Samuel F.B. Morse. His system used a key (which looked something like a stapler) to make and break an electric circuit. Morse developed a code in which short bursts of current (dots) and longer bursts (dashes) stood for letters.

By 1850, all the major cities in the eastern United States were connected by telegraph lines. In 1851, a telegraph cable was laid under the English Channel to connect London and Paris. In 1866, the first successful transatlantic cable was completed, linking Newfoundland and Ireland. By 1875, it was possible to send messages around the world—from London to Calcutta, from New York to Melbourne, from Paris to Tokyo—in less than five minutes.

Business leaders formed corporations.

As world trade and industry expanded so did the size of businesses. Building transcontinental railroads and telegraph systems took a huge supply of money for investment, or capital. Many entrepreneurs needed help in raising the capital to start their businesses. To raise this money, an entrepreneur could sell shares of **stock** in the new company. Everyone who bought stock became a part-owner of the business.

By the mid-1800's, most major companies had thousands of owners. For example, Ferdinand de Lesseps set up a corporation to raise money to build the Suez Canal. He sold nearly 400,000 shares, which were purchased by several governments and more than 20,000 individuals. Many new railroads were financed in the same way.

If a company did well, stockholders stood to make money in two ways. First, each stockholder shared in the company's profits in proportion to the amount of stock he or she owned. Second, stockholders could often sell their shares of stock at a higher price than they had paid for them, because other people were eager to own a share of a thriving business.

On the other hand, if the company did poorly, stockholders might lose the money they had invested. However, they could never lose more than they had originally paid for the stock. According to new laws that were passed in all the industrial countries, stockholders were not personally responsible for the debts of companies in which they held stock.

Businesses organized in this new way were called **corporations**. Countless businesses formed corporations and added the term *incorporated* (in the United States) or *limited liability* (in Great Britain) to their names.

Businesses were soon operating on a larger scale than ever before. Some corporations were so successful that they drove nearly all their rivals out of business. For example, American John D. Rockefeller began his rise to wealth by building an oil refinery in 1863. His business incorporated as the Standard Oil Company of Ohio in 1870. Soon Rockefeller owned not only oil refineries but also oil wells, oil pipelines, and oil sales agencies. He controlled every step of the business from the ground to the customer. By the 1880's, Standard Oil was the only major oil company in the United States. When a single company controls an entire industry, the situation is called a **monopoly.** In the late 1800's, monopolies arose in many industries, both in the United States and in Europe.

Economic ties circled the globe.

The transportation revolution, the growth of trade, and the huge increase in industrial production brought countries around the world into closer contact than ever before. A shirt manufacturer in Britain, for example, could have 1,000 bales of cotton delivered from New Orleans to his factory in Manchester in 10 days. The finished shirts might be on sale in shops in Vienna and St. Petersburg three weeks after they left the factory.

Industrial countries depended on a steady stream of imports from many parts of the world. To keep their factories running, most industrial countries needed far more raw materials than they themselves could provide. As their cities swelled in size and population, most industrial countries also needed more food than they could grow. By 1875, for example, Britain imported more than 75 percent of the wheat its people consumed.

Much of this food and the resources for industry came from countries that had few factories of their own. In turn, those countries bought their manufactured goods from the industrial countries. The world was rapidly becoming interdependent.

The growth of a world economy brought risks along with benefits. In 1857, for example, the collapse of a major insurance company in the United States led to the failure of dozens of other businesses across the country. Within months, this financial crisis had shaken businesses in Britain, France, Argentina, and Australia. Such "crashes" took place repeatedly in the late 1800's. Crop failures or financial problems in one part of the world now had international impact.

People relocated in search of work.

As we saw in Chapter 22, the Industrial Revolution was accompanied by a population explosion. In 1850, about 266 million people lived in Europe. By the end of the century, the population had risen above 400 million, an increase of more than 50 percent. That figure would have been even larger if many Europeans had not left the continent for other lands.

The 1800's were marked by great shifts in population. Some parts of the world had large-scale **emigration**—that is, many people left those places to settle elsewhere. In other places, there was large-scale **immigration**—that is, many people settled in that area. Between 1850 and 1900, an estimated 25 million people sought to escape poverty or oppression by emigrating to the United States, Canada, South Africa, Australia, New Zealand, and Latin America.

The migration within Europe, as rural people flocked to the cities, was even greater. For every seven children born in the rural areas of western Europe after 1850, one stayed at home, one emigrated to another country, and five moved to cities in their own country. These massive shifts in population played a large part in the development of the modern world.

These immigrants faced a 250-mile trip down the North Saskatchewan River to their new home in Canada. Like many others, they hoped for a fresh start.

Section Review 1

Define: (a) stock, (b) corporation, (c) monopoly, (d) emigration, (e) immigration
Identify: (a) Great Exhibition, (b) Victoria, (c) Fulton, (d) Suez Canal, (e) Morse
Answer:
1. How did industrialization encourage the demand for goods?
2. (a) What changes occurred in transportation? (b) How did the growth of transportation affect other industries?
3. What changes took place in communications?
4. (a) How did entrepreneurs raise money for investment? (b) In what two ways could stockholders make money?
5. (a) What were the advantages of the increase in world trade? (b) What were the drawbacks of the world economy?
6. Briefly describe the major shifts in Europe's population in the late 1800's.

Critical Thinking
7. The text describes three ceremonial occasions—the Great Exhibition, the opening of the Suez Canal, and the driving of the golden spike at Promontory Point. (a) What was the significance of each for trade? (b) What do these celebrations suggest about the spirit of the age?

Working people gained more influence.

2

By 1850, some of the worst abuses of the Industrial Revolution were slowly being corrected. From a modern point of view, however, workers still had many grievances. A number of people tried to solve these problems in new ways.

At first, many reformers came from the middle and upper classes. For example, a few British aristocrats championed laws limiting child labor (page 485). Such upper-class reformers saw themselves as protecting the common people from the greed of the new entrepreneurs. In the late 1800's, however, working people themselves became more active in politics. Gradually, they made their voices heard.

During the 1800's, demands for reform grew louder. However, reformers often disagreed with one another on how to improve society.

Socialists planned to share wealth.

Industrial society "may truly be said to be a miserly, selfish system," wrote a British reformer named Robert Owen in 1857. "Under this system, to support life you must be tyrant or slave. It is all about individual wealth and power, with which the most successful are maintained with considerable hazard and gross injustice." A French writer, Pierre Joseph Proudhon (proo-DON), put it more simply. "Property," he said, "is theft."

The ideas of Owen, Proudhon, and similar thinkers came to be called **socialism**. Socialists believe that the wealth of a country should be shared equally among all its citizens. Under a socialist system, society as a whole owns most factories and businesses. Some socialists believe that there should be no private property at all.

Robert Owen tried to put his socialist ideals into practice. Owen began his working life as a shop clerk. By the time he was 30, he was the owner of a cotton mill with 2,000 employees at New Lanark, Scotland. Owen treated his workers well. He built houses near the factory and rented them to his employees at low rates. He did away with child labor, giving his workers' children free schooling instead.

New Lanark prospered, but Owen's later attempts to set up socialist villages failed. His most ambitious experiment was the cooperative village of New Harmony, Indiana, founded in 1825. It lasted only four years and then broke up from constant quarrels about the sharing of goods and profits.

Marx urged workers to revolt.

Robert Owen preached cooperation among social classes. A later socialist, Karl Marx (1818–1883), said that such cooperation was impossible. "The history of all . . . society is the history of class struggles," wrote Marx in 1848. "Freeman and slave, patrician and plebeian, lord and serf . . . stood in constant opposition to one another."

Marx called Owen and others like him *utopian socialists*. As you may recall, the word *utopia* means "nowhere" and was the title of a book

Karl Marx

describing an ideal society (page 346). Marx described his own ideas as *scientific socialism* because he claimed that they were based on the scientific study of history.

Marx was born in Germany in 1818. While a student, he became a radical activist and a journalist. Marx outlined his ideas in *The Communist Manifesto*, published in 1847. A short book, it sowed the seeds for several later revolutions. By 1848, Marx had been exiled from France, Belgium, and Germany. He finally found a haven in Britain, where he spent the rest of his life writing. His major work was *Das Kapital*, a three-volume study of economics and political power.

Marx's co-author for both the *Communist Manifesto* and *Das Kapital* was a fellow German socialist, Friedrich Engels (page 486). Engels came from a well-to-do family with international economic interests. Indeed, Marx and his family were so poor that they often depended on Engels for support.

Marx believed that economics was the key to understanding both the past and the present. Economic goals—the need for food, shelter, clothing, and other goods—were the forces that determined people's actions, said Marx. Thus, the most basic question in history was this: Who controls the means of producing goods? In a farming society, Marx reasoned, land was the most important source of wealth. Therefore, landowners dominated society and government. In an industrial society, factory owners had the greatest economic power. As a result, they soon won political power as well.

Marx said that work was the true source of all value. For example, the work of a shoemaker changed a piece of leather into a pair of shoes for which a buyer would pay money. Without the shoemaker, the leather had no value. According to Marx, workers were being cheated out of the wealth created through their efforts. Workers in a shoe factory got only part of the money for which each pair of shoes sold. The rest of the money went to the factory owner as profit.

According to Marx, the Industrial Revolution was making the rich richer and the poor poorer. Marx used the word *bourgeoisie* to describe the factory-owning middle class. These people were capitalists, people who invest money in businesses. Marx used the Latin word *proletariat* to describe the urban working class. These workers, said Marx, had nothing to sell but their labor. They had no choice but to work for whatever wages the bourgeoisie offered.

Sooner or later, Marx predicted, workers would join together to overthrow the bourgeoisie and establish a true socialist society. "Workers of the world, unite!" wrote Marx. "You have nothing to lose but your chains."

Despite Marx's predictions, however, workers showed little sign of rebelling. Except for a brief outburst in Paris in 1871 (page 524), there were no large workers' revolts in the late 1800's. Most workers did not want to overthrow the system but to share in its benefits.

Moreover, some of Marx's key ideas proved wrong. The gap between the rich and the poor did not widen as he had expected. The rich certainly got richer, but the lives of the poor also improved. The tremendous growth of trade and production brought benefits to almost everyone. Marx also underestimated the noneconomic forces that influence people. He ignored the importance of religion, nationalism, ethnic loyalties, and other ideals in people's lives.

Working men won the vote.

Although workers did not revolt, many did strive for changes in society. Brought together in factories, mines, and mills, workers soon saw that there was strength in numbers.

As you have read, workers began to form trade unions in the early 1800's (page 487). Trade unions did not try to remake society, as the socialists did. Instead, unions tried to raise wages and improve working conditions. By 1875, British trade unions had won the right to strike and picket peacefully and had built up a membership of 1 million people. In many other European countries, however, unions remained illegal.

The basis for workers' growing influence was the right to vote. The right to vote is often called **suffrage**. By the end of the 1800's, several industrial countries had universal manhood suffrage (the right of all adult men to vote). No country, however, allowed women to vote.

In the United States, nearly all adult white men had the right to vote by 1850. However, the great numbers of blacks who were slaves had no voting rights. In some places, free blacks had once had the right to vote, but it was taken away from them. As you will read later in this chapter, black men won the right to vote after the Civil War. It was many years, however, before either black or white women could vote.

In Great Britain, as you have read, the Reform Bill of 1832 (page 505) gave the vote to most men in the middle class. In 1867 and 1875, further reform bills gave the vote to nearly all men.

In France, Napoleon III (page 507) broadened voting rights during the 1850's and 1860's. In 1871, France became the first European country to allow universal manhood suffrage.

Realism replaced romanticism in art.

Just as the working class was becoming more important in politics, it was also becoming more visible in the arts. Artists and writers turned away from romantic, idealized views of the past and of nature. Instead, novels and paintings began to reflect the lives of ordinary people and current social issues. This new artistic approach is called realism. Realists tried to observe and report what they saw in a precise, objective fashion.

Realism in painting In 1855, artists in Paris held a grand exhibit of French paintings. The works on display were mainly romantic landscapes, formal portraits, battle scenes, and figures from ancient myths.

Just outside the exhibit hall, an artist named Gustave Courbet (koor-**BAY**) set up a large wooden shack labeled the Pavilion of Realism. The paintings within were all by Courbet and included a huge, stark funeral scene that had been turned

The realist painters emphasized everyday life, especially among the lower classes. This painting by Daumier shows travelers in a third-class railroad carriage. Compare it with the romantic painting on page 498.

down by the official exhibit. Realist painters such as Courbet scorned romantic art. Courbet called the romantics "painters of angels" and asked, "What do those look like? I've never had the luck to see one in the flesh."

Another outstanding artist of the realist school was Honoré Daumier (doh-MYAY). He became famous for his scathing pictures of what he saw as the pompous and self-satisfied middle class.

Realism in literature Realist authors turned to the novel as the form best suited to their goals. "The only reason for the existence of a novel," wrote American author Henry James, "is that it does attempt to represent life." Many European countries produced realist authors. France had Gustave Flaubert (floh-BAIR) and Honoré de Balzac (BAHL-zak). In Russia, there were Fyodor Dostoevsky (DAHS-tuh-YEF-skee) and Leo Tolstoy (tahl-STOY). William Thackeray, Charles Dickens, and Thomas Hardy wrote in Britain.

Section Review 2

Define: (a) socialism, (b) bourgeoisie, (c) proletariat, (d) suffrage, (e) realism
Identify: (a) Robert Owen, (b) Karl Marx
Answer:
1. (a) What were the general beliefs of socialists? (b) How did Marx's approach to socialism differ from Owen's?
2. Marx stressed the importance of work as the source of value. Explain what he meant.
3. (a) According to Marx, how did bourgeois business owners take advantage of workers? (b) What did he predict would happen? (c) Give two reasons why the events he predicted failed to occur.
4. How did trade unions increase the power of working people?
5. (a) Briefly describe how the right to vote grew broader in Europe and the United States.

Voice from the Past · *An Industrial City*

Charles Dickens was the most widely read of the English realists, largely because he mixed his realism with plenty of sentiment and melodrama. At the same time, he vividly reminded his readers that they lived in a world where much was grim, ugly, and unjust. Here is how he describes an industrial town in his 1854 novel, *Hard Times*.

It was a town of red brick, or of brick that would have been red if the smoke and ashes had allowed it; but, as matters stood, it was a town of unnatural red and black, like the painted face of a savage. It was a town of machinery and tall chimneys, out of which interminable [endless] serpents of smoke trailed themselves for ever and ever, and never got uncoiled. It had a black canal in it, and a river that ran purple with ill-smelling dye, and vast piles of buildings full of windows where there was a rattling and a trembling all day long, and where the piston of the steam-engine worked monotonously up and down, like the head of an elephant in a state of melancholy madness. It contained several large streets all very like one another, and many small streets still more like one another, inhabited by people equally like one another, who all went in and out at the same hours, with the same sound upon the same pavements, to do the same work, and to whom every day was the same as yesterday and tomorrow, and every year the counterpart of the last and the next.

1. Dickens uses strong sensory words. What adjectives relate to each of the following senses? (a) sight (b) hearing (c) smell
2. What real social problems does Dickens mention in this description?
3. (a) Which seems more alive and powerful, the city or the people in it? (b) How does Dickens create this impression?

(b) What groups were still denied the vote?

6. What new themes did art and literature begin to portray in the mid-1800's?

Critical Thinking

7. How might each of the following people have reacted to Proudhon's statement, "Property is theft"? (a) Robert Owen (b) Karl Marx (c) a trade unionist (d) a stockholder in a business

8. How was the change in socialist ideas from Owen to Marx similar to the change in literary styles during this period?

Italy and Germany formed nations. 3

Many early nationalists had been romantics like Byron and Mazzini. In politics as in art, however, realism was replacing romanticism. During the late 1800's, a new group of national leaders practiced what they called *realpolitik*. This German term meant "the politics of reality." People used the word to describe a tough, calculating brand of politics in which idealism played no part.

As nationalism grew in strength, it destroyed the balance of power that Metternich had so carefully set up in 1815. In France, Napoleon III was bent on reviving French glory. In Germany and Italy, people were determined to form united nation-states. Austria wanted to preserve its empire. These conflicting goals touched off five wars among the Great Powers between 1854 and 1871.

Cavour united Italy.

The Congress of Vienna left Italy divided and almost entirely under foreign control. In the north, Austria ruled Venetia and Lombardy and also dominated the small states of Tuscany, Modena, Parma, and Lucca. In the south, Spain ruled the Kingdom of the Two Sicilies (map, page 520).

During the fateful year of 1848, revolts broke out in eight separate states on the Italian peninsula. Giuseppe Mazzini, the early leader of Italian nationalism (page 496), briefly headed a republican government at Rome. However, the 1848 rebellions failed in Italy just as they did elsewhere in Europe. Within months, the former rulers of the Italian states returned and drove Mazzini and other nationalist leaders into exile.

After 1848, Italian nationalists looked to the Kingdom of Sardinia for leadership. Sardinia was the only Italian state ruled by an Italian dynasty. This kingdom included the Piedmont, Nice, and Savoy as well as the island of Sardinia. It was the largest and most powerful of the Italian states and had the most liberal government.

In 1852, Sardinia's King Victor Emmanuel II named Count Camillo di Cavour (kuh-VOOR) his prime minister. Cavour (1810–1861) was a wealthy aristocrat and a moderate nationalist. He made uniting Italy his highest priority.

Cavour considered Mazzini and the earlier nationalists vague and impractical. He believed that careful diplomacy and well-chosen alliances were more useful than grand proclamations and romantic rebellions. In turn, nationalists such as Mazzini called Cavour a "pale ghost of Machiavelli." They feared his main goal was not to unite Italy but to broaden the power of Sardinia.

An alliance with Napoleon III The greatest roadblock to Italian unity was Austria. Cavour knew that Sardinia was going to need help from another Great Power to drive Austria out of northern Italy.

Cavour found an ally in France. Napoleon III hoped to make France Europe's greatest power, as it had been under his uncle, Napoleon I. However, Napoleon III lacked his uncle's brilliance, and most of his schemes backfired.

Napoleon III believed that France could dominate Italy if Austria were out of the way. In 1858, the French emperor and Cavour had a secret meeting at which Napoleon agreed to help drive Austria out of Lombardy and Venetia. In return, Cavour promised to give France the border regions of Nice and Savoy.

Cavour soon provoked a war with Austria. A combined French-Sardinian army won two quick victories against the Austrians. Meanwhile, Italian nationalists staged revolts against Austria all across northern Italy. They demanded that Sardinia take over their lands.

A strong, united Italy was not what Napoleon III had expected. For a time, he considered going to war against Sardinia. However, Cavour had been careful to maintain good relations with the other Great Powers so that France was isolated.

The Unification of Italy, 1850–1870

KEY

- ▨ Kingdom of Sardinia, 1858
- ▨ Added to Sardinia, 1859-1860
- ▨ Added to Italy, 1866
- ▨ Added to Italy, 1870

0 — 100 Miles

Map Study

By skillful maneuvers, Cavour (above) led Italy to national unity. What border territories did he give up in 1860? What territory was the last to be added to Italy?

Napoleon backed down, accepting Nice and Savoy as Cavour had promised. In 1860, Sardinia annexed all of northern Italy except Venetia.

Garibaldi and the Red Shirts While Cavour was uniting the north, he was also secretly helping nationalist rebels in southern Italy. In May 1860, a small army of about 1,100 Italian nationalists sailed from Genoa to Sicily. They were led by a bold and romantic soldier, Giuseppe Garibaldi (GAR-uh-BAHL-dee). In battle, Garibaldi always wore a bright red shirt. Since his followers imitated him, they became known as the "Red Shirts."

Garibaldi was victorious in Sicily and began marching north. Volunteers flocked to his banner. Everywhere he was greeted as a liberator. Garibaldi spoke excitedly of freeing the rest of Italy, especially his beloved birthplace, Nice.

Now it was Cavour's turn to feel that his schemes had backfired. He had given Nice to France as a consolation prize, and he did not want to provoke Napoleon III again. "Garibaldi has become intoxicated with success," Cavour complained to an adviser. "He is planning the wildest schemes."

Knowing that war against France would lead to disaster, Cavour arranged for King Victor Emmanuel II to meet Garibaldi in Naples. "The Red One" willingly agreed to step aside and let the Sardinian king rule the areas he conquered.

In March 1861, an Italian parliament met at Turin and declared Victor Emmanuel II king of Italy. The new nation thus had a government headed by a constitutional monarch and an elected parliament.

A united Italy faced problems.

Worn out by years of work, Cavour died shortly after Victor Emmanuel II became king. He never saw his country fully united. Venetia did not become part of the new nation until 1866. In 1871, Italy took over the Papal States. Rome became the national capital of a united Italy.

(According to a treaty called the Law of Guarantees, the pope kept the section of Rome known as Vatican City.)

The movement of the capital to Rome was a triumphant moment for Italian nationalists. However, unification did not cure all the country's problems. Many centuries had passed since the peninsula had last been united, and fierce rivalries flared between different provinces. The greatest tension arose between the industrialized north and the agricultural south. The people of these two regions had very different ways of living. They scarcely understood each other's versions of the Italian language.

After Cavour's death, Italy lacked strong national leadership. Garibaldi tried to head a government, but he lacked the political skill. Within the Italian parliament, there were no well-organized parties with clear-cut policies. As a result, prime ministers and cabinets changed frequently.

Italy also faced severe economic problems. There were bloody peasant revolts in the south and strikes and riots in the northern cities. One result of Italy's problems was massive emigration, particularly from the south. Between 1860 and 1910, 4 million Italians moved to the United States and another 1 million went to Argentina. "I had hoped to evoke the soul of Italy," wrote the old patriot Mazzini shortly before his death in 1872, "but all I can see is a corpse."

Austria and Prussia were rivals.

Like Italy, Germany finally achieved unity in the mid-1800's. Since 1815, 39 German states had formed a German Confederation. The two largest states, Austria and Prussia, dominated this loose grouping.

Austria, earlier the home of the Holy Roman emperor, was still considered the natural leader of Germany. Vienna, Austria's capital, was an important cultural center for German music, art, and literature. However, Austria faced serious problems. Most of the people in the Austrian empire were non-Germans who yearned to break away. Austria also lagged behind Prussia in industrial development.

Prussia, on the other hand, had everything to gain from nationalism. It had a mainly German population. As early as 1834, Prussia had taken the lead by forming the Zollverein (TSOHL-vur-eyn), a free-trade area that included all the major German states except Austria. Prussia was also the most industrial of the German states. Moreover, Prussia's army was by far the most powerful in central Europe.

Prussia was a conservative state. Although most adult men could vote, the Prussian parliament had little control over policies. The king, William I of the Hohenzollern family, had almost unlimited power. His ministers and army officers all came from Prussia's wealthy landlord class, the junkers. Prussia's middle class, although wealthy, had little political influence.

In 1862, William I chose as his prime minister a junker and a staunch conservative named Otto von Bismarck (1815–1898). A master of realpolitik, Bismarck set out to make Prussia the head of a united Germany. He saw Austria as Prussia's major rival. "Germany," he said, "is clearly too small for us both."

Bismarck had only contempt for the liberals who had led the movement for German unity in 1848. In his first speech as prime minister, he told the Prussian parliament, "The great questions of our day cannot be solved by speeches and majority votes—that was the great mistake of 1848 and 1849—but by blood and iron."

Bismarck united Germany by blood and iron.

In 1864, Bismarck took the first step toward increasing Prussian power. He led Prussia into war against Denmark to win two border provinces, Schleswig and Holstein. The quick victory increased national pride among Prussians and won Prussia new respect from other Germans.

The Seven Weeks' War In 1866, Bismarck purposely provoked Austria into declaring war on Prussia. This conflict was known was the Seven Weeks' War. As the name suggests, the war was quickly over. Thanks to Prussia's efficient railroad network, Prussian generals could move their troops to the battlefield more quickly than Austrian leaders could. Once there, the Prussians used their superior training and equipment to win one smashing victory after another.

Austria was humiliated. It lost some German lands to Prussia. It also lost Venetia to Italy, which had fought alongside Prussia. Worst of all,

The Unification of Germany, 1865–1871

DENMARK

SCHLESWIG

HOLSTEIN

MECKLENBURG

Baltic Sea

Memel

North Sea

OLDENBURG

Hamburg

BRANDENBURG

• Berlin

WEST PRUSSIA

EAST PRUSSIA

RUSSIAN

EMPIRE

• Warsaw

NETHERLANDS

H A N O V E R

Oder River

Niemen River

Vistula River

WESTPHALIA

Ruhr River

Rhine River

Elbe River

SAXONY

SILESIA

BELGIUM

HESSE

Ems

• Frankfort

BOHEMIA

• Prague

LUX

Sedan •

BAVARIA

AUSTRIAN

LORRAINE

Danube

WÜRTTEMBURG
HOHENZOLLERN

River

Vienna •

FRANCE

ALSACE

• Munich

EMPIRE

ITALY

KEY

Prussia, 1865

Annexed by Prussia, 1866

Joined Prussia in North German Confederation, 1867

South German States (joined Prussia to form German empire, 1871)

Conquered from France, 1871

—— German empire, 1871

0   100 Miles

Adriatic Sea

Map Study

Prussia's chancellor, Otto von Bismarck (right), created a united German empire under Prussian leadership. When did Prussia take over Hanover? Saxony and Mecklenburg? What were some of the German states that joined with Prussia to form the German empire in 1871? What territories were conquered from France?

Austria was forced to withdraw from the German Confederation.

Prussia now took control of northern Germany. For the first time, the eastern and western parts of the Prussian kingdom were joined. In 1867, the remaining states in the north joined the North German Confederation, which Prussia dominated completely.

Reeling from this defeat, the Austrian empire set out to rebuild its strength. The empire's biggest problem was the discontent of the many nationalities it ruled. The Hungarians, who had rebelled in 1848, were the largest of these groups. They wanted more independence.

In 1867, Austria agreed to a *dual monarchy.* Austria and Hungary became two independent and equal states with one ruler. Each state had its own parliament and officials. The two states still had a united army, however, and they acted as one in foreign policy. The new empire was known as Austria-Hungary.

The Franco-Prussian War By 1867, only a few southern German states remained independent of Prussia. Because most people in southern Germany were Catholics, they did not want to be dominated by Prussia, which was largely Protestant. However, Bismarck felt certain he could win their support if they faced a threat from outside Germany. He believed his best chance was to provoke a war with France.

Napoleon III of France, whose clumsy diplomacy had helped Cavour unite Italy, soon gave Bismarck a chance to win southern Germany. In 1868, Spanish revolutionaries overthrew Spain's Queen Isabella II and offered the throne to Leopold of Hohenzollern, a distant cousin of Prussia's William I. Napoleon III protested, as he did not want France surrounded by Hohenzollern rulers. The Prussian prince turned down the Spanish offer, but tensions remained high.

During this crisis, the French ambassador met with the Prussian king. Bismarck deliberately gave German newspapers a misleading account of the two men's conversation. Bismarck made it sound as if the king and the ambassador had insulted each other.

As Bismarck hoped, this news story caused an uproar. Soon public opinion in both countries demanded war. On July 15, 1870, France declared war on Prussia.

The Prussian army struck at once. Before most French soldiers had even left their hometowns, Prussian troops poured into northern France. In September 1870, the Prussian army surrounded the main French force at Sedan. Among the 100,000 French prisoners was Napoleon III himself, a beaten and broken man.

Only the city of Paris held out against the Germans. For four months, Parisians withstood a German siege. Finally, hunger forced them to surrender.

France was crushed. It had to pay Prussia the huge sum of 5 billion francs. As an even greater blow to French pride, France had to give Prussia the two border provinces of Alsace and Lorraine, which contained France's richest coal and iron deposits.

The Franco-Prussian War was the final step in German unification. Now people in southern Germany as well as those in the north were caught up in nationalistic fever. Despite their earlier doubts, they accepted Prussian leadership.

The Second Reich On January 18, 1871, at the conquered French palace of Versailles, King William I of Prussia was crowned *kaiser* (KYE-zuhr), or emperor, of the newly formed German empire. To Germans, the empire was known as the Second Reich (ryke). (They considered the Holy Roman Empire the First Reich.) Bismarck became the new nation's first prime minister.

The new German nation had a solid economic foundation. By 1870, Germany was the world's third biggest producer of manufactured goods, after Britain and the United States. After unification, German industry grew even faster. Soon it overtook Britain.

Footnote to History

Food was so scarce in besieged Paris that people ate sawdust, leather, and rats. Even the animals in the Paris zoo were slaughtered for food by starving Parisians.

France formed the Third Republic.

In the aftermath of the Franco-Prussian War, France went through a series of crises. After being released by Prussia, Napoleon III spent his last years in exile in Britain. France's National Assembly met to decide on a new government.

Meanwhile, in March 1871, a radical government called the Paris Commune took control of Paris. Once again, Paris faced war, this time a war against France's own National Assembly. When the assembly's troops marched into the city, Parisian workers threw up barricades in the streets and fought block by block. Thousands died, and much of the city burned. In May 1871, the National Assembly defeated the last Communards, as supporters of the Commune were called. The following week, more than 20,000 Parisians were executed.

Not until 1875 could the National Assembly agree on a new government. Eventually, the members voted to set up a republic. In the words of a leading French politician, it was "the system of government that divides us least." The Third Republic, as this new system was called, lasted nearly 60 years. However, France remained bitterly divided, with a dozen political parties jockeying for power. Between 1871 and 1914, France averaged a change of government every ten months.

Despite these divisions, the French were united in their hatred of Germany. Nearly all French people agreed that France must regain Alsace and Lorraine. As French political leader Léon Gambetta declared, "We shall demand each day before Europe our rights and our ravished provinces. France is at the mercy of Germany. We are in a state of latent war; neither peace or freedom nor progress is any longer possible in Europe."

The balance of power broke down.

For 40 years after the Congress of Vienna in 1815, the countries of Europe had remained at peace with one another. The first crack in the peace settlement had come with the Crimean (krye-MEE-uhn) War in 1853. That war pitted Britain and France against Russia. These three countries had competing interests in the Ottoman empire, now weak and crumbling. In a pointless struggle, British and French armies attacked the Crimea, a Russian peninsula in the Black Sea. Although the Crimean War cost the lives of 500,000 men, it was fought far from most European capitals. It did not lead to general warfare in Europe. Its most important result was to reveal the military weakness of the huge but backward Russian empire.

The first battles after 1815 to strike close to home were the wars of Italian and German unification. However, these wars were short, and many countries took no part in them. Europe had not known a major war since the fall of Napoleon.

Meanwhile, the political situation in Europe had changed greatly since 1815. At the Congress of Vienna, there had been five Great Powers—Britain, France, Austria, Prussia, and Russia. The wars of the late 1800's changed one Great Power, as Prussia became Germany, and added a sixth, Italy.

In 1815, all the Great Powers had been fairly equal in strength. By 1871, however, Britain and

Daily Life · *Balloons in War*

When Prussian troops surrounded Paris in 1870, French political leader Léon Gambetta was desperate to escape. If only he could get out of the city, he hoped to raise new armies to defend France. Gambetta took the only way not blocked by the Prussians—he left Paris by balloon. More than 160 other people did the same. During the four months of the siege, balloons also carried ten tons of mail in and out of Paris.

For a brief period, balloons were very important in war. During the United States Civil War, the North used its balloon corps to observe enemy troops and direct cannon fire. After the Franco-Prussian War, many countries added balloon corps to their armies.

Germany were clearly the strongest, both economically and militarily. Austria, Russia, and Italy lagged far behind. France struggled along somewhere in between. The balance of power had broken down, and the risk of a major war was increasing.

It is no coincidence that Britain and Germany, the two countries with the greatest military power, were also the industrial leaders. The Industrial Revolution had military as well as economic impact. In war, industrial countries had enormous advantages over nonindustrial countries. Victory usually went to the side with the most advanced weapons and the best transportation network.

As war became industrialized, it also became nationalized. France built a citizen-army during the French Revolution. By the end of the 1800's, all industrial countries relied on such armies.

Germany's military leader, Count Helmuth von Moltke, wrote:

> The days are gone by when, for dynastic ends, small professional armies went to war to conquer a city or a province. The wars of the present day call whole nations to arms. The entire financial resources of the state are appropriated to the purpose. In the interest of humanity, it is to be hoped that wars will become less frequent, as they have become more terrible.

Section Review 3

Define: (a) realpolitik, (b) junker, (c) dual monarchy, (d) kaiser
Identify: (a) Mazzini, (b) Cavour, (c) Victor Emmanuel II, (d) Napoleon III, (e) Garibaldi, (f) Bismarck, (g) Zollverein, (h) Seven Weeks' War, (i) Franco-Prussian War, (j) Second Reich, (k) Third Republic
Answer:
1. What made Sardinia the leader in the Italian nationalist movement?
2. (a) Why did Cavour make an agreement with Napoleon III? (b) What were the terms? (c) What were the results?
3. (a) How was the kingdom of Italy established? (b) What additional territories were joined to it later?

4. What problems did the united Italy face?
5. Why did Prussia rather than Austria take the lead in uniting Germany?
6. Briefly describe the major steps that Bismarck took to unify Germany.
7. What lasting effect did the Franco-Prussian War have on relations between France and Germany?
8. What political problems did France face under the Third Republic?
9. How had the balance of power in Europe changed since 1815?

Critical Thinking
10. (a) In what ways were the unification of Italy and Germany alike? (b) How was the outcome different for the two countries? Explain.

The United States spread westward. 4

Across the Atlantic Ocean from Europe, another country was also establishing itself as a nation. When the United States of America declared its independence in 1776, all 13 states lay along the Atlantic coast. By the time the nation celebrated its hundredth birthday in 1876, its borders had reached the Pacific coast. To unite this territory, Americans fought bitter wars with the Indians and with Mexico. The bloodiest war of all on the path to nationhood, however, was a war the people of the United States fought among themselves. It is known as the Civil War (1861–1865). Within ten years after the Civil War, it was clear that the United States was on its way to becoming a world power to rival Britain and Germany.

Americans moved westward.

At the end of the Revolutionary War, the Mississippi River marked the western boundary of the United States. Surprisingly, it was Napoleon who gave the United States its first chance to expand west of this river.

The Louisiana Purchase Ever since 1763, when Great Britain drove France out of North America, Spain had held the lands west of the Mississippi. Then in 1800, Spain made a secret treaty with

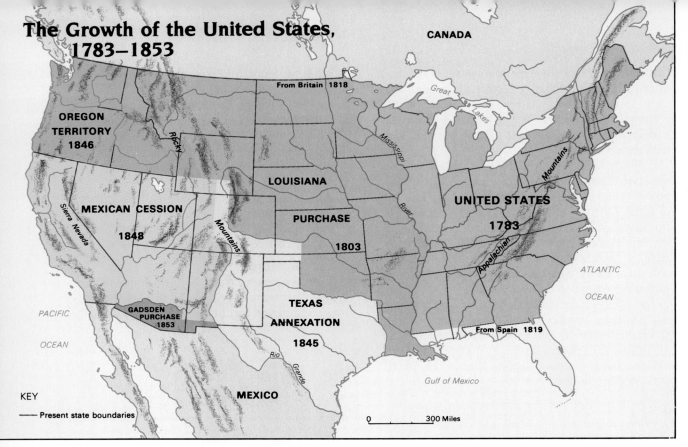

The Growth of the United States, 1783–1853

CANADA

OREGON TERRITORY 1846

From Britain 1818

Great Lakes

Rocky

Mississippi

Mountains

LOUISIANA

MEXICAN CESSION 1848

Sierra Nevada

Mountains

PURCHASE 1803

River

UNITED STATES 1783

Appalachian

ATLANTIC OCEAN

PACIFIC OCEAN

GADSDEN PURCHASE 1853

TEXAS ANNEXATION 1845

From Spain 1819

Rio Grande

Gulf of Mexico

MEXICO

KEY
—— Present state boundaries

0 _____ 300 Miles

Map Study

What was the first territory to be added to the United States after 1783? What lands were added between 1805 and 1840? Between 1840 and 1860?

Napoleon, giving those lands to France. The region was known as the Louisiana Territory.

Napoleon dreamed of building a French empire in the Americas as well as in Europe. However, as you read in Chapter 23, Toussaint L'Ouverture led a revolt against French rule in Haiti. Toussaint's fighters and yellow fever all but wiped out a French army of 10,000 soldiers. Discouraged, Napoleon gave up the idea of an American empire and decided to sell the Louisiana Territory. The United States, under President Thomas Jefferson, was eager to buy.

In 1803, the United States bought the entire territory—828,000 square miles—at the bargain price of $15 million. The cost came to about three cents per acre.

The war with Mexico For the next 40 years, the Rocky Mountains were the western boundary of the United States. Then, during the 1840's, a new idea took hold. Some Americans began to argue that the Pacific Ocean was the country's natural boundary.

The lands west of the Louisiana Territory belonged to Mexico, which had won its independence from Spain in 1821 (page 503). However, a number of people from the United States had settled in the area, with Mexico's acceptance. Some settlers were unhappy with Mexican rule.

The largest number of American settlers were in Texas. In 1836, Texans revolted against Mexican rule. For nine years, Texas was an independent country. Then, in 1845, it joined the United States.

Mexico was angered by the United States' decision to annex Texas. The two countries soon quarreled over the new state's southern boundary. Both sides sent troops into the disputed area near the Rio Grande. In 1846, there was a skirmish between Mexican and American soldiers. Within a few days, the United States Congress declared war on Mexico.

The war lasted from May 1846 to September 1847. American troops invaded Mexico and advanced on Mexico City. In bitter fighting, they

526

captured the city, and Mexico was forced to surrender. The United States won not only the western part of Texas but also all the land between the Rio Grande and Canada.

Just as the war began, people in California revolted against Mexico and set up their own republic. In the treaty that ended the war, California too became part of the United States.

Meanwhile, the United States had been negotiating with Great Britain over the Oregon Territory in the northwest. In 1846, the two countries agreed to set the northern boundary of the United States at 49° north latitude.

Conflict grew between North and South.

As people settled these western lands, questions arose over the laws and customs to be followed there. Ever since the nation's early days, the northern and southern parts of the United States had followed different ways of life. Each section wanted to extend its own way of life to the western lands.

The North had a diversified economy with both farms and industry. Northern farmers raised a variety of crops that fed the thriving northern cities. Mills and factories in the North competed with Britain in making cloth, shoes, iron, and machinery. For both its farms and factories, the North depended on free workers. Such workers could move from place to place to meet the needs of industry. They could also be laid off when business slumped.

The South depended on just a few cash crops, mainly cotton. To raise cotton, planters needed a large labor force year round. They relied on slave labor. Southerners traded their cotton for manufactured goods from Europe, especially Great Britain. The South had little industry of its own.

The economic differences between the two sections soon led to political conflicts. The bitterest of these conflicts arose over slavery. Many people in the North considered slavery morally wrong. They wanted laws that would outlaw slavery in the new western territories. Some wanted to abolish slavery altogether. Most white southerners believed slavery was necessary for their economy. They wanted laws to protect slavery in the west so that they could raise cotton on the fertile soil there.

Southerners feared the North's rising industrial power and growing population. Soon, they reasoned, the North would completely dominate the federal government. The election of 1860 seemed to confirm their worst fears. Abraham Lincoln, a northern candidate who opposed the spread of slavery, was elected president.

In the months after the election, 11 southern states made the fateful decision to withdraw from the United States. They established a separate nation called the Confederate States of America. On April 12, 1861, Confederate guns opened fire on Fort Sumter, a fort in South Carolina held by soldiers of the federal government.

The Civil War preserved the Union and ended slavery.

The Civil War lasted from 1861 to 1865. Counting losses on both sides, about 720,000 Americans died in the war. Many were killed in combat, but even more died of diseases such as yellow fever and dysentery that swept through army camps. No other war has taken so many American lives.

Clara Barton (1821–1912) helped the wounded in the American Civil War and the Franco-Prussian War. She founded the American Red Cross.

In part, the North and the South fought over their different views of the Union (the country as a whole). The South believed that the states had formed the Union. Therefore, said southerners, states were free to leave the Union if they wished to do so. Northerners believed that the Constitution of the United States had established the Union once and for all.

To European observers, it was clear that the struggle between North and South was a war for the survival of the United States. It was as much a war of nationalism as the conflict between Prussia and Austria over the future of Germany.

From the beginning of the war, President Abraham Lincoln was determined to preserve the Union. In his inaugural speech, Lincoln reminded his hearers that he had taken an oath to "preserve, protect, and defend" the Union.

Although Lincoln was deeply opposed to slavery, he said repeatedly that the purpose of the war was to save the Union and not to end slavery. Yet many northerners believed that the war was a crusade against slavery. Lincoln eventually decided that ending slavery would help to save the Union. In late 1862, he issued the Emancipation Proclamation, declaring that all slaves in the Confederate states were free.

At first, the proclamation freed no slaves, because the Confederate states did not accept it as law. As Union armies advanced into the South, however, they freed slaves in the lands they conquered. The Emancipation Proclamation also made clear to people in Europe that the war was being fought against slavery. The proclamation made many Europeans, especially the British, less sympathetic to the South. They did not send the money and supplies that the South had hoped they would.

The longer the war went on, the more important the North's advantages in population and industry became. Its bigger population allowed it to raise larger armies. Its factories and railroads kept those armies supplied.

Worn down by lack of food and supplies, the major Confederate army surrendered on April 8, 1865. The Civil War was over.

The Union had been preserved at a tremendous cost. In the aftermath of the war, Congress passed

Lincoln visited the Union army near Antietam, soon after the bloodiest battle of the war. He had just decided to issue the Emancipation Proclamation.

the Thirteenth Amendment to the Constitution. That amendment forever abolished slavery in all parts of the United States.

Industry developed rapidly.

After the war, the American economy expanded at a rate never before seen in the history of the world. There were three main reasons for this rapid growth. First, the United States had a wealth of raw materials. Second, it had a rapidly growing population to provide workers. (During the 1870's, immigrants arrived at the rate of nearly 2,000 a day.) Third, the nation had a democratic political system that put few restraints on its business development.

As early as 1870, the United States had 53,000 miles of railroad track and 5.5 million horsepower in steam engines, more than any other country in the world. American factories led the world in the production of clocks, rifles, sewing machines, and copper wire. American farms led world production of corn, wheat, cotton, and cattle. Never before had so much real and potential wealth been concentrated within one country.

The nation celebrated its first century.

Americans were proud of their country and its achievements. They celebrated its hundredth birthday in 1876 with a magnificent Centennial Exposition in Philadelphia. Like the British exhibition of 1851, this celebration drew visitors from all over the world.

The exposition stood in an enormous 400-acre park on the outskirts of Philadelphia. The main exhibition hall—the United States' answer to the Crystal Palace—covered more than 21 acres. At the time, it was the largest building in the world. Another enormous building, the Machine Hall, held mechanical marvels from all over the world. Among them were several "automatic-writing machines" (the first typewriters) and an amazing new invention that could transmit a human voice by wire. Its inventor, Alexander Graham Bell, called it the telephone.

In the Agriculture Hall, visitors could watch self-rising flour in action and marvel at Gail Borden's new product, canned condensed milk. Other buildings included a Shoe and Leather Hall, a glassworks, a butter and cheese factory, an art gallery, and a Women's Building. In this last building, among exhibits of embroidery, knitted work, and other domestic arts, there were also machines invented by women. These included a machine for washing blankets, a steam iron, and an early dishwashing machine.

Between May and November 1876, more than 9 million people attended the Centennial Exposition—more than had visited any previous world's fair. Most were Americans, of course, but those who came from abroad undoubtedly went away impressed. The United States had made remarkable progress during the 100 years since its founding. Over the next 50 years, it would take its place as a major power in the world.

Section Review 4

Define: (a) diversified economy, (b) cash crop
Identify: (a) Louisiana Purchase, (b) Abraham Lincoln, (c) Confederate States of America, (d) Civil War, (e) Emancipation Proclamation, (f) Thirteenth Amendment
Answer:
1. What part did Napoleon play in the expansion of the United States?
2. (a) How did Texas become part of the United States? (b) How did the annexation of Texas lead to war between the United States and Mexico? (c) What additional territories did the United States gain as a result?
3. How did the economies of the North and the South differ?
4. How was the issue of slavery related to the new western lands that the United States had gained?
5. How did the North and the South differ in their views of the Union?
6. (a) Briefly describe the political events that led to the outbreak of fighting. (b) What was the outcome of the war?
7. How was slavery ended in the United States?
8. What three factors promoted rapid industrial growth after the Civil War?

Critical Thinking
9. How might the Civil War be viewed as a conflict over nationalism?

Chapter Review 24

Summary

1. Industrialism created a global economy. Industry boomed in the mid-1800's. Railroads, the Suez Canal, and the development of steamships speeded transportation. The telegraph made global communication possible. Many businesses became corporations to get new funds for investment. Production and the demand for raw materials soared, causing the growth of worldwide trade. Industrialization also brought about great shifts in population.

2. Working people gained more influence. As industry spread, socialists urged equal distribution of wealth. While Robert Owen tried to set up cooperative villages, Karl Marx called for a revolt against capitalists. Workers made gains through trade unions, and working men won the right to vote in some countries. The working class also became more visible culturally as realism replaced romanticism.

3. Italy and Germany formed nations. Under the leadership of Cavour, Italy formed a united kingdom. Problems plagued the new nation, however. Guided by Bismarck, Prussia became the center of a new German nation after winning wars against Austria and France. The rise of Germany signaled the collapse of the balance of power in Europe.

4. The United States spread westward. During the 1800's, the United States bought the Louisiana Territory, annexed Texas and California, won vast lands from Mexico, and negotiated with Britain for the Oregon Territory. Conflict between the industrial North and the agricultural South led to a Civil War. The North's victory ended slavery. After the war, the economy of the United States grew rapidly.

Reviewing the Facts

1. Define the following terms:
a. stock
b. corporation
c. emigration
d. immigration
e. socialism
f. suffrage

2. Explain the importance of each of the following names, dates, places, or terms:
a. Victoria
b. Fulton
c. 1869
d. Morse
e. Owen
f. Marx
g. utopian socialism
h. scientific socialism
i. proletariat
j. realpolitik
k. Cavour
l. Garibaldi
m. Napoleon III
n. Bismarck
o. Seven Weeks' War
p. Franco-Prussian War
q. Louisiana Purchase
r. Lincoln
s. Civil War
t. Emancipation Proclamation
u. Bell

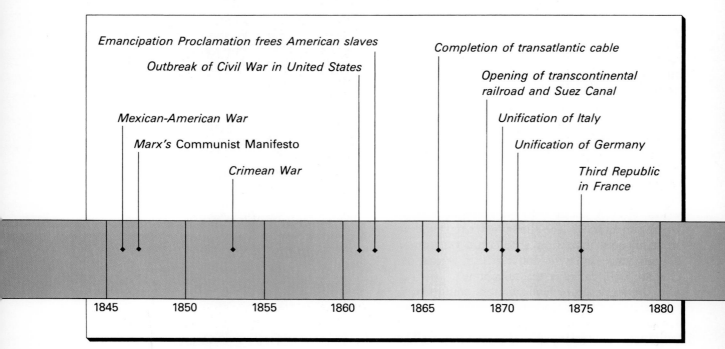

Emancipation Proclamation frees American slaves

Outbreak of Civil War in United States

Completion of transatlantic cable

Opening of transcontinental railroad and Suez Canal

Mexican-American War

Unification of Italy

Marx's Communist Manifesto

Unification of Germany

Crimean War

Third Republic in France

1845   1850   1855   1860   1865   1870   1875   1880

3. Give examples of the way industry expanded after 1850.
4. (a) What advances took place in transportation? (b) Communication?
5. (a) What was the advantage of incorporation for a business? (b) For stockholders?
6. Give specific examples to show that a world economy had developed by the late 1800's.
7. Briefly summarize Marx's ideas on the following topics. (a) relations between social classes (b) work and economic value (c) the bourgeoisie (d) the proletariat
8. (a) How did Marx expect workers to win political power? (b) What methods did they actually use?
9. How did realism differ from romanticism in art?
10. How did Cavour succeed in uniting Italy?
11. Briefly describe the part each of the following played in the unification of Germany. (a) German Confederation (b) Schleswig-Holstein (c) Seven Weeks' War (d) Franco-Prussian War
12. Describe the problems that France and Italy faced after 1870.
13. How did the balance of power change between 1815 and 1875?
14. (a) What led to war between the United States and Mexico? (b) What was the outcome?
15. (a) How did the North and the South differ economically? (b) Why was the issue of slavery especially divisive?
16. Why was the North victorious in the Civil War?

Thinking about History

1. Why is the right to vote critical to the improvement of a group's social and economic conditions?
2. (a) Bismarck and Cavour both practiced realpolitik. Give examples from both Italy and Germany. (b) Evaluate the importance of realism and idealism in politics.
3. Compare the growth of trade in the late Middle Ages and during the Industrial Revolution. What similarities and differences were there?

Writing and Speaking about History

1. As a British worker in the mid-1850's, prepare a placard to carry in a demonstration protesting current working conditions.
2. Prepare a courtroom setting and mock trial to hear the following indictment: "Bismarck deliberately provoked France to declare war on Prussia."

3. Conduct a series of interviews between any two of the following people:
   a. Owen and Marx on the workers' dilemma
   b. Bismarck and Napoleon III on the Franco-Prussian War
   c. Cavour and Garibaldi on Italian unification

Practicing Skills

1. Use the card catalog of the school library to prepare a partial working bibliography on this research topic: "The United States Civil War was a conflict over nationalism."
2. Compare the map of the United States in 1853 (page 526) with a present-day map. Name a state that meets the following criterion:
   a. part of the United States in 1783
   b. part of the Louisiana Purchase on 1803
   c. part of the Texas annexation in 1845
   d. part of Oregon Country in 1846
   e. part of the Mexican Cession in 1848
3. Make a timeline of events that led to the unification of Italy and Germany. Extend your timeline from 1845 to 1875 in five-year increments.

Investigating History

1. As the Great Exhibition showed, Queen Victoria was very interested in new technology. One of the developments she supported was photography. Research the early history of photography. Where was it developed? By whom? How does photography differ today? Find examples in books of early photographs. Look for the work of Mathew B. Brady, who photographed the Civil War.
2. Choose one of the realist authors mentioned in this chapter and read a book or short story by that author. Identify the features that make the work realistic.
3. Find out about one of the tycoons of industry in the United States during this period, such as Andrew Carnegie, Cornelius Vanderbilt, John D. Rockefeller, or Leland Stanford.
4. Soon after the Civil War, the United States added Alaska. Prepare a report that describes how Alaska was acquired.

Decision Making in History

How would Metternich have viewed the wars for unification in Italy and Germany? As Metternich, what advice would you give to Bismarck and Cavour?

The Age of Imperialism

Red-coated British soldiers stand at attention around a royal pavillion during a ceremony in India. Britain's Queen Victoria took the title Empress of India in 1876.

1. **Nations competed for overseas empires.**
2. **Imperialists divided Africa.**
3. **The British dominated South Asia.**
4. **Imperialism threatened China.**
5. **Japan built a modern nation.**
6. **Imperialism reached the Western Hemisphere.**

On a warm November afternoon in 1875, the H.M.S. *Serapis* steamed into Bombay harbor as British battleships formed two long lines to greet the vessel. On the bridge stood His Royal Highness Edward, Prince of Wales. He was Queen Victoria's eldest son and the heir to the British throne. Smiling, he waved to the cheering sailors and bowed to the captain of each ship as his own glided by.

When the *Serapis* finally docked, brass bands played and cannons fired salutes. Lord Northbrook, the queen's representative in India, welcomed the future king. Together they rode through streets crowded with cheering Indians. The *Times* of London reported, "The whole population of Bombay swarmed along the road," giving the Prince "a welcome such as an Indian city has seldom seen."

The following day, his thirty-fourth birthday, Prince Edward officially greeted dozens of Indian princes who came to pay their respects. Seated on a silver throne, dressed in royal robes, and flanked by British officials in scarlet and gold uniforms, the prince received his guests one by one. Each was magnificently dressed for the occasion. One guest, the nine-year-old ruler of Baroda, wore so many jewels that he was compared to "a crystallized rainbow."

The prince spent four days in Bombay, attending state banquets, receiving visitors, and watching a spellbinding performance by magicians and snake charmers. Then he began a grand tour. Over the next three months, he visited Calcutta, Madras, and other major Indian cities. At each stop, he reviewed troops, inspected railway lines and stations, visited prisons, palaces, and sacred ruins, and attended countless balls, banquets, and fireworks displays.

Throughout his stay, the heir to the British throne was treated as if he were the next emperor of India. In many respects, he was. Shortly after his return home, Parliament would add *Empress of India* to his mother's long list of titles.

Only a century earlier, the British East India Company had been building a trading network based on forts in major Indian cities. Now this enormous country was part of the British empire. In the words of Prime Minister Benjamin Disraeli, India was "the brightest jewel in Her Majesty's Crown."

Disraeli had not always viewed British colonies as jewels. In 1852, he referred to India and other colonies as a "millstone round our neck." In this chapter, we will see why Disraeli and other Europeans changed their views of colonies in the late 1800's. The chapter will also explain how the empires Europeans built affected people around the world.

Nations competed for overseas empires. 1

In 1901, when Queen Victoria died and Edward became king, Britain and other industrialized nations controlled virtually the entire world. They ruled some lands directly; they governed others indirectly through treaties or trade agreements. As empires grew in size and number, people needed a word to describe this new policy of conquering and ruling other lands. The word they invented was **imperialism**.

Imperialists proudly displayed world maps with their nation's empire in bright colors. The British empire usually appeared in red. It was the largest empire the world had ever known, covering an area nearly 100 times larger than Britain, with a population of more than 400 million. Britain controlled territory on every continent but Antarctica. About one fourth of the world's land and people lived under British rule.

Britain's lead was challenged.

As late as 1870, many Britons believed that colonies were more trouble than they were worth. They noted that trade with their former colonies in North America had grown tremendously since the United States won its independence. Many Britons were eager to rid themselves of their remaining colonies.

Throughout the 1800's, Britain granted many of its colonies more freedom. By the 1840's, Canadians had a measure of self-rule. Soon after, Australians also won the right to govern themselves. Yet even as the British were granting some colonies more freedom, the British empire was adding more territory elsewhere. By the turn of the century, a majority of Britons had come to believe that colonies were essential to their nation's prosperity and prestige.

Britain's attitude toward empires changed as Britain's role in the world changed. In the mid-1800's, Britain was the most powerful nation in the world. Its factories produced more goods than those of any other country, and the British navy guarded the oceans so that those goods could be shipped safely to ports around the world. The British exported more than just goods. They also exported capital, the money needed to build factories, mines, railroads, and other businesses. Britain became the world's banker. The money its banks loaned came from the profits earned by manufacturers, merchants, and shippers.

By the late 1800's, however, Germany and the United States were challenging Britain's economic leadership. Although British factories continued to increase their output each year, Britain's share of the world's total production fell sharply. In 1870, it produced one third of the world's total. By 1900, British factories were turning out just one fifth.

At the same time, countries that had once welcomed British goods were now taxing those goods to protect their own factories. Increasingly, Britain had to find new markets for its goods or protect existing markets. It also had to safeguard sources of raw materials. The British Isles had only a few of the resources its factories needed. Most were imported.

Faced with economic decline, Britain looked to its colonies for markets and resources. In the late 1800's, the British government tightened its hold over India and other colonies. It also added new colonies in hopes of guarding critical trade routes and business interests.

Imperialism fostered rivalries.

Other countries followed Britain's lead. They too came to see colonies as necessary for their economic well-being. France, which had been a colonial power since the 1600's, greatly expanded its holdings in the late 1800's. By 1900, it had an empire second in size only to Britain's. The Dutch expanded too. Spain and Portugal, both of which had lost most of their original empires, tried to build new empires in Africa. At the same time, Austria-Hungary moved into the Balkans, and Russia expanded into the Caucasus, Central Asia, and eastern Siberia.

Countries that had no colonies set out to acquire them. Belgium, Italy, and Germany all took over lands in Africa. Germany also tried to control parts of East Asia and islands in the south Pacific. At the same time, German bankers made loans to governments in Latin America, and German capitalists were building a Berlin-to-Baghdad railway. Their hope was that where business went, the German flag would soon follow.

Two non-European countries, the United States and Japan, also became involved in overseas expansion during this period. Both were interested in East Asia. The United States was also deeply involved in Latin America.

Increasingly, Europeans viewed an empire as a measure of national stature. "There has never been a great power without great colonies," proclaimed one French writer. Thus the race for colonies grew out of a strong sense of national pride as well as from economic competition. As the competition for colonies intensified, many countries claimed land that had little economic value. Pride, not profit, was their motive. Each country was determined to plant its flag on as much of the world as possible.

Europe believed in its own superiority.

Thanks to the Industrial Revolution, each European country had not only the weapons needed to win an empire but also the means to control it. Steamers, railroads, telegraph cables, and other inventions allowed nations to keep in close touch with even the most distant colony.

At the same time, the new technology encouraged Europeans to think that they had a right to conquer other countries. They regarded their steamships and factories as proof of their progress. They believed that they had the right and the duty to bring the results of that progress to other peoples.

Many Europeans went abroad with a strong sense of mission. One such European was Cecil Rhodes, a young Englishman who became rich in the diamond mines of South Africa. He boasted:

> I contend that we Britons are the first race in the world, and the more of the world we inhabit, the better it is for the human race. I believe it is my duty to God, my Queen, and my country to paint the whole map of Africa red [the color of the British empire on maps], red from the Cape of Good Hope to Cairo.

The push for expansion also came from missionaries who worked among the peoples of Asia, Africa, and the Pacific islands. Many missionaries believed that European rule was the best way to end evil practices such as the slave trade.

Perhaps the most famous of these missionaries was David Livingstone (1813–1873). A minister from Scotland, Livingstone went to Africa in 1841 to preach the Gospel and heal the sick. He grieved to see East Africans carried off to be sold as slaves in Arabian, Turkish, and Persian lands. Over the years, he became convinced that only the British government was strong enough to end the trade. As a result of his efforts and those of his followers, the slave trade was abolished in East Africa in the 1880's. At the same time, much of the region became part of the British empire.

Imperialism had mass appeal.

Stories of adventure in distant places have always appealed to people. In the late 1800's, Europeans and Americans were eager to read about soldiers who guarded the empire against fierce enemies in far-off lands, sailors who roamed the open sea, and merchants who traded for silks and spices in mysterious Asian ports. When David Livingstone wrote a book about his work in Africa, thousands of people in Europe and the United States bought copies.

Newspapers competed for readers by hiring reporters to search the globe for stories of adventure, mystery, or excitement. For example, in the late 1860's, David Livingstone and a group of Africans traveled deep into the heart of the continent in search of evidence against the slave trade. When several years passed with no word from him or his party, many people feared he was dead. An American newspaper hired reporter Henry Stanley to find Livingstone. Stanley arrived in Zanzibar in January 1871. Ten months later, he caught up with Livingstone on the shores of Lake Tanganyika.

Stanley's account of the meeting made headlines around the world. Stanley became a celebrity. Queen Victoria gave him a jeweled snuffbox. Cities across the United States held banquets in his honor.

Novels and poetry also glorified imperialism. The most popular writer of the day was Joseph Rudyard Kipling (1865–1936). Children and adults alike were fascinated by his poems and stories, many of which were set in India. Kipling appealed not only to his readers' spirit of adventure but

also to their feelings of superiority. He saw imperialism as a mission to "civilize non-Europeans" and urged his readers to:

> Take up the White Man's Burden—
>   Send forth the best ye breed—
> Go bind your sons to exile
>   To serve your captives' need . . .

In answering the call of imperialism, Europeans altered life on every continent.

Section Review 1

Define: imperialism
Identify: (a) Prince Edward, (b) Rhodes, (c) Livingstone, (d) Stanley, (e) Kipling
Answer:
1. (a) What countries challenged Britain's economic leadership? (b) How was the search for colonies a response to Britain's declining share in world trade?
2. What part did each of the following play in imperialism? (a) markets (b) raw materials (c) national pride
3. (a) What countries joined the competition for colonies? (b) How did this competition set up a potentially explosive situation?
4. What attitude did people in industrialized countries have toward other peoples?
5. (a) What part did missionaries play in imperialism? (b) How did newspapers and writers encourage imperialism?

Critical Thinking
6. Reread the lines from Kipling's poem on this page. (a) What did he mean by "the White Man's Burden"? (b) What was the exile of which he spoke? (c) What does the word *captives* indicate?

Footnote to History

When Stanley finally reached Livingstone's camp, he reported that his first impulse was to rush over and throw his arms around Livingstone. Then, perhaps remembering that he had come without an invitation and that the missionary was a reserved Scot, Stanley settled for a simpler greeting. He held out his hand and said, "Dr. Livingstone, I presume?"

Imperialists divided Africa. 2

Nowhere was the competition for colonies more intense than in Africa. When the Age of Imperialism began in 1875, Europeans controlled less than 10 percent of the continent. By 1900, 90 percent of Africa was divided into colonies.

Europeans explored Africa.

For centuries, Europeans had considered Africa the "dark continent" because they knew so little about it. Although European ships had traded at ports along the coasts for centuries, the vast interior of the continent was unknown to Europeans until well into the 1800's.

Beginning with the Scotsman Mungo Park's exploration of the Niger River in 1805 and 1806, European explorers slowly penetrated the African interior. The Frenchman René Caillié (kah-YAY) was the first European to cross the Sahara (1827–1828), while the German Heinrich Barth traveled widely in western Africa during the 1850's. Best-known of the explorers was David Livingstone, the Scottish missionary who spent 30 years in central Africa.

Explorers such as Barth and Livingstone gave Europeans their first detailed information about Africa and its peoples. In the mid-1800's, Africa south of the Sahara contained more than 700 different ethnic groups, each with its own language and customs. Most were organized into communities based on ties of tradition and kinship. Occasionally, a powerful group formed a state that was strong enough to conquer neighboring groups and form an empire.

These communities and states had been trading with Europeans for hundreds of years. Africans had no reason to expect any change in those relationships. Yet by the late 1800's, traditional relationships were changing rapidly.

Europeans scrambled for colonies.

The scramble for African territory began after 1879. In that year, Henry Stanley, the reporter who found David Livingstone, returned to Africa and claimed most of the Congo River valley in the name of King Leopold II of Belgium. The Belgian Congo, as the colony later became known, was 80 times larger than Belgium.

Leopold's action alarmed France. The French responded in 1882 by taking the north bank of the Congo River. Soon Britain, Germany, Italy, Portugal, and Spain were also staking claims to parts of Africa.

The competition was so fierce that countries feared a war. To prevent fighting, representatives from European countries met in Berlin in 1884 and 1885 to lay down rules for this new competition. No African ruler attended this meeting, yet it sealed Africa's fate. Europeans agreed that any European country could claim land in Africa simply by sending troops to occupy strategic points there. As a result, by 1913 a map of the continent looked like a patchwork quilt of imperial colors.

North Africa Europeans had already moved into North Africa. There, the once-powerful Ottoman empire had become too weak to prevent local rulers from taking control in Morocco, Algeria, Tunisia, and Egypt. These local rulers were no match for the Europeans bent on conquest.

As early as 1830, France had invaded Algeria. Its aim was to build its prestige and to stop Algerian pirates who attacked French ships. Until 1869, no other European country paid much attention to North Africa. That year, a French company built a canal across the Isthmus of Suez at the northern end of the Red Sea. The canal linked the Mediterranean and Red Seas, providing a much shorter route from Europe to the Indian Ocean.

As the fastest route to India and Australia, the Suez Canal was crucial to Britain. It was so important that the British government bought stock in the company that owned the canal in 1875. Guarding the canal became a critical part of Britain's foreign policy. Therefore, when fighting broke out in Egypt in 1882, Britain took over the area. Egypt became a British **protectorate**—a country whose foreign policy is controlled by an outside government.

Next the British turned their attention to Sudan, which lay along the Nile River south of Egypt. Because water from the Nile was essential to the people of Egypt, the British believed that they had to control the headwaters of the Nile to guard Egypt and the canal. Many Britons also now shared Rhodes's dream of ruling all of Africa from Cairo to Cape Town. Thus, in 1896, Britain and Egypt invaded Sudan. The Sudanese defended their country fiercely, but in 1898, General Horatio Kitchener conquered the country. The following year, Britain and Egypt made Sudan a **condominium**—a country ruled jointly by two other countries.

France also dreamed of a great African empire. It would stretch from Dakar in the west to French Somaliland in the east. To fulfill that dream, the

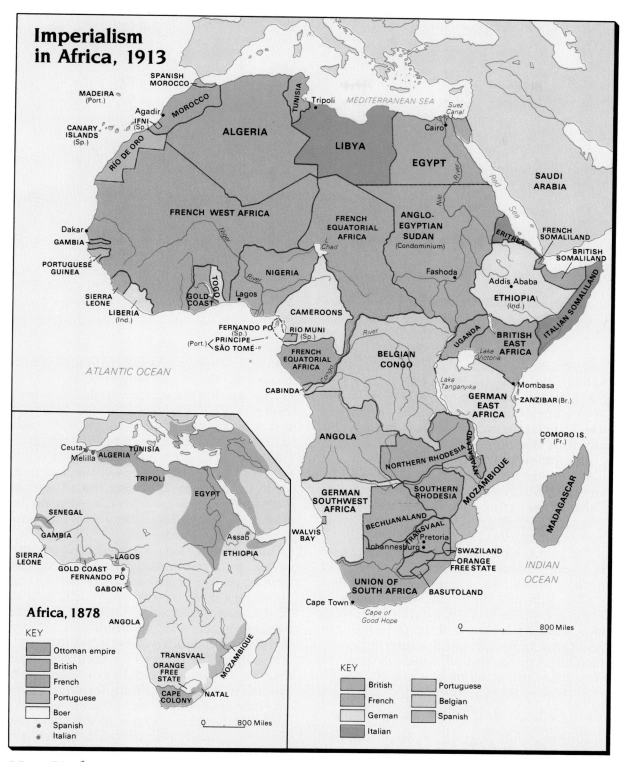

Imperialism in Africa, 1913

SPANISH MOROCCO
MADEIRA (Port.)
Agadir
MOROCCO
IFNI (Sp.)
CANARY ISLANDS (Sp.)
RIO DE ORO
ALGERIA
TUNISIA
Tripoli
MEDITERRANEAN SEA
Suez Canal
Cairo
LIBYA
EGYPT
Red Sea
Nile River
SAUDI ARABIA

FRENCH WEST AFRICA
Dakar
GAMBIA
PORTUGUESE GUINEA
Niger River
SIERRA LEONE
LIBERIA (Ind.)
GOLD COAST
TOGO
NIGERIA
Lagos
L. Chad
FRENCH EQUATORIAL AFRICA
ANGLO-EGYPTIAN SUDAN (Condominium)
Fashoda
ERITREA
FRENCH SOMALILAND
BRITISH SOMALILAND
Addis Ababa
ETHIOPIA (Ind.)
ITALIAN SOMALILAND

ATLANTIC OCEAN
FERNANDO PO (Sp.)
PRINCIPE (Port.)
SÃO TOMÉ
RIO MUNI (Sp.)
CAMEROONS
FRENCH EQUATORIAL AFRICA
River
BELGIAN CONGO
Congo River
CABINDA
UGANDA
Lake Victoria
BRITISH EAST AFRICA
Lake Tanganyika
GERMAN EAST AFRICA
Mombasa
ZANZIBAR (Br.)

ANGOLA
NORTHERN RHODESIA
NYASALAND
MOZAMBIQUE
COMORO IS. (Fr.)
MADAGASCAR

GERMAN SOUTHWEST AFRICA
SOUTHERN RHODESIA
WALVIS BAY
BECHUANALAND
TRANSVAAL
Pretoria
Johannesburg
SWAZILAND
ORANGE FREE STATE
UNION OF SOUTH AFRICA
BASUTOLAND
Cape Town
Cape of Good Hope
INDIAN OCEAN

0   800 Miles

Africa, 1878

Ceuta
Melilla
ALGERIA
TUNISIA
TRIPOLI
EGYPT
SENEGAL
GAMBIA
SIERRA LEONE
GOLD COAST
FERNANDO PO
LAGOS
GABON
Assab
ETHIOPIA
ANGOLA
MOZAMBIQUE
TRANSVAAL
ORANGE FREE STATE
CAPE COLONY
NATAL

KEY
- Ottoman empire
- British
- French
- Portuguese
- Boer
- • Spanish
- • Italian

0   800 Miles

KEY
- British
- French
- German
- Italian
- Portuguese
- Belgian
- Spanish

Map Study

Britain long planned a Cairo-to-Cape-Town railroad. In 1913, what British colonies could it have gone through? What other powers blocked its way?

At the Battle of Omdurman in 1898, 26,000 British troops defeated about 50,000 Sudanese. The key to victory was Britain's 20 machine guns.

French gradually took over Tunisia and Morocco. In 1898, they also pushed east into Sudan. There they encountered British troops at Fashoda. For weeks, Britain and France were at the edge of war. Then France suddenly backed down. It now turned its attention south of the Sahara.

Africa south of the Sahara European control south of the Sahara began in the mid-1800's around trading posts such as the French port of Dakar in the west or the British port of Cape Town in the south. From such outposts, European control spread inland.

The push toward colonization often came from European officials and merchants. Many were tempted to use force whenever they came into conflict with an African state. Often, Europeans found it easier to shoot first and ask questions later than to negotiate with the group involved. As a result, home governments sometimes found themselves in the middle of wars about which they knew little or nothing.

European conquest took many forms.

Equipped with superior weapons, European armies usually had no great difficulty defeating African soldiers. Such defeats, however, did not always result in an easy conquest. It might take years to conquer a large empire. Samori Touré,

a Malinke, built an empire that stretched across the northern Ivory Coast into present-day Ghana. To protect that empire, he bought arms from Europeans along the coast. He also set up his own weapons factory. As a result, he was able to hold off the French for more than six years.

Some parts of Africa were not organized into states or empires. Here, each village was independent. Therefore, Europeans had to conquer every community to take over the region. Britain made 500 separate treaties before it won control of eastern Nigeria.

Other African states accepted European rule without going to war. In some cases, an alliance with Europeans seemed to be a smaller threat than conquest by a neighboring people. Such alliances, however, gradually led to a European takeover. In this way, for example, the British won control of Africa's Gold Coast.

Elsewhere, Europeans were sometimes invited into a region to protect a leader or a group against internal enemies. One of the best-known examples is Buganda, the African kingdom on the north shore of Lake Victoria. In the 1880's and 1890's, Buganda was in the midst of civil war as Muslims, Catholics, Protestants, and followers of the traditional Ganda religion competed for power. With British help, however, the two Christian groups removed the king and seized power. In 1900, they signed an agreement that gave them a privileged position in the British colony of Uganda.

Africa became a continent of colonies.

By 1900, Europeans controlled most of Africa. Only two countries remained free from European control, Liberia and Ethiopia.

Liberia, founded during the 1820's by former American slaves, was closely allied with the United States. This alliance kept the West African nation safe from conquest.

The kingdom of Ethiopia in East Africa owed its independence to a variety of factors. Geography gave it some protection. It was located at a place where the rival empires of Britain, France, and Italy met. Each was determined to keep the others from expanding further, and Ethiopia could stand as a buffer state. Ethiopia also had the natural protection of mountains. Most important, it had a leader capable of using these advantages to protect his kingdom.

Menelik II, who ruled Ethiopia from 1889 to 1913, took advantage of international rivalries to get the most modern weapons. With these, he turned back an Italian invasion in 1896. Then he went on to conquer neighboring peoples to create an empire.

Colonial rule European rule of the rest of Africa was mostly indirect. Relatively few Europeans settled in their African colonies, except in Algeria and South Africa. In 1900, for example, only 2,000 of Uganda's 3 million people were British. Thus, all colonial governments had to have some African administrators.

Wherever possible, Europeans turned to Africans already in authority. Many traditional rulers continued to hold office. However, this policy did not mean that life continued as usual for the people of Africa.

Europeans wanted African workers for mines and plantations. At first, Europeans simply used their superior weapons to force Africans into work crews. Later, however, most colonial governments used an economic weapon—taxes. Africans had long paid taxes to their rulers in goods and services. Now, however, they were required to pay taxes in money. The need for money forced many Africans to work on plantations or in mines, all owned by Europeans.

Other Africans began to raise crops that Europeans wanted to buy rather than food crops for themselves. This shift marked the beginning of a money economy.

Colonial governments used tax money to provide a range of services that led to better health care, improved farming methods, European-style education, and other changes. In some cases, Africans benefited from these services. Often, however, the new services were only for European settlers or traders.

The African people were now second-class citizens in their own lands. Many African leaders came to believe that only by borrowing from European cultures could they regain control over their own country. "The blacks had slept long; perhaps too long," observed Blaise Diagne, a Senegalese leader. "But beware! Those who have slept long and soundly, when once they wake up, will not easily fall back to sleep again."

Europeans were fearful of such an awakening. To guard against it, some colonial officials encouraged rivalries among ethnic groups. As long as Africans were divided, Europeans could keep control. Many nations also kept education to a minimum in their colonies. Rather than train Africans, Europeans often brought in Indians, Chinese, and other Asians to handle jobs requiring special skills.

In setting up their colonies, Europeans had two main goals. One was to keep order and prevent rebellions. The other was to see to it that their colonies paid for themselves.

Economic disappointments When the scramble for Africa began, many believed that the African people would soon be buying European goods in great quantities. Shortly after his return from Africa in 1872, Henry Stanley, for example, told a group of Manchester business leaders, "There are 40 million people beyond the gateway of the Congo, and the cotton spinners of Manchester are waiting to clothe them." Stanley estimated that if each of these Africans bought just one Sunday dress or suit every year, the merchants of Manchester would enjoy a tremendous boost in sales.

However, those sales never materialized. Most Africans were too poor to buy European goods. Europeans also found that much of Africa was too wet or too dry for commercial farming to succeed. Minerals and good farmland were often too far from transportation routes to ship goods profitably to market. Only a few powerful business groups such as traders and shippers prospered from imperialism. Leaders in those businesses urged governments to continue imperialism.

Few European nations grew rich from their colonies. Only in South Africa did Europeans find the wealth of which they dreamed. As a result, South Africa's history differed sharply from that of the rest of the continent.

South Africa supplied great wealth.

The British first took control of the Cape of Good Hope in 1806, during the Napoleonic wars. They called the region Cape Colony. There the British found not only a variety of African peoples but also a well-established community of about 40,000 Dutch settlers. The Dutch called themselves *Boers* (from the Dutch word for farmer). Most Boers were strict Calvinists who believed that God had selected a small group, of which they were a part, for salvation. They used this belief to justify their harsh treatment of African peoples in the region.

The Boers disliked being ruled by Britain. They wanted their own government. Thousands migrated from Cape Colony during the 1830's into the African interior. This Great Trek brought the Boers into conflict with the Zulu people, who had built a great empire in southern Africa. After years of fighting, the Boers finally defeated the Zulu and set up three countries—Natal, Transvaal, and the Orange Free State.

At first, Britain accepted the independence of the three Boer states. At the time, Britain's main interest was the Cape Colony, which was an important stop on the route around Africa to India. In 1845, the British annexed Natal to guard Africa's southern coast but allowed the other two states to remain independent.

Then, in 1867, diamonds were discovered on a farm at Kimberley, on the border of the Orange Free State. Within weeks, Kimberley became a boom town. "Men who set out to work in the morning, not knowing where their dinner was to come from," noted one reporter, "became richer than any member of their family had ever been before it was time for an eleven o'clock snack."

Most of the miners were British. Among them was Cecil Rhodes, who gradually won control of the entire Kimberley diamond field. By 1889, his company controlled 90 percent of the world's diamond output.

As British miners crowded onto Boer land, tension between the Boers and the British mounted. In 1886, gold was discovered in a ridge of mountains called the Rand in the heart of Transvaal. Again British fortune-seekers stampeded into Boer territory. By 1895, the Boers were outnumbered by *uitlanders* (AYT-lahn-duhrz), the Boer term for foreign settlers.

When the Boers tried to keep their way of life by restricting uitlanders, the newcomers were outraged. They had the support of Cecil Rhodes. In 1895, one of his associates tried to overthrow the government of Transvaal. Although the attempt failed, the Boers blamed Britain for the uprising. As tensions mounted, the Boers took up arms against Britain in 1899.

On the surface, it appeared a hopelessly uneven match—100,000 Boers against the largest empire the world had ever known. The Boers, however, successfully used guerilla tactics against the British army. Britain struck back by burning farms and destroying food supplies in the Boer regions. British troops captured and imprisoned Boer women and children. At last, the Boers were forced to make peace in 1902.

To prevent future trouble with the Boers, the British allowed the Dutch-speaking settlers to keep their language in both schools and courts. The British even helped Boers rebuild their farms. (On the other hand, the British did nothing to help Africans whose farms had been destroyed.)

Both the Transvaal and the Orange Free State became self-governing British colonies, much like Australia and Canada. In 1910, they were joined with Cape Colony and Natal. The new country had equal status with Canada and Australia within the British empire.

After the mining boom tapered off, the Boers were once more the majority of the Europeans in the new state. Two Boers, Louis Botha and Jan Christian Smuts, served as South Africa's first prime ministers.

In the end, the British bought peace with the Boers at the expense of the black African population. Blacks made up 75 percent of South Africa's people. Under Boer rule, the millions of black Africans who lived in the country were reduced to a life little better than slavery.

Section Review 2

Define: (a) protectorate, (b) condominium, (c) uitlander

Identify: (a) Suez Canal, (b) Kitchener, (c) Menelik II, (d) Cape Colony, (e) Boers, (f) Great Trek

Answer:

1. (a) How did the scramble for colonies in Africa begin? (b) Why did representatives of European countries meet in Berlin? (c) What was the result of the meeting?
2. Briefly describe France's expansion in North Africa.
3. (a) What were the effects of the building of the Suez Canal on Egypt? (b) What were the effects on Sudan?
4. How did each of the following exhibit a different pattern of colonization? (a) the empire of Samori Touré (b) Nigeria (c) Buganda
5. (a) What two African countries remained free of European control? (b) Why?
6. (a) What did the policy of indirect rule mean for Africa? (b) What were some of the effects of colonial rule on African society?
7. (a) How did the Boers and the British come into conflict? (b) What were the results? (c) What concessions did the British make to the Boers?

Critical Thinking

8. How did colonization make Africans second-class citizens in terms of role in politics, taxation, ethnic rivalry, and education?

The British dominated South Asia. 3

India was the cornerstone of the British empire. The Industrial Revolution had turned Britain into the world's workshop, and India was a major supplier of raw materials for that workshop. Its 300 million people were also a large potential market for British-made goods. It is not surprising, then, that the British valued India above their other colonies and that other nations envied Britain's control of that country.

British rulers in India built English-style homes where they lived surrounded by Indian servants.

Britain expanded control over India.

British economic interest in India began in the 1600's, when the British East India Company set up trading posts at Bombay, Madras, and Calcutta. At first, India's ruling Mughal dynasty kept European traders under control. By 1700, however, the Mughal empire was collapsing. Dozens of small states, each headed by a ruler or *maharajah*, broke away from Mughal control.

The growth of the East India Company The East India Company was quick to take advantage of the growing weakness of the Mughals. By 1757, the company was the leading power in India. It governed directly or indirectly an area that included modern Bangladesh, most of southern India, and nearly all the territory along the Ganges River in the north.

Officially, the British government regulated the company's efforts both in London and in India. In fact, the company ruled India with little interference from the British government. The company even had its own army, which was led by British officers and staffed by *sepoys* (SEE-poyz), or Indian soldiers. One early company official referred to this army as "a delicate and dangerous machine, which with a little mismanagement may easily turn against us."

The Great Rebellion The army did indeed turn against the company in 1857. In that year, word spread among the sepoys that their British-made rifle cartridges were sealed with beef and pork fat. Soldiers had to bite off the seal to use the cartridges. Both Hindu and Muslim soldiers were outraged by the news. (Muslims are forbidden to eat pork, and Hindus are not allowed to eat beef.) Although the British quickly corrected the error, they could not quiet the soldiers' suspicions.

On May 10, 1857, the sepoys at Meerut rebelled. They marched to Delhi, where they were joined by Indian soldiers stationed there. Together, the soldiers captured the city. From Delhi, the rebellion spread to much of northern and central India. Fighting was widespread and fierce.

The British called this outbreak the Sepoy Mutiny, but in fact it was a full-scale rebellion. Muslim rebels even tried to place a descendant of the last Mughal emperor on the throne.

It took the East India Company more than a year of hard fighting to regain control of the country. The British government sent troops to help the company. The British were also helped by serious splits between Hindus and Muslims. Hindus did not want the Mughal empire restored. Indeed, many Hindus preferred British rule to Muslim rule.

At the same time, nearly all the princes and maharajahs who had made alliances with the East India Company remained loyal. Also loyal were the Sikhs, a religious group that had long been hostile to the Mughals (page 291). Indeed, from then on, the bearded and turbaned Sikhs became the mainstay of Britain's army in India and fought loyally for the British.

India after 1857 The mutiny marked a turning point in Indian history. In 1858, the British government took direct command of India. A cabinet minister in London directed policy, and a British governor-general in India carried out the government's orders. (After 1877, this official held the title of viceroy.)

To reward the many princes who had remained loyal to Britain, the British promised to respect all treaties the East India Company had made with them. They also promised that the Indian states that were still free would remain independent. Unofficially, however, Britain won greater and greater control of those states. For example, if rival princes claimed a throne, the British often interfered to make sure the prince they preferred won.

The part of India that was under direct British rule was called the *Raj*. The Raj was divided into 10 provinces and some 250 districts. Sometimes a handful of district officials were the only Britons among the million or more people in their districts.

Convinced that they knew what was best for India, British officials set out to improve the country. They built bridges, dams, canals, and European-style public buildings. Their irrigation projects opened millions of acres of land to farming. The British also created a network of telegraph lines and railroads that linked major Indian cities. By 1900, India had more than 30,000 miles of track—the third largest rail network in the world.

As in Europe, the development of railroads boosted trade, especially in inland areas that now were directly connected with seaports. The tea industry, for example, blossomed almost overnight

Daily Life · A New Look for the Army

In 1850, a British soldier's uniform had a brilliant red coat, a shiny black hat, and white breeches. Such uniforms made a splendid sight on the parade ground—and a splendid target on the battlefield. During the sepoy revolt, British soldiers in India found that they were much safer after their bright uniforms were covered with a layer of yellow-brown dust (in the dry season) or mud (in the wet season). Dirt-colored uniforms made fine camouflage. Eventually, the British adopted this drab color as their official combat uniform. They called it *khaki,* from the Indian word for dust.

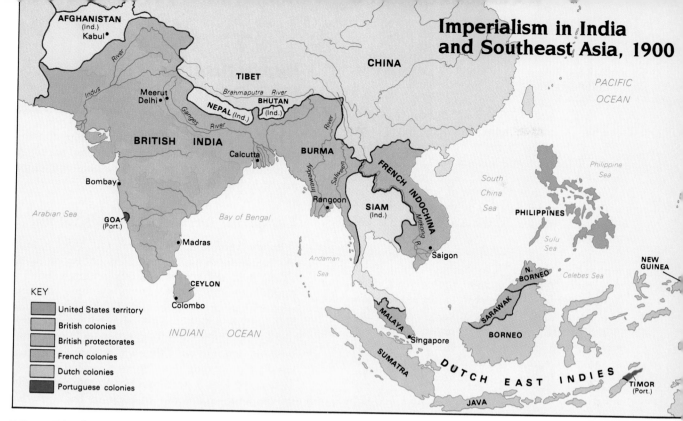

Imperialism in India and Southeast Asia, 1900

KEY

- United States territory
- British colonies
- British protectorates
- French colonies
- Dutch colonies
- Portuguese colonies

Map Study

What country separated British and French colonies? What was its status?

in the hilly regions of the northeast. Between 1850 and 1871, Indian tea exports soared from 200,000 pounds to more than 6 million pounds annually. Other major export crops such as jute, cotton, and indigo also benefited from railway development.

The beginning of Indian nationalism The British were proud of the changes they brought to India. They boasted of the many improvements they had made. Indians quietly noted, however, that money for the new roads, telegraph cables, and irrigation projects came from Indian taxpayers. Only the railroads were built by private British companies. Yet they too got help from taxpayers. Nor did the British do the work of digging roadbeds and laying track. Rather, they directed the projects and supplied the technical skills. Indians did the hard work. Yet the Indians had no opportunity to manage future projects.

Increasingly, Indians resented a system that made them second-class citizens in their own country. They resented the many signs that read, "For Europeans only." Such signs were everywhere—at doorways, in railroad cars and waiting

rooms, and even on park benches. Even Indians with a European education faced discrimination. They were barred from top posts in the Indian Civil Service. Those who managed to get middle-level jobs were paid less than Europeans. A British engineer on the East India Railway, for example, made nearly 20 times as much money as his Indian counterpart.

A spirit of Indian nationalism slowly began to grow. This feeling led to the founding of the Indian National Congress in 1885 and the Muslim League in 1906. At first, such groups were mainly concerned with winning equal opportunities for Indians in the civil service. Gradually, however, their demands broadened. By the early 1900's, they were calling for self-government.

Britain protected the Raj.

Britain had no desire to give the Indians more control over their own country. Instead, as the competition for colonies in other parts of the world grew more fierce, the British tightened their control in South and Southeast Asia. The

543

British saw two threats to their control of India—France on the southeast and Russia on the northwest.

In the late 1800's, France took over much of what is now Vietnam, Laos, and Kampuchea. To keep the French from advancing farther west, the British moved into Burma. By 1885, Burma was a province of India. The British also helped protect the independence of Siam, now Thailand. Britain hoped Siam would be a buffer between French colonies in the east and British colonies in the west.

The British were also concerned about India's northern border. There they feared a Russian advance. As early as 1839, the East India Company had invaded Afghanistan in the hope of creating a buffer zone, but the invasion failed. In 1878, the British decided to try again. The Second Afghan War, which lasted three years, finally established India's northern border. It also checked Russian influence in the region.

Section Review 3

Define: (a) maharajah, (b) sepoy
Identify: (a) Mughal, (b) Sikhs, (c) Raj, (d) Indian National Congress, (e) Muslim League
Answer:
1. How did the British East India Company win control of much of India?
2. (a) What caused the sepoys to revolt? (b) What groups supported the British during the revolt? (c) What were the results?
3. (a) From a British point of view, how did British rule benefit India? (b) From an Indian point of view, what were the drawbacks of British rule?
4. What were the goals of the Indian National Congress and the Muslim League?
5. What steps did Britain take to protect its control of India?

Critical Thinking
6. What point of view might each of the following people have taken on British rule of India? (a) a textile manufacturer in Britain (b) a British railroad executive in India (c) an Indian official in the civil service (d) a Sikh soldier (e) a maharajah educated in Britain

Imperialism threatened China. 4

To the east of India lay China. Here too Europeans were eager to win colonies. Indeed, at one time it seemed as if a scramble for China might follow the one for Africa.

Europeans forced treaties on China.

In the 1800's, the Manchus still ruled China as the Ch'ing dynasty (page 274). For many years, China had been a prosperous country, with a highly developed agricultural system. Farming was critical because, by 1800, China had some 300 million people—more than the entire population of Europe. China was not industrial, but workers in small workshops were able to produce most of the goods the Chinese needed.

Because China was practically self-sufficient, its emperors had little interest in trading with Europeans. For decades, Europeans could do business only at the port of Canton. Despite pleas from Britain and other nations, China refused to open other ports to foreigners. The Chinese regarded European goods as inferior to their own and bought few goods from the European merchants at Canton.

European merchants were determined to find a product the Chinese would buy in large quantities. Eventually, the British East India Company discovered such a product—opium. Opium is a habit-forming narcotic made from the poppy plant. The use of opium was strictly controlled in India, Europe, and China. Now, however, British merchants smuggled in so much opium that the weak Chinese government was powerless to control its flow.

In 1836, the Chinese government tried to stop the opium trade by appealing to Queen Victoria for help. A leading official wrote to her:

Suppose there were people from another country who carried opium for sale to England and seduced your people into buying and smoking it; certainly your honorable ruler would deeply hate it and be bitterly aroused.

When such pleas went unanswered, the quarrel over opium grew into a war. The Opium War

Canton was the first port where China granted Europeans trading rights. By 1800, flags of many European countries flew over Canton's busy harbor. In the harbor were both Chinese and European vessels.

of 1839 was fought mostly at sea. Chinese fleets, armed with a type of cannon in use since the 1300's, proved to be no match for well-armed British gunboats. In 1842, the two sides signed a treaty at Nanking.

For China, the Treaty of Nanking marked the beginning of a century of humiliation. The treaty was a clear victory for Britain. The British won the right to trade at four Chinese ports besides Canton. In each of these ports, British citizens would enjoy *extraterritorial* rights. That is, Britons did not have to obey Chinese law. They were subject only to British law and to British courts. Furthermore, China was required to pay damages for the opium it had destroyed. The trade in the deadly drug continued.

The Treaty of Nanking was the first of many unequal treaties China would be forced to make as one European country after another established **spheres of influence**. These were regions in which the economic interests of a foreign nation came before those of China. In these regions, foreigners did much as they pleased.

A revolt weakened southern China.

By 1850, the Ch'ing dynasty was losing control of the country. The government was riddled with corruption. China was on the verge of bankruptcy as a result of the unequal treaties. Most serious of all, the population was increasing quickly while food production grew little. China's population reached about 430 million in 1850, nearly half again as large as 50 years before. The result was widespread hunger even in good years. In a bad year, such as 1852 when the Yellow River flooded, millions starved. As one Chinese official lamented:

Today there are law-breaking soldiers and greedy officials everywhere who encourage the bandits and indulge them. Whenever one thinks of it, one's heart goes cold. Right and wrong are turned upside down.

It was in this upside-down world that a man named Hung Hsiu-ch'uan (hoong sh'yoo-chwan) attracted a following. Hung, a teacher in a small village in southern China, claimed to have a divine mission to save the world. He told the peasants that with their help he would establish on Earth a "Heavenly Kingdom of Great Peace." Hung's revolt was called the Taiping Rebellion from the Chinese words for "great peace." By 1853, his ragtag army had about 1 million people.

Chinese officials were unable to keep the rebels from taking control of all of southern China. In Nanking, Hung established a government for his Heavenly Kingdom, but it did not stay in power long. With British help, the imperial army won back the south from the rebels in a 10-year war that took 20 million lives.

The rebellion convinced many Chinese officials that modernization was the country's only hope

545

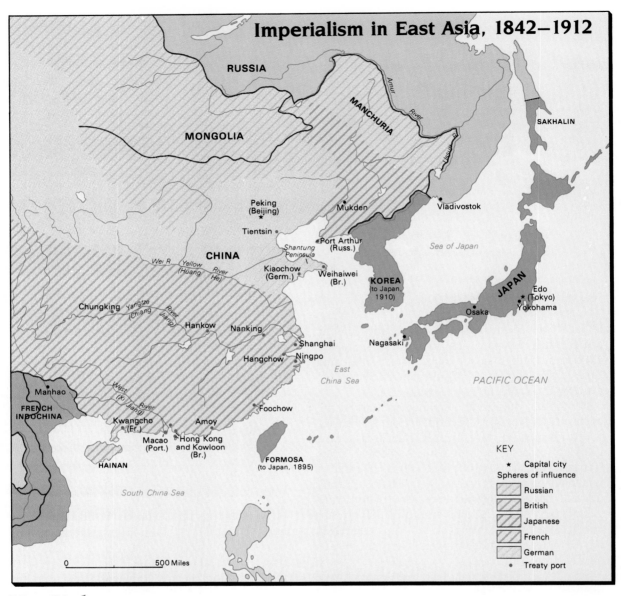

Imperialism in East Asia, 1842–1912

KEY

★ Capital city

Spheres of influence

	Russian
	British
	Japanese
	French
	German
•	Treaty port

Map Study

What European power might rival Japan in northern China and Korea?

for survival. During the 1860's and 1870's, these officials tried to upgrade the army and navy, improve transportation and communication, and broaden China's educational system to include technical subjects and foreign languages.

Such efforts, however, met with strong opposition. A number of officials believed that China should borrow little if anything from the West. China's emperors seemed to agree. As a result, China continued to weaken.

Foreign influence expanded.

Outsiders were quick to take advantage of China's weakness. A second opium war with Britain and France from 1857 to 1860 gave foreigners even more trading rights. About the same time, the Russians forced China to give up the Ussuri territory, where the Russians built their major Pacific naval base of Vladivostok. In 1879, Japan annexed the Ryukyu Islands.

546

By 1885, much of China's empire was gone. The rest fell in the 1890's when Japan took over Formosa and the Liaotung Peninsula. Japan was able to keep only Formosa, as several European countries joined together to force Japan out of the peninsula. Once they did so, however, the Europeans demanded some Chinese territory for themselves. Russia took Port Arthur and the Liaotung Peninsula in 1896, and France took Kwangchow. By 1898, Germany controlled Kiaochow, and Britain held Weihaiwei.

The United States began to fear that China would be carved into colonies and American traders would be shut out. Therefore, in 1899, the United States declared the Open-Door Policy. This policy proposed an "open door" to China for merchants of all nations. A number of nations agreed to the policy. As a result, American trade rights were protected in China, and China was protected from colonization. Yet, though it was not carved into colonies, China remained at the mercy of outsiders.

In this French cartoon, Britain, Germany, Russia, France, and Japan carve up China.

Nationalism grew in China.

Although China kept its freedom, Europeans dominated most of China's largest cities. There, resentment simmered beneath the surface as some Chinese formed secret societies pledged to rid the country of the "foreign devils."

The most famous of these secret groups was the Society of Righteous and Harmonious Fists, better known simply as the Boxers. In 1900, the Boxers rebelled in Peking, shouting the slogan, "Death to the Foreign Devils." The Boxers surrounded the European section of the city and kept it under siege for several months. Eventually, an army made up of troops from eight nations (Britain, France, Germany, Austria, Italy, Russia, Japan, and the United States) arrived. It quickly defeated the Boxers.

Despite the failure of the Boxer uprising, a nationalist movement began to take shape in China. It drew its strength from the many humiliations the Chinese suffered at the hands of imperialists. Its goals were nationalism, republicanism, and land reform.

Section Review 4

Define: (a) extraterritorial rights, (b) sphere of influence
Identify: (a) Opium War, (b) Hung Hsiuch'uan (c) Open-Door Policy, (d) Boxer Rebellion
Answer:
1. Why were China's emperors uninterested in trading with Europe?
2. (a) Why did the British import opium to China? (b) What was the Chinese response? (c) What did the British gain from the treaty ending the Opium War?
3. (a) What conditions led to the Taiping Rebellion? (b) What change in outlook did the revolt cause among China's leaders?
4. (a) What events caused the United States to announce the Open-Door Policy? (b) What did this policy protect?
5. What were the goals of Chinese nationalists?

Critical Thinking
6. Despite its losses in the 1800's, China remained an independent country. Why was China not carved into colonies as Africa was?

Japan built a modern nation. 5

When imperialists threated China, the Chinese fought to keep their traditional way of life. Japan chose a different course. It responded by becoming a powerful rival of European nations.

Americans ended Japanese isolation.

Japan in 1850 was almost as it had been in the 1600's when the Tokugawa family took control of the country and ushered in an era of peace. For 250 years, Tokugawa shoguns ruled over a remarkably stable society. During this period, the Japanese had almost no contact with the industrialized countries of the world. Japan continued to trade with China, but the only Europeans allowed in the country were Dutch traders who kept an outpost at Nagasaki.

Then, in 1853, four United States ships commanded by Commodore Matthew Perry steamed into what is now Tokyo harbor. Perry came to ask the Japanese to open their country to foreign trade. The Japanese who lined the harbor were astounded by the foreigners' black ships made of iron and powered by steam. They were also shocked by the cannons and rifles that could have wiped out hundreds of the fiercest samurai in a matter of seconds.

The Japanese felt that they had no choice but to give in to Perry's demands and sign a treaty with the United States. They were not strong enough to force the foreigners to leave. The treaty the Japanese signed was the first of many with the Western powers. By 1860, Japan, like China, had granted permission to trade and extraterritorial rights to many foreign nations.

The Japanese feared that foreigners would take over Japan unless some changes took place. Therefore, in 1868, a new group of leaders overthrew the last of the Tokugawa shoguns. The new leaders ruled in the name of Emperor Mutsuhito, who was just 15 years old. Mutsuhito chose the name *Meiji* for his reign, meaning "enlightened rule."

Industrialization transformed Japan.

The Meiji era was a revolutionary time in Japan. During the 45 years of Mutsuhito's reign, one change followed another. Feudalism was ended,

Commodore Matthew Perry arrived in Japan in 1853. His huge warships dwarfed the Japanese boats that went out to meet them. With this show of strength, Perry forced Japan to open its ports to American merchants.

Japan responded to the threat from the West by developing its own industries.

and Japan adopted a constitution much like Germany's. As in Germany, real power was in the hands of a small group of men who were determined to build a powerful nation.

Industrialization in Japan "Open the country to drive out the barbarians" was the slogan of leaders such as Tomomi Iwakura (toh-moh-mee ee-wah-koo-rah). To do so, he vowed to seek knowledge throughout the world. In 1873, Iwakura led the first of many missions to Europe and North America. On these missions, the Japanese studied foreign ways of life and chose the best Western civilization had to offer. Observed one Japanese leader:

Are we to delay the using of steam machinery until we have discovered the principles of steam for ourselves? If we can select examples from them [Westerners] and adopt their contrivances, why should we not be successful in working them out?

Over the next 30 years, the Japanese economy became as modern as any in the world. The country's first railroad line was built in 1872, connecting Tokyo, the nation's capital, with the port of Yokohama some 20 miles away. By 1914, Japan had more than 7,000 miles of railroad track. Coal production grew from half a million tons in 1875 to more than 21 million tons in 1913. Meanwhile, large state-supported companies built thousands of factories. Japan's government took an active part in the development of industry.

Little help came from the outside. Fearful of economic dependence, the Japanese borrowed as little money as possible from European or American bankers. Any money they did borrow was quickly repaid. Japan earned most of the capital it needed to modernize by the sale of such traditional products as silk.

Japanese imperialism Economic development was only one part of Japan's plan to become a world power. Another part of the plan was military reform. Japan's new leaders believed that military strength was essential for a strong and independent nation. In modernizing its army and building a navy, the Japanese chose the best that Europe had to offer. Japanese leaders patterned their army after Germany's and their navy after

Britain's. By 1890, Japan had several dozen war-ships and 500,000 soldiers.

Japan was now strong enough to renegotiate the unequal treaties it had signed in the 1850's. In 1899, the Japanese persuaded Western powers to give up their extraterritorial privileges in Japan.

As Japan became stronger, it also became more imperialistic. Like many European nations, Japan saw empire building as a way of meeting its economic needs. As in Europe, national pride also played a large part in Japan's imperialism. The Japanese were determined to show the world that theirs was a powerful nation.

From the start, Japan's leaders saw opportunities to expand at China's expense. In 1894, the two countries went to war. As a result of that war, China was forced to grant Korea independence. Soon, the Japanese began to take over Korea. They also moved into Manchuria, China's north-eastern province, which was rich in iron and coal. Japan's growing interest in Manchuria alarmed the Russians, who were also eager to take over the province. In 1904, the conflict exploded in the Russo-Japanese War.

Most Europeans expected Russia to defeat Japan easily. To their surprise, the Japanese won victory after victory. At the Battle of Tsushima (soo-shee-muh), fought in the straits between Japan and Korea, the Japanese navy sank 38 of the 40 ships in the Russian Far Eastern Fleet.

With their victory in the war, the Japanese won control of all Russian business interests in southern Manchuria. Though still technically part of China, Manchuria was now a part of Japan's sphere of influence. More important, Japan won recognition as a great power. It was the only Asian country that was able to deal with the West as an equal.

Section Review 5

Identify: (a) Matthew Perry, (b) Mutsuhito, (c) Meiji, (d) Battle of Tsushima, (e) Russo-Japanese War
Answer:
1. (a) What was the policy of the Tokugawa shoguns toward other nations? (b) What changed this policy?
2. How did the reign of the Tokugawa shoguns come to an end?

3. What changes took place in Japan during the Meiji era?
4. (a) How did Japan become an imperialist nation? (b) What was the importance of the Russo-Japanese War?

Critical Thinking
5. Reread the quotation on page 549. What attitude toward modernization did Japanese leaders take?

Imperialism reached the Western Hemisphere. 6

Europeans and Americans brought many changes to countries such as China and Japan. Contact with the West also changed life in places that once seemed very remote and isolated. In some of these places, Westerners took political control and started colonies. In others, they were interested only in economic power.

Outsiders dominated Latin America.

By 1870, a number of European nations were eyeing Latin America with new interest. It had many of the resources their factories needed. Suddenly there was a demand for tin from Bolivia and copper from Chile. There was also a market for Latin American food products. The revolution in land and sea transportation helped open those markets. For example, the development of refrigerated railroad cars and refrigerated ships enabled countries such as Argentina to ship huge quantities of refrigerated beef and mutton to Europe.

Latin Americans responded to the growing demand for raw materials and crops by increasing their output. In doing so, however, they needed capital to build railroads, docks, processing plants, and other facilities. Latin American governments borrowed money for improvements from banks in Europe and the United States. Latin American landowners and business people also borrowed money to expand their enterprises.

Gradually, however, outsiders took over ownership of plantations, mines, processing plants, and other key businesses in Latin America. By

1914, Britain had invested more than $5 billion in Latin America. The United States, which had only a very tiny investment in the region in 1870, had more than $1.6 billion invested by 1914. As outsiders became more involved in Latin America's economy, their political influence also increased.

The United States had the greatest stake in Latin America. Leaders in the United States believed that unrest in the region threatened the security not only of American businesses there but also the security of the United States itself. These leaders were especially fearful that Europeans might take over unstable governments in Latin America to protect their investments.

Since the 1820's, the United States had been using the Monroe Doctrine (page 504) to keep foreigners out of the Americas. In the 1890's, the United States began to use that doctrine in new ways. The United States government acted as a negotiator in disputes between Latin American nations and European powers. It was even willing to go to war to protect its interests in the region.

Spain and the United States fought a war.

Cuba was one of the last Spanish colonies in the Americas. The Cubans rose up against Spain in 1895. American newspapers printed daily reports of the conflict, shocking their readers with tales of Spanish brutality and Cuban heroism. While the Spanish efforts to put down the revolt were indeed brutal, many of the news accounts were exaggerated. As a result of these stories, the American public clamored for war against Spain to free Cuba.

The United States had several reasons for watching the revolution closely. A number of Americans did business in Cuba. They had plantations, factories, and warehouses on the island. In fact, the United States bought most of its sugar from Cuba. Cuba had strategic importance as well. It guarded the entrance to the Gulf of Mexico.

Many people in the United States identified with the Cubans. They saw Cuba's fight for freedom as similar to their own war for independence.

United States' interest in Latin America increased after 1900 with the building of the Panama Canal. Here, workers dig the 8-mile-long Gaillard Cut.

Thus, when the United States battleship *Maine* mysteriously blew up in Havana harbor on February 15, 1898, the United States was quick to blame Spain. On April 24, the two nations went to war.

The war lasted five months. When it was over, the United States had won much of Spain's empire in the Caribbean and the Pacific. Although Cuba was allowed its independence, the United States insisted on the right to intervene in Cuban affairs. The United States also claimed the right to build naval bases on the island.

The United States built a canal.

In the years after the Spanish-American War, the United States increased its involvement in Latin American affairs. The United States government worked closely with investors to protect and expand trade in the region.

No president was more enthusiastic about expanding American interests abroad than Theodore Roosevelt, who led the nation from 1901 to 1909. He was especially eager to build a canal across the narrow Isthmus of Panama, which was then part of Colombia. Such a canal would shorten the sea route from New York to San Francisco by more than 5,000 miles. The United States Navy could move more quickly to defend either of the nation's coasts.

In 1903, the United States offered Colombia $10 million plus a yearly payment for the right to build a canal across Panama. The Colombian senate thought the price was ridiculously low for what would soon be an extremely valuable trade route. They demanded a higher price.

Roosevelt responded by encouraging a revolution in Panama. Panamanians had often tried to break away from Colombia. With help from the United States Navy, rebels in Panama quickly

Voice from the Past · A View of Imperialism

Carl Schurz came to the United States from Germany after fighting in the revolutions of 1848. He was elected to the United States Senate in 1869. The following excerpt is from a speech he gave in 1899, when the United States was preparing to take over the Philippines, Pacific islands that had belonged to Spain.

If we take those new regions, we shall be well entangled in that contest for territorial aggrandizement [expansion], which distracts other nations and drives them far beyond their original design. So it will be . . . with us. We shall want new conquests to protect that which we already possess. The greed of speculators, working upon our government, will push us from one point to another, and we shall have new conflicts on our hands, almost without knowing how we got into them . . . We are told that our industries are gasping for breath; that we are suffering from over-production; that our products must have new outlets, and that we need colonies and dependencies the world over to give us more markets. More markets? Certainly. But do we, civilized beings, indulge in the absurd and barbarous notion that we must own the countries with which we wish to trade? Here are our official reports before us telling us that of late years our export trade has grown enormously . . . Trade is developed, not by the best guns, but by the best merchants.

1. What does Schurz predict will happen if the United States begins to follow an imperialist policy?
2. (a) What economic argument in favor of imperialism does he summarize? (b) How does he respond to it?
3. If Schurz had still been a senator, how do you think he would have voted on the annexation of the Philippines? Explain your answer.

won their independence. They then leased the United States a ten-mile-wide zone in which to build a waterway.

For the next ten years, American engineers battled floods, heat, and mosquitos while building the canal. In 1914, the canal was finally opened. Ships from all nations began to use it. Latin America become a crossroads of world trade.

As interest in Latin America grew, Roosevelt issued a *corollary* to the Monroe Doctrine. (A corollary is a natural result of another statement.) In 1823, the Monroe Doctrine had warned Europeans that the Americas were closed to further colonization. Now, Roosevelt's corollary said that as a result of that warning, the United States had the right to act as an international police officer in the Americas.

The Roosevelt Corollary was used to justify American intervention in Latin America on several occasions. The United States sent troops to such countries as Haiti, Nicaragua, the Dominican Republic, and Cuba.

The situation in Latin America showed the link between political and economic independence. To be truly independent, a country needed to control both its own economy and its own government. The presence of foreign interests spurred a new growth of nationalism in Latin America.

Interest in Pacific islands grew.

Even before the Panama Canal opened, interest in the islands that dotted the Pacific was growing. By the late 1800's, Europeans and Americans were competing fiercely for control of the larger islands and island groups.

Rivalry grew for a variety of reasons. Some islands were rich in resources. Others were valued as coaling stations and naval bases. Steamships ran on large amounts of coal. Therefore, every trading nation needed places where its huge freighters could stop and refuel. Naval bases were also needed, where a ship could stop for repairs if necessary. The great engines that powered steamships required trained technicians with special equipment. Few nations were willing to rely on their rivals for coal or repairs. Each country wanted its own islands in the Pacific.

In 1876, Europeans and Americans controlled fewer than half the islands in the Pacific. By 1900, nearly all the islands had lost their independence. Britain was the leader here as elsewhere. It held Australia, New Zealand, Fiji, the southern Solomons, and many other islands in the Pacific. Germany took the northern Solomons and a number of islands once held by Spain. France controlled Tahiti.

The United States was mainly interested in Hawaii. By the 1880's, Americans dominated the islands and were eager for the United States to annex them. When Queen Liliukalani refused to give up her country's freedom, she was overthrown. In 1898, Hawaii became part of the United States. The following year, as a result of the Spanish-American War, the United States also won control of Guam and the Philippines.

No part of the world was too remote for trade and colonization. The industrial nations were willing to compete for even the most distant island. By the early 1900's, explorers from several nations were racing to claim even the frozen wastes of Antarctica.

Section Review 6

Define: Roosevelt corollary
Identify: (a) Latin America, (b) Spanish-American War, (c) Theodore Roosevelt, (e) Panama, (f) Liliukalani
Answer:
1. (a) Why were European countries interested in Latin America? (b) How did European economic influence in Latin America increase?
2. Why was the United States concerned about events in Latin America?
3. (a) Give four reasons for the United States' interest in the Cuban revolt. (b) What was the result of the war between the United States and Spain?
4. How did the United States gain the right to build a canal in Panama?
5. Why were industrialized nations interested in Pacific islands?

Critical Thinking
6. (a) How are political and economic independence linked? (b) If two countries, such as Brazil and Great Britain, are trading, how can one trading partner be more dependent than the other?

Chapter Review 25

Summary

1. Nations competed for overseas empires. The need for new markets, the desire to foster national pride and spread European values, and the lure of adventure all fostered imperialism. By 1900, European powers, the United States, and Japan had colonial empires in Africa, India, China, and the Pacific islands.

2. Imperialists divided Africa. Armed with superior weapons, European nations conquered all of Africa except Liberia and Ethiopia. Under colonial rule, Africans became second-class citizens.

3. The British dominated South Asia. By 1757, the British East India Company was the leading power in India. In 1857, following the Sepoy Mutiny, the British government forced the East India Company to turn over the rule of India to the British crown. Benefits of British rule were reaped mainly by Europeans. Discrimination against Indians caused the rise of nationalism in the late 1800's.

4. Imperialism threatened China. Defeat in the Opium War of 1839 forced China to open its ports to British traders. In the following years, one country after another established spheres of influence in China. By 1850, China was on the verge of bankruptcy. Corruption in the civil service, foreign control, and famine lead to a rebellion against the Ch'ing dynasty.

In 1899, the United States proposed the Open-Door Policy to protect American trading rights in the country. Resentment of imperialism fostered secret societies and nationalism in China.

5. Japan built a modern nation. Japan's isolation ended when American Commodore Matthew Perry sailed into Tokyo Harbor in 1853. The Meiji era of modernization that followed gave Japan a strong economy. Military reforms fostered imperialism.

6. Imperialism reached the Western Hemisphere. Although Latin American countries maintained their independence, foreign investments tied Latin American economies to outside powers. United States control of Latin America increased after a war with Spain in the late 1800's. In 1904, the United States used the Roosevelt Corollary to justify intervention in Latin American affairs. Not long after, the United States began work on the Panama Canal. By the late 1800's, outsiders were also competing for control of Pacific islands.

Reviewing the Facts

1. Define the following terms:
   a. imperialism
   b. protectorate
   c. condominium
   d. extraterritorial rights
   e. sphere of influence

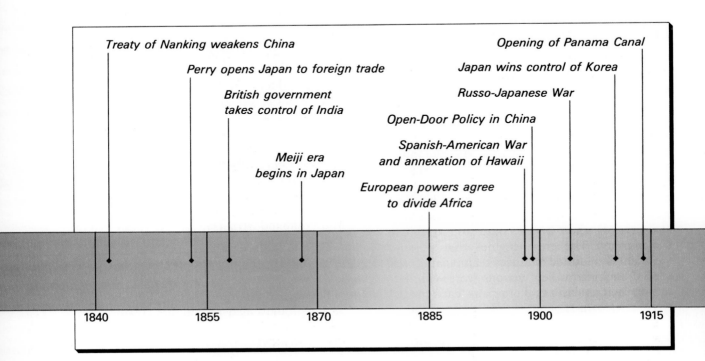

Treaty of Nanking weakens China

Perry opens Japan to foreign trade

British government takes control of India

Meiji era begins in Japan

European powers agree to divide Africa

Open-Door Policy in China

Spanish-American War and annexation of Hawaii

Russo-Japanese War

Japan wins control of Korea

Opening of Panama Canal

1840   1855   1870   1885   1900   1915

2. Explain the importance of each of the following names, places, or terms:

a. Livingstone
b. Leopold II
c. Suez Canal
d. Menelik II
e. Boer
f. uitlander
g. East India Company
h. Sepoy Mutiny
i. Sikh
j. Indian National Congress
k. Muslim League
l. Opium War
m. Open-Door Policy
n. Boxer Rebellion
o. Perry
p. Meiji era
q. Russo-Japanese War
r. Latin America
s. Spanish-American War
t. Panama Canal
u. Roosevelt Corollary

3. (a) How did the need for new markets and raw materials affect imperialism? (b) What part did nationalism play?
4. (a) How did the scramble for colonies in Africa begin? (b) Why did European countries meet in Berlin in 1884 and 1885?
5. (a) How did France gain control of parts of North Africa and West Africa? (b) How did Britain gain control of Egypt and the Sudan?
6. (a) Why did the history of South Africa differ from that of the rest of the continent? (b) How did European rule affect Africans?
7. (a) What led to war between the British and the Boers? (b) What was the outcome?
8. (a) What led to the rise of nationalism in India? (b) How did the Raj respond?
9. (a) Describe China in 1800. (b) How did the British use opium to gain power there?
10. (a) How did colonization in China differ from colonization in Africa? (b) What were the goals of Chinese nationalists?
11. (a) How did Japan keep from becoming a colonized nation? (b) How did it become an imperialistic power?
12. (a) How did outsiders gain control of Latin America? (b) Name two ways the United States increased its power there.

Thinking about History

1. In the early 1900's, the British boasted that the sun never set on their empire. What did they mean? Support your answer with information from the maps in this chapter.
2. Explain why the Suez Canal has been called Britain's lifeline.

3. On page 553, the text states that "to be truly independent, a country needed to control both its own economy and its own government." Apply this statement to each of the following regions. (a) Latin America (b) China (c) India (d) South Africa

Writing and Speaking about History

1. Write an essay based on one of the following:
   a. India was the brightest jewel in Her Majesty's crown.
   b. India was a millstone around the necks of the British.
2. Write five sentences that support the following thesis statement: "Imperialism benefits the Mother Country at the expense of the colonies."
3. Debate the following topic: "The United States had the right to enforce the Monroe Doctrine."

Practicing Skills

1. Review the maps on pages 537 and 546. (a) What European countries moved into African lands once claimed by the Ottomans? (b) What foreign power claimed the East Asian treaty port of Hong Kong? (c) Of Macao? (d) Of Port Arthur?
2. (a) What group of islands in Southeast Asia did the United States claim (page 543)? (b) Use a present-day map of Southeast Asia (page 737) to tell what modern countries lie in the region once known as French Indochina.

Investigating History

1. Prepare a data base file on colonies using these fields: (a) colony, (b) location, (c) colonial power, (d) date of colonization. Update this file later on by including a field for the present-day name of the colony and a field for the date of independence.
2. Many of Rudyard Kipling's poems provide insights into the way Kipling and the British viewed imperialism. Find examples from Kipling's writing that reflect these views.

Decision Making in History

As a Japanese government official in the 1850's, you are torn between adopting European ways and maintaining ancient Japanese traditions. What recommendations will you make to the emperor? What arguments will you present for modernization?

The Turn of the Century

Photography was in vogue at the turn of the century, whether it was the work of professional portrait photographers (as shown in the poster above) or enthusiastic amateurs such as young Jacques Lartigue.

1. **Inventions changed ways of life.**

2. **Science presented new ideas.**

3. **Women sought rights and freedoms.**

4. **Art and entertainment took new forms.**

5. **Europe faced rising tensions.**

"Photography is a magic thing! A magic thing with all sorts of mysterious smells, a bit strange and frightening, but something you learn to love very quickly." So wrote seven-year-old Jacques Lartigue (lahr-**TEEG**) in his diary in 1901. His father, a wealthy Parisian banker, bought Jacques his first camera.

Photography had come a long way since Louis Daguerre (duh-**GARE**) had made the first hazy photographs in the 1830's. By the 1850's, homes all over the world were decorated with solemn, black and white family photographs. Known as daguerreotypes, such pictures cost as little as 25 cents each. By 1900, simple box cameras like the one Jacques owned could produce black and white photographs as good as those today.

Armed with his camera, young Jacques set out to capture the world around him. His pictures give a glimpse of life in a well-to-do family of the time.

By 1900, the upper classes in France and other industrialized countries had luxuries that earlier generations had never known. Electric lights or gaslights lit their houses at night. Coal furnaces or gas heaters warmed them in winter. Hot and cold running water, flush toilets, and bathtubs made their lives easier, cleaner, and more comfortable than ever before. The telephone kept them in touch with distant friends and relatives. Their servants—for even middle-class households had "help"—cooked meals on huge, iron stoves and washed clothes in machines.

Jacques's photos show not only his friends and relatives but also the new machines of the early 1900's. With his father, Jacques went to the military airfield outside Paris and saw France's first flimsy airplanes take to the sky. Most of all, however, Jacques loved automobiles. In 1912, his father bought a 35-horsepower Peugeot—"a big, open monster," Jacques called it. The Lartigue family, wearing goggles and rubber coats in case it rained, roared along the dirt roads at 30 miles per hour.

Sitting next to Yves, the family chauffeur, Jacques waited eagerly for the chance to pass another car.

We see a car ahead of us. Yves accelerates. We are coming closer . . . We see the white cloud behind the wheels of the car, smell the dust . . . Oh, what a fantastic moment . . . There we go, past the other car! I feel cut off from the rest of the world, wonderfully superior to everybody else; I wish we would never stop!

Such an event, Jacques wrote sadly, "doesn't happen too often . . . there are still so few cars on the road."

In this chapter, we will see some of the new inventions and scientific developments that altered Jacques Lartigue's life in the early 1900's. We will also see how the writers and artists of this exciting age viewed their world. Finally, we will see how governments responded to the challenge of this new age.

Jacques Lartigue (left) skillfully photographed scenes from daily life in the early 1900's. At right, the Lartigue's chauffeur changes a flat tire.

557

Inventions changed ways of life. 1

Worldwide industrial production more than tripled between 1870 and 1914. The Industrial Revolution touched lands from Europe to Japan and Australia. Three countries dominated the world economy—Great Britain, Germany, and the United States. Together, these countries produced two thirds of all the world's manufactured goods in 1913. This economic growth was accompanied by rapid advances in technology.

Bessemer began an Age of Steel.

In the mid-1800's, despite all the advances of science and industry, iron was still the basic metal for tools and machines. In the 3,000 years since the Iron Age began (page 38), nothing had replaced iron. In the late 1800's, however, a new age began—the Age of Steel.

Steel is a mixture of purified iron and a small amount of carbon. It is tougher, lighter, and more flexible than iron. For hundreds of years, metalworkers made steel in small quantities for swords and knives. (Steel can hold a sharp edge, and iron cannot.) Purifying steel took weeks of steady heating, making the metal very expensive.

In the 1850's, an Englishman named Henry Bessemer developed a less costly way to make steel. He forced blasts of hot air through the molten iron to burn out impurities. Bessemer began using this new "blast furnace" in 1859 in his factories at Sheffield. Operating around the clock, the huge furnaces lit up the night sky with an eerie glare.

By the turn of the century, steel was widely used for machinery, ships, and railroad track. Steel rails lasted up to 15 times longer than iron ones. Steel girders replaced stone and iron as the supports for buildings. The first building with a steel frame was Chicago's ten-story Home Insurance Building, completed in 1884.

New sources of power came into use.

Before 1890, the tallest buildings stood about 20 stories high. With steel girders, architects could plan much taller buildings, but how would people reach the top floors? In 1889, the invention of the electric elevator made possible a new kind of building for crowded cities—the skyscraper. By 1913, New York City was a city of skyscrapers. Its 60-story Woolworth Building, completed that year, was the world's tallest building. It rose 792 feet above the shadowy streets.

Electricity was one of the new kinds of energy that were coming into use in the late 1800's. Just as iron was giving way to steel for some uses, coal and steam were giving way to electricity, oil, gasoline, and natural gas.

To many people, electricity seemed the most magical of the new kinds of energy. Early in the 1800's, Alessandro Volta and Michael Faraday had discovered ways to make small amounts of electricity. In 1872, the Belgian electrician Zenobe Gramme developed the first industrial dynamo. Dynamos generated electric power by using steam engines to spin electromagnets. With the invention of the dynamo, electricity moved out of the laboratory and into daily life.

Edison set up a research laboratory.

If electricity seemed like magic, without doubt its greatest magician was the American inventor, Thomas Alva Edison (1847–1931). Edison worked on everything from movie projectors to household irons, from phonographs to doorbells. Altogether, he patented more than 1,000 inventions.

As a 12-year-old boy in Michigan, Edison had sold newspapers and candy on commuter trains to and from Detroit. While the commuters were at work, he taught himself mathematics and science in the public library. He also set up a laboratory in one of the boxcars on the train.

By the time he was 20 years old, Edison was working as a telegrapher, but he regarded inventing as his real career. In 1870, he went from poverty to wealth in a single bound when he sold his invention of a stock ticker for $40,000.

The wizard of Menlo Park Edison used his money to start a laboratory in Menlo Park, New Jersey, where he worked full-time as an inventor. Indeed, the idea of a laboratory for industrial research and development was Edison's most important invention.

A steady stream of inventions flowed from Edison's laboratory. People began calling him "the wizard of Menlo Park." Actually, Edison was not

Daily Life · *Music for the Home*

"Mary had a little lamb," bellowed Thomas Edison into the mouthpiece of his newest invention. The device recorded the sound vibrations on a sheet of tin foil wrapped around a cylinder. When Edison turned the crank, a scratchy imitation of his own voice came back through the funnel-shaped speaker. It was the first phonograph.

Like Edison's prototype, the earliest record players needed no electricity. To hear a record, you simply wound up the phonograph with a crank. It played until it ran down. The earliest records were wax cylinders, later replaced by disks. On such recordings, people could hear all kinds of music, from music-hall entertainers to world-famous opera singers, in their own homes.

so much an inventor as a perfecter of already existing inventions. "The first thing," he said, "is to find out what everyone else knows and begin where they leave off."

The electric light In 1879, Edison developed the first practical electric light bulb. As early as 1808, an English scientist named Humphrey Davy had made a bulb in which a piece of thin metal would glow. The problem, which baffled inventors for years, was to find something that would glow but would not quickly burn itself out.

After months of trial and error, Edison discovered an answer—thin cotton thread coated with carbon. Making sure that a vacuum existed inside the bulb, Edison turned on the current.

It lit up . . . We sat and looked, and the lamp continued to burn. None of us could go to bed, and there was no sleep for any of us for 40 hours. We sat and just watched it, with anxiety growing into elation.

Within three years, Edison perfected light bulbs that would burn for 1,400 hours. He also designed and guided the construction of New York City's first electrical system. On September 4, 1882, as the sun set, New York's first electric streetlight glowed to life.

Telephones and radios carried voices.

Electricity had powered the first great advance in modern communications, the telegraph. In the late 1800's, it powered two more advances, the telephone and the radio.

Bell and the telephone Alexander Graham Bell (1847–1922) was a Scot who emigrated to the United States. He studied speech and sound to teach deaf students to talk. He was also interested in transmitting sound electrically. After several years of experimenting, he succeeded in changing the sound waves of the human voice into electric impulses, sending them through a wire and then changing them back to sound waves at the other end. Bell patented his invention, which he called a telephone, in 1876.

At the Philadelphia Exposition in 1876, Bell displayed his telephone to the astonished crowd. Among those watching was the emperor of Brazil, who used Bell's machine to speak with an aide in another room. "My word!" the emperor exclaimed when his aide answered, "It speaks Portuguese!"

The telephone quickly became an essential part of modern life. By 1900, there were nearly 2 million telephones in the United States, and by 1912, there were 8.7 million. The telephone also spread rapidly in the cities of western Europe, especially in Germany and Britain.

Marconi and the radio The next challenge was to send messages without using wires. Many people contributed to the invention of the radio. Physicists James C. Maxwell and Heinrich Hertz made the theoretical discoveries about electromagnetic waves, or radio waves. Then, in 1895, inventor Guglielmo Marconi used these waves to send telegraph signals directly through the air, without the use of wires. He used transmitters that sent out electromagnetic signals at certain frequencies and receivers that could be "tuned in" to pick up the signals. In 1901, Marconi's wireless telegraph sent Morse code across the Atlantic. Primitive radios were soon standard equipment for ships at sea. Not until later could radios transmit human voices.

A new engine burned gasoline.

During the 1870's, many inventors experimented with an engine that would run on gasoline. Like the steam engine, the gasoline engine had a piston that moved inside a cylinder. Instead of steam pressure to move the piston, the gasoline engine used a series of small explosions inside the cylinder. Because the gasoline burned inside the cylinder, the new machine came to be called an *internal combustion engine*. It was much smaller than a steam-powered engine. Steam-powered vehicles were large because they had to carry coal, water, and a furnace in which the coal burned to heat the water. By contrast, the gasoline engine needed no furnace and no water, only a tank to hold the gasoline.

In 1885, German inventor Gottlieb Daimler mounted a gasoline engine on a bicycle to produce the world's first motorcycle. In 1890, he founded the Daimler Motor Company. He manufactured cars that he named for a friend's daughter, Mercedes.

Ford built cars on an assembly line.

By 1900, about 13,000 automobiles were sputtering and clattering along the roads of Europe and North America. Some of these vehicles could reach speeds of 10 to 15 miles per hour. Nearly all of them had been assembled by hand. Such cars were expensive to buy and to repair. As a result, they remained luxuries that the average worker never dreamed of buying.

One of the mechanics who built such cars was an American named Henry Ford. Ford decided to make cars that many people could buy. "The way to make automobiles is to make them all alike," he said, "just as one pin is like another pin when it comes from the pin factory, or one match is like another." Ford's solution was the Model T, a homely but reliable car. By 1913, it was selling for just $500, less than half the usual price of a car.

How did Ford lower prices? Part of the answer was mass production. Ford's Tin Lizzies were made from standardized, interchangeable parts. Thus, they were easier to assemble and repair than other cars.

Ford's major innovation was to improve efficiency in his factory. He watched his workers and noticed that they spent much of their time carrying parts and tools to the car they were working on. To put an end to this wasted time and motion, Ford set up an **assembly line**.

The assembly line was a moving conveyor belt that rolled unfinished automobiles past the workers. Workers did their tasks one after the other while the chassis moved slowly past. By 1914, workers on Ford's assembly line could put a car together from start to finish in less than two hours. Soon, Ford's Detroit factory was producing 2,000 cars every hour.

By 1914, there were more than 600,000 cars in operation around the world. Of these, 75 percent were in the United States, where the Automobile Age had gotten off to a roaring start.

The Wrights built an airplane.

Meanwhile, in 1903, two brothers from Dayton, Ohio, had put the gasoline engine to a spectacular new use. At Kitty Hawk, North Carolina, on a cold, windy December morning, Wilbur and Orville Wright launched the age of powered flight. This first airplane flight lasted only 12 seconds and covered 120 feet. By 1905, the Wrights' third plane, *Flyer III*, could do all kinds of maneuvers and stay aloft for half an hour.

In 1908, Wilbur Wright went to Paris to demonstrate the airplane. The American pilot was greeted as a conquering hero. Crowds cheered as they watched him fly rings around the Eiffel Tower and stay aloft as long as two hours at a time.

Unlike the automobile, which blossomed almost overnight, the airplane developed slowly. Even in 1914, the total number of airplanes in the world was less than 1,000.

Inventions became group efforts.

The Wright brothers were among the last in a long line of independent inventors. Many early inventions of the Industrial Revolution were the

In the Wright Flyer, the pilot lay prone to minimize wind resistance. To take off, the plane rolled along a track made of two-by-four boards.

work of one or two people experimenting in their basements, backyards, or small workshops. After 1900, however, most major technical advances resulted from group effort. Technology had become too complex and too expensive for one person to undertake a project from start to finish.

Therefore, after 1900, it is seldom accurate to name one person as *the* inventor of a complex device such as the computer or the television. As the twentieth century progressed, most new inventions came from research laboratories such as the one that Edison founded at Menlo Park.

Section Review 1

Define: (a) steel, (b) dynamo, (c) assembly line
Identify: (a) Henry Bessemer, (b) Thomas Edison, (c) Alexander Graham Bell, (d) Guglielmo Marconi, (e) Henry Ford, (f) Orville and Wilbur Wright
Answer:
1. What countries dominated world industry in the year 1900?
2. (a) Why did steel become more common in the late 1800's? (b) What were some of its most important uses?
3. (a) What were the major sources of energy in the early Industrial Revolution? (b) In the later Industrial Revolution?
4. Briefly describe the contributions of Thomas Edison.
5. How did communications change in the late 1800's and early 1900's?
6. What changes did Henry Ford bring to the auto industry?

Critical Thinking
7. (a) Using the quotation from Ford on page 560, explain how his attitude on making goods differed from those of a traditional craftsperson. (b) From a worker's point of view, what would be the advantages and disadvantages of an assembly line?

Science presented new ideas. 2

Theoretical scientists such as Volta, Faraday, Maxwell, and Hertz laid the groundwork for Edison and Marconi. In a similar way, other scientists in the late 1800's and early 1900's were pushing the frontiers of knowledge forward.

561

Medical discoveries saved lives.

At the beginning of the 1800's, doctors had few weapons in the fight against disease. Some of their "cures"—such as bloodletting—did more harm than good. Thanks to advances during the 1800's, more and more diseases could be cured or even prevented. By 1875, Europeans lived an average of 15 years longer than their grandparents had lived.

As you have read, Edward Jenner discovered a way to prevent smallpox (page 432). By 1875, widespread inoculation had nearly wiped out smallpox in western Europe.

Another major discovery came in the 1840's. Several American doctors and dentists began using the gases ether and chloroform to "knock out" their patients during painful operations. With this discovery of anesthesia, surgery became a routine part of medical care rather than a last-resort remedy.

Lister Although anesthesia made surgery less painful, nearly half of all surgical patients still died of infection. No one knew why. A Scottish surgeon, Joseph Lister (1827–1912), suggested that infection might be connected with the filthy conditions that were normal in hospitals. Patients were seldom bathed. Doctors worked in their street clothes and went from one patient to the next without even cleaning their instruments.

In 1865, Lister began a new program of cleanliness in his hospital ward. He insisted that his staff keep the place spotlessly clean. He began using carbolic acid to clean medical instruments. As a result, 85 percent of his patients survived. By 1890, other European and American hospitals were trying to live up to Lister's standard of cleanliness.

Pasteur Although Lister believed that tiny, invisible particles caused infection, he had no proof at first. Then, in 1865, Lister read of the work that French scientist Louis Pasteur (pas-**TUHR**) was doing. (The two scientists later became good friends.)

Pasteur (1822–1895) was experimenting to find out why milk soured and alcohol fermented. He discovered that the causes were microscopic organisms he called bacteria. He found that heat could destroy many harmful bacteria. The process of heating a liquid to kill the bacteria in it is now called *pasteurization*.

Pasteur also found ways to weaken the micro-organisms that caused disease. Among other diseases, he worked with the virus that caused rabies, which was always fatal. In 1885, grief-stricken parents brought him their nine-year-old son who had been bitten by a rabid dog. Pasteur hesitated to use his new methods on a person without more tests, but there was no other hope. He inoculated the boy, and the youngster recovered.

Armed with the new knowledge of bacteria, later scientists found the causes of many diseases. Slowly, they also began to find cures. Moreover, when people saw how closely disease and filth were connected, they began to be more careful with city water supplies and food products. As a result, such diseases as cholera and typhus claimed fewer lives.

Darwin developed the theory of evolution.

No scientific idea of the 1800's caused a greater upheaval than the work of British biologist Charles Darwin (1809–1882). Darwin's research dated from the mid-1800's, but the controversy about his writings reached a peak in the latter part of the century. The cause of the controversy was Darwin's answer to the most challenging and important question that faced biologists: How can we explain the tremendous variety of plants and animals on Earth?

The most widely accepted answer in the 1800's was the idea of *special creation*. According to this view, every kind of plant and animal had been created by God at the beginning of the world and had remained the same since then.

Darwin challenged the idea of special creation. In 1859, he published a book titled *The Origin of Species by Means of Natural Selection*. Interest was so great that the book sold out immediately. In his book, Darwin put forward three major premises:

1. Within every species, more individuals are born than can survive. Therefore, every living thing takes part in a constant struggle for survival.
2. Variations—differences among individuals—make some members of a species better fitted to their environment than others. The fittest individuals are most likely to survive. Darwin called this idea *natural selection*.

3. Because the fittest individuals are more likely to live to become adults, they are therefore more likely to have offspring. Thus, they pass on their differences to a new generation.

This process, Darwin reasoned, explains how species change over time and how new species gradually arise from old ones. Thus, over time, many different kinds of living things could have developed from a few early ones. Darwin's idea of change through natural selection came to be called the *theory of evolution.* (Darwin himself did not use the term evolution.)

The Origin of Species caused great excitement among scientists. Naturalist Thomas Henry Huxley wrote, "It is doubtful if any single book, except the *Principia* [of Sir Isaac Newton], ever worked so great and rapid a revolution in science." By 1900, nearly all biologists and botanists accepted the theory of evolution as the best explanation of variety among living things.

At the same time, Darwin's ideas roused a storm of debate outside the scientific community. Many people believed that the idea of evolution directly contradicted the account of creation in the Bible. The bishop of Oxford, for example, accused Darwin of "a tendency to limit God's glory in creation." In 1871, Darwin fueled the conflict when he published *The Descent of Man.* In this new book, he said that humans too had evolved from earlier forms of life.

The evolution controversy continued for decades. Even today, well over 100 years after *The Origin of Species* was first published, Darwin's ideas are not universally accepted.

Social Darwinists favored competition.

Darwin was a biologist, but a number of nineteenth-century thinkers applied his ideas about plants and animals to economics and politics. The leader in this movement was Herbert Spencer, an English sociologist.

Footnote to History

In 1901, a London newspaper polled its readers, asking for lists of the 10 most influential books of the past 100 years. Of the hundreds of different lists that the paper received, every one included *The Origin of Species.*

Free economic competition, Spencer argued, was natural selection in action. The best companies, for example, make profits, while inefficient ones go bankrupt. Spencer applied the same rules to individuals. Those who were fittest for survival enjoyed wealth and success, while the poor remained poor because they were unfit. This idea became known as *social Darwinism.* Social Darwinists believed that governments should not upset the "natural" system of rich and poor.

Others carried Darwin's ideas even further. The German philosopher Friedrich Nietzsche (NEE-chuh) believed that some humans could and should evolve to a higher level by the use of willpower and courage. Such people would become *übermenschen* (supermen) above the common herd. "I am opposed," Nietzsche wrote, "to parliamentary government . . . because [it is] the means whereby cattle become masters."

Many nationalists and imperialists seized on both Darwin's and Nietzsche's ideas to support their own views. They argued that their own nation should prove its superiority through power, especially military power. As we will see in later chapters, several dictators used nationalism and scorn for democracy to justify their oppressive governments.

Science advanced in many fields.

Just as Copernicus and Galileo began a scientific revolution around 1600, Darwin was part of a new age of science that began in the late 1800's. Thanks to the work of many men and women, the foundations of modern biology, chemistry, and physics were established by 1914.

Biology Although Darwin said that living things passed on their variations from one generation to the next, he did not know how they did so. In the 1860's, Gregor Mendel discovered that there is a pattern to the way that certain traits are inherited. Although his work was not widely known until 1900, Mendel laid the groundwork for the science of genetics.

Other biologists took up the study of bacteria where Louis Pasteur left off. The German scientist Robert Koch, for example, discovered the organisms that caused tuberculosis and cholera.

Chemistry In chemistry, most of the major elements and compounds found in nature had been identified by the end of the 1800's. In 1803,

Marie Curie was Polish, born in a part of Poland ruled by Russia. She named the mineral polonium in honor of her country.

the British chemist John Dalton had theorized that all matter is made of tiny particles called atoms. Dalton showed that elements contain only one kind of atom, which has a specific weight. Compounds, on the other hand, contain more than one kind of atom.

In 1869, Dmitri Mendeleev (MEN-duh-LAY-yef), a Russian chemist, organized a chart on which all the known elements were arranged in order of weight, from lightest to heaviest. He left gaps where he predicted that new elements would be discovered. Later, his predictions proved correct. Mendeleev's chart, called the Periodic Table, is still used by scientists today.

A husband and wife team working in Paris discovered two of the missing elements. Marie and Pierre Curie found that a mineral called pitchblende released a powerful form of energy. In 1898, Marie Curie gave this energy the name *radioactivity*. The Curies discovered two new

elements that they named radium and polonium. Both were highly radioactive. In 1903, the Curies shared the Nobel Prize for Physics for their work on radioactivity. In 1911, Marie won the Nobel Prize for Chemistry for the discovery of radium and polonium. The prizes awarded to the Curies show how closely the fields of chemistry and physics were linked.

Physics Physicists around 1900 were trying to unravel the secrets of the atom. Among the leaders in this field were two British physicists, Ernest Rutherford and J. J. Thomson. Earlier scientists believed that the atom was the smallest particle that existed. Rutherford suggested that atoms were made up of yet smaller particles. Each atom, he said, had a nucleus surrounded by one or more particles called electrons.

Soon other physicists such as Max Planck, Neils Bohr, and Albert Einstein were studying the forces that held atoms together. Their discoveries, as we shall see in Chapter 30, were fully as revolutionary as Darwin's ideas.

Section Review 2

Define: (a) anesthesia, (b) bacteria, (c) natural selection, (d) element, (e) atom, (f) radioactivity
Identify: (a) Joseph Lister, (b) Louis Pasteur, (c) Charles Darwin, (d) special creation, (e) theory of evolution, (f) social Darwinism, (g) Friedrich Nietzsche, (h) Gregor Mendel, (i) Dmitri Mendeleev, (j) Marie and Pierre Curie
Answer:
1. List four developments that improved health care during the 1800's.
2. (a) How did the theory of special creation explain the variety of living things? (b) How did the theory of evolution explain this variety?
3. Why did Darwin's ideas arouse controversy?
4. How did some thinkers apply Darwin's ideas to industrial society?
5. How were the contributions of Dalton, Mendeleev, and the Curies related?

Critical Thinking
6. Darwin did not fully agree with the social Darwinists. How do natural selection and economic competition differ?

Women sought rights and freedoms. 3

In 1906, Marie Curie became the first woman ever to teach at France's prestigious Sorbonne. She won two Nobel Prizes and was acknowledged as one of the foremost scientists of her time. Yet she could never become a member of the French Academy of Sciences because she was a woman. During the years when she was making her great discoveries, she could not even vote.

The massive changes that the 1800's brought to Europe and North America affected everyone's lives. By the late 1800's, however, it was clear that the Industrial Revolution and the social changes that went with it had had different results for women than for men.

Women faced economic problems.

In some ways, the Industrial Revolution opened economic opportunities to women. Factory work offered higher wages than work done at home. Women spinners in Manchester's cotton factories, for example, received much higher pay than women who spun cotton thread at home.

On the other hand, women factory workers usually earned only half as much as men. Employers claimed that women needed less money than men because women did not have to support families. This argument ignored the many women who worked because their husbands had died or deserted them or were too ill to work.

Trade unions began to win better wages for working men in the mid-1800's. However, these unions seldom accepted women as members. Unions fought to keep women out of skilled jobs that offered better pay. Men feared that if women worked at such jobs, employers would lower the wages for everyone doing the work. During the mid-1800's, women formed several unions of their own in the trades where they dominated. Still, by 1907, only 15 percent of the unions in Great Britain admitted women.

When reformers began demanding better conditions for workers, the laws often applied first to women and children. Lawmakers were more willing to protect women and children than men. Beginning in the 1830's, some laws limited the hours women and children could work. Other laws set health and safety standards in factories.

Sometimes, these laws backfired against women. If the law said that women could not work 16 hours a day, some employers simply fired women and hired men instead. Eventually, however, the reforms spread to all workers and benefited both men and women.

Women entered new fields.

The years around 1900 were a watershed for working women. A gradual shift took place in the kinds of jobs that were open to them. In the late 1800's, working women were clustered in three kinds of jobs. The largest share worked as servants in other people's homes. In industry, most women were either garment workers or textile workers.

Middle-class women with an education had other job possibilities. Some were teachers. There was a demand for teachers in the late 1800's because countries in western Europe were beginning to offer free public schooling. France began public education in the 1860's. The British government began to organize schools in 1870, although they were not free to all children until 1891.

Nursing was another career open to women. British nurse Florence Nightingale (1820–1910) took the lead in winning professional training

Florence Nightingale organized British army hospitals during the Crimean War.

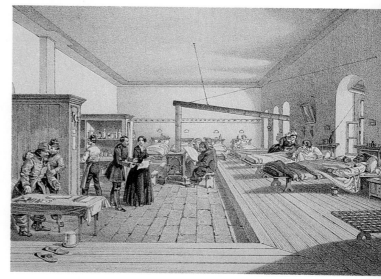

for women as nurses. In 1854, she went to Turkey and later Russia to help British soldiers in the Crimean War. Making her night rounds in the hospitals, she became known to hundreds of sick and wounded soldiers as "The Lady with the Lamp." When she returned to Britain, she used money that was donated in her honor to found the Nightingale School for Nurses. It was the first school of professional nursing in the world.

Teaching, nursing, library work, and social work were service professions in which many women worked. Opportunities for women in other professions were limited. In 1898, for example, there were only two women lawyers in all France.

In the late 1800's, a number of women's medical schools opened. Faced with this competition, several large medical schools for men began to admit women as well. By 1900, 10 percent of the medical students in the United States were women.

New jobs were also appearing for less educated women. After 1900, many women worked as shop clerks and office workers. (Before 1870, nearly all office clerks were men.)

While jobs in offices, stores, and schools were opening to women, jobs in industry were closing. The traditional women's industries—textiles and garment making—fell on hard times after 1900. Thus, the share of women in manufacturing jobs dropped sharply.

Women had few legal rights.

Working women of the middle 1800's faced yet another problem. They had no legal right to the money they earned. An unmarried woman's wages legally belonged to her father. If she married, everything she owned or earned became her husband's property.

Women could not sue or make contracts. Often, if a woman's husband died, she could not even act as guardian of her children.

In 1900, no country in Europe allowed women to vote. Even in Britain, where Queen Victoria was perhaps the most popular monarch the country had ever had, women could not vote or serve in Parliament. "Women are creatures of impulse and emotion," declared one British member of Parliament in 1906. "They do not decide questions on the ground of reason as men do." Thousands of women (and men) throughout the developed world disagreed.

Women sought the right to vote.

In the United States, women such as Lucretia Mott and Susan B. Anthony organized a campaign for women's rights as early as 1848. By the 1880's, women were working internationally to win more rights. In 1888, women activists founded the International Council for Women. Delegates and

By 1900, women in many countries were organizing to demand the right to vote. They believed that this right was the basis for other steps toward legal equality.

observers from 27 countries attended the council's 1899 meeting, coming from lands as far apart as the United States, New Zealand, Argentina, Iceland, Persia, and China.

Even among activist women, however, the question of suffrage (voting rights) for women remained controversial. Not all women were in favor of it; not all men were against it.

In Britain and the United States, there had been decades of peaceful efforts to win the right to vote for women. Around 1900, more militant organizations sprang up. In the United States, Carrie Chapman Catt headed the North American Woman Suffrage Association. In Britain, Emmeline Pankhurst formed the Women's Social and Political Union (WSPU) in 1903.

The WSPU became the most militant organization for women's rights. Besides peaceful demonstrations and parades, its members cut telegraph wires, heckled government speakers, chained themselves to railings at public buildings, and smashed windows. Their goal was to draw attention to the cause of woman's suffrage.

Emmeline Pankhurst and her daughters Christabel and Sylvia were arrested and imprisoned dozens of times. When she was jailed, Emmeline Pankhurst turned to hunger strikes to keep her cause before the public. British officials force-fed her to keep her alive.

The authorities could not stop another woman who was determined to become a martyr to the cause of woman's suffrage. In June 1913, the cream of European society was watching the English Derby at Epsom Downs. Suddenly, a young WSPU member, Emily Davison, threw herself in front of the king's horse and was killed.

Voice from the Past · A Citizen's Right to Vote

In 1872, Susan B. Anthony and 50 other women were arrested for trying to vote in the presidential election. After she was found guilty, Anthony made the following statement.

Of all my prosecutors, from the corner grocery politician who entered the complaint, to the United States marshal, commissioner, district-attorney, district-judge, your honor on the bench—not one is my peer, but each and all are my political superiors; and had your honor submitted my case to the jury . . . even then I should have had just cause of protest, for not one of those men was my peer but, native or foreign born, white or black, rich or poor, educated or ignorant, sober or drunk, each and every man of them was my political superior; hence in no sense my peer . . .

Precisely as no disfranchised person [person without the right to vote] is entitled to sit upon a jury, and no woman is entitled to the franchise, so none but a regularly admitted lawyer is allowed to practice in the courts, and no woman can gain admission to the bar—hence, jury, judge, counsel, all must be of the superior class.

[Here, the judge stated that the trial had been handled according to the established forms of law.]

Yes, your honor, but by forms of law all made by men, interpreted by men, administered by men, in favor of men and against women; and hence your honor's ordered verdict of guilty, against a United States citizen for the exercise of the "citizen's right to vote," simply because that citizen was a woman and not a man.

1. (a) According to Susan B. Anthony, why are none of the people who brought her to trial her peers? (b) What right do they have that makes them her political superiors?

2. What traditional right in American and British law does she imply she was denied in her trial?

3. Besides the right to vote, what other opportunities and civic responsibilities were closed to women, according to this speech?

At her funeral, thousands of women in white dresses carried banners supporting woman's suffrage. "Thoughts have gone forth whose power can sleep no more," read one banner. "Victory! Victory!"

In fact, victory was still many years away. Though the woman's suffrage movement commanded wide attention between 1880 and 1914, its successes were few. Women won the right to vote in New Zealand (1893) and Australia (1902). Only in two European territories—Finland (1906, then part of the Russian empire) and Norway (1913)—did women gain voting rights before World War I. Several western states in the United States also granted women the right to vote. Often, women won voting rights for local elections before they won statewide or national rights.

On other issues, women's rights made faster progress. Britain and most states in the United States enacted laws giving married women the right to own property. In Britain, women began to serve as safety inspectors in factories where women worked. Women also served on local boards to oversee schools and hospitals.

Section Review 3

Define: suffrage
Identify: (a) Florence Nightingale, (b) Susan B. Anthony, (c) Carrie Chapman Catt, (d) Emmeline Pankhurst
Answer:
1. What economic problems did women face?
2. (a) What fields of work employed most women in the late 1800's? (b) What new fields opened around 1900?
3. What were some of the restrictions on women's legal and political rights?
4. How did women try to secure their rights?
5. (a) In what areas did they achieve some success by 1914? (b) In what areas were they less successful?

Critical Thinking

6. In the 1850's, teaching, office work, and professional nursing were unusual jobs for women. (a) From the point of view of an employer of that time, explain why each of these jobs is "unsuitable" for women. (b) From the point of view of an employer in 1900, explain why each job is a "natural" one for women.

Art and entertainment took new forms. 4

The late 1800's and early 1900's saw great changes in the world of the arts. The period was also marked by new forms of art and entertainment for a mass audience.

New styles in art replaced realism.

"Come right away to the fourth floor of my house, and before your eyes I'll make a picture as exact, as true, as brilliant as Raphael himself could ever have made." So Louis Daguerre told a French reporter in 1839, shortly after he had developed the first successful photographic process. "From today, painting is dead," lamented a French painter after seeing Daguerre's photographs. Painting certainly was not dead, but it would never be quite the same again.

Impressionism During the 1870's and 1880's, French painters launched a new style of art called impressionism. Influenced partly by photography, these artists tried to capture the impression of a scene at a certain instant. Leading impressionists included Edouard Manet (man-**NAY**), Auguste Renoir (ren-**WAHR**), Claude Monet (mon-**NAY**), and Camille Pissarro (puh-**SAHR**-oh).

Impressionists wanted above all to show the effects of light at a given moment. "Light is the principal personage of a painting," asserted Manet. Natural light blends all the colors of the spectrum. Therefore, the impressionists turned away from the somber browns, blacks, and grays of realism (page 517). Instead, impressionists painted with dabs of pure color—reds, oranges, yellows, bright blues. Impressionist works seem to shimmer and sparkle.

Postimpressionism During the 1890's, a new group of painters, sometimes called the postimpressionists, carried this emphasis on light and color even further. Among these artists were Vincent van Gogh (van **GOH**) and Paul Gauguin (goh-**GAN**). Gauguin explained his colorful style this way:

By the combination of lines and colors, under the pretext of some motif taken from nature, I create symphonies and harmonies that represent nothing absolutely real in

Like many impressionists, Monet favored outdoor scenes for their natural light. A detail from his "Gladioli" (left), a tranquil garden scene, shows the impressionists' use of light and color. In "Starry Night" (right), the postimpressionist Van Gogh painted the sky as an overwhelming display of fireworks.

the ordinary sense of the word but are intended to give rise to thoughts as music does.

Expressionism Other early twentieth-century painters, such as the Norwegian Edvard Munch and the Russian Vasily Kandinsky, were mainly concerned with expressing the feelings that a scene aroused. They were therefore known as expressionists. Because the feelings they expressed were often grim and anguished, their paintings were unsettling and frightening.

New directions Even with wild colors and distortions, the paintings of Van Gogh and Munch could still be recognized as objects from the real world. Other artists, however, were beginning to change the shapes they painted beyond all recognition. One group of painters, for example, was nicknamed the cubists because their work featured geometric planes and angles. A picture of a person might look at first sight like an intricate stack of boxes.

One of the cubists was a young Spaniard working in Paris, Pablo Picasso. He explained why he rejected realism: "Nature and art, being two different things, cannot be the same thing, period. Through art, we express our concept of what nature is not."

Music often took nationalistic themes.

Romanticism was still the leading style of music in the late 1800's. These years were a golden age of opera. Composers such as Giuseppe Verdi (**VERD**-ee) and Giacomo Puccini (poo-**CHEE**-nee) wedded their emotional music to melodramatic plots.

Nationalism also played a strong role in music. The German composer Richard Wagner (**VAHG**-nuhr), for example, based many of his operas on old German legends. Nearly every European country had a composer whose work gave people a heightened sense of national identity.

Just as painters were branching out from tradition, some composers began to experiment with different kinds of music. The French composers Claude Debussy (deb-yoo-**SEE**) and Maurice Ravel (ruh-**VEL**) wrote loosely structured musical impressions such as *The Sea* (Debussy) and *The*

Waltz (Ravel). In fact, music critics compared them to the impressionist painters.

Other composers, such as the Russians Alexander Scriabin (skree-**AHB**-uhn) and Igor Stravinsky (struh-**VIHN**-skee), produced even more complex harmonies and rhythms. The Austrian Arnold Schönberg (**SHUHN**-buhrg) began to base his music on mathematical patterns rather than upon sounds that were pleasing to the ear.

Most of this experimental music did not appeal to a wide public. When Stravinsky's ballet *The Rite of Spring* was first performed in Paris in 1913, the audience rioted against what they thought was an insult to their ears.

The turn of the century also saw the beginnings of modern popular music. In Britain, singers with Cockney accents sang ballads at popular theaters known as music halls. In the United States, ragtime—a musical style based on a rapid melody and strong beat—was becoming very popular thanks to black musicians such as Scott Joplin.

The arts reached new audiences.

In earlier periods, art, music, and most theater had been largely the concern of the upper classes. By 1900, however, artists, writers, and musicians were appealing to a much larger audience. For the first time, we can speak of *mass culture.* There were at least three causes for the rise of mass culture around the turn of the century.

First, the spread of public education broadened literacy in both Europe and North America. The millions of new readers created an enormous market for newspapers, magazines, and books that were written in simple, colorful language.

Second, improvements in communication made it possible to meet this broad demand for information and entertainment. The new, high-speed presses and linotype machines could turn out thousands of pages in a few hours. The phonograph brought music directly into people's homes.

The third cause was a gradual reduction in working hours. By 1900, most industrial countries had limited the working day to ten hours. Most people worked Monday through Friday and half a day on Saturday. Thus, men and women of the lower and middle classes had more leisure time than ever before. They could take part in activities that their grandparents never had time to enjoy.

Sports entertained millions.

The five-and-a-half-day work week created the "weekend," a special time of relaxation and fun. All kinds of new leisure activities became popular. Millions flocked to beaches on summer weekends. Golf and tennis were a hit among the well-to-do, who could afford to join clubs with playing areas. People with less money took up soccer or baseball, which they could play with simple equipment on vacant lots.

For every person who played sports, there were 20 who enjoyed watching. In the United States, football and baseball skyrocketed in popularity. Teams from the rival American and National leagues played baseball's first World Series in 1903. Soccer became popular in Europe.

As a result of the growing interest in sports, the international Olympic Games began in 1896. They revived the Greek tradition of holding an athletic competition among states every four years. Fittingly, the first modern Olympics were held in Athens.

Baseball's popularity grew swiftly in the 1890's.

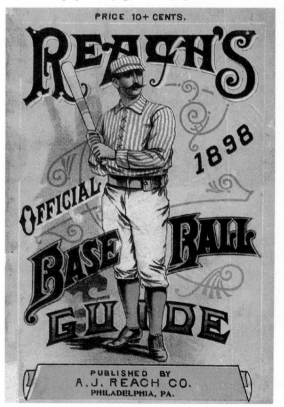

PRICE 10+ CENTS.

REACH'S

1898

OFFICIAL

BASE BALL

GUIDE

PUBLISHED BY
A. J. REACH CO.
PHILADELPHIA, PA.

People flocked to see movies.

One of the most popular new leisure activities was an evening visit to the movie theater or the music hall. With names such as the Gaiety, the Grand, or the Orpheum, music halls offered a dozen or more different acts. Such variety shows often included singers, dancers, comedians, acrobats, and even trained parakeets.

During the 1880's, dozens of inventors worked on moving-picture cameras and projectors. One successful design came from France. Another came from Thomas Edison's laboratory.

The earliest films caused a sensation only because of their novelty. They were in black and white, lasted less than a minute, and had no plot. One, for example, showed a man sneezing—that was all!

In 1903, an American filmmaker named Edwin S. Porter offered the first feature film. As the lights dimmed, a fierce bandit appeared on the screen and fired his revolver directly at the audience. People shrieked with fear and delight. In the next eight minutes, they watched as a band of outlaws held up a train and fled, only to be hunted down by a white-hatted sheriff and his hard-riding posse. The film was *The Great Train Robbery*, and it packed theaters on both sides of the Atlantic.

Movies quickly became big business. By 1910, 5 million Americans attended some 10,000 theaters across the country each day. The European movie industry enjoyed similar growth.

The people who saw *The Great Train Robbery* were watching the beginnings of both a new industry and a new art form. Movies made possible a new kind of visual storytelling. Moving images, together with recorded sound, came to dominate mass culture in the twentieth century.

Section Review 4

Define: mass culture
Identify: (a) impressionism, (b) expressionism
Answer:
1. (a) What were the major characteristics of impressionist and postimpressionist painting? (b) Name the leading painters of these schools.
2. What trends in painting followed the impressionist period?
3. How did some music of the late 1800's reflect political trends of the time?
4. (a) What were the causes of the development of mass culture around 1900? (b) Give some examples of the new forms of art and entertainment for wide audiences.

Critical Thinking
5. (a) How did the development of photography change the function of painting? (b) What is the importance of each today?
6. Reread the statement by Gauguin on pages 568–569. (a) What purpose do painting and music share? (b) In your opinion, what is the importance of the arts in society?

Europe faced rising tensions. 5

More than ever before, the views of ordinary people were making an impact on society. By 1914, most industrialized countries allowed all adult men to vote. This development brought about two major changes in European politics.

First, political parties became more tightly organized than before. In earlier times, political parties had been loose-knit clubs. Now they were (or tried to be) well-oiled machines for winning elections. Major parties had branches in every election district. Those branches reported to a central committee. The central committee set party policies and made sure that party members in parliament supported those policies.

Second, the spread of democracy brought forward a new kind of political leader. Besides commanding the respect and support of fellow party leaders, a successful politician now had to appeal to large numbers of voters. As a result, politicians found they had to be part actors and part salespersons, able to win widespread support.

By itself, the right to vote did not guarantee democratic government. Much depended on the political system of each country. Even in the United States, for example, only the House of Representatives was elected directly by the voters. Senators were not directly elected. Until 1913, they were chosen by the state legislatures. France had a similar system with a Chamber of Deputies and a Senate. In Britain, members of the House of Lords were not elected at all.

Such *upper houses* could reject bills passed by the *lower houses* and also frame bills of their own. In some other countries, the powers of elected legislatures were restricted both by an upper house and by a monarch who still made many major governmental decisions.

Germany had a hollow democracy.

Germany was a good example of the limits on democracy. The Reichstag (RYKES-tahg) was the lower house of the German parliament. It was elected by universal manhood suffrage. Members of the upper house, the Bundesrat (BOON-duhs-raht), were appointed by each of Germany's 25 states. Often, they were chosen by local princes and dukes.

Furthermore, the German kaiser (emperor) named his own chancellor (prime minister). Neither the Reichstag nor the Bundesrat had any control over the chancellor. Thus, if the Reichstag voted against raising the army budget, the chancellor might simply raise the budget anyway. "The Reichstag does not make history," said one German political leader, "but is merely playing a comedy."

Otto von Bismarck continued to govern Germany as chancellor until 1890. As we have seen, Bismarck was a staunch conservative who distrusted both democracy and socialism. However, he was shrewd enough to know that his government needed popular support. During the 1880's, therefore, Bismarck gave Germany the world's first large-scale welfare program. His laws included insurance to help workers in case of accident or sickness. Soon he added old-age pensions for every German worker.

By passing these laws, Bismarck hoped to take support away from his enemies, the socialists. "Anybody who has before him the prospect of a pension, be it ever so small," Bismarck noted, "is much happier and more content with his lot, much more tractable and easy to manage, than he whose future is absolutely uncertain." Bismarck's goal was not so much to help the workers as to prevent revolution, and he succeeded.

Bismarck's political career ended abruptly. In 1888, Kaiser William II came to the throne. The young kaiser was headstrong, quarrelsome, and

determined to rule Germany himself. Accordingly, he forced Bismarck to resign in 1890. However, Bismarck's system of state socialism, as he called his social programs, remained in effect. So did his military and nationalist policies. With their economic needs met, most Germans supported these policies even though Germany's government was basically undemocratic.

Britain faced two political crises.

Germany had half a dozen political parties, as did France and Italy. In Britain, two major parties dominated politics—the Liberals and the Conservatives. In the late 1800's, both parties produced prime ministers who were enormously popular, the Conservatives' Benjamin Disraeli and the Liberals' William Gladstone.

The Irish question The two parties differed little on questions of imperialism or reform. The issue on which the two parties were most seriously split was the Irish question. Ireland had been controlled by the British government for nearly 300 years. It had been ruled directly from London since 1801.

During the 1870's, nationalists in Ireland organized an Irish Home Rule Party. Its members sought a measure of independence for Ireland. In general, Conservatives opposed Irish Home Rule, while Liberals favored it. Liberal prime minister William Gladstone brought forward two home rule bills in parliament, but both were defeated.

Meanwhile, in Ireland, a drop in the prices for farm products made it impossible for thousands of people to pay their rents. In just one year, landlords forced more than 2,000 families out of their homes. Some angry farmers and other nationalists turned to violence, burning barns and beating landlords' agents.

Footnote to History

As a peaceful form of protest, the Irish decided to shun anyone who bought a farm after its tenant had been unfairly evicted. No neighbor would speak to or do business with the new owner. The first person to be treated this way was Charles Boycott. His name came to stand for breaking off all day-to-day dealings with a person or group.

During the 1870's and 1880's, both Protestants and Catholics in Ireland worked for home rule. By the 1900's, however, many Irish Protestants had turned against it. Most Irish Protestants lived in the northern part of Ireland, known as Ulster. They feared being a minority in a country dominated by Catholics.

In 1914, Parliament finally approved a home rule bill. By then, Irish Protestants were gathering weapons and holding military drills to fight against home rule.

Just one month before home rule was to take effect, World War I broke out in Europe. The problem of Irish independence was left to wait and to fester.

The issue of the House of Lords In 1909, Britain's Liberal finance minister was David Lloyd George. Orphaned as a child, he had been raised by his uncle, a shoemaker. Lloyd George became the champion of social welfare programs. Under his leadership, the Liberals put forward a program to provide old-age pensions, accident and illness insurance for workers, and even some unemployment benefits. To pay for these benefits, Lloyd George called for an income tax that would hit hardest at the wealthy. He called his program the "People's Budget."

The People's Budget easily passed in the House of Commons, but the House of Lords vetoed it. The House of Lords seldom opposed the Commons, but many lords were wealthy landowners who stood to lose money from Lloyd George's new taxes.

Lloyd George and the Liberals turned the budget issue into a question on the place of the House of Lords in British government. The Liberal party wanted to limit the powers of the House of Lords. Liberals won the next two elections, but still the lords refused to accept reforms. Finally, the king threatened to name enough new, reform-minded lords to pass the changes that the Commons demanded. The threat was enough. Rather than accept dozens of new members, the House of Lords voted to limit its own powers.

Henceforth, the House of Lords could only *delay* bills passed by the House of Commons. After two years, such bills became law whether or not the Lords approved of them. Britain had taken one more step toward a fully democratic form of government.

Queen Victoria (center front) was called "the grandmother of Europe." Her many children married into royal families all over the continent. Here she is surrounded by her royal relatives. At left are her grandson, Kaiser William II (seated), Britain's future George V (in black hat), and Victoria's son, soon to be Edward VII (in light coat).

In Vienna at the turn of the century, all the most fashionable people could be seen walking or driving along the Ringstrasse ("ring street").

Social divisions marked life in "the beautiful era."

Despite the growth of democracy in some countries, by 1900, both Europe and the United States had a tiny but fabulously wealthy upper class. Its members seemed, in the words of one French writer, "to live upon a golden cloud, spending their riches as indolently [lazily] and naturally as the leaves grow green."

For the wealthy, the years around 1900 were *la belle epoque* (the beautiful era). Ladies and gentlemen of the upper class lived surrounded by servants. They maintained several homes, some in town and some in the country. All of Europe was their playground. In March, the wealthy went to the French seaside resort of Biarritz. In April, they visited the yearly exhibition of the French art society in Paris. In June, they flocked to the English Derby at Epsom Downs. The summer months found them at mountain spas such as Germany's Marienbad. In the fall, they went hunting at splendid country estates.

Only 1 or 2 percent of the European population belonged to the upper class. About 25 to 35 percent were members of the middle class. The middle class, as we have seen, had been growing since the Middle Ages and included a wide range of people—merchants, shopkeepers, doctors,

lawyers, teachers, and government employees. Industrialization created new middle-class positions—factory supervisors, sales representatives, and thousands of office workers. Middle-class families had enough money to buy such labor-saving gadgets as washing and sewing machines and to take summer vacations. Many middle-class families built comfortable houses in the fast-growing neighborhoods just outside the city. With the coming of electric streetcars, middle-class people began to live outside the city and commute to work each day. Some even bought Henry Ford's new Model T's.

The urban lower class, as well as the peasantry in eastern Europe, still lived on the edge of poverty. Despite major medical advances during the 1800's, tuberculosis and other deadly diseases were still a menace in slums and tenements from Moscow to Chicago.

As the representative of the workers, trade unions were growing stronger. Although strikes were not always successful, workers sometimes won higher wages and better working conditions. In 1889, for example, Ben Tillett led a walkout of 10,000 London dockworkers. For a month, no cargoes were loaded or unloaded. Then the shipowners agreed to pay the dockworkers higher wages and cut the work week from 55 to 48 hours.

Despite such gains, some radicals still believed that only a revolution would improve the lives of the working class. One group of revolutionaries called themselves **anarchists**. Anarchists believed that all governments were evil and should be overthrown. These radicals committed a number of assassinations around the turn of the century, including that of the czar of Russia in 1881, the French president in 1894, the king of Italy in 1900, and President William McKinley of the United States in 1901. However, the number of anarchists and revolutionary socialists remained very small in every country.

Crises shook Europe's fragile peace.

In different ways, Britain and Germany had both achieved stability by 1900. France too was fairly stable under the Third Republic (page 523). For the countries in the heartland of Europe, the age of nation building was over.

Around the edges of Europe, nationalism was still a deeply troubling issue. Ireland was one example. Norway was another. Norwegians finally won their independence from Sweden in 1905. The greatest conflicts over nationalism, however, were arising in eastern Europe.

Austria-Hungary, Russia, and the Ottoman empire were all multinational empires. All three lagged behind western Europe industrially and militarily. (The once powerful Ottoman empire was now so weak that it was known as "the sick man of Europe.") All three included peoples who wanted their own nations.

Ethnic minorities in these empires faced the risk of persecution. Bulgarians were massacred by their Ottoman rulers in the 1870's. In 1895, Ottoman ruler Abdul Hamid II turned on the Armenian minority in his empire, beginning a series of massacres that eventually took more than 1 million lives. Jews in Russia lived under the threat of *pogroms*, mob attacks in which many were killed and still more had their homes and businesses destroyed.

The most complex national conflicts arose on the Balkan Peninsula. There, Serbs, Bosnians, Montenegrins, Croats, Slovenes, Albanians, Bulgarians, and Romanians all hoped to build their own countries. Many of these groups spoke Slavic languages, but they maintained their separate identities.

Between 1900 and 1914, repeated uprisings and crises in the Balkans threatened both Austria-Hungary and the Ottoman empire. Russia saw itself as protector of all the Slavic peoples and often encouraged the nationalism of Slavic groups in the Balkans. In this role, Russia was a constant threat to Austria-Hungary.

Crises also arose in western Europe. France was still bitter about the loss of Alsace and Lorraine (page 523). In 1911, France and Germany came to the brink of war when a German gunboat threatened Morocco, a French colony in Africa.

War in the Balkans, hostility along the Rhine, saber rattling in North Africa—all made peace difficult to keep. Yet a strange optimism grew in Europe. As each crisis was solved without a general war, people began to think that war had been banished forever.

Section Review 5

Define: (a) upper house, (b) lower house, (c) pogrom, (d) anarchist
Identify: (a) Reichstag, (b) Bundesrat, (c) William II, (d) David Lloyd George
Answer:
1. How did wider voting rights affect political parties and their leaders?
2. Why was Germany not a true democracy?
3. (a) What programs did Bismarck enact as his policy of state socialism? (b) What were his reasons for doing so?
4. (a) What was "the Irish question"? (b) How did the political situation in Ireland change between 1870 and 1900?
5. How did Britain's House of Lords lose its last political powers?
6. (a) What European countries were still multinational empires? (b) What groups were still frustrated in hopes for nations of their own?
7. How did each of the following create crises in this era? (a) Slavic nationalism (b) hostility between France and Germany (c) anarchists

Critical Thinking
8. Both Bismarck and Lloyd George passed social welfare programs. Did their actions reflect the same political philosophies? Explain.
9. (a) How is the phrase *la belle epoque* a good description of this era in Europe? (b) In what ways is the phrase a poor description?

Chapter Review 26

Summary

1. Inventions changed ways of life. Between 1870 and 1914, numerous practical inventions made people's lives more comfortable. Bessemer's blast furnace brought on the Age of Steel. Thomas Edison invented new uses for electricity. The telephone, radio, and combustion engine transformed transportation and communication. Ford's assembly line established the modern manufacturing process.

2. Science presented new ideas. New standards of cleanliness, the introduction of pasteurization, and the widespread use of inoculation decreased the number of deaths from disease. Darwin proposed the theory of evolution to explain the variety of living things. Later, a number of thinkers applied his ideas to economics and politics. The development of genetics and theories about the composition of elements led to advances in chemistry and physics.

3. Women sought rights and freedoms. Although by the late 1800's more women worked outside the home, they still faced economic and political restrictions. Many women in the United States and Britain believed that the right to vote would improve their status. Although women used a variety of tactics to call attention to their cause, they achieved only limited success by 1914.

4. Art and entertainment took new forms. The spread of public education, improved communications, and more leisure time helped create mass culture in the late 1800's. Sports and movies became especially popular. Painting styles shifted from realism to increasingly abstract forms, and composers experimented with new harmonies and rhythms.

5. Europe faced rising tensions. By 1900, the views of ordinary people were impacting society. Democratic rights expanded in Britain when the House of Lords lost its last political power. However, the controversy over Irish home rule divided British voters and produced rising tensions. In the early 1900's, democracy in Germany was severely limited, although Bismarck's state socialism recognized increasing public interests in politics. In eastern Europe, independence movements among persecuted minorities caused rising tensions.

Reviewing the Facts

1. Define the following terms:
   a. assembly line
   b. anarchist
2. Explain the importance of each of the following names, places, or terms:
   a. blast furnace   b. Edison

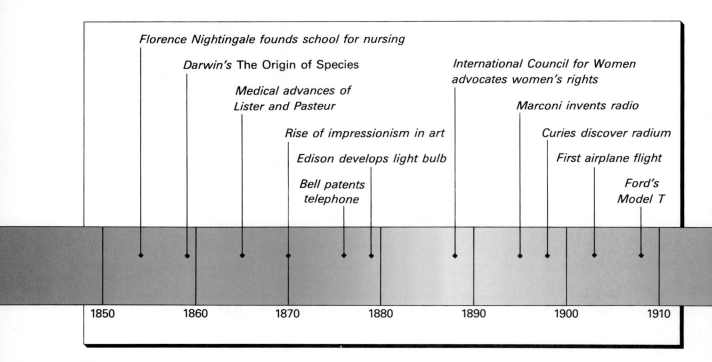

Florence Nightingale founds school for nursing

Darwin's The Origin of Species

Medical advances of Lister and Pasteur

Rise of impressionism in art

Edison develops light bulb

Bell patents telephone

International Council for Women advocates women's rights

Marconi invents radio

Curies discover radium

First airplane flight

Ford's Model T

1850   1860   1870   1880   1890   1900   1910

c. Bell
d. Marconi
e. internal combustion engine
f. Model T
g. Kitty Hawk
h. anesthesia
i. pasteurization
j. theory of evolution
k. social Darwinism
l. Periodic Table
m. radioactivity

n. Nightingale
o. Anthony
p. Pankhurst
q. mass culture
r. impressionism
s. expressionism
t. Wagner
u. upper house
v. lower house
w. Bismarck
x. Lloyd George
y. pogrom

3. (a) What metal largely replaced iron in the late 1800's? (b) What new source of energy came into use?

4. (a) Describe two communication advances. (b) Two transportation advances. (c) Two medical discoveries that increased life span.

5. (a) How was Darwin's theory of evolution received? (b) Describe two ideas that were derived from it.

6. What contributions did each of the following scientists make? (a) Mendeleev (b) Dalton (c) Marie Curie (d) Rutherford

7. (a) What steps did women take to win wider rights? (b) In what areas did they succeed before 1914? (c) In what areas did they fail?

8. (a) Describe three art forms that replaced realism. (b) What movements influenced music?

9. (a) What three factors contributed to the rise of mass culture around 1900? (b) What two forms of entertainment did people enjoy as a result of leisure time?

10. Describe how the views of ordinary people impacted European politics.

11. Describe the social welfare program that developed in Germany.

12. (a) What was the Irish question? (b) Describe the status of the Irish question in 1914.

13. How did the power of Britain's House of Lords decline?

14. (a) What issues threatened peace in eastern Europe? (b) What conflict threatened peace in western Europe?

Thinking about History

1. How did inventions such as the electric light and the telephone gradually help to diminish class distinctions?

2. How did the Industrial Revolution form the impetus for the women's rights movement? Why did the right to vote become a central issue in the movement?

Writing and Speaking about History

1. Prepare a resolution for the 1899 Meeting of the International Council for Women, addressing the plight of women and suggesting remedies.

2. Make a chart that shows either the inventions or the scientific and medical advances described in this chapter. Include the person or persons responsible, the date, and the importance of the invention or discovery.

3. Choose one of the inventions or discoveries that you listed in the preceding exercise. Prepare a five-minute speech explaining its importance or significance.

Practicing Skills

1. As the researcher for a paper on the rights and freedoms of women, prepare ten information note cards from the chapter section on women. (See Research Skills Handbook, page 578.)

2. What event on the timeline on page 576 occurred in the same year as each of the following events from this chapter? (a) first feature film (b) first World Series

Investigating History

1. In the library, find examples of the works of one or more of the following painters: Edouard Manet, Auguste Renoir, Camille Pissarro, Vincent van Gogh, Paul Gauguin, Pablo Picasso. How does the artist's work reflect the movements you studied in this chapter?

2. Continue the data base file of inventions that you began in Chapter 22 (page 489).

3. Trace the expansion of women's suffrage from the Industrial Revolution through the civil rights movement of the 1900's. Focus your research on the United States and Great Britain.

Decision Making in History

As a member of the British House of Lords in 1909, you have just voted to limit the powers of the House (page 573). How do you justify your decision to those members of the House who oppose the vote?

Research Skills

The Research Paper: Gathering Materials

Gathering material for your research paper involves two steps: preparing a working bibliography and notetaking.

The working bibliography is a list of all materials that may be appropriate to the topic. To develop a working bibliography, first create a list of subject headings or descriptors for the topic, such as *industry, Great Britain,* and *economics* for a paper on the Industrial Revolution. Use these descriptors to find material in the library's reference tools.

The library has many reference tools. These include encyclopedias, atlases, almanacs, biographical dictionaries, *Readers' Guide to Periodical Literature,* and the card catalog.

The card catalog is a file of drawers that contain cards for every book in the library. Each book usually has an author card, a title card, and a subject card. The cards are arranged alphabetically. Each nonfiction book has a call number. The call number is a kind of address that tells you in what section of the library the book is located.

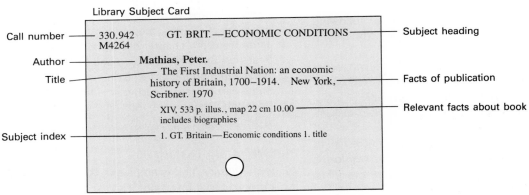

When you find an appropriate book, prepare a working bibliography card as shown below. Once you have compiled your working bibliography, you can begin taking notes and preparing a tentative outline. Finalize your outline at the end of notetaking.

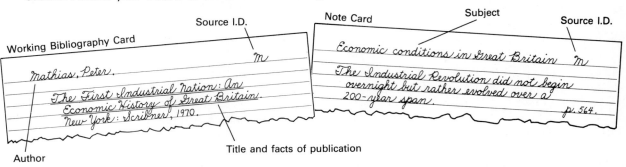

578

Unit Review VII

1. Describe the significance of the invention or discovery made by each of the following:
   a. Kay
   b. Whitney
   c. Watt
   d. Trevithick
   e. Morse
   f. Bell
   g. Marconi
   h. Ford
   i. Wright brothers
   j. Lister
   k. Pasteur
   l. Marie Curie

2. Explain the relationship of the terms in each of the following groups:
   a. conservative; liberal; radical
   b. laissez-faire; industrialization
   c. industrialization; realism
   d. nationalism; romanticism; liberalism
   e. entrepreneur; stock; corporation; monopoly
   f. imperialism; social Darwinism

3. With what artistic movement (romanticism, realism, impressionism) is each of the following people associated?
   a. Beethoven
   b. Courbet
   c. Delacroix
   d. Renoir
   e. Dickens
   f. Manet
   g. Monet

4. Describe the role that each of the following men played in nationalistic movements within their country:
   a. Mazzini
   b. Cavour
   c. Garibaldi
   d. Bolívar
   e. San Martín
   f. Dom Pedro
   g. Hidalgo
   h. L'Ouverture
   i. Bismarck

5. (a) Where did the Industrial Revolution begin? (b) What factors aided industrial growth there?

6. (a) How did industrialization affect life in the cities? (b) The role of children? (c) The rise of the middle class? (d) Tensions between the classes?

7. (a) What did the delegates at the Congress of Vienna in 1815 hope to accomplish? (b) How did the Congress strike a balance between punishing France and destroying it?

8. (a) In what way were Latin American revolutions of the early 1800's similar to the American Revolution? (b) How were they different?

9. (a) What did the revolutions of 1848 achieve at first? (b) What happened in the counter-revolutions?

10. (a) How was socialism a response to industrialization? (b) How did Karl Marx's approach to socialism differ from Robert Owen's?

11. (a) How did trade unions increase the power of working people? (b) How did suffrage affect the worker's growing influence?

12. (a) What problems did Italy face after unification? (b) What were the strengths of Germany in 1870?

13. (a) What economic differences existed between the North and South in the United States? (b) How was the issue of slavery related to the westward expansion of the United States? (c) How was slavery ended?

14. (a) How was imperialism an outgrowth of industrialization? (b) What attitude did people in industrialized countries have toward other people?

15. Give one effect of imperialism on each of the following groups of people: (a) Indians (b) Africans (c) Chinese

16. (a) How did Japan's response to imperialism differ from China's? (b) How did imperialism in Latin America differ from imperialism in Africa and parts of Asia?

17. (a) In what areas had the women's movement achieved some success by 1914? (b) In what areas was the movement less successful?

18. How did each of the following create crises at the end of the 1800's? (a) Slavic nationalism (b) enmity between France and Germany (c) anarchists

Unit VIII
Years of Crisis

CHAPTERS

When the twentieth century began, Europe dominated the globe both economically and politically. Yet within 50 years, Europe's worldwide empires crumbled. A global economic crisis dealt a serious blow to the dreams of endless wealth created by industrialism. Several of the oldest ruling families in Europe, including the Romanovs in Russia, lost their thrones. Moreover, the countries of Europe nearly destroyed one another in two terrible wars that left millions dead.

During these years of turmoil, nationalism spread to many parts of the world. People in China, India, Africa, and the Middle East began to demand nations of their own. Other regions, such as Latin America, sought freedom from foreign economic control.

Out of the crises from 1900 to 1945, a new world emerged. It was a world dominated by two great powers, the United States and the Soviet Union. Yet it was also a world in which the people of many regions won new rights of self-determination.

Abandoned army camp, Verdun, France

World War I

Soon after the assassination at Sarajevo, French newspaper readers saw this picture with a report of the event. The picture's romantic tone undoubtedly caught the eye of many newsstand customers.

1. **Conflicts divided Europe.**

2. **Europe plunged into war.**

3. **The war dragged on for four years.**

4. **Peace stood on shaky foundations.**

June 28, 1914, was a hot, sultry day in Sarajevo (SAHR-uh-yeh-voh), capital of the Austrian province of Bosnia. Despite the heat, crowds had jammed the streets for hours. They were hoping to catch a glimpse of Archduke Franz Ferdinand, heir to the throne of Austria-Hungary. As nephew of the aged Emperor Franz Josef, Franz Ferdinand expected to rule Austria soon.

Not everyone in Sarajevo was pleased with this royal visit. Most Bosnians were Serbs, a Slavic people. Many wanted Bosnia to be part of Serbia, a neighboring Slavic country, instead of a province in the Austro-Hungarian empire. On this June morning, a handful of young

Serbian nationalists were scattered among the crowds awaiting the archduke's arrival. They were determined to give Franz Ferdinand their own terrible greeting.

The royal train arrived in Sarajevo shortly before 10 A.M. An honor guard of Austrian troops stood at attention while the archduke and his wife, Sophie, got into the open car that would take them to the official welcoming ceremonies at the town hall. A six-car motorcade left the station, led by the mayor of Sarajevo. Franz Ferdinand and Sophie rode in the second car. The royal couple smiled and waved while people cheered and threw flowers to them.

One of the Serbian nationalists, however, threw something else—a bomb. As it hurtled through the air, Franz Ferdinand threw up his arm to protect himself and his wife. The bomb struck his upraised arm and bounced off, exploding in the street. The blast injured a dozen people and sent a dark cloud of smoke into the sky.

After a brief pause, the motorcade continued at top speed toward the town hall. Although unhurt, Franz Ferdinand was furious. "Mr. Mayor," barked the archduke after the party had arrived safely at the hall, "we come to visit you, and we are greeted with bombs! This is outrageous!"

Before any further ceremonies, Franz Ferdinand wanted to go to the hospital to visit those who had been hurt by the bomb blast. Sophie insisted on going with him.

It was just after 11 A.M. when the motorcade resumed. Once again, the archduke and his wife were in the second car, riding behind the mayor. Unfortunately, no one had told the mayor's chauffeur about the visit to the hospital. Holding to the original plan, he turned down a side street. "You've gone the wrong way!" screamed the mayor. The driver braked and began to back up. So did the archduke's chauffeur.

It was too late. Standing at this intersection, no more than two steps from the archduke, was Gavrilo Princip (PREEN-tseep). The slightly built young Serb was a member of the Black Hand, a secret society of Slavic extremists. Princip drew a small pistol and from point-blank range fired two shots. The first struck Sophie, and the second hit the archduke. Both died within minutes.

News of the assassination spread quickly across Europe. People everywhere were horrified, yet not really surprised. After all, there had been

Compare this photo, taken shortly before the assassination, with the painting on page 582.

more than 40 assassinations of political leaders—kings, generals, prime ministers, presidents—between 1900 and 1914.

Yet the assassination in Sarajevo was different from the others. It started a chain of events that, within five weeks, dragged almost all the countries of Europe into war—the first major war in more than a century. Two people died that June morning in Bosnia, but the terrible conflict that followed claimed the lives of more than 8 million soldiers and 6 million civilians.

In this chapter, we will look at both the immediate and the underlying causes of the war. Then we will see why neither side was able to win the quick victory that all leaders expected. Finally, we will see how the war's death and destruction left a bitter legacy for victors and vanquished alike.

Conflicts divided Europe. 1

How did the assassination of Franz Ferdinand trigger a world war? The answers are not simple. By itself, the murder of Franz Ferdinand could never have started such a vast conflict. However, tensions had been building in Europe for more than 50 years. Rivalry among the Great Powers—

Kaiser William II liked nothing better than to review his troops. He is shown here dressed in his army greatcoat and spiked helmet.

Austria-Hungary, Great Britain, Germany, France, Italy, and Russia—had led to crisis after crisis. The assassination at Sarajevo was merely the last step on the long road to war, a road down which Europe had been drifting for decades.

Bismarck shaped European alliances.

The conflict grew in part from a network of alliances going back to the 1870's. Ironically, these alliances had been designed to keep peace.

Between 1865 and 1871, Prussia's blood-and-iron chancellor, Otto von Bismarck, freely used war to unify Germany (page 521). After 1871, however, Bismarck turned to a policy of peace. Germany, he said, was a "satisfied power." Bismarck's new goal was to prevent war because war might shatter his newly created German empire. From 1871 to 1890, Bismarck worked to keep peace in Europe.

Bismarck saw France as the greatest threat to peace, because the French wanted revenge for their defeat in the Franco-Prussian War (page 523). Bismarck's first goal, therefore, was to isolate France. "As long as it is without allies," Bismarck stressed, "France poses no danger to us."

In 1879, Bismarck succeeded in partially isolating France by forming the Dual Alliance between Germany and Austria-Hungary. Three years later, these two countries were joined by Italy, making the Triple Alliance. In 1887, Bismarck took yet another possible ally away from France by making a treaty with Russia.

Bismarck's alliances were a fragile network. Germany had ties to both Austria-Hungary and Russia. Yet those two empires were locked in a struggle over the Balkans. Could Germany hold both its allies? And what part would Britain play? For the moment, the British seemed content to stand proudly alone. However, it was clear that a shift in the diplomatic winds might blow apart the web of treaties.

Shifting alliances threatened peace.

In 1890, Germany's foreign policy changed abruptly. In that year, Kaiser William II forced Bismarck to resign. Unlike his grandfather, who had let Bismarck rule Germany for more than 20 years, the new kaiser was determined to be his own master. A proud and stubborn man, William II was eager to show the world just how mighty Germany had become. The army was his greatest pride. "I and the army were born for each other," said William II at his coronation in 1888.

William II set Germany on a new course. Shortly after coming to power, he let the treaty of friendship between Russia and Germany lapse. The French were delighted. For years, France had been loaning Russia money for industrial development, hoping to earn the goodwill of the Russian government. The French reaped their reward in 1894 when Russia made an alliance with France.

According to the terms of the treaty, France and Russia promised to come to each other's aid if either was attacked by a third country. Such a treaty had been Bismarck's greatest fear. A war with either Russia or France would make Germany the enemy of both. Germany would then be forced to fight on both its eastern and western borders.

The impulsive kaiser made an even greater mistake in his dealings with Great Britain. Britain and Germany were economic rivals, but they had remained on fairly friendly terms during much of the 1800's. The kaiser himself was half English, as his mother was Queen Victoria's eldest daughter. Nevertheless, he held a lifelong grudge against Britain. He envied its worldwide empire and its mighty navy. The kaiser decided that Germany should challenge Britain. During the 1890's, Germany built its own small colonial empire, threatening British and French dominance. At the same time, William II started a tremendous ship-building program, planning to make the German navy equal to Britain's.

Alarmed, Great Britain began to enlarge its own fleet, joining Germany in a naval arms race. Moreover, the British government ended its policy of isolation and sought allies.

In 1904, Britain signed a treaty of friendship with France. In 1907, it signed a second treaty, this time with France and Russia. These treaties were *ententes* (friendly understandings) rather than alliances. Although the Triple Entente did not bind Britain to fight alongside France and Russia, it did ensure that Britain would almost certainly not fight against them.

By 1907, two rival camps existed in Europe. On one side was the Triple Alliance—Germany, Austria-Hungary, and Italy. On the other side was the Triple Entente—Great Britain, France, and Russia. A dispute between any two powers could draw the entire continent into war.

The Balkans were a powder keg.

Nowhere was the situation more tense than on the Balkan Peninsula. With good reason, this area was called the powder keg of Europe. For nearly 100 years, many Balkan groups had been trying to free themselves from the Ottoman empire. As that empire weakened, several Balkan groups broke away. By the early 1900's, these breakaway groups had formed a half-dozen new nations—Albania, Bulgaria, Greece, Montenegro, Romania, and Serbia. Nationalism was a powerful force in all of these countries, each of which longed to extend its borders. For example, Serbia, which had a large Slavic population, hoped to absorb all the Slavs on the peninsula into its own nation.

Such nationalist movements threatened Austria-Hungary, which ruled many Slavic peoples. At the same time, Austria-Hungary saw the decline of the Ottoman empire as an opportunity to extend its own sphere of influence on the Balkan Peninsula.

Europe before World War I

KEY
- Triple Alliance
- Triple Entente

0 — 300 Miles

Map Study

To which alliance system did Italy belong? France? Belgium?

While Austria felt threatened by nationalism in the Balkans, Russia was delighted. The Russians were Slavs, part of the same large language family as the Serbs, Bulgarians, and many other Balkan peoples. Russia encouraged these Slavic groups in their struggles for independence. Russia had selfish reasons for supporting these countries. By gaining influence in the Balkans, Russia hoped to win access to the warm-water ports of the Mediterranean Sea.

Thus, Russia and Austria were on a collision course in the Balkans. The two countries almost went to war in 1908. In that year, Austria annexed Bosnia and Herzegovina, two Balkan areas with large Slavic populations. Serbian officials, who had hoped to take over the two provinces themselves, were outraged. Russia offered Serbia full support, but the Russian threat proved hollow. Russia was totally unprepared for war. When Germany stood firmly behind Austria, the Russians had no choice but to back down.

In the following years, one crisis after another broke out on the Balkan Peninsula. Each time, peace was maintained, but one nation or another felt humiliated. After 1913, no one was willing to yield again.

585

A *warlike mood spread in Europe.*

By the summer of 1914, many Europeans believed that war was inevitable. There were some leaders in every country who thought that war was the best way to settle international problems. As a result, all the Great Powers except Britain kept large standing armies. With such an army, every government now felt it had the muscle to back up its demands in a crisis.

Generals in each country tried to perfect their plans for war. Many military leaders yearned for a chance to put their plans into practice. Most believed that their weapons were so advanced that no war could last longer than six months. A number of generals feared that if war did not begin soon, other countries might grow stronger. They urged political leaders not to delay.

Militarism, the glorification of armed strength, won support from ordinary civilians too. To many people, war seemed the purest kind of patriotism. "Happy are those who have died in great battles, lying on the ground before the face of God," wrote a French poet in the summer of 1914. Millions of Europeans appeared to share such feelings. In the 100 years since the Napoleonic wars, Europeans had forgotten the horrors of war and remembered only its glories.

Section Review 1

Define: (a) entente, (b) militarism
Identify: (a) Sarajevo, (b) Franz Ferdinand, (c) Triple Alliance, (d) William II, (e) Triple Entente
Answer:
1. What factors led to the assassination of Archduke Franz Ferdinand?
2. (a) What were Bismarck's major goals after 1871? (b) What alliances did he make?
3. How was the Triple Entente formed?
4. How did Austria and Russia become rivals in the Balkans?
5. How did each of the following encourage the drift toward war in 1914? (a) political leaders (b) military leaders (c) popular opinion

Critical Thinking
6. Do you think World War I would have occurred if the archduke had not been assassinated? Explain your answer.

Europe plunged into war.   2

By 1914, rival alliances, nationalism, imperialism, and an arms race had brought Europe to the brink of war. All that was needed was a spark to light the fuse. The spark came with the killing of Franz Ferdinand on June 28, 1914, as you read at the beginning of this chapter.

Because the killer was a Serbian, Austria-Hungary decided to use the murder as an excuse to teach Serbia a lesson. "Serbia must learn to fear us again," one Austrian diplomat said bluntly.

Before acting, Austria consulted its main ally, Germany. Would the kaiser stand behind Austria if a war with Serbia involved other powers? Yes, came the kaiser's reply on July 5, and he set no limits on his support. The kaiser had given Austria-Hungary what amounted to a blank check. Germany would back its ally all the way.

Austria-Hungary made the first move.

On July 23, nearly a month after the assassination, Austria-Hungary sent Serbia an **ultimatum,** a set of demands that, if not met, would end negotiations and lead to war. The ultimatum was deliberately harsh. Serbia was to stop all anti-Austrian activity. In addition, the Serbian government would have to allow Austrian officials into Serbia to investigate the killing and judge those accused of the crime. Serbia had 48 hours to respond.

Serbian leaders hesitated. They knew that refusing the ultimatum would lead to a war with Austria-Hungary, a larger and more powerful country than Serbia. At the same time, they knew that they would be giving up their nation's independence if they allowed Austrian officials into Serbia. Serbia had no choice but to say no to this condition. Four days later, on July 28, Austria declared war on Serbia.

Russia mobilized for war.

Serbia, although weaker than Austria-Hungary, had a powerful friend of its own. As protector of the Slavic peoples in southeastern Europe, the Russian government announced that it would stand behind the Serbs. This time, Russia would make up for backing down in 1908.

At this point, railroad timetables played a crucial part in turning the conflict between Austria and Serbia into a full-scale European war. Because armies were larger than ever before, moving soldiers into battle took days of travel in thousands of railroad cars. Russia faced special difficulties because it had few railroads and a large army. Russia needed many weeks to **mobilize**—that is, to get its army into position for war. The Russians felt they could not afford to wait.

By July 30, the Russian government had begun moving its army toward the Russian-Austrian border. Expecting Germany to join Austria, Russia also mobilized along the German border. At the same time, Czar Nicholas II of Russia told the kaiser (who was his cousin) that the army moves were just a precaution. Yet to German eyes, Russia's mobilization amounted to a declaration of war. On August 1, the German government declared war on Russia.

Russia looked to its ally, France, for help. Germany did not wait for France to act. Two days after declaring war on Russia, Germany also declared war on France.

The Great Powers took sides.

Germany now faced Bismarck's nightmare—a two-front war. It would have to fight France on its western border and Russia in the east. However, Germany's generals had long had plans for such a war. During the 1890's, General Alfred von Schlieffen (SHLEE-fuhn) drew up a master plan that called for a lightning-quick attack against France while Russia slowly mobilized. Under the Schlieffen Plan, almost the entire German army would race west to knock France out of action before the Russian army was ready to fight in the east.

Speed was vital to the German plan. The French had troops and forts all along their border with Germany, and the Germans knew that breaking through this border would be slow work. There was another route, however. France's northern border with Belgium was unprotected.

Germany demanded that its troops be allowed to cross through Belgium on the way to France. Belgium, whose neutrality had been guaranteed by the Great Powers since 1839, refused. The Germans paid no attention to the refusal and marched into Belgium on August 4. Britain was

Posters were important in the war effort. Britain used Lord Kitchener, hero of the Sudan, on a recruiting poster (left). A poster with the medieval knight Siegfried urged Germans to buy war bonds (right).

especially concerned, because of its closeness to Belgian ports. Outraged, Great Britain declared war on Germany.

By mid-August 1914, the battle lines were clearly drawn. On one side were Germany and Austria-Hungary, known as the Central Powers because of their geographic location in the heart of Europe. On the other side were Great Britain, France, and Russia. They were known as the Allied Powers or the Allies.

Other powers soon joined the war. In October, Turkey joined the Central Powers. A year later, Bulgaria did the same. In the beginning, Italy stayed neutral. The Italians said that the Triple Alliance was a defensive alliance and Germany had been the aggressor. However, nine months later, Italy joined the Allies against Germany and Austria.

In the late summer of 1914, millions of soldiers marched happily off to battle, convinced that the war would be short. Only a few people foresaw the horrors ahead. Staring out over London at nightfall, Britain's foreign minister, Sir Edward Grey, said sadly to a friend, "The lamps are going out all over Europe. We shall not see them lit again in our lifetime."

The German army invaded France.

Throughout August, 1.5 million German soldiers tramped over Belgium into northern France. There they encountered about the same number of French soldiers plus a small British force. (Britain did not keep a large peacetime army, so few British soldiers reached France until early 1915.) As summer turned to fall, these two sides formed a battle line that became known as the Western Front. (See map, page 593.)

At first, the French underestimated German strength. For years, French generals had stressed the importance of *élan* (ay-**LAHN**), or spirit, in battle. To attack the enemy boldly was all that counted. There was no need for defensive tactics, French army leaders reasoned, because victory would go to the army that attacked more vigorously.

Élan, however, was no match for the German fighting machine. All along the Western Front, German soldiers pushed back French forces. By September 2, German units were nearing the outskirts of Paris.

Germany now seemed within days of a victory on the Western Front. Problems quickly developed for Germany, however. The Germans had always feared Russia far more than they feared France, and now Russia was mobilizing more quickly than expected. Therefore, the German high command decided to send thousands of men to the east. This move weakened the western army just at the time when the rapid advance into France had stretched German supply lines to the limit. Moreover, as the French retreated toward Paris, their lines of communication were becoming shorter and shorter. As a result, the French and British were able to concentrate their forces.

The Allies struck back.

On September 6, the Allies attacked a gap in the German lines northwest of Paris in the valley of the Marne River. Every available soldier was hurled into the struggle. When the French army ran out of trucks, hundreds of taxicabs from Paris rushed more soldiers to the battlefield.

At the Marne, the German advance was stopped dead in its tracks. On September 12, German generals gave the order to retreat. The German army fell back to a new line about 40 miles north of the Marne. Paris was saved.

Although it was only the first major clash on the Western Front, the Battle of the Marne was perhaps its most important single event. The German retreat left the Schlieffen Plan in ruins. A quick victory in the west was no longer possible.

Germany had no hope of a quick victory in the east either. Although the Germans won several battles against the Russians in 1914, Russia was simply too big for overnight conquest. Germany's generals now faced the fearful prospect of a long war on two fronts.

Section Review 2

Define: (a) ultimatum, (b) mobilize, (c) élan
Identify: (a) Schlieffen Plan, (b) Central Powers, (c) Allies, (d) Western Front, (e) Eastern Front, (f) Battle of the Marne
Answer:
1. (a) What was Austria-Hungary's goal in sending Serbia an ultimatum? (b) Why did Serbia refuse? (c) What was the result?

2. (a) Why did Russia face particular difficulties in preparing for war? (b) What action did these difficulties lead Russia to take?
3. (a) What brought Germany into the war? (b) How did France become involved?
4. (a) How did Germany plan to solve the problem of a two-front war? (b) What development thwarted this plan?
5. Why did Great Britain enter the war?
6. How did the war become a stalemate?

Critical Thinking

7. It is sometimes said that in 1914 each side was pulled into war by its weakest member. (a) What were the weaknesses of Austria-Hungary and Russia? (b) How might the alliance system have encouraged them to act irresponsibly?

The war dragged on for four years.

3

After the Battle of the Marne, the war on the Western Front settled into a stalemate. Both sides dug in and held their existing positions. By early 1915, each army had built an elaborate system of tunnels, shelters, and trenches. These battle lines stretched more than 600 miles from the English Channel to the Swiss border. The space between the two sets of trenches won the grim name of "no-man's-land." As soldiers settled into the trenches for weeks and then months and then years, people began to realize that this war was unlike any other in history.

World War I was an industrialized war.

During World War I, countries on both sides used the technology of the Industrial Revolution to help their armies. They invented new weapons and made older ones more deadly.

New weapons on land One of these new weapons was the automatic machine gun. It fired so rapidly that a soldier's only protection was to take cover in the trenches. The machine gun played a major part in the deadlock and slaughter on the ground. Once the machine guns opened fire, neither side could advance.

In 1915, Germany turned to another new weapon, poison gas. It was a mixture that choked and blinded its victims. The Allies quickly began using gas too. Gas was an unpredictable weapon because winds blew it in random directions. In time, the invention of gas masks gave troops some protection from the burning clouds of mustard and chlorine gas.

In 1916, yet another invention, the tank, came into use. The British, who designed this armored motor vehicle, hoped it would smash through enemy lines. However, the first tanks had so many mechanical difficulties that they bogged down in mud or got stuck in shell holes. As a result, tanks were not used effectively until late in 1917.

New inventions in the air While millions of soldiers struggled on the ground, a handful of fighting men launched a new kind of battle in the air. Here, airplanes took part in war for the first time in history.

At first, planes were used mainly for scouting and taking photographs of enemy lines. Before

Daily Life · Wartime Shortages

During World War I, every country in Europe faced food shortages. For example, in Britain, milk, bread, tea, and bacon were very scarce; sugar and butter were almost unobtainable. To give everyone a fair chance at scarce goods, governments issued ration booklets. Each booklet held coupons for scarce items. The coupons were good until a certain date. Anyone who used all the coupons before that date had to wait until the next rationing period to receive more. The coupons at right belonged to King George V.

long, both sides also used them to drop bombs. The Germans, for example, used a kind of blimp to bomb the city of London. In 1915, they devised a way of timing machine guns with an airplane engine so that German pilots could fire forward through the spinning propellor. The Allies quickly did the same. The age of the dogfight, or aerial battle, began.

New inventions on the sea New weapons also changed the war at sea. Early in the war, Great Britain used its navy to blockade the North Sea coast. Britain hoped to keep food and war materials from reaching Germany. The Germans fought back with a new invention, the submarine or U-boat (*U* for *Untersee,* or "under the sea"). In September 1914, a German U-boat sank three armored British cruisers off the coast of the Netherlands. From then on, Germany used its large fleet of U-boats to attack ships carrying food and war supplies to Britain.

World War I *changed ways of life.*

World War I was a total war—that is, countries put all their resources into the war effort. Both human and industrial resources were turned to the demands of war.

The roles of civilians In the past, most wars had been fought by professional soldiers. World War I was different. The long trench lines were manned by drafted civilians. As the war went on, governments called for more and more soldiers. In every country, the vast majority of men between 20 and 40 years of age were in military service for the duration of the war.

As more and more men went to war, millions of women replaced them in factories, offices, and shops. Women also plowed fields, paved streets, dug ditches, and kept the soldiers supplied with food, clothing, and weapons. Before the war, most people had believed that only men could handle certain jobs. For example, few people believed that a woman could build a tank or run a hospital. During the war, many people changed these views as they watched women tackle jobs that had once been considered men's work.

The role of government In each country, the wartime government took much greater control of the economy than ever before. Governments told companies what to produce and in what quantities. Workers were assigned to specific factories. People with special skills such as welding or engineering were ordered to use them. Many inefficient factories and those producing luxuries were closed. So many goods were in short supply that governments turned to **rationing.** Under this system, people could buy only small amounts of goods that were needed for the war effort. Eventually, rationing covered a wide range of items from butter to shoe leather.

Early in the war, each side dug one set of trenches. Later, soldiers added second and third trenches to which they could retreat if the first lines failed to hold. Eventually, some armies boasted complete underground towns with kitchens, storage rooms, and sleeping quarters.

Blinded by poison gas, British soldiers grope their way past fallen comrades.

The role of propaganda Governments controlled the news. Leaders feared that honest reporting of battles might turn voters against the war. Governments also tried to keep up a fighting spirit by using all kinds of **propaganda**. Propaganda is one-sided information that aims to convince people of a certain point of view. All the warring countries used books, posters, and news reports to arouse hatred of the enemy.

The death toll mounted in the west.

Despite propaganda and news blackouts, the truth about the war could not be hidden forever. Casualty lists in the newspapers grew longer and longer. Wounded soldiers came home with tales of horror. Those still on the battlefield confirmed those stories in their letters.

"The men slept in mud, washed in mud, ate mud, and dreamed mud," wrote one soldier on the Western Front. The trenches swarmed with rats and insects. Fresh food was nonexistent. Soldiers lived on canned meat that was often spoiled, bread that was hard as rock, and limited supplies of drinking water. Between repairing the trenches by day and sentry duty at night, soldiers rarely slept more than an hour or two at a time.

Day and night, every man lived in fear. When their officers ordered an attack, the men went "over the top" of their trenches, usually into murderous machine-gun fire. One did not have to go over the top to die, however. A sniper's bullet or an artillery bombardment could bring death into the trenches. "Shells of all calibers kept raining on our sector," wrote one French soldier. "The trenches disappeared, filled with earth . . . The air was unbreathable. Our blinded, wounded, crawling, and shouting soldiers kept falling on top of us and died splashing us with blood. It was living hell."

The slaughter reached a peak in 1916. That February, the Germans launched a massive attack against the French near Verdun on the Meuse River. It lasted more than five months, at the end of which each side had lost more than 300,000 men.

In July, the British army tried to relieve the pressure on the French by attacking the Germans northwest of Verdun in the valley of the Somme River. Thousands of tons of explosives rained from the sky, and the rat-tat-tat of machine guns echoed for hours at a time. In the first day of battle alone, more than 20,000 British soldiers were killed. Before the Battle of the Somme trailed off several months later, each side had suffered over half a million casualties.

What did each side gain from these two great battles? Near Verdun, the Germans advanced about four miles. In the Somme valley, the British advanced about five miles.

Footnote to History

For many years, the war that began in 1914 was called simply the Great War. People hoped it would be "the war to end war" and that there would never be another. Only when another equally savage conflict broke out did people begin to number the wars—World War I and World War II.

Voice from the Past · *Bombardment in the Trenches*

The novel *All Quiet on the Western Front* by Erich Maria Remarque tells of the war through the eyes of an 18-year-old German soldier. Here he waits in the trenches through days of artillery shelling, knowing that an attack will come afterward.

We wake up in the middle of the night. The earth booms. Heavy fire is falling on us. We crouch into corners . . .

The dug-out heaves, the night roars and flashes. We look at each other in the momentary flashes of light, and with pale faces and pressed lips shake our heads . . .

The attack does not come, but the bombardment continues. Slowly we become mute. Hardly a man speaks. We cannot make ourselves understood . . .

Our company commander scrambles in . . . He says that an attempt will be made to bring up food this evening . . .

We pull in our belts tighter and chew every mouthful three times as long. Still the food does not last out; we are damnably hungry. I take out a scrap of bread, eat the white and put the crust back in my knapsack; from time to time I nibble at it . . .

Towards morning, while it is still dark, there is some excitement. Through the entrance rushes in a swarm of fleeing rats that try to storm the walls. Torches [flashlights] light up the confusion. Everyone yells and curses and slaughters. The madness and despair of many hours unloads itself in this outburst. Faces are distorted, arms strike out, the beasts scream; we stop just in time to avoid attacking one another . . .

Night again. We are deadened by the strain—a deadly tension that scrapes along one's spine like a gapped knife. Our legs refuse to move, our hands tremble, our bodies are a thin skin stretched painfully over repressed madness . . . So we shut our teeth—it will end—it will end—perhaps we will come through.

1. Why would one army bombard the other for many hours before attacking?
2. How did the artillery shelling affect supplies for men in the trenches?
3. (a) What probably drove the rats into the trench? (b) How did the soldiers react?
4. How did the days of shelling affect these soldiers mentally and emotionally?

War raged on other fronts.

Even as war raged in the west, both sides were sending millions of men to fight on other fronts. These fronts played a crucial role in tipping the balance between the Allies and the Central Powers.

The Eastern Front The biggest of those other fronts was in the east, where Russians and Serbs battled Austrians, Turks, and Germans. The war in the east was more a war of movement than in the west, but here too stalemate was common.

At the outbreak of the war, Russian forces penetrated both Austria and Germany. In August 1914, the Germans crushed the invading Russians at the Battle of Tannenberg. Afterward, the Germans gradually pressed the Russians back into their own land.

Russia never recovered from its defeat at Tannenberg. Short of food, guns, boots, and even blankets, the Russian army had only one asset—numbers. Russia's enormous population was used to refill the ranks of the army despite overwhelming casualties. For more than three years,

World War I in Europe

Map Study
Name two battles that took place along the Eastern Front.

that army tied up hundreds of thousands of German troops in the east. Thus, Germany could never hurl its full fighting force at the west.

The Ottoman front In October 1914, the Ottoman Turks entered the war on the side of the Central Powers, thus opening up a third front. The following February, the British and French struck at the Ottoman nerve center, the straits linking the Black and Mediterranean seas. The Allies hoped to open the straits to send much-needed supplies to Russia. The Allied assault, known as the Gallipoli campaign, was a disaster. After almost a year of fighting, the Allies were forced to give up.

Later, the British mounted more indirect campaigns against the Ottomans by organizing Arab

nationalists in the Middle East. These campaigns were more successful than the direct attack on Turkey had been. The Arabs were eager to revolt against their Turkish overlords. Gradually, Allied forces took control of Baghdad, Jerusalem, and Damascus.

The Italian front Another major front opened in May 1915 when Italy joined the war on the side of the Allies. Italy did not help the Allies as much as they had hoped. The Italian army lacked equipment, and public opinion in Italy was divided as to which side to support. However, fighting on the Italian front diverted some Austrian forces from the war in the east.

The war in Asia and Africa Far from the battlefields of Europe, places in Asia and Africa also saw fighting. Japan declared war against Germany within a few weeks after war had broken out in Europe. The Japanese quickly overran German possessions in China and captured most of Germany's Pacific island colonies. In Africa, the British and French conquered most of Germany's possessions. In German East Africa (modern Tanzania), however, Germany managed to hold out to the bitter end.

The Russian war effort weakened.

By 1917, Europe had lost more men in 3 years of fighting than in all the wars of the previous 300 years. Still there was no end in sight. Nowhere were the effects of war more sorely felt than in Russia. The Russians had poured all their resources into the war, but they were not enough. Russian soldiers faced the well-armed Germans with little more than their courage. They lacked guns, ammunition, warm clothes, and food. Badly led and lacking supplies, the Russian army felt betrayed by its leaders.

Discontent with the czar's government had been brewing for decades. In March 1917, Russian revolutionaries drove the czar from power and set up a provisional (temporary) government. (See Chapter 28.) Although the new government promised the Allies to go on fighting, few Russians were willing to fight any longer.

The United States entered the war.

Germany in 1917 also had its share of problems. Although the Central Powers had won important military successes in 1916, those efforts had nearly exhausted their resources and manpower. Food shortages were already critical because of the British blockade. Worse, Germany's potato crop failed in the summer of 1916.

Desperate to strike a decisive blow, Germany decided to take a new risk. On January 31, 1917, the Germans announced that their submarines would sink without warning any ship in the waters around Britain. This policy was called unrestricted submarine warfare.

The Germans had tried this policy earlier in the war. On May 7, 1915, a German U-boat had sunk the British passenger ship *Lusitania*, killing 1,198 people including 139 United States citizens. The attack had outraged people in the United States. President Woodrow Wilson had sent a strong protest to Germany. The Germans, fearing that the United States would declare war, backed down. They agreed to give warning to ships of a neutral country before firing.

When the Germans returned to unrestricted submarine warfare in 1917, they knew their decision would lead to war with the United States. However, they hoped to starve Britain into defeat before the United States could mobilize.

In fall 1916, Britain secretly shipped 47 of its fearsome new tanks to the Western Front for use in the Battle of the Somme.

Three days after Germany announced its plans, President Wilson warned Germany that the United States would take any action necessary to protect its citizens. Soon after, German U-boats sank three American ships bound for Great Britain.

In February 1917, another event added fuel to the fire. The British intercepted a telegram from Germany's foreign secretary, Arthur Zimmermann, to the German minister in Mexico. The message said that Germany would help Mexico get back its lost land in New Mexico, Texas, and Arizona if Mexico would side with Germany. The British quickly decoded the message and gave it to the United States government.

Many Americans demanded war against Germany. On April 2, 1917, President Wilson asked Congress to declare war. With this declaration, the United States entered the war on the side of the Allies.

The war came to an end.

At first, the German U-boat campaign went well. In April 1917 alone, German submarines sank over 800,000 tons of Allied shipping. However, the Allies quickly worked out a way to guard their ships. They organized convoys—large, specially equipped fleets designed to guard merchant ships. The convoy system dashed Germany's hopes for a quick defeat of Britain.

Yet the Germans were far from beaten. On the Eastern Front, they were making every effort to drive Russia out of the war. Although Russia was in chaos after the overthrow of the czar, its armies struggled on.

One party of Russian revolutionaries, the Bolsheviks, had pledged to make peace. The leader of the Bolsheviks, a man known as Lenin, was living as an exile in Switzerland. In March 1917, the Germans arranged for a special train to carry Lenin secretly back to Russia. Just as the Germans had hoped, Lenin quickly led his party to power. In November 1917, the Bolsheviks took control of Russia. In March 1918, Germany and Russia signed the Treaty of Brest Litovsk, which ended the war between those two countries.

Victory in the east allowed Germany to send nearly all its forces to the Western Front. For the first time since 1914, Germany now had more soldiers in northern France than did the Allies. Soon, however, the arrival of American troops would again tip the balance in the Allies' favor. Thus, Germany needed to act quickly.

The Germans prepared one final attack on the Western Front. They formed crack units of "shock troops" by putting veterans from the east alongside those who had fought in the west. In March 1918, 6,000 German cannons opened the attack with the largest artillery barrage of the entire war. The combination of artillery, skilled troops, and dense fog helped the Germans win victory after victory. By early June, they had once again reached the banks of the Marne. Paris was only 50 miles away.

Just as victory seemed within reach, the German drive stalled. The effort of reaching the Marne had exhausted supplies and men alike. Soldiers stopped advancing to loot shops for food. Germany had no more trained troops to replace those who had been killed or wounded. The only soldiers left were 15- and 16-year-old boys.

Meanwhile, American troops began arriving in France at a rate of about 250,000 a month. Marshal Ferdinand Foch (fawsh), the French general in command of the Allied forces, used the Americans to fill the gaps in his ranks. The "Yanks" were inexperienced but courageous and eager for action. With each passing day, the German army grew weaker while the Allied forces increased in strength.

In August 1918, the decisive battle of the war took place around Amiens. Leading the attack were some 300 Allied tanks that rumbled forward at a snail's pace, smashing through the German lines. The Germans continued to fight through September, but their resources were strained to the breaking point.

The other Central Powers were crumbling as well. First the Bulgarians and then the Ottoman Turks sued for peace. In November, a revolution in Austria-Hungary brought the empire to an end. Germany itself was on the very brink of revolution.

On November 9, 1918, Kaiser William II abdicated, and Germany became a republic. On the same day, a representative of the new government met with Marshal Foch. In a railway car in a forest not far from Paris, the two signed an **armistice,** an agreement to stop fighting. Two days later on November 11, World War I came to an end.

The cost of the war was staggering.

World War I had shaken the economic and social foundations of European society. A whole generation of young men had been struck down. France lost 20 percent of its men between the ages of 20 and 44, and Germany lost 15 percent. Almost every family in Europe had a son, a husband, or a brother who had been killed or maimed.

The war also left deep scars in the memories of those who survived. Among them were writers, painters, and composers who passed on their experiences to others through their works. Their bitterness and pessimism ran through much of the art and literature of the 1920's and 1930's. Disillusioned and disheartened, these young people became known as the Lost Generation.

Although the war had ended, it was foolish to speak of winners, said Winston Churchill, Britain's under-secretary of the navy. Victory, he said, had been "bought so dear as to be indistinguishable from defeat."

Section Review 3

Define: (a) no-man's-land, (b) U-boat, (c) rationing, (d) propaganda, (e) convoy, (f) armistice
Identify: (a) Woodrow Wilson, (b) *Lusitania*, (c) Treaty of Brest Litovsk
Answer:
1. What new weapons came into use in World War I?
2. Why is World War I called a total war?
3. How did the war affect the role of women in society?
4. What was the role of government during the war years?
5. (a) How did the war progress on the Western Front? (b) On the Eastern Front?
6. What part did each of the following countries play? (a) Ottoman empire (b) Italy (c) Japan (d) the United States
7. What factors led to Germany's defeat?

Critical Thinking
8. Restate Winston Churchill's evaluation of the Allies' victory in your own words. What evidence supports his statement?

Peace stood on shaky foundations.

4

The leaders of the victorious Allied Powers met at Versailles in January 1919 to hammer out the peace treaties that would officially end World War I. People hoped that these treaties would mark the beginning of a lasting era of peace. Yet even before the treaties were ready to sign, those hopes were dashed.

Wilson proposed a plan for peace.

It was largely because of one man that hopes had risen so high. That man was President Woodrow Wilson of the United States. Americans had fought this war, said Wilson, not for their own selfish ends but "to make the world safe for democracy."

In January 1918, while the war was still raging, Wilson had drawn up a series of proposals. Known as the Fourteen Points, they outlined his goals for a just and lasting peace.

Of the Fourteen Points, the first five set general goals for the postwar world. They were these:
1. Ending secret treaties
2. Agreeing to freedom of the seas
3. Removing economic barriers to trade
4. Reducing the size of national armies and navies
5. Adjusting colonial claims with fairness toward the colonial peoples

The sixth through the thirteenth points were specific suggestions on changing national borders and creating new nations. Wilson's guiding idea in these points was **self-determination**—allowing people to decide for themselves under what government they wished to live.

Finally, the fourteenth point proposed a "general association of nations" that would protect "great and small states alike." To Wilson, this was the most important point. He hoped for an organization that would keep peace by encouraging its members to solve problems through negotiation. This proposal eventually led to the formation of the League of Nations.

The world hailed Wilson's Fourteen Points as a landmark in the quest for world peace. Both the Allies and the Germans accepted Wilson's proposal as the basis for peace negotiations.

Conflicting demands dominated the conference.

When Wilson arrived in France for the peace conference in December 1918, people greeted him as an angel of peace. "Here and there along the way," wrote a reporter who traveled on Wilson's train, "peasant families were seen kneeling beside the track to pray for him and his mission."

The task facing Wilson at Versailles was not easy. Groups that had once been part of the Ottoman and Austro-Hungarian empires wanted the peacemakers to give them their own independent nations. However, many groups claimed the same lands. Not since Napoleon's defeat in 1815 had Europe faced such a task of rebuilding.

There were other problems as well. At first, both France and Britain had agreed with Wilson's ideas for a just peace. Now, however, both countries wanted to make the German people pay for the suffering the war had caused. Italy too had its own demands. In 1915, the Allies had lured Italy into the war by promising it parts of Austria-Hungary where many Italian-speaking people lived. Now Italy wanted its reward.

With so many conflicting ambitions, the peace talks at Versailles were stormy. Although more than two dozen countries were represented, the major decisions were hammered out in private by France, Britain, and the United States. Italy played only a minor part. Russia, which had suffered perhaps the greatest loss of life, was in the midst of a civil war and was not invited to attend the conference.

The Allies dictated peace terms.

Spring came late to northern France in 1919. April was dreary, cold, and damp. May at last brought sunshine and warmth. The finches and nightingales began to return to the gardens and parks at Versailles, the magnificent estate built by Louis XIV.

On the afternoon of May 7, about 4 months after the conference had begun, some 70 delegates representing 27 countries gathered in the ornate conference room. In the front, on a raised platform, sat the Big Three, the men whose views had dominated the peace conference. These were Georges Clemenceau (kleh-mahn-SOH) of France,

Wilson, Clemenceau, and Lloyd George (center three seated) look on as the treaty is signed.

David Lloyd George of Britain, and Woodrow Wilson of the United States. None of the defeated countries had been allowed to take part in the discussions. Their representatives were present now only to hear the verdict.

The verdict was indeed harsh. Back in Germany, officials were horrified as they studied the Versailles treaty. Several resigned in protest. In the end, however, they had no choice but to sign.

The final signing ceremony took place in the Hall of Mirrors at Versailles, the same room in which the Germans had forced the French to sign a humiliating treaty in 1871 (page 523). The date was June 28, 1919—five years to the day after Franz Ferdinand's assassination at Sarajevo.

The treaty fell far short of a just and lasting peace. These were its terms:

Territorial losses Germany lost 13 percent of its land, where nearly 10 percent of its people lived. France, Poland, Belgium, and Denmark all received some of the territory.

France regained Alsace-Lorraine, which Germany had taken in 1871. France also won the

597

Europe after World War I

KEY
Territory lost by:
- Austria-Hungary
- Russia
- Germany
- Bulgaria

0   300 Miles

Map Study

Which of the Central Powers were forced to cede land to Poland? Which of the Allies?

right to work the rich mines of the Saar basin for 15 years. After that time, the people of the Saar region were to have the right to rejoin Germany if they so wished.

Poland, which had not appeared on a map of Europe since it was partitioned in the 1790's, once again became an independent nation. The new Poland received a large strip of German land called the Polish corridor. This strip cut off East Prussia from the rest of Germany and gave Poland access to the Baltic Sea.

All of Germany's territories in Africa and the Pacific were given as **mandates** to Britain, France, and Japan. A mandate was a territory that was administered on behalf of the League of Nations. The Allies were to govern these lands until they were judged fit for independence.

Military restrictions The treaty had many clauses designed to keep Germany from ever again threatening the peace. The size of the German army was strictly limited. Germany could not manufacture war material. Submarines and airplanes were also banned. Furthermore, the Germans were forbidden to place any troops in the Rhineland, a strip of land in western Germany between the Rhine River and the French border.

War guilt The most severe part of the Treaty, however, was Article 231, the "war-guilt" clause. This clause placed sole blame for World War I on Germany's shoulders. As a result, the Germans were obliged to pay **reparations** to the Allies—that is, money to compensate for the enormous costs of the war. The final reparations bill came to $31 billion, which Germany was to pay over the next 30 years.

The League of Nations Although the peace conference dashed many of Wilson's hopes for a just and lasting peace, he did win one major victory. The Allies agreed to create a League of Nations. Five large nations—the United States, Britain, France, Italy, and Japan—were to be permanent members of its Executive Council. The League would also have a general assembly at which representatives of 42 Allied and neutral nations would meet. Germany was deliberately left out. So was Russia, which was then in the midst of civil war and revolution.

Other treaties created new nations.

The treaty with Germany was just one of five signed in Paris during 1919 and 1920. The other Central Powers also suffered losses in territory. However, out of the ashes of these old empires, Wilson's idea of national self-determination guided the creation of several new nations.

The Turkish treaty The treaty with the Ottoman Turks forced them to give up almost all of their old empire. Their territory was limited to what is now the country of Turkey.

The lands that the Ottomans lost in Southwest Asia were formed into several new territories—Iraq, Lebanon, Palestine, Transjordan, and Syria. Like the former German colonies, these areas became mandates. The League of Nations assigned control of Palestine, Iraq, and Transjordan to Great

Footnote to History

In 1918, one of the worst epidemics in history swept around the globe. It was a worldwide outbreak of influenza. In a year, it killed 10 million people—more than all the combat deaths of the war. The epidemic was partly a result of the war because troop movements carried the flu to every continent.

Britain. Syria and Lebanon went to France. Some Turkish territory went to Greece. The treaty also recognized the independence of Arabia.

The break-up of Austria-Hungary Several new countries were carved out of the Austro-Hungarian empire. Austria and Hungary were both recognized as independent nations. However, they lost some territory to the newly formed countries of Poland, Czechoslovakia, and Yugoslavia. Trieste and southern Tyrol went to Italy. Finally, Romania received a large area, thus doubling its size.

The Bulgarian treaty By this treaty, the defeated Bulgaria gave up land to Romania, Yugoslavia, and Greece. Bulgaria had to pay almost a half-billion dollars in reparations.

Russian losses Even before the peace treaty was signed, Germany had to cancel the severe Treaty of Brest Litovsk in which Germany had taken about a fourth of Russia's European territory. Even so, Russia ended by losing more land than Germany.

The Allies, fearful of Russia's new revolutionary government, wanted to protect Russia's neighbors on the west. As a result, Russia lost the province of Bessarabia in the southwest to Romania. Poland also gained much Russian territory. Finland, Estonia, Latvia, and Lithuania, which had all declared their independence from Russia in 1918, were recognized as nations.

In several of these other treaties, the Allies added clauses aimed at further limiting Germany's size and power. The new country of Czechoslovakia, for example, included a region called the Sudetenland (soo-**DAYT**-uhn-LAND). Some 3 million Germans lived in this border region. Furthermore, the treaties forbade any *anschluss* (union) between Germany and the now tiny state of Austria, whose 6 million people were nearly all German speaking.

The United States rejected the treaty.

Across the Atlantic, many Americans objected to the Treaty of Versailles, especially to the League of Nations. Some believed that the United States' best hope for peace was to stay out of European affairs. Other Americans feared the League might undermine the powers of Congress in foreign affairs. They wanted to be sure, for example, that no American soldiers could be ordered to fight without Congress's consent.

After a bitter debate, the United States Senate refused to join the League of Nations or accept the Treaty of Versailles. The United States worked out a separate treaty with Germany and its allies several years later.

In the end, the Treaty of Versailles did little to build a lasting peace. Instead, it left a legacy of bitterness and hatred in the hearts of the German people. Other countries felt cheated and betrayed by the peace settlements. Lacking the support of several world powers, the League of Nations was in no position to take action on these complaints. It was, as one observer described it, "a peace built on quicksand."

Section Review 4

Define: (a) self-determination, (b) mandate, (c) reparations
Identify: (a) Versailles, (b) Fourteen Points, (c) League of Nations, (d) Big Three
Answer:
1. What were the general goals of the Fourteen Points?
2. What attitudes did Britain, France, and Italy take at the peace conference?
3. (a) Whom did the Treaty of Versailles blame for the war? (b) What role did the Central Powers play in the negotiations?
4. (a) What territory did Germany lose to France? (b) What new countries were created in eastern Europe from lands lost by Austria-Hungary and Russia?
5. What changes took place in Southwest Asia as a result of the war?
6. (a) Describe the organization of the League of Nations. (b) What powerful nations did not become members?
7. Why did the United States reject the Treaty of Versailles?

Critical Thinking
8. Review the proposals of the Fourteen Points (page 596). Which of these points, if they had been accepted around 1900, might have prevented war from beginning in 1914? Explain your answer.

Chapter Review 27

Summary

1. Conflicts divided Europe. By 1913, nationalism and the race for empires had divided Europe into two opposing camps. On one side was the Triple Alliance—Germany, Austria-Hungary, and Italy. On the other side was the Triple Entente—Great Britain, France, and Russia. Many Europeans felt that the only answer to the conflicts lay in armed might.

2. Europe plunged into war. The spark that set off the war was the assassination of Austrian Archduke Franz Ferdinand by a Serbian nationalist. When Serbia rejected Austria's ultimatum, Russia leaped to Serbia's defense. The mobilization of Russian forces led to a German declaration of war. Defeat at the Battle of Marne dashed German hopes for a quick victory.

3. The war dragged on for four years. The war in the west turned into a stalemate that lasted for four years. During these years, new technologies of warfare and the total involvement of citizens and governments made World War I unlike any earlier war. In 1917, heavy Russian losses contributed to a revolution that overthrew the czar. The entrance into the war of the United States turned the tide for the Allies in 1917. On November 11, 1918, Germany surrendered.

4. Peace stood on shaky foundations. Even before the war ended, President Wilson proposed Fourteen Points for a just and lasting peace. In the end, however, the Allies dictated harsh peace terms to the defeated powers, causing extreme bitterness, especially among the Germans. However, Wilson's proposal to form a League of Nations was accepted. Strong isolationist sentiment led the United States to reject both the treaty and the League.

Reviewing the Facts

1. Define the following terms:
   - a. militarism
   - b. ultimatum
   - c. mobilize
   - d. rationing
   - e. propaganda
   - f. armistice
   - g. self-determination
   - h. mandate
   - i. reparations

2. Explain the importance of each of the following names, places, dates, or terms:
   - a. Franz Ferdinand
   - b. 1914
   - c. Bismarck
   - d. William II
   - e. Ottoman empire
   - f. Triple Alliance
   - g. Triple Entente
   - h. Schlieffen Plan
   - i. Western Front
   - j. Battle of the Marne
   - k. Allies
   - l. U-boat
   - m. Zimmermann note
   - n. Treaty of Brest Litovsk
   - o. Woodrow Wilson
   - p. Versailles
   - q. war guilt

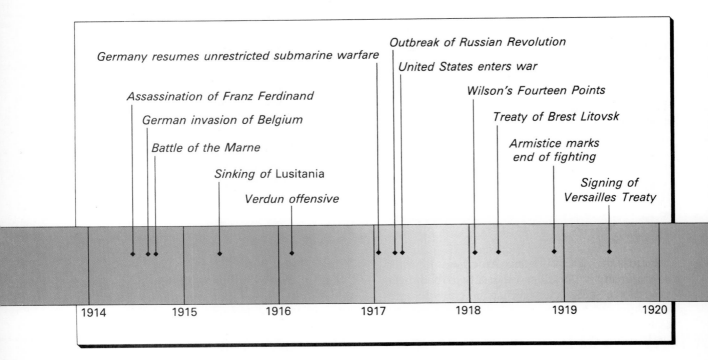

Germany resumes unrestricted submarine warfare

Outbreak of Russian Revolution

United States enters war

Assassination of Franz Ferdinand

Wilson's Fourteen Points

German invasion of Belgium

Treaty of Brest Litovsk

Battle of the Marne

Armistice marks end of fighting

Sinking of Lusitania

Signing of Versailles Treaty

Verdun offensive

1914 1915 1916 1917 1918 1919 1920

3. (a) In what way did Kaiser William II undermine Bismarck's policies? (b) Describe the two sets of alliances that resulted.
4. (a) What powers were on a collision course in the Balkans? (b) How did Slavic nationalism intensify the conflict?
5. Briefly describe the chain of events that resulted in the outbreak of World War I.
6. (a) Why did the Schlieffen Plan fail? (b) How did its failure affect Germany's plans for the war?
7. Describe three ways in which World War I differed from earlier wars.
8. (a) Describe war along the Western Front. (b) How did it differ from war in the east?
9. (a) What happened during the war along the Ottoman front? (b) Along the Italian front? (c) In Asia and Africa?
10. (a) What happened in Russia in 1917? (b) How had the war contributed to this event?
11. Why did the United States enter the war in 1917?
12. (a) List five general goals that Wilson proposed in his Fourteen Points. (b) How did the demands of France and Britain conflict with these goals?
13. (a) Describe Germany's territorial losses. (b) What new countries were created in eastern Europe? (c) What changes took place in Southwest Asia?
14. (a) What military restrictions were placed on Germany? (b) How did the Sudetenland and the prohibition of *anschluss* limit German power?
15. (a) Describe the League of Nations. (b) Which major powers did not belong? (c) Why?

Thinking about History

1. Why did European generals believe in 1914 that the war would be a short one? What factors did they neglect to consider?
2. King Edward VII of England died in 1910, four years before the outbreak of war. Historian Barbara Tuchman wrote, "Edward's funeral turned out to be the funeral of royalty itself; a final grand curtain-call of kings before they marched off the stage forever." Do you think Tuchman's statement is accurate in view of the changes that took place in Europe after World War I? Give examples.

Writing and Speaking about History

1. Prepare a memorandum from a Russian official to a French official describing the effects of the war on the Russian people. In your memorandum, mention the threat of a Russian revolution and how it might affect the Allied war effort.
2. Design a propaganda poster supporting either the Allies or the Central Powers. Include a visual and a slogan in the poster.
3. Conduct a telephone conversation between *one* of the following soldiers and his parents. In the conversation, discuss life on the front as well as the problems the war has created at home.
   Russian soldier at Tannenberg, 1914
   French soldier at the Marne, 1914
   German soldier at Verdun, 1916
   British soldier at the Somme, 1916

Practicing Skills

1. Describe the status of each of the following countries on the maps of Europe on pages 585 and 598. (a) Serbia (b) Hungary (c) Yugoslavia (d) Poland (e) Czechoslovakia (f) Bosnia
2. (a) What territorial changes on the map on page 598 were made to limit Germany's power? (b) To limit Russia's power? (c) How does the map help explain why the Treaty of Versailles was a peace built on quicksand?
3. Use the information on pages 584 and 585 to make a timeline of events that led up to World War I.

Investigating History

1. Prepare a report on one of the new weapons used in World War I. Tell how it developed from earlier technological advances and include a model or drawing as an illustration.
2. Report on one of the new countries that came into being after World War I. Where was it located? What countries were its neighbors? What part, if any, had it played in the earlier history of the region? Did it conflict with the nationalist goals of any other nation?

Decision Making in History

Rewrite one or more of the following sections of the Treaty of Versailles so that it is less punitive toward Germany. Consider that the treaty must restrict Germany without antagonizing the German people.
   territorial losses
   military restrictions
   war guilt

Russia in Revolution

This painting by a Russian artist shows the revolutionary leader Lenin speaking to a crowd of rebellious workers, soldiers, and sailors. In Russian art since 1917, Lenin always appears as a forceful, dynamic leader—the hero of the revolution.

1. **Russia struggled to reform.**

2. **Russia moved toward revolution.**

3. **The Bolsheviks led a second revolution.**

4. **Stalin became dictator.**

It was cold, bitterly cold, in St. Petersburg on the morning of February 25, 1917. As the sun rose over the frozen Neva River, thousands of women huddled in the doorways of the city's bakeries, waiting, as they waited almost every morning, for bread. By the time sleepy-eyed workers began to trudge through the snow to factories and offices, the lines to some bakeries were several blocks long.

Then came the news: There was no bread. The bakers could not bake without flour, and there were no trains to bring flour to the city. Russia had been at war for nearly three years, and the country's railroads were under enormous strain. Nearly every boxcar was needed to carry food and supplies to the army.

During past shortages, the women of St. Petersburg had quietly returned home without their bread. This time they refused to leave. Instead, they milled about the streets, shouting, "We want bread! We want bread!" They gathered on trolley tracks, stopping traffic. They forced passengers off streetcars and even turned over a few cars. Some women began throwing rocks through store windows.

The women did not consider themselves revolutionaries. They were just tired—tired of waiting for bread that never came, tired of watching their sons and husbands march off to die in war. They were tired of poverty—tired of seeing the carriages of the rich glide by while their own families huddled around grimy stoves in dark, crowded tenements.

Within hours, the women were joined by workers from several textile factories and the huge Putilov steelworks on the outskirts of the city. By early afternoon, great crowds had gathered along St. Petersburg's main street. The demonstrators shouted and sang. Many held up banners proclaiming "We want Bread!" or "End the War!" Others held a more menacing slogan—"Down with the Czar!"

Nicholas II, Russia's czar, did not pay much attention to the protesters. He was far more concerned with the war against Germany. On that same Thursday morning, Nicholas left St. Petersburg for his headquarters at the front. He felt certain that the police would easily handle the disturbances. Yet even as his train rumbled across the snowy Russian plains, unrest spread through the capital city.

By Monday, St. Petersburg was in the hands of rebellious workers and the many soldiers who had joined them. The czar soon realized that this was no ordinary disturbance, and he tried desperately to return to the capital. The uprising, however, had by then reached far beyond St. Petersburg. Railroad workers along the czar's route would not let his train pass. Meanwhile, at the front, soldiers refused to fight. Thousands deserted from the army daily. In this crisis, Nicholas called a meeting of his generals. They presented Nicholas with a bleak decision: He must **abdicate** (resign as ruler).

On March 2, 1917, Nicholas II gave up the throne that his family, the Romanovs, had held for more than three centuries. In this chapter, we will see that this revolution had been building for almost 100 years. We will also see why the czar's abdication did not bring peace or democracy to Russia.

Russia struggled to reform. 1

"Three centuries to build it up, and three days for it to vanish," wrote one observer in March 1917, speaking of the Russian monarchy. His comment was misleading. The old regime was not destroyed in a few days. The Russian Revolution was like a firecracker with a very long fuse. The explosion came in 1917, but the fuse had been burning for years.

To understand the revolution, it is necessary to go back in time at least to 1825. That year, Czar Alexander I, who had helped defeat Napoleon (page 464), died. With his death, Russia entered a period of turmoil that lasted nearly 100 years.

Most Russians lived as serfs.

In the early 1800's, while the Industrial Revolution was changing western Europe, Russia remained an agricultural country. More than 90 percent of all Russians depended on farming for their livelihood. A few owned large estates, but the vast majority—more than 80 percent of the people—were serfs. These men, women, and children worked for the owners of the large estates.

Serfdom had developed in Russia during the late Middle Ages (page 415). By the 1800's, serfs were permanently bound to the noble whose land they worked. Nobles had almost unlimited power over their serfs. They could buy and sell serfs in open markets like cattle. Landholders could beat their serfs or even exile them to Siberia. (Siberia is the bleak region of northeastern Russia that lies in Asia.)

By the 1820's, many Russians believed that serfdom must be ended. They argued that the system was morally wrong and also kept the empire economically backward. Serfs had no incentives to better themselves or learn new ways of farming. Why should they produce more food to fatten the landlords? Why should they learn

603

Harnessed like oxen, Russian serfs haul a barge up the Volga River. In more industrialized countries, steam engines did such work.

new skills or start new businesses? Educated Russians were convinced that freeing the serfs was the first and most necessary step toward modernizing Russia.

In Russia, all it would have taken to end serfdom was the command of the czar. The czar was an absolute ruler. He had complete control over the lives and property of his subjects. He was the sole source of all laws. The czar was an **autocrat**, a ruler with unlimited power. (The word comes from Greek words meaning "rule by oneself.")

For a time, Czar Alexander I toyed with the idea of freeing the serfs. He even took a few slight steps in that direction. Yet he did not do so. When he died suddenly of a fever in 1825, an important chance for peaceful reform died with him.

The Decembrists revolted.

Alexander's death brought on a revolt in December 1825. The army officers who led it became known to history as the Decembrists, after the month in which their revolt took place.

The officers were all veterans of the long wars against Napoleon. While fighting in western Europe, they had come into contact with such ideas as bills of rights for citizens. When they returned to Russia, they found that the czar's government still ruled with unlimited powers. With no legal way to work for reform or even to express their ideas, a few young officers organized secret revolutionary societies. Their goal was to win a written constitution for Russia that allowed some of the rights of western Europe.

These secret groups were plotting an uprising when Alexander I died. No one was certain which of his several brothers would become the next czar. The oldest brother was Constantine, but he did not want to rule Russia.

Some young officers in St. Petersburg decided to take advantage of the confusion. They threw their support behind Constantine, even though he had already agreed to step aside for a younger brother, Nicholas. When it was time for the army to take the oath of loyalty to the new czar, the officers ordered their troops to shout "Constantine and Constitution." In their ignorance, many of the soldiers apparently believed that "Constitution" was Constantine's wife.

Troops loyal to Nicholas forcefully put down the Decembrists' revolt. Its leaders were executed or sent to forced labor in Siberia. Nicholas I never forgot the revolt. He ruled Russia with an iron hand for 30 years.

Nicholas I resisted change.

Nicholas I was determined to fight the "revolutionary spirit." He once said, "Revolution stands on the threshold of Russia, but I swear it will never enter Russia while my breath lasts."

When some educated Russians called for him to free the serfs, the czar refused. He agreed that serfdom was wrong, but he believed that he needed the support of the landlords to prevent peasant revolts. The czar explained, "The landlord is the most faithful, the unsleeping watchdog guarding the state; he is the natural police magistrate." Between 1825 and 1854, those faithful landlords and the czar crushed at least 500 peasant uprisings.

Nicholas also set out to combat any sign of political opposition among upper-class Russians. He did so by limiting education. After all, he argued, the government needed only a few educated officials. To end the demands for change, the czar's government strictly censored books, newspapers, and pamphlets. Nicholas also set up a secret police force to hunt out any person who dared to speak of change or reform.

Although Nicholas I succeeded in keeping revolution out of Russia, his foreign policy was less successful. In his efforts to take over parts of the Ottoman empire, he found himself at war not only with Turkey but also with Great Britain and France. The Crimean War (1853–1856) was a disaster for Russia. Russia's defeat on its own soil showed the weaknesses of the czar's autocratic government. The war also revealed that Russian technology was far behind that of Britain and France.

Alexander II freed the serfs.

In 1855, Nicholas I died, and his son Alexander II succeeded him. The new czar accepted the need for reforms. In fact, he commented that it was better to offer reforms from above than to have them forced on the government from below. Almost everyone agreed that the first step was the abolition of serfdom.

On March 3, 1861 (the day before Abraham Lincoln became president of the United States), Alexander issued a decree freeing the serfs. The new law left about half the farmable land in the hands of the nobles. The other half was parceled out to the serfs, who were required to pay the government for it. The government in turn paid the nobles for their lost lands.

The new law worked to the nobles' advantage. Most of them had heavily mortgaged their land. With the money the government gave them, they could pay off their debts. Moreover, they were also free of their old duties to feed, clothe, and house the serfs.

The newly freed peasants did not own their land outright as private property. Instead, the land became the property of the peasant community. Each peasant community was called a *mir* (meer). The mir as a whole owned the land, worked the land, and paid taxes to the government. It was almost impossible for a peasant to leave the mir, because then others would have to pay an extra share of taxes. Peasants remained tied to the mir much as serfs had been tied to their owners.

Freeing the serfs was only the first of Alexander's reforms. He also gave Russians a few more rights. For the first time, people charged with crimes could have public trials and a lawyer of their own choice. Alexander II also set up elected councils known as *zemstvos* to deal with local matters such as education and road maintenance. In addition, he expanded educational opportunities.

Reforms encouraged unrest.

Although some people were pleased with the reforms, many Russians believed that they fell far short of what was needed. In comparison with the people of western Europe, most Russians were still oppressed.

The peasants, for example, continued to bear many burdens. They alone paid a poll tax. They alone were subject to the death penalty if found guilty of a crime. They alone were bound to their mir by a system that kept them from moving freely from one place to another. To add to their discontent, few peasants had enough land to support their families. Russia's population was growing rapidly. Yet the amount of land available to peasants was limited. As a result, there were hundreds of peasant riots in the late 1800's.

Some educated Russians were also dissatisfied. Censorship still forced them to discuss their political ideas in secret. Their secret societies became increasingly radical as the years went by. A few favored **nihilism** (from the Latin word *nihil* meaning "nothing"). Michael Bakunin, a nihilist leader, described their aims:

> *Our first work must be destruction and annihilation of everything as it now exists. You must accustom yourself to destroying everything; the good with the bad; for if but an atom of this old world remains, the new will never be created.*

Some idealistic students put their faith in the *narod.* (*Narod* means "people" in Russian.) Known as *narodniki,* these young students went among the peasants to teach them to read, to provide medical services, and to spread the idea of revolution. Hundreds of narodniki were arrested and shipped to Siberia. Those who remained grew more radical. Their goal soon became the assassination of the czar.

On March 13, 1881, as Alexander II rode in his carriage, a student threw a bomb at him. The bomb missed the czar but wounded several of his guards. As Alexander stepped down to help the injured, another radical threw a second bomb. His body shattered, Alexander could only whisper, "Home to the palace to die."

Alexander III *upheld the autocracy.*

Alexander III succeeded his father to the throne. Placing his faith in the "power and right of autocracy," he completely rejected reform. Alexander reduced the power of the zemstvos and put even stricter limits on what could be published. His secret police carefully watched both secondary schools and universities. Teachers were ordered to send detailed reports on every student.

Alexander set out to strengthen "autocracy, orthodoxy, and nationality." In other words, anyone who questioned the absolute power of the czar, who worshiped outside the Russian Orthodox Church, or who spoke a language other than Russian was regarded as dangerous. Finns, Poles, and other national groups within Russia were oppressed.

No group was treated more harshly than the Jews. They were forced to live in a special region in the southwestern part of the empire. Schools were closed to them. They were also subject to new laws that encouraged prejudice. As a result, pogroms (riots against Jews) broke out in many parts of Russia. Police and soldiers stood by and watched as Jewish homes, stores, and synagogues were looted and destroyed.

Nicholas II *became czar.*

When Alexander III died in 1894, most Russians breathed a sigh of relief. They hoped the new czar, Nicholas II, would lead a new era of reform. Once again, they were disappointed. When a number of zemstvos demanded a constitution, Nicholas told them to forget "such foolish dreams." "I shall maintain the principle of autocracy," he announced at his coronation, "just as firmly and unflinchingly as it was preserved by my unfortunate dead father."

Cultural changes Nonetheless, Russia was changing despite Nicholas's attempts to hold it back. In universities, students argued over the ideas of foreign thinkers such as Charles Darwin, Karl Marx, and Louis Pasteur. At the same time, Russian artists, thinkers, and scientists were making their own unique contributions. Novelists such as Leo Tolstoy and Fyodor Dostoevsky became great literary figures. For the first time, Russian authors were widely read in translation outside their own country. Sergei Diaghilev (dee-**AHG**-uh-lehf) helped give Russian ballet its reputation as the finest in the world. Composer Peter Ilyich Tchaikovsky (chy-**KAHF**-skee) wrote music for the ballet (*The Nutcracker Suite*), as well as for the concert hall. His *1812 Overture* celebrated Napoleon's defeat at Moscow.

Economic developments Russia moved closer to the European mainstream in other ways as well. Although more than 85 percent of the population still lived in rural areas, Russian cities were growing rapidly. Between 1861 and 1870, the population of cities and towns had increased 45 percent.

The czar's government encouraged the growth of industries by investing national funds directly or by loaning money to local businesses. The czar also ordered tariffs to protect Russian products from foreign competition. Most of the new industries were concentrated in such cities as St. Petersburg, Moscow, Lodz, Baku, and various Black Sea ports.

The czar also encouraged foreign investment. With the help of British and French investors,

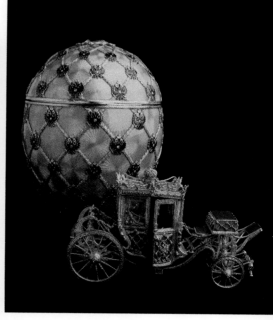

Inept as a ruler, Nicholas II was devoted to his wife and five children. Each Easter, the czar gave his wife a gem-encrusted egg such as the one above.

work began in 1891 on the Trans-Siberian Railway to connect European Russia with Russian ports on the Pacific. When it was completed in 1904, this railroad was the longest in the world.

Russia, however, was still far behind the West. In 1914, even after decades of expansion, the country's coal output was only one twentieth that of the United States. At the same time, the vast majority of the Russian people continued to live much as their ancestors had, tending small fields in the countryside. Those who did get jobs in the cities were not much better off. Working conditions in Russian factories were poor, and wages were miserably low. Trade unions were outlawed.

Russia was facing many of the same problems that Britain and other countries had faced in the early stages of the Industrial Revolution. The gap between rich and poor was enormous. As Leo Tolstoy wrote:

All our palaces, all our theaters, all these riches of ours, we owe to the effort of these same hungry people who make these things . . . The common people are hungry because we [lucky ones] are too full.

In the West, later stages of the Industrial Revolution brought a slow but steady improvement in the standard of living for all. Perhaps the same thing would have happened in Russia. We will never know. Events moved too swiftly toward a crisis.

Section Review 1

Define: (a) czar, (b) abdicate, (c) autocrat, (d) mir, (e) zemstvo, (f) nihilism, (g) narodniki
Identify: (a) St. Petersburg, (b) Nicholas II, (c) Romanov, (d) Siberia, (e) Decembrists, (f) Nicholas I, (g) Alexander II, (h) Alexander III
Answer:
1. (a) What group made up the largest share of Russia's population in the 1800's? (b) Describe their social and economic position.
2. What were the goals of the Decembrists?
3. (a) What attitude did Nicholas I take toward reform? (b) Toward freeing the serfs?
4. What reforms did Alexander II make?

607

5. (a) How did the position of the peasants change after they were freed? (b) How were their rights and freedom of movement still limited?
6. Describe Alexander III's policy of "autocracy, orthodoxy, and nationality."
7. (a) By 1900, how did Russia compare economically with western Europe? (b) What economic changes were taking place in Russia?

Critical Thinking

8. What opinion might each of the following people have expressed about Alexander II's reforms? (a) an old Decembrist (b) a serf in one of the new mirs (c) a nihilist (d) a narodnik

Russia moved toward revolution.

2

When the twentieth century began, Russia was still an autocracy. Yet a number of groups were trying to bring about change. Some were moderates, such as the Constitutional Democrats. This group hoped to limit the czar's power and create a constitutional monarchy like Britain's.

Other groups were interested not in reform but in revolution. Ever since the Decembrists of 1825, a handful of men and women in each generation had worked secretly for revolution. Only a few of these radicals were peasants or workers. Most were from middle-class backgrounds, sons and daughters of shopkeepers and teachers.

The revolutionaries were divided.

The radicals could be divided into two groups: those who appealed to the peasants and those who appealed to industrial workers. By the early 1900's, these two groups were known as the Social Revolutionaries (the SR's) and the Social Democrats (the SD's).

Social Revolutionaries The Social Revolutionaries believed the force to overthrow the czar's government would come from Russia's peasants. Unlike most European socialists, the SR's did not think that the revolution would begin with the urban working class. Instead, they considered

Russia a special case because of its enormous peasant class. The SR's believed that Russia could develop its own special kind of rural socialism. Their goal was a government that would distribute the land fairly among the peasants. The SR's also wanted to replace the czar with a democratically elected government.

Social Democrats The Social Democrats were Marxists. Karl Marx (page 515) was a German philosopher who argued that the workers of the world would one day overthrow the ruling classes and share equally in society's wealth. Like Marxists in other countries, the Social Democrats were convinced that future revolutions would be led by an urban working class.

Among the leaders of the SD's was a short, balding man in his early 30's who called himself Lenin. Lenin (1870–1924) not only planned to overthrow the czar but also hoped to spark a worldwide Marxist revolution. The son of a prosperous school inspector, Lenin was born Vladimir Ilyich Ulyanov (ool-YAH-nof). He took the name Lenin for his underground activities. Lenin became a revolutionary after his older brother was executed in 1887 for plotting to assassinate Alexander III.

Lenin worked tirelessly for revolution. He was arrested, sent to Siberia, and eventually forced to live in exile outside Russia. Yet his faith in Marxism never wavered. Speaking of Lenin, an early colleague wrote:

There is no other man who is absorbed by the revolution 24 hours a day, who has no thoughts but thoughts of revolution, and even in his sleep dreams of nothing but revolution.

Bolsheviks and Mensheviks In 1903, Lenin's eagerness to act was the direct cause of a split in Social Democratic ranks. Most SD's thought that Russia would have to be industrialized before a Marxist revolution could take place.

Lenin believed the revolution could go forward at once. He admitted that Russia's working class was too small and too poorly educated to stage a revolution. Therefore, he argued, the workers needed a tiny, determined group of Marxists to show them the way. After overthrowing the czar, said Lenin, these radicals would establish a "dictatorship of the proletariat" until the people were able to take charge of society themselves.

Lenin presented these views at a stormy party conference in London, where many SD's gathered in exile. At that meeting, his policy was approved by a margin of one vote. From then on, Lenin and his followers called themselves Bolsheviks (BOHL-shuh-vihks), from the Russian word meaning "majority." Lenin's opponents who preferred to move more slowly were called Mensheviks (MEHN-shuh-vihks), from the word meaning "minority."

Actually, outside the convention the Mensheviks were by far the larger of the two groups within the Social Democrats. Most Russian SD's believed that Lenin's ideas contradicted those of Marx. Yet the names *Bolshevik* and *Menshevik* stuck with the two groups.

In 1903, such debates seemed academic—of interest to only a few political thinkers. None of the revolutionary parties posed a serious threat to the Russian government. Most of the radical leaders were either in prison or, like Lenin, in exile. None commanded wide popular support. These leaders were like officers in search of an army. They needed more than speeches and debates to enlist troops.

The czar made serious mistakes.

Between 1900 and 1914, Russia faced a series of crises that showed its weaknesses. Yet Czar Nicholas II still resisted change. Pressed by several moderate leaders, he grudgingly allowed some reforms. If World War I had not broken out, these changes might slowly have turned Russia into a constitutional monarchy. When the war came, however, time ran out for the Romanovs.

The Russo-Japanese War In 1904, Nicholas II decided that a victorious war would shift Russians' attention from problems within the country. Therefore, he declared war on Japan, Russia's neighbor in East Asia. Russia and Japan were both imperialist powers, and they were competing for control of Korea.

Russian soldiers and sailors marched off to war enthusiastically, but the result came as a complete surprise. They were soundly beaten. Defeat in war increased unrest at home and led to the revolution of 1905.

The revolution of 1905 On January 22, 1905, about 200,000 workers and their families approached the czar's Winter Palace with a petition.

They were asking for better working conditions, more personal freedom, and an elected national legislature. They were unarmed. Some carried pictures of the "Little Father," as they fondly called the czar. Nicholas was not at the palace, but his generals and police chiefs were. They ordered the soldiers to fire on the crowd. Between 500 and 1,000 people were killed. Russians called the day Bloody Sunday.

Bloody Sunday provoked a wave of strikes that spread across the country. By October 1905, the czar could no longer ignore the demands for change. He reluctantly promised more freedom. He also approved the creation of a Russian parliament, or *Duma* (DOO-muh).

The first Duma took office in May 1906. Its leaders were moderates who wanted Russia to become a constitutional monarchy more like Britain. The Constitutional Democrats, a middle-class party, held the largest number of seats. If Nicholas had chosen to work closely with the group, the history of Russia might have been different. The czar, however, hesitated to share his power with a parliament. Three months after the Duma opened, he dissolved it and sent its members home. There would be other Dumas, but none would have real power.

What were Nicholas's motives? He believed he was doing his duty to God and to the Russian

Russian troops leaving for the war with Japan knelt to the czar and the icon he displayed.

people by "being firm." In this opinion, he had the complete support of his closest adviser—his wife, the Czarina Alexandra. The czar was devoted to his "Alix." A German princess by birth, the czarina passionately loved her adopted country. She was determined to protect the Romanov dynasty's autocratic power and pass it on in full to her son, Alexis.

World War I ended Romanov rule.

In 1914, the assassination of Archduke Franz Ferdinand touched off a crisis (page 583). The long-standing feud between Russia and Austria-Hungary over the Balkans came to a head. Czar Nicholas made the fateful decision to go to war. It was this decision, more than any other single factor, that cost Nicholas his throne.

Few Russians understood why their country went to war with Austria and Germany in 1914. Nonetheless, they answered the call for volunteers with patriotic fervor. Millions of soldiers marched west, singing "God Save the Czar!"

Before the year was over, however, the dreams of glory had turned into a nightmare. Although they fought bravely, the poorly equipped Russians were no match for the German army. Germany's advanced artillery destroyed whole Russian battalions. German machine guns mowed down advancing Russians by the thousands. Defeat followed defeat. Before 1914 was over, more than 4 million Russian soldiers were killed, wounded, or taken prisoner.

The czarina and Rasputin's influence When more defeats followed in 1915, the czar made another mistake. Nicholas moved his headquarters to the front so that he could inspire his troops to victory. He left the government of Russia in Alexandra's hands. The czarina, unfortunately, was strongly influenced by her friend, the mysterious Rasputin (ra-SPYOOT-uhn).

Rasputin was a Siberian peasant who claimed to be a holy man. Burly, uncouth, and commanding, he won the confidence of Nicholas and Alexandra by seeming to cure their only son of a dangerous blood disease, hemophilia. For ten years, Rasputin wielded great influence at the court, nearly all of it bad. He obtained powerful positions for dozens of his friends, even though they were unqualified for the jobs. He urged the czarina to ignore demands for reform.

Most Russian nobles resented the influence of this upstart peasant. In December 1916, three young aristocrats decided he must be killed. They lured Rasputin to a mansion and fed him poisoned cakes. The poison seemed to have no effect on his bull-like strength, so the conspirators shot him a dozen times. Thinking he was finally dead, they then threw him in the Neva River. When his body was found three days later, he had died of drowning. The murderers confessed their crime, but they had such widespread support in the capital that they were never punished.

A nation in chaos By the winter of 1916–1917, conditions in Russia were desperate. Food and fuel were in short supply, and prices were wildly inflated. Most of the best soldiers had long since died, and the ranks of the army were filled with unwilling men gathered up by the draft. In St. Petersburg, the first strikes had begun.

With Rasputin out of the way, people began to grumble about Alexandra. Rumors spread that the German-born empress was spying for the enemy. At the palace, the czarina mourned Rasputin. She ignored those who advised her to withdraw from politics and allow the czar to choose ministers and advisers who better understood the public mood.

Nicholas himself seemed unable to make any decisions. "Is it possible," he wearily asked an adviser, "that for 22 years I have tried to act for the best, and that for 22 years I have been wrong?" Perhaps Nicholas already knew the answer. Back at his headquarters at the front, he spent hours playing dominoes, as if he knew that the real game was already over.

A provisional government tried to rule.

In February 1917 came the bread riots and strikes that forced Nicholas from his throne (pages 602–603). After he abdicated, no one was certain who ruled St. Petersburg, let alone Russia. The czar had delivered his abdication to members of the Duma. Accordingly, the Duma chose several leaders to act as a provisional, or temporary, government.

The members of the Duma were mostly conservative or moderate men. Their main goal was to create a constitution for Russia. They had taken no part in the demonstrations and strikes

As in other countries, women in Russia held many crucial factory jobs during World War I. Women factory workers played a large part in the revolts of February 1917 that overthrew the czar's government.

that led to the downfall of the czar. As a result, radicals in the capital ignored both the Duma and the provisional government.

The power of the soviets Gradually, another political organization began to develop. Workers and soldiers in the capital gathered to form **soviets.** A soviet (SOHV-ee-EHT) was an elected workers' council. Many such councils had been formed during the 1905 revolution. Throughout the turbulent winter of 1916–1917, workers set up more councils to organize protests and plan demonstrations.

Every factory and military barracks in the city sent representatives to the St. Petersburg Soviet. Most of those representatives were socialists. Many were revolutionaries recently released from prison or just back from exile. They belonged to the major radical groups—the Social Revolutionaries, the Mensheviks, and the Bolsheviks.

Because most workers and soldiers obeyed its commands, the St. Petersburg Soviet was more powerful locally than the provisional government. Yet its members were seriously divided on many issues. For the time being, therefore, the soviet let the provisional government try to run the country.

Kerensky as leader The dominant figure in the provisional government was Alexander Kerensky (KEHR-uhn-skee), a young lawyer born in the same town as Lenin. Their fathers had been friends. Kerensky, however, became a Social

Revolutionary rather than a Bolshevik. He was the only Duma deputy who was also a member of the St. Petersburg Soviet. Because he commanded the respect of both groups, he led the provisional government.

The provisional government failed.

Almost immediately, Kerensky and the provisional government made a fateful mistake. They chose to continue the war against Germany. Many Duma leaders felt honor-bound by treaties Russia had made with the Allies. Others feared that the Germans might seize St. Petersburg and restore the czar to his throne. Thus, they made the foolhardy decision to keep on fighting.

The Russian army was no more willing to fight and die for the provisional government than for the czar. Desertions continued. Peasants were eager to return home and obtain a share of the lands from the great estates, which were being divided. They ignored Kerensky's plea to forget land distribution until the war was over. "Let the officers do the fighting for themselves," a ragged soldier was heard to say on a train near Moscow. "I don't care who wins the war. It's only for a lot of capitalists anyhow. My house is far from the front, and the Germans will never get to my village."

While the Russian army was falling apart, the Germans launched their own "secret weapon."

611

They helped Lenin return to Russia. He traveled through Germany in a sealed passenger car. On April 3, 1917, he arrived at the Finland Station in St. Petersburg. A wild and happy crowd gathered to welcome the Bolshevik leader back to Russia. Lenin was home after 17 years in exile.

Section Review 2

Define: soviet
Identify: (a) Karl Marx, (b) Lenin, (c) Bolsheviks, (d) Mensheviks, (e) Bloody Sunday, (f) Duma, (g) Alexandra, (h) Rasputin, (i) Alexander Kerensky
Answer:
1. How did the ideas of the Social Revolutionaries differ from those of the Social Democrats?
2. (a) What course of action did Lenin support? (b) How did his proposal split the party?
3. (a) What was the czar's goal in the Russo-Japanese War? (b) What territory was in dispute? (c) What were the results of the war?
4. (a) Briefly describe the revolution of 1905. (b) What were its results?
5. How did World War I lead to the downfall of the czar?
6. After the czar's abdication, what part did the following play in government? (a) the Duma (b) St. Petersburg Soviet (c) Kerensky
7. Why was it a mistake for the provisional government to continue the war?

Critical Thinking
8. If Nicholas II had been a more competent ruler, could he have prevented the Russian Revolution? Or was it the result of events beyond his control? Present your viewpoint with evidence to support it.

The Bolsheviks led a second revolution. 3

Germany's strategy in helping Lenin return to Russia made sense. The Bolsheviks were strongly opposed to continuing the war. Lenin's return would certainly contribute to unrest in Russia, which in turn would help Germany's war effort.

Lenin, however, had bigger plans than simply pulling Russia out of the war. In a speech to the crowd that greeted him, he hurled abuse at the provisional government:

The people need peace, the people need bread . . . We must fight for the social revolution, fight to the end, till the complete victory of the proletariat. Long live the world social revolution!

The Bolsheviks gained support.

Later, Lenin met privately with his fellow Bolsheviks. The February revolution was only a modest beginning, he told them. It was now time to plan the Bolshevik takeover.

Lenin's plans seemed outrageous even to many of his followers. The Bolsheviks were not very popular. They had almost no support among the peasants. Even in St. Petersburg, most workers considered the Bolsheviks too narrow and undemocratic. There were only a few Bolsheviks among the St. Petersburg Soviet's deputies.

Revolutionaries soon toppled the statue of tyrannical Alexander III, the most hated czar.

The very narrowness of their party proved to be the Bolsheviks' greatest advantage. Among the dozens of parties that sprang up after the czar was overthrown, only the Bolsheviks were tightly organized and well disciplined. They were more like a tiny army than a political party. As a result, in the chaos of 1917, the Bolsheviks were able to exert more influence than larger but less organized groups.

During the summer and fall of 1917, events played into the hands of the Bolsheviks. First, the war went from bad to worse, and the provisional government still insisted on fighting it. Second, in September, General Lavr Kornilov (kawr-NEE-luhf) tried to seize power. As commander-in-chief of the army, he was much admired by the upper and middle classes, who felt that the revolution had gone too far. Some people even said that Kornilov would restore the czar. Gathering troops loyal to his cause, the general led an army toward St. Petersburg.

The revolutionaries stopped Kornilov in the same way that they had stopped Nicholas's attempt to return to St. Petersburg in February. Marshaled by the Bolsheviks, railroad workers tore up tracks and diverted trains, making it impossible for Kornilov's troops to advance. The Bolsheviks also organized Red Guard units to defend the capital. Meanwhile, groups of workers and soldiers met with the general's troops, urging them to join the revolution. Within a few days, Kornilov had no army left.

The Bolsheviks had saved St. Petersburg. Throughout September, popular support swung suddenly to the Bolsheviks. Party membership increased rapidly. Public opinion was clear on two things: Russians did not want the czar to return, and they did not want the war to continue.

Lenin's slogan of "Peace, Land, and Bread" captured the popular imagination. The Bolsheviks were the only party that seemed strong enough to protect the revolution against generals and czarists. They were the only party that seemed willing to end the war. They were the only party that promised land reform at once.

By late September, a majority of the deputies in the St. Petersburg Soviet supported the Bolsheviks. Leon Trotsky, second only to Lenin in popularity within the party, became the chairman of the soviet. Within days, soviets in Moscow and other cities also came under Bolshevik control.

Lenin took control.

Lenin decided that it was time to act. "History will not forgive us," he wrote, "if we do not seize power now." On the night of October 24, Bolshevik Red Guards took over government offices. The St. Petersburg Soviet ordered the arrest of the leaders of the provisional government.

The Bolshevik takeover was practically bloodless. The streetcars kept running, and the restaurants and theaters remained open. There were no loyal troops left to defend the provisional government. Kerensky and his colleagues disappeared as quickly and as completely as the czarist regime they had replaced.

The next evening, Lenin addressed the All-Russian Congress of Soviets, a group of representatives from soviets all over the country. They greeted him with thunderous cheers. After minutes of deafening applause, he told the crowd, "We shall now proceed to construct the socialist order!"

What was this new socialist order? The government ordered all farmland to be divided among the peasants. The Bolshevik government signed a truce with Germany, and peace talks began between the two countries. The new government also took over all major industries. From now on, workers' councils were to run the factories.

Lenin had long planned on a dictatorship of the proletariat, under which a small group would rule in the name of the people. He wanted Bolsheviks, and only Bolsheviks, to govern Russia. Yet other parties still had much popular support. When elections were held later in November 1917, the Social Revolutionary party won a majority in the new national assembly. In response, the Bolsheviks closed the assembly at once. The only democratically elected body in Russian history had a life span of a single day.

Footnote to History

Long before the rise of the Russian Bolsheviks, revolutionaries used the color red as their symbol. In one sense, it stood for the common blood of all people, regardless of social rank. In another sense, it stood for the bloodshed of violent revolution. The Bolsheviks' use of red has led many people to link it specifically with communism.

Lenin was pleased. "The dissolution of the Constituent Assembly," he bluntly told Trotsky, "means a complete and frank liquidation of the idea of democracy by the idea of dictatorship. It will serve as a good lesson."

Many Russians objected to the Bolsheviks and their policies. There was widespread unrest. Discontent increased when Russians learned about the Treaty of Brest Litovsk, which the Bolshevik government signed with Germany in March 1918. In the treaty, the Bolsheviks surrendered one fourth of Russia's European territory to Germany. They also gave up many of the country's mines and factories. Many patriotic Russians were outraged.

Lenin was unconcerned about the lost lands. He was certain that the socialist revolution soon would spread to Germany and the treaty would be set aside. (He was half right. Russia got most of its territory back later in 1918. However, the land was returned because the Allies defeated Germany, not because of a revolution.)

Voice from the Past · *An Argument about Lenin*

A young American reporter, John Reed, arrived in St. Petersburg in August 1917. In his book, *Ten Days that Shook the World*, he wrote a vivid description of the Bolshevik rise to power. Soon after the Bolshevik coup, he heard the following argument between two Russians.

"Now brother," answered the soldier earnestly, *"you don't understand. There are two classes, don't you see, the proletariat and the bourgeoisie. We—"*

"Oh, I know that silly talk!" broke in the student rudely . . . *"I'm a Marxian student. And I tell you that this isn't Socialism you are fighting for. It's just plain pro-German anarchy . . . I suppose [the student went on] . . . that you believe Lenin is a real friend of the proletariat?"*

"Yes, I do," answered the soldier . . .

"Well, my friend, do you know that Lenin was sent through Germany in a closed car? Do you know that Lenin took money from the Germans?"

"Well, I don't know much about that," answered the soldier stubbornly, *"but it seems to me that what he says is what I want to hear, and all simple men like me. Now there are two classes, the bourgeoisie and the proletariat—"*

"You are a fool! Why, my friend, I spent two years in [the czar's prison] for revolutionary activity, when you were still . . . singing 'God Save the Czar!' . . . Didn't you ever hear of me?"

"I'm sorry to say I never did," answered the soldier with humility . . . *"You are probably a great hero."*

"I am," said the student with conviction. *"And I am opposed to the Bolsheviki, who are destroying our Russia, our free Revolution. Now how do you account for that?"*

The soldier scratched his head. "I can't account for it at all," he said . . . *"but then, I'm not well educated. It seems to me that there are only two classes, the proletariat and the bourgeoisie—"*

1. (a) What political group did the soldier support? (b) How can you tell what group the student probably supported?
2. What accusations did the student make against Lenin and the Bolsheviks?
3. What issue seemed to concern the soldier the most?
4. Toward which person was the reporter, John Reed, more sympathetic? Give evidence from the report for your answer.

Civil war divided Russia.

By summer, the Bolsheviks' opponents formed several "White" armies, so-called to distinguish them from the Bolshevik Red Army. Several Western nations, including the United States, sent small armies to Russia to help the Whites, a fact that the Bolsheviks later recalled bitterly.

Russia's civil war between the Whites and the Reds proved more deadly than any of the earlier revolutions. It lasted from 1918 to 1920, leaving an estimated 15 million Russians dead. Many died of hunger. Others were killed in the fighting. Still others fell victim to a worldwide flu epidemic that swept the globe beginning in 1918. Several thousand were shot by the Bolsheviks as suspected enemies of the new regime. Among the dead were the former czar, the czarina, and their five children. They were shot by the Bolsheviks in July 1918.

Victory eventually went to the Red Army, capably led and organized by Trotsky. The Whites might have won if they had not been deeply divided among themselves. They also lost support among peasants and workers because they threatened to restore farms and factories to their former owners.

In the aftermath of the civil war, Lenin and the Bolsheviks faced overwhelming problems. War and revolution had left the Russian economy in ruins. Trade was at a standstill. In the upheaval, factories had been destroyed. Many of the people who knew how to run those factories had been killed or imprisoned. Other skilled workers returned to farming just to survive.

Lenin restored order.

The socialist order of Lenin's plans seemed to be coming apart. Unrest spread. The Cheka, the Bolshevik secret police, became more and more ruthless toward "enemies of the revolution." Even some former Bolshevik supporters now turned against the new government.

The Kronstadt revolt For example, in March 1921, the sailors at Kronstadt, a major naval base on the outskirts of Petrograd, staged a revolt. In 1917, the sailors had been strong Bolshevik supporters. They had played a key role in overthrowing the czar. Now their list of complaints were almost the same as in 1917. They demanded free elections, freedom of speech, and the abolition of the secret police.

The Bolsheviks ignored the sailors' demands. Lenin and his colleagues brutally crushed the Kronstadt uprising. A former Lenin supporter was distressed. "What can I do now in this life?" he asked. "I cannot live outside this Russia of ours, and I cannot breathe within it."

The New Economic Policy Even Lenin realized that changes would have to be made if the Bolshevik regime were to survive. Late in 1921, he outlined what came to be known as the New Economic Policy (NEP). It called for a temporary compromise with capitalism.

Under the NEP, farmers were allowed to sell their surplus crops, livestock, and dairy goods on the free market. (Until this time, the Bolshevik government had simply taken whatever surpluses the peasants produced.) Individuals were permitted to buy and sell goods for profit. The government even allowed private ownership of some small businesses. At the same time, Lenin tried to encourage foreign investment.

A new name and a new party Lenin began some political reforms as well. Russia included many different national groups. Acknowledging these differences, Lenin created a number of autonomous (self-governing) republics within the country.

In 1922, the Bolsheviks gave Russia a new name. The country became the Union of Soviet Socialist Republics (USSR), a name sometimes shortened to the Soviet Union.

By 1922, the USSR had a new capital as well. During the civil war, Lenin had moved the capital from Petrograd (today called Leningrad) to Moscow, mainly because the inland city was safer from foreign invasion.

The Bolsheviks also gave their group a new name. It became the Communist party. The name came from the writings of Karl Marx. He used the word *communism* to describe the economic system that would exist after workers had seized power.

Thanks partly to the new policies and to the peace that followed the civil war, the USSR slowly recovered. By 1928, the country's farms and factories were producing as much as they had before World War I. After a decade of turmoil, life seemed to have returned to normal for most people in the Soviet Union.

Two men struggled to succeed Lenin.

Lenin did not live to see this recovery. He died in 1924 after spending the last two years of his life as a semi-invalid owing to a series of strokes. In the year before Lenin's death, a quiet struggle took place within the Communist party to determine who would succeed Lenin.

Trotsky The most obvious candidate was Lev Davidovich Bronstein (1879–1940). He was better known as Leon Trotsky, the name he had used in the Bolshevik underground. Trotsky had been an important figure in the revolutionary movement since the revolution of 1905. He was the organizer of the 1917 takeover, founder of the Red Army, and a capable, popular leader.

Trotsky, however, had many enemies within the party. Some feared that he would become a dictator. They likened him to Napoleon in the French Revolution. Therefore, more and more party members gave their support to Joseph Stalin, secretary of the Communist party.

Stalin Stalin was a quiet man who rarely received much public notice. He had been born in 1879 in Georgia, the mountainous region on the southern border of the Russian empire. During his early days as a Bolshevik, he changed his name from Djugashvili (joo-guhsh-VEE-lee) to Stalin. It was an appropriate choice, since *Stalin* means "man of steel" in Russian. Joseph Djugashvili was certainly that: cold, hard, and impersonal. One Communist who worked with him during this period described him as "just a gray blur, looming up now and then darkly."

Stalin worked behind the scenes. As party secretary, he was responsible for hundreds of important appointments. By 1924, he had placed many of his supporters in key positions.

As he lay dying, Lenin realized that Stalin, not Trotsky, was the more dangerous man. "Comrade Stalin has concentrated enormous power in his hands," wrote Lenin in a secret document that was not published until long after his death, "and I am not sure that he always knows how to use that power with sufficient caution."

Other Communist leaders did not see the danger. After Lenin's death, most allied themselves with Stalin against Trotsky. Indeed, Trotsky was expelled and forced to leave the USSR in 1929.

Having disposed of Trotsky, Stalin turned against his recent allies. He used his enormous power within the party to isolate them one by one. By 1928, Stalin stood alone, as totally in command of the party—and therefore the government—as Lenin had been.

Section Review 3

Define: dictatorship of the proletariat
Identify: (a) Lavr Kornilov, (b) Treaty of Brest Litovsk, (c) White Army, (d) Red Army, (e) Kronstadt revolt, (f) New Economic Policy, (g) Union of Soviet Socialist Republics, (h) Communist party, (i) Leon Trotsky, (j) Joseph Stalin
Answer:
1. (a) What disadvantages did the Bolsheviks face in trying to take power in 1917? (b) What advantages did they have?
2. How did Kornilov's attempted coup help the Bolsheviks?
3. How did the Bolsheviks actually take control of the government?
4. What policies did the new government follow in each of these areas? (a) land (b) industry (c) democratic government (d) the war against Germany
5. What were the results of Russia's civil war?
6. (a) How did Lenin deal with political discontent after the civil war? (b) How did he deal with the country's economic problems?
7. How did Stalin rise to power between 1922 and 1928?

Critical Thinking
8. Why did Lenin's slogan of "Peace, Land, and Bread" win wide support? To what group or groups did each word appeal?

Stalin became dictator. 4

Although Trotsky and Stalin had much in common, their political views differed in one important way. Like Lenin, Trotsky was dedicated to the idea of *world* revolution. To him, the Russian Revolution was merely the first act in a worldwide uprising of the proletariat. Stalin, on the other hand, was not as concerned with developments outside the Soviet Union. He coined the phrase "socialism in one country" to describe his aims. To Stalin, the Soviet Union was the revolution, and it was up to the Soviet people to fashion a perfect Communist state. The rest of the world could wait.

Stalin blended Marxism with old-fashioned Russian nationalism. He was convinced that, sooner or later, foreign enemies would attack the Soviet Union. In the past, he observed, "Russia was ceaselessly beaten for her backwardness . . . She was beaten because to beat her was profitable and went unpunished." Stalin was determined to keep history from repeating itself. Thus, he set out to make his country powerful enough to withstand an attack. "We are 50 or 100 years behind the advanced countries," he said. "We must make good this lag in 10 years. Either we do it, or they crush us."

Stalin launched two new revolutions.

In 1928, Stalin broke with the policies of Lenin to create what were in effect two new Soviet revolutions. One revolution took place in industry and the other in agriculture.

An industrial revolution In 1928, Stalin outlined a Five-Year Plan for the development of the USSR's economy. The plan called for industrial growth in all parts of the country, especially in resource-rich eastern Siberia. He also set specific production targets for each industry.

The targets were deliberately set high. Many economists, including some in the USSR, were convinced that Stalin's goals were impossible to achieve. However, Stalin was determined to make the Soviet Union a great industrial power quickly, whatever the cost. The entire Soviet work force was thrown into the effort to industrialize.

From the start, the government decided who worked, where they worked, and for how long. It controlled every aspect of the worker's life. The secret police were ready to imprison or execute those who did not contribute.

Stalin's grim methods produced fantastic results. Although most of the targets of the first Five-Year Plan were not met, the Soviets made impressive gains. A second plan, launched in 1933, proved equally successful. Between 1928 and 1938, there was construction everywhere.

For a time, Stalin was glorified as much as Lenin. Later, however, he was partly discredited.

The amount of electricity generated each year increased by nearly 800 percent. Over the same ten-year period, coal production jumped from 32 million tons per year to 115 million tons. Steel production increased from 4 million tons to 18 million tons annually. By 1938, the USSR was on the verge of becoming a major industrial power.

An agricultural revolution Stalin's agricultural revolution was as complete and far more brutal than his industrial revolution. There were more than 25 million small farms in the USSR in 1928. That year, the government announced that these privately owned farms would be abolished.

They would be replaced by collective farms, large units worked by hundreds of families. The government expected that these large farms, equipped with modern machinery, would produce more food with fewer workers.

The peasants, many of whom had only recently won their own land, resisted fiercely. For centuries, they had struggled against the nobles. Now they were being forced to submit to yet another landlord, the Soviet government.

Stalin showed no mercy. Between 5 million and 10 million peasants died. Millions more were shipped to Siberia. Many farmers destroyed their crops and livestock in protest against collectivization. The government confiscated what remained of the harvest to feed city workers. Thus, for the peasants, the winters of 1931 and 1932 brought one of the greatest famines in the country's history.

Eventually, Stalin got his way. By 1938, more than 90 percent of all peasants lived on collective farms. Agricultural production was recovering. That year the country produced about as much wheat as it had in 1928, before collectivization.

The human cost of these forced changes was enormous. A British writer traveling in the country during this period met a secret-police colonel who had taken part in forcing peasants onto collective farms. The colonel told him:

I am an old Bolshevik. I worked in the underground against the czar, and then I fought in the civil war. Did I do all that in order that I should now surround villages with machine guns and order my men to fire indiscriminately into crowds of peasants? Oh, no, no!

The USSR *became a totalitarian state.*

If Stalin's government was this brutal, how did he stay in power? Why was there no rebellion? One answer is that people were afraid to speak out. The Soviet Union in the 1930's had become a **totalitarian** state—a country in which a dictator or a small group controls every part of the lives of its citizens. Not even the slightest dissent was tolerated by the government.

Joseph Stalin was an absolute dictator, more powerful than the most autocratic czar. He crushed his enemies and anyone whom he thought might become an enemy. The secret police arrested and executed millions of suspected traitors.

One of Stalin's first targets was religion. The Bolsheviks had tried but failed to repress religion in 1921. In 1929, the government again struck at religion. Many churches, synagogues, and mosques were closed or put to other uses. Schools, which had been ordered to ignore religion, were now required to teach lessons presenting religion as backward and harmful. Yet many people in the Soviet Union remained devoutly religious.

In 1934, Stalin even turned against members of the Communist party itself. During the late 1930's, thousands of old Bolsheviks were brought to trial and executed for "crimes against the Soviet

Daily Life • *Tractors and Politics*

Tractors came to play both an economic and a political role in the USSR under Stalin. In 1928, there were only 7,000 tractors in the entire Soviet Union, even though most of the country's 150 million people were farmers. Tractors were far too expensive for individual peasant families. One of Stalin's goals in setting up large, state-run farms was to mechanize Soviet farming. By 1931, the need for tractors was even more serious. Angry peasants had killed about half the plow horses in the country as a desperate protest against Stalin's policy. During the 1930's, the government set up Machine-Tractor Stations throughout the countryside. They were more than equipment centers. They were also the rural political headquarters of the Communist party.

ОРУЖИЕМ МЫ ДОБИЛИ ВРАГА
ТРУДОМ МЫ ДОБУДЕМ ХЛЕБ
ВСЕ ЗА РАБОТУ, ТОВАРИЩИ!

Much Soviet art in the Stalinist era celebrated the strength and importance of working men and women. This poster urges, "Let's all get to work, comrades."

state." Most of the accused had been longtime Communists who had fought in the revolution and the civil war. Indeed, many had helped Stalin become the party's leader. Among the accused were *all* the Bolsheviks who had held positions in Lenin's first government except Stalin himself.

People were arrested for having friends in foreign countries, for practicing their religion, for casual remarks overheard by police informers. Factory and farm managers who failed to meet their targets were in particular danger. Even the director of the Moscow Zoo was arrested because his monkeys got tuberculosis. The police themselves were not safe, especially if they didn't discover enough criminals.

Every family came to fear the knock on the door in the early hours of the morning. Such a visit might mean a son, father, mother, or daughter taken prisoner and not heard from again for months or years—or ever.

Only once during his long career did Stalin show any hesitancy. In 1932, after a bitter argument over the brutality of his campaign against the peasants, his wife Nadia killed herself. Grief-stricken, Stalin offered to resign. The party's leaders sat in shocked silence. No one wanted to be the first to agree that Stalin should step down. Finally, they asked him to stay in office. Never again did he offer to resign.

For almost 25 years, Joseph Stalin kept a firm grip on the USSR's destiny. More than any other individual, he was responsible for the Soviet Union's rise to a position as a great world power. Without his forced industrialization, the USSR might not have been able to stand up to Germany in World War II.

During Stalin's years in power, the Soviet Union became a modern state. Its people saw their standard of living rise. They became better educated and mastered the ever-changing world of science and technology.

The Soviet people paid a heavy price for the progress they made in the 1930's. In writing his autobiography, Soviet novelist Boris Pasternak refused to go any further than 1930. "To continue it would be immeasurably difficult," he said. "One would have to talk in a manner that would grip the heart and make the hair stand on end." In the end, the people of the USSR were less free in the 1930's than they had been in the days of the czars.

Section Review 4

Define: totalitarianism
Identify: Five-Year Plan
Answer:
1. How did Stalin's ideas on communism differ from Trotsky's?
2. (a) How did Stalin revolutionize Soviet industry? (b) What were his policies in agriculture?
3. What are the features of a totalitarian state?
4. What steps did Stalin take in the 1930's to stamp out all possible dissent?

Critical Thinking
5. What features of Stalin's government were similar to czarist government?

619

Summary

1. Russia struggled to reform. While the Industrial Revolution was transforming western Europe, Russia remained largely agricultural. Most Russian peasants were bound to the land as serfs. A series of uprisings in the early 1800's caused Nicholas I to increase controls. The freeing of serfs in 1861 by Alexander II failed to end discontent. Alexander III tightened controls once again. Limited industrialization under Nicholas II brought some changes, but Russia still lagged far behind.

2. Russia moved toward revolution. In the early 1900's, Russian radicals worked secretly for revolution. Social revolutionaries favored a peasants' revolt, whereas Social Democrats, or Marxists, favored the revolt of urban workers. Lenin's call for a dictatorship of the proletariat split Marxists into Bolsheviks (Lenin's supporters) and Mensheviks (his opponents). Russia's defeat in the Russo-Japanese War, Bloody Sunday, and World War I all added fuel to the fire. Riots and strikes in March 1917 forced the abdication of the czar. When Kerensky's provisional government continued to fight in World War I, Germany helped Lenin return to Russia.

3. The Bolsheviks led a second revolution. In November 1917, Lenin's Bolsheviks came to power. The new government ended the war, divided land among the peasants, and took control of major industries. The following summer, civil war broke out as Reds (Bolsheviks) battled Whites, who were opposed to Lenin's reforms. After the Reds emerged victorious, Lenin instituted a New Economic Policy that offered a compromise with capitalism. The new government also changed the name of Russia to the USSR. Lenin's death provoked an internal struggle between Trotsky and Stalin, which Stalin won.

4. Stalin became a dictator. Determined to make the Soviet Union a world power, Stalin forced rapid industrialization and collectivization of agriculture. Millions of peasants were killed when they offered fierce resistance to Lenin's agricultural reforms. Stalin instituted a totalitarian state.

Reviewing the Facts

1. Define the following terms:
   a. abdicate
   b. autocrat
   c. nihilism
   d. soviet
   e. totalitarian
2. Explain the importance of each of the following names, places, or terms:
   a. czar
   b. serf
   c. Decembrist revolt
   d. Crimean War

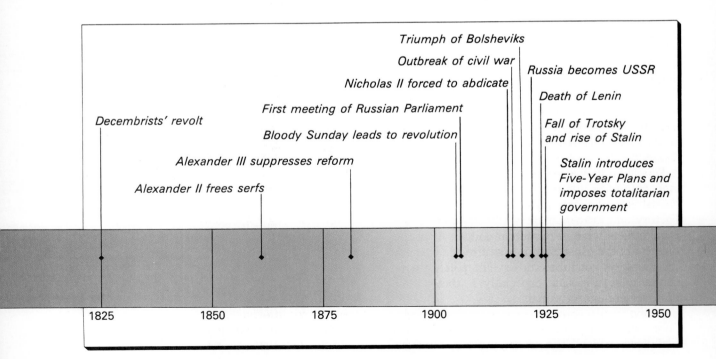

Triumph of Bolsheviks

Outbreak of civil war

Nicholas II forced to abdicate

Russia becomes USSR

Death of Lenin

First meeting of Russian Parliament

Decembrists' revolt

Bloody Sunday leads to revolution

Fall of Trotsky and rise of Stalin

Alexander III suppresses reform

Alexander II frees serfs

Stalin introduces Five-Year Plans and imposes totalitarian government

1825   1850   1875   1900   1925   1950

e. Social Revolutionary   m. Bloody Sunday
f. Social Democrat   n. Duma
g. Marx   o. Rasputin
h. Lenin   p. Kerensky
i. Bolshevik   q. Trotsky
j. Menshevik   r. Kronstadt revolt
k. Nicholas II   s. USSR
l. Russo-Japanese   t. Communist party
   War   u. Stalin

3. Describe social conditions in Russia in 1800.
4. What was the attitude toward reform of each of the following czars? (a) Nicholas I (b) Alexander II (c) Alexander III (d) Nicholas II
5. (a) What changes took place in Russia under Nicholas II? (b) What signs of backwardness remained?
6. (a) To what social class did Russia's radicals belong in the early 1900's? (b) Describe the goals of the two groups to which they belonged. (c) Into what two groups did the Social Democrats split?
7. How did each of the following contribute to the czar's downfall? (a) Russo-Japanese War (b) World War I (c) Rasputin and Alexandra
8. Describe the role of each of the following in the provisional government of 1917. (a) Duma (b) Petrograd Soviet (c) Kerensky
9. (a) How did Lenin institute a dictatorship of the proletariat? (b) What economic reforms did he bring about?
10. (a) Briefly describe the Russian civil war that followed Lenin's takeover. (b) What was the result of the war?
11. (a) How did Lenin restore political order? (b) Economic order?
12. (a) Describe the struggle between Trotsky and Stalin. (b) How did their views differ?
13. (a) Describe Stalin's changes in industry and agriculture. (b) How did he rule?

Thinking about History

1. The text states that the Russian Revolution was like a firecracker with a long fuse. Explain.
2. What did the slogan "autocracy, orthodoxy, nationalism" mean to the czars? How might the same ideas have served as a slogan for Stalin's rule?
3. The Communists often compared their revolution to the French Revolution (page 448). What similarities can you find? What differences? Were the Communists right to fear the rise of a Napoleon?

Writing and Speaking about History

1. An obituary is an announcement of the death of a person, usually with brief biographical notes. Write a 100-word obituary for one of the following czars:
   a. Nicholas I
   b. Alexander II
   c. Alexander III
2. Prepare a mock trial for either Nicholas II or Stalin based on one of these charges:
   a. Nicholas II is accused of suppressing the rights of the Russian people.
   b. Stalin is accused of undermining the goals of the Russian Revolution.

Practicing Skills

1. Use information in this text to write two paragraphs on Lenin. In the first paragraph, trace Lenin's rise to power. In the second, describe Lenin's policies while in power. Use footnotes or parenthetical references to document your facts. (See Research Skills Handbook, page 686.)
2. Tell in what year each of the following events from Russian history occurred. Who ruled Russia at the time of each event?
   a. Treaty of Brest Litovsk
   b. Kronstadt revolt
   c. Outbreak of World War I
   d. Russia becomes the USSR
   e. Abolishment of privately owned farms

Investigating History

1. Research the life and works of: (a) Pushkin, (b) Tolstoy, (c) Dostoevsky, (d) Chekhov. What is the background of this Russian writer? What themes did he stress? What influence has his work had outside Russia?
2. The autonomous republics that comprise the Soviet Union today were drawn up largely on ethnic lines. Use an almanac to find out the names of the Soviet republics. What ethnic group occupies each one? What is the history of that ethnic group within the Soviet Union? What place do Russian Jews occupy within this structure?

Decision Making in History

As an adviser to Alexander II, you favor the emancipation of the serfs. How will you convince the czar to follow this course of action?

Shifts in World Power

By 1930, massive demonstrations in support of independence were taking place all across India. This crowd carries a banner showing the wheel of Ashoka, a Buddhist symbol associated with the ancient ruler who had united much of India. India's flag carries the same symbol today.

1. **Indians organized for independence.**

2. **Nationalism spread to the Middle East.**

3. **Latin America faced difficult changes.**

4. **China overthrew its emperor.**

On March 30, 1919, and again on April 6, Hindus and Muslims came to the ancient city of Amritsar to fast and pray in protest against British rule in India. Amritsar was the capital city of the Punjab, a province in north central India. The organizer of these protests was Mohandas Gandhi (GAHN-dee), leader of India's growing movement for *swaraj*, or self-rule.

Gandhi's appeal for self-rule won wide support in the Punjab. Most of the Indian soldiers who had fought for Great Britain in World War I had come from this province. Treated as valuable allies during the war, they had returned home only to find themselves once again second-class citizens.

The British were alarmed by the protests in Amritsar, especially by the cooperation between Hindus and Muslims. Often, the two groups had been hostile to each other. On April 10, the British deputy commissioner decided to take a stand against the protests. He arrested two leaders of the protest movement—one Hindu, the other Muslim—and had them jailed without a trial. When their supporters petitioned for their release, British troops opened fire on them. As word of the British action spread, an enraged Indian mob took revenge by burning British banks and killing several British people.

To restore order, British officials called for army troops under General R. E. H. Dyer. Dyer had been born in India and had spent much of his military career there. Like many Britons, he thought that Indian nationalists needed to be taught a lesson. He got his chance on April 13, 1919.

That day, Indian peasants, dressed in their best holiday clothes, poured into the city for a Hindu festival. About 10,000 celebrators gathered in a walled park called Jillianbagh near the center of the city. A small group of nationalists was also meeting there, defying Dyer's ban on public gatherings.

Late in the afternoon, General Dyer arrived at the park with about 90 Indian soldiers. Some were armed with rifles, others with knives. Without a word of warning, Dyer ordered his men to open fire on the unarmed men, women, and children in the park. The terror-stricken crowd had no way to escape because Dyer's soldiers blocked the only exit.

The shooting, which lasted for ten minutes, was a slaughter. Nearly 400 Indians were killed. More than 1,200 lay wounded. Dyer ordered his troops to withdraw, leaving the injured on the ground without medical care.

News of the massacre spread quickly throughout India and to Britain. The British government ordered an inquiry. When questioned, Dyer expressed no regrets for his actions. He admitted that his men could have scattered the crowd simply by firing into the air. Instead, he had ordered them to shoot to kill. "I was going to punish them," he said. "My idea from the military point of view was to make a wide impression."

In this sense, Dyer's murderous behavior was completely successful. Never had a single British action made such a "wide impression" on the people of India. Almost overnight, millions of Indians changed from loyal British subjects into revolutionaries who demanded independence.

India was not the only country that set out to rid itself of foreign rule in the years after World War I. In this chapter, we will study the growing importance of nationalism not only in India but in the Middle East and China as well. We will also examine developments in Latin America, where countries faced intervention from outsiders as well as internal struggles.

Indians organized for independence. 1

By the early 1900's, British merchants, soldiers, and officials had been in India for more than 200 years. During those years, the British had gradually gained more and more control of India. By 1858, Great Britain ruled most of the country (page 542).

The British government boasted of the many improvements it had brought to India—bridges, canals, irrigation projects, and railroads. Many Indians, however, were not impressed. Their tax money had paid for most of those improvements. At the same time, many upper-class Indians were educated in British schools. There they discovered such European political ideas as nationalism, socialism, and democracy. Soon Western-educated Indian leaders began to apply these ideas to their own country.

In 1885, a group of Indian nationalists formed the Indian National Congress. Most but not all of its members were Hindus. In 1906, Muslims formed their own nationalist group, the Muslim League. Muslims made up a quarter of the Indian population and lived side by side with Hindus in many places.

The Congress party wanted self-rule.

At first, the Indian National Congress—later called the Congress party—spoke of "unswerving loyalty to the British Crown." The party was concerned mainly with winning equal opportunities for Indians in the civil service. Gradually, however, the demands of the Congress party broadened. Its supporters wanted Indians to have greater control of their own government.

After 1900, radicals within the Congress party called for an end to cooperation with Britain. "Every Englishman knows they are a mere handful in this country," a party leader told his colleagues in 1906, "and it is the business of every one of them to befool you into believing that you are weak and they are strong. [You must] realize that the future rests entirely in your own hands."

Yet, while the British may have been a mere handful in India, the number of Congress party supporters was not much larger. The vast majority of Indians were uneducated and uninterested in politics. In a country of 325 million people, there were only 8,000 university graduates. These educated lawyers, doctors, teachers, and journalists formed the nucleus of the Congress party. Often, they were as out of touch with ordinary villagers as were the British.

Gandhi led the independence movement.

The person who breathed life into Indian nationalism and brought it to the common people was Mohandas Karamchand Gandhi (1869–1948). As a young man, Gandhi studied law in Britain. Then he went to South Africa, where Indians filled many positions in the British colonial government. Like black Africans, Indians in South Africa suffered from the country's harsh racial laws (page 540). His sense of injustice aroused, Gandhi took a stand against these laws. In South Africa, he developed the religious and political ideas that made him one of the most influential leaders of the twentieth century.

While very conscious of his Hindu roots, Gandhi belonged to no specific religious group. He borrowed freely from all of the major world religions, including Christianity and Islam. His philosophy of action was based upon these four general principles:

1. Live simply, never seeking material rewards.
2. Be tolerant of the religious beliefs of others.
3. Spend life in the service of others.
4. Battle injustice in all its forms but never by resorting to violence.

Gandhi practiced what he preached. He lived an almost monastic existence, fasting regularly and giving up all possessions. Yet he did not retreat from the world. In 1914, at the age of 45, Gandhi returned to India. There he was welcomed as a leader in the Indian movement for independence.

Gandhi did not limit his campaigns to fighting British injustice. He also worked to end the injustice of his fellow Indians toward the untouchables, the lowest group in Hindu society (page 72). Gandhi treated the untouchables as equals. He called them *harijans* (hahr-ih-JAHNS), meaning "people of God."

Gandhi built his philosophy around peace and love. Everywhere he went, "this great soul in a beggar's garb," as the poet Rabindranath Tagore called him, won the hearts of the Indian people. Soon they were calling him the *Mahatma* (muh-HAHT-muh), meaning "Great Soul."

When World War I broke out in 1914, Gandhi and millions of other Indians put aside their discontent with Britain. Indian soldiers helped Great Britain defeat Germany. Gandhi, in keeping with his principles of nonviolence, served as an ambulance driver and received a medal for bravery. In return for India's help, the British government promised to begin reforms in India that would eventually lead to self-government.

Tensions rose after World War I.

In 1918, Indian troops returned home from the war. They expected Britain to fulfill its promise. However, British reforms fell far short of Indian hopes. As a result, acts of anti-British terrorism erupted in parts of India. The British struck back with the Rowlatt Act, a law that gave the government the right to jail protesters without trial for as long as two years.

To protest the Rowlatt Act, Gandhi called for days of fasting and prayer in the spring of 1919, as you read at the beginning of this chapter. Then the Amritsar massacre took place, sparking an explosion of anger across India. After the massacre, Gandhi wrote, "Cooperation in any shape or form with this satanic government is sinful."

In December, Britain tried to soothe tensions by passing the Government of India Act. This law set up a dual system of administration in which the British governor-general shared power with an Indian legislature. Although the law gave Indians more voice in domestic affairs, the

British kept control over foreign policy and national security. Gandhi and many other nationalist leaders felt that the new law was a token offer. They rejected the British reforms.

Gandhi saw clearly that India could not defeat Britain by force of arms. Instead, he called on Indians to use nonviolent moral force. He called his policy *satyagraha*, meaning "hold fast to the truth." In English, it is called passive resistance or civil disobedience.

Gandhi argued that Indians did not need guns or weapons to bring the mighty British empire to its knees. He reasoned that Great Britain could not govern India if Indians peacefully refused to cooperate. Therefore, he urged Indians to boycott British goods and to refuse to pay British taxes, obey British laws, or attend British courts.

For example, Gandhi urged all Indians to boycott British cloth and make their own. Gandhi himself devoted two hours each day to spinning his own yarn on a simple handwheel. He wore nothing but *khadi* (homespun cloth) and urged millions of Indians to follow his example. The result was that the sale of British cloth in India fell sharply.

Civil disobedience took no money, no physical strength, no skill with weapons. It took only courage. Men and women, young and old, weak and strong—all could join in Gandhi's movement. Millions did so.

Throughout 1920, there were dozens of strikes, demonstrations, and protests. Thousands of Indians were arrested by the British, who struggled to keep trains running, factories open, and jails from bursting. Despite Gandhi's pleas to avoid violence, protests often led to riots. Sometimes, hundreds were killed or wounded. Alarmed by the violence, Gandhi called off civil disobedience in February, 1922. One month later, he was arrested and sentenced to six years in prison.

Hindus and Muslims drifted further apart.

Gandhi remained in prison for only two years. He was released in 1924 because his health was poor. What he found on his release horrified him. Unity between Hindus and Muslims, which he had worked so hard to achieve in 1920, had all but disappeared. Hatred between the two groups threatened to tear India apart.

Gandhi urged Indians to live simply. He spun cotton thread to make his own clothing and wore only a dhoti *in peasant style.*

Conflict between Hindus and Muslims was not new in India. The two groups differed sharply both in their religious ideas and in their social traditions. Muslims believed in one God. Hindus believed that God was manifest in many forms. Muslims believed that all followers of Islam were equal before God. Hinduism accepted the division of society into castes that were not considered equal.

Besides such basic beliefs, each group had a number of customs and traditions that antagonized the other. Muslims, for example, ate beef, and Hindus considered the cow sacred. Some Hindus drank alcoholic beverages, a practice that was forbidden among Muslims. In towns where Hindu temples and Muslim mosques were close together, Muslims sometimes complained that Hindu music and processions disturbed their prayers. Hindus complained of hearing the Muslim calls to prayer five times a day.

Tensions increased as India became more urbanized during the early 1900's. Hindus and Muslims competed for jobs and housing in cities such as Calcutta and Delhi.

Hatred and distrust between the two groups erupted in riots. During the 1920's, there were more than 90 such outbursts, in which hundreds of Indians were killed and thousands wounded.

As early as 1906, some Muslims formed the Muslim League to ensure that their interests would be considered in discussions about India's future. The British encouraged the leaders of the Muslim League. They saw the Muslims as important allies in the British struggle to keep control of India.

Gandhi worked hard to heal the rift between Muslims and Hindus. He often spoke of the need for Indian unity. "There is no force in the cry of driving out the English if the substitute is to be Hindu domination," he said. "That will be no swaraj." Despite his urgings, however, by 1930 the Muslim League was calling for a separate Muslim nation.

Indians called for full independence.

During the 1920's and 1930's, British and Indian leaders held numerous conferences and round-table meetings. Meanwhile, both violent and nonviolent protests continued. Finally, in 1935, Britain passed a new Government of India Act. It called for a democratically elected national legislature to govern India. Each province was also to have its own assembly for local government.

The new act allowed Indians home rule—that is, complete control over domestic affairs. In 1918, Indians might have welcomed such a law. By 1935, however, home rule was no longer enough for most Indian nationalists. The Congress party was committed to full independence. "Between Indian nationalism, Indian freedom, and British imperialism there can be no common ground," said Jawaharlal Nehru, the leading figure in the Congress party in the 1930's.

The British reforms were not popular with Muslims either. The 1935 law provided safeguards for Muslim interests. However, the Muslim

Voice from the Past · Gandhi's Plan of Action

In 1920, Gandhi and the Congress party set a goal of winning swaraj within a year. Here were the steps Gandhi asked of all Indians.

Firstly, we must acquire greater mastery over ourselves and secure an atmosphere of perfect calm, peace, and good will . . .

Secondly, we must still further cleanse our hearts, and we Hindus and Muslims must cease to suspect one another's motives, and we should believe ourselves incapable of wronging one another.

Thirdly, we Hindus must call no one unclean or mean or inferior to ourselves, and must therefore cease to regard the "Pariah" class to be untouchable. We must consider it sinful to regard a fellow-being as untouchable.

These three things are matters of inward transformation, and the result will be seen in our daily dealings.

The fourth is the curse of drink . . . A supreme effort should be made . . . [to lead] liquor-sellers to give up their licenses, and the habitual visitors to these shops to give up the habit . . .

The fifth thing is the introduction of the spinning wheel in every home, larger production and use of khadi, and complete giving up of foreign cloth.

1. What inner changes of mind and spirit did Gandhi ask of Indians?
2. What outward changes in habits did he want?
3. What major social divisions did he think Indians had to heal to achieve swaraj?
4. How was Gandhi's way of seeking swaraj different from a purely political approach?

League had decided to settle for nothing less than a separate Muslim nation. They had already chosen a possible name for their country—Pakistan (Land of the Pure).

Members of the league wanted Pakistan to be carved out of the parts of India where most Muslims lived. "It is a dream that the Hindus and Muslims can ever evolve a common nationality," said Muhammad Jinnah, leader of the Muslim League. Muslims, he said, were "a nation according to any definition of a nation, and they must have their homelands, their territory, and their state."

Thus, there was no easy answer for the British. To give in to either side would mean almost certain civil war. Meanwhile, Hindu-Muslim tensions continued to build. Riots became increasingly common. "We neither govern nor misgovern," wrote one British observer in the 1930's. "We're just hanging on."

Section Review 1

Define: (a) swaraj, (b) harijan, (c) Mahatma, (d) satyagraha
Identify: (a) Amritsar massacre, (b) Indian National Congress, (c) Muslim League, (d) Mohandas Gandhi
Answer:
1. (a) How did the goals of the Congress party change from the time of its founding to 1935? (b) Why did the Congress party have little popular support in its early days?
2. What were Gandhi's four basic principles?
3. (a) How did World War I affect Indian nationalism? (b) What was the effect of the Amritsar massacre?
4. What course of action did Gandhi suggest against the British?
5. (a) What were some of the issues that divided Hindus and Muslims? (b) What course of action did Gandhi support? (c) What did the Muslims want?
6. (a) How did Britain try to solve the problem in 1935? (b) Why did their solution fail?

Critical Thinking
7. In your opinion, why was Gandhi able to win popular support for Indian independence when earlier nationalist leaders had not been able to do so?

Nationalism spread to the Middle East.   2

Nationalism was also on the rise in the region known today as the Middle East. The Middle East includes the part of Asia that stretches from Turkey to Afghanistan. When Europeans began trading with Asia, they called this region the Middle East because it lay between their homes and the more distant eastern lands of India, China, and Japan. Today, North Africa is also considered part of the Middle East because it has strong cultural ties to the Middle Eastern countries.

The Middle East is the birthplace of three great religions—Islam, Judaism, and Christianity. Islam is the youngest of the three and has by far the most followers in the region. During the 700's, warriors from the Arabian Peninsula turned much of the Middle East into a Muslim empire. Later, Seljuk Turks and then Ottoman Turks conquered the region and adopted the Muslim faith. By the 1400's, much of the Middle East was ruled by the Ottoman empire. Only Persia did not come under Ottoman control.

The Ottomans ruled the Middle East for about 500 years. After the 1500's, their empire began a long, slow decline that lasted into the twentieth century. The Scientific Revolution and the Industrial Revolution, which dramatically changed life in Europe, made little impact in Ottoman lands. The sultans, or rulers, of the empire were not interested in factories or new inventions. Thus, the Middle East fell behind Europe economically, but it preserved its traditional ways.

By the end of World War I, the Ottomans had lost control of all their lands outside present-day Turkey (page 598). Great Britain received the lands called Palestine, Transjordania, and Iraq as mandates (lands to be governed on behalf of the League of Nations). France received Syria and Lebanon as mandates.

Many people in the Middle East did not want to be ruled by France or Great Britain. Just as the people of India fought to have their own nation after World War I, the people of the Middle East also launched independence movements during this period. Each group in the Middle East chose a different path toward nation building.

Several countries chose modernization.

At the end of World War I, two countries in the Middle East chose to break with many of their Islamic traditions. Those countries were Turkey and Persia.

The Republic of Turkey In 1918, Turkey was all that remained of the Ottoman empire. It included the old Turkish homeland of Anatolia and a small strip of land around Istanbul.

In 1919, Greek soldiers invaded Turkey and threatened to conquer it. The Turkish sultan, weak and corrupt, was powerless to stop them. Many Turks believed that their country's only hope for survival lay in the overthrow of the sultan. In 1922, a group of Turkish nationalists overthrew the last Ottoman emperor. The leader of the revolution was an able army officer named Mustafa Kemal (1881–1938).

In 1923, Kemal and other nationalists established the Republic of Turkey, the first republic in the Middle East. As its president, Kemal set out to make Turkey a modern nation.

As a first step in modernization, Kemal broke the close connection between church and state that had existed under the sultans. He wanted to separate the laws of Islam from the laws of the nation. Kemal replaced Islamic laws with laws from various European nations. He replaced Islamic religious courts with secular ones.

Kemal also gave Turkish women equal legal and political rights, including the right to vote and to be elected to office. He had nothing but scorn for the Islamic custom that required women to wear veils in public. "What is the sense in this behavior?" Kemal asked. "Do the mothers and daughters of a civilized nation assume this barbarian posture? It makes the nation look ridiculous." Kemal himself made a point of dressing in European style.

Kemal believed that the future of his country lay in the education of its young people. He closed traditional Islamic religious schools and set up secular public ones. Students in the new schools learned to read and write the Roman alphabet, not the Arabic script.

Despite the limited natural resources of Turkey, Kemal also pushed for economic growth. He built railroads and factories in many parts of the country.

Mustafa Kemal (Atatürk), founder of modern Turkey.

By the time of Kemal's death in 1938, Turkey had a firm sense of national identity. It was also committed to modernization in the pattern of Europe and the United States. Kemal's influence was so strong that the Turkish people gave him the name Atatürk, meaning "father of the Turks."

The change from Persia to Iran Unlike the rest of the Middle East, the ancient country of Persia never came under the control of the Ottoman Turks. However, both Great Britain and Russia established spheres of influence there in the 1800's. By the early 1900's, the two countries virtually controlled the Persian government.

In 1921, a Persian army officer named Reza Khan seized control of the weak Persian government. By 1925, he had deposed the ruling shah and taken the title for himself. He ruled as Reza Shah Pahlavi.

Reza Shah set out to modernize his country and free it from foreign rule. He was remarkably successful in both these goals. As Atatürk had done in Turkey, Reza Shah set up public schools, built roads and railroads, encouraged industrial growth, and gave women more rights. Unlike Atatürk, however, the shah kept all power in his own hands. In 1935, he changed the name of his country from Persia to Iran.

628

Saudi Arabia kept Islamic traditions.

While Turkey and Iran broke with many Islamic traditions, another new country held strictly to Islamic law. Soon after World War I, much of the Arabian peninsula was united under a single ruler who ruled in traditional fashion.

Arabia is a harsh desert land where water can be as precious as gold. For thousands of years, the Arabian desert was home to groups of nomads who traveled from place to place in search of water and grazing for their herds. These nomads were known as Bedouin (page 174).

The Bedouin lived in family groups. Members were related through their fathers and grandfathers. At the head of each group was a **shaykh**— a man usually chosen from one leading family within the group. The shaykh commanded tremendous respect from those he led. They looked on him as both a father and a ruler.

In 1902, a shaykh named Abd al-Aziz Ibn Saud (sah-**OOD**) set out to extend his power. His early support came from a small sect of Islamic traditionalists. By military skill and well-planned marriages to the daughters of neighboring shaykhs, he gradually won control of eastern Arabia. After World War I, he began advancing westward. One by one, he overthrew the local ruling families.

In 1926, Ibn Saud proclaimed himself king of an Arab nation. Six years later, he renamed the country Saudi Arabia after his family.

Ibn Saud held firmly to Arab and Islamic traditions. He ran his country much like a Bedouin shaykhdom. Loyalty to the Saudi government was based on custom, religion, and family ties. Unlike Atatürk, who chose to separate church and state, Ibn Saud made the laws of Islam the laws of his kingdom. Women in Saudi Arabia had to wear veils in public as Islamic law required. Alcoholic drinks were banned. Legal penalties for crimes were set according to the Koran. For years, the Saudi government frowned on much modern technology, including telephones, automobiles, and even bicycles.

Jews and Arabs fought over Palestine.

After World War I, the British and the French held Lebanon, Syria, Transjordania, Iraq, and Palestine as mandates. The people of these lands faced a different problem from the people of Turkey or Saudi Arabia. Most people in the mandates were mainly concerned with breaking free from European control.

Worn out from World War I, France and Britain could not halt the force of Arab nationalism.

The banners of Ibn Saud's army proclaimed the basic beliefs of Islam: "There is no god but God, and Muhammad is his prophet."

Iraq became independent of Britain in 1922, Transjordania in 1923. France signed treaties accepting the independence of Syria and Lebanon in 1936. Only Palestine was not yet free.

Until about 2,000 years ago, Palestine was the homeland of the Jewish people. Around 1000 B.C., Jewish kings ruled the country from Jerusalem (page 37). Twice the Jewish kingdom was destroyed, once by the Babylonians in 586 B.C. and again by the Romans in A.D. 70. Each time, many Jews fled Palestine and settled in other countries. Only a few managed to remain in their ancient homeland. Jews continued to live in Palestine even after the country came under Arab and later Ottoman rule.

Jewish nationalists The exiled Jews faced centuries of persecution and anguish. Still, they held on to their beliefs and traditions. For many Jews, these traditions were not enough. They wanted a homeland, a place where Jewish laws and traditions would also be the laws and traditions of their nation.

During the 1800's, the desire for a homeland grew stronger among many Jews. Pogroms in eastern Europe and Russia forced thousands of Jews to escape to Great Britain, France, Germany, and the United States. Thousands also emigrated to Palestine. There they bought large parcels of land, which they organized into socialist farming communities, called *kibbutzim* (kih-boo-TSEEM).

At first, most of the new Jewish settlers in Palestine came from eastern Europe. In the 1890's, however, a scandal in the French army fanned the flames of Jewish nationalism in western Europe as well.

In 1894, Captain Alfred Dreyfus, one of the few Jewish officers in the French army, was accused of selling secrets to Germany. The evidence against him was flimsy, but some other officers disliked him because he was Jewish. The army found Dreyfus guilty and sentenced him to life in prison. For 12 years, his family and friends worked tirelessly to clear his name. The French army and its political supporters tried to hush up the issue. At last, another man was found to have been the spy, and Dreyfus was declared innocent.

The Dreyfus case showed the strength of anti-Jewish feeling in France and other parts of western Europe. In response, western European Jews too began to work for a Jewish homeland in Palestine.

Their leading spokesperson was Theodor Herzl (1860–1904), a writer and journalist in Vienna. These Jewish nationalists were known as Zionists. (Zion is another name for Israel, the Jewish homeland.)

The Balfour Declaration Chaim Weizmann (VYTES-mahn), a Russian-born university professor, was the leader of the Zionist movement in Britain. Weizmann succeeded in winning the support of Britain's foreign secretary, Sir Arthur Balfour. In 1917, at the height of World War I, the secretary issued a document known as the Balfour Declaration. It stated:

> His Majesty's Government views with favor the establishment in Palestine of a national home for the Jewish people, and will use their best endeavors to facilitate the achievement of that object, it being clearly understood that nothing shall be done which may prejudice the civil and religious rights of existing non-Jewish communities in Palestine or the rights and political status enjoyed by Jews in any other country.

Balfour worded his document carefully, fearing the loss of either Jewish or Arab support in the British war effort. According to the declaration, Britain favored a Jewish homeland but not at the expense of the Arabs in Palestine. The ambiguity of the Balfour Declaration laid the foundation for conflicts that would dominate the Middle East for the next 30 years.

British rule Britain took control of Palestine in 1920 as a mandate. Immediately, both Arab nationalists and Jewish nationalists asked the British to fulfill the promises of the Balfour Declaration. Each group wanted its own country in Palestine. Each side believed it had the support of the British government.

While the British looked for an answer to the problem, Jews continued to immigrate to Palestine. Weizmann often spoke of creating a Palestine "just as Jewish as England is English." This trend alarmed Palestinian Arabs, who feared that Jews might become a majority. In 1929, a riot broke out between Jews and Arabs in Jerusalem. Over 100 people on each side were killed.

Jewish immigration increased during the 1930's. In 1933, Hitler came to power in Germany and began persecuting Jews (Chapter 30). Thousands of Jews fled Germany and settled in Palestine.

In 1908, Jewish settlers in Palestine drew lots for land in the desert where they planned to build a new city. Today, that city is Tel-Aviv.

By 1939, Jewish settlers had founded 200 kibbutzim in Palestine. The number of Jews living in the region had increased from 85,000 in 1914 to 445,000. Jews now made up about one fourth of Palestine's population.

Palestinian Arabs, alarmed at the growing number of Jews, staged violent demonstrations against the British. Britain, fearful of alienating the Arab community, tightened restrictions on Jewish immigration into Palestine. Thousands of Jews were left stranded in Germany. Jewish terrorism against the British became increasingly common. By the outbreak of World War II in 1939, many despaired of ever finding an answer to the Palestinian conflict.

Oil brought outsiders to the Middle East.

While nationalism simmered in many Middle Eastern countries, the region's economy was also taking a new direction. Even while traditional Islamic kingdoms such as Saudi Arabia and Iraq frowned on modern machines, they were sitting on top of great deposits of oil to fuel those machines.

The knowledge that oil existed in the Middle East was not new. Since ancient times, people there had noticed places where petroleum seeped to the surface of the ground. In those days, however, people had little use for the sticky, foul-smelling liquid. That situation changed in the late 1800's and early 1900's when people found that oil could be used as fuel. Soon, oil was a valuable resource for industrialized countries.

The Middle Eastern countries themselves had little use for oil. They had few factories or machines to use it, nor did they have the technology to drill their own oil wells. Therefore, most Middle Eastern rulers were willing to rent drilling rights to foreign oil companies.

In the early 1900's, European and American companies began to drill for oil in the Middle East. In 1901, William Knox D'Arcy, a British speculator, made a deal with the shah of Persia, paying him a share of the profits in exchange for the right to drill oil wells in Persia. In 1908, D'Arcy made the first big oil strike in the Middle East. Soon his company, the Anglo-Iranian Oil Company, completely controlled the industry in that country.

During the 1920's and 1930's, European and American companies found huge deposits of oil in Iran, Iraq, Saudi Arabia, and Kuwait. Geologists later learned that the land around the Persian Gulf has nearly two thirds of the world's known supply of oil.

Although foreign companies paid some money to the leaders of each country where oil was found, most of the profits went to the companies. The discovery of oil in the Middle East intensified old quarrels over boundaries and spheres of influence. It also, as you will see in later chapters, created new pressures on Middle Eastern society.

Section Review 2

Define: (a) mandate, (b) shaykh, (c) kibbutz
Identify: (a) Middle East, (b) Mustafa Kemal, (c) Reza Shah Pahlavi, (d) Abd al-Aziz Ibn Saud, (e) Zionism, (f) Balfour Declaration
Answer:
1. (a) Why did the Middle East lag behind Europe economically? (b) What were the political results of World War I in the Middle East?
2. (a) How did Turkey become a republic? (b) Describe Atatürk's general policy for Turkey and give two specific examples.
3. (a) How were Reza Shah Pahlavi's policies like Atatürk's? (b) How were they different?
4. (a) Describe the Bedouin way of life. (b) How did Ibn Saud combine nationalism and Islamic tradition?
5. (a) What was the goal of the Zionist movement? (b) How did the movement begin?
6. What problems did the Balfour Declaration create?
7. Why did the discovery of oil lead to the growth of foreign influence in the Middle East?

Critical Thinking
8. Evaluate the leaders described in this section. (a) Which probably was considered most successful by Europeans? Explain. (b) Which probably was the most admired by traditional Muslims? Explain.

Latin America faced difficult changes. 3

By 1900, most of Latin America had been free of foreign rule for about 80 years. Although free, Latin American countries still faced problems that hindered their efforts at nation building.

Politically, Latin American countries remained isolated. None of them played a large part in World War I. Economically, on the other hand, Latin America had many ties to other lands. Latin American resources and products were sold worldwide: beef from Argentina, coffee from Brazil and Colombia, oil from Venezuela and Mexico, tin from Bolivia, nitrates and copper from Chile, and sugar from Cuba.

Few countries had democratic governments.

In many Latin American countries, political strongmen called caudillos ruled as dictators (page 504). These men did little to help the common people. Together with a small group of wealthy aristocrats, they alone enjoyed the benefits of independence.

To further their own interests, many caudillos and their supporters encouraged foreigners to invest in Latin American mines, plantations, and other businesses. The money from these investments lined the pockets of the caudillos and the outsiders. The common people of Latin America gained nothing.

There were, of course, exceptions. Reform-minded presidents such as Uruguay's Lorenzo Batlle (BAHT-yay) and Hipólito Irigoyen (EE-reh-GOH-yane) in Argentina tried to improve education and welfare in their countries. Benito Juarez brought an era of reform to Mexico in the 1860's.

However, such reformers made few lasting changes. Sooner or later, the caudillos returned to power. Usually, they had the support of the upper classes, who felt threatened by programs to give more power to ordinary people. One typical caudillo was Juan Vicente Gómez, a ruthless man who ruled Venezuela for nearly 30 years after seizing power in 1908. "All Venezuela is my cattle ranch," he once boasted.

Mexicans revolted in 1910.

Mexico suffered from the same problems as other Latin American countries. In 1910, 800 wealthy aristocrats (in a country of 15 million people) owned more than 90 percent of the rural land. Peasants in rural villages lived at the mercy of the landowners. Conditions in the cities were not much better. Factory workers labored 12 to 15 hours a day for very low wages. No laws protected their rights.

The rule of Díaz Mexico's ruler at the turn of the century was Porfirio Díaz (1830–1915). Díaz was an army officer who came to power in 1876. Although he called for elections regularly between 1876 and 1910, they were not free elections. Díaz controlled who could run, who could vote, and how the votes were counted. He was reelected seven times.

These Zapatistas (followers of Zapata) were peasant men and women who fought in the Mexican Revolution. Their strength and unity shows in this painting by one of Mexico's foremost artists, José Orozco. Orozco did many paintings in support of the revolution.

During his rule, Díaz brought Mexico economic progress. Under his leadership, railroads spread across the country and foreign business people set up new factories in the countryside. To many outsiders, Mexico seemed to be a stable, prospering country. They did not see the anger that seethed beneath the surface.

Revolution In 1910, that anger erupted as poor workers and farmers rose up against the government. Roving bands of fighters killed rich land-owners and burned their houses.

The revolution had no single leader. In each part of Mexico, local leaders gathered their own armies. Often they fought with one another as well as with the government soldiers. One of the most famous fighters was Emiliano Zapata (sah-**PAH**-tah), a mestizo. "It is better to die on your feet than to live on your knees," Zapata told the peasants who joined him.

Revolution raged in the cities as well. There, protestors demanded better working conditions. Some leaders criticized foreign ownership of businesses in Mexico. Others attacked the wealth of the Catholic Church. Nearly all Mexicans were Catholics, but Church leaders were closely allied with the rich and powerful.

The government of Díaz toppled in 1911. Unfortunately, no single figure could command enough support to unite the country. The result was a bitter civil war that dragged on for nearly a decade.

Reform In 1917, a revolutionary leader named Venustiano Carranza took control in Mexico. He called for a convention to draft a new constitution for the country.

The constitution of 1917 was a revolutionary document. It provided for the breakup of large estates. It set up a labor code to protect the rights of workers. It set rules for foreign investments but did not eliminate them. It also limited the Catholic Church's role in politics and education and forced the Church to give up some of its property.

Although he had called for the constitution, Carranza failed to carry out its measures. Instead, he ruled as a dictator. Peasant armies under Zapata and other rebel leaders continued their revolutionary struggle. In 1920, Carranza was overthrown.

In the fall of 1920, a moderate leader named Alvaro Obregón came to power. His presidency marked the end of civil war and the beginning of reform. Obregón put into effect many of the ideas of the 1917 constitution. Gradually, peasant villages took over lands from wealthy landlords. Public schools were established. Although poverty and corruption continued to plague Mexico, the country remained stable politically. President succeeded president in an orderly way, without the coups that troubled other parts of Latin America.

The United States interfered in Latin America.

The Mexican revolution drew the interest of many countries in the Western Hemisphere. None was more interested than Mexico's powerful neighbor to the north, the United States.

The United States' interest in Latin American affairs was not new. As early as 1823, its government had issued the Monroe Doctrine, warning European countries to keep hands off the newly formed Latin American countries (page 504). Many Latin Americans did not welcome the Monroe Doctrine. They believed that the United States itself was interfering in their countries by issuing such a declaration.

In the early 1900's, President Theodore Roosevelt aroused further fears in Latin America by his Roosevelt Corollary (page 553). This policy gave the United States the role of international police officer in the Americas.

By 1900, the United States was replacing Great Britain, Germany, and France as the major foreign investor in Latin America. Anxious about its economic interests, the United States used the Roosevelt Corollary to intervene in Latin American affairs time and time again.

The small republics in Central America and the Caribbean bore the brunt of United States intervention. These countries were Panama, Nicaragua, Haiti, Cuba, and the Dominican Republic.

For example, in the early 1900's, United States businesses owned large farms for growing tobacco, sugar cane, cotton, coffee, and bananas in Nicaragua. When rebels in Nicaragua took up arms against the government in 1912, the United States government sent marines to protect American business interests. The United States also wanted its troops to stop the fighting from spreading to nearby Panama, where the canal was being built. The marines stayed in Nicaragua until 1933.

Investments by United States businesses in Latin America grew rapidly between 1914 and 1929. At the outbreak of World War I, United States businesses jumped at the chance to buy British and German property in the region. By 1929, these businesses had invested nearly $5.4 billion in Latin America. This figure amounted to 35 percent of all United States investments in foreign lands.

Much of this money was invested in the oil business. In the early 1900's, deposits of petroleum were found in Mexico, Venezuela, Peru, and Colombia. United States companies channeled millions of dollars into Latin America. Other United States investments went into Chilean copper and nitrate, Argentinian beef and Cuban sugar.

Latin American nationalists resented the way in which the United States protected its interests

Daily Life · *Art on Walls*

Mexico's democratic revolution brought a revolution in art as well. No longer was art mainly for the rich. Instead, Obregón brought art to the people by offering the walls of public buildings for murals of Mexico's past. Mexican artists such as Diego Rivera, David Alfaro Siqueiros, and José Clement Orozco took up the offer and won worldwide fame for their powerful murals. Not only was this art in new places, but it had new subjects as well. Under Porfirio Díaz, Mexican artists had imitated Spanish and French painters. The new revolutionary artists turned instead to Mexico's Indian heritage. Their murals glorified the long-ago battle of the Aztecs against Cortés and also the ongoing struggle of the Indian peasants against the landowners.

in the region. Time and time again, they pointed out that the profits from United States businesses helped keep dictators in power. In Venezuela, for example, United States oil companies were on friendly terms with dictator Juan Vicente Gómez. When Gómez died in 1935, millions of Venezuelans hoped that the United States businesses would go as well.

Roosevelt announced the Good Neighbor Policy.

By 1935, however, the United States was taking steps to improve its relations with Latin America. In 1933, Franklin D. Roosevelt took office as president of the United States. (He was a cousin of the earlier president, Theodore Roosevelt.) The newly elected president announced a change of policy toward Latin America. The new plan was called the Good Neighbor Policy. Under this policy, the United States promised to respect the rights of Latin American countries.

True to his word, Roosevelt withdrew United States troops from Latin American countries where they had been posted. The last marines left Haiti in 1936. For the first time in 30 years, there were no United States armed forces anywhere in Latin America.

The damage to relations between Latin America and the United States, however, lasted after the troops went home. Latin Americans did not forget how the United States had treated them. Moreover, United States businesses still controlled millions of dollars' worth of property in the region. People in Latin America remained uneasy over the enormous power the United States had in their countries.

Latin American economies were weak.

Foreign ownership of Latin American businesses was only one part of a larger economic problem. In many Latin American countries, the entire national economy depended on a single export. For example, oil was the key to Venezuela's prosperity. Brazil and Colombia depended on coffee.

Countries that depend on a single resource have little control over their own economies. When the price of that resource falls on the world market, the economy of the country may collapse.

In the 1930's, many Latin American countries faced just such a crisis. During those years, the world economy slumped into a deep, long-lasting depression (Chapter 30). The crisis had widespread effects in Latin America.

Brazil is a good example. During the hard times of the 1930's, many people could no longer afford to drink coffee. World coffee consumption fell so sharply that more than 3 billion pounds of coffee sat in the warehouses of São Paulo, Brazil. Coffee workers lost their jobs. Unable to sell its coffee, Brazil had no money to buy the manufactured goods it needed from other countries.

Some Latin American governments reacted to the decline in foreign markets by encouraging the growth of national industries. Mexico went a step further. In 1938, it seized foreign oil properties and **nationalized** them—that is, it brought the oil industry under government control. Several other countries did the same. Later, Mexico compensated the foreign companies whose assets it had seized. Today, Mexicans celebrate March 18, the date of the oil takeover, as their declaration of economic independence.

Section Review 3

Define: (a) caudillo, (b) nationalize
Identify: (a) Porfirio Díaz, (b) Alvaro Obregón, (c) Monroe Doctrine, (d) Roosevelt Corollary, (e) Good Neighbor Policy
Answer:
1. (a) What political problems did most Latin American countries face in the early 1900's? (b) What economic problems?
2. (a) Describe Porfirio Díaz's rule in Mexico. (b) How did he fall from power?
3. What changes were called for by Mexico's constitution of 1917?
4. How did Mexico regain political stability?
5. How did economic interests lead the United States to intervene in Latin America?
6. How did United States policy toward Latin America change during the 1930's?
7. What problems did reliance on a single resource create for many Latin American economies?

Critical Thinking
8. How is political independence related to economic independence? Use examples from Latin America in your answer.

635

China overthrew its emperor. 4

In the early 1900's, China was independent in name only. Although the Chinese civilization was one of the oldest in the world, it had faced years of humiliation at the hands of outsiders (pages 544–547). Foreign countries had spheres of influence in China. Foreigners controlled China's trade and economic resources.

Many people in China believed that their country's only chance for survival lay in modernization and nationalism. They urged government officals to improve the army and navy, to build modern factories, and to reform education. Yet while some leaders wanted change, others feared it. They believed that China's greatness lay in its traditional ways.

Chinese nationalists overthrew the Ch'ing dynasty.

Among the groups pushing for modernization and nationalization was the Kuomintang, or Nationalist People's party. Its founder and leader was Sun Yat-sen. In 1911, the Nationalists succeeded in overthrowing the last emperor of the Ch'ing dynasty, which had ruled China since 1644. Sun Yat-sen became president of the new Republic of China.

Sun, a physician who had spent many years in the United States, hoped to establish a modern government based on what he called the Three Principles of the People. The three principles were (1) nationalism (meaning an end to foreign control); (2) people's rights (democracy); and (3) people's livelihood (meaning a form of non-Marxist socialism and land reform to benefit the peasant farmers).

Sun and his followers quickly discovered that it was easier to destroy an old government than to build a new one. The end of imperial rule, after 2,000 years, left China weak and disunited. Civil war broke out as one powerful group battled another. Provincial warlords ruled territories as large as their armies could conquer.

As always during times of unrest, the Chinese peasants suffered most. Warlord armies terrorized the countryside, pillaging and looting everywhere. Roads and bridges fell into disrepair, and crops were destroyed. Famine took the lives of millions. This was the situation in China when World War I broke out in 1914.

Sun Yat-sen's government, though practically powerless, sided with the Allies against Germany. Sun and other leaders hoped that the Allies, in gratitude, would return control of China to the Chinese.

On May 4, 1919, some 3,000 angry students—the first generation of young Chinese to receive a Western-style education—gathered in the center of Peking. They had just heard infuriating news from the peace conference at Versailles. The Allied leaders had refused to give up their territories and commercial interests in China. Even worse for China, Japan was to be allowed to keep the Chinese territory it had seized during the war. "Down with the European imperialists!" the students shouted. "Boycott Japan!"

The May Fourth protests spread to other cities and became a truly national movement. It was not a revolution as such—that would come later—but it showed how much China's young people wanted a strong, modern nation. "What should we fear?" asked Mao Tse-tung (MOW zuh-DUNG), a young schoolteacher from the countryside who supported the Peking students.

> We should not fear the militarists. We should not fear the capitalists. What is the greatest force? The greatest force is the union of the popular masses.

As you will read, Mao later turned the masses into a powerful revolutionary army.

A Communist party arose in China.

China's humiliation at the hands of the Allied powers left a deep scar on many young Chinese intellectuals. Many turned away from Sun's belief in Western-style democracy. They turned instead to the ideals and beliefs of a powerful new leader. That leader was Lenin of the Soviet Union (Chapter 28).

Lenin was willing to help China's Nationalist government. He believed that the Soviet Union and China had common enemies—the European powers and the United States. Early in 1920, Lenin began sending military advisers and equipment to the Nationalists. Several of the Chinese Nationalist leaders traveled to Moscow for military training.

In 1921, the Chinese set up their own Communist party. In the beginning, the Communist party was closely allied with the Nationalist (Kuomintang) party of Sun Yat-sen.

In 1925, Sun Yat-sen died, and leadership of the Nationalists passed to his brother-in-law, a Japanese-trained general named Chiang Kai-shek (jee-**AHNG** kye-shehk). Chiang set out to defeat the warlords and unite all of China under the Nationalists.

Although the Communists supported him, Chiang distrusted them. He believed that the Soviet Union was supporting the Nationalists only until the Communists grew strong enough to take over. Chiang, the son of a well-to-do landowner, did not agree with the Communists' goal of creating a socialist economy. Many of Chiang's supporters were bankers and business people in the coastal cities. They feared a revolution like the one that brought the Communists to power in the Soviet Union.

Together, Chiang's Nationalist forces and the Communists fought the warlords. Chiang led a successful march from Canton to Shanghai.

Then Chiang decided that time had come to strike at the Communists. At dawn on April 12, 1927, Nationalist troops and armed gangs moved into Shanghai. They killed many Communist leaders and trade union members in the streets of the city. Similar killings took place in other cities. The Chinese Communist party was nearly wiped out. Its few survivors went into hiding.

In 1928, Chiang became president of the Nationalist Republic of China. Great Britain and the United States both formally recognized the new government. The Soviet Union, as a result of the Shanghai massacre, did not.

Mao Tse-tung preached revolution.

The Nationalist government of Chiang promised democracy and political rights for all Chinese. As time went by, however, Chiang was not able to fulfill his promises. His government became less democratic and more corrupt. Those that disagreed with its policies were thrown into jail or killed.

In the cities, the Nationalist government set up new factories and businesses. It also built

Chiang Kai-shek (right) and Mao Tse-tung (left) were once allies but later became enemies.

railroads, updated China's laws, and opened new schools and hospitals. These improvements helped city people.

However, the Nationalists did nothing to improve life for China's rural peasants. Many peasants turned away from Chiang and the Nationalist government. They looked instead to the Chinese Communist party.

One of the leaders of the Communists in the late 1920's was Mao Tse-tung (1893–1976). Mao came from a prosperous peasant family. His father forced him to leave school to work when he was 13. Mao ran away and went to school whenever he could, finally finishing high school when he was 25. Afterward, he worked as a librarian and a teacher. He began his political activities in his student days and became a member of the Communist party.

When the Communists were nearly wiped out in 1927, Mao fled to the countryside. He had already begun to develop his own brand of communism. Karl Marx (pages 515–516) had written that the revolution would begin among urban workers. Lenin had already shown that a Marxist revolution could take place in a largely rural

637

country, but he had based his organization in Russia's cities. Mao went one step further. He believed he could bring Marxist revolution to a rural country and the peasants could be the true revolutionaries. Mao predicted:

In a very short time, several hundred million peasants will rise like a tornado or tempest, a force so swift and violent that no power, however great, will be able to suppress it. They will break all trammels [bonds] that now bind them and rush forward along the road to liberation. They will send all imperialists, warlords, corrupt officials, local bullies, and bad gentry to their graves.

Civil war broke out.

By 1930, civil war raged in China. The Communists set up strongholds in the southern Chingkang Mountains. The Nationalists attacked them repeatedly but failed to drive them out. From their mountain hideouts, the Communists waged a guerrilla war against Chiang's armies. Mao outlined his strategy:

1. Retreat when the enemy advances.
2. Harass when the enemy encamps.
3. Attack when the enemy hesitates.
4. Pursue when the enemy retreats.

Such tactics were only possible with the support of the peasants in the area where the guerrillas were fighting. "The people are the water, the soldiers are the fish," Mao observed. "The fish cannot live without water."

Mao ensured support for his army by dividing land the Communists won among local farmers. He also made sure that Communist soldiers respected peasant property by helping farmers with their harvest and protecting women and children. As a result, more and more Chinese farmers joined Mao's Red Army, as it came to be called.

The Red Army retreated.

In 1933, Chiang Kai-shek launched a huge campaign to destroy the Communists. He gathered an army of nearly a million men, surrounded the Communists' mountain stronghold, and began tightening the noose. Outnumbered nearly ten to one, Mao realized that battle was hopeless. In 1934, he and his followers fled the mountains.

This was the beginning of an epic journey called the Long March. Over the next year, the Communists covered about 6,000 miles, keeping one step ahead of Chiang's forces. They often traveled at night to escape being seen from Nationalist airplanes. The chase lasted more than a year. About 100,000 Communists began the march. No more than 30,000—perhaps as few as 10,000—reached safety in northwestern China. There they were beyond the reach of Chiang's forces.

Mao and the other Communists who survived the march settled in caves cut into hillsides of northwestern China. They quickly gained new followers. Meanwhile, as civil war between Nationalists and Communists continued, Japan invaded China.

Japan invaded Manchuria.

The Japanese had taken advantage of the fighting in China as early as 1931. In that year, Japanese forces invaded the northeast part of China, Manchuria. This attack marked the beginning of World War II in Asia.

In 1937, the Japanese attacked other parts of China. Thousands of Chinese lost their lives as cities and villages were bombed. Many more died of starvation because farms were destroyed. By 1938, Japan controlled a large part of China.

The Japanese invasion forced the Nationalists and the Communists to unite against this new enemy. Yet Chiang and Mao remained rivals with different goals for China. Although allied, they fought the Japanese in different ways.

Chiang was more concerned with fighting the Communists than with driving out the Japanese. He believed that the Communists were the greater threat. Although he received money and weapons

Footnote to History

In the course of the Long March, members of the Red Army crossed at least 24 rivers. They climbed over 18 mountain ranges, some of them deep in snow. They fought 15 major battles and faced minor skirmishes almost every day. They crossed miles of swampland where they had to sleep sitting up, leaning back to back in pairs, to keep from sinking into the mud and drowning.

With the Red Army, Mao (on horseback) and his wife, Chiang Ch'ing (in round hat), made the grueling Long March to safety in western China.

from the United States to fight Japan, Chiang saved those resources to use against Mao.

On the other hand, Mao and his Red Army fought the Japanese in every way they knew how. More and more Chinese peasants joined Mao's army to help his fight. They looked to the Communists as heroes who were defending China from foreigners. As we shall see in Chapter 32, the loyalty Mao won from the peasants was a powerful weapon against the Nationalists.

Section Review 4

Identify: (a) Sun Yat-sen, (b) Mao Tse-tung, (c) Nationalist party (Kuomintang), (d) Chiang Kai-shek, (e) Long March
Answer:
1. (a) What were the three principles of Sun Yat-sen's new government? (b) What problems did China face during his presidency?
2. Why were Chinese students angry over the terms of the Versailles settlement?
3. How did the Soviet Union gain influence in China?
4. (a) Why did Chiang turn against his Communist allies? (b) What did he do?
5. (a) What improvements did Chiang's government bring to China? (b) What were the weaknesses of his government?
6. How was Mao's form of communism different from Marx's and Lenin's?
7. (a) What military methods did Mao use to weaken the Nationalists? (b) What political methods did he use to win support from the people? (c) What events led to the Long March, and what were its results?
8. (a) How did the Japanese react to the civil war in China? (b) Contrast Chiang's and Mao's policies toward the Japanese.

Critical Thinking
9. What did Mao mean by his statement, "The people are the water, the soldiers are the fish"? What kinds of support does a guerrilla army need to fight successfully?

Summary

1. Indians organized for independence. Following World War I, Indian nationalists increased their demands for self-rule. When hundreds of Indians were killed at Amritsar, Gandhi led a program of civil disobedience and economic boycott. Although Gandhi hoped to unite Muslims and Hindus, Muslim leaders called for a separate state.

2. Nationalism spread to the Middle East. The collapse of the Ottoman empire in World War I led to independence movements in the Middle East. In 1923, Turkish nationalists, led by Kemal, established the Republic of Turkey. In 1921, Reza Khan seized control of what is now Iran and set out to modernize the country. Saudi Arabia, unified by Ibn Saud, was governed according to Islamic law. By 1936, only Palestine was not yet free of foreign rule. The Palestinian issue was complicated by conflict between Jews and Arabs, each of which wanted their own country.

3. Latin America faced difficult changes. Although politically independent, Latin American countries depended economically on foreign investors. Dictatorial governments did little to improve living conditions. In 1910, discontent led to a revolution in Mexico that turned into civil war. By 1920, Mexico had a stable government. Beginning in the early 1900's, the United States intervened in Latin American affairs to protect its investments. Although the Good Neighbor Policy of 1935 eased tensions, resentments against the United States continued.

4. China overthrew its emperor. In 1911, Chinese nationalists, led by Sun Yat-sen, overthrew the emperor and set up a republic. When the Nationalists were unable to maintain order, civil war broke out in the north. China's humiliation in the Treaty of Versailles convinced many Chinese to break with the West and embrace communism. In 1925, leadership of the Nationalists passed to Chiang Kai-shek, who came to mistrust the Communists. Led by Mao Tse-tung, Communists won the support of the people. In 1933, Chiang forced Mao's army into retreat. From their hiding places in the northern mountains, the Communists launched a campaign against invading Japanese, thus winning even more peasant support.

Reviewing the Facts

1. Define the following terms:
   a. shaykh   b. nationalize
2. Explain the importance of each of the following names, places, or terms:
   a. swaraj   c. Mahatma
   b. harijan   d. satyagraha

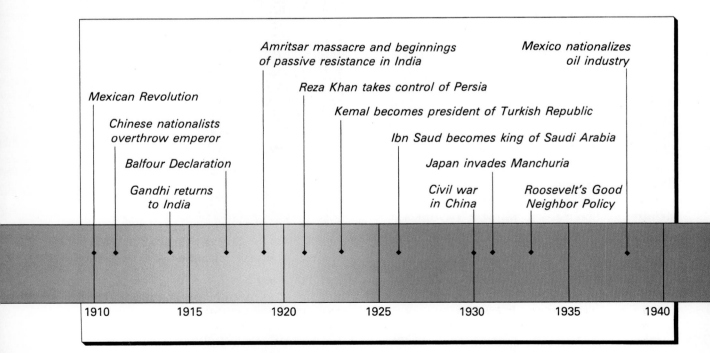

Mexican Revolution

Chinese nationalists overthrow emperor

Balfour Declaration

Gandhi returns to India

Amritsar massacre and beginnings of passive resistance in India

Reza Khan takes control of Persia

Kemal becomes president of Turkish Republic

Ibn Saud becomes king of Saudi Arabia

Japan invades Manchuria

Civil war in China

Mexico nationalizes oil industry

Roosevelt's Good Neighbor Policy

| 1910 | 1915 | 1920 | 1925 | 1930 | 1935 | 1940 |

e. Amritsar
f. Indian National Congress
g. Muslim League
h. Middle East
i. mandate
j. Kemal
k. Reza Khan
l. Ibn Saud
m. Zionism
n. Balfour Declaration
o. caudillo
p. Díaz
q. Obregón
r. Good Neighbor Policy
s. Sun Yat-sen
t. Mao Tse-tung
u. Chiang Kai-shek
v. Long March

3. How was Indian nationalism affected by each of the following? (a) Gandhi (b) World War I (c) the Amritsar massacre
4. (a) What were the goals of Hindu nationalists in 1930? (b) Of Muslim nationalists?
5. (a) What two nations in the Middle East chose a path toward modernization? (b) Which nation held strictly to Islamic law?
6. Describe the conflict over Palestine from the Jewish and Arab point of view.
7. (a) Why did the Mexican revolution of 1910 turn into civil war? (b) In what way was the constitution of 1917 a revolutionary document?
8. How did United States policy toward Latin America change between 1900 and 1935?
9. (a) What happened in China in 1911? (b) What problems did the new government face?
10. (a) How did the Treaty of Versailles contribute to the Communist movement in China? (b) Why did Chiang break from the Communists?
11. (a) How did Mao's brand of communism differ from that of Marx and Lenin? (b) How did Mao gain the support of Chinese peasants?

Thinking about History

1. At various times in their development, Mexico, Turkey, and Iran each took steps to separate church and state. The United States was also founded on this principle. Why does a nation restrict the power of religion in government?
2. The French Revolution, Mexican Revolution, and Russian Revolution each caused massive political and social changes. Compare the three revolutions. What changes did each bring?

Writing and Speaking about History

1. Prepare an outline that traces the nationalist movement from 1900 to 1939 in *one* of the countries you studied in this chapter.

2. Use the information in your outline to write a feature story that discusses how nationalism affected ways of life during this period.
3. Plan an interview with Atatürk of Turkey and Ibn Saud of Saudi Arabia. Focus your interview on the role of modernization and tradition in the Middle East.

Practicing Skills

1. Use information from Chapters 14, 17, 23, and 29 to make a timeline of Mexican history. Extend your timeline from 1500 B.C. to A.D. 2000 in 500-year increments. Include these events on your timeline:
   a. Rise of Olmecs
   b. Rise of Mayas
   c. Height of Aztecs
   d. Conquest of Aztecs
   e. Independence
   f. Revolt against Díaz
2. On an outline map of the Middle East, draw in the boundaries of the following empires:
   Islamic empire 750 (page 177)
   Ottoman empire 1500 (page 812)
   (a) What parts of the Middle East did each empire control? (b) How did the presence of these empires affect nationalism?

Investigating History

1. Gandhi and Nehru were both ardent nationalists. Yet they differed greatly in their approach. Find out more about these leaders. How did their backgrounds differ? How did each feel about the nationalist movement in India?
2. Report on life on a kibbutz. Include information about the social and economic structure of a kibbutz.
3. Research and report on the life of one of the nationalist leaders discussed in this chapter. Describe his early life. What policies did he later adopt? What hardships did he overcome?

Decision Making in History

How might the independence movement in India have turned out if the Indian people had chosen war as the path to independence? Did civil disobedience bring independence faster than violence might have? What were the advantages of civil disobedience for the Indian people?

641

The Years between the Wars

The anger and discontent of German workers show in this picture of a Communist gathering of the 1920's by German artist George Grosz.

1. Europe recovered from World War I.

2. Society faced rapid change.

3. Wall Street's crash opened the Depression.

4. Fascist leaders formed dictatorships.

5. The world drifted toward war.

In the summer of 1923, the printing presses at Germany's mints were rolling, and they were turning out money. Germans counted their currency in *marks,* and the presses printed 400 quadrillion (400,000,000,000,000,000) marks a day! Crushed by its huge war expenses and burdened with heavy payments to the Allies, Germany was in the midst of disastrous inflation. From 1918 to 1923, the value of the mark fell, slowly at first and then with terrifying speed.

What did inflation mean for the people of Germany? At the war's end, a loaf of bread cost two marks in Berlin. By December 1921, the price had risen to 40 marks, and just 1 year later a loaf cost more than 1,500 marks.

Bad as inflation already was, it went completely out of control in 1923. By that summer, a glass of beer cost 2 million marks and a loaf of bread 4 million. Workers collected their pay twice a day so that they could rush out to buy the things they needed before prices rose even higher. People took cartons and wheelbarrows full of money to buy food for supper. By autumn, the mark was worthless. Bank notes for billions of marks lay in street gutters.

Upper-class Germans suffered least from inflation because their lands and factories rose in value, keeping up with rising prices. Ordinary people faced harder times. Prices rose faster than wages, so people could not buy as much food or clothing as before. The inflation was a great shock to Germany's middle class. Civil servants, professionals, and people with fixed incomes or pensions saw their life savings become worthless. People discovered that the money they had saved to buy a house now barely covered the cost of a table.

What was the good of saving or planning for the future? Germans asked one another. What was the good of Germany's new democratic government, asked many, if people lost everything they had worked for? Germany eventually strengthened the mark, but the confidence of the German people was harder to rebuild.

In Germany and throughout Europe, the 1920's were a time of doubts and uncertainties. Embittered by the past war, people also feared the future. Some artists and writers expressed this bitterness in their work. Many people hid their fears by living for the pleasure of the moment. Thus, a thin shell of gaiety covered dark doubts and unanswered questions.

Europe recovered from World War I. 1

In human suffering, the cost of World War I had been staggering. The economic losses were also immense. The Allied and Central Powers had spent about $200 billion fighting the war. By 1918, every major European country was nearly bankrupt.

Only two world powers came out of the Great War in better financial shape than they entered it—Japan and the United States. Neither country had suffered fighting on its own soil. Both had expanded their international trade during the war.

These economic changes showed one of the major effects of World War I—the decline of European dominance in world affairs. Much wealth and power was still concentrated in Europe, of course, but the war had drained the continent's resources. The European Allies and the Central Powers were like two boxers who had battered each other in a long and brutal fight.

A second effect of the war was the sudden rise of new democracies. Between 1914 and 1918, Europe's last absolute rulers—the Hohenzollerns in Germany, the Hapsburgs in Austria-Hungary, and the Romanovs in Russia—were all overthrown. In Russia, the new democratic government soon fell to a Communist dictatorship. Even so, for the first time in history, most European countries were ruled by democratic governments.

New democracies were unstable.

Many citizens of the new democracies had little experience with parliamentary government. Germany and the new countries formed from Austria-Hungary, for example, had been ruled by kings and emperors for generations. There were problems even in France and Italy, whose parliaments pre-dated World War I. There, the large number of political parties made effective government difficult.

Democratic government is based on the principle of majority rule. In countries where there are only two or three major parties, it is fairly easy for one party to win a working majority. In countries with a dozen or more political groups, however, it is difficult for one party to win enough support to govern effectively.

In such countries, the largest party usually forms a **coalition** government. A coalition is a temporary alliance of several parties to form a parliamentary majority. Because the parties disagree on so many policies, coalitions seldom last long. In France, for example, there were some 40 changes of government in the 20 years between 1919 and 1939.

Coalition governments have other problems as well. Because they are in office for short times and because their members do not agree on important issues, such governments find it hard to provide leadership toward any long-term goals. People may accept this weak leadership as long as a country faces no major problems. When difficulties arise, however, the weaknesses of a coalition government are magnified. People may then be willing to sacrifice democracy in exchange for strong leadership. Such a course of events is exactly what happened in Italy, Germany, and several other countries in the 1920's and 1930's.

The German republic was weak.

The new democratic government set up in Germany in 1919 was known as the Weimar (VYE-mahr) Republic after the city where the national assembly met. The Weimar Republic had serious weaknesses from the start. Under Bismarck and William II, few democratic traditions had had a chance to take root. Furthermore, postwar Germany had seven major political parties and many minor ones.

Worst of all, the democratic government bore the burden of defeat. It was not the Hohenzollerns who had signed the Treaty of Versailles but representatives of the new republic. As a result, millions of Germans always viewed the Weimar government and its supporters as traitors.

Germany also faced enormous economic problems that had begun during the war. Unlike Britain and France, Germany did not increase taxes greatly during the war. Thus, while Germany spent $37 billion fighting World War I, its government collected only $1.5 billion in taxes. To make up the difference, the Germans simply printed money when they needed it. This paper money began to collapse after Germany's defeat in 1918. The result was a time of skyrocketing inflation (page 642).

Most Germans blamed the Weimar government and its weak leaders for Germany's problems. They failed to see that the war had caused most of their difficulties. As far as many Germans were concerned, Germany had made only one wartime mistake: It had lost. Next time, they swore, the result would be different.

The Dawes Plan brought stability.

Germany recovered swiftly from the 1923 inflation, thanks largely to the work of an international committee headed by Charles Dawes, an American banker and statesman. The committee worked out a financial plan to strengthen Germany's economy. The Dawes Plan provided for a $200 million loan from American banks to stabilize German currency. The plan also set a more realistic schedule for Germany's reparations payments.

Put into effect in 1924, the Dawes Plan worked extremely well. As the German economy began to recover, it attracted further loans and investments from the United States. By 1929, Germany's factories were producing as much as they had in 1913.

Treaties raised hopes for peace.

As prosperity returned, Germany began again to take an active part in European affairs. Germany's foreign minister, Gustav Stresemann (SHTRAY-zeh-mahn), tried to undo the worst features of the Versailles settlement through careful diplomacy. He was helped by France's foreign minister, Aristide Briand (bree-AHN), a moderate who favored better relations with Germany.

In 1925, Briand and Stresemann met in the Swiss town of Locarno, together with representatives from Belgium, Italy, and Great Britain. They signed a treaty promising that France and Germany would never again make war against each other. Germany also promised to respect the existing borders of France and Belgium. In return for this concession, Germany was admitted to the League of Nations.

In 1928, the "spirit of Locarno" led to the Kellogg-Briand peace pact. Frank Kellogg, the American secretary of state, arranged this agreement with France's Briand. Countries that signed the treaty pledged "to renounce war as an instrument of national policy." Almost every country in the world, including the Soviet Union, eventually signed.

Unfortunately, there was no realistic way to punish a country that broke its promise of peace. The League of Nations was the obvious choice to enforce the treaty, but it had no armed forces of its own.

Nonetheless, hopes were high in Europe in the late 1920's. Besides the peace treaties, Europeans were enjoying an economic boom. Industrial production rose to its pre–World War I level. However, much of the boom depended on massive American investment. As long as the American economy stayed healthy, the sun would shine on Europe.

Section Review 1

Define: (a) inflation, (b) coalition
Identify: (a) Weimar Republic, (b) Dawes Plan, (c) Kellogg-Briand pact
Answer:

1. How did World War I change the balance of economic power in the world?
2. (a) How did the war change forms of government in Europe? (b) Why were many of the new governments weak?
3. (a) What political problems did the Weimar Republic face? (b) What economic problems? (c) How were the economic problems solved?
4. (a) How did relations improve between France and Germany in the 1920's? (b) Among nations worldwide?

Critical Thinking

5. Explain what leaders in the 1920's meant by "the spirit of Locarno." What policies would such a spirit have encouraged?

Society faced rapid change.

2

Amid all the havoc World War I caused, it did have one positive result. It quickened the pace of invention. During the war, scientists developed new drugs and medical treatments that helped millions of people after the war. The principles of tank construction were put to use in building better automobiles, trucks, and tractors. The war's technological advances did not go to waste in the postwar years.

Technology made the world seem smaller.

During the war, millions of people communicated across battle zones and moved supplies thousands of miles. Therefore, many of the greatest improvements came in communication and transportation.

The spread of the automobile The automobile benefited from a host of wartime improvements— electric fuel pumps and starters, air-filled tires, and more powerful engines. "Check now what

Fliers such as Katherine Stinson and Charles Lindbergh became celebrities in the 1920's.

the new, roomier Austin offers you! Dependability! Performance! Style! Comfort!" This British newspaper advertisement from the late 1920's showed how far the automobile industry had come since 1900. Cars no longer looked like buggies on wheels. They were sleek and brightly polished, complete with chrome-plated bumpers, headlights, and shock absorbers.

The beginnings of air travel The war also brought spectacular improvements in aircraft. By 1918, planes could fly several hundred miles.

During the 1920's, airplanes were put to many new uses. Daring pilots carried the first airmail letters. Wartime fliers became "barnstormers," visiting country fairs to perform aerial acrobatics and take people for their first airplane rides.

In 1919, two British pilots, John Alcock and Arthur Brown, made the first successful flight across the Atlantic Ocean, flying from Newfoundland to Ireland. The next major crossing came in 1927, when a young American pilot named Charles Lindbergh captured worldwide attention with his 33-hour solo flight from New York to Paris.

Most of the world's major passenger airlines were established during the 1930's, though air travel was too expensive for all but the rich. Still, everyone could enjoy the thrilling exploits of aviation pioneers such as Amelia Earhart, the first woman to fly across the Atlantic.

Radio for millions Marconi's first successful experiments with radio were in 1895 (page 559). The first voice transmission took place in 1906. The real push for radio development, however, came during World War I. The advantages of wireless communication in battle were so great that all countries gave radio research a high priority. By the end of the war, armies had developed a wide range of radio equipment.

In 1920, the world's first commercial radio station, KDKA in Pittsburgh, began broadcasting. Almost overnight, radio mania swept the United States. Radio receivers were mass-produced, and by 1925 a family could buy one for as little as $25. Soon every major city had stations broadcasting news, plays, and music. In 1921, KDKA and several other stations carried live, play-by-play descriptions of the World Series.

Science challenged old ideas.

Just as studies of electricity had begun long before practical uses for it were known, scientific research in the early 1900's was far ahead of technology. The two most important thinkers of the era had begun their work at the turn of the century. However, their ideas became much more widely known during the 1920's and 1930's. These two thinkers were a German physicist named Albert Einstein and an Austrian physician named Sigmund Freud.

Taken together, Einstein and Freud challenged some of the most deeply rooted ideas that people held about themselves and the world in which they lived. They were part of a scientific revolution that was as profound as that of Copernicus and Galileo (pages 358–360).

Einstein's theory of relativity Einstein offered new and startling ideas on space, time, energy, and matter. He began by tackling a problem that baffled physicists at the turn of the century. The speed of light had been measured very carefully. Scientists found that light travels at exactly the same speed no matter what direction it moves in relation to Earth. Yet this finding seemed to break the laws of motion described by Sir Isaac Newton, because Earth itself moves through space. Why did Earth's movement have no effect on the speed at which light seemed to move?

In 1905, Einstein put forward the idea that the speed of light is constant (unchanging). At the same time, other things that seem constant, such as space and time, are not. Space and time can change, said Einstein, when measured in relation to an object moving at high speeds. Such changes take place only near the speed of light—about 186,000 miles per second. Thus, we never notice such changes in our everyday world. Because relative motion is the key to Einstein's ideas, they are called the *theory of relativity*.

Einstein's ideas had wide implications. For example, he said that matter could be changed into energy according to the formula $E = mc^2$. E stands for energy, m for mass, and c^2 for the speed of light multiplied by itself. Because the speed of light is such an enormous number, the formula shows that even a tiny atom contains an enormous amount of energy. This idea, which

Daily Life · *Form and Function*

In architecture, simplicity was the rule. The American Frank Lloyd Wright and the Swiss Le Corbusier (luh kor-boo-ZYAY) rejected the showy decoration of most prewar buildings. Instead, they chose bold but simple outlines. Their goal was to fit their buildings to the needs of the people who lived or worked in them.

In 1919, the German architect Walter Gropius created a special school to spread the ideals of simplicity and functionalism—that is, fitness for use. This school, called the *Bauhaus* (Building House), revolutionized not only architecture but also the design of such everyday items as printers' typefaces, furniture, and household appliances.

seemed fantastic in the early 1900's, became terrifyingly real when the atom bomb was developed in the 1940's.

Freud Freud's ideas were fully as revolutionary as Einstein's. Freud drew a new and, to some people, shocking picture of the workings of the human mind.

Freud began to develop his ideas while treating people with psychological problems. He found that some of these problems could be traced back to events in the patient's childhood. However, the patients had repressed (blocked) the happenings from their conscious memories. When a patient was able to uncover the repressed memory, the psychological problem was eased or cured.

From these experiences, Freud constructed a theory about the way the human mind worked. He called part of the mind the *unconscious*. In the unconscious, there were drives, especially sexual drives, of which the conscious mind was unaware.

Freud's theories ran into strong opposition. Many people were shocked by the idea that part of their mind was beyond their conscious control. Many were also shocked by the importance Freud gave to sex. All the same, his basic ideas had widespread influence.

Society became more open.

New ideas and new ways of life led to a new kind of individual freedom during the 1920's. Many people were willing to break with the past, to question traditional values, to consider new and different ideas.

This new spirit of independence was partly the result of World War I, which had disrupted customs and social patterns. Not surprisingly, young people were generally more willing to change than their elders. "What's the matter with kids today?" asked one popular song of the 1920's. The "matter" was that young people were experimenting with values that often differed from their parents'.

The new independent spirit showed clearly in the changes that women were making in their lives. Their work in the war effort was the decisive factor that won women the right to vote. After World War I, women's suffrage became law in the United States, Britain, Germany, Sweden, Austria, Hungary, Czechoslovakia, and elsewhere.

Women in Washington, D.C., unfurled the banner of the National Women's Party in 1920.

Most women still followed traditional paths of marriage and family. However, growing numbers began to choose a different lifestyle. These women wanted greater freedom in their personal lives. Wives should not be second-class members of the family, feminists argued, but equal partners with their husbands. Margaret Sanger and Emma Goldman risked arrest by speaking in favor of birth control. As women sought wider career choices in the 1920's, the numbers of women in medicine, education, journalism, and other professions increased.

Art reflected society's doubts.

During the 1920's, new attitudes also appeared in art and literature.

'My nerves are bad to-night. Yes, bad. Stay with me.
'Speak to me. Why do you never speak? Speak.
'What are you thinking of? What thinking? What?
'I never know what you are thinking. Think.'

I think we are in rats' alley
Where the dead men lost their bones.

King Oliver's Creole Jazz Band in the 1920's included Baby Dodds on drums, Louis Armstrong on trumpet, and Lil Hardin at the piano.

These lines come from poet T.S. Eliot's "The Waste Land" (1922). This long poem conjured up a picture of a world drained of hope and faith. The horror of World War I had made a deep impression on many artists and writers.

A Czech writer named Franz Kafka wrote eerie novels about people caught in threatening circumstances that they could neither understand nor escape. Kafka started writing before World War I, but much of his work was published after his death in 1922. It struck a chord among many readers in the uneasy postwar years.

Also in 1922, Irish-born novelist James Joyce caused a stir with *Ulysses*. This 1,500-page novel focused on a single day in the lives of three Dubliners. Joyce broke with normal sentence structure and vocabulary in an attempt to mirror the workings of the human mind.

One group of writers and artists was inspired directly by the ideas of Sigmund Freud. Calling themselves Surrealists, they tried to draw on the unconscious rather than the conscious part of their minds. The paintings of the German Max Ernst and the Spaniard Salvador Dali were closer to dreams and nightmares than to everyday reality.

American cultural influences spread.

World War I showed that the United States was a world power both politically and economically. Soon it was clear that the United States had world influence culturally as well.

Perhaps the most distinctly American contribution to the 1920's was jazz. This music had developed during the 1880's and 1890's in the southern United States, particularly among the black musicians of New Orleans and Memphis. The development of the phonograph and radio helped bring jazz to other parts of the world. The lively, loose beat of jazz seemed to capture the new freedom of the age. Jazz swept the United States and Europe.

In New York, black writers, artists, and composers were also achieving worldwide recognition. This cultural movement was known collectively as the Harlem Renaissance. (Harlem was the major black neighborhood of New York City.) Among the best-known writers were the poets Countee Cullen and Langston Hughes as well as the novelist Claude McKay.

Another art form in which Americans took the lead was the motion picture. Movies began to draw large audiences before World War I (page 571). By the 1920's, the movies had become a major industry. Many countries around the world, from Cuba to Japan, produced movies. However, 90 percent of all films came from one place—the Los Angeles suburb of Hollywood.

Americans turned to isolationism.

Although proud of their country's achievements, many Americans were uncomfortable with their new position as world leaders. **Isolationism—**

the idea that Americans should avoid political ties to other countries—won wide support. It was this feeling that led the United States to reject the Treaty of Versailles and remain outside the League of Nations.

Economically, however, the United States was not isolated at all. Under the Dawes Plan, loans from American banks helped Germany recover from the disastrous 1923 inflation. Other European countries had borrowed heavily from the United States during the war. In the 1920's, American businesses greatly expanded their overseas operations, especially in Latin America. The United States became a major trading partner for countries around the world.

By 1929, the world economy was like a delicately balanced house of cards. The key card that held up all the rest was American economic prosperity. If something happened to the United States' economy, the whole card house might come tumbling down. In 1929, something did happen.

Section Review 2

Define: isolationism
Identify: (a) Albert Einstein, (b) Sigmund Freud, (c) Franz Kafka, (d) James Joyce, (e) Surrealists, (f) Bauhaus, (g) Harlem Renaissance
Answer:
1. (a) What advances were made in transportation during the 1920's and the 1930's? (b) In communication?
2. (a) What generalization did Einstein set forth about light, space, and time? (b) About matter and energy?
3. Why were Freud's ideas revolutionary?
4. How did the changes of the postwar years affect women?
5. (a) What new trends appeared in art and literature during the 1920's? (b) Give examples of American contributions to world culture during this era.
6. How did the United States' return to political isolationism contradict its economic position?

Critical Thinking
7. (a) What features of life in the 1920's suggest a mood of optimism? (b) Of pessimism?

Wall Street's crash opened the Depression. 3

In 1929, a narrow street in New York City near the southern tip of Manhattan Island was the financial capital of the world. This was Wall Street. Coal merchants in Liverpool, factory owners in Berlin, wheat dealers in Winnipeg, and steel importers in Tokyo all paid close attention to events on Wall Street. Along its sidewalks were the offices of banks and investment companies that dominated the world economy.

The stock market fell in 1929.

The heart of Wall Street was an imposing gray building, the New York Stock Exchange. Here optimism about the United States' booming economy showed in soaring stock prices. Between January 1924 and September 1929, the *New York Times* average of stock prices rose from $110 to $455. Many people began to think stock prices would go up forever.

On Thursday, October 24, the New York Stock Exchange opened for what brokers hoped would be a profitable day of rising prices. Within an hour, their hopes were dashed. Everyone wanted to sell stocks, and no one wanted to buy them. Prices went down and down and down.

Overwhelmed by the record-breaking number of orders to sell, the stock ticker could not display the latest prices. By 1 P.M., the ticker had fallen 92 minutes behind transactions on the floor. Thus, frightened brokers could not get a true picture of what was happening. The wild shouting of the 1,000 brokers and their assistants became what one observer called a "weird roar." Great crowds gathered on the street outside the Stock Exchange. Rumors of business failures and attempted suicides swept through the crowd.

In the week following Black Thursday, as October 24 was soon called, stock prices continued to drop. Billions of dollars in paper wealth simply vanished.

At first, the crash appeared to have hurt only the million or so people who had gambled and lost on the stock market. The United States' vast industrial and agricultural resources were physically unhurt. There seemed to be no reason for prosperity to end. Yet, within a few months of the crash, unemployment rates began to rise. Meanwhile, industrial production, prices, and wages fell sharply. A long business slump known as the Great Depression had begun.

The Great Depression touched every corner of the American economy. By 1932, factory production had been cut in half. More than 86,000 businesses failed, and 9,000 banks closed. Around 9 million people lost their savings accounts. Unemployment soared from 3.2 percent in 1929 to 25 percent in 1933.

America, traditionally the land of opportunity, now seemed to have nothing to offer millions of its citizens. One writer recalled:

The jobless were the most conspicuous feature of that dismal landscape. They clustered about poolrooms and taverns, sat in the parks when the weather was fair, stood in empty doorways to get out of the wind, panhandled for nickels and dimes on the streets, and sat for hours over a nickel cup of coffee in dingy restaurants, staring out the window.

The world economy had weaknesses.

The Great Depression showed clearly that there were serious economic weaknesses in the United States and, indeed, throughout the world. Although the causes of the Great Depression are complex, three weaknesses in the economy were especially important.

Overproduction and underconsumption American industry became fabulously productive during the 1920's. By 1929, American factories turned out nearly half of the world's industrial goods. Rising productivity led to enormous profits.

This new wealth, however, was not evenly distributed. For example, the richest 5 percent of the population earned 33 percent of all personal income in 1929. Meanwhile, at the other end of the scale, fully 60 percent of all American families earned less than $2,000 a year. Thus, most families were too poor to buy the record number of goods being produced.

In short, supply raced ahead of demand. There was both overproduction by business and underconsumption by consumers.

As a result, store owners could not sell all the goods they had on hand. They cut back their orders from factories. Factories began to cut back production and lay off workers. These actions started a downward economic spiral. As more workers lost their jobs, families bought even fewer goods. In turn, factories made further cuts in production and laid off more workers.

The plight of the farmer During the 1920's, American farmers also became increasingly productive. Scientific farming methods and new farm machinery dramatically increased the yield of crops per acre. Farmers tried to maximize their profits by raising just a few cash crops. Farming became more and more like industry. Thus, farmers became more dependent on the market prices of wheat, corn, and pork.

At the same time, American farmers faced new competition from abroad. For the first time, countries such as Australia and Argentina were exporting large amounts of grain. European farmers were increasing production too.

As a result, a worldwide surplus of agricultural products drove prices and profits down. In 1930, for example, the price of a bushel of wheat (in terms of gold) fell to its lowest level in 400 years.

Unable to sell their crops at a profit, many farmers could not pay off their loans. These bad debts weakened banks and forced some to close.

Speculation in stocks The danger signs of overproduction by factories and farms should have warned people against speculating wildly in the stock market. Yet no one heeded the warning.

The stock market crash dashed the hopes of thousands of investors. Between September 1929 and July 1932, the *New York Times* industrial average fell from $455 to an all-time low of $58. Stockholders lost a staggering $74 billion.

The losses on Wall Street had both economic and psychological consequences. Economically, they swept away fortunes among the upper class. Consumer spending dropped sharply. Psychologically, Americans' spirit of optimism was replaced with a sense of doubt and fear.

The Depression spread worldwide.

When the American economy collapsed, the shock waves were felt around the world. After the stock market crash, worried American investors began to call back their loans abroad to cope with the crisis at home. This withdrawal dealt a hard blow to the economy of western Europe.

As weeks of unemployment stretched into months, jobless people searched the help-wanted ads and waited in unemployment offices for a chance to work. Their despair shows in this painting by Isaac Soyer.

Because of their war debts and dependence on American loans, Germany and Austria were particularly hard hit. A large Austrian bank, the Creditanstalt, failed, starting a financial panic in central Europe. As in the United States, this crisis began a downward spiral in the economy.

The effects of the Depression were felt throughout the world. Between 1929 and 1932, world manufacturing production fell by 38 percent. International trade dropped by an incredible 65 percent. Unemployment rates skyrocketed to record levels. In the United States, Great Britain, Germany, and Japan, more than 25 million angry, jobless people began to demand sweeping economic and political changes.

The Depression confronted democracies with a serious challenge to their economic and political systems. Each country tried to meet the crisis in its own way.

Roosevelt began the New Deal.

In the first presidential election after the Depression began, Americans elected Franklin Delano Roosevelt (1882–1945). At first glance, Roosevelt seemed an unlikely leader for such a grave crisis. Yet he proved to be a dynamic and effective president.

Born into a wealthy New York family, Roosevelt had held several positions in state and national government. In 1920, he ran unsuccessfully for vice president. Suddenly, in 1921, he was stricken with polio and paralyzed. After months of effort, he regained the use of his hands and arms. Next he struggled to walk. Eventually, wearing braces, he was able to take a few steps. Then he resumed his political career. In 1928, he was elected governor of New York.

Roosevelt's confident manner appealed to millions of Americans who felt bewildered and betrayed by the Depression. "If you have spent two years in bed trying to wiggle your big toe," he said, "everything else seems easy."

As president, Roosevelt immediately began a program of relief, recovery, and reform that he called the New Deal. Large public works projects helped to provide jobs for the unemployed. New government agencies gave financial help to businesses and farms. The Social Security Act of 1935 provided insurance for the elderly and the disabled. For the first time, the United States government spent large amounts of public money on welfare and relief programs.

Roosevelt and his advisers believed firmly in the capitalist free-enterprise system. However, they also believed that government spending was the best way to create jobs and start an economic recovery. They were willing to spend more money than the government raised through taxes, creating a national debt.

651

Franklin Delano Roosevelt in 1936

The New Deal strategists also took steps to remove some of the economic problems that had caused the Depression. For example, the new Securities and Exchange Commission regulated the workings of the stock market. The banking system was reorganized, and the federal government insured bank deposits up to $5,000.

Roosevelt's policies were widely popular. He won reelection in 1936 and 1940. (He was the only American president to be elected to a third term.) Yet recovery from the Depression was slow. Unemployment in the late 1930's remained around 14 percent. National income, while on the rise, was still well below its 1929 level.

While the New Deal reformed America's economic system, Roosevelt's strong leadership preserved the country's faith in its democratic political system. Taking office at a time of grave national crisis, Roosevelt made a special point of explaining his policies to the American people. He became the first president to make frequent use of the radio, broadcasting informal speeches known as "fireside chats." His compassionate style, democratic values, and reform programs established Roosevelt as a leader of democracy in a world that was increasingly threatened by ruthless dictators.

Britain and France struggled to rebuild.

Coming less than a dozen years after World War I, the Depression struck hard at Europe. Despite hardship, however, Britain and France preserved democratic government.

"Muddling through" in Britain Because the British economy depended on foreign trade, the Depression hit Britain with great force. To meet the emergency, British voters in 1931 overwhelmingly elected an all-party coalition cabinet known as the National Government. Its prime minister was Ramsay MacDonald. MacDonald was the leader of the Labour party, which had replaced the Liberals as the main opposition to the Conservatives since World War I.

The National Government passed high protective tariffs, increased taxes, regulated the currency, and lowered interest rates to encourage industrial growth. These measures brought about a slow but steady recovery of the economy. By 1937, the unemployment rate had been cut in half, and production had risen above 1929 levels.

These gains, however, failed to lift Britain's mood of discouragement in the 1930's. Neither MacDonald nor his Conservative party successor, Stanley Baldwin, was a dynamic leader like Roosevelt. Nonetheless, the British avoided political extremes. Their moderate course allowed them to "muddle through" the Depression.

Weakness in France Unlike Britain, France in 1930 was still a heavily agricultural country. It was less dependent on foreign trade than was Britain. Thus, France was somewhat cushioned against the Depression. Nevertheless, by 1935, 1 million French people were out of work.

As we will see in the next section, the Depression brought anti-democratic groups to power in some European countries. In France too there were groups that wanted to end democracy and set up a dictatorship. This movement frightened both moderates and radicals. Therefore, moderates, Socialists, and Communists united to form a coalition. Known as the Popular Front, the coalition won power in the 1936 elections.

The Popular Front passed a series of reforms to help the workers. These reforms included pay increases, holidays with pay, and a 40-hour work week. Unfortunately, price increases quickly offset wage gains, and unemployment remained high.

Section Review 3

Identify: (a) Wall Street, (b) Great Depression, (c) Franklin D. Roosevelt, (d) New Deal, (e) National Government, (f) Popular Front
Answer:

1. (a) Briefly describe Black Thursday. (b) What other changes in the American economy showed that a major economic slump had begun?
2. What were the three major weaknesses in the economy that led to the Depression?
3. Explain how overproduction and underconsumption began a downward spiral in the economy.
4. How did the crisis in the United States' economy lead to problems in other countries?
5. (a) What policies did Roosevelt begin to help the victims of the Depression? (b) To prevent similar crises in banking and stocks from occurring again?
6. (a) How did Britain respond to the Depression? (b) How did France?

Critical Thinking

7. (a) What do you think Roosevelt hoped to suggest by using the term *New Deal* for his policies? (b) Was the term a good description? Why or why not?

Fascist leaders formed dictatorships.

4

The crisis of the Depression brought on political upheavals in many countries. Millions of people lost faith in democratic government. In many countries, people turned to extremist political groups. Some turned to communism, hoping for a workers' revolution that would begin a new era. Others turned to a new political movement known as **fascism** (FASH-ihzm).

Fascism glorified the state.

Unlike communism, fascism had no clearly defined theory or program. Fascists acted first and devised theories later. According to Benito Mussolini, the first of Europe's Fascist dictators,

"Fascism was not the nursling of a doctrine worked out beforehand with detailed elaboration: it was born of the need for action."

Nevertheless, most Fascists shared several ideas. They believed in an extreme form of nationalism. Unlike more peaceful nationalists, however, Fascists were not content to serve their own nation and let others do the same. Fascists believed that nations must struggle. Peaceful states, they said, were doomed to be conquered and enslaved by more warlike ones.

Fascists looked to an authoritarian leader to guide the state and rally the people. Loyalty to the leader was considered the same as loyalty to the state.

The trappings of fascism were also similar from country to country. Fascists wore uniforms or shirts of a certain color. They had special salutes and war cries. They held mass rallies and ceremonies that glorified the nation.

In some surprising ways, fascism was similar to its archenemy, communism. Both systems advocated dictatorial one-party rule. Both denied individual rights and insisted on the supremacy of the state. Both scorned democracy.

However, there were also differences between fascism and communism. Fascists, unlike Communists, did not seek a classless society. Rather, they believed that each class had its distinct place and function. Communism claimed to be a dictatorship of the workers. Fascist parties allied themselves, in most cases, with aristocrats and industrialists. Many Communists were internationalists, hoping to unite workers of all countries in a class struggle. Fascism, in contrast, was openly nationalistic.

Mussolini took power in Italy.

Italy was the first country to have a Fascist government. Fascism arose in Italy during the 1920's, even before the Depression struck. Italy had entered World War I in hopes of winning some Austrian territories in the Alps and around the Adriatic Sea, as well as German and Turkish areas. However, the Versailles settlement did not give Italy as much land as it had wanted. Millions of Italians felt betrayed.

Italians also faced a severe economic crisis. The war drove up expenses, and the cost of living shot up 500 percent between 1914 and 1919. To

653

make matters worse, unemployment was rising. As a result, there was widespread social unrest.

Italy's upper and middle classes feared that this unrest might lead to a Communist revolution, as had just happened in Russia. To many Italians, their democratic government seemed helpless to deal with the country's problems. Growing numbers turned to a new leader, Benito Mussolini.

The rise of Mussolini Mussolini (1883–1944) favored monarchy, nationalism, and militarism. After World War I, he gathered a group of war veterans to combat communism. Known as the Blackshirts, Mussolini's supporters roamed the streets beating up Communists and Socialists. By attacking leftists, the Fascists won support from the middle classes, the aristocracy, and the industrialists.

By 1922, the Fascists were ready to take over Italy's government. Mussolini declared, "Either they will give us the government or we shall take it by descending on Rome." In October 1922, the Blackshirts began to march on Italy's capital. King Victor Emmanuel III and the government gave in and named Mussolini premier. He held emergency powers to restore order and make new laws.

Following the German style of goose-stepping, Mussolini led his troops on parade in 1938.

Mussolini was now Il Duce (**DOO**-cheh), the Leader, of Italy. Il Duce was a dazzling orator. Although of modest height, he towered above the Italian masses as he addressed them from the balcony of his office in Rome. His black eyes ablaze, Mussolini stood with his massive jaw thrust forward and his hands on his hips. His deep emotional delivery enthralled the crowd as he promised a great future for Italy.

Fascist policies With Mussolini in power, parliamentary democracy was quickly swept away. Before long, all political parties except the Fascists were abolished. The press was strictly censored. Mussolini's secret police clamped down on all opposition.

Mussolini believed that capitalists and workers must be forced to cooperate for the good of the state. He set up 22 state corporations to run all parts of Italy's economy. These corporations dealt with wages, prices, and working conditions. Strikes were against the law.

Italy became the model for Fascists in other countries. Later Fascist leaders, including Adolf Hitler in Germany and Francisco Franco in Spain, looked to Mussolini. Many Fascist governments came to power in eastern Europe in the late 1920's and early 1930's. All borrowed ideas and institutions from Italy.

The Nazi party arose in Germany.

No country suffered more from the Depression than did Germany. Factories ground to a halt. Banks closed. By 1932, nearly 40 percent of Germany's work force was unemployed. The jobless roamed the streets shouting, "Give us bread."

In such conditions, the moderate Weimar government lost support to extremists of the left and right. Some people turned to communism. Others, especially among the upper and middle classes, turned to a German brand of fascism known as nazism (**NAHT**-**SIHZ**-uhm).

The Nazis blamed the Treaty of Versailles for Germany's troubles. They condemned democracy as a foreign system forced on Germany by the victors. They declared that Germany's economic problems stemmed from the loss of its European territories and overseas colonies and from the burden of reparations. Germany would never be prosperous, they said, until it regained its military power.

Hitler led the Nazis.

The leader of the Nazis was Adolf Hitler. Hitler was born in a small town in Austria in 1889. After dropping out of high school, he moved to Vienna, planning to study art or architecture.

At the time, Vienna was still the capital of the vast, multi-ethnic Austrian empire. Many Jews were among the city's intellectual and financial leaders. There were also Slavic people from other parts of the Austro-Hungarian empire. Hitler later claimed that his hatred of Jews and Slavs began there.

Most of Hitler's ideas and attitudes crystallized in Vienna. In the public library, he eagerly read books on German history and mythology. He favored writers who called the Germans a master race with the right and duty to conquer other peoples. Slavic peoples, Latin peoples, and Jews were labeled inferior.

Hitler led an aimless life, living in hostels and doing odd jobs, until World War I broke out. Then he volunteered for the German army and fought well, twice winning the Iron Cross.

At the end of the war, Hitler went to the German city of Munich, where he joined a right-wing political group. This group later named itself the National Socialist German Workers' Party, called the Nazis for short. In 1920, the party adopted the *swastika*, or bent cross, as its symbol. The Nazis also set up a private army called storm troopers.

By 1921, Hitler's success as an organizer and speaker had won him the role of *führer* (leader) of the Nazi party. Although he was undistinguished looking, Hitler was a spellbinding speaker. His style was less polished than Mussolini's but even more filled with hatred. He would begin a speech in a normal voice, getting louder and louder as anger swelled up. Finally, he would seem to lose all self-control. His face would puff with fury, his voice rise to a screech, and his hands flail the air. Then he would suddenly stop, smooth his hair, and look quite calm again.

In 1923, Hitler led the Nazis in an attempted coup in Munich. The coup failed, and Hitler was imprisoned. While in jail, he wrote *Mein Kampf* (My Struggle), setting forth his views on the superiority of the Germans, the inferiority of other peoples, and the decadence of democracy. *Mein Kampf* became the guidebook of nazism.

Hitler became dictator.

During the prosperity of the mid-1920's, Nazi strength declined. During the Depression, however, many Germans came to think that they had to choose between communism and nazism. Most chose the Nazis. Monarchists, nationalists, conservatives, aristocrats, army officers, and industrialists backed Hitler. The Nazis became the largest party in Germany, although they were still not a majority.

In 1933, in a coalition government, Germany's president named Hitler chancellor. Conservative leaders believed that they could control Hitler and use him for their purposes. They were mistaken, and millions paid for that mistake.

One of Hitler's first acts as chancellor was to call for new Reichstag elections to be held in March 1933. On February 27, someone set fire to the Reichstag building in Berlin. The Nazis blamed the Communists. (Today, most historians believe that the Nazis themselves set the fire.) By stirring up fear of the Communists, the Nazis and their allies won a majority of the seats in the next election. (In addition, the presence of Nazi storm troopers at voting centers intimidated many voters.)

The Nazi revolution Once they had control of the Reichstag, the Nazis began their revolution. First, they excluded Communists from the Reichstag. With the Communists gone, the Nazis won a two-thirds vote to pass a law called the Enabling Act. It gave Hitler the right to declare laws for the next four years without the approval of the Reichstag. This act was the legal basis for Hitler's dictatorship.

As dictator, Hitler banned competing political parties. First the Social Democrats, then the Catholic parties, and finally the monarchists were outlawed.

Hitler ruled through his secret police, the black-shirted Gestapo, who pledged absolute loyalty

Footnote to History

The term *fascism* was supposed to conjure up memories of Rome. In Latin, *fasces* meant a bundle of wooden rods tied around an ax handle. Some Roman officials carried such bundles as symbols of state power.

Voice from the Past · *The Nazi Party Program*

In 1920, the National Socialist German Workers' Party published a list of 25 demands. Here are some of the demands that appeared on that list.

1. We demand the union of all Germans to form a Great Germany . . .

2. We demand equality of rights for the German people in its dealings with other nations, and abolition of the Peace Treaties of Versailles . . .

4. . . . None but those of German blood, whatever their creed, may be members of the nation. No Jew, therefore, may be a member of the nation . . .

8. All further non-German immigration must be prevented. We demand that all non-Germans who entered Germany [after] August 2nd, 1914, shall be compelled forthwith to depart . . .

23. We demand . . .

(a) that all editors and their co-workers on newspapers using the German language must be members of the nation;

(b) that special permission from the State shall be necessary before non-German newspapers may appear . . .

It must be forbidden to publish newspapers that do not [work toward] the national welfare. We demand legal prosecution of all tendencies in art and literature of a kind likely to [destroy] our life as a nation . . .

1. Which demand suggested that the Nazis were not satisfied with Germany's current borders?

2. What group was specifically excluded from "the nation"?

3. (a) What groups could not write for a German newspaper? (b) What restrictions were put on non-German newspapers?

4. (a) What overall policy did Nazis advocate toward art and literature? (b) Who do you think would decide what writings and art were harmful to the nation?

to the Führer. By the mid-1930's, the Nazis had set up special prisons called concentration camps to jail anyone whose political ideas were unacceptable to Hitler.

Anti-Jewish laws Jews made up about 1 percent of the German population. They included many distinguished people who had contributed to Germany's international renown. Among them were such leading scientists as Albert Einstein (page 646). Yet Hitler and the Nazis labeled the Jews as inferior, unfit to be part of the great Nazi reich (empire).

In 1935, the Nazis passed the Nuremberg laws, depriving Jews of German citizenship. Jews were not allowed to fly the German flag, to write or publish, to act on stage or in films, to teach, to work in hospitals or in banks, or to sell books. All Jews were required to wear a yellow Star of David to identify themselves.

Nazi violence against Jews increased. Many Jews were imprisoned in concentration camps. In November 1938, Nazi mobs looted Jewish shops, burned synagogues, and beat Jews on the streets and in their homes.

Censorship and totalitarian rule The Nazi government controlled the press, broadcasting, literature, drama, music, painting, and film. The Nazis destroyed forbidden books in huge bonfires.

The art and music of Nazi Germany reflected Hitler's tastes. The Führer condemned almost all modern art, favoring classical and romantic styles. In music, Hitler had a passion for the operas of Richard Wagner, which were based on German myths. He claimed to have seen several of Wagner's operas more than 100 times.

German mythology found great favor among Nazis. In fact, some Nazi leaders wanted to close Christian churches and return to the worship of the old Germanic gods. However, Hitler believed that persecuting Christians would only strengthen them. Still, Christian clergy were forbidden to criticize the Nazi party or the government. Parents were discouraged from sending their children to religious schools.

The Nazis used the public schools to spread their own ideas. Schoolchildren were required to join Hitler's youth movement. Boys learned to be ready to fight and die for the Führer. Girls prepared for motherhood so that Germany would have plenty of young soldiers.

The Third Reich In *Mein Kampf*, Hitler had set forth his plan for a "Greater Germany." First, Germany was to take over neighboring lands with sizable German populations. These lands were Austria and large parts of Poland and Czechoslovakia. Next, Germans would conquer and settle much of eastern Europe, driving out or enslaving the Slavic peoples who lived there.

Hitler called his proposed German empire the Third Reich. (The Holy Roman Empire had been the First Reich and the German empire of 1871–1918 the Second Reich.) Proudly, Hitler boasted that the Third Reich would last 1,000 years.

Militarists ruled Japan.

As fascism spread in Europe, one of Asia's leading nations moved toward a similar system. Following a period of reform and progress in the 1920's, Japan fell under military rule.

During the 1920's, liberals were a majority in Japan's parliament. In 1922, Japan signed an international treaty agreeing to respect the territorial integrity of China. The Japanese also signed the Kellogg-Briand pact renouncing war.

Japan's parliamentary government had several weaknesses, however. The constitution put strict limits on the powers of the prime minister and the cabinet. Most importantly, these civilian leaders had almost no control over the armed forces. Instead, army leaders were responsible only to the emperor.

As long as Japan remained prosperous, the civilian government kept power. However, when the Depression struck, military leaders soon won control of the country. Their plan for solving Japan's economic problems was to build a Pacific empire. Such an empire, they said, would give Japan raw materials, win markets for Japan's goods, and find space for its growing population.

Japanese businesses had already invested heavily in China's northeast province, Manchuria. Manchuria was rich in natural resources such as iron and coal. In 1931, the Japanese army seized Manchuria, despite objections from the parliamentary government. Japanese technicians and capital poured in to build mines and factories. Japan's new empire had begun.

The growing power of the military also had a great impact within Japan. Instead of a forceful leader like Mussolini or Hitler, the militarists encouraged the cult of the emperor. The Japanese considered their emperor divine. This cult helped to win popular support for the army leaders who ruled in the emperor's name.

Dictators promised easy answers.

By the mid-1930's, it was clear to everyone that Woodrow Wilson's dream of a world "made safe for democracy" had turned into a nightmare. In country after country across Europe, democracy had been destroyed. Only in those places with solid democratic traditions—Britain, France, and the Scandinavian countries—did democracy remain strong. Where such traditions were lacking, elections and political parties quickly gave way to dictators and secret police. By 1935, for example, only one democracy, Czechoslovakia, remained in eastern Europe.

Remarkably, most of these new dictators, including Hitler, were actually voted into power. Why were people willing to sacrifice their freedom? Economic distress was certainly part of the answer. During the Depression, many people lost faith in democratic government. To some, the loss of freedom seemed a small price to pay for putting ample food on the table.

Hitler, Mussolini, and other dictators offered simple answers to complicated questions: Trust the leader. Think only of the glory of the nation. Believe in the superiority of one's own race above all others. The dictators appealed to the crudest of human emotions, hatred and fear.

In Italy, Germany, and Japan, the new dictators did solve some of their countries' economic problems. There was a catch, however. They boosted the economy with huge increases in military spending. In Germany, for example, the military budget grew from $8 million in 1933 to $135 million in 1939. Moreover, the dictators were not spending these vast sums simply to provide jobs. Hitler and Mussolini fully intended to use the armies they were so carefully assembling. "A minute on the battlefield," asserted Mussolini, "is worth a lifetime of peace."

657

Section Review 4

Define: (a) fascism, (b) Il Duce, (c) führer
Identify: (a) Benito Mussolini, (b) Nazi party, (c) Adolf Hitler, (d) *Mein Kampf*, (e) Gestapo, (f) Third Reich
Answer:
1. (a) What ideas did most Fascists share? (b) How were fascism and communism alike? (c) How did they differ?
2. (a) What factors led to the rise of fascism in Italy? (b) How did Mussolini take control of the government?
3. What conditions led to the growth of extremist political groups in Germany?
4. What basic political ideas did Hitler develop during his stay in Vienna?
5. How did Hitler come to power in Germany?
6. (a) How did the Enabling Act increase Hitler's power? (b) What were the Nuremberg laws?
7. What plans did Hitler have for expansion of Germany?
8. (a) How did political power change hands in Japan during the Depression? (b) What policies did the new leaders advocate?

Critical Thinking
9. Compare the rise of Hitler with the rise of Mussolini. How did the following factors contribute to the each dictator's power? (a) economic conditions (b) political ideas (c) personal styles (d) private armies
10. (a) What "easy answers" did Hitler and Mussolini offer? (b) Why are such answers appealing in a time of crisis? (c) What steps can voters take to avoid being misled by such tactics?

The world drifted toward war. 5

By the mid-1930's, it was quite clear that the powerful countries of the world had split into two camps. On one side were dictatorships such as Germany and Italy whose leaders were bent on military conquest. On the other side were democracies such as Britain, France, and the United States whose leaders longed to keep peace.

One powerful nation—the Soviet Union—fit in neither category. During the 1930's, the Soviet Union took little part in world affairs while Stalin brutally forced the country through major economic changes (page 617). Nonetheless, the Soviet Union with its Communist government loomed large in the plans and fears of other countries.

The fear of a Communist revolution helped both Hitler and Mussolini in their rise to power. The Western democracies also deeply feared the Soviet Union. Indeed, many political leaders in Britain and the United States considered the Communist Soviet Union a greater threat than Nazi Germany. As the 1930's passed, however, it became obvious that fascism was a far more immediate danger. The democracies and the Soviet dictatorship temporarily set aside their differences to meet the Fascist threat.

The League of Nations was weak.

Many people pinned their hopes for world peace on the League of Nations. The League enjoyed high prestige in the 1920's. France and Germany signed the Locarno pact (page 644) in 1925. In 1926, Germany joined the League. For a brief period, it seemed that the League was indeed helping to create a more peaceful world. Unfortunately, these hopes collapsed as dictatorships encouraged militarism in the 1930's.

Ironically, the three countries that posed the greatest threats to peace—Germany, Japan, and Italy—were all members of the League of Nations in 1933. At the same time, the two countries that were strong enough to stand up to the dictators—the United States and the Soviet Union—were not members. (The Soviet Union joined in 1934.) Thus, the burden of supporting the League fell mainly on Great Britain and France.

Britain and France had been the two leading world powers of the 1800's. However, World War I had weakened them both severely. The French were still determined to uphold the terms of the Versailles treaty, but France was not strong enough to stand up to Germany alone. Many British people, on the other hand, believed that the Versailles treaty had been unfair and that Germany was entitled to some geographic and military expansion. Above all, Britain's leaders wanted to avoid a war that would further weaken their economy.

During the 1930's, therefore, Britain and France did not take a firm stand against Fascist aggression. Instead, they followed a policy of **appeasement**. That is, they made concessions to the Fascists in hopes of keeping peace.

Japan invaded China.

The first direct challenge to the League of Nations came in 1931 when the Japanese army invaded the Chinese province of Manchuria (page 657). The Japanese set up a *puppet government*—that is, a government controlled by an outside power—in Manchuria.

Japan's attack on Manchuria clearly violated the Kellogg-Briand peace pact, which Japan had signed. Other members of the League protested vigorously, as did the United States. However, the League had no armed forces of its own. Thus, it could do little. Japan ignored the protests and withdrew from the League in March 1933.

In 1937, a border incident touched off a full-scale war between Japan and China. On July 7, the Japanese and the Chinese exchanged shots at a railroad bridge 20 miles from Peking. One Japanese soldier was found dead near the bridge. Given this excuse, Japanese forces swept into northern China. These events marked the beginning of World War II in Asia.

China's leader, Chiang Kai-shek, had an army of more than 1 million soldiers, but it was no match for the superior equipment and training of the Japanese. Peking and other northern cities fell to the Japanese in less than a week. The capital, Nanking, fell by the end of 1937. Between 100,000 and 200,000 people in Nanking were executed within 6 weeks.

Yet the Chinese did not surrender. Forced to retreat westward, Chiang Kai-shek set up a new capital at Szechwan (sech-wahn). At the same time, Chinese guerrillas continued to fight within the area conquered by the Japanese. Many of the guerrilla fighters were organized by China's Communist leader, Mao Tse-tung (page 637).

Mussolini attacked Ethiopia.

Meanwhile, other dictators were also pursuing aggressive policies. Ever since coming to power in 1922, Mussolini had dreamed of building an Italian colonial empire in Africa. However, most of Africa had long ago been carved into British and French territories. Therefore, Mussolini decided to move against the independent African nation of Ethiopia.

In October 1935, Italy launched a massive invasion of Ethiopia. Mussolini used airplanes, tanks, guns, and poison gas against the Ethiopian army, many of whose soldiers still fought only with spears. The Ethiopians fought courageously, but their situation was hopeless. By the middle of 1936, Ethiopia was conquered.

Once again, the League was faced with a clear case of armed aggression. Once again, the League condemned the attack, but its members did nothing. The British government, for example, spoke out strongly against Italy's actions. Yet Britain continued to let Italian troops and supplies pass through the British-controlled Suez Canal on their way to Ethiopia.

No doubt the British and the French hoped that, by treating Mussolini gently, they could keep peace in Europe. Haile Selassie, the Ethiopian emperor, knew better. When he spoke at a League of Nations meeting in Switzerland, he said, "It is us today. It will be you tomorrow."

Hitler and Mussolini joined forces.

Even while Italy was conquering Ethiopia, Europeans faced the threat of war closer to home. Since becoming chancellor of Germany, Hitler had secretly strengthened the German army. In March 1935, he announced that Germany would no longer obey the military limits set by the Treaty of Versailles. France and Britain did nothing to stop this military buildup.

German troops in the Rhineland A year later, in March 1936, Hitler made his most daring move. The Nazi leader announced that he had sent German troops into the Rhineland. The Treaty of Versailles forbade Germany to place troops in this region along the French border.

The French might have challenged Hitler, but once again Britain's prime minister, Neville Chamberlain, urged appeasement. Why, asked Chamberlain, should Germany not station soldiers wherever it liked within its own borders?

Hitler later said that he would have been forced to back down if Britain or France had challenged his move into the Rhineland. "If the French had then marched into the Rhineland," he said, "we

Pablo Picasso's Guernica *expressed his anguish at the wanton bombing of that village. The artist ordered that the painting should not go to Spain until democracy was restored there, as it was in the 1970's.*

would have had to withdraw with our tails between our legs." Whether that was true or not, the British and the French did nothing.

The Rome-Berlin Axis Hitler's growing strength convinced Mussolini that he should seek an alliance with Germany. In October 1936, Italy and Germany reached an agreement that became known as the Rome-Berlin Axis. An axis is a straight line around which an object rotates. Hitler and Mussolini expected their alliance to become the axis around which Europe would rotate. A month later, Germany also made an agreement with Japan. Thus, Germany, Italy, and Japan were called the Axis Powers.

Civil war broke out in Spain.

Hitler and Mussolini soon found another chance to test their strength against the democracies of Europe. In July 1936, civil war had broken out in Spain. The Fascist powers decided to support the Spanish general Francisco Franco.

Spain had been a monarchy until 1931. Between 1931 and 1936, a democratic government held office amid a series of crises. Many army leaders, however, favored a Fascist-style government. In July 1936, General Francisco Franco led a revolt against the elected government. Thus began a civil war that dragged on for three bloody years.

Hitler and Mussolini sent tanks, cannons, and airplanes to Franco's forces, called the Nationalists. German and Italian troops even fought alongside Nationalist troops.

The Republican army, as supporters of Spain's elected government were called, received little help from abroad. The Soviet Union sent some aid. The Western democracies remained neutral. An International Brigade of volunteers fought with gallantry on the Republican side, but it could do little against a professional army.

Early in 1939, the Republicans collapsed. Franco became Spain's Fascist dictator and remained in power for more than 30 years.

In many ways, the Spanish Civil War was a precursor of World War II. It showed what kind of war was soon to burst upon the world. In April 1937, a squadron of German planes appeared above the small village of Guernica (ger-NEE-kuh) in northern Spain. The planes dropped their load of bombs, killing hundreds of villagers, most of them women and children. There was no military reason for this attack. Several German pilots who took part later admitted that the bombing had been conducted as a "test." One of Franco's officers said of Guernica, "We bombed it, and bombed it, and bombed it, and *bueno*, why not?" Countless more bombs and immeasurably more agony lay in store for Europe and the world.

Hitler demanded more lands.

By 1938, Hitler was ready for his next move. He planned to take over areas around Germany that had large German populations. His first target was his native Austria.

The takeover of Austria The Versailles treaty prohibited a union between Austria and Germany. Nevertheless, in March 1938, Hitler threatened to attack Austria. The Austrian chancellor was forced to resign, and an Austrian Nazi leader took his place. The new Nazi chancellor immediately asked Hitler to send troops into Austria to "keep order." On March 11, German troops crossed the border. On March 13, Austria became a German province. Again Britain and France did nothing.

The move into Czechoslovakia Hitler's next target was Czechoslovakia. Czechoslovakia had a large German minority, living mostly in the mountainous border area called the Sudetenland (soo-**DAYT**-uhn-LAND). The Sudetenland was very heavily fortified. It was Czechoslovakia's main defense against German attack.

Hitler demanded that Czechoslovakia give up the Sudetenland and let Germany send in troops.

British Prime Minister Chamberlain (left) tried to appease Hitler (right) at Munich in 1938.

To settle the issue, four of Europe's Great Powers met in September 1938. The leaders of Germany, Great Britain, France, and Italy gathered at Munich in Czechoslovakia. However, Czechoslovakia had no representative.

At the Munich conference, Britain and France agreed to allow Germany to take the Sudetenland. Hitler promised that the rest of Czechoslovakia would remain independent. The leader of appeasement, Prime Minister Neville Chamberlain, returned to Britain and announced that the Munich agreement ensured "peace in our time."

Six months later, in March 1939, Hitler broke the Munich agreement and took over the rest of Czechoslovakia. Clearly, the British and French policy of appeasement was a failure. Only war would stop Hitler.

Section Review 5

Define: (a) appeasement, (b) puppet government
Identify: (a) League of Nations, (b) Rhineland, (c) Neville Chamberlain, (d) Axis powers, (e) Francisco Franco, (f) Sudetenland, (g) Munich conference
Answer:
1. How did the attitude of the democracies toward the Soviet Union change during the 1930's?
2. What were some of the factors that weakened the League of Nations?
3. Why did France and Britain fail to take a strong stand against Hitler time after time?
4. How did World War II begin in Asia?
5. How did Mussolini try to create an Italian colonial empire?
6. (a) Why was the Spanish Civil War a test of strength between the Fascist powers and the democracies? (b) What was the outcome?
7. What part did each of the following play in Hitler's growing power? (a) the Rhineland (b) the Rome-Berlin Axis (c) Austria (d) the Munich conference

Critical Thinking
8. (a) What is the difference between appeasement and compromise? (b) What were the results of appeasement in Asia, Africa, and Europe? (c) Do you think a peaceful compromise was possible? Explain your answer.

661

Summary

1. Europe recovered from World War I. World War I brought an end to European dominance and saw the rise of new democracies. One of these, the Weimar Republic in Germany, faced severe economic problems as a result of the war. These problems were resolved in part by loans offered by the Dawes Plan of 1924. As prosperity returned, Germany improved its relations with France.

2. Society faced rapid change. During the 1920's, automobiles, commercial air travel, and radios widened social contacts. Albert Einstein's theory of relativity caused a revolution in scientific thought, while Sigmund Freud provided insights into the workings of the human mind. A growing spirit of independence was reflected in the women's movement. American jazz and movies spread American culture, although politically the United States turned to isolationism.

3. Wall Street's crash opened the Depression. Stock prices in the United States soared in the 1920's, until a crash on Wall Street brought on the Great Depression. The effects of the Depression spread worldwide. In the United States, President Franklin Roosevelt introduced the New Deal. In Britain, the government raised tariffs and lowered interest rates. France passed temporary reforms to help workers.

4. Fascist leaders formed dictatorships. The crisis of the Depression brought on political upheavals in many countries. In Italy, Mussolini established a Fascist government in 1922. In Germany, Hitler came to power in 1933 and instituted a Nazi revolution. Japanese military leaders began empire building.

5. The world drifted toward war. During the 1930's, a weak League of Nations and Anglo-French appeasement opened the way for Fascist aggression. Japan invaded Manchuria in 1931 and China in 1937. Italy invaded Ethiopia in 1935. In 1936, Hitler moved into the Rhineland and made a formal alliance with Italy. Their combined forces helped Franco form a Fascist dictatorship in Spain. In 1938, Hitler claimed Austria and the Sudetenland.

Reviewing the Facts

1. Define the following terms:
   a. coalition
   b. isolationism
   c. fascism
   d. appeasement
2. Explain the importance of each of the following names, places, or terms:
   a. inflation
   b. Weimar Republic
   c. Dawes Plan
   d. Kellogg-Briand Pact
   e. Einstein
   f. Surrealists
   g. Harlem Renaissance

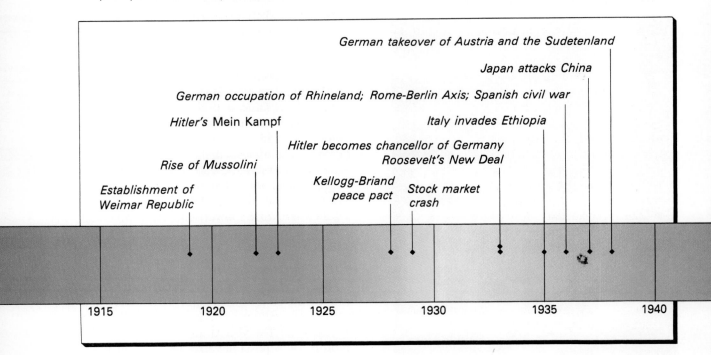

German takeover of Austria and the Sudetenland

Japan attacks China

German occupation of Rhineland; Rome-Berlin Axis; Spanish civil war

Hitler's Mein Kampf

Italy invades Ethiopia

Hitler becomes chancellor of Germany
Roosevelt's New Deal

Rise of Mussolini

Kellogg-Briand peace pact

Stock market crash

Establishment of Weimar Republic

1915   1920   1925   1930   1935   1940

h. Wall Street
i. Great Depression
j. New Deal
k. Mussolini
l. Nazi party
m. Hitler
n. *Mein Kampf*
o. Gestapo
p. Third Reich
q. Chamberlain
r. Rome-Berlin Axis
s. Franco
t. Munich conference

3. (a) What economic difficulties did the Weimar Republic face? (b) How were they resolved?
4. (a) Describe Einstein's theory of relativity. (b) Describe Freud's revolutionary idea.
5. What changes occurred in the status of women in the postwar years?
6. (a) What cultural trends reflected the growing power of the United States? (b) What political viewpoint did the country adopt?
7. (a) How did growing supply and diminishing demand affect industry? (b) Agriculture?
8. (a) How did speculation lead to the stock market crash? (b) Why did the economic crisis in the United States have a worldwide impact?
9. (a) How did the Treaty of Versailles contribute to the rise of fascism in Italy? (b) In Germany?
10. (a) What political changes did Mussolini institute? (b) What economic changes?
11. (a) How did the enabling acts increase Hitler's power? (b) How did the Nuremberg laws reflect his racial ideas?
12. Describe the aggressions taken by each of the following countries between 1931 and 1938. (a) Italy (b) Japan (c) Germany
13. (a) How did Franco come to power in Spain? (b) In what way was the Spanish civil war a precursor of World War II?

Thinking about History

1. Explain how each of the following might help create an artificial demand for goods that leads to overproduction. (a) assembly line (b) installment buying (c) commercial advertisements
2. Mussolini and Hitler both created special organizations for young people. Why do dictators frequently try to appeal to young people?

Writing and Speaking about History

1. Identify the reasons for the rise of fascism in the early 1930's. From this list, develop a thesis statement about the rise of fascism, with major facts to support it.

2. Write a paragraph that compares fascism and communism.
3. President Franklin Roosevelt frequently conducted radio "fireside chats" to reassure the American people. Prepare a fireside chat to be delivered either by Franklin Roosevelt, Ramsay MacDonald, or the president of France in 1931.

Practicing Skills

1. How does the map of Africa on page 537 help explain why Mussolini chose to invade Ethiopia rather than another country in Africa?
2. The information in the following table shows unemployment in Germany and Britain between 1929 and 1939. Use the information to answer the questions.

	Germany	Great Britain
1929	1,899,000	1,216,000
1931	4,520,000	2,630,000
1933	4,804,000	2,521,000
1935	2,151,000	2,036,000
1937	912,000	1,484,000
1939	119,000	1,514,000

(a) In what year was unemployment greatest in Germany? In Britain? (b) What years show a decline in the unemployment rates for each country? What might account for this decline? (c) Which nation shows the greatest decline in unemployment between 1929 and 1939?

Investigating History

1. In the 1980's, hundreds of farm families in the United States faced bankruptcy. Find out about the causes of the crisis. How were the causes similar to and different from those that contributed to the Great Depression? Compare the response of government in each case.
2. Extreme nationalism such as that practiced by the Nazis is sometimes called *chauvinism.* Look up the derivation of the term. How does chauvinism differ from nationalism?

Decision Making in History

Neville Chamberlain chose to appease Hitler rather than fight. As an adviser to Chamberlain, what advice would you offer based on these two considerations: (a) the impact of another war on Britain, and (b) Germany's concerns and aspirations?

World War II

In World War II, airplanes carried the war far from the battle front, bombing cities and towns and killing many civilians.

1. **Germany overran much of Europe.**
2. **Japan conquered an Asian empire.**
3. **World War II was a total war.**
4. **The Allies launched a drive to victory.**

Only 21 years after the end of World War I, a second world war broke out in Europe. A Pole named Martin Gray was 14 years old in September 1939 when he heard the shuddering screams of German dive-bombers over the Polish capital of Warsaw. Years later, Gray recorded his grim memories of the beginning of World War II:

The sirens wailed, the bombers skimmed the rooftops, their shadows glided across the road, and in the streets the people were running, clutching their heads . . . We went downstairs to the cellar, the walls were shaking and flakes of white plaster fell on our hair. My mother was deathly pale, my eyes stung, women screamed.

Day after day, Warsaw's buildings crumbled and burned from the merciless hammering of German tanks and planes. Martin Gray's family huddled around their radio to find out what was happening in their city and elsewhere in Poland. Germans had taken over some of the Polish radio stations. As a Polish Jew, Martin Gray was shocked by their broadcasts:

We listen to German broadcasts: they're announcing thousands of prisoners, tomorrow Hitler will be in Warsaw. "Poles," says the cheerful voice, "it's the Jews who are the cause of your troubles, the Jews who wanted the war, the Jews who are going to pay" . . . Then the bombers come back . . . the cellar shakes.

In two weeks, German tanks surrounded Warsaw and choked off all supplies. Civilians in the city could endure the bombing but not the lack of food. On September 27, 1939, the starving people of Warsaw surrendered to German troops. Martin Gray watched as the Germans took over the Polish capital:

They marched slowly, their heels ringing on the cobbles of the narrow streets. I was walking along the pavement, behind the rows of curious bystanders. Their planes were skimming the rooftops above Jerusalem Avenue. Patrols moved along the pavement; they didn't seem to notice the people, everyone drew aside. For a moment I followed three soldiers in ankle boots with long black bayonets. Yes, we were going to suffer.

The Poles suffered through six years of Nazi terror and oppression. Indeed, all of Europe suffered. Between 1939 and 1945, people in almost every major city of Europe heard what Martin Gray had heard—the sound of German bombers and tanks.

In Asia, the sounds were much the same. There the aggressor was not Germany but its ally in the east, Japan. Together the two countries hoped to dominate the world. They almost succeeded.

This chapter is the story of the drive by the so-called Axis countries—mainly Germany, Italy, and Japan—for world conquest. Opposing them were the Allies—Great Britain, France, the USSR, China, and the United States.

Germany overran much of Europe. 1

In the 1930's, the German dictator Adolf Hitler said over and over that Germany desired only peace and justice. Those who opposed Germany's reasonable desires, he said, were the enemies of peace. Yet all the while, he was preparing for war.

All during the 1930's, Britain and France followed a policy of appeasement. That is, they made concessions to Hitler in hopes of keeping peace. As a result, Hitler took the Sudetenland in 1938. One year later, German troops marched into western Czechoslovakia and seized it as well (page 661). The Italian dictator Mussolini, striving to keep up with his German ally, moved into the Balkans and took over Albania. Encouraged by these victories, Hitler abandoned his talk of peace. He talked instead of war and conquest.

Hitler prepared for war.

On April 28, 1939, Hitler stood before the Reichstag (Germany's parliament) and announced his newest plan. This time, he wanted the Polish Corridor. This strip of land had been cut from Germany after World War I to give Poland access to the sea (page 598). Hitler demanded that the seaport of Danzig within the Polish Corridor be returned to Germany. Furthermore, he wanted a German railway and highway route through the corridor.

Hitler's demands convinced Britain and France that appeasement was no longer possible. The governments of both countries pledged to defend Poland if Hitler threatened its independence. At the same time, they asked the Soviet Union to join them in stopping Hitler's aggression.

The Soviets were still smarting from their exclusion at the Munich conference (page 661). Soviet dictator Joseph Stalin was not eager to ally himself with the West. Furthermore, Hitler too was secretly seeking an agreement with Stalin.

In August 1939, Germany and the Soviet Union announced a ten-year nonaggression pact. In public, Hitler and Stalin pledged never to attack each other. In private, they agreed to divide eastern Europe. The Soviet Union was to have the Baltic countries of Lithuania, Latvia, and Estonia. Germany and the USSR would each take over a part of Poland.

News of the agreement stunned the world. Hitler's Nazis had come to power by attacking communism and German Communists. Communist sympathizers around the world were shocked that Stalin would deal with Hitler. Even Hitler's Nazi supporters were taken aback. Hitler had written, "Never forget that the rulers of present-day Russia are common blood-stained criminals." Yet the advantage of the agreement for Hitler was clear. Germany need not fear a two-front war like the one it had faced in 1914.

In August 1939, Hitler ordered his generals to prepare to invade Poland in September. On the night of August 31, 1939—only hours before the planned attack—a small band of German soldiers disguised themselves in Polish uniforms. Then they pretended to seize a German radio station on the German-Polish border. They fired their pistols in the air and smeared blood over the face of a drugged prisoner. This phony raid was Hitler's excuse for attacking Poland. The Poles, he said, had violated Germany's borders.

Germany invaded Poland.

Early the next morning (September 1, 1939), wave upon wave of German planes roared over Poland. Swooping low over Polish airfields, squadrons of German dive-bombers strafed (raked

Map Study
Name the Axis Powers. What lands did Germany take over in 1938?

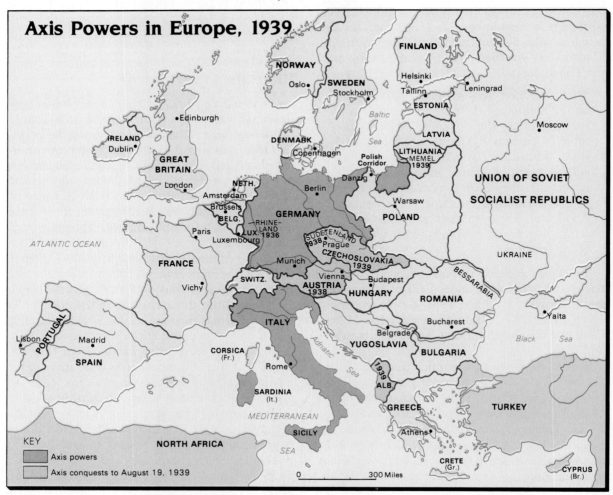

Axis Powers in Europe, 1939

KEY
- Axis powers
- Axis conquests to August 19, 1939

0   300 Miles

with gunfire) and bombed Polish planes, which were still on the ground. In less than 48 hours, the Germans wiped out the Polish air force. At the same time, German tanks and troop trucks crossed the Polish border, carrying an army of about 1,250,000 men. Long columns of German tanks rolled swiftly and easily over the flat Polish land, destroying everything in their path.

In a matter of days, the Poles lost their air force, their army, their railroads and telegraph centers, and their factories. They were demoralized, stunned, defeated.

The Germans called their sudden, massive attack *blitzkrieg* (**BLITS**-kreeg), meaning "lightning war." The fast-moving weapons of modern war—the armored tank and the airplane—were central to this new kind of warfare.

If Hitler thought that France and Britain would not honor their pledge to Poland, he was mistaken. Although not yet equipped to fight, they warned Hitler to stop his attack by 11 A.M. of September 3. The deadline passed, and Germany's armies rolled on. Britain and France declared war.

By the end of September 1939, Poland was conquered. Nazi armies occupied the western half. As agreed, the Soviet Union occupied the east. Warsaw held out until September 27 but finally surrendered. Meanwhile, Britain and France mobilized for war.

Hitler won support with hate-filled speeches at massive Nazi rallies.

The Soviets made their move.

For six months after the fall of Poland, there was a strange lull in the fighting. Although German submarines began to attack British merchant and passenger ships, there was no fighting on land between the Allies (France and Britain) and Germany. Newspapers called it a "phony war."

The only aggression in Europe during this time took place in the north. Hitler had agreed that the three Baltic countries would be Soviet spheres of influence. One week after the fall of Poland, Stalin threatened to attack Estonia, Latvia, and Lithuania unless they yielded to his demands. Under pressure, all three signed treaties allowing Soviet military bases on their soil.

Next, Stalin demanded territory from Finland. The Finnish government promptly refused. In November 1939, nearly 1 million Soviet troops crossed the Finnish border. The Finns defended their country fiercely, attacking swiftly on skis

while Soviet troops struggled through the deep snow. In the end, however, the Soviets won through sheer force of numbers. In March 1940, Finland was forced to accept Stalin's terms.

Germany overwhelmed Scandinavia.

For Hitler, the winter of waiting was over. In the spring of 1940, he made his next move. Again he did the unexpected. Most people, including the French, thought Hitler would attack France. However, Hitler was not yet ready to do so. First, he wanted to control Denmark and Norway. There he planned to set up airfields and naval bases from which he could strike at Britain and British shipping.

On April 9, 1940, German tanks rolled into Denmark. German troops that had been hidden on a merchant ship in Copenhagen's harbor marched ashore. They captured the Danish king and his ministers. Denmark surrendered within 24 hours.

On the same day, bombers of the German *Luftwaffe* (air force) attacked Norway. A German invasion force scrambled onto Norway's rocky shores. The Norwegians were better prepared than

German artillery pounded Dunkirk's docks and beaches while British rescue ships steered through the smoke to save Allied soldiers.

the Danes had been. Even so, Norway's major seaports and its capital city, Oslo, fell to the Germans within two days.

German troops blitzed the west.

As war moved closer to Britain, a new leader came to power in Parliament. In May 1940, Neville Chamberlain, the leader of appeasement, was forced to resign as prime minister. His successor was Winston Churchill (1874–1965), who had long warned that Britain must make a stand against Hitler. In his first speech as prime minister, Churchill told the nation that there was no quick road to victory. "I have nothing to offer," he said, "but blood, toil, tears, and sweat." The next five years would prove how right he was.

In June 1940, a month after the Scandinavian attacks, Hitler prepared to strike at France. Along their border with Germany, the French had built an elaborate set of fortifications known as the Maginot (mah-jih-NOH) Line. The French expected this war to be a defensive one, as World War I had been, and the French army was well prepared for trench warfare. It was totally unprepared, however, for the German blitzkrieg.

France's 2 million soldiers stood ready to fight along the Maginot Line. Once more Hitler fooled

them. As in World War I, the German army swung west around the French defenses and struck through Belgium.

On the morning of May 10, 1940, German parachutists dropped from the skies over the Low Countries—the Netherlands, Luxembourg, and Belgium. Luxembourg collapsed in only a few hours. On May 14, Germany threatened to destroy all Dutch cities if the Netherlands did not surrender. As proof, the Luftwaffe pounded Rotterdam to rubble even as talks about surrender were in progress. One day later, Belgium fell.

Columns of German tanks moved into northern France, driving Allied troops back toward the port of Dunkirk on the English Channel. There the Allied troops were trapped with their backs to the sea. The Germans closed in for the kill.

The seafaring people of Britain set out to rescue their trapped army. The fleet that sailed for Dunkirk from British ports on May 26, 1940, was perhaps the strangest naval expedition in history. Bobbing on the choppy sea were private yachts, ferries, lifeboats, motorboats, paddle steamers, fishing boats, and dockyard tugs. At the helm of these 850 craft were civilian volunteers. Their task was to help the British navy carry stranded soldiers across the Channel.

For eight days, from May 28 to June 4, this hodgepodge fleet sailed back and forth between

Britain and the burning, bombed-out docks of Dunkirk. When the operation ended on June 4, an incredible 338,000 battle-weary soldiers had been carried safely to Britain.

France fell to the Nazis.

Even as the Nazi blitzkrieg swept through France, Italian armies were also on the march. At first, Italy's Fascist dictator, Benito Mussolini, had hesitated to take part in the war. Now, with France about to fall, Mussolini decided to grab for conquest and glory. On June 10, he declared war against both Britain and France. Italy then attacked France from the south.

France seemed doomed. As German forces neared Paris, masses of people fled the city. Cars, bicycles, carts, and taxis jammed the roads leading south from Paris. German planes screamed overhead, firing into the snarled traffic.

As the end approached, the French government asked Marshall Henri Pétain (pay-TAN), an aged hero from World War I, to become prime minister. On June 16, 1940, he told the French army, "We must cease to fight."

Hitler demanded that the French leaders surrender at Compiègne in the same railroad car where Germans had been forced to sign the armistice ending World War I. On June 22, 1940, the meeting took place. Hitler walked from the railroad car giddy with triumph.

According to the terms of surrender, France was divided into two parts. The Germans were to occupy the northern two thirds of France and control the coastline. Pétain's government was to hold the southern part.

Pétain and his ministers moved to the city of Vichy (VISH-ee) in southern France. Their government became known as the Vichy Regime. Many French people regarded Pétain as a traitor. Others believed he had acted to save France from destruction. As time went on, however, the Vichy government cooperated more and more closely with the Nazis.

In time, French freedom fighters found their own way to combat the Nazis. Led by General Charles de Gaulle, they formed an underground movement known as the Free French. Although capture meant certain death, French resistance fighters made heroic efforts to sabotage the Nazis for the rest of the war.

Germany attacked Great Britain.

In all of Europe, only one country still held out against Hitler. That country was Great Britain. In a speech after Dunkirk, Churchill had already made clear that the British would never give in to the Nazis. Foreseeing the grim possibility of a German invasion, Churchill said:

> . . . [W]e shall fight in the seas and oceans, we shall fight with growing confidence and growing strength in the air; we shall defend our Island, whatever the cost may be. We shall fight on the beaches, we shall fight on the landing grounds, we shall fight in the fields and in the streets, we shall fight in the hills; we shall never surrender.

French resistance fighters used gadgets such as these to travel secretly behind German lines and communicate with others in the Free French. They hid a compass in a bootheel, a radio transmitter in a wine carrier, and news bulletins in a hollowed log.

On April 13, 1941, Prime Minister Winston Churchill visited the British town of Bristol a few hours after German bombers struck. "We shall give it them back," he said to the cheers of the townspeople.

Ignoring the advice of his generals, Hitler decided to invade Britain. During the summer of 1940, the Germans prepared for Operation Sea Lion, a seaborne attack on Britain that would begin in mid-September. First, however, Hitler sent the Luftwaffe bombers to knock out Britain's defenses, particularly its Royal Air Force (RAF).

To face the Germans' 900 fighter planes and 1,300 bombers, the British had only 650 fighters. The fate of Britain rested on the skill and raw courage of its 1,400 pilots.

Against these overwhelming odds, Britain had two secret weapons. One was an electronic tracking device known as radar. Blips on their radar screens warned the British as German planes approached. Britain's second secret weapon was the ability to crack German codes (page 680). Together, these warning systems gave RAF fliers the time they needed to scramble into their planes and rise to the attack.

The Battle of Britain began on August 8, 1940. Night and day, the RAF and the Luftwaffe battled for control of the skies. At first, the Germans concentrated their attacks on naval bases and airfields, although some bombing raids hit London. The RAF not only defended Britain but also struck back at Germany. In late August, British bombers flew over Germany, hitting Berlin and other cities.

Furious that Berlin had been bombed, Hitler ordered attacks against London and other British cities. The piercing wail of air-raid sirens filled the air as bomb after bomb exploded in city streets, setting buildings ablaze. The cost to British civilians was terrible—300 to 600 lives lost per day and from 1,000 to 3,000 injured daily.

Despite the fire-filled days and nights, the people of Britain fought on, more determined than ever not to give in. By the end of 1940, Hitler knew he could neither wipe out the RAF nor break the spirit of the British people. As a result, he abandoned Operation Sea Lion. Churchill expressed the gratitude of the British people to the RAF pilots when he said, "Never was so much owed by so many to so few."

Hitler invaded the Soviet Union.

The failure to take Britain stunned Hitler. It did not, however, defeat him. His next step was to break the pact he had made with Stalin less than two years earlier. Like Napoleon 150 years earlier, Hitler decided to strike eastward before finishing off Great Britain. Like Napoleon, Hitler was making a great mistake.

For Hitler, the Soviet Union was a tempting prize. There, he believed, his German master race would find the living space to prosper and expand. There too the Germans would win valuable mineral resources.

Hitler's first step was to take over the Balkans. In April 1941, Germany attacked both Greece and Yugoslavia on the same day. Yugoslavia fell in 11 days, Greece in 24. In Athens, the Nazis celebrated their victory by hanging swastikas on the Parthenon. By the end of the year, Bulgaria, Romania, and Hungary had all allied themselves with Germany.

With the Balkans in his power, Hitler was ready for war against the USSR. Early on Sunday morning, June 22, 1941, as the Soviet people slept, the roar of tanks and planes announced the beginning of the German blitzkrieg. In the first hours of the attack, Luftwaffe bombs destroyed 1,000 Soviet planes on the ground. Taken by surprise, the lines of the Red Army were smashed in a dozen places.

The invasion rolled on week after week. Like the pincers of a giant crab, two columns of the German army would crash through Russian defenses and surround whole divisions. In this way, the Germans moved steadily closer to their three goals—Leningrad in the north, Moscow in the center, and the rich grain and oil fields in the south.

By mid-November 1941 (five months after the assault began), Leningrad was surrounded by German armies. Hitler then tried to starve the 3 million inhabitants of the city into submission. More than 500,000 Leningraders died during the winter of 1941–1942. Yet the city refused to surrender.

Meanwhile, other German armies reached the outskirts of Moscow. There they met stiff resistance from Soviet troops. They also faced the brutal cold of a Soviet winter. The Germans, clad only in summer uniforms, were not ready for the cold. In his arrogance, Hitler had believed he would defeat the Soviet Union before winter set in. Hitler had underestimated the determination of Soviet troops.

Like Napoleon, Hitler faced a winter war near Moscow. Napoleon, however, had had the good sense to retreat when the snows started falling. Hitler instead sent a stunning order to his freezing generals: "No retreat!"

The German troops obeyed. They dug in to face the long winter. Indeed, even a retreat would have been difficult, as crankcases froze in their tanks and trucks. The Soviets, on the other hand, were well trained for winter warfare. For both sides, it now appeared the war would be a long one.

Section Review 1

Define: (a) appeasement, (b) blitzkrieg
Identify: (a) Polish Corridor, (b) Luftwaffe, (c) Winston Churchill, (d) Maginot Line, (e) Dunkirk, (f) Vichy Regime, (g) Free French, (h) Charles de Gaulle, (i) RAF
Answer:

1. (a) What new demands did Hitler make in the spring of 1939? (b) How did Britain and France end their policy of appeasement?
2. (a) Why was the Hitler-Stalin nonaggression pact unexpected? (b) Why was it important to Hitler?
3. How did World War II begin in Europe?
4. What territories did the USSR take in 1939?
5. Why did Hitler want control of Scandinavia?
6. (a) In what way was the German attack on France similar to the beginning of World War I? (b) What key difference between the two wars led to the French defeat?
7. How was France governed after its fall?
8. (a) How did Hitler plan to defeat Britain? (b) Why did he fail?
9. (a) What were Hitler's goals in attacking the Soviet Union? (b) What successes did the Germans achieve? (c) How did the campaign turn into a disaster for Germany?

Critical Thinking

10. Suppose you had been a news analyst in 1940. Write a short summary of the reasons why you expect Hitler to attack the USSR soon. Then take the opposite point of view and write a similar summary of the reasons why you would not expect him to do so.

Japan conquered an Asian empire. 2

While the German advance froze to a halt in the Soviet Union, the Japanese were making their plans in the east. Just as Hitler envisioned Europe ruled by the Aryan race, Japan had its own dreams of glory. Japan hoped to drive Western imperialists from Asian lands and establish its own broad sphere of influence. Japan called its planned empire the Greater East Asia Co-Prosperity Sphere.

Stretching from Manchuria in the north to Australia in the south, this new empire would be forced to serve the economic needs of its conqueror, Japan.

Japan's conquest of Asia began in 1931 when Japanese troops took over Manchuria, China's northeastern province. Six years later, in 1937, Japanese armies were once more on the march. This time they moved south into the ancient heartland of China.

The Japanese believed that the farmlands and rich resources of China would soon be theirs. They were wrong. As one Chinese general said, "China can exterminate the population of Japan while losing 105 million men. We shall still have 300 million left."

By 1939, the war between China and Japan had dragged on for three years. Japan's economy was strained to the breaking point. Japanese military leaders grew alarmed by their dwindling supplies of oil, iron, rubber, and tin. They began to eye the lands of Southeast Asia, where rich supplies of these resources lay.

The United States aided Great Britain.

In 1940, the only obstacle to Japanese expansion was the United States. Although thousands of miles away, Americans had been watching events in Asia and Europe with growing horror.

From the beginning, Hitler's aggression in Europe had sparked fierce debate in the United States. Many Americans reacted by vowing to keep their country out of war. Between 1935 and 1937, these isolationists succeeded in passing laws known as the neutrality acts. These laws made it illegal to sell arms to countries at war. They also made it illegal for Americans to lend money or sell on credit to such countries.

Franklin Roosevelt, then president of the United States, recognized the strong feelings of the isolationists. He also knew that the United States could not stand by helplessly as the Axis powers conquered country after country.

In 1939, Roosevelt persuaded Congress to allow the sale of weapons and other goods to fighting nations by a cash-and-carry policy. Thus, countries at war could buy such goods as long as they paid for them immediately and took them away on their ships. Because the British still controlled the sea routes, this act was a great help to them.

In September 1940, during the Battle of Britain, Roosevelt went a step further. He gave Britain 50 destroyers in return for 99-year leases on bases in Newfoundland, Bermuda, and Jamaica. That same year, Congress approved a Selective Service Act providing for the United States' first military draft during peacetime.

In the presidential election of 1940, Roosevelt tried to calm Americans' fears over the country's growing involvement in the war. He promised parents that their "boys were not going to be sent into any foreign wars." All he was doing, he argued, was helping the British defend themselves. Roosevelt stressed that the United States could serve as the "arsenal of democracy," supplying arms but not soldiers to the free countries of the world.

Soon after Roosevelt won reelection, Churchill told him that the British needed more help. By then, the entire northern coast of Europe was under Nazi control. Hitler's submarines were sinking British ships that carried food and war supplies to the island nation.

After a fierce debate, Congress passed Roosevelt's Lend-Lease Act in the spring of 1941. This act authorized the president to send war supplies to any country whose defenses he considered vital to the United States. Those countries could pay for the supplies after the war.

By the fall of 1941, the United States was arming merchant ships and using its navy to protect British ships across the Atlantic. In September, after a German submarine fired on an American ship, Roosevelt ordered navy commanders to shoot German submarines on sight. In effect, the United States was now engaged in an undeclared naval war against Hitler.

Japan threatened American interests in Asia.

Relations between the United States and Japan were also moving toward a crisis. Roosevelt was determined to keep Japan from taking over China. In addition, Japan threatened the American-controlled Philippine islands, the British colonies of Singapore and Malaya, and the oil-rich Dutch colonies in Indonesia.

To put pressure on the Japanese, Roosevelt banned the shipment of American fuel, scrap iron, and steel to Japan. This loss of vital supplies made it difficult for Japan to continue its war in China. In effect, Japan's military rulers had two choices. One choice was to pull out of China and admit defeat. The other was to obtain more war materials by striking south against Indochina, Malaya, and the East Indies. The Japanese foresaw that the second choice would provoke war with the United States. In a fateful conference with Emperor Hirohito in September 1940, Japanese generals decided on the second choice—attack.

At the same time, Japan, Italy, and Germany signed the Tripartite (three-part) or Axis pact. Hitler now formally supported Japan's war plan.

The Japanese bombed Pearl Harbor.

War between Japan and the United States now seemed inevitable. To prepare for it, one of Japan's boldest leaders, Admiral Isoroku Yamamoto, made a daring plan. Yamamoto hoped to destroy American naval power in the Pacific by sinking the American fleet at Pearl Harbor, Hawaii.

On November 25, 1941, the Japanese First Air Fleet set sail. It included aircraft carriers, battleships, cruisers, and submarines. It moved secretly, sending no radio signals for anyone to trace.

American officials knew that a large Japanese fleet had gone to sea in late November. They braced themselves for an attack, perhaps on the Philippines or Malaya. Almost no one thought the Japanese could attack Hawaii, 3,000 miles distant from Japan.

By early Sunday morning, December 7, 1941, the Japanese fleet lay north of Hawaii. From the decks of its aircraft carriers, the first attack wave of 183 planes roared over the dark ocean as American sailors slept in their bunks. When the last planes returned to the carriers, Japan had blown up 200 American planes, sunk or damaged 8 American battleships, and killed more than 3,000 sailors and marines.

It was 2:30 P.M. in Washington, D.C., when stunned listeners on the United States mainland heard the first radio reports of the disaster at Pearl Harbor. For this "unprovoked and dastardly attack," as President Roosevelt called it, the

Voice from the Past · *Four Freedoms*

Even before the United States entered World War II, President Roosevelt set forth American aims for the postwar world. Addressing Congress on January 6, 1941, Roosevelt described the goals for which Americans would work and fight.

In future days, which we seek to make secure, we look forward to a world founded upon four essential human freedoms.

The first is freedom of speech and expression, everywhere in the world.

The second is freedom of every person to worship God in his own way—everywhere in the world.

The third is freedom from want—which, translated into world terms, means economic understandings which will secure to every nation a healthy peacetime life for its inhabitants—everywhere in the world.

The fourth is freedom from fear—which, translated into world terms, means a worldwide reduction of armaments to such a point and in such a thorough fashion that no nation will be in a position to commit an act of physical aggression against any neighbor—anywhere in the world.

1. List the freedoms that Roosevelt believed were essential for a secure world.
2. (a) Which freedoms can the government of a single country guarantee to its citizens? (b) Which freedoms, according to Roosevelt, require international cooperation?
3. Consider the conflicts you have read about in history. If everyone in the world enjoyed these four freedoms, do you think all war would end? Support your answer with reasons.

At Pearl Harbor, a small boat picked up survivors from the burning USS West Virginia.

United States declared war against Japan on December 8, 1941. Soon after, Japan's allies, Germany and Italy, declared war on the United States.

Japan overran the Pacific.

Only ten hours after the attack on Pearl Harbor, planes from a second Japanese fleet pounded American military bases in the Philippines. The Japanese marched into the city of Manila in January 1942 and overwhelmed the American and Filipino defenders at Bataan (April 1942) and Corregidor (May 1942).

Meanwhile, the Japanese had been striking out in other directions. During December 1941, they took Hong Kong from the British and added the American islands of Guam and Wake to their empire. More important for their drive to the south, they also attacked the Malay Peninsula.

By February 1942, the Japanese had hacked their way through Malayan rain forests to Singapore and forced the surrender of some 70,000 British defenders. Possession of both Malaya and the Philippines gave the Japanese an ideal base from which to launch attacks against the Dutch East Indies to the south. By March 1942, Japan had conquered the oil-rich Dutch islands of Java, Borneo, Sumatra, and Celebes. By May 1942,

they had established full control of Burma, threatening both China and British India.

By mid-1942, Japan's red and white banner with its rising sun flew over most lands and islands of the western Pacific Ocean. Since the attack at Pearl Harbor, the Japanese had conquered a vast expanse of land and ocean. Their empire measured 5,000 miles from north to south and 6,000 miles from east to west. Now they hoped to push their conquests even farther, to Australia and perhaps Hawaii as well.

The Allies turned the tide in the Pacific.

The main Allied forces in the Pacific were the Americans and the Australians. In May 1942, they succeeded in stopping the Japanese drive toward Australia in the five-day Battle of the Coral Sea. During this battle, the fighting was done by airplanes that took off from enormous aircraft carriers. Not a single shot was fired by surface ships.

Japan's next thrust was toward Midway Island, which lies west of Hawaii. Here again, the Allies succeeded in stopping the Japanese. Americans had broken the Japanese code and learned that Midway was to be the target.

Admiral Chester W. Nimitz, the American commander in chief in the Pacific, moved to defend the island. On June 3, 1942, his scout planes found the Japanese fleet. The Americans sent torpedo planes and dive-bombers to the attack. The Japanese were caught with their planes still on the decks of their carriers. American fliers destroyed 322 Japanese planes, 4 aircraft carriers, and several other ships. Stripped of its air force, the Japanese fleet was forced to withdraw. Hawaii was never again seriously threatened.

The Allies went on the offensive.

The Battle of Midway was a turning point in the Pacific war. Soon the Allies began "island hopping." Island by island, they won back territory from the Japanese. With each island, Allied forces moved closer to Japan.

The first Allied offensive was at Gaudalcanal in the Solomon Islands. The savage struggle in the sweltering forests and tall grasses of Guadalcanal lasted from July 1942 to February 1943.

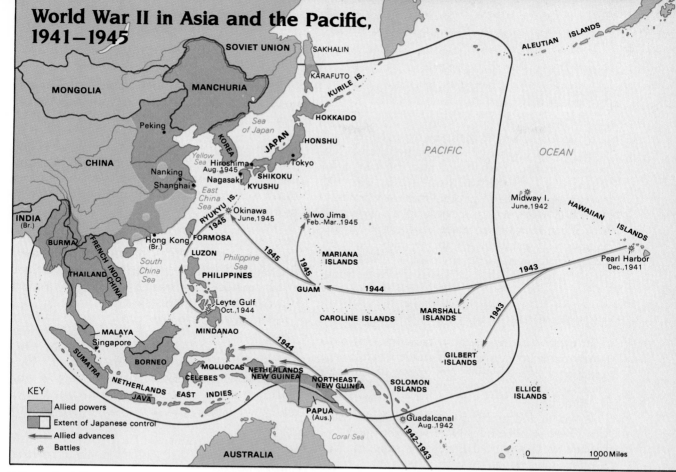

World War II in Asia and the Pacific, 1941–1945

MONGOLIA
MANCHURIA
SOVIET UNION
SAKHALIN
KARAFUTO IS.
KURILE IS.
ALEUTIAN ISLANDS
Peking
CHINA
Sea of Japan
HOKKAIDO
KOREA
JAPAN
HONSHU
PACIFIC OCEAN
Nanking
Shanghai
Hiroshima Aug. 1945
Nagasaki
SHIKOKU
KYUSHU
Tokyo
Yellow Sea
East China Sea
Midway I. June,1942
HAWAIIAN ISLANDS
INDIA (Br.)
RYUKYU IS.
1945
Okinawa June,1945
Iwo Jima Feb.-Mar.,1945
BURMA
FORMOSA
Hong Kong (Br.)
1945
MARIANA ISLANDS
Pearl Harbor Dec.,1941
FRENCH INDO-CHINA
LUZON
Philippine Sea
South China Sea
PHILIPPINES
1945
1943
THAILAND
GUAM
1944
1943
Leyte Gulf Oct.,1944
CAROLINE ISLANDS
MARSHALL ISLANDS
1943
MALAYA
Singapore
MINDANAO
1944
SUMATRA
BORNEO
MOLUCCAS
CELEBES
NETHERLANDS NEW GUINEA
NORTHEAST NEW GUINEA
1944
GILBERT ISLANDS
NETHERLANDS EAST INDIES
JAVA
SOLOMON ISLANDS
ELLICE ISLANDS
PAPUA (Aus.)
Guadalcanal Aug.,1942
Coral Sea
1942-1943
AUSTRALIA
0   1000 Miles

KEY
Allied powers
Extent of Japanese control
Allied advances
Battles

Map Study

What countries on mainland Southeast Asia did Japan rule at the height of its power? What two islands did the Allies attack after the Marianas?

Six times United States cruisers and battleships fought the Japanese navy to a stalemate. Finally, after losing thousands of men, Japan gave up the island.

The Japanese offensive in the Pacific had been halted. In the remaining years of the war, as we shall see, Japan was forced to yield all it had conquered to the relentless counterattack of the United States and other Allied powers.

Section Review 2

Define: isolationists
Identify: (a) Lend-Lease Act, (b) Isoroku Yamamoto, (c) December 7, 1941, (d) Chester W. Nimitz, (e) Battle of Midway
Answer:
1. How did World War II begin in Asia?
2. What steps did the United States take to help

the Allies before actually entering the war?
3. (a) What economic issues led to conflict between the United States and Japan? (b) How did Japan decide to solve its economic problems?
4. How did war break out between the United States and Japan?
5. Briefly describe the course of the war in the Pacific.
6. (a) What was the result of the Battle of the Coral Sea? (b) Of the Battle of Midway?

Critical Thinking
7. Admiral Yamamoto, who had visited the United States, warned Japanese leaders against provoking war with that country. If Pearl Harbor had not been attacked, do you think the United States would have remained the arsenal of democracy without actually entering the war? Explain your answer.

World War II was a total war.

3

By 1942, some 60 nations on 6 continents were at war. Thus, more than half of the world's population had been drawn into the war. Like World War I, World War II was a total war. Nations poured all their resources into the war effort. Men and women joined the armed services or worked in factories to meet wartime needs. Civilians also faced danger in air raids, besieged cities, and concentration camps. Total war brought death and destruction to the home front.

Production rose to meet war needs.

In every warring country, factories that ordinarily made consumer goods suddenly shifted to producing war supplies. Yet many of Europe's richest economic regions were soon devastated by fighting.

As more and more of Europe's factories were destroyed or fell under Nazi control, the Allies looked to the United States for supplies. The United States responded with a massive war effort.

In 1939, when the German blitzkrieg struck Poland, the United States was unprepared for a major war. Among the armies of the world, the United States army ranked nineteenth in size— one notch below Portugal, one above Bulgaria. Moreover, the United States economy was still lagging from the Great Depression.

The changes in the next two years were phenomenal. Suddenly the productive energies of the nation were channeled toward a common goal. The Selective Service Act of 1940 placed 1,600,000 young Americans in uniform by the time of the Pearl Harbor attack and 15,145,000 by the end of the war.

Even more astonishing were the gigantic month-to-month leaps in factory output. By the end of 1942, the United States was turning out as much war material as Germany, Italy, and Japan combined. By 1944, United States factories were making twice as many weapons and war goods as the Axis countries. Even the Soviet leader, Joseph Stalin, admitted in 1943, "this war would have been lost" without United States production.

The war effort provided jobs.

If more than 15 million Americans were in uniform, who was available to work in American defense factories? To a great extent, the answer was women. Since the 1800's, the number of women working for wages had been growing. The Depression, however, had hit working women especially hard. Employers had forced many women—especially married ones—to give up their jobs to men.

Once the war began, however, factory owners hired and trained more women than ever before. By the war's end in 1945, 6 million women were working in war-related jobs. They riveted airplane wings, molded tank treads, harvested crops, and did thousands of other tasks.

Other groups who had been unable to find jobs also joined the work force. Some had lost their jobs during the Great Depression. In 1939, the United States had 7 million unemployed. Many found work in defense industries. Groups who had been denied jobs because of discrimination, including blacks and the disabled, found that new opportunities were suddenly open.

For the first time since the Depression began, many Americans had dollars in their pockets. Unfortunately, consumer goods—everything from diapers to waffle irons—were in short supply. With demand growing and supplies dropping, Americans faced a new problem. Prices began shooting upward.

The government tried to ward off inflation. Prices for some goods were limited by law. The government also set up a rationing system. Families used booklets of ration coupons to get scarce goods such as meat, milk, and butter.

In 1942, President Roosevelt asked Congress for a large increase in the income tax. The new tax helped to pay for the war and also curbed inflation by reducing the money consumers could spend. World War II introduced Americans to the burdens of paying for a huge war effort with a substantial yearly tax on their incomes.

Governments fought a propaganda war.

In all the warring countries, governments bombarded their citizens with propaganda messages. Over the radio, in newspapers, and at neighborhood movie theaters, people were constantly reminded of their duty to support the war effort.

Much of this propaganda was simple and practical. In Britain, where sailors risked their lives to bring in food and other necessities, the government campaigned against waste. People were also urged to grow vegetables in backyard "victory gardens."

Propaganda was also used to assure people that fighting the war was necessary. In the United States, for example, Hollywood moviemakers worked for the federal government to produce a series of short films called "Why We Fight." Using newsreels, documentary footage, and other sources, these films traced the rise of the Nazi party in Germany, the Fascists in Italy, and Japanese militarism.

There was, of course, a fine line between hating Nazis or Japanese militarists and hating all Germans or Japanese. Unfortunately, many people crossed this line during the war.

After the attack on Pearl Harbor, many Americans became suspicious of Japanese Americans, especially those living on the West Coast. As a result, the United States government forced more than 110,000 Japanese Americans to abandon their homes, businesses, and jobs. They were sent to internment camps where they lived in cramped quarters surrounded by barbed wire until the war ended in 1945.

Hitler ordered the Holocaust.

As a total war, World War II endangered civilians as well as soldiers. The killing in World War I, though horrible, had been limited mainly to troops fighting in trenches. In World War II, however, the use of bomber planes brought entire countries into the destruction zone.

The most frightful example of war against civilians took place under the Nazis. Hitler's government turned the machinery of war against whole groups of civilians, especially the Jews.

Nazis divided humankind into two groups—a "master race" composed of Aryans (Germanic peoples) and a lesser race composed of everyone else. Hitler planned to enslave the non-Aryan peoples of Europe such as the Russians and the Poles. However, he had other plans for the group he hated most, the Jews.

Soon after coming to power, Hitler deprived German Jews of their property and political rights (page 656). Later, as one country after another came under German control, Hitler set out to achieve what he called the "final solution"—the total destruction of the Jewish people.

Beginning in 1941, Hitler began a program of **genocide**—the killing of an entire people. Millions of Jews from all parts of Europe fell under Hitler's power. Nazi officers arrested whole families of Jews, simply because they were Jews, and crammed them into railroad boxcars. Carload after carload rolled toward special prisons known as concentration camps. These tightly guarded prisons were run by black-uniformed guards from a special Nazi army unit, the SS.

The SS leaders prided themselves on the efficiency with which they carried out Hitler's wishes to destroy the Jews. When the victims arrived, they were divided into two groups. In one group were those judged healthy enough to do heavy labor for the Nazi Reich. In the other were those who were to die at once. Always included in this second group were babies, young children, and aging grandparents. They might be shot, bayoneted, or gassed. Any who were merely wounded were buried alive.

At some camps, those selected for death were stripped of their clothes and herded into a chamber that their guards called a shower room. With chilling candor, the director of the Auschwitz (OWSH-vits) camp in Poland described his system for killing people:

I used Zyklon B, which was a crystallized prussic acid, which we dropped into the death chamber from a small opening. It took 3 to 15 minutes to kill the people in the death chamber, depending upon climatic conditions. We knew when the people were dead because their screaming stopped. We usually waited about a half hour before we opened the doors and removed the bodies.

In such ways, Nazi officials at Auschwitz and 30 other death camps killed thousands of people a day.

Before World War II, there were about 11 million Jews living in Europe. By the end of the war, about 6 million had been deliberately and systematically murdered by the Nazis. Today,

On April 10, 1945, American troops reached Buchenwald, a concentration camp with 20,000 prisoners. Many were too near death to be saved.

this horrible destruction is known as the Holocaust.

Jews were not the only victims of Nazi brutality. About 4 million other prisoners died in German concentration camps, including Poles, Russians, Czechs, and many Gypsies of southeastern Europe.

Squads of Nazi police rounded up Slavs by the thousands, packed them like cattle into boxcars, and hauled them to slave labor camps. Hundreds of thousands perished there from hunger, cold, exhaustion, and disease. "The Slavs are to work for us," commented one Nazi official. "Insofar as we don't need them, they may die."

In Asia, civilians and prisoners of war also suffered terrible casualties. After the Battle of Bataan in the Philippines, 35,000 American and Filipino soldiers were taken prisoner by the Japanese in April 1942. Thousands of these prisoners died of hunger, thirst, torture, and disease on the "death marches" to Japanese prison camps. Likewise, hundreds of thousands of Chinese civilians died in bombing raids and zones under Japanese control.

Massive bombings and death-filled concentration camps took a high toll in civilian lives. By the war's end, more than 30 million civilians had died—twice the number of soldiers killed in battle.

Section Review 3

Define: (a) inflation, (b) propaganda, (c) genocide
Identify: (a) Selective Service Act, (b) Aryan, (c) Holocaust
Answer:
1. What steps did the United States take between 1939 and 1942 to prepare for war?
2. (a) How did the shift to a wartime economy change the work force? (b) How were prices and consumer goods affected?
3. What role did propaganda play in the war?
4. (a) What was Hitler's plan for the Aryan or Germanic peoples? (b) For the Slavs?
5. How did Hitler try to destroy the Jews of Europe?

6. (a) How could a single leader such as Hitler be responsible for such a massive crime as the Holocaust? (b) Who else might bear part of the responsibility?

The Allies launched a drive to victory.

4

On December 8, 1941, in his war message to Congress, President Roosevelt described December 7—the day on which Pearl Harbor had been bombed—as "a date which will live in infamy." To Prime Minister Winston Churchill of Great Britain, however, the date represented something quite different. It marked the beginning of an alliance between Great Britain and the United States that would in time, he believed, ensure the very survival of Britain. Churchill knew that pain and agony lay in the years ahead, but he was now confident of an Allied victory.

Allied forces trapped the Desert Fox.

In October 1942, British and American forces began their first major campaign together, in North Africa. The stakes there were high. The Suez Canal, Britain's lifeline to India, would go to the victor.

Since 1939, control of North Africa had see-sawed back and forth between Germany and Great Britain. Then, early in 1942, German General Erwin Rommel had begun a massive offensive in the region. A genius in tank warfare, Rommel was known as the Desert Fox. He had slowly but surely pushed British forces east across Egypt. By summer, the British were holding on by a thread in the strategic city of El Alamein (el AHL-uh-MAYN), their backs to the Suez Canal.

In August 1942, General Bernard Montgomery arrived in the North African desert to command the British forces. Small, lean, and steely-eyed, Montgomery planned not to defend but to attack. He spent two months amassing artillery and tanks. Finally, in October, Montgomery was ready to strike. So swift and overwhelming was his attack that Rommel lost 60,000 men, 500 tanks, and 400 large artillery pieces in less than a week.

The Battle of El Alamein marked a turning point in North Africa and a major shift in the war as a whole. It was the beginning of the Allied drive to seize the North African coast.

American and British forces closed in on the staggering Axis army from two directions. From the west, American General Dwight D. Eisenhower led Allied troops through Morocco and Algeria. From the east, Montgomery continued to roll back the German army. In May 1943, the two pincers of the drive came together in Tunisia, trapping 250,000 Germans and Italians. The coast of North Africa was in Allied hands.

Soviet forces took the offensive.

For Hitler, the news from the North African desert was bad, but the news that had been coming from the Soviet Union was even worse. The Germans had been fighting in the Soviet Union for nearly two years, since June 1941. In November 1941, the bitter cold of winter had stopped them dead in their tracks outside Leningrad and Moscow (page 671). When spring came, the German tanks were ready to roll again.

In the spring of 1942, the Germans took the offensive in the southern Soviet Union. Hitler hoped to capture Soviet oil fields in the Caucasus. He also wanted to wipe out the city of Stalingrad, named in honor of the Soviet leader.

The Battle of Stalingrad began in August 1942. From Stalin came the order to defend his namesake city at all costs. Soon the costs were appallingly high. Night after night and day after day, Soviet defenders holed up in bombed-out apartments and courtyards. From there, they fought the Germans with knives, guns, bayonets, and even clubs. Only death forced them to yield. Even so, after months of brutal house-to-house fighting, the Germans appeared to be in control. Then another winter set in.

Soviet commander Georgi Zhukov saw the cold as an opportunity to roll fresh tanks across the frozen landscape and begin a counterattack. Like a giant vise, Zhukov's army closed around Stalingrad, trapping the Germans in the city and cutting off their supplies. The Germans' situation was hopeless, but Hitler's order came: "Stay and fight! I am not leaving the Volga!"

The Germans did their best to follow the impossible order. When they finally surrendered on

January 31, 1943, defying Hitler's orders even then, there were only 91,000 Germans left out of an original army of 280,000. Dazed and frostbitten, the German captives trudged through the snow to Soviet prison camps.

After Stalingrad, it was the Germans who were thrown on the defensive. Up and down the 1,800-mile front, Soviet tanks and artillery hammered Hitler's armies. By now, many German military leaders realized what Hitler refused to admit—that the Nazi empire was collapsing. The Third Reich's days were numbered.

Fascist rule crumbled in Italy.

By the spring of 1943, it was clear that the tide had turned in favor of the Allies. The question was where the Allied armies should attack next. Stalin urged the British and Americans to attack the Germans in western Europe, thus relieving pressure on the Soviet front. Churchill disagreed. Fearful of launching a full-scale invasion of western Europe too soon, he favored attacking Italy from the North African coast.

On July 9, 1943, an Allied invasion force of 160,000 soldiers and marines crossed the Mediterranean and approached the southern shore of Sicily. After a ferocious naval bombardment, they clambered into flat-bottomed landing craft, charged through knee-deep water, and won a beachhead on Sicily. Sicily fell to the Allies in August after a bloody but brief struggle lasting only 39 days.

Stunned by their army's collapse in Sicily, the Italian people forced the dictator Mussolini to resign. On July 25, 1943, he was placed under arrest. A new premier, Pietro Badoglio (bah-**DOHL**-yoh), took power. He renounced his country's pact with Hitler and urged the Italian people "to fight the Germans in every way, everywhere, and all the time."

Italy's sudden change of loyalties did not save it from invasion. Hitler was determined to stop the Allies in Italy rather than fight on German soil. For almost two years, German armies occupied much of Italy, fiercely opposing Allied landings on Italy's western coast. The effort to free Italy did not succeed until 1945, when Germany itself was close to collapse.

The Allies invaded France.

Even as the Allies were battling for Italy in 1943, they began work on a daring plan to invade France and free western Europe from the Nazis. The enormous task of commanding the invasion fell to American General Dwight D. Eisenhower. Under his direction, the Allies gathered a force of 2 million British, American, and Canadian troops together with mountains of military equipment and supplies. Another million stood ready to give sea and air support to the attack.

Hitler knew that such a force was being trained in Britain. The question was when the invasion would take place and where on the French coast it would strike.

Daily Life · The Broken Code

All during the war, hundreds of British men and women lived with a carefully guarded secret. They could read the coded radio messages that the German army beamed back and forth. The Germans generated their codes with a complex electrical device like the one at the right. They thought these codes were unbreakable. However, early in the war, a few daring Poles smuggled a copy of the machine to Britain. The British name for this secret source of information was "Ultra."

Ultra was vital to Montgomery in North Africa. From it, he learned that Rommel was ill and the German army was desperately short of fuel. Without Ultra, Montgomery might not have been the victor at El Alamein.

World War II in Europe and North Africa, 1939–1945

Map Study

List the nations under Axis control in Europe in 1941. By what three major routes did the Allies close in on the Axis powers after 1943?

The Allies planned to attack Normandy in northern France. To keep their plans secret, the Allies set up a huge phantom army with its own headquarters and equipment. In radio messages they knew the Germans could read, Allied commanders sent orders to this make-believe army to attack the French port of Calais. Hitler was completely fooled and ordered his generals to keep a large army at Calais.

The Allied invasion began on June 6, 1944, code-named D day. In the dead of night, an immense fleet of 5,300 ships set sail for their target, the beaches of Normandy. Shortly after midnight, 13,000 airborne troops parachuted into France. They were followed in the early morning hours by thousands upon thousands of seaborne soldiers—history's largest amphibious attack. After 5 days of fighting, the Allies held a strip of France

80 miles long. Less than 3 weeks later, 1 million men were ashore and moving steadily inland.

By the beginning of August 1944, German troops were pulling out of Paris to escape the Allied onslaught. Several units of the Free French movement led by Charles de Gaulle joined the Allies in their race toward Paris. Finally, on August 24, 1945, the Allies entered the city in triumph. Parisians were delirious with joy.

Footnote to History

American paratroopers who landed in France on D day carried a simple signaling device to help them find one another in the dark. Each man had a metal "cricket" toy to click. No German radio operator could intercept these messages!

The German Reich collapsed.

Hitler now faced the old German nightmare—war on two fronts. The Soviet army, 5 million strong, advanced against Germany from the east. To the west, British and American forces were sweeping across the Rhine River into Germany itself. The German armies retreated.

The end was near for Hitler's Reich, but Hitler refused to recognize it. Germany must fight on, he said. "We shall never capitulate—never. We may be destroyed, but if we are, we shall drag a world with us—a world in flames." Yet, when Soviet tanks stood at the very gates of Berlin, the thought of falling into Soviet hands proved too much for him. On April 30, 1945, Hitler killed himself.

Mussolini, the overthrown Fascist dictator of Italy, was dead too. He had been assassinated on April 25.

The Allies too lost a leader in the same month. Franklin Roosevelt had just begun his fourth term as president. On April 12, 1945, an artist was drawing the president's portrait. Suddenly Roosevelt said, "I have a terrific headache." He never spoke again. A few hours later, Americans were stunned to learn that Roosevelt had died from a cerebral hemorrhage. Across the United States, people wept at the news. Wartime allies from Britain to China mourned.

Roosevelt's successor, Harry Truman, was president when the German Reich finally collapsed. On May 2, 1945, Berlin formally surrendered to the Soviet army. On May 7, the commanders of the German army and navy signed papers declaring the unconditional surrender of their forces. The war in Europe was over.

A final horror ended the Pacific war.

Meanwhile, Allied forces in the Pacific were closing in on Japan. By 1945, the Allies had reclaimed much of the Pacific, including the Philippines. From strategic bases such as Saipan in the Mariana Islands, the Allies launched long-range bombing missions against Japan. Still, they wanted to get closer.

In February, American marines landed on Iwo Jima, an island only 750 miles from Tokyo. The marines took the island after a month of bitter fighting and heavy losses. Then they moved on to the Ryukyu Islands just south of Japan. They captured Okinawa on April 1. The ordeal cost 45,000 American lives.

The taking of Iwo Jima and Okinawa opened the way for an invasion of Japan. However, Allied leaders knew that such an invasion would be a desperate struggle. Japan still had a large army that would defend every inch of its homeland. Moreover, thousands of Japanese pilots volunteered for suicide missions. These *kamikazes*, as they were called, crashed their explosive-filled planes into Allied ships, killing themselves at the same time.

President Truman saw only one way to avoid an invasion of Japan. He decided to use a powerful new weapon called the atom bomb.

By the 1930's, nuclear physicists had shown that the splitting of uranium atoms let loose tremendous energy. During the war, American scientists had urged President Roosevelt to develop a bomb using the energy of the atom before the Germans did so. Among the international team of scientists who urged the building of such a bomb were a Jewish refugee from Nazi Germany named Albert Einstein and a refugee from Fascist Italy named Enrico Fermi.

The first test of the new bomb took place on July 16, 1945, at Alamogordo in the New Mexican desert. The blinding burst of light and awesome roar of the first explosion was described by one witness as "magnificent, beautiful, stupendous, and terrifying."

Truman was delighted that the testing of this secret weapon had been successful. From the German city of Potsdam, where he was meeting with Churchill and Stalin, Truman issued a declaration on July 26, 1945. He warned the Japanese that they faced "prompt and utter destruction" unless they surrendered at once. The Japanese government did not reply.

On the morning of August 6, 1945, an American B-52 bomber released an atom bomb nicknamed "Little Boy" over Japan. The bomb drifted by parachute toward its target, Hiroshima, a city of 343,000 people. Two thirds of Hiroshima was instantly destroyed by the blast. About 80,000 people perished in the searing heat. Three days later, on August 9, a second atom bomb destroyed the city of Nagasaki and killed 40,000 people.

Aghast at these horrors, Japan's Emperor Hirohito urged his generals to surrender. He told them,

Victims of the atom bomb at Hiroshima waited for help at a first-aid station. Many of the city's medical facilities had been destroyed.

"I cannot bear to see my innocent people suffer any longer." The formal surrender took place on September 2, 1945, on the wide deck of the American battleship *Missouri* in Tokyo Bay. Representatives of the Allied powers—China, Britain, Australia, France, the Soviet Union, and the United States—watched as the Japanese foreign minister signed the papers of surrender.

Section Review 4

Define: kamikaze
Identify: (a) Erwin Rommel, (b) Bernard Montgomery, (c) Dwight D. Eisenhower, (d) Georgi Zhukov, (e) D day, (f) Hiroshima
Answer:
1. (a) Why was North Africa vital to the British? (b) What did Rommel accomplish there? (c) Why was El Alamein a turning point?
2. How were the Germans defeated at Stalingrad?
3. What were the results of the Allied invasion of Sicily?
4. How was the invasion of France carried out?
5. How did the war in Europe draw to a close?
6. (a) How did the development of the atom bomb change Allied plans for the defeat of Japan? (b) When and where were the atom bombs used?

Critical Thinking
7. Evaluate Truman's decision to use the atomic bomb. How could it be justified as saving more lives than it cost? What alternatives might have been considered?
8. There is a saying that generals are always well prepared to fight the past war. Explain how this saying does or does not apply to each of the following countries in World War II. (a) Germany (b) France (c) Britain (d) USSR

Summary

1. Germany overran much of Europe. In the spring of 1939, Hitler announced his intention to take over the Polish Corridor. Britain and France responded by ending appeasement. Soon after, Hitler signed a nonaggression pact with Stalin. World War II in Europe began when Germany overran Poland. The Soviets followed by taking over the Baltic nations. By June 1940, Germany had overwhelmed Scandinavia and moved into France. On June 10, Italy joined the war on the side of Germany. After the fall of France, Germany began an unsuccessful air attack on Britain. Germany next invaded the Soviet Union but was halted by the severe Russian winter.

2. Japan conquered an Asian empire. Japan's conquests in Asia began in 1931 with the takeover of Manchuria. Six years later, Japan moved into China proper. The war in China was slowed by dwindling Japanese resources even as the United States was aiding the Allies with war supplies. When the United States cut off shipments of resources to Japan, Japan prepared to move into Southeast Asia. On December 7, 1941, Japan bombed Pearl Harbor in Hawaii and brought the United States into the war. Soon Japan held most of the western Pacific, but Allied victories at Midway and in the Coral Sea halted Japan.

3. World War II was a total war. Production rose dramatically in the United States. The war effort provided jobs for the jobless and opened new opportunities for women. Both sides used propaganda to promote the war effort. In the United States, fear of the Japanese led to the internment of Japanese-American civilians. In Germany, Hitler waged a program of genocide against the Jewish people. Devastating air raids caused civilian deaths.

4. The Allies launched a drive to victory. After defeating German forces in North Africa, Allied troops successfully invaded southern Europe, thus causing the collapse of Mussolini's government. To the east, defeat at Stalingrad gave rise to the threat of invasion of Germany on two fronts. A major Allied offensive began on D day, resulting in German surrender. The Allies ended the war in the Pacific by dropping atomic bombs on Hiroshima and Nagasaki.

Reviewing the Facts

1. Define the following terms:
   a. isolationist   b. genocide
2. Explain the importance of each of the following names, dates, places, or terms:
   a. appeasement   c. radar
   b. blitzkrieg   d. Polish Corridor

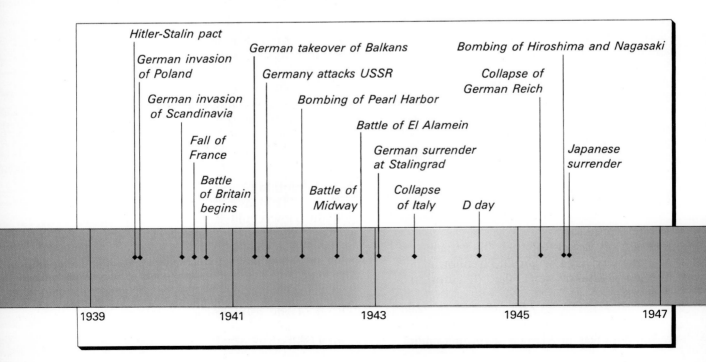

Hitler-Stalin pact

German invasion of Poland

German takeover of Balkans

Bombing of Hiroshima and Nagasaki

German invasion of Scandinavia

Germany attacks USSR

Collapse of German Reich

Fall of France

Bombing of Pearl Harbor

Battle of El Alamein

Japanese surrender

Battle of Britain begins

Battle of Midway

German surrender at Stalingrad

Collapse of Italy

D day

1939   1941   1943   1945   1947

e. Luftwaffe
f. Churchill
g. Maginot Line
h. Dunkirk
i. Vichy Regime
j. Free French
k. De Gaulle
l. RAF
m. Roosevelt
n. Lend-Lease Act

o. December 7, 1941
p. Battle of Midway
q. Selective Service
Act
r. Holocaust
s. Rommel
t. Montgomery
u. June 6, 1944
v. Eisenhower
w. Truman

3. (a) How did the war in Europe begin? (b) What territory had Hitler conquered by June 1940?
4. (a) What factors led to the fall of France? (b) How was France governed after its fall?
5. (a) Describe the Battle of Britain. (b) What was its outcome?
6. (a) Why did Hitler break his pact with the Soviets? (b) Why did the invasion stall?
7. How did World War II in Asia begin?
8. (a) What did Roosevelt do to help the Allies between 1939 and 1941? (b) What brought the United States into the war?
9. (a) Describe Japan's victories in the Pacific. (b) What two battles stopped the Japanese advance?
10. (a) Why did the Allies look to the United States for supplies? (b) How did wartime propaganda harm Japanese-Americans?
11. (a) Describe Hitler's racial policies. (b) How did he apply them to the Jewish people?
12. (a) What was the significance of El Alamein? (b) Of the Battle of Stalingrad?
13. (a) What were the results of the Allied invasion of southern Europe? (b) How was the invasion of western Europe carried out?
14. (a) Describe the end of the war in Europe. (b) Describe the end of the war in the Pacific.

Thinking about History

1. Although Dunkirk was a defeat for the Allies, it also marked a turning point in the war. Explain.
2. Compare World War I and World War II in each of the following areas. (a) causes (b) participants (c) methods of warfare (d) destruction caused
3. Reread Roosevelt's statement of the Four Freedoms on page 673. Compare it with Wilson's Fourteen Points (page 596). In what ways were the goals of the two presidents similar? In what ways were they different?

Writing and Speaking about History

1. Complete one of the following statements. Then use the statement as a topic sentence for a paragraph.
   a. France fell to Germany because _____.
   b. Hitler failed to take Great Britain because _____.
   c. Hitler's Soviet campaign failed because _____.
   d. Japan bombed Pearl Harbor because _____.

2. Conduct a talk-show interview between any two of the following people:
   a. De Gaulle and Pétain on the fall of France
   b. Churchill and Chamberlain on appeasement
   c. Hitler and Stalin on the nonaggression pact
   d. Mussolini and Badoglio on the fall of Italy

Practicing Skills

1. (a) Use the map on page 675 to make a timeline of crucial battles in the Pacific. (b) How does the map help to explain why the policy of island hopping was vital to an Allied victory in the Pacific?
2. (a) According to the map on page 681, why was victory in North Africa crucial to an invasion of southern Europe? (b) How does this map explain why Hitler feared a two-front war?

Investigating History

1. Find out more about the role of planes during World War II.
2. During and after the war, Hollywood turned out hundreds of movies that depicted World War II. If possible, view some of these movies. What messages do the movies convey?
3. Report on one of the following people during the war. (a) Roosevelt (b) Churchill (c) De Gaulle (d) Eisenhower (e) Montgomery (f) MacArthur (g) Rommel (h) Zhukov

Decision Making in History

Hitler made ill-advised decisions during the war. Evaluate the list below. Which do you feel was most instrumental in Germany's defeat? What alternative course of action might Hitler have taken?
   a. the decision to bomb Great Britain
   b. the decision to invade the Soviet Union
   c. the decision not to retreat from the Soviet Union

Research Skills

The Research Paper: Writing

The last stage in the research process is the actual writing of the paper. This stage is simple if you have done a good job of notetaking and outlining (page 578). Like the historical essay, your research paper should have an introduction, a developmental section, and a conclusion (page 318). You will probably find yourself writing several drafts. Check each draft for flow of ideas, transitions, organization, spelling, grammar, and punctuation.

Your research paper includes an additional stage not found in the historical essay. In a research paper, you must document your sources. Use documentation not only when you quote an author directly but also when you summarize what someone else has said. Documentation is not necessary when you are simply repeating something that is widely known or believed.

There are two types of documentation: footnotes and parenthetical references. Check with your teacher to see what form you should follow.

To footnote a quotation or a statement in your paper, follow it with a number placed slightly above the line. Then use that number to introduce your footnote at the foot of the page. (You may also group footnotes together at the end of the paper.)

Parenthetical references fall within the body of the report. Each reference refers to a source listed in the bibliography. Note the difference in style between the two forms:

Footnote Format

> Appeasement had many roots, most evident in France. The French had lost 1,400,000 soldiers in World War I. They feared repeating another such disaster.[1]
>
> [1] R.R. Palmer and Joel Colton, A History of the Modern World (New York: Alfred A. Knopf, 1965), p. 818.

Parenthetical Format

> Appeasement had many roots, most evident in France. The French had lost 1,400,000 soldiers in World War I. They feared repeating another such disaster (Palmer and Colton 818).

The final stage in the research process is compiling the selected bibliography. The selected bibliography lists only those sources that were used. Pull out all note cards that contain sources not used. Arrange the remaining cards alphabetically by author within categories: books, periodicals, and so forth. Copy each source exactly as it appears on the bibliography card. Place the final bibliography at the end of the paper.

Unit Review VIII

1. Explain how each of the following contributed to the start of World War I: (a) rival alliances (b) nationalism (c) imperialism (d) militarism

2. Explain the significance to World War I of each term listed below:
   a. Schlieffen Plan
   b. Serbia
   c. U-boat
   d. Allied Powers
   e. Central Powers
   f. Western Front
   g. Eastern Front
   h. Battle of the Marne
   i. Treaty of Brest Litovsk
   j. Fourteen Points

3. Tell whether each of the following places existed on a map of Europe *before* World War I or *after* World War I.
   a. Serbia
   b. Bosnia
   c. Yugoslavia
   d. USSR
   e. Austria-Hungary
   f. Ottoman empire
   g. Czechoslovakia
   h. Estonia

4. (a) What was the Great Depression? (b) How did it impact the rise of dictators? (c) Name three dictators who arose after World War I.

5. Explain how each of the following contributed to the start of World War II: (a) Treaty of Versailles (b) fascism (c) appeasement

6. (a) What brought the United States into World War I? (b) Into World War II?

7. (a) What was Germany's greatest fear in both wars? (b) How was this fear realized in World War I? (c) In World War II?

8. (a) How did the battles of World War II differ from World War I? (b) In what way were both wars total wars?

9. Explain the importance to World War II of each term listed below:
   a. blitzkrieg
   b. Polish Corridor
   c. Luftwaffe
   d. RAF
   e. Maginot Line
   f. Vichy Regime
   g. Lend Lease
   h. Battle of Stalingrad
   i. Battle of Midway
   j. D day

10. Tell whether the following events happened before or after the Russian Revolution of 1917.
    a. Freeing of the serfs
    b. Civil war between the Reds and Whites
    c. Treaty of Brest Litovsk
    d. Decembrist revolt
    e. Bloody Sunday
    f. Russo-Japanese War
    g. Kronstadt revolt

11. Explain the significance of each of the following terms either to Kerensky's government, Lenin's government, or Stalin's government:
    a. Petrograd Soviet
    b. "Peace, Land, Bread"
    c. New Economic Policy
    d. Five-Year Plan

12. Explain the origin of each of the following names or terms:
    a. Bolsheviks
    b. Mensheviks
    c. dictatorship of the proletariat
    d. communism
    e. USSR

13. How did each of the following people impact nationalistic movements in the early 1900's?
    a. Gandhi
    b. Jinnah
    c. Kemal
    d. Reza Khan
    e. Ibn Saud
    f. Weizmann
    g. Zapata
    h. Carranza
    i. Obregón
    j. Sun Yat-sen
    k. Chiang Kai-shek
    l. Mao Tse-tung

14. (a) How did World War I affect nationalism in India? (b) How did the end of the Ottoman empire affect nationalism in the Middle East?

15. (a) Describe the Arab-Israeli conflict over Palestine. (b) What role did the Balfour declaration play in this conflict?

16. (a) What impact did the Treaty of Versailles have on Chinese Nationalists? (b) Why did civil war erupt in China in the 1920's?

Unit IX

The Modern World

After World War II, the United States and the Soviet Union emerged as the most powerful countries in the world. While the rivalry between the two superpowers stopped short of direct warfare, they competed politically, economically, and militarily. The United States and the Soviet Union also took opposite sides in regional conflicts around the world from Korea to El Salvador.

Meanwhile, Europe's worldwide empires began to crumble, and many new countries were formed in Asia and Africa. These newly independent nations faced a variety of challenges. Chief among them were the need for economic development and political stability. Similar issues confronted the countries of Latin America, although they had been independent for a much longer time. As communication, alliances, and trade forged new links among nations, developments in every part of the world had far-reaching effects.

Skyline of Dallas, Texas

The Cold War

Winston Churchill (left), Franklin Roosevelt (center), and Joseph Stalin (right) met at Yalta in the Soviet Union as World War II was drawing to a close.

1. **Two superpowers arose after the war.**

2. **The war left Europe divided.**

3. **China became a Communist country.**

Traces of pink were lighting the pre-dawn sky when hundreds of Soviet soldiers heard the roar of planes approaching the airfield. During the next hour, about 25 aircraft landed at Saki airfield on the Crimean Peninsula along the northern shores of the Black Sea.

The planes bore the insignias of the Soviet Union's two major wartime allies, Great Britain and the United States. They carried about 700 passengers, including Winston Churchill, the British prime minister, and Franklin D. Roosevelt, the American president. The date was February 3, 1945.

At the airport, a Red Army band greeted the leaders, playing each country's national anthem. Soviet officials led their visitors to three nearby tents where they dined on smoked salmon and caviar. Then they set out on a six-hour automobile ride over winding mountain roads to the small Black Sea resort city of Yalta.

Yalta had once been a popular spot with Russian royalty. Dozens of palaces lined the coast. One 45-room mansion that had belonged to Czar Nicholas II became Roosevelt's headquarters. Ten miles away, Churchill and his staff settled into another luxurious villa. In yet another palace resided their host, Joseph Stalin, the dictator of the Soviet Union.

Roosevelt, Churchill, and Stalin represented the Big Three among the Allied countries fighting Nazi Germany. Germany's defeat was now certain. At their first meeting at Yalta, Churchill toasted "the broad sunlight of victorious peace."

However, "victorious peace" meant different things to each of the three leaders. For Churchill, it meant a free and democratic Europe that Britain would lead, thanks to its centuries-old parliamentary traditions and its mighty empire. For Stalin, victorious peace meant increased Soviet power and a chance to safeguard the USSR against any further invasions from the West. For Roosevelt, victorious peace meant a world in which democracy could thrive under the leadership of the United States.

The discussions and debates at Yalta reflected these different viewpoints. For example, the three leaders disagreed sharply over Poland. Churchill wanted the Polish government-in-exile, which had operated in London during the war, to take power. Stalin had other ideas. The Soviet army already controlled most of Poland and had set up a pro-Soviet government there. Stalin wanted recognition for this Communist government. "Throughout history, Poland has always been a corridor for attacks on Russia," Stalin said at Yalta, explaining his point of view. "It is not only a question of honor for Russia, but one of life and death."

Roosevelt played the part of mediator. While he agreed in principle with Churchill that Poland should have a free, democratic government, he was prepared to make concessions to Stalin for two reasons. First, he hoped that the Soviet Union would quickly join the war against Japan in the Pacific. He expected that struggle to be long and difficult. Soviet help could shorten the war and save American lives. (The first test of the atom bomb was still five months away, and Roosevelt could not foresee how soon Japan would surrender.) Second, Roosevelt wanted Stalin's support for a new world peace organization, the United Nations.

Yalta was the last face-to-face meeting of the Big Three. About two months later, on April 12, 1945, Roosevelt died suddenly. Vice President Harry S. Truman succeeded him as president.

In later years, the Yalta conference became the subject of heated controversy. Should the United States have treated the USSR as a wartime ally or as a future rival? Had Roosevelt "given" Poland and other countries in the eastern half of Europe to Stalin? Or had Roosevelt and Churchill made fair agreements that Stalin later broke to take over eastern Europe?

At the time, Roosevelt and his staff had high hopes. "We really believed in our hearts that this was the dawn of the new day we had all been praying for and talking about for so many years," recalled Harry Hopkins, one of Roosevelt's closest advisers at Yalta. "We were absolutely certain that we had won the first great victory of the peace—and, by 'we,' I mean all of us, the whole civilized race."

In this chapter, we will see how the United States and the USSR changed from wartime allies to unfriendly rivals. Their rivalry, which was neither true peace nor outright war, was called the Cold War.

Two superpowers arose after the war. 1

In spring of 1945, American troops rolled eastward across Germany. Soviet troops marched westward. On April 25, 1945, American and Soviet forces met at Torgau on the Elbe River in Germany. Nazi Germany had been crushed between the two great powers.

After months of fighting, the two armies were ready to celebrate. They saluted each other, drank toasts, danced jigs, sang, and shouted. "Today is the happiest day in all our lives," proclaimed a Soviet major to the Americans. "Long live your great leader! Long live our great leader!"

The United States and the Soviet Union now stood forth as the most powerful nations in the world. Unfortunately, all too soon the good feelings between Americans and Soviets came to an end. Almost before the last Nazi guns were silenced, a great rift began to develop between the United States and the Soviet Union.

The United States disarmed quickly.

At the war's end, the United States was both the most powerful and the most prosperous of all the countries that had taken part in the war. Many Americans had suffered during the war. About 400,000 had died in battle, and many more were injured. However, no bombs had fallen on American cities. American factories were unscathed. Few other industrialized countries were as lucky.

In 1945, the United States had the biggest navy and the best-equipped army and air force in the world. The United States was also the only country to possess the war's most formidable weapon, the atom bomb. Militarily, the United States was the unchallenged leader of the world.

However, Americans were eager to return to peace. Families wanted their sons, husbands, or fathers home from the army. Therefore, the United States demobilized as soon as the war was over. Between 1945 and 1947, the number of Americans in the armed forces dropped from 12 million to 1.5 million.

"No nation in history," President Truman wrote in his memoirs, "had ever won so great a victory and asked for so little in return." It was also true that no country had ever emerged from a war so prosperous. In 1947, the United States produced half of the world's manufactured goods, 57 percent of its steel, 43 percent of its electricity, and 62 percent of its oil. Never before in history had so large a percentage of the world's wealth been concentrated in a single country.

After World War I, as we saw in Chapter 30, the United States had turned to political isolationism (page 648). After World War II, however, the American attitude was different. The United States even offered to make New York City the permanent headquarters of the new United Nations. Shortly before his death, Franklin Roosevelt had said, "We have learned that we cannot live alone, at peace; that our own well-being is dependent on the well-being of other nations."

American soldiers (left) met their Soviet allies (right) on a ruined bridge over the Elbe River at Torgau in defeated Germany.

Daily Life · *Television*

The late 1940's and early 1950's saw a great change in American living rooms. In more and more homes, chairs were circled around a large cabinet with a glass screen that showed a flickering, black and white picture. Television, which had been in the experimental stages before World War II, had arrived.

By the early 1950's, Americans were buying 250,000 televisions a month. Comedy shows, game shows, and sports drew millions of viewers. Movie houses and radio stations suddenly faced financial ruin as people turned to television for entertainment. Even restaurants found their business dropping off because people hated to leave home and miss their favorite shows. Politicians timed their statements to make the nightly news. Television began a new age in mass communication.

The USSR *demanded a buffer zone.*

Like the United States, the Soviet Union emerged from the war as a nation of enormous economic and military strength. In fact, it was second in power only to the United States.

Unlike the United States, however, the USSR had suffered heavy fighting on its own soil. Large areas of the Soviet Union had been occupied by brutal Nazi armies. Many Soviet cities were destroyed. Fields around the cities were filled with mass graves. Soviet war losses have been estimated at 20 million, of whom half were civilians. For every American killed in World War II, 50 Soviets died.

These losses help to explain why the United States and the Soviet Union acted differently after the war. While American leaders were most concerned about building a peaceful world, Soviet leaders were most concerned about protecting their country against future wars.

The best protection the USSR could have, Stalin reasoned, was a **buffer zone** along its western border. A buffer zone is a region that lies between two rivals, cutting down the threat of conflict. The area Stalin wanted as a buffer zone was eastern Europe. By dominating this region, Stalin hoped to ensure that the Soviets could stop any future invasion before the Soviet Union itself was hurt. Moreover, Soviet control of eastern Europe would bring about 100 million more people into the Communist system.

Stalin's plans ignored the wishes of the people who lived in eastern Europe. Like the USSR, most countries in eastern Europe lacked strong democratic traditions. Thus, the Soviet Union could hope to push Communist governments into power without effective opposition.

The United Nations was founded.

One of Roosevelt's chief goals at Yalta had been to win Soviet support for a worldwide peacekeeping organization. Even before the war was over, plans for such an organization began.

An international conference in San Francisco between April and June 1945 drew up a charter (constitution) for the United Nations. In signing this charter, 51 countries pledged to work together "to save succeeding generations from the scourge of war, which twice in our lifetime has brought untold sorrow to mankind."

The charter provided the United Nations (or UN) with a main representative body known as the General Assembly. Every member nation could cast a vote in the General Assembly. The General Assembly approved new members, discussed a broad range of issues, and made recommendations and agreements.

A second group, the Security Council, was in charge of investigating disputes, peacekeeping, and emergency action. Five countries—Britain, China, France, the United States, and the Soviet Union—were permanent members of the council.

In the UN General Assembly, each member country has one vote. Votes are tallied on the electric voting boards at the front of the room with different colors standing for yes, no, or abstain.

Six other members were chosen from the UN membership at large. These members served two-year terms on the council. (Later, the number of other members was increased to 10, so that the Security Council now has 15 members.)

Both the United States and the Soviet Union insisted on being permanent council members when the UN charter was written. The two countries also agreed that each permanent member would have veto power. In other words, the Security Council could take no action unless all five permanent members agreed.

Besides the General Assembly and the Security Council, the UN included many other organizations and agencies. For example, an International Court of Justice dealt with questions of international law. The Secretariat, headed by the Secretary-General, organized the daily business of the United Nations.

From the start, the United Nations enjoyed at least two advantages over the old League of Nations. First, no major powers refused to join. Second, the charter provided for a UN peacekeeping force, an armed group that could be drawn from the troops of member countries. The UN could use these troops to enforce its decisions or to separate warring groups.

Despite these advantages, the UN also faced a major stumbling block. Unless all five permanent members of the Security Council agreed on a course of action, the UN could do nothing. Time and again, one permanent member or another used its veto power to paralyze the United Nations.

The United Nations proved more effective on social and economic issues than in solving political crises. Agencies such as UNESCO (United Nations Education, Scientific, and Cultural Organization), FAO (Food and Agriculture Organization), and WHO (World Health Organization) helped to coordinate worldwide efforts to battle disease, feed the hungry, and improve literacy.

Overall, the United Nations had a mixed record of successes and failures. However, the UN proved powerless to deal with one great threat that hung over the entire world after 1945—the threat of nuclear war.

Nuclear weapons spread.

Of all the new weapons of World War II, one stood out for its overwhelming power—the atom bomb. At Hiroshima and Nagasaki, just two of these murderous weapons killed 120,000 people. "The primary reaction of the populace to the bomb," as the official American report on its use noted, "was fear, uncontrolled terror, strengthened by the sheer horror of the destruction and suffering witnessed and experienced by the survivors."

The destructive power of the atom bomb was not limited to its tremendous blast. First came a heat flash that could burn, blind, and kill. Later, in the days and weeks after the blast, came radioactive fallout that spread sickness and slow death across a much broader area.

Once the United States had such a bomb, the Soviet Union was determined not to be left with weaker weapons. The Soviets began a crash program to develop their own atom bomb immediately after World War II. In 1949, they tested their first atom bomb in a remote part of Siberia. That test marked the end of the American monopoly on such bombs.

Now that both superpowers possessed such weapons, the world faced a new situation. Winston Churchill called it "a balance of terror." He meant that both countries would be so terrified of destruction that they would avoid war.

The atom bomb was the first example of a *nuclear* weapon. Weapons of this type get their power from reactions involving the center or *nucleus* of an atom.

In 1952, American scientists produced an even more destructive nuclear weapon, the hydrogen bomb. Soviet scientists quickly followed suit, testing their country's first hydrogen bomb in 1953. In a contest that came to be called the arms race, the two superpowers continued to compete in making more and larger nuclear weapons. Knowing that such a race might end in worldwide disaster, leaders in both countries also searched from time to time for ways to limit or slow this arms race.

Section Review 1

Define: (a) demobilize, (b) buffer zone, (c) veto, (d) nuclear weapon
Identify: (a) Yalta conference, (b) Cold War, (c) Harry S. Truman, (d) United Nations, (e) General Assembly, (f) Security Council, (g) arms race
Answer:
1. (a) Why was the United States in a stronger economic position than other countries at the end of World War II? (b) Why was it in the strongest military position?
2. How was the United States' attitude in 1945 different from its attitude after World War I?
3. (a) What was the major Soviet goal in 1945? (b) Why was that goal important to Soviet leaders?
4. (a) What features made the UN stronger than the League of Nations had been? (b) What weakness sometimes kept the UN from taking effective action?
5. How did the arms race develop?

Critical Thinking
6. Compare and contrast the situations of the United States and the Soviet Union in 1945. What factors help to explain why they became rivals instead of allies?

The war left Europe divided. 2

In 1945, Europe, which had once dominated the globe, was struggling to survive. "What is Europe now?" Winston Churchill asked at the end of World War II. "It is a rubble-heap, a charnel house, a breeding ground of pestilence and hate."

Europe faced dark days indeed. Hunger and want stalked the land from Bulgaria to Belgium. Tens of millions of Europeans were homeless, classified by bureaucrats as "displaced persons." To make matters worse, the winter of 1946–1947 was the coldest in living memory, and fuel supplies were disastrously low.

Germany was defeated and divided.

Hitler's policies of destruction had, like a boomerang, come back to destroy Germany. Some 4 million Germans had died in the war. Cities lay in ruins. Transportation was at a standstill. Every bridge across such major rivers as the Rhine and the Main had been destroyed in Allied bombing raids. So too had most of the country's businesses. In the Ruhr valley, only one factory in ten was still operating at the war's end.

East-West split Germany's postwar fate was decided in part at Yalta. There Stalin argued that Germany should be permanently divided to prevent its ever again making war. Roosevelt and Churchill agreed to divide Germany into four occupation zones, expecting that the division would be temporary. The United States, Great Britain, France, and the USSR were each to control a zone.

The western Allies encouraged the growth of democratic government in their three occupation zones. In 1949, Britain, France, and the United States allowed their zones to join. The three zones became the Federal Republic of Germany.

This self-governing democratic state is now known as West Germany.

However, Stalin was not prepared to lose control over the Soviet zone. This was the easternmost section of Germany, including the capital, Berlin. Under a Communist government, this section became the German Democratic Republic, known as East Germany. It remained under Soviet domination.

The Nuremberg trials Besides geographic division, Germany had another price to pay for the war. The discovery of Hitler's death camps (page 677) led the Allies to put 22 surviving Nazi leaders on trial for "crimes against humanity." The trials were held in the southern German town of Nuremberg during 1946.

"The wrongs which we seek to condemn and punish," said one prosecutor about the Nazis, "have been so calculated, so malignant, and so devastating that civilization cannot tolerate their being ignored—because it cannot survive their being repeated." In the end, 12 Nazis were sentenced to death. Seven Nazi leaders received long prison sentences, and three were acquitted. The greatest war criminal of all, Adolf Hitler, had taken his own life during the last days of the war in Berlin.

Europe was split between East and West.

As Germany collapsed in defeat, armies from the Soviet Union had pushed the Nazis back across eastern Europe. By the end of the war, Soviet troops occupied the countries of Bulgaria, Romania, Hungary, Poland, Czechoslovakia, and eastern Germany.

In most of these countries, local Communists had fought hard against the Nazis in resistance movements. Many of these Communists had spent at least part of the war in Moscow and were closely allied with the Soviets.

In 1945, with the support of the Soviet army, Communists won powerful posts in eastern European governments. As the Nazis had done earlier, they often won control of the police, the newspapers, and the radio stations. Soon they took over completely.

Stalin had promised Roosevelt to allow free elections in Poland and other parts of eastern

Europe "as soon as possible." By July 1945, however, it was clear he would not keep this promise. "A freely elected government in any of these East European countries would be anti-Soviet," Stalin said bluntly, "and that we cannot allow."

By 1948, Communist governments were in power in Albania, Bulgaria, Romania, Poland, Hungary, and Czechoslovakia. These countries were sometimes called Soviet **satellites**. In this sense, a satellite is a country whose policies are dictated or heavily influenced by another country.

Tito and Yugoslavia As in the other countries of eastern Europe, Communists came to power in Yugoslavia. However, Yugoslavia followed a somewhat different path from its neighbors and did not become a Soviet satellite.

The leader of Yugoslavia's Communists was Josip Broz, better known by his wartime name of Tito (TEE-toh). Tito had led Yugoslav *partisans* (guerrillas) against the Nazis. By the time the Red Army arrived in Yugoslavia in late 1944, much of the country had already been freed by Tito's fighters. Although he was a Communist, Tito was above all a fierce Yugoslav nationalist. He was determined that the Soviets should not dominate his country.

Geography gave Tito a strong position. Yugoslavia's rugged mountains offered protection against Soviet tanks. Likewise, the country's long coastline on the Adriatic had plenty of harbors through which Tito could get supplies from the West if the need arose. With these advantages and his own army behind him, Tito refused to obey orders from Stalin. "We demand," said Tito, "that everyone shall be master in his own house."

"I will shake my little finger," Stalin boasted in 1948, "and there will be no more Tito." Yet Tito long outlasted Stalin. The Yugoslav leader remained in power until his death in 1980 and kept his country independent of the Soviet Union.

An iron curtain Europe was now divided into two political regions: a mostly democratic Western Europe and a Communist Eastern Europe. Winston Churchill described this new situation in 1946:

A shadow has fallen upon the scenes so lately lighted by the Allied victory. From Stettin in the Baltic to Trieste in the Adriatic, an iron curtain has descended across the continent. Behind that line lie all the capitals of the ancient states of Central

and Eastern Europe . . . These famous cities and the populations around them lie in what I must call the Soviet sphere, and all are subject in one form or another, not only to Soviet influence but to a very high and, in many cases, increasing measure of control from Moscow.

The phrase "iron curtain" came to stand for the division of Europe.

Stalin had achieved one of his long-term goals. Eastern Europe had become a buffer zone between the West and the USSR.

The Truman Doctrine blocked communism.

President Truman agreed with Churchill that communism was a spreading threat in Europe. Against this threat, Truman favored a vigorous policy of containment. By containment he meant stopping any Soviet attempt to force Communist rule in new areas.

Truman's ideas were first put to the test in Greece. In 1946 and 1947, a bitter civil war was raging between the Greek government and Communist guerrillas supported by the Soviets.

In March 1947, Truman asked Congress for $400 million in military and economic aid for Greece and neighboring Turkey, another country facing Soviet pressures. Congress approved the money, and American aid proved vital in defeating the Communist rebels in Greece. Thus, Greece remained part of Western Europe politically, even though it lay to the east geographically.

American policy toward communism came to be called the Truman Doctrine. Under this policy, the United States did not try to overthrow Communist governments where they already existed. It did, however, do everything short of war to prevent further Communist takeovers. "The free peoples of the world look to us for support in maintaining their freedoms," said President Truman. "If we falter in our leadership, we may endanger the peace of the world."

Amid the ruins of postwar Europe, homeless families struggled to stay together. Bombs destroyed these children's home in Alsace, France.

The Marshall Plan aided Western Europe.

In the late 1940's, communism seemed to threaten Western as well as Eastern Europe. Throughout Western Europe, shaky economies and political unrest seemed to make countries easy targets for Communist takeovers.

To help rebuild Europe and stop communism, American Secretary of State George Marshall had a bold plan. He wanted to offer European countries massive economic aid immediately. In the spring of 1948, Congress approved the European Recovery Program, often called the Marshall Plan. During the next 5 years, this plan funneled more than $13 billion in food, fuel, and manufactured goods to 16 countries in Western Europe.

The Marshall Plan also offered aid to the countries of Eastern Europe, including the Soviet Union. However, the USSR turned down the aid and forced its satellites to do likewise. Only Yugoslavia accepted.

European countries were free to use the Marshall Plan aid however they saw fit. There were no strings attached to the help. The United States asked only that the participating countries cooperate rather than compete with one another economically.

The United States hoped that the funds would bring three specific benefits to each nation.
1. Stable currency—that is, money with firm value, not subject to runaway inflation
2. Increased agricultural and industrial production
3. Expanded exports

By all these standards, the Marshall Plan was a smashing success. Within four years, for example, industrial production in the countries receiving aid was 41 percent *higher* than it had been on the eve of World War II. At the same time, currencies had been stabilized and exports were rising rapidly.

Economic cooperation was also increasing. In 1951, six Western European countries formed the European Coal and Steel Community. Members abolished all tariffs on coal and steel and set common price levels for exports. As we shall see in Chapter 33, this organization formed the nucleus around which the European Common Market later developed.

The Marshall Plan benefited the United States as well. As the American government bought food and goods to send to Europe, American farms and factories raised production to record levels. As a result, the American economy continued its wartime boom without faltering. Moreover, Western Europeans soon became good customers for American exports.

Rival alliances arose.

Both the United States and the Soviet Union feared that the Cold War might suddenly turn hot. Both countries met the threat of war by organizing alliances.

Voice from Our Time · *Against Hunger and Poverty*

On June 5, 1947, Secretary of State George C. Marshall delivered a speech at Harvard University. In it, Marshall explained the goals of the United States in providing aid to Europe.

... *It is logical that the United States should do whatever it is able to do to assist in the return of normal economic health in the world, without which there can be no political stability and no assured peace. Our policy is directed not against any country or doctrine, but against hunger, poverty, desperation, and chaos. Its purpose should be the revival of a working economy in the world so as to permit the emergence of political and social conditions in which free institutions can exist.*

1. How does Marshall deny that the American goal is simply to stop communism?
2. In your own words, explain the results that Marshall hopes his plan will achieve.

The United States built up its armed forces in Western Europe. Meanwhile, the draft was continued in the United States to keep the army and navy at record peacetime size. Likewise, the Soviet Union kept a huge standing army and required its satellites to do the same.

The NATO *alliance* In 1949, the United States joined Canada and ten Western European countries to form the North Atlantic Treaty Organization (NATO). The European members were Great Britain, Belgium, Denmark, France, Iceland, Italy, Luxembourg, the Netherlands, Norway, and Portugal.

The 12 members of NATO pledged military support to one another in case any member was attacked. This alliance marked the United States' first *peacetime* military commitment since the country's founding in 1776.

Greece and Turkey joined NATO in 1952, and West Germany joined in 1955. By then, NATO kept a standing military force of more than 500,000 troops as well as thousands of planes, tanks, and other equipment.

The *Warsaw Pact* The USSR, for its part, saw NATO as a threat. In 1955, the Soviets developed an alliance system of their own, known as the Warsaw Pact. The Warsaw Pact linked the USSR and seven Eastern European countries—Poland, East Germany, Czechoslovakia, Hungary, Romania, Bulgaria, and Albania.

Conflict developed at Berlin.

During the 1950's, several hotspots developed in the Cold War. One place where East and West faced each other directly was Berlin. The former German capital lay deep within East Germany. Like Germany itself, Berlin had been divided into American, French, British, and Soviet sections. The presence of Western powers in Berlin irritated and threatened the Soviets. West Berlin was like a non-Communist island in the middle of East Germany.

In June 1948, the Soviets decided to starve West Berlin into submission. They blocked all roads to the city. No food, fuel, or other vital supplies could reach West Berlin. For 2 million West Berliners, a desperate siege had begun.

The Western Allies refused to be forced out of Berlin. "The United States is going to stay. Period," said President Truman. Within hours,

the American, British, and French governments were making plans to keep West Berlin alive by airlifting supplies to the city. Western transport planes, filled to the brim with food, coal, medicine, and other necessities, began around-the-clock flights to Berlin.

The task was immense, and so were the difficulties. The airlift brought some 4,500 tons of supplies into West Berlin every day. At the city's three major airports, planes landed and took off at an average rate of one per minute.

Soviet fighter planes harassed the airlift pilots, buzzing across their paths as they came and went from Berlin. However, Stalin knew that shooting down an American plane would almost certainly lead to war. When the Western Allies did not back down, Soviet leaders decided that West Berlin was not worth the risk of World War III. In May 1949, after nearly a year, the Soviets ended their blockade of Berlin.

Map Study

What Communist country was not a member of the Warsaw Pact? What nations were neutral? Which alliance had greater access to the seas?

Postwar Europe

KEY
- NATO members, 1955
- Warsaw Pact member, 1955
- Other communist countries
- Nonaligned countries

0   500 Miles

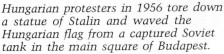
Hungarian protesters in 1956 tore down a statue of Stalin and waved the Hungarian flag from a captured Soviet tank in the main square of Budapest.

The Hungarian revolt failed.

Even while the Soviet Union challenged the West, challenges to Soviet dominance arose in Eastern Europe. Many people in the satellite countries resented Soviet control and looked for a chance to end it. Some thought their chance had come when Stalin died in 1953.

Stalin's death brought to power a new, more moderate group of Soviet leaders. The most powerful of them was Nikita Khrushchev (kroosh-CHOF). The new leaders allowed the satellite countries a little more independence as long as they remained firmly Communist and wholeheartedly allied to the Soviet Union.

This small gain only whetted people's desire for more freedom in Eastern Europe. Beginning in East Germany in 1953, a wave of strikes and protests swept across Czechoslovakia, Hungary, and Poland.

In Hungary, the protests grew to a major crisis. In October 1956, the Hungarian army joined with the protesters to oust Hungary's Soviet-controlled government. Angry mobs stormed through Budapest, waving Hungarian flags with the Communist hammer-and-sickle emblems cut out. The rioters beat and killed as many members of the Soviet-supported secret police as they could catch. "From the youngest child to the oldest man,"

said one Hungarian, "no one wants communism. We have had enough of it, enough of it forever."

Imre Nagy (nahj), the most popular and liberal Hungarian Communist leader, formed a new government. Nagy promised free elections, denounced the Warsaw Pact, and demanded that all Soviet troops leave Hungary.

Such reforms were far more than the USSR would allow. In early November, Soviet tanks rolled into Budapest, backed by crack infantry units of the Red Army. Armed only with pistols and bottles, thousands of Hungarian "freedom fighters" threw up barricades in the streets and fought the invaders but to no avail. The Soviets overthrew the Nagy government and replaced it with pro-Soviet leaders. Nagy himself was executed. Some 200,000 Hungarians fled west.

Although the Truman Doctrine had promised to support free peoples who resisted communism, the United States did nothing to help Hungary break free of Soviet control. Many Hungarians were bitterly disappointed. The American policy of containment did not extend to driving the Soviet Union out of its satellites.

No help came to Hungary from the United Nations either. Although the UN passed one resolution after another condemning the USSR, the Soviet veto in the Security Council stopped the UN from taking any action.

Europe's overseas empires crumbled.

As we have seen, the countries of Europe were barely able to support themselves in 1945, let alone rule overseas colonies. At the same time, nationalist movements in Asia and later in Africa gained strength. Together, these developments brought down the curtain on the age of European imperialism.

Great Britain made the most dramatic exit from empire. This island nation once ruled a fourth of the world's land and 500 million of its people. In 1947, Britain gave up the "brightest jewel" of its empire, India. Britain also withdrew from the bitterly divided Middle Eastern state of Palestine (page 754). Thereafter, Britain continued to divest itself of its colonies.

The shift away from empire was marked by a sudden turnaround in British politics. In July 1945, British voters turned their great war leader, Winston Churchill, out of office. Churchill's Conservative party was replaced in power by the Labour party under Clement Attlee.

Why did the British vote against Churchill? Despite his inspired leadership, voters saw him as a symbol of the country's past, and many Britons believed that the country needed new directions. The Labour party leaders believed that imperial rule was wrong. They also thought that the government should spend its increasingly limited resources closer to home. They wanted better schools and hospitals as well as welfare benefits for those who needed them. Under Attlee's government, Britain made fairly peaceful agreements for independence with many of its former colonies.

Like Britain, France faced the loss of its overseas lands. Unlike Britain, however, France struggled to hold on to its empire. As a result, the French found themselves trapped in long, bloody, expensive conflicts in Indochina and North Africa. Eventually, however, the French were forced to accept the end of the imperial era.

One by one, other European countries also lost their colonies. Yet Europe's influence survived in the places it had once ruled. Often, former colonies kept English or French as their official language. Many newly independent countries kept close economic ties with their former rulers. As Europe recovered its prosperity, new trading partnerships replaced the old imperialism.

Section Review 2

Define: (a) satellite, (b) containment
Identify: (a) Nuremberg trials, (b) Tito, (c) North Atlantic Treaty Organization, (d) Warsaw Pact, (e) Nikita Khrushchev
Answer:
1. (a) How was Germany divided in 1945? (b) How did that division lead to the development of two separate countries?
2. Give at least two reasons why Communists were in a strong position to take over governments in Eastern Europe.
3. How did the outcome of the Communist takeover in Yugoslavia differ from the outcome elsewhere in Eastern Europe?
4. (a) What was the Truman Doctrine? (b) How was it applied in Greece?
5. (a) What were the three goals of the Marshall Plan? (b) What were the results?
6. (a) What promise did NATO members make to one another? (b) How did the Communist countries respond?
7. (a) Why was Berlin a likely spot for trouble to develop in the Cold War? (b) What crisis arose there in 1948?
8. (a) What changes did Hungarians try to make in their government in 1956? (b) What were the results?
9. (a) How did Europe's world influence change after 1945? (b) How did the British and the French differ in their reactions?

Critical Thinking
10. If you were asked to write a definition of "crimes against humanity," what important considerations would you want to include?

China became a Communist country. 3

Except for the Soviet Union, no country suffered such high casualties in World War II as China. Japanese forces occupied half the country, including most of China's major cities. The total number of Chinese civilians who were killed in the fighting or died of famine brought on by the war may be as high as 22 million.

China's war effort was not united.

As we saw in Chapter 29, a bitter civil war between the Nationalists (Kuomintang) and the Communists divided China on the eve of the 1937 Japanese invasion. During the world war, the Nationalists and the Communists claimed to be fighting the Japanese together, yet they continued to jockey for position within China. The two groups fought the Japanese in very different ways.

Mao and the Communists Under their leader, Mao Tse-tung, the Communists had their stronghold in northwestern China. From there, they mobilized Chinese peasants for guerrilla war against the Japanese in the northeast. Communist guerrillas ambushed Japanese truck convoys, attacked small Japanese forces, and blew up Japanese supply posts. At the same time, Communist leaders set up political groups in villages throughout northern China.

In the areas they controlled, the Communists worked to win widespread peasant support. For example, they strictly limited the amount of rent landlords could collect. They encouraged peasants to learn to read. They helped to improve food production. As a result, more and more recruits flocked to the Communists' Red Army. By 1945, much of northern China was under Communist control.

Chiang and the Nationalists Meanwhile, the Nationalist forces under Chiang Kai-shek had set up their stronghold in southwestern China. Chiang made the city of Chungking his wartime capital, protected from the Japanese by a series of formidable mountain ranges. Here he gathered an army of 2.5 million men. Between 1942 and 1945, this army received $1.5 billion in aid from the United States.

American advisers, sent to help Chiang modernize his army, reported widespread corruption among the Nationalists. Supplies of food and medicine intended for the whole army often ended up in the hands of a few officers. Nationalist leaders were also out of touch with the ordinary people. Chiang deeply distrusted the peasants and refused to arm them.

Chiang's army fought occasional battles against the Japanese along the Yangtze River. In general, however, the Nationalist army saved its strength for the battle Chiang expected soon against the Communists. There was little doubt that the uneasy truce between the Communists and the Nationalists would collapse if Japan were defeated.

China faced renewed civil war.

World War II in Asia ended suddenly with the flash of atom bombs at Hiroshima and Nagasaki. Japan's sudden surrender caught both Chiang and Mao by surprise. The United States urged Chiang and Mao to negotiate a political settlement of their differences. Yet even as the Japanese were surrendering, both the Nationalists and the Communists were stockpiling weapons and preparing for civil war.

The civil war between Nationalist and Communist forces lasted from 1946 to 1949. At the beginning, the Nationalists appeared to have a huge advantage. Their army outnumbered the Communists' army three to one. The Nationalists were also better equipped. Chiang's forces received nearly $2 billion in aid from the United States between 1946 and 1949.

After Japan's surrender in 1945, Chiang's Nationalist troops moved back into southern and central China. However, they did little to win popular support. "They stole and looted freely," reported General Albert Wedemeyer, an American adviser.

Chiang's government stumbled from one crisis to another. Famine still stalked the land. China's economy was close to collapse. Inflation made Chinese currency nearly worthless.

As the Nationalists weakened, the Communists gained strength. Mao and his colleagues avoided pitched battles. They allowed Chiang to hold the cities while the Red Army spread through the countryside. As thousands of Nationalist soldiers deserted to the Communists, the two armies became roughly equal in size.

The Communists were victorious.

In the spring of 1949, China's major cities fell one by one to the Communists. What was left of Chiang's once enormous army fled south. By the fall of 1949, Chiang and other Nationalist leaders had fled to the island of Taiwan.

On October 1, 1949, Mao Tse-tung stood on the balcony of the ancient Imperial Palace in Peking. The immense square below was filled

In Taiwan, the Nationalist Chinese maintained a strong military force, both in fear of a Communist attack and in hope of someday retaking the mainland. On training exercises in 1954, these Nationalist troops wore heavy camouflage, making them hard to spot from the air.

by a crowd that had come to see its country's new leader. "Our nation will never again be an insulted nation," Mao told his listeners. "We have stood up." After more than 20 years of almost constant struggle, the Communists ruled all of mainland China. They established a new government, the People's Republic of China.

It was a moment of triumph few could have predicted. Both the Nationalists and the Japanese had tried to destroy the Communists. The United States had also thrown its weight against the Communists. The world's major Communist power, the Soviet Union, had been locked in a struggle with Hitler and had given Mao very little help. Moreover, the Soviets objected to Mao's policies because he drew his strength from rural peasants, not from urban workers as Marx and Lenin had predicted. The peasants had become the backbone of Mao's movement. They had brought Mao his victory.

The United States refused to recognize Communist China.

For many years, the United States refused to accept the People's Republic of China as China's true government. After Chiang Kai-shek fled to Taiwan, the United States helped him set up a Nationalist government on that small island. Both

Chiang and the United States called Taiwan the Republic of China. With American support, the Taiwan government continued to represent China in the United Nations until 1972.

Why did the United States continue to support Chiang despite Nationalist corruption and defeat? The answer lies in the Cold War. Even though the Soviet Union had done little to help Mao win, the fact remained that Mao was a Communist. Moreover, the Soviets soon sent massive aid to the People's Republic of China. To an American government already locked into a bitter struggle with the Soviet Union, Mao's victory in China seemed to be a giant step forward in a Communist campaign to conquer the world. This American suspicion of Communist China was soon strengthened by the outbreak of the Korean War.

War split Korea into north and south.

Korea had been occupied by the Japanese since the early 1900's. After World War II, Japan was driven out. Soviet forces occupied the northern half of Korea, while American troops held the south. The dividing line was the thirty-eighth parallel of latitude.

At the United Nations, the United States argued for unifying Korea under a single government.

The Korean War, 1950–1953

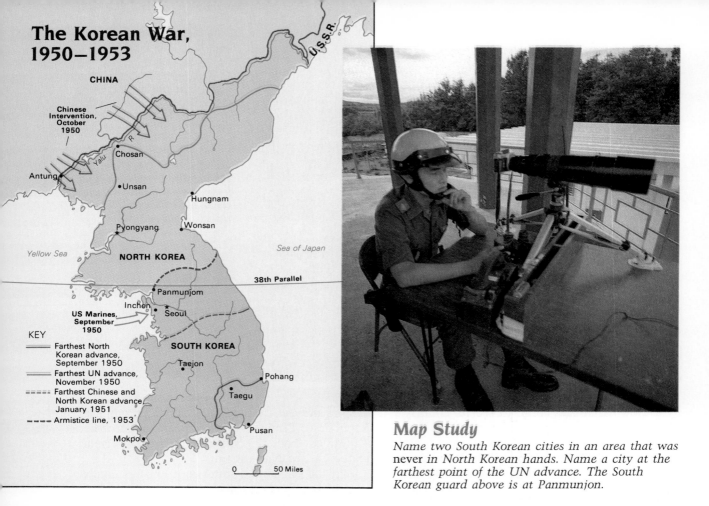

CHINA

Chinese Intervention, October 1950

Antung

Yalu R.

Chosan

•Unsan

•Hungnam

Pyongyang ★

•Wonsan

Yellow Sea

NORTH KOREA

Sea of Japan

38th Parallel

Panmunjom

Inchon

US Marines, September 1950

★ Seoul

KEY

— Farthest North Korean advance, September 1950

— Farthest UN advance, November 1950

----- Farthest Chinese and North Korean advance, January 1951

- - - Armistice line, 1953

SOUTH KOREA

Taejon

•Pohang

Taegu

Pusan

Mokpo•

0   50 Miles

Map Study

Name two South Korean cities in an area that was never in North Korean hands. Name a city at the farthest point of the UN advance. The South Korean guard above is at Panmunjon.

The Soviets, fearful that such a government would be pro-American, refused. They set up their own puppet government in the north. In the south, an American-supported government took control.

Soon after World War II, the United States cut back its armed forces in South Korea. By the beginning of 1949, there were only 500 American troops there. The Soviets concluded that the United States would not fight to defend South Korea. They prepared to back North Korea with tanks, airplanes, and money in an attempt to take over all of the peninsula.

On June 25, 1950, the North Koreans swept across the thirty-eighth parallel in a surprise attack on South Korea. Within a few days, North Korean troops had penetrated deep into South Korea. On June 27, President Truman ordered American troops stationed in Japan to support the South Koreans. He also sent an American fleet into the waters between Taiwan and China.

South Korea also called on the United Nations to stop the North Korean invasion. When the

matter came to a vote in the Security Council, the USSR was not there. The Soviets were boycotting the council in protest over the presence of Nationalist China (Taiwan). Thus, the Soviets could not veto the UN's plan of action.

The United Nations voted to send an international force to Korea to stop the invasion. All together, 15 nations, including Britain and Canada, sent troops to Korea. Because the Security Council had approved this military action, the troops that supported South Korea fought under the UN flag. General Douglas MacArthur, an American hero of World War II, commanded the United Nations forces.

Meanwhile, the North Koreans continued their advance. By September 1950, they controlled the entire Korean peninsula except for a tiny area in the far southeast.

In that month, however, MacArthur pulled a surprise attack of his own. A small force of marines landed at the port of Inchon behind North Korean lines. More and more UN troops followed the first landing. The North Koreans found themselves with enemies on two sides. Within two weeks, the North Koreans were driven back almost to their homeland.

The UN army chased the retreating North Korean troops across the thirty-eighth parallel into North Korea. In late November, UN troops approached the Yalu River, the border between North Korea and China. It seemed as if North and South Korea were about to become a single country again by force of arms.

Then, in late November 1950, 300,000 Chinese troops joined the war on the side of North Korea. The Chinese wanted North Korea as a Communist buffer state to protect their northeastern province of Manchuria. They also felt threatened by the American fleet off their coast. The fight between North and South Korea had escalated into a war in which the main opponents were the Chinese and the Americans.

By sheer force of numbers, the Chinese drove the UN troops (most of which were Americans) southward. At some points along the battlefront, the Chinese outnumbered them ten to one. By early January 1951, all UN and South Korean troops had been pushed out of North Korea. The Chinese advanced to the south, capturing the South Korean capital, Seoul.

"We face an entirely new war," declared General MacArthur. Convinced that Korea was the place "where the Communist conspirators have elected to make their play for global conquest," MacArthur called for the use of nuclear weapons against Chinese cities.

President Truman disagreed. He viewed MacArthur's proposals as reckless. "We are trying to prevent a world war, not start one," said Truman. He dismissed MacArthur.

Footnote to History

Americans first became familiar with the term *brainwashing* in the Korean War. Some American prisoners of war in Korea were isolated, threatened, and mistreated. At the same time, they were constantly questioned and lectured about communism. Eventually, such treatment led some men to accept Communist ideas. Since then, forcing new ideas on a person by extreme treatment has been called brainwashing.

Over the next two years, UN forces fought a limited war. In such a war, one or both sides aim at less than all-out victory over the enemy. The UN goal was to drive the North Koreans back to the thirty-eighth parallel. By 1952, UN troops had recaptured Seoul and were in firm control of South Korea.

Finally, in July 1953, North and South Korea signed a cease-fire agreement. With minor changes, the border between the two Koreas remained what it had been before the conflict. Counting both civilians and soldiers, the war had cost an estimated 5 million lives.

Although the Korean War ended in a stalemate, it did have several important results. First, the war showed that Communist China was a great power. The Chinese had been able to match the military strength of the West, at least in a nonnuclear war fought in Asia.

Second, the Korean War set a pattern for later conflicts between the great superpower rivals, the United States and the USSR. Each side would have gains and losses, but neither side could attain a clear-cut victory. Both sides lived in an atmosphere of uncertainty.

Section Review 3

Identify: (a) Mao Tse-tung, (b) Chiang Kai-shek, (c) Taiwan, (d) Korean War, (e) Douglas MacArthur
Answer:
1. How did the Chinese Communists increase their power during World War II?
2. What course of action did the Nationalists follow during and after the war?
3. What policy did the United States follow toward China from 1949 to 1972?
4. (a) What was the situation in Korea in 1945? (b) How did the Korean War begin?
5. What part did each of the following play in the war? (a) the UN (b) the United States (c) China
6. What was the outcome of the war?

Critical Thinking
7. (a) What advantages did each side have in China's civil war? (b) What factor do you think was most important in producing a victory for Mao?

Summary

1. Two superpowers arose after the war. After the war, the western Allies hoped to spread democracy, whereas Stalin sought to increase Soviet power. The United States and the Soviet Union emerged from the war as rival superpowers engaged in a nuclear arms race. Although the founding of the United Nations symbolized a desire for peace, its efforts were hampered by the veto powers of the Security Council.

2. The war left Europe divided. World War II left Europe in ruins. A defeated Germany was divided into four occupied zones. In time, the zones occupied by the western Allies became a democratic state known as the Federal Republic of Germany, or West Germany. East Germany remained under Communist control, and much of Eastern Europe also fell to the Soviets. The United States instituted a course of containment to block the further spread of communism, set up the Marshall Plan to aid economic recovery in Western Europe, and joined NATO, a mutual defense pact. The Soviet Union responded with the Warsaw Pact and the Berlin blockade to starve West Berlin into submission. Although the Soviets loosened controls after Stalin's death, they quickly suppressed a revolution in Hungary. A final outcome of the war was the loss of overseas empires for Europe.

3. China became a Communist country. At the end of World War II, civil war once again broke out in China between Nationalists and Communists. Defeated Nationalists fled to Taiwan in 1949. Led by Mao Tse-tung, Communists set up the People's Republic of China, which the United States refused to recognize. After the war, Korea was occupied by Soviets in the north and United States troops in the South. In 1950, North Koreans, aided by Chinese Communists, swept into South Korea. The United Nations sent a peacekeeping force to stop the invasion. The war ended in a stalemate in 1953.

Reviewing the Facts

1. Define the following terms:
   a. buffer zone
   b. satellite
2. Explain the importance of each of the following names, places, or terms:
   a. Yalta conference
   b. Cold War
   c. Truman
   d. United Nations
   e. arms race
   f. Nuremberg trials
   g. Tito

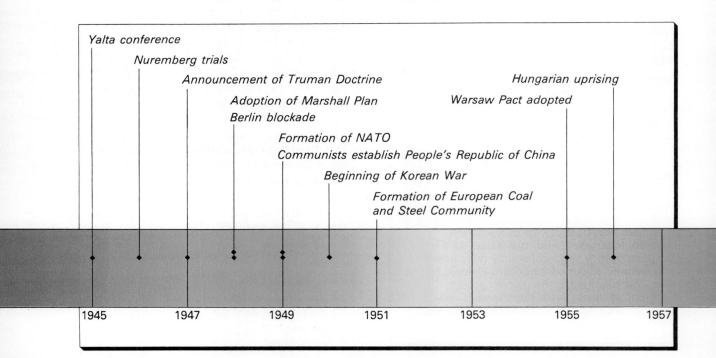

Yalta conference

Nuremberg trials

Announcement of Truman Doctrine

Hungarian uprising

Adoption of Marshall Plan

Warsaw Pact adopted

Berlin blockade

Formation of NATO

Communists establish People's Republic of China

Beginning of Korean War

Formation of European Coal and Steel Community

1945   1947   1949   1951   1953   1955   1957

h. iron curtain
i. Truman Doctrine
j. Marshall Plan
k. NATO
l. Warsaw Pact
m. West Berlin
n. Khrushchev
o. Imre Nagy
p. Mao Tse-tung
q. Chiang Kai-shek
r. Taiwan

3. (a) What two nations arose as superpowers after the war? (b) How did their goals differ?
4. (a) What two advantages over the League of Nations did the United Nations enjoy? (b) What hampered action by the UN?
5. How did the development of nuclear weapons affect the balance of power?
6. How did the division of Germany after the war lead to two separate nations?
7. (a) Explain how the USSR created a buffer zone in Eastern Europe. (b) How was Yugoslavia able to remain outside Soviet control?
8. How did each of the following reflect the policy of containment? (a) Truman Doctrine (b) NATO (c) Marshall Plan
9. (a) How did the USSR respond to the formation of NATO? (b) To West Berlin?
10. (a) How did the Allies respond to the Berlin blockade? (b) To the Hungarian revolt?
11. (a) How did the British respond to the shift away from empires after the war? (b) How did the French respond?
12. (a) How did Chinese Communists increase their power during and after the war? (b) How did the United States respond to the Communist victory in China?
13. (a) Describe the division of Korea after World War II. (b) Describe the war that arose in Korea in 1950. (c) What was the outcome of the conflict?

Thinking about History

1. Churchill originated two key phrases of the Cold War era—"iron curtain" and "balance of terror." Explain what each phrase suggests about political developments after 1945.
2. Look at the map on page 699. (a) What geographic advantages helped Yugoslavia avoid domination by the Soviets? (b) What geographic disadvantages faced other countries such as Romania, Hungary, and Czechoslovakia?

Writing and Speaking about History

1. Write two paragraphs. In the first paragraph, summarize the causes of the Cold War. In the second paragraph, list some of the results.
2. In chart form, compare Yugoslavia's challenge to Soviet domination with the Hungarian revolt of 1956. Include the advantages and disadvantages faced by each country, leaders involved, and the outcome.
3. Prepare a courtroom setting and mock trial to hear the following indictment: "Chiang Kai-shek destroyed the chance for democracy in China."

Practicing Skills

1. In the library, find a biography of one of the political leaders mentioned in this chapter. Follow the preliminary steps for writing a review of this book. (See Research Skills Handbook, page 802.)
2. Use information from Chapters 25 (page 547) and 29 (page 636) and information from this chapter to make a timeline that traces the events leading up to the formation of the People's Republic of China. Extend the timeline from 1900 to 1950 in ten-year increments.
3. According to the map on page 704, how long did it take for the Chinese to advance from the Yalu River in North Korea to Pohang in South Korea?

Investigating History

1. Investigate one of the United Nations' agencies. Why was it formed? What have been some of its achievements? What problems has it faced?
2. Report on the history of Korea. How has its location affected its history? What influence has Korea had on the rest of East Asia?

Decision Making in History

Although the United Nations sent forces to Korea in 1950, it failed to send forces to help Hungary in 1956. Evaluate these two decisions. In what ways were the situations different? In what ways were they alike? How might the actions of the UN be justified to the Hungarian people?

Cooperation and Division in Europe

Economic cooperation has brought prosperity to much of Western Europe. Here, shops line a pedestrian mall in the West German city of Aachen, which was Charlemagne's capital nearly 1,200 years ago.

1. **Western Europe moved toward cooperation.**

2. **Eastern Europe was linked to the USSR.**

In Europe's long and war-torn history, few cities have seen more of war than Strasbourg on the eastern edge of France. In the days of the Roman empire, it was an army outpost guarding the Rhine River. When the Roman empire crumbled, the Franks took over Strasbourg. During much of the Middle Ages, it was a free city in the Holy Roman Empire. Then France's Louis XIV seized the city in 1681.

Strasbourg remained part of France until the Prussian army besieged the city for seven weeks and captured it in 1870. Strasbourg and all of Alsace and Lorraine then passed into German hands for nearly 50 years. The French triumphantly retook Strasbourg after World War I, only to lose it again to Germany at the outbreak of World War II. After the war, Strasbourg became part of France once again.

Strasbourg changed hands many times because it stood near the Rhine, an important boundary in European geography. For centuries,

Europe has been a continent of boundaries. Boundaries between countries were often battle zones. Even in times of peace, borders were often heavily fortified. Travelers had to show their documents—passports, visas, or other permits—to cross from one country into another.

Arrival at a border also signaled price changes. The same item might cost the equivalent of $5.00 in Britain, $5.60 in France, and $6.00 in Italy. The differences arose because each country had different tariff laws. The paperwork involved in doing business across European frontiers was immense.

Then, in 1957, something happened to change this situation. Several countries in Western Europe formed a *Common Market* to encourage trade by eliminating tariffs among members. The Common Market countries also agreed to charge the same import duties on goods brought from other countries. This agreement made prices more uniform.

The Common Market has made a difference in Strasbourg. "For centuries," explained the city's mayor, "we in the border areas have known nothing but fear and insecurity. Now that nightmare has ended. The Common Market and the concept of Europe have made a basic and fundamental change in our lives."

Before the Common Market, the people of Strasbourg could not work in neighboring German towns even though there were plenty of jobs there. The Common Market agreement, however, allowed workers to travel freely among member countries.

By the early 1970's, some 26,000 French workers were making daily trips across the Rhine to German factories. On returning home, they could shop at supermarkets and department stores that offered a selection of food, clothing, and appliances from all over Western Europe. Before the Common Market, only about 1 percent of the goods in French department stores had been imported. Every day, about 10,000 Germans drove into Alsace, where many loaded their cars with food, which was cheaper in France than in West Germany. The Common Market was an economic success. It also fostered a spirit of international cooperation in Western Europe.

The Eastern European countries formed an economic organization of their own called Comecon. However, it was not as successful as the Common Market. The Soviet Union dominated Comecon and set industrial goals for each member. After many years of real hardship, the people of Eastern Europe began to enjoy a rising standard of living in the late 1970's and 1980's. Soviet control relaxed a little—but only to a point.

Western Europe moved toward cooperation. 1

Over the course of European history, conquerors from Charlemagne to Hitler tried unsuccessfully to unite Europe. After World War II, a French statesman began a peaceful revolution to unite Europe economically. Jean Monnet (zhahn moh-NEH) saw economic cooperation as a first step toward a politically united Europe. He prophesied in the 1950's, "Once a common market has been created, then political union will come naturally." Most European leaders, however, were more interested in the immediate practical benefits of economic cooperation than in long-range plans for political unity.

Western Europe formed a Common Market.

In 1950, Monnet and French Foreign Minister Robert Schumann suggested a tariff-free market in coal and steel. These were the key products Europe needed for rebuilding after the war. Six countries—West Germany, France, Italy, Belgium, the Netherlands, and Luxembourg—agreed to form such a market. The European Coal and Steel Community (ECSC) proved a great success. By 1960, steel production in its member nations had doubled.

In 1957, the six nations took a further step toward economic cooperation. By the Treaty of Rome, they created the European Economic Community (EEC), usually called the Common Market. Member nations pledged to remove trade barriers among themselves by gradually ending tariffs and **import quotas.** An import quota is a limit that one country sets on the amount of goods that may be brought in from another country.

709

While encouraging trade among themselves, the Common Market countries continued to trade with nonmembers as well. Goods coming into the Common Market from outside were subject to a common tariff.

The Common Market quickly became one of the most important economic units in the world. The rising prosperity of its members led other countries to apply for membership. In 1973, the Common Market expanded, admitting Great Britain, Denmark, and Ireland. The group continued to grow in the 1980's. Greece became a member in 1981, and Spain and Portugal joined in 1986.

As yet, Monnet's dream of a politically united Europe remains only a dream. In fact, the increase in membership of the Common Market has made political unity even more remote. The membership of such diverse countries as Greece and Ireland has magnified the political and social differences among members. While encouraging economic cooperation, the countries of Western Europe have maintained their unique identities, including strengths and troubles.

West Germany prospered in peace.

The most dramatic political and economic transformation in postwar Europe took place in West Germany. Within a few years of the war, the West Germans had built a stable democratic government. Soon they also enjoyed the most prosperous economy in Europe.

West Germany's political rebirth began in 1949. The German Federal Republic (or West Germany) was formed when Britain, France, and the United States combined the parts of Germany that their troops occupied (pages 695–696). The new German republic was headed by a chancellor who was responsible to a democratically elected legislature.

West Germany's first chancellor was Konrad Adenauer, a former mayor of Cologne who had been jailed several times by the Nazis. Adenauer took office in 1949 at the age of 73. The "Old Man," as he was known, dominated West German politics until he retired in 1963.

The most pressing problem that Adenauer faced was rebuilding West Germany's ruined economy. More than $3 billion of economic aid from the Marshall Plan helped to get the wheels of industry turning again. German business leaders rebuilt their bombed-out factories, installing new, efficient equipment. Germany soon had some of the most up-to-date factories in the world. By 1958, West German industry was producing nearly twice as much as the German factories of 1938, even though West Germany was only about half the size of prewar Germany. West Germany became the foremost industrial nation in Europe.

Between West and East Another major problem facing Adenauer was West Germany's place in the Cold War. "Our country," he noted, "is the point of tension between two world blocs . . . Long ago I made a great decision: we belong to the West, and not the East." Adenauer used his long term of office to steer his country into a close alliance with the United States and the countries of Western Europe. West Germany joined NATO in 1955 and the Common Market in 1957. In 1963, the West Germans signed a Treaty of Cooperation with France. Under Adenauer's leadership, West Germany rose from shame and defeat to a new position of respect.

Ostpolitik While West Germany enjoyed close ties with the West, it remained isolated from Eastern Europe and the Soviet Union for 20 years. Neither Adenauer nor his immediate successors recognized East Germany. In 1969, however, a new chancellor, Willy Brandt, decided to improve relations with the Soviet Union and Eastern Europe. His program was called *Ostpolitik* (eastern policy).

Brandt visited both Moscow and Warsaw in 1970. With the Soviet Union, he negotiated a treaty calling for normal relations between the two countries. In a similar agreement with Poland, West Germany formally accepted the loss of once-German lands. Ostpolitik led to a diplomatic breakthrough in 1973: East and West Germany formally recognized each other as sovereign states.

New problems In 1979, West Germany celebrated its thirtieth anniversary of democratic government. Chancellor Helmut Schmidt pointed not only to West Germany's democracy but also to its economic development and international prestige.

Over the next three years, however, Germany dropped into its worst economic slump since the end of World War II. Schmidt's party, the Social Democrats, had ruled since 1969. The opposition party, the Christian Democrats, charged that

Supporters of the Green party (in German, Die Grünen) paraded before the opening of the Bundestag with a giant globe to show their concern for worldwide issues such as disarmament and the environment.

government spending had grown enormously and that many Germans had grown overdependent on government programs. The Christian Democrats came to power in 1983, pledging to lower government spending and place fewer restrictions on businesses.

Defense was also an issue in German politics. Some people questioned Germany's role in NATO and its close cooperation with the United States. German protesters opposed the presence of United States troops and missiles in West Germany. Many West Germans feared being caught in a war between the Soviet Union and the United States. The new chancellor, Helmut Kohl, pledged to hold fast to NATO. He also agreed to allow the United States to place new missiles in Germany, despite strong opposition from many West Germans.

One of the leading groups to oppose the missiles was a new political party calling itself the Greens. The Greens focused on two main issues, peace and the environment. In later elections, they won a small but growing number of seats in the German legislature. Similar parties arose in other European countries as well.

As the earliest region to industrialize, Europe had long suffered from air and water pollution. Germans and other Europeans made great efforts to clean up the environment. Yet a single disaster could undo years of work. In 1986, for example, tons of pesticides were accidentally poured into the Rhine River during a fire at a Swiss chemical plant, poisoning the river from Switzerland to the Netherlands.

Great Britain faced difficulties.

Great Britain's postwar economic plight stood in sharp contrast to West Germany's vigorous growth. World War II left Britain victorious on the battlefield but with a weak economy and a restless empire.

A *welfare state* The Labour party, which came to power just as the war was ending in 1945, responded to the crisis with a sweeping program of economic and social change. Within two years, the government had nationalized railroads, coal mines, airlines, the Bank of England, and the electric and gas utilities. At the same time, new laws extended unemployment and old-age insurance and gave the public a broad program of free medical services. As a result of these far-reaching changes, Great Britain became a **welfare state**—that is, a country in which government

Margaret Thatcher (above), the leader of the Conservative or Tory party, became the first woman to serve as Britain's prime minister. Her government's spending cuts and limits on wage increases led to confrontations such as a strike by miners (left).

assumes basic responsibility for people's social and economic well-being.

During the 1950's and 1960's, government changed hands between the Labour and Conservative parties. The Conservatives accepted most of the Labour party's changes, although they did end the nationalization program.

Economic changes During the 1950's, Britain's economy slowly improved. The unemployment rate dropped. At the same time, the average worker's income nearly doubled, bringing a rise in the standard of living.

In the 1960's, however, Britain's economy again ran into difficulties, and the decline lasted well into the 1980's. Many of Britain's factories were old, and factory equipment was outdated. British business was also plagued by low **productivity**.

Productivity is a worker's hourly output of goods and services. Britain had one of the lowest levels of productivity in the industrialized world. Britain's exports fell, but the cost of its imports remained high.

Economic growth was also hampered because thousands of highly trained scientists and engineers left Great Britain for more promising opportunities in the United States, Canada, and Australia. This migration was sometimes called the "brain drain."

After a long period of Labour dominance, the Conservatives took control of Parliament in 1979. Their leader, Margaret Thatcher, became prime minister, the first woman to be elected to this office. Thatcher warned Britons that tough measures were needed to revive their economy. She reduced government spending and borrowing. She also lowered interest rates and cut taxes on higher income groups. Some nationalized businesses were reorganized as private companies.

By 1985, 3 million Britons were unemployed, and many workers suffered from reduced social services. Inflation reached 22 percent before heading down again. As a result of such hardships, riots broke out among the poor and unemployed.

There was one bright spot amid these shadows. Rich deposits of oil and natural gas had been discovered under the North Sea. They helped Britain meet its growing need for energy. By 1981, Britain had become the world's sixth largest oil-producing nation.

The breakup of the empire Britain's economic woes went hand in hand with a decline in British power around the world. One by one, the countries of the British empire sought their independence. At first, most of the former colonies kept close ties to Great Britain through the Commonwealth of Nations. Slowly, however, many withdrew from the Commonwealth.

Independence brought political and economic turmoil to some former parts of the empire. Therefore, some people from former colonies moved to Britain to start new lives. People who had been born in Britain feared that the newcomers would compete with them for jobs and housing. Some Britons turned against the newcomers because they were of different ethnic and cultural backgrounds. Outbreaks of violence took place in several cities between the new arrivals and people born in Britain.

Social changes within Britain Other changes in postwar Britain caused less conflict. There were more educational and social opportunities for people from a variety of backgrounds. There were also new roads to success for people who were not from Britain's traditional upper class. This greater openness brought an upsurge in creativity. The Beatles, who gave a new direction to popular music, came from a working-class background. So did the playwright John Osborne, the actor Michael Caine, and countless other new names of the period. For many people, these broader opportunities helped to cushion the impact of the nation's problems.

Northern Ireland One of Britain's thorniest problems was on its neighboring island. There was ongoing unrest in Northern Ireland. This region, sometimes called Ulster, had remained part of Great Britain when Ireland became an independent republic in 1921.

Most people in Northern Ireland were Protestants, but Catholics made up a large minority. Protestants dominated the government. During the late 1960's and 1970's, Catholics demanded more political power. Demonstrations and violence increased. In 1969, Britain sent soldiers to keep order, but violence continued in Northern Ireland and spread to England as well. Bombs exploded in London shopping districts and hotels. Between 1969 and 1986, more than 2,500 people were killed.

In November 1985, the prime ministers of Britain and Ireland signed an agreement that gave the Irish Republic a say in the way Northern Ireland was governed. Radical Protestants in Northern Ireland reacted with rage. Extremists on both sides continued their terrorist acts.

Betty Williams (left) and Mairead Corrigan won the Nobel Peace Prize for founding the Women's Peace Movement in Northern Ireland.

France took an independent route.

World War II dealt France a devastating blow. Many homes, factories, and towns lay in ruins at the war's end. About 600,000 French people had been killed. The survivors were bitterly divided between those who had cooperated with their German conquerors and those who had resisted. The war left wounds that would have challenged any government.

The Fourth Republic In the fall of 1946, French voters approved a new constitution. The government it set up was known as the Fourth Republic. Unfortunately, this new system had a built-in weakness. It lacked strong executive leadership. The president of the republic was mainly a ceremonial figure. Nearly all power lay in the hands of a legislative body called the National Assembly.

In the Assembly, many small political parties continually struggled for control. No one party was strong enough to form a stable government. Between 1946 and 1958, 21 different administrations tried to govern the country.

Despite such political problems, the Fourth Republic did succeed in restoring economic prosperity. By 1952, French industry was producing half again as much as it had just before the war.

Colonial wars Like Britain, France faced the breakup of its colonial empire. Unlike the British, however, the French chose to resist independence movements in several of their colonies.

France fought bitterly to hold on to its colonies in Southeast Asia. The French withdrew from Indochina only after a disastrous defeat at Dien Bien Phu in 1954.

That same year, Algerian nationalists launched a widespread rebellion against French rule. As a colony, Algeria was particularly important to France. The French government regarded Algeria as an overseas part of France itself. There were 1 million French settlers in Algeria, far more than in any other French colony. These settlers made up about 10 percent of the total population there. They enjoyed a privileged life that they were determined to protect. Moreover, the French army vowed to avenge its defeat in Indochina by destroying the Algerian rebels.

By 1958, more than 400,000 French soldiers were engaged in a bloody and seemingly endless war in Algeria. The Algerians fought as guerrillas, striking and then withdrawing before the French army could respond.

As the war lost support in France, the French government began to discuss making peace with the rebel forces. This idea infuriated the army, and in May 1958, the French army seized control of the government in Algeria.

Faced with an open revolt that might lead to a civil war, the National Assembly turned to the one man who could unite the country—General Charles de Gaulle. On June 2, 1958, the National Assembly granted De Gaulle full powers of government for six months. They asked him to end

Daily Life • *The Most Popular Sport*

The most popular sport in Europe—in fact in the world—is football, not American-style football but the game that in the United States is called soccer. People in ancient China, Japan, and Rome played games resembling soccer. However, the game as it is today got its start in England. In the Middle Ages, whole towns played soccer on Shrove Tuesday, the day before Ash Wednesday. Goals were set up at opposite ends of town, and hundreds of people might play on each side. Such games were more like full-scale brawls than organized sports. The first side to score a goal won. Then both sides tended to the wounded. The rules of the game as we know it today were drawn up in the late 1800's at British boarding schools. Today, nearly every European country has a national soccer team.

To prove his commitment to settling the Algerian issue, French president Charles de Gaulle visited Algeria soon after he took office.

the crisis and supervise the writing of a new constitution.

De Gaulle and the Fifth Republic De Gaulle was virtually a living legend. During World War II, he had led the French government-in-exile and championed resistance to the Nazis. To the French, he stood for courage, determination, and patriotism. In 1944, De Gaulle had become head of the provisional government. However, in 1946, he had resigned in protest over the weak executive branch of the new Fourth Republic.

When he returned to power in 1958, De Gaulle's first priority was to replace the Fourth Republic. Under his guidance, a new constitution was written. The Fifth Republic, as the new government was called, gave more power to the executive. In late 1958, French voters approved the new constitution and elected De Gaulle president for a seven-year term.

De Gaulle's great prestige as a military leader won back the loyalty of the French army. He brought the army revolt in Algeria to a peaceful end. Then he began peace talks with the Algerian nationalists. After lengthy negotiations, Algeria finally received its independence in 1962.

De Gaulle wanted France to play a powerful and independent role in world politics. In particular, he did not want France to seem tied to the United States. To show its independence, France developed its own atom bomb, joining the "nuclear club" of the United States, the Soviet Union, and Great Britain in 1960. France also became the first Western European country to recognize the People's Republic of China. As a further show of independence, France withdrew from NATO in 1966.

De Gaulle's nationalist policies won the support of many French people. His economic policies were also successful. France remained the leading agricultural producer of Western Europe, and its industries prospered as well.

With these many successes, De Gaulle was taken by surprise in 1968 when rioting students called for his resignation. They took over parts of Paris around the university, blocking streets with barricades and fighting with police. The number of college students had tripled in France between 1958 and 1968. Yet the universities had not expanded or changed their programs to meet the needs of a new generation. Workers joined

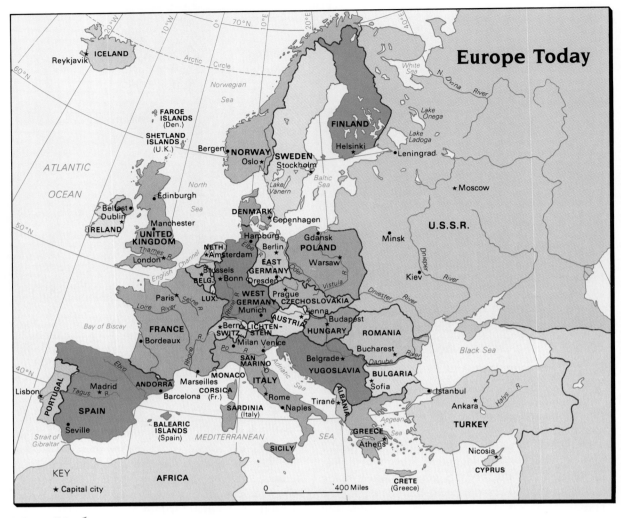

Europe Today

KEY
★ Capital city

Map Study

Compare this map with the one on page 666. How have Germany and Poland changed? (Note that the German Danzig has become the Polish Gdansk.)

the protests in widespread strikes. They wanted a shorter work week and higher wages.

The specific demands of the protesters were less important than the general mood of discontent. Many people were simply tired of leaders whose ideas came from the 1930's and 1940's.

De Gaulle won reelection after promising raises for workers and reforms in the universities. However, he soon lost an important vote in the Assembly. He resigned in 1969 and died a year later.

After De Gaulle De Gaulle's influence on France's government survived through the 1970's. The next two presidents, Georges Pompidou and

Valéry Giscard d'Estaing, followed most of the same foreign policies as De Gaulle.

In 1981, the French elected the first Socialist president of the Fifth Republic, François Mitterand. Mitterand's sympathies were with the unemployed workers, but his plans to create jobs were not as successful as he hoped. A scholar of international politics concluded that Mitterand had been elected for much the same reason that conservative leaders came to power in Britain and Germany. "It's not a question of conservatism or socialism being ascendant [on the rise]," he said. "It's that people have been voting for a change."

Dictatorships ended in Western Europe.

Parliamentary democracy was well established in the northern countries of Western Europe. However, three countries in the south—Spain, Portugal, and Greece—spent long periods under the rule of dictators. These countries were also among the least industrialized in Europe. During the 1970's, all three countries won democratic governments.

Spain Francisco Franco had been dictator of Spain since the 1930's. However, Franco kept a member of the ruling family as king for ceremonial purposes.

When Franco died in 1975, King Juan Carlos took control of the government. Juan Carlos moved Spain carefully toward democracy, mindful that the army might try to seize power if it lost confidence in him. In 1976, the king called for an election, the first free election in Spain since 1936. He allowed political parties, including the Communist party, to take part. Moderate democratic parties won the support of most voters.

In the late 1970's, Spain elected a Socialist government, alarming the army. In 1981, a group of officers tried to take over the government. However, most of the army remained loyal to Juan Carlos. Democracy in Spain had survived a major challenge.

Portugal Portugal had also been under dictatorial rule since the 1930's. In 1974, a group of army officers took control of the government. They promised a return to democracy. The elections of April 1975 brought a democratic government to power.

Greece After World War II, the king of Greece resumed his reign. Greece had close ties to the United States and Western Europe, joining NATO in 1952.

Then, in 1967, a small group of army officers seized control of the government. The king fled into exile. This army group, known as "the colonels," set up a harsh and dictatorial regime that lasted until 1974.

In that year, a long-simmering quarrel between Greece and Turkey over the island of Cyprus broke out again. The threat of war led to the collapse of Greece's military government. Civilian leaders took over and called for elections. The voters chose to have a republic.

Section Review 1

Define: (a) tariff, (b) import quota, (c) welfare state, (d) productivity, (e) guerrillas
Identify: (a) Common Market, (b) Comecon, (c) Jean Monnet, (d) Konrad Adenauer, (e) Ostpolitik, (f) Margaret Thatcher, (g) Charles de Gaulle, (h) Francisco Franco, (i) Juan Carlos
Answer:
1. Describe some of the changes that the Common Market brought to Strasbourg.
2. (a) What was the first postwar effort at economic cooperation in Europe? (b) How was the Common Market formed?
3. (a) What were Adenauer's major accomplishments? (b) How did German foreign policy change under Willy Brandt? (c) What political issues arose in West Germany in the 1980's?
4. (a) How did Britain become a welfare state? (b) What economic problems did Britain face beginning in the 1960's? (c) How did Thatcher's government try to solve them?
5. Describe the issues that led to violence in Northern Ireland.
6. (a) What serious weakness undermined France's Fourth Republic? (b) What problems did France face abroad?
7. (a) How did De Gaulle come to power? (b) What stand did he take in foreign policy?
8. In what Western European countries were new democracies established in the 1970's?

Critical Thinking
9. Why has it proved much harder to unite Europe politically than economically? Briefly suggest three reasons. Compare your ideas with those of others in your class.

Eastern Europe was linked to the USSR. 2

After World War II, the countries of Eastern Europe were dominated by the Soviet Union (page 696). The USSR did not allow them to accept aid from the Marshall Plan. However, the aid that the Soviets offered through Comecon (the Council for Mutual Economic Assistance) was

Before East Germany built the Berlin Wall in 1961, only a barbed-wire barricade separated East and West Berlin. This East German soldier was one of many people who fled to the West simply by jumping across the barricade.

far too little to repair the war's damages. Moreover, the USSR did not allow Eastern Europeans to choose their own economic priorities. Instead, the USSR insisted that they concentrate on developing industries that fit Soviet needs.

Such obstacles made Eastern Europe's economic recovery slower than Western Europe's. Gradually, however, industrialization spread more widely in Eastern Europe. East Germany and Czechoslovakia took the lead, with Albania remaining the least developed. By the 1970's, the standard of living in Eastern Europe had improved.

Most Eastern Europeans were loyal to their Communist governments. Yet there was a constant undercurrent of discontent with Soviet control. Sometimes these feelings erupted in protests.

Footnote to History

Humor can be a form of protest, and Eastern Europeans often make jokes about their economic shortages. One joke tells of an East German who sees a coffin being delivered to her neighbor's house. "Oh," she says, "I didn't realize that there was a death in your family." "There wasn't," replies her friend, "but you have to buy what you can when you can."

East Germany led in industry.

Life in East Germany, as the German Democratic Republic is known, was bleak for many years after World War II. In East Berlin, whole blocks of bombed-out buildings stood as grim reminders of the war. East German stores and markets had few consumer goods. Meat and fresh vegetables were often in short supply. Meanwhile, in nearby West Berlin, new construction had replaced the ruins, and the standard of living was steadily rising.

Faced with this contrast, more than 3 million East Germans fled to West Germany between 1949 and 1961. Most of these refugees escaped by going from East Berlin to West Berlin. Suddenly, on August 13, 1961, the Communists built a barrier between the two halves of Berlin. Known as the Berlin Wall, the barrier eventually became a 28-mile wall of concrete and barbed wire. Escape to the West became much more difficult, although a few East Berliners still try it each year.

In the meantime, life in East Germany has improved. Its economy is the strongest in Eastern Europe and continues to expand. East German leaders have begun to make some economic contacts with the West.

Like parts of Western Europe, East Germans have paid a price for their industrial growth. East Germany suffers from the highest levels of water, air, and ground pollution of any European country. Chemicals such as DDT that have been banned in the United States and Western Europe are still used in Eastern Europe. East German citizens have little information on pollution levels because the government-controlled press carries few reports on environmental issues.

Reforms were stamped out in Czechoslovakia.

In 1968, students staged protests in many parts of Europe, both East and West. In Czechoslovakia, a new Communist leader, Alexander Dubcek (DOOB-chek), responded with a program of reforms.

He loosened controls on writings and discussions. Dubcek said he wanted to create "socialism with a human face" but without giving up the basic ideas of communism. The time of Dubcek's reforms is often called "Prague Spring," when new ideas bloomed in Czechoslovakia's capital.

Dubcek's new policies alarmed the Soviets. They called on the other Warsaw Pact countries to take action with them against Czechoslovakia. On August 20, armed forces from the USSR, Poland, East Germany, Hungary, and Bulgaria invaded Czechoslovakia over four frontiers. Dubcek remained in power briefly but was soon replaced by a leader more in tune with the USSR.

Since its Prague Spring, Czechoslovakia has had one of the strictest governments in Eastern Europe. Its leaders even resisted orders from Moscow to reform in 1986.

Voice from Our Time • A *Czechoslovak Protest*

During the occupation of Czechoslovakia in 1968, a group of Czechoslovakian scientists and writers living in Austria issued this *Manifesto against Aggression.*

... In the fateful hours of the occupation of ... Czechoslovakia, we consider it necessary to proclaim certain basic convictions which we hold in common as intellectuals, as Czechs and Slovaks, as citizens of the Czechoslovak Socialist Republic.

1. We believe that as intellectuals we have one basic duty to our nation: to speak the truth ...

2. We trust the strength of ideas, and we distrust power ... We have no weapons but words and ideas, yet we are convinced that no force of oppression can withstand the thrust of thought. Today more than ever, we realize that an attack on ideas is an attack on man himself.

3. People may be deprived of all their civil rights, but they cannot be deprived of their freedom to think. Totalitarian dictatorships may rob people of everything except their will to resist. Tanks can occupy territory but not the minds of men ...

7. The violent acts of recent days have demonstrated again that totalitarian dictatorship represents the greatest danger to mankind. It is a matter of indifference under what ideology the dictators send their tanks into peaceful countries and for what ostensible motives soldiers shoot unarmed citizens.

1. Why was this document not issued in Czechoslovakia?
2. What do the authors say is the basic duty of intellectuals to their country?
3. Why do the authors claim that dictatorships cannot totally defeat a people?

Polish workers formed Solidarity.

Poles rebelled in 1956 to protest harsh working conditions and plans to form collective farms. At that time, the Soviets installed Wladyslaw Gomulka (goh-MOOL-kuh) as head of Poland's government. He stopped the move to collectivization, gave more freedom to the Roman Catholic Church, and loosened government control of industry. Discontent among the Poles quieted but did not disappear.

Over the years, Gomulka's regime became more restrictive. Poles resented his government because it had been forced on them by the Soviets. His economic policies did not bring prosperity to Poland. Food prices were high, and meat was scarce. One Polish consumer complained,

> Products appear and disappear, reappear ... And then sometimes they just disappear for good. It used to be that our stores were stocked with many different kinds of cheese. I haven't seen cheese in six months.

The Poles continued to hope for change. Their national spirit soared in 1979 when the Roman Catholic Church selected a Pole, John Paul II,

as the new pope. In June 1979, when the popular pope visited his homeland, millions of Poles turned out to greet him and receive his blessing.

National pride soon led the Poles to defy Soviet dominance again. When the Polish Communist government announced another increase in meat prices, protests broke out in several cities.

Workers at the shipyard in Gdansk (guh-DAHNSK) took the lead. They declared a strike in August 1980. The workers shut themselves inside the shipyard and refused to work until the government recognized their union, called Solidarity. Both the union and the strike were illegal under Poland's Communist regime. Nonetheless, Solidarity and its leader, Lech Walesa (vah-WEHN-suh), received the fervent support of millions of Poles.

Eventually, the government agreed to the most important of Walesa's demands. Solidarity won the right to exist as an independent trade union, and Polish workers won the right to strike. These were astonishing concessions for an Eastern European government.

For several months in 1981, Solidarity's workers moved aggressively to win even more reforms. Watching and waiting from abroad, the Western democracies feared that Soviet tanks might crush

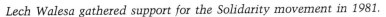

Lech Walesa gathered support for the Solidarity movement in 1981.

the union. Instead, the Soviets urged Polish authorities themselves to crack down on the protesters.

In December 1981, the Polish government declared **martial law**. Under martial law, military authorities rule the civilian population as if the country were in a state of war. Army tanks rolled into Poland's major cities. Walesa and other Solidarity leaders were arrested. The union was declared illegal. Many of the reforms were reversed.

Solidarity continued in secret as a strong opponent to the Soviet system. In 1983, Walesa was released from prison. That same year, he won the Nobel Peace Prize. In August 1986, some other imprisoned leaders were released. However, their travels and meetings were closely watched. Walesa expressed worries about his future in Poland.

Some countries weakened ties with the Soviet Union.

Although all the countries of Eastern Europe have Communist governments, not all are equally close in their ties to the Soviet Union. Three countries—Albania, Romania, and Yugoslavia—have taken different paths away from Soviet dominance.

Yugoslavia The leader of Yugoslavia's Communist government after World War II was Josip Broz, known as Tito (page 696). Although he was a Communist, Tito was also a Yugoslavian patriot. He did not intend to allow the Soviets to dominate his country. In 1948, he broke with the USSR.

Yugoslavia has used its independent position to build economic ties with both Communist and non-Communist countries. It trades with Western Europe and the United States. Tourists from many countries visit its picturesque coast.

When Tito died in 1980, many observers expected a crisis in Yugoslavia. No other leader had the personal prestige and power that seemed necessary to unite the country and overcome rivalries among its ethnic groups. However, national leaders set up a system of sharing power that has seemed to satisfy all groups.

Albania Albania took a very different path in breaking with the Soviet Union. Instead of strengthening ties with Western Europe, Albania looked to China as an ally. In 1960, when a split developed between the USSR and China, Albania sided with the Chinese. In return, the Albanians received economic aid from China as well as political support against the Soviets.

Relations between China and Albania later cooled. Today, Albania has no close links with any other country. Economically, it remains the least developed country in Europe.

Romania Romania shares a long border with the Soviet Union. Thus, it lacks the geographic advantages that helped Yugoslavia take an independent stand. Nonetheless, the Romanians have taken some careful steps away from Soviet dominance.

When China and the Soviet Union quarreled, Romania refused to take either side. Instead, Romanian leaders said that no country should tell another what to do within its own borders. Despite its stand against the USSR, however, Romania allows its own citizens few personal freedoms.

Section Review 2

Define: martial law
Identify: (a) Berlin Wall, (b) Alexander Dubcek, (c) Prague Spring, (d) Wladyslaw Gomulka, (e) Solidarity, (f) Lech Walesa, (g) Tito
Answer:
1. (a) How were conditions in East Germany different from those in West Germany in the 1950's? (b) How has East Germany changed since 1961?
2. (a) What changes did Dubcek try to make in Czechoslovakia? (b) How did the Soviets react?
3. (a) What factors led to protests in Poland in 1980? (b) What gains did the Poles achieve? (c) How did the period of reform in Poland come to an end?
4. (a) What political development helped Albania take an independent stand? (b) What other Eastern European countries have weakened their ties to the USSR?

Critical Thinking
5. How have the following issues contributed to uneasy relations between Eastern Europe and the Soviet Union? (a) economic policies (b) nationalism

Summary

1. Western Europe moved toward cooperation. After World War II, many countries in Western Europe joined the Common Market, which achieved economic unity by abolishing tariffs and import quotas. Postwar West Germany became a prosperous industrialized nation with a democratic form of government and strong ties to the West. Postwar Britain, on the other hand, suffered major economic problems, which the Labour government tried to solve with a massive welfare program. In the 1960's, Britain faced a renewed economic crisis that has continued into the 1980's. Like Britain, France also faced political and economic problems after the war. Wartime hero Charles de Gaulle restored stability. In Spain and Portugal, prewar dictatorships came to an end, as did repressive military rule in Greece.

2. Eastern Europe was linked to the USSR. Eastern Europe, which was dominated by the Soviet Union, experienced slow economic growth after the war. Recently, however, East Germany has industrialized and made economic progress. In 1968, Dubcek's reforms in Czechoslovakia led to tightening of Soviet controls. In Poland, a severe economic crisis led to workers' strikes and the formation of a labor union called Solidarity, which has been banned by Poland's Communist government. Albania, Yugoslavia, and Romania have weakened their ties with the Soviet Union.

Reviewing the Facts

1. Define the following terms:
   a. import quota
   b. welfare state
   c. productivity
   d. martial law
2. Explain the importance of each of the following names, places, or terms:
   a. Common Market
   b. Adenauer
   c. Comecon
   d. Ostpolitik
   e. Brandt
   f. Schmidt
   g. Thatcher
   h. Northern Ireland
   i. De Gaulle
   j. Mitterand
   k. Juan Carlos
   l. Berlin Wall
   m. Dubcek
   n. Solidarity

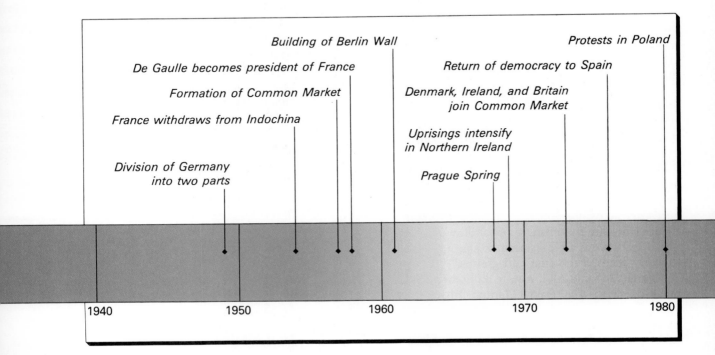

Building of Berlin Wall

De Gaulle becomes president of France

Formation of Common Market

France withdraws from Indochina

Division of Germany into two parts

Protests in Poland

Return of democracy to Spain

Denmark, Ireland, and Britain join Common Market

Uprisings intensify in Northern Ireland

Prague Spring

1940   1950   1960   1970   1980

3. (a) What step did Monnet take in 1950 to bring about economic unity in Europe? (b) How was the Common Market formed in 1957?
4. (a) Describe two problems that West Germany's Adenauer faced after the war. (b) How did he deal with each problem? (c) What change in foreign policy did Brandt make?
5. (a) How did the Labour government address Britain's economic problems after the war? (b) How did Thatcher address the country's economic problems in the late 1970's?
6. Describe the conflict in Northern Ireland between Catholics and Protestants.
7. (a) Describe the political and economic problems that France's Fourth Republic faced after the war. (b) What steps did De Gaulle take to strengthen France?
8. How did dictatorships come to an end in each of the following countries? (a) Spain (b) Portugal (c) Greece
9. (a) What economic problems did East Germany face after the war? (b) How has life improved there in recent years?
10. (a) What changes did Dubcek make in Czechoslovakia in the 1960's? (b) What happened as a result of those changes?
11. (a) What crisis threatened Poland in the 1980's? (b) What course of action did Polish workers take? (c) How did the government respond?
12. Describe the path that each of the following countries has taken in order to break away from Soviet dominance. (a) Yugoslavia (b) Albania (c) Romania

Thinking about History

1. Contrast Britain's welfare state with the concept of laissez-faire that prevailed in nineteenth-century Britain (page 486).
2. Like Monnet, Metternich (page 491) and Napoleon (page 461) also saw the advantages of a united Europe. What steps have been taken in recent years toward this goal? How does this approach differ from Napoleon's? From Metternich's?

Writing and Speaking about History

1. Write a feature story that focuses on Charles de Gaulle as either a war hero or president of the Fifth Republic.

2. Write a letter to the editor that either supports or opposes one of the following:
   a. the granting of independence to Great Britain's colonies after World War II
   b. the granting of independence to France's colonies after World War II
3. As a German adult living in East Germany or West Germany in 1950, what will you say to a group of young people regarding the changes you have seen in Germany since 1930?

Practicing Skills

1. Describe the status of Poland on each of the following maps:
   a. Europe in 1715 (page 420)
   b. Europe in 1815 (page 493)
   c. Europe before World War I (page 585)
   d. Europe after World War I (page 598)
   e. Postwar Europe (page 699)
   For about how many years did Poland as an independent nation disappear from the map of Europe?
2. Review the timeline on page 722. (a) About how many years passed between the division of Germany and the building of the Berlin Wall? (b) Which event on the timeline refers to a temporary loosening of controls in Czechoslovakia?

Investigating History

1. On page 713, the text talks about a popular singing group known as the Beatles. Investigate the impact of the Beatles.
2. Find out which governments in Western Europe are still headed by a king or a queen. What role does the monarch play in the government?
3. Each of the following people has won a Nobel Peace Prize since 1970: (a) Lech Walesa, (b) Mairead Corrigan, (c) Betty Williams, and (d) Willy Brandt. Find out about one of these people. What did he or she do to win this honor?

Decision Making in History

Adenauer and Brandt each had different policies regarding West Germany's acceptance of East Germany. Evaluate their policies within the context of the times. Do you agree or disagree with their viewpoints. If you agree, why? If you disagree, what advice would you offer?

Change and Conflict in Asia

At Expo 70 in Japan, pedestrians strolled amid futuristic architecture while a gondola car (far left) offered others an aerial view of the fair.

1. Japan became an industrial giant.

2. China changed under a Communist government.

3. India and Pakistan became independent.

4. Southeast Asia faced revolution and war.

For the people of Japan, March 14, 1970, was a long-awaited day of national pride. That day, Emperor Hirohito opened Expo 70 on the outskirts of the city of Osaka. It was the first World's Fair ever held in Asia.

For the emperor, the occasion marked a triumph in a reign that had seen both triumphs and tragedies. He had been his country's ruler for almost half a century, since 1926. He had reigned during Japan's expansion in East Asia in the 1930's, its early military successes during World War II, and its final defeat.

Now Japan had risen again to take its place among the world's richest and most powerful nations. This time, its power was based on economic, not military, strength. As Expo 70 showed the world,

Japan had become an industrial powerhouse. Out of the ashes of defeat, the Japanese had created an economic miracle. The results of this miracle were on display at Expo 70. During the six months of the exhibition, more than 50 million visitors marveled at its sights.

At the steel pavilion, 1,300 loudspeakers stunned visitors with a "Song of Steel." In 1970, Japan produced more steel than any other country except the United States and the USSR—despite having almost no iron ore deposits. In steel and many other industries, Japan had become the new "workshop of the world," as Britain had once been. The Japanese imported raw materials and exported quality finished goods.

The millions of Japanese who visited Expo 70 showed at least as much interest in what the rest of the world had to offer as in their own exhibits. Perhaps the favorite display of all was the United States' pavilion. It included not only some moon rocks brought back to Earth by the *Apollo* astronauts in 1969 but also Babe Ruth's baseball uniform.

The Japanese had achieved a workable blend between their own culture and the ways of the Western nations. Economically, Japan seemed poised to challenge the two great superpowers. One American futurologist (a specialist who estimates future developments) believed that this dream would become a reality. "It would not be surprising," he said, "if the twenty-first century turned out to be the Japanese century."

In this chapter we will see how Japan and China changed after World War II. We will also see how a third major Asian nation, India, faced independence. Finally, we will examine events in Southeast Asia, where almost constant warfare posed threats not only to that region but also to the whole world.

Japan became an industrial giant. 1

In August 1945, Hirohito became the first Japanese emperor in centuries to speak publicly to his subjects. Atom bombs had just destroyed the cities of Hiroshima and Nagasaki. The whole country was on the brink of ruin. Over the radio,

Hirohito asked all loyal Japanese to "bear the unbearable"—defeat. On September 2, his country formally surrendered to the Allies.

The once prosperous Japanese economy was in ruins. Moreover, Japan itself was soon occupied by foreign forces. Most Japanese felt that their world had been turned upside down.

The United States occupied Japan.

From 1945 to 1952, about 30,000 American soldiers and civilians were based in Japan. General Douglas MacArthur, hero of the war in the Pacific, was in charge. MacArthur ran his army with an iron hand, and during the occupation he ran Japan the same way. The Japanese, devastated by the war, accepted the occupation as the price of defeat. In fact, many were pleased that the changes MacArthur ordered were not as harsh as those that had been forced on the losing countries after World War I.

The leaders of the United States had three goals for Japan. First, they planned to *demilitarize* the country (that is, to disband its armed forces and remove its military equipment). Second, they wanted to give Japan a stable, democratic government. Third, they hoped to revive the Japanese economy and make Japan a vital part of the capitalist world. All three efforts succeeded.

Demilitarization Japan lost not only the war but also any chance to make war in the future. The Japanese armed forces were disbanded except for a small police force. All arms production was halted. Japan's new constitution, adopted in 1947, included a special clause. "The Japanese people," it stated, "forever renounce war as a sovereign right of the nation, or use of force as a means of settling international disputes."

Democracy Not surprisingly, the 1947 Japanese constitution made Japan much more democratic than before. All Japanese aged 20 and over had the right to vote. For the first time, Japanese women could take part in elections. Under the new constitution, the emperor became a constitutional monarch like the ruler of Britain. Real political power rested in the hands of a Diet, as the Japanese parliament was called. The majority of the Diet chose a prime minister, who became the country's head of government.

Land reform One of the most sweeping economic changes made under the occupation was

Many Japanese companies offer daily exercise classes to help employees stay fit and alert.

throughout the world. During the 1950's and 1960's, the Japanese economy expanded at the almost unheard-of rate of 10 percent per year.

Between 1950 and 1970, Japan's **gross national product** (GNP) soared from $10 billion to $200 billion. The gross national product is the total value of goods and services produced by a country in a year. By the time of Expo 70, Japan had roared past Britain, France, and West Germany to become the world's third leading industrial nation. In 1984, Japan's GNP was $1.235 trillion!

What accounts for the extraordinary success of Japanese industry and commerce? There are at least four key factors.

Effective use of imported technology In the Meiji Era (page 548), the Japanese began adopting the technology of Europe and the United States. After the war, they continued to borrow the best of Western technology. For example, the Sony Corporation bought the rights to manufacture transistors from an American company. Within 20 years, Sony had built a business empire based on the transistor. Sony sold radios, stereo equipment, and television sets worldwide.

A *productive labor force* Company loyalty was a key ingredient in Japan's economic success. In factories and offices across Japan, employees began their workday with songs such as this one:

For building a new Japan,
Let's put our strength and minds together,
Sending our goods to the people of the world,
Endlessly and continuously
Like water from a fountain.
Grow, industry, grow, grow!
Harmony and Sincerity!
Matsushita Electric!

Because workers felt a part of their company, they took pride in their work. Japanese companies set high standards for their products, and the workers tried hard to meet those standards.

Job security was one key to this strong loyalty. Japan's largest companies often guaranteed their most important workers lifetime jobs. Strikes were rare, and absentee rates were among the lowest in the world. With their jobs secure, Japanese workers also proved willing to change with the times. They eagerly adopted new technology.

High rates of saving and investment People in Japan saved a large part of their wages. In 1970, for example, Japanese workers saved 19.4 percent

land reform. Before World War II, only 30 percent of all Japanese farmers actually owned the land they worked. The others worked as tenants for large landowners. After 1945, the government took over all large estates and sold the land on easy terms to the farmers who had been renting it.

Independence By 1950, Japan was both peaceful and democratic. Gradually, partly because of Japan's support for the United States during the Korean War (pages 703–705), the former enemies became allies. In September 1951, the United States and 47 other nations signed a peace treaty with Japan, officially restoring Japanese independence. Six months later, the last occupation troops withdrew.

Japan's economy boomed.

During and after the occupation, the Japanese economy recovered from the war. By 1953, Japanese industrial production had climbed back to prewar levels.

All this progress, however, simply set the stage for Japan's economic miracle. Japan developed one new industry after another. Soon Japanese steel, ships, motorcycles, cars, bicycles, cameras, and even pianos edged out their competition of their yearly incomes. (By contrast, American workers saved less than 6 percent.) Japanese banks used these deposits to lend businesses money for new equipment and projects.

The role of government The Japanese government has actively supported business since the 1950's. The government does not control industries, which are owned privately. However, the success of Japanese businesses is a major government goal. To encourage investments, the government sets few regulations and keeps taxes on business low.

Economic growth brought problems.

While the Japanese made great strides in business and industry, they neglected some social problems. Japan rapidly became a crowded, polluted, urban nation.

Urban growth Between 1950 and 1970, the percentage of the Japanese population living in rural areas dropped from 60 percent to just 18 percent. Millions of people moved into already overcrowded cities. Other people found that the sprawling cities spread out to absorb their homes and farms.

By 1970, more than half of Japan's 100 million people lived in the Tokaido Corridor. This is a narrow, 350-mile-long strip that stretches along the Pacific coast of the island of Honshu from Tokyo to Kobe. It includes Japan's six largest cities.

Pollution Thousands of factories and millions of automobiles give the Tokaido Corridor worse smog levels than any other urban area in the world. Sometimes Japanese schoolchildren have to wear face masks simply to play outdoors.

Water pollution is also a severe problem. In the 1960's, a number of people in the city of Minamata died of mercury poisoning. The poison came from the fish that make up a large part of the Japanese diet. Fish in Minamata Bay had absorbed high levels of mercury from chemical pollution. Since that time, Japan's government and industry have made great strides in reducing pollution.

Japanese society is changing.

While industrialism has brought some problems to Japan, it has not led to widespread class tensions. Japan has little poverty. However, economic growth has had other effects on society.

A homogeneous society Japan is a homogeneous (hoh-muh-JEE-nee-uhs) society. That is, most of its people belong to the same ethnic group. Japan rarely accepts immigrants. Some 600,000 Koreans live and work in Japan, but they cannot become citizens and are poorly treated by the Japanese. Another group that suffers from prejudice are called *burakumin*. These people are descended from outcasts of the 1800's and earlier, under the Tokugawa shoguns.

Today, Japan's leading economic position is bringing more and more foreigners to Tokyo and other Japanese cities. There is pressure for more openness in Japanese society.

Changing roles for women New opportunities are opening for Japanese women. Besides winning

Daily Life • *Packing the Subway*

Tokyo has more than 11 million residents. The city's streets are jammed with a chaotic mass of automobiles, trucks, buses, taxis, motorcycles, and bicycles. Getting to and from work is an ordeal, and many workers spend several hours each day commuting. Many residents ride Tokyo's modern subway system. The subways too are crowded. In fact, in order to pack each car with its maximum number of riders, the subway hires teams of professional pushers who shove passengers inside the doors. In 1973, during a gasoline shortage, thousands of new riders turned to the subways. The crowds were so great that 2,000 emergency pushers were hired.

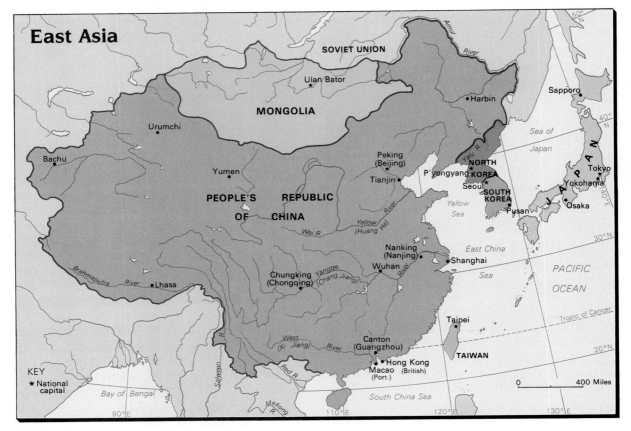

East Asia

KEY
★ National capital

Map Study

What are the two ways of spelling the name of China's capital city? Of what country is Taipei the capital?

the right to vote in 1947, women also won the right to own property in their own name. Until recently, it was the custom for Japanese women to marry and spend full time raising their children. In the 1970's, however, women began to enter the work force in larger numbers. By 1980, more than half the women of Japan held jobs. However, most high-ranking jobs were still closed to women.

Despite the incredible speed of change in postwar Japan, many traditions have remained. In cobblestoned side streets away from traffic jams and shopping districts, delicate wooden teahouses still serve customers in the age-old tea ceremony. Buddhist monks still chant prayers beneath the softly curving roofs of ancient temples. And while thousands of Japanese fans attend baseball games, thousands also flock to *sumo* wrestling matches and martial arts programs.

Section Review 1

Define: (a) demilitarize, (b) gross national product, (c) homogeneous society
Identify: (a) Hirohito, (b) Douglas MacArthur, (c) Diet
Answer:
1. Why was Expo 70 significant for Japan?
2. (a) What goals did the United States set for Japan in 1945? (b) How was each achieved?
3. What factors help to account for Japan's "economic miracle"?
4. Briefly describe some of the problems rapid growth has brought to Japan.
5. How have the changes since 1945 affected the lives of women in Japan?

Critical Thinking
6. Some historians have called the 1800's the British century and the 1900's the American

century. The futurologist quoted on page 725 said that the next century might be the Japanese century. What factors make a century "belong" to any given power? To what extent can such a statement be accurate?

China changed under a Communist government. 2

The triumph of the Red Army and Mao's Communist party in 1949 ended nearly half a century of revolution, civil war, and chaos for China. Their victory also marked the beginning of a new era in Chinese history. Over the next 20 years, Mao and his colleagues strove to change China into both a Communist society and a modern industrial nation. To reach these goals, China's leaders experimented with a number of different—and often conflicting—policies.

Communist leaders made reforms.

In its early years of power, the Chinese Communist party was quite small. Its 4.5 million members were only about 1 percent of China's whole population. However, party members were dedicated and highly disciplined.

Government organization As a first step after taking power in 1949, Communist leaders set out to solidify their hold on the country. They set up new governments for all of China's provinces, cities, towns, and villages.

The Chinese Communists closely modeled their new system on that of the Soviet Union. As the Soviets had done, the Chinese set up two parallel organizations, the Communist party and the national government. There was considerable overlap between the two. This system remains in force today. The party sets policy, and the government carries it out. The party is the more powerful institution, and government officials do nothing without the party's approval.

Until 1959, Mao Tse-tung was both head of state and chairman of the Communist party's Central Committee. His rule was authoritarian, but it also provided stability after years of turmoil.

Land reform The new government's most pressing task was to improve China's economy.

Half a century of wars and general chaos had left the country in ruins. Inflation was so bad that Chinese money was almost worthless.

Mao was determined to reshape the economy along socialist lines. Party leaders made economic plans for the whole country. At first, they followed the model of the Soviet Union but tried to adapt it to Chinese needs. In later years, they tried other systems.

In a country where more than 80 percent of the population still lived in rural areas, farming was the obvious place to start. Most farmers owned no land. Just 10 percent of the rural population owned 70 percent of the country's farmland. The poorer farmers rented land from these wealthy landlords. One of the new government's first acts was an Agrarian Reform Law (1950). Under this law, the government took the holdings of landlords and divided them among the peasants.

The process of redividing the land often turned bloody. Peasants had long suffered at the hands of the landlords, and now the poor took the law into their own hands. Many landlords and others accused of exploiting the poor were stoned to death in town squares or condemned to forced labor. Altogether, about 2 million people were killed during the first 5 years of Communist control.

Mao never intended that peasant families keep the farmland as private property. He had a vision of a new rural China based on peasants owning and working the land in groups, or collectively.

Between 1953 and 1957, the government tried to increase food production by combining many small farms into larger, more efficient ones. These large collective farms were usually several thousand acres in size. Several hundred peasant families lived on each of them. The state controlled the use of equipment, labor, and the land itself, but families still worked their own small plots.

Industry The Communists were also concerned with industry and business. They wanted to set up centralized planning for the whole economy. Gradually, the government took over, or nationalized, all private industries and businesses.

In 1953, Mao launched a Soviet-style Five-Year Plan, which set production targets for industry and stressed rapid growth. The plan was a striking success. By 1957, steel production had quadrupled, and the output of coal, cement, and electricity had doubled.

The Great Leap Forward The success of the first Five-Year Plan encouraged Chinese leaders to plan an even more ambitious program. Mao thought that China could make "great leaps" toward both a truly socialist society and a stronger economy. He hoped to harness the energy of millions of peasants and workers to make great progress.

Early in 1958, Mao proclaimed what he called "the Great Leap Forward." The plan called for still larger collective farms called communes. These communes were expected to increase efficiency. By pooling labor and land, peasants on communes could buy equipment and set up local industries.

By the end of 1958, some 26,000 of these self-sufficient *people's communes* had been set up. The average commune was more than 15,000 acres in size and had a work force of more than 25,000 people. Each commune had small factories as well as farmlands. Local groups even tried to produce their own iron and steel with backyard blast furnaces.

All workers on a commune earned nearly the same amount of money, no matter how much or how little work they did. Workers ate in communal dining rooms, slept in communal dormitories, and raised their children in communal nurseries. The peasants hated living this way and eventually gave up most of the communal arrangements.

During the Great Leap Forward, China tried to make steel with small blast furnaces such as these.

Cities too formed collective groups. In urban areas, each neighborhood formed a street association. These street associations assigned people to jobs and housing, ran health programs, and enforced laws.

The Great Leap Forward was a failure. Poor planning slowed industrial growth. The local blast furnaces, for example, could not produce usable steel. Productivity dropped. Crops failed in 1958, in 1959, and again in 1960, causing famine all across China. Vast numbers of people starved to death. Faced with such disaster, the government officially gave up the Great Leap Forward in 1961.

China and the USSR split.

Between 1949 and 1960, the USSR was the only nation to send aid to China. The Soviets sent workers and money to help the Chinese meet their goals. The leaders of the USSR assumed that the Chinese would follow the Soviet model of communism. Mao, however, wanted China to develop its own form of communism. His experiments in policy angered the Soviets.

In 1960, the growing rift between the countries reached a climax. The Soviet government suddenly called home all its workers and advisers in China. In some cases, they took with them the blueprints for factories that were only half-built. All Soviet aid stopped.

After 1960, relations between the two countries remained tense. China and the USSR share the longest border in the world, and troops from the two countries began to threaten and harass each other along that border. In 1969, fighting broke out in Manchuria. Although peace was quickly restored, the conflict showed how wide the split had become.

A Cultural Revolution swept China.

After the failure of the Great Leap Forward and the split with the USSR, Mao took a less active part in leadership for a while. Other leaders tried to modernize China in less drastic ways.

The new leaders modified the communal system. For example, farm families were allowed to live in their own homes and to keep or sell crops they grew on their small private plots. Factory workers could earn wage increases, bonuses, and promotions if they exceeded production goals. China also modernized its army. In 1964, China exploded its first atom bomb, a dramatic sign of modern technology.

While such policies brought steady progress, Mao disapproved of them. He believed that rewards such as higher wages weakened workers' revolutionary spirit. Such policies, he claimed, also created a new privileged class, undercutting the Communist goal of social equality.

Though Mao was now more than 70 years old, he still held the powerful position of chairman of the Communist party. He was still extremely popular as the hero of the revolution throughout China. Mao decided to use his standing and go directly to the people. He called on them to restore the purity of the revolution.

In 1966, Mao launched a "great revolution to establish proletarian culture." He appealed directly to the country's youth, calling on them "to learn revolution by making revolution." Mao told students to destroy all "feudal" elements in Chinese culture—that is, all the remaining traces of the old upper classes. Young people left their classrooms by the thousands to form revolutionary units called Red Guards.

Over the next 18 months, the Cultural Revolution swept through every part of Chinese society. The Red Guards shut down colleges and schools. They lashed out at professors, government officials, factory managers, even their own parents—anyone who seemed to have special privileges. Some of the people accused by the Red Guards were beaten to death. Others died in jail. Scientists and doctors were sent to the countryside to do farm work. Meanwhile, other young fanatics destroyed Buddhist temples, books, and other reminders of pre-1949 China.

The result of this outbreak was that the Chinese economy headed for collapse. Factories were shut down, and farm production stopped almost completely in some places.

By 1967, even Mao had to admit that matters had gone too far. He tried to use the army to restore order. Soldiers disbanded Red Guard units and reopened schools and colleges. Zhou Enlai*

*In 1958, the Chinese adopted a new method of spelling Chinese words in the roman alphabet. Under the new system, called Pinyin, *Mao Tse-tung* became *Mao Zedong. Peking* became *Beijing.* Because many newspapers in the United States have now adopted the new form, Pinyin spellings are used hereafter for the names of contemporary leaders.

Red Guards devotedly studied Mao's sayings, collected in a small red book. (Masks were protection from the dusty winds of the winter monsoon.)

(joh ehn-lye), one of the founders of the Chinese Communist party and a veteran of the Long March, played a key role in these events. During the early 1970's, Zhou worked to restore order in China. However, turmoil continued until 1976. The effect on the country and on the Communist party was devastating.

China made broader world contacts.

During the Cultural Revolution, China's borders were closed to most foreigners, and China played little part in world affairs. Zhou Enlai ended this isolationist policy.

One major part of Zhou's foreign policy after 1969 was better relations with the United States. The United States and China had had almost no contact since the Korean War. Throughout the 1950's and 1960's, the Chinese had called the United States their most dangerous enemy. However, as relations between China and the Soviet Union grew colder, Zhou saw the advantage of closer ties with the United States. The United States was also eager to take advantage of the split between China and the USSR.

The first American group to pay an official visit to China was a table-tennis team in 1971. Its tour was such a success that it was called "ping-pong diplomacy." In the same year, the United States allowed the People's Republic of China to join the United Nations. (Since 1949, the United States had used its veto in the Security Council to keep out the Communist government.)

Chinese-American relations warmed greatly in February 1972, when President Richard Nixon paid a visit to China. Politically, of course, the two countries remained far apart. However, they were now at least on speaking terms. Some trade agreements also came from the official visit.

A new leader emerged after Mao.

In 1976, both Mao and Zhou Enlai died. Deng Xiaoping (dung shah-oh-ping) became the most powerful figure in the new government. A veteran of the Long March, Deng had been driven from power twice by party radicals. Deng planned to quadruple Chinese output in industry and agriculture by the year 2000. To meet this goal, he looked to contacts with Japan, the United States, and Europe. He negotiated new trade agreements with the industrial countries, took loans from them, and sent students to study their technology.

These changes affected everyday life in China. Scientists who had been sent to plow fields during the Cultural Revolution were urged to do research again. Deng also allowed a limited amount of private enterprise to spur production. For example, peasants could sell any food they produced over their quota in newly opened free markets.

In January 1980, China adopted a new constitution and some new laws. Their purpose, in part, was to prevent anything like the Cultural Revolution from happening again. In 1981, four leaders of the Cultural Revolution, including Mao's widow, Jiang Qing, were brought to trial. Called the "Gang of Four," they were accused of "defaming, torturing, and killing thousands of opponents in an attempt to usurp party power and state leadership."

During the 1980's, China's relations with non-Communist countries continued to improve,

Voice from Our Time · Mao on Education

Mao delivered these remarks on education to party leaders in February 1964. He charged that China's system of formal education placed too much emphasis on simple memorization and repetition. Many Chinese educators and students shared his views.

The current examination methods contain many surprises, unusual questions, and difficult problems ... I do not approve of them ... I suggest taking some sample examination problems and having them published. Let the students study and do them with open books ... In examinations, students should be allowed to whisper to each other and to hire others to take the examinations for them. If your answer is right, I copy yours. Copying is good too. In the past, whispering and hiring of examinees was done on the sly. Now let them be open. When I cannot do what you have done, then let me copy ... Teachers giving lectures should allow the students to fall asleep ... Sleeping may help one to recover from fatigue. Students should be given the choice of not listening to monotonous lectures ... We should not read too many books. We must read Marxist books but not too many of them ... Reading too many books will lead the readers to take opposing views ...

1. (a) How does Mao think examinations should be conducted? (b) If Mao's system were adopted, what grade would all students receive?
2. (a) How would Mao's system keep all students equal? (b) Why would Mao approve of that result?
3. (a) What does Mao think about reading? (b) What reason does he give for not reading many books?
4. What is Mao's opinion of school?

while those with the USSR remained tense. The border between the USSR and China remains heavily guarded by both countries.

Life in China has improved.

Despite the political turmoil in China since the 1940's, some aspects of Chinese life have greatly improved. Overall, people in both the countryside and the cities are better fed and better housed than they were before 1949.

Farm communes offer services that peasants never had before, such as hospitals, schools, banks, and traveling entertainers. Most rural families own their own homes, although they do not own the land on which the house stands.

Most city families live in apartment buildings. An average family of four shares two rooms. Because cities are crowded and jobs there are hard to find, the government keeps tight control over who can move to the cities.

Schools Education has improved throughout China. Before 1949, there were almost no schools in rural areas. Now most rural children are supposed to finish grade school, although not all children do. Some rural young people also finish middle school, but few go on to high school.

In the cities, nearly all children complete grade school. Most students finish middle school and at least one year of high school. The top students attend special schools. Competition is keen for admittance to college. Only 3 or 4 percent of China's 18-year-olds go to college.

The changing role of women Perhaps the most dramatic changes since 1949 have been in the lives of women. This story by an older Chinese woman vividly describes the harsh lives of some women in the early 1900's. "When I was 22, I was sold. He [my husband] came one day and fetched me and my daughter and took us to a slave dealer called Yang. My husband sold us."

Footnote to History

A very popular result of President Nixon's visit to China was the arrival of two special immigrants to the National Zoological Park in Washington, D.C. China sent the United States two giant pandas, Ling-ling and Hsing-hsing, in exchange for two rare musk oxen. The pandas soon became the zoo's most popular residents.

The Communist government radically changed the lives of Chinese women. Women were officially guaranteed full equality under the law. In 1950, the New Marriage Law ended traditional practices such as arranged marriages, the sale of women and children, child brides, and polygamy (the practice of having more than one wife). The law also gave widows the right to remarry.

Since 1950, Chinese women have made rapid progress. Over half the nation's doctors, factory workers, and communal workers now are women. By the mid-1980's, female managers were operating several of China's largest textile mills. Nonetheless, full equality had not yet been achieved. For example, men still dominate the Communist party and run the educational system.

Section Review 2

Identify: (a) Mao Tse-Tung, (b) Five-Year Plan, (c) Great Leap Forward, (d) Cultural Revolution, (e) Zhou Enlai, (f) Pinyin, (g) Deng Xiaoping
Answer:
1. (a) How is the Communist party related to the government in China? (b) What powerful positions did Mao hold?
2. (a) Why was land reform an important issue for China? (b) How did the ownership of land change under communism?
3. (a) What were the results of Mao's Five-Year Plan? (b) Of the Great Leap Forward?
4. (a) Give examples of the relationship between the USSR and China from 1949 to 1959. (b) How did the relationship change after 1960?
5. (a) Why did Mao call for a Cultural Revolution? (b) Briefly describe what followed.
6. How did China's policy toward the United States change around 1970?
7. What changes did Deng Xiaoping encourage?
8. How has life in China changed since 1949 in each of the following areas? (a) rural life and farming (b) education (c) the role of women

Critical Thinking
9. Chinese Communist leaders have sought both economic modernization and total social equality. (a) Which of Mao's policies stressed economic progress? (b) Which stressed total social equality? (c) Which goal seemed more important to Deng Xiaoping? Explain.

India and Pakistan became independent. 3

The people of India had been working since the early 1900's to win their independence from Great Britain (pages 622–627). Under their great leader, Mohandas Gandhi, many Indians had waged a peaceful struggle of marches, boycotts, and noncooperation against their British rulers. At the end of World War II, British public opinion turned against imperialism. It was clear that India would soon be free. It was not clear, however, whether independence could be achieved without bloodshed among Indians themselves.

Independence brought partition.

In February 1947, British Prime Minister Clement Attlee announced that Britain would turn over the government of India "into responsible Indian hands" no later than June 1948.

Attlee later explained why he had set this deadline:

I had come to the conclusion that it was useless to try to get agreement by discussion between leaders of rival [Indian] communities. Unless these men were faced with the urgency of a time limit, there would always be procrastination.

The Indian leaders who had been negotiating with Attlee included Jawaharlal Nehru of the Congress party and Muhammad Ali Jinnah of the Muslim League. As you have read in Chapter 29, India's Hindus and Muslims were bitterly divided. The Muslim League stated that it would never accept Indian independence if it meant rule by the Hindu-dominated Congress party. Jinnah said, "The only thing the Muslim has in common with the Hindu is his slavery to the British."

The Muslim League demanded *partition*, the division of British India into two countries, one Hindu and one Muslim. Muslims planned for an independent country to be called Pakistan.

At first, the British disagreed, insisting that a single Indian government take over when they withdrew. However, Hindus and Muslims were already clashing with each other. In August 1946, four days of rioting in Calcutta left more than 5,000 people dead and more than 15,000 hurt.

British leaders decided that partition was the best way to limit bloodshed. A boundary commission hastily drew the borders of the two new countries. Pakistan consisted of two Muslim regions 1,000 miles apart. One lay to the northeast of India, the other to the northwest. In the words of one historian, Pakistan "hung like elephant's ears from the body of India."

The new borders made little economic sense. East Pakistan included many jute-growing regions, for example. The jute mills were in Calcutta, which remained in India. Moreover, the boundaries left millions of Hindus in Pakistan and millions of Muslims in India.

On August 15, 1947, India and Pakistan became independent. Nehru became prime minister of India, and Jinnah became prime minister of Pakistan.

As Gandhi and others had feared, a bloodbath followed. Millions of people struggled to cross from one side of the India-Pakistan border to the other. Trainloads of refugees were massacred on both sides of the border. In all, more than 500,000 Hindus and Muslims died.

Gandhi himself fell victim to the violence of Hindu against Hindu. In January 1948, he was shot to death by a young Hindu who opposed Gandhi's efforts to win equal treatment for Harijans (untouchables). His death deprived India of its most honored leader.

Nehru sought to modernize India.

For the first 17 years after independence, India had one prime minister—Jawaharlal Nehru, who had been one of Gandhi's most devoted followers. Educated in Britain, Nehru described himself as a "mixture of East and West, out of place everywhere, at home nowhere." Nehru was a brilliant and skillful politician who won great popularity among all groups in India. He emphasized democracy, unity, and economic modernization for India.

In foreign affairs, Nehru took a strong stand against colonialism. He tried to reach an agreement with the Portuguese to end their control of Goa, the last colony on the Indian subcontinent. When negotiations failed, he drove them out by force. He also tried to follow a policy of nonalignment—that is, taking neither side in the Cold War.

Economic difficulties The most difficult problems facing India were economic. India remained primarily an agricultural country. Nearly 80 percent of the population lived in some 550,000 villages. Most Indians also remained poor, with a **per capita income** of $150 per year in 1980. (A country's per capita income is its gross national product divided by the population.)

Nehru and later leaders strove to modernize the country's economy. India began to adopt modern farming techniques in the 1960's. New strains of seed, for example, greatly increased crop yields. Likewise, India's industries grew slowly but steadily.

Despite great progress, major obstacles remained. One problem was the unequal distribution of land. More than 35 percent of India's farmland was owned by the wealthiest 5 percent of the rural population, while half the people owned no land at all.

Another obstacle was India's constantly growing population. The government set up birth control clinics around the country. Posters urged couples to have no more than two children. Such programs, however, had little success. Large families were a tradition in India, and poor couples counted on children for care in their old age. By 1970, India was home to about 525 million people—50 percent more than in 1947. That number was growing by 40,000 *every day*! "It's like a flood," one government official declared. "Every year we need an additional 2.5 million tons of grain—just to stay even."

Conflict with China and Pakistan Trouble on its borders distracted India from its domestic issues. India and China share a 1500-mile border. In 1962, the two countries went to war briefly over a disputed area. China's forces surprised and overpowered those of India and occupied most of the land in question.

India's relations with neighboring Pakistan were almost always hostile. Indian leaders thought that partition had mutilated their country. The Pakistanis, for their part, were dismayed that their country did not include Kashmir, a large province in northern India where 75 percent of the people were Muslims. Clashes in Kashmir and other spots along the border led to full-scale war in 1965. After three weeks of fighting, India and Pakistan signed a truce that established an uneasy peace.

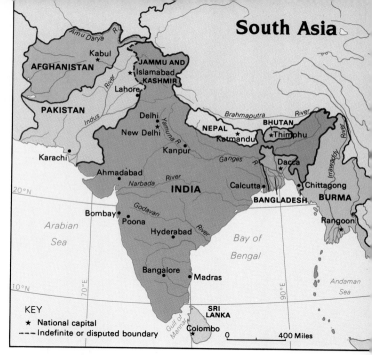

Map Study
What nations have a border disagreement? Which South Asian nations are landlocked?

Indira Gandhi governed India.

Nehru's death in 1964 left the Congress party with no leader strong enough to hold together its many factions. Then in 1966, Nehru's daughter Indira Gandhi (no relation to the Mahatma) was chosen prime minister. Over the next ten years, she proved a forceful leader in her own right.

Under Indira Gandhi, India made economic progress. Both industrial and agricultural production grew during the 1970's. India became one of the world's top ten industrial nations. However, only some of this progress trickled down to the poor. Meanwhile, India's birthrate dropped slightly but remained among the highest in the world. In 1983, India had a population of about 746 million—nearly 15 percent of the world's population.

Like Nehru, Indira Gandhi often pointed out that her country was the world's largest democracy. India also sought the status of a world power by exploding its first nuclear device in 1974.

Indira Gandhi was a controversial figure. In 1975, she was found guilty of illegal campaign practices, but she refused to step down as prime minister. Instead, she declared a state of emergency, arrested political opponents, and clamped

Indira Gandhi governed India for nearly 20 years.

down on the press. In 1977, her party lost the parliamentary elections, and she was ousted from office. However, she was reelected in 1980.

Fighting among religious and ethnic groups continued in some parts of India. Muslims and Hindus battled in Assam, a northeastern province. Sikh separatists turned to violence as they demanded their own independent state in northern India. In October 1984, Indira Gandhi was assassinated by two of her own bodyguards, who were Sikhs. In the following riots, Hindus killed more than 2,500 Sikhs. Meanwhile, Indira Gandhi's son Rajiv Gandhi was elected the new prime minister.

Pakistan became two countries.

In the years after independence, Pakistan faced the same kinds of social and political issues as India. It also faced two problems all its own.

One problem was a lack of strong leadership. Muhammad Ali Jinnah, the Muslim leader most responsible for the creation of Pakistan, died in 1948. No strong leader took his place.

Pakistan's second problem was geographic. East and West Pakistan were separated by more than 1,000 miles of Indian territory. Except that their populations were mainly Muslim, the two regions had very little in common. The western section of the country had a variety of ethnic groups, mainly Punjabi. Almost all people in East Pakistan belonged to the Bengali ethnic group.

East Pakistan was poorer and more densely populated than the west. Most of Pakistan's industry was in the western part. West Pakistan also controlled the army. After 1958, a military dictatorship centered in the west ruled the entire country.

Not surprisingly, resentment built in East Pakistan. "We have never been anything but a colony of the west," one Bengali leader asserted in 1970. Widespread rioting broke out in East Pakistan in 1970. The Pakistani army struck ruthlessly at the rebels. During the grim summer of 1971, about half a million Bengalis were killed. Millions of others fled to India, which supported the Bengali rebels.

In December, full-scale war broke out between Pakistan and India. The Indian army, larger and better equipped, smashed the Pakistani forces. Pakistan formally surrendered on December 16, 1971. Soon after, East Pakistan became an independent nation called Bangladesh, meaning "land of the Bengalis."

Bangladesh was the world's eighth most populous nation and also the world's poorest. In 1975, Bangladesh became a military dictatorship.

Section Review 3

Define: (a) partition (b) per capita income, (c) nonalignment
Identify: (a) Jawaharlal Nehru, (b) Kashmir, (c) Indira Gandhi, (d) Bangladesh
Answer:
1. (a) What were Nehru's goals within India? (b) In relations with other countries?
2. (a) What economic progress did India make under Nehru and Indira Gandhi? (b) What problems hindered progress?
3. (a) Why was there hostility between India and Pakistan? (b) What was the result?
4. (a) What did East and West Pakistan have in common? (b) What issues divided them?
5. How did East Pakistan become the independent country of Bangladesh?

Critical Thinking
6. Review the definition of *nationalism* in the glossary. Do you think nationalism is a strong force in South Asia? Explain your answer.

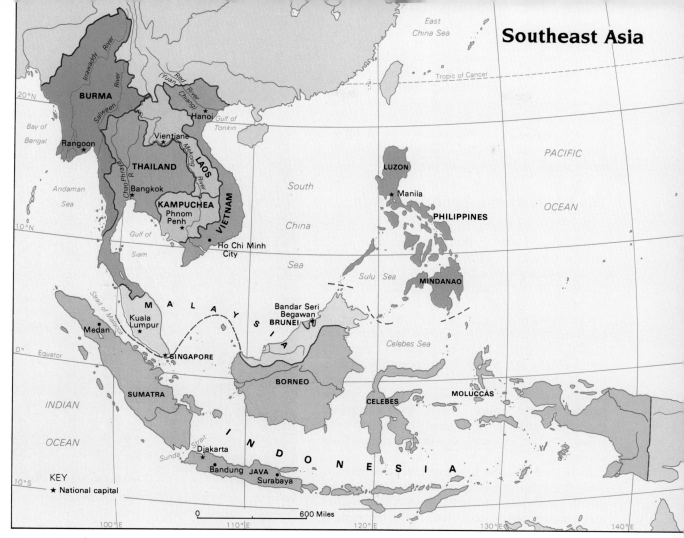

BURMA

Irawaddy River

Salween River

20°N

Bay of
Bengal

Rangoon ★

Andaman
Sea

10°N

Gulf of
Siam

Hanoi ★

Vientiane ★

Red River
(Yuan Chiang)

THAILAND

Bangkok ★

Chao Phraya R

Mekong River

LAOS

KAMPUCHEA

Phnom
Penh ★

VIETNAM

Ho Chi Minh
City ●

Gulf of
Tonkin

M   A   L   A   Y   S   I   A

Kuala
Lumpur ★

Medan ●

0°   Equator

★ SINGAPORE

SUMATRA

Strait of Malacca

Bandar Seri
Begawan
BRUNEI ●

BORNEO

INDIAN

OCEAN

10°S

KEY
★ National capital

Sunda Strait

Djakarta ★

Bandung ●

JAVA

Surabaya ●

0   600 Miles

100°E   110°E   120°E   130°E   140°E

East
China Sea

Tropic of Cancer

LUZON

Manila ★

PHILIPPINES

PACIFIC

OCEAN

South

China

Sea

Sulu Sea

MINDANAO

Celebes Sea

CELEBES

MOLUCCAS

I   N   D   O   N   E   S   I   A

Map Study
Name Southeast Asia's island nations. Which of them is the largest in area?

Southeast Asia faced revolution and war.   4

During the early 1900's, foreign powers controlled all of Southeast Asia except Siam (now Thailand). The British ruled Burma and Malaya. The United States controlled the Philippines. The Dutch held the East Indies. France ruled Indochina, a region including today's Laos, Kampuchea, and Vietnam. During the early part of World War II, Japanese forces conquered much of Southeast Asia.

The defeat of Japan in 1945 created a power vacuum in Southeast Asia. The European colonial nations hoped to regain control, but the peoples of Southeast Asia had other ideas. Within each region, competing groups struggled for power. The result was a tragic wave of wars and revolutions in many parts of Southeast Asia.

Former colonies became independent.

The independence struggle that followed World War II was most quickly settled in the former Dutch colony of the East Indies. By 1949, that colony had become the independent country of Indonesia. A Dutch-trained engineer, Sukarno, led the Indonesian nationalist movement. He became Indonesia's first president but later became a dictator. Sukarno held power until 1968. Since then, army leaders have dominated the government.

737

Among the British colonies, Burma became fully independent in 1948 and Malaya in 1957. In 1963, Malaya joined with other former British colonies in the area, including Singapore, to form a new independent nation known as Malaysia. Singapore, with its largely Chinese population, broke away in 1965 as a separate state.

The Philippines sought democracy.

Before World War II began, the United States had promised the Philippines complete independence by 1946. That promise was kept. The Japanese occupation ended in 1945, and the new Republic of the Philippines officially began on July 4, 1946.

The major problem in the Philippines, despite huge amounts of aid from the United States, has been the economy. Most Filipinos are extremely poor, while a few people have enormous wealth. Rebels known as Huks, with Communist support, appealed to poor farmers eking out a living on tiny plots. The Huks tried to seize control in the 1940's and 1950's. Fighting continued until 1954, but the government finally stamped out the rebellion.

In 1965, Ferdinand E. Marcos was elected president. He promised reforms and programs to improve education and agriculture. The United States supported Marcos as a strong opponent of communism. Despite his promises, however, problems continued to plague the Philippines. Marcos's government was charged with fraud and corruption. During the late 1960's and early 1970's, Communists renewed their guerrilla war. Conflicts between Christians and Muslims also erupted. In 1973, Marcos declared martial law. He also proclaimed a new constitution, giving himself an unlimited term of office.

Charges of misrule mounted against Marcos in the 1980's. In August 1983, Benigno Aquino (uh-KEE-noh), a popular leader who opposed Marcos, was assassinated as he got off an airplane bringing him back from exile in the United States. Most people suspected that Marcos and the military were responsible for the killing.

On November 3, 1985, Marcos gave in to pressure from the United States to hold elections. Corazón Aquino, widow of Benigno Aquino, ran for president against Marcos. She waged a forceful campaign and seemed the definite winner. Yet,

Filipinos overwhelmingly supported Corazón Aquino when she became president in 1986.

after an obviously rigged election, the National Assembly declared Marcos president. Aquino resisted and held her own inauguration on February 25, 1986. Finally, when two important army leaders pledged their support to Aquino, Marcos and his family fled the country.

The French were driven out of Indochina.

In French Indochina, independence was not won easily, nor did it bring peace. More than 40 years after World War II, war still haunts Laos, Kampuchea, and Vietnam.

The richest part of French Indochina was Vietnam, the narrow coastal region that runs for nearly 1,000 miles beside the South China Sea. Vietnam had iron and coal mines in the north, rubber plantations and rice fields in the south. This wealth, combined with French national pride, gave France strong reasons for wanting to hold the area after World War II.

However, a strong nationalist movement had grown up in Vietnam. Its foremost leader was Ho Chi Minh, a Communist guerrilla who had helped drive out the Japanese. Ho and other nationalists formed the Vietminh (Independence) League. The Vietminh was strongest in northern Vietnam.

War in Indochina, 1946–1954 When France tried to reassert its control over Vietnam, both nationalists and Communists fought the French armies. The French held most of the major cities, but French forces were nearly powerless in the countryside, where the Vietminh had the support of most peasants. The Vietminh used hit-and-run tactics to bottle up the French in the cities and a few strongholds. Ho called this way of fighting "the war of the flea."

Meanwhile, the Indochina War was becoming increasingly unpopular with French voters. Many French people felt that Vietnam was not worth the lives and money it was costing. "For every ten men you kill," Ho Chi Minh had warned the French, "we will kill one of yours. And it is you who will have to give up in the end."

Ho proved to be right. In 1954, the French suffered a major defeat at Dien Bien Phu. After that loss, France agreed to a settlement. An international peace conference was scheduled to discuss the future of Indochina in general and of Vietnam in particular.

The role of the United States The United States government had sent arms and money to the French to help them defeat the Communists. The United States government saw Ho's victory as a threat to the rest of Asia. John Foster Dulles, American secretary of state, explained the government's viewpoint:

> If Indochina falls, Thailand and Burma would be in extreme danger; Malaya, Singapore, and even Indonesia would become vulnerable to the Communist power drive.

This belief that the fall of one Southeast Asian nation to communism would lead to the fall of its neighbors was known as the *domino theory.* This idea became a cornerstone of United States foreign policy.

A divided Vietnam At the peace conference in Geneva, the United States tried to limit the Communist influence to the northern part of Vietnam. According to the peace terms, Vietnam was divided along the seventeenth parallel of latitude. North of that line, Ho Chi Minh's forces governed. To the south, the United States and France set up a separate government under Ngo Dinh Diem (noh dihn d'yem).

Unfortunately, Diem was neither popular nor capable. He did little to appeal to the people, unlike Ho Chi Minh, who began a program of land redistribution in the north. Instead, Diem ruled as a dictator.

Communist guerrillas, called Viet Cong, began to gain strength in the south. Some were trained soldiers from North Vietnam. Others were South Vietnamese who opposed Diem. Gradually, the Viet Cong won control of large areas of the countryside.

In 1963, a group of South Vietnamese generals— with the quiet backing of the United States— planned a coup. Meeting almost no resistance, they overthrew and killed Diem. The new leaders, however, had no more popular support than Diem. A Communist takeover seemed sure to follow.

The United States entered the Vietnam War.

Faced with this dilemma, the United States decided to step into the conflict directly. Americans had been serving as advisers to the South Vietnamese since the late 1950's. Now the number of those advisers steadily increased. The United States also sent more and more planes, tanks, and other military equipment to South Vietnam.

In August 1964, United States President Lyndon Johnson told Congress that North Vietnamese patrol boats had attacked two American destroyers in the Tonkin Gulf. As a result, Congress gave the president authority to send American troops into Vietnam. By late 1965, more than 185,000 United States soldiers were on the ground in South Vietnam. Meanwhile, American planes bombed North Vietnam.

Escalation The war escalated—that is, the number of troops and the amount of fighting increased step by step. By 1968, more than half a million American soldiers had been thrown into the battle in Vietnam.

The United States had the best-equipped, most advanced army in the world. However, the Americans faced two major difficulties. First, they were not fighting an open battle but a guerrilla war. Second, the Viet Cong had great popular support, while the South Vietnamese government became steadily more unpopular.

Unable to win a clear-cut victory on the ground, the United States turned more and more to air power. Trying to destroy enemy hideouts, American forces bombed millions of acres of farmland and forest. The bombing brought widespread misery to the peasants, turning them even more against the South Vietnamese government. Yet the American goal was to win support for that government. "It was as if we were trying to build a house with a bulldozer and wrecking crane," one American official later said.

The close of the war During the late 1960's, the war became increasingly unpopular in the United States. By 1973, a large share of Americans opposed the war. Bowing to intense pressure, President Richard Nixon began withdrawing United States troops from Vietnam. However, he also authorized secret bombing in neighboring Cambodia to wipe out Viet Cong supply routes and hiding places.

Nixon hoped to strengthen the South Vietnamese government so that it could stand on its own. The United States sent South Vietnam the best equipment money could buy. However, equipment was not enough to save the corrupt and unpopular government in the south.

The North Vietnamese struck with a massive attack in the spring of 1975. Within six weeks, Communist troops took control of Saigon. All Vietnam came under a Communist government. Hanoi, once the capital of North Vietnam, became the capital of the whole country. Saigon, former capital of the south, was renamed Ho Chi Minh City in honor of the Communist leader.

Fighting continued elsewhere in Southeast Asia.

The Vietnam War also involved Laos and Cambodia. Although Cambodia's leader Norodom Sihanouk (SEE-uh-nook) tried to remain neutral, the Viet Cong used Cambodia for supply routes

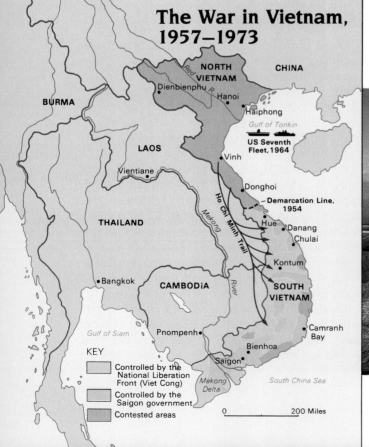

The War in Vietnam, 1957–1973

KEY

Controlled by the National Liberation Front (Viet Cong)

Controlled by the Saigon government

Contested areas

0   200 Miles

Map Study

By what route did North Vietnam move supplies and soldiers into South Vietnam? Through what countries did they pass? What information from the map and the photograph helps to explain why American troops relied heavily on helicopters?

War turned millions of Southeast Asians into homeless refugees.

and bases. In 1970, the United States helped to replace Sihanouk with an anti-Communist leader, Lon Nol. This changeover triggered a civil war that lasted for five years. In 1975, Cambodian Communists, known as the Khmer Rouge, won control of the country. They renamed it Kampuchea. Laos also fell to local Communists, the Pathet Lao, in 1975.

In all three Indochinese states—Vietnam, Laos, and Kampuchea—the new governments launched wholesale attacks against their non-Communist enemies. Many who had worked with the Americans were rooted out. Thousands were killed, and millions were sent to harsh "reeducation" camps. Refugees fled their homelands in small, overcrowded vessels. These "boat people" hoped to reach a safe harbor or to be rescued at sea. Thousands drowned. Other refugees fled to camps in neighboring Thailand.

Kampuchea suffered the most. In 1976, the Khmer Rouge leader, Pol Pot, sealed the country's borders and launched a reign of terror. More than a million Kampucheans—nearly 20 percent of the country's people—died of starvation or in mass executions.

Meanwhile, the Khmer Rouge and the Vietnamese Communists became bitter enemies. In 1977, a Vietnamese army invaded Kampuchea and overthrew the Khmer Rouge, although the guerrillas are still fighting.

Section Review 4

Identify: (a) Sukarno, (b) Ferdinand Marcos, (c) Corazón Aquino, (d) Ho Chi Minh, (e) Ngo Dinh Diem, (f) Gulf of Tonkin incident, (g) Norodom Sihanouk, (h) Pol Pot
Answer:
1. (a) What new nation replaced the former Dutch colony of the East Indies? (b) What British colonies in Southeast Asia became independent?
2. (a) How did the Philippines gain independence? (b) What problems did the country face?
3. (a) How did Marcos win control of the government? (b) How did he lose power?
4. How did Vietnam come to be divided into two warring parts?
5. (a) What part did the United States play in Vietnam before 1954? (b) Between 1954 and 1964? (c) From 1964 to 1973?
6. (a) How did the Khmer Rouge come to power in Cambodia? (b) What did they do?

Critical Thinking
7. Many countries in Southeast Asia have suffered guerrilla warfare. (a) How can guerrillas successfully wage war against larger, better-equipped government armies? (b) What underlying problems can make a government vulnerable to such a war?

741

Summary

1. Japan became an industrial giant. Under United States occupation, Japan adopted a democratic form of government, pledged itself to disarmament, and instituted land reforms. Industrialization and postwar prosperity produced an economic miracle in the country. At the same time, rapid economic growth led to severe social problems, including pollution and crowding. Changing roles for women and an influx of foreigners has affected Japanese society.

2. China changed under a Communist government. In 1949, the Chinese Communist party reorganized the government, instituted massive land reforms, and centralized planning of industry and business. In 1958, Mao announced the Great Leap Forward, which established communes. Slowed industrialization led Mao to launch a purge called the Cultural Revolution that nearly destroyed China. Since 1976, China's leader, Deng Xiaoping, has encouraged both contacts with the West and some private enterprise.

3. India and Pakistan faced new problems. In 1947, division between Muslims and Hindus led to the creation of two separate nations, India and Pakistan. Progress in India has been hampered by unequal distribution of land, a rapidly expanding population, conflicts with China and Pakistan, and conflicts between Hindus and Muslims. Muslim Pakistan became two nations in 1971, Pakistan and Bangladesh.

4. Southeast Asia faced revolution and war. Indonesia, Burma, Malaya, and the Philippines gained independence after World War II. The government of Ferdinand Marcos in the Philippines lasted for 20 years before he was ousted for misrule in 1985. Vietnam was divided into North and South Vietnam after Communist forces ousted the French in 1954. Although the United States aided South Vietnam, the South Vietnamese could not defeat the Viet Cong, who had wide popular support. The United States withdrew from the war in 1973. Soon after, the Viet Cong united the country and supported Communist takeovers in Kampuchea and Laos.

Reviewing the Facts

1. Define the following terms:
   a. gross national product
   b. per capita income
2. Explain the importance of each of the following names, places, or terms:
   a. MacArthur
   b. demilitarize
   c. Diet

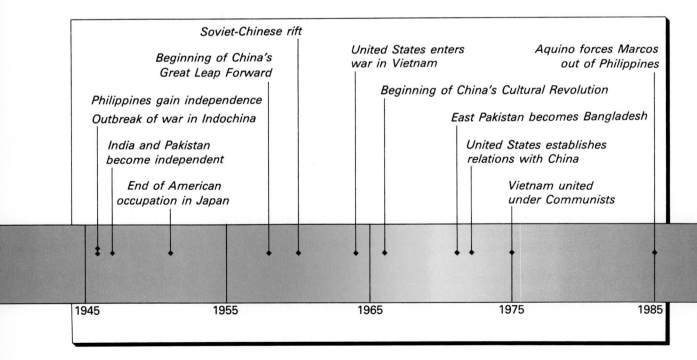

Soviet-Chinese rift

Beginning of China's Great Leap Forward

United States enters war in Vietnam

Aquino forces Marcos out of Philippines

Philippines gain independence
Outbreak of war in Indochina

Beginning of China's Cultural Revolution

East Pakistan becomes Bangladesh

India and Pakistan become independent

United States establishes relations with China

End of American occupation in Japan

Vietnam united under Communists

1945   1955   1965   1975   1985

d. homogeneous society
e. Mao Tse-tung
f. Great Leap Forward
g. Cultural Revolution
h. Zhou Enlai
i. Deng Xiaoping
j. Nehru
k. Indira Gandhi
l. Rajiv Gandhi
m. Bangladesh
n. Sukarno
o. Marcos
p. Aquino
q. Ho Chi Minh
r. Viet Cong
s. Ngo Dinh Diem
t. Gulf of Tonkin
u. Khmer Rouge
v. Pathet Lao

3. (a) Describe Japan's economic miracle. (b) What problems did it cause?
4. (a) What political changes did the Communists make in China in 1949? (b) Economic changes? (c) Industrial changes?
5. (a) What changes in city and country life were instituted by the Great Leap Forward? (b) What was Mao's goal in the Cultural Revolution? (c) What was its outcome?
6. (a) How did China move further away from the Soviet Union? (b) Closer to the United States?
7. (a) What economic progress has India made since independence? (b) Describe the obstacles that have hindered growth.
8. How did East Pakistan become Bangladesh?
9. (a) What political change took place in the Philippines in 1946? (b) In 1973? (c) In 1985?
10. (a) Why did the United States enter the conflict in Vietnam? (b) Why did the United States begin withdrawing its forces in 1973? (c) What is the status of Vietnam today?
11. How did communism spread from Viet Nam to neighboring Kampuchea and Laos?

Thinking about History

1. Compare the Korean conflict with the war in Vietnam. How did the end of World War II contribute to division in each country? What role did the United States play in each war? How were the outcomes similar? How were they different?

2. Although Communists in China and the Soviet Union set out initially to totally abolish private enterprise, both countries have somewhat modified their attitudes toward private ownership in recent years. Why?

Writing and Speaking about History

1. Prepare an appropriate book cover for a book on postwar Japan, postwar China, or postwar India. On the front cover, include the title, author's name, and a drawing or photograph related to the theme. Write a 250-word dust jacket that summarizes the major features of the book. (See Research Skills Handbook, page 802.)
2. Conduct a meet-the-press interview in 1952 with Nehru of India, Mao Tse-tung of China, and the prime minister of Japan. Focus your questions on the strengths and weaknesses of each country and the future of Asia.

Practicing Skills

1. How does the map on page 735 help explain the statement, "India was once much larger than it is today"?
2. How does the map on page 728 help explain why Korea has been both a bridge and a battleground for much of its history?

Investigating History

1. Make a survey of ads in magazines and newspapers to determine Japan's status as a major industrial nation. What products are among its exports? How have Japanese imports affected business in the United States?
2. Report on current events in one of the countries discussed in this chapter. Include information on the economy, political changes, new trends, and ways of life.
3. Add to the data base file on colonies that you began on page 555.

Decision Making in History

Evaluate United States relations with Ferdinand Marcos during his years in power. What governed American attitudes toward his government in 1965? What caused a change in those attitudes? What recommendations would you make for American policy toward the Philippines today?

Nationalism in Africa and the Middle East

Ghana's independence ceremony in 1957 was attended by representatives from many countries. Britain's Duchess of Kent and Ghana's new president, Kwame Nkrumah, were at the forefront of the ceremony. The white wigs worn by some officials are a tradition from British courtrooms.

1. **Africans resumed the fight for independence.**

2. **African nations took diverse paths.**

3. **Nationalism sparked Mideast conflicts.**

Church bells pealed joyously through the night air in the African city of Accra. It was midnight, March 6, 1957. The bells marked the end of the British colony of Gold Coast and the birth of the new nation of Ghana, named in honor of the ninth-century African kingdom. As the red, green, and yellow flag of Ghana was hoisted atop the parliament building in Accra, 50,000 people cheered. The new country's president, Kwame Nkrumah (KWAHM-ee en-KROO-muh), wept for joy.

The next day, a week-long celebration began. Accra was host to 2,000 foreign visitors. Among them was a Soviet delegation that presented Ghana with a jet plane and several automobiles. Vice President Richard Nixon headed the United States' delegation. With him were UN representative Ralph Bunche and the Reverend Martin Luther King, Jr. They gave the new country a library of technical books.

The most honored guest at the state dinner celebrating independence was the Duchess of Kent, representing Elizabeth II, queen of Britain. Wearing a white chiffon gown and a jeweled tiara, the duchess danced with President Nkrumah, who wore a prisoner's robe. The robe was a reminder that six years earlier, Nkrumah had been in a British jail for demanding independence.

Ghana was one of the first African nations to gain independence. Its self-rule was an important symbol throughout Africa. It brought hope to other groups under colonial rule.

In this chapter, we shall see how the nations of Africa and the Middle East won their independence and struggled to maintain it. We shall also see how the growth of nationalism led to conflicts throughout Africa and the Middle East.

Africans resumed the fight for independence. 1

Between World War I and World War II, an educated, westernized African middle class appeared in cities throughout the continent. These Africans studied at schools run by missionaries and colonial governments. Often such middle-class Africans went abroad to Europe or the United States to attend college. From this educated elite came the first nationalist leaders who worked to end colonial rule.

After World War II, these leaders gained new support. About 200,000 Africans fought alongside British and French soldiers in North Africa, Asia, and Europe. Those soldiers helped free France, Burma, and Ethiopia. They returned home eager for their own freedom.

The Atlantic Charter raised hopes.

For many Africans, the most important event of the war took place in August 1941. British Prime Minister Winston Churchill and United States President Franklin Roosevelt met secretly on a warship off the coast of Canada. The two leaders agreed on their goals for the postwar world. This agreement was called the Atlantic Charter.

From an African point of view, the key clause in the charter dealt with self-government.

[The United States and Britain] respect the right of all peoples to choose the form of government under which they will live; and they wish to see sovereign rights and self-government restored to those who have been forcibly deprived of them.

Africans saw those words as a promise by the leading Allies to end colonial rule throughout the world. As soon as the war was over in 1945, Africans demanded that the Allies keep their word.

African hopes were soon frustrated, however. European countries with colonies in Africa—Britain, France, Belgium, Spain, and Portugal—did not immediately disband their empires. Winston Churchill went so far as to say that the Atlantic Charter had applied only to European countries under Nazi rule.

Disillusioned, Africans set out to win their freedom for themselves. The returning soldiers joined with older leaders who had long been working for independence. They now resumed that struggle.

Africans reacted to the new nationalism.

The struggle for freedom took different forms in different parts of Africa. Nationalist leaders drew on their own African traditions and also on the experiences of other people who had fought for freedom.

The Islamic reaction The first African countries to win their freedom were in North Africa. That region has a strong Islamic tradition and close ties to the Middle East. When the Ottoman empire collapsed after World War I, Muslims in the Middle East began to build their own nations. Muslim nationalists in North Africa watched enviously. Their struggle for independence drew on the Islamic idea of the jihad or holy war.

During World War II, the Allies drove the Germans and Italians out of North Africa. The result was freedom for the former Italian colony of Libya. Ethiopia, conquered by Italy, also regained its independence.

Soon after the war, a new and more nationalistic government also came to power in Egypt. Egypt had been a British protectorate in the late 1800's, and the British had recognized its independence in 1922. Egypt's king continued to cooperate closely with Britain—too closely, some Egyptians thought. In 1952, a group of young army officers overthrew the king and declared a republic. Their leader, Colonel Gamal Abdel Nasser, became its president. In 1956, Nasser took over the Suez Canal, breaking Britain's last hold on Egypt.

France resisted demands for independence in its colonies of Morocco, Tunisia, and Algeria. Soon Muslim nationalists in all three countries revolted. The French gave in fairly quickly in Morocco and Tunisia, using all their energies to keep Algeria. There, a bitter war dragged on until 1962, when the French finally withdrew.

With the peace settlement in Algeria, all Africa north of the Sahara was independent. The region maintained its close ties with other Islamic nations in the Middle East.

The traditional reaction Groups working for independence south of the Sahara drew on a different set of traditions. Nationalists sometimes used traditional African forms of organization. The Mau Mau of Kenya were a secret society whose members were bound together by oaths and rituals. During the 1950's, the Mau Mau attacked both European settlers and other Africans who cooperated with Europeans. Although the British stamped out the Mau Mau, its terrorist tactics pushed Britain toward granting independence to Kenya.

The Indo-Western reaction Other African nationalists had watched India's successful drive for independence. They saw how effective Gandhi's efforts had been, combining mass protest with political organization.

Leaders such as Nkrumah in Gold Coast and Kenneth Kaunda in Northern Rhodesia formed political parties to demand independence. Through such parties, Africans organized strikes, demonstrations, protests, and boycotts. They combined Western-style political skills with the kind of mass action that Gandhi had popularized in India. "There is a new African in the world," said Nkrumah, "and that new African is ready to fight his own battle."

Nationalist leaders promised that independence would bring great benefits to all Africans. Hopes were high for a new age of development and prosperity. Not all those hopes were realistic. Indeed, the promise of independence raised many hopes that were not fulfilled.

Independence spread across Africa.

In 1952, the map of Africa showed only four independent countries: Ethiopia, Egypt, Liberia, and white-controlled South Africa. By 1956, Libya, the Sudan, Tunisia, and Morocco had also won independence.

In the late 1950's, the focus of the independence movement shifted south of the Sahara. The new nation of Ghana marked the beginning of this shift (page 744). By 1960, there were 18 more independent countries on the map of Africa. By the 1980's, all of Africa was independent except Namibia, which was controlled by South Africa. South Africa itself, while politically independent, remained under the rule of a white minority (pages 752–753).

Thus, for most of Africa, the bitter age of European colonial rule had lasted less than 100 years. Yet the changes brought by colonialism were not so quickly wiped out.

Even after independence, African countries faced problems caused by years of colonial rule. Europeans had drastically altered Africa's economy. They had imposed governments that had no relation to the culture of the Africans they controlled. Often colonial rule was harsh and authoritarian.

Only in the last years of their rule did the French and British make some attempts to prepare their colonies for self-government. The Belgians made no such effort at all. Thus the new nations had difficulty running schools, maintaining transportation systems, building armed forces, and managing economic growth.

Africans faced economic crises.

Africa has the potential for great wealth. It has many valuable minerals, including gold, cobalt, platinum, uranium, and diamonds. Yet foreigners have benefited from these riches far more than have Africans. The wealth from Africa's mines has usually gone to industrial countries such as Britain, the United States, and Japan.

Dependence on a few exports The colonial powers had no interest in building industry in Africa. They were interested mainly in exporting minerals, timber, and cash crops. Most African countries thus had economies based on only one or two crops or minerals. For example, coffee and tea were important cash crops in colonial Kenya and remained vital for independent Kenya. However, when world demand for coffee or tea declined, Kenya had few other products to sell.

Industrial problems Many African countries have tried to make their economies more balanced by developing new industries. Many times, however, they have tackled large projects for which they have had to borrow money from abroad.

For example, Nkrumah hoped to build industry in Ghana using electric power from a great dam on the Volta River. With electric power from the dam, Nkrumah planned to run an aluminum mill and canning factories. He hired European and American engineers, borrowed money from abroad, and poured funds into the project. Yet because some of the calculations were wrong, the dam has never had enough water to make all the power that was expected. Drought made the problem worse. Economic problems plagued the factories. The result was a costly failure and a large foreign debt for Ghana.

Without foreign loans and foreign markets, many of the new African nations would have collapsed. The goods they produced for export, such as cocoa, coffee, peanuts, copper, tin, and zinc, rarely sold for prices high enough to pay for the goods they imported, such as machinery, fertilizers, and gasoline. Thus most African nations were chronically in debt.

Farming and famine Two thirds of the people of Africa live in rural areas. However, farming is difficult. The soil is poor in much of the continent, and the tsetse fly, which attacks people and livestock, infests almost a third of Africa.

Colonial rule put new pressures on the land, pressures that lasted after independence. Colonial rulers forced African farmers to raise crops for export instead of food crops. Acres and acres of cotton and peanuts replaced small family plots of grains and vegetables. Growing the same cash crops year after year wore out the soil faster than traditional farming methods.

Even after they gained independence, many African governments encouraged the planting of cash crops. Countries needed exports to trade with industrial nations. They needed income to pay the interest on their foreign debts.

With less land devoted to food crops, food supplies dwindled. At the same time, the population grew. Severe famine now threatens much of Af-

Famine victims in Ethiopia search for grain after sacks broke on being dropped from relief planes.

rica, including Ethiopia, Somalia, Mozambique, Zambia, Kenya, and the Sudan. According to UN estimates, 30 of the hungriest countries in the world are in Africa. Even with help from abroad, famine will endanger the lives of Africans, especially children, for another generation.

Building nations proved difficult.

When the countries of Africa became independent, they kept the borders set during colonial times. Yet European countries had drawn those borders without regard for the African groups living within them. Some borders split groups that shared the same language and culture. Other borders joined groups whose cultures clashed. African governments faced a daunting task—to bind their citizens into a single nation.

Many colonial governments followed a policy of "divide and conquer." By encouraging ethnic loyalties, Europeans often played one African group against another. This rivalry has made unity harder to achieve for the new nations.

In Nigeria, for example, there are some 250 different ethnic groups and about 400 different languages. At independence, the concept of "Nigeria" had little meaning for an Ibo family living in an isolated village. However, as family members traveled to other parts of the country to schools and jobs, they relied on other Ibos for help and support. Soon the family felt a strong allegiance to Ibos throughout Nigeria. Naturally, the family would support Ibo candidates for political office.

The growth of ethnic loyalty in Africa resembled in some ways the experience of newly arrived immigrants to the United States. Those immigrants tended to settle near other newcomers from their homeland. They supported the efforts of fellow immigrants to win political office and to advance in other ways. However, unlike people in the United States, few Africans had strong national loyalties to offset their regional or ethnic ties. Ethnic loyalty can be a stepping stone toward loyalty to a nation, but building toward a larger loyalty takes time.

Section Review 1

Define: (a) jihad, (b) cash crop
Identify: (a) Ghana, (b) Kwame Nkrumah, (c) Atlantic Charter, (d) Gamal Abdel Nasser
Answer:
1. (a) What groups of Africans took the lead in nationalism? (b) Why was the Atlantic Charter important to African nationalists?
2. How did colonial rule end in each of the following North African countries? (a) Libya (b) Egypt (c) Algeria
3. How did African leaders carry on the struggle for independence south of the Sahara?
4. During what years did most African countries win their independence?
5. (a) How did holdovers from the colonial period weaken Africa economically? (b) How did attempts to industrialize sometimes backfire? (c) What problems affect agriculture?
6. How have regional and ethnic ties made nation building difficult?

Critical Thinking
7. Is it harder for a country to industrialize now than it was in the early 1800's when the Industrial Revolution was just beginning? Why or why not? (Be sure to consider the role of foreign trade and competition, both as a help and a hindrance.)

African nations took diverse paths. 2

When they became independent, most African countries patterned their new governments and economic systems after those of Western Europe and the United States. They set up representative democracies with capitalist economies. Some African countries such as Gabon succeeded in following the Western model. They were successful because they had fairly solid economic bases and a growing middle class. These countries also relied heavily on their former colonial rulers for support. Gabon, for instance, kept close ties with France.

The Western model, however, was not successful in many African countries. In some cases, an elite upper class ran the country for their own benefit, ignoring the needs of the people. Sometimes, the new governments made grandiose promises that they were unable to keep. When the promises were not met, coups and uprisings followed.

Thus, within a decade of independence, there were a variety of governments in power in Africa. Some were democracies. Others were ruthless dictatorships. African countries also tried a variety of economic systems. The examples that follow show some of the issues that Africans have faced since independence.

Ivory Coast prospered as a one-party democracy.

Ivory Coast (so-called because of its once-large elephant population) became independent of France on August 7, 1960. Since then, it has enjoyed more prosperity and stability than most of its neighbors.

Ivory Coast's new government had a national assembly with 120 members. The members were elected for five-year terms in a nationwide election. Ivory Coast's president also served a five-year term. The Ivory Coast Democratic Party was the only political party. Within it are people from all the 60 ethnic groups of Ivory Coast.

Ivory Coast's president was the leader of its independence movement, Felix Houphouet-Boigny (HOO-fway-BWAH-nyee). Quiet, idealistic, and extremely popular, he was elected to six consecutive five-year terms. His leadership was crucial to Ivory Coast. He won his sixth term in 1985 when he was 80, leading many people to wonder who would succeed him.

Ivory Coast's economy is based mostly on capitalism. Much of its trade is with France, and many French settlers stayed after independence. These ties with France helped keep Ivory Coast's economy stable. Ivory Coast benefited from French investments, technology, and management skills.

Agriculture remained the basis of the country's economy. Small farms were common. For example, the country's coffee and cocoa crops come from some 400,000 farms. With many small farms rather than a few large plantations, Ivory Coast has a solid middle class.

In 1980, when the world price for cocoa and coffee dropped sharply, Ivory Coast was badly

Map Study

Name the nations through which the Nile River flows from its sources.

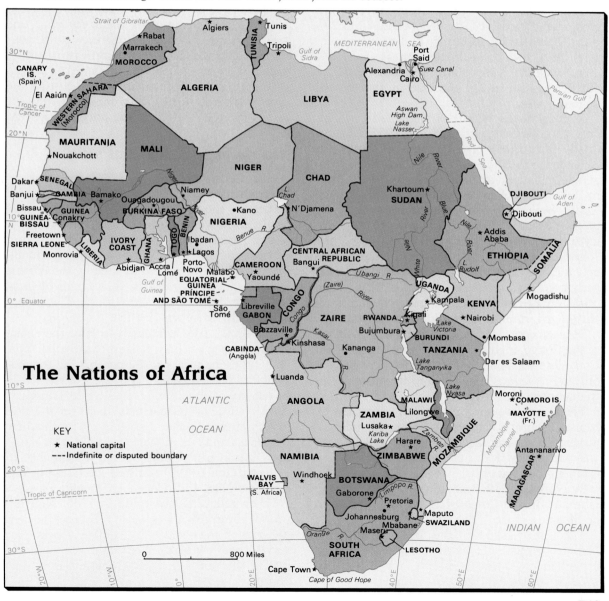

The Nations of Africa

KEY
★ National capital
‒‒‒ Indefinite or disputed boundary

0   800 Miles

749

hurt. The government urged farmers to diversify their crops. Pineapples, coconuts, bananas, sugarcane, cotton, and rubber trees were among the new crops. Ivorians hoped to make their country less dependent on one or two crops.

The country's slow but steady industrialization was tied to agriculture. For example, factories were planned to refine sugar, can fruit, make wood into pulp, turn rubber into tires, and make cotton cloth.

Zaire came under one-man rule.

The Congo (now called Zaire) faced severe problems in its drive for independence from Belgium. The Belgians had made no attempt to prepare the Congo for self-government. By 1960, there were only 16 college graduates in all of the Congo, a country the size of the eastern United States.

As neighboring countries won their freedom, unrest in the Congo increased. In 1956, Belgium finally put forth a plan offering the Congo independence in 30 years. African nationalists demanded changes much sooner. Suddenly, early in 1960, the Belgians announced that the Congo would become independent in less than six months. Clearly, Belgian leaders hoped the country would collapse in chaos.

Immediately, dozens of leaders began to compete for votes in the upcoming election. Political parties sprang up everywhere. The first prime minister, Patrice Lumumba, put together a coalition government of 16 different parties.

Belgians continued to hold many key positions in the Congo, including running the army. When Congolese soldiers rebelled against their Belgian officers, a wave of violence and terrorism swept the country.

The situation grew worse when a local leader, Moise Tshombe (CHOM-bay), claimed independence for a region called Katanga. Soon the Congo was torn by civil war between the central government and Katanga.

By November 1960, there were four rival governments in the Congo. The country seemed to be breaking apart.

The Congo asked for the help of the United Nations, which sent in troops. With UN help, a civilian government reunited the country in 1963. Then the UN forces withdrew.

In 1965, the leader of the army, General Joseph Mobutu, seized power. Mobutu set up a highly authoritarian, one-party government. As president, he could declare war, make treaties, and declare a state of emergency on his own command. The country's legislature had almost no power. He and his allies enriched themselves from the national treasury. Corruption takes nearly half the government's income.

In 1975, Mobutu changed the country's name and the name of its great river to Zaire, as it was called before the colonial era. He changed his own name to Mobutu Sese Seko and forced all citizens to replace their European or foreign names with African ones. One effect of this change was to make people more aware of their ethnic differences and thus to increase disunity, which Mobutu has encouraged.

Mobutu maintained one of the longest-lasting governments in Africa. His one-party rule put an end to civil war but at the price of freedom.

Nigeria formed a federal union.

Like Ghana, Nigeria was a British colony. Nigerian nationalists began organizing political parties in the 1920's, and by 1945 the independence movement was quite strong.

There were, in fact, three strong political parties representing different regional and ethnic groups. Northern Nigeria was dominated by the Islamic Fulani and Hausa peoples. In western Nigeria, the Yoruba formed the largest group. The leading group in the east was the Ibo.

The British had deliberately isolated the Fulani and Hausa peoples from the rest of the population, denying them access to European-style schools. The Ibo, on the other hand, were educated in British-style schools and were literate in English. As a result, Ibo people held many of the best jobs throughout Nigeria, even in the north where the Hausa and Fulani were strongest. The Hausa and Fulani feared domination by the better-educated and better-organized Ibo. Despite this disunity, plans for independence went ahead.

When independence came in 1960, Nigeria's central government was weak, reflecting the deep divisions in the country. The different geographic regions had few links. Not one paved road connected the northern and southern parts of the country.

In 1966, a group of Ibo army officers staged a coup, killing many government leaders. In response, military officers from the north struck back with a coup of their own. They killed the Ibo head of government. In the following months, thousands of Ibos who lived in northern Nigeria were killed. Thousands more fled southward to their homeland.

In 1967, Ibo leaders tried to break away from Nigeria. They declared their homeland the independent country of Biafra. A 30-month war between Nigeria and Biafra followed. As bombing destroyed crops and the Biafran army slowly lost ground, famine killed thousands, mostly children. Biafra finally surrendered in 1970.

To reunite the country, Nigeria set up a new federal government. Within the federal union, there were 12 states, each with a fair measure of self-government. (Seven new states were formed in 1976.) This division helped to overcome ethnic conflict. The new government played down old rivalries. Despite fears, there was no bloodbath in the defeated Biafra.

An oil boom in the 1970's temporarily helped Nigeria. Nigeria sought to use the oil profits to build up its industries. However, each of Nigeria's states tried to develop its own economy with little central planning or control. As a result, waste and inefficiency mounted. Meanwhile, in its drive for industry, Nigeria neglected its farmers. Thus, when the oil boom ended, the country faced an economic crisis.

As Nigeria's economy worsened, its democratic government collapsed too. In 1983, after elections marred by violence and fraud, the military took over the government. A second coup in 1985 brought new army leaders to power. However, the new leaders released many political prisoners and allowed the press greater freedom. The future of democracy in Nigeria was uncertain.

Tanzania tried economic experiments.

The East African country of Tanzania followed a different path, both politically and economically, to national unity. In 1961, the former colony of Tanganyika won its independence peacefully. In 1964, Tanganyika united with the island country of Zanzibar to form Tanzania.

The widespread use of the Swahili language helped to unify Tanzania. The country also had a single political party, the party that had organized the independence movement. Its leader, Julius Nyerere (nye-uh-RAIR-ee), was Tanzania's president from 1961 until his resignation in 1985.

Like Houphouet-Boigny in Ivory Coast, Nyerere used one-party rule to unite his country. He believed that winning agreement by discussion within one party was closer to African traditions than elections among competing parties.

Nyerere also had strong ideas about Tanzania's economy. At independence, Tanzania was a poor agricultural country. In 1966, Nyerere decided to take drastic steps to try to improve the economy. He feared that Tanzania was developing "an economic and social elite whose prime concern was profits for themselves and not the needs of the majority." He urged people to be guided by ideals of self-sacrifice and self-reliance.

Nyerere wanted to develop a socialist economy based on traditional African village life. He downplayed industry and instead concentrated on farming. Moreover, he tried to avoid asking other countries for aid. Government officials were required to follow a strict code of ethics.

To accomplish his goals, Nyerere called for building *ujamaa* villages. (*Ujamaa* is a Swahili word meaning "familyhood.") In these villages, each person was expected to work for the common good. In return, the government promised to supply medical care and education. Nyerere's system has been called "an African form of socialism."

Many Tanzanians shared Nyerere's dream for a new society. Nyerere was popular among the ordinary people of the countryside. However, his ujamaa villages were less popular. People who were forced to move to the villages were unhappy. Sometimes wealthy peasants tried to take over leadership of the ujamaa villages.

By 1977, even Nyerere admitted that the ujamaa villages were a failure. The country was poorer after ten years of his economic experiment. Food production was not keeping up with the increasing population. Since Nyerere had discouraged foreign investment in Tanzania, there were few industrial jobs.

Nyerere began to make reforms. He allowed private farms and outside investment. Nyerere's successor as president, Ali Hassan Mwinyi, returned some businesses to private control. Unlike Nigeria, Tanzania weathered its economic crisis without a military coup.

South African blacks sought freedom.

Great Britain granted South Africa independence in 1931, more than a quarter of a century before Ghana won its freedom. Yet Africans throughout the continent did not cheer South Africa's independence as they did Ghana's. The reason was simple: Although South Africa was free of *British* rule, it remained under *white* rule. Black Africans, who made up about 75 percent of the country's population, had no voice in its government. Indeed, their situation grew worse after independence.

The apartheid system The South African government classified its population in four groups—whites, blacks, Asians, and "coloreds" (people of mixed ancestry). In 1948, the white-controlled government set up a system called **apartheid** (uh-**PAHR**-tayt). Under apartheid, the people of different groups were rigidly separated.

The government justified apartheid by saying that each group was free to develop in its own way. In practice, however, apartheid kept power and wealth in the hands of the white minority. Whites controlled the economy, using blacks as a low-paid labor force.

Apartheid touched every part of life in South Africa. Nonwhites could have homes only in certain areas. There were separate schools and hospitals for blacks and whites, and those for whites were much better equipped. Parks, playgrounds, and beaches were separate.

The "homelands" policy In 1959, South Africa went even further in separating blacks and whites. The government passed a law called the Group Areas Act. This law set aside certain parts of the country for the black ethnic groups within South Africa such as the Zulu, the Xhosa, the Sotho, and others. These areas were known as "homelands" or *bantustans*.

Under the homelands policy, about 13 percent of the land was set aside for blacks, who made up 75 percent of the population. About 87 percent of the country—including its best farmland and its fabulously rich mines—remained for the whites, who made up 14 percent of the population.

The government forced thousands of blacks to settle in these homelands. Many black families had to leave farms where their parents and grandparents had lived. They were "returning" to homelands neither they nor their ancestors had ever seen.

Many black South Africans continued to live outside the homelands. They did so because their jobs were in the white-controlled areas. South Africa's economy would have collapsed without

Johannesburg, South Africa, (left) is one of the most prosperous cities in Africa. Outside it lie black townships such as Crossroads (right).

Voice from Our Time · *The Effects of Banning*

Bakone Moloto, a young South African black, was active in a movement to increase literacy among blacks. One day, without warning, the police seized him and sent him to a distant town. He was placed under a banning order. Here his mother describes what banning means.

My son was banned to [the town of] Mafekeng. I hardly knew any person I could request to . . . give him moral support . . . Word had already reached me that my son had been dumped in an empty house somewhere in Mafekeng . . . [Later] he described in detail the restrictions of his banning order and some of its limitations. He highlighted the following points:

That he was allowed only one visitor at a time. If he spoke to more than one person at a time, it was an offence for which he could be charged, convicted, and imprisoned.

That he might not enter any school, church, or publishing office.

That he must remain within Montshioa township, except on his way to work, when he must not stop anywhere.

All of these restrictions had far-reaching implications. Mafekeng being such a small town . . . he was compelled to take the first [job] offer he received. He was never quite certain of whether he could use a shared taxi.

1. What is the purpose of the banning rules?
2. Why was Bakone never sure if he could use a shared taxi?
3. How would banning restrict a normal family life?

---

these workers. Yet the government made no real provisions for the blacks who work in South Africa's cities. As a result, millions of blacks crowded into slums called townships around major cities. Soweto, on the outskirts of Johannesburg, was one such township.

Family members who were not employed, including children, could not legally enter the cities. Thus, families were often separated. The parents might work in white areas while the children lived far away with a grandparent. To be together, families had to live in the shanty towns illegally.

A *rising tide of protest* In 1960, black South Africans organized a large protest. Government troops fired into a crowd of demonstrators in the black township of Sharpeville, killing 70 unarmed people and wounding hundreds more. Immediately afterward, the government outlawed the black political groups that had been asking for reforms.

South Africa's government relied on force, using its powerful army and police to crush protests

from the black majority. People the government considered troublemakers—white or black—were jailed without trial. Those who spoke out against apartheid were arrested, forced to leave the country, or *banned*. A person who was banned was not allowed to publish, attend public meetings, or speak publicly.

After 1960, violence increased on both sides. In 1976, a bitter riot broke out in the black township of Soweto. Police fired into the crowds with automatic weapons, killing 176 young blacks. Between 1983 and 1986, there were more than 2,300 such killings.

After the Soweto riots, blacks turned increasingly to violence. Fearful white citizens armed themselves and regularly practiced with their guns. Some black groups murdered other blacks for cooperating with the white government. An American journalist in South Africa during the early 1980's summed up the situation this way: "This is a country no longer at peace and not yet at war."

Section Review 2

Define: (a) ujamaa, (b) apartheid, (c) bantustan
Identify: (a) Felix Houphouet-Boigny,
(b) Mobutu Sese Seko, (c) Julius Nyerere
Answer:

1. (a) What type of government did Ivory Coast set up when it became independent? (b) What economic policies did it follow?
2. (a) Why did the Congo face more severe problems than many other African nations on becoming independent? (b) What factors threatened the Congo's unity? (c) Briefly describe Mobutu's rule.
3. (a) What problems for unity did Nigeria face? (b) What events led to civil war? (c) How did Nigeria try to satisfy its many groups? (d) How did the country come under military rule?
4. (a) How did Nyerere justify one-party rule? (b) What were his goals for Tanzania's economy? (c) What were the results?
5. Why did other Africans not consider South Africa's independence cause for celebration?
6. (a) What share of South Africa's population did whites make up? (b) What share did blacks make up?
7. Describe the policy that the South African government instituted in 1948.
8. What was the homelands policy?
9. What methods did the white government use to maintain control in South Africa?

Critical Thinking

10. (a) Based on the examples in this section, what problems seem to threaten an African country with several political parties? (b) What problems might arise in a country with a single party?

Nationalism sparked Mideast conflicts.

3

As you have read, nationalism in northern Africa was closely linked to nationalism in an overlapping area, the Middle East. There are many definitions for the term *Middle East*, the name used by Europeans for the lands between Europe and Asia. Today, the most useful definition of *Middle East* includes Southwest Asia from Iran in the east to the Arabian Peninsula in the west. The countries of North Africa that border the Mediterranean Sea are also considered part of the Middle East.

The majority, but not all, of the people in the Middle East are Muslim. As you have learned, three great religions began in the Middle East: Judaism, Christianity, and Islam.

For centuries, the peoples of the Middle East passed from the control of one empire to another. With the collapse of the Ottoman empire after World War I, however, nationalism became a growing force in the region. As each group struggled to establish its own nation, the region became a powder keg of conflicting loyalties.

Moreover, in the 1970's, the price of oil, the Middle East's most valuable resource, skyrocketed. Industrial countries around the world relied on oil as a source of energy. Therefore, oil-rich countries in the Middle East were able to use oil as a weapon in global politics.

Israel became a nation.

After World War I, Britain took over Palestine as a mandate on behalf of the League of Nations (pages 629–630). In the Balfour Declaration, the British promised to support the creation of a Jewish homeland in Palestine. At the same time, they promised to safeguard the rights of Arabs who lived there.

Since the late 1800's, many Jewish settlers had migrated to Palestine from Europe. After World War II, when the world learned how millions of Jews had died in the Nazi Holocaust, there was an outpouring of support for such a homeland. Even the United States and the USSR agreed on this issue.

Arabs, however, made up 70 percent of Palestine's population. They wanted Palestine to become an Arab nation-state. They opposed the creation of a Jewish state. Why, Arabs asked, should Arab land be taken because of what the Nazis had done? "Give them [the Jews] and their descendants the choicest lands and homes of the Germans who oppressed them," suggested King Ibn Saud of Saudi Arabia in 1945.

In Palestine as in India, the British found themselves caught between two groups with radically different goals. Again as in India, the British

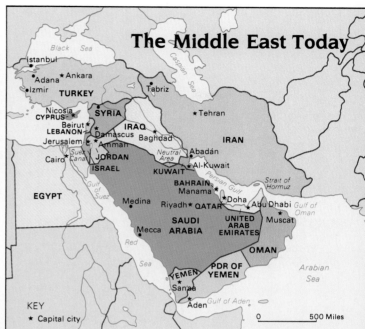

The Middle East Today

Map Study

Oil and oil refineries (left) have brought sudden wealth to much of the Middle East, especially to countries along the Persian Gulf. What countries border the gulf? What strait controls entrance into the Persian Gulf?

decided to withdraw. Early in 1947, Prime Minister Clement Attlee announced that the British would leave Palestine by the end of the year. They left the responsibility for the region in the hands of the United Nations.

The UN at once formed a special 11-nation committee to hammer out a solution that both Jews and Arabs could accept. After months of debate, the committee decided on partition. Palestine would be divided into two states, one Jewish, the other Arab.

While the Jews were not completely satisfied, they were ready to accept the UN plan. The Arabs, on the other hand, were furious. The new Jewish state would include more than half the total land of Palestine, even though less than a third of the population was Jewish.

Nevertheless, the UN General Assembly approved the plan. Both the United States and the Soviet Union voted in favor of it. In later years, however, the USSR often supported the Arab countries, especially Syria. The United States, on the other hand, based much of its Middle Eastern policy on support for Israel.

In May 1948, David Ben-Gurion, longtime leader of the Palestinian Jews, announced the creation of the independent nation of Israel. Within hours, six Arab states—Egypt, Iraq, Lebanon, Saudi Arabia, Jordan, and Syria—attacked Israel. The war quickly became a victory march for the Israelis. By the end of 1948, they controlled nearly three fourths of Palestine. When the fighting stopped, Egypt and Jordan divided what remained of Palestine. The Jews had a homeland, but the Palestinian Arabs were left without a country.

Palestinians sought a nation.

Faced with Israeli rule, thousands of Arab families took as many of their belongings as they could carry and fled from Israel. By 1949, some 500,000 Palestinian Arabs had left the country. Most settled in refugee camps that ringed the borders of their former homeland. There they remained, becoming pawns in the struggle between the Arab countries and Israel. New generations of children grew up in the camps.

Israel, 1967–1973

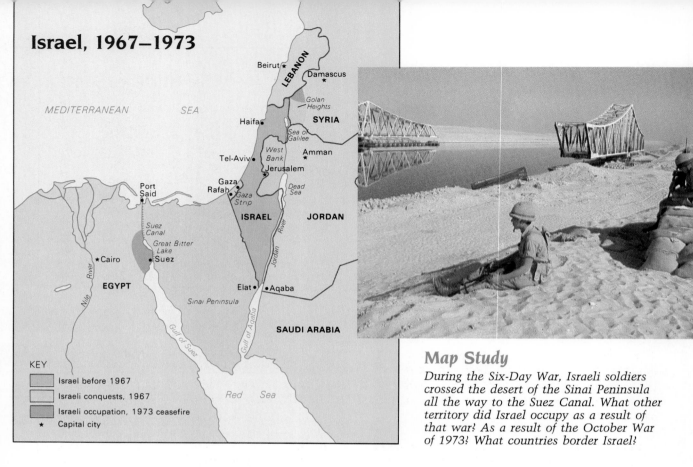

MEDITERRANEAN SEA

Beirut ★
Damascus ★
LEBANON
Golan Heights
SYRIA
Haifa
Sea of Galilee
West Bank
Amman ★
Tel-Aviv
Jerusalem ☆
Gaza
Rafah
Gaza Strip
Dead Sea
Port Said
Suez Canal
Great Bitter Lake
ISRAEL
JORDAN
★ Cairo
• Suez
EGYPT
Elat •
• Aqaba
Sinai Peninsula
SAUDI ARABIA
Gulf of Suez
Gulf of Aqaba
Red Sea
Nile River
Jordan River

KEY
Israel before 1967
Israeli conquests, 1967
Israeli occupation, 1973 ceasefire
★ Capital city

Map Study

During the Six-Day War, Israeli soldiers crossed the desert of the Sinai Peninsula all the way to the Suez Canal. What other territory did Israel occupy as a result of that war? As a result of the October War of 1973? What countries border Israel?

Palestinian nationalism remained a powerful force in the Middle East. A group called the Palestinian Liberation Organization (PLO) waged a guerrilla war against Israel. Many Palestinians supported the PLO, and its leaders demanded a voice in any peace settlement in the Middle East. Meanwhile, other groups also claimed to speak for the Palestinians. Some groups formed their own armies and turned to terrorism.

Egypt and Israel made peace.

No peace treaty ended the war between the Arab nations and Israel because the Arabs refused to recognize Israel as a nation. The uneasy truce was broken frequently by sniping and raids.

The Six-Day War War broke out again in 1967. Egypt closed the Gulf of Aqaba to Israel, and Israel responded by attacking Egypt. In six days, the Israelis masterfully defeated the armies of Egypt, Syria, and Jordan. Israel also occupied much new territory (map, above).

The October War After the Six-Day War, there was again a fragile peace for five years. Then, on October 6, 1973, while Israelis observed Yom

Kippur, the holiest day of the year for Jews, Egypt and Syria attacked. Taken by surprise, the Israeli army lost ground at first but quickly recovered. They surrounded the Egyptians in the Sinai Peninsula and forced the Syrians back across the border.

A peace treaty With help from American Secretary of State Henry Kissinger, Egyptian President Anwar el-Sadat and Israeli Prime Minister Golda Meir reached an agreement in 1974. Under its terms, Israel withdrew east of the Suez Canal and returned part of the Sinai Peninsula to Egypt. Egypt, in turn, agreed not to put troops there.

In 1977, Sadat went to Jerusalem to meet with the newly elected Israeli prime minister, Menachim Begin. His action was a great shock to

Footnote to History

Henry Kissinger traveled back and forth between Israel and Egypt so many times when he was negotiating the settlement to the October War that the term *shuttle diplomacy* was coined to describe his work.

756

the Arab world. Egypt, like other Arab states, had declared repeatedly that Israel had no right to exist. Now Sadat and Begin were trying to make peace.

When Sadat and Begin could not reach an agreement, President Carter of the United States invited both men to the presidential retreat at Camp David, Maryland. For 13 days, the three leaders stayed in cabins there. They jogged, chatted, and argued along the paths of a pine-scented forest. At last, a beaming Carter announced that Sadat and Begin had agreed to sign a preliminary peace treaty.

In 1979, Sadat and Begin signed an official peace treaty. Egypt became the only Arab nation to recognize Israel's right to exist. Many Arabs called Sadat a traitor. Other Arab countries broke ties with Egypt. In October 1981, Sadat was assassinated by Egyptians who wanted a strict Islamic government. For a time, Egypt lost its position of leadership among Islamic countries. In the mid-1980's, however, several Arab nations again sought ties with Egypt.

Relations between Israel and the rest of its neighbors have remained tense. Terrorists have bombed buildings and buses in Israel. The Israelis have struck deep within Syria and Lebanon at suspected guerrilla camps. Both sides have killed civilians. Israeli troops intervened in the Lebanese civil war. The conflicting nationalism of the Israelis and the Palestinian Arabs has made a peace settlement difficult to achieve.

Reaction followed change in Iran.

Nationalism also led to strife in Iran. There, within a single country, leaders had conflicting national ideals. Iran's political leader, the shah, wanted a modern, industrial nation like the countries of Western Europe. The country's conservative Muslim leaders, known as *ayatollahs*, had a different goal. They wanted an Islamic republic, a nation based on strict obedience to the teachings of Islam.

In 1925, Reza Khan, an army officer, became the shah, or ruler, of Iran (page 628). He took the name Reza Shah Pahlavi. He tried to modernize his country in the European style. He built Iran's first railroad and gave women more rights. His son, Muhammad Reza Shah Pahlavi, became ruler during World War II.

In 1953, Iran was caught in a power struggle between the shah and the popular leader of the parliament, Prime Minister Muhammad Mossadeq. When the shah tried to force Mossadeq out of office, crowds rioted in the streets of Tehran. The shah fled, and Mossadeq took over the government.

In this crisis, the United States supported the shah. It was the height of the Cold War, and the shah was a staunch anti-Communist, whatever his other failings. With American money and arms, the shah returned to his throne, more powerful than before.

The shah's rule was a mixture of brutality and enlightenment. He allowed his secret police to

Daily Life • *Veiled Faces*

In many Muslim nations, women wear veils called *chadors* in public. The strictness of rules about veiling varies greatly from country to country. In Turkey, for example, veils are rare. In Iran, however, women who leave home without veils risk severe penalties. Most women in Saudi Arabia do not wear veils in public. In Qatar, women are not photographed even for passports. The wife of the ruler of Abu Dhabi has never been seen by a man outside her immediate family. Yet she is president of the Abu Dhabi women's association, whose members try to improve the lives of desert women. The organization publishes a magazine for women and runs a bank that is managed, staffed, and patronized entirely by women.

use torture and murder. At the same time, he set up schools and distributed some land to peasants. As industry grew, workers shared in the profits. Women began to hold jobs outside the home and to dress in Western-style clothes. In 1963, women won the right to vote.

The money for modernization came from the sale of more than 6 million barrels of oil that flowed daily from Iran's wells. In 1974, Iran's oil output was second only to that of Saudi Arabia.

Oil wealth created great contrasts in Iranian society. Modern skyscrapers gleamed in Tehran's business center. The shah paid handsome salaries to technical experts who came from abroad to modernize Iran's industries. Outside the city, however, many Iranians lived in mud huts. Poor Iranians bitterly resented the wealthy foreigners and their Western influence. Conservative Muslims saw modernization as an attack on Islam.

The overthrow of the shah By the late 1970's, millions of Iranians were eager to be rid of the shah. He kept his throne only by armed force and support from the United States.

The leader of the shah's opponents was a 78-year-old religious leader, Ayatollah Ruhollah Khomeini (koh-MAY-nee). From exile in France, Khomeini sent stirring calls for revolt on tape cassettes played over telephones. At Khomeini's command, oil workers went on strike. Riots broke out in the cities.

Finally, in January 1979, the shah fled from Iran. In February, the Ayatollah Khomeini returned from exile. He set up a new government, an Islamic republic, under the direction of leading ayatollahs.

Khomeini made it clear that he considered the revolution to be a religious crusade. The new government quickly banned alcohol and American-style music. Women were again separated from men at schools, swimming pools, and other public places. Judges sentenced criminals based on the Koran. For example, thieves were punished by cutting off their right hands. The new government jailed or executed thousands of Iranians.

Above all, Khomeini's government preached hatred for the United States. In November 1979, a group of Iranian revolutionaries stormed the United States embassy in Tehran and seized more than 60 American citizens as hostages. The Iranians held most of the American hostages until January 1981.

The Ayatollah Khomeini directed the Iranian revolution from exile in France.

The Iran-Iraq war The religious leaders who came to power in Iran belonged to the branch of Islam known as the Shi'ites (page 179). There were Shi'ites in most parts of the Middle East, but in most countries they were a minority. Often they had been oppressed by the Sunni majority.

The new rulers of Iran encouraged revolts among Shi'ites elsewhere. For example, Khomeini openly called on Shi'ites in Iraq to overthrow their government and set up an Islamic republic like the one in Iran. Angered by such tactics and thinking that Iran was too weak to defend itself, Iraqi leaders attacked an Iranian border region in 1980.

The border fighting quickly became a full-scale, vicious war. Iran declared it a holy war and sent teenage boys to the front to use up the enemy's ammunition. Iranians accused Iraq of using poison gas. Fearful of Iran's revolutionary influence, the Muslim nations of Jordan and Saudi Arabia gave aid to Iraq.

The explosive mixture of religion and nationalism in the Middle East had taken a new direction. In the name of Islamic nationalism, Muslim was fighting Muslim.

Civil war destroyed Lebanon.

One of the most tragic examples of the link between Middle Eastern conflicts and world politics has been Lebanon. Struggles between Muslims and Christians, Sunnis and Shi'ites, and Israelis and Palestinians all became intertwined within a single country.

Lebanon became a French mandate after World War I. In 1943, Lebanon's many religious groups drew up a constitution under which they shared political power. The Maronites, a Christian group, made up a slight majority of the population, according to a 1932 census. Therefore, the president was to be a Christian. The prime minister was to be a Sunni Muslim, and the speaker of the legislature was to be a Shi'ite Muslim. Other offices in Lebanon's government were allotted to Greek Orthodox Christians and to the Druze, a secretive Islamic sect.

This system of government worked well until the mid-1950's. By that time, the Muslim population had increased, but the Christians would not allow a new census. Muslims demanded more power in government, and civil war erupted in 1958. The United States, fearing Soviet power in the Middle East, sent in marines to end the fighting. The basic issues, however, remained unsolved.

In the 1970's, the Arab-Israeli conflict spilled over into Lebanon. Many Muslim refugees from Palestine came to Lebanon. The PLO also made its headquarters in Lebanon. The Lebanese government was unable to control the private armies of the Palestinians. By the late 1970's, the PLO virtually ruled much of southern Lebanon. From bases there, Palestinian groups launched guerrilla raids against Israel.

In 1975, civil war again broke out in Lebanon. Other countries quickly became involved. The United States and Israel aided the Maronite Christians. Syria and Libya sent aid to the Muslims and the PLO. Many of the weapons supplied by Syria came originally from the Soviet Union. Later in the war, however, Syria switched to supporting some of the Christian groups, apparently to prevent any group from winning a clear victory.

In 1982, Israel invaded Lebanon to drive out the PLO. Israeli troops destroyed much of southern Lebanon and then advanced to Beirut. While Israeli troops besieged PLO strongholds, thousands of PLO fighters went to other Muslim countries. An international force, including soldiers from the United States and France, tried to establish peace in war-torn Beirut.

Fighting continued daily in Lebanon during the 1980's. Terrorists blew up the United States embassy in April 1983. Later that year, 250 American marines and 58 French soldiers died in a bomb attack by Muslim terrorists. American and European teachers, doctors, and reporters were kidnapped by terrorist groups.

Lebanon had become a battleground in which each small faction looked out for its own interests. No leader could speak with authority for any group. Under such circumstances, negotiations were almost impossible. As a nation, Lebanon stood on the brink of destruction.

Section Review 3

Define: (a) Middle East, (b) ayatollah
Identify: (a) Palestine, (b) Israel, (c) PLO, (d) Shi'ites
Answer:
1. (a) Why was there widespread support for the creation of Israel? (b) What groups opposed the idea?
2. How was the state of Israel created?
3. (a) What was the result for the Palestinian Arabs? (b) How did other Arab nations respond?
4. Why was the treaty between Egypt and Israel a major diplomatic achievement?
5. (a) What were the goals of the shah for Iran? (b) What were the goals of the ayatollahs? (c) How was the shah overthrown?
6. Why did war break out between Iran and Iraq?
7. (a) How did Lebanon try to keep peace among its many religious groups in the 1940's? (b) How did that agreement break down? (c) What outside powers became involved in fighting in Lebanon?

Critical Thinking
8. (a) How are nationalism and religion linked in the conflict over Palestine? (b) In the conflict within Iran? (c) In the conflict between Iran and Iraq? (d) How does such a link make reaching an agreement more difficult?

Chapter Review 35

Summary

1. Africans resumed the fight for independence. In the 1920's, a westernized African middle class took the lead in independence movements. The struggle for independence began in North Africa, where it took many forms and spread south. African countries faced economic and political crises brought on by colonial rule.

2. African nations took diverse paths. After independence, African nations patterned their new countries after Western democracies. When the Western model failed, Africans experimented with a variety of political and economic systems, including one-party democracy in Ivory Coast, one-man rule in Zaire, and a federal republic in Nigeria. In Nigeria, a military coup in 1985 brought democracy to an end. Tanzania was led by Julius Nyerere, who worked hard to bring economic stability. South Africa remained under white rule after independence in 1931. In 1948, South Africa set up apartheid to segregate the black majority and keep power in the hands of the whites. In 1959, South Africa forced the black majority to settle in homelands. The white government uses brute force to crush resistance.

3. Nationalism sparked Mideast conflicts. Although the partition of Israel in 1948 provided Jews with a homeland, it led to the loss of a homeland for Palestinian Arabs and sparked several Arab-Israeli wars. In 1979, Egypt and Israel signed a peace accord, but relations in the region remain tense. In Iran, a revolution ended modernization and brought Shi'ite Muslim religious leaders to power. Iran has tried to spread a Shi'ite revolution to neighboring Iraq. Division in Lebanon led to civil war in 1958. Fighting has intensified because of the presence of the PLO, which has launched attacks against Israel.

Reviewing the Facts

1. Define the following terms:
   a. jihad
   b. cash crop
   c. ethnic group
   d. ujamaa
   e. apartheid
   f. homeland
   g. Middle East
   h. ayatollah
2. Explain the importance of each of the following names, places, or terms:
   a. Ghana
   b. Nkrumah
   c. Atlantic Charter

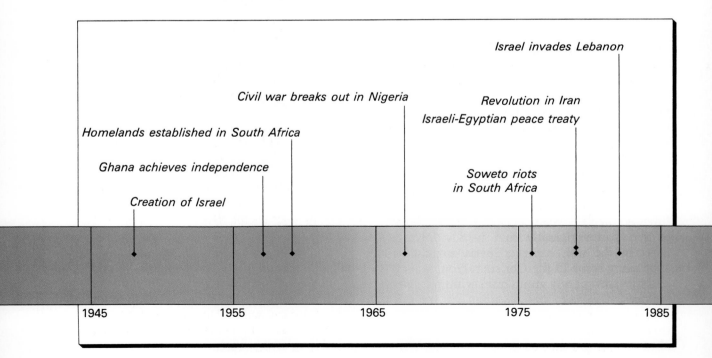

Israel invades Lebanon

Civil war breaks out in Nigeria

Revolution in Iran

Israeli-Egyptian peace treaty

Homelands established in South Africa

Ghana achieves independence

Soweto riots
in South Africa

Creation of Israel

1945   1955   1965   1975   1985

d. Nasser
e. Ivory Coast
f. Houphouet-Boigny
g. Katanga
h. Mobutu
i. Nigeria
j. Nyerere
k. Soweto
l. Israel
m. PLO
n. Shi'ite
o. Lebanon

3. (a) How did colonial rule end in Libya? (b) In Egypt? (c) In Algeria?
4. (a) How did the effects of colonial rule weaken African countries economically? (b) What problems did they face in agriculture? (c) In nation building?
5. (a) What helped stabilize the economy of Ivory Coast? (b) Why did the Congo face more severe problems in nation building than other African nations? (c) What problems did Nigeria face in 1960? (d) How was Tanzania able to weather its economic crisis?
6. (a) Who controls South Africa today? (b) What methods has the South African government used to keep control?
7. (a) How was the state of Israel created? (b) What was the result for Palestinian Arabs?
8. (a) How did the ayatollahs come to power in Iran? (b) What changes did they make? (c) What are their policies toward the United States? (d) Toward Iraq?
9. (a) Why did civil war break out in Lebanon in 1958? (b) How did the Arab-Israeli conflict spill over into Lebanon?

Thinking about History

1. In both Africa and India, independence movements originated with an educated Westernized middle class. Yet the outcomes were very different. Compare the independence movements in these two places. How did Gandhi give unity to the movement in India? Would it have been possible for one man to unite Africans in a similar way?
2. A traditional Islamic society has many customs and ideas that conflict with modernization. What are some of these customs and ideas? How has the presence of oil intensified the conflict? In what other parts of the world have people feared the loss of tradition in the face of modernization?

Writing and Speaking about History

1. Choose two of the statements below. Write a paragraph giving three or more reasons to explain each statement.
    a. Building nations proved difficult for Africans.
    b. African nations face difficulty raising food.
    c. Ivory Coast has enjoyed more stability than many of its neighbors.
2. In chart form, contrast each of the following conflicts in the Middle East:
    a. Iran-Iraq
    b. Arab-Israeli
    c. Civil war in Lebanon
    For each conflict, describe the cause and the groups fighting.
3. Use the information in your chart to prepare a brief oral report on the differences that divide people in the Middle East.

Practicing Skills

Use the map on page 755 to answer the following questions: (a) What waterway connects the Red Sea and the Mediterranean Sea? (b) On what sea does Israel lie? (c) What nation lies to the north of Israel? (d) To the east of Israel?

Investigating History

1. Research one of the following Middle Eastern cities: Jerusalem, Mecca, Medina, or Istanbul. Find out why that city is important to Muslims, Christians, or Jews.
2. Although many people in the Middle East speak Arabic and believe in Islam, not all of these people are Arabs. At the same time, there are some people in the Middle East (Palestinian Christians, for example) who consider themselves Arabs even though they are not followers of Islam. Find out more about what it means to be an Arab. What definition can you offer?

Decision Making in History

Evaluate Nyerere's African form of socialism. What were its positive aspects? Its negative aspects? Why did Nyerere succeed in the long run, even though this program failed?

761

Latin America and Canada in the Modern World

The Pan-American Highway crosses rugged terrain ranging from the rain forests of Brazil and Guatemala to the tundra of Canada. Here it descends from the Andes Mountains of Peru to a river valley.

1. **Mexico and Central America face change.**

2. **Caribbean nations take different paths.**

3. **South American nations seek solutions.**

4. **Canada confronts a changing world.**

In August 1929, the Brazilian coastal city of Rio de Janeiro buzzed with excitement. Despite sweltering heat and oppressive humidity, thousands of Brazilians waited in long lines to see the first International Highways Exposition ever held in the Americas. The Exposition celebrated a bold proposal made at the Conference of American States six years earlier. That proposal called for the building of a highway that would link the countries of the Americas. As the long line of spectators filed through the Exposition Building, they saw displays of modern highway-building techniques, demonstrations of the latest highway construction equipment, and films showing workers carving roads through dense jungles and over lofty mountains.

The Exposition was a huge success. Brazilians leaving the exhibits talked excitedly about the plans. Meanwhile, delegates from countries throughout the Americas were meeting in another part of Rio de Janeiro to discuss the details of building the highway.

For 10 days, 200 delegates from 19 countries in the Western Hemisphere discussed plans for the Pan-American Highway. (*Pan* comes from the Greek word meaning "all.") They agreed on building methods, highway laws, trucking regulations, and ways to raise money for the huge project. A spirit of friendship among the delegates filled the air.

The building of the highway began seven years later in 1936. For the next 27 years, each country along the route worked to complete its section of the highway.

Today, the dream of a single highway connecting the Americas is nearly complete. More than 17,000 miles of international highway run south from Alaska, across Canada and the United States, through Central America, and south to Argentina. The highway also connects the west and east coasts of South America, passing through Bolivia, Argentina, Uruguay, and Brazil. The only section not yet complete is a 250-mile stretch across dense rain forest between Panama and Colombia.

The Pan-American Highway brings hundreds of small villages and large cities, once separated by a day's walk, to within half an hour of each other. It also fosters trade, tourism, and communication among the countries it crosses. To many people, the highway is a symbol of the countless ways in which the countries of the Western Hemisphere are linked. It is a symbol too of what the people of the Americas can accomplish when they work together.

Mexico and Central America face change.   1

Mexico and Central America make up a region of Latin America that extends from the Rio Grande in the north to the Isthmus of Panama in the south. Mexico is the largest country in the region. The seven countries of Central America—Guatemala, Belize, El Salvador, Honduras, Nicaragua, Costa Rica, and Panama—are much smaller.

Over the years, the countries of this region have seen many changes. In the 1500's, they changed from Indian kingdoms to Spanish colonies (pages 363–365). In the 1800's, they changed from Spanish colonies to independent nations (pages 499–504).

Dramatic changes continue to occur in the region today. Many countries, of which Nicaragua is one example, have faced civil strife and political instability. Mexico, while politically stable, has seen its economy go up and down like a dizzying roller coaster. The United States is often deeply concerned with those changes. Historically, Mexico and Central America are closely linked to the United States.

Mexico faced economic challenges.

The 2,000-mile border between Mexico and the United States is like few other borders in the world. On one side is the world's wealthiest and most industrialized nation. On the other side is a struggling nation striving hard to feed, clothe, and house its citizens.

Plans for development During the 1950's and 1960's, Mexico's government invited foreign companies to invest in Mexico. Huge European, Japanese, and United States companies helped pay for and build factories in Mexico. Such companies with branches in many countries are called **multinational corporations.** Many Mexicans found jobs building automobiles, processing foods, and making electrical appliances in the new factories.

Mexico's economy grew by leaps and bounds. Skyscrapers sprang up in Mexico City, Monterrey, and Guadalajara. New freeways cut across the jammed streets of these cities. By 1964, people throughout the world were marveling at Mexico's "economic miracle."

Yet the miracle masked some serious problems. One was Mexico's explosive population growth. The country's population jumped from 20 million in 1940 to 51 million in 1970 to 77 million in 1984. Another problem was poverty. Nearly all the economic growth was concentrated in a few booming cities. The economic miracle had done little to help people in the countryside. The great majority of Mexicans still lived in drafty homes without running water, ate meager meals, and struggled to find jobs that paid no more than $3 or $4 a day.

Mexico City prospered during the oil boom of the late 1970's but faced hard times in the 1980's.

In the 1970's, Mexican leaders searched for ways to help the poor. Mexico's new president, Luis Echeverría, was critical of the multinational corporations. He charged that they were taking too much money out of Mexico. He convinced Mexico's congress to tax these companies more heavily and to limit the amount of business they could do in Mexico. The tax money was used to build roads, schools, and health clinics. Yet the new tax money was not enough to solve the deep-rooted problem of poverty.

In search of more money to meet the country's needs, Mexico borrowed from foreign banks. Soon Mexico's national debt almost doubled from $13 billion in 1970 to $23 billion in 1976.

The oil boom Miraculously, in 1976, a solution to all Mexico's economic problems seemed to appear. That year, geologists made spectacular discoveries of oil along Mexico's eastern coastline and offshore in the Gulf of Mexico. Within a short time, Mexico became one of the world's largest producers of petroleum.

As oil production increased, the country's export earnings jumped from $500 million in 1976 to a sensational $16 *billion* in the early 1980's. Because Mexico had nationalized its oil industry in 1938 (page 635), much of the money went directly into the national treasury.

The Mexican government, confident that its oil earnings would allow it to repay all loans easily, borrowed even more money from foreign banks. The Mexican government spent lavishly on social programs and new factories. At the same time, the free flow of money brought on a wave of corruption. Some government officials built magnificent mansions and created hundreds of phony jobs for their friends.

Then the oil boom collapsed. Beginning in 1981, the world price for oil began to plummet. So did Mexico's economy. In August 1982, the Mexican government shocked the banks of the world by announcing that it could not make the payments on its national debt of $80 billion. Mexico, in other words, was virtually bankrupt. At the last minute, international banks and foreign governments came to Mexico's rescue with emergency loans. These loans were enough to save Mexico temporarily from economic collapse.

In December 1982, Mexicans elected a new president, Miguel de la Madrid. He vowed to end government corruption, deal with the foreign debt, and help Mexico's poor. Yet his stringent efforts to cut government costs threatened the gains that Mexicans had made in wages, education, housing, and health care.

Urban and rural issues The new economic crisis showed clearly that poverty is still a widespread problem. Many Mexican cities have gleaming office buildings in their centers and rings of slums around the edges. In these slums, which the Mexicans call "lost cities," people live in wooden or cardboard shacks. Yet even in the lost cities, people have a better chance for jobs, health care, and education than they do in the countryside.

Opinions vary as to why poverty is so widespread in Mexico's countryside. Some say it is because farmers lack modern equipment. Others point out that foreign farming corporations grow food for export rather than for the Mexican people. Still others blame the lack of government spending in the countryside.

In recent years, many of Mexico's peasants have simply given up on the countryside. Some crowd into Mexico's growing cities in search of jobs and a better way of life. There, they often find exactly what they left behind—poverty and

The Nations of Latin America

UNITED STATES

• Monterrey

Rio Grande

Gulf of Mexico

• Puerto Vallarta

Mexico City ★
• Veracruz

Acapulco •

MEXICO

ATLANTIC OCEAN

Tropic of Cancer

★ Nassau

Havana ★

THE BAHAMAS

CUBA

Belmopan
★ **BELIZE**

GUATEMALA
HONDURAS

Guatemala
★ • Tegucigalpa

San Salvador ★

EL SALVADOR

Managua •

NICARAGUA

COSTA
RICA **PANAMA**

San José ★

Panama
City

JAMAICA

Kingston •

HAITI

Port-
au-Prince

DOMINICAN
REPUBLIC

Santo Domingo •
★ San Juan

PUERTO
RICO
(U.S.)

Caribbean Sea

Maracaibo •

Caracas •

Lake
Maracaibo

VENEZUELA

Orinoco River

GRENADA

TRINIDAD
AND TOBAGO

Panama
Canal

Medellín •
• Bogotá

• Cali

COLOMBIA

Georgetown
★ **SURINAME**
GUYANA • Paramaribo
★ ★ Cayenne
FRENCH
GUIANA
(Fr.)

20°N

10°N

GALÁPAGOS
ISLANDS
(Ecuador)

Quito ★
ECUADOR

Guayaquil •

Negro

Amazon River

Equator 0°

PACIFIC

Andes

PERU

Lima ★
• Cuzco

La Paz
• L. Titicaca
• Arequipa

Mountains

OCEAN

BOLIVIA

★ Sucre

São Francisco River

BRAZIL

• Recife

Brasília •

Belo •
Horizonte

10°S

PARAGUAY

Paraguay R.

Tucumán •

Asunción ★

Río de Janeiro
São Paulo •

20°S

Valparaíso •
Santiago •

CHILE

Paraná R.

ARGENTINA

Buenos Aires ★

Bahía
Blanca •

Uruguay R.

URUGUAY

★ Montevideo

Río de la
Plata

Tropic of Capricorn

Concepción •

ATLANTIC

OCEAN

30°S

KEY

★ Capital city

40°S

0   1000 Miles

FALKLAND ISLANDS
(United Kingdom)

Strait of
Magellan

Cape
Horn

120°W 110°W 100°W 90°W 80°W 70°W 60°W 50°W 40°W 30°W 20°W

30°N

Map Study

What countries border Mexico? What is the largest island in the Caribbean?
What country's capital lies almost directly on the equator? What is the largest
country in Latin America?

unemployment. Others choose a different route. They migrate north to the United States.

Tensions with the United States The number of Mexicans crossing illegally into the United States has risen sharply in the past two decades. Many thousands of Mexicans now cross the border illegally every year. Some hope to stay permanently. Other workers come to find temporary jobs. They plan to return to Mexico once they have earned some money.

The number of Mexican workers illegally entering the United States has created tension between the two countries. Mexico benefits from the millions of dollars its workers send home each year. At the same time, the United States government claims that these workers take jobs away from its citizens and put strains on social services such as public clinics and schools.

On the other hand, the Mexican government asserts that the United States reaps great benefit from the workers from Mexico. A Mexican economist explained:

> We provide the United States with a huge labor force. Most of the farms and many of the businesses in the United States Southwest depend on Mexican labor. Yet our workers . . . are poorly treated up north.

Despite such conflicts, however, the two countries continue to work hard at improving relations. In 1986, Mexican President Miguel de la Madrid emerged from a meeting with United States President Ronald Reagan stating that their talks "were an extraordinary effort to better the atmosphere of our relations."

Nicaragua erupted into a civil war.

Like Mexico, every country in Central America suffers from poverty and unemployment. Most Central American farmers have little land. They lack modern equipment. Cities are crowded and offer few jobs. Wealth rests in the hands of a few families. Every Central American country except Costa Rica also has a long history of rule by dictators. In recent years, there have been violent demonstrations and bloody civil wars in several Central American countries. Sometimes the conflicts were resolved. More often, they bred more violence.

Nicaragua is the largest country in Central America. Here too the United States has played an active role in the country's affairs. As early as 1912, United States Marines entered Nicaragua to help maintain order. When they withdrew in 1933, they left the government under the protection of a national police force known as the National Guard. The leader of the National Guard was General Anastasio Somoza (soh-MOH-sah). Somoza set out to win political power for himself.

Somoza's main opponent was Augusto Cesar Sandino (san-DEE-noh). Sandino was a strong nationalist who wanted to reduce foreign influence—including that of the United States—in Nicaragua. The National Guard killed Sandino in 1934.

Three years later, in 1937, Somoza became president and dictator of the country. In all, the Somoza family ruled Nicaragua for 42 years, the longest rule by one family in Latin American history. The Somoza family owned a huge busi-

Daily Life · Pottery Old and New

Pieces of pre-Columbian pottery from Central America are prized for their beauty and rarity. Throughout rural Central America, however, potters still make fine jars, bowls, pitchers, and bottles using some of the same methods and designs used by pre-Columbian artisans. The Spanish conquerors introduced the use of glazes and the potter's wheel. Some of the styles and methods of production used today in remote villages are unique. However, as roads are built and villagers have more contact with outsiders, folk-art pottery will probably become more uniform and may even be replaced by manufactured items.

ness empire that included about one tenth of Nicaragua's farmland, the country's only airline, a television station, a newspaper, a textile mill, and several sugar refineries. To keep control of its empire, the family fixed elections and assassinated political rivals. Many Nicaraguans came to believe that only a revolution would end the Somoza dictatorship.

In the early 1970's, Nicaraguan rebel groups joined together to form an army called the Sandinista National Liberation Front (FSLN). The Sandinistas took their name from the rebel leader Sandino who had been killed in 1934. Although the Sandinistas included many groups, many of the leaders were Marxists.

Between 1977 and 1979, Nicaragua was engulfed by a civil war between Somoza's National Guard and the Sandinista rebels. The United States government supported Somoza because the Sandinistas were receiving aid from the Soviet Union and Cuba. Most of the Sandinista's support, however, came from the angry Nicaraguan people themselves. Nicaraguan men and women took up arms to fight the hated dictatorship.

In 1979, the Sandinistas were victorious. They overthrew the Somoza government and forced its leaders to leave the country. On July 19, 1979, jubilant Sandinista fighters and their supporters clogged the streets of Managua, the capital city, to celebrate their victory.

Nicaragua's new government set out to rebuild the country and to make revolutionary social and economic changes. The government gave land formerly owned by the Somoza family to landless peasants. It encouraged high school students to teach peasants to read and write. It also set up clinics to give people free health care. Food was distributed to the most needy.

Soon, however, the Sandinistas ran into problems. The war, which had taken 50,000 lives and cost $500 million, had left the country with huge debts. The Sandinistas were forced to borrow heavily from other nations. Much of the aid came from the Soviet Union and Cuba.

The Nicaraguan economy was weak, and many goods were in short supply. People waited in long lines to buy their weekly groceries and then found store shelves bare. As criticism of the government grew, the Sandinistas responded by shutting down newspapers and radio stations that voiced protests.

El Salvador was also split by civil war between guerrillas and government troops. Some guerrillas, as in this photo, were as young as 12.

Meanwhile, rebels called *contras* continued to fight against the new government. (*Contra* comes from the Spanish word for "against.") Contra guerrillas attacked government soldiers. They also staged attacks on coffee plantations and other businesses to disrupt the economy.

In response, Sandinista officials took military aid from the Soviet Union and Cuba. With this aid, the Nicaraguan army quickly became the biggest and best supplied in Central America.

Nicaragua's ties to Communist countries alarmed leaders in the United States. President Ronald Reagan charged that Nicaragua was being used as a staging ground for a Communist takeover of all Central America. By 1986, the United States had sent millions of dollars to the contras.

Contra activity has clearly weakened the Sandinista government. However, a 1984 election showed that the Sandinista government could still count on the support of most Nicaraguans.

Section Review 1

Define: multinational corporation
Identify: (a) Pan-American Highway, (b) Central America, (c) Miguel de la Madrid, (d) Anastasio Somoza, (e) Sandinista, (f) contra

Answer:

1. (a) What economic successes did Mexico achieve between 1945 and 1975? (b) What economic problems remained?
2. (a) What short-term effects did the oil boom have for Mexico? (b) What long-term effects?
3. (a) Why do many Mexican workers cross illegally into the United States? (b) What position does each country take on the issue?
4. (a) How did the Somoza family gain and keep control of Nicaragua? (b) How was the family overthrown?
5. (a) What policies did the Sandinistas follow after they were in power? (b) What problems did they face? (c) Why did the United States support their opponents?

Critical Thinking

6. Scan the section for examples of different ways the United States has interacted with Mexico and Central America. What ways do you find? Where possible, evaluate the results.

Caribbean nations take different paths. 2

The Caribbean islands stretch for more than 2,000 miles from the western tip of Cuba to the coast of Venezuela. Three mainland countries are also part of the Caribbean region. These are Guyana, Suriname, and French Guiana.

Like Mexico and Central America, every country in the Caribbean was once a colony of a larger power. Spain, Great Britain, France, the Netherlands, and the United States all managed to gain a foothold in the region.

Most Caribbean nations had won political independence by the 1960's. Yet they were far from being economically independent. The countries of the Caribbean have followed different paths toward economic development.

Puerto Rico drew closer to the United States.

Until 1898, Puerto Rico was a colony of Spain. In that year, however, the United States went to war with Spain and won much of Spain's empire in the Caribbean and Pacific. For all practical purposes, Puerto Rico became a colony of the United States.

United States rule brought many changes to the island. In the past, Puerto Rican farmers had planted a variety of crops. Now large sugar companies from the United States bought up the best farmland. There they planted sugarcane. Soon, most Puerto Ricans depended on the sugar industry for their living. Dependence on a single industry is always dangerous. When that industry fails, everyone suffers. Thus, when the price of sugar fell in the 1930's, Puerto Ricans faced unemployment and poverty. Many Puerto Ricans blamed the United States. A movement for independence gained strength.

In 1948, Puerto Ricans won the right to elect their own governor. The voters chose Luis Muñoz Marin (MOON-YOHS muh-REEN). Muñoz Marin wanted Puerto Rico to be strong and prosperous. He developed a plan called Operation Bootstrap. (An old saying describes people who get rich by hard work as "lifting themselves up by their own bootstraps.")

Under Operation Bootstrap, low tax rates encouraged United States businesses to invest in Puerto Rico. Soon hundreds of new factories dotted the island. The people of Puerto Rico were able to find many kinds of work besides cutting sugarcane. The average yearly income for a Puerto Rican worker rose from $121 in 1940 to $900 in 1965. Today, it is about $3,865. That is higher than any nation in Latin America but lower than any state in the United States.

Many Puerto Ricans were satisfied with the economic progress on their island. In 1952, they voted to become an "Associated Free State" of the United States. The Commonwealth of Puerto Rico, as it is called, has the power to elect its own government. Puerto Ricans are citizens of the United States. However, they cannot vote in national elections, and they do not have voting representatives in Congress.

Operation Bootstrap had many successes, but some serious economic and social problems emerged in the 1970's. One was the government's neglect of farming. Once, Puerto Ricans had grown more than enough crops to feed themselves. However, few farmers wanted to work the land when they could take higher paying jobs in factories. As a result, many Puerto Ricans abandoned

By a statue of Columbus in Puerto Rico, the flags of Puerto Rico and the United States fly together.

their farms, forcing the island to begin importing much of its food.

Another current problem is unemployment. Industrialization did not create all the jobs needed. Therefore, many Puerto Rican young people travel to the mainland in search of work. In 1986, about 2 million Puerto Ricans lived in the United States. (The population of Puerto Rico itself is about 3.5 million.)

Puerto Rico is still torn between its Caribbean traditions and its connection with the United States. As one Puerto Rican put it:

> We have a split personality . . . We're proud to be Latin Americans who speak Spanish and have a distinctive culture, but we know life would be very difficult for us if our close ties with the United States were suddenly cut.

Cuba became a Communist nation.

Like Puerto Rico, Cuba was also a Spanish colony until the late 1800's. Cuba became independent from Spain in 1899, after the Spanish-American War (pages 551–552).

Although Cuba did not become a United States colony, the United States kept tight control over the island. In time, United States business people owned most of Cuba's mines, plantations, and factories. Between 1898 and 1934, the United States sent soldiers to Cuba several times to help various dictators stay in power and to protect its business interests.

During the 1950's, the dictator of Cuba was Fulgencio Batista (buh-TEES-tuh). Batista ruled the island cruelly with little concern for the people. However, he did not interfere with United States businesses on the island. Therefore, he had strong support from the United States government.

Castro in control By the 1950's, many Cubans had had enough of the dictator. In 1959, guerrilla fighters led by a young Cuban lawyer named Fidel Castro finally overthrew Batista's corrupt dictatorship.

At first, Castro was praised throughout Latin America and the United States for bringing democracy to Cuba. When he came to New York to speak at the United Nations, crowds cheered him and showered confetti on his motorcade.

However, within a year of taking power, Castro suspended all elections and named himself president. He shut down radio stations and newspapers that criticized his government. Cubans who opposed the government were jailed or executed. The United States government became convinced that Cubans had traded one bad dictator for another.

Then Castro made revolutionary changes in Cuba's economy. These changes antagonized the United States and caught the attention of all Latin America. In 1960, the Cuban government nationalized United States–owned oil refineries, mines, stores, and even soft-drink bottling plants. Moreover, Cuba made no payment for the properties. United States business leaders were outraged.

The United States embargo In response to Castro's actions, President Dwight Eisenhower placed an economic **embargo** on Cuba. An embargo is a government order forbidding trade with a country. The United States would no longer sell goods to Cuba or buy Cuban products.

The embargo threatened to ruin Cuba's economy. The United States had been Cuba's biggest customer, buying nearly all its sugar crop. Cuba imported most of its manufactured goods—everything from toothpaste to machinery—from the United States.

After the embargo, Cuba turned to other nations for help. The Soviet Union promised to buy Cuba's sugar harvest at a fixed rate and also offered other aid. The United States grew alarmed when Cuba and the Soviet Union signed a far-reaching military and trade agreement.

The Bay of Pigs Within two years, the United States was actively working to drive Castro from power. President John F. Kennedy approved a plan to attack Cuba in the spring of 1961. The United States Central Intelligence Agency (CIA) trained and armed anti-Castro Cuban refugees in Guatemala. In April 1961, the forces landed at a beach called Playa Girón. (It was known in the United States as the Bay of Pigs.) The attackers expected many Cubans to join them and bring down the Castro government.

The attack at the Bay of Pigs was a total failure. Cubans rallied to the defense of Castro, and the invaders were quickly captured. The incident seriously embarrassed the United States in the eyes of other countries.

After the Bay of Pigs, Castro openly declared that Cuba, like the Soviet Union, was a Communist country. Soon Castro's links to the Soviet Union brought on a new crisis with the United States.

The missile crisis In October 1962, a United States spy plane flying over Cuba brought back photographs of Soviet missiles there. The missiles were capable of carrying nuclear warheads. Castro claimed that Cuba needed the missiles to defend itself against attacks such as the Bay of Pigs. President Kennedy and his advisers feared that the Soviet Union would use the weapons against United States cities.

Kennedy demanded that the Soviet Union remove the missiles. The world held its breath as it waited for the Soviet response. Nuclear war seemed possible. In the end, however, the Soviets agreed to remove the missiles if the United States would promise never again to invade Cuba. Although the crisis ended peacefully, relations between the United States and Cuba did not improve.

Cuba under Castro Today, no one can dispute the fact that communism is firmly entrenched in Cuba. During his 30 years in power, Castro has tried to make Cuba a stronger country. Supporters of the revolution point to its many successes. Life expectancy is greater now for the average Cuban than it was in 1959. Birthrates and infant death rates have declined. Diseases such as malaria and polio have been eliminated. Illiteracy has been wiped out.

Yet the Cuban economy remains fragile. It would collapse without economic aid from the Soviet Union that averages $1 million dollars per day.

Meanwhile, Castro allows virtually no criticism of the government. Discontented Cubans tried to escape the island throughout the 1960's and 1970's. In 1980, Castro temporarily opened the doors to emigration. Some 125,000 Cubans boarded yachts, and small freighters, and even ski boats and sought refuge in Florida.

Despite such discontent, Castro's revolution remains popular with many Cubans. As one Cuban farmer commented,

Before the Revolution, my family was poor and without land. Now I help run a cooperative farm. The government built me an apartment, sent my children to school and provided my family with free health care. Of course I support the Revolution.

Section Review 2

Define: embargo
Identify: (a) Luis Muñoz Marin, (b) Operation Bootstrap, (c) Fulgencio Batista, (d) Fidel Castro, (e) Bay of Pigs
Answer:
1. (a) What was the dominant industry in Puerto Rico before 1948? (b) How did Puerto Rico improve its economy?
2. Describe the political position of Puerto Rico in relation to the United States.
3. How did Castro come to power in Cuba?
4. (a) What political policies did Castro follow? (b) What economic policies?
5. (a) What economic step did the United States take against Castro? (b) What military action? (c) What were the results?
6. How did a confrontation develop between the United States and the Soviet Union in Cuba?

Critical Thinking
7. Suppose you were a journalist trying to write an objective evaluation of life in Cuba under Castro. What groups of people should you interview? Why might it prove difficult to reach a fair conclusion?

South American nations seek solutions. 3

After winning their independence in the early 1800's, many South American countries came under the rule of military strongmen called caudillos (page 504). Many countries went through cycles of dictatorship and democracy. Democratic governments often failed to keep peace or provide economic stability. Dictatorships offered stability but also brought brutality and oppression.

Brazil ended military rule.

Brazil covers nearly half of South America and is almost the size of the United States. Among the countries of the world, Brazil ranks fifth in area and eighth in population. It is often called the "Giant of South America."

During the 1950's and early 1960's, Brazil had a democratic government. In 1961, Brazilians chose João Goulart as president. Although no one knew it at the time, Goulart would be the last democratically elected president to rule Brazil for more than 20 years.

Goulart inherited many problems. Inflation was high, and the nation owed foreign banks huge loans. Goulart added to Brazil's problems by his inexperience, weakness, and uncertainty.

Near the end of his term, Goulart took an unexpected step. He allowed peasants to move onto the empty farmland of some wealthy landowners. The landowners, who did not want to lose their land, convinced army leaders to overthrow Goulart.

In 1964, army officers seized control of the government. They immediately canceled all elections and named a general to the presidency.

Brazil's economic miracle To solve the country's pressing economic problems, the army leaders then did what no democratic government had dared to do. They cut workers' wages and slowed rising prices. In the process, they also created a stable government. Soon foreign companies and governments were investing millions of dollars in Brazil's future. By 1974, the world was praising the "Brazilian miracle."

Gleaming skyscrapers rose in cities such as Rio de Janeiro and São Paulo. A 3,500-mile high-

This Japanese-owned pepper plantation is an example of the foreign investment in Brazil.

way was cut through the Amazon Basin to link Brazil's Atlantic coast with the interior. Factories sprang up throughout the countryside.

Yet the economic boom had a dark side as well. Some of the worst pollution in the world hung over Brazil's cities and seeped into its water. In certain neighborhoods, a frightening number of babies were born dead, and people suffered from headaches and sickness as a result of pollution. Moreover, the spectacular growth of the economy had been partly financed by keeping workers' wages low.

After ten years of military rule, Brazil's workers and peasants were poorer than ever. In that same period, the military government drastically cut education, welfare, and health programs. While a few Brazilians grew extremely wealthy, the great majority of people were underfed and poorly housed. Discontent began to grow.

Political repression Brazilians who dared speak out against the army government took great risks. Police arrested opponents and dragged them to secret jails where they were tortured and sometimes killed. Terror squads roamed the streets and openly shot people suspected of opposing the government.

771

Such abuses of human rights created an outcry throughout the world. In 1976, the United States threatened to cut back its military aid to Brazil until the generals showed more respect for human rights. Slowly, abuses of human rights became less frequent in Brazil. Other changes were also occurring.

The end of the miracle By the end of the 1970's, Brazil's economic miracle was beginning to fade. Inflation was running over 100 percent a year. Unemployment spread thoughout the country. São Paulo, the industrial heartland of the country, was hit especially hard. Brazil's national debt rose to $87 billion, the largest in the world. The army's economic plan no longer seemed to be working.

The return of democracy In 1982, the army named a new president, General João Figueiredo. He promised to "open the country up to democracy," and he kept his word. After 21 years of military rule, Brazil finally returned to democracy in 1985.

On January 15, 1985, Brazilians overwhelmingly elected Tancredo Neves president. Before Neves was sworn in as president, however, he became extremely ill. Brazilians waited tensely and hoped for his recovery. It did not come, and Neves died without ever taking office. Vice President José Sarney, once a political opponent of Neves, became president. Despite fears of an uprising, Brazil's transition from military rule to democratic rule proved to be peaceful. Many were hopeful for the future.

Chile's socialist experiment failed.

Chile is a long, narrow country stretching 2,700 miles along the Pacific coast of South America, In the 1950's and 1960's, Chile had a democratic government similar to that of the United States. In fact, Chile had the longest and strongest tradition of democratic rule in South America.

Nevertheless, Chile faced a host of nagging problems. Although it had a larger middle class than any other South American country, there were still many poor farmers and miners. Its economy was barely growing. Chile had to import much of its food because wealthy landowners

Voice from Our Time · *Literature* Is Fire

Many Latin American writers are actively involved in social reform and revolutionary politics. The Peruvian writer Mario Vargas Llosa explained his view of literature.

[I]t is necessary to remind our societies what awaits them [if they encourage writers]. To warn them that literature is fire, that it signifies non-conformism and rebellion, that the writer's very reason for being is protest, contradiction, and criticism . . . Literature is a form of permanent [rebellion] and recognizes no straitjackets . . . Literature may perish but it will never conform.

Only if this condition is fulfilled is literature useful to society . . . Its mission is to agitate, disturb, alarm, keep men constantly dissatisfied with themselves: its function is to unconditionally stimulate the will to change and improve, even though in order to achieve this the most deadly and poisonous weapons must be employed. It must be understood once and for all that the more terrible and cruel an author's writings against his country, the more intense the passion that binds him to it.

1. Why does the author compare literature to fire?
2. According to Llosa, what is the purpose of literature?
3. What might he mean by "deadly and poisonous weapons" in literature?
4. With what groups might such a writer come into conflict?
5. Do you agree or disagree with this evaluation of literature? Explain.

exported many crops for profit. In addition, three large copper mines produced over two thirds of Chile's copper. These mines were owned by United States companies, so their profits too were sent out of Chile.

Facing these problems, Chilean voters turned to a man with more radical ideas than their leaders of the 1960's. In 1970, Chileans elected as their president a Marxist candidate named Salvador Allende (ah-YEHN-day). This democratic election of a Marxist president was a new turn in Latin American politics. The world watched Chile as never before.

Allende's experiment Allende moved rapidly to carry out his radical program of "transition to socialism." The government set up medical clinics and food programs for the poor. Large landowners were forced to distribute much of their land to the rural poor. The government supported workers' rights to form unions and strike for higher pay. Workers and peasants enthusiastically welcomed such changes. However, Allende's programs won little support among the middle and upper classes.

Then, Allende nationalized the copper mines owned by the United States. Arguing that "the United States has already taken too much wealth out of Chile," he did not repay their owners. The United States government was so angered by these moves that it cut off all loans to the Allende government. Chile's economy went rapidly downhill.

As the economy worsened, Allende faced growing opposition at home. The opposition reached a boiling point in 1973. On September 11, the guards at the presidential palace in Santiago deserted their posts, leaving Allende and a few supporters inside without protection. Santiago was strangely quiet. Suddenly air force planes screamed over the city. Rockets hit the presidential palace. It burst into flames. Allende was killed. Chile's long tradition of democracy came to a sudden end.

Pinochet's regime General Augusto Pinochet (pee-noh-SHAY) headed the new military government. He rapidly made himself dictator. Pinochet silenced Allende's supporters with arrests, torture, and murder. Late at night, Chileans could hear rifle shots as soldiers in armored cars patrolled city streets. In all, between 5,000 and 15,000 Chileans were killed.

The military government banned all political parties. Newspapers, radio, and television were strictly censored. The army even took control of the universities.

Pinochet quickly undid most of Allende's socialist changes. He returned the copper mines to the United States businesses. He also allowed wealthy landowners to regain their holdings. The government strongly discouraged strikes.

Pinochet established close ties with the United States, which rewarded Chile with millions in economic and military aid. Inflation dropped from 600 percent per year in 1973 to just under 10 percent in 1981, the lowest in Latin America. Foreign investments rose dramatically.

Despite these limited successes, however, Pinochet did little to improve the condition of the poor. Abuses of human rights continued. As opposition to Pinochet grew in the mid-1980's, the increasingly unpopular dictator had to fight harder and harder to stay in power.

Perón shaped modern Argentina.

Like Brazil and Chile, Argentina has traveled a stormy path in search of a stable government. At times, elections were held and civilian governments ruled. At other times, the military seized control of the government. Yet one remarkable leader has left an enduring mark on the nation's government in the modern period. That leader was Juan Perón (pay-ROHN), who ruled Argentina between 1946 and 1955 and again briefly between 1973 and 1974. As one Argentine said, "The shadow of Juan Perón fell on every leader of our nation."

The Peróns in control Perón was first elected president of Argentina in 1946. Although the army and most wealthy Argentines were against him, Perón had the support of the workers and their labor unions. Perón's government redistributed income in favor of poor factory workers, promoted industrialization, and nationalized several foreign-owned companies. Perón created a powerful political party that in some ways resembled the Fascist parties that Hitler and Mussolini had built (pages 653–655). Perón's actions were sometimes those of a dictator.

Juan Perón's wife, Eva Perón, took an active part in government. She set up a charitable foundation in a huge marble building, personally giving out money and gifts to the needy. As a long line of poor Argentines filed into her office, she granted each a favor. To a hungry family, she gave food. To a nearly blind grandmother, she gave a pair of glasses. She also led a successful fight to win votes for Argentine women.

The Peróns formed a powerful pair. "Evita," as Eva Perón was fondly called by the masses, enhanced her husband's popularity with the common people. When she died in 1952, the nation mourned for weeks. Millions of Argentines wept as they passed her open coffin. Juan Perón had lost his greatest ally.

A *time of crisis* After Evita's death, Perón's high-handed actions began to anger more and more Argentines. He strengthened his own party by outlawing other political parties. He organized young people into armed groups, telling them that Perónism was the one true faith of the people. The Roman Catholic Church was outraged when mobs of these young people attacked and burned several famous churches in Perón's name. Wealthy Argentines were upset by Perón's heavy taxes and his nationalization of industries.

Finally, Perón's opponents joined forces. With the support of the Church and upper-class Argentines, a group of army officers forced Perón to resign and leave the country.

Following Perón's overthrow, Argentina was governed by eight presidents, only two of them elected. The army overthrew one leader after another. No one was able to restore order. When Perón was allowed to return to Argentina in 1972, the country was still in turmoil.

The *return of Perón* Perón ran for president in 1973. His new wife, Isabel, ran for vice president. They won with 62 percent of the vote. However, Perón's return to power at age 78 was troubled and short-lived. In July 1974, the aged Perón died. Isabel Perón became Latin America's first female head of state.

Isabel Perón's new government was not able to deal with the nation's pressing economic and social problems. Perón was politically inexperienced. She waited too long to make key decisions. Members of her government fought among themselves. Argentina again plunged into chaos, and fighting broke out among rival groups.

Finally, on March 24, 1976, the military staged a coup. Isabel Perón was placed under house arrest, and a group of generals took power.

Military rule The military leaders launched a vicious campaign against anyone who disagreed with their government. Thousands of suspected guerrillas were arrested, tortured, and killed. Some 20,000 Argentines simply vanished. They were known as *desaparecidos*, or "missing ones." Most were probably seized and killed by off-duty soldiers. Argentines called this period of violence "the dirty war."

The military had no better results running the country than the earlier elected governments. Prices rose and wages fell. Many businesses closed.

In 1982, a new general took control. General Leopoldo Galtieri faced a nation that was seriously divided. He decided on a bold move to unite the people of Argentina. Lying 400 miles east of Patagonia is a group of rocky, windswept islands known as the Falkland Islands. These islands, settled long ago by the British, were home to 1,800 British citizens and their 600,000 sheep. However, many Argentines felt the Falklands belonged to them. Galtieri decided it was time for the Argentines to make good their claim.

Argentine troops seized the Falkland Islands on April 2, 1982. People in Argentina turned out for massive demonstrations of national pride. The British government, however, did not intend to give up the Falklands. In the ten-week war that followed, the Argentines were soundly defeated. General Galtieri's gamble had failed. Now angry crowds gathered in downtown Buenos Aires shouting, "Nail Galtieri to the wall!"

General Galtieri left office, and the military promised to hold elections. In 1983, Argentines elected Raul Alfonsin as president. For the first time in 40 years, the Perónist party had been defeated in a free election.

President Alfonsin set out to heal some of Argentina's political wounds. Many army and police officers were put on trial for committing torture and murder. Workers' wages were raised slightly. Inflation was brought under control. It was a hopeful time for Argentines.

Section Review 3

Identify: (a) João Goulart, (b) Salvador Allende, (c) Augusto Pinochet, (d) Juan Perón, (e) Eva Perón, (f) Isabel Perón, (g) Falkland Islands

Answer:

1. (a) What events led to an army takeover of Brazil in 1964? (b) How did the military create an economic miracle in Brazil?
2. (a) What happened in Brazil when the economic miracle began to fade? (b) How did democracy return to Brazil in 1985?
3. (a) Why did Allende's election as president of Chile win worldwide attention? (b) Describe his socialist experiment.
4. (a) What factors helped bring about Allende's downfall? (b) Describe the military regime that replaced him.
5. (a) What group of people formed Perón's power base in Chile? (b) What mistakes helped to bring about his downfall in 1955?
6. (a) How did the military come to power in Argentina in 1976? (b) Why did Argentina decide to invade the Falkland Islands? (c) What was the outcome?

Critical Thinking

7. Compare the cases of the three countries described in this section. (a) What causes have led to the overthrow of democratic governments? (b) What factors have led to the restoration of democracy?

Canada confronts a changing world. 4

Canada is often referred to by people in the United States as "our friendly neighbor to the north." Canada, which covers more than half of North America, has a long history of cooperation and peace with the United States. Yet, despite close ties between the two nations, many Canadians are puzzled when their country is referred to as a friendly neighbor. As one Canadian put it, "How could we be true friends? You hardly know us."

Since 1960, Canada has faced many economic and political changes. Some changes have raised questions about relations between Canada and the United States. These issues have made people in the United States pay closer attention to their northern neighbor. Recent history shows the many ties that bind the two nations.

Canada took an active role in world affairs.

Canada's prestige and economic strength after World War II convinced many Canadians that the nation was ready to take an active role in foreign affairs. In 1945, Canada became a founding member of the United Nations. Four years later, in 1949, it joined NATO (page 699).

During the early 1950's, Canada sent troops to Korea under the UN flag (page 704). In 1957, Canadian statesman Lester Pearson temporarily helped ease friction in the Middle East, for which he won the Nobel Peace Prize.

Also in 1957, Canada and the United States combined their air defense systems to defend North America against possible attack. They created the North American Air Defense Command (NORAD). Some Canadians opposed NORAD, saying that it committed Canada to United States policies. Other Canadians believed that NORAD was necessary for Canada's defense against its other close neighbor, the USSR.

Canada resolved conflicts with the United States.

By 1960, Canadians were proud of their growing economy and accomplishments in foreign affairs. Many felt that it was now time for Canada to take a more independent stand toward the United States. Some members of the Canadian government began to voice reluctance to follow the lead of the United States.

The Cuban missile crisis (page 770) highlighted strains between the United States and Canada. At that time, Canadian Prime Minister John Diefenbaker refused to place Canada's nuclear bombers on alert, as required by the NORAD treaty. United States President John Kennedy sent an angry letter challenging the government of

Footnote to History

Canada's flag had long carried the British Union Jack, showing the country's British heritage. In 1964, Canadians adopted a new flag. It features an eleven-point red maple leaf. The change was a welcome one to French Canadians, who disliked reminders of Canada's ties to Britain.

Canada

Map Study
What Canadian provinces or territories do not border the United States?

Canada to live up to its agreements. A few months later, a great debate broke out in Canada's Parliament over the same issue.

The controversy over Canada's commitment to nuclear arms reached a peak in 1963. Diefenbaker refused to accept nuclear warheads from the United States for use in defending North America, although Canada had promised to do so several years earlier.

Debate over whether or not to accept the warheads became so heated that Diefenbaker was forced to call a general election in 1963. His party lost, and opposition leader Lester Pearson became the new prime minister. Prime Minister Pearson accepted the warheads from the United States. In so doing, he dramatically improved relations between the two countries.

French nationalists sought rights.

Pearson's government also faced a serious domestic challenge to Canada's national unity. In the 1960's, conflict erupted in Quebec Province between French-speaking and English-speaking Canadians.

French Canadians are proud of their heritage. Although French rule in Canada ended in 1763, French Canadians have maintained their culture. They still speak French, send their children to French schools, and support the Roman Catholic Church. Today, descendants of the early French settlers live throughout Canada. In the province of Quebec, they form a majority. Yet in the 1960's, they did not feel they had a fair share of jobs, businesses, or political power.

In 1960, Jean Lesage, prime minister of Quebec, began a movement to defend French Canadian rights. That movement became known as the Quiet Revolution. Lesage wanted the English-speaking people of Canada to respect Quebec's French language and heritage. He also wanted French Canadians to take control of Quebec businesses that were owned by English Canadians and foreign companies.

Lesage's Quiet Revolution was much too slow-paced for some French Canadians. They supported **separatism**. They wanted Quebec to separate from Canada and become an independent state. A few French Canadians used violence to try to win Quebec's independence from Canada. They called themselves the Front de Liberation de Quebec (FLQ). The FLQ used terrorist tactics, planting bombs in public buildings.

The Pearson government tried to find solutions to the separatist movement. It moved to give Quebec a "special status" in Canada by allowing the province to keep a greater share of federal taxes, make some foreign policy decisions, and control its own natural resources. Many Canadians, however, criticized Pearson for granting special privileges to Quebec. In April 1968, Pearson retired as prime minister. His successor was Pierre E. Trudeau (troo-DOH), a dashing and dynamic man.

Although Trudeau himself was a French Canadian, he was alarmed by the growing separatist movement in Quebec. He planned to give French Canadians more rights but to keep Quebec as part of Canada.

In 1969, the Canadian Parliament passed a law that made French, along with English, an official language of Canada. Huge sums of money were spent to teach French to English-speaking public officials, clerks, teachers, and other government employees.

In 1980, the people of Quebec had a chance to vote on separatism. All Canadians nervously awaited election day. In the end, 60 percent of the voters rejected the idea of an independent Quebec. Canada had survived its most serious challenge to unity. French Canadians remain very proud of their heritage.

Today Canada faces many of the same concerns and issues as other countries in the Western Hemisphere, including the United States. It too is fighting inflation and unemployment. Yet a

Quebec buses carried signs in French urging voters to say yes *or* no *to separatism in 1980.*

recent opinion poll revealed that four out of five Canadians are optimistic about the future. The optimism was apparent at the dazzling World's Fair in Vancouver. Expo 86 attracted millions of visitors to Canada and further enhanced the nation's international image.

Section Review 4

Define: separatism
Identify: (a) NORAD, (b) Lester Pearson, (c) Jean Lesage, (d) Pierre Trudeau
Answer:
1. (a) Describe the dramatic economic changes that took place in Canada after World War II. (b) How did Canada extend its involvement in world affairs during this same period?
2. (a) What was the attitude of Diefenbaker's government toward the United States and nuclear arms? (b) How did Pearson's attitude differ?
3. (a) What was the Quiet Revolution? (b) How were its goals different from those of the separatist movement?
4. How was the issue of separatism resolved?

Critical Thinking
5. Suggest a list of topics on which United States citizens should seek more information if they truly want to call Canada their "friendly neighbor to the north."

Summary

1. Mexico and Central America face change. During the 1950's, Mexico's economic miracle masked severe rural poverty. Mexico borrowed heavily to help the poor, even after the discovery of oil, until world oil prices plummeted in 1981. In Nicaragua, the United States has recently supported contra rebels against the Sandinista government.

2. Caribbean nations take different paths. In the early 1900's, United States sugarcane plantations imposed a single-resource economy on Puerto Rico. After World War II, Operation Bootstrap improved the Puerto Rican economy, although problems still remained. In 1959, Fidel Castro set up a Communist government in Cuba. Today, Cuba remains tied to the Soviet Union.

3. South American nations seek solutions. In 1964, Brazilian military officers overthrew the republic and set up a dictatorship, which achieved an economic miracle in the cities but left extreme poverty in the countryside. In 1985, democratic government returned to Brazil. In the early 1970's, President Allende of Chile experimented with socialism. Military leaders, supported by the upper class, overthrew Allende in 1973 and set up a harsh dictatorship. Abuses of human rights continue in Chile. Argentina was controlled by

Juan Perón from 1946 to 1955 and again between 1973 and 1974. In 1976, the military took over but was not able to unite the country. In 1983, Argentines elected a new president who has attempted to stabilize the economy.

4. Canada confronts a changing world. Canada's prestige and economic strength after World War II led the country to assume an active role in world affairs. Although conflicts developed between the United States and Canada over NORAD, the two countries were able to resolve their differences in the early 1960's. Demands for more economic and political power among French Canadians led to a separatist movement. The issue was resolved in a general election when the people of Quebec voted to remain a part of Canada.

Reviewing the Facts

1. Define the following terms:
   a. multinational corporation
   b. embargo
   c. separatism
2. Explain the importance of each of the following names, places, or terms:
   a. Pan-American Highway
   b. Miguel de la Madrid

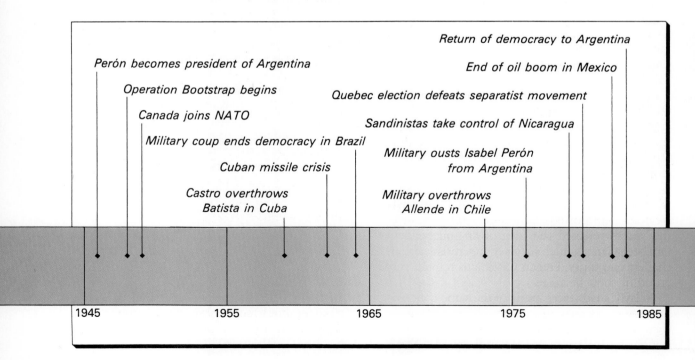

Return of democracy to Argentina

Perón becomes president of Argentina

End of oil boom in Mexico

Operation Bootstrap begins

Quebec election defeats separatist movement

Canada joins NATO

Military coup ends democracy in Brazil

Sandinistas take control of Nicaragua

Cuban missile crisis

Military ousts Isabel Perón from Argentina

Castro overthrows Batista in Cuba

Military overthrows Allende in Chile

1945   1955   1965   1975   1985

c. Somoza
d. Sandinistas
e. contras
f. Operation Bootstrap
g. Associated Free State
h. Batista
i. Castro
j. Bay of Pigs
k. Figueiredo
l. Allende
m. Pinochet
n. Juan Perón
o. Eva Perón
p. Isabel Perón
q. desaparecidos
r. Falkland Islands
s. Alfonsin
t. Pearson
u. NORAD
v. Lesage
w. Trudeau

3. (a) What problems persisted in Mexico despite the economic miracle? (b) What happened when oil prices plummeted in 1981?
4. How has rural poverty in Mexico affected relations with the United States?
5. (a) How did the Sandinistas come to power in Nicaragua? (b) What changes did they make? (c) Why does the United States support their opponents?
6. (a) What changes did the United States bring to Puerto Rico after 1900? (b) How did Puerto Rico improve its economy? (c) What is the status of Puerto Rico today?
7. (a) What changes did Castro bring to Cuba? (b) Describe relations between Cuba and the United States.
8. (a) Why did the military overthrow the Brazilian government in 1964? (b) What did the military accomplish? (c) Why has democratic government returned to Brazil in recent years?
9. (a) Why did Chile's socialist experiment fail? (b) Describe the regime that replaced Allende.
10. (a) What led to the overthrow of Perón in 1955? (b) Of Isabel Perón in 1976? (c) Of the military government that replaced her?
11. What changes took place in Canada's role in foreign affairs after World War II?

12. (a) Describe the conflict between Canada and the United States that arose in the 1960's. (b) Describe separatism and its outcome.

Thinking about History

1. Every country in South America except Guyana has at one time in its history been governed by the military. Why have South Americans often been willing to accept army rule? What conditions within a country precipitate military coups?
2. The Pan-American Highway serves as a link that brings the people of the Americas together. How did each of the following either unite the people of ancient times or keep ancient peoples apart? (a) Roman roads (b) the Nile River (c) the geography of Greece

Writing and Speaking about History

1. In chart form, compare military rule in Chile, Argentina, and Brazil. For each country, list conditions leading to the takeover, the characteristics of military rule, and the outcome.
2. Debate the following topic: "Puerto Rico should weaken its ties to the United States."

Practicing Skills

1. How does the map on page 765 help explain the United States' reaction to Soviet missiles in Cuba?
2. Label the territories, provinces, provincial capitals, and the national capital of Canada on an outline map of the country.

Investigating History

1. The Amazon Basin is the world's largest rain forest. Find out more about the Amazon Basin. Why is it important to the ecology of the Western Hemisphere? What plants and animals can be found there? Why is it in danger today?
2. Research some of the cultural ties that link peoples of the Americas. These include music, language, sports, and food.

Decision Making in History

Evaluate the issue of Mexicans illegally entering the United States from the point of view of both countries. To what conclusion do you come? What recommendations can you make?

World Leaders: The USSR and the United States

Soviet General Secretary Mikhail Gorbachev (left) and American President Ronald Reagan met in Iceland in the fall of 1986. Iceland was chosen because it lies about halfway between the United States and the Soviet Union.

1. **Policies changed within the USSR.**

2. **The USSR has goals abroad.**

3. **Americans sought new opportunities at home.**

4. **Americans differed on foreign policy.**

The two leaders shook hands, posed for photographers, and then sat down with interpreters and note takers in a small, secluded room in a simple guesthouse. They discussed a plan for *arms control*— that is, limits on the nuclear weapons each country would build. They proposed drastic cuts in such weapons, with the goal of eventually eliminating them entirely. If the two men had agreed, the meeting would have produced the most powerful arms control agreement since the explosion of the first atom bomb.

Outside the meeting room, Reykjavik, the capital of the small, quiet country of Iceland, was transformed for the event. There were a few demonstrators in the streets, but they were outnumbered by shoppers buying souvenirs such as T-shirts, scarves, and ashtrays, all with pictures of the two leaders. There was even a small parade of Icelandic ponies, their riders carrying the Icelandic flag and those of the countries of the two leaders.

There were intense questions of protocol. One of the leaders arrived for a meeting a minute early. The other leader was not ready for the ceremonial greeting and rushed out a little flustered. Both men looked at their watches and then smiled for the cameras. One leader stayed at his country's embassy in Reykjavik. The other stayed on one of his country's ships in the harbor. The aides of one leader rejected the china tea service provided by their Icelandic hosts. A more elaborate set was produced.

The meeting began on a Saturday morning and lasted far longer into Sunday than had been expected. And when it was all over, the meeting had not been a success. There was no agreement on arms control, and there were no clear plans for another meeting. Both leaders went home tired and grim.

The leaders who met at Reykjavik in October 1986 were President Ronald Reagan of the United States and General Secretary Mikhail Gorbachev of the Soviet Union. Despite the disappointing end of the talks, both Gorbachev and Reagan offered hope that future meetings might be more successful.

The United States and the USSR are alike in many ways. Both are large countries, covering much of their continents. Size has given both countries many natural resources that have helped them to build strong economies. Both countries have citizens of many ethnic groups, so that each national government must deal with variety in language and culture among its citizens.

Finally, each country has a powerful **ideology**—a system of beliefs—that influences its political, social, and economic actions. The Soviet ideology is based on the writings of Marx and Lenin. This ideology calls for government control of the economy, political control by the Communist party, and support for worldwide Communist revolution. The American ideology includes democratic government with free elections, private enterprise in the economy, and support for the worldwide spread of democracy. Neither country has been completely consistent in following its ideology, either at home or abroad.

Since the two countries first became rivals in the Cold War, both nations have changed in many ways. Yet both countries have continued to follow paths suggested by their history. Each country has goals and problems that grow from deep historic roots. In this chapter, we see how long-standing trends are linked to new developments in the USSR and the United States.

Policies changed within the USSR. 1

On March 5, 1953, Joseph Stalin died. His death marked the end of an era in Soviet history. During Stalin's 29 years of leadership, he had transformed the Soviet Union into a global power. The Soviet people, however, had paid a high price for this success. They not only endured constant shortages of consumer goods and food but also lived in almost constant fear of the secret police. His death raised hopes that new leaders would improve the Soviet standard of living and reduce the powers of the secret police.

Since Stalin's death, the Soviet Union has had a number of leaders. Yet certain issues that faced Stalin, Lenin, and in some cases even the czars have remained the same. The questions of political leadership, economic development, the right to dissent, religious freedom, and ethnic variety have long been crucial and remain major questions in the Soviet Union today.

Khrushchev rose to power.

Stalin's death made clear a basic problem in the Soviet system. There is no legal, well-defined way for one leader to succeed another. No public election identifies winners or losers in the struggle for power. Instead, party leaders compete with one another, maneuvering for important posts within the party and trying to win supporters.

For the first few years after Stalin's death, a group of leaders shared power. Many party members had suffered under Stalin's dictatorial rule, so they hoped to prevent any single person from gaining such control again.

As time went by, however, one man did gain more and more power. That man was Nikita

While touring the United States in 1959, Soviet leader Khrushchev (right) visited a farm in Iowa.

Khrushchev (1894–1971). Few people would have predicted Khrushchev's rise. The son of a coal miner, he first worked as a metalworker and mechanic. He had little formal education before he joined the Communist party in 1918 when he was 24. During the next 20 years, Khrushchev rose in the party. In 1939, he became a full member of the Politburo, the political bureau of the Communist party's central committee. This elite group of about 20 leaders makes policy decisions for the party.

Although his bluff, earthy manners led some Soviet leaders to underestimate him, Khrushchev was shrewd, tough, and at times ruthless. By 1956, he had pushed aside his rivals. By 1958, he was both first secretary of the Communist party and premier of the Soviet Union, the two most powerful positions in the country. Once more, a single leader was in control.

De-Stalinization Khrushchev boldly demonstrated his power at a secret session of the Twentieth Communist Party Congress in Moscow in February 1956. Before an astounded audience, he attacked Stalin and his policies. He accused the late dictator of jailing and killing loyal Soviet citizens.

Khrushchev's speech signaled the beginning of a policy called "de-Stalinization." Party workers destroyed pictures and monuments of the former dictator. Stalin's body was moved from its place of honor next to Lenin and buried outside the Kremlin wall. The city of Stalingrad was renamed Volgograd.

Khrushchev's overthrow Khrushchev called for a number of economic and political reforms that eventually led to his undoing. Many party leaders disliked the changes he was making in party organization, which threatened to reduce their power. They were worried by the greater intellectual freedom he allowed. Khrushchev also faced crises abroad. Several times, he confronted the United States and then was forced to back down, as happened in the Cuban missile crisis (page 770). Such problems in foreign policy weakened his power at home.

In 1964, party leaders voted to remove Khrushchev from his powerful position as first secretary of the party. Later, Khrushchev noted with some pride that a simple vote had ended his power. He was not arrested or put on trial. The USSR had indeed changed since Stalin's time.

The "old guard" held power until 1985.

Again, party leaders maneuvered for power. Again, there was a period in which several leaders shared power.

Brezhnev By the late 1960's, however, Leonid Brezhnev (1906–1982) had established himself as the top Soviet leader, the first among equals. He was a less colorful leader than Khrushchev and aroused less controversy within the party. Brezhnev reversed many of Khrushchev's policies. For example, he clamped down on dissent within the Soviet Union. Brezhnev held power until his death in 1982.

Many Soviets thought that their country suffered from a general lack of direction during Brezhnev's last years. The economy was stagnant. Soviet troops were bogged down in a war in Afghanistan (page 788). When Brezhnev died at the age of 76, many people were ready for a leader from a younger generation. Yet most members of the Politburo came from Brezhnev's generation. This "old guard" managed to delay changes in policy for several years.

Andropov and Chernenko Brezhnev's successor was Yuri Andropov (1914–1984). Andropov did replace some aging leaders in the government and party with younger people. However, Andropov himself did not hold office long. In poor health, he stopped appearing in public in August 1983. Rumors circulated that he was seriously ill. He died in February 1984.

Konstantin Chernenko (1911–1985), a member of the "old guard" in the party, was chosen to replace Andropov. He held office for less than a year. His death was announced in March 1985.

A new generation On March 11, 1985, Mikhail Gorbachev succeeded Chernenko as general secretary of the Communist party. His rise to power marked a new era in the Soviet Union. At 54, he was the youngest member of the Politburo and the first top Soviet leader who had not been born under czarist rule. Many of Gorbachev's most pressing problems, however, were the same ones that had confronted earlier leaders. Chief among those problems was the economy.

The USSR has a planned economy.

Even before the revolution of 1917, Russian leaders were trying to catch up with the West economically. All Soviet leaders since that time have faced the same problem.

The role of planning The Soviet system calls for the government to make most economic decisions. Officials make plans and set goals for both agriculture and industry. In theory, such a plan tells managers at every factory and farm how much to produce. The plan also sets the price that farms and factories will receive for their output.

In practice, the Soviet government has changed its attitude toward plans from time to time. Under Lenin's New Economic Policy (page 615), for example, farmers and factory managers had more freedom to make their own decisions. Stalin's Five-Year Plans, on the other hand, were rigid, and their goals were often unrealistically high.

In his last year in power, Khrushchev supported the idea of allowing factory managers to make more decisions on their own. From 1965 to 1970, the Soviets experimented with such a system. Factory efficiency improved, and wages rose as well. However, some party leaders objected because the new system gave them less control. Brezhnev returned to strict central plans in 1970.

In the mid-1980's, Gorbachev seemed to be trying to make the central plans more flexible again. He clearly favored economic reforms. However, many party conservatives feared reforms would conflict with the Communist party's centralized control.

Priorities in industry Since 1917, the USSR has almost always given top priority to "heavy" industries—basic industries that produce metals, farm machinery, trucks, and weapons. Soviet economic planners have given much lower priority to consumer goods—clothing, refrigerators, washing machines, and wristwatches.

By putting its efforts into heavy industry, the USSR became a world leader in the production

Soviet grocery shoppers line up to buy fresh produce, which is often scarce. Usually, shoppers in the USSR must wait in one line to select their purchases, in a second line to pay for them, and in a third line to pick them up.

of coal, steel, cement, and in many types of mining. Such progress came with a price, however. Consumers grew more and more discontent with shortages of such items as toothpaste, towels, rugs, and shoes. People who had enough money to buy a refrigerator or television waited months until the appliances were available. When shoppers did find goods to purchase, their quality was generally poor. Gorbachev promised to raise the amount and quality of consumer goods.

Environmental issues   In their drive for rapid economic growth, Soviet planners paid little attention to environmental issues such as pollution in air and water. Long after Western Europe and the United States had begun to work toward cleaner air and water, the Soviet Union continued to ignore the issue.

In 1986, however, a disastrous event forced the USSR to take a new look at environmental concerns. In April 1986, the most serious accident in the history of nuclear power occurred at the Chernobyl nuclear plant 60 miles north of Kiev. A reactor caught fire, spewing radioactive smoke into the air. About 30 people were killed, and thousands faced the risk of developing cancer later. Winds carried the radiation across Europe and beyond. Some observers expected that this event would strengthen the influence of Soviet groups concerned about the environment.

Dissent has gone in cycles.

Since Stalin's time, freedom of expression has risen and fallen in cycles. Such shifts affect people in many fields—poets, moviemakers, reporters, artists, scientists, religious leaders, and ordinary people who wish to discuss issues freely.

During de-Stalinization, Khrushchev loosened the ties of censorship. For example, in 1962, Alexander Solzhenitsyn (SOHL-zuh-**NEET**-suhn) published a novel titled *One Day in the Life of Ivan Denisovich*. The book exposed the brutality of Stalin's labor camps, where workers had to scheme and struggle to get a crust of bread.

Under Brezhnev, government censors severely limited what could be published. When Solzhenitsyn won the Nobel Prize for literature in 1970, he was not allowed to go to Sweden to accept it. He was also expelled from the writers' union, which meant that his works could no longer be published in the USSR.

Dissident Andrei Sakharov and his wife Yelena Bonner were allowed to return to their Moscow apartment in 1986 after years of internal exile to the distant city of Gorky.

In response to such censorship, some writers passed around their works secretly. This system was called *samizdat*, or "self-publishing." Some writers smuggled their works out of the Soviet Union to be published abroad. Such actions were risky. When Solzhenitsyn's detailed account of life in Soviet prison camps, *The Gulag Archipelago*, was published in Europe, the author was forced to leave the Soviet Union.

Some leading **dissidents** came from the Soviet scientific community. A dissident is a person who expresses a differing opinion. For example, Andrei Sakharov is a distinguished physicist who helped to build the USSR's first hydrogen bomb. After speaking out against Soviet policy, Sakharov was forced to leave Moscow to live in the remote city of Gorky. Other dissidents have been imprisoned or sent to psychiatric hospitals.

Gorbachev seemed to offer more freedom of expression for Soviet intellectuals. As a symbol of this policy, in December 1986 Sakharov was allowed to return to his home in Moscow and continue his work in physics.

Religion is controversial in the USSR.

Although Soviet authorities frown on organized religion, many religions still flourish in the USSR. Foreign observers estimate that about 40 percent of the Soviet people believe in some religion, although many never attend services.

The Russian Orthodox Church has about 50 million members, and it is the best treated of the organized religions in the country. Islam is also strong, especially in the Central Asian republics of the USSR, and Muslims are generally free to practice their religion. Baptists and Jews, on the other hand, face many difficulties in practicing their religions, and hold their services secretly.

Jews are viewed not only as a religious group but also as a national minority. Thousands of Jews have left the USSR for Israel and other countries. However, the USSR has denied exit permits to thousands more who wish to leave.

The USSR *has many nationalities.*

Another challenge to the Soviet government arises from the many different groups that live within its borders. Like the United States, the USSR has a variety of ethnic groups. In the United States, the great variety of ethnic groups is the result of years of immigration. The situation is different in the USSR. There, most groups still live in their traditional homelands. Beginning in czarist times, Russia's borders expanded to take in these lands. Altogether, the USSR today includes more than 100 ethnic groups.

For the country as a whole, Russians were the dominant ethnic group under the czars and remained so under the Communist regime. Several czars followed a policy of "russification." That is, they tried to force other ethnic groups to accept the Russian language and culture. The Bolsheviks promised to end that policy. However, they continued to favor the Russian language for use in schools and government.

The strength of national feeling in one Soviet republic, Kazakhstan, burst out in late 1986. When Gorbachev replaced a local Kazakh leader in the Communist party with a Russian, riots broke out in the capital city of Kazakhstan. The Kazakhs are one of the largest minorities within the USSR.

The ethnic issue is a growing problem for the USSR. Birthrates are higher among the Muslim groups of Central Asia than they are among Russians. In the most recent census, Russians made up a little more than half the Soviet Union's population. By the year 2000, Russians may be outnumbered by other nationalities.

Since czarist times, Russian ballet has been famous. The Moscow company often tours abroad.

Section Review 1

Define: (a) ideology, (b) de-Stalinization, (c) heavy industry, (d) samizdat, (e) dissident, (f) russification

Identify: (a) Nikita Khrushchev, (b) Politburo, (c) Leonid Brezhnev, (d) Mikhail Gorbachev, (e) Chernobyl, (f) Alexander Solzhenitsyn

Answer:

1. (a) What basic problem in the Soviet political system did Stalin's death reveal? (b) Why did it take three years for Khrushchev to emerge as the new leader?
2. What events led to Khrushchev's loss of power?
3. What changes in policy did Brezhnev make?
4. What new policies did Gorbachev seem to support?
5. (a) How has Soviet policy on economic planning shifted from time to time? (b) What problems has the country faced in industry?
6. (a) During what periods has a greater measure of dissent been allowed in the USSR? (b) What are some of the risks dissidents face?

7. (a) How does the USSR regard its various religious groups? (b) Its ethnic groups?

Critical Thinking

8. Suppose a Soviet citizen and an American citizen were discussing the Soviet way of choosing leaders. What advantages might the Soviet see in the USSR's way? What disadvantages might the American point out?

The USSR *had goals abroad.*

2

Just as certain themes have been important in Soviet domestic affairs, several main issues have influenced Soviet foreign policy over the years. One such issue is a concern for protecting its borders. Another is support for Communist governments abroad. A third has been its relations with the other superpower, the United States.

Khrushchev shifted policies.

Stalin always insisted that sooner or later the USSR and the Western countries would fight an all-out war. This belief was one reason he was quick to break ties with the West after World War II.

Peaceful coexistence Khrushchev disagreed. He firmly believed that communism would take over the world, but he thought it could triumph peacefully. He favored a policy of peaceful coexistence in which the two superpowers would compete economically and scientifically.

Khrushchev's policies led to a slight thaw in the Cold War of the 1950's. In September 1959, Khrushchev became the first Soviet premier to visit the United States. He toured New York City and Pittsburgh, ate lunch with Hollywood stars, and saw a farm in Iowa.

The space race In the competition for international prestige, the Soviets leaped to an early lead in the space race. On October 4, 1957, they launched the world's first artificial satellite, *Sputnik.* Although the silvery sphere was only about the size of a volley ball, its launch was a triumph for Soviet technology.

Americans were shocked at being beaten and promptly poured money into their own space program. From then on, space became a major arena for competition between the two superpowers.

Renewed confrontation In 1960, Khrushchev's policy of peaceful coexistence came to an abrupt end. Just before a scheduled meeting between Khrushchev and President Dwight Eisenhower, the Soviets shot down an American U-2 spy plane over their territory. Khrushchev demanded that Eisenhower apologize and promise to cancel all

Daily Life · *Blue Jeans*

The durable denim pants called blue jeans have become a status symbol and sometimes a sign of dissent in the USSR. Blue jeans were first worn by miners in the days of the 1849 California Gold Rush. Over the years, they became the uniform of American farmers and blue-collar workers. Then, in the 1960's, young Americans began to wear blue jeans almost everywhere. Blue jeans even caught on with noted fashion designers.

Love of blue jeans spread to Europe and to the USSR, where jeans were linked to rock-and-roll music and other Western styles. In the Soviet Union, jeans are scarce, and American jeans are smuggled in for sale on the black market. American tourists have been startled by offers from Soviet citizens to trade valuable antiques and handcrafts for a humble pair of blue jeans.

The Soviet Union

Murmansk
LITHUANIAN SSR
ESTONIAN SSR
RUSSIAN SFSR
LATVIAN SSR
Leningrad
Minsk
MOLDAVIAN SSR
BYELORUSSIAN SSR
Archangel
Kiev
Moscow ★
UKRAINIAN SSR
Odessa
Gorky
RUSSIAN SOVIET FEDERATED SOCIALIST REPUBLIC
Yakutsk
Kazan
Perm
Volgograd
Chelyabinsk
GEORGIAN SSR
ARMENIAN SSR
Yerevan
Omsk
Novosibirsk
Krasnoyarsk
AZERBAIJAN SSR
Baku
KAZAKH SSR
Karaganda
Lake Baikal
Vladivostok
TURKMEN SSR
UZBEK SSR
Tashkent
Lake Balkhash
Samarkand
KIRGHIZ SSR
TADZHIK SSR

North Sea
ARCTIC OCEAN
Barents Sea
Baltic Sea
Kara Sea
Yenisey
Kolyma R.
Kamchatka Peninsula
Sea of Okhotsk
Don River
Dnieper
Black Sea
Volga
Ural River
Ob River
Irtysh R.
Lena River
Amur River
Sea of Japan
Caspian Sea
Aral Sea
Persian Gulf
Bering Strait
Bering Sea

KEY
★ National capital
0   600 Miles

Map Study
Which is the largest of the Soviet Republics? Which border the Caspian Sea?

such flights. When Eisenhower refused, the meeting between the two leaders was canceled.

At this point, Khrushchev began a series of direct confrontations with the United States. First came the Berlin Wall in 1961 (page 718). A little more than a year later, Khrushchev prepared to send nuclear missiles to Cuba (page 770). The two superpowers came close to war, but Khrushchev backed down and removed the missiles.

The USSR supported Communists elsewhere.

Since the 1917 revolution, the USSR has had a long-term goal of supporting Marxist governments elsewhere in the world. Soviet followers of Marx believe that such revolutions are the logical path of history.

The first example of such a revolution took place in China in 1949. At first, the Soviets played the role of elder brother to the Communist Chinese government. The Chinese, however, did not wish to be dominated by the USSR. In 1960, a serious rift developed between the two countries (page 730). As tensions worsened, both sides massed troops along their shared border. Today, that border bristles with weapons and fortifications. At times, incidents along the border have led to fighting.

Castro's revolution in Cuba (page 769) offered the Soviets a showcase for communism in the Western Hemisphere. Yet the results were not completely successful from the Soviet point of view. Cuba proved to be a costly showcase. The USSR poured economic aid into the country. Castro was not completely satisfied either. In 1984, he accused the Soviet Union of doing too little for the world's poverty-stricken countries.

When the Marxist-led Sandinistas took power in Nicaragua (page 766), the Soviet Union hailed the takeover as a triumph. The Sandinistas hoped for aid of all kinds from the USSR, but they

787

were disappointed. Soviet leaders turned down many of their requests.

The Soviet Union has expressed support for revolutionary movements in Nicaragua, El Salvador, Angola, Ethiopia, and other countries. On the other hand, Soviet leaders are not willing to spend large sums to prop up Marxist governments everywhere. With tough economic problems facing the USSR itself, the Soviets have limited their commitments abroad.

The USSR intervened in neighboring countries.

For centuries, the land now known as the Soviet Union has suffered repeatedly from invasions. Thus, secure borders are a major concern for Soviet leaders. This concern for safety was one reason that Stalin was determined to set up a Communist buffer zone in Eastern Europe after World War II (page 693).

Eastern Europe When Khrushchev denounced Stalin, his speech had a great impact in Eastern Europe. Soon afterward, some Eastern European countries took a more independent stand than

An Afghan guerrilla with a machine gun guards a rebel camp against Soviet forces.

the USSR would accept. To stop this trend, Khrushchev sent troops to restore Soviet control in Hungary in 1956 (page 700). While willing to make some reforms, Khrushchev did not intend to lose the Soviet Union's buffer zone.

In 1968, the official Soviet newspaper, *Pravda*, published an article outlining the Soviet view on Eastern Europe. The article said that Eastern European countries had only limited sovereignty. In other words, they did not have all the rights of fully independent countries. This idea became known as the Brezhnev Doctrine. Soviet leaders used this idea to justify sending troops to Czechoslovakia in 1968 (page 719).

Afghanistan The Soviet Union has always maintained a deep interest in Afghanistan, a small nation on the USSR's southern border. Even in czarist times, Russia competed with Great Britain for a sphere of power in this region.

In December 1978, a coup in Afghanistan brought a group of Communists to power. The Communists had little support among the Afghan people, however, and rebellions against the new government broke out across the country. For many Afghans, the revolt became a *jihad*, or holy war in the name of Islam.

In 1979, the USSR sent 80,000 Soviet troops to Afghanistan to prop up the Communist regime. By 1986, the number of Soviet troops had risen to at least 125,000. Yet the Soviets found that large forces and advanced weaponry do not succeed in a guerrilla war. The guerrillas fought on, despite Soviet bombs, land mines, and artillery. By 1987, the Soviets were seeking a way to withdraw their troops without causing the Communist government to collapse.

The superpowers discussed arms.

Since the early 1960's, there have been several "thaws" and "freezes" in relations between the USSR and the United States. Even during times of great tension, however, both countries sought progress on arms control. Both countries know that a war between them would have disastrous worldwide consequences. Both also know that the money they spend on arms limits progress in other parts of their economies.

In 1963, President John Kennedy declared that a "shaft cut through the darkness" after he and Khrushchev agreed to a limited ban on testing nuclear weapons. Thereafter, the two countries held many discussions about weapons, hoping to lessen the risk of nuclear war. Though such talks slowed the arms race, they did not end it. As the 1986 meeting between Reagan and Gorbachev showed, arms control is a difficult issue for both countries.

Section Review 2

Define: (a) guerrilla, (b) buffer zone
Identify: (a) *Sputnik*, (b) Sandinista, (c) *Pravda*, (d) Brezhnev Doctrine
Answer:
1. (a) How was Khrushchev's foreign policy different from Stalin's? (b) How did Khrushchev's approach change after 1960?
2. Briefly describe the USSR's relations with each of the following countries. (a) China (b) Cuba (c) Nicaragua
3. How did Khrushchev and Brezhnev each assert control over Eastern Europe?
4. Summarize the events that led the USSR to send troops to Afghanistan.
5. Why have the United States and the USSR continued to seek an arms control agreement?

Critical Thinking
6. Give an example of how domestic issues can affect Soviet foreign policy.

Americans sought new opportunities at home. 3

After World War II, the United States was the acknowledged world leader in industry. Americans enjoyed a time of unprecedented prosperity. Yet the United States also faced crises within its own borders. Some of these conflicts were deeply rooted in the nation's past, including the struggle for equal rights for all Americans. Other problems arose from postwar changes in the economy and the population.

Some crises divided the American people. However, in other ways, the country became more unified as citizens saw the strength of their government to survive challenges.

Political power changed hands.

In the 40 years after World War II, the two major political parties in the United States—the Republicans and the Democrats—vied for power in the government. Each won the presidency several times. Because voters were free to choose a new president every four years, power changed hands often. Yet even when political crises arose, leaders succeeded each other in the order set forth by the Constitution.

Truman Harry S. Truman, the Democratic vice president who succeeded Roosevelt in 1944, was elected in his own right in 1948. He remained president until 1953.

Eisenhower In the 1952 election, voters chose the Republican candidate, the popular World War II general Dwight D. Eisenhower. The stability and prosperity of the 1950's made it easy for Eisenhower to win a second term, and he held office until 1961.

Kennedy The 1960 election was a hard-fought one between Eisenhower's vice president, Richard M. Nixon, and a Democratic senator, John F. Kennedy. Kennedy won, becoming the youngest man ever elected president. He challenged Americans, "Ask not what your country can do for you. Ask what you can do for your country." Tragically, Kennedy was shot to death by an assassin on November 22, 1963.

Johnson Kennedy's vice president, Lyndon B. Johnson, a former senator from Texas, stepped into the presidency. He was elected in his own right by a wide majority in 1964. Johnson's time in office was marked by many reforms in civil rights (page 792). He also called for many new social programs in a "war on poverty." More and more, however, the attention of the country turned to the Vietnam War (page 797).

Nixon The winner of the 1968 election was Republican Richard M. Nixon, who had narrowly lost to Kennedy in 1960. Nixon was reelected in 1972. He had noteworthy successes in foreign policy, including ending American involvement in Vietnam and renewing diplomatic ties with China. However, his efforts to cover up crimes by his supporters led to a political scandal known as the Watergate affair. The scandal grew until Nixon was forced to resign as president in 1974.

Ford Although no president had ever resigned before, power passed smoothly to Vice President

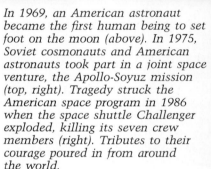

In 1969, an American astronaut became the first human being to set foot on the moon (above). In 1975, Soviet cosmonauts and American astronauts took part in a joint space venture, the Apollo-Soyuz mission (top, right). Tragedy struck the American space program in 1986 when the space shuttle Challenger exploded, killing its seven crew members (right). Tributes to their courage poured in from around the world.

Gerald Ford. He held office for two years and helped heal the bitterness that resulted from the Watergate scandal. However, Ford lost his bid to be elected president in 1976.

Carter In 1976, the Democratic candidate, James Earl Carter, won. Carter set an idealistic policy of encouraging human rights throughout the world. At home, however, he proved ineffective in dealing with Congress. His presidency was also marked by economic problems such as high inflation. He lost the 1980 election to Republican Ronald Reagan.

Reagan Reagan was a staunch conservative, opposed to many of the social programs enacted since the 1950's. He promised lower taxes and less government spending in all fields except defense. He was overwhelmingly reelected in 1984. While Reagan achieved his goal of lowering taxes, government spending continued to rise. The result was a huge government debt that proved difficult to reduce.

Since 1945, the American presidency has changed hands much more often than leadership in the Soviet Union. Yet all the changes in the United States have been orderly, even in times of tragedy or political crisis.

The population increased rapidly.

Some of the biggest changes in the United States since 1945 have been demographic changes. **Demography** is the study of population statistics, including what groups make up the population, where people live, birthrates, and death rates.

The baby boom During World War II, Americans had fewer children, in part because the war separated young couples. After the war, the birthrate shot upward. In 1940, the population was 132 million. In 1950, it was 151 million, and in 1960, it was over 179 million. So many children were born between 1945 and 1960 that the period became known as the "baby boom."

Schools, hospitals, and other services struggled to keep pace with such growth.

The move to the suburbs During the Depression of the 1930's, few families had been able to buy homes or cars. When the war came, civilian goods of all kinds, including cars and building materials, were in short supply. Thus, when the war ended, many people were eager for cars, houses, and other goods. With the postwar boom in the economy, people also had money to spend.

Workers with cars were free to live farther from their jobs than people who had to walk to work. Moreover, with a car a worker could live anywhere, not just along streetcar lines or bus routes.

With this new freedom to choose where to live, many American families moved from cities to **suburbs.** Suburbs were areas around a city that depended on the city for jobs, shopping, banking, and other services. By 1970, 37 percent of Americans lived in suburbs.

A mobile society Moving became a frequent event for many American families. People moved from place to place in search of new jobs and better opportunities. Many companies expected their employees to move every few years.

Frequently, Americans' moving vans headed for a part of the country called the sunbelt. Composed of states with warm climates, the sunbelt stretches from Georgia and the Carolinas to California. In the 1960's, an economic boom drew many white Americans to that region in search of jobs.

Black Americans, on the other hand, continued a trend started in the 1920's of moving northward. By 1980, only 19 percent of black Americans lived in the South.

The economy underwent changes.

For 20 years after World War II, Americans enjoyed a time of general prosperity. The United States' GNP (gross national product) went from $200 billion in 1945 to $500 billion in 1960. By 1970, the GNP hit $1 trillion.

A market economy In contrast to the Soviet Union, the United States does not have a planned economy. Instead of making what government planners order, American factory managers turn out goods that they think people want to buy. Businesses that correctly judge the "market" (that

is, customer wants) make profits. Thus, the American economy is called a market economy. It is based on the principles of free enterprise set forth by Adam Smith (page 434).

The postwar boom Consumer demand played a large part in American prosperity after the war. The growing population wanted homes. The housing boom spurred growth throughout the economy as people bought paint, plumbing, furniture, appliances, and all the other items needed in a new house. Economist John Kenneth Galbraith called the postwar United States the "affluent society." (*Affluent* means "having a plentiful supply of goods.")

For the first time, young people became an important part of the consumer market. During the 1950's, economists estimated that the average teenager spent more than $500 per year on items such as records, movie tickets, and cosmetics.

The problem of poverty The new affluence did not reach all Americans, however. About 20 percent of the population fell below the poverty line—that is, they lacked the money for basics such as adequate food, shelter, and clothing. President Johnson attacked poverty with programs for job training, education, community development, and medical insurance. Such programs were costly, and later administrations cut most

In the postwar building boom, single-family homes sprang up in suburbs across the country.

of them. However, medical benefits for the poor and elderly remained in effect.

Decline in manufacturing In the 1970's, the American economy suddenly seemed to slow down. Productivity declined. Unemployment and inflation rose. American industry had dominated the world market for years. Since 1945, however, Germany and Japan had built new factories to replace those the war had destroyed. Their new factories were highly efficient. American industries with older factories could not compete as successfully in the world market.

The changes hit hard at industries that had once been the backbone of American prosperity. The steel industry went into a steep decline. The United States, which once exported 60 percent of the world's iron and steel, began to import much of the iron and steel it used. Likewise, the American automobile industry lost sales to imported cars. Steel mills closed, and carmakers laid off thousands of workers. Employment levels also declined. In 1982, almost 11 percent of the nation's workers—some 12 million people—were without jobs. About 20 percent of the black population was unemployed.

A shift to service industries In general, the United States was moving from an economy based on manufacturing to one based on service industries. Service industries include restaurants, stores, banks, insurance, advertising, and communications. Also included in the service sector are a number of high-technology businesses such as computer programming and information processing.

In a service economy, there are few jobs for unskilled workers. Most unskilled jobs, such as those in the fast-food industry, are low paying and offer little chance for advancement.

Some observers feared an increasing split in the American work force. They saw a bright future for highly skilled, highly paid decision makers. Meanwhile, unskilled workers risked low pay and dead-end jobs.

Black Americans sought civil rights.

The problems of unemployment and poverty affected a higher percentage of black Americans than of whites. Prejudice and unfair laws deprived blacks of economic and political advantages that other Americans enjoyed. In the 1950's and 1960's, blacks launched a massive movement to win **civil rights**, the rights that the United States Constitution promised to all citizens.

After the war By the 1950's, the armed forces and the departments of the federal government were integrated. That is, they accepted both black and white citizens on an equal footing. However, the United States was far from offering full equality. In the South, local laws and threats of force blocked three out of four black adults from voting. Laws in 21 states called for **segregation** (separation of blacks and whites) in public schools. Blacks were barred from public libraries, restaurants, hotels, and many other places. Segregation was most common in the South, but many hotels and restaurants in the North also refused to admit blacks. Employers discriminated against black workers.

Segregation and the schools In 1954, black Americans won a stunning victory that overturned laws supporting segregated schools. In the case *Brown v. Board of Education of Topeka*, the Supreme Court ruled that towns could no longer have one public school for white children and another for black children. When a high school in Little Rock, Arkansas, refused to accept black students, President Eisenhower sent federal troops to see that the law was obeyed.

The *Brown* decision was a landmark in the black struggle for equality. Many more cases were brought to court in an effort to end segregation in other parts of American life.

The leadership of Martin Luther King, Jr. On December 1, 1955, in Montgomery, Alabama, a black woman named Rosa Parks was arrested for refusing to give up her bus seat to a white man. In protest, Montgomery blacks organized a year-long bus boycott. The boycott forced white city leaders to recognize the blacks' determination and economic power.

One of the organizers of the bus boycott was a Baptist minister, the Reverend Martin Luther King, Jr. King soon became a national leader in the growing civil rights movement. With stirring speeches and personal courage, he urged blacks to demand their rights. At the same time, he was completely committed to nonviolence. Like Gandhi (page 625), he believed that justice could triumph through moral force.

In April 1963, King began a drive to end segregation in Birmingham, Alabama. He and his followers boycotted segregated businesses and held peaceful marches and demonstrations. Against them, the Birmingham police used electric cattle prods, attack dogs, clubs, and fire hoses to break up marches.

Television cameras brought those scenes into the living rooms of millions of Americans, who were shocked by what they saw. On May 10, Birmingham's city leaders gave in. A committee of blacks and whites oversaw the gradual desegregation of the city and tried to open more jobs for blacks. The victory was later marred by grief, however, when a bomb exploded at a Birmingham church, killing four black children.

Civil rights legislation In 1964, Congress passed a Civil Rights Act. The new law outlawed discrimination in all projects receiving federal funds and in public facilities such as theaters and hotels.

King addressed marchers at the Lincoln Memorial.

Voice from Our Time · A *Dream* to *Follow*

In August 1963, Martin Luther King, Jr., organized a mammoth march on Washington, D.C., to demand "freedom now" for black Americans. More than 200,000 Americans, both blacks and whites, gathered before the Lincoln Memorial to hear him speak. His speech expressed the heart and soul of the civil rights movement.

I have a dream that one day this nation will rise up and live out the true meaning of its creed: "We hold these truths to be self-evident; that all men are created equal."

I have a dream that one day on the red hills of Georgia the sons of former slaves and the sons of former slaveowners will be able to sit down together at the table of brotherhood . . .

I have a dream that my four little children will one day live in a nation where they will not be judged by the color of their skin but by the content of their character . . .

This is our hope . . . With this faith we will be able to work together, to pray together, to struggle together, to go to jail together, to stand up for freedom together, knowing that we will be free one day . . .

When we let freedom ring, when we let it ring from every village and every hamlet, from every state and every city, we will be able to speed up that day when all of God's children, black men and white men, Jews and Gentiles, Protestants and Catholics, will be able to join hands and sing in the words of the old Negro spiritual, "Free at last! Free at last! Thank God almighty, we are free at last."

1. Summarize King's dream in your own words.
2. What did King say he and his supporters were prepared to do in order to achieve the dream?
3. (a) Why do you think he called his goal a dream? (b) How did this speech support King's emphasis on non-violence?
4. What is the importance of a "dream" for a reform movement such as this?

The following year, Congress passed the Voting Rights Act of 1965. Under this law, federal examiners went into the South to register black voters. The number of blacks who went to the polls tripled in just four years.

Such laws did not end racial discrimination and violence. In 1968, in Memphis, Tennessee, Martin Luther King, Jr., was assassinated. In cities all across the country, riots exploded in black neighborhoods. Yet the new laws did open the doors to better education and more jobs for blacks. Voting rights gave blacks more political power. In the 1970's and 1980's, the number of elected black officials in the nation grew rapidly. Blacks won positions of leadership in many regions of the country.

Civil rights for other groups Inspired by the black civil rights movement, other groups began to press for change. American Indians tried to protect what remained of their ancestral lands by demonstrations and court cases.

Hispanics, or Spanish-speaking Americans, also sought recognition. Cesar Chávez organized migrant farm workers in a union that won nationwide attention with a strike against California grape growers. In recent years, a number of Hispanics have won high elected and appointed government offices.

Americans debated the role of religion.

Many black civil rights leaders, including Martin Luther King, Jr., were also ministers. Church leaders all across the country, both black and white, supported the civil rights movement. They considered civil rights a moral issue as well as a political one.

Religion has always been a major force in American life. The United States' Constitution promises Americans freedom of religion. It also guarantees that the government will not support any church. The idea of the separation of church and state has a long history in the United States.

Americans thus face a dilemma. They want to preserve the separation of church and state. At the same time, deep religious convictions lead many to take public stands on issues. The line between political issues and moral or religious issues is often impossible to draw.

In the late 1970's, church membership rose rapidly. The fastest-growing churches were Protestant groups that stressed a literal interpretation of the Bible. These groups were called fundamentalist churches. Their members sought to bring their values into the forefront of American life. Issues such as allowing daily prayers in the public schools, prohibiting abortions, banning pornography, and opposing communism were all important to them. By the mid-1980's, fundamentalist groups had become a significant political force.

Women took new roles in society.

American women also organized to make changes in society. Although women in the United States had equal political rights with men, they faced discrimination in education and employment. In 1963, for example, the average female worker earned only 63 percent as much as the average male worker. The women's movement demanded "equal pay for equal work."

The National Organization for Women (NOW) fought discrimination in the courts, using the 1964 Civil Rights Law. That law included an amendment prohibiting discrimination by sex. (The amendment had been added by opponents of the bill who hoped the addition would ensure its defeat.)

As the women's movement gained strength, it worked for passage of an equal rights amendment to the Constitution. In 1972, Congress passed an amendment stating, "Equality of rights under law shall not be denied or abridged by the United States or any state on account of sex." However, the amendment never became law because it was not approved by enough states.

Many men and women opposed the women's movement and the Equal Rights Amendment. They believed that women's traditional roles as wives and mothers were threatened.

Despite opposition, women had made great progress in the job market by 1980. There were at least a few women in almost every line of work. However, women still earned much less than men. Women workers were paid about 68 cents for every dollar that men received.

Women's representation in government increased. Women had been elected to both houses of Congress. Nationally, women were serving as

The United States Today

Map labels:

CANADA

Olympia ★ WASHINGTON
Columbia R.
Salem ★
OREGON
Boise ★ IDAHO
Helena ★ MONTANA
NORTH DAKOTA
Bismarck ★
SOUTH DAKOTA
Pierre ★
MINNESOTA
St. Paul ★ WISCONSIN
Madison ★
MICHIGAN
Lansing ★
GREAT LAKES
St. Lawrence River
MAINE
★ Augusta
VT. Mont- pelier ★ Concord
N.H.
Albany ★ MASS. ★ Boston
NEW YORK ★ Providence
R.I.
CT. Hartford

Carson City ★
Sacra- mento ★
NEVADA
Great Salt Lake
Salt Lake City ★
UTAH
WYOMING
Cheyenne ★
Denver ★
River
COLORADO
NEBRASKA
IOWA
Des Moines ★
Lincoln ★
Topeka ★ KANSAS
ILLINOIS INDIANA
Springfield ★ Indian- apolis ★
OHIO
Columbus ★
PENNSYLVANIA N.J.
Harrisburg ★ ★ Trenton
MD. DEL.
★ Dover
Annapolis ★ Washington D.C.
W.VA. Charleston ★
VIRGINIA ★ Richmond
Frankfort ★ KENTUCKY

CALIFORNIA
PACIFIC OCEAN
Sacramento
Santa Fe ★
ARIZONA
Phoenix ★
NEW MEXICO
Colorado
MISSOURI
Jefferson City ★
Nashville ★
TENNESSEE
NORTH CAROLINA
Raleigh ★
SOUTH CAROLINA
Columbia ★
ATLANTIC OCEAN

OKLAHOMA
Oklahoma City ★
ARKANSAS
Little Rock ★
MISSIS- SIPPI
Jackson ★
ALABAMA
Mont- gomery ★
GEORGIA
Atlanta ★

TEXAS
Austin ★
LOUISIANA
Baton Rouge ★
Tallahassee ★

Rio Grande
Gulf of Mexico
FLORIDA

State boundary
⊛ National capital
★ State capital

U.S.S.R.
Bering Strait
ARCTIC OCEAN
CANADA
MEXICO
ALASKA
Bering Sea
Juneau ★
PACIFIC OCEAN
0   500 Miles

PACIFIC OCEAN
HAWAII
Honolulu ★
0   100 Miles

ATLANTIC OCEAN
PUERTO RICO
(U.S. Comm.)
Caribbean Sea
San Juan ★
0   100 Miles

0   400 Miles

Map Study

On which map does an inch stand for the most miles? If all four maps used the same scale, would Alaska look larger or smaller in comparison?

governors and mayors. In 1981, Sandra Day O'Connor became the first female justice on the Supreme Court. In 1984, Geraldine Ferraro ran for vice president of the United States on the Democratic ticket.

Americans worried about pollution.

The United States' economy relied on a plentiful supply of resources, including fertile soil, water, forests, and minerals. For most of their history as a nation, Americans were confident that these resources would last forever.

During the prosperity of the 1950's, businesses forged ahead with little thought for the environment. Smoke poured from factory chimneys, and pipes carried polluted wastewater directly into rivers. The great numbers of new automobiles filled the air with exhaust fumes. In some cases,

the results were deadly. In New York City, for example, unusual weather conditions trapped pollution over the city in 1953 and again in 1963, leading to 600 deaths.

During the 1960's, many Americans became concerned about the effects of pollution. They put pressure on state and federal governments to enact laws against pollution. In 1970, Congress set up the Environmental Protection Agency to see that national laws for clean air and clean water were enforced.

As a result of such actions, many rivers and lakes became cleaner. Fish returned to lakes that had been declared "dead" in the 1960's. Air quality improved too. Yet cleanup programs were costly. They cut into business profits and also led to higher taxes. Thus, they remained controversial even though nearly everyone agreed that the goals were worthwhile.

795

Section Review 3

Define: (a) demography, (b) suburb, (c) market economy, (d) civil rights, (e) segregation
Identify: (a) Harry Truman, (b) Dwight Eisenhower, (c) John Kennedy, (d) Lyndon Johnson, (e) Richard Nixon, (f) Gerald Ford, (g) James Carter, (h) Ronald Reagan, (i) Martin Luther King, Jr., (j) Rosa Parks, (k) Sandra Day O'Connor, (l) Geraldine Ferraro
Answer:

1. (a) How did the office of the presidency change hands in normal circumstances? (b) What crises led to the presidency's changing hands? (c) How did these crises show the stability of the American political system?
2. (a) What was the baby boom? (b) How did residential patterns shift after 1945?
3. (a) Why could the United States of the 1950's be characterized as an affluent society? (b) How did the American economy slow down and change in the 1970's?
4. (a) What was the importance of *Brown v. Board of Education of Topeka?* (b) Of the Montgomery bus boycott? (c) The Civil Rights Act of 1964? (d) The Voting Rights Act?
5. How have religion and politics sometimes become intertwined?
6. (a) What problems did women face in employment? (b) How did women's groups benefit from the Civil Rights Act?
7. (a) How was economic growth linked to environmental problems? (b) Why are efforts to protect the environment still controversial?

Critical Thinking

8. Choose one of the issues discussed in this section and explain why it shows a basic change in American life. Compare your reasons with those of your classmate.

Americans differed on foreign policy.

4

Throughout the history of the United States, conflicting goals have created debate over American foreign policy. Since its founding as a democracy, the United States has often tried to help other people win democratic freedoms. Americans honor the rights they have under their Constitution, and they want to support the cause of human rights abroad. These values are basic to the American ideology.

At the same time, the United States has national interests that sometimes conflict with its democratic ideals. Like any other great power, it sometimes ignores the rightful interests of weaker countries.

Americans have also disagreed on how active their country should be in world affairs. Sometimes they have called for the United States to assert itself as a world leader. At other times, especially after a setback, they have turned to isolationism.

The Vietnam War divided Americans.

The most important, and the most devastating, foreign problem for the United States in the 1960's and early 1970's was the war in Vietnam. The war began in part as an effort to support democracy in Vietnam. Yet it was also a question of power politics in the United States' rivalry with communism.

As you read in Chapter 34, the United States supported an anti-Communist regime in South Vietnam against its Communist opponents (pages 739–740). Under President Eisenhower, about 650 American military advisers went to Vietnam. President Kennedy increased the number of advisers to 15,000.

In August 1964, President Johnson announced that North Vietnamese gunboats had attacked an American destroyer in the Gulf of Tonkin. At the president's urging, Congress passed the Gulf of Tonkin Resolution. It gave the president power "to repel attacks on American forces" and help the government of South Vietnam.

Johnson used the Gulf of Tonkin Resolution to order the bombing of North Vietnam, although the United States never declared war on that country. He also sent combat troops to Vietnam. By 1968, there were about 500,000 American soldiers there.

American and South Vietnamese forces failed to defeat the Communist rebels, known as Viet Cong. The Viet Cong waged a guerrilla war with sudden attacks, mines, booby traps, and sniper fire. American military leaders, however, were

The Vietnam War Memorial lists all the soldiers who died in combat. At its dedication, people searched for the names of friends and relatives.

convinced that the war could be won if the United States used its full strength.

As the number of American troops in Vietnam grew, the number of American deaths rose too. In 1967, almost 7,500 Americans died in battle there. The next year, that number jumped to more than 12,500.

In 1965, when the troop buildup first began, some 82 percent of all Americans felt that the United States should stay in Vietnam until the Communists withdrew. By 1967, however, opposition to the war was widespread among Americans. Many people charged that the war was both immoral and unwinnable. Antiwar protesters held marches and demonstrations all across the country. Some former soldiers who had served in Vietnam joined the peace movement. In late 1969, massive antiwar protests swept the country. About 250,000 people marched in Washington, D.C., calling for an end to the war.

Other Americans strongly supported the war and called the demonstrators unpatriotic cowards. During a peace march in New York, angry construction workers attacked the marchers with clubs and pipes. The country was bitterly divided.

News of the 1968 My Lai (mee lye) massacre, in which United States Marines killed 300 Vietnamese civilians, shocked Americans. So did events at Kent State University in Ohio, where National Guard troops opened fire on protesters, killing four students and wounding nine. Then, in 1971, publication of the top-secret Pentagon Papers revealed that President Johnson had distorted the Gulf of Tonkin incident to win the vote in Congress.

In 1971, a poll showed that 65 percent of the American people thought that the United States should not be fighting in Vietnam. The army itself was troubled. Morale and discipline sank to an all-time low.

When the last of the American troops finally withdrew from Vietnam in 1973, they were not welcomed home with parades and celebrations. Vietnam seemed to be a major failure in American foreign policy, and many people wanted simply to forget it. Veterans resented what they saw as callous indifference to their sacrifices.

In 1982, in belated recognition of those sacrifices, the country raised a monument to the memory of Americans who died in Vietnam. Thousands of Vietnam veterans, their families, and the families of those who died in the war attended its dedication. At last, it seemed, some of the wounds of the long and terrible war were healing.

Problems in the Middle East affected the United States.

The Middle East was another region in which the United States faced conflict. The United States strongly supported the state of Israel, in part because Israel was a democracy. However, American industry also needed Arab oil. In addition, the United States opposed any growth of Soviet influence in the Middle East.

Arab-Israeli relations Frequently, the United States tried to act as a peacemaker in the region. President Carter brought Prime Minister Menachim Begin of Israel and President Anwar el-Sadat of Egypt together to work out a peace accord in September 1978 (page 757). The next spring, the three leaders negotiated a peace treaty, ending 30 years of war between Egypt and Israel.

Other Arab states were less willing than Egypt to work with the United States. Many Arabs

797

accused the United States of ignoring Arab interests and favoring Israel.

The Iranian hostage crisis In 1979, the shah of Iran was overthrown (page 758). The shah had ruled tyrannically, but he had been a staunch anti-Communist and thus had received much aid from the United States. Many Iranians blamed the United States for the shah's harsh rule. Soon after his fall, an Iranian mob invaded the United States embassy in Tehran and seized about 60 hostages (page 758). Months went by, and the United States could do nothing to free the hostages. The United States looked weak and helpless. Only when a new president, Ronald Reagan, took office, did Iran's leaders free the hostages.

The issue of terrorism The hostage crisis raised American awareness of the tactics of international terrorism. Terrorist groups hijacked passenger planes and ships, bombed public buildings, and kidnapped people. Although many such acts were the work of extremist groups from the Middle East, the attacks took place worldwide. The terrorist goals ranged from winning recognition for their cause to freeing jailed members of their groups.

Terrorism presented a serious problem for democratic countries including the United States. President Reagan accused certain countries such as Iran and Libya of sponsoring terrorism. In 1986, after a terrorist bombing killed American soldiers in Europe, Reagan ordered a bombing raid on Libya. He urged other leaders to take a tougher stand against terrorists.

However, in November 1986, news broke that the United States had had secret dealings with Iran. The deals linked the sale of arms to Iran with the freeing of hostages held by terrorist groups under Iran's influence. Many Americans were angry that their government, despite all its declarations, had bargained with a terrorist regime.

Latin American conflicts won new prominence.

Although nationalist movements in the Middle East have created difficulties for the United States, such movements in Latin America have created even greater controversy about United States policy.

Presidents Eisenhower and Kennedy worried about the presence of a pro-Soviet government in Cuba under Fidel Castro. Kennedy authorized the disastrous 1961 Bay of Pigs invasion of Cuba in the hope of eliminating Castro (page 770). Instead, the attack made Castro stronger and encouraged him to forge even tighter links with the Soviet Union.

The Alliance for Progress Kennedy's main hope for stopping any spread of communism in Latin America was the Alliance for Progress. The alliance was designed to use United States aid to help Latin American countries develop economically and foster democratic governments in the region. Kennedy was extremely popular in Latin America, and there was great enthusiasm for his programs.

Human rights In general, during the late 1960's and 1970's, the United States supported anti-Communist governments in Latin America. At times, that policy meant supporting harsh military dictatorships, such as that of General Pinochet in Chile (page 773).

President Carter hoped to make human rights the focal point of United States foreign policy throughout the world. He threatened to withdraw support from governments that did not respect the rights of their citizens. However, Carter found that in reality he was forced to maintain ties with authoritarian regimes. For example, he suspended aid to the military government of El Salvador, but he resumed that aid when he became convinced that Communist nations were supplying the rebels with arms.

Carter did achieve one major policy victory in Latin America. He won Senate approval for a treaty settling a long-standing dispute over the Canal Zone with Panama.

Opposition to communism President Reagan firmly believed that Soviet power was a growing threat in Latin America. When a Marxist government took control of the small island nation of Grenada, Reagan ordered a surprise attack with United States troops that brought down the government. The invasion of Grenada, while criticized by some as an unnecessary use of force, was welcomed by most Grenadians and by the neighboring Caribbean islands.

Reagan was also determined to oppose Communists in El Salvador and Nicaragua. He called for military and economic aid to the right-wing

In December 1986, test pilots Jeana Yeager and Dick Rutan set a new aviation record by flying nonstop around the world. "What kind of world would there be," asked Rutan, "if there were no daring?"

government of El Salvador, which was fighting a civil war against leftist guerrillas. However, the conflict in El Salvador continued. Reagan also supported the Nicaraguan contras, the guerrillas opposed to the Sandinista government there (page 767).

Many Americans were against United States intervention in either El Salvador or Nicaragua. They believed that the United States was increasing the bloodshed in those countries. Some feared that Central America could become another Vietnam.

History puts events in perspective.

Since World War II, Americans have accepted great responsibilities in the world. Through idealistic efforts such as the Peace Corps, ordinary Americans have tried to help people in developing nations. The United States supplies much of the money for United Nations programs for health care, farming improvements, and education.

As one of the world's leading powers, the United States has a highly visible role in international affairs. Its actions have far-reaching effects. People in other countries hail it as a champion or denounce it as a villain. These extreme views make it hard to form a realistic judgment of American policies.

Yet the study of history is mostly an effort to see the larger trends behind each separate event. By looking at the major trends in history, historians can also try to put modern events in perspective.

Section Review 4

Identify: (a) Gulf of Tonkin Resolution, (b) Alliance for Progress
Answer:
1. (a) How did the United States become involved in Vietnam? (b) How did American involvement increase beginning in 1965?
2. (a) How did public opinion about the war change? (b) Why did the Vietnam War divide Americans?
3. (a) What major success did the United States help achieve in the Middle East? (b) What major problem did the United States face with Iran after the shah was overthrown?
4. What were the main features of each of the following presidents' foreign policy toward Latin America? (a) Kennedy (b) Carter (c) Reagan

Critical Thinking
5. Discuss the following question: What is the role of a superpower in the world today?

Summary

1. Policies changed within the USSR. In 1958, five years after Stalin's death, Nikita Khrushchev emerged as the leader of the Soviet Union. Failures in his internal program and a loss of prestige abroad led to his fall in 1964. For the next 20 years, a succession of Soviet leaders reversed many of Khrushchev's policies. In 1985, Mikhail Gorbachev took power. Gorbachev has seemed to favor flexible central plans and a relaxation of censorship. Crucial problems continue to arise because of the government's views toward ethnic minorities and religion. Recently, environmental issues have also arisen.

2. The USSR had goals abroad. Soviet foreign policy has been concerned with protection of the country's borders, support for Communist governments abroad, and relations with the United States. Both Khrushchev and Brezhnev asserted control over Eastern Europe. In 1978, the Soviet Union invaded Afghanistan. The United States and the USSR continue to seek an arms control agreement.

3. Americans sought new opportunities at home. Since 1945, the American presidency has changed hands in an orderly democratic fashion, despite several crises. Population has increased rapidly, and society has become more mobile. Despite a postwar boom, most black Americans suffered from unemployment and poverty. Martin Luther King, Jr., began a drive to end segregation in the South. The black civil rights movement won important legislation and spread to other minorities. By the mid-1980's, fundamentalist groups had become a significant political force, and women had taken on new roles in society. Environmental issues have remained controversial.

4. Americans differed on foreign policies. Conflicting goals over American foreign policy have centered on the war in Vietnam in the 1960's and on continued United States involvement in Latin American affairs. In the Middle East, the United States has supported Israel. Several Arab groups have used terrorism to win recognition of their goals.

Reviewing the Facts

1. Define the following terms:
   a. ideology
   b. dissident
   c. demography
   d. suburb
   e. civil rights
   f. segregation
2. Explain the importance of each of the following names, places, or terms:
   a. Khrushchev
   b. de-Stalinization

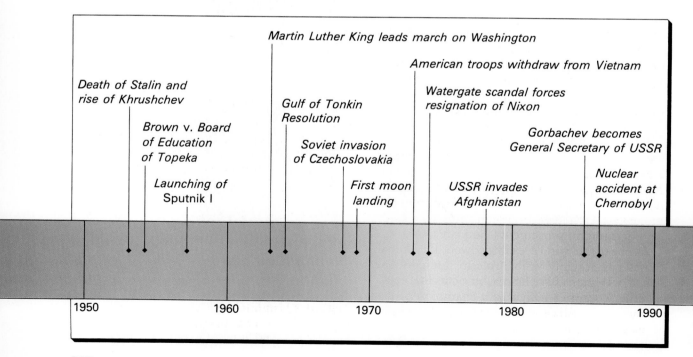

Martin Luther King leads march on Washington

American troops withdraw from Vietnam

Death of Stalin and rise of Khrushchev

Watergate scandal forces resignation of Nixon

Gulf of Tonkin Resolution

Brown v. Board of Education of Topeka

Gorbachev becomes General Secretary of USSR

Soviet invasion of Czechoslovakia

Launching of Sputnik I

First moon landing

USSR invades Afghanistan

Nuclear accident at Chernobyl

1950   1960   1970   1980   1990

c. Brezhnev
d. Gorbachev
e. Solzhenitsyn
f. Sakharov
g. peaceful coexistence
h. *Sputnik*
i. *Pravda*
j. Watergate
k. Reagan
l. baby boom
m. market economy
n. planned economy
o. service industry
p. Martin Luther King, Jr.
q. Rosa Parks
r. Geraldine Ferraro
s. Gulf of Tonkin Resolution
t. Alliance for Progress

3. (a) How has the issue of succession caused instability in the Soviet Union. (b) How does the American method differ?

4. How has Soviet policy toward each of the following shifted from time to time? (a) economic development (b) dissent

5. (a) What three main issues have influenced Soviet foreign policy over the years? (b) Give an example of how the Soviet Union has dealt with each issue.

6. Why is arms control a major issue between the USSR and the United States?

7. (a) What factors contributed to postwar prosperity in the United States after 1945? (b) To an economic slump in the 1970's?

8. (a) Why did blacks launch a civil rights movement in the United States in the 1950's? (b) Describe the gains they made in 1964 and 1965.

9. (a) How did the Vietnam war divide Americans? (b) Why are Americans divided over United States intervention in Latin American countries?

10. (a) What has been the role of the United States in the Middle East? (b) How has the United States reacted to terrorism?

Thinking about History

1. Compare the civil rights movement of Martin Luther King, Jr., with Mohandas Gandhi's program of civil disobedience in India (page 624). In what ways were the issues similar? In what ways were they different?

2. Compare the problem of succession within the Soviet Union with the problem of choosing an emperor in the Roman empire (page 143). What happens when a nation lacks a legal well-defined way for one ruler to succeed another? How has the existence of such a method benefited the United States? How did the lack of such a method contribute to Rome's downfall?

Writing and Speaking about History

1. Write an essay of compare and contrast (Research Skills Handbook, page 384) that looks at some of the similarities and differences between the United States and the USSR. Include these topics in your essay:
   a. size
   b. ethnic minorities
   c. ideology
   d. role in world affairs

2. Suppose a Soviet teenager and an American teenager were comparing ways of life. What might they say?

Practicing Skills

Label each of the following places on an outline map of the world. On a separate sheet of paper, explain how the United States, the USSR, or both have been involved in each place in recent years.
   a. Cuba
   b. Nicaragua
   c. Afghanistan
   d. Israel
   e. Iran
   f. Vietnam
   g. El Salvador

Investigating History

1. Despite its vast size, the USSR has little land that is good for farming. Research the climates and vegetation zones found in the Soviet Union. In what part of the country do most farms lie? What has the government done to increase farmland?

2. In an atlas, find out the land area, population, largest cities, ethnic composition, life expectancy, resources, and per capita income of the United States and the USSR. What do these statistics tell you about each country in relation to the other?

Decision Making in History

Evaluate the factors involved in arms control. Why is it difficult for the superpowers to reach an agreement. What advice would you offer them?

Research Skills

Writing a Book Review

During the course of the year, you may be asked to write a book review of a historical novel or biography. Unlike a book report that calls for a summary of the book, a book review calls for analysis, evaluation, and criticism. The *New York Times Book Review* contains some excellent models as does the *American Historical Review,* the journal of the American Historical Association. Other models might be found in the *Book Review Digest,* which indexes book reviews and quotes a sentence or so to give the essence of each review.

Here are the preliminary steps for preparing a book review:

1. Note carefully the full name of the author, the exact title of the book, the publisher, and the date of publication, as on a bibliography card.
2. Read about the author to determine his or her background. Try to find out whether or not the author is an authority on the subject. Some information about the author can usually be found in the preface or on the dust jacket of the book.
3. Read the book carefully. As you read, take notes on the author's style and coverage. Read for enjoyment but read critically as well.

A book review has the following four sections:

1. Begin the review with a clear summary of the book. The summary does not need to go chapter by chapter. Rather it should present an overview of the book with special attention to important sections. The summary should make up no more than one third of the total review.
2. Identify the method of treatment. In this section, answer such questions as: Is the book arranged chronologically or topically? Is it based on primary or secondary sources? Is the work written in a popular or a scholarly style?
3. Present a critical analysis of the content of the book. Was the book complete in its coverage, or did the author neglect some important aspect of the topic? To what extent does bias contribute to or detract from the quality of the book? Is the quality of the book consistent or do some parts seem to be more thoroughly researched than others?
4. Conclude with personal reflections on the book. This section deals with the work in terms of its relationship to you as the reader. It might answer such questions as: What did I learn? Did the book change my mind about the topic? Did my appreciation for the topic change? Did I learn to think better or analyze better from this work. Specific errors should be accurately cited, and any corrections should be carefully documented. Your own biases as a reviewer should be noted.

Unit Review IX

1. Explain the origin and purpose of each of the following agreements or policies:
   - a. Truman Doctrine
   - b. Marshall Plan
   - c. NATO
   - d. Warsaw Pact
   - e. Common Market
   - f. Comecon
   - g. Ostpolitik
   - h. Solidarity
   - i. Brezhnev Doctrine

2. Each of the following countries has experienced unrest since World War II. Match each country with the correct geographic location: (a) Eastern Europe (b) Middle East (c) Africa (d) East Asia (e) South Asia (f) Southeast Asia (g) Latin America
   - a. Bangledesh
   - b. Cuba
   - c. Iran
   - d. Israel
   - e. Korea
   - f. Vietnam
   - g. Poland
   - h. Nigeria
   - i. Nicaragua
   - j. Chile
   - k. Lebanon
   - l. Zaire

3. With what country is each of the following people associated? What role did that person play in the country after independence?
   - a. Nehru
   - b. Gandhi
   - c. Nkrumah
   - d. Nasser
   - e. Mobutu
   - f. Houphouet-Boigny
   - g. Nyerere
   - h. Meir

4. With what country is each of the following people associated? What stand against oppression or inequality has each person taken?
   - a. Nagy
   - b. Dubcek
   - c. Walesa
   - d. Tito
   - e. Jean Lesage
   - f. Solzhenitsyn
   - g. Martin Luther King, Jr.

5. (a) What two superpowers arose after World War II? (b) What is the Cold War?

6. (a) Describe the division of Germany into East Germany and West Germany. (b) Describe the division of Europe into East and West.

7. (a) What happened in China in 1949? (b) How did the United States react to this event?

8. (a) Describe the division of Korea into North Korea and South Korea. (b) What part did the United States play in the ensuing conflict?

9. Match the name or term in the left column with the correct country in the right.
   - 1. economic miracle
   - 2. Cultural Revolution
   - 3. conflict with Pakistan
   - 4. Sukarno
   - 5. Marcos
   - 6. Diem
   - 7. Khmer Rouge
   - a. Indonesia
   - b. Kampuchea
   - c. Philippines
   - d. South Vietnam
   - e. China
   - f. Japan
   - g. India

10. In recent years, both Gorbachev of the Soviet Union and Deng Xiaoping of China seem to have loosened some controls within their country. Give examples of some changes they have made that point in this direction.

11. (a) Explain how regional and ethnic divisions weakened Nigeria in 1960. (b) Describe one other problem that new African nations faced.

12. (a) Who rules South Africa today? (b) How has that government used apartheid to stay in power?

13. (a) How has the conflict over Israel spilled over into Lebanon? (b) How has the conflict between tradition and modernization affected Iran?

14. (a) What economic challenges has Mexico faced in recent years? (b) What two groups are fighting a civil war in Nicaragua?

15. (a) What is the current political status of Puerto Rico? (b) To what nation does Cuba have close ties today?

16. Decide whether each of the following statements describes (a) Brazil, (b) Argentina, or (c) Chile.
    - a. A military coup ousted Allende and brought democracy to an end.
    - b. Juan Perón ruled between 1946 and 1955.
    - c. Army leaders brought on an economic miracle in the 1960's.

The World about 1700 B.C.

Stonehenge

KEY

China under the Shang dynasty
Babylonian empire under Hammurabi
Indus Valley civilization
Egypt during the Middle Kingdom
Minoan and Mycenaean civilizations
Fertile Crescent
• City

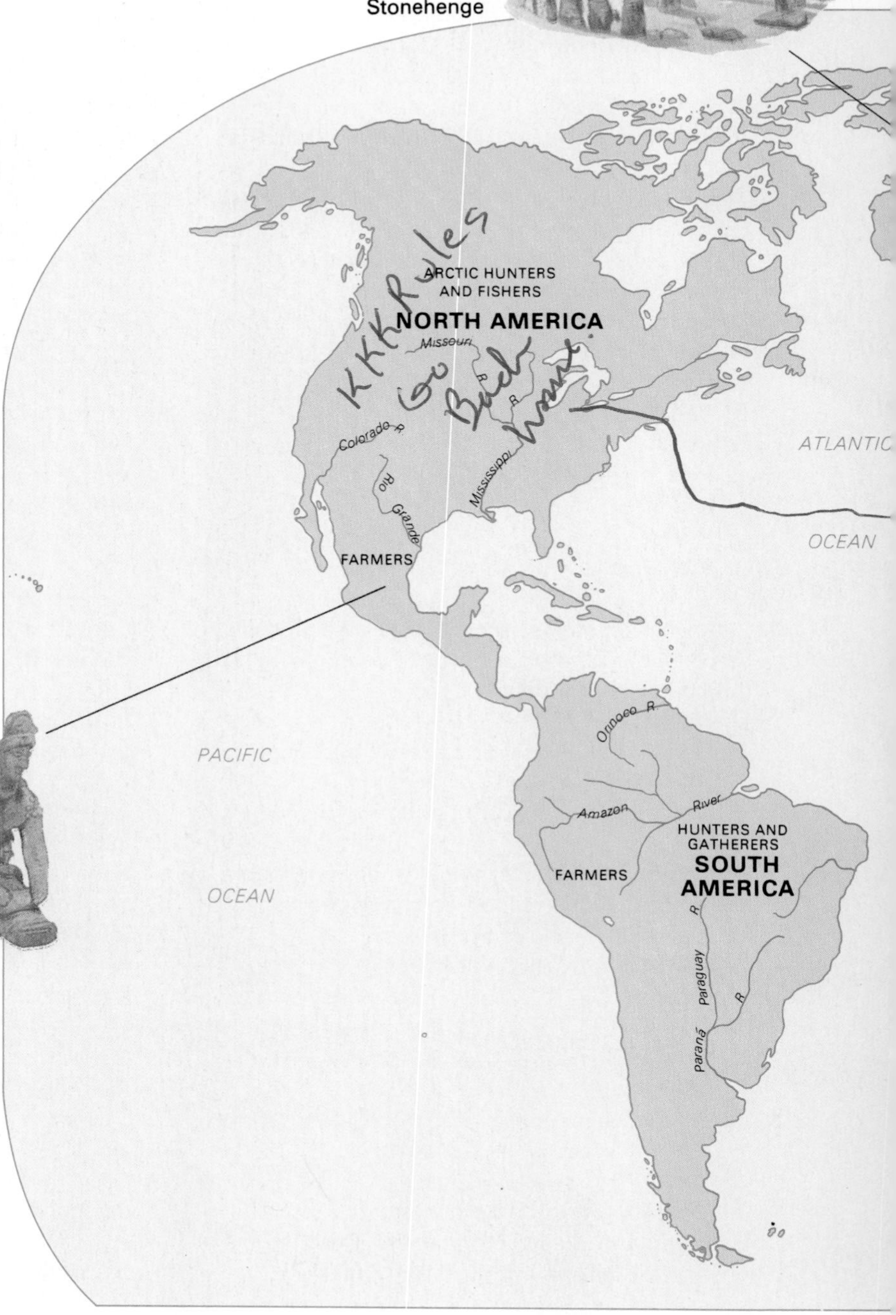

Clay figurine grinding corn

ARCTIC HUNTERS
AND FISHERS
NORTH AMERICA
Missouri
Colorado R.
Rio Grande
Mississippi

FARMERS

ATLANTIC

OCEAN

PACIFIC

OCEAN

Orinoco R.
Amazon
River
HUNTERS AND
GATHERERS
**SOUTH
AMERICA**
FARMERS
Paraguay
Paraná
R.

Historical Atlas

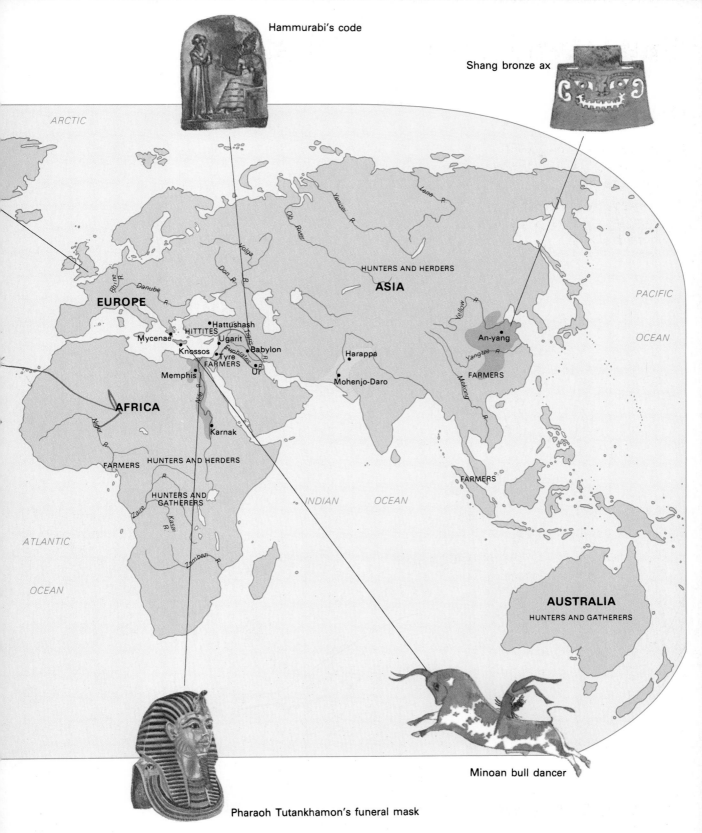

Hammurabi's code

Shang bronze ax

ARCTIC

EUROPE

Rhine R.

Danube R.

Volga R.

Don R.

Ob River

Yenisei R.

Lena R.

ASIA

HUNTERS AND HERDERS

PACIFIC

OCEAN

HITTITES

Hattushash

Mycenae

Ugarit

Knossos

Tyre

Babylon

FARMERS

Ur

Tigris R.

Euphrates R.

Memphis

Harappa

Yellow R.

An-yang

Yangtze R.

FARMERS

Mohenjo-Daro

AFRICA

Nile R.

Karnak

Mekong R.

FARMERS

Niger R.

FARMERS

HUNTERS AND HERDERS

HUNTERS AND
GATHERERS

Zaire R.

Kasai R.

INDIAN

OCEAN

FARMERS

ATLANTIC

OCEAN

Zambezi R.

AUSTRALIA

HUNTERS AND GATHERERS

Minoan bull dancer

Pharaoh Tutankhamon's funeral mask

The World about 200 B.C.

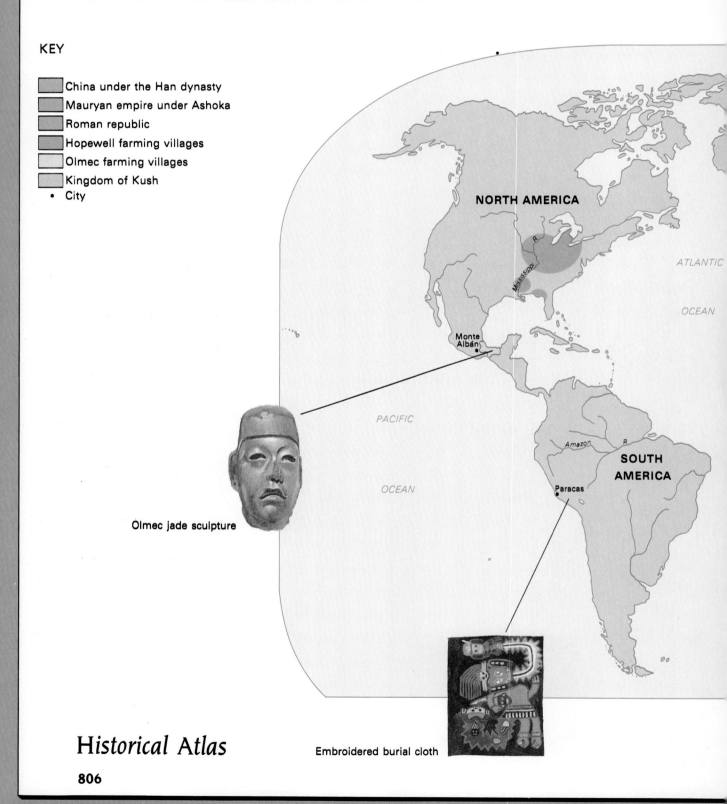

KEY

China under the Han dynasty
Mauryan empire under Ashoka
Roman republic
Hopewell farming villages
Olmec farming villages
Kingdom of Kush
• City

NORTH AMERICA

R.

MISSISSIPPI

ATLANTIC

OCEAN

Monte
Albán

PACIFIC

OCEAN

Amazon   R.

SOUTH
AMERICA

Paracas

Olmec jade sculpture

Embroidered burial cloth

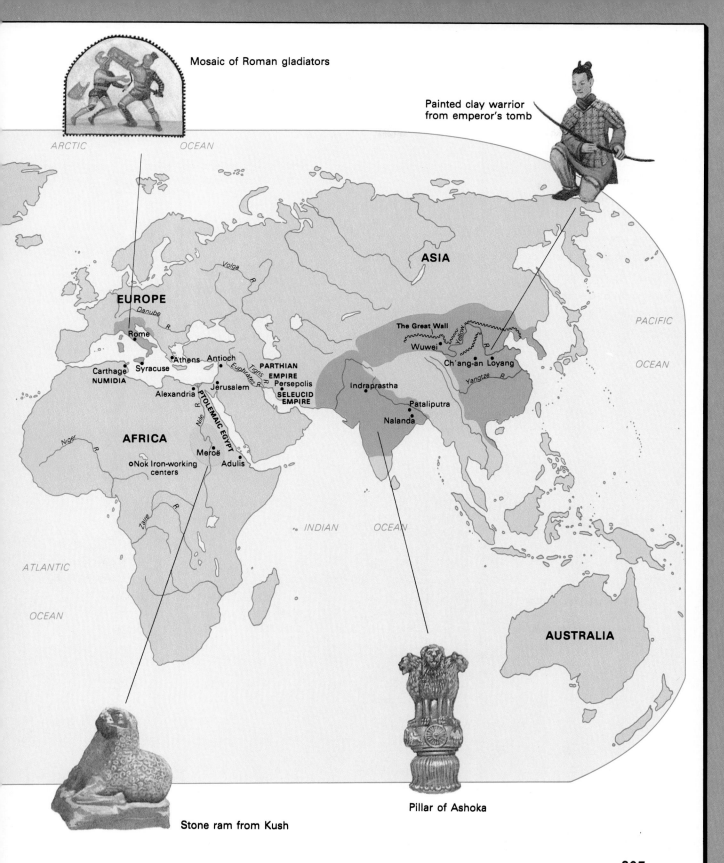

Mosaic of Roman gladiators

Painted clay warrior
from emperor's tomb

ARCTIC   OCEAN

Volga R.

ASIA

PACIFIC

OCEAN

EUROPE

Danube R.

Rome

The Great Wall

Athens   Antioch   Wuwei   Yellow R.

Carthage   Syracuse   PARTHIAN   Ch'ang-an Loyang
NUMIDIA   EMPIRE
                      Jerusalem   Persepolis   Yangtze R.
       Alexandria   SELEUCID
                                       EMPIRE   Indraprastha

Niger R.   Pataliputra
            AFRICA   Nalanda

       oNok Iron-working   Meroë
            centers   Adulis

Zaire R.

ATLANTIC   INDIAN   OCEAN

OCEAN

AUSTRALIA

Stone ram from Kush

Pillar of Ashoka

The World about 800

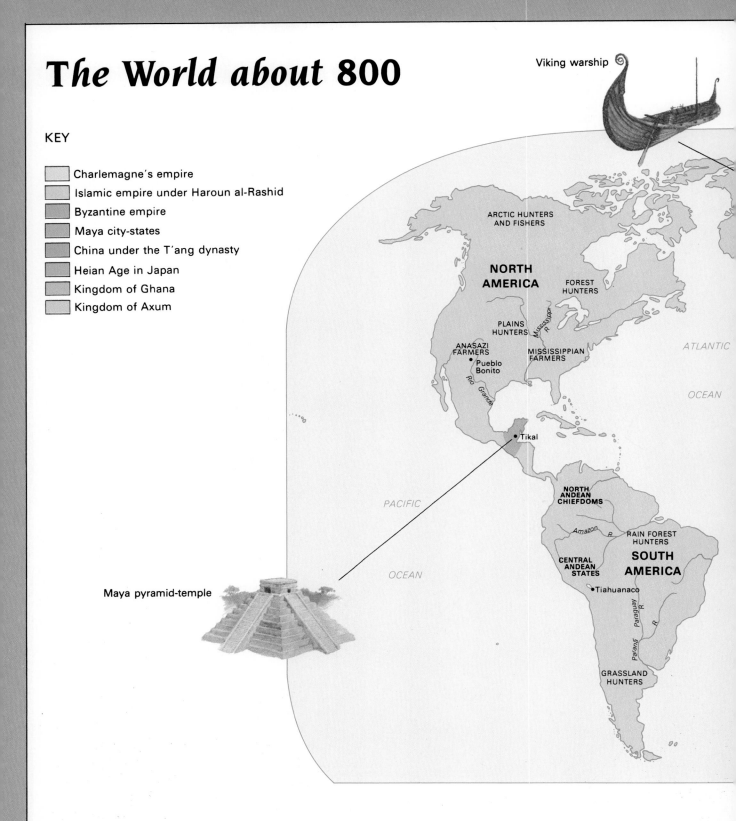

Viking warship

KEY

- Charlemagne's empire
- Islamic empire under Haroun al-Rashid
- Byzantine empire
- Maya city-states
- China under the T'ang dynasty
- Heian Age in Japan
- Kingdom of Ghana
- Kingdom of Axum

ARCTIC HUNTERS AND FISHERS

NORTH AMERICA

FOREST HUNTERS

PLAINS HUNTERS

MISSISSIPPIAN FARMERS

ANASAZI FARMERS

• Pueblo Bonito

Mississippi R.

Rio Grande

ATLANTIC

OCEAN

• Tikal

NORTH ANDEAN CHIEFDOMS

Amazon R.

RAIN FOREST HUNTERS

CENTRAL ANDEAN STATES

SOUTH AMERICA

PACIFIC

• Tiahuanaco

OCEAN

Paraguay R.

Paraná R.

GRASSLAND HUNTERS

Maya pyramid-temple

Historical Atlas

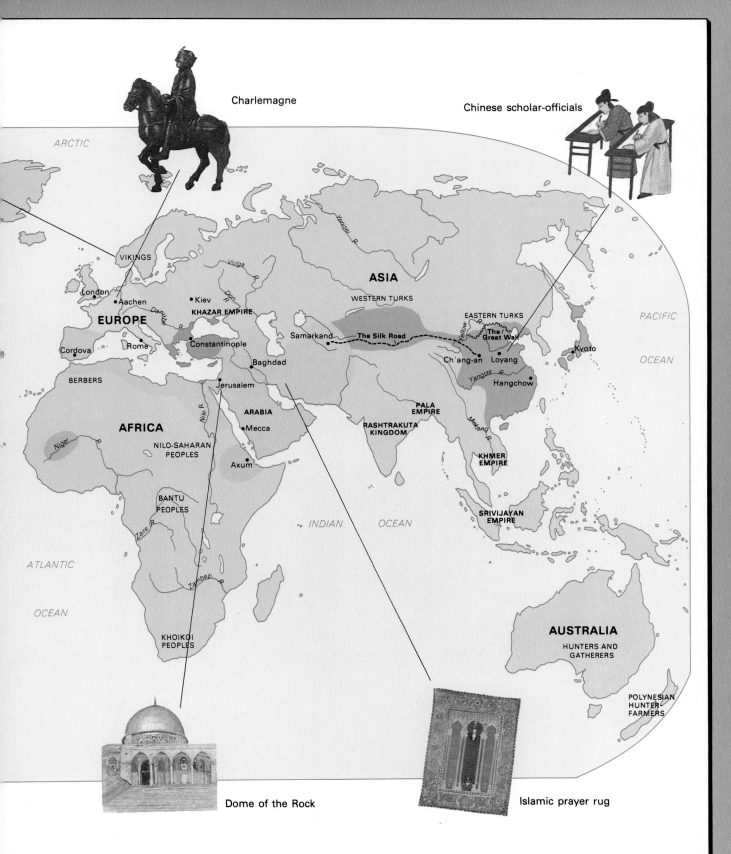

Charlemagne

Chinese scholar-officials

ARCTIC

ASIA

VIKINGS

WESTERN TURKS

EASTERN TURKS

PACIFIC

London
Aachen
Kiev
Volga R.
KHAZAR EMPIRE
Samarkand
The Silk Road
Yellow R.
The Great Wall

EUROPE

Danube R.
Don R.
Constantinople

Cordova
Rome
Baghdad

BERBERS
Jerusalem
Nile R.
ARABIA
Mecca

AFRICA
Niger R.
NILO-SAHARAN PEOPLES
Axum

BANTU PEOPLES
Zaire R.

ATLANTIC

OCEAN
Zambezi R.

KHOIKOI PEOPLES

Ch'ang-an
Loyang
Kyoto

OCEAN

Yangtze R.
Hangchow

PALA EMPIRE
RASHTRAKUTA KINGDOM
Mekong R.
KHMER EMPIRE

INDIAN   OCEAN

SRIVIJAYAN EMPIRE

AUSTRALIA
HUNTERS AND GATHERERS

POLYNESIAN HUNTER-FARMERS

Dome of the Rock

Islamic prayer rug

809

The World about 1250

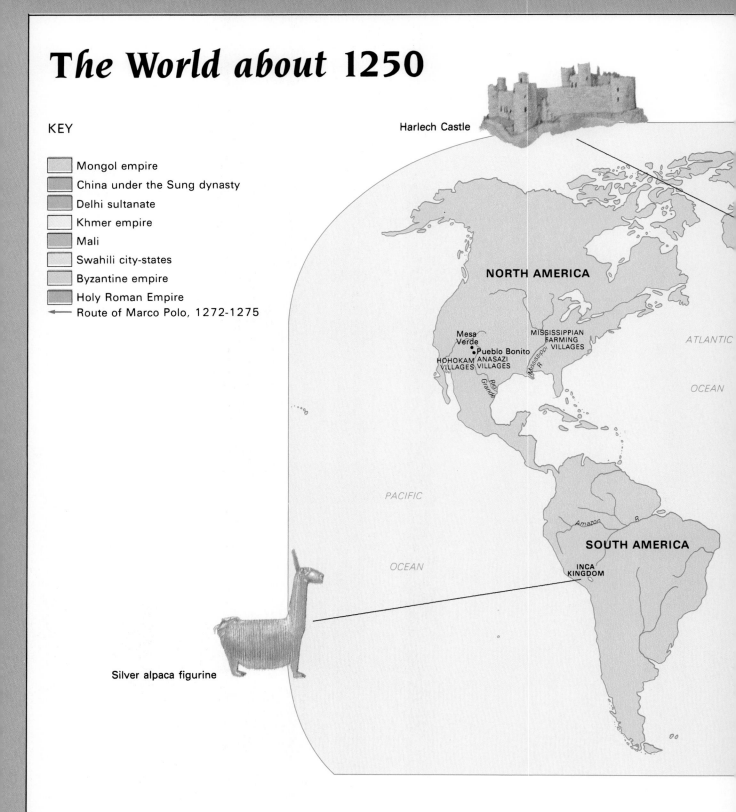

Harlech Castle

NORTH AMERICA

Mesa Verde

MISSISSIPPIAN FARMING VILLAGES

Pueblo Bonito

HOHOKAM VILLAGES   ANASAZI VILLAGES

Mississippi R

Rio Grande

ATLANTIC

OCEAN

PACIFIC

OCEAN

SOUTH AMERICA

Amazon R

INCA KINGDOM

Silver alpaca figurine

Historical Atlas

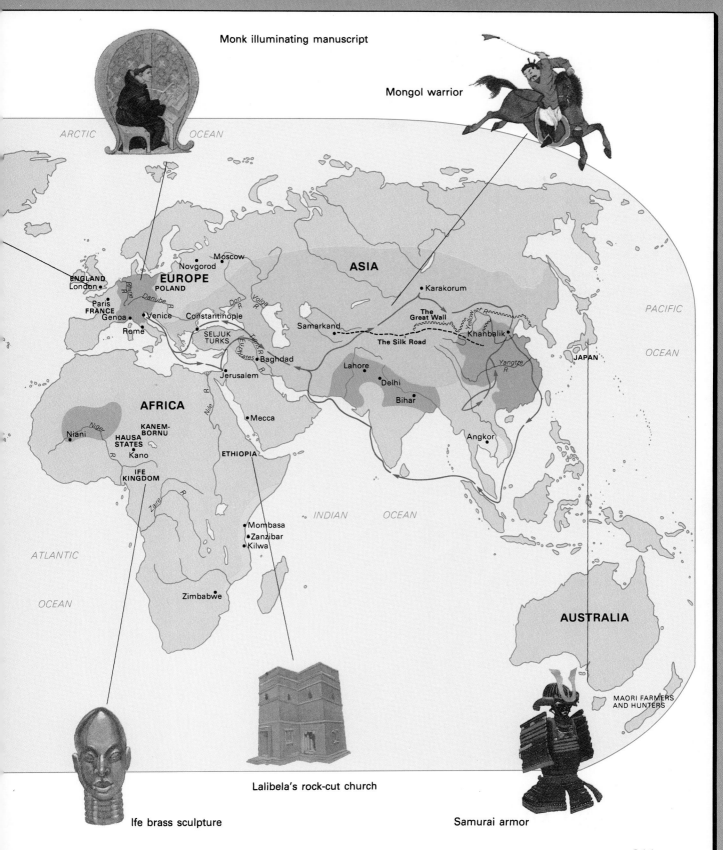

Monk illuminating manuscript

Mongol warrior

ARCTIC   OCEAN

ENGLAND
London

EUROPE
POLAND

Moscow

Novgorod

ASIA

Karakorum

PACIFIC

Paris
FRANCE
Genoa
Rome

Rhine R.

Danube R.

Venice

Constantinople

Don R.

Volga R.

Samarkand

The
Great Wall

Yellow R.

Khanbalik

OCEAN

SELJUK
TURKS

Tigris R.

Euphrates R.

Baghdad

The Silk Road

JAPAN

Jerusalem

Lahore

Delhi

Yangtze R.

AFRICA

Nile R.

Mecca

Bihar

Niani

Niger R.

KANEM-
BORNU

HAUSA
STATES

Kano

ETHIOPIA

Angkor

IFE
KINGDOM

Zaire R.

INDIAN   OCEAN

ATLANTIC

Mombasa
Zanzibar
Kilwa

OCEAN

AUSTRALIA

Zimbabwe

MAORI FARMERS
AND HUNTERS

Lalibela's rock-cut church

Ife brass sculpture

Samurai armor

The World about 1500

KEY

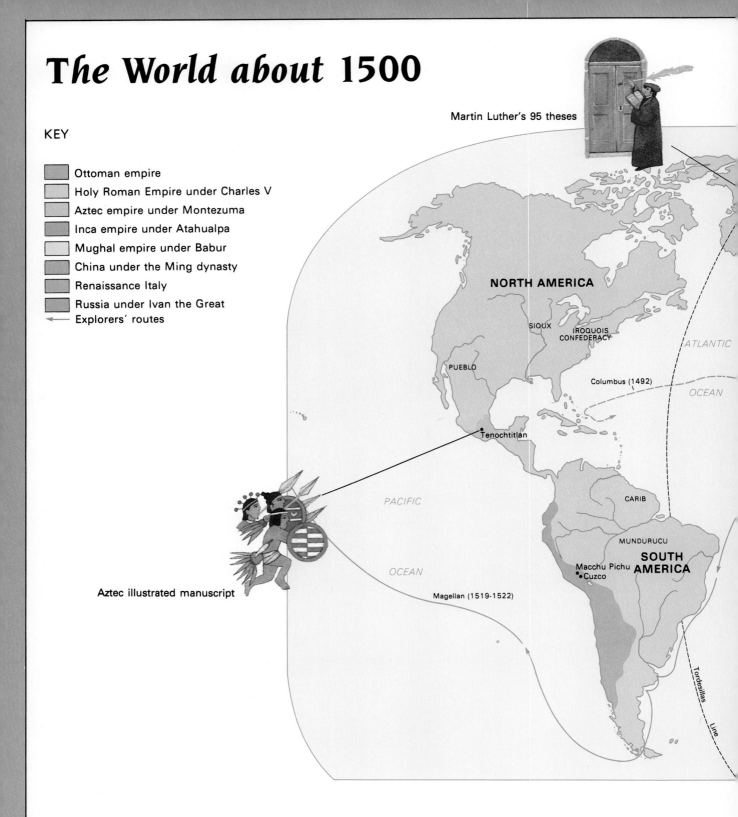

Martin Luther's 95 theses

- ▮ Ottoman empire
- ▮ Holy Roman Empire under Charles V
- ▮ Aztec empire under Montezuma
- ▮ Inca empire under Atahualpa
- ▮ Mughal empire under Babur
- ▮ China under the Ming dynasty
- ▮ Renaissance Italy
- ▮ Russia under Ivan the Great
- ← Explorers' routes

NORTH AMERICA

SIOUX

IROQUOIS CONFEDERACY

ATLANTIC

PUEBLO

OCEAN

Columbus (1492)

Tenochtitlan

PACIFIC

CARIB

MUNDURUCU

Aztec illustrated manuscript

OCEAN

SOUTH AMERICA

Macchu Pichu

Cuzco

Magellan (1519-1522)

Tordesillas Line

Historical Atlas

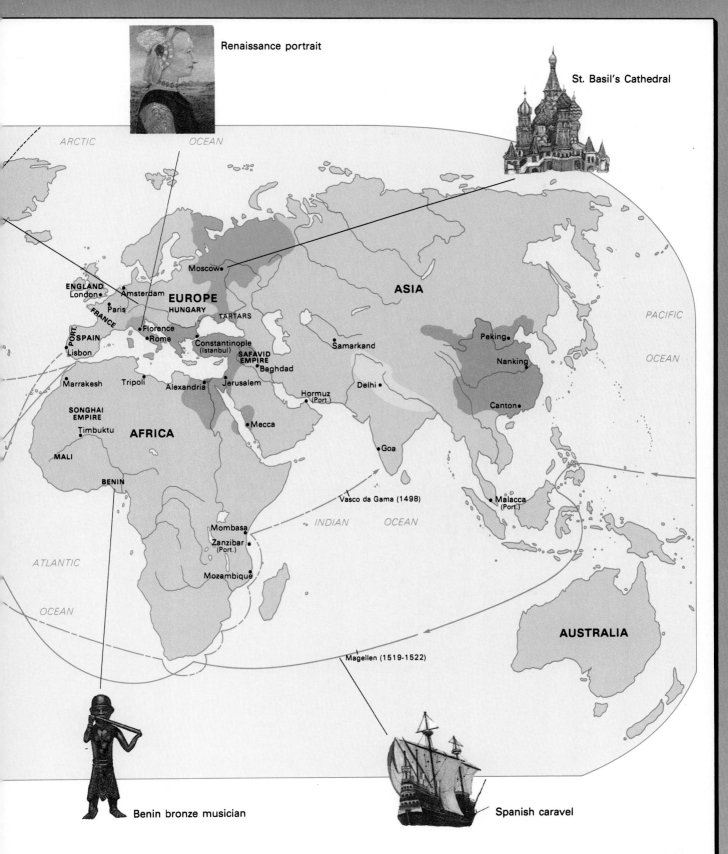

Renaissance portrait

St. Basil's Cathedral

ARCTIC OCEAN

ASIA

PACIFIC OCEAN

Moscow•

ENGLAND
London•
• Amsterdam
Paris•
FRANCE
PORT.
SPAIN
Lisbon•
EUROPE
HUNGARY
TARTARS
• Florence
• Rome
Constantinople
(Istanbul)
SAFAVID
EMPIRE
• Baghdad

• Samarkand

Peking•

Nanking•

Marrakesh•
Tripoli
Alexandria•
Jerusalem•
Hormuz
(Port.)
Delhi •
Canton•

SONGHAI
EMPIRE
• Timbuktu
AFRICA
• Mecca

• Goa

MALI

BENIN

Vasco da Gama (1498)

• Malacca
(Port.)

Mombasa•
Zanzibar•
(Port.)
INDIAN   OCEAN

ATLANTIC

Mozambique•

OCEAN

AUSTRALIA

Magellen (1519-1522)

Benin bronze musician

Spanish caravel

813

The World about 1800

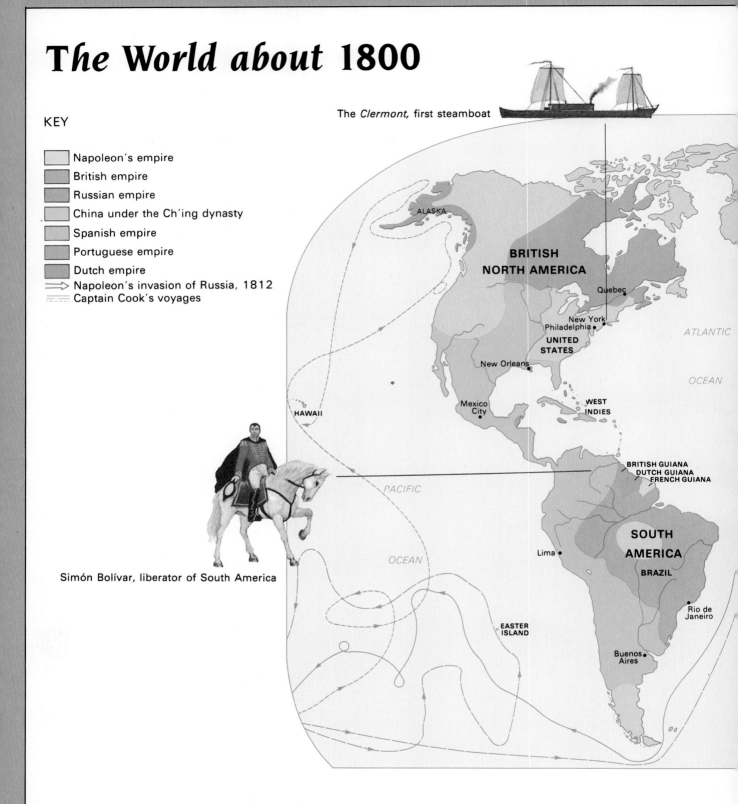

KEY

- ☐ Napoleon's empire
- ▢ British empire
- ▢ Russian empire
- ☐ China under the Ch'ing dynasty
- ☐ Spanish empire
- ▢ Portuguese empire
- ▢ Dutch empire
- ⇒ Napoleon's invasion of Russia, 1812
- ═ Captain Cook's voyages

The *Clermont,* first steamboat

ALASKA

BRITISH
NORTH AMERICA

Quebec

New York
Philadelphia

UNITED
STATES

New Orleans

Mexico
City

HAWAII

WEST
INDIES

ATLANTIC

OCEAN

BRITISH GUIANA
DUTCH GUIANA
FRENCH GUIANA

PACIFIC

OCEAN

Simón Bolívar, liberator of South America

Lima

SOUTH
AMERICA

BRAZIL

Rio de
Janeiro

EASTER
ISLAND

Buenos
Aires

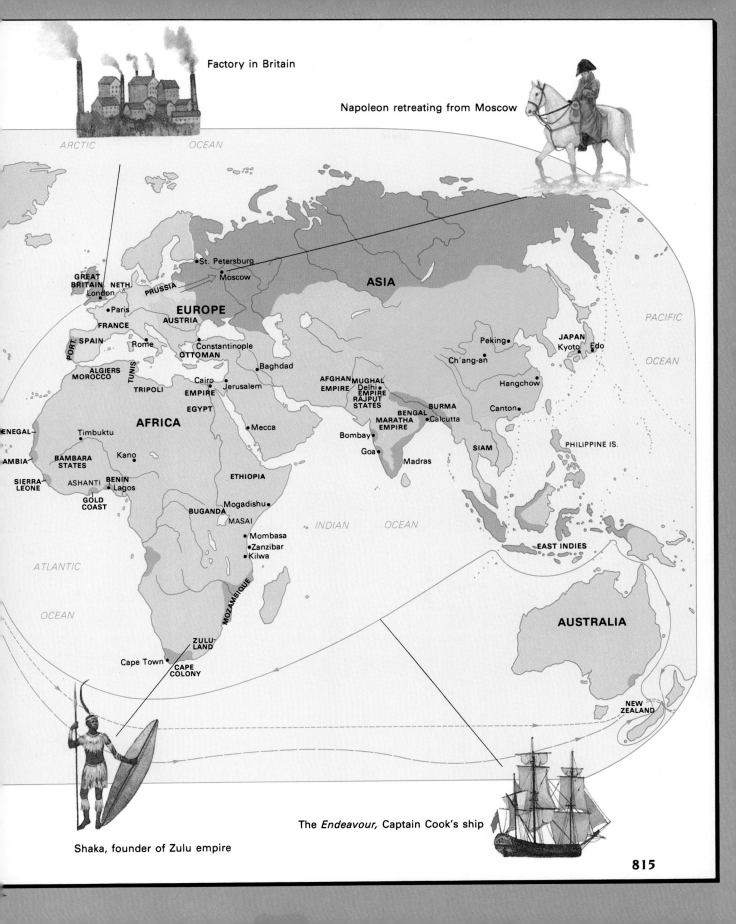

Factory in Britain

Napoleon retreating from Moscow

ARCTIC   OCEAN

GREAT
BRITAIN   NETH.
London
• Paris
FRANCE
PORT. SPAIN
Rome
EUROPE
AUSTRIA
PRUSSIA
• St. Petersburg
• Moscow

ASIA

PACIFIC

JAPAN
Peking •   Kyoto • Edo
Ch'ang-an
OCEAN

ALGIERS
MOROCCO
TUNIS
TRIPOLI
Constantinople
OTTOMAN
EMPIRE
EGYPT
Cairo
Jerusalem
Baghdad
Mecca

AFGHAN
EMPIRE
MUGHAL
EMPIRE
RAJPUT
STATES
Delhi
Hangchow
Canton •

AFRICA

SENEGAL
GAMBIA
SIERRA
LEONE
BAMBARA
STATES
ASHANTI
GOLD
COAST
Timbuktu
Kano
BENIN
Lagos
ETHIOPIA
BUGANDA
MASAI
Mogadishu
Mombasa
Zanzibar
Kilwa

BENGAL
MARATHA
EMPIRE
BURMA
Calcutta
Bombay
Goa
Madras
SIAM

PHILIPPINE IS.

INDIAN   OCEAN

EAST INDIES

AUSTRALIA

ATLANTIC

OCEAN

MOZAMBIQUE

ZULU-
LAND
Cape Town
CAPE
COLONY

NEW
ZEALAND

The *Endeavour,* Captain Cook's ship

Shaka, founder of Zulu empire

The World about 1900

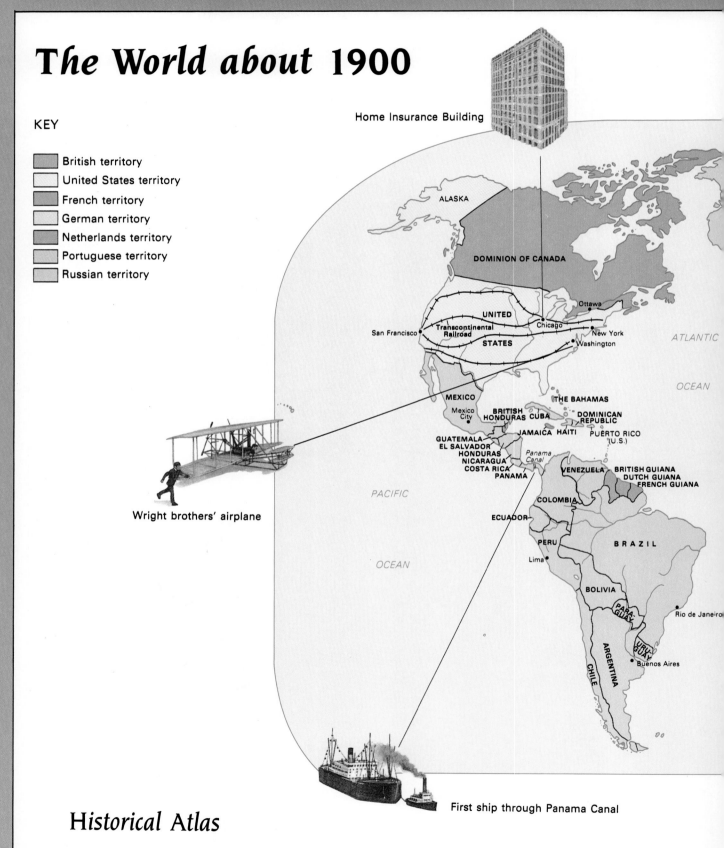

KEY

- British territory
- United States territory
- French territory
- German territory
- Netherlands territory
- Portuguese territory
- Russian territory

Home Insurance Building

Wright brothers' airplane

First ship through Panama Canal

ALASKA

DOMINION OF CANADA

Ottawa

UNITED

Transcontinental
Railroad

Chicago

San Francisco

STATES

New York

Washington

ATLANTIC

OCEAN

MEXICO

Mexico
City

THE BAHAMAS

BRITISH
HONDURAS CUBA

DOMINICAN
REPUBLIC

GUATEMALA
EL SALVADOR
HONDURAS
NICARAGUA
COSTA RICA
PANAMA

JAMAICA HAITI

PUERTO RICO
(U.S.)

Panama
Canal

VENEZUELA

BRITISH GUIANA
DUTCH GUIANA
FRENCH GUIANA

COLOMBIA

PACIFIC

ECUADOR

PERU

Lima

BRAZIL

BOLIVIA

OCEAN

PARA-
GUAY

Rio de Janeiro

URU-
GUAY

ARGENTINA

CHILE

Buenos Aires

Women's suffrage movement

Trans-Siberian Railroad

Japanese factory

ARCTIC OCEAN

REENLAND
(Den.)

ICELAND

KINGDOM
OF SWEDEN
AND
NORWAY

RUSSIAN EMPIRE

• St. Petersburg
• Moscow

PACIFIC

GREAT
BRITAIN NETH.
BELG.
London•

DEN.

GERMANY

Trans-Siberian
Railroad

OCEAN

Paris•

FRANCE

AUSTRIA-
HUNGARY
SWITZ.

ROMANIA

Peking•

• Vladivostok

JAPAN

Rome•

PORT.

SPAIN

ITALY

SERBIA

BULGARIA

• Tokyo

OTTOMAN EMPIRE

ISTANBUL

• Shanghai

GREECE

CHINA

OCEAN

RIO DE ORO

MOROCCO

ALGERIA

TUNIS

TRIPOLI
(Ott.)

Baghdad•
Suez
Canal•

Jerusalem•

Cairo•

PERSIA

AFGHAN
ISTAN

Delhi•

Canton•

EGYPT

ARABIA

BRITISH INDIA

Calcutta•

SIAM

INDOCHINA

PHILIPPINE IS.

FRENCH WEST AFRICA

Mecca•

Bombay•

AMBIA
GUINEA

TOGO-
LAND

NIGERIA

ERITREA

ADEN

FRENCH
SOMALILAND

SUMATRA

Singapore•

BORNEO

NEW
GUINEA

RRA LEONE
LIBERIA

GOLD
COAST

SP.
GUINEA

CAMEROON

SUDAN

ETHIOPIA

BRITISH
SOMALILAND

INDIAN   OCEAN

JAVA

TIMOR

BELGIAN
CONGO

ITALIAN
SOMALILAND

EAST
AFRICA

CABINDA

GERMAN
EAST
AFRICA

ATLANTIC

ANGOLA

RHODESIA

MOZAMBIQUE

MADAGASCAR

COMMONWEALTH
OF AUSTRALIA

OCEAN

GERMAN
S.W.
AFRICA

BECHUANALAND

Perth•

• Brisbane

CAPE
COLONY

TRANSVAAL

ORANGE
FREE STATE

• Sydney

Cape Town•

Melbourne•

NEW
ZEALAND

British rule in India

817

The Modern World

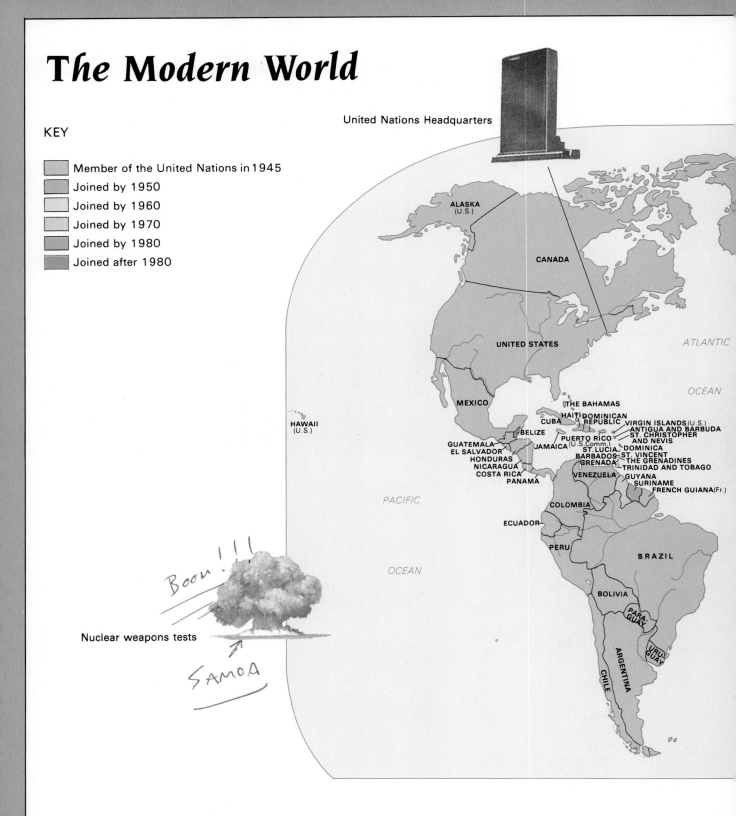

United Nations Headquarters

KEY

- Member of the United Nations in 1945
- Joined by 1950
- Joined by 1960
- Joined by 1970
- Joined by 1980
- Joined after 1980

ALASKA (U.S.)

CANADA

UNITED STATES

ATLANTIC

OCEAN

MEXICO

HAWAII (U.S.)

THE BAHAMAS

CUBA

HAITI DOMINICAN REPUBLIC

VIRGIN ISLANDS (U.S.)

ANTIGUA AND BARBUDA

ST. CHRISTOPHER AND NEVIS

BELIZE

PUERTO RICO (U.S. Comm.)

DOMINICA

GUATEMALA

EL SALVADOR

HONDURAS

NICARAGUA

COSTA RICA

PANAMA

JAMAICA

ST. LUCIA

BARBADOS

GRENADA

ST. VINCENT

THE GRENADINES

TRINIDAD AND TOBAGO

VENEZUELA

GUYANA

SURINAME

FRENCH GUIANA (Fr.)

COLOMBIA

ECUADOR

PERU

BRAZIL

BOLIVIA

PARAGUAY

URUGUAY

ARGENTINA

CHILE

PACIFIC

OCEAN

Boom!!!

Nuclear weapons tests

SAMOA

Historical Atlas

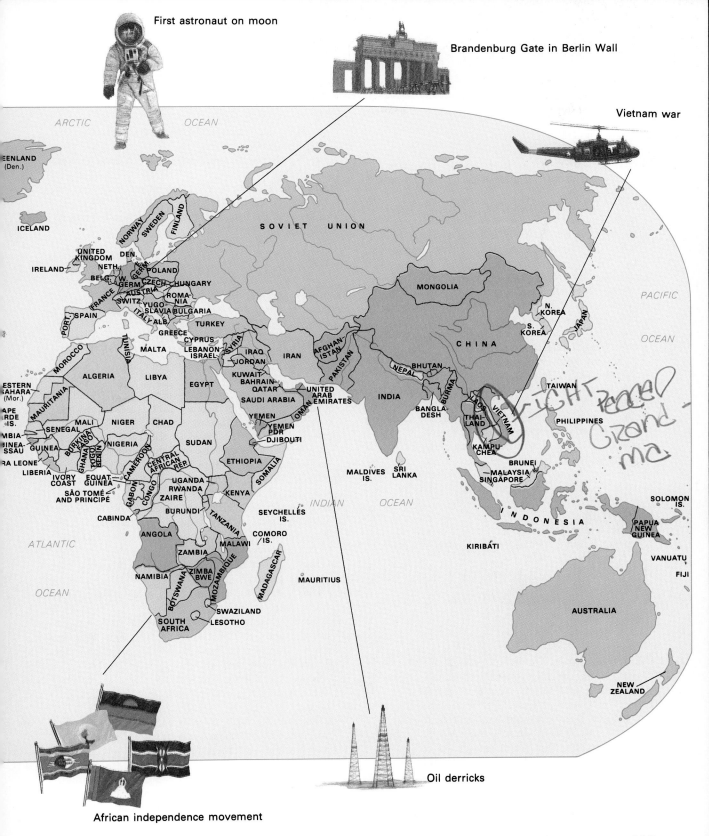

First astronaut on moon

Brandenburg Gate in Berlin Wall

Vietnam war

ARCTIC OCEAN

GREENLAND (Den.)

ICELAND

ATLANTIC OCEAN

NORWAY
SWEDEN
FINLAND

UNITED KINGDOM
IRELAND
DEN.
NETH.
BELG.
E. GERM.
POLAND
W. GERM
CZECH
HUNGARY
FRANCE
AUSTRIA
SWITZ.
YUGO-SLAVIA
ROMA-NIA
BULGARIA
ITALY
ALB.
PORT.
SPAIN
GREECE
TURKEY
CYPRUS
MALTA

SOVIET UNION

MONGOLIA

CHINA

N. KOREA
S. KOREA
JAPAN

PACIFIC OCEAN

TAIWAN

MOROCCO
WESTERN SAHARA (Mor.)
ALGERIA
TUNISIA
LIBYA
EGYPT
MAURITANIA
CAPE VERDE IS.
SENEGAL
GAMBIA
GUINEA-BISSAU
GUINEA
SIERRA LEONE
LIBERIA
IVORY COAST
MALI
BURKINA FASO
GHANA
TOGO
BENIN
NIGER
NIGERIA
CHAD
SUDAN
CENTRAL AFRICAN REP.
CAMEROUN
EQUAT. GUINEA
SÃO TOMÉ AND PRINCIPE
GABON
CONGO
CABINDA
ZAIRE
UGANDA
RWANDA
BURUNDI
ETHIOPIA
SOMALIA
KENYA
TANZANIA
ANGOLA
ZAMBIA
MALAWI
ZIMBA BWE
MOZAMBIQUE
NAMIBIA
BOTSWANA
MADAGASCAR
COMORO IS.
SEYCHELLES IS.
MAURITIUS
SOUTH AFRICA
SWAZILAND
LESOTHO

LEBANON
ISRAEL
SYRIA
JORDAN
IRAQ
IRAN
KUWAIT
BAHRAIN
QATAR
SAUDI ARABIA
UNITED ARAB EMIRATES
OMAN
YEMEN
YEMEN PDR
DJIBOUTI

AFGHAN-ISTAN
PAKISTAN
NEPAL
BHUTAN
INDIA
BANGLA-DESH
BURMA
LAOS
THAI-LAND
VIETNAM
KAMPU-CHEA

FIGHT Peace! Grand ma.

PHILIPPINES

BRUNEI
MALAYSIA
SINGAPORE
INDONESIA

MALDIVES IS.
SRI LANKA

INDIAN OCEAN

KIRIBATI

SOLOMON IS.
PAPUA NEW GUINEA
VANUATU
FIJI

AUSTRALIA

NEW ZEALAND

Oil derricks

African independence movement

819

Glossary

a

abdicate: To resign as ruler. (p. 603)

absolute monarch: A ruler with unlimited power. (p. 409)

aid: A grant of money that a vassal gives to a lord. (p. 203)

anarchist: A person who believes that all governments are evil and therefore should be overthrown. (p. 575)

apartheid: South Africa's legal system of rigid separation between blacks and whites. (p. 752)

appeasement: The policy of making concessions in the hope of avoiding war. (p. 659)

apprentice: A person who is learning a trade or craft from a master and who works without pay except for room and board. (p. 213)

archaeologist: A person who studies the remains of ancient societies to learn about past ways of life. (p. 12)

arete: The ideal of striving for excellence, showing courage, and winning fame and honor. (p. 99)

aristocracy: A government dominated by a small group of noble families. (p. 101)

armistice: An agreement to stop fighting. (p. 595)

artisan: A skilled worker who makes goods by hand. (p. 28)

assembly line: A line of factory workers and machinery along which a product passes with each worker doing a specialized task until the product is complete. (p. 560)

autocrat: A ruler with unlimited power; an absolute ruler. (p. 604)

b

balance of power: A defensive strategy in which weak countries join together to match or exceed the power of a stronger country. (p. 413)

balance of trade: The difference in value between a country's imports and its exports. (p. 410)

barter: A form of trade in which people exchange goods without the use of money. (p. 31)

bishop: A church official who sets moral standards and supervises the finances of several local churches. (p. 153)

bourgeoisie: In medieval France, people who live in burghs or towns rather than in rural areas (p. 211); according to Marx, the factory-owning middle class. (p. 516)

boyar: A Russian noble who owns a large estate. (p. 253)

buffer zone: A region that lies between two rivals, cutting down the threat of conflict. (p. 693)

burgher: A person who lives in a walled town, or a burgh. (p. 211)

c

cabinet: An executive committee chosen by the head of a country to help make government decisions. (p. 439)

caliph: An Islamic leader who holds both political and religious power. (p. 178)

canon law: The law of the Roman Catholic Church. (p. 216)

capitalism: An economic system characterized by the investment of money in business ventures with the goal of making a profit. (p. 373)

caravel: A ship developed in the 1400's with triangular sails for tacking into the wind and square sails for running before the wind. (p. 335)

cardinal: A leading bishop in the Roman Catholic Church. (p. 215)

caste: A rigid social group, membership in which is determined at birth and never changes during a person's life; in Hinduism, caste is linked to religious purity. (p. 72)

cataract: A set of rapids in a river, blocking the passage of boats. (p. 48)

caudillo: A dictator, usually an army officer, of a Latin American country. (p. 504)

chivalry: A code of ideals demanding that a knight aid the poor, defend the weak, and fight bravely for his three masters—his earthly feudal lord, his heavenly Lord, and his chosen lady. (p. 226)

city-state: A political unit made up of a city and the surrounding countryside that is under the control of the city. (p. 30)

civilization: A form of culture that includes cities, specialized workers, writing, advanced technology, and complex institutions. (p. 27)

civil rights: Full rights of citizenship. (p. 792)

civil service: Workers employed by a government to carry out its daily functions such as repairing roads, delivering mail, collecting taxes, and so on. (p. 142)

clan: A group of people who are descended from the same ancestor. (p. 275)

coalition: A temporary alliance between groups who are usually on different sides. (p. 455)

colony: A settlement in a new territory by a group of people who keep their ties to their home government; a region governed by a foreign power. (p. 101)

common law: The unified body of law that developed, case by case, from the rulings of England's royal judges and became common to the whole kingdom. (p. 221)

condominium: A country ruled jointly by two other countries. (p. 536)

conquistador: A Spanish soldier and fortune hunter who took part in the conquest of the Americas. (p. 364)

constitutional monarchy: A government led by a ruler whose power is limited by law. (p. 439)

consul: A powerful official in the Roman republic who commanded the army and directed the government. (p. 126)

corporation: A business owned by stockholders who share in its profits but are not personally responsible for its debts. (p. 513)

count: A powerful landowner who ruled a county in a king's name, administered justice, and raised armies. (p. 196)

coup: A sudden takeover of a country's government. (p. 458)

crop rotation: The system of growing a different crop in a field each year to preserve the fertility of the land. (p. 473)

crusader: A person who fights on behalf of a religious or moral cause. (p. 228)

culture: The way of life that a group of people develops and passes on to its children; culture includes language, tools, skills, beliefs, and traditions. Every human group has a culture. Civilization is one form of culture. (p. 14)

cuneiform: An ancient form of writing that used wedge-shaped symbols. (p. 28)

czar: The Russian emperor. (p. 252)

d

daimyo: A feudal lord in Japan who commanded a private army of samurai. (p. 278)

delta: A broad, triangular, marshy region at the mouth of a river. (p. 48)

democracy: A government in which the citizens hold the final power. (p. 103)

demography: The study of population statistics. (p. 790)

dictator: In Rome, a political leader elected for a limited time and given absolute power to make laws and command the army; later any political leader who takes on such powers, usually without legal basis. (p. 126)

dissident: A person who expresses an opinion that differs from those held by the general society. (p. 784)

divine right: The idea that rulers receive their authority from God and are answerable only to God. (p. 398)

dynasty: A series of rulers from a single family. (p. 52)

e

edict: A public announcement of a policy. (p. 75)

embargo: A government order forbidding trade with another country. (p. 769)

emigration: The departure from a country to live elsewhere. (p. 514)

empire: A state that conquers other lands and then rules them. (p. 34)

enclosure: The process by which wealthy landowners buy the open fields in a village, fence them, and then rent them to tenant farmers who work the land. (p. 473)

enlightened despot: An absolute ruler who uses his or her power for the good of the people he or she rules. (p. 436)

entrepreneur: A person who organizes, manages, and takes on the risks of running a business. (p. 477)

epic: A long poem that tells the story of a historical or legendary hero. (p. 98)

excommunicate: To cut off from the church. (p. 173)

executive: Having to do with the branch of government that carries out the laws. (p. 434)

f

factory: A building where goods are manufactured. (p. 476)

fair: A gathering of people at a regular time and place to buy, sell, and trade goods. (p. 212)

fascism: A political movement that believes in an extreme form of nationalism—denying individual rights, insisting upon the supremacy of the state, and advocating dictatorial one-party rule. (p. 653)

federal: A form of government in which power is shared between the national government and the governments of the separate states. (p. 445)

821

feudalism: A political and military system based on the holding of land, with an emphasis on local protection, local government, and local self-sufficiency. (p. 201)

fief: The piece of land given to a vassal by a lord. (p. 202)

friar: A member of a Roman Catholic religious order who takes the same vows as a monk but travels about preaching instead of living in a monastery. (p. 217)

g

genocide: The killing of an entire people. (p. 677)

gentry: A social class ranking below nobles but above common people; in Chinese society, the class of scholar-officials. (p. 263)

gravitas: The Roman virtue of weightiness or seriousness, related to the qualities of discipline, strength, and loyalty. (p. 123)

gross national product: The total value of goods and services produced by a country in a year. (p. 726)

guerrillas: Bands of fighters who are not part of a formal army and who usually attack by surprise and withdraw swiftly. (p. 463)

guild: An association of people who work at the same occupation. (p. 213)

h

heretic: A person whose ideas are incorrect in the opinion of the Church. (p. 173)

hieroglyphics: A form of writing based on pictorial characters that developed in Egypt. (p. 62)

hoplite: A soldier of ancient Greece who fought on foot with a shield and a spear. (p. 101)

humanist: One who studies classical texts. (p. 326)

i

ideology: A system of beliefs that influences political, social, and economic actions. (p. 781)

immigration: The act of entering and settling in a country other than one's native country. (p. 514)

imperialism: The policy of extending one country's rule over many lands. (p. 533)

import quota: A limit that one country sets on the amount of goods that may be brought in from another country. (p. 709)

inflation: An overall rise in the prices of goods and services. (p. 155)

institution: A long-lasting pattern of organization in a society. Governments, families, education systems, and organized religions are examples of institutions. (p. 29)

interdict: An order from the pope prohibiting Church ceremonies in the lands of a ruler who is disobedient to the pope. (p. 216)

investiture: A feudal ceremony in which a vassal receives land or a bishop takes office; an act that symbolically confirms an agreement through the exchange of objects. (p. 202)

isolationism: The idea that a country should avoid political or military alliances with other countries. (p. 648)

j

jihad: In Islam, a holy war. (p. 177)

joint-stock company: A business arrangement in which many investors together raise money for a venture too large for any of them to undertake alone. They share the profits in proportion to the amount they invested. (p. 392)

journeyman: A person who, after completing an apprenticeship, works at a craft for wages under the supervision of a master. (p. 213)

judicial: Having to do with the branch of government that interprets the laws. (p. 434)

jury: A group of people sworn to give a verdict based on evidence in a court of law; in medieval England, usually 12 neighbors who answered questions about the facts of a case for a royal judge. (p. 221)

k

khan: The leader of a group of Mongols. (p. 268)

knight: An armored warrior who fought on horseback. (p. 193)

l

legislative: Having to do with the branch of government that makes the laws. (p. 434)

lineage: A group of families—including past generations, living members, and future generations—descended from a common ancestor. (p. 300)

literacy: The ability to read and write. (p. 36)

lord: In the feudal system, the person who makes a grant of land to another person (the vassal). (p. 202)

m

maat: In ancient Egypt, the idea of goodness that included justice, right, truth, and order. (p. 60)

mandate: A territory that was administered on behalf of the League of Nations until it was judged ready for independence. (p. 598)

manor: A small estate from which a lord's family gained its livelihood. (p. 204)

martial law: Law that is enforced by military authorities over the civilian population of a country as if the country were in a state of war. (p. 721)

mercantilism: An economic theory under which a country increases its wealth by exporting more goods than it imports. (p. 410)

mercenary: A soldier who fights in any country's army for pay. (p. 128)

militarism: Glorification of armed strength. (p. 586)

mobilize: To position an army for war. (p. 587)

monastery: A religious community of men or women who give up all their possessions and devote their lives to worship and prayer. (p. 191)

monopoly: The situation in which a single company controls an entire industry. (p. 513)

monotheist: A person who believes in one God. (p. 36)

monsoon: A seasonal wind that blows dry air part of the year and then shifts directions, bringing heavy rainfall the other part of the year. (p. 67)

multinational corporation: A company that has branches in many countries. (p. 763)

n

nationalism: A feeling of loyalty to one's own land and people (p. 245); the belief that one's greatest loyalty should be to a nation-state. (p. 495)

nationalize: To bring under government control. (p. 635)

nation-state: A group of people who share similar traditions, history, and language, who occupy a definite territory, and who are united under one government. (p. 240)

nihilism: A belief that the existing society and government must be destroyed so that a better society can be created. (p. 606)

nomad: A person who has no permanent home and moves from place to place. (p. 16)

o

oasis: A place in a desert where underground water comes to the surface in a spring or well. (p. 299)

p

patriarch: The bishop of Constantinople, head of the Eastern Orthodox Church. (p. 173)

patrician: In ancient Rome, a member of the privileged upper class. (p. 123)

per capita income: A country's gross national product divided by its population. (p. 735)

phalanx: A Greek army unit made up of soldiers standing side by side, their shields forming a solid wall. (p. 101)

pharaoh: A king of Egypt, considered a god. (p. 52)

philosophes: A group of thinkers in the early 1700's who believed in reason, liberty, natural law, progress, and human happiness. (p. 429)

plebeian: A common farmer, artisan, or merchant in ancient Rome; a plebeian was a free citizen with the right to vote. (p. 124)

plebiscite: An election in which all citizens vote yes or no on an issue. (p. 459)

polis: A Greek city-state. (p. 100)

polytheist: A person who believes in more than one god. (p. 32)

pope: The bishop of Rome, head of the Roman Catholic Church. (p. 154)

predestination: The doctrine that God has known since the beginning of time who will be saved. (p. 354)

prehistory: The period of time before the beginning of written records. (p. 13)

prime minister: The leader of the majority party in a country's parliament. The prime minister heads the cabinet. (p. 440)

productivity: A worker's hourly output of goods and services. (p. 712)

proletariat: The poorest class in ancient Rome (p. 131); according to Marx, the urban working class. (p. 516)

propaganda: One-sided information designed to convince people of a certain point of view. (p. 591)

prophet: A messenger sent to reveal God's will. (p. 38)

protectorate: A country whose foreign policy is controlled by an outside government. (p. 536)

purdah: The practice of keeping women in seclusion. (p. 291)

pyramid: An immense structure used as a tomb by the pharaohs. (p. 52)

r

rationing: A system limiting the amount of goods people can buy during a time of shortage. (p. 590)

reincarnation: The idea that the inner self is reborn in another form. (p. 71)

reparations: Compensation paid after a war by a defeated nation for the damages it caused other nations. (p. 598)

republic: A government under which citizens with the right to vote choose their leaders. (p. 123)

s

samurai: A Japanese warrior who fought for his lord and lived according to the code of bushido. (p. 277)

satellite: A country whose policies are dictated or heavily influenced by another country. (p. 696)

satire: Literature that mocks society for its foolishness and wickedness. (p. 147)

savanna: A grassy plain with a few scattered trees. (p. 299)

segregation: The policy of separating by race in schools and other public facilities. (p. 792)

self-determination: Free choice of people in a territory to decide under what government they wish to live. (p. 596)

senate: In ancient Rome, the aristocratic branch of government. (p. 126)

separation of powers: The idea that governmental power should be divided among three branches—executive, legislative, and judicial—so that no single branch can become a threat to liberty. (p. 434)

separatism: a movement for the creation of an independent state (p. 777)

serf: A peasant who was bound to a manor and owed duties to the lord of the manor. (p. 204)

shaykh: The leader of a group of Bedouin. (p. 629)

shogun: The supreme general of Japan's army, having the powers of a military dictator. (p. 277)

socialism: The belief that the wealth of a country should be shared equally among all its citizens. (p. 515)

society: A lasting group of people who have a network of relationships with one another. (p. 14)

soviet: A workers' council that has political powers and organizes political activities. (p. 611)

sphere of influence: A region dominated but not directly ruled by a foreign nation. (p. 543)

steppe: A vast stretch of dry grassland in Asia and eastern Europe. (p. 267)

stock: A share in the ownership of a business. (p. 513)

subcontinent: A large region that is part of a continent, yet separated from the rest of the continent in some way. (p. 67)

suburbs: Areas around a city that depend on the city for jobs and services. (p. 791)

suffrage: The right to vote. (p. 517)

sultan: An Islamic ruler who has political power but not religious authority. (p. 183)

t

tariff: A tax on goods imported from another country. (p. 410)

technology: The part of a culture that includes tools and the skills to make and use them. (p. 16)

theocracy: A government controlled by church leaders. (p. 354)

totalitarianism: A political system in which the government has total control over the lives of individual citizens. (p. 618)

tragedy: A play that portrays men and women of heroic character whose very strength leads to their downfall. (p. 109)

tribune: A Roman official elected by the assembly to speak on behalf of the plebeians. (p. 132)

triumvirate: A group of three political leaders who ruled Rome. (p. 135)

tyrant: In ancient Greece, a man who took over the government by force but usually supported the interest of the common people against the nobles. (p. 101)

u

ultimatum: A final demand that, if not met, will end negotiations and lead to war. (p. 586)

union: A group of workers in a trade or industry who join together to bargain for better working conditions and higher wages. (p. 487)

v

vassal: A person who receives land from a lord and pledges military service in return. (p. 202)

vernacular: The everyday language of a region or country. (p. 325)

veto: To overrule another's decision. (p. 126)

viceroy: A person who governs on behalf of a king; in Spain's empire, a noble who governed a part of Spain's territory in the Americas. (p. 367)

villa: A country estate. (p. 150)

w

welfare state: A country in which the government assumes basic responsibility for people's social and economic well-being. (p. 711)

Belgian Congo, 536
Belgium, 414, 465; under Spain, 372; industrialization in, 481–482; imperialism of, 534, 536, 746, 750; and World War I, 588, 597; and World War II, 668; after World War II, 699, 709
Belisarius, 168–169
Belize, 763
Bell, Alexander Graham, 529, 559
Benedict, 190–191
Benedictine rule, 191
Bengali, 736
Ben-Gurion, David, 755
Benin, 301
Berbers, 178, 304, 306
Berlin: after Thirty Years' War, 422; Napoleon in, 460; in World War II, 670, 718; division of, after World War II, 699; airlift, 699
Berlin Wall, 718, 787
Bermuda, 672
Berserkrs, 198
Bessarabia, 599
Bessemer, Henry, 558
Bethlehem, 151
Biafra, 751
Bible, 37, 43, 348, 794; historic information in, 42; reason and, 225; translations of, 242, 349; first printing of, 347; and science, 358, 563; King James version, 398
Bill of Rights, English, 404
Biology, 563
Bishops, 153–154, 190, 203, 215, 216
Bismarck, Otto von, 521–522, 523, 572, 584, 587, 644
Black Death, 244, 324
Blacks: in Latin America, 500; voting rights of, 517, 792–794; in South Africa, 540, 752–753; in U.S., civil rights of, 791, 792–794
Black Sea, 95, 157, 167, 251, 417, 438
Blackshirts, 654
Black Stone of Mecca, 174, 175
Blanc, Louis, 507
Blanche of Castile, 238
Blitzkrieg, 667, 668–669, 671
Blue jeans, 786
Boers, 540
Bohemia, 242, 380, 421, 424
Bohr, Neils, 564
Boleyn, Anne, 351–352, 353
Bolívar, Simón, 501–502, 504
Bolivia, 550, 632, 634
Bolsheviks, 595, 608, 611, 612–616, 618–619, 785
Bombay, 532, 541
Boniface VIII, pope, 240–241
Book of the Dead, 61
Borneo, 674
Bosnia, 575, 582–583
Bosporus, 157, 167, 438

Boston, 399, 441, 443
Boston Tea Party, 443
Bosworth, Battle of, 248
Boulton, Matthew, 477
Bourbon, House of, 377, 378, 379, 380, 409, 413, 414, 423, 494, 505
Bourgeoisie, 211, 450, 516
Boxers, 547
Boyars, 253, 415, 417
Boycott, Charles, 572
Brahman, 71, 72, 287
Brahmins, 72, 73, 294
Brainwashing, 705
Brandenburg, 421–422
Brandt, Willy, 710
Brassey, Thomas, 512
Brazil, 341, 504, 632, 635, 762–763; claimed by Portugal, 338–339; independence of, 503; government in, 771
Brest Litovsk, Treaty of, 595, 599, 614
Brethren of the Common Life, 345
Brezhnev, Leonid, 782, 784, 788
Briand, Aristide, 644
Brighton, England, 480
Britain. See England; Great Britain
Britain, Battle of, 669–670, 672
British West Indies, 440
Brontë, Emily, 498
Bronze, 29, 38, 39, 54, 79, 98, 101
Bronze Age, 29, 39, 97–98
Brown, Arthur, 645
Brown, Moses, 481
Brunelleschi, Filippo, 329
Brutus, Marcus, 136
Budapest, 700
Buddha (Gautama), 66–67, 73, 75, 81, 275
Buddhism: in China, 66–67, 262; in India, 73–76, 286, 287; in Japan, 275, 278; in Southeast Asia, 294
Buenos Aires, 501
Buganda, 538–539
Bulgaria, 676; in Ottoman empire, 575; nationalism in, 585; and World War I, 588, 595, 599; and World War II, 671, 676; after World War II, 696, 699
Bunche, Ralph, 744
Bundesrat, 572
Burbage, James, 396
Burghers, 211, 213–214, 237
Burgundians, 157, 158, 159, 190
Burials: Paleolithic, 18; Egyptian, 47–48, p51, 52, 54, 55, 56; Chinese, 84, p87; Greek, 98; Hopewell, 310
Burma, 293, 544, 674, 737, 738
Bushido, 277
Business: industrialization and, 513; failure, 514
Byron, Lord, 496, 497, 519
Byzantine empire: formation of, 159; extent of, 166, 168, m169, 174, 182, m184; trade in, 167,

170–171; Muslims and, 167, 173, 177, 178, 182, 228; emperor's power in, 168, 197; reconquering of Roman lands, 168–169, 192; laws and government in, 169–170; culture of, 170–172, 182–183; religion in, 167, 172–173, 182–184, 228; threats to, 173, 177, 182; Slavs and, 182–184, 251; Turks and, 183, 228, 252; decline of, 183–184
Byzantium, 157, 167. See also Constantinople

Cabral, Pedro Alvarez, 339
Caesar, Julius, 125, 135–136, 137, 141, 142, 189
Caillié, René, 536
Calais, 247, 248, 681
Calas, Jean, 427, 428
Calcutta, 533, 541, 626, 734
Calendar, 8; Jewish, 8; Muslim, 8, 175; prehistoric, 19; Chaldean, 41; Egyptian, 63; Roman, 136; Mayan, 313; Russian, 416–417
California, 527
Caligula, Roman emperor, 143, 146
Caliphs, 178–179, 183
Calvin, John, 351, 354
Calvinism, 354, 372, 377, 380, 381
Cambyses, Persian king, 43
Camp David agreements, 757, 797
Canaan, 36, 37
Canada, 680, m776; France surrenders, 424, 440; England claims, 399, 424; self-rule in, 533; relations with U.S., 775–777; separatism in, 776–777
Canal(s): in ancient Egypt, 54; Grand, in Sui China, 261; in Hohokam culture, 312; in Holland, 374; British, during Industrial Revolution, 478; See also Panama Canal; Suez Canal
Candide (Voltaire), 430
Cannon, invention of, 245
Canon law, 216
Canossa, 216, 222
Canterbury Tales, The (Chaucer), 239
Canton, 273, 544, p545
Cape Colony, 540
Cape of Good Hope, 336, m337, 540
Capet, Hugh, 221–222
Capetian dynasty, 221–222, 235
Capitalism, 373, 651
Caracalla, Roman emperor, 150
Caravans, 50
Caravel, 335
Cardinals, 215, 241
Caribbean Islands, 309, 499, 768–770, 798; explorations of, 337, 338. See also British West Indies
Carolingian dynasty, 194, 196, 198, 221

Carolingian miniscule, 196
Carranza, Venustiano, 633
Carter, Howard, 47–48, 56, 62
Carter, James Earl, 757, 790, 797, 798
Carthage, 35, m129, 168, 177; in Punic Wars, 127–131
Cartwright, Edmund, 476
Caspian Sea, 251
Cassius, Gaius, 136
Caste system, 72, 287, 294, 624
Castiglione, Baldassare, 326
Castro, Fidel, 769, 787, 798
Çatal Hüyük, 21
Cataracts, 48
Catherine II (the Great), czarina, 436–439, 460
Catherine de Medici, 377
Catherine of Aragon, 351–352
Catholicism: in England, 351–353, 390, 393, 403; in Scotland, 354, 390; versus Protestantism, 356–358, 364, 368; in Spain, 364, 368–371, 372; in France, 377–379; Richelieu's rule in France, 378–379; and Thirty Years' War, 381; under Napoleon, 459; in Ireland, 573, 713; in Mexico, 633; in Poland, 720. See also Roman Catholic Church
Cato, 130
Catt, Carrie Chapman, 567
Cattle, 20, 69
Caudillos, 504, 632, 771
Cavaliers, 400–401
Cave paintings, p12, 13, 18
Cavour, Camillo di, 519–520, 521, 523
Celebes, 674
Celsius, Anders, 359
Celtic peoples, 188
Centennial Exposition, 529
Central America, 763; early civilizations in, 23, 298; geography of, 309, m309; Mayas in, 313; Europeans in, 338, 340; revolutions in, 499; U.S. and, 634, 753, 766, 787–788, 798–799; political instability in, 763, 766; Soviet Union and, 787–788
Central Powers, 588
Cervantes, Miguel de, 370
Ceylon, 76, 374
Chaeronea, 115
Chaldeans, 40–42
Chamberlain, Neville, 659, 661, 668
Chamber of Deputies, France, 494, 505, 506, 571
Champollion, Jean François, 63
Chandra Gupta I, 285
Chandra Gupta II, 286
Chandragupta Maurya, 74–75, 285
Ch'ang-an, 262, 263, 264, 265, 267, 276
Chanson de geste, 225
Charlemagne, 194–198, m195, m197, 223

Charles V, Holy Roman emperor, 344, 349, 351, 357–358, 367, 368, 372
Charles VI, Holy Roman emperor, 420, 421
Charles I, king of England, 399–400, 405
Charles II, king of England, 402–404
Charles VI, king of France, 245
Charles VII (the Dauphin), king of France, 246, 247, 248
Charles VIII, king of France, 330
Charles IX, king of France, 377
Charles X, king of France, 505
Charles I, king of Spain. See Charles V, Holy Roman emperor
Charles II, king of Spain, 413
Charles XII, king of Sweden, 417–418
Charles Martel, Frankish ruler, 176–177, 193
Charles the Bald, Frankish king, 197, 198
Charles the Bold, Duke of Burgundy, 248
Charles the Simple, Frankish king, 201, 202
Chartres, 209–210, 212; cathedral at, 209–210, 218, p219
Chaucer, Geoffrey, 239, 325
Chávez, Cesar, 794
Chemistry, 563–564
Cheng Ho, 273
Ch'eng-twu, Ming ruler, p272
Chernenko, Konstantin, 783
Chernobyl, 784
Chess, p187, 241
Chiang Kai-shek, 637, 638, 639, 659, 702, 703
Chicago, 558
Chichimecs, 314
Child labor, 485–486, 515, 565
Chile, 367, 501, 550, 632, 634, 772–773, 798
China: ancient, 67, 76–82, m77; geography of, 76–77, 79, 84; culture of, 78, 79–80, 81, 85, 86, 261–267, 272–274, 546, 733; Shang dynasty, 78–79, 80, m81, 261; early cities in, 79; Chou dynasty, m81, 83; Confucianism in, 67, 81–82, 86, 262, 263; Taoism in, 82; Legalists, 82; Ch'in dynasty, 83–85; Great Wall of, 83, 84–85, 261; Han dynasty, 85–87, m86, 261, 295; Great Silk Road of, 86, 87, 263; Buddhism in, 87, 262; Golden Age in, 260–274; Sui dynasty, 261, m262; T'ang dynasty, 261–264, m262, 295; choosing of scholar-officials in, 262–263; Sung dynasty, 264–265, m265; trade with, 265, 273; under the Mongols, 267–271; Ming dynasty, 271–272, m271, 273, 274; Europeans in, 273–274, 544–547;

Ch'ing dynasty, 274, 544, 545; Vietnam under, 295; European imperialism in, 544–547, m546; Taiping Rebellion, 545–546; nationalism in, 547; Boxer Rebellion, 547; and Japan, 546, 547, 550, 636–638, 672, 701; and World War I, 594, 636; Ch'ing dynasty overthrown, 636; communism in, 636–638, 639, 701–705, 729–733; Nationalists in, 636–637, 638, civil war in, 638, 702; Japanese invasion of, 659, 702; and World War II, 674, 701; People's Republic of, 703, 715; U.S. recognition of, 703; and U.N., 703, 704; and Soviet Union, 703, 730, 787; and Korean War, 703, 705; and Eastern Europe, 721; Five Year Plan, 729; Great Leap Forward, 730; cultural revolution, 730–732, 789; and India, 735
Ch'in dynasty, 78, 83–85
Ch'ing dynasty, 274, 544, 545, 636
Chivalry, 226–227, 371
Chou dynasty, 78, 81, m81, 83, 261
Christendom, concept of, 192, 197
Christian Era, 8
Christianity: rise of, 141, 151–154, m153; in Roman empire, 152–154, 156–157; Constantine's conversion to, 156–157; in Byzantine empire, 167; conversion of Slavs, 182; in Middle Ages, 190–192, 201, 215; Clovis' conversion to, 190; in Japan, 279, 280; in Africa, 303; in Nazi Germany, 656. See also Religion
Chungking, 702
Churches: Byzantine, 166, 171, 181; of the Middle Ages, 218, p219, 231–232, 247, p253, 326; of the Renaissance, 329, 333; of England, p394–395
Churchill, Winston, 237, 701, 745; and World War II, 596, 668, 669, 670, 672, 679, 680, 682, 695, 696; and Yalta conference, 690–691, 691
Church of England, 352, 354, 390, 393, 398, 399, 402
Cicero, 136, 325, 326
Cincinnatus, Roman dictator, 127
Cistercian order, 215
Cities, 27, 29; of Fertile Crescent, 27–28, 29–30; in Indus Valley, 67–70; of Shang China, 79; Roman, 147 (see also Rome); Byzantine, 157, 167–173, 179, 183, 230; of Russia, 251, 418, 606; of T'ang China, 263; of Sung China, 265, 269–270, of Japan, 276, 727; of India, 288, 289, 533; Mayan, 313–314; Aztec, 314; of Renaissance Italy, 323–324, 328–331; of Americas, 367;

841

692, 789; and Great Depression, 651–652; and World War II, 672, 673, 676, 679, 693, 745; and Yalta conference, 690–691, 693, 695, 696

Roosevelt, Theodore, 552–553, 634

Roosevelt Corollary, 553, 634

Rosetta Stone, p62, 63

Rotterdam, 668

Roundheads, 400–401

Rousseau, Jean Jacques, 434, 435

Rowlatt Act, 624

Royal Society of London, 432, 475

Rubáiyát **(Khayyám),** 181

Rubicon River, 135

Ruhr Valley, 482, 505, 695

Rurik, Russian prince, 182

Russia: early kingdoms of, 182, m183, 251–252; religion in, 182, 415; Mongols in, 251, m252, 268, 415; czarist, 252–253, 415, 417, 604–608, 609, 785; under Peter the Great, 414–419; isolation of, 414–415; serfdom in, 415, 603–604, 605; expansion of the empire, 417–418, 437–438, m438, 439, 534, 544, 546, 547; in the Great Northern War, 417–418; under Catherine the Great, 436–439; in 1800's, 603–607; and Napoleonic Wars, 460, 461, 463–464, 606; and the Congress of Vienna, 492, 495; Decembrist Revolt, 604, 608; in Crimean War, 605; Nationalism in, 575; revolutionaries in, 594, 595, 608–609, 611, 613; in the Russo-Japanese War, 550, 609; revolution of 1905, 609–610; in World War I, 584, 585–588, 592–596, 599, 610, 611–612, and Treaty of Brest-Litovsk, 595, 599, 614; provisional government in, 594, 610–611; Bolshevik revolution, 594, 595, 598, 599, 603, 612–616, 785; civil war in, 598, 615. *See also* Soviet Union

Russian Orthodox Church, 252, 785

Russo-Japanese War, 550, 609

Rutherford, Ernest, 564

Saar basin, 598

Sadat, Anwar el-, 756, 797

Sahara, desert, 49, 299, 304

Saigon, 740

St. Bartholomew's Day massacre, 377

St. Basil's Cathedral, p253

St. Helena, 465

St. Petersburg, 418–419, 603, 612, 613, 615. *See also* Leningrad

Sakharov, Andrei, 784

Saladin, 230, 231

Salamis, Battle of, 106, 107

Sallust, 133

Salons, 430–431

Salt, 305

Samarkand, 263, 289

Samudraupta, 285–286

Samurai, 277, 278

Sand, George, 498

Sandinistas, 767, 787, 799

Sandino, Augusto Cesar, 766, 767

Sanger, Margaret, 647

San Martin, José, 501

Sans-culottes, 450, 454, 459, 494

Sanskrit, 70

Santiago, 367

São Paulo, 771, 772

Sappho, p110

Sarajevo, 582–583

Sardinia, 414, 458, 492, 519, 520

Sarney, José, 772

Satire, 147

Satrap, 44

Saudi Arabia, 629, 631, 757, 758

Savannas, 299–300, 304–306, 308

Savonarola, Girolamo, 346

Savoy, 414, 519, 520

Saxons, 157, 159, 188, 190, 192, 195

Saxony, 195

Scandinavia, 182, 199, 201, 243; in World War II, 667–668. *See also* Denmark; Norway; Sweden

Scherm, 18

Schleswig, 521

Schlieffen, Alfred von, 587, 588

Schliemann, Heinrich, 98

Schmalkaldic League, 357

Schmidt, Helmut, 710

Scholastica, 191

Schönberg, Arnold, 570

"School of Athens, The" (Raphael), p326, 334

Schumann, Robert, 499, 709

Schurz, Carl, 552

Science: in ancient Greece, 117; under the caliphs, 179–181; under the Guptas, 286; revolution, 345, 358–360, 428; and the Enlightenment, 428–429, 431–432, 513; in early 1900's, 556–564; after World War I, 646–647; during World War II, 682. *See also* Industrial Revolution

Scientific Revolution, 345, 358–360, 428

Scipio Aemilianus, 130

Scipio Africanus, 129, 130, 131

Scotland, p21; under the Romans, 131, 188; Reformation in, 354, 390; under the Stuarts, 390, 398, 399; part of Great Britain, 398, n413, 439, 495; factories in, 483

Scott, Sir Walter, 497

Scriabin, Alexander, 570

Scribes, 27, 28, 37, 59, 62

Scythians, 105

Second Afghan War, 544

Secret History **(Procopius),** 168

Sedan, 523

Seeds, 20

Sekigahara, Battle of, 280

Selassie, Haile, 659

Selective Service Act, 672, 676

Seleucid dynasty, 129, 130, 151

Seleucus, 116

Self-determination, 596

Seljuk Turks, 183, 201, 228, 627

Senate, Roman, 126

Seoul, 705

Separation of powers, 434–435

Separatists, Canadian, 776–777

Sepoy Mutiny, 542

Sepoys, 541–542

Serbia, 575, 582–583, 585–588, 592

Serfs: in feudal Europe, 204, 213, 244, 415, 418, 437; in Russia, 415, 418, 437, 603–605

Sesshu, 281

Seven Weeks' War, 521–523

Seven Years' War, 423, 440, 441

Seymour, Jane, 353

Sforza, Caterina, 327

Shah Jahan, 284, 285, 290, 291, 292

Shakespeare, William, 286, 396, 412

Shakuntala **(Kalidasa),** 286

Shang dynasty, 78–79, 80, 261

Shanghai, 637

Shih Huang-ti, Chinese emperor, 83–84, 85

Shi'ites, 179, 758, 759

Shikibu, Murasaki, 275, 277

Shinto, 275

Shiva, 287, 294, 299

Shoguns, 277–278, 280, 548

Shotoku, Prince, 275–276

Shudras, 72

Siam. *See* Thailand

Siberia, 251, 603

Sicilies, Kingdom of the Two, 492, 496, 506, 519

Sicily: colony of Greece, 112, 122; under Carthage, 127; under Rome, 128, 131; under Byzantium, 182; Muslims in, 198; in World War II, 680

Sieyès, Abbé, 451

Sigismund, Holy Roman emperor, 242

Sihanouk, Norodom, 740, 741

Sikhs, 291, 542, 736

Silesia, 422–423, 424

Silk, 79, 80, 86, 260, 265, 273

Sinai Peninsula, 756

Singapore, 672, 674, 738

Sistine Chapel, 333

Six-Day War, 756

Skyscraper, 558

Slater, Samuel, 481

Slavery: in Sumer, 32–33; in ancient Egypt, 36, 53, 55, 60; in Babylon, 41–42; in Indus Valley,

Slavery (continued)
70; in Greece, 110; in Rome, 132; in North Africa, 159; of the Indians in the Americas, 367–368; in the French Caribbean, 460, 500; revolt in Haiti, 500; in the U.S., 517, 527–529
Slave trade: in Roman republic, 132; in the 1500's, 340–341; African, 534–535
Slavs: in the Middle Ages, 195, 222; in Russia, 182–184, 251; culture of, 182–184, 195; under Austrian rule, 495; and World War I, 575, 582, 585; Nazis and, 655, 678
Slovaks, 719
Slovenes, 575
Slums: Roman, 150; disease in, 484, 574; and industrialization, 486; in South Africa, 753; in Mexico, 764
Smallpox, 180, 339, 365, 562
Smith, Adam, 434, 442, 486, 791
Smyth, Sir Thomas, 393
Social class. *See* Class structure
Social Contract, The (Rousseau), 435
Social Darwinism, 563
Social Democrats, 608–609
Socialism, 515–516, 572, 614; in Tanzania, 751
Social Revolutionaries, 608, 611, 613
Social Security Act, 651
Society, 14. *See also* Class structure
Socrates, 112–113
Solidarity, 720–721
Solomon, 37–38, 167
Solomon Islands, 553, 674
Solon, 103–104
Solzhenitsyn, Alexander, 784
Somalia, 747
Somaliland, 536
Somme, Battle of the, 591
Somoza, Anastasio, 766, 767
Songhai, 304, 307–308
Song of Roland, 195, 220, 225–226, 226, 227, 325
Soninke people, 306
Sophocles, 109, 412
South Africa, 534, 539, 540, 746; apartheid in, 7520753
South America, m309; Indians of, 310, 315; explorations of, 338, 339–340; independence in, 499–504, m502, 771; governments and economies of, 771–774
Southeast Asia, m737; early kingdoms in, 293–295; trade in, 294, 295; Islam in, 295; French in, 544; British in, 544, 737; colonies become independent, 737; war in, 737–741
Soviet, 611
Soviet Union, 615, m787; under Lenin, 613–616, 783; under Stalin, 616–619, 658, 781, 783;

industrial and agricultural revolution, 617–618, 619; totalitarianism in, 618–619; communism in, 637, 781–782, 783, 786; in World War II, 665–666, 667, 670–671, 679–680, 682, 788; and Yalta conference, 690–691, 786; and Cold War, 691–705, 781, 786; and Eastern Europe, 693, 696, 700, 719, 721, 788; and arms race, 694–695; and Berlin blockade, 699; and Hungarian revolt, 700; and Communist China, 703, 730, 787; and Korea, 703; and Comecon, 709; and Cuba, 767, 769–770, 782, 787; Middle East interests of, 759, 797; relations with U.S., 780–781, 788–789; under Khrushchev, 781–782, 786; de-Stalinization in, 782, 784; and Afghanistan, 782, 788; planned economy in, 783–784; Chernobyl incident, 784; dissent in, 784; religion in 784–785; ethnic groups in, 785; support for communism abroad, 786–789; space program, 786. *See also* Russia
Soweto, 753
Space race, 786
Spain, 12; under Carthage, 128; under the Romans, 134, p142, 148; barbarian invasions of, 159, 169; Muslims in, 169, 174, 176, 177, 178, 183, 193, 224, 249, 250; Visigoths in, 188; under Charlemagne, 195; government in, 238; plague in, 243; kingdoms of, 249–250, m250; Inquisition in, 250, 253; explorations by, 273, 339, 367; empire of, 363–367, m367, 392, 500–504, 525, 553; Catholicism in, 364, 369–370; European power, 368–371; golden age of culture in, 370–371; Netherland's revolt against, 369–370, 372–373, 391; defeat of the Armada, 370, 388–389, 390–392; and War of the Spanish Succession, 413–414; declares war on Britain, 445; and the Napoleonic Wars, 455, 463, 500; and Congress of Vienna, 492, 519; and revolutions in South America, 500–504; in the late 1800's, 523; independence of Mexico from, 503, 526; and Spanish-American War, 551–552; civil war in, 660; after World War II, 710, 717
Spanish-American War, 551–552, 768, 769
Sparta, 95, 100, 102–103, 106, p110, 111–112
Spartacus, 132
Spencer, Herbert, 563
Spheres of influence, 545
Spices, 292, 335, 336, 338, 374

Spiritual Exercises (St. Ignatius), 356
Sports, 313, 570, 714, 728
Sri Lanka (Ceylon), 76
SS, 677
Stalin, Joseph, 700; rise to power, 616–619, 658; and World War II, 658, 665, 667, 670, 676, 679, 680, 682; and Eastern Europe, 691, 693, 696; and Yalta conference, 690–691, 695, 696; after World War II, 699, 781, 786
Stalingrad, 679, 782; Battle of, 679
Stamp Act, 441–442
Standard Oil Company, 513
Stanley, Henry, 535, 536, 539
Starry Messenger (Galileo), 359
States General (Netherlands), 373
Steam power, 473, 477–478, 512, 560
Steel, 558, 709, 725, 792
Stephen II, pope, 194
Stephenson, George, 479
Steppe, 267–268
Stock market crash, 649–650
Stoicism, 145–147, 149
Stone Age, 9, 15. *See also* Neolithic Age; Paleolithic Age
Stonehenge, p7
Storm Troopers, 655
Strait of Magellan, 339, 391
Strasbourg, 708–709
Stravinsky, Igor, 570
Stresemann, Gustav, 644
Stuart dynasty, 354, 389, 398, 399, 440
Suarez, Ines, 367
Suburbs, 791
Sudan, 536, 538, 746, 747
Sudentenland, 599, 665; Hitler's invasion of, 661
Suez, Isthmus of, 50
Suez Canal, 512, 536, 659, 679, 746
Suffrage, 517. *See also* Voting rights
Sugar, 440, 551, 632, 634, 768, 769
Suger, abbot, 218
Sui dynasty, 261
Sukarno, 737
Sulieman the Magnificent, sultan, 419
Sulla, 133, 134
Sultan, 183, 288
Sumanguru, 306
Sumatra, 295, 674
Sumerian civilization, 27–33
Summa Theologiae (Aquinas), 225
Sundiata, 306, 307
Sung dynasty, 264–265, 266, 267, 268, 269, 281
Sunni Ali, 307
Sunni Muslims, 179, 183, 758, 759
Sun Yat-sen, 636, 637
Supply and demand, law of, 434
Surnames, 213

Acknowledgments

Text Credits

p. 50 From James B. Pritchard, ed., *The Ancient Near East: An Anthology of Texts and Pictures*. Copyright © 1958 by Princeton University Press. Excerpts reprinted with permission of Princeton University Press.

p. 75 From *The Edicts of Asoka* edited by Nakam and Mckeon. By permission of the University of Chicago Press.

p. 133 From *Sallust* translated by J.C. Rolfe and published by Harvard University Press. Reprinted by permission of Harvard University and the Loeb Classical Library.

p. 143 From *Roman Civilization* edited by Naphtali Lewis and Meyer Reinhold. By permission of Columbia University Press.

p. 365 From *The Broken Spears* by Miguel Leon-Portilla, copyright © 1962 by the Beacon Press. Reprinted by permission of Beacon Press.

p. 592 From *All Quiet on the Western Front*, Erich Maria Remarque, copyright 1929, 1930 by Little, Brown, and Company, copyright renewed 1957, 1958 by Erich Maria Remarque.

p. 614 From *Ten Days that Shook the World* by John Reed, © 1960, published by Random House.

p. 647 From "The Waste Land" by T.S. Eliot from *Collected Poems 1900–1935*, © 1963 by T.S. Eliot, published by Faber and Faber, Ltd.

pp. 664, 665 From *For Those I Loved*, Martin Gray, translated from the French by Anthony White, © 1972 by Little, Brown, and Company, and the Bodley Head.

p. 793 Reprinted by permission of Joan Daves. From *I Have a Dream*, copyright © 1963 by Martin Luther King, Jr.

Art Credits

Photo research: Carole Frohlich
Art editor: Penny Peters
Maps: Charthouse/Richard D. Pusey
Illustrations: pp. 31, 53, 101, 108, 148, 202, 205, 211, 219, 272, 397, 804–818, Tony Smith, Virgil Pomfret Agency
Graphs and **charts:** pp. 36, 62r, 330, 479, 483, James R. Hamilton; Graph p. 464, after Charles Joseph Minard, 1861
Time lines: James R. Hamilton
Calligraphy in *Voices from the Past:* Mary Stevenson Keefe

Photo Credits

Cover: Robert Frerck/Odyssey Productions
Title page: R. Vroom/Photo Researchers

Introduction: 7 Dallas & John Heaton/CLICK/Chicago. 8*l* Michael Holford; *m* Courtesy, Audemars Piguet, NY; *r* Science Museum, London/A.C. Cooper Ltd., photographer.

Unit I: (opener) 10–11 Georg Gerster/Photo Researchers. 12 Amplicaciones y Reproducciones "MAS." 14 Peter Menzel. 16*tl* Courtesy, Institut Royal des Sciences Naturelles de Belgique, Brussels; *bl* Michael Holford; *tr* Courtesy, Wiltshire Archaeological & Natural History Society, Devizes, England; *br* Lee Boltin Picture Library. 17 Michael Holford. 18 Irven DeVore/Anthro-Photo. 19 © Alexander Marshack 1972. 21 Elizabeth Zeschin. 22*l* Courtesy of The Oriental Institute of the University of Chicago; *r* By courtesy of the Board of Trustees of the Victoria and Albert Museum, London. 23 Reproduced by Courtesy of the Trustees of the British Museum (**BM**). 26 Standard of Ur, peace panel. BM. 29*t* Michael Holford; *b* Hirmer Verlag München. 32 Scala/Art Resource (**AR**). 33 Courtesy of The Oriental Institute of the University of Chicago. 35 Hirmer Verlag München. 37 Yale Babylonian Collection. 38 Louis Goldman/Photo Researchers.

40 BM. 41 Erich Lessing/Magnum. 47 Lee Boltin Picture Library. 51*t* (detail) Egyptian Expedition of The Metropolitan Museum of Art (**MMA**), Rogers Fund, 1930 (30.4.44). *b* Jean Vertut. 53 Michael Holford. 55 John G. Ross/Mediterranean Archives. 56 George Holton/Photo Researchers. 58*t* BM/Michael Holford; *bl, m, r* Michael Holford. 59*t* BM; *b* Reproduced by permission of the Syndics of the Fitzwilliam Museum, Cambridge. 60 Egyptian Museum, Cairo. 61*l* Ny Carlsberg Glyptotek, Copenhagen; *m* Staatliche Museen, Berlin/Hirmer Verlag München; *r* John G. Ross/Newsweek Books Picture Collection. 62*l* BM. 66 Roland & Sabrina Michaud/Woodfin Camp & Associates. 69*tl* Paolo Koch/Photo Researchers; *tr, b* Jehangir Gazdar/Woodfin Camp & Associates. 71 The British Library (**BL**)/Michael Holford. 73 C.M. Dixon Colour Photo Library. 76 © Raghubir Singh 1972. 79*l* Michael Holford; *r* Cultural Relics Bureau, Beijing, and MMA. 80 The Seattle Art Museum, Eugene Fuller Memorial Collection. 82 Collection of The National Palace Museum, Taipei, Taiwan, Republic of China. 84 Dallas & John Heaton/CLICK/Chicago. 85 Pang Weiliang/Xinhua News Agency. 87 Robert Harding Picture Library.

Unit II: (opener) 92–3 H. Armstrong Roberts, Inc. 94 R. Manley/Shostal Associates. 97 Fresco, Palace of Knossos. Archaeologisches Museum Stierspringer/Hirmer Verlag München. 99*l* MMA, Dodge Fund, 1907 (07.96); *m, r* BM. 104 MMA, Rogers Fund, 1917 (17.230.14a,b). 107 BM. 109*l* Robert Frerck/Odyssey Productions; *r* Archaeological Museum, Piraeus/Ekdotike Athenon S.A. 110*l* © Caecilia H. Moessner; *m* BM; *r* Museo Nazionale, Taranto. Giraudon/AR. 113 MMA, Catharine Lorillard Wolfe Fund, 1931 (31.45). 115 (detail) "La Battaglia di Alessandro." Museo Nazionale, Naples. Scala/AR. 120 Josephine Powell. 122 Emmett Bright/Photo Researchers. 124 Giraudon/AR. 126*l* Courtesy, Soprintendenza Archeologica di Ostia; *r* Stela of Lucius Erennius Praesens. Musée Calvet, Avignon. 132 (detail) Mosaic of Dar Bue Ammera, from Aliten. Musée des Antiquities, Tripoli. Pierre Belzeaux/Photo Researchers. 134 © M. Grimoldi. 137 BM. 140 Josephine Powell. 142 Robert Frerck/Odyssey Productions. 144*b* Thomas B. Hollyman/Photo Researchers. 149*l* MMA, Rogers Fund, 1903 (03.14.13); *m, r* Museo Nazionale, Naples/Fotografia Foglia, photographer. 150 Michael Holford. 157 Claus Hansmann, Stockdorf.

Unit III: (opener) 164–5 John Sims/CLICK/Chicago. 166 Alon Reininger/Contact Press Images. 168 Constantinople, *Notitia Dignitatum*, 1436. MS. Canon. Misc. 378, f. 84. Bodleian Library, Oxford. 170*l, r* (detail) Scala/AR. 172 K. Scholz/Shostal Associates. 175 Camerapix, Nairobi. 176 Page from a Qur'an, late 11th c. Courtesy of The Harvard University Art Museums (Arthur M. Sackler Museum). Private collection. 178 MMA, The James F. Ballard Collection, Gift of James F. Ballard, 1922. Otto Nelson, photographer. 180*l* From an Ottoman illuminated manuscript, late 16th c. The Granger Collection, NY; *r* Astrolabe, 1291. MMA, Bequest of Edward C. Moore, 1891. The Edward C. Moore Collection (91.1.535 a–h). 187 C.M. Dixon Colour Photo Library. 191 Foto Biblioteca Vaticana. 192 Lindisfarne Gospels, Northumbria, c. 1700. Initial page at the beginning of the Gospel according to Saint John. Cotton MS, Nero D, IV. BL. 193 BM. 195*r* Metz Cathedral. Giraudon/AR. 199*l* Statens Historiska Museet, Stockholm/Werner Forman Archive; *m* Viking Ship Museum, Bygdøy, Oslo/Werner Forman Archive; *r* © University Museum of National Antiquities, Oslo, Norway. Eirik Irgens Johnsen, photographer. 206 Luttrell Psalter, AD 1335–40. Add. MS 42130, f. 171. BM. 209 (detail) #E 2432-c, Cod 2549, fol. 164. Österreichische Nationalbibliothek, Vienna. 210 *Hours of the Virgin*, MS 399 (September). Pierpont Morgan Library, NY. 212 (detail) *Ethiques politiques et économiques d'Aristote*. Ms 927, fol 145 R. Musée Municipal, Rouen. Giraudon/AR. 217 *Livre de la vie active des religieuses de l'Hotel-Dieu*, 15th c. Musée de l'Assistance Publique, Paris. 219*bl* Sonia Halliday; *br* Michael Holford. 221 (detail)

Michael Holford. 225 Pietro di Pavia illuminating an initial. *Naturalis historia*, Pliny, 1389. MS E. 24 inf., f 332. Biblioteca Ambrosiana, Milan. 226 MS 5073, fol 140 v. Bibliothèque Arsenal, Paris. Giraudon/AR. 227 *Heures de la Bienheureuse Vierge Marie* (November). Dutuit B. 37, fol 15r. Petit Palais, Paris/Bulloz. 230*l* Bildarchiv Foto Marburg/AR; *r* R. Manley/Shostal Associates. 234 Painting by Antoine Dufour, c. 1505. Musée Dobrée, Nantes. Giraudon/AR. 237 Add. MS 4838, The Article of Barons, 1215. BL. 238 Reproduced by gracious permission of Her Majesty Queen Elizabeth II. 241 C.M. Dixon Colour Photo Library. 243 MS 13076–77, FOL 24verso. © Bibliothèque royale Albert 1er, Brussels. 245 *Chronique d'Angleterre*, Jean de Wavrin. Royal 14 E IV fol. 59. Flemish, late 15th c. BL. 249 Portrait by M. Sittow. National Portrait Gallery, London. 253 TASS/Sovfoto.

Unit IV: (opener) 258–9 Ric Ergenbright. 260 (detail) Edimedia. 263 From a Ch'ing album. OE 5 a fol p. 31/RcC 1486. Bibliothèque Nationale, Paris. 264 Wan-go H.C. Weng. 266*l* "Pine and Mountains in Spring," Mi Fei. National Palace Museum, Taipei, Taiwan, Republic of China; *r* Courtesy of The Harvard University Art Museums (The Arthur M. Sackler Museum). Gift of Ernest B. Dane, 1892 and Helen P. Dane. 268 By courtesy of the Board of Trustees of the Victoria and Albert Museum, London. 272*b* Wan-go H.C. Weng/Collection of the National Palace Museum, Taipei, Taiwan, Republic of China. 276 Benrido Company, Ltd., Kyoto. 278 The Board of Trustees of the Royal Armouries, London. 280 Courtesy of the Freer Gallery of Art, Smithsonian Institution, Washington, D.C. (67.20). 281 Bob Brudd/CLICK/Chicago. 283 Ric Ergenbright. 287 Robert Ivey/Ric Ergenbright Photography. 291 Reproduced by permission of The India Office Library (BL). 292 (detail) India, Golconda or northern Madras. Painting on cotton, 1630–1640 A.D. The Brooklyn Museum (14.719.2), Museum Collection Fund. 295 Shostal Associates. 298 Norman Prince. 301 MMA, The Michael C. Rockefeller Memorial Collection, Gift of Nelson A. Rockefeller, 1972 (1978.412.310). 303*r* Kal Muller/Woodfin Camp & Associates. 307*l* Lee Boltin Picture Library; *r* Bibliothèque Nationale, Paris. 310 Gemini Smith Inc. La Jolla © Bradley Smith. 312 Courtesy of Museum of the American Indian, Heye Foundation, NY. 313 Gemini Smith Inc. La Jolla © Bradley Smith. 315 MS. Arch. Selden A.1, f. 2. Bodleian Library, Oxford.

Unit V: (opener) 320–1 Robert Frerck/Odyssey Productions. 322 "Copy of Map of Catena," Florence 1490, S. Buonsignori. Museum of Florence. Scala/AR. 323 Bibliothèque, L'Institut de France. 326 "The School of Athens," 1509–11, Raphael. Stanza della Segnatura, Vatican. Scala/AR. 327*l* "Battista Sforza," Piero della Francesca. Galleria degli Uffizi. Scala/AR; *r* "Federico da Montefeltro, Duke of Urbino," Piero della Francesca. Uffizi. Scala/AR. 330 "Story of St. Peter: Resurrection of Tabitha, and Healing of the Cripple," c. 1425, Masaccio. Brancacci Chapel, S. Maria del Carmine, Florence. Scala/AR. 332 "Pieta," 1497–9, Michelangelo. St. Peter's Rome. Scala/AR. 333*l* "David," 1501–4, Michelangelo. Accademia, Florence. Scala/AR; *r* Scala/AR. 334 "Mona Lisa," 1503, Leonardo da Vinci. Musée de Louvre. Scala/AR. 337*t* Painting by Ridolfo Ghirlandaio (attr.). Museo Navale, Pegli. Scala/AR; *b* Michael Holford. 338 "Treatise of Piero de Cresienzi," end 15th c. *Le Livre de Rustican des Proiffiz rurals*. BL. 340 The Granger Collection, NY. 344 Courtesy, Dr. Henning Schleifenbaum, Siegen, Germany. 347 Giraudon/AR. 348 Painting by Lucas Cranach the Elder, 1526. Nationalmuseum, Stockholm. 352 Painting from studio of Hans Holbein. By kind permission of Warwick Castle, England. 353 Musée Condé, Chantilly. Giraudon/AR. 357*l* Bibliothèque publique et universitaire, Geneva; *r* Papal Coronation of Pius II, 3 Sept., 1458, Siena. Duomo, Libreria Piccolomini. Scala/AR. 359*l* Museo della Scienza, Florence. Scala/AR; *r* Gal. 48 c. 29v. Biblioteca Nazionale Centrale, Florence/Guido Sansoni, photographer. 360 Courtesy, Museum of Our National Heritage, Lexington. 363 Cat. #2183, Anon. Government Art Collection, London. 366 R. Manley/Shostal Associates. 339*l* Reproduced by permission of Patrimonio Nacional. Amplicaciones y Reproducciones "MAS"; *r* Portrait by Alonson Sanchez. © Museo del Prado, Madrid. 370 Museo-Casa Greco. Amplicaciones y Reproducciones "MAS." 373 Rijksmuseum-Stichting, Amsterdam. 374 (detail) "Flowers and Baluser, Motifs," 17th c. CAT #77. Philadelphia Museum of Art. Gift of Mrs. Francis P. Garvan. Eric Mitchell, photographer.

375 Rijksmuseum-Stichting, Amsterdam. 376 "Young Woman with a Water Jug," Johannes Vermeer. MMA, Gift of Henry G. Marquand, 1889. Marquand Collection (89.15.21). 378 Painting by Philippe de Campaigne. Musée de Louvre. Giraudon/AR.

Unit VI: (opener) 386–7 M. Schneiders/H. Armstrong Roberts, Inc. 388 "Armada Portrait," George Gower (attr.), c. 1588. By kind permission of the Marquess of Tavistock, and the Trustees of the Bedford Estates. 391 By permission of the Folger Shakespeare Library. 393 Painting by Cornelius Vroom. Tiroler Landesmuseum Ferdinandeum. 394–5 Visscher's View of London, MAP L85c no. 7 c.1. By permission of the Folger Shakespeare Library. 396 National Portrait Gallery, London. 399 (detail) The National Portrait Gallery, Smithsonian Institution (NPG. 65.61). 401 Historical Pictures Service, Chicago. 404 S. Vidler/Leo de Wys Inc. 408 Giraudon/AR. 411 Painting by H. Rigaud. Musée de Louvre. Scala/AR. 412 Scala/AR. 415 Rijksmuseum-Stichting, Amsterdam. 416 New York Public Library, Slavonic Division. 418 Bibliothèque Nationale, Paris/Bulloz. 421 Painting by Möller. Kunsthistorische Museum, Vienna. 423 "Die Wachtparade," Daniel Chodowiecki. Staatliche Museen, Berlin/Bildarchiv Preussischer Kulturbesitz. Jörg P. Anders, photographer. 427 "Die Tafelrunde," J. Tietze. Bildarchiv Preussischer Kulturbesitz. 430 "First Reading of *L'Orphelin de Chine* at the home of Mme Geoffrin." Musée des Beaux-Arts, Rouen. Giraudon/AR. 432 Courtesy, Wellcome Institute, London. 433 "Mozart as a Child with his Father and his Sister," Louis Carmotelle. Musée Condé, Chantilly. Giraudon/AR. 435 Portrait by Allan Ramsay, 1766. National Galleries of Scotland. 437 Painting by Groot, 1745. Leningrad Russian Museum/Novosti Press Agency. 444*l* Independence National Historical Park Collection; *tr, br* Robert Llewellyn. 448 "Pillage des Invalides," J.-B. Lallemand fils. Musée Carnavalet, Paris/Bulloz. 451 "Le Serment du Jeu de Paume," d'après Jacques-Louis David. Musée Carnavalet, Paris/Bulloz. 452*l* "La Maraichère," Jacques-Louis David. Musée des Beaux-Arts, Lyons; *r* Painting by Gautier d'Agoty. Bulloz. 456 "Execution of Louis XVI, January 21, 1793," anon. Musée Carnavalet/Gemini Smith Inc. La Jolla © Bradley Smith. 459 "Napoleon in His Study," Jacques-Louis David. National Gallery of Art, Washington, D.C. Samuel H. Kress Collection. 462 Bibliothèque Nationale, Paris/ Jean-Loup Charmet. 463 © Museo del Prado, Madrid.

Unit VII: (opener) 470–1 Dave Forbert/Shostal Associates. 472 Ann Ronan Picture Library, Somerset, England. 474 Henlow Enclosure, from a map by John Goodman Maxwell, 1798. Bedfordshire County Record Office, England. 477*l, r* Mansell Collection. 480 Ann Ronan Picture Library, Somerset, England. 485 Illustration appended to British Parliamentary Commission's report on work in mines, 1844. 486 Mary Evans Picture Library/Photo Researchers. 490 "Redoute paree am 10. November 1814," J.N. Hochle. Österreichische Nationalbibliothek, Vienna. 491 Copyright reserved to Her Majesty Queen Elizabeth II. 494 (detail) "Court Ball in the Ceremonial Ballroom, New Year," Wilhelm Gauss. Historisches Museum der Stadt Wien. 496 National Portrait Gallery, London. 498*l* Bodleian Library, Oxford; *mt* Portrait by Eugène Delacroix. Jean-Loup Charmet; *mb* Mansell Collection; *r* "Wanderer über dem Nebelmeer," Caspar David Friedrich. Hamburger Kunsthalle. 500 The Granger Collection, NY. 501 Organization of American States, Washington, D.C. 506 "Am 13. Marz 1848 vor dem Landhaus," J. Albert. Historisches Museum der Stadt Wien. 510 The Bridgeman Art Library/AR. 512 "A Race for the Buckhorns," Currier & Ives, 1866. The Granger Collection, NY. 514 Provincial Archives of Alberta, Photograph Collection (B5628)/E. Brown, photographer. 516 The Bettmann Archive. 517 MMA, Bequest of Mrs. H.O. Havemeyer, 1929. The H.O. Havemeyer Collection (29.100.129). 520*r* Portrait by Francesco Hayez. Giraudon/AR. 522*b* The Bettmann Archive. 524 The Granger Collection, NY. 527 Historical Pictures Service, Chicago. 528 Library of Congress/Alexander Gardner, photographer. 532 "Celebrations in India 1897," M.E. Caddy. The Bridgeman Art Library/AR. 538 "Battle of Omdurman, 6:30 a.m., Sept. 2, 1898." ET Archive Ltd. 541 Lawrence Impey, Hampshire, England. 542 (detail) Scots Guards, attached to Guards Camel Corps, Nile Expedition, 1885; painting by Lt. Frank Baden-Powell. National Army Museum, London. 545 Peabody Museum of Salem. 547 Jean-Loup Charmet. 548 "Commodore Perry Landing in Japan," Tsukioki Yoshitoshi. BM. 549 Exterior of the Tomioka silk reeling factory, c. 1870. Tsuneo Tamba Collection, Yokahama,

Japan. Japan Information Bureau, London. 551 The Granger Collection, NY. 556 Musée Toulouse-Lautrec, Albi. 557*l, r* Association des Amis de Jacques Henri Lartigue, Paris. 559 Science Museum, London/Michael Holford. 561 From *Milestones of History* (George Weidenfeld and Nicolson Ltd., publishers). Reproduced with permission. 564 Brown Brothers. 565 Mary Evans Picture Library/Photo Researchers. 566 Museum of London. 569*l* (detail) "Gladioli" 1873, Claude Monet. French 1840–1926. Oil on canvas. 22 × 32½". The Detroit Institute of Arts, City of Detroit (21.71); *r* "The Starry Night," Vincent van Gogh 1889. Oil on canvas, 29 × 36¼". Collection, The Museum of Modern Art, NY. Acquired through the Lillie P. Bliss Bequest. 570 National Baseball Hall of Fame and Museum, Inc. 573 Mary Evans Picture Library/Photo Researchers. 574 "Sirk-Ecke," Maximilian Lenz, 1900. Historisches Museum der Stadt Wien.

Unit VIII: (opener) 580–1 Leonard Freed/Magnum. 582 *Le Petit Journal*, July 19. Jean-Loup Charmet. 583 © Librairie Larousse. 584 Culver Pictures. 587*l, m* ET Archive Ltd. 587*r*, 589 Trustees of the Imperial War Museum (**IWM**). 590 "Over the Top," John Nash. IWM. 591 "Gassed," John Singer Sargent. IWM. 594 IWM. 597 "Peace Conference," Orpen. IWM. 602 Painting by Axenov. TASS/Sovfoto. 604 "Volga's Barge Haulers," 1870–73. I. Repin. Novosti Press Agency. 607*l* Brown Brothers; *t* © The Forbes Magazine Collection, NY. Larry Stein, photographer. 609 Popperfoto. 611 H. Roger-Viollet. 612 New York Public Library Collection. 617, 618 TASS/Sovfoto. 619 From *Art of the October Revolution*, Mikhail Guerman (Aurora Publishers, Leningrad). Reproduced with permission. 622 The Bettmann Archive. 625 "The Spinner," 1946, Margaret Bourke-White, Life Magazine © Time Inc. 628 The Bettman Archive. 629 Royal Geographical Society Picture Library, London. 631 Zionist Archives and Library, NY. 633 "Zapatistas," José Clemente Orozco, 1931. Oil on canvas, 45 × 55". Collection, The Museum of Modern Art, NY. Given anonymously. 634 Peter Menzel. 637 Jack Wilkes, Life Magazine © Time Inc. 639 PRC/Sovfoto. 642 "KPA Versammlung, 1932," Hans Grundig. Staatliche Museen zu Berlin (DDR), Nationalgalerie. 645*t* © Heritage Press/Underwood, Collinge & Associates; *b* Hake's Americana & Collectibles, York, PA. 646 "Wassily" Chair, Marcel Breuer, 1902–1981. Courtesy of The Harvard University Art Museums (Busch-Reisinger). Anonymous Gift. 647 The Bettmann Archive. 648 Courtesy of the William Ransom Hogan Jazz Archives, Tulane University.

651 "Employment Agency," Isaac Soyer, 1937. Oil. 34½ × 45". Collection of Whitney Museum of American Art. Purchase (37.44). 652 Brown Brothers. 654 Wide World Photos. 660 "Guernica," Pablo Picasso, 1937. © Museo del Prado, Madrid. © ARS, New York/SPADEM, Paris 1987. 661 The Bettmann Archive. 664 Painting by Junghaus. U.S. Air Force Art Collection. 667 H. Roger-Viollet. 668 "The Withdrawal from Dunkirk," Charles Cundall. IWM. 669*l, m, r* © 1987 Erich Lessing-Culture and Fine Arts Archives/Magnum. 670 Mansell Collection. 674 National Archives. 678 "Buchenwald, 1945," Margaret Bourke-White, Life Magazine © Time Inc. 680 Polish Institute and Sikorski Museum/A.C. Cooper Ltd., photographer. 683 Wide World Photos.

Unit IX: (opener) 688–9 © Wes Thompson 1986/The Stock Market. 690 Franklin D. Roosevelt Library, Hyde Park, NY. 692 Wide World Photos. 694 Owen Franken/Sygma. 600*l, r*, 697, 703 Wide World Photos. 704*r* Suzanne Engelmann/Shostal Associates. 708 Milt & Joan Mann/Cameramann International. 711 Regis Bossu/Sygma. 712*l* Stuart Franklin/Sygma; *r* Jacob Sutton/Gamma-Liaison. 713 Wide World Photos. 714 S. Brown/Leo de Wys Inc. 715 Erich Lessing/Magnum. 718 Wide World Photos. 720 Chris Niedenthal/Black Star. 724 Milt & Joan Mann/Cameramann International. 726 Diego Goldberg/Sygma. 727 A. Stawicki/Woodfin Camp & Associates. 730 Henri Cartier-Bresson/Magnum. 731 Harry Redl/Black Star. 736 Bartholomew/Gamma-Liaison. 738 A. Hernandez/Sygma. 740*r* Gamma-Liaison. 741 Wide World Photos. 744 Mark Kauffman, Life Magazine © Time Inc. 747 Camerapix/Gamma-Liaison. 752*l* Abbas/Magnum; *r* A. Tannenbaum/Sygma. 755*l* Alain Nogues/Sygma. 756*r* Wide World Photos. 757 Bill Strode/Woodfin Camp & Associates. 758 Gamma-Liaison. 762 Betty Crowell. 764 Peter Menzel. 766 Girard Foundation Collection, Museum of International Folk Art, a unit of the Museum of New Mexico, Santa Fe. © Cradoc Bagshaw. 767 Claude Urraca/Sygma. 769 Bill Wassman/The Stock Market. 771 Tony Linck/Shostal Associates. 777 Canapress Photo Service. 780 Gamma-Liaison. 782 Wide World Photos. 783 Paolo Bosio/Gamma-Liaison. 784 F. Hibon/Sygma. 785 A. Andanson/Sygma. 786 TASS/Sovfoto. 788 P. Franceschi/Sygma. 790*l* NASA/Johnson Space Center, Houston; *tr* NASA; *br* Sygma. 791 Ralph Krubner/H. Armstrong Roberts, Inc. 793 Wide World Photos. 797 Medford Taylor/Black Star. 799 Ron Siddle/Sygma.

SEATTLE EVENING HIGH SCHOOL
SEATTLE PUBLIC SCHOOLS